THE AMERICAN CRIMINAL JUSTICE PROCESS

SELECTED RULES, STATUTES AND GUIDELINES

WEST PUBLISHING CO.
ST. PAUL, MINN., 1989

COPYRIGHT © 1989 By WEST PUBLISHING CO.
                    50 West Kellogg Boulevard
                    P.O. Box 64526
                    St. Paul, MN 55164–0526

All rights reserved
Printed in the United States of America
**[No claim of copyright is made for official
U.S. government statutes, rules, or regulations.]**
Library of Congress Cataloging-in-Publication Data

United States. Supreme Court.
    The American criminal justice process.
    1. Criminal procedure—United States. 2. Court rules—United
States. I. Title.
    KF9607 1989   345.73′05   89–14744
                        347.3055

ISBN 0–314–54059–8

Am.Crim.Just.Pro.

PUBLISHER'S PREFACE

While the American criminal justice process is not as "statutory" in origin as some segments of law, its modern implementation of evolved common law concepts and constitutional mandates is largely directed by statutes, rules and administrative regulations.

Designed as a broad supplementary resource, this pamphlet does not pretend to attach relative importance to comparable provisions by their inclusion or exclusion, or even to compile the most widely-emulated models. An editorial decision to include the Federal Rules of Criminal Procedure, rather than the significant 1987 Revision of the Uniform Rules of Criminal Procedure, is hardly more defensible than the decision to depict a sentencing and corrections structure through the Model Sentencing and Corrections Act rather than through complete reproduction of the Model Penal Code. Likewise, excerpts from the Federal Sentencing Guidelines might be no more instructive than illustrations drawn from the sentencing guidelines of Minnesota, Pennsylvania, or any other state that has developed a comprehensive guideline scheme.

In any case, we invite your ongoing comments, on content or its balance, in an effort to keep this compilation as useful a resource as possible.

Such a variegated body of laws regulates operation of our criminal justice system that no one-volume statutory collection could hope to support a detailed study of the subject in all, or even most, jurisdictions. Nevertheless, we believe that this collection of illustrative state and federal statutes, rules and guidelines, together with the introductory comments of leading legal scholars, provides a stable foundation of primary sources for study of the American criminal justice process . . . from initial apprehension to final release.

*

TABLE OF CONTENTS

*

TIME TABLE FOR LAWYERS
IN
FEDERAL CRIMINAL CASES

Amended to February 1, 1989

This table indicates the time for the various steps in a criminal action as provided by the Federal Rules of Criminal Procedure, the Federal Rules of Appellate Procedure, the 1980 Revised Rules of the Supreme Court, and, where applicable, Titles 18 and 28 of the United States Code. Most of these time limitations may be enlarged by the court under the conditions and with the exceptions indicated under "Enlargement of time" in the table. Citations are to the supporting Rules and are in the form "Crim.R. __" for the Rules of Criminal Procedure and "App.R. __" for the Rules of Appellate Procedure. Citations to the 1980 Revised Rules of the Supreme Court are not abbreviated.

ACQUITTAL

Motion for judgment of	After evidence on either side is closed. If motion is made at close of all the evidence, the court may reserve decision and decide motion either before verdict is returned or after jury returns verdict of guilty or is discharged without verdict. Motion may be made or renewed within 7 days after discharge of jury or within such further time as court may fix during the 7-day period. Crim.R. 29.

ALIBI

Notice by defendant	Upon written demand of government, defendant to serve within 10 days or at such different time as court directs. Crim.R. 12.1(a). Exceptions for good cause shown. Crim.R. 12.1(e).
Disclosure by government	Within 10 days after service of defendant's notice of alibi, government to serve written notice stating names and addresses of rebuttal witnesses. Crim.R. 12.1(b). Exceptions for good cause shown. Crim.R. 12.1(e).
Continuing duty to disclose	Either party to promptly notify of existence and identity of additional witness learned of prior to or during trial whose identity, if known, should have been included in information furnished under Crim.R. 12.1(a) or (b). Crim.R. 12.1(c). Exceptions for good cause shown. Crim.R. 12.1(e).

ALLOCUTION

	Before sentence is imposed, court to afford counsel for defendant an opportunity to speak on behalf of defendant and to address defendant personally and ask if the defendant wishes to make statement or to present information in mitigation. Crim.R. 32(a)(1).

APPEAL	See, also, "Certiorari".
Notification of right	After imposing sentence following plea of guilty or nolo contendere of right to appeal sentence. Crim.R. 32(a)(2).
	After imposing sentence in case which has gone to trial on plea of not guilty. Crim.R. 32(a)(2).
By defendant	Within 10 days after entry of (i) judgment or order appealed from or (ii) a notice of appeal by the Government. If a timely motion in arrest of judgment or for new trial on any ground other than newly discovered evidence has been made, appeal may be taken within 10 days after entry of order denying the motion; motion for new trial based on newly discovered evidence will similarly extend time if made before or written 10 days after entry of judgment. Time may be extended for not more than 30 additional days on a showing of excusable neglect. App.R. 4(b).
By government	When authorized by statute, within 30 days after entry of (i) judgment or order appealed from or (ii) a notice of appeal by any defendant. Time may be extended for not more than 30 additional days on a showing of excusable neglect. App.R. 4(b).
To Supreme Court	See 28 U.S.C.A. Rules, 1980 Revised Rules of the Supreme Court, Rule 11.
Record (appellant)	Within 10 days after filing notice of appeal: Appellant to place written order for transcript and file copy of order with clerk; if none to be ordered, file a certificate to that effect; unless entire transcript to be included, file a statement of issues and serve appellee a copy of order or certificate and of statement. App.R. 10(b).
Record (appellee)	Within 10 days of service of appellant's order or certificate or statement, appellee to file and serve on appellant a designation of additional parts of transcript to be included. Unless within 10 days after designation appellant has ordered such parts and so notified appellee, appellee may within following 10 days either order the parts or move in district court for order requiring appellant to do so. App.R. 10(b).
Record (costs)	At time of ordering, party to make satisfactory arrangements with reporter for payment of cost of transcript. App.R. 10(b)(4).
Record (reporter)	If transcript cannot be completed within 30 days of receipt of order, reporter shall request extension of time from clerk of court of appeals. App.R. 11(b).
Setting appeal for argument	The clerk will advise the parties. A request for postponement of argument or for allowance of additional time must be made by motion filed reasonably in advance of the date fixed for hearing. App.R. 34(b).

TIME TABLE FOR LAWYERS

APPEARANCE

    Before magistrate   Without unnecessary delay after an arrest without warrant or an arrest under a warrant issued on a complaint. Crim.R. 5(a).

ARREST of judgment

    Motion in   Within 7 days after verdict or finding of guilty, or after plea of guilty or nolo contendere, or within such further time as the court may fix during the 7-day period. Crim.R. 34.

ARRESTED persons   See, also, "CUSTODY".

    Under warrant upon complaint or without warrant   To be taken without unnecessary delay before nearest federal magistrate, or, if none available, before state or local judicial officer authorized by 18 U.S.C.A. § 3041. Crim.R. 5(a). If person arrested without warrant is brought before magistrate, complaint shall be filed forthwith. Crim.R. 5(a).

    Under warrant upon indictment or information   To be brought promptly before the court or before a United States magistrate. Crim.R. 9(c)(1).

    Commitment to another district   Person arrested (1) in a district other than that in which the offense is alleged to have been committed, or (2) for a probation violation in a district other than the district of supervision, or (3) on a warrant (issued for failure to appear pursuant to subpoena or terms of release) in a district other than that in which the warrant was issued, shall be taken without unnecessary delay before the nearest available federal magistrate. Crim.R. 40.

BILL of particulars   Before arraignment. Crim.R. 7(f).

    Amendment   At any time subject to such conditions as justice requires. Crim.R. 7(f).

    Motion for   Before arraignment or within 10 days after arraignment or at such later time before as court may permit. Crim.R. 7(f).

CERTIORARI

    Petition for writ   See 28 U.S.C.A. Rules, 1980 Revised Rules of the Supreme Court, Rule 20.

CHANGE of venue   See "Transfer".

CLERICAL mistakes   Corrected at any time and after such notice, if any, as the court orders. Crim.R. 36.

CLERK'S office   Open during business hours on all days except Saturdays, Sundays, legal holidays and on days on which weather or other conditions have made office of clerk inaccessible. Crim.R. 45(a), 56; App.R. 45(a).

COMMITMENT to another district	Person arrested (1) in a district other than that in which the offense is alleged to have been committed, or (2) for a probation violation in a district other than the district of supervision, or (3) on a warrant (issued for failure to appear pursuant to subpoena or terms of release) in a district other than that in which the warrant was issued, shall be taken without unnecessary delay before the nearest available federal magistrate. Crim.R. 40.
COMPLAINT	When person arrested without a warrant is brought before a magistrate, a complaint must be filed forthwith. Crim.R. 5(a).
COMPUTATION of time	Exclude day of the act or event from which designated period of time begins to run. Include last day of the period so computed unless it is a Saturday, Sunday, or legal holiday, or, when act to be done is the filing of some paper in court, a day on which weather or other conditions have made the office of the clerk of the district court inaccessible, in which event period runs until end of the next day which is not one of the aforementioned days. Crim.R. 45(a).
	Intermediate Saturdays, Sundays, and legal holidays are excluded if the period is less than 11 days. Crim.R. 45(a).
	Exclude day of the act, event, or default from which designated period of time begins to run. Include last day of the period unless Saturday, Sunday, or legal holiday, in which event period extends until end of next day which is not a Saturday, Sunday, or legal holiday. App.R. 26(a).
	Intermediate Saturdays, Sundays, and legal holidays are excluded if the period is less than 7 days. App.R. 26(a).
	Service by mail adds 3 days to a period computed from time of such service. Crim.R. 45(e); App.R. 26(c).
	Supreme Court matters, see 28 U.S.C.A. Rules, 1980 Revised Rules of the Supreme Court, Rule 29.
COUNSEL	
Joint representation of defendants jointly charged or joined for trial	Court shall promptly inquire into such joint representation and shall personally advise each defendant of right to effective assistance of counsel, including separate representation. Crim.R. 44(c).
COURTS	Always open except when weather or other conditions make court inaccessible. Crim.R. 45(a).
	District courts always open. Crim.R. 56.
CUSTODY	See, also, "ARRESTED PERSONS".
Release prior to trial	In accordance with 18 U.S.C.A. §§ 3142 and 3144. Crim.R. 46(a).

CUSTODY—Cont'd

Release during trial | Person released before trial to continue on release during trial unless court determines otherwise. Crim.R. 46(b).

Release pending sentence or pending notice of appeal | In accordance with 18 U.S.C.A. § 3143. Crim.R. 46(c).

Witness | Witness who has been detained pursuant to 18 U.S.C.A. § 3144 and whose deposition is taken pursuant to Crim.R. 15(a) may be discharged by court after deposition has been subscribed. Crim.R. 15(a).

Reports | Attorney for government shall make biweekly report to court listing defendants and witnesses held in excess of 10 days and shall make statement of reasons why each witness should not be released and why each defendant is still in custody. Crim.R. 46(g).

DEFENSES and objections

Raising of motion | Time for making pretrial motions or requests (and, if required, a later date of hearing) may be set by court at time of arraignment or as soon thereafter as practicable. Crim.R. 12(c). Defenses and objections which may be, and those which must be, raised before trial. Crim.R. 12(b).

Ruling on motion | Motion made before trial must be determined before trial unless court orders that it be deferred for determination at the trial of the general issue or until after verdict. Crim.R. 12(e).

Alibi | See "ALIBI".

Insanity | Written notice of intention to rely on defense of insanity to attorney for government and copy filed with clerk within time provided for filing of pretrial motions or at such time as court directs. Court may for cause shown allow late filing or grant additional time or make other order as appropriate. Crim.R. 12.2(a).

Mental condition | Written notice of intention to introduce expert testimony to attorney for government and copy filed with clerk within time provided for filing of pretrial motions or at such later time as court directs. Court may for cause shown allow late filing or grant additional time or make other order as appropriate. Crim.R. 12.2(b).

DEPOSITIONS

Notice of taking | Reasonable written notice. The court for cause shown may extend or shorten the time. Crim.R. 15(b).

Taking of | By order of court whenever due to exceptional circumstances of the case it is in interest of justice that testimony of prospective witness of party be taken and preserved for use at trial upon motion of such party. Crim.R. 15(a).

DISCOVERY or inspection	
Motion	Motion for discovery under Crim.R. 16 must be raised prior to trial. Crim.R. 12(b).
Notice by government of intention to use evidence	At arraignment or as soon thereafter as practicable, defendant may request notice of government's intention to use (in evidence-in-chief at trial) any evidence defendant may (under Crim.R. 16) be entitled to discover. Crim.R. 12(d).
Statements or report by government witnesses	Shall not be subject of subpena, discovery, or inspection until witness has testified on direct examination in the trial of the case. 18 U.S.C.A. § 3500(a).
Continuing duty to disclose	Party who, prior to or during trial, discovers additional evidence or material previously requested or ordered, which is subject to discovery or inspection shall promptly notify other party or attorney or the court. Crim.R. 16.
DISMISSAL	If there is unnecessary delay in presenting charge to grand jury or in filing an information against defendant held to answer to district court or in bringing defendant to trial, the court may dismiss the indictment, information, or complaint. Crim.R. 48(b).
ENLARGEMENT of time	Extension of time when day on which weather or other conditions have made office of clerk inaccessible. Crim.R. 45(a).
Criminal procedure	When act required or allowed to be done at or within specified time, court for cause shown may (1) with or without motion or notice, order period enlarged if request is made before expiration of period originally prescribed or as extended by previous order or (2) upon motion made after expiration of specified period permit act to be done if failure to act was result of excusable neglect. Crim.R. 45(b). See, however, "Motion for judgment of acquittal", "Motion for new trial", "Motion in arrest of judgment," and "Correction of sentence", this heading.
Appeal	Extension of time for filing notice of appeal for period not to exceed 30 days from expiration of time otherwise prescribed by App.R. 4(b), upon showing of excusable neglect, before or after time has expired. App.R. 4(b). In cases on appeal, for good cause shown, court may enlarge time prescribed by rules of appellate procedure or by its order for doing any act, or may permit an act to be done after expiration of such time. Court may not, however, enlarge time for filing notice of appeal (but see provision in App.R. 4(b) for extension of time), petition for allowance, or petition for permission to appeal. App.R. 26(b).
Supreme Court	See 28 U.S.C.A. Rules, 1980 Revised Rules of the Supreme Court, Rule 29.
Motion for judgment of acquittal	No enlargement of the 7-day period except as fixed by the court within that time. Crim.R. 29, 45(b).

ENLARGEMENT of time—Cont'd

Motion for new trial	No enlargement of the 7-day period except as fixed by the court within that time. Crim.R. 33, 45(b).
Motion in arrest of judgment	No enlargement of the 7-day period except as fixed by the court within that time. Crim.R. 34, 45(b).
Correction of sentence	No enlargement. Crim.R. 35, 45(b).

EVIDENCE

Suppression	Motion must be raised prior to trial. Crim.R. 12(b).
Notice by government of intention to use evidence	At arraignment or as soon thereafter as practicable, either (1) at discretion of government respecting specified evidence or (2) at request of defendant respecting intention to use (in evidence-in-chief at trial) any evidence defendant may (under Crim.R. 16) be entitled to discover. Crim.R. 12(d).
Notice by defendant of intention to introduce expert testimony of mental condition	Written notice to attorney for government and copy filed with clerk within time provided for filing of pretrial motions or at such time as court directs. Court may for cause shown allow late filing or grant additional time or make order as appropriate. Crim.R. 12.2(b).

EXECUTION, stay of   Stay of execution pending appeal. Crim.R. 38(a).

FOREIGN law   Reasonable written notice required of party intending to raise an issue concerning the law of a foreign country. Crim.R. 26.1.

GRAND jury

Challenges	Challenges to the array or to individual jurors must be made before administration of the oath to the jurors. (If not previously determined upon challenge, objections may be made by motion to dismiss indictment.) Crim.R. 6(b). In any event challenge must be made before the voir dire examination begins, or within 7 days after the grounds of challenge are discovered or could have been discovered, whichever is earlier. 28 U.S.C.A. § 1867(a), (b).
Excuse of juror	At any time for cause shown court may excuse a juror either temporarily or permanently. Crim.R. 6(g).
Summoning	Grand juries must be summoned at such times as the public interest requires. Crim.R. 6(a).
Tenure	Until discharged by court but not more than 18 months unless court extends service for period of 6 months or less when the extension is in the public interest. Crim.R. 6(g).

HOLIDAYS   New Year's Day, Birthday of Martin Luther King, Jr., Washington's Birthday, Memorial Day, Independence Day, Labor Day, Columbus Day, Veterans Day, Thanksgiving Day, Christmas Day, and any other day appointed as a holiday by the President

HOLIDAYS—Cont'd

or the Congress of the United States or by the state in which the district court is held. Crim.R. 45(a); App.R. 26(a).

INDICTMENT

Defects	Defenses and objections based on defects (other than failure to show jurisdiction in the court or to charge offense which objections shall be noticed at any time during pendency of proceedings) must be raised prior to trial. Crim.R. 12(b).
Delivery of copy to defendant	Before called upon to plead. Crim.R. 10.
Failure to find	If complaint or information is pending, failure to find indictment must be reported to magistrate forthwith. Crim.R. 6(f).
Sealing and secrecy	Federal magistrate to whom an indictment is returned may direct that indictment shall be kept secret until defendant is in custody or has been released pending trial; clerk thereupon to seal and no person to disclose except when necessary for issuance and execution of warrant or summons. Crim.R. 6(e)(4).

INFORMATION

Amendment	At any time before verdict or finding if no additional or different offense is charged and substantial rights are not prejudiced. Crim.R. 7(e).
Defects	Defenses and objections based on defects (other than failure to show jurisdiction in the court or to charge an offense which objections shall be noticed by the court at any time during pendency of proceedings) must be raised prior to trial. Crim.R. 12(b).
Delivery of copy to defendant	Before called upon to plead. Crim.R. 10.

INSTRUCTIONS

Action on requests	Court must inform counsel of its proposed action prior to arguments to jury. Court may instruct jury before or after arguments are completed or at both times. Crim.R. 30.
Filing requests for	At close of evidence or at such earlier time during trial as court reasonably directs. Copies must be furnished adverse parties at same time. Crim.R. 30.
Objections	Before jury retires to consider verdict. Crim.R. 30.

JUDGE, disability of

Any other judge regularly sitting in or assigned to the court may (1) during trial, upon certifying familiarity with record of trial, proceed with and finish trial and (2) after verdict or finding of guilt, perform duties of judge before whom defendant has been tried. Crim.R. 25.

JUDGMENT of acquittal

Motion for — After evidence on either side is closed. If motion is made at close of all the evidence, court may reserve decision and decide motion either before verdict is returned or after jury returns verdict of guilty or is discharged without verdict. Motion may be made or renewed within 7 days after discharge of jury or within such further time as court may fix during the 7-day period. Crim.R. 29.

JURY

See, also, "Grand jury".

Alternate jurors — Replace jurors who are found to be unable or disqualified prior to the time jury retires to consider its verdict. Alternate jurors who do not replace regular jurors are discharged after that time. Crim.R. 24(c).

Array, challenge of — Must be made before voir dire examination begins, or within 7 days after the grounds for the challenge are discovered or could have been discovered, whichever is earlier. 28 U.S.C.A. § 1867(a), (b).

Less than 12 — By stipulation in writing at any time before verdict. Even absent stipulation, if court finds it necessary to excuse juror for just cause after jury has returned, a valid verdict may be returned by remaining 11 jurors in discretion of court. Crim.R. 23(b).

Poll of jury — When verdict is returned and before it is recorded, at request of any party or on court's own motion. Crim.R. 31(d).

LEGAL HOLIDAYS — See "Holidays", this table.

MAIL — Service by mail adds 3 days to a period computed from the time of such service. Crim.R. 45(e); App.R. 26(c).

MENTAL condition (defense) — Written notice and copy filed with clerk within time provided for filing of pretrial motions or at such later time as court directs. Court may for cause shown allow late filing or grant additional time or make other order as appropriate. Crim.R. 12.2(a), (b).

MOTIONS

Service of — Written motions, supporting affidavits, and notice of hearing must be served not later than 5 days before time specified for hearing unless a different period is fixed by rule or order of court. For cause shown, such an order may be made on ex parte application. Crim.R. 45(d).

Opposing affidavits may be served not less than 1 day before hearing, except as permitted by court. Crim.R. 45(d).

NEW trial

Motion generally — Within 7 days after verdict or finding of guilt or within such further time as the court may fix during the 7-day period. Crim.R. 33.

Newly discovered evidence — Before or within two years after final jugment. If appeal is pending motion may be granted only on remand of case. Crim.R. 33.

OBJECTIONS — See "Defenses and objections."

PLEA of guilty or nolo contendere

Agreement procedure — Court to require disclosure of agreement at time plea is offered. Crim.R. 11(e)(2). Except for good cause shown, notice to court of existence of agreement to be given at arraignment or at such other time prior to trial as fixed by court. Crim.R. 11(e)(5).

Appeal — Notification following sentence of right to appeal sentence. Crim.R. 32.

Motion to withdraw — If motion is made before sentence is imposed, court may permit withdrawal upon showing of any fair and just reason. At any later time, only on direct appeal or by motion under 28 U.S.C.A. § 2255. Crim.R. 32(d).

PRELIMINARY examination

Defendant in custody — Preliminary examination within a reasonable time but not later than 10 days following initial appearance. Crim.R. 5. See, also, 18 U.S.C.A. § 3060.

Defendant not in custody — Preliminary examination within a reasonable time but not later than 20 days following initial appearance. Crim.R. 5. See, also, 18 U.S.C.A. § 3060.

Extension — With consent of defendant, one or more times, by federal magistrate, upon showing of good cause, taking into account public interest in prompt disposition. Without consent of defendant, by judge of the United States only upon showing that extraordinary circumstances exist and that delay is indispensable to interests of justice. Crim.R. 5. See, also, 18 U.S.C.A. § 3060(c).

No examination — Preliminary examination shall not be held if defendant is indicted or information against defendant is filed in district court before date set for preliminary examination. Crim.R. 5. See, also, 18 U.S.C.A. § 3060(e).

PRESENTENCE investigation and report — Before imposition of sentence or granting of probation unless court otherwise directs.

At reasonable time before imposing sentence, court to permit defendant and counsel to read report. Crim.R. 32(c).

PRETRIAL conference   At any time after the filing of the indictment or information. Crim.R. 17.1.

PROBATION

Hearings relating to revocation   Preliminary hearing—Prompt, whenever probationer held in custody on ground that probationer has violated condition of probation. Crim.R. 32.1(a)(1).

Revocation hearing—Unless waived, within a reasonable time. Crim.R. 32.1(a)(2).

REMOVAL proceedings   See "Commitment to Another District".

SATURDAYS   Exclusion in computation of time. Crim.R. 45(a); App.R. 26(a).

SEARCH warrant

Service   Search warrant must be served in the daytime, unless the issuing authority, by appropriate provision in the warrant, and for reasonable cause shown, authorizes its execution at times other than daytime. Crim.R. 41(c).

Execution and return   Must be executed within the time specified in the warrant, which time is not to exceed 10 days. Crim.R. 41(c). Must be returned promptly, accompanied by written inventory. Crim.R. 41(d).

SENTENCE   See, also, "PRESENTENCE investigation and report".

Pre-imposition remarks of counsel and statement by defendant   Before sentence is imposed: counsel to have opportunity to speak on behalf of defendant; court to address defendant personally and ask if defendant wishes to make statement or present information in mitigation; government to have equivalent opportunity to speak. Crim.R. 32(a)(1).

Notification of right to appeal   After imposing sentence following plea of guilty or nolo contendere of right to appeal sentence. Crim.R. 32(a)(2).

After imposing sentence in case which has gone to trial on plea of not guilty. Crim.R. 32(a)(2).

Correction on remand or for changed circumstances   Court shall correct sentence found on appeal as imposed in violation of law, or as a result of incorrect application of sentencing guidelines, or found to be unreasonable. Crim.R. 35(a).

Within one year after imposition of sentence on motion of Government to reflect defendant's subsequent, substantial assistance. Crim.R. 35(b). See, also, 18 U.S.C.A. § 3553 note.

Imposition   Must be imposed without unnecessary delay, but, upon motion by defendant and Government jointly, may postpone for reasonable time to determine factor important to sentencing determination. Crim.R. 32(a).

XVII

SENTENCE—Cont'd

Vacation, setting aside, or correction, motion for — At any time. 28 U.S.C.A. § 2255.

SEVERANCE — Motion for severance of charges or defendants under Crim.R. 14 must be raised prior to trial. Crim.R. 12(b).

SUBPOENA — Court may direct that books, papers, documents, or objects designated in subpoena be produced before court prior to trial or prior to time they are to be offered in evidence and may upon their production permit them to be inspected by parties or their attorneys. Crim.R. 17(c).

SUMMONS

Reissue — At request of government attorney made at any time while complaint, indictment, or information is pending, if summons was returned unserved. Crim.R. 4(d)(4), 9(c)(2).

Return — On or before the return day. Crim.R. 4(d)(4), 9(c)(2).

SUNDAYS — Exclusion in computation of time. Crim.R. 45(a); App.R. 26(a).

TERM of court — Terms of court have been abolished. 28 U.S.C.A. § 138.

TRANSFER

Motion for — At or before arraignment or at such other time as the court or the rules may prescribe. Crim.R. 22.

VERDICT, return of — In case of more than one defendant, jury may return verdicts with respect to the one or more as to whom it has agreed at any time during its deliberations. Crim.R. 31(b).

WARRANT (arrest) — See, also, "ARRESTED PERSONS".

Reissue — At request of government attorney made at any time while complaint, indictment, or information is pending, if warrant was returned unexecuted and not cancelled. Crim.R. 4(d)(4), 9(c)(2).

Showing to defendant — Officer who does not have warrant in possession at time of arrest must show it to defendant as soon as possible upon request. Crim.R. 4(d)(3), 9(c)(1).

AN INTRODUCTION TO THE AMERICAN CRIMINAL JUSTICE PROCESS

Reprinted from LaFave and Israel, Criminal Procedure (1985).

Variations in the Structure of the Process

A useful description of the American criminal justice process must begin by acknowledging that there is no single set of criminal justice procedures applied uniformly throughout this country. Variations exist both from jurisdiction to jurisdiction and from one type of case to another within the same jurisdiction. In our overview, we will take note of a few of the more significant variations, but our primary focus will be on the procedural pattern followed for most cases in most jurisdictions. In this section, we will briefly examine three structural elements that account for many of the variations in the process. If the overview is read with these three elements in mind, the potential for minor or major variations at each of the various steps in the process will be readily apparent.

(a) Allocation of State and Federal Authority. Under our system of federalism, states bear the primary responsibility for defining and controlling criminal behavior. While the federal government has adopted its own criminal code to deal with activities that extend beyond state boundaries or have a special impact upon the operation of the federal government, the vast majority of all criminal prosecutions in this country are based on violations of state law, rather than federal law. Just as each state can shape its substantive criminal code to fit the value judgments and traditions shared by its people, each can also shape the procedures that will be used in enforcing that code. As a result, in many respects, we have fifty-one different criminal justice processes, one for each of the states and one for the federal government. Each jurisdiction's process must comply with federal constitutional standards, but those standards, notwithstanding broad interpretation by the courts, still cover only the most basic elements of the process. Individual jurisdictions retain considerable autonomy in formulating their own procedural systems within the framework of the constitutional standards.

Of course, the allocation of primary responsibility to the states does not necessarily have to result in substantial variations from one jurisdiction to another. Though given considerable autonomy, the states could seek on their own initiative to achieve uniformity. In many other fields, the states have done exactly that, usually by adopting model acts or by modeling their law after a dominant federal provision. In the criminal justice field, however, only a relatively small number of procedures have been standardized.[1] The states

---

1. Roughly half the states have adopted court rules or codes of criminal procedure modeled after the Federal Rules of Criminal Procedure, but only a half-dozen of those states largely track the provisions of the Federal Rules. See Israel, On Recognizing Variations in State Criminal Procedure, 15 Mich.J.L.Ref. 465, 485–86 (1982). Most of the "Federal Rules states" borrow substantially from the Federal Rules but differ from the Federal Rules in their treatment of various procedures. Id. at 486–490. Similarly, while certain Federal statutes (e.g., the Federal Bail Reform Act of 1966) have

served as a model for numerous state provisions, the states relying upon a federal model frequently depart from one or more of its basic provisions. Id. at 490.

The limited influence of federal models in shaping state standards is attributable to several factors, but the most significant probably are the differences in the substantive law enforced at the federal and state level and the differences in the institutional setting in which that law is enforced. The crimes investigated and prosecuted by the federal government tend to have a somewhat different character than the crimes typically started with a common grounding provided by the English common law, but each state then molded its procedure to fit its own needs. The result is fifty-one criminal procedure systems that reflect a common core, but also reveal, at each step in the process, anywhere from a few to a great many variations. Consider, for example, the jury utilized as a factfinder in all fifty-one jurisdictions. In some aspects of jury practice, such as jury size, the law of the different jurisdictions can be neatly categorized as following one of several basic patterns. In other aspects of jury practice, however, such as the selection of jurors, state laws reflect a wide range of variations.

The importance of particular differences in state laws, as they affect the overall process, differs markedly from one variation to another. Some variations are major, having an impact upon many other steps in the jurisdiction's overall process. Other variations, however, are narrow and largely confined in impact. Indeed some have almost no impact, since they relate primarily to terminology rather than substance.

(b) The Role of Discretion. Variations in the administration of the criminal justice process exist not only between jurisdictions, but also within individual jurisdictions. The variations that occur within a single jurisdiction are commonly the product of the significant role of discretionary authority in criminal justice administration. In most jurisdictions, substantial discretion is granted to officials at several key steps in the process. At the very outset, police are given discretion in determining whether to expend their scarce resources in the investigation of a particular complaint. If they do decide to investigate, they then face a series of choices in their exercise of further discretionary authority. While they may not use investigative practices prohibited by law, they also are not required to use a particular investigative procedure simply because it is allowed under the law. Similarly, while police may not arrest without proper grounds, they need not arrest simply because they have proper grounds. If the police do arrest, the case then is presented to the prosecuting attorney, who also has broad discretion. The prosecuting attorney has discretion as to whether to prosecute, and if he does prosecute, whether to do so to the maximum extent permitted by law. The magistrate, who next receives the case, is granted considerable leeway in setting the terms of pretrial release (i.e., bail), although this discretionary authority is subject to certain broad limitations. The trial judge also has considerable discretionary authority, often subject only to prohibitions against arbitrary misuse. Indeed, in some jurisdictions, the scope of most of the major aspects of pretrial procedure, such as discovery and voir dire examination, depends largely on the discretion of the trial judge.

The extensive grants of discretion found throughout the criminal justice process necessarily produce some case-by-case diversity in the application of the process. The degree of diversity will depend upon the extent to which similar officials share the same value judgments, but it is almost certain that not all officials will exercise their discretionary authority in the same way. In some instances, a particular agency, such as a prosecutor's office, may seek to obtain uniformity in the exercise of discretion through administrative regulations. Even if the individual agency is fairly successful, however, considerable diversity will remain as between similar officials employed by different agencies. In our step-by-step description of the process, we will note the major points at which discretionary authority plays a significant role. At each of these points, it should be kept in mind, the

treated in the state systems. Federal prosecutions, for example, involve a substantially smaller portion of offenses that might be classified as street crimes and a substantially higher portion of offenses involving embezzlement or fraud. Illustrative of the differences in institutional setting is the federal court criminal caseload which, though substantial, is considerably less than that carried by courts in almost all of the larger states.

manner in which the process is administered will vary considerably from one community to another, and even from one official to another within the same community.

(c) Misdemeanor–Felony Distinctions. Another source of variations in the process, particularly variations within a single jurisdiction, is the division commonly drawn between the process applicable to major and minor crimes.[2] For the purpose of putting the overview in proper perspective, it is sufficient to recognize a few of the more significant distinctions, starting with the apprehension of the offender. In many jurisdictions, police are subject to a more restrictive arrest standard in making arrests for minor offenses. On the other hand, in dealing with a minor offense, police often also have greater discretion to release the offender upon issuance of a citation in lieu of taking him into custody. At the prosecution stage, a distinction is drawn in the review of the prosecutor's decision to charge. The defendant accused of a minor offense ordinarily is not entitled to either a preliminary hearing or grand jury review—the two procedures commonly utilized in major offenses to provide independent screening of the charging decision. At the trial stage, further differences appear. The charge on a minor offense will be triable before a lower court magistrate, rather than a judge of a court of general jurisdiction. This distinction often carries with it a wide range of procedural consequences. For example, in trials before a magistrate, the jurisdiction may provide a smaller jury, deny pretrial discovery, and even relax the ordinarily applicable rules of evidence.

In many jurisdictions, the line used to distinguish between minor and major offenses is the substantive law's designation of an offense as a misdemeanor or felony.[3] Other jurisdictions treat as minor crimes only certain misdemeanors, usually those punishable by not more than a certain term of imprisonment (commonly six months or ninety days); misdemeanors carrying higher terms are then treated in much the same manner as felonies. Some jurisdictions will draw different lines for different purposes. Thus, the police officer's authority to release on a citation may be limited to ninety-day misdemeanors while the magistrate's trial authority may extend to all misdemeanors. For the sake of brevity, our discussion of the separate treatment of minor offenses will assume a single dividing line under which all misdemeanors are treated as minor crimes.

Variations in Chronology and Personnel

Along with variations in structure, our overview also will largely ignore variations in both the chronology of the process and the personnel administering the process. Those

---

2. Our discussion of the treatment of minor crimes excludes the ordinary traffic violation. In many jurisdictions, all but the most serious traffic violations (e.g., driving while intoxicated) have been decriminalized. Indeed, even in those jurisdictions in which all traffic violations are technically misdemeanors, the less serious traffic offenses often are governed by somewhat different procedures than minor misdemeanors generally. On the other hand, our discussion does encompass city ordinance violations in those jurisdictions in which ordinances largely duplicate in substance and penalty state misdemeanor provisions governing such offenses as assault, petty theft, etc. Such ordinances commonly are used as a basis for prosecution in lieu of the state misdemeanor provisions (often because the fines collected for ordinance violations go to the city), with the prosecution brought by the city attorney rather than the local prosecutor. In jurisdictions of this type, the procedure applied to ordinance violations is basically the same as that applied to minor misdemeanors generally. See e.g., People v. Burnett, 55 Mich.App. 649, 223 N.W.2d 110 (1974); Ill.—S.H.A. ch. 38, ¶¶ 102–15.

3. American jurisdictions commonly use one of two different standards in distinguishing between felonies and misdemeanors. Some classify as felonies all offenses punishable by a maximum term of imprisonment of more than one year; offenses punishable by imprisonment for one year or less are then misdemeanors. Others look to the location of the possible imprisonment. If the offense is punishable by imprisonment in a penitentiary, it is a felony; if punishable only by a jail term, it is a misdemeanor. See W. LaFave and A. Scott, Criminal Law § 26 (1972). As a matter of practice, both dividing lines frequently produce the same result since state correction codes commonly provide for imprisonment in the penitentiary if a sentence exceeds one year and for imprisonment in jail if the sentence is for one year or less.

differences, however, may also substantially affect the character of the process. Two jurisdictions may use the same procedure, but if each uses the procedure at a different stage in the process, that procedure is likely to have a somewhat different role and impact in each of the jurisdictions. Similarly, differences in personnel will produce differences in administrative style that affect the impact of a variety of procedures, particularly those dependent upon the exercise of discretionary authority.

(a) **Chronology.** Our overview uses the sequence of procedural steps followed in the typical criminal case. Certain cases, because of their special qualities, are not likely to follow this typical chronology. For example, there are cases in which the prosecutor will want to approve the police decision to proceed before the arrest is made. As a result, both the prosecutor's screening and the magistrate's screening (through the magistrate's issuance of an arrest warrant) will have come before rather than after the arrest. Similarly, where the grand jury's investigative authority is utilized, grand jury review occurs at the outset and defendant usually will have been indicted before he is arrested. Such differences in chronology mean that the arrest will play a more limited role than in the typical case, where the police officer's warrantless arrest, made on his own initiative, constitutes the first step in the decision to charge. This, in turn, has a bearing on the review procedure that follows the arrest, and may also affect other elements of the subsequent procedure (e.g., the setting of bail).

Putting aside exceptional cases, variations in chronology also will exist from one jurisdiction to another. While the overview recognizes some of the more substantial differences among jurisdictions, it ignores minor variations and even significant variations followed in only a small group of jurisdictions. Thus, it should be kept in mind that both the chronological variations mentioned in our step-by-step overview and many others not mentioned there may play a fairly substantial role in determining the overall shape of the process in a particular jurisdiction.[4]

(b) **Personnel.** Throughout most of the overview, we will not be drawing distinctions between persons who occupy a particular position in the administration of the process. We will refer simply to "police," "prosecutors," "defense counsel," "magistrates," and "trial judges," without further description of the individual official. It should be kept in mind, however, that each of these groupings encompasses a wide range of officials. Even within a single jurisdiction, there may be several different types of agencies assigned to policing, judging, and lawyering, and the performance of the particular role is often influenced by the structure of the agency as well as the actor's own attitudes and capabilities.

Perhaps the broadest range of organizational differences is found in police agencies. The term "police" encompasses all governmental officials who have been given primary responsibility for the enforcement of one or more criminal statutes and the special enforcement authority (e.g., arrest authority) that goes with that responsibility. Included within this group are officers of such varied agencies as the Federal Bureau of Investigation, the state police, the county sheriff's department, and the local township or city police department. The term also encompasses officers of various "specialized" agencies that have authority to

---

4. In addition to ignoring variations in chronology for exceptional cases and atypical jurisdictions, a step-by-step overview, such as that presented here, also suffers from its treatment of each step as if it were started and completed at a single point in the process. While some steps have definite starting and ending points, others are ongoing procedures. Investigatory procedures, for example, do not always stop with the filing of charges, but may continue on through to the time of trial. Similarly, the prosecutor's decision to go forward with the charges, though made initially at a particular point in the proceeding, is ongoing in the sense that it is subject to reconsideration at various subsequent stages in the proceedings.

4

enforce only a limited group of criminal laws (e.g., state conservation officers or federal secret service agents) or to enforce the criminal code in a quite limited geographic area (e.g., park police).[5] Altogether, there are approximately 20,000 different police agencies in this country.

While the police role is performed by the widest variety of officials, there also is considerable diversity among prosecuting agencies. In most state cases, the prosecuting agency will be the office of the local prosecuting attorney (also called a "district attorney," "state's attorney" or "county attorney"). The local prosecutor ordinarily is elected from, and has jurisdiction over all crimes committed within, a local prosecutorial district consisting of one or more counties. In a large number of states, however, the local prosecutor's jurisdiction is not exclusive; the attorney general also has the authority to initiate prosecutions for at least certain types of crimes. Indeed, in three states, there are no locally elected prosecutors, and the attorney general has full responsibility for all prosecutions. Also, where local ordinance prosecutions are used in lieu of state misdemeanor prosecutions, the prosecutor ordinarily will be the city or township attorney rather than the local prosecuting attorney. In federal prosecutions, the prosecutor usually will be an assistant United States Attorney, but certain types of prosecutions also are brought by other divisions of the Justice Department (e.g., antitrust).

In both federal and state systems, the role of the defense lawyer is performed by basically two groups of lawyers, private practitioners and attorneys in public defender agencies. Private practitioners vary considerably in their practice arrangements both as to the type of clients and type of criminal cases handled. Public defender agencies, on the other hand, represent only indigents and ordinarily handle a wide range of offenses. Those agencies usually are part of the state or local government, though some are private, nonprofit organizations that contract with the government to provide defender services.

Within the judiciary, the widest diversity is found among those judicial officials we will describe as "magistrates." Magistrates commonly exercise full jurisdiction, including trial jurisdiction, over minor offenses, and jurisdiction over the preliminary steps (usually warrant issuance, first appearance, and preliminary hearing) in the processing of higher level offenses. In the federal system, the magistrate's functions are performed by United States magistrates, judicial officers appointed by the District Court. In several state judicial systems, magistrates are judges of courts of general jurisdiction, assigned to a special magistrate's division of that court. More frequently, magistrates are judges of courts of limited jurisdiction, commonly titled "justice of the peace courts." In many states, a magistrate court will be a court "not-of-record," and convictions for minor offenses in that court therefore will be subject to review by a trial *de novo* before the general trial court rather than by the traditional form of appellate review on the trial record.[6]

---

5. Substantial variations exist not only among the different types of police agencies, but also among the officers employed by particular agencies. For example, within local police agencies, there will be considerable variation among officers, depending in part upon their unit, in their experience in dealing with the various police investigative practices noted in our step-by-step overview. In most local departments, the bulk of the police manpower tends to be assigned to the patrol division, and patrol officers perform an especially wide range of functions, including many related to social services and traffic control. Typically, less than 10 percent of that division's time is devoted to the investi-

gation of major crimes. On the other hand, officers in the detective division will devote a substantial percentage of their efforts to criminal investigation. The end result is that only a small portion of the officers in a local police department may have substantial experience in felony investigations.

6. Historically, courts not-of-record lacked the capacity to prepare a transcript of their trials. Without that record, their convictions could not be subjected to the traditional form of appellate review. Accordingly, when the conviction was appealed, the higher court simply gave the case *de novo* consideration through a

Considerably less variation exists among the general trial courts. These are the courts with trial jurisdiction over felonies and over any misdemeanor cases that may be beyond the jurisdiction of the magistrate court. In the state systems, the general trial courts commonly are known as "superior courts," "district courts," or "circuit courts." In the federal system, the general trial court is, of course, the United States District Court.

An Overview: The Steps in the Process

In this section, we will describe briefly the major steps taken in the processing of a criminal case. Our focus, as noted previously, is on the processing of a "typical case" in a "typical jurisdiction." This means that our description basically is limited to those procedures employed by most states in processing most of their felony and misdemeanor cases. Where no single procedural pattern is followed by a substantial majority of the states, we will note the major alternatives followed by significant groups of states. However, variations adopted by only a few states, or variations applied only to a limited class of cases, are largely ignored.

While our primary objective in this section is to provide an overview of the interrelated procedural steps that constitute the total process, we have also sought to provide some indication of the significance of the different steps as measured in quantitative terms. This hopefully will assist the reader in gauging the practical significance of the various legal standards discussed in the subsequent chapters. While some of these standards relate to procedures employed in the vast majority of criminal prosecutions, others concern procedures utilized in fewer than even one percent of all prosecutions.

(a) Step 1: The Report of the Crime. The criminal justice process usually starts when the police receive information concerning the possible commission of a crime. The police may obtain that information either through their own observations or from the reports of interested citizens. In either case, if it appears likely that a crime was committed, the offense will be recorded in the police files as a "reported" crime (and will be listed statistically as an offense "known to the police").[7]

Surprisingly, we have somewhat limited data on the exact distribution of reported crimes in this country. The data is adequate, however, to provide a rough estimate of the likely distribution of reported offenses in a typical industrial state. Approximately 60 percent of all reported crimes will relate to the taking or destruction of property. The major offenses in this group will include the various forms of theft (perhaps 50 percent of all property offenses), burglary (15 percent), and vandalism (15 percent). Assaults of all varieties, ranging from assaults with weapons to simple assaults, may provide an additional 10 percent of the reported crimes. Offenses relating to the use of alcohol and drugs (e.g., public drunkenness, possession of drugs, and driving under the influence) are likely to constitute

---

new trial. Today, magistrate courts not-of-record often have the facilities to provide a verbatim transcript of their proceedings, but convictions in those courts remain subject to review by a trial *de novo* before a trial court of general jurisdiction. The trial *de novo* procedure has been retained, in large part, due to concern that a person convicted of a misdemeanor should be entitled to a more formal and thorough trial than is provided in courts not-of-record. Magistrates in such courts often are not lawyers, and they may apply the rules governing trials only in a rather loose fashion. In over half of the states, at least some of the state's magistrate courts are not-of-record.

7. The National Crime Survey (a study based on a sample of 60,000 households) indicates that, at least as to the seven offense categories covered in the F.B.I.'s annual summary of reported offenses (The Uniform Crime Reports), less than half of the offenses committed are reported to the police. However, the ratio of reported to actual crimes varies substantially with the offense. Thus, while there may be three burglaries committed for each one reported, almost every motor vehicle theft is reported.

another 10 percent of the reported offenses. The remaining 20 percent of the reported crimes will be spread over a variety of offenses. Included in this group are the most serious violent felonies, such as robbery (likely to constitute 2 to 4 percent of all reported offenses), and murder and forcible rape (each likely to fall below one-half of one percent).

(b) **Step 2: Pre-arrest Investigation.** Once the police become aware of the possible commission of a crime, they must determine (1) whether the crime actually was committed and (2) if it was, whether there is sufficient information pointing to the guilt of a particular person to justify arresting and charging him. Pre-arrest investigative procedures are designed to answer these questions and to collect evidence that may be helpful in establishing guilt at trial.[8] The particular procedures used will vary with the circumstances of the crime. In some instances, a police officer will observe a crime being committed in his presence and will make an arrest "on the spot." In such cases, the pre-arrest investigation consists of no more than the officer's initial observation. In other cases, the officer will observe activity that is suspicious, though not necessarily criminal, and will seek further information to determine whether to make an arrest. Where an alleged offense has been called to the officer's attention by an interested citizen, the officer also is likely to seek further information.

Where additional information is sought, the officer may utilize a variety of investigatory techniques to gather that information. Perhaps the most common is to question the suspect. Pre-arrest questioning may be accompanied by the temporary detention of the suspect on the street or at home, but does not involve taking him into custody, as occurs with an arrest. The scope of the officer's questioning may range from merely asking the suspect to identify himself to asking him to respond to an accusation made by others. Where the crime investigated involved violence, or there is some other reason to believe the suspect could be armed, the officer may undertake some sort of search of the temporarily detained suspect (usually a pat-down or "frisk" of the suspect's outer clothing). In a small percentage of these police-suspect encounters, the officer also may search the car of a suspect who was stopped while driving.

Along with the police-suspect encounter, the other common pre-arrest investigatory techniques are the interviewing of witnesses (including the victim) and the examination of the scene of the crime. In certain types of cases (e.g., homicides and burglaries), that examination may include the collection of physical evidence (e.g., fingerprints) that will be subjected to scientific analysis. For other offenses, commonly those committed by specialized professional criminals, police informants may be contacted for information concerning possible offenders. Thorough searches of homes and offices, and electronic eavesdropping through wiretaps and similar devices, are also used in certain types of investigations. These procedures, however, commonly require prior judicial authorization through the issuance of a search warrant.

(c) **Step 3: The Arrest.** Once the officer has acquired sufficient information to justify arresting a suspect, the arrest ordinarily is the next step in the criminal justice process. An

---

8. Not all pre-arrest investigations are aimed at previously committed offenses. In dealing with certain crimes, such as vice offenses, the police often use undercover agents and other investigative techniques aimed more at anticipated future crimes than at previously committed offenses. Also, not all pre-arrest investigations directed at past offenses are conducted by the police. The prosecutor, utilizing the aid of the grand jury, will conduct investigations of those offenses that are most readily solved through the use of grand jury's special investigative powers, such as its subpoena authority. Both the future-offense investigation and the grand jury investigation are exceptions to the general rule, however, and represent a very small percentage of all pre-arrest investigations.

7

arrest generally occurs when the officer takes the suspect into custody for the purpose of transporting him to the station and there charging him with a crime.[9] Although an arrest may be authorized in advance by a judicially issued warrant, the vast majority of all arrests are made on the officer's own initiative, without a warrant.

As with reported crimes, arrests will be distributed over a variety of offenses. The distribution of arrests will differ substantially from the distribution of reported crimes, however, because some reported crimes are more likely to lead to arrests than others.[10] While the exact distribution will vary with the individual jurisdiction, a general pattern emerges that roughly fits most jurisdictions. Typically, only 20 to 30 percent of the arrests will be for felonies, with the remainder being for misdemeanors. Though the theft group of offenses constitutes the number one category of reported crimes, it will rank behind the alcohol/drug offenses as a basis for arrests. In those jurisdictions that continue to treat public drunkenness as a crime, that offense alone, even where not enforced with full vigor, can account for 20 percent of all arrests. When that 20 percent is added to arrests for driving under the influence and for possession or sale of drugs, over one-third of all arrests are likely to be attributable to alcohol/drug offenses. The theft offenses are then likely to account for an additional 25–30 percent of the arrests. A substantial percentage of the arrests, perhaps as high as 20 percent, will be for public disorder misdemeanors, such as simple assaults, vandalism, and disorderly conduct. Less than 10 percent will be for serious felony offenses against the person, with aggravated assault and robbery likely to account for 2 percent each and forcible rape and murder for less than one-half of one percent each. The remaining arrests, approximately 10 percent, will be spread over a wide variety of offenses, including arson, nonviolent sex offenses, and possession of weapons.

A substantial percentage of the persons arrested, typically 20 to 30 percent, will be within the age limit for juvenile court jurisdiction. Ordinarily, juvenile arrestees will be separated from the adult arrestees shortly after their arrest. From this point on, we will assume that we are dealing only with the adult arrestees.

(d) Step 4: Booking. Immediately after making an arrest, the arresting officer usually will search the arrestee's person and remove any weapons, contraband, or evidence relating to a crime. He then will arrange for the transportation of the arrestee to the police station, a centrally located jail, or some similar "holding" facility. It is at this facility that the arrestee will be taken through a process known as "booking." Initially, the arrestee's name, the time of his arrival, and the offense for which he was arrested are noted in the police "blotter" or "log." The arrestee then will be photographed and fingerprinted. Typically, he also will be informed of the charge on which he has been booked and will be allowed to make at least one telephone call. When booked on a minor offense, he may be able to obtain his release on "stationhouse bail," i.e., by posting cash as a security payment and promising to appear before a magistrate at a specified date. Persons arrested on

---

9. As an alternative to the traditional "custodial arrest," many jurisdictions grant the officer discretion to briefly detain a person subject to arrest and to then release him upon issuance of a citation (sometimes called an "appearance ticket"). This alternative is most commonly authorized for misdemeanor offenses, and sometimes is limited to particular types of misdemeanors.

10. The "arrest-clearance" rate for reported crimes (which is basically the percentage of reported offenses resulting in the arrest of a suspected offender) varies from over 90 percent for some offenses to less than 20 percent for others. Those crimes that tend to come to the attention of a police officer through his personal observation of the crime usually have the highest arrest-clearance rates. Substantially lower rates are found for offenses that become known to the police primarily through victim reports. Here, the most significant factor will be the victim's ability to identify the offender. Thus, the arrest-clearance rate for burglary (20 percent) is far less than that for aggravated assault (over 60 percent).

serious offenses, and those arrested on minor offenses but unable to gain their release, will remain at the holding facility until ready to be presented before a magistrate (see step 8). Ordinarily, they will be placed in a "lockup," which usually is some kind of cell. Before entering the lockup, they will be subjected to another search, more thorough than that conducted at the point of arrest. This search is designed primarily to inventory the arrestee's personal belongings and to prevent the introduction of contraband into the lockup.

(e) Step 5: Post-arrest Investigation. The extent of the post-arrest investigation will vary with the fact situation. In some situations, such as where the arrestee was caught "red-handed," there will be little left to be done. In other situations, police will utilize many of the same kinds of investigative procedures as are used before arrest (e.g., interviewing witnesses, searching the suspect's home, and viewing the scene of the crime). Post-arrest investigation does offer one important investigative source, however, that ordinarily is not available prior to the arrest—the person of the arrestee. Thus, the arrestee may be placed in a lineup or simply taken to a place where a witness can view him individually (a "showup"). He may be required to provide handwriting or hair samples that can be compared with evidence the police have found at the scene of the crime. He also may be questioned at length about the crime for which he was arrested and any other crime thought to be related. Although we do not have precise data on these post-arrest procedures involving the arrestee, the best available estimates indicate they are not applied to the vast majority of arrestees. In most communities, they are used almost exclusively in the investigation of felony cases and even then not in most of those investigations.

(f) Step 6: The Decision to Charge. Sometime between the booking of the arrestee and his presentation before a magistrate, there will be a review of the decision to file charges. Initially, the police officer making the arrest fills out an arrest report, which is reviewed by a higher ranking police officer. That officer may conclude either that charges should not be brought or that they should be based on a lower level offense than that for which the arrestee was booked. The decision not to charge may be based upon the officer's conclusion that there is insufficient evidence or that the particular offense can more appropriately be handled by a "stationhouse adjustment" (e.g., in the case of a fight among acquaintances, a warning and lecture may be deemed sufficient). If the officer decides against prosecution, the arrestee may be released from the lockup on the officer's direction (although some departments follow the practice of seeking prosecutor approval before releasing felony arrestees). In some jurisdictions, the police will drop as many as 10 to 15 percent of their arrests (predominantly misdemeanor arrests) at this point.

The second review of the decision to charge is usually the review by the prosecuting attorney. Prosecutor offices vary considerably, however, both as to the timing and extent of their review. In some jurisdictions, prosecutors regularly screen all felony and misdemeanor cases before charges are filed with the court. In other jurisdictions, pre-charge prosecutorial review is limited to exceptional cases, primarily those in which the police seek the prosecutor's advice. Here, the primary prosecutorial screening occurs sometime after charges have been filed. In the case of felonies, the prosecutor may not review the case until he is required to present it at a preliminary hearing or a grand jury screening. In misdemeanor cases, the prosecutor may not review the case until it goes to trial (and thus he may never screen misdemeanor charges to which the defendant pleads guilty). Still other jurisdictions prefer a midway position, with prosecutors undertaking a pre-charge screening of all felony cases, but utilizing a post-charge review for all but the most serious misdemeanors.

The timing of the screening is likely to have an impact upon the scope of the screening, as prosecutors tend to have less information available to them the earlier their review is undertaken. However, even among prosecutors utilizing the most prompt post-arrest screening, there is considerable variation in the sources considered in deciding whether to charge. The practice ranges from prosecutors who read only the police reports to those who regularly interview the police officer and often the victim of the crime as well.

Prosecutor offices also vary in the weight that will be given to a particular factor in determining whether to prosecute. The most significant factor, of course, is the strength of the evidence. If the evidence clearly is insufficient to gain a conviction, the case will be dropped. Similarly, if the evidence will support only a lesser offense than that suggested by the police, the charge will be reduced. Where the evidence arguably is sufficient to support the requested charge, the prosecutor will then turn to other factors that might suggest the case is inappropriate for prosecution in light of the equities of the situation and the overall caseload of the prosecutor's office. Such factors include the harm caused by the offense, the victim's attitude toward pressing the case, the arrestee's criminal record, and the adequacy of alternative remedies.[11] It is in the consideration of these factors that differences between prosecutors are most likely to be significant.

Though we can hardly characterize any particular pre-charge screening program as typical of most jurisdictions, a fairly common pattern is found in the eventual results of the overall screening carried on through the entire criminal justice process. In the end, at least as to felonies, the cases against 30 to 60 percent of all arrestees will be dropped as a result of such screening.[12] If only a small percentage of the felony cases are rejected at pre-charge screening, then there will be a much higher percentage rejected at subsequent stages when the prosecutor engages in more thorough screening.

To some extent, the prosecutor's post-charge screening will give greater weight to the sufficiency of the evidence, but the prosecutor is still free to consider all of the factors that are considered in pre-charge screening. If the prosecutor decides in his post-charge screening that the case does not merit prosecution, he will file a motion to terminate the prosecution (a *nolle prosequi* motion), which will be granted almost automatically by the court. In jurisdictions in which pre-charge screening is not extensive, post-charge screening may account for the disposition of more charges than any other step in the criminal justice process. In New York City, for example, where only one percent of all felony arrestees are rejected for prosecution at the pre-charge stage, approximately 40 percent of all charges are subsequently rejected through post-charge screening, usually before the cases reach the trial court. Secondary screening also can be quite significant in jurisdictions with extensive pre-charge screening. In the District of Columbia, for example, the cases against 21 percent

---

11. Many prosecutor offices have developed pre-charge "diversion programs" that provide a formal structure for the prosecutor's refusal to charge notwithstanding sufficient evidence. Under these programs, certain types of charges (usually misdemeanors) will not be prosecuted if the arrestee agrees to comply with specified "rehabilitative conditions" (e.g., making restitution to the victim, maintaining regular employment, etc.). Other prosecutors prefer not to tie the decision to charge to such conditions. They will bring charges and then seek to have the rehabilitative conditions imposed as conditions of probation following conviction.

12. The limited data available on the disposition of misdemeanor arrests indicates that a high percentage of misdemeanor cases also are rejected as a result of prosecutorial screening, but those figures are much more difficult to evaluate. In some jurisdictions, for example, post-charge dismissals may include situations in which defendants charged with offenses such as public drunkenness are allowed to forfeit their bail, with the charges against them then being dismissed—a practice that amounts, in effect, to imposing a fine without a conviction record.

of the arrestees are rejected by an initial decision not to charge, but then an additional 29 percent are dismissed after charges are brought on *nolle prosequi* motions.[13]

Statistics on charge reductions reflect a less consistent pattern than that characterizing dismissals. The percentage of reductions attributable to the screening process varies considerably, but prosecutors have been known to reduce the offense from that designated in the police booking in as many as 30 percent of the felony cases subjected to pre-charge screening. In many jurisdictions, certain types of felony arrests, most notably those involving non-professional thefts, are almost automatically reduced to misdemeanors (e.g., first-offense shoplifting reduced to petty theft). While most reductions occur before the initial charge is filed, a substantial number of reductions often occur later in the proceedings on the prosecutor's motion. Where plea bargaining takes the form of a charge bargain rather than a sentence bargain (see step 12), most of the later reductions are likely to be attributable to plea bargaining rather than post-charge prosecutorial screening.

(g) Step 7: Filing the Complaint. Assuming that the pre-charge screening results in a decision to prosecute, the next step in the criminal justice process is the filing of charges with the magistrate court. Typically, the initial charging instrument will be called a "complaint." In misdemeanor cases, which may be tried before the magistrate court, the complaint will serve as the charging instrument throughout the proceedings. In felony cases, on the other hand, the complaint serves to set forth the charges only before the magistrate court; an information or indictment will replace the complaint as the charging instrument when the case reaches the general trial court. The complaint ordinarily includes a brief description of the offense and is sworn to by a complainant. The complainant usually will be either the victim or the investigating officer. When an officer-complainant did not observe the offense being committed, but relied on information received from the victim or other witnesses, he will note that the facts alleged in the complaint are based on "information and belief."

In most jurisdictions, at some point between the filing of the complaint and the first appearance (see step 8), the magistrate will conduct an *ex parte* review of the case. The purpose of this review is to ensure that the arrest and complaint are supported by sufficient incriminating information to establish probable cause to believe the defendant committed the crime charged. The magistrate's review may be based on the complaint itself where the complaint alleges the facts establishing probable cause (e.g., that the complainant observed the offense). In other cases, it may be based on a police officer's affidavit setting forth available information establishing probable cause. In some jurisdictions, the magistrate also may base his determination upon a brief oral statement presented by the complainant. If the magistrate finds that probable cause has not been established, he will direct the prosecution to promptly produce more information or release the arrested person. Such instances tend to be quite rare, however.[14]

---

13. Vera Institute, Felony Arrests: Their Prosecution and Disposition in New York City's Courts 6–19 (2d ed. 1981); B. Forst, J. Lucanovic, and S. Cox, What Happens After Arrest? 39 (1977). One factor that often leads to the dismissal of a case that was approved at pre-charge screening is a "change of heart" by the victim. Id. at 23–77. This factor is especially significant for those cases in which the victim is likely to have had a previous acquaintance with the arrestee (a common situation, for example, in aggravated assault cases). See Vera Institute, supra, at 27–42, 65–76.

14. In many states, if the defendant was arrested without a warrant (as is usually the case), the magistrate will issue an arrest warrant after finding probable cause. Since the defendant has already been arrested, the warrant is not being used here for its traditional function of obtaining prior judicial approval for the arrest. Instead, the post-arrest warrant serves simply to provide judicial authorization for continuing to hold the arrestee in custody. In most jurisdictions, the post-arrest issuance of a warrant is viewed as an unnecessary formality, and the magistrate's finding of probable

(h) Step 8: The First Appearance. After the complaint has been filed and reviewed, the arrestee (who is now formally a defendant) is presented before the magistrate. This proceeding before the magistrate usually is described as the "first appearance," although some jurisdictions call it the "initial presentment" or the "arraignment on the warrant." Where the arrested person was released by police on a citation or stationhouse bail, the first appearance will not be scheduled until several days after the arrest. In most instances, however, the arrestee will still be in custody, and state law will require that he be brought before the magistrate without unnecessary delay. Ordinarily, the time consumed in booking, transportation, reviewing the decision to charge, and limited post-arrest investigation makes it unlikely that the arrestee will be presented before the magistrate until at least several hours after his arrest. Thus, if the magistrate court does not have an evening session, a person arrested in the afternoon or evening will not be presented before the magistrate until the next day. If arrested on a Friday or a weekend, he will not be presented until the next Monday, unless the magistrate court has a special weekend session.

The first appearance often is a quite brief proceeding. Initially, the magistrate will make certain that the person before him is the person named in the complaint. The magistrate then will inform the defendant of the charge in the complaint and will note various rights that the defendant may have in further proceedings. The range of rights mentioned will vary from one jurisdiction to another. Commonly, the magistrate will inform the defendant of his right to remain silent and warn him that anything he says in court or to the police may be used against him at trial. The magistrate also will inform the defendant of his right to be represented by counsel and his right to appointed counsel if he is indigent. Although the timing varies, most jurisdictions at least initiate the process of providing counsel for the indigent at the first appearance. The magistrate first will determine that the defendant is indigent and desires the assistance of appointed counsel. The magistrate then will either himself arrange for representation by the public defender or appointed private counsel or notify the judge in charge of appointments.

Other aspects of the first appearance are likely to depend upon whether the defendant is charged with a felony or misdemeanor. In the felony case, the magistrate will advise the defendant of the next step in the process, the preliminary hearing, and will set a date for that hearing unless the defendant desires to waive it. If the defendant is charged with a misdemeanor, he will not be entitled to a preliminary hearing (or a subsequent grand jury review). The misdemeanor charge is triable to the magistrate, and the magistrate therefore can proceed with a misdemeanor case in the same fashion as a general trial court receiving a felony case. For the misdemeanor, the first appearance becomes an arraignment on the complaint, equivalent to the arraignment on the information or indictment in a felony case (see step 12).[15]

---

cause will combine with the complaint to authorize continuing custody.

15. The initial step in the magistrate's arraignment of the misdemeanor defendant involves an explanation of available pleas to the charge stated in the complaint and an entry of a plea to that charge. While most misdemeanor defendants eventually plead guilty, many will not do so at the first appearance since they have not yet had the opportunity to consult with counsel or others (e.g., relatives) whose advice might be sought. They will plead not guilty or will be allowed to defer

entry of their plea to a later date. In a jurisdiction relying primarily on post-charge screening, a substantial percentage of the misdemeanor cases will be reviewed by the prosecutor and dismissed on his motion prior to the defendant's next scheduled court appearance. For the cases that survive this screening, the rate of guilty pleas is likely to be between 80 and 95 percent. For these defendants, the next step in the process is sentencing (see step 15). For the 5 to 20 percent of the surviving cases that go to trial, the next step will be the filing of pretrial motions (see step 13).

The final function of the magistrate at the first appearance is to set bail (i.e., set the conditions under which the defendant can obtain his release from custody pending the final disposition of his case). If the defendant obtained his release previously by posting stationhouse bail, the magistrate will merely review that bail. In felony cases, the defendant ordinarily will still be in custody and the magistrate will be making the initial decision on bail. At one time, bail was limited almost entirely to the posting of cash or a secured bond, purchased from a professional bondsman. Today, the defendant may also be able to obtain his release by depositing with the court cash equal to 10 percent of the amount of the bond set by the magistrate. Indeed, several states make such extensive use of the 10 percent alternative that they have effectively eliminated the role of the professional bondsman. In addition, courts today frequently authorize release upon the defendant's unsecured promise to appear (commonly called "release on personal recognizance" or "personal bond"). In some jurisdictions, as many as one-third of all defendants are released under this procedure. Overall, however, even in jurisdictions that make liberal use of the various bail alternatives, as many as 30 percent of all felony defendants are unable to make bail and therefore remain in jail pending the disposition of their case. In misdemeanor cases, the percentage remaining in custody will be much lower, very often less than 10 percent.

(i) Step 9: Preliminary Hearing. Following the first appearance, the next scheduled step in a felony case ordinarily is the preliminary hearing. In many jurisdictions, however, a substantial portion of the felony caseload will be disposed of during the period (usually one or two weeks) between the first appearance and the scheduled preliminary examination. As mentioned previously, where the primary screening by the prosecutor occurs after charges are filed, a substantial number of felony charges are likely to be dismissed or reduced to a misdemeanor during this period. Even for those felony charges that remain, a preliminary hearing will not necessarily be held. The defendant ordinarily may waive his right to a preliminary hearing, and it is not unusual for a substantial percentage (e.g., 20–30 percent) to waive, usually because they intend to plead guilty. Also, even if the defendant desires a preliminary hearing, state law allows the prosecutor to bypass the hearing in a significant number of states.[16]

Where the preliminary hearing is held, it will provide, like grand jury review, a screening of the decision to charge by a neutral body. In the preliminary hearing, that neutral body is the magistrate, who must determine whether, on the evidence presented, there is probable cause to believe that defendant committed the crime charged. Ordinarily, the magistrate will already have determined that probable cause exists as part of the *ex parte* screening of the complaint (see step 7). The preliminary hearing, however, provides screening in an adversary proceeding in which both sides are represented by counsel. Jurisdictions vary in the evidentiary rules applicable to the preliminary hearing, but most require that the parties rely primarily on live witnesses rather than affidavits. Typically, the prosecution will present its key witnesses and the defense will limit its response to the cross-examination of those witnesses. The defendant has the right to present his own

---

16. In almost all of the "indictment jurisdictions" (see step 10), the prosecutor can bypass the preliminary hearing by taking the case directly before the grand jury. In the federal courts, this route is taken so frequently that preliminary hearings are a rarity in many districts. In the typical indictment jurisdiction, however, preliminary hearings are bypassed only in a limited class of cases (e.g., murder prosecutions), and most felony cases go through both a preliminary hearing and grand jury screening. In several indictment states, almost all cases are given this double review. In information states (see step 11), since alternative screening by the grand jury is not utilized, the felony defendant commonly has a right to a preliminary hearing.

evidence at the hearing, but traditional defense strategy advises against subjecting defense witnesses to prosecution cross-examination in any pretrial proceeding.

If the magistrate concludes that the evidence presented establishes probable cause, he will "bind the case over" to the next stage in the proceedings. In an indictment jurisdiction (see step 10), the case is boundover to the grand jury, and in a jurisdiction that permits the direct filing of an information (see step 11), the case is boundover directly to the general trial court. If the magistrate finds that the probable cause supports only a misdemeanor charge, he will reject the felony charge and allow the prosecutor to substitute the lower charge, which will then be set for trial in the magistrate court. If the magistrate finds that the prosecution's evidence does not support any charge, he will order that the defendant be released. The rate of dismissals at the preliminary hearing quite naturally varies with the degree of previous screening exercised by the prosecutor. In a jurisdiction with fairly extensive screening, the percentage of dismissals is likely to fall in the range of 5 to 15 percent of the cases heard.

(j) **Step 10: Grand Jury Review.** Although all American jurisdictions still have provisions authorizing grand jury screening of felony charges, such screening is mandated only in those states requiring felony prosecutions to be instituted by an indictment, a charging instrument issued by the grand jury. About half of the states currently require grand jury indictments for at least some classes of felony prosecutions. In several of these "indictment states," prosecution by indictment is required only for felonies subject to the most severe punishment (life imprisonment and capital punishment). In the remaining indictment jurisdictions, including the federal system, a grand jury indictment is required in all felony prosecutions (unless waived by the defendant). If there has been a preliminary hearing, the magistrate's decision at that hearing is not binding on the grand jury. It can reject prosecution notwithstanding a preliminary hearing bindover, or reinstitute prosecution even though the magistrate concluded that the prosecution's evidence was inadequate.

The grand jury is composed of a group of private citizens who are selected to review cases presented over a term that may range from one to several months. Traditionally the grand jury consisted of 23 persons with the favorable vote of a majority needed to indict. Today, many states use a somewhat smaller grand jury (e.g., 12) and some require more than a simple majority to indict. As in the case of the magistrate at the preliminary hearing, the primary function of the grand jury is to determine whether there is sufficient evidence to justify a trial on the charge sought by the prosecution. The grand jury, however, participates in a screening process quite different from the preliminary hearing. It meets in a closed session and hears only the evidence presented by the prosecution. The defendant has no right to offer his own evidence or to be present during grand jury proceedings. If a majority of the grand jurors conclude that the prosecution's evidence is sufficient, the grand jury will issue the indictment requested by the prosecutor. The indictment will set forth a brief description of the offense charged, and the grand jury's approval of that charge will be indicated by its designation of the indictment as a "true bill." If the grand jury majority refuses to approve a proposed indictment, the charges against the defendant will be dismissed. In most indictment jurisdictions, grand juries refuse to indict in only a small percentage (e.g., 3 to 8 percent) of the cases presented before them.

(k) **Step 11: The Filing of the Indictment or Information.** If an indictment is issued, it will be filed with the general trial court and will replace the complaint as the accusatory instrument in the case. Where grand jury review either is not required or has been waived in the particular case, an information will be filed with the trial court. Like the indictment, the information is a charging instrument which replaces the complaint, but it is issued by the prosecutor rather than the grand jury. Approximately half of the states do not require prosecution by indictment, and prosecutors in these jurisdictions proceed by information in the vast majority of their prosecutions. In these "information states," the charge in the information ordinarily must be supported by a preliminary hearing bindover (unless the preliminary hearing was waived).

(*l*) **Step 12: Arraignment on the Information or Indictment.** After the indictment or information has been filed, the defendant is arraigned—i.e., he is brought before the trial court, informed of the charges against him, and asked to enter a plea of guilty, not guilty, or, as is permitted under some circumstances, *nolo contendere*. Most of the cases that reach the arraignment stage will not go to trial. Depending upon the quality of pre-arraignment screening, anywhere from 10 to 30 percent of the cases will be dismissed as a result of a *nolle prosequi* or a successful defense motion. Of the remaining felony cases, 70 to 90 percent will be resolved by a guilty plea in most jurisdictions.[17] Whether the guilty plea rate in a particular jurisdiction is closer to 70 percent or 90 percent depends upon several factors. One very significant variable may be the extent to which the prosecutor is willing to plea bargain—i.e., grant concessions in return for a guilty plea. While the vast majority of prosecutors make substantial use of plea bargaining, they vary markedly both as to the type of cases in which they will grant major concessions and as to the nature of those concessions. One of the most common concessions is the reduction of the offense charged in return for a guilty plea to a lesser offense. Thus, in a jurisdiction with extensive plea bargaining, it is not unusual to find that only a small percentage of the defendants plead guilty to the original charge. In other jurisdictions, prosecutors will offer concessions that deal directly with the sentence as opposed to the level of the charge. Such sentencing concessions often take the form of a prosecution recommendation of a lenient sentence (which will be given great weight by the sentencing judge) or a promise of a specific sentence agreed to by the judge.

(m) **Step 13: Pretrial Motions.** In most jurisdictions, a broad range of objections must be raised by a pretrial motion. Those motions commonly present challenges to the institution of the prosecution (e.g., claims regarding the grand jury), attacks upon the sufficiency of the charging instrument, requests for discovery of the prosecution's evidence, and requests for the suppression of evidence allegedly obtained through a constitutional violation. While some pretrial motions are made only by defendants who intend to go to trial, other motions are advanced almost as frequently by defendants expecting to plead guilty even if the motion succeeds. Nevertheless, pretrial motions are likely to be made in no more than 10 percent of all felony cases that reach the trial court. In misdemeanor cases, pretrial motions may be made in less than one percent of the cases before the magistrate court. The use of pretrial motions varies, of course, with the nature of the case. In narcotics cases, for example, motions to suppress are quite common. In the typical forgery case, on the other hand, pretrial motions of any type are quite rare.

As a group, pretrial motions are likely to result in the dismissal of not substantially more than 5 percent of all of the felony cases before the trial judge (and they are likely to

---

17. There are several jurisdictions, however, which present a quite different pattern. In Baltimore, for example, defendants commonly demand trial, but waive their right to jury trial. The guilty plea rate (excluding dismissals) is quite low (e.g., 15 percent), but the percentage of jury trials is even lower. See McIntyre and Lippman, Prosecutors and Early Dispositions of Felony Cases, 56 A.B.A.J. 1154 (1970) (also noting substantial variations among other urban districts in post-arraignment dismissals, guilty pleas, and jury and bench trials).

have even less impact on the misdemeanor docket). The pretrial motion most likely to produce a dismissal is the motion to suppress. Quite frequently, if the defendant gains suppression of unconstitutionally obtained evidence, there will be insufficient remaining evidence to continue with the prosecution.

(n) Step 14: The Trial. As noted previously, most felony and misdemeanor cases are likely to be disposed of either by a guilty plea or by a dismissal. Quite commonly, only 10 to 15 percent of the felony cases that reach the trial court actually will go to trial. Misdemeanor cases tend to have an even lower trial rate. Magistrate courts often have trials in less than 5 percent of the cases presented before them. Most trials will not be lengthy affairs. Misdemeanor trials typically last less than one day. Felony trials may occupy somewhat more time, particularly when tried to a jury, but most will be completed within a few days.

In all jurisdictions, the defendant will have a right to a jury trial for all felony offenses and for misdemeanors punishable by more than 6 months imprisonment (although the jury trial right in the misdemeanor cases may exist only through a trial *de novo*). Most states also provide a jury trial for lesser misdemeanors as well. Juries traditionally were composed of 12 persons, but many states now utilize 6 person juries in misdemeanor cases and several use the smaller juries in non-capital felony cases as well. Of course, the right to a jury trial can be waived, and in most jurisdictions, a significant number of defendants will waive the jury in favor of a bench trial. Over the country as a whole, however, a clear majority (perhaps 60–65 percent) of all felony trials are tried to a jury. In several jurisdictions, the percentage of jury trials comes close to 80 percent, although in at least one state, it is as low as 13 percent. In misdemeanor cases, bench trials often are in the majority even in jurisdictions that extend the defendant's jury trial right to all misdemeanors. In all but a few jurisdictions, the jury verdict in misdemeanor and felony cases, whether for acquittal or conviction, must be unanimous. Where the jurors cannot agree, no verdict is entered and the case may be retried. Such "hung juries" occur in a small percentage of cases (e.g., 3–6 percent).

The criminal trial resembles the civil trial in many respects. There are, however, several distinguishing features that are either unique to criminal trials or of special importance in such trials. These include (1) the presumption of defendant's innocence, (2) the requirement of proof beyond a reasonable doubt, (3) the right of the defendant not to take the stand, (4) the exclusion of evidence obtained by the state in an illegal manner, and (5) the more frequent use of incriminating statements of defendants. In most jurisdictions, the misdemeanor trial will be almost indistinguishable from a felony trial. In some jurisdictions, however, misdemeanor trials tend to be less formal, with rules of evidence applied in a rather loose fashion.

Whether a criminal case is tried to the bench or to a jury, the odds favor conviction over acquittal. The acquittal rate for felonies generally does not exceed one-third. At the misdemeanor level, the rate of acquittals often is somewhat lower. A substantial variation exists, however, among the different types of crimes. Acquittal rates for rape and robbery tend to be considerably higher, for example, than acquittal rates for forgery or assault. Where the offense is one that is not likely to produce either an offender caught "red-handed," more than one eyewitness, or contraband discovered in the defendant's possession, the acquittal rate for the offense is likely to be higher than the average for offenses generally.

(o) Step 15: Sentencing. If the defendant pleads guilty or is found guilty at trial, the judge will enter a judgment of conviction and set the case for sentencing. The structure of the sentence and the discretion of the judge in choosing among sentencing alternatives will be controlled by statute. For misdemeanors a judge ordinarily has discretion to impose a fine, probation, suspended sentence, or fixed jail term not to exceed a statutorily prescribed maximum. For felony offenses, the choice ordinarily is between imprisonment and probation although the legislature is likely to have prohibited probation for some offenses. When imprisonment is imposed, a majority of the states require that the sentence be indeterminate, i.e., the court sets a minimum and maximum term, with the parole board determining the actual release date between the minimum and maximum. State law will set the highest maximum sentence permissible for the particular crime and will also require that the minimum be no greater than a certain percentage (e.g., one-half) of the maximum. Some jurisdictions also impose other restrictions upon the court (e.g., sentencing guidelines) in its setting of the maximum and minimum terms. In recent years, many states have moved from indeterminate to determinate prison sentences for most felonies. Under determinate sentencing, the judge sets a single fixed term of imprisonment, which must fall within a fairly narrow range set by the legislature for the particular crime. This sentencing structure eliminates earlier parole release except for limited good-behavior credits.

Among misdemeanor convictions, there often is a substantial difference in the pattern of sentences for those cases that were originally filed as misdemeanors and those that started as felonies but were reduced to misdemeanors as part of a plea bargain. In the former group, the vast majority of the defendants will be fined, placed on probation, or receive a suspended sentence. Where the initial charge was at a felony level, the defendant convicted of a misdemeanor is more likely to receive a jail sentence (often combined with probation). Defendants convicted on felony charges also are likely to be incarcerated for at least a short period. Prison sentences usually are imposed in anywhere from one-third to one-half of the felony convictions. Many jurisdictions also make extensive use of short jail sentences, combined with probation, in felony cases. Of course, the likelihood of incarceration and the length of incarceration will vary with the seriousness of the offense for which conviction was obtained (and, in guilty plea cases, often the seriousness of the original charge).

(p) Step 16: Appeals. In felony cases, initial appeals will be taken to the intermediate appellate court or to the state supreme court if there is no intermediate appellate court. Initial appeals in misdemeanor cases will be taken to the general trial court, and in some jurisdictions will consist of a trial *de novo.* Although all convicted defendants are entitled to appeal their convictions, appeals are taken predominantly by those defendants who were sentenced to imprisonment. In several states, a fairly substantial portion of felony appeals (perhaps as many as 20 percent) come from imprisoned defendants who pled guilty and are challenging their pleas. Most felony appeals, however, are taken by imprisoned defendants who are seeking review of a trial conviction. In some jurisdictions, as many as 90 percent of the defendants who were convicted after trial and sentenced to imprisonment will appeal their convictions. Even with almost automatic appeals by this group of defendants, however, the total number of felony appeals is still not likely to exceed 15 percent of all felony convictions. In misdemeanor cases, the appeal rate is much lower.

The rate of reversals on appeal varies with the particular appellate court, but tends to fall within the range of 10 to 20 percent of the cases heard. In many jurisdictions, the most common objection raised on appeal is the trial court's admission of evidence obtained through an allegedly unconstitutional search. That objection also provides the most common basis for reversal. Other grounds raised quite frequently (but with much less success) are the insufficiency of the evidence, the incompetency of counsel, constitutional violations in identification procedures, and challenges to the admission of defendant's incriminating statements made to the police.

(q) Step 17: Postconviction Remedies. After the appellate process is exhausted, imprisoned defendants may be able to use postconviction remedies to challenge their convictions on limited grounds. In particular, federal postconviction remedies allow state as well as federal prisoners to challenge their convictions in the federal courts on certain constitutional grounds. The federal district courts receive roughly 9,000 such postconviction applications each year. Relief is granted on less than 4 percent of these petitions, however, and the relief often is limited to requiring a further hearing. In the state systems, postconviction remedies are used far less frequently.

(r) The Criminal Justice Funnel. If one drew a diagram of the criminal justice process, charting the numbers of persons processed at each stage, the shape of the diagram would be roughly that of a funnel. A great number of persons are subjected to the process at its initial stage (pre-arrest investigation), and at each subsequent stage, fewer and fewer persons are involved. There are more persons investigated as suspects than arrested, more persons arrested than charged, more persons charged than finally brought to adjudication, more persons adjudicated than found guilty, and more persons found guilty than subjected to incarceration. As the caseload moves through it, the criminal justice process sifts out cases in much the same manner as a sieve. This "sieve effect" or "funnel analogy" is aptly illustrated by a rough model of the distribution of a cross-section of felony cases in a typical jurisdiction. While our model probably is not duplicated in any particular jurisdiction, available figures suggest it is roughly approximated in many urban communities.

We start with 5,000 possible felonies that come to the attention of the police either through citizen complaint or officer observations. Although the investigation of some of these possible felonies will not point to any suspects, the investigation of others will require police encounters with more than one suspect. As a result, the police investigation process for 5,000 felonies can readily produce more than 5,000 police-suspect encounters. Assuming a typical mix of reported felonies (i.e., with a heavy emphasis on property crimes), the investigation of the 5,000 felonies is likely to lead to the arrest of no more than 1,500 persons. Out of this group of arrestees, approximately 400 will be juveniles. They will be transferred to the juvenile process, leaving 1,100 adult arrestees for possible criminal prosecution. After the police and prosecutor have reviewed the cases against these arrestees, about 350 will be released without any charges being pressed. In an additional 150 cases, the charges will be reduced to misdemeanors. Thus, of 1,500 felony arrestees, only 600 will have felony charges filed against them.

The 600 felony charges will then be screened at preliminary hearings or grand jury proceedings, and will be subject to challenge by defense motions of various sorts. These procedures are likely to result in the dismissal of roughly 50 cases. Still another 50 cases may be dismissed by the prosecutor as a result of his review of the case once it reaches the trial court. Of the 500 felony cases that are left, approximately 400 will be resolved by guilty pleas. Perhaps half of those pleas will be to misdemeanor charges, and the others will be to the felony charged or to a lesser felony. There remain roughly 100 felony cases that will go to trial. Approximately 70 of the trials will result in convictions, although not necessarily for felonies.

In the end, of the 1,100 adult arrestees, approximately 250 will be convicted on a felony charge (including felonies lesser than that originally charged) and 300 will be convicted of misdemeanor charges. Of the 550 arrestees eventually convicted, as many as 250 may receive a sentence that includes some incarceration, but for most of the 250, incarceration will be limited to a short jail term, typically combined with probation. Approximately 100 will be sentenced to prison terms.

For a detailed treatment of the legal course through which a criminal proceeding passes, from detection and initial investigation of a crime through post-conviction review, see LaFave and Israel's Criminal Procedure, Hornbook Series, Student Edition (West Publishing Company, St. Paul, 1985), with current annual pocket part, ... from pages 2–20 of which this Introduction is drawn.

*

THE UNITED STATES CONSTITUTION

SELECTED PROVISIONS OF THE UNITED STATES CONSTITUTION

*

INTRODUCTION

*Reprinted from Israel and LaFave, Criminal Procedure:
Constitutional Limitations, 4th Ed. (1988).*

The Constitution and Criminal Procedure

To understand how constitutional limitations came to play such a significant role in the legal regulation of the criminal justice process, one must start with the Constitution itself. As originally proposed, the Constitution had only a few provisions relating to the administration of criminal law. But with the addition of the Bill of Rights, designed to ensure that the federal government did not encroach upon the rights of individuals, the criminal justice process took on a special significance in the Constitution.

Of the 23 separate rights noted in the first eight Amendments, 12 concern criminal procedure. The Fourth Amendment guarantees the right of the people to be secure against unreasonable searches and seizures and prohibits the issuance of warrants unless certain conditions are met. The Fifth Amendment requires prosecution by grand jury indictment for all infamous crimes (excepting certain military prosecutions) and prohibits placing a person "twice in jeopardy" or compelling him to be a "witness against himself." The Sixth Amendment lists several rights that apply "in all criminal prosecutions"—the rights to a speedy trial, to a public trial, to an impartial jury of the state and district in which the crime was committed, to notice of the "nature and cause of the accusation," to confrontation of opposing witnesses, to compulsory process for obtaining favorable witnesses, and to the assistance of counsel. The Eighth Amendment adds a prohibition against requiring excessive bail. Finally, aside from these guarantees directed specifically at criminal procedure, there is the due process clause of Fifth Amendment. That clause encompasses the criminal justice process, along with other legal processes, in its general prohibition against the "deprivat[ion] of life, liberty or property without due process of law."

Taken together, the various Bill of Rights provisions offer an obvious potential for extensive constitutional regulation of the criminal justice process. Constitutional provisions, however, are not self-defining. Their ultimate impact is dependent, in large part, upon how they are interpreted by the judiciary in the course of adjudicating individual cases. Thus, it was not until the Supreme Court came to adopt certain critical interpretations of the Constitution's criminal procedure guarantees that the potential for substantial constitutionalization of the criminal justice process was realized.

Constitutionalization and Judicial Interpretation

Two important doctrinal developments were prerequisites to establishing, through Supreme Court rulings, extensive constitutional regulation of the nation's criminal justice procedures. First, the relevant guarantees in the Bill of Rights had to be made applicable in large part to state proceedings. Although federal criminal jurisdiction has been expanding over the years, more than 95% of all prosecutions still are brought in the state systems. For the Constitution to have a major impact upon criminal justice administration, its criminal procedure provisions had to be held applicable to state as well as federal proceedings. That result eventually was reached through various Supreme Court rulings interpreting the Fourteenth Amendment's due process clause. Those rulings did not come, however, until the Warren Court (i.e., the Court of Chief Justice Earl Warren's tenure) adopted the "selective incorporation" interpretation of the Fourteenth Amendment in the 1960's, almost 100 years after the adoption of the Fourteenth Amendment.

The second major doctrinal prerequisite for the extensive constitutionalization of criminal procedure was adoption of expansive interpretations of individual guarantees. Even though applied to the states, the Bill of Rights guarantees, if interpreted narrowly, would have only a limited impact upon the criminal justice process. A narrow construction of each of the guarantees would produce a constitutional regulatory scheme that governs only a small portion of the total process and imposes there limitations fairly restricted in scope and unlikely to have a significant impact upon traditional state and federal criminal justice practices. Consider, for example, the Fifth Amendment clause stating that "no person * * * shall be compelled in any criminal case to be a witness against himself." Read narrowly, that provision might be said simply to prohibit the state from compelling the defendant to testify in his criminal trial as to any incriminating aspects of his involvement in the offense charged. Such an interpretation would make constitutional an important structural element of an accusatorial process, but its significance would be limited to the trial, and even then, it would only restate a prohibition well accepted in all of the states and the federal system. The Supreme Court has, in fact, adopted a much broader view of the self-incrimination privilege, a view that gives rise to a wide-range of constitutional limitations. Reading the privilege to be "as broad as the mischief against which it seeks to guard," *Counselman v. Hitchcock* (1892), the Court has construed the self-incrimination clause to: guarantee to the accused an absolute right not to give any testimony at his trial; bar procedural restrictions that require an early decision as to the exercise of that right not to testify; prohibit comment by the prosecutor upon the defendant's failure to testify; prohibit the use of compulsory process in other proceedings besides the criminal trial (e.g., grand jury proceedings) to compel a witness to give testimony that could conceivably be used against that witness in a later criminal prosecution; prohibit admission at trial of statements of the accused obtained by the state through the use of means deemed coercive, such as the threat of removal from public office, *Garrity v. N.J.* (1967); prohibit admission at trial of statements of the accused given in response to custodial interrogation by police unless the accused had been advised of certain rights (including the right to remain silent) and voluntarily waived those rights; and prohibit the compulsory production of personal documents under some circumstances.

As evidenced by the Court's Fifth Amendment rulings, an expansive interpretation of a constitutional guarantee can result in the establishment of restrictions that have a bearing upon numerous aspects of the process. Such an interpretation can also produce, as did the Court's Fifth Amendment rulings on custodial interrogation, the prescription of a series of procedures designed to safeguard the constitutional right. So too, when expansive interpretations of various different constitutional guarantees are combined, the end product can be a series of interrelated constitutional limitations that extend throughout the process.

The adoption of expansive interpretations of the Constitution's criminal procedure guarantees is not a new phenomenon. *Counselman*, supra, held in 1892 that the prohibition against compulsory self-incrimination was not limited to barring prosecution compulsion of defendant's testimony at trial but extended to "any proceeding" in which a witness would otherwise be compelled to give testimony that might incriminate him in a subsequent criminal case. Indeed, it is debatable whether any Supreme Court ruling has adopted a broader view of the Fourth Amendment than did *Boyd v. U.S.* (1886), also decided before the turn of the century. Over the first century and a half of constitutional interpretation, however, Supreme Court opinions adopting strikingly expansive interpretations of criminal procedure guarantees were fairly infrequent. It was not until the 1960's—the same period that saw the application of the various Bill of Rights guarantees to the states—that expansive rulings became relatively commonplace. Application of the criminal procedure guarantees to state proceedings gave the Court many more opportunities to rule on the scope of those guarantees, and in numerous instances, the Court responded with an expansive, far reaching interpretation of the particular guarantee.

Even during the Warren Court period of the 1960's, which might be described as the heyday of expansionist interpretation, not every ruling adopted an especially broad view of the particular criminal procedure guarantee before the Court. Moreover, during the 1970's and 1980's, the results were much more mixed. Decisions during that period not infrequently refused to expand upon broad readings of guarantees adopted by the Warren Court, and in several instances, partially withdrew from those rulings. Quite often, however, such changes in direction dealt with issues at the margin or edges of the prior interpretation rather than core concepts, which remained unchallenged. Also, still other decisions of the 1970's and 1980's adopted new, expansive interpretations applicable to areas barely touched by earlier rulings, or further extended constitutional limitations consistent with expansive Warren Court rulings.

It should be kept in mind, of course, that any characterization of a Supreme Court ruling as "expansive" or "narrow" rests, in considerable part, upon the eyes of the beholder. A decision that one observer characterizes as broadly expansive because it goes far beyond previous rulings will be seen by another as simply taking a minor step beyond a very restricted starting point because it falls short of rejecting the conceptual grounding of those earlier rulings and leaves the law with a less than sweeping view of the right involved. A decision that some would characterize as a major retreat from past expansive rulings others would characterize as largely consistent with those rulings but simply refusing to extend them at the edges.

For a succinct analysis of the constitutional standards of major current significance governing criminal procedure, see Israel and LaFave's Criminal Procedure in a Nutshell: Constitutional Limitations, 4th Ed., Nutshell Series (West Publishing Company, St. Paul, 1988) ... from pages 2–9 of which this Introduction is drawn.

SELECTED PROVISIONS OF THE UNITED STATES CONSTITUTION

Preamble

We the People of the United States, in Order to form a more perfect Union, establish Justice, insure domestic Tranquility, provide for the common defence, promote the general Welfare, and secure the Blessings of Liberty to ourselves and our Posterity, do ordain and establish this Constitution for the United States of America.

Article I

Section 1. All legislative Powers herein granted shall be vested in a Congress of the United States, which shall consist of a Senate and House of Representatives.

. . .

[6] The Senate shall have the sole Power to try all Impeachments. When sitting for that Purpose, they shall be on Oath or Affirmation.

When the President of the United States is tried, the Chief Justice shall preside: And no Person shall be convicted without the Concurrence of two thirds of the Members present.

[7] Judgment in Cases of Impeachment shall not extend further than to removal from Office, and disqualification to hold and enjoy any Office of Honor, Trust, or Profit under the United States: but the Party convicted shall nevertheless be liable and subject to Indictment, Trial, Judgment, and Punishment, according to Law.

. . .

Section 6. [1] The Senators and Representatives shall receive a Compensation for their Services, to be ascertained by Law, and paid out of the Treasury of the United States. They shall in all Cases, except Treason, Felony and Breach of the Peace be privileged from Arrest during their Attendance at the Session of their respective Houses, and in going to and returning from the same; and for any Speech or Debate in either House, they shall not be questioned in any other Place.

. . .

Section 8. [1] The Congress shall have Power To lay and collect Taxes, Duties, Imposts and Excises, to pay the Debts and provide for the common Defence and general Welfare of the United States; but all Duties, Imposts and Excises shall be uniform throughout the United States;

. . .

[6] To provide for the Punishment of counterfeiting the Securities and current Coin of the United States;

. . .

[9] To constitute Tribunals inferior to the supreme Court;

[10] To define and punish Piracies and Felonies committed on the high Seas, and Offenses against the Law of Nations;

. . .

[17] To exercise exclusive Legislation in all Cases whatsoever, over such District (not exceeding ten Miles square) as may, by Cession of particular States, and the Acceptance of Congress, become the Seat of the Government of the United States, and to exercise like Authority over all Places purchased by the Consent of the Legislature of the State in which the Same shall be, for the Erection of Forts, Magazines, Arsenals, dock-Yards, and other needful Buildings;—And

[18] To make all Laws which shall be necessary and proper for carrying into Execution the foregoing Powers, and all other Powers vested by this Constitution in the Government of the United States, or in any Department or Officer thereof.

Section 9. . . .

[2] The privilege of the Writ of Habeas Corpus shall not be suspended, unless when in Cases of Rebellion or Invasion the public Safety may require it.

[3] No Bill of Attainder or ex post facto Law shall be passed.

. . .

Section 10. [1] No State shall enter into any Treaty, Alliance, or Confederation; grant Letters of Marque and Reprisal; coin Money; emit Bills of Credit; make any Thing but gold and silver Coin a Tender in Payment of Debts; pass any Bill of Attainder, ex post facto Law, or Law impairing the Obligation of Contracts, or grant any Title of Nobility.

. . .

Article II

Section 1. [1] The executive Power shall be vested in a President of the United States of America. . . .

. . .

[8] Before he enter on the Execution of his Office, he shall take the following Oath or Affirmation: "I do solemnly swear (or affirm) that I will faithfully execute the Office of President of the United States, and will to the best of my Ability, preserve, protect and defend the Constitution of the United States."

Section 2. [1] The President shall be Commander in Chief of the Army and Navy of the United States, and of the militia of the several States, when called into the actual Service of the United States; he may require the Opinion, in writing, of the principal Officer in each of the Executive Departments, upon any Subject relating to the Duties of their respective Offices, and he shall have Power to grant Reprieves and Pardons for Offenses against the United States, except in Cases of Impeachment.

[2] He shall have Power, by and with the Advice and Consent of the Senate to make Treaties, provided two thirds of the Senators present concur; and he shall nominate, and by and with the Advice and Consent of the Senate, shall appoint Ambassadors, other public Ministers and Consuls, Judges of the supreme Court, and all other Officers of the United States, whose Appointments are not herein otherwise provided for, and which shall be established by Law; but the Congress may by Law vest the Appointment of such inferior Officers, as they think proper, in the President alone, in the Courts of Law, or in the Heads of Departments.

[3] The President shall have Power to fill up all Vacancies that may happen during the Recess of the Senate, by granting Commissions which shall expire at the End of their next Session.

Section 3. He shall from time to time give to the Congress Information of the State of the Union, and recommend to their Consideration such Measures as he shall judge necessary and expedient; he may, on extraordinary Occasions, convene both Houses, or either of them, and in Case of Disagreement between them, with Respect to the Time of Adjournment, he may adjourn them to such Time as he shall think proper; he shall receive Ambassadors and other public Ministers; he shall take Care that the Laws be faithfully executed, and shall Commission all the Officers of the United States.

Section 4. The President, Vice President and all civil Officers of the United States, shall be removed from Office on Impeachment for, and Conviction of, Treason, Bribery, or other high Crimes and Misdemeanors.

Article III

Section 1. The judicial Power of the United States, shall be vested in one supreme Court, and in such inferior Courts as the Congress may from time to time ordain and establish. The Judges, both of the supreme and inferior Courts, shall hold their Offices during good Behaviour, and shall, at stated Times, receive for their Services a Compensation, which shall not be diminished during their Continuance in Office.

Section 2. [1] The judicial Power shall extend to all Cases, in Law and Equity, arising under this Constitution, the Laws of the United States, and Treaties made, or which shall be made, under their Authority;—to all Cases affecting Ambassadors, other public Ministers and Consuls;—to all Cases of admiralty and maritime Jurisdiction;—to Controversies to which the United States shall be a Party;—to Controversies between two or more States;—between a State and Citizens of another State;—between Citizens of different States;—between Citizens of the same State claiming Lands under the Grants of different States, and between a State, or the Citizens thereof, and foreign States, Citizens or Subjects.

[2] In all Cases affecting Ambassadors, other public Ministers and Consuls, and those in which a State shall be a Party, the supreme Court shall have original Jurisdiction. In all the other Cases before mentioned, the supreme Court shall have appellate Jurisdiction, both as to Law and Fact, with such Exceptions, and under such Regulations as the Congress shall make.

[3] The trial of all Crimes, except in Cases of Impeachment, shall be by Jury; and such Trial shall be held in the State where the said Crimes shall have been committed; but when not committed within any State, the Trial shall be at such Place or Places as the Congress may by Law have directed.

Section 3. [1] Treason against the United States, shall consist only in levying War against them, or, in adhering to their Enemies, giving them Aid and Comfort. No Person shall be convicted of Treason unless on the Testimony of two Witnesses to the same overt Act, or on Confession in open Court.

[2] The Congress shall have Power to declare the Punishment of Treason, but no Attainder of Treason shall work Corruption of Blood, or Forfeiture except during the Life of the Person attainted.

Article IV

Section 1. Full Faith and Credit shall be given in each State to the public Acts, Records, and judicial Proceedings of every other State. And the Congress may by general Laws prescribe the Manner in which such Acts, Records and Proceedings shall be proved, and the Effect thereof.

Section 2. [1] The Citizens of each State shall be entitled to all Privileges and Immunities of Citizens in the several States.

[2] A Person charged in any State with Treason, Felony, or other Crime, who shall flee from Justice, and be found in another State, shall on

demand of the executive Authority of the State from which he fled, be delivered up, to be removed to the State having Jurisdiction of the Crime.

[3] No Person held to Service or Labour in one State, under the Laws thereof, escaping into another, shall, in Consequence of any Law or Regulation therein, be discharged from such Service or Labour, but shall be delivered up on Claim of the Party to whom such Service or Labour may be due.

Section 3. ...

[2] The Congress shall have Power to dispose of and make all needful Rules and Regulations respecting the Territory or other Property belonging to the United States; and nothing in this Constitution shall be so construed as to Prejudice any Claims of the United States, or of any particular State.

Section 4. The United States shall guarantee to every State in this Union a Republican Form of Government, and shall protect each of them against Invasion; and on Application of the Legislature, or of the Executive (when the Legislature cannot be convened) against domestic Violence.

Article V

The Congress, whenever two thirds of both Houses shall deem it necessary, shall propose Amendments to this Constitution, or, on the Application of the Legislatures of two thirds of the several States, shall call a Convention for proposing Amendments, which, in either Case, shall be valid to all Intents and Purposes, as part of this Constitution, when ratified by the Legislatures of three fourths of the several States, or by Conventions in three fourths thereof, as the one or the other Mode of Ratification may be proposed by the Congress; Provided that no Amendment which may be made prior to the Year One thousand eight hundred and eight shall in any Manner affect the first and fourth Clauses in the Ninth Section of the first Article; and that no State, without its Consent, shall be deprived of its equal Suffrage in the Senate.

Article VI

. . .

[2] This Constitution, and the Laws of the United States which shall be made in Pursuance

thereof; and all Treaties made, or which shall be made, under the Authority of the United States, shall be the supreme Law of the Land; and the Judges in every State shall be bound thereby, any Thing in the Constitution or Laws of any State to the Contrary notwithstanding.

[3] The Senators and Representatives before mentioned, and the Members of the several State Legislatures, and all executive and judicial Officers, both of the United States and of the several States, shall be bound by Oath or Affirmation, to support this Constitution; but no religious Test shall ever be required as a Qualification to any Office or public Trust under the United States.

Article VII

The Ratification of the Conventions of nine States shall be sufficient for the Establishment of this Constitution between the States so ratifying the Same.

ARTICLES IN ADDITION TO, AND AMENDMENT OF, THE CONSTITUTION OF THE UNITED STATES OF AMERICA, PROPOSED BY CONGRESS, AND RATIFIED BY THE LEGISLATURES OF THE SEVERAL STATES PURSUANT TO THE FIFTH ARTICLE OF THE ORIGINAL CONSTITUTION.

Amendment I [1791]

Congress shall make no law respecting an establishment of religion, or prohibiting the free exercise thereof; or abridging the freedom of speech, or of the press; or the right of the people peaceably to assemble, and to petition the Government for a redress of grievances.

Amendment II [1791]

A well regulated Militia, being necessary to the security of a free State, the right of the people to keep and bear Arms, shall not be infringed.

Amendment III [1791]

No Soldier shall, in time of peace be quartered in any house, without the consent of the Owner, nor in time of war, but in a manner to be prescribed by law.

Amendment IV [1791]

The right of the people to be secure in their persons, houses, papers, and effects, against unreasonable searches and seizures, shall not be violated, and no Warrants shall issue, but upon probable cause, supported by Oath or affirmation, and particularly describing the place to be searched, and the persons or things to be seized.

Amendment V [1791]

No person shall be held to answer for a capital, or otherwise infamous crime, unless on a presentment or indictment of a Grand Jury, except in cases arising in the land or naval forces, or in the Militia, when in actual service in time of War or public danger; nor shall any person be subject for the same offence to be twice put in jeopardy of life or limb; nor shall be compelled in any criminal case to be a witness against himself, nor be deprived of life, liberty, or property, without due process of law; nor shall private property be taken for public use, without just compensation.

Amendment VI [1791]

In all criminal prosecutions, the accused shall enjoy the right to a speedy and public trial, by an impartial jury of the State and district wherein the crime shall have been committed, which district shall have been previously ascertained by law, and to be informed of the nature and cause of the accusation; to be confronted with the witnesses against him; to have compulsory process for obtaining witnesses in his favor, and to have the Assistance of Counsel for his defence.

Amendment VII [1791]

In Suits at common law, where the value in controversy shall exceed twenty dollars, the right of trial by jury shall be preserved, and no fact tried by jury, shall be otherwise re-examined in any Court of the United States, than according to the rules of the common law.

Amendment VIII [1791]

Excessive bail shall not be required, nor excessive fines imposed, nor cruel and unusual punishments inflicted.

Amendment IX [1791]

The enumeration in the Constitution, of certain rights, shall not be construed to deny or disparage others retained by the people.

Amendment X [1791]

The powers not delegated to the United States by the Constitution, nor prohibited by it to the States, are reserved to the States respectively, or to the people.

. . .

Amendment XIII [1865]

Section 1. Neither slavery nor involuntary servitude, except as a punishment for crime whereof the party shall have been duly convicted, shall exist within the United States, or any place subject to their jurisdiction.

Section 2. Congress shall have power to enforce this article by appropriate legislation.

Amendment XIV [1868]

Section 1. All persons born or naturalized in the United States, and subject to the jurisdiction thereof, are citizens of the United States and of the State wherein they reside. No State shall make or enforce any law which shall abridge the privileges or immunities of citizens of the United States; nor shall any State deprive any person of life, liberty, or property, without due process of law; nor deny to any person within its jurisdiction the equal protection of the laws.

Section 2. Representatives shall be apportioned among the several States according to their respective numbers, counting the whole number of persons in each State, excluding Indians not taxed. But when the right to vote at any election for the choice of electors for President and Vice President of the United States, Representatives in Congress, the Executive and Judicial officers of a State, or the members of the Legislature thereof, is denied to any of the male inhabitants of such State, being twenty-one years of age, and citizens of the United States, or in any way abridged, except for participation in rebellion, or other crime, the basis of representation therein shall be reduced in the proportion which the number of such male citizens shall bear to the whole number of male citizens twenty-one years of age in such State.

Section 3. No person shall be a Senator or Representative in Congress, or elector of President and Vice President, or hold any office, civil or military, under the United States, or under any State, who having previously taken an oath, as a member of Congress, or as an officer of the United States, or as a member of any State legislature, or as an executive or judicial officer of any State, to support the Constitution of the United

States, shall have engaged in insurrection or rebellion against the same, or given aid or comfort to the enemies thereof. But Congress may by a vote of two-thirds of each House, remove such disability.

Section 4. The validity of the public debt of the United States, authorized by law, including debts incurred for payment of pensions and bounties for services in suppressing insurrection or rebellion, shall not be questioned. But neither the United States nor any State shall assume or pay any debt or obligation incurred in aid of insurrection or rebellion against the United States, or any claim for the loss or emancipation of any slave; but all such debts, obligations and claims shall be held illegal and void.

Section 5. The Congress shall have power to enforce, by appropriate legislation, the provisions of this article.

. . .

Amendment XV [1870]

Section 1. The right of citizens of the United States to vote shall not be denied or abridged by the United States or by any State on account of race, color, or previous condition of servitude.

Section 2. The Congress shall have power to enforce this article by appropriate legislation.

SELECTED STATE PROVISIONS

Table of Contents

Model Penal Code
Selected Uniform Laws

*

MODEL PENAL CODE
INTRODUCTION

Reprinted from Low, Criminal Law (1984).

With a few exceptions, the American States did not systematically codify their criminal law until late in the 20th Century. Rather, criminal codes grew in a hodge-podge, catch-as-catch-can fashion. Whenever something bad happened, the legislature passed a law against it. The result in many places was incredible inconsistency, caused by the fact that the legislature that passed a new statute often paid no attention to what was already on the books. A good example is the law in California that authorized a 15–year maximum sentence for a person who broke into a car to steal something inside. Another statute on the books at the same time authorized a maximum of 10 years for stealing the entire car. The law in several other States punished a person who tried to get another to commit perjury by a 5–year maximum, while another provision in the same Codes established a 1–year maximum if the attempt was successful.

The American Law Institute is a private organization of lawyers, judges, and law professors, formed in 1923. Beginning in 1952, after years of false starts, the Institute began to draft a "model" criminal code, designed to encourage States to revise their penal codes to eliminate inconsistency and redundancy. Tentative Drafts emerged for comment and criticism during the period between 1953 and 1962, and finally in 1962 the Proposed Official Draft was approved. Several volumes of commentary to Part II of the Model Penal Code (the specific crimes) were finally published in 1980, and another several volumes on Part I (the general provisions) were published in 1985.

The Model Penal Code is studied by students of the criminal law for two reasons. First, it was prepared over a 10–year period by the best minds this country (and others) have to offer. As an academic document, it is a first-rate attempt to state what a modern criminal law ought to look like. Second, it has been remarkably successful. In many respects it *is* the law in many American jurisdictions, and will dominate the American criminal law in the near future and for many years to come. There is no State that has done nothing in response to the Model Penal Code. After nearly 200 years in which virtually no State enacted a systematic criminal code, most States have enacted substantial revisions of their criminal codes since 1962, based largely on the Model Penal Code. Many others have revisions in progress. [Among the enacted codes, incidentally, the one in New York has been the most influential in other States.]

But the Model Penal Code has not only been noticed in legislative halls. The judges have taken account of it too, and it has had a significant influence on both reasoning and results in criminal cases, from the United States Supreme Court on down through the rest of the State and Federal court systems. The result is that an educated criminal lawyer today has to speak two languages, the language of the common law and the language of the Model Penal Code. In virtually all States the language of the common law is on the way out and the language of the Model Penal Code on the way in. There is much in common between the two systems but they do indeed speak in a different tongue.

It is appropriate to add a word about federal criminal law. The job of combating crime, particularly street violence, is primarily for the States in this country. There is, however, a substantial body of federal criminal law that exists independently of the criminal law of the States. It speaks to many of the same subjects, but also addresses distinctly federal interests. For present purposes, two points should be made.

First, all criminal cases in the federal system must be based on a specific statute enacted by the Congress. There are no common law crimes. [The same is true in many States today, by the way, but not all. Note what the Model Penal Code has to say on this subject in § 1.05(1). Many modern State codes have a similar provision.]

Second, there was a substantial effort to enact a new federal criminal code based on the Model Penal Code, but it has not yet commanded sufficient political support to get enacted and it is now doubtful whether it ever will. There are, in any event, a number of drafts of a new federal criminal code floating around, and you may see references to them from time to time. [The same thing has happened in several States, by the way, including California.] But this does not mean that the Model Penal Code is irrelevant to federal practice. Every federal Circuit Court had at one time adopted the Model Penal Code insanity test, and more and more the federal judges, including those on the Supreme Court, are thinking and talking in the language of the Model Code. The federal lawyer too, then, needs to know about the Model Penal Code.

For a concise outline of substantive American criminal law, juxtaposing the common law and the Model Penal Code, see Low's Criminal Law, Black Letter Series (West Publishing Company, St. Paul, 1984) ... from pages 58–60 of which this Introduction is drawn.

AMERICAN LAW INSTITUTE MODEL PENAL CODE

Table of Contents

MODEL PENAL CODE

PART I. GENERAL PROVISIONS

ARTICLE 1. PRELIMINARY

MODEL PENAL CODE

SELECTED STATE PROVISIONS

MODEL PENAL CODE

PART II. DEFINITION OF SPECIFIC CRIMES
Offenses Against Existence or Stability of the State

Offenses Involving Danger to the Person

ARTICLE 210.   CRIMINAL HOMICIDE

ARTICLE 211.   ASSAULT; RECKLESS ENDANGERING; THREATS

ARTICLE 212.   KIDNAPPING AND RELATED OFFENSES; COERCION

ARTICLE 213.   SEXUAL OFFENSES

Offenses Against Property
ARTICLE 220.   ARSON, CRIMINAL MISCHIEF, AND OTHER PROPERTY DESTRUCTION

ARTICLE 221.   BURGLARY AND OTHER CRIMINAL INTRUSION

ARTICLE 222.   ROBBERY

SELECTED STATE PROVISIONS

ARTICLE 223. THEFT AND RELATED OFFENSES

ARTICLE 224. FORGERY AND FRAUDULENT PRACTICES

Offenses Against the Family

ARTICLE 230. OFFENSES AGAINST THE FAMILY

Offenses Against Public Administration

ARTICLE 240. BRIBERY AND CORRUPT INFLUENCE

ARTICLE 241. PERJURY AND OTHER FALSIFICATION IN OFFICIAL MATTERS

PART III. TREATMENT AND CORRECTION [OMITTED]

PART IV. ORGANIZATION OF CORRECTION [OMITTED]

SELECTED STATE PROVISIONS

EDITOR'S NOTE: Respecting the general subject of PARTS III and IV, see the more recent Uniform Law Commissioners' Model Sentencing and Corrections Act, this pamphlet.

PART I

GENERAL PROVISIONS

ARTICLE 1

PRELIMINARY

Section 1.01 Title and Effective Date

(1) This Act is called the Penal and Correctional Code and may be cited as P.C.C. It shall become effective on _____ .

(2) Except as provided in Subsections (3) and (4) of this Section, the Code does not apply to offenses committed prior to its effective date and prosecutions for such offenses shall be governed by the prior law, which is continued in effect for that purpose, as if this Code were not in force. For the purposes of this Section, an offense was committed prior to the effective date of the Code if any of the elements of the offense occurred prior thereto.

(3) In any case pending on or after the effective date of the Code, involving an offense committed prior to such date:

(a) procedural provisions of the Code shall govern, insofar as they are justly applicable and their application does not introduce confusion or delay;

(b) provisions of the Code according a defense or mitigation shall apply, with the consent of the defendant;

(c) the Court, with the consent of the defendant, may impose sentence under the provisions of the Code applicable to the offense and the offender.

(4) Provisions of the Code governing the treatment and the release or discharge of prisoners, probationers and parolees shall apply to persons under sentence for offenses committed prior to the effective date of the Code, except that the minimum or maximum period of their detention or supervision shall in no case be increased.

Section 1.02 Purposes; Principles of Construction

(1) The general purposes of the provisions governing the definition of offenses are:

(a) to forbid and prevent conduct that unjustifiably and inexcusably inflicts or threatens substantial harm to individual or public interests;

(b) to subject to public control persons whose conduct indicates that they are disposed to commit crimes;

(c) to safeguard conduct that is without fault from condemnation as criminal;

(d) to give fair warning of the nature of the conduct declared to constitute an offense;

(e) to differentiate on reasonable grounds between serious and minor offenses.

(2) The general purposes of the provisions governing the sentencing and treatment of offenders are:

(a) to prevent the commission of offenses;

(b) to promote the correction and rehabilitation of offenders;

(c) to safeguard offenders against excessive, disproportionate or arbitrary punishment;

(d) to give fair warning of the nature of the sentences that may be imposed on conviction of an offense;

(e) to differentiate among offenders with a view to a just individualization in their treatment;

(f) to define, coordinate and harmonize the powers, duties and functions of the courts and of administrative officers and agencies responsible for dealing with offenders;

(g) to advance the use of generally accepted scientific methods and knowledge in the sentencing and treatment of offenders;

(h) to integrate responsibility for the administration of the correctional system in a State Department of Correction [or other single department or agency].

(3) The provisions of the Code shall be construed according to the fair import of their terms but when the language is susceptible of differing constructions it shall be interpreted to further the general purposes stated in this Section and the special purposes of the particular provision involved. The discretionary powers conferred by the Code shall be exercised in accordance with the criteria stated in the Code and, insofar as such criteria are not decisive, to further the general purposes stated in this Section.

Section 1.03 Territorial Applicability

(1) Except as otherwise provided in this Section, a person may be convicted under the law of this State of an offense committed by his own conduct or the conduct of another for which he is legally accountable if:

(a) either the conduct which is an element of the offense or the result which is such an element occurs within this State; or

(b) conduct occurring outside the State is sufficient under the law of this State to constitute an attempt to commit an offense within the State; or

(c) conduct occurring outside the State is sufficient under the law of this State to constitute a conspiracy to commit an offense within the State and an overt act in furtherance of such conspiracy occurs within the State; or

(d) conduct occurring within the State establishes complicity in the commission of, or an attempt, solicitation or conspiracy to commit, an offense in another jurisdiction which also is an offense under the law of this State; or

(e) the offense consists of the omission to perform a legal duty imposed by the law of this State with respect to domicile, residence or a relationship to a person, thing or transaction in the State; or

(f) the offense is based on a statute of this State which expressly prohibits conduct outside the State, when the conduct bears a reasonable relation to a legitimate interest of this State and the actor knows or should know that his conduct is likely to affect that interest.

(2) Subsection (1)(a) does not apply when either causing a specified result or a purpose to cause or danger of causing such a result is an element of an offense and the result occurs or is designed or likely to occur only in another jurisdiction where the conduct charged would not constitute an offense, unless a legislative purpose plainly appears to declare the conduct criminal regardless of the place of the result.

(3) Subsection (1)(a) does not apply when causing a particular result is an element of an offense and the result is caused by conduct occurring outside the State which would not constitute an offense if the result had occurred there, unless the actor purposely or knowingly caused the result within the State.

(4) When the offense is homicide, either the death of the victim or the bodily impact causing death constitutes a "result," within the meaning of Subsection (1)(a) and if the body of a homicide victim is found within the State, it is presumed that such result occurred within the State.

(5) This State includes the land and water and the air space above such land and water with respect to which the State has legislative jurisdiction.

Section 1.04 Classes of Crimes; Violations

(1) An offense defined by this Code or by any other statute of this State, for which a sentence of [death or of] imprisonment is authorized, constitutes a crime. Crimes are classified as felonies, misdemeanors or petty misdemeanors.

(2) A crime is a felony if it is so designated in this Code or if persons convicted thereof may be sentenced [to death or] to imprisonment for a term which, apart from an extended term, is in excess of one year.

(3) A crime is a misdemeanor if it is so designated in this Code or in a statute other than this Code enacted subsequent thereto.

(4) A crime is a petty misdemeanor if it is so designated in this Code or in a statute other than this Code enacted subsequent thereto or if it is defined by a statute other than this Code which now provides that persons convicted thereof may be sentenced to imprisonment for a term of which the maximum is less than one year.

(5) An offense defined by this Code or by any other statute of this State constitutes a violation if it is so designated in this Code or in the law defining the offense or if no other sentence than a fine, or fine and forfeiture or other civil penalty is authorized upon conviction or if it is defined by a statute other than this Code which now pro-

vides that the offense shall not constitute a crime. A violation does not constitute a crime and conviction of a violation shall not give rise to any disability or legal disadvantage based on conviction of a criminal offense.

(6) Any offense declared by law to constitute a crime, without specification of the grade thereof or of the sentence authorized upon conviction, is a misdemeanor.

(7) An offense defined by any statute of this State other than this Code shall be classified as provided in this Section and the sentence that may be imposed upon conviction thereof shall hereafter be governed by this Code.

Section 1.05   All Offenses Defined by Statute; Application of General Provisions of the Code

(1) No conduct constitutes an offense unless it is a crime or violation under this Code or another statute of this State.

(2) The provisions of Part I of the Code are applicable to offenses defined by other statutes, unless the Code otherwise provides.

(3) This Section does not affect the power of a court to punish for contempt or to employ any sanction authorized by law for the enforcement of an order or a civil judgment or decree.

Section 1.06   Time Limitations

(1) A prosecution for murder may be commenced at anytime.

(2) Except as otherwise provided in this Section, prosecutions for other offenses are subject to the following periods of limitation:

   (a) a prosecution for a felony of the first degree must be commenced within six years after it is committed;

   (b) a prosecution for any other felony must be commenced within three years after it is committed;

   (c) a prosecution for a misdemeanor must be commenced within two years after it is committed;

   (d) a prosecution for a petty misdemeanor or a violation must be commenced within six months after it is committed.

(3) If the period prescribed in Subsection (2) has expired, a prosecution may nevertheless be commenced for:

   (a) any offense a material element of which is either fraud or a breach of fiduciary obligation within one year after discovery of the offense by an aggrieved party or by a person who has legal duty to represent an aggrieved party and who is himself not a party to the offense, but in no case shall this provision extend the period of limitation otherwise applicable by more than three years; and

   (b) any offense based upon misconduct in office by a public officer or employee at any time when the defendant is in public office or employment or within two years thereafter, but in no case shall this provision extend the period of limitation otherwise applicable by more than three years.

(4) An offense is committed either when every element occurs, or, if a legislative purpose to prohibit a continuing course of conduct plainly appears, at the time when the course of conduct or the defendant's complicity therein is terminated. Time starts to run on the day after the offense is committed.

(5) A prosecution is commenced either when an indictment is found [or an information filed] or when a warrant or other process is issued, provided that such warrant or process is executed without unreasonable delay.

(6) The period of limitation does not run:

   (a) during any time when the accused is continuously absent from the State or has no reasonably ascertainable place of abode or work within the State, but in no case shall this provision extend the period of limitation otherwise applicable by more than three years; or

   (b) during any time when a prosecution against the accused for the same conduct is pending in this State.

Section 1.07   Method of Prosecution When Conduct Constitutes More Than One Offense

(1) **Prosecution for Multiple Offenses; Limitation on Convictions.** When the same conduct of a defendant may establish the commission of more than one offense, the defendant may be prosecuted for each such offense. He may not, however, be convicted of more than one offense if:

   (a) one offense is included in the other, as defined in Subsection (4) of this Section; or

(b) one offense consists only of a conspiracy or other form of preparation to commit the other; or

(c) inconsistent findings of fact are required to establish the commission of the offenses; or

(d) the offenses differ only in that one is defined to prohibit a designated kind of conduct generally and the other to prohibit a specific instance of such conduct; or

(e) the offense is defined as a continuing course of conduct and the defendant's course of conduct was uninterrupted, unless the law provides that specific periods of such conduct constitute separate offenses.

(2) Limitation on Separate Trials for Multiple Offenses. Except as provided in Subsection (3) of this Section, a defendant shall not be subject to separate trials for multiple offenses based on the same conduct or arising from the same criminal episode, if such offenses are known to the appropriate prosecuting officer at the time of the commencement of the first trial and are within the jurisdiction of a single court.

(3) Authority of Court to Order Separate Trials. When a defendant is charged with two or more offenses based on the same conduct or arising from the same criminal episode, the Court, on application of the prosecuting attorney or of the defendant, may order any such charge to be tried separately, if it is satisfied that justice so requires.

(4) Conviction of Included Offense Permitted. A defendant may be convicted of an offense included in an offense charged in the indictment [or the information]. An offense is so included when:

(a) it is established by proof of the same or less than all the facts required to establish the commission of the offense charged; or

(b) it consists of an attempt or solicitation to commit the offense charged or to commit an offense otherwise included therein; or

(c) it differs from the offense charged only in the respect that a less serious injury or risk of injury to the same person, property or public interest or a lesser kind of culpability suffices to establish its commission.

(5) Submission of Included Offense to Jury. The Court shall not be obligated to charge the jury with respect to an included offense unless there is a rational basis for a verdict acquitting the defendant of the offense charged and convicting him of the included offense.

Section 1.08 When Prosecution Barred by Former Prosecution for the Same Offense

When a prosecution is for a violation of the same provision of the statutes and is based upon the same facts as a former prosecution, it is barred by such former prosecution under the following circumstances:

(1) The former prosecution resulted in an acquittal. There is an acquittal if the prosecution resulted in a finding of not guilty by the trier of fact or in a determination that there was insufficient evidence to warrant a conviction. A finding of guilty of a lesser included offense is an acquittal of the greater inclusive offense, although the conviction is subsequently set aside.

(2) The former prosecution was terminated, after the information had been filed or the indictment found, by a final order or judgment for the defendant, which has not been set aside, reversed, or vacated and which necessarily required a determination inconsistent with a fact or a legal proposition that must be established for conviction of the offense.

(3) The former prosecution resulted in a conviction. There is a conviction if the prosecution resulted in a judgment of conviction which has not been reversed or vacated, a verdict of guilty which has not been set aside and which is capable of supporting a judgment, or a plea of guilty accepted by the Court. In the latter two cases failure to enter judgment must be for a reason other than a motion of the defendant.

(4) The former prosecution was improperly terminated. Except as provided in this Subsection, there is an improper termination of a prosecution if the termination is for reasons not amounting to an acquittal, and it takes place after the first witness is sworn but before verdict. Termination under any of the following circumstances is not improper:

(a) The defendant consents to the termination or waives, by motion to dismiss or otherwise, his right to object to the termination.

(b) The trial court finds that the termination is necessary because:

(i) it is physically impossible to proceed with the trial in conformity with law; or

(ii) there is a legal defect in the proceedings which would make any judgment entered upon a verdict reversible as a matter of law; or

(iii) prejudicial conduct, in or outside the courtroom, makes it impossible to proceed with the trial without injustice to either the defendant or the State; or

(iv) the jury is unable to agree upon a verdict; or

(v) false statements of a juror on voir dire prevent a fair trial.

Section 1.09 When Prosecution Barred by Former Prosecution for Different Offense

Although a prosecution is for a violation of a different provision of the statutes than a former prosecution or is based on different facts, it is barred by such former prosecution under the following circumstances:

(1) The former prosecution resulted in an acquittal or in a conviction as defined in Section 1.08 and the subsequent prosecution is for:

(a) any offense of which the defendant could have been convicted on the first prosecution; or

(b) any offense for which the defendant should have been tried on the first prosecution under Section 1.07, unless the Court ordered a separate trial of the charge of such offense; or

(c) the same conduct, unless (i) the offense of which the defendant was formerly convicted or acquitted and the offense for which he is subsequently prosecuted each requires proof of a fact not required by the other and the law defining each of such offenses is intended to prevent a substantially different harm or evil, or (ii) the second offense was not consummated when the former trial began.

(2) The former prosecution was terminated, after the information was filed or the indictment found, by an acquittal or by a final order or judgment for the defendant which has not been set aside, reversed or vacated and which acquittal, final order or judgment necessarily required a determination inconsistent with a fact which must be established for conviction of the second offense.

(3) The former prosecution was improperly terminated, as improper termination is defined in Section 1.08, and the subsequent prosecution is for an offense of which the defendant could have been convicted had the former prosecution not been improperly terminated.

Section 1.10 Former Prosecution in Another Jurisdiction: When a Bar

When conduct constitutes an offense within the concurrent jurisdiction of this State and of the United States or another State, a prosecution in any such other jurisdiction is a bar to a subsequent prosecution in this State under the following circumstances:

(1) The first prosecution resulted in an acquittal or in a conviction as defined in Section 1.08 and the subsequent prosecution is based on the same conduct, unless (a) the offense of which the defendant was formerly convicted or acquitted and the offense for which he is subsequently prosecuted each requires proof of a fact not required by the other and the law defining each of such offenses is intended to prevent a substantially different harm or evil or (b) the second offense was not consummated when the former trial began; or

(2) The former prosecution was terminated, after the information was filed or the indictment found, by an acquittal or by a final order or judgment for the defendant which has not been set aside, reversed or vacated and which acquittal, final order or judgment necessarily required a determination inconsistent with a fact which must be established for conviction of the offense of which the defendant is subsequently prosecuted.

Section 1.11 Former Prosecution Before Court Lacking Jurisdiction or When Fraudulently Procured by the Defendant

A prosecution is not a bar within the meaning of Sections 1.08, 1.09 and 1.10 under any of the following circumstances:

(1) The former prosecution was before a court which lacked jurisdiction over the defendant or the offense; or

(2) The former prosecution was procured by the defendant without the knowledge of the appropriate prosecuting officer and with the

purpose of avoiding the sentence which might otherwise be imposed; or

(3) The former prosecution resulted in a judgment of conviction which was held invalid in a subsequent proceeding on a writ of habeas corpus, coram nobis or similar process.

Section 1.12 Proof Beyond a Reasonable Doubt; Affirmative Defenses; Burden of Proving Fact When Not an Element of an Offense; Presumptions

(1) No person may be convicted of an offense unless each element of such offense is proved beyond a reasonable doubt. In the absence of such proof, the innocence of the defendant is assumed.

(2) Subsection (1) of this Section does not:

(a) require the disproof of an affirmative defense unless and until there is evidence supporting such defense; or

(b) apply to any defense which the Code or another statute plainly requires the defendant to prove by a preponderance of evidence.

(3) A ground of defense is affirmative, within the meaning of Subsection (2)(a) of this Section, when:

(a) it arises under a section of the Code which so provides; or

(b) it relates to an offense defined by a statute other than the Code and such statute so provides; or

(c) it involves a matter of excuse or justification peculiarly within the knowledge of the defendant on which he can fairly be required to adduce supporting evidence.

(4) When the application of the Code depends upon the finding of a fact which is not an element of an offense, unless the Code otherwise provides:

(a) the burden of proving the fact is on the prosecution or defendant, depending on whose interest or contention will be furthered if the finding should be made; and

(b) the fact must be proved to the satisfaction of the Court or jury, as the case may be.

(5) When the Code establishes a presumption with respect to any fact which is an element of an offense, it has the following consequences:

(a) when there is evidence of the facts which give rise to the presumption, the issue of the existence of the presumed fact must be submitted to the jury, unless the Court is satisfied that the evidence as a whole clearly negatives the presumed fact; and

(b) when the issue of the existence of the presumed fact is submitted to the jury, the Court shall charge that while the presumed fact must, on all the evidence, be proved beyond a reasonable doubt, the law declares that the jury may regard the facts giving rise to the presumption as sufficient evidence of the presumed fact.

(6) A presumption not established by the Code or inconsistent with it has the consequences otherwise accorded it by law.

Section 1.13 General Definitions

In this Code, unless a different meaning plainly is required:

(1) "statute" includes the Constitution and a local law or ordinance of a political subdivision of the State;

(2) "act" or "action" means a bodily movement whether voluntary or involuntary;

(3) "voluntary" has the meaning specified in Section 2.01;

(4) "omission" means a failure to act;

(5) "conduct" means an action or omission and its accompanying state of mind, or, where relevant, a series of acts and omissions;

(6) "actor" includes, where relevant, a person guilty of an omission;

(7) "acted" includes, where relevant, "omitted to act";

(8) "person," "he" and "actor" include any natural person and, where relevant, a corporation or an unincorporated association;

(9) "element of an offense" means (i) such conduct or (ii) such attendant circumstances or (iii) such a result of conduct as

(a) is included in the description of the forbidden conduct in the definition of the offense; or

(b) establishes the required kind of culpability; or

(c) negatives an excuse or justification for such conduct; or

(d) negatives a defense under the statute of limitations; or

(e) establishes jurisdiction or venue;

(10) "material element of an offense" means an element that does not relate exclusively to the statute of limitations, jurisdiction, venue or to any other matter similarly unconnected with (i) the harm or evil, incident to conduct, sought to be prevented by the law defining the offense, or (ii) the existence of a justification or excuse for such conduct;

(11) "purposely" has the meaning specified in Section 2.02 and equivalent terms such as "with purpose," "designed" or "with design" have the same meaning;

(12) "intentionally" or "with intent" means purposely;

(13) "knowingly" has the meaning specified in Section 2.02 and equivalent terms such as "knowing" or "with knowledge" have the same meaning;

(14) "recklessly" has the meaning specified in Section 2.02 and equivalent terms such as "recklessness" or "with recklessness" have the same meaning;

(15) "negligently" has the meaning specified in Section 2.02 and equivalent terms such as "negligence" or "with negligence" have the same meaning;

(16) "reasonably believes" or "reasonable belief" designates a belief which the actor is not reckless or negligent in holding.

ARTICLE 2

GENERAL PRINCIPLES OF LIABILITY

Section 2.01 Requirement of Voluntary Act; Omission as Basis of Liability; Possession as an Act

(1) A person is not guilty of an offense unless his liability is based on conduct which includes a voluntary act or the omission to perform an act of which he is physically capable.

(2) The following are not voluntary acts within the meaning of this Section:

(a) a reflex or convulsion;

(b) a bodily movement during unconsciousness or sleep;

(c) conduct during hypnosis or resulting from hypnotic suggestion;

(d) a bodily movement that otherwise is not a product of the effort or determination of the actor, either conscious or habitual.

(3) Liability for the commission of an offense may not be based on an omission unaccompanied by action unless:

(a) the omission is expressly made sufficient by the law defining the offense; or

(b) a duty to perform the omitted act is otherwise imposed by law.

(4) Possession is an act, within the meaning of this Section, if the possessor knowingly procured or received the thing possessed or was aware of his control thereof for a sufficient period to have been able to terminate his possession.

Section 2.02 General Requirements of Culpability

(1) Minimum Requirements of Culpability. Except as provided in Section 2.05, a person is not guilty of an offense unless he acted purposely, knowingly, recklessly or negligently, as the law may require, with respect to each material element of the offense.

(2) Kinds of Culpability Defined.

(a) *Purposely.*

A person acts purposely with respect to a material element of an offense when:

(i) if the element involves the nature of his conduct or a result thereof, it is his conscious object to engage in conduct of that nature or to cause such a result; and

(ii) if the element involves the attendant circumstances, he is aware of the existence of such circumstances or he believes or hopes that they exist.

(b) *Knowingly.*

A person acts knowingly with respect to a material element of an offense when:

(i) if the element involves the nature of his conduct or the attendant circumstances, he is aware that his conduct is of that nature or that such circumstances exist; and

(ii) if the element involves a result of his conduct, he is aware that it is practically certain that his conduct will cause such a result.

(c) *Recklessly.*

A person acts recklessly with respect to a material element of an offense when he consciously disregards a substantial and unjustifiable risk that the material element exists or will result from his conduct. The risk must be of such a nature and degree that, considering the nature and purpose of the actor's conduct and the circumstances known to him, its disregard involves a gross deviation from the standard of conduct that a law-abiding person would observe in the actor's situation.

(d) *Negligently.*

A person acts negligently with respect to a material element of an offense when he should be aware of a substantial and unjustifiable risk that the material element exists or will result from his conduct. The risk must be of such a nature and degree that the actor's failure to perceive it, considering the nature and purpose of his conduct and the circumstances known to him, involves a gross deviation from the standard of care that a reasonable person would observe in the actor's situation.

(3) Culpability Required Unless Otherwise Provided. When the culpability sufficient to establish a material element of an offense is not prescribed by law, such element is established if a person acts purposely, knowingly or recklessly with respect thereto.

(4) Prescribed Culpability Requirement Applies to All Material Elements. When the law defining an offense prescribes the kind of culpability that is sufficient for the commission of an offense, without distinguishing among the material elements thereof, such provision shall apply to all the material elements of the offense, unless a contrary purpose plainly appears.

(5) Substitutes for Negligence, Recklessness and Knowledge. When the law provides that negligence suffices to establish an element of an offense, such element also is established if a person acts purposely, knowingly or recklessly. When recklessness suffices to establish an element, such element also is established if a person

acts purposely or knowingly. When acting knowingly suffices to establish an element, such element also is established if a person acts purposely.

(6) Requirement of Purpose Satisfied if Purpose Is Conditional. When a particular purpose is an element of an offense, the element is established although such purpose is conditional, unless the condition negatives the harm or evil sought to be prevented by the law defining the offense.

(7) Requirement of Knowledge Satisfied by Knowledge of High Probability. When knowledge of the existence of a particular fact is an element of an offense, such knowledge is established if a person is aware of a high probability of its existence, unless he actually believes that it does not exist.

(8) Requirement of Wilfulness Satisfied by Acting Knowingly. A requirement that an offense be committed wilfully is satisfied if a person acts knowingly with respect to the material elements of the offense, unless a purpose to impose further requirements appears.

(9) Culpability as to Illegality of Conduct. Neither knowledge nor recklessness or negligence as to whether conduct constitutes an offense or as to the existence, meaning or application of the law determining the elements of an offense is an element of such offense, unless the definition of the offense or the Code so provides.

(10) Culpability as Determinant of Grade of Offense. When the grade or degree of an offense depends on whether the offense is committed purposely, knowingly, recklessly or negligently, its grade or degree shall be the lowest for which the determinative kind of culpability is established with respect to any material element of the offense.

Section 2.03 Causal Relationship Between Conduct and Result; Divergence Between Result Designed or Contemplated and Actual Result or Between Probable and Actual Result

(1) Conduct is the cause of a result when:

(a) it is an antecedent but for which the result in question would not have occurred; and

(b) the relationship between the conduct and result satisfies any additional causal requirements imposed by the Code or by the law defining the offense.

(2) When purposely or knowingly causing a particular result is an element of an offense, the element is not established if the actual result is not within the purpose or the contemplation of the actor unless:

(a) the actual result differs from that designed or contemplated, as the case may be, only in the respect that a different person or different property is injured or affected or that the injury or harm designed or contemplated would have been more serious or more extensive than that caused; or

(b) the actual result involves the same kind of injury or harm as that designed or contemplated and is not too remote or accidental in its occurrence to have a [just] bearing on the actor's liability or on the gravity of his offense.

(3) When recklessly or negligently causing a particular result is an element of an offense, the element is not established if the actual result is not within the risk of which the actor is aware or, in the case of negligence, of which he should be aware unless:

(a) the actual result differs from the probable result only in the respect that a different person or different property is injured or affected or that the probable injury or harm would have been more serious or more extensive than that caused; or

(b) the actual result involves the same kind of injury or harm as the probable result and is not too remote or accidental in its occurrence to have a [just] bearing on the actor's liability or on the gravity of his offense.

(4) When causing a particular result is a material element of an offense for which absolute liability is imposed by law, the element is not established unless the actual result is a probable consequence of the actor's conduct.

Section 2.04   Ignorance or Mistake

(1) Ignorance or mistake as to a matter of fact or law is a defense if:

(a) the ignorance or mistake negatives the purpose, knowledge, belief, recklessness or negligence required to establish a material element of the offense; or

(b) the law provides that the state of mind established by such ignorance or mistake constitutes a defense.

(2) Although ignorance or mistake would otherwise afford a defense to the offense charged, the defense is not available if the defendant would be guilty of another offense had the situation been as he supposed. In such case, however, the ignorance or mistake of the defendant shall reduce the grade and degree of the offense of which he may be convicted to those of the offense of which he would be guilty had the situation been as he supposed.

(3) A belief that conduct does not legally constitute an offense is a defense to a prosecution for that offense based upon such conduct when:

(a) the statute or other enactment defining the offense is not known to the actor and has not been published or otherwise reasonably made available prior to the conduct alleged; or

(b) he acts in reasonable reliance upon an official statement of the law, afterward determined to be invalid or erroneous, contained in (i) a statute or other enactment; (ii) a judicial decision, opinion or judgment; (iii) an administrative order or grant of permission; or (iv) an official interpretation of the public officer or body charged by law with responsibility for the interpretation, administration or enforcement of the law defining the offense.

(4) The defendant must prove a defense arising under Subsection (3) of this Section by a preponderance of evidence.

Section 2.05   When Culpability Requirements Are Inapplicable to Violations and to Offenses Defined by Other Statutes; Effect of Absolute Liability in Reducing Grade of Offense to Violation

(1) The requirements of culpability prescribed by Sections 2.01 and 2.02 do not apply to:

(a) offenses which constitute violations, unless the requirement involved is included in the definition of the offense or the Court determines that its application is consistent with effective enforcement of the law defining the offense; or

(b) offenses defined by statutes other than the Code, insofar as a legislative purpose to impose absolute liability for such offenses or with respect to any material element thereof plainly appears.

(2) Notwithstanding any other provision of existing law and unless a subsequent statute otherwise provides:

(a) when absolute liability is imposed with respect to any material element of an offense defined by a statute other than the Code and a conviction is based upon such liability, the offense constitutes a violation; and

(b) although absolute liability is imposed by law with respect to one or more of the material elements of an offense defined by a statute other than the Code, the culpable commission of the offense may be charged and proved, in which event negligence with respect to such elements constitutes sufficient culpability and the classification of the offense and the sentence that may be imposed therefor upon conviction are determined by Section 1.04 and Article 6 of the Code.

Section 2.06 Liability for Conduct of Another; Complicity

(1) A person is guilty of an offense if it is committed by his own conduct or by the conduct of another person for which he is legally accountable, or both.

(2) A person is legally accountable for the conduct of another person when:

(a) acting with the kind of culpability that is sufficient for the commission of the offense, he causes an innocent or irresponsible person to engage in such conduct; or

(b) he is made accountable for the conduct of such other person by the Code or by the law defining the offense; or

(c) he is an accomplice of such other person in the commission of the offense.

(3) A person is an accomplice of another person in the commission of an offense if:

(a) with the purpose of promoting or facilitating the commission of the offense, he

(i) solicits such other person to commit it; or

(ii) aids or agrees or attempts to aid such other person in planning or committing it; or

(iii) having a legal duty to prevent the commission of the offense, fails to make proper effort so to do; or

(b) his conduct is expressly declared by law to establish his complicity.

(4) When causing a particular result is an element of an offense, an accomplice in the conduct causing such result is an accomplice in the commission of that offense, if he acts with the kind of culpability, if any, with respect to that result that is sufficient for the commission of the offense.

(5) A person who is legally incapable of committing a particular offense himself may be guilty thereof if it is committed by the conduct of another person for which he is legally accountable, unless such liability is inconsistent with the purpose of the provision establishing his incapacity.

(6) Unless otherwise provided by the Code or by the law defining the offense, a person is not an accomplice in an offense committed by another person if:

(a) he is a victim of that offense; or

(b) the offense is so defined that his conduct is inevitably incident to its commission; or

(c) he terminates his complicity prior to the commission of the offense and

(i) wholly deprives it of effectiveness in the commission of the offense; or

(ii) gives timely warning to the law enforcement authorities or otherwise makes proper effort to prevent the commission of the offense.

(7) An accomplice may be convicted on proof of the commission of the offense and of his complicity therein, though the person claimed to have committed the offense has not been prosecuted or convicted or has been convicted of a different offense or degree of offense or has an immunity to prosecution or conviction or has been acquitted.

Section 2.07 Liability of Corporations, Unincorporated Associations and Persons Acting, or Under a Duty to Act, in Their Behalf

(1) A corporation may be convicted of the commission of an offense if:

(a) the offense is a violation or the offense is defined by a statute other than the Code in which a legislative purpose to impose liability on corporations plainly appears and the conduct is performed by an agent of the corporation acting in behalf of the corporation within the scope of his office or employment, except that if the law defining the offense designates the agents for whose conduct the corporation is accountable or the circumstances under which it is accountable, such provisions shall apply; or

(b) the offense consists of an omission to discharge a specific duty of affirmative performance imposed on corporations by law; or

(c) the commission of the offense was authorized, requested, commanded, performed or recklessly tolerated by the board of directors or by a high managerial agent acting in behalf of the corporation within the scope of his office or employment.

(2) When absolute liability is imposed for the commission of an offense, a legislative purpose to impose liability on a corporation shall be assumed, unless the contrary plainly appears.

(3) An unincorporated association may be convicted of the commission of an offense if:

(a) the offense is defined by a statute other than the Code which expressly provides for the liability of such an association and the conduct is performed by an agent of the association acting in behalf of the association within the scope of his office or employment, except that if the law defining the offense designates the agents for whose conduct the association is accountable or the circumstances under which it is accountable, such provisions shall apply; or

(b) the offense consists of an omission to discharge a specific duty of affirmative performance imposed on associations by law.

(4) As used in this Section:

(a) "corporation" does not include an entity organized as or by a governmental agency for the execution of a governmental program;

(b) "agent" means any director, officer, servant, employee or other person authorized to act in behalf of the corporation or association and, in the case of an unincorporated association, a member of such association;

(c) "high managerial agent" means an officer of a corporation or an unincorporated association, or, in the case of a partnership, a partner, or any other agent of a corporation or association having duties of such responsibility that

his conduct may fairly be assumed to represent the policy of the corporation or association.

(5) In any prosecution of a corporation or an unincorporated association for the commission of an offense included within the terms of Subsection (1)(a) or Subsection (3)(a) of this Section, other than an offense for which absolute liability has been imposed, it shall be a defense if the defendant proves by a preponderance of evidence that the high managerial agent having supervisory responsibility over the subject matter of the offense employed due diligence to prevent its commission. This paragraph shall not apply if it is plainly inconsistent with the legislative purpose in defining the particular offense.

(6)(a) A person is legally accountable for any conduct he performs or causes to be performed in the name of the corporation or an unincorporated association or in its behalf to the same extent as if it were performed in his own name or behalf.

(b) Whenever a duty to act is imposed by law upon a corporation or an unincorporated association, any agent of the corporation or association having primary responsibility for the discharge of the duty is legally accountable for a reckless omission to perform the required act to the same extent as if the duty were imposed by law directly upon himself.

(c) When a person is convicted of an offense by reason of his legal accountability for the conduct of a corporation or an unincorporated association, he is subject to the sentence authorized by law when a natural person is convicted of an offense of the grade and the degree involved.

Section 2.08   Intoxication

(1) Except as provided in Subsection (4) of this Section, intoxication of the actor is not a defense unless it negatives an element of the offense.

(2) When recklessness establishes an element of the offense, if the actor, due to self-induced intoxication, is unaware of a risk of which he would have been aware had he been sober, such unawareness is immaterial.

(3) Intoxication does not, in itself, constitute mental disease within the meaning of Section 4.01.

(4) Intoxication which (a) is not self-induced or (b) is pathological is an affirmative defense if by reason of such intoxication the actor at the time

of his conduct lacks substantial capacity either to appreciate its criminality [wrongfulness] or to conform his conduct to the requirements of law.

(5) **Definitions.** In this Section unless a different meaning plainly is required:

(a) "intoxication" means a disturbance of mental or physical capacities resulting from the introduction of substances into the body;

(b) "self-induced intoxication" means intoxication caused by substances which the actor knowingly introduces into his body, the tendency of which to cause intoxication he knows or ought to know, unless he introduces them pursuant to medical advice or under such circumstances as would afford a defense to a charge of crime;

(c) "pathological intoxication" means intoxication grossly excessive in degree, given the amount of the intoxicant, to which the actor does not know he is susceptible.

Section 2.09 Duress.

(1) It is an affirmative defense that the actor engaged in the conduct charged to constitute an offense because he was coerced to do so by the use of, or a threat to use, unlawful force against his person or the person of another, which a person of reasonable firmness in his situation would have been unable to resist.

(2) The defense provided by this Section is unavailable if the actor recklessly placed himself in a situation in which it was probable that he would be subjected to duress. The defense is also unavailable if he was negligent in placing himself in such a situation, whenever negligence suffices to establish culpability for the offense charged.

(3) It is not a defense that a woman acted on the command of her husband, unless she acted under such coercion as would establish a defense under this Section. [The presumption that a woman, acting in the presence of her husband, is coerced is abolished.]

(4) When the conduct of the actor would otherwise be justifiable under Section 3.02, this Section does not preclude such defense.

Section 2.10 Military Orders

It is an affirmative defense that the actor, in engaging in the conduct charged to constitute an offense, does no more than execute an order of his superior in the armed services which he does not know to be unlawful.

Section 2.11 Consent

(1) **In General.** The consent of the victim to conduct charged to constitute an offense or to the result thereof is a defense if such consent negatives an element of the offense or precludes the infliction of the harm or evil sought to be prevented by the law defining the offense.

(2) **Consent to Bodily Injury.** When conduct is charged to constitute an offense because it causes or threatens bodily injury, consent to such conduct or to the infliction of such injury is a defense if:

(a) the bodily injury consented to or threatened by the conduct consented to is not serious; or

(b) the conduct and the injury are reasonably foreseeable hazards of joint participation in a lawful athletic contest or competitive sport or other concerted activity not forbidden by law; or

(c) the consent establishes a justification for the conduct under Article 3 of the Code.

(3) **Ineffective Consent.** Unless otherwise provided by the Code or by the law defining the offense, assent does not constitute consent if:

(a) it is given by a person who is legally incompetent to authorize the conduct charged to constitute the offense; or

(b) it is given by a person who by reason of youth, mental disease or defect or intoxication is manifestly unable or known by the actor to be unable to make a reasonable judgment as to the nature or harmfulness of the conduct charged to constitute the offense; or

(c) it is given by a person whose improvident consent is sought to be prevented by the law defining the offense; or

(d) it is induced by force, duress or deception of a kind sought to be prevented by the law defining the offense.

Section 2.12 De Minimis Infractions

The Court shall dismiss a prosecution if, having regard to the nature of the conduct charged to constitute an offense and the nature of the attendant circumstances, it finds that the defendant's conduct:

(1) was within a customary license or tolerance, neither expressly negatived by the person whose interest was infringed nor inconsistent with the purpose of the law defining the offense; or

(2) did not actually cause or threaten the harm or evil sought to be prevented by the law defining the offense or did so only to an extent too trivial to warrant the condemnation of conviction; or

(3) presents such other extenuations that it cannot reasonably be regarded as envisaged by the legislature in forbidding the offense.

The Court shall not dismiss a prosecution under Subsection (3) of this Section without filing a written statement of its reasons.

Section 2.13 Entrapment

(1) A public law enforcement official or a person acting in cooperation with such an official perpetrates an entrapment if for the purpose of obtaining evidence of the commission of an offense, he induces or encourages another person to engage in conduct constituting such offense by either:

(a) making knowingly false representations designed to induce the belief that such conduct is not prohibited; or

(b) employing methods of persuasion or inducement which create a substantial risk that such an offense will be committed by persons other than those who are ready to commit it.

(2) Except as provided in Subsection (3) of this Section, a person prosecuted for an offense shall be acquitted if he proves by a preponderance of evidence that his conduct occurred in response to an entrapment. The issue of entrapment shall be tried by the Court in the absence of the jury.

(3) The defense afforded by this Section is unavailable when causing or threatening bodily injury is an element of the offense charged and the prosecution is based on conduct causing or threatening such injury to a person other than the person perpetrating the entrapment.

ARTICLE 3

GENERAL PRINCIPLES OF JUSTIFICATION

Section 3.01 Justification an Affirmative Defense; Civil Remedies Unaffected

(1) In any prosecution based on conduct which is justifiable under this Article, justification is an affirmative defense.

(2) The fact that conduct is justifiable under this Article does not abolish or impair any remedy for such conduct which is available in any civil action.

Section 3.02 Justification Generally: Choice of Evils

(1) Conduct which the actor believes to be necessary to avoid a harm or evil to himself or to another is justifiable, provided that:

(a) the harm or evil sought to be avoided by such conduct is greater than that sought to be prevented by the law defining the offense charged; and

(b) neither the Code nor other law defining the offense provides exceptions or defenses dealing with the specific situation involved; and

(c) a legislative purpose to exclude the justification claimed does not otherwise plainly appear.

(2) When the actor was reckless or negligent in bringing about the situation requiring a choice of harms or evils or in appraising the necessity for his conduct, the justification afforded by this Section is unavailable in a prosecution for any offense for which recklessness or negligence, as the case may be, suffices to establish culpability.

Section 3.03 Execution of Public Duty

(1) Except as provided in Subsection (2) of this Section, conduct is justifiable when it is required or authorized by:

(a) the law defining the duties or functions of a public officer or the assistance to be rendered to such officer in the performance of his duties; or

(b) the law governing the execution of legal process; or

(c) the judgment or order of a competent court or tribunal; or

(d) the law governing the armed services or the lawful conduct of war; or

(e) any other provision of law imposing a public duty.

(2) The other sections of this Article apply to:

(a) the use of force upon or toward the person of another for any of the purposes dealt with in such sections; and

(b) the use of deadly force for any purpose, unless the use of such force is otherwise expressly authorized by law or occurs in the lawful conduct of war.

(3) The justification afforded by Subsection (1) of this Section applies:

(a) when the actor believes his conduct to be required or authorized by the judgment or direction of a competent court or tribunal or in the lawful execution of legal process, notwithstanding lack of jurisdiction of the court or defect in the legal process; and

(b) when the actor believes his conduct to be required or authorized to assist a public officer in the performance of his duties, notwithstanding that the officer exceeded his legal authority.

Section 3.04 Use of Force in Self–Protection

(1) **Use of Force Justifiable for Protection of the Person.** Subject to the provisions of this Section and of Section 3.09, the use of force upon or toward another person is justifiable when the actor believes that such force is immediately necessary for the purpose of protecting himself against the use of unlawful force by such other person on the present occasion.

(2) **Limitations on Justifying Necessity for Use of Force.**

(a) The use of force is not justifiable under this Section:

(i) to resist an arrest which the actor knows is being made by a peace officer, although the arrest is unlawful; or

(ii) to resist force used by the occupier or possessor of property or by another person on his behalf, where the actor knows that the person using the force is doing so under a claim of right to protect the property, except that this limitation shall not apply if:

(1) the actor is a public officer acting in the performance of his duties or a person lawfully assisting him therein or a person making or assisting in a lawful arrest; or

(2) the actor has been unlawfully dispossessed of the property and is making a re-entry or recaption justified by Section 3.06; or

(3) the actor believes that such force is necessary to protect himself against death or serious bodily harm.

(b) The use of deadly force is not justifiable under this Section unless the actor believes that such force is necessary to protect himself against death, serious bodily harm, kidnapping or sexual intercourse compelled by force or threat; nor is it justifiable if:

(i) the actor, with the purpose of causing death or serious bodily harm, provoked the use of force against himself in the same encounter; or

(ii) the actor knows that he can avoid the necessity of using such force with complete safety by retreating or by surrendering possession of a thing to a person asserting a claim of right thereto or by complying with a demand that he abstain from any action which he has no duty to take, except that:

(1) the actor is not obliged to retreat from his dwelling or place of work, unless he was the initial aggressor or is assailed in his place of work by another person whose place of work the actor knows it to be; and

(2) a public officer justified in using force in the performance of his duties or a person justified in using force in his assistance or a person justified in using force in making an arrest or preventing an escape is not obliged to desist from efforts to perform such duty, effect such arrest or prevent such escape because of resistance or threatened resistance by or on behalf of the person against whom such action is directed.

(c) Except as required by paragraphs (a) and (b) of this Subsection, a person employing protective force may estimate the necessity thereof under the circumstances as he believes them to be when the force is used, without retreating, surrendering possession, doing any other act which he has no legal duty to do or abstaining from any lawful action.

(3) Use of Confinement as Protective Force. The justification afforded by this Section extends to the use of confinement as protective force only if the actor takes all reasonable measures to terminate the confinement as soon as he knows that he safely can, unless the person confined has been arrested on a charge of crime.

Section 3.05   Use of Force for the Protection of Other Persons

(1) Subject to the provisions of this Section and of Section 3.09, the use of force upon or toward the person of another is justifiable to protect a third person when:

(a) the actor would be justified under Section 3.04 in using such force to protect himself against the injury he believes to be threatened to the person whom he seeks to protect; and

(b) under the circumstances as the actor believes them to be, the person whom he seeks to protect would be justified in using such protective force; and

(c) the actor believes that his intervention is necessary for the protection of such other person.

(2) Notwithstanding Subsection (1) of this Section:

(a) when the actor would be obliged under Section 3.04 to retreat, to surrender the possession of a thing or to comply with a demand before using force in self-protection, he is not obliged to do so before using force for the protection of another person, unless he knows that he can thereby secure the complete safety of such other person; and

(b) when the person whom the actor seeks to protect would be obliged under Section 3.04 to retreat, to surrender the possession of a thing or to comply with a demand if he knew that he could obtain complete safety by so doing, the actor is obliged to try to cause him to do so before using force in his protection if the actor knows that he can obtain complete safety in that way; and

(c) neither the actor nor the person whom he seeks to protect is obliged to retreat when in the other's dwelling or place of work to any greater extent than in his own.

Section 3.06   Use of Force for the Protection of Property

(1) Use of Force Justifiable for Protection of Property. Subject to the provisions of this Section and of Section 3.09, the use of force upon or toward the person of another is justifiable when the actor believes that such force is immediately necessary:

(a) to prevent or terminate an unlawful entry or other trespass upon land or a trespass against or the unlawful carrying away of tangible, movable property, provided that such land or movable property is, or is believed by the actor to be, in his possession or in the possession of another person for whose protection he acts; or

(b) to effect an entry or re-entry upon land or to retake tangible movable property, provided that the actor believes that he or the person by whose authority he acts or a person from whom he or such other person derives title was unlawfully dispossessed of such land or movable property and is entitled to possession, and provided, further, that:

(i) the force is used immediately or on fresh pursuit after such dispossession; or

(ii) the actor believes that the person against whom he uses force has no claim of right to the possession of the property and, in the case of land, the circumstances, as the actor believes them to be, are of such urgency that it would be an exceptional hardship to postpone the entry or re-entry until a court order is obtained.

(2) Meaning of Possession. For the purposes of Subsection (1) of this Section:

(a) a person who has parted with the custody of property to another who refuses to restore it to him is no longer in possession, unless the property is movable and was and still is located on land in his possession;

(b) a person who has been dispossessed of land does not regain possession thereof merely by setting foot thereon;

(c) a person who has a license to use or occupy real property is deemed to be in possession thereof except against the licensor acting under claim of right.

(3) Limitations on Justifiable Use of Force.

(a) *Request to Desist.* The use of force is justifiable under this Section only if the actor first requests the person against whom such force is used to desist from his interference with the property, unless the actor believes that:

(i) such request would be useless; or

(ii) it would be dangerous to himself or another person to make the request; or

(iii) substantial harm will be done to the physical condition of the property which is sought to be protected before the request can effectively be made.

(b) *Exclusion of Trespasser.* The use of force to prevent or terminate a trespass is not justifiable under this Section if the actor knows that the exclusion of the trespasser will expose him to substantial danger of serious bodily harm.

(c) *Resistance of Lawful Re-entry or Recaption.* The use of force to prevent an entry or re-entry upon land or the recaption of movable property is not justifiable under this Section, although the actor believes that such re-entry or recaption is unlawful, if:

(i) the re-entry or recaption is made by or on behalf of a person who was actually dispossessed of the property; and

(ii) it is otherwise justifiable under paragraph (1)(b) of this Section.

(d) *Use of Deadly Force.* The use of deadly force is not justifiable under this Section unless the actor believes that:

(i) the person against whom the force is used is attempting to dispossess him of his dwelling otherwise than under a claim of right to its possession; or

(ii) the person against whom the force is used is attempting to commit or consummate arson, burglary, robbery or other felonious theft or property destruction and either:

(1) has employed or threatened deadly force against or in the presence of the actor; or

(2) the use of force other than deadly force to prevent the commission or the consummation of the crime would expose the actor or another in his presence to substantial danger of serious bodily harm.

(4) Use of Confinement as Protective Force. The justification afforded by this Section extends to the use of confinement as protective force only if the actor takes all reasonable measures to terminate the confinement as soon as he knows that he can do so with safety to the property, unless the person confined has been arrested on a charge of crime.

(5) Use of Device to Protect Property. The justification afforded by this Section extends to the use of a device for the purpose of protecting property only if:

(a) the device is not designed to cause or known to create a substantial risk of causing death or serious bodily harm; and

(b) the use of the particular device to protect the property from entry or trespass is reasonable under the circumstances, as the actor believes them to be; and

(c) the device is one customarily used for such a purpose or reasonable care is taken to make known to probable intruders the fact that it is used.

(6) Use of Force to Pass Wrongful Obstructor. The use of force to pass a person whom the actor believes to be purposely or knowingly and unjustifiably obstructing the actor from going to a place to which he may lawfully go is justifiable, provided that:

(a) the actor believes that the person against whom he uses force has no claim of right to obstruct the actor; and

(b) the actor is not being obstructed from entry or movement on land which he knows to be in the possession or custody of the person obstructing him, or in the possession or custody of another person by whose authority the obstructor acts, unless the circumstances, as the actor believes them to be, are of such urgency that it would not be reasonable to postpone the entry or movement on such land until a court order is obtained; and

(c) the force used is not greater than would be justifiable if the person obstructing the actor were using force against him to prevent his passage.

Section 3.07 Use of Force in Law Enforcement

(1) Use of Force Justifiable to Effect an Arrest. Subject to the provisions of this Section and of Section 3.09, the use of force upon or toward the person of another is justifiable when the actor is making or assisting in making an arrest and the actor believes that such force is immediately necessary to effect a lawful arrest.

(2) Limitations on the Use of Force.

(a) The use of force is not justifiable under this Section unless:

(i) the actor makes known the purpose of the arrest or believes that it is otherwise known by or cannot reasonably be made known to the person to be arrested; and

(ii) when the arrest is made under a warrant, the warrant is valid or believed by the actor to be valid.

(b) The use of deadly force is not justifiable under this Section unless:

(i) the arrest is for a felony; and

(ii) the person effecting the arrest is authorized to act as a peace officer or is assisting a person whom he believes to be authorized to act as a peace officer; and

(iii) the actor believes that the force employed creates no substantial risk of injury to innocent persons; and

(iv) the actor believes that:

(1) the crime for which the arrest is made involved conduct including the use or threatened use of deadly force; or

(2) there is a substantial risk that the person to be arrested will cause death or serious bodily harm if his apprehension is delayed.

(3) Use of Force to Prevent Escape from Custody. The use of force to prevent the escape of an arrested person from custody is justifiable when the force could justifiably have been employed to effect the arrest under which the person is in custody, except that a guard or other person authorized to act as a peace officer is justified in using any force, including deadly force, which he believes to be immediately necessary to prevent the escape of a person from a jail, prison, or other institution for the detention of persons charged with or convicted of a crime.

(4) Use of Force by Private Person Assisting an Unlawful Arrest.

(a) A private person who is summoned by a peace officer to assist in effecting an unlawful arrest, is justified in using any force which he would be justified in using if the arrest were lawful provided that he does not believe the arrest is unlawful.

(b) A private person who assists another private person in effecting an unlawful arrest, or who, not being summoned, assists a peace officer in effecting an unlawful arrest, is justified in using any force which he would be justified in using if the arrest were lawful, provided that (i) he believes the arrest is lawful, and (ii) the arrest would be lawful if the facts were as he believes them to be.

(5) Use of Force to Prevent Suicide or the Commission of a Crime.

(a) The use of force upon or toward the person of another is justifiable when the actor believes that such force is immediately necessary to prevent such other person from committing suicide, inflicting serious bodily harm upon himself, committing or consummating the commission of a crime involving or threatening bodily harm, damage to or loss of property or a breach of the peace, except that:

(i) any limitations imposed by the other provisions of this Article on the justifiable use of force in self-protection, for the protection of others, the protection of property, the effectuation of an arrest or the prevention of an escape from custody shall apply notwithstanding the criminality of the conduct against which such force is used; and

(ii) the use of deadly force is not in any event justifiable under this Subsection unless:

(1) the actor believes that there is a substantial risk that the person whom he seeks to prevent from committing a crime will cause death or serious bodily harm to another unless the commission or the consummation of the crime is prevented and that the use of such force presents no substantial risk of injury to innocent persons; or

(2) the actor believes that the use of such force is necessary to suppress a riot or mutiny after the rioters or mutineers have been ordered to disperse and warned, in any particular manner that the law may require, that such force will be used if they do not obey.

(b) The justification afforded by this Subsection extends to the use of confinement as preventive force only if the actor takes all reasonable measures to terminate the confinement as soon as he knows that he safely can, unless the person confined has been arrested on a charge of crime.

Section 3.08 Use of Force by Persons With Special Responsibility for Care, Discipline or Safety of Others

The use of force upon or toward the person of another is justifiable if:

(1) the actor is the parent or guardian or other person similarly responsible for the general care and supervision of a minor or a person acting at the request of such parent, guardian or other responsible person and:

(a) the force is used for the purpose of safeguarding or promoting the welfare of the minor, including the prevention or punishment of his misconduct; and

(b) the force used is not designed to cause or known to create a substantial risk of causing death, serious bodily harm, disfigurement, extreme pain or mental distress or gross degradation; or

(2) the actor is a teacher or a person otherwise entrusted with the care or supervision for a special purpose of a minor and:

(a) the actor believes that the force used is necessary to further such special purpose, including the maintenance of reasonable discipline in a school, class or other group, and that the use of such force is consistent with the welfare of the minor; and

(b) the degree of force, if it had been used by the parent or guardian of the minor, would not be unjustifiable under Subsection (1)(b) of this Section; or

(3) the actor is the guardian or other person similarly responsible for the general care and supervision of an incompetent person; and:

(a) the force is used for the purpose of safeguarding or promoting the welfare of the incompetent person, including the prevention of his misconduct, or, when such incompetent person is in a hospital or other institution for his care and custody, for the maintenance of reasonable discipline in such institution; and

(b) the force used is not designed to cause or known to create a substantial risk of causing death, serious bodily harm, disfigurement, extreme or unnecessary pain, mental distress, or humiliation; or

(4) the actor is a doctor or other therapist or a person assisting him at his direction, and:

(a) the force is used for the purpose of administering a recognized form of treatment which the actor believes to be adapted to promoting the physical or mental health of the patient; and

(b) the treatment is administered with the consent of the patient or, if the patient is a minor or an incompetent person, with the consent of his parent or guardian or other person legally competent to consent in his behalf, or the treatment is administered in an emergency when the actor believes that no one competent to consent can be consulted and that a reasonable person, wishing to safeguard the welfare of the patient, would consent; or

(5) the actor is a warden or other authorized official of a correctional institution, and:

(a) he believes that the force used is necessary for the purpose of enforcing the lawful rules or procedures of the institution, unless his belief in the lawfulness of the rule or procedure sought to be enforced is erroneous and his error is due to ignorance or mistake as to the provisions of the Code, any other provision of the criminal law or the law governing the administration of the institution; and

(b) the nature or degree of force used is not forbidden by Article 303 or 304 of the Code; and

(c) if deadly force is used, its use is otherwise justifiable under this Article; or

(6) the actor is a person responsible for the safety of a vessel or an aircraft or a person acting at his direction, and

(a) he believes that the force used is necessary to prevent interference with the operation of the vessel or aircraft or obstruction of the execution of a lawful order, unless his belief in the lawfulness of the order is erroneous and his error is due to ignorance or mistake as to the law defining his authority; and

(b) if deadly force is used, its use is otherwise justifiable under this Article; or

(7) the actor is a person who is authorized or required by law to maintain order or decorum in a vehicle, train or other carrier or in a place where others are assembled, and:

(a) he believes that the force used is necessary for such purpose; and

(b) the force used is not designed to cause or known to create a substantial risk of causing death, bodily harm, or extreme mental distress.

Section 3.09 Mistake of Law as to Unlawfulness of Force or Legality of Arrest; Reckless or Negligent Use of Otherwise Justifiable Force; Reckless or Negligent Injury or Risk of Injury to Innocent Persons

(1) The justification afforded by Sections 3.04 to 3.07, inclusive, is unavailable when:

(a) the actor's belief in the unlawfulness of the force or conduct against which he employs protective force or his belief in the lawfulness of an arrest which he endeavors to effect by force is erroneous; and

(b) his error is due to ignorance or mistake as to the provisions of the Code, any other provision of the criminal law or the law governing the legality of an arrest or search.

(2) When the actor believes that the use of force upon or toward the person of another is necessary for any of the purposes for which such belief would establish a justification under Sections 3.03 to 3.08 but the actor is reckless or negligent in having such belief or in acquiring or failing to acquire any knowledge or belief which is material to the justifiability of his use of force, the justification afforded by those Sections is unavailable in a prosecution for an offense for which recklessness or negligence, as the case may be, suffices to establish culpability.

(3) When the actor is justified under Sections 3.03 to 3.08 in using force upon or toward the person of another but he recklessly or negligently injures or creates a risk of injury to innocent persons, the justification afforded by those Sec-

tions is unavailable in a prosecution for such recklessness or negligence towards innocent persons.

Section 3.10 Justification in Property Crimes

Conduct involving the appropriation, seizure or destruction of, damage to, intrusion on or interference with property is justifiable under circumstances which would establish a defense of privilege in a civil action based thereon, unless:

(1) the Code or the law defining the offense deals with the specific situation involved; or

(2) a legislative purpose to exclude the justification claimed otherwise plainly appears.

Section 3.11 Definitions

In this Article, unless a different meaning plainly is required:

(1) "unlawful force" means force, including confinement, which is employed without the consent of the person against whom it is directed and the employment of which constitutes an offense or actionable tort or would constitute such offense or tort except for a defense (such as the absence of intent, negligence, or mental capacity; duress; youth; or diplomatic status) not amounting to a privilege to use the force. Assent constitutes consent, within the meaning of this Section, whether or not it otherwise is legally effective, except assent to the infliction of death or serious bodily harm.

(2) "deadly force" means force which the actor uses with the purpose of causing or which he knows to create a substantial risk of causing death or serious bodily harm. Purposely firing a firearm in the direction of another person or at a vehicle in which another person is believed to be constitutes deadly force. A threat to cause death or serious bodily harm, by the production of a weapon or otherwise, so long as the actor's purpose is limited to creating an apprehension that he will use deadly force if necessary, does not constitute deadly force;

(3) "dwelling" means any building or structure, though movable or temporary, or a portion thereof, which is for the time being the actor's home or place of lodging.

ARTICLE 4

RESPONSIBILITY

Section 4.01 Mental Disease or Defect Excluding Responsibility

(1) A person is not responsible for criminal conduct if at the time of such conduct as a result of mental disease or defect he lacks substantial capacity either to appreciate the criminality [wrongfulness] of his conduct or to conform his conduct to the requirements of law.

(2) As used in this Article, the terms "mental disease or defect" do not include an abnormality manifested only by repeated criminal or otherwise anti-social conduct.

Section 4.02 Evidence of Mental Disease or Defect Admissible When Relevant to Element of the Offense; [Mental Disease or Defect Impairing Capacity as Ground for Mitigation of Punishment in Capital Cases]

(1) Evidence that the defendant suffered from a mental disease or defect is admissible whenever it is relevant to prove that the defendant did or did not have a state of mind which is an element of the offense.

[(2) Whenever the jury or the Court is authorized to determine or to recommend whether or not the defendant shall be sentenced to death or imprisonment upon conviction, evidence that the capacity of the defendant to appreciate the criminality [wrongfulness] of his conduct or to conform his conduct to the requirements of law was impaired as a result of mental disease or defect is admissible in favor of sentence of imprisonment.]

Section 4.03 Mental Disease or Defect Excluding Responsibility is Affirmative Defense; Requirement of Notice; Form of Verdict and Judgment When Finding of Irresponsibility is Made

(1) Mental disease or defect excluding responsibility is an affirmative defense.

(2) Evidence of mental disease or defect excluding responsibility is not admissible unless the defendant, at the time of entering his plea of not guilty or within ten days thereafter or at such later time as the Court may for good cause permit, files a written notice of his purpose to rely on such defense.

(3) When the defendant is acquitted on the ground of mental disease or defect excluding responsibility, the verdict and the judgment shall so state.

Section 4.04 Mental Disease or Defect Excluding Fitness to Proceed

No person who as a result of mental disease or defect lacks capacity to understand the proceedings against him or to assist in his own defense shall be tried, convicted or sentenced for the commission of an offense so long as such incapacity endures.

Section 4.05 Psychiatric Examination of Defendant With Respect to Mental Disease or Defect

(1) Whenever the defendant has filed a notice of intention to rely on the defense of mental disease or defect excluding responsibility, or there is reason to doubt his fitness to proceed, or reason to believe that mental disease or defect of the defendant will otherwise become an issue in the cause, the Court shall appoint at least one qualified psychiatrist or shall request the Superintendent of the Hospital to designate at least one qualified psychiatrist, which designation may be or include himself, to examine and report upon the mental condition of the defendant. The Court may order the defendant to be committed to a hospital or other suitable facility for the purpose of the examination for a period of not exceeding sixty days or such longer period as the Court determines to be necessary for the purpose and may direct that a qualified psychiatrist retained by the defendant be permitted to witness and participate in the examination.

(2) In such examination any method may be employed which is accepted by the medical profession for the examination of those alleged to be suffering from mental disease or defect.

(3) The report of the examination shall include the following: (a) a description of the nature of the examination; (b) a diagnosis of the mental

condition of the defendant; (c) if the defendant suffers from a mental disease or defect, an opinion as to his capacity to understand the proceedings against him and to assist in his own defense; (d) when a notice of intention to rely on the defense of irresponsibility has been filed, an opinion as to the extent, if any, to which the capacity of the defendant to appreciate the criminality [wrongfulness] of his conduct or to conform his conduct to the requirements of law was impaired at the time of the criminal conduct charged; and (e) when directed by the Court, an opinion as to the capacity of the defendant to have a particular state of mind which is an element of the offense charged.

If the examination can not be conducted by reason of the unwillingness of the defendant to participate therein, the report shall so state and shall include, if possible an opinion as to whether such unwillingness of the defendant was the result of mental disease or defect.

The report of the examination shall be filed [in triplicate] with the clerk of the Court, who shall cause copies to be delivered to the district attorney and to counsel for the defendant.

Section 4.06   Determination of Fitness to Proceed; Effect of Finding of Unfitness; Proceedings if Fitness is Regained[; Post–Commitment Hearing]

(1) When the defendant's fitness to proceed is drawn in question, the issue shall be determined by the Court. If neither the prosecuting attorney nor counsel for the defendant contests the finding of the report filed pursuant to Section 4.05, the Court may make the determination on the basis of such report. If the finding is contested, the Court shall hold a hearing on the issue. If the report is received in evidence upon such hearing, the party who contests the finding thereof shall have the right to summon and to cross-examine the psychiatrists who joined in the report and to offer evidence upon the issue.

(2) If the Court determines that the defendant lacks fitness to proceed, the proceeding against him shall be suspended, except as provided in Subsection (3) [Subsections (3) and (4)] of this Section, and the Court shall commit him to the custody of the Commissioner of Mental Hygiene [Public Health or Correction] to be placed in an appropriate institution of the Department of Mental Hygiene [Public Health or Correction] for

so long as such unfitness shall endure. When the Court, on its own motion or upon the application of the Commissioner of Mental Hygiene [Public Health or Correction] or the prosecuting attorney, determines, after a hearing if a hearing is requested, that the defendant has regained fitness to proceed, the proceeding shall be resumed. If, however, the Court is of the view that so much time has elapsed since the commitment of the defendant that it would be unjust to resume the criminal proceeding, the Court may dismiss the charge and may order the defendant to be discharged or, subject to the law governing the civil commitment of persons suffering from mental disease or defect, order the defendant to be committed to an appropriate institution of the Department of Mental Hygiene [Public Health].

(3) The fact that the defendant is unfit to proceed does not preclude any legal objection to the prosecution which is susceptible of fair determination prior to trial and without the personal participation of the defendant.

[Alternative: (3) At any time within ninety days after commitment as provided in Subsection (2) of this Section, or at any later time with permission of the Court granted for good cause, the defendant or his counsel or the Commissioner of Mental Hygiene [Public Health or Correction] may apply for a special post-commitment hearing. If the application is made by or on behalf of a defendant not represented by counsel, he shall be afforded a reasonable opportunity to obtain counsel, and if he lacks funds to do so, counsel shall be assigned by the Court. The application shall be granted only if the counsel for the defendant satisfies the Court by affidavit or otherwise that as an attorney he has reasonable grounds for a good faith belief that his client has, on the facts and the law, a defense to the charge other than mental disease or defect excluding responsibility.

[(4) If the motion for a special post-commitment hearing is granted, the hearing shall be by the Court without a jury. No evidence shall be offered at the hearing by either party on the issue of mental disease or defect as a defense to, or in mitigation of, the crime charged. After hearing, the Court may in an appropriate case quash the indictment or other charge, or find it to be defective or insufficient, or determine that it is not proved beyond a reasonable doubt by the evidence, or otherwise terminate the proceedings on the evidence or the law. In any such case, unless all defects in the proceedings are promptly cured, the Court shall terminate the commitment ordered under Subsection (2) of this Section and order the defendant to be discharged or, subject to the law governing the civil commitment of persons suffering from mental disease or defect, order the defendant to be committed to an appropriate institution of the Department of Mental Hygiene [Public Health].]

Section 4.07 Determination of Irresponsibility on Basis of Report; Access to Defendant by Psychiatrist of His Own Choice; Form of Expert Testimony When Issue of Responsibility is Tried

(1) If the report filed pursuant to Section 4.05 finds that the defendant at the time of the criminal conduct charged suffered from a mental disease or defect which substantially impaired his capacity to appreciate the criminality [wrongfulness] of his conduct or to conform his conduct to the requirements of law, and the Court, after a hearing if a hearing is requested by the prosecuting attorney or the defendant, is satisfied that such impairment was sufficient to exclude responsibility, the Court on motion of the defendant shall enter judgment of acquittal on the ground of mental disease or defect excluding responsibility.

(2) When, notwithstanding the report filed pursuant to Section 4.05, the defendant wishes to be examined by a qualified psychiatrist or other expert of his own choice, such examiner shall be permitted to have reasonable access to the defendant for the purposes of such examination.

(3) Upon the trial, the psychiatrists who reported pursuant to Section 4.05 may be called as witnesses by the prosecution, the defendant or the Court. If the issue is being tried before a jury, the jury may be informed that the psychiatrists were designated by the Court or by the Superintendent of the Hospital at the request of the Court as the case may be. If called by the Court, the witness shall be subject to cross-examination by the prosecution and by the defendant. Both the prosecution and the defendant may summon any other qualified psychiatrist or other expert to testify, but no one who has not examined the defendant shall be competent to testify to an expert opinion with respect to the mental condition or responsibility of the defendant, as distinguished from the validity of the procedure

followed by, or the general scientific propositions stated by, another witness.

(4) When a psychiatrist or other expert who has examined the defendant testifies concerning his mental condition, he shall be permitted to make a statement as to the nature of his examination, his diagnosis of the mental condition of the defendant at the time of the commission of the offense charged and his opinion as to the extent, if any, to which the capacity of the defendant to appreciate the criminality [wrongfulness] of his conduct or to conform his conduct to the requirements of law or to have a particular state of mind which is an element of the offense charged was impaired as a result of mental disease or defect at that time. He shall be permitted to make any explanation reasonably serving to clarify his diagnosis and opinion and may be cross-examined as to any matter bearing on his competency or credibility or the validity of his diagnosis or opinion.

Section 4.08 Legal Effect of Acquittal on the Ground of Mental Disease or Defect Excluding Responsibility; Commitment; Release or Discharge

(1) When a defendant is acquitted on the ground of mental disease or defect excluding responsibility, the Court shall order him to be committed to the custody of the Commissioner of Mental Hygiene [Public Health] to be placed in an appropriate institution for custody, care and treatment.

(2) If the Commissioner of Mental Hygiene [Public Health] is of the view that a person committed to his custody, pursuant to paragraph (1) of this Section, may be discharged or released on condition without danger to himself or to others, he shall make application for the discharge or release of such person in a report to the Court by which such person was committed and shall transmit a copy of such application and report to the prosecuting attorney of the county [parish] from which the defendant was committed. The Court shall thereupon appoint at least two qualified psychiatrists to examine such person and to report within sixty days, or such longer period as the Court determines to be necessary for the purpose, their opinion as to his mental condition. To facilitate such examination and the proceedings thereon, the Court may cause such person to be confined in any institution located near the

place where the Court sits, which may hereafter be designated by the Commissioner of Mental Hygiene [Public Health] as suitable for the temporary detention of irresponsible persons.

(3) If the Court is satisfied by the report filed pursuant to paragraph (2) of this Section and such testimony of the reporting psychiatrists as the Court deems necessary that the committed person may be discharged or released on condition without danger to himself or others, the Court shall order his discharge or his release on such conditions as the Court determines to be necessary. If the Court is not so satisfied, it shall promptly order a hearing to determine whether such person may safely be discharged or released. Any such hearing shall be deemed a civil proceeding and the burden shall be upon the committed person to prove that he may safely be discharged or released. According to the determination of the Court upon the hearing, the committed person shall thereupon be discharged or released on such conditions as the Court determines to be necessary, or shall be recommitted to the custody of the Commissioner of Mental Hygiene [Public Health], subject to discharge or release only in accordance with the procedure prescribed above for a first hearing.

(4) If, within [five] years after the conditional release of a committed person, the Court shall determine, after hearing evidence, that the conditions of release have not been fulfilled and that for the safety of such person or for the safety of others his conditional release should be revoked, the Court shall forthwith order him to be recommitted to the Commissioner of Mental Hygiene [Public Health], subject to discharge or release only in accordance with the procedure prescribed above for a first hearing.

(5) A committed person may make application for his discharge or release to the Court by which he was committed, and the procedure to be followed upon such application shall be the same as that prescribed above in the case of an application by the Commissioner of Mental Hygiene [Public Health]. However, no such application by a committed person need be considered until he has been confined for a period of not less than [six months] from the date of the order of commitment, and if the determination of the Court be adverse to the application, such person shall not be permitted to file a further application until [one year] has elapsed from the date of any preceding hearing on an application for his release or discharge.

Section 4.09 Statements for Purposes of Examination or Treatment Inadmissible Except on Issue of Mental Condition

A statement made by a person subjected to psychiatric examination or treatment pursuant to Sections 4.05, 4.06 or 4.08 for the purposes of such examination or treatment shall not be admissible in evidence against him in any criminal proceeding on any issue other than that of his mental condition but it shall be admissible upon that issue, whether or not it would otherwise be deemed a privileged communication [, unless such statement constitutes an admission of guilt of the crime charged].

Section 4.10 Immaturity Excluding Criminal Conviction; Transfer of Proceedings to Juvenile Court

(1) A person shall not be tried for or convicted of an offense if:

(a) at the time of the conduct charged to constitute the offense he was less than sixteen years of age [, in which case the Juvenile Court shall have exclusive jurisdiction *]; or

(b) at the time of the conduct charged to constitute the offense he was sixteen or seventeen years of age unless:

(i) the Juvenile Court has no jurisdiction over him, or,

(ii) the Juvenile Court has entered an order waiving jurisdiction and consenting to the institution of criminal proceedings against him.

(2) No court shall have jurisdiction to try or convict a person of an offense if criminal proceedings against him are barred by Subsection (1) of this Section. When it appears that a person charged with the commission of an offense may be of such an age that criminal proceedings may be barred under Subsection (1) of this Section, the Court shall hold a hearing thereon, and the burden shall be on the prosecution to establish to the satisfaction of the Court that the criminal proceeding is not barred upon such grounds. If the Court determines that the proceeding is barred, custody of the person charged shall be surrendered to the Juvenile Court, and the case, includ-

ing all papers and processes relating thereto, shall be transferred.

* The bracketed words are unnecessary if the Juvenile Court Act so provides or is amended accordingly.

ARTICLE 5

INCHOATE CRIMES

Section 5.01 Criminal Attempt

(1) **Definition of Attempt.** A person is guilty of an attempt to commit a crime if, acting with the kind of culpability otherwise required for commission of the crime, he:

(a) purposely engages in conduct which would constitute the crime if the attendant circumstances were as he believes them to be; or

(b) when causing a particular result is an element of the crime, does or omits to do anything with the purpose of causing or with the belief that it will cause such result without further conduct on his part; or

(c) purposely does or omits to do anything which, under the circumstances as he believes them to be, is an act or omission constituting a substantial step in a course of conduct planned to culminate in his commission of the crime.

(2) **Conduct Which May Be Held Substantial Step Under Subsection (1)(c).** Conduct shall not be held to constitute a substantial step under Subsection (1)(c) of this Section unless it is strongly corroborative of the actor's criminal purpose. Without negativing the sufficiency of other conduct, the following, if strongly corroborative of the actor's criminal purpose, shall not be held insufficient as a matter of law:

(a) lying in wait, searching for or following the contemplated victim of the crime;

(b) enticing or seeking to entice the contemplated victim of the crime to go to the place contemplated for its commission;

(c) reconnoitering the place contemplated for the commission of the crime;

(d) unlawful entry of a structure, vehicle or enclosure in which it is contemplated that the crime will be committed;

(e) possession of materials to be employed in the commission of the crime, which are specially designed for such unlawful use or which can serve no lawful purpose of the actor under the circumstances;

(f) possession, collection or fabrication of materials to be employed in the commission of the crime, at or near the place contemplated for its commission, where such possession, collection or fabrication serves no lawful purpose of the actor under the circumstances;

(g) soliciting an innocent agent to engage in conduct constituting an element of the crime.

(3) **Conduct Designed to Aid Another in Commission of a Crime.** A person who engages in conduct designed to aid another to commit a crime which would establish his complicity under Section 2.06 if the crime were committed by such other person, is guilty of an attempt to commit the crime, although the crime is not committed or attempted by such other person.

(4) **Renunciation of Criminal Purpose.** When the actor's conduct would otherwise constitute an attempt under Subsection (1)(b) or (1)(c) of this Section, it is an affirmative defense that he abandoned his effort to commit the crime or otherwise prevented its commission, under circumstances manifesting a complete and voluntary renunciation of his criminal purpose. The establishment of such defense does not, however, affect the liability of an accomplice who did not join in such abandonment or prevention.

Within the meaning of this Article, renunciation of criminal purpose is not voluntary if it is motivated, in whole or in part, by circumstances, not present or apparent at the inception of the actor's course of conduct, which increase the probability of detection or apprehension or which make more difficult the accomplishment of the criminal purpose. Renunciation is not complete if it is motivated by a decision to postpone the criminal conduct until a more advantageous time or to transfer the criminal effort to another but similar objective or victim.

Section 5.02 Criminal Solicitation

(1) **Definition of Solicitation.** A person is guilty of solicitation to commit a crime if with the purpose of promoting or facilitating its commission he commands, encourages or requests anoth-

er person to engage in specific conduct which would constitute such crime or an attempt to commit such crime or which would establish his complicity in its commission or attempted commission.

(2) Uncommunicated Solicitation. It is immaterial under Subsection (1) of this Section that the actor fails to communicate with the person he solicits to commit a crime if his conduct was designed to effect such communication.

(3) Renunciation of Criminal Purpose. It is an affirmative defense that the actor, after soliciting another person to commit a crime, persuaded him not to do so or otherwise prevented the commission of the crime, under circumstances manifesting a complete and voluntary renunciation of his criminal purpose.

Section 5.03 Criminal Conspiracy

(1) Definition of Conspiracy. A person is guilty of conspiracy with another person or persons to commit a crime if with the purpose of promoting or facilitating its commission he:

(a) agrees with such other person or persons that they or one or more of them will engage in conduct which constitutes such crime or an attempt or solicitation to commit such crime; or

(b) agrees to aid such other person or persons in the planning or commission of such crime or of an attempt or solicitation to commit such crime.

(2) Scope of Conspiratorial Relationship. If a person guilty of conspiracy, as defined by Subsection (1) of this Section, knows that a person with whom he conspires to commit a crime has conspired with another person or persons to commit the same crime, he is guilty of conspiring with such other person or persons, whether or not he knows their identity, to commit such crime.

(3) Conspiracy With Multiple Criminal Objectives. If a person conspires to commit a number of crimes, he is guilty of only one conspiracy so long as such multiple crimes are the object of the same agreement or continuous conspiratorial relationship.

(4) Joinder and Venue in Conspiracy Prosecutions.

(a) Subject to the provisions of paragraph (b) of this Subsection, two or more persons charged

with criminal conspiracy may be prosecuted jointly if:

(i) they are charged with conspiring with one another; or

(ii) the conspiracies alleged, whether they have the same or different parties, are so related that they constitute different aspects of a scheme of organized criminal conduct.

(b) In any joint prosecution under paragraph (a) of this Subsection:

(i) no defendant shall be charged with a conspiracy in any county [parish or district] other than one in which he entered into such conspiracy or in which an overt act pursuant to such conspiracy was done by him or by a person with whom he conspired; and

(ii) neither the liability of any defendant nor the admissibility against him of evidence of acts or declarations of another shall be enlarged by such joinder; and

(iii) the Court shall order a severance or take a special verdict as to any defendant who so requests, if it deems it necessary or appropriate to promote the fair determination of his guilt or innocence, and shall take any other proper measures to protect the fairness of the trial.

(5) Overt Act. No person may be convicted of conspiracy to commit a crime, other than a felony of the first or second degree, unless an overt act in pursuance of such conspiracy is alleged and proved to have been done by him or by a person with whom he conspired.

(6) Renunciation of Criminal Purpose. It is an affirmative defense that the actor, after conspiring to commit a crime, thwarted the success of the conspiracy, under circumstances manifesting a complete and voluntary renunciation of his criminal purpose.

(7) Duration of Conspiracy. For purposes of Section 1.06(4):

(a) conspiracy is a continuing course of conduct which terminates when the crime or crimes which are its object are committed or the agreement that they be committed is abandoned by the defendant and by those with whom he conspired; and

(b) such abandonment is presumed if neither the defendant nor anyone with whom he conspired does any overt act in pursuance of the conspiracy during the applicable period of limitation; and

(c) if an individual abandons the agreement, the conspiracy is terminated as to him only if and when he advises those with whom he conspired of his abandonment or he informs the law enforcement authorities of the existence of the conspiracy and of his participation therein.

Section 5.04 Incapacity, Irresponsibility or Immunity of Party to Solicitation or Conspiracy

(1) Except as provided in Subsection (2) of this Section, it is immaterial to the liability of a person who solicits or conspires with another to commit a crime that:

(a) he or the person whom he solicits or with whom he conspires does not occupy a particular position or have a particular characteristic which is an element of such crime, if he believes that one of them does; or

(b) the person whom he solicits or with whom he conspires is irresponsible or has an immunity to prosecution or conviction for the commission of the crime.

(2) It is a defense to a charge of solicitation or conspiracy to commit a crime that if the criminal object were achieved, the actor would not be guilty of a crime under the law defining the offense or as an accomplice under Section 2.06(5) or 2.06(6)(a) or (b).

Section 5.05 Grading of Criminal Attempt, Solicitation and Conspiracy; Mitigation in Cases of Lesser Danger; Multiple Convictions Barred

(1) **Grading.** Except as otherwise provided in this Section, attempt, solicitation and conspiracy are crimes of the same grade and degree as the most serious offense which is attempted or solicited or is an object of the conspiracy. An attempt, solicitation or conspiracy to commit a [capital crime or a] felony of the first degree is a felony of the second degree.

(2) **Mitigation.** If the particular conduct charged to constitute a criminal attempt, solicitation or conspiracy is so inherently unlikely to result or culminate in the commission of a crime that neither such conduct nor the actor presents a public danger warranting the grading of such offense under this Section, the Court shall exercise its power under Section 6.12 to enter judgment and impose sentence for a crime of lower grade or degree or, in extreme cases, may dismiss the prosecution.

(3) **Multiple Convictions.** A person may not be convicted of more than one offense defined by this Article for conduct designed to commit or to culminate in the commission of the same crime.

Section 5.06 Possessing Instruments of Crime; Weapons

(1) **Criminal Instruments Generally.** A person commits a misdemeanor if he possesses any instrument of crime with purpose to employ it criminally. "Instrument of crime" means:

(a) anything specially made or specially adapted for criminal use; or

(b) anything commonly used for criminal purposes and possessed by the actor under circumstances which do not negative unlawful purpose.

(2) **Presumption of Criminal Purpose from Possession of Weapon.** If a person possesses a firearm or other weapon on or about his person, in a vehicle occupied by him, or otherwise readily available for use, it is presumed that he had the purpose to employ it criminally, unless:

(a) the weapon is possessed in the actor's home or place of business;

(b) the actor is licensed or otherwise authorized by law to possess such weapon; or

(c) the weapon is of a type commonly used in lawful sport.

"Weapon" means anything readily capable of lethal use and possessed under circumstances not manifestly appropriate for lawful uses which it may have; the term includes a firearm which is not loaded or lacks a clip or other component to render it immediately operable, and components which can readily be assembled into a weapon.

(3) **Presumptions as to Possession of Criminal Instruments in Automobiles.** Where a weapon or other instrument of crime is found in an automobile, it shall be presumed to be in the possession of the occupant if there is but one. If there is more than one occupant, it shall be presumed to be in the possession of all, except under the following circumstances:

(a) where it is found upon the person of one of the occupants;

(b) where the automobile is not a stolen one and the weapon or instrument is found out of view in a glove compartment, car trunk, or other enclosed customary depository, in which case it shall be presumed to be in the possession of the occupant or occupants who own or have authority to operate the automobile;

(c) in the case of a taxicab, a weapon or instrument found in the passengers' portion of the vehicle shall be presumed to be in the possession of all the passengers, if there are any, and, if not, in the possession of the driver.

Section 5.07 Prohibited Offensive Weapons

A person commits a misdemeanor if, except as authorized by law, he makes, repairs, sells, or otherwise deals in, uses, or possesses any offensive weapon. "Offensive weapon" means any bomb, machine gun, sawed-off shotgun, firearm specially made or specially adapted for concealment or silent discharge, any blackjack, sandbag, metal knuckles, dagger, or other implement for the infliction of serious bodily injury which serves no common lawful purpose. It is a defense under this Section for the defendant to prove by a preponderance of evidence that he possessed or dealt with the weapon solely as a curio or in a dramatic performance, or that he possessed it briefly in consequence of having found it or taken it from an aggressor, or under circumstances similarly negativing any purpose or likelihood that the weapon would be used unlawfully. The presumptions provided in Section 5.06(3) are applicable to prosecutions under this Section.

ARTICLE 6

AUTHORIZED DISPOSITION OF OFFENDERS

Section 6.01 Degrees of Felonies

(1) Felonies defined by this Code are classified, for the purpose of sentence, into three degrees, as follows:

(a) felonies of the first degree;

(b) felonies of the second degree;

(c) felonies of the third degree.

A felony is of the first or second degree when it is so designated by the Code. A crime declared to be a felony, without specification of degree, is of the third degree.

(2) Notwithstanding any other provision of law, a felony defined by any statute of this State other than this Code shall constitute for the purpose of sentence a felony of the third degree.

Section 6.02 Sentence in Accordance With Code; Authorized Dispositions

(1) No person convicted of an offense shall be sentenced otherwise than in accordance with this Article.

[(2) The Court shall sentence a person who has been convicted of murder to death or imprisonment, in accordance with Section 210.6.]

(3) Except as provided in Subsection (2) of this Section and subject to the applicable provisions of the Code, the Court may suspend the imposition of sentence on a person who has been convicted of a crime, may order him to be committed in lieu of sentence, in accordance with Section 6.13, or may sentence him as follows:

(a) to pay a fine authorized by Section 6.03; or

(b) to be placed on probation [, and, in the case of a person convicted of a felony or misdemeanor to imprisonment for a term fixed by the Court not exceeding thirty days to be served as a condition of probation]; or

(c) to imprisonment for a term authorized by Sections 6.05, 6.06, 6.07, 6.08, 6.09, or 7.06; or

(d) to fine and probation or fine and imprisonment, but not to probation and imprisonment [, except as authorized in paragraph (b) of this Subsection].

(4) The Court may suspend the imposition of sentence on a person who has been convicted of a violation or may sentence him to pay a fine authorized by Section 6.03.

(5) This Article does not deprive the Court of any authority conferred by law to decree a forfeiture of property, suspend or cancel a license, remove a person from office, or impose any other civil penalty. Such a judgment or order may be included in the sentence.

Section 6.03 Fines

A person who has been convicted of an offense may be sentenced to pay a fine not exceeding:

(1) $10,000, when the conviction is of a felony of the first or second degree;

(2) $5,000, when the conviction is of a felony of the third degree;

(3) $1,000, when the conviction is of a misdemeanor;

(4) $500, when the conviction is of a petty misdemeanor or a violation;

(5) any higher amount equal to double the pecuniary gain derived from the offense by the offender;

(6) any higher amount specifically authorized by statute.

Section 6.04 Penalties Against Corporations and Unincorporated Associations; Forfeiture of Corporate Charter or Revocation of Certificate Authorizing Foreign Corporation to Do Business in the State

(1) The Court may suspend the sentence of a corporation or an unincorporated association which has been convicted of an offense or may sentence it to pay a fine authorized by Section 6.03.

(2)(a) The [prosecuting attorney] is authorized to institute civil proceedings in the appropriate court of general jurisdiction to forfeit the charter of a corporation organized under the laws of this State or to revoke the certificate authorizing a foreign corporation to conduct business in this State. The Court may order the charter forfeited or the certificate revoked upon finding (i) that the board of directors or a high managerial agent acting in behalf of the corporation has, in conducting the corporation's affairs, purposely engaged in a persistent course of criminal conduct and (ii) that for the prevention of future criminal conduct of the same character, the public interest requires the charter of the corporation to be forfeited and the corporation to be dissolved or the certificate to be revoked.

(b) When a corporation is convicted of a crime or a high managerial agent of a corporation, as defined in Section 2.07, is convicted of a crime committed in the conduct of the affairs of the corporation, the Court, in sentencing the corporation or the agent, may direct the [prosecuting attorney] to institute proceedings authorized by paragraph (a) of this Subsection.

(c) The proceedings authorized by paragraph (a) of this Subsection shall be conducted in accordance with the procedures authorized by law for the involuntary dissolution of a corporation or the revocation of the certificate authorizing a foreign corporation to conduct business in this State. Such proceedings shall be deemed additional to any other proceedings authorized by law for the purpose of forfeiting the charter of a corporation or revoking the certificate of a foreign corporation.

Section 6.05 Young Adult Offenders

(1) **Specialized Correctional Treatment.** A young adult offender is a person convicted of a crime who, at the time of sentencing, is sixteen but less than twenty-two years of age. A young adult offender who is sentenced to a term of imprisonment which may exceed thirty days [alternatives: (1) ninety days; (2) one year] shall be committed to the custody of the Division of Young Adult Correction of the Department of Correction, and shall receive, as far as practicable, such special and individualized correctional and rehabilitative treatment as may be appropriate to his needs.

(2) **Special Term.** A young adult offender convicted of a felony may, in lieu of any other sentence of imprisonment authorized by this Article, be sentenced to a special term of imprisonment without a minimum and with a maximum of four years, regardless of the degree of the felony involved, if the Court is of the opinion that such special term is adequate for his correction and rehabilitation and will not jeopardize the protection of the public.

[(3) **Removal of Disabilities; Vacation of Conviction.**

(a) In sentencing a young adult offender to the special term provided by this Section or to any sentence other than one of imprisonment, the Court may order that so long as he is not convicted of another felony, the judgment shall not constitute a conviction for the purposes of any disqualification or disability imposed by law upon conviction of a crime.

(b) When any young adult offender is unconditionally discharged from probation or parole before the expiration of the maximum term thereof, the Court may enter an order vacating the judgment of conviction.]

[(4) **Commitment for Observation.** If, after pre-sentence investigation, the Court desires additional information concerning a young adult offender before imposing sentence, it may order that he be committed, for a period not exceeding ninety days, to the custody of the Division of Young Adult Correction of the Department of Correction for observation and study at an appropriate reception or classification center. Such Division of the Department of Correction and the [Young Adult Division of the] Board of Parole shall advise the Court of their findings and recommendations on or before the expiration of such ninety-day period.]

Subsection (3) should be eliminated if Section 306.6, dealing with removal of disabilities generally, is adopted.

Subsection (4) should be eliminated if Subsection (1) of Section 7.08, dealing with commitments for observation generally, is adopted.

Section 6.06 Sentence of Imprisonment for Felony; Ordinary Terms

A person who has been convicted of a felony may be sentenced to imprisonment, as follows:

(1) in the case of a felony of the first degree, for a term the minimum of which shall be fixed by the Court at not less than one year nor more than ten years, and the maximum of which shall be life imprisonment;

(2) in the case of a felony of the second degree, for a term the minimum of which shall be fixed by the Court at not less than one year nor more than three years, and the maximum of which shall be ten years;

(3) in the case of a felony of the third degree, for a term the minimum of which shall be fixed by the Court at not less than one year nor more than two years, and the maximum of which shall be five years.

Alternate Section 6.06 Sentence of Imprisonment for Felony; Ordinary Terms

A person who has been convicted of a felony may be sentenced to imprisonment, as follows:

(1) in the case of a felony of the first degree, for a term the minimum of which shall be fixed by the Court at not less than one year nor more than ten years, and the maximum at not more than twenty years or at life imprisonment;

(2) in the case of a felony of the second degree, for a term the minimum of which shall be fixed by the Court at not less than one year nor more than three years, and the maximum at not more than ten years;

(3) in the case of a felony of the third degree, for a term the minimum of which shall be fixed by the Court at not less than one year nor more than two years, and the maximum at not more than five years.

No sentence shall be imposed under this Section of which the minimum is longer than one-half the maximum, or, when the maximum is life imprisonment, longer than ten years.

Section 6.07 Sentence of Imprisonment for Felony; Extended Terms

In the cases designated in Section 7.03, a person who has been convicted of a felony may be sentenced to an extended term of imprisonment, as follows:

(1) in the case of a felony of the first degree, for a term the minimum of which shall be fixed by the Court at not less than five years nor more than ten years, and the maximum of which shall be life imprisonment;

(2) in the case of a felony of the second degree, for a term the minimum of which shall be fixed by the Court at not less than one year nor more than five years, and the maximum of which shall be fixed by the Court at not less than ten nor more than twenty years;

(3) in the case of a felony of the third degree, for a term the minimum of which shall be fixed by the Court at not less than one year nor more than three years, and the maximum of which shall be fixed by the Court at not less than five nor more than ten years.

Section 6.08 Sentence of Imprisonment for Misdemeanors and Petty Misdemeanors; Ordinary Terms

A person who has been convicted of a misdemeanor or a petty misdemeanor may be sentenced to imprisonment for a definite term which shall be fixed by the Court and shall not exceed one year in the case of a misdemeanor or thirty days in the case of a petty misdemeanor.

Section 6.09 Sentence of Imprisonment for Misdemeanors and Petty Misdemeanors; Extended Terms

(1) In the cases designated in Section 7.04, a person who has been convicted of a misdemeanor or a petty misdemeanor may be sentenced to an extended term of imprisonment, as follows:

(a) in the case of a misdemeanor, for a term the minimum of which shall be fixed by the Court at not more than one year and the maximum of which shall be three years;

(b) in the case of a petty misdemeanor, for a term the minimum of which shall be fixed by the Court at not more than six months and the maximum of which shall be two years.

(2) No such sentence for an extended term shall be imposed unless:

(a) the Director of Correction has certified that there is an institution in the Department of Correction, or in a county, city [or other appropriate political subdivision of the State] which is appropriate for the detention and correctional treatment of such misdemeanants or petty misdemeanants, and that such institution is available to receive such commitments; and

(b) the [Board of Parole] [Parole Administrator] has certified that the Board of Parole is able to visit such institution and to assume responsibility for the release of such prisoners on parole and for their parole supervision.

Section 6.10 First Release of All Offenders on Parole; Sentence of Imprisonment Includes Separate Parole Term; Length of Parole Term; Length of Recommitment and Reparole After Revocation of Parole; Final Unconditional Release

(1) **First Release of All Offenders on Parole.** An offender sentenced to an indefinite term of imprisonment in excess of one year under Section 6.05, 6.06, 6.07, 6.09 or 7.06 shall be released conditionally on parole at or before the expiration of the maximum of such term, in accordance with Article 305.

(2) **Sentence of Imprisonment Includes Separate Parole Term; Length of Parole Term.** A sentence to an indefinite term of imprisonment in excess of one year under Section 6.05, 6.06, 6.07, 6.09 or 7.06 includes as a separate portion of the sentence a term of parole or of recommitment for violation of the conditions of parole which governs the duration of parole or recommitment after the offender's first conditional release on parole. The minimum of such term is one year and the maximum is five years, unless the sentence was imposed under Section 6.05(2) or Section 6.09, in which case the maximum is two years.

(3) **Length of Recommitment and Reparole After Revocation of Parole.** If an offender is recommitted upon revocation of his parole, the term of further imprisonment upon such recommitment and of any subsequent reparole or recommitment under the same sentence shall be fixed by the Board of Parole but shall not exceed in aggregate length the unserved balance of the maximum parole term provided by Subsection (2) of this Section.

(4) **Final Unconditional Release.** When the maximum of his parole term has expired or he has been sooner discharged from parole under Section 305.12, an offender shall be deemed to have served his sentence and shall be released unconditionally.

Section 6.11 Place of Imprisonment.

(1) When a person is sentenced to imprisonment for an indefinite term with a maximum in excess of one year, the Court shall commit him to the custody of the Department of Correction [or other single department or agency] for the term of his sentence and until released in accordance with law.

(2) When a person is sentenced to imprisonment for a definite term, the Court shall designate the institution or agency to which he is committed for the term of his sentence and until released in accordance with law.

Section 6.12 Reduction of Conviction by Court to Lesser Degree of Felony or to Misdemeanor

If, when a person has been convicted of a felony, the Court, having regard to the nature and circumstances of the crime and to the history and character of the defendant, is of the view that it would be unduly harsh to sentence the offender in accordance with the Code, the Court may enter judgment of conviction for a lesser degree of felony or for a misdemeanor and impose sentence accordingly.

Section 6.13 Civil Commitment in Lieu of Prosecution or of Sentence

(1) When a person prosecuted for a [felony of the third degree,] misdemeanor or petty misdemeanor is a chronic alcoholic, narcotic addict [or prostitute] or person suffering from mental abnormality and the Court is authorized by law to order the civil commitment of such person to a hospital or other institution for medical, psychiatric or other rehabilitative treatment, the Court may order such commitment and dismiss the prosecution. The order of commitment may be made after conviction, in which event the Court may set aside the verdict or judgment of conviction and dismiss the prosecution.

(2) The Court shall not make an order under Subsection (1) of this Section unless it is of the view that it will substantially further the rehabilitation of the defendant and will not jeopardize the protection of the public.

ARTICLE 7

AUTHORITY OF COURT IN SENTENCING

Section 7.01 Criteria for Withholding Sentence of Imprisonment and for Placing Defendant on Probation

(1) The Court shall deal with a person who has been convicted of a crime without imposing sentence of imprisonment unless, having regard to the nature and circumstances of the crime and the history, character and condition of the defendant, it is of the opinion that his imprisonment is necessary for protection of the public because:

(a) there is undue risk that during the period of a suspended sentence or probation the defendant will commit another crime; or

(b) the defendant is in need of correctional treatment that can be provided most effectively by his commitment to an institution; or

(c) a lesser sentence will depreciate the seriousness of the defendant's crime.

(2) The following grounds, while not controlling the discretion of the Court, shall be accorded weight in favor of withholding sentence of imprisonment:

(a) the defendant's criminal conduct neither caused nor threatened serious harm;

(b) the defendant did not contemplate that his criminal conduct would cause or threaten serious harm;

(c) the defendant acted under a strong provocation;

(d) there were substantial grounds tending to excuse or justify the defendant's criminal conduct, though failing to establish a defense;

(e) the victim of the defendant's criminal conduct induced or facilitated its commission;

(f) the defendant has compensated or will compensate the victim of his criminal conduct for the damage or injury that he sustained;

(g) the defendant has no history of prior delinquency or criminal activity or has led a law-abiding life for a substantial period of time before the commission of the present crime;

(h) the defendant's criminal conduct was the result of circumstances unlikely to recur;

(i) the character and attitudes of the defendant indicate that he is unlikely to commit another crime;

(j) the defendant is particularly likely to respond affirmatively to probationary treatment;

(k) the imprisonment of the defendant would entail excessive hardship to himself or his dependents.

(3) When a person who has been convicted of a crime is not sentenced to imprisonment, the Court shall place him on probation if he is in need of the supervision, guidance, assistance or direction that the probation service can provide.

Section 7.02 Criteria for Imposing Fines

(1) The Court shall not sentence a defendant only to pay a fine, when any other disposition is authorized by law, unless having regard to the nature and circumstances of the crime and to the history and character of the defendant, it is of the opinion that the fine alone suffices for protection of the public.

(2) The Court shall not sentence a defendant to pay a fine in addition to a sentence of imprisonment or probation unless:

(a) the defendant has derived a pecuniary gain from the crime; or

(b) the Court is of opinion that a fine is specially adapted to deterrence of the crime involved or to the correction of the offender.

(3) The Court shall not sentence a defendant to pay a fine unless:

(a) the defendant is or will be able to pay the fine; and

(b) the fine will not prevent the defendant from making restitution or reparation to the victim of the crime.

(4) In determining the amount and method of payment of a fine, the Court shall take into account the financial resources of the defendant and the nature of the burden that its payment will impose.

Section 7.03   Criteria for Sentence of Extended Term of Imprisonment; Felonies

The Court may sentence a person who has been convicted of a felony to an extended term of imprisonment if it finds one or more of the grounds specified in this Section. The finding of the Court shall be incorporated in the record.

(1) The defendant is a persistent offender whose commitment for an extended term is necessary for protection of the public.

The Court shall not make such a finding unless the defendant is over twenty-one years of age and has previously been convicted of two felonies or of one felony and two misdemeanors, committed at different times when he was over [insert Juvenile Court age] years of age.

(2) The defendant is a professional criminal whose commitment for an extended term is necessary for protection of the public.

The Court shall not make such a finding unless the defendant is over twenty-one years of age and:

(a) the circumstances of the crime show that the defendant has knowingly devoted himself to criminal activity as a major source of livelihood; or

(b) the defendant has substantial income or resources not explained to be derived from a source other than criminal activity.

(3) The defendant is a dangerous, mentally abnormal person whose commitment for an extended term is necessary for protection of the public.

The Court shall not make such a finding unless the defendant has been subjected to a psychiatric examination resulting in the conclusions that his mental condition is gravely abnormal; that his criminal conduct has been characterized by a pattern of repetitive or compulsive behavior or by persistent aggressive behavior with heedless indifference to consequences; and that such condition makes him a serious danger to others.

(4) The defendant is a multiple offender whose criminality was so extensive that a sentence of imprisonment for an extended term is warranted.

The Court shall not make such a finding unless:

(a) the defendant is being sentenced for two or more felonies, or is already under sentence of imprisonment for felony, and the sentences of imprisonment involved will run concurrently under Section 7.06; or

(b) the defendant admits in open court the commission of one or more other felonies and asks that they be taken into account when he is sentenced; and

(c) the longest sentences of imprisonment authorized for each of the defendant's crimes, including admitted crimes taken into account, if made to run consecutively would exceed in length the minimum and maximum of the extended term imposed.

Section 7.04   Criteria for Sentence of Extended Term of Imprisonment; Misdemeanors and Petty Misdemeanors

The Court may sentence a person who has been convicted of a misdemeanor or petty misdemeanor to an extended term of imprisonment if it finds one or more of the grounds specified in this Section. The finding of the Court shall be incorporated in the record.

(1) The defendant is a persistent offender whose commitment for an extended term is necessary for protection of the public.

The Court shall not make such a finding unless the defendant has previously been convicted of two crimes, committed at different times when he was over [insert Juvenile Court age] years of age.

(2) The defendant is a professional criminal whose commitment for an extended term is necessary for protection of the public.

The Court shall not make such a finding unless:

(a) the circumstances of the crime show that the defendant has knowingly devoted himself to criminal activity as a major source of livelihood; or

(b) the defendant has substantial income or resources not explained to be derived from a source other than criminal activity.

(3) The defendant is a chronic alcoholic, narcotic addict, prostitute or person of abnormal mental condition who requires rehabilitative treatment for a substantial period of time.

The Court shall not make such a finding unless, with respect to the particular category to which the defendant belongs, the Director of Correction has certified that there is a specialized institution or facility which is satisfactory for the rehabilitative treatment of such persons and which otherwise meets the requirements of Section 6.09, Subsection (2).

(4) The defendant is a multiple offender whose criminality was so extensive that a sentence of imprisonment for an extended term is warranted.

The Court shall not make such a finding unless:

(a) the defendant is being sentenced for a number of misdemeanors or petty misdemeanors or is already under sentence of imprisonment for crime of such grades, or admits in open court the commission of one or more such crimes and asks that they be taken into account when he is sentenced; and

(b) maximum fixed sentences of imprisonment for each of the defendant's crimes, including admitted crimes taken into account, if made to run consecutively, would exceed in length the maximum period of the extended term imposed.

Section 7.05   Former Conviction in Another Jurisdiction; Definition and Proof of Conviction; Sentence Taking into Account Admitted Crimes Bars Subsequent Conviction for Such Crimes

(1) For purposes of paragraph (1) of Section 7.03 or 7.04, a conviction of the commission of a crime in another jurisdiction shall constitute a previous conviction. Such conviction shall be deemed to have been of a felony if sentence of death or of imprisonment in excess of one year was authorized under the law of such other jurisdiction, of a misdemeanor if sentence of imprisonment in excess of thirty days but not in excess of a year was authorized and of a petty misdemeanor if sentence of imprisonment for not more than thirty days was authorized.

(2) An adjudication by a court of competent jurisdiction that the defendant committed a crime constitutes a conviction for purposes of Sections 7.03 to 7.05 inclusive, although sentence or the execution thereof was suspended, provided that the time to appeal has expired and that the defendant was not pardoned on the ground of innocence.

(3) Prior conviction may be proved by any evidence, including fingerprint records made in connection with arrest, conviction or imprisonment, that reasonably satisfies the Court that the defendant was convicted.

(4) When the defendant has asked that other crimes admitted in open court be taken into account when he is sentenced and the Court has not rejected such request, the sentence shall bar the prosecution or conviction of the defendant in this State for any such admitted crime.

Section 7.06   Multiple Sentences; Concurrent and Consecutive Terms

(1) **Sentences of Imprisonment for More Than One Crime.** When multiple sentences of imprisonment are imposed on a defendant for more than one crime, including a crime for which a previous suspended sentence or sentence of probation has been revoked, such multiple sentences shall run concurrently or consecutively as the Court determines at the time of sentence, except that:

(a) a definite and an indefinite term shall run concurrently and both sentences shall be satisfied by service of the indefinite term; and

(b) the aggregate of consecutive definite terms shall not exceed one year; and

(c) the aggregate of consecutive indefinite terms shall not exceed in minimum or maximum length the longest extended term authorized for the highest grade and degree of crime for which any of the sentences was imposed; and

(d) not more than one sentence for an extended term shall be imposed.

(2) Sentences of Imprisonment Imposed at Different Times. When a defendant who has previously been sentenced to imprisonment is subsequently sentenced to another term for a crime committed prior to the former sentence, other than a crime committed while in custody:

(a) the multiple sentences imposed shall so far as possible conform to Subsection (1) of this Section; and

(b) whether the Court determines that the terms shall run concurrently or consecutively, the defendant shall be credited with time served in imprisonment on the prior sentence in determining the permissible aggregate length of the term or terms remaining to be served; and

(c) when a new sentence is imposed on a prisoner who is on parole, the balance of the parole term on the former sentence shall be deemed to run during the period of the new imprisonment.

(3) Sentence of Imprisonment for Crime Committed While on Parole. When a defendant is sentenced to imprisonment for a crime committed while on parole in this State, such term of imprisonment and any period of reimprisonment that the Board of Parole may require the defendant to serve upon the revocation of his parole shall run concurrently, unless the Court orders them to run consecutively.

(4) Multiple Sentences of Imprisonment in Other Cases. Except as otherwise provided in this Section, multiple terms of imprisonment shall run concurrently or consecutively as the Court determines when the second or subsequent sentence is imposed.

(5) Calculation of Concurrent and Consecutive Terms of Imprisonment.

(a) When indefinite terms run concurrently, the shorter minimum terms merge in and are satisfied by serving the longest minimum term and the shorter maximum terms merge in and are satisfied by discharge of the longest maximum term.

(b) When indefinite terms run consecutively, the minimum terms are added to arrive at an aggregate minimum to be served equal to the sum of all minimum terms and the maximum terms are added to arrive at an aggregate maximum equal to the sum of all maximum terms.

(c) When a definite and an indefinite term run consecutively, the period of the definite term is added to both the minimum and maximum of the indefinite term and both sentences are satisfied by serving the indefinite term.

(6) Suspension of Sentence or Probation and Imprisonment; Multiple Terms of Suspension and Probation. When a defendant is sentenced for more than one offense or a defendant already under sentence is sentenced for another offense committed prior to the former sentence:

(a) the Court shall not sentence to probation a defendant who is under sentence of imprisonment [with more than thirty days to run] or impose a sentence of probation and a sentence of imprisonment [, except as authorized by Section 6.02(3)(b)]; and

(b) multiple periods of suspension or probation shall run concurrently from the date of the first such disposition; and

(c) when a sentence of imprisonment is imposed for an indefinite term, the service of such sentence shall satisfy a suspended sentence on another count or a prior suspended sentence or sentence to probation; and

(d) when a sentence of imprisonment is imposed for a definite term, the period of a suspended sentence on another count or a prior suspended sentence or sentence to probation shall run during the period of such imprisonment.

(7) Offense Committed While Under Suspension of Sentence or Probation. When a defendant is convicted of an offense committed while under suspension of sentence or on probation and such suspension or probation is not revoked:

(a) if the defendant is sentenced to imprisonment for an indefinite term, the service of such sentence shall satisfy the prior suspended sentence or sentence to probation; and

(b) if the defendant is sentenced to imprisonment for a definite term, the period of the suspension or probation shall not run during the period of such imprisonment; and

(c) if sentence is suspended or the defendant is sentenced to probation, the period of such suspension or probation shall run concurrently with or consecutively to the remainder of the prior periods, as the Court determines at the time of sentence.

Section 7.07 Procedure on Sentence; Presentence Investigation and Report; Remand for Psychiatric Examination; Transmission of Records to Department of Correction

(1) The Court shall not impose sentence without first ordering a pre-sentence investigation of the defendant and according due consideration to a written report of such investigation where:

(a) the defendant has been convicted of a felony; or

(b) the defendant is less than twenty-two years of age and has been convicted of a crime; or

(c) the defendant will be [placed on probation or] sentenced to imprisonment for an extended term.

(2) The Court may order a pre-sentence investigation in any other case.

(3) The pre-sentence investigation shall include an analysis of the circumstances attending the commission of the crime, the defendant's history of delinquency or criminality, physical and mental condition, family situation and background, economic status, education, occupation and personal habits and any other matters that the probation officer deems relevant or the Court directs to be included.

(4) Before imposing sentence, the Court may order the defendant to submit to psychiatric observation and examination for a period of not exceeding sixty days or such longer period as the Court determines to be necessary for the purpose. The defendant may be remanded for this purpose to any available clinic or mental hospital or the Court may appoint a qualified psychiatrist to make the examination. The report of the examination shall be submitted to the Court.

(5) Before imposing sentence, the Court shall advise the defendant or his counsel of the factual contents and the conclusions of any pre-sentence investigation or psychiatric examination and afford fair opportunity, if the defendant so requests, to controvert them. The sources of confidential information need not, however, be disclosed.

(6) The Court shall not impose a sentence of imprisonment for an extended term unless the ground therefor has been established at a hearing after the conviction of the defendant and on written notice to him of the ground proposed. Subject to the limitation of Subsection (5) of this Section, the defendant shall have the right to hear and controvert the evidence against him and to offer evidence upon the issue.

(7) If the defendant is sentenced to imprisonment, a copy of the report of any pre-sentence investigation or psychiatric examination shall be transmitted forthwith to the Department of Correction [or other state department or agency] or, when the defendant is committed to the custody of a specific institution, to such institution.

Section 7.08 Commitment for Observation; Sentence of Imprisonment for Felony Deemed Tentative for Period of One Year; Re-sentence on Petition of Commissioner of Correction

(1) If, after pre-sentence investigation, the Court desires additional information concerning an offender convicted of a felony or misdemeanor before imposing sentence, it may order that he be committed, for a period not exceeding ninety days, to the custody of the Department of Correction, or, in the case of a young adult offender, to the custody of the Division of Young Adult Correction, for observation and study at an appropriate reception or classification center. The Department and the Board of Parole, or the Young Adult Divisions thereof, shall advise the Court of their findings and recommendations on or before the expiration of such ninety-day period. If the offender is thereafter sentenced to imprisonment, the period of such commitment for observation shall be deducted from the maximum term and from the minimum, if any, of such sentence.

(2) When a person has been sentenced to imprisonment upon conviction of a felony, whether for an ordinary or extended term, the sentence shall be deemed tentative, to the extent provided in this Section, for the period of one year following the date when the offender is received in custody by the Department of Correction [or other state department or agency].

(3) If, as a result of the examination and classification by the Department of Correction [or other state department or agency] of a person under sentence of imprisonment upon conviction of a

felony, the Commissioner of Correction [or other department head] is satisfied that the sentence of the Court may have been based upon a misapprehension as to the history, character or physical or mental condition of the offender, the Commissioner, during the period when the offender's sentence is deemed tentative under Subsection (2) of this Section shall file in the sentencing Court a petition to resentence the offender. The petition shall set forth the information as to the offender that is deemed to warrant his re-sentence and may include a recommendation as to the sentence to be imposed.

(4) The Court may dismiss a petition filed under Subsection (3) of this Section without a hearing if it deems the information set forth insufficient to warrant reconsideration of the sentence. If the Court is of the view that the petition warrants such reconsideration, a copy of the petition shall be served on the offender, who shall have the right to be heard on the issue and to be represented by counsel.

(5) When the Court grants a petition filed under Subsection (3) of this Section, it shall resentence the offender and may impose any sentence that might have been imposed originally for the felony of which the defendant was convicted. The period of his imprisonment prior to re-sentence and any reduction for good behavior to which he is entitled shall be applied in satisfaction of the final sentence.

(6) For all purposes other than this Section, a sentence of imprisonment has the same finality when it is imposed that it would have if this Section were not in force.

(7) Nothing in this Section shall alter the remedies provided by law for vacating or correcting an illegal sentence.

Section 7.09 Credit for Time of Detention Prior to Sentence; Credit for Imprisonment Under Earlier Sentence for the Same Crime

(1) When a defendant who is sentenced to imprisonment has previously been detained in any state or local correctional or other institution following his [conviction of] [arrest for] the crime for which such sentence is imposed, such period of detention following his [conviction] [arrest] shall be deducted from the maximum term, and from the minimum, if any, of such sentence. The officer having custody of the defendant shall furnish a certificate to the Court at the time of sentence, showing the length of such detention of the defendant prior to sentence in any state or local correctional or other institution, and the certificate shall be annexed to the official records of the defendant's commitment.

(2) When a judgment of conviction is vacated and a new sentence is thereafter imposed upon the defendant for the same crime, the period of detention and imprisonment theretofore served shall be deducted from the maximum term, and from the minimum, if any, of the new sentence. The officer having custody of the defendant shall furnish a certificate to the Court at the time of sentence, showing the period of imprisonment served under the original sentence, and the certificate shall be annexed to the official records of the defendant's new commitment.

PART II

DEFINITION OF SPECIFIC CRIMES

OFFENSES AGAINST EXISTENCE OR STABILITY OF THE STATE

[This category of offenses, including treason, sedition, espionage and like crimes, was excluded from the scope of the Model Penal Code. These offenses are peculiarly the concern of the federal government. The Constitution itself defines treason: "Treason against the United States shall consist only in levying War against them, or in adhering to their Enemies, giving them Aid and Comfort. * * * " Article III, Section 3; cf. Pennsylvania v. Nelson, 350 U.S. 497 (supersession of state sedition legislation by federal law). Also, the definition of offenses against the stability of the state is inevitably affected by special political considerations. These factors militated against the use of the Institute's limited resources to attempt to draft "model" provisions in this area. However we provide at this point in the Plan of the Model Penal Code for an Article 200, where definitions of offenses against the existence or stability of the state may be incorporated.]

OFFENSES INVOLVING DANGER TO THE PERSON

ARTICLE 210

CRIMINAL HOMICIDE

Section 210.0 Definitions

In Articles 210–213, unless a different meaning plainly is required:

(1) "human being" means a person who has been born and is alive;

(2) "bodily injury" means physical pain, illness or any impairment of physical condition;

(3) "serious bodily injury" means bodily injury which creates a substantial risk of death or which causes serious, permanent disfigurement, or protracted loss or impairment of the function of any bodily member or organ;

(4) "deadly weapon" means any firearm, or other weapon, device, instrument, material or substance, whether animate or inanimate, which in the manner it is used or is intended to be used is known to be capable of producing death or serious bodily injury.

Section 210.1 Criminal Homicide

(1) A person is guilty of criminal homicide if he purposely, knowingly, recklessly or negligently causes the death of another human being.

(2) Criminal homicide is murder, manslaughter or negligent homicide.

Section 210.2 Murder

(1) Except as provided in Section 210.3(1)(b), criminal homicide constitutes murder when:

(a) it is committed purposely or knowingly; or

(b) it is committed recklessly under circumstances manifesting extreme indifference to the value of human life. Such recklessness and indifference are presumed if the actor is engaged or is an accomplice in the commission of, or an attempt to commit, or flight after committing or attempting to commit robbery, rape or deviate sexual intercourse by force or threat of force, arson, burglary, kidnapping or felonious escape.

(2) Murder is a felony of the first degree [but a person convicted of murder may be sentenced to death, as provided in Section 210.6].

Section 210.3 Manslaughter

(1) Criminal homicide constitutes manslaughter when:

(a) it is committed recklessly; or

(b) a homicide which would otherwise be murder is committed under the influence of extreme mental or emotional disturbance for which there is reasonable explanation or excuse. The reasonableness of such explanation or excuse shall be determined from the viewpoint of a person in the actor's situation under the circumstances as he believes them to be.

(2) Manslaughter is a felony of the second degree.

Section 210.4 Negligent Homicide

(1) Criminal homicide constitutes negligent homicide when it is committed negligently.

(2) Negligent homicide is a felony of the third degree.

Section 210.5 Causing or Aiding Suicide

(1) **Causing Suicide as Criminal Homicide.** A person may be convicted of criminal homicide for causing another to commit suicide only if he purposely causes such suicide by force, duress or deception.

(2) **Aiding or Soliciting Suicide as an Independent Offense.** A person who purposely aids or solicits another to commit suicide is guilty of a felony of the second degree if his conduct causes such suicide or an attempted suicide, and otherwise of a misdemeanor.

[Section 210.6 Sentence of Death for Murder; Further Proceedings to Determine Sentence

(1) **Death Sentence Excluded.** When a defendant is found guilty of murder, the Court shall impose sentence for a felony of the first degree if it is satisfied that:

(a) none of the aggravating circumstances enumerated in Subsection (3) of this Section was established by the evidence at the trial or will be established if further proceedings are initiated under Subsection (2) of this Section; or

(b) substantial mitigating circumstances, established by the evidence at the trial, call for leniency; or

(c) the defendant, with the consent of the prosecuting attorney and the approval of the Court, pleaded guilty to murder as a felony of the first degree; or

(d) the defendant was under 18 years of age at the time of the commission of the crime; or

(e) the defendant's physical or mental condition calls for leniency; or

(f) although the evidence suffices to sustain the verdict, it does not foreclose all doubt respecting the defendant's guilt.

(2) Determination by Court or by Court and Jury. Unless the Court imposes sentence under Subsection (1) of this Section, it shall conduct a separate proceeding to determine whether the defendant should be sentenced for a felony of the first degree or sentenced to death. The proceeding shall be conducted before the Court alone if the defendant was convicted by a Court sitting without a jury or upon his plea of guilty or if the prosecuting attorney and the defendant waive a jury with respect to sentence. In other cases it shall be conducted before the Court sitting with the jury which determined the defendant's guilt or, if the Court for good cause shown discharges that jury, with a new jury empanelled for the purpose.

In the proceeding, evidence may be presented as to any matter that the Court deems relevant to sentence, including but not limited to the nature and circumstances of the crime, the defendant's character, background, history, mental and physical condition and any of the aggravating or mitigating circumstances enumerated in Subsections (3) and (4) of this Section. Any such evidence, not legally privileged, which the Court deems to have probative force may be received, regardless of its admissibility under the exclusionary rules of evidence, provided that the defendant's counsel is accorded a fair opportunity to rebut such evidence. The prosecuting attorney and the defendant or his counsel shall be permitted to present argument for or against sentence of death.

The determination whether sentence of death shall be imposed shall be in the discretion of the Court, except that when the proceeding is conducted before the Court sitting with a jury, the Court shall not impose sentence of death unless it submits to the jury the issue whether the defendant should be sentenced to death or to imprisonment and the jury returns a verdict that the sentence should be death. If the jury is unable to reach a unanimous verdict, the Court shall dismiss the jury and impose sentence for a felony of the first degree.

The Court, in exercising its discretion as to sentence, and the jury, in determining upon its verdict, shall take into account the aggravating and mitigating circumstances enumerated in Subsections (3) and (4) and any other facts that it deems relevant, but it shall not impose or recommend sentence of death unless it finds one of the aggravating circumstances enumerated in Subsection (3) and further finds that there are no mitigating circumstances sufficiently substantial to call for leniency. When the issue is submitted to the jury, the Court shall so instruct and also shall inform the jury of the nature of the sentence of imprisonment that may be imposed, including its implication with respect to possible release upon parole, if the jury verdict is against sentence of death.

Alternative formulation of Subsection (2):

(2) Determination by Court. Unless the Court imposes sentence under Subsection (1) of this Section, it shall conduct a separate proceeding to determine whether the defendant should be sentenced for a felony of the first degree or sentenced to death. In the proceeding, the Court, in accordance with Section 7.07, shall consider the report of the pre-sentence investigation and, if a psychiatric examination has been ordered, the report of such examination. In addition, evidence may be presented as to any matter that the Court deems relevant to sentence, including but not limited to the nature and circumstances of the crime, the defendant's character, background, history, mental and physical condition and any of the aggravating or mitigating circumstances enumerated in Subsections (3) and (4) of this Section. Any such evidence, not legally privileged, which the Court deems to have probative force may be received, regardless of its admissibility under the exclusionary rules of evidence, provided that the defendant's counsel is accorded a fair opportunity to rebut such evidence. The prosecuting attorney and the defendant or his counsel shall be permitted to present argument for or against sentence of death.

The determination whether sentence of death shall be imposed shall be in the discretion of the Court. In exercising such discretion, the Court shall take into account the aggravating and mitigating circumstances enumerated in Subsections (3) and (4) and any other facts that it deems relevant but shall not impose sentence of death unless it finds one of the aggravating circumstances enumerated in Subsection (3) and further finds that there are no mitigating circumstances sufficiently substantial to call for leniency.

(3) Aggravating Circumstances.

(a) The murder was committed by a convict under sentence of imprisonment.

(b) The defendant was previously convicted of another murder or of a felony involving the use or threat of violence to the person.

(c) At the time the murder was committed the defendant also committed another murder.

(d) The defendant knowingly created a great risk of death to many persons.

(e) The murder was committed while the defendant was engaged or was an accomplice in the commission of, or an attempt to commit, or flight after committing or attempting to commit robbery, rape or deviate sexual intercourse by force or threat of force, arson, burglary or kidnapping.

(f) The murder was committed for the purpose of avoiding or preventing a lawful arrest or effecting an escape from lawful custody.

(g) The murder was committed for pecuniary gain.

(h) The murder was especially heinous, atrocious or cruel, manifesting exceptional depravity.

(4) Mitigating Circumstances.

(a) The defendant has no significant history of prior criminal activity.

(b) The murder was committed while the defendant was under the influence of extreme mental or emotional disturbance.

(c) The victim was a participant in the defendant's homicidal conduct or consented to the homicidal act.

(d) The murder was committed under circumstances which the defendant believed to provide a moral justification or extenuation for his conduct.

(e) The defendant was an accomplice in a murder committed by another person and his participation in the homicidal act was relatively minor.

(f) The defendant acted under duress or under the domination of another person.

(g) At the time of the murder, the capacity of the defendant to appreciate the criminality [wrongfulness] of his conduct or to conform his conduct to the requirements of law was impaired as a result of mental disease or defect or intoxication.

(h) The youth of the defendant at the time of the crime.]

ARTICLE 211

ASSAULT; RECKLESS ENDANGERING; THREATS

Section 211.0   Definitions

In this Article, the definitions given in Section 210.0 apply unless a different meaning plainly is required.

Section 211.1   Assault

(1) **Simple Assault.** A person is guilty of assault if he:

(a) attempts to cause or purposely, knowingly or recklessly causes bodily injury to another; or

(b) negligently causes bodily injury to another with a deadly weapon; or

(c) attempts by physical menace to put another in fear of imminent serious bodily injury.

Simple assault is a misdemeanor unless committed in a fight or scuffle entered into by mutual consent, in which case it is a petty misdemeanor.

(2) **Aggravated Assault.** A person is guilty of aggravated assault if he:

(a) attempts to cause serious bodily injury to another, or causes such injury purposely, knowingly or recklessly under circumstances manifesting extreme indifference to the value of human life; or

(b) attempts to cause or purposely or knowingly causes bodily injury to another with a deadly weapon.

Aggravated assault under paragraph (a) is a felony of the second degree; aggravated assault under paragraph (b) is a felony of the third degree.

Section 211.2 Recklessly Endangering Another Person

A person commits a misdemeanor if he recklessly engages in conduct which places or may place another person in danger of death or serious bodily injury. Recklessness and danger shall be presumed where a person knowingly points a firearm at or in the direction of another, whether or not the actor believed the firearm to be loaded.

Section 211.3 Terroristic Threats

A person is guilty of a felony of the third degree if he threatens to commit any crime of violence with purpose to terrorize another or to cause evacuation of a building, place of assembly, or facility of public transportation, or otherwise to cause serious public inconvenience, or in reckless disregard of the risk of causing such terror or inconvenience.

ARTICLE 212

KIDNAPPING AND RELATED OFFENSES; COERCION

Section 212.0 Definitions

In this Article, the definitions given in Section 210.0 apply unless a different meaning plainly is required.

Section 212.1 Kidnapping

A person is guilty of kidnapping if he unlawfully removes another from his place of residence or business, or a substantial distance from the vicinity where he is found, or if he unlawfully confines another for a substantial period in a place of isolation, with any of the following purposes:

(a) to hold for ransom or reward, or as a shield or hostage; or

(b) to facilitate commission of any felony or flight thereafter; or

(c) to inflict bodily injury on or to terrorize the victim or another; or

(d) to interfere with the performance of any governmental or political function.

Kidnapping is a felony of the first degree unless the actor voluntarily releases the victim alive and in a safe place prior to trial, in which case it is a felony of the second degree. A removal or confinement is unlawful within the meaning of this Section if it is accomplished by force, threat or deception, or, in the case of a person who is under the age of 14 or incompetent, if it is accomplished without the consent of a parent, guardian or other person responsible for general supervision of his welfare.

Section 212.2 Felonious Restraint

A person commits a felony of the third degree if he knowingly:

(a) restrains another unlawfully in circumstances exposing him to risk of serious bodily injury; or

(b) holds another in a condition of involuntary servitude.

Section 212.3 False Imprisonment

A person commits a misdemeanor if he knowingly restrains another unlawfully so as to interfere substantially with his liberty.

Section 212.4 Interference With Custody

(1) **Custody of Children.** A person commits an offense if he knowingly or recklessly takes or entices any child under the age of 18 from the custody of its parent, guardian or other lawful custodian, when he has no privilege to do so. It is an affirmative defense that:

(a) the actor believed that his action was necessary to preserve the child from danger to its welfare; or

(b) the child, being at the time not less than 14 years old, was taken away at its own instigation without enticement and without purpose to commit a criminal offense with or against the child.

Proof that the child was below the critical age gives rise to a presumption that the actor knew the child's age or acted in reckless disregard thereof. The offense is a misdemeanor unless the actor, not being a parent or person in equivalent relation to the child, acted with knowledge that his conduct would cause serious alarm for the child's safety, or in reckless disregard of a likelihood of causing such alarm, in which case the offense is a felony of the third degree.

(2) Custody of Committed Persons. A person is guilty of a misdemeanor if he knowingly or recklessly takes or entices any committed person away from lawful custody when he is not privileged to do so. "Committed person" means, in addition to anyone committed under judicial warrant, any orphan, neglected or delinquent child, mentally defective or insane person, or other dependent or incompetent person entrusted to another's custody by or through a recognized social agency or otherwise by authority of law.

Section 212.5   Criminal Coercion

(1) Offense Defined. A person is guilty of criminal coercion if, with purpose unlawfully to restrict another's freedom of action to his detriment, he threatens to:

    (a) commit any criminal offense; or

    (b) accuse anyone of a criminal offense; or

    (c) expose any secret tending to subject any person to hatred, contempt or ridicule, or to impair his credit or business repute; or

    (d) take or withhold action as an official, or cause an official to take or withhold action.

It is an affirmative defense to prosecution based on paragraphs (b), (c) or (d) that the actor believed the accusation or secret to be true or the proposed official action justified and that his purpose was limited to compelling the other to behave in a way reasonably related to the circumstances which were the subject of the accusation, exposure or proposed official action, as by desisting from further misbehavior, making good a wrong done, refraining from taking any action or responsibility for which the actor believes the other disqualified.

(2) Grading. Criminal coercion is a misdemeanor unless the threat is to commit a felony or the actor's purpose is felonious, in which cases the offense is a felony of the third degree.

ARTICLE 213

SEXUAL OFFENSES

Section 213.0   Definitions

In this Article, the definitions given in Section 210.0 apply unless a different meaning plainly is required. Sexual intercourse includes intercourse per os or per anum, with some penetration however slight; emission is not required.

Deviate sexual intercourse means sexual intercourse per os or per anum between human beings who are not husband and wife, and any form of sexual intercourse with an animal.

Section 213.1   Rape and Related Offenses

(1) Rape. A male who has sexual intercourse with a female not his wife is guilty of rape if:

    (a) he compels her to submit by force or by threat of imminent death, serious bodily injury, extreme pain or kidnapping, to be inflicted on anyone; or

    (b) he has substantially impaired her power to appraise or control her conduct by administering or employing without her knowledge drugs, intoxicants or other means for the purpose of preventing resistance; or

    (c) the female is unconscious; or

    (d) the female is less than 10 years old.

Rape is a felony of the second degree unless (i) in the course thereof the actor inflicts serious bodily injury upon anyone, or (ii) the victim was not a voluntary social companion of the actor upon the occasion of the crime and had not previously permitted him sexual liberties, in which cases the offense is a felony of the first degree.

(2) Gross Sexual Imposition. A male who has sexual intercourse with a female not his wife commits a felony of the third degree if:

    (a) he compels her to submit by any threat that would prevent resistance by a woman of ordinary resolution; or

    (b) he knows that she suffers from a mental disease or defect which renders her incapable of appraising the nature of her conduct; or

(c) he knows that she is unaware that a sexual act is being committed upon her or that she submits because she mistakenly supposes that he is her husband.

Section 213.2 Deviate Sexual Intercourse by Force or Imposition

(1) By Force or Its Equivalent. A person who engages in deviate sexual intercourse with another person, or who causes another to engage in deviate sexual intercourse, commits a felony of the second degree if:

(a) he compels the other person to participate by force or by threat of imminent death, serious bodily injury, extreme pain or kidnapping, to be inflicted on anyone; or

(b) he has substantially impaired the other person's power to appraise or control his conduct, by administering or employing without the knowledge of the other person drugs, intoxicants or other means for the purpose of preventing resistance; or

(c) the other person is unconscious; or

(d) the other person is less than 10 years old.

(2) By Other Imposition. A person who engages in deviate sexual intercourse with another person, or who causes another to engage in deviate sexual intercourse, commits a felony of the third degree if:

(a) he compels the other person to participate by any threat that would prevent resistance by a person of ordinary resolution; or

(b) he knows that the other person suffers from a mental disease or defect which renders him incapable of appraising the nature of his conduct; or

(c) he knows that the other person submits because he is unaware that a sexual act is being committed upon him.

Section 213.3 Corruption of Minors and Seduction

(1) Offense Defined. A male who has sexual intercourse with a female not his wife, or any person who engages in deviate sexual intercourse or causes another to engage in deviate sexual intercourse, is guilty of an offense if:

(a) the other person is less than [16] years old and the actor is at least [4] years older than the other person; or

(b) the other person is less than 21 years old and the actor is his guardian or otherwise responsible for general supervision of his welfare; or

(c) the other person is in custody of law or detained in a hospital or other institution and the actor has supervisory or disciplinary authority over him; or

(d) the other person is a female who is induced to participate by a promise of marriage which the actor does not mean to perform.

(2) Grading. An offense under paragraph (a) of Subsection (1) is a felony of the third degree. Otherwise an offense under this section is a misdemeanor.

Section 213.4 Sexual Assault

A person who has sexual contact with another not his spouse, or causes such other to have sexual intercourse with him, is guilty of sexual assault, a misdemeanor, if:

(1) he knows that the contact is offensive to the other person; or

(2) he knows that the other person suffers from a mental disease or defect which renders him or her incapable of appraising the nature of his or her conduct; or

(3) he knows that the other person is unaware that a sexual act is being committed; or

(4) the other person is less than 10 years old; or

(5) he has substantially impaired the other person's power to appraise or control his or her conduct, by administering or employing without the other's knowledge drugs, intoxicants or other means for the purpose of preventing resistance; or

(6) the other person is less than [16] years old and the actor is at least [4] years older than the other person; or

(7) the other person is less than 21 years old and the actor is his guardian or otherwise responsible for general supervision of his welfare; or

(8) the other person is in custody of law or detained in a hospital or other institution and the actor has supervisory or disciplinary authority over him.

Sexual contact is any touching of the sexual or other intimate parts of the person for the purpose of arousing or gratifying sexual desire.

Section 213.5   Indecent Exposure

A person commits a misdemeanor if, for the purpose of arousing or gratifying sexual desire of himself or of any person other than his spouse, he exposes his genitals under circumstances in which he knows his conduct is likely to cause affront or alarm.

Section 213.6   Provisions Generally Applicable to Article 213

(1) **Mistake as to Age.** Whenever in this Article the criminality of conduct depends on a child's being below the age of 10, it is no defense that the actor did not know the child's age, or reasonably believed the child to be older than 10. When criminality depends on the child's being below a critical age other than 10, it is a defense for the actor to prove by a preponderance of the evidence that he reasonably believed the child to be above the critical age.

(2) **Spouse Relationships.** Whenever in this Article the definition of an offense excludes conduct with a spouse, the exclusion shall be deemed to extend to persons living as man and wife, regardless of the legal status of their relationship. The exclusion shall be inoperative as respects spouses living apart under a decree of judicial separation. Where the definition of an offense excludes conduct with a spouse or conduct by a woman, this shall not preclude conviction of a spouse or woman as accomplice in a sexual act which he or she causes another person, not within the exclusion, to perform.

(3) **Sexually Promiscuous Complainants.** It is a defense to prosecution under Section 213.3 and paragraphs (6), (7) and (8) of Section 213.4 for the actor to prove by a preponderance of the evidence that the alleged victim had, prior to the time of the offense charged, engaged promiscuously in sexual relations with others.

(4) **Prompt Complaint.** No prosecution may be instituted or maintained under this Article unless the alleged offense was brought to the notice of public authority within [3] months of its occurrence or, where the alleged victim was less than [16] years old or otherwise incompetent to make complaint, within [3] months after a parent, guardian or other competent person specially interested in the victim learns of the offense.

(5) **Testimony of Complainants.** No person shall be convicted of any felony under this Article upon the uncorroborated testimony of the alleged victim. Corroboration may be circumstantial. In any prosecution before a jury for an offense under this Article, the jury shall be instructed to evaluate the testimony of a victim or complaining witness with special care in view of the emotional involvement of the witness and the difficulty of determining the truth with respect to alleged sexual activities carried out in private.

OFFENSES AGAINST PROPERTY

ARTICLE 220

ARSON, CRIMINAL MISCHIEF, AND OTHER PROPERTY DESTRUCTION

Section 220.1   Arson and Related Offenses

(1) **Arson.** A person is guilty of arson, a felony of the second degree, if he starts a fire or causes an explosion with the purpose of:

(a) destroying a building or occupied structure of another; or

(b) destroying or damaging any property, whether his own or another's, to collect insurance for such loss. It shall be an affirmative defense to prosecution under this paragraph that the actor's conduct did not recklessly endanger any building or occupied structure of another or place any other person in danger of death or bodily injury.

(2) **Reckless Burning or Exploding.** A person commits a felony of the third degree if he purposely starts a fire or causes an explosion, whether on his own property or another's, and thereby recklessly:

(a) places another person in danger of death or bodily injury; or

(b) places a building or occupied structure of another in danger of damage or destruction.

(3) **Failure to Control or Report Dangerous Fire.** A person who knows that a fire is endan-

gering life or a substantial amount of property of another and fails to take reasonable measures to put out or control the fire, when he can do so without substantial risk to himself, or to give a prompt fire alarm, commits a misdemeanor if:

(a) he knows that he is under an official, contractual, or other legal duty to prevent or combat the fire; or

(b) the fire was started, albeit lawfully, by him or with his assent, or on property in his custody or control.

(4) **Definitions.** "Occupied structure" includes a ship, trailer, sleeping car, airplane, or other vehicle, structure or place adapted for overnight accommodation of persons or for carrying on business therein, whether or not a person is actually present. Property is that of another, for the purposes of this section, if anyone other than the actor has a possessory or proprietory interest therein. If a building or structure is divided into separately occupied units, any unit not occupied by the actor is an occupied structure of another.

Section 220.2 Causing or Risking Catastrophe

(1) **Causing Catastrophe.** A person who causes a catastrophe by explosion, fire, flood, avalanche, collapse of building, release of poison gas, radioactive material or other harmful or destructive force or substance, or by any other means of causing potentially widespread injury or damage, commits a felony of the second degree if he does so purposely or knowingly, or a felony of the third degree if he does so recklessly.

(2) **Risking Catastrophe.** A person is guilty of a misdemeanor if he recklessly creates a risk of catastrophe in the employment of fire, explosives or other dangerous means listed in Subsection (1).

(3) **Failure to Prevent Catastrophe.** A person who knowingly or recklessly fails to take reasonable measures to prevent or mitigate a catastrophe commits a misdemeanor if:

(a) he knows that he is under an official, contractual or other legal duty to take such measures; or

(b) he did or assented to the act causing or threatening the catastrophe.

Section 220.3 Criminal Mischief

(1) **Offense Defined.** A person is guilty of criminal mischief if he:

(a) damages tangible property of another purposely, recklessly, or by negligence in the employment of fire, explosives, or other dangerous means listed in Section 220.2(1); or

(b) purposely or recklessly tampers with tangible property of another so as to endanger person or property; or

(c) purposely or recklessly causes another to suffer pecuniary loss by deception or threat.

(2) **Grading.** Criminal mischief is a felony of the third degree if the actor purposely causes pecuniary loss in excess of $5,000, or a substantial interruption or impairment of public communication, transportation, supply of water, gas or power, or other public service. It is a misdemeanor if the actor purposely causes pecuniary loss in excess of $100, or a petty misdemeanor if he purposely or recklessly causes pecuniary loss in excess of $25. Otherwise criminal mischief is a violation.

ARTICLE 221

BURGLARY AND OTHER CRIMINAL INTRUSION

Section 221.0 Definitions

In this Article, unless a different meaning plainly is required:

(1) "occupied structure" means any structure, vehicle or place adapted for overnight accommodation of persons, or for carrying on business therein, whether or not a person is actually present.

(2) "night" means the period between thirty minutes past sunset and thirty minutes before sunrise.

Section 221.1 Burglary

(1) **Burglary Defined.** A person is guilty of burglary if he enters a building or occupied structure, or separately secured or occupied portion thereof, with purpose to commit a crime therein, unless the premises are at the time open to the

public or the actor is licensed or privileged to enter. It is an affirmative defense to prosecution for burglary that the building or structure was abandoned.

(2) Grading. Burglary is a felony of the second degree if it is perpetrated in the dwelling of another at night, or if, in the course of committing the offense, the actor:

(a) purposely, knowingly or recklessly inflicts or attempts to inflict bodily injury on anyone; or

(b) is armed with explosives or a deadly weapon.

Otherwise, burglary is a felony of the third degree. An act shall be deemed "in the course of committing" an offense if it occurs in an attempt to commit the offense or in flight after the attempt or commission.

(3) Multiple Convictions. A person may not be convicted both for burglary and for the offense which it was his purpose to commit after the burglarious entry or for an attempt to commit that offense, unless the additional offense constitutes a felony of the first or second degree.

Section 221.2 Criminal Trespass

(1) Buildings and Occupied Structures. A person commits an offense if, knowing that he is not licensed or privileged to do so, he enters or surreptitiously remains in any building or occupied structure, or separately secured or occupied portion thereof. An offense under this Subsection is a misdemeanor if it is committed in a dwelling at night. Otherwise it is a petty misdemeanor.

(2) Defiant Trespasser. A person commits an offense if, knowing that he is not licensed or privileged to do so, he enters or remains in any place as to which notice against trespass is given by:

(a) actual communication to the actor; or

(b) posting in a manner prescribed by law or reasonably likely to come to the attention of intruders; or

(c) fencing or other enclosure manifestly designed to exclude intruders.

An offense under this Subsection constitutes a petty misdemeanor if the offender defies an order to leave personally communicated to him by the owner of the premises or other authorized person. Otherwise it is a violation.

(3) Defenses. It is an affirmative defense to prosecution under this Section that:

(a) a building or occupied structure involved in an offense under Subsection (1) was abandoned; or

(b) the premises were at the time open to members of the public and the actor complied with all lawful conditions imposed on access to or remaining in the premises; or

(c) the actor reasonably believed that the owner of the premises, or other person empowered to license access thereto, would have licensed him to enter or remain.

ARTICLE 222

ROBBERY

Section 222.1 Robbery

(1) Robbery Defined. A person is guilty of robbery if, in the course of committing a theft, he:

(a) inflicts serious bodily injury upon another; or

(b) threatens another with or purposely puts him in fear of immediate serious bodily injury; or

(c) commits or threatens immediately to commit any felony of the first or second degree.

An act shall be deemed "in the course of committing a theft" if it occurs in an attempt to commit theft or in flight after the attempt or commission.

(2) Grading. Robbery is a felony of the second degree, except that it is a felony of the first degree if in the course of committing the theft the actor attempts to kill anyone, or purposely inflicts or attempts to inflict serious bodily injury.

ARTICLE 223

THEFT AND RELATED OFFENSES

Section 223.0 Definitions

In this Article, unless a different meaning plainly is required:

(1) "deprive" means: (a) to withhold property of another permanently or for so extended a period as to appropriate a major portion of its economic value, or with intent to restore only upon payment of reward or other compensation; or (b) to dispose of the property so as to make it unlikely that the owner will recover it.

(2) "financial institution" means a bank, insurance company, credit union, building and loan association, investment trust or other organization held out to the public as a place of deposit of funds or medium of savings or collective investment.

(3) "government" means the United States, any State, county, municipality, or other political unit, or any department, agency or subdivision of any of the foregoing, or any corporation or other association carrying out the functions of government.

(4) "movable property" means property the location of which can be changed, including things growing on, affixed to, or found in land, and documents although the rights represented thereby have no physical location. "Immovable property" is all other property.

(5) "obtain" means: (a) in relation to property, to bring about a transfer or purported transfer of a legal interest in the property, whether to the obtainer or another; or (b) in relation to labor or service, to secure performance thereof.

(6) "property" means anything of value, including real estate, tangible and intangible personal property, contract rights, choses-in-action and other interests in or claims to wealth, admission or transportation tickets, captured or domestic animals, food and drink, electric or other power.

(7) "property of another" includes property in which any person other than the actor has an interest which the actor is not privileged to infringe, regardless of the fact that the actor also has an interest in the property and regardless of the fact that the other person might be precluded from civil recovery because the property was used in an unlawful transaction or was subject to forfeiture as contraband. Property in possession of the actor shall not be deemed property of another who has only a security interest therein, even if legal title is in the creditor pursuant to a conditional sales contract or other security agreement.

Section 223.1 Consolidation of Theft Offenses; Grading; Provisions Applicable to Theft Generally

(1) **Consolidation of Theft Offenses.** Conduct denominated theft in this Article constitutes a single offense. An accusation of theft may be supported by evidence that it was committed in any manner that would be theft under this Article, notwithstanding the specification of a different manner in the indictment or information, subject only to the power of the Court to ensure fair trial by granting a continuance or other appropriate relief where the conduct of the defense would be prejudiced by lack of fair notice or by surprise.

(2) **Grading of Theft Offenses.**

(a) Theft constitutes a felony of the third degree if the amount involved exceeds $500, or if the property stolen is a fire-arm, automobile, airplane, motorcycle, motorboat or other motor-propelled vehicle, or in the case of theft by receiving stolen property, if the receiver is in the business of buying or selling stolen property.

(b) Theft not within the preceding paragraph constitutes a misdemeanor, except that if the property was not taken from the person or by threat, or in breach of a fiduciary obligation, and the actor proves by a preponderance of the evidence that the amount involved was less than $50, the offense constitutes a petty misdemeanor.

(c) The amount involved in a theft shall be deemed to be the highest value, by any reasonable standard, of the property or services which the actor stole or attempted to steal. Amounts involved in thefts committed pursuant to one scheme or course of conduct, whether from the same person or several persons, may be aggregated in determining the grade of the offense.

(3) Claim of Right. It is an affirmative defense to prosecution for theft that the actor:

(a) was unaware that the property or service was that of another; or

(b) acted under an honest claim of right to the property or service involved or that he had a right to acquire or dispose of it as he did; or

(c) took property exposed for sale, intending to purchase and pay for it promptly, or reasonably believing that the owner, if present, would have consented.

(4) Theft from Spouse. It is no defense that theft was from the actor's spouse, except that misappropriation of household and personal effects, or other property normally accessible to both spouses, is theft only if it occurs after the parties have ceased living together.

Section 223.2   Theft by Unlawful Taking or Disposition

(1) Movable Property. A person is guilty of theft if he unlawfully takes, or exercises unlawful control over, movable property of another with purpose to deprive him thereof.

(2) Immovable Property. A person is guilty of theft if he unlawfully transfers immovable property of another or any interest therein with purpose to benefit himself or another not entitled thereto.

Section 223.3   Theft by Deception

A person is guilty of theft if he purposely obtains property of another by deception. A person deceives if he purposely:

(1) creates or reinforces a false impression, including false impressions as to law, value, intention or other state of mind; but deception as to a person's intention to perform a promise shall not be inferred from the fact alone that he did not subsequently perform the promise; or

(2) prevents another from acquiring information which would affect his judgment of a transaction; or

(3) fails to correct a false impression which the deceiver previously created or reinforced, or which the deceiver knows to be influencing

another to whom he stands in a fiduciary or confidential relationship; or

(4) fails to disclose a known lien, adverse claim or other legal impediment to the enjoyment of property which he transfers or encumbers in consideration for the property obtained, whether such impediment is or is not valid, or is or is not a matter of official record.

The term "deceive" does not, however, include falsity as to matters having no pecuniary significance, or puffing by statements unlikely to deceive ordinary persons in the group addressed.

Section 223.4   Theft by Extortion

A person is guilty of theft if he purposely obtains property of another by threatening to:

(1) inflict bodily injury on anyone or commit any other criminal offense; or

(2) accuse anyone of a criminal offense; or

(3) expose any secret tending to subject any person to hatred, contempt or ridicule, or to impair his credit or business repute; or

(4) take or withhold action as an official, or cause an official to take or withhold action; or

(5) bring about or continue a strike, boycott or other collective unofficial action, if the property is not demanded or received for the benefit of the group in whose interest the actor purports to act; or

(6) testify or provide information or withhold testimony or information with respect to another's legal claim or defense; or

(7) inflict any other harm which would not benefit the actor.

It is an affirmative defense to prosecution based on paragraphs (2), (3) or (4) that the property obtained by threat of accusation, exposure, lawsuit or other invocation of official action was honestly claimed as restitution or indemnification for harm done in the circumstances to which such accusation, exposure, lawsuit or other official action relates, or as compensation for property or lawful services.

Section 223.5   Theft of Property Lost, Mislaid, or Delivered by Mistake

A person who comes into control of property of another that he knows to have been lost, mislaid, or delivered under a mistake as to the nature or amount of the property or the identity of the recipient is guilty of theft if, with purpose to deprive the owner thereof, he fails to take reasonable measures to restore the property to a person entitled to have it.

Section 223.6 Receiving Stolen Property

(1) **Receiving.** A person is guilty of theft if he purposely receives, retains, or disposes of movable property of another knowing that it has been stolen, or believing that it has probably been stolen, unless the property is received, retained, or disposed with purpose to restore it to the owner. "Receiving" means acquiring possession, control or title, or lending on the security of the property.

(2) **Presumption of Knowledge.** The requisite knowledge or belief is presumed in the case of a dealer who:

(a) is found in possession or control of property stolen from two or more persons on separate occasions; or

(b) has received stolen property in another transaction within the year preceding the transaction charged; or

(c) being a dealer in property of the sort received, acquires it for a consideration which he knows is far below its reasonable value.

"Dealer" means a person in the business of buying or selling goods, including a pawnbroker.

Section 223.7 Theft of Services

(1) A person is guilty of theft if he purposely obtains services which he knows are available only for compensation, by deception or threat, or by false token or other means to avoid payment for the service. "Services" includes labor, professional service, transportation, telephone or other public service, accommodation in hotels, restaurants or elsewhere, admission to exhibitions, use of vehicles or other movable property. Where compensation for service is ordinarily paid immediately upon the rendering of such service, as in the case of hotels and restaurants, refusal to pay or absconding without payment or offer to pay gives rise to a presumption that the service was obtained by deception as to intention to pay.

(2) A person commits theft if, having control over the disposition of services of others, to which he is not entitled, he knowingly diverts such services to his own benefit or to the benefit of another not entitled thereto.

Section 223.8 Theft by Failure to Make Required Disposition of Funds Received

A person who purposely obtains property upon agreement, or subject to a known legal obligation, to make specified payment or other disposition, whether from such property or its proceeds or from his own property to be reserved in equivalent amount, is guilty of theft if he deals with the property obtained as his own and fails to make the required payment or disposition. The foregoing applies notwithstanding that it may be impossible to identify particular property as belonging to the victim at the time of the actor's failure to make the required payment or disposition. An officer or employee of the government or of a financial institution is presumed: (i) to know any legal obligation relevant to his criminal liability under this Section, and (ii) to have dealt with the property as his own if he fails to pay or account upon lawful demand, or if an audit reveals a shortage or falsification of accounts.

Section 223.9 Unauthorized Use of Automobiles and Other Vehicles

A person commits a misdemeanor if he operates another's automobile, airplane, motorcycle, motorboat, or other motor-propelled vehicle without consent of the owner. It is an affirmative defense to prosecution under this Section that the actor reasonably believed that the owner would have consented to the operation had he known of it.

ARTICLE 224

FORGERY AND FRAUDULENT PRACTICES

Section 224.0 Definitions

In this Article, the definitions given in Section 223.0 apply unless a different meaning plainly is required.

Section 224.1 Forgery

(1) **Definition.** A person is guilty of forgery if, with purpose to defraud or injure anyone, or with

knowledge that he is facilitating a fraud or injury to be perpetrated by anyone, the actor:

(a) alters any writing of another without his authority; or

(b) makes, completes, executes, authenticates, issues or transfers any writing so that it purports to be the act of another who did not authorize that act, or to have been executed at a time or place or in a numbered sequence other than was in fact the case, or to be a copy of an original when no such original existed; or

(c) utters any writing which he knows to be forged in a manner specified in paragraphs (a) or (b).

"Writing" includes printing or any other method of recording information, money, coins, tokens, stamps, seals, credit cards, badges, trademarks, and other symbols of value, right, privilege, or identification.

(2) **Grading.** Forgery is a felony of the second degree if the writing is or purports to be part of an issue of money, securities, postage or revenue stamps, or other instruments issued by the government, or part of an issue of stock, bonds or other instruments representing interests in or claims against any property or enterprise. Forgery is a felony of the third degree if the writing is or purports to be a will, deed, contract, release, commercial instrument, or other document evidencing, creating, transferring, altering, terminating, or otherwise affecting legal relations. Otherwise forgery is a misdemeanor.

Section 224.2 Simulating Objects of Antiquity, Rarity, Etc.

A person commits a misdemeanor if, with purpose to defraud anyone or with knowledge that he is facilitating a fraud to be perpetrated by anyone, he makes, alters or utters any object so that it appears to have value because of antiquity, rarity, source, or authorship which it does not possess.

Section 224.3 Fraudulent Destruction, Removal or Concealment of Recordable Instruments

A person commits a felony of the third degree if, with purpose to deceive or injure anyone, he destroys, removes or conceals any will, deed, mortgage, security instrument or other writing for which the law provides public recording.

Section 224.4 Tampering With Records

A person commits a misdemeanor if, knowing that he has no privilege to do so, he falsifies, destroys, removes or conceals any writing or record, with purpose to deceive or injure anyone or to conceal any wrongdoing.

Section 224.5 Bad Checks

A person who issues or passes a check or similar sight order for the payment of money, knowing that it will not be honored by the drawee, commits a misdemeanor. For the purposes of this Section as well as in any prosecution for theft committed by means of a bad check, an issuer is presumed to know that the check or order (other than a post-dated check or order) would not be paid, if:

(1) the issuer had no account with the drawee at the time the check or order was issued; or

(2) payment was refused by the drawee for lack of funds, upon presentation within 30 days after issue, and the issuer failed to make good within 10 days after receiving notice of that refusal.

Section 224.6 Credit Cards

A person commits an offense if he uses a credit card for the purpose of obtaining property or services with knowledge that:

(1) the card is stolen or forged; or

(2) the card has been revoked or cancelled; or

(3) for any other reason his use of the card is unauthorized.

It is an affirmative defense to prosecution under paragraph (3) if the actor proves by a preponderance of the evidence that he had the purpose and ability to meet all obligations to the issuer arising out of his use of the card. "Credit card" means a writing or other evidence of an undertaking to pay for property or services delivered or rendered to or upon the order of a designated person or bearer. An offense under this Section is a felony of the third degree if the value of the property or services secured or sought to be secured by means of the credit card exceeds $500; otherwise it is a misdemeanor.

Section 224.7 Deceptive Business Practices

A person commits a misdemeanor if in the course of business he:

(1) uses or possesses for use a false weight or measure, or any other device for falsely determining or recording any quality or quantity; or

(2) sells, offers or exposes for sale, or delivers less than the represented quantity of any commodity or service; or

(3) takes or attempts to take more than the represented quantity of any commodity or service when as buyer he furnishes the weight or measure; or

(4) sells, offers or exposes for sale adulterated or mislabeled commodities. "Adulterated" means varying from the standard of composition or quality prescribed by or pursuant to any statute providing criminal penalties for such variance, or set by established commercial usage. "Mislabeled" means varying from the standard of truth or disclosure in labeling prescribed by or pursuant to any statute providing criminal penalties for such variance, or set by established commercial usage; or

(5) makes a false or misleading statement in any advertisement addressed to the public or to a substantial segment thereof for the purpose of promoting the purchase or sale of property or services; or

(6) makes a false or misleading written statement for the purpose of obtaining property or credit; or

(7) makes a false or misleading written statement for the purpose of promoting the sale of securities, or omits information required by law to be disclosed in written documents relating to securities.

It is an affirmative defense to prosecution under this Section if the defendant proves by a preponderance of the evidence that his conduct was not knowingly or recklessly deceptive.

Section 224.8 Commercial Bribery and Breach of Duty to Act Disinterestedly

(1) A person commits a misdemeanor if he solicits, accepts or agrees to accept any benefit as consideration for knowingly violating or agreeing to violate a duty of fidelity to which he is subject as:

(a) agent or employee of another;

(b) trustee, guardian, or other fiduciary;

(c) lawyer, physician, accountant, appraiser, or other professional adviser or informant;

(d) officer, director, manager or other participant in the direction of the affairs of an incorporated or unincorporated association; or

(e) arbitrator or other purportedly disinterested adjudicator or referee.

(2) A person who holds himself out to the public as being engaged in the business of making disinterested selection, appraisal, or criticism of commodities or services commits a misdemeanor if he solicits, accepts or agrees to accept any benefit to influence his selection, appraisal or criticism.

(3) A person commits a misdemeanor if he confers, or offers or agrees to confer, any benefit the acceptance of which would be criminal under this Section.

Section 224.9 Rigging Publicly Exhibited Contest

(1) A person commits a misdemeanor if, with purpose to prevent a publicly exhibited contest from being conducted in accordance with the rules and usages purporting to govern it, he:

(a) confers or offers or agrees to confer any benefit upon, or threatens any injury to a participant, official or other person associated with the contest or exhibition; or

(b) tampers with any person, animal or thing.

(2) **Soliciting or Accepting Benefit for Rigging.** A person commits a misdemeanor if he knowingly solicits, accepts or agrees to accept any benefit the giving of which would be criminal under Subsection (1).

(3) **Participation in Rigged Contest.** A person commits a misdemeanor if he knowingly engages in, sponsors, produces, judges, or otherwise participates in a publicly exhibited contest knowing that the contest is not being conducted in compliance with the rules and usages purporting to govern it, by reason of conduct which would be criminal under this Section.

Section 224.10 Defrauding Secured Creditors

A person commits a misdemeanor if he destroys, removes, conceals, encumbers, transfers or otherwise deals with property subject to a security interest with purpose to hinder enforcement of that interest.

Section 224.11 Fraud in Insolvency

A person commits a misdemeanor if, knowing that proceedings have been or are about to be instituted for the appointment of a receiver or other person entitled to administer property for the benefit of creditors, or that any other composition or liquidation for the benefit of creditors has been or is about to be made, he:

(a) destroys, removes, conceals, encumbers, transfers, or otherwise deals with any property with purpose to defeat or obstruct the claim of any creditor, or otherwise to obstruct the operation of any law relating to administration of property for the benefit of creditors; or

(b) knowingly falsifies any writing or record relating to the property; or

(c) knowingly misrepresents or refuses to disclose to a receiver or other person entitled to administer property for the benefit of creditors, the existence, amount or location of the property, or any other information which the actor could be legally required to furnish in relation to such administration.

Section 224.12 Receiving Deposits in a Failing Financial Institution

An officer, manager or other person directing or participating in the direction of a financial institution commits a misdemeanor if he receives or permits the receipt of a deposit, premium payment or other investment in the institution knowing that:

(1) due to financial difficulties the institution is about to suspend operations or go into receivership or reorganization; and

(2) the person making the deposit or other payment is unaware of the precarious situation of the institution.

Section 224.13 Misapplication of Entrusted Property and Property of Government or Financial Institution

A person commits an offense if he applies or disposes of property that has been entrusted to him as a fiduciary, or property of the government or of a financial institution, in a manner which he knows is unlawful and involves substantial risk of loss or detriment to the owner of the property or to a person for whose benefit the property was entrusted. The offense is a misdemeanor if the amount involved exceeds $50; otherwise it is a petty misdemeanor. "Fiduciary" includes trustee, guardian, executor, administrator, receiver and any person carrying on fiduciary functions on behalf of a corporation or other organization which is a fiduciary.

Section 224.14 Securing Execution of Documents by Deception

A person commits a misdemeanor if by deception he causes another to execute any instrument affecting or purporting to affect or likely to affect the pecuniary interest of any person.

OFFENSES AGAINST THE FAMILY

ARTICLE 230

OFFENSES AGAINST THE FAMILY

Section 230.1 Bigamy and Polygamy

(1) **Bigamy.** A married person is guilty of bigamy, a misdemeanor, if he contracts or purports to contract another marriage, unless at the time of the subsequent marriage:

(a) the actor believes that the prior spouse is dead; or

(b) the actor and the prior spouse have been living apart for five consecutive years throughout which the prior spouse was not known by the actor to be alive; or

(c) a Court has entered a judgment purporting to terminate or annul any prior disqualifying marriage, and the actor does not know that judgment to be invalid; or

(d) the actor reasonably believes that he is legally eligible to remarry.

(2) **Polygamy.** A person is guilty of polygamy, a felony of the third degree, if he marries or cohabits with more than one spouse at a time in purported exercise of the right of plural marriage. The offense is a continuing one until all

cohabitation and claim of marriage with more than one spouse terminates. This Section does not apply to parties to a polygamous marriage, lawful in the country of which they are residents or nationals, while they are in transit through or temporarily visiting this State.

(3) Other Party to Bigamous or Polygamous Marriage. A person is guilty of bigamy or polygamy, as the case may be, if he contracts or purports to contract marriage with another knowing that the other is thereby committing bigamy or polygamy.

Section 230.2 Incest

A person is guilty of incest, a felony of the third degree, if he knowingly marries or cohabits or has sexual intercourse with an ancestor or descendant, a brother or sister of the whole or half blood [or an uncle, aunt, nephew or niece of the whole blood]. "Cohabit" means to live together under the representation or appearance of being married. The relationships referred to herein include blood relationships without regard to legitimacy, and relationship of parent and child by adoption.

Section 230.3 Abortion

(1) Unjustified Abortion. A person who purposely and unjustifiably terminates the pregnancy of another otherwise than by a live birth commits a felony of the third degree or, where the pregnancy has continued beyond the twenty-sixth week, a felony of the second degree.

(2) Justifiable Abortion. A licensed physician is justified in terminating a pregnancy if he believes there is substantial risk that continuance of the pregnancy would gravely impair the physical or mental health of the mother or that the child would be born with grave physical or mental defect, or that the pregnancy resulted from rape, incest, or other felonious intercourse. All illicit intercourse with a girl below the age of 16 shall be deemed felonious for purposes of this subsection. Justifiable abortions shall be performed only in a licensed hospital except in case of emergency when hospital facilities are unavailable. [Additional exceptions from the requirement of hospitalization may be incorporated here to take account of situations in sparsely settled areas where hospitals are not generally accessible.]

(3) Physicians' Certificates; Presumption from Non-Compliance. No abortion shall be performed unless two physicians, one of whom may be the person performing the abortion, shall have certified in writing the circumstances which they believe to justify the abortion. Such certificate shall be submitted before the abortion to the hospital where it is to be performed and, in the case of abortion following felonious intercourse, to the prosecuting attorney or the police. Failure to comply with any of the requirements of this Subsection gives rise to a presumption that the abortion was unjustified.

(4) Self-Abortion. A woman whose pregnancy has continued beyond the twenty-sixth week commits a felony of the third degree if she purposely terminates her own pregnancy otherwise than by a live birth, or if she uses instruments, drugs or violence upon herself for that purpose. Except as justified under Subsection (2), a person who induces or knowingly aids a woman to use instruments, drugs or violence upon herself for the purpose of terminating her pregnancy otherwise than by a live birth commits a felony of the third degree whether or not the pregnancy has continued beyond the twenty-sixth week.

(5) Pretended Abortion. A person commits a felony of the third degree if, representing that it is his purpose to perform an abortion, he does an act adapted to cause abortion in a pregnant woman although the woman is in fact not pregnant, or the actor does not believe she is. A person charged with unjustified abortion under Subsection (1) or an attempt to commit that offense may be convicted thereof upon proof of conduct prohibited by this Subsection.

(6) Distribution of Abortifacients. A person who sells, offers to sell, possesses with intent to sell, advertises, or displays for sale anything specially designed to terminate a pregnancy, or held out by the actor as useful for that purpose, commits a misdemeanor, unless:

(a) the sale, offer or display is to a physician or druggist or to an intermediary in a chain of distribution to physicians or druggists; or

(b) the sale is made upon prescription or order of a physician; or

(c) the possession is with intent to sell as authorized in paragraphs (a) and (b); or

(d) the advertising is addressed to persons named in paragraph (a) and confined to trade or professional channels not likely to reach the general public.

(7) Section Inapplicable to Prevention of Pregnancy. Nothing in this Section shall be deemed applicable to the prescription, administration or distribution of drugs or other substances for avoiding pregnancy, whether by preventing implantation of a fertilized ovum or by any other method that operates before, at or immediately after fertilization.

Section 230.4　Endangering Welfare of Children

A parent, guardian, or other person supervising the welfare of a child under 18 commits a misdemeanor if he knowingly endangers the child's welfare by violating a duty of care, protection or support.

Section 230.5　Persistent Non-support

A person commits a misdemeanor if he persistently fails to provide support which he can provide and which he knows he is legally obliged to provide to a spouse, child or other defendant.

OFFENSES AGAINST PUBLIC ADMINISTRATION

ARTICLE 240

BRIBERY AND CORRUPT INFLUENCE

Section 240.0　Definitions

In Articles 240–243, unless a different meaning plainly is required:

(1) "benefit" means gain or advantage, or anything regarded by the beneficiary as gain or advantage, including benefit to any other person or entity in whose welfare he is interested, but not an advantage promised generally to a group or class of voters as a consequence of public measures which a candidate engages to support or oppose;

(2) "government" includes any branch, subdivision or agency of the government of the State or any locality within it;

(3) "harm" means loss, disadvantage or injury, or anything so regarded by the person affected, including loss, disadvantage or injury to any other person or entity in whose welfare he is interested;

(4) "official proceeding" means a proceeding heard or which may be heard before any legislative, judicial, administrative or other governmental agency or official authorized to take evidence under oath, including any referee, hearing examiner, commissioner, notary or other person taking testimony or deposition in connection with any such proceeding;

(5) "party official" means a person who holds an elective or appointive post in a political party in the United States by virtue of which he directs or conducts, or participates in directing or conducting party affairs at any level of responsibility;

(6) "pecuniary benefit" is benefit in the form of money, property, commercial interests or anything else the primary significance of which is economic gain;

(7) "public servant" means any officer or employee of government, including legislators and judges, and any person participating as juror, advisor, consultant or otherwise, in performing a governmental function; but the term does not include witnesses;

(8) "administrative proceeding" means any proceeding other than a judicial proceeding the outcome of which is required to be based on a record or documentation prescribed by law, or in which law or regulation is particularized in application to individuals.

Section 240.1　Bribery in Official and Political Matters

A person is guilty of bribery, a felony of the third degree, if he offers, confers or agrees to confer upon another, or solicits, accepts or agrees to accept from another:

(1) any pecuniary benefit as consideration for the recipient's decision, opinion, recommendation, vote or other exercise of discretion as a public servant, party official or voter; or

(2) any benefit as consideration for the recipient's decision, vote, recommendation or other exercise of official discretion in a judicial or administrative proceeding; or

(3) any benefit as consideration for a violation of a known legal duty as public servant or party official.

It is no defense to prosecution under this section that a person whom the actor sought to influence was not qualified to act in the desired way whether because he had not yet assumed office, or lacked jurisdiction, or for any other reason.

Section 240.2 Threats and Other Improper Influence in Official and Political Matters

(1) **Offenses Defined.** A person commits an offense if he:

(a) threatens unlawful harm to any person with purpose to influence his decision, opinion, recommendation, vote or other exercise of discretion as a public servant, party official or voter; or

(b) threatens harm to any public servant with purpose to influence his decision, opinion, recommendation, vote or other exercise of discretion in a judicial or administrative proceeding; or

(c) threatens harm to any public servant or party official with purpose to influence him to violate his known legal duty; or

(d) privately addresses to any public servant who has or will have an official discretion in a judicial or administrative proceeding any representation, entreaty, argument or other communication with purpose to influence the outcome on the basis of considerations other than those authorized by law.

It is no defense to prosecution under this Section that a person whom the actor sought to influence was not qualified to act in the desired way, whether because he had not yet assumed office, or lacked jurisdiction, or for any other reason.

(2) **Grading.** An offense under this Section is a misdemeanor unless the actor threatened to commit a crime or made a threat with purpose to influence a judicial or administrative proceeding, in which case the offense is a felony of the third degree.

Section 240.3 Compensation for Past Official Behavior

A person commits a misdemeanor if he solicits, accepts or agrees to accept any pecuniary benefit as compensation for having, as public servant, given a decision, opinion, recommendation or vote favorable to another, or for having otherwise exercised a discretion in his favor, or for having violated his duty. A person commits a misdemeanor if he offers, confers or agrees to confer compensation acceptance of which is prohibited by this Section.

Section 240.4 Retaliation for Past Official Action

A person commits a misdemeanor if he harms another by any unlawful act in retaliation for anything lawfully done by the latter in the capacity of public servant.

Section 240.5 Gifts to Public Servants by Persons Subject to Their Jurisdiction

(1) **Regulatory and Law Enforcement Officials.** No public servant in any department or agency exercising regulatory functions, or conducting inspections or investigations, or carrying on civil or criminal litigation on behalf of the government, or having custody of prisoners, shall solicit, accept or agree to accept any pecuniary benefit from a person known to be subject to such regulation, inspection, investigation or custody, or against whom such litigation is known to be pending or contemplated.

(2) **Officials Concerned with Government Contracts and Pecuniary Transactions.** No public servant having any discretionary function to perform in connection with contracts, purchases, payments, claims or other pecuniary transactions of the government shall solicit, accept or agree to accept any pecuniary benefit from any person known to be interested in or likely to become interested in any such contract, purchase, payment, claim or transaction.

(3) **Judicial and Administrative Officials.** No public servant having judicial or administrative authority and no public servant employed by or in a court or other tribunal having such authority, or participating in the enforcement of its decisions, shall solicit, accept or agree to accept any pecuniary benefit from a person known to be interested in or likely to become interested in any

matter before such public servant or a tribunal with which he is associated.

(4) Legislative Officials. No legislator or public servant employed by the legislature or by any committee or agency thereof shall solicit, accept or agree to accept any pecuniary benefit from any person known to be interested in a bill, transaction or proceeding, pending or contemplated, before the legislature or any committee or agency thereof.

(5) Exceptions. This Section shall not apply to:

(a) fees prescribed by law to be received by a public servant, or any other benefit for which the recipient gives legitimate consideration or to which he is otherwise legally entitled; or

(b) gifts or other benefits conferred on account of kinship or other personal, professional or business relationship independent of the official status of the receiver; or

(c) trivial benefits incidental to personal, professional or business contacts and involving no substantial risk of undermining official impartiality.

(6) Offering Benefits Prohibited. No person shall knowingly confer, or offer or agree to confer, any benefit prohibited by the foregoing Subsections.

(7) Grade of Offense. An offense under this Section is a misdemeanor.

Section 240.6 Compensating Public Servant for Assisting Private Interests in Relation to Matters Before Him

(1) Receiving Compensation. A public servant commits a misdemeanor if he solicits, accepts or agrees to accept compensation for advice or other assistance in preparing or promoting a bill, contract, claim, or other transaction or proposal as to which he knows that he has or is likely to have an official discretion to exercise.

(2) Paying Compensation. A person commits a misdemeanor if he pays or offers or agrees to pay compensation to a public servant with knowledge that acceptance by the public servant is unlawful.

Section 240.7 Selling Political Endorsement; Special Influence

(1) Selling Political Endorsement. A person commits a misdemeanor if he solicits, receives, agrees to receive, or agrees that any political party or other person shall receive, any pecuniary benefit as consideration for approval or disapproval of an appointment or advancement in public service, or for approval or disapproval of any person or transaction for any benefit conferred by an official or agency of government. "Approval" includes recommendation, failure to disapprove, or any other manifestation of favor or acquiescence. "Disapproval" includes failure to approve, or any other manifestation of disfavor or nonacquiescence.

(2) Other Trading in Special Influence. A person commits a misdemeanor if he solicits, receives or agrees to receive any pecuniary benefit as consideration for exerting special influence upon a public servant or procuring another to do so. "Special influence" means power to influence through kinship, friendship or other relationship, apart from the merits of the transaction.

(3) Paying for Endorsement or Special Influence. A person commits a misdemeanor if he offers, confers or agrees to confer any pecuniary benefit receipt of which is prohibited by this Section.

ARTICLE 241

PERJURY AND OTHER FALSIFICATION IN OFFICIAL MATTERS

Section 241.0 Definitions

In this Article, unless a different meaning plainly is required:

(1) the definitions given in Section 240.0 apply; and

(2) "statement" means any representation, but includes a representation of opinion, belief or other state of mind only if the representation clearly relates to state of mind apart from or in addition to any facts which are the subject of the representation.

Section 241.1 Perjury

(1) Offense Defined. A person is guilty of perjury, a felony of the third degree, if in any official proceeding he makes a false statement under oath or equivalent affirmation, or swears or affirms the truth of a statement previously made, when the statement is material and he does not believe it to be true.

(2) Materiality. Falsification is material, regardless of the admissibility of the statement under rules of evidence, if it could have affected the course or outcome of the proceeding. It is no defense that the declarant mistakenly believed the falsification to be immaterial. Whether a falsification is material in a given factual situation is a question of law.

(3) Irregularities No Defense. It is not a defense to prosecution under this Section that the oath or affirmation was administered or taken in an irregular manner or that the declarant was not competent to make the statement. A document purporting to be made upon oath or affirmation at any time when the actor presents it as being so verified shall be deemed to have been duly sworn or affirmed.

(4) Retraction. No person shall be guilty of an offense under this Section if he retracted the falsification in the course of the proceeding in which it was made before it became manifest that the falsification was or would be exposed and before the falsification substantially affected the proceeding.

(5) Inconsistent Statements. Where the defendant made inconsistent statements under oath or equivalent affirmation, both having been made within the period of the statute of limitations, the prosecution may proceed by setting forth the inconsistent statements in a single count alleging in the alternative that one or the other was false and not believed by the defendant. In such case it shall not be necessary for the prosecution to prove which statement was false but only that one or the other was false and not believed by the defendant to be true.

(6) Corroboration. No person shall be convicted of an offense under this Section where proof of falsity rests solely upon contradiction by testimony of a single person other than the defendant.

Section 241.2 False Swearing

(1) False Swearing in Official Matters. A person who makes a false statement under oath or equivalent affirmation, or swears or affirms the truth of such a statement previously made, when he does not believe the statement to be true, is guilty of a misdemeanor if:

(a) the falsification occurs in an official proceeding; or

(b) the falsification is intended to mislead a public servant in performing his official function.

(2) Other False Swearing. A person who makes a false statement under oath or equivalent affirmation, or swears or affirms the truth of such a statement previously made, when he does not believe the statement to be true, is guilty of a petty misdemeanor, if the statement is one which is required by law to be sworn or affirmed before a notary or other person authorized to administer oaths.

(3) Perjury Provisions Applicable. Subsections (3) to (6) of Section 241.1 apply to the present Section.

Section 241.3 Unsworn Falsification to Authorities

(1) In General. A person commits a misdemeanor if, with purpose to mislead a public servant in performing his official function, he:

(a) makes any written false statement which he does not believe to be true; or

(b) purposely creates a false impression in a written application for any pecuniary or other benefit, by omitting information necessary to prevent statements therein from being misleading; or

(c) submits or invites reliance on any writing which he knows to be forged, altered or otherwise lacking in authenticity; or

(d) submits or invites reliance on any sample, specimen, map, boundary-mark, or other object which he knows to be false.

(2) Statements "Under Penalty." A person commits a petty misdemeanor if he makes a written false statement which he does not believe to be true, on or pursuant to a form bearing notice, authorized by law, to the effect that false statements made therein are punishable.

(3) Perjury Provisions Applicable. Subsections (3) to (6) of Section 241.1 apply to the present Section.

Section 241.4 False Alarms to Agencies of Public Safety

A person who knowingly causes a false alarm of fire or other emergency to be transmitted to or within any organization, official or volunteer, for dealing with emergencies involving danger to life or property commits a misdemeanor.

Section 241.5 False Reports to Law Enforcement Authorities

(1) **Falsely Incriminating Another.** A person who knowingly gives false information to any law enforcement officer with purpose to implicate another commits a misdemeanor.

(2) **Fictitious Reports.** A person commits a petty misdemeanor if he:

(a) reports to law enforcement authorities an offense or other incident within their concern knowing that it did not occur; or

(b) pretends to furnish such authorities with information relating to an offense or incident when he knows he has no information relating to such offense or incident.

Section 241.6 Tampering With Witnesses and Informants; Retaliation Against Them

(1) **Tampering.** A person commits an offense if, believing that an official proceeding or investigation is pending or about to be instituted, he attempts to induce or otherwise cause a witness or informant to:

(a) testify or inform falsely; or

(b) withhold any testimony, information, document or thing; or

(c) elude legal process summoning him to testify or supply evidence; or

(d) absent himself from any proceeding or investigation to which he has been legally summoned.

The offense is a felony of the third degree if the actor employs force, deception, threat or offer of pecuniary benefit. Otherwise it is a misdemeanor.

(2) **Retaliation Against Witness or Informant.** A person commits a misdemeanor if he harms another by any unlawful act in retaliation for anything lawfully done in the capacity of witness or informant.

(3) **Witness or Informant Taking Bribe.** A person commits a felony of the third degree if he solicits, accepts or agrees to accept any benefit in consideration of his doing any of the things specified in clauses (a) to (d) of Subsection (1).

Section 241.7. Tampering With or Fabricating Physical Evidence

A person commits a misdemeanor if, believing that an official proceeding or investigation is pending or about to be instituted, he:

(1) alters, destroys, conceals or removes any record, document or thing with purpose to impair its verity or availability in such proceeding or investigation; or

(2) makes, presents or uses any record, document or thing knowing it to be false and with purpose to mislead a public servant who is or may be engaged in such proceeding or investigation.

Section 241.8 Tampering With Public Records or Information

(1) **Offense Defined.** A person commits an offense if he:

(a) knowingly makes a false entry in, or false alteration of, any record, document or thing belonging to, or received or kept by, the government for information or record, or required by law to be kept by others for information of the government; or

(b) makes, presents or uses any record, document or thing knowing it to be false, and with purpose that it be taken as a genuine part of information or records referred to in paragraph (a); or

(c) purposely and unlawfully destroys, conceals, removes or otherwise impairs the verity or availability of any such record, document or thing.

(2) **Grading.** An offense under this Section is a misdemeanor unless the actor's purpose is to defraud or injure anyone, in which case the offense is a felony of the third degree.

Section 241.9 Impersonating a Public Servant

A person commits a misdemeanor if he falsely pretends to hold a position in the public service with purpose to induce another to submit to such pretended official authority or otherwise to act in reliance upon that pretense to his prejudice.

ARTICLE 242

OBSTRUCTING GOVERNMENTAL OPERATIONS; ESCAPES

Section 242.0 Definitions

In this Article, unless another meaning plainly is required, the definitions given in Section 240.0 apply.

Section 242.1 Obstructing Administration of Law or Other Governmental Function

A person commits a misdemeanor if he purposely obstructs, impairs or perverts the administration of law or other governmental function by force, violence, physical interference or obstacle, breach of official duty, or any other unlawful act, except that this Section does not apply to flight by a person charged with crime, refusal to submit to arrest, failure to perform a legal duty other than an official duty, or any other means of avoiding compliance with law without affirmative interference with governmental functions.

Section 242.2 Resisting Arrest or Other Law Enforcement

A person commits a misdemeanor if, for the purpose of preventing a public servant from effecting a lawful arrest or discharging any other duty, the person creates a substantial risk of bodily injury to the public servant or anyone else, or employs means justifying or requiring substantial force to overcome the resistance.

Section 242.3 Hindering Apprehension or Prosecution

A person commits an offense if, with purpose to hinder the apprehension, prosecution, conviction or punishment of another for crime, he:

(1) harbors or conceals the other; or

(2) provides or aids in providing a weapon, transportation, disguise or other means of avoiding apprehension or effecting escape; or

(3) conceals or destroys evidence of the crime, or tampers with a witness, informant, document or other source of information, regardless of its admissibility in evidence; or

(4) warns the other of impending discovery or apprehension, except that this paragraph does not apply to a warning given in connection with an effort to bring another into compliance with law; or

(5) volunteers false information to a law enforcement officer.

The offense is a felony of the third degree if the conduct which the actor knows has been charged or is liable to be charged against the person aided would constitute a felony of the first or second degree. Otherwise it is a misdemeanor.

Section 242.4 Aiding Consummation of Crime

A person commits an offense if he purposely aids another to accomplish an unlawful object of a crime, as by safeguarding the proceeds thereof or converting the proceeds into negotiable funds. The offense is a felony of the third degree if the principal offense was a felony of the first or second degree. Otherwise it is a misdemeanor.

Section 242.5 Compounding

A person commits a misdemeanor if he accepts or agrees to accept any pecuniary benefit in consideration of refraining from reporting to law enforcement authorities the commission or suspected commission of any offense or information relating to an offense. It is an affirmative defense to prosecution under this Section that the pecuniary benefit did not exceed an amount which the actor believed to be due as restitution or indemnification for harm caused by the offense.

Section 242.6 Escape

(1) **Escape.** A person commits an offense if he unlawfully removes himself from official detention or fails to return to official detention following temporary leave granted for a specific purpose or limited period. "Official detention" means arrest, detention in any facility for custody of persons under charge or conviction of crime or alleged or found to be delinquent, detention for extradition or deportation, or any other detention

for law enforcement purposes; but "official detention" does not include supervision of probation or parole, or constraint incidental to release on bail.

(2) Permitting or Facilitating Escape. A public servant concerned in detention commits an offense if he knowingly or recklessly permits an escape. Any person who knowingly causes or facilitates an escape commits an offense.

(3) Effect of Legal Irregularity in Detention. Irregularity in bringing about or maintaining detention, or lack of jurisdiction of the committing or detaining authority, shall not be a defense to prosecution under this Section if the escape is from a prison or other custodial facility or from detention pursuant to commitment by official proceedings. In the case of other detentions, irregularity or lack of jurisdiction shall be a defense only if:

(a) the escape involved no substantial risk of harm to the person or property of anyone other than the detainee; or

(b) the detaining authority did not act in good faith under color of law.

(4) Grading of Offenses. An offense under this Section is a felony of the third degree where:

(a) the actor was under arrest for or detained on a charge of felony or following conviction of crime; or

(b) the actor employs force, threat, deadly weapon or other dangerous instrumentality to effect the escape; or

(c) a public servant concerned in detention of persons convicted of crime purposely facilitates or permits an escape from a detention facility.

Otherwise an offense under this section is a misdemeanor.

Section 242.7 Implements for Escape; Other Contraband

(1) Escape Implements. A person commits a misdemeanor if he unlawfully introduces within a detention facility, or unlawfully provides an inmate with, any weapon, tool or other thing which may be useful for escape. An inmate commits a misdemeanor if he unlawfully procures, makes, or otherwise provides himself with, or has in his possession, any such implement of escape. "Unlawfully" means surreptitiously or contrary to law, regulation or order of the detaining authority.

(2) Other Contraband. A person commits a petty misdemeanor if he provides an inmate with anything which the actor knows it is unlawful for the inmate to possess.

Section 242.8 Bail Jumping; Default in Required Appearance

A person set at liberty by court order, with or without bail, upon condition that he will subsequently appear at a specified time and place, commits a misdemeanor if, without lawful excuse, he fails to appear at that time and place. The offense constitutes a felony of the third degree where the required appearance was to answer to a charge of felony, or for disposition of any such charge, and the actor took flight or went into hiding to avoid apprehension, trial or punishment. This Section does not apply to obligations to appear incident to release under suspended sentence or on probation or parole.

ARTICLE 243

ABUSE OF OFFICE

Section 243.0 Definitions

In this Article, unless a different meaning plainly is required, the definitions given in Section 240.0 apply.

Section 243.1 Official Oppression

A person acting or purporting to act in an official capacity or taking advantage of such actual or purported capacity commits a misdemeanor if, knowing that his conduct is illegal, he:

(a) subjects another to arrest, detention, search, seizure, mistreatment, dispossession, assessment, lien or other infringement of personal or property rights; or

(b) denies or impedes another in the exercise or enjoyment of any right, privilege, power or immunity.

Section 243.2 Speculating or Wagering on Official Action or Information

A public servant commits a misdemeanor if, in contemplation of official action by himself or by a governmental unit with which he is associated, or in reliance on information to which he has access in his official capacity and which has not been made public, he:

(1) acquires a pecuniary interest in any property, transaction or enterprise which may be affected by such information or official action; or

(2) speculates or wagers on the basis of such information or official action; or

(3) aids another to do any of the foregoing.

OFFENSES AGAINST PUBLIC ORDER AND DECENCY

ARTICLE 250

RIOT, DISORDERLY CONDUCT, AND RELATED OFFENSES

Section 250.1 Riot; Failure to Disperse

(1) **Riot.** A person is guilty of riot, a felony of the third degree, if he participates with [two] or more others in a course of disorderly conduct:

(a) with purpose to commit or facilitate the commission of a felony or misdemeanor;

(b) with purpose to prevent or coerce official action; or

(c) when the actor or any other participant to the knowledge of the actor uses or plans to use a firearm or other deadly weapon.

(2) **Failure of Disorderly Persons to Disperse Upon Official Order.** Where [three] or more persons are participating in a course of disorderly conduct likely to cause substantial harm or serious inconvenience, annoyance or alarm, a peace officer or other public servant engaged in executing or enforcing the law may order the participants and others in the immediate vicinity to disperse. A person who refuses or knowingly fails to obey such an order commits a misdemeanor.

Section 250.2 Disorderly Conduct

(1) **Offense Defined.** A person is guilty of disorderly conduct if, with purpose to cause public inconvenience, annoyance or alarm, or recklessly creating a risk thereof, he:

(a) engages in fighting or threatening, or in violent or tumultuous behavior; or

(b) makes unreasonable noise or offensively coarse utterance, gesture or display, or addresses abusive language to any person present; or

(c) creates a hazardous or physically offensive condition by any act which serves no legitimate purpose of the actor.

"Public" means affecting or likely to affect persons in a place to which the public or a substantial group has access; among the places included are highways, transport facilities, schools, prisons, apartment houses, places of business or amusement, or any neighborhood.

(2) **Grading.** An offense under this section is a petty misdemeanor if the actor's purpose is to cause substantial harm or serious inconvenience, or if he persists in disorderly conduct after reasonable warning or request to desist. Otherwise disorderly conduct is a violation.

Section 250.3 False Public Alarms

A person is guilty of a misdemeanor if he initiates or circulates a report or warning of an impending bombing or other crime or catastrophe, knowing that the report or warning is false or baseless and that it is likely to cause evacuation of a building, place of assembly, or facility of public transport, or to cause public inconvenience or alarm.

Section 250.4 Harassment

A person commits a petty misdemeanor if, with purpose to harass another, he:

(1) makes a telephone call without purpose of legitimate communication; or

(2) insults, taunts or challenges another in a manner likely to provoke violent or disorderly response; or

(3) makes repeated communications anonymously or at extremely inconvenient hours, or in offensively coarse language; or

(4) subjects another to an offensive touching; or

(5) engages in any other course of alarming conduct serving no legitimate purpose of the actor.

Section 250.5 Public Drunkenness; Drug Incapacitation

A person is guilty of an offense if he appears in any public place manifestly under the influence of alcohol, narcotics or other drug, not therapeutically administered, to the degree that he may endanger himself or other persons or property, or annoy persons in his vicinity. An offense under this Section constitutes a petty misdemeanor if the actor has been convicted hereunder twice before within a period of one year. Otherwise the offense constitutes a violation.

Section 250.6 Loitering or Prowling

A person commits a violation if he loiters or prowls in a place, at a time, or in a manner not usual for law-abiding individuals under circumstances that warrant alarm for the safety of persons or property in the vicinity. Among the circumstances which may be considered in determining whether such alarm is warranted is the fact that the actor takes flight upon appearance of a peace officer, refuses to identify himself, or manifestly endeavors to conceal himself or any object. Unless flight by the actor or other circumstance makes it impracticable, a peace officer shall prior to any arrest for an offense under this section afford the actor an opportunity to dispel any alarm which would otherwise be warranted, by requesting him to identify himself and explain his presence and conduct. No person shall be convicted of an offense under this Section if the peace officer did not comply with the preceding sentence, or if it appears at trial that the explanation given by the actor was true and, if believed by the peace officer at the time, would have dispelled the alarm.

Section 250.7 Obstructing Highways and Other Public Passages

(1) A person, who, having no legal privilege to do so, purposely or recklessly obstructs any highway or other public passage, whether alone or with others, commits a violation, or, in case he persists after warning by a law officer, a petty misdemeanor. "Obstructs" means renders impassable without unreasonable inconvenience or hazard. No person shall be deemed guilty of recklessly obstructing in violation of this Subsection solely because of a gathering of persons to hear him speak or otherwise communicate, or solely because of being a member of such a gathering.

(2) A person in a gathering commits a violation if he refuses to obey a reasonable official request or order to move:

(a) to prevent obstruction of a highway or other public passage; or

(b) to maintain public safety by dispersing those gathered in dangerous proximity to a fire or other hazard.

An order to move, addressed to a person whose speech or other lawful behavior attracts an obstructing audience, shall not be deemed reasonable if the obstruction can be readily remedied by police control of the size or location of the gathering.

Section 250.8 Disrupting Meetings and Processions

A person commits a misdemeanor if, with purpose to prevent or disrupt a lawful meeting, procession or gathering, he does any act tending to obstruct or interfere with it physically, or makes any utterance, gesture or display designed to outrage the sensibilities of the group.

Section 250.9 Desecration of Venerated Objects

A person commits a misdemeanor if he purposely desecrates any public monument or structure, or place of worship or burial, or if he purposely desecrates the national flag or any other object of veneration by the public or a substantial segment thereof in any public place. "Desecrate" means defacing, damaging, polluting or otherwise physically mistreating in a way that the actor knows will outrage the sensibilities of persons likely to observe or discover his action.

Section 250.10 Abuse of Corpse

Except as authorized by law, a person who treats a corpse in a way that he knows would outrage ordinary family sensibilities commits a misdemeanor.

Section 250.11 Cruelty to Animals

A person commits a misdemeanor if he purposely or recklessly:

(1) subjects any animal to cruel mistreatment; or

(2) subjects any animal in his custody to cruel neglect; or

(3) kills or injures any animal belonging to another without legal privilege or consent of the owner.

Subsections (1) and (2) shall not be deemed applicable to accepted veterinary practices and activities carried on for scientific research.

Section 250.12 Violation of Privacy

(1) **Unlawful Eavesdropping or Surveillance.** A person commits a misdemeanor if, except as authorized by law, he:

(a) trespasses on property with purpose to subject anyone to eavesdropping or other surveillance in a private place; or

(b) installs in any private place, without the consent of the person or persons entitled to privacy there, any device for observing, photographing, recording, amplifying or broadcasting sounds or events in such place, or uses any such unauthorized installation; or

(c) installs or uses outside a private place any device for hearing, recording, amplifying or broadcasting sounds originating in such place which would not ordinarily be audible or comprehensible outside, without the consent of the person or persons entitled to privacy there.

"Private place" means a place where one may reasonably expect to be safe from casual or hostile intrusion or surveillance, but does not include a place to which the public or a substantial group thereof has access.

(2) **Other Breach of Privacy of Messages.** A person commits a misdemeanor if, except as authorized by law, he:

(a) intercepts without the consent of the sender or receiver a message by telephone, telegraph, letter or other means of communicating privately; but this paragraph does not extend to (i) overhearing of messages through a regularly installed instrument on a telephone party line or on an extension, or (ii) interception by the telephone company or subscriber incident to enforcement of regulations limiting use of the facilities or incident to other normal operation and use; or

(b) divulges without the consent of the sender or receiver the existence or contents of any such message if the actor knows that the message was illegally intercepted, or if he learned of the message in the course of employment with an agency engaged in transmitting it.

ARTICLE 251

PUBLIC INDECENCY

Section 251.1 Open Lewdness

A person commits a petty misdemeanor if he does any lewd act which he knows is likely to be observed by others who would be affronted or alarmed.

Section 251.2 Prostitution and Related Offenses

(1) **Prostitution.** A person is guilty of prostitution, a petty misdemeanor, if he or she:

(a) is an inmate of a house of prostitution or otherwise engages in sexual activity as a business; or

(b) loiters in or within view of any public place for the purpose of being hired to engage in sexual activity.

"Sexual activity" includes homosexual and other deviate sexual relations. A "house of prostitution" is any place where prostitution or promotion of prostitution is regularly carried on by one person under the control, management or supervision of another. An "inmate" is a person who engages in prostitution in or through the agency of a house of prostitution. "Public place" means any place to which the public or any substantial group thereof has access.

(2) **Promoting Prostitution.** A person who knowingly promotes prostitution of another commits a misdemeanor or felony as provided in Subsection (3). The following acts shall, without limitation of the foregoing, constitute promoting prostitution:

(a) owning, controlling, managing, supervising or otherwise keeping, alone or in association with others, a house of prostitution or a prostitution business; or

(b) procuring an inmate for a house of prostitution or a place in a house of prostitution for one who would be an inmate; or

(c) encouraging, inducing, or otherwise purposely causing another to become or remain a prostitute; or

(d) soliciting a person to patronize a prostitute; or

(e) procuring a prostitute for a patron; or

(f) transporting a person into or within this state with purpose to promote that person's engaging in prostitution, or procuring or paying for transportation with that purpose; or

(g) leasing or otherwise permitting a place controlled by the actor, alone or in association with others, to be regularly used for prostitution or the promotion of prostitution, or failure to make reasonable effort to abate such use by ejecting the tenant, notifying law enforcement authorities, or other legally available means; or

(h) soliciting, receiving, or agreeing to receive any benefit for doing or agreeing to do anything forbidden by this Subsection.

(3) Grading of Offenses Under Subsection (2). An offense under Subsection (2) constitutes a felony of the third degree if:

(a) the offense falls within paragraph (a), (b) or (c) of Subsection (2); or

(b) the actor compels another to engage in or promote prostitution; or

(c) the actor promotes prostitution of a child under 16, whether or not he is aware of the child's age; or

(d) the actor promotes prostitution of his wife, child, ward or any person for whose care, protection or support he is responsible.

Otherwise the offense is a misdemeanor.

(4) Presumption from Living off Prostitutes. A person, other than the prostitute or the prostitute's minor child or other legal dependent incapable of self-support, who is supported in whole or substantial part by the proceeds of prostitution is presumed to be knowingly promoting prostitution in violation of Subsection (2).

(5) Patronizing Prostitutes. A person commits a violation if he hires a prostitute to engage in sexual activity with him, or if he enters or remains in a house of prostitution for the purpose of engaging in sexual activity.

(6) Evidence. On the issue whether a place is a house of prostitution the following shall be admissible evidence: its general repute; the repute of the persons who reside in or frequent the place; the frequency, timing and duration of visits by non-residents. Testimony of a person against his spouse shall be admissible to prove offenses under this Section.

Section 251.3 Loitering to Solicit Deviate Sexual Relations

A person is guilty of a petty misdemeanor if he loiters in or near any public place for the purpose of soliciting or being solicited to engage in deviate sexual relations.

Section 251.4 Obscenity

(1) Obscene Defined. Material is obscene if, considered as a whole, its predominant appeal is to prurient interest, that is, a shameful or morbid interest, in nudity, sex or excretion, and if in addition it goes substantially beyond customary limits of candor in describing or representing such matters. Predominant appeal shall be judged with reference to ordinary adults unless it appears from the character of the material or the circumstances of its dissemination to be designed for children or other specially susceptible audience. Undeveloped photographs, molds, printing plates, and the like, shall be deemed obscene notwithstanding that processing or other acts may be required to make the obscenity patent or to disseminate it.

(2) Offenses. Subject to the affirmative defense provided in Subsection (3), a person commits a misdemeanor if he knowingly or recklessly:

(a) sells, delivers or provides, or offers or agrees to sell, deliver or provide, any obscene writing, picture, record or other representation or embodiment of the obscene; or

(b) presents or directs an obscene play, dance or performance, or participates in that portion thereof which makes it obscene; or

(c) publishes, exhibits or otherwise makes available any obscene material; or

(d) possesses any obscene material for purposes of sale or other commercial dissemination; or

(e) sells, advertises or otherwise commercially disseminates material, whether or not obscene, by representing or suggesting that it is obscene.

A person who disseminates or possesses obscene material in the course of his business is presumed to do so knowingly or recklessly.

(3) **Justifiable and Non–Commercial Private Dissemination.** It is an affirmative defense to prosecution under this Section that dissemination was restricted to:

(a) institutions or persons having scientific, educational, governmental or other similar justification for possessing obscene material; or

(b) non-commercial dissemination to personal associates of the actor.

(4) **Evidence; Adjudication of Obscenity.** In any prosecution under this Section evidence shall be admissible to show:

(a) the character of the audience for which the material was designed or to which it was directed;

(b) what the predominant appeal of the material would be for ordinary adults or any special audience to which it was directed, and what effect, if any, it would probably have on conduct of such people;

(c) artistic, literary, scientific, educational or other merits of the material;

(d) the degree of public acceptance of the material in the United States;

(e) appeal to prurient interest, or absence thereof, in advertising or other promotion of the material; and

(f) the good repute of the author, creator, publisher or other person from whom the material originated.

Expert testimony and testimony of the author, creator, publisher or other person from whom the material originated, relating to factors entering into the determination of the issue of obscenity, shall be admissible. The Court shall dismiss a prosecution for obscenity if it is satisfied that the material is not obscene.

ADDITIONAL ARTICLES

[At this point, a State enacting a new Penal Code may insert additional Articles dealing with special topics such as narcotics, alcoholic beverages, gambling and offenses against tax and trade laws. The Model Penal Code project did not extend to these, partly because a higher priority on limited time and resources was accorded to branches of the penal law which have not received close legislative scrutiny. Also, in legislation dealing with narcotics, liquor, tax evasion, and the like, penal provisions have been so intermingled with regulatory and procedural provisions that the task of segregating one group from the other presents special difficulty for model legislation.]

*

SELECTED UNIFORM LAWS

Table of Contents

INTRODUCTION

These acts were drafted by the National Conference of Commissioners on Uniform State Laws and (like the American Law Institute's Model Penal Code) have been recommended for adoption or adaption in all states.

The National Conference of Commissioners on Uniform State Laws is composed of Commissioners from each of the states, the District of Columbia and Puerto Rico. The Commissioners are lawyers and judges of standing and experience, and teachers of law in some of the leading law schools. The object of the National Conference, as stated in its constitution, is "to promote uniformity in state laws on all subjects where uniformity is deemed desirable and practicable." If the National Conference decides to take up a proposed subject, tentative drafts of acts are submitted from year to year and are discussed section by section. Each uniform act is thus the result of one or more tentative drafts subjected to the criticism, correction, and emendation of the Commissioners, who represent the experience and judgment of a select body of lawyers chosen from every part of the United States. When finally approved by the National Conference, the uniform acts are recommended for general adoption throughout the jurisdiction of the United States and are submitted to the American Bar Association for its approval.

The notes or comments prepared by the Commissioners on Uniform State Laws in explanation of a particular Act appear under the Commissioners' Prefatory Note preceding the text of such Act. Also preceding the text of each act is a table indicating those states that have substantially adopted the act into law. In this vein, it should be noted that many states may not have incorporated wholesale a given Uniform Act, but have nevertheless found its instruction invaluable in their legislative deliberations.

The following Uniform Acts are presented in their entirety. It should be noted, however, that the often extensive explanatory comments of the Commissioners on each section of these acts have not been carried into this pamphlet, for their sheer volume. However, like the Advisory Committee and Amendment Notes that accompany the Federal Rules, the

Comments relating to a Uniform Act provide unique insight into the underlying intent of many of the sections. For the full text of these Comments, as well as statutory constructions by the courts, and references to informative law review articles, see Volumes 10 and 11 of Uniform Laws Annotated, available in most large law libraries.

Acknowledgment is gratefully made to the National Conference of Commissioners on Uniform State Laws for permission to reproduce the following model and uniform statutes.

UNIFORM ACT TO SECURE THE ATTENDANCE OF WITNESSES FROM WITHOUT A STATE IN CRIMINAL PROCEEDINGS

Table of Jurisdictions Wherein Act Has Been Adopted

Jurisdiction	Laws	Effective Date	Statutory Citation
Alabama	1977, No. 638, p. 1084		Code 1975, §§ 12–21–280 to 12–21–285.
Alaska	1962, c. 34	3–23–1962*	AS 12.50.010 to 12.50.080.
Arizona	1937, c. 74	3–25–1937*	A.R.S. §§ 13–4091 to 13–4096.
Arkansas	1935, No. 65	2–20–1935*	Ark.Stats. §§ 43–2005 to 43–2009.
California	1937, p. 562	8–27–1937	West's Ann.Cal.Penal Code, §§ 1334 to 1334.6.
Colorado	1939, c. 99	4–10–1939	C.R.S. 16–9–201 to 16–9–205.
Connecticut	1937, c. 333	4–16–1937	C.G.S.A. § 54–82i.
Delaware	1937, c. 214	4–7–1937	11 Del.C. §§ 3521 to 3526.
District of Columbia	1952, Stat. 15	3–5–1952	D.C.Code 1981, §§ 23–1501 to 23–1504.
Florida	1941, c. 20458	5–26–1941*	West's F.S.A. §§ 942.01 to 942.06.
Georgia	1976, No. 1351	3–31–1976	O.C.G.A. §§ 24–10–90 to 24–10–97.
Hawaii	1972, c. 9	1–1–1973	HRS §§ 836–1 to 836–6.
Idaho	1935, c. 10	2–11–1935*	I.C. § 19–3005.
Illinois	1959, p. 2147	7–23–1959	S.H.A. ch. 38, ¶¶ 156–1 to 156–6.
Indiana	1935, c. 21	7–1–1935	West's A.I.C. 35–37–5–1 to 35–37–5–9.
Iowa			I.C.A. §§ 819.1 to 819.5.
Kansas	1951, c. 354	3–31–1951*	K.S.A. 22–4201 to 22–4206.
Kentucky	1952, c. 132	6–19–1952	KRS 421.230 to 421.270.
Louisiana	1936, No. 285	7–9–1936*	LSA—C.Cr.P. arts. 741 to 745.
Maine	1939, c. 9	2–21–1939*	15 M.R.S.A. §§ 1411 to 1415.
Maryland	1955, c. 333	6–1–1955	Code, Courts and Judicial Proceedings, §§ 9–301 to 9–306.
Massachusetts	1937, c. 210	4–16–1937*	M.G.L.A. c. 233, §§ 13A to 13D.
Michigan	1970, No. 232	12–3–1970	M.C.L.A. §§ 767.91 to 767.95.
Minnesota	1935, c. 140	4–11–1935*	M.S.A. §§ 634.06 to 634.09.
Mississippi	1938, c. 261	4–7–1938	Code 1972, §§ 99–9–27 to 99–9–35.
Missouri	1959, H.B. 295	6–12–1959*	V.A.M.S. §§ 491.400 to 491.450.
Montana	1937, c. 188	3–18–1937	MCA 46–15–111 to 46–15–114.
Nebraska	1937, c. 71	5–13–1937*	R.R.S. 1943, §§ 29–1906 to 29–1911.
Nevada	1957, c. 41	2–18–1951	N.R.S. 174.395 to 174.445.
New Hampshire	1937, c. 65	4–15–1937	RSA 613:1 to 613:6.
New Jersey	1941, c. 88	4–28–1941	N.J.S.A. 2A:81–18 to 2A:81–23.
New Mexico	1937, c. 66	3–5–1937*	NMSA 1978, §§ 31–8–1 to 31–8–6.
New York	1936, c. 387	5–1–1936	McKinney's CPL § 640.10.
North Carolina	1937, c. 217	3–17–1937	G.S. §§ 15A–811 to 15A–816.
North Dakota	1933, c. 217	3–3–1933*	NDCC 31–03–25 to 31–03–31.
Ohio	1937, p. 668	8–23–1937	R.C. §§ 2939.25 to 2939.29.
Oklahoma	1949, p. 205	4–21–1949	22 Okl.St.Ann. §§ 721 to 727.
Oregon	1937, c. 124	2–26–1937*	ORS 136.623 to 136.637.
Pennsylvania	1941, P.L. 147	6–23–1941	42 Pa.C.S.A. §§ 5961 to 5965.
Puerto Rico	1934, No. 60	8–11–1934	34 L.P.R.A. §§ 1471 to 1475.
Rhode Island	1936, c. 2382	5–1–1936*	Gen.Laws 1956, §§ 12–16–1 to 12–16–13.
South Carolina	1948, p. 1810	4–8–1948	Code 1976, §§ 19–9–10 to 19–9–130.
South Dakota	1937, c. 259	3–6–1937*	SDCL 23A–14–1 et seq.
Tennessee	1939, c. 148	3–7–1939*	T.C.A. §§ 40–17–201 to 40–17–210.
Texas	1951, c. 441	6–15–1951	Vernon's Ann.Texas C.C.P. art. 24.28.
Utah	1937, c. 147	3–17–1937	U.C.A.1953, 77–21–1 to 77–21–5.
Vermont	1937, No. 46	3–9–1937	13 V.S.A. §§ 6641 to 6649.
Virgin Islands	1957, No. 160	9–1–1957	5 V.I.C. §§ 3861 to 3865.
Virginia	1938, c. 397	4–1–1938*	Code 1950, §§ 19.2–272 to 19.2–282.
Washington	1943, c. 218	3–20–1943*	West's RCWA 10.55.010 to 10.55.130.

Jurisdiction	Laws	Effective Date	Statutory Citation
West Virginia	1937, c. 41	3–12–1937*	Code, 62–6A–1 to 62–6A–6.
Wisconsin	1969, c. 255	7–1–1970	W.S.A. 976.02.
Wyoming	1935, c. 120	2–20–1935	W.S.1977, §§ 7–11–407 to 7–11–409.

* Date of approval.

Historical Note

The Uniform Act to Secure the Attendance of Witnesses from Without a State in Criminal Proceedings was approved by the National Conference of Commissioners on Uniform State Laws, and the American Bar Association, in 1936. It is a revision of the former Uniform Act to Secure the Attendance of Witnesses from Without the State in Criminal Cases, which was promulgated in 1931.

Commissioners' Prefatory Note

1936 Revision

At its annual meeting in Boston in August, 1936, the Conference approved two significant changes of substance and several minor changes of form in this Uniform Act. The Uniform Act as originally adopted had been subject to criticism on the ground that it provided for the compulsory attendance of witnesses only when a criminal action was pending. It was pointed out that occasionally the ability to secure a warrant for arrest or an indictment before a Grand Jury may depend upon the testimony of witnesses outside the state. Accordingly, the first important change adopted in 1936 extends the application of the act so as to provide for the possibility of securing the attendance of witnesses in connection with Grand Jury proceedings as well as in criminal cases.

The second major change approved by the Conference in 1936 was to provide that, when expedient, a witness may be arrested, held in custody, and delivered over to an officer of the requesting state.

This act should be adopted by every state. Its adoption will facilitate the administration of the criminal law. Officers engaged in the enforcement of criminal laws have long contended that there should be some statutory authority for securing the attendance of a witness from without the state in which the criminal proceeding is pending.

It is worthy of note that The Interstate Commission on Crime, at its annual meeting in Boston, in August, 1936, approved this Uniform Act in the form in which it is here printed, and is cooperating with the Conference in attempting to secure its adoption in all of the states.

1931 Act

The National Conference of Commissioners on Uniform State Laws at its Conference in Atlantic City in September, 1931, after careful consideration, adopted the Uniform Act to Secure the Attendance of Witnesses from Without the State in Criminal Cases. The act was thereafter approved by the American Bar Association.

For the past four years various drafts of an act on this subject were before the conference for consideration. During this time, and before the act was finally adopted, the American Law Institute in the preparation of its Code of Criminal Procedure prepared a tentative draft of a chapter on this subject. Through conferences of committees representing the American Law Institute and the National Conference of Commissioners on Uniform State Laws an act was agreed upon which was thereafter adopted by both organizations. Hence this act will be found as a chapter in the Code of Criminal Procedure referred to above.

There are now [1931] ten states that have statutes providing for the securing of the attendance of witnesses from other states in criminal prosecutions. They are Connecticut, Iowa, Maine, Massachusetts, New Hampshire, New York, Rhode Island, South Dakota, Vermont and Wisconsin.

The statutes in question apply, in Connecticut to any "criminal prosecution"; in Iowa, South Dakota and Wisconsin to a "criminal action"; in Maine and Massachusetts to a "criminal case," and in New Hampshire, Rhode Island and Vermont to a "criminal cause."

The statutes in Connecticut, New Hampshire and Vermont provide unconditionally for the summoning of any person in the state who is wanted as a material witness in any other state. In Iowa, South Dakota and Wisconsin the statutes provide that this may be done if the state asking for the witness has a similar statute. In Maine and Rhode Island the statutes provide for the summoning of witnesses wanted in any of the New England States. The statute of Massachusetts provides for the summoning of witnesses wanted in adjoining states and in Maine.

The statutes provide that the summons or subpoena shall be issued in New York and Wisconsin by a judge of a court of record, in Iowa by the district court, in South Dakota by the circuit court, in Connecticut by a justice of the peace or judge having authority to commit persons to prison, in Vermont by a justice or municipal or city judge, in Maine and Massachusetts by a justice of the peace and in New Hampshire by any justice.

The [1931] Uniform Act designates the case to which the act is applicable as a "criminal prosecution." It allows the summoning of a witness who will not be compelled to travel more than one thousand miles to reach the place of trial. It provides that the summons or subpoena shall be issued by a judge of a court of record, and that the pending prosecution shall be in a court of record. It exempts the witness from prosecution for crime or from a civil suit in connection with any matter which arose before the entrance of the witness into the state in response to the summons.

1936 ACT

Be it enacted . . . .

§ 1. Definitions

"Witness" as used in this act shall include a person whose testimony is desired in any proceeding or investigation by a Grand Jury or in a Criminal Action, Prosecution or Proceeding.

The word "State" shall include any Territory of the United States and the District of Columbia.

The word "summons" shall include a subpoena, order or other notice requiring the appearance of a witness.

§ 2. Summoning Witness in this State to Testify in Another State

If a judge of a court of record in any state which by its laws has made provision for commanding persons within that state to attend and testify in this state certifies under the seal of such court that there is a criminal prosecution pending in such court, or that a grand jury investigation has commenced or is about to commence, that a person being within this state is a material witness in such prosecution, or grand jury investigation, and that his presence will be required for a specified number of days, upon presentation of such certificate to any judge of a court of record in the county in which such person is, such judge shall fix a time and place for a hearing, and shall make an order directing the witness to appear at a time and place certain for the hearing.

If at a hearing the judge determines that the witness is material and necessary, that it will not cause undue hardship to the witness to be com-

pelled to attend and testify in the prosecution or a grand jury investigation in the other state, and that the laws of the state in which the prosecution is pending, or grand jury investigation has commenced or is about to commence, [and of any other state through which the witness may be required to pass by ordinary course of travel], will give to him protection from arrest and the service of civil and criminal process, he shall issue a summons, with a copy of the certificate attached, directing the witness to attend and testify in the court where the prosecution is pending, or where a grand jury investigation has commenced or is about to commence at a time and place specified in the summons. In any such hearing the certificate shall be prima facie evidence of all the facts stated therein.

If said certificate recommends that the witness be taken into immediate custody and delivered to an officer of the requesting state to assure his attendance in the requesting state, such judge may, in lieu of notification of the hearing, direct that such witness be forthwith brought before him for said hearing; and the judge at the hearing being satisfied of the desirability of such custody and delivery, for which determination the certificate shall be prima facie proof of such desirability may, in lieu of issuing subpoena or summons, order that said witness be forthwith taken into custody and delivered to an officer of the requesting state.

If the witness, who is summoned as above provided, after being paid or tendered by some properly authorized person the sum of 10 cents a mile for each mile by the ordinary traveled route to and from the court where the prosecution is pending and five dollars for each day, that he is required to travel and attend as a witness, fails without good cause to attend and testify as directed in the summons, he shall be punished in the manner provided for the punishment of any witness who disobeys a summons issued from a court of record in this state.

§ 3. Witness from Another State Summoned to Testify in This State

If a person in any state, which by its laws has made provision for commanding persons within its borders to attend and testify in criminal prosecutions, or grand jury investigations commenced or about to commence, in this state, is a material witness in a prosecution pending in a court of record in this state, or in a grand jury investigation which has commenced or is about to commence, a judge of such court may issue a certificate under the seal of the court stating these facts and specifying the number of days the witness will be required. Said certificate may include a recommendation that the witness be taken into immediate custody and delivered to an officer of this state to assure his attendance in this state. This certificate shall be presented to a judge of a court of record in the county in which the witness is found.

If the witness is summoned to attend and testify in this state he shall be tendered the sum of 10 cents a mile for each mile by the ordinary traveled route to and from the court where the prosecution is pending and five dollars for each day that he is required to travel and attend as a witness. A witness who has appeared in accordance with the provisions of the summons shall not be required to remain within this state a longer period of time than the period mentioned in the certificate, unless otherwise ordered by the court. If such witness, after coming into this state, fails without good cause to attend and testify as directed in the summons, he shall be punished in the manner provided for the punishment of any witness who disobeys a summons issued from a court of record in this state.

§ 4. Exemption from Arrest and Service of Process

If a person comes into this state in obedience to a summons directing him to attend and testify in this state he shall not while in this state pursuant to such summons be subject to arrest or the service of process, civil or criminal, in connection with matters which arose before his entrance into this state under the summons.

If a person passes through this state while going to another state in obedience to a summons to attend and testify in that state or while returning therefrom, he shall not while so passing through this state be subject to arrest or the service of process, civil or criminal, in connection with matters which arose before his entrance into this state under the summons.

§ 5. Uniformity of Interpretation

This act shall be so interpreted and construed as to effectuate its general purpose to make uniform the law of the states which enact it.

§ 6. Short Title

This act may be cited as "Uniform Act to Secure the Attendance of Witnesses from Without a State in Criminal Proceedings."

§ 7. Repeal

All acts or parts of acts inconsistent with this act are hereby repealed.

§ 8. Constitutionality

If any provision of this act or the application thereof to any person or circumstances is held invalid, such invalidity shall not affect other provisions or applications of the act which can be given effect without the invalid provision or application, and to this end the provisions of this act are declared to be severable.

§ 9. Time of Taking Effect

This act shall take effect _____.

UNIFORM CRIMINAL EXTRADITION ACT

Table of Jurisdictions Wherein Act Has Been Adopted

Jurisdiction	Laws	Effective Date	Statutory Citation
Alabama	1931, p. 559	7–22–1931 *	Code 1975, §§ 15–9–20 to 15–9–65.
Alaska	1962, c. 34	3–23–1962 *	AS 12.70.010 to 12.70.290.
Arizona	1937, c. 10	2–24–1937 *	A.R.S. §§ 13–3841 to 13–3868.
Arkansas	1935, No. 126	3–19–1935 *	Ark.Stats. §§ 43–3001 to 43–3030.
California	1937, p. 1582	8–27–1937	West's Cal.Penal Code, §§ 1547 to 1556.2.
Colorado	1953, c. 117	4–1–1953	C.R.S. 16–19–101 to 16–19–133.
Connecticut	1957, c. 362		C.G.S.A. §§ 54–157 to 54–185.
Delaware	1937, c. 213	4–7–1937 *	11 Del.C. §§ 2501 to 2530.
Florida	1941, c. 20460	5–26–1941 *	F.S.A. §§ 941.01 to 941.30.
Georgia	1951, p. 726	3–1–1951	O.C.G.A. §§ 17–13–20 to 17–13–49.
Hawaii	1941, c. 99	4–24–1941	HRS §§ 832–1 to 832–27.
Idaho	1927, c. 29	7–1–1927	I.C. §§ 19–4501 to 19–4527.
Illinois	1955, p. 1982	7–14–1955	S.H.A. ch. 60, 18 to 49.
Indiana	1935, c. 49	7–1–1935	West's A.I.C. 35–33–10–3.
Iowa	1949, c. 244	4–21–1949	I.C.A. §§ 820.1 to 820.29.
Kansas	1937, c. 273	3–29–1937	K.S.A. 22–2701 to 22–2730.
Kentucky	1960, c. 135	6–16–1960	KRS 440.150 to 440.420.
Louisiana	1966, No. 310	1–1–1967	LSA–C.Cr.P. arts. 261 to 280.
Maine	1929, c. 124	3–23–1929	15 M.R.S.A. §§ 201 to 229.
Maryland	1937, c. 179	5–18–1937	Code 1957, art. 41, §§ 16 to 43.
Massachusetts	1937, c. 304	10–1–1937	M.G.L.A. c. 276, §§ 11 to 20R.
Michigan	1937, No. 144	10–29–1937	M.C.L.A. §§ 780.1 to 780.31.
Minnesota	1939, c. 240	4–14–1939 *	M.S.A. §§ 629.01 to 629.29.
Missouri	1953, p. 425	90 days after 5–31–1953	V.A.M.S. §§ 548.011 to 548.300.
Montana	1937, c. 190	3–18–1937	MCA 46–30–101 to 46–30–413.
Nebraska	1963, c. 159	4–2–1963 *	R.R.S.1943, §§ 29–729 to 29–758.
Nevada	1967, c. 1098		N.R.S. 179.177 to 179.235.
New Hampshire	1937, c. 70	4–21–1937	RSA 612:1 to 612:30.
New Jersey	1936, c. 42	3–30–1936 *	N.J.S.A. 2A:160–6 to 2A:160–35.
New Mexico	1937, c. 65	3–5–1937	N.M.S.A.1978, §§ 31–4–1 to 31–4–30.
New York	1936, c. 892	9–1–1936	McKinney's CPL §§ 570.02 to 570.66.
North Carolina	1937, c. 273	3–20–1937	G.S. §§ 15A–721 to 15A–750
Ohio	1937, p. 588	8–20–1937	R.C. §§ 2963.01 to 2963.29.
Oklahoma	1949, p. 207	3–25–1949	22 Okl.St.Ann. §§ 1141.1 to 1141.30.
Oregon	1935, c. 77	2–23–1935 *	ORS 133.743 to 133.857.
Pennsylvania	1941, P.L. 288	7–8–1941 *	42 Pa.C.S.A. §§ 9121 to 9148.
Puerto Rico	1960, No. 4	6–23–1960	34 L.P.R.A. §§ 1881 to 1881bb.
Rhode Island	1947, c. 1890	6–1–1947	Gen.Laws 1956, §§ 12–9–1 to 12–9–35.
South Dakota	1953, c. 200	2–18–1953 *	SDCL 23–24–1 to 23–24–39.
Tennessee	1951, c. 240	3–16–1951 *	T.C.A. §§ 40–9–101 to 40–9–130.
Texas	1951, c. 438	6–15–1951	Vernon's Ann.C.C.P. art. 51.13.
Utah	1937, c. 146	3–22–1937	U.C.A.1953, 77–30–1 to 77–30–28.
Vermont	1933, No. 36	2–17–1933 *	13 V.S.A. §§ 4941 to 4969.
Virgin Islands	1957, No. 160	9–1–1957	5 V.I.C. §§ 3801 to 3829.
Virginia	1940, c. 305	3–28–1940 *	Code 1950, §§ 19.2–85 to 19.2–118.
Washington	1971, Ex.Sess. c. 46	7–1–1971	West's RCWA 10.88.200 to 10.88.930.
West Virginia	1937, c. 42	90 days after 3–12–1937	Code, 5–1–7 to 5–1–13.
Wisconsin	1933, c. 40	3–22–1933 *	W.S.A. 976.03.
Wyoming	1935, c. 122	2–20–1935	W.S.1977, §§ 7–3–201 to 7–3–22.

* Date of approval.

UNIFORM ACTS

The Uniform Criminal Extradition Act was superseded by the new Uniform Extradition and Rendition Act approved by the National Conference of Commissioners on Uniform State Laws in 1980. The text of this new Act is set out infra.

Historical Note

The revised Uniform Criminal Extradition Act was approved by the National Conference of Commissioners on Uniform State Laws, and the American Bar Association, in 1936. It derived from a prior Uniform Criminal Extradition Act, approved in 1926, and amended in 1932.

Commissioners' Prefatory Note

The Federal Constitution, adopting substantially the language of the earlier articles of Confederation between the thirteen colonies provides, in section 2 of Article IV, U.S.C.A. Const., art. IV, § 2, cl. 2, that "A person charged in any state with treason, felony, or other crime, who shall flee from justice, and be found in another state, shall on demand of the executive authority of the state from which he fled, be delivered up to be removed to the state having jurisdiction of the crime."

But notwithstanding the clarity of the above provision, the federal Congress, acting upon an opinion of Attorney–General Randolph, decided in 1793 that the section of the constitution was not self-executing, chiefly because it provided no machinery for its execution, and passed in 1793 an act which has been brought forward as sections 5278 and 5279 of the U.S. Revised Statutes of 1875, 18 U.S.C.A. §§ 662, 663 [18 U.S.C.A. §§ 3182, 3194, and 3195], as follows:

"5278. Whenever the executive authority of any State or Territory demands any person as a fugitive from justice, of the executive authority of any state or territory to which such person has fled, and produces a copy of an indictment found or an affidavit made before a magistrate of any state or territory, charging the person demanded with having committed treason, felony, or other crime, certified as authentic by the Governor or Chief Magistrate of the state or territory from whence the person so charged has fled; it shall be the duty of the executive authority of the state or territory to which such person has fled to cause him to be arrested and secured, and to cause notice of the arrest to be given to the executive authority making such demand, or to the agent of such authority appointed to receive the fugitive, and to cause the fugitive to be delivered to such agent when he shall appear. If no such agent appears within six months from the time of the arrest, the prisoner may be discharged. All costs and expenses incurred in the apprehending, securing and transmitting such fugitive to the state or territory making such demand, shall be paid by such state or territory.

"5279. Any agent so appointed who receives the fugitive into his custody, shall be empowered to trans-port him to the State or Territory from which he has fled. And every person who by force, sets at liberty or rescues the fugitive from such agent while so transporting him, shall be fined not more than five hundred dollars or imprisoned not more than one year."

The above section of the Constitution and the above federal law form the basis of the interstate extradition of fugitive criminals in all the states. The Constitution creates the right to demand the fugitive, and the federal law creates the machinery, and they thus distinguish interstate extradition from international extradition which rests entirely upon treaties and is defined by treaty limitations.

But the Act of Congress did not create machinery to cover all the exigencies which arise; and as the federal law of 1793 has never been enlarged by Congress, except to a limited extent in the District of Columbia, to authorize the bringing back of fugitive offenders against the laws of the United States applicable there, it has come to be recognized that the several states may provide machinery for applying the law of extradition in respect to matters not covered by the Act of Congress. Thus the states can legislate upon the method of applying for the writ of habeas corpus, upon the method of arrest and detention of the fugitive before extradition is demanded, upon the mode of preliminary trial, upon the manner of applying for a requisition, upon the extent of asylum allowed a prisoner when brought back to the state from which he has fled, and upon his exemption from civil process; not to mention other points less important which have always been regulated by local law.

These and many other subjects collateral to the main right to extradition have been the subjects of quite diversified legislation and judicial decision in the various states, and the bodies of law thus built up are quite different throughout America. It therefore appeared wise to the Conference of Commissioners on Uniform State Laws to prepare an act embracing what appear to be the best features of all the various laws of the several states as well as the judicial law applicable, and to offer it as a practicable law for all the states to adopt, thus codifying the practice and promoting uniformity at the same time. Footnotes below the text of most of the sections give the origin of the language where statutory, and the judicial decisions upon which it is based when the sections involve restatement or codification of judicial law.

Section 6 and part of Section 5 of the Act, however, originated with the National Conference of Commissioners on Uniform State Laws and are designed to cover cases not clearly reached by existing extradition laws. Hitherto, it has been possible to extradite only those criminals who could be said to be "fugitives", that is, who had been physically present in the state in which the crime was committed and had fled therefrom. One who commits a crime against the laws of a state by acts done outside of that state has been held not to be a "fugitive." Courts have been in conflict as to whether one whose criminal acts were done within the state can be said to be a "fugitive" when his departure from the state was under the legal compulsion of an extradition proceeding.

Sections 5 and 6 have been drafted to meet the practical need of authority for the extradition of both of these classes of criminals who, perhaps, cannot technically be called "fugitives." Section 6, as approved by the Conference in 1926, provided for the extradition of a criminal from the state in which he acted to the state in which his acts had criminal effect. By an amendment, approved by the Conference in 1932, this section now permits the extradition of that person not only from the state in which he acted, but from any state into which he thereafter moves. It is true that the Constitution does not put upon the states the obligation to extradite criminals who are not fugitives. But, though the Constitution requires that fugitives shall be extradited, it does not prohibit states from endeavoring to enforce the criminal law by the extradition of those persons who

have violated the law of the demanding state but who cannot be called "fugitives" from that state. The effectiveness of Section 6, therefore, depends upon comity between the states, rather than upon the mandatory effect of the Constitution.

Section 5 contains two paragraphs, added by the Conference in 1936. The second of these paragraphs authorizes the extradition of a criminal who, under the decisions of some states, has been held not to be a "fugitive" because his departure from the state in which the crime was committed was under compulsory process. The first paragraph is intended to cover the situation of a man who is wanted for trial in one state and who is already serving a prison sentence in another state.

The Uniform Criminal Extradition Act, as printed in the following pages, is in the form in which it was approved by the Conference at its meeting in Boston in August, 1936. In addition to the revision of Section 5, as already stated, the Conference, at that meeting, approved many minor changes.

Attention should be called to the fact that The Interstate Commission on Crime, at its meeting in Boston in August, 1936, approved this Uniform Act in the form in which it is here printed, and is cooperating with the Conference in recommending its adoption in the several states.

UNIFORM CRIMINAL EXTRADITION ACT

An Act relating to the extradition of persons charged with crime, and to make uniform the law with reference thereto.

Be it enacted ....

---

§ 1. Definitions

Where appearing in this act, the term "Governor" includes any person performing the functions of Governor by authority of the law of this state. The term "Executive Authority" includes the Governor, and any person performing the functions of Governor in a state other than this state, and the term "State," referring to a state other than this state, includes any other state or territory, organized or unorganized, of the United States of America.

§ 2. Fugitives from Justice; Duty of Governor

Subject to the provisions of this act, the provisions of the Constitution of the United States controlling, and any and all acts of Congress enacted in pursuance thereof, it is the duty of the Governor of this state to have arrested and delivered up to the Executive Authority of any other state of the United States any person charged in that state with treason, felony, or other crime, who has fled from justice and is found in this state.

§ 3. Form of Demand

No demand for the extradition of a person charged with crime in another state shall be recognized by the Governor unless in writing alleging, except in cases arising under Section 6, that the accused was present in the demanding state at the time of the commission of the alleged crime, and that thereafter he fled from the state, and accompanied by a copy of an indictment found or by information supported by affidavit in the state having jurisdiction of the crime, or by a copy of an affidavit made before a magistrate there, together with a copy of any warrant which was issued thereupon; or by a copy of a judgment of conviction or of a sentence imposed in execution thereof, together with a statement by the Executive Authority of the demanding state that the person claimed has escaped from confinement or has broken the terms of his bail, probation or parole. The indictment, information, or affidavit made before the magistrate must substantially charge the person demanded with having committed a crime under the law of that state; and the copy of indictment, information, affidavit, judgment of conviction or sentence must be authenticated by the Executive Authority making the demand.

§ 4. Governor May Investigate Case

When a demand shall be made upon the Governor of this state by the Executive Authority of another state for the surrender of a person so charged with crime, the Governor may call upon the Attorney–General or any prosecuting officer in this state to investigate or assist in investigating the demand, and to report to him the situation and circumstances of the person so demanded, and whether he ought to be surrendered.

§ 5. Extradition of Persons Imprisoned or Awaiting Trial in Another State or Who Have Left the Demanding State Under Compulsion

When it is desired to have returned to this state a person charged in this state with a crime, and such person is imprisoned or is held under criminal proceedings then pending against him in another state, the Governor of this state may agree with the Executive Authority of such other state for the extradition of such person before the conclusion of such proceedings or his term of sentence in such other state, upon condition that such person be returned to such other state at the expense of this state as soon as the prosecution in this state is terminated.

The Governor of this state may also surrender on demand of the Executive Authority of any other state any person in this state who is charged in the manner provided in Section 23 of this act with having violated the laws of the state whose Executive Authority is making the demand, even though such person left the demanding state involuntarily.

§ 6. Extradition of Persons not Present in Demanding State at Time of Commission of Crime

The Governor of this state may also surrender, on demand of the Executive Authority of any other state, any person in this state charged in such other state in the manner provided in Section 3 with committing an act in this state, or in

a third state, intentionally resulting in a crime in the state whose Executive Authority is making the demand, and the provisions of this act not otherwise inconsistent, shall apply to such cases, even though the accused was not in that state at the time of the commission of the crime, and has not fled therefrom.

§ 7. Issue of Governor's Warrant of Arrest; Its Recitals

If the Governor decides that the demand should be complied with, he shall sign a warrant of arrest, which shall be sealed with the state seal, and be directed to any peace officer or other person whom he may think fit to entrust with the execution thereof. The warrant must substantially recite the facts necessary to the validity of its issuance.

§ 8. Manner and Place of Execution

Such warrant shall authorize the peace officer or other person to whom directed to arrest the accused at any time and any place where he may be found within the state and to command the aid of all peace officers or other persons in the execution of the warrant, and to deliver the accused, subject to the provisions of this act to the duly authorized agent of the demanding state.

§ 9. Authority of Arresting Officer

Every such peace officer or other person empowered to make the arrest, shall have the same authority, in arresting the accused, to command assistance therein, as peace officers have by law in the execution of any criminal process directed to them, with like penalties against those who refuse their assistance.

§ 10. Rights of Accused Person; Application for Writ of Habeas Corpus

No person arrested upon such warrant shall be delivered over to the agent whom the Executive Authority demanding him shall have appointed to receive him unless he shall first be taken forthwith before a judge of a court of record in this state, who shall inform him of the demand made for his surrender and of the crime with which he is charged, and that he has the right to demand and procure legal counsel; and if the prisoner or his counsel shall state that he or they desire to test the legality of his arrest, the judge of such court of record shall fix a reasonable time to be allowed him within which to apply for a writ of habeas corpus. When such writ is applied for, notice thereof, and of the time and place of hearing thereon, shall be given to the prosecuting officer of the county in which the arrest is made and in which the accused is in custody, and to the said agent of the demanding state.

§ 11. Penalty for Non–Compliance with Preceding Section

Any officer who shall deliver to the agent for extradition of the demanding state a person in his custody under the Governor's warrant, in wilful disobedience to the last section, shall be guilty of a misdemeanor and, on conviction, shall be fined [not more than $1,000.00 or be imprisoned not more than six months, or both].

§ 12. Confinement in Jail When Necessary

The officer or persons executing the governor's warrant of arrest, or the agent of the demanding state to whom the prisoner may have been delivered may, when necessary, confine the prisoner in the jail of any county or city through which he may pass; and the keeper of such jail must receive and safely keep the prisoner until the officer or person having charge of him is ready to proceed on his route, such officer or person being chargeable with the expense of keeping.

The officer or agent of a demanding state to whom a prisoner may have been delivered following extradition proceedings in another state, or to whom a prisoner may have been delivered after waiving extradition in such other state, and who is passing through this state with such a prisoner for the purpose of immediately returning such prisoner to the demanding state may, when necessary, confine the prisoner in the jail of any county or city through which he may pass; and the keeper of such jail must receive and safely keep the prisoner until the officer or agent having charge of him is ready to proceed on his route, such officer or agent, however, being chargeable with the expense of keeping; provided, however, that such officer or agent shall produce and show to the keeper of such jail satisfactory written evidence of the fact that he is actually transporting such prisoner to the demanding state after a requisition by the Executive Authority of such demanding state. Such prisoner shall not be entitled to demand a new requisition while in this state.

§ 13. Arrest Prior to Requisition

Whenever any person within this state shall be charged on the oath of any credible person before any judge or magistrate of this state with the commission of any crime in any other state and, except in cases arising under Section 6, with having fled from justice, or with having been convicted of a crime in that state and having escaped from confinement, or having broken the terms of his bail, probation or parole, or whenever complaint shall have been made before any judge or magistrate in this state setting forth on the affidavit of any credible person in another state that a crime has been committed in such other state and that the accused has been charged in such state with the commission of the crime, and, except in cases arising under Section 6, has fled from justice, or with having been convicted of a crime in that state and having escaped from confinement, or having broken the terms of his bail, probation or parole and is believed to be in this state, the judge or magistrate shall issue a warrant directed to any peace officer commanding him to apprehend the person named therein, wherever he may be found in this state, and to bring him before the same or any other judge, magistrate or court who or which may be available in or convenient of access to the place where the arrest may be made, to answer the charge or complaint and affidavit, and a certified copy of the sworn charge or complaint and affidavit upon which the warrant is issued shall be attached to the warrant.

§ 14. Arrest Without a Warrant

The arrest of a person may be lawfully made also by any peace officer or a private person, without a warrant upon reasonable information that the accused stands charged in the courts of a state with a crime punishable by death or imprisonment for a term exceeding one year, but when so arrested the accused must be taken before a judge or magistrate with all practicable speed and complaint must be made against him under oath setting forth the ground for the arrest as in the preceding section; and thereafter his answer shall be heard as if he had been arrested on a warrant.

§ 15. Commitment to Await Requisition; Bail

If from the examination before the judge or magistrate it appears that the person held is the person charged with having committed the crime alleged and, except in cases arising under Section 6, that he has fled from justice, the judge or magistrate must, by a warrant reciting the accusation, commit him to the county jail for such a time not exceeding thirty days and specified in the warrant, as will enable the arrest of the accused to be made under a warrant of the Governor on a requisition of the Executive Authority of the state having jurisdiction of the offense, unless the accused give bail as provided in the next section, or until he shall be legally discharged.

§ 16. Bail; in What Cases; Conditions of Bond

Unless the offense with which the prisoner is charged is shown to be an offense punishable by death or life imprisonment under the laws of the state in which it was committed, a judge or magistrate in this state may admit the person arrested to bail by bond, with sufficient sureties, and in such sum as he deems proper, conditioned for his appearance before him at a time specified in such bond, and for his surrender, to be arrested upon the warrant of the Governor of this state.

§ 17. Extension of Time of Commitment; Adjournment

If the accused is not arrested under warrant of the Governor by the expiration of the time specified in the warrant or bond, a judge or magistrate may discharge him or may recommit him for a further period not to exceed sixty days, or a judge or magistrate judge may again take bail for his appearance and surrender, as provided in Section 16, but within a period not to exceed sixty days after the date of such new bond.

§ 18. Forfeiture of Bail

If the prisoner is admitted to bail, and fails to appear and surrender himself according to the conditions of his bond, the judge, or magistrate by proper order, shall declare the bond forfeited and order his immediate arrest without warrant if he be within this state. Recovery may be had on such bond in the name of the state as in the case of other bonds given by the accused in criminal proceedings within this state.

§ 19. Persons under Criminal Prosecution in This State at Time of Requisition

If a criminal prosecution has been instituted against such person under the laws of this state

and is still pending the Governor, in his discretion, either may surrender him on demand of the Executive Authority of another state or hold him until he has been tried and discharged or convicted and punished in this state.

§ 20. Guilt or Innocence of Accused, When Inquired Into

The guilt or innocence of the accused as to the crime of which he is charged may not be inquired into by the Governor or in any proceeding after the demand for extradition accompanied by a charge of crime in legal form as above provided shall have been presented to the Governor, except as it may be involved in identifying the person held as the person charged with the crime.

§ 21. Governor May Recall Warrant or Issue Alias

The Governor may recall his warrant of arrest or may issue another warrant whenever he deems proper.

§ 22. Fugitives from This State; Duty of Governors

Whenever the Governor of this State shall demand a person charged with crime or with escaping from confinement or breaking the terms of his bail, probation or parole in this state, from the Executive Authority of any other state, or from the chief justice or an associate justice of the Supreme Court of the District of Columbia authorized to receive such demand under the laws of the United States, he shall issue a warrant under the seal of this state, to some agent, commanding him to receive the person so charged if delivered to him and convey him to the proper officer of the county in this state in which the offense was committed.

§ 23. Application for Issuance of Requisition; by Whom Made; Contents

I. When the return to this state of a person charged with crime in this state is required, the prosecuting attorney shall present to the Governor his written application for a requisition for the return of the person charged in which application shall be stated the name of the person so charged, the crime charged against him, the approximate time, place and circumstances of its commission, the state in which he is believed to be, including the location of the accused therein at the time the application is made and certifying that, in the opinion of the said prosecuting attorney the ends of justice require the arrest and return of the accused to this state for trial and that the proceeding is not instituted to enforce a private claim.

II. When the return to this state is required of a person who has been convicted of a crime in this state and has escaped from confinement or broken the terms of his bail, probation or parole, the prosecuting attorney of the county in which the offense was committed, the parole board, or the warden of the institution or sheriff of the county, from which escape was made, shall present to the Governor a written application for a requisition for the return of such person, in which application shall be stated the name of the person, the crime of which he was convicted, the circumstances of his escape from confinement or of the breach of the terms of his bail, probation or parole, the state in which he is believed to be, including the location of the person therein at the time application is made.

III. The application shall be verified by affidavit, shall be executed in duplicate and shall be accompanied by two certified copies of the indictment returned, or information and affidavit filed, or of the complaint made to the judge or magistrate, stating the offense with which the accused is charged, or of the judgment of conviction or of the sentence. The prosecuting officer, parole board, warden or sheriff may also attach such further affidavits and other documents in duplicate as he shall deem proper to be submitted with such application. One copy of the application, with the action of the Governor indicated by endorsement thereon, and one of the certified copies of the indictment, complaint, information, and affidavits, or of the judgment of conviction or of the sentence shall be filed in the office of [the secretary of state] to remain of record in that office. The other copies of all papers shall be forwarded with the Governor's requisition.

§ 24. Costs and Expenses

[When the punishment of the crime shall be the confinement of the criminal in the penitentiary, the expenses shall be paid out of the state treasury, on the certificate of the Governor and warrant of the Auditor; and in all other cases they shall be paid out of the county treasury in the county wherein the crime is alleged to have been committed. The expenses shall be the fees paid to the officers of the state on whose Gover-

nor the requisition is made, and not exceeding ... cents a mile for all necessary travel in returning such prisoner.]

§ 25. Immunity from Service of Process in Certain Civil Actions

A person brought into this state by, or after waiver of, extradition based on a criminal charge shall not be subject to service of personal process in civil actions arising out of the same facts as the criminal proceeding to answer which he is being or has been returned, until he has been convicted in the criminal proceeding, or, if acquitted, until he has had reasonable opportunity to return to the state from which he was extradited.

§ 25–A. Written Waiver of Extradition Proceedings

Any person arrested in this state charged with having committed any crime in another state or alleged to have escaped from confinement, or broken the terms of his bail, probation or parole may waive the issuance and service of the warrant provided for in sections 7 and 8 and all other procedure incidental to extradition proceedings, by executing or subscribing in the presence of a judge of any court of record within this state a writing which states that he consents to return to the demanding state; provided, however, that before such waiver shall be executed or subscribed by such person it shall be the duty of such judge to inform such person of his rights to the issuance and service of a warrant of extradition and to obtain a writ of habeas corpus as provided for in Section 10.

If and when such consent has been duly executed it shall forthwith be forwarded to the office of the Governor of this state and filed therein. The judge shall direct the officer having such person in custody to deliver forthwith such person to the duly accredited agent or agents of the demanding state, and shall deliver or cause to be delivered to such agent or agents a copy of such consent; provided, however, that nothing in this Section shall be deemed to limit the rights of the accused person to return voluntarily and without formality to the demanding state, nor shall this waiver procedure be deemed to be an exclusive procedure or to limit the powers, rights or duties of the officers of the demanding state or of this state.

§ 25–B. Non-Waiver by This State

Nothing in this act contained shall be deemed to constitute a waiver by this state of its right, power or privilege to try such demanded person for crime committed within this state, or of its right, power or privilege to regain custody of such person by extradition proceedings or otherwise for the purpose of trial, sentence or punishment for any crime committed within this state, nor shall any proceedings had under this act which result in, or fail to result in, extradition be deemed a waiver by this state of any of its rights, privileges or jurisdiction in any way whatsoever.

§ 26. No Right of Asylum. No Immunity from Other Criminal Prosecutions while in This State

After a person has been brought back to this state by, or after waiver of extradition proceedings, he may be tried in this state for other crimes which he may be charged with having committed here as well as that specified in the requisition for his extradition.

§ 27. Interpretation

The provisions of this act shall be so interpreted and construed as to effectuate its general purposes to make uniform the law of those states which enact it.

§ 28. Constitutionality

If any provision of this act or the application thereof to any person or circumstances is held invalid, such invalidity shall not affect other provisions or applications of the act which can be given effect without the invalid provision or application, and to this end the provisions of this act are declared to be severable.

§ 29. Repeal

All acts and parts of acts inconsistent with the provisions of this act and not expressly repealed herein are hereby repealed.

§ 30. Short Title

This act may be cited as the Uniform Criminal Extradition Act.

§ 31. Time of Taking Effect

This act shall take effect on the _____ day of _____, 19__.

UNIFORM EXTRADITION AND RENDITION ACT

Table of Jurisdictions Wherein Act Has Been Adopted

Jurisdiction	Laws	Effective Date	Statutory Citation
North Dakota..........1985, c. 364		6–30–1985	NDCC 29–30.3–01 to 29–30.3–25.

Historical Note

The Uniform Extradition and Rendition Act was approved by the National Conference of Commissioners on Uniform State Laws in 1980. This new Act supersedes the Uniform Criminal Extradition Act.

PREFATORY NOTE

This is the first opportunity for the Conference to examine the Uniform Criminal Extradition Act promulgated in 1926. The strong rationale in favor of uniformity in state law governing interstate retrieval of fugitives led 27 states to adopt the Act by 1939 and 12 more to do so by 1951. Presently, fifty-one states and territories of the United States have adopted the Act or a variation of it. (See 11 U.L.A.Crim.Law and Proc. (Master ed., cum. annual pocket part 1980)).

Concerns about the Act began to surface within the past two decades and these concerns centered upon the proposition that the Act had become too cumbersome in its operation. These concerns have been publicly expressed by officials who are centrally involved in the operation of the Act, such as the governors and the attorneys general of the states. (See, Policy Positions of the National Governors' Conference, Policy A–12 at p. 10 (June 1973); and Report on the Office of the Attorney General, p. 332, National Association of Attorneys General, Raleigh, North Carolina, (February 1971).) Critics observed that, under the Act, action must occur by at least 9 agencies from the asylum and demanding states before the wanted person is available for the first step in the criminal justice process in the demanding state.[1] Many of these agencies have no interest or only a minimal interest in the prosecution underlying the retrieval. The critics conclude that the Act is unnecessarily cumbersome because its requirements exceed the needs of interstate harmony and of protection to individuals from mistaken or improvident retrievals.

The Act has become cumbersome because of social changes that have occurred subsequent to the extensive adoption of the Act by the states, including demographic changes, technological changes in police information systems, and the increased opportunities for mobility. Pressure for change in the Act continue to mount because of the following factors:

1. Integration of fugitive retrieval with ordinary police patrol resulting from technological changes in police information systems.

2. Increase in the percentage of the nation's population that live in socially and economically integrated areas that are intersected by state lines.

3. Disharmony among the states in interpreting the Act, e.g., whether the demanding documents should manifest probable cause, thereby, seriously weakening the uniformity of extradition procedures. (See Comment to Sections 3–101 and 3–102 for a discussion of this conflict in state interpretation of the Act.)

4. Social advantages of decreasing the dependency by states upon professional bondsmen by modernizing extradition procedures, thereby enhancing the capability of official state agencies to effectuate fugitive retrievals.

Recent technological changes in police information systems have two characteristics: (1) the advent, since 1967, of a network of connected state, regional, and national computerized data bases on persons subject to arrest warrants, and (2) the ability to equip police on automobile or foot patrol with mobile terminals that provide direct electronic access to computerized data based on wanted persons.

A study by the federal government in 1972 located 101 discrete automated information systems that served police agencies with computerized data bases on wanted persons. (Directory of Automated Criminal Justice Information Systems, (U.S. Dept. of Justice, LEAA, 1972).) There has been a decided shift from the early emphasis

[1] These nine agencies include: (1) police in asylum state, Uniform Criminal Extradition Act §§ 14 and 15 (hereinafter referred to as "Act"); (2) magistrate or judge in asylum state, §§ 13 and 15 Act; (3) prosecutor in demanding state, § 23 Act; (4) attorney general in demanding state (The attorney general by practice advises the governor on the adequacy of the prosecutor's request to extradite a person from another state. See Kansas Governor's Extradition Manual (1972), p. 5); (5) governor in demanding state, § 3 Act; (6) secretary of state in demanding state (attestation of demanding state's documents; see Kansas Governor's Extradition Manual (1972), p. 5; (7) attorney general of asylum state, § 4 Act; (8) governor of asylum state, § 7 Act; (9) judge of asylum state, § 10 Act.

on computer applications for crime statistics reporting and crime record keeping to rapid retrieval of information for patrol officers, particularly information on wanted persons. (K. Colton, The Use of Computers By Police: Patterns of Successes and Failures, International Symposium on Criminal Justice Information and Statistics Systems, p. 139 (Project Search, October 1972).) This development reflects an earlier soothsaying study the American Telephone and Telegraph Co. in 1966 that predicted widespread police use of computers relating to wanted persons in the 1970–75 period. (Law Enforcement Communications, 1970–75, A Long Range Study (A.T. & T. Co., July 1966, IACP Library).)

Associated with the computerization of wanted persons files has been the development of vehicle-installed terminals that provide patrol officers with direct electronic access to the computerized files on wanted persons. Currently, there are approximately 1000 operational mobile digital terminals that have been installed in police patrol vehicles. (State Criminal Justice Telecommunications Analysis, p. 5–30 (Jet Propulsion Laboratory, Calif. Inst. of Tech., June 1977).) Earlier studies projected police adoption of mobile digital terminals for half of the 75,000 police patrol units by 1983. (Nat'l Crim. Just. Communications Requirements, n. 47 at 6–29 (Jet Propulsion Laboratory, Calif. Inst. of Tech., June 28, 1974).) These studies have been somewhat tempered by the cost of the in-car terminals, but planners continue to agree that large municipal police departments will find that mobile digital terminals are cost effective and will equip their police cars with them. (State Criminal Justice Telecommunications Analysis, p. 5–30 (Jet Propulsion Laboratory, Calif. Ins. of Tech., June 1977).)

Computerized files on wanted persons, interconnected regionally and nationally and directly accessible to patrol police, will greatly enlarge the geographical range of police information on wanted persons. Studies have already established the increasing police dependency upon these technological changes in information systems about wanted persons. (See J. Murphy, Arrest by Police Computer, 1–10 (Lexington Books 1976).) Pressure on the cumbersome extradition procedure will continue to mount as police increase their activities in retrieval of wanted persons across state lines.

Technological changes in police information systems are by no means the only source of pressure upon the extradition process. Substantial demographic changes have occurred since the Act was promulgated in 1926 and adopted by most of the states nearly three decades ago. Approximately 25% of the nation's population

now live in socially and economically integrated areas that spread across state lines. (J. Murphy, Arrest by Police Computer, Appendix, Population Centers Crossing State Borders, pp. 89–90 (Lexington Books 1976).) In these metropolitan areas, a substantial number of retrievals are for a short distance, albeit across state borders.[2] Each state border, however, marks the territorial limitation on the execution of the state's policy on criminal justice expressed in its criminal and penal statutes. Without a less cumbersome process for retrieving persons indispensable to a state's policy on justice, and consistent with civil liberties, the state's policy in criminal justice is frustrated.

One positive reason for examining the Criminal Extradition Act is the possibility of decreasing the dependency by states upon professional bondsmen. Since 1963, significant gains have been made in bail reform by the states and congress in increasing non-monetary forms of bail. Although many of the changes in bail were designed specifically to eliminate bondsmen, who are known in bail lore as fugitive hunters, there has been little analysis of the retrieval of fugitives who failed to appear after bail release. Matched against the official system of fugitive retrieval under the Uniform Criminal Extradition Act is the system of bondsmen with more legal power to retrieve fugitives than either federal or state police. Unless the official retrieval system is examined and improved, there is a risk that current bail reform efforts will be retarded, and the danger of reversion to a system dependent upon bondsmen will increase. Revision of the extradition process for more efficiency without loss of civil liberties will encourage the final replacement of bondsmen with police in fugitive retrieval—a socially desirable goal. (See, W. Thomas, Bail Reform in America, pp. 254–256 (Univ. of California Press 1976); J. Murphy, Arrest by Police Computer, pp. 35–46 (Lexington Books 1976).)

The Uniform Extradition and Rendition Act is structured to present a choice to the states in the procedure to be used for the retrieval of wanted persons found in another state. A state has a choice of extradition in Article III, which follows the procedures formerly set forth in the Uniform Criminal Extradition Act. Alternatively, the state may choose the less cumbersome procedure of rendition in Article IV. Both the rendition and extradition procedures are supplemented by the provisions found in Articles II and V that set forth the rules governing transfer and proceedings prior to extradition and rendition.

2. In 1973 the Washington, D.C., police had 1,064 requests from states for extradition of fugitives; 846 were from Virginia and Maryland counties that comprise the Washington, D.C., metropolitan area. (Statistics supplied by Lieutenant Glenn Ramey, Fugitive Unit, Metropolitan Police Department, Washington,

D.C.) Sixty percent of extradition requests received by Johnson County, Kansas, are from police in Kansas City, Missouri, a distance of ten miles. (Telephone interview with J. Marques, Assistant District Attorney, Johnson County, Kansas, July 11, 1974.)

Both the extradition and rendition procedures set forth in this Act reflect three basic policy decisions of the Committee bearing upon the process of fugitive retrieval. First, the historic role of the governor in the process of fugitive retrieval has been retained. In the extradition process set forth in Article III, demands for the return of fugitives continue to be issued by the governor of the demanding state, and arrest warrants continue to be issued by the governor of the asylum state. The rendition process set forth in Article IV is more expeditious than extradition, but the rendition process is subject to the right on the part of the governor of the asylum state to terminate the use of rendition procedure at any time prior to the execution of an order to transfer custody.

Second, it was decided that all demands or requests for the retrieval of a fugitive, either under the extradition or rendition procedures, must include a certified copy of an arrest warrant issued after a determination of probable cause. This requirement will resolve two conflicts that have appeared in the cases interpreting the Uniform Criminal Extradition Act. By this requirement, the retrieval process must be initiated by a finding of probable cause. Furthermore, the probable cause determination will be made by the demanding or requesting state, not by the asylum state. The forums of the asylum state will be entitled to rely on the representations of a person authorized to issue arrest warrants in the demanding or requesting state that an arrest warrant has been issued for the fugitive after a determination of probable cause. This structure will reflect the Supreme Court's recent interpretation of the provision on extradition found in the Constitution, Article IV, Section 2. "Under Article III, Section 2, the courts of the asylum state are bound to accept the demanding state's judicial determination since the proceedings of the demanding state are clothed with the traditional presumption of regularity. In short, when a judicial officer of the demanding state has determined that probable cause exists, the courts of the asylum state are without power to review the determination." Michigan v. Doran, 99 S.Ct. 530 (1978). (See Comment to Sections 3–101 and 3–102 for an extensive discussion of the requirement of the finding of probable cause in the demanding or requesting state.)

The third major policy decision that is reflected in the Extradition and Rendition Act is the establishment of a new right to a judicial extradition hearing to contest the arrest under the governor's warrant during the extradition procedure set forth in Article III. Under the Uniform Criminal Extradition Act, the ordinary method of challenge is by application for the extraordinary writ of habeas corpus. The idea of a judicial hearing prior to transfer is also included in the more summary process of rendition in Article IV—the procedure proposed as an alternative to extradition.

There are two reasons to support the decision to establish a judicial extradition hearing, rather than a writ of habeas corpus, as the method to test an extradition arrest. First is the impropriety of using an extraordinary writ as the statutorily mandated method to challenge confinement during the operation of the ordinary procedures of the statute. None of the other compacts or uniform acts that bear on the transfer of persons across state lines for the administration of criminal justice utilize the extraordinary writ of habeas corpus as the statutorily mandated method of challenging confinement. Rather, many of these acts of compacts set forth a hearing on issues that reflects the operation of the particular act or compact. (See, e.g., Section 2 of the Uniform Act To Secure the Attendance of Witnesses, and Sections 2 and 3 of the Uniform Rendition of Accused Persons Act.) An additional reason for establishing a judicial extradition hearing is the opportunity to define the issues to be presented at the hearing—an opportunity which is not available with the writ of habeas corpus. The Extradition and Rendition Act defines the issues that can be raised at the hearing, and these issues reflect the operation of the proposed Act.

Thirdly, the opportunity for an ordinary judicial hearing, albeit subject to waiver, prior to transfer by extradition in Article III and rendition in Article IV answers the current constitutional objections to interstate transfers without pre-transfer hearings. These objections have been raised to interstate transfers of prisoners without hearings under the Interstate Agreement on Detainers. Sisbarro v. Warden, 592 F.2d 1 (1st Cir.1979); Atkinson v. Hanberry, 589 F.2d 917 (5th Cir.1979); Cuyler v. Adams, 592 F.2d 720 (3rd Cir.1979, certiorari granted Feb. 19, 1980). In all of these cases the courts reasoned that a prisoner's constitutionally protected "liberty" interest was not breached by an interstate transfer without an opportunity for a hearing. For cases to the contrary, see e.g., Moen v. Wilson, 536 P.2d 1129 (Colo.1975). By contrast, most of the persons subject to the extradition or rendition process under this Act would not be imprisoned. A sufficient "liberty" interest would, presumably, be present to challenge a transfer without the opportunity for a hearing. Therefore, an opportunity for a pre-transfer hearing is available to a person whose custody is sought by extradition or rendition.

1980 ACT

ARTICLE I
GENERAL PROVISIONS

Section

Be it enacted ...

ARTICLE I

GENERAL PROVISIONS

§ 1-101. [Definitions]

As used in this Act:

(1) "Arrest warrant" means any document that authorizes a peace officer to take custody of a person.

(2) "Certified copy" means a copy of a document accompanied by a statement of a custodian authorized by the law of a state to maintain the document that the copy is a complete and true copy of an official record filed and maintained in a public office.

(3) "Demanded person" means a person whose return to a demanding state is sought from another state by extradition under Article III.

(4) "Demanding state" means a state that is seeking the return of a person from another state through the process of extradition under Article III.

(5) "Executive authority" means the Chief Executive in a state other than this State, any person performing the functions of Chief Executive, or a representative designated by the Chief Executive.

(6) "Governor" means the Governor of this State, any person performing the functions of Governor or a representative designated by the Governor.

(7) "Issuing authority" means any person who may issue or authorize the issuance of an arrest warrant.

(8) "Requested person" means a person whose return to a requesting state is sought from another state by rendition under Article IV.

(9) "Requesting state" means a state that is seeking the return of a person from another state through the process of rendition under Article IV.

(10) "State" means any state of the United States, the District of Columbia, the Commonwealth of Puerto Rico, or any territory or pos-

session subject to the legislative authority of the United States.

§ 1–102. [Conditions of Release]

The law of pre-trial release of this State governs release of a person pursuant to Sections 2–103, 3–106, 4–105, and 5–101.

§ 1–103. [Non–Waiver by This State]

This Act and proceedings under it are not exclusive and do not affect the authority of this State to:

(1) try a demanded or requested person for a crime committed within this State;

(2) take custody of a demanded or requested person by extradition or rendition proceedings for the purpose of trial, sentence, or punishment for a crime committed within this State;

(3) take custody of a person under other provisions of law, including interstate agreements; or

(4) release a person from custody upon any valid conditions.

ARTICLE II

PROCEEDINGS PRIOR TO EXTRADITION AND RENDITION

§ 2–101. [Arrest Without a Warrant]

(a) A peace officer may arrest a person without an arrest warrant upon probable cause to believe that the person is the subject of another state's arrest warrant issued for (i) commission of a crime punishable by death or imprisonment for a term exceeding one year, (ii) escape from confinement, or (iii) violation of any term of bail, probation, parole, or an order arising out of a criminal proceeding.

(b) The arrested person must be brought forthwith before a judge of the [_____] court.

(c) The judge of the [_____] court shall issue an order to continue custody or other process to assure the appearance of the person, if testimony or affidavit shows probable cause to believe the person is the subject of another state's arrest warrant issued for (i) the commission of a crime punishable by death or imprisonment for a term exceeding one year (ii) escape from confinement, or (iii) violation of any term of bail, probation, parole, or an order arising out of a criminal proceeding.

§ 2–102. [Issuance of Process or Arrest Warrant Prior to Receipt of Demand or Request]

(a) [Upon application of a prosecuting official] a judge of the [_____] court shall authorize the issuance of an arrest warrant or other process to obtain the appearance of a person, if testimony or affidavit shows probable cause to believe:

(1) the person is in this State; and

(2) the person is the subject of another state's arrest warrant issued for (i) the commission of a crime punishable by death or imprisonment for a term exceeding one year, (ii) escape from confinement, or (iii) violation of any term of bail; probation, parole, or order arising out of a criminal proceeding.

(b) Other process to obtain the appearance of a person must require the appearance before a judge of the [_____] court.

(c) The arrest warrant must require that the person be brought forthwith before a judge of the [_____] court.

§ 2–103. [Appearance Prior to Receipt of Demand or Request]

(a) The judge shall inform the person appearing pursuant to Section 2–101 or 2–102 of:

(1) the name of the other state that has subjected the person to an arrest warrant;

(2) the basis for the arrest warrant in the other state;

(3) the right to assistance of counsel; and

(4) the right to require a judicial hearing under this Act before transfer of custody to the other state.

(b) After being informed by the judge of the effect of a waiver, the arrested person may waive the right to require a judicial hearing under this Act and consent to return to the other state by executing waiver in the presence of the judge. If the waiver is executed, the judge shall issue an order to transfer custody pursuant to Section 5–101 or, with the consent of the official upon whose application the arrest warrant was issued in the other state, authorize the voluntary return of the person to that state.

(c) Unless a waiver is executed pursuant to subsection (b), the judge shall (i) release the person upon conditions that will reasonably assure availability of the person for arrest pursuant to Section 3–105 or 4–104, or (ii) direct a law enforcement officer to maintain custody of the person. Subject to Section 2–104, the period of conditional release or custody may not exceed 30 days.

§ 2–104. [Extension of Time]

(a) If the person is not arrested pursuant to Section 3–105 or 4–104 within the period specified in the arrest warrant or other process, the judge for good cause may issue further orders under Section 2–103(c) for additional periods not exceeding a total of 60 days. Further extensions of orders may be requested by the person under Section 2–103(c).

(b) If the person is not arrested pursuant to Section 3–105 or 4–104 within the time specified by the judge, the person may not be subjected to any further order in this State under Section 2–103(c). If the person is subsequently arrested in this State under Section 2–101 or 2–102 on the basis of the same arrest warrant of the other state, the person may not be subjected to the issuance of orders under Section 2–103(c) and must be released from custody. However, the person may be arrested thereafter pursuant to Section 3–105 or 4–104.

ARTICLE III

EXTRADITION

§ 3–101. [Demand for Extradition]

(a) The Governor may recognize a written demand by an executive authority for the extradition of a person, alleging that the person:

(1) is charged with a crime in the demanding state; or,

(2) having been charged with or convicted of a crime in the demanding state has (i) escaped from confinement or (ii) violated any term of bail, probation, parole, or an order arising out of a criminal proceeding in the demanding state.

(b) The Governor may demand the extradition of a person from another state in accordance with the Constitution of the United States and may comply with the requirements of the other state for recognition of a demand.

§ 3–102. [Supporting Documentation]

The demand for extradition must be accompanied by a certified copy of an arrest warrant and one of the following:

(1) a statement by the issuing authority that the arrest warrant was issued after a determination of probable cause to believe that a crime has been committed and the demanded person committed the crime, together with a copy of the provisions of law defining the crime and fixing the penalty therefor;

(2) a certified copy of the indictment upon which the arrest warrant is based;

(3) a statement by the issuing authority that the arrest warrant was issued after a determination of probable cause to believe that the demanded person has violated any term of bail, probation, or an order arising out of a criminal proceeding; or

(4) a certified copy of a judgment of conviction or a sentencing order accompanied by a statement by the issuing authority that the demanded person has escaped from confinement or violated any term of parole.

§ 3–103. [Governor's Investigation]

The Governor may:

(1) investigate the demand for extradition and the circumstances of the demanded person;

(2) request the Attorney General or any [other] prosecuting official to investigate; or

(3) hold a hearing.

§ 3–104. [Extradition of Persons Imprisoned or Awaiting Trial]

(a) If a demanded person is being prosecuted, is imprisoned, is on parole or probation, or is subject to an order arising out of a criminal proceeding, in this State, the Governor may:

(1) grant extradition;

(2) delay action; or

(3) agree with the executive authority of the demanding state to grant extradition upon conditions.

(b) The Governor may agree with an executive authority of another state for the extradition of a person who is being prosecuted, is imprisoned, is on parole or probation, or is subject to an order arising out of a criminal proceeding, in that state upon conditions prescribed by the agreement.

§ 3-105. [Governor's Warrant]

(a) If the Governor decides to comply with the demand for extradition, he shall issue a warrant for the arrest and extradition of the demanded person. The Governor's warrant must recite the name of the state demanding extradition and the crime charged or other basis for the demand.

(b) The Governor may specify the time and manner is which the warrant is executed.

(c) At any time before the transfer of custody of the demanded person to the agent of the demanding state, the Governor may recall the warrant or issue another warrant.

(d) The warrant must be directed to any law enforcement officer and require compliance with Section 3-106.

(e) The law relating to assistance in the execution of other arrest warrants in this State applies to the execution of the Governor's warrant.

§ 3-106. [Rights of Demanded Person]

(a) A person arrested under a Governor's warrant must be brought forthwith before a judge of the [_____] court of this State who shall receive the warrant and inform the person of:

(1) the name of the state demanding extradition;

(2) the crime charged or other basis for the demand;

(3) the right to assistance of counsel; and

(4) the right to a judicial hearing under Section 3-107.

(b) After being informed by the judge of the effect of a waiver, the demanded person may waive the right to a judicial hearing and consent to return to the demanding state by executing a written waiver in the presence of the judge. If the waiver is executed, the judge shall issue an order to transfer custody pursuant to Section 5-101 or, with the consent of the executive authority of the demanding state, authorize the voluntary return of the person.

(c) If a hearing is not waived, the judge shall hold it within 10 days after the appearance. The demanded person and the prosecuting official of the [county] in which the hearing is to be held must be informed of the time and the place of the hearing. The judge shall (i) release the person upon conditions that will reasonably assure availability of the person for the hearing, or (ii) direct a law enforcement officer to maintain custody of the person.

§ 3-107. [Judicial Extradition Hearing]

(a) If the judge after hearing finds that the Governor has issued a warrant supported by the documentation required by Sections 3-101(a) and 3-102, the judge shall issue an order to transfer custody pursuant to Section 5-101 unless the arrested person establishes by clear and convincing evidence that he is not the demanded person.

(b) If the judge does not order transfer of custody, he shall order the arrested person to be released. If the agent of the demanding state has not taken custody within the time specified in the order to transfer custody, the demanded person must be released. Thereafter, an order to transfer custody may be entered only if a new arrest warrant is issued as a result of a new demand for extradition or a new request for rendition.

(c) An order to transfer custody is not appealable.

(d) An order denying transfer is appealable.

ARTICLE IV

RENDITION

§ 4-101. [Request for Rendition]

(a) Subject to subsections (b) and (c), this State may grant a written request by an issuing authority of another state for the rendition of a person in this State.

(b) The request must be refused if the requested person is:

(1) being prosecuted or is imprisoned in this State for a criminal offense;

(2) the subject of a pending proceeding in a juvenile court of this State brought for the purpose of adjudicating the person to be a delinquent child; [or]

(3) in the custody of an agency of this State pursuant to an order of disposition of a juvenile court of this State as a delinquent child[; or]

[(4) under the supervision of the juvenile court of this State pursuant to informal adjustment or an order of disposition of the court].

(c) The request must allege that the person:

(1) is charged with a crime punishable in the requesting state by death or imprisonment for a term exceeding one year in the requesting state, or

(2) having been charged with or convicted of a crime in the requesting state, has escaped from confinement or violated any term of bail, probation, parole, or an order arising out of a criminal proceeding in the requesting state.

(d) Upon application of a prosecuting official of this State, an issuing authority may request rendition of a person from another state and may comply with requirements of that state for the granting of the request. A correction official who is also an issuing authority may request rendition from another state of a person described in subsection (c)(2), and subject to the jurisdiction of the correction official.

§ 4–102. [Supporting Documentation]

The request for rendition must be accompanied by a certified copy of the arrest warrant and one of the following:

(1) a statement by the issuing authority that the arrest warrant was issued after a determination of probable cause to believe that a crime has been committed and the requested person committed the crime, together with a copy of the provisions of law defining the crime and fixing the penalty therefor;

(2) a certified copy of the indictment upon which the arrest warrant is based;

(3) a statement by the issuing authority that the warrant was issued after a determination of probable cause to believe that the requested person has violated any term of bail, probation,

or other judicial order arising out of a criminal proceeding; or

(4) a certified copy of a judgment of conviction or a sentencing order accompanied by a statement by the issuing authority that the requested person has escaped from confinement or violated any term of parole.

§ 4–103. [Filing of Request]

A request for rendition under Section 4–101 must be filed with [an office of this State designated by the Governor for the receipt of requests for rendition], which office shall forward the request to the proper prosecuting official of this State. The Governor by written order may terminate the use of rendition at any time before the issuance of an order to transfer custody.

§ 4–104. [Issuance of Arrest Warrant or Process]

Upon receipt of a request under Section 4–103, the prosecuting official shall apply to a judge of the [_____] court for the issuance of an arrest warrant, or other process, to obtain the appearance of the requested person. If the judge finds that the provisions of Sections 4–101 and 4–102 have been complied with, he shall issue the warrant or other process. The warrant must require that the person be brought forthwith before a judge of the [_____] court. Other process to obtain the appearance of a person must require the appearance before a judge of the [_____] court.

§ 4–105. [Rights of Requested Person]

(a) The judge shall inform the person appearing pursuant to Section 4–104 of:

(1) the name of the state requesting rendition;

(2) the basis for the arrest warrant in the other state;

(3) the right to assistance of counsel; and

(4) the right to require a judicial hearing pursuant to Section 4–106.

(b) After being informed by the judge of the effect of a waiver, the requested person may waive the right to a judicial hearing and consent to return to the requesting state by executing a written waiver in the presence of the judge. If the waiver is executed, the judge shall issue an order to transfer custody pursuant to Section 5–101 or with consent of the official upon whose

127

application the request was issued authorize the voluntary return of the person.

(c) If a hearing is not waived, the judge shall hold it within 10 days after the appearance. The requested person and the prosecuting official of the [county] in which the hearing is to be held must be informed of the time and place of the hearing. The judge shall (i) release the person upon conditions that will reasonably assure availability of the person for the hearing, or (ii) direct a law enforcement officer to maintain custody of the person.

§ 4-106. [Judicial Rendition Hearing]

(a) If the judge after hearing finds that Sections 4-101 and 4-102 have been complied with, he shall issue an order to transfer custody pursuant to Section 5-101 unless the arrested person establishes by clear and convincing evidence that he is not the requested person.

(b) If the judge does not order transfer of custody, he shall order the arrested person to be released. If the agent of the requesting state has not taken custody within the time specified in the order to transfer custody, the requested person must be released. Thereafter, an order to transfer custody may be entered only if a new arrest warrant is issued as a result of a new demand for extradition or a new request for rendition.

(c) An order to transfer custody is not appealable.

(d) An order denying transfer is appealable.

ARTICLE V

MISCELLANEOUS

§ 5-101. [Order to Transfer Custody]

(a) Except as provided in subsection (b), a judicial order to transfer custody issued pursuant to Section 2-103, 3-106, 3-107, 4-105, or 4-106 must direct a law enforcement officer to take or retain custody of the person until an agent of the other state is available to take custody. If the agent of the other state has not taken custody within 10 days, the judge may:

(1) order the release of the person upon conditions that will assure the person's availability on a specified date within 30 days; or

(2) extend the original order for an additional 10 days upon good cause shown for the failure of an agent of the other state to take custody.

(b) If the agent of the other state has not taken custody within the time specified in the order, the person must be released. Thereafter, an order to transfer custody may be entered only if a new arrest warrant or other process to obtain appearance of a person is issued as a result of a new demand for extradition or a new request for rendition.

(c) The judge in the order may authorize the voluntary return of the person with consent of the executive authority or with the consent of the official upon whose application the request for rendition was made.

§ 5-102. [Confinement]

An agent who has custody of a person pursuant to an order to transfer custody issued in any state may request confinement of the person in any detention facility in this State while transporting him pursuant to the order. Upon production of proper identification of the agent and a copy of the order, the detention facility shall confine the person for that agent. The person is not entitled to another extradition or rendition proceeding in this State.

§ 5-103. [Cost of Return]

Unless the states otherwise agree, the state to which the person is being returned shall pay the cost of returning the person incurred after transfer of custody to its agent.

§ 5-104. [Applicability of Other Law]

(a) A person returned to this State is subject to the law of this State as well as the provisions of law that constituted the basis for the return.

(b) This Act does not limit the powers, rights, or duties of the officials of a demanding, or requesting, state or of this State.

§ 5-105. [Payment of Transportation and Subsistence Costs]

If a person returned to this State is found not to have violated the law that constituted the basis for the return, the judge may order the [county] to pay the person the cost of transportation and subsistence to:

(1) the place of the person's initial arrest; or

(2) the person's residence.

§ 5–106. [Uniformity of Application and Construction]

This Act shall be applied and construed to effectuate its general purpose to make uniform the law with respect to the subject of this Act among states enacting it.

§ 5–107. [Short Title]

This Act may be cited as the Uniform Extradition and Rendition Act.

§ 5–108. [Severability]

If any provision of this Act or its application to any person or circumstance is held invalid, the invalidity does not affect other provisions or applications of the Act which can be given effect without the invalid provision or application, and to this end the provisions of this Act are severable.

ARTICLE VI

EFFECTIVE DATE AND REPEAL

§ 6–101. [Time of Taking Effect]

This Act takes effect _____.

§ 6–102. [Repeal]

The following Acts and parts of Acts are repealed

(1) Uniform Rendition of Accused Persons Act, and,

(2) Uniform Criminal Extradition Act.

UNIFORM CRIME VICTIMS REPARATIONS ACT

Table of Jurisdictions Wherein Act Has Been Adopted

Jurisdiction	Laws	Effective Date	Statutory Citation
Kansas ....1978, c. 130		7–1–1978	K.S.A. §§ 74–7301 to 74–7321.
Louisiana.............1982, No. 250		7–17–1982	LSA–R.S. 46:1801 to 46:1823.
Montana ....1977, c. 527		1–1–1978	MCA 53–9–101 to 53–9–133.
North Dakota.........1975, c. 587		7–1–1975	NDCC 65–13–01 to 65–13–20.
Ohio.................1974, H.B. 185		1–1–1975	R.C. §§ 2743.51 to 2743.72.
Texas................1979, c. 189		1–1–1980	Vernon's Ann.Texas Civ.St. art. 8309–1.

Historical Note

The Uniform Crime Victims Reparations Act was approved by the National Conference of Commissioners on Uniform State Laws, and the American Bar Association, in 1973.

Commissioners' Prefatory Note

This Act establishes a state-financed program of reparations to persons who suffer personal injury and dependents of those who are killed by criminally injurious conduct or in attempts to prevent criminal conduct or to apprehend criminals. Reparations are measured by economic loss such as medical expenses, loss of earnings, and costs incurred in obtaining services as a substitute for those the victim would have provided. Throughout, the emphasis is on the victim rather than the perpetrator of the crime.

The civil and criminal liability of the offender is not covered by this Act, save for provisions directing the offender to reimburse the State. The actual financial return to the State through this mechanism is not anticipated to be large, and a realistic appraisal is that the costs of the program will be borne by the State and its citizens. A variety of limitations and exclusions stated in the Act are designed to limit those costs. The suggested maximum allowance of $50,000 per victim, the exclusion of motor vehicle accidents (with some exceptions) and elimination of pain and suffering as an element of awards are illustrations.

Probably the most perplexing policy choice to be made by any state instituting a program of this sort relates to the relevance, if any, of the financial condition of the victim. Some would further reduce costs by denying reparations to victims able to bear the economic loss caused by crime. Others would conclude that the victim's losses should be borne by the State irrespective of his financial resources. This Act is drafted to accommodate either choice, but the clear preference is to eliminate any "financial needs" or "financial stress" test as a condition precedent to receipt of benefits. For those states taking the other view, the Act contains a provision including this condition but defining it in terms of financial hardship or stress rather than "need." The objective of that definition is to ensure that the program is not an unnecessary substitute for welfare but is a program to protect against substantial changes in life style caused by losses through crime.

A kindred issue is that of allocation of criminally caused loss through personal injury among competing sources of payment such as insurance, workmen's compensation and Social Security. This Act reflects the policy choice that these programs are primary. Implementation of that policy occurs in two ways. First, insurers are not entitled to claim reimbursement from the State for their expenditures. Second, victims who have been paid, or who are entitled to be paid, by insurers will have their claims against the State fund reduced by the amount of available insurance. In somewhat overly simplistic terms, the policy of the Act is to preclude double recovery for any criminal incident.

Administration of the Act is entrusted to a three-man Board whose members will serve full or part time, depending upon the expectable workload in any state. The Act includes procedural details which will be seen to parallel provisions of the Uniform Administrative Procedures Act. Any State legislature in a state having such an administrative procedures act will be well advised to eliminate the duplicate provisions herein.

1973 ACT

Sec.
1. Definitions.
2. Award of Reparations.
3. Crime Victims Reparations Board.
4. Powers and Duties of the Board.
5. Application for Reparations; Awards; Limitations on Awards.
6. Notice to Attorney General; Function of Attorney General.
7. Informal Disposition; Contested Cases.
8. Contested Cases; Notice; Hearing; Records.
9. Evidence of Physical Condition.
10. Enforcement of Board's Order.
11. Award and Payment of Reparations.

Be it enacted ....

§ 1. Definitions

(a) As used in this Act, the words and phrases in this Section have the meanings indicated.

(b) "Board" means the Crime Victims Reparations Board created under Section 3.

(c) "Claimant" means any of the following claiming reparations under this Act: a victim, a dependent of a deceased victim, a third person other than a collateral source, or an authorized person acting on behalf of any of them.

(d) "Collateral source" means a source of benefits or advantages for economic loss otherwise reparable under this Act which the victim or claimant has received, or which is readily available to him, from:

(1) the offender;

(2) the government of the United States or any agency thereof, a state or any of its political subdivisions, or an instrumentality of two or more states, unless the law providing for the benefits or advantages makes them excess or secondary to benefits under this Act;

(3) Social Security, Medicare, and Medicaid;

(4) state required temporary non-occupational disability insurance;

(5) workmen's compensation;

(6) wage continuation programs of any employer;

(7) proceeds of a contract of insurance payable to the victim for loss which he sustained because of the criminally injurious conduct; or

(8) a contract providing prepaid hospital and other health care services, or benefits for disability.

(e) "Criminally injurious conduct" means conduct that (1) occurs or is attempted in this State, (2) poses a substantial threat of personal injury or death, and (3) is punishable by fine, imprisonment, or death, or would be so punishable but for the fact that the person engaging in the conduct lacked capacity to commit the crime under the laws of this State. Criminally injurious conduct does not include conduct arising out of the ownership, maintenance, or use of a motor vehicle except when intended to cause personal injury or death.

(f) "Dependent" means a natural person wholly or partially dependent upon the victim for care or support and includes a child of the victim born after his death.

(g) "Economic loss" means economic detriment consisting only of allowable expense, work loss, replacement services loss, and, if injury causes death, dependent's economic loss and dependent's replacement services loss. Noneconomic detriment is not loss. However, economic detriment is loss although caused by pain and suffering or physical impairment.

(1) "Allowable expense" means reasonable charges incurred for reasonably needed products, services, and accommodations, including those for medical care, rehabilitation, rehabilitative occupational training, and other remedial treatment and care. The term includes a total charge not in excess of $500 for expenses in any way related to funeral, cremation, and burial. It does not include that portion of a charge for a room in a hospital, clinic, convalescent or nursing home, or any other institution engaged in providing nursing care and related services, in excess of a reasonable and customary charge for semi-private accommodations, unless other accommodations are medically required.

(2) "Work loss" means loss of income from work the injured person would have performed if he had not been injured, and expenses reasonably incurred by him in obtaining services in lieu of those he would have performed for income, reduced by any income from substitute work actually performed by him or by income he would have earned in available appropriate

substitute work he was capable of performing but unreasonably failed to undertake.

(3) "Replacement services loss" means expenses reasonably incurred in obtaining ordinary and necessary services in lieu of those the injured person would have performed, not for income but for the benefit of himself or his family, if he had not been injured.

(4) "Dependent's economic loss" means loss after decedent's death of contributions of things of economic value to his dependents, not including services they would have received from the decedent if he had not suffered the fatal injury, less expenses of the dependents avoided by reason of decedent's death.

(5) "Dependent's replacement services loss" means loss reasonably incurred by dependents after decedent's death in obtaining ordinary and necessary services in lieu of those the decedent would have performed for their benefit if he had not suffered the fatal injury, less expenses of the dependents avoided by reason of decedent's death and not subtracted in calculating dependent's economic loss.

(h) "Non-economic detriment" means pain, suffering, inconvenience, physical impairment, and other non-pecuniary damage.

(i) "Victim" means a person who suffers personal injury or death as a result of (1) criminally injurious conduct, (2) the good faith effort of any person to prevent criminally injurious conduct, or (3) the good faith effort of any person to apprehend a person suspected of engaging in criminally injurious conduct.

§ 2. Award of Reparations

The Board shall award reparations for economic loss arising from criminally injurious conduct if satisfied by a preponderance of the evidence that the requirements for reparations have been met.

§ 3. Crime Victims Reparations Board

(a) A Crime Victims Reparations Board is created [in the executive branch], consisting of three members appointed by the Governor [with the advice and consent of the Senate]. At least one member shall be a person admitted to the bar of this State.

(b) The term of office of each member shall be [six] years and until his successor is appointed and qualified, except that of the members first appointed one each shall be appointed to serve for terms of [two], [four], and [six] years. A person appointed to fill a vacancy shall be appointed for the remainder of the unexpired term.

(c) The Governor shall designate a member who is admitted to the bar of this State to serve as chairman at the pleasure of the Governor.

(d) Members shall [serve full time, receive an annual salary prescribed by the Governor within the available appropriation not exceeding [ ] dollars,] [serve part time, and receive [ ] dollars per diem,] and be reimbursed for actual expenditures incurred in performance of their duties in the same manner as State officials generally.

§ 4. Powers and Duties of the Board

(a) In addition to the powers and duties specified elsewhere in this Act, the Board has the powers and duties specified in this section.

(b) The duty to establish and maintain a principal office and other necessary offices within this state, appoint employees and agents as necessary, and prescribe their duties and compensation.

(c) The duty to adopt by rule a description of the organization of the Board stating the general method and course of operation of the Board.

(d) The duty to adopt rules to implement this Act, including rules for the allowance of attorney's fees for representation of claimants; and to adopt rules providing for discovery proceedings, including medical examination consistent with Sections 9 and 10. Rules shall be statements of general applicability which implement, interpret, or prescribe policy, or describe the procedure or practice requirements of the Board.

(e) The duty to prescribe forms for applications for reparations.

(f) The duty to hear and determine all matters relating to claims for reparations, and the power to reinvestigate or reopen claims without regard to statutes of limitations or periods of prescription.

(g) The power to request from prosecuting attorneys and law enforcement officers investigations and data to enable the Board to determine whether, and the extent to which, a claimant qualifies for reparations. A statute providing confidentiality for a claimant's or victim's juvenile court records does not apply to proceedings under this Act.

(h) The duty, if it would contribute to the function of the Board, to subpoena witnesses and other prospective evidence, administer oaths or affirmations, conduct hearings, and receive relevant, nonprivileged evidence.

(i) The power to take notice of judicially cognizable facts and general, technical, and scientific facts within their specialized knowledge.

(j) The duty to make available for public inspection all Board decisions and opinions, rules, written statements of policy, and interpretations formulated, adopted, or used by the Board in discharging its functions.

(k) The duty to publicize widely the availability of reparations and information regarding the filing of claims therefor.

§ 5. Application for Reparations; Awards; Limitations on Awards

(a) An applicant for an award of reparations shall apply in writing in a form that conforms substantially to that prescribed by the Board.

(b) Reparations may not be awarded unless the claim is filed with the Board within one year after the injury or death upon which the claim is based.

(c) Reparations may not be awarded to a claimant who is the offender or an accomplice of the offender, nor to any claimant if the award would unjustly benefit the offender or accomplice. [Unless the Board determines that the interests of justice otherwise require in a particular case, reparations may not be awarded to the spouse of, or a person living in the same household with, the offender or his accomplice or to the parent, child, brother, or sister of the offender or his accomplice.]

(d) Reparations may not be awarded unless the criminally injurious conduct resulting in injury or death was reported to a law enforcement officer within 72 hours after its occurrence or the Board finds there was good cause for the failure to report within that time.

(e) The Board, upon finding that the claimant or victim has not fully cooperated with appropriate law enforcement agencies, may deny, reconsider, or reduce an award of reparations.

(f) Reparations otherwise payable to a claimant shall be reduced or denied

(1) to the extent the economic loss upon which the claim is based is recouped from other persons, including collateral sources, and

(2) to the extent the Board deems reasonable because of the contributory misconduct of the claimant or of a victim through whom he claims.

[(g)(1) Reparations may be awarded only if the Board finds that unless the claimant is awarded reparations he will suffer financial stress as the result of economic loss otherwise reparable. A claimant suffers financial stress only if he cannot maintain his customary level of health, safety, and education for himself and his dependents without undue financial hardship. In making its finding the Board shall consider all relevant factors, including:

(i) the number of claimant's dependents;

(ii) the usual living expenses of the claimant and his family;

(iii) the special needs of the claimant and his dependents;

(iv) the claimant's income and potential earning capacity; and

(v) the claimant's resources.

(2) Reparations may not be awarded if the claimant's economic loss does not exceed ten per cent of his net financial resources. A claimant's net financial resources do not include the present value of future earnings and shall be determined by the Board by deducting from his total financial resources:

(i) one year's earnings;

(ii) the claimant's equity, up to $30,000 in his home;

(iii) one motor vehicle; and

(iv) any other property exempt from execution under [the general personal property exemptions statute of this State].

(3) Notwithstanding paragraph (2):

(i) the board may award reparations to a claimant who possesses net financial resources in excess of those allowable under paragraph (2) if, considering the claimant's age, life expectancy, physical or mental condition, and expectancy of income including future earning power, it finds that the claimant's financial resources will become exhausted during his lifetime; or

(ii) the Board may (A) reject the claim finally, or (B) reject the claim and reserve to the claimant the right to reopen his claim, if it appears that the exhaustion of claimant's financial resources is probable, in which event the Board may reopen pursuant to an application to reopen if it finds that the resources available to the claimant from the time of denial of an award were prudently expended for personal or family needs.]

[(h)] Reparations may not be awarded if the economic loss is less than [$100].

[(i) ALTERNATIVE A: Reparations for work loss, replacement services loss, dependent's economic loss, and dependent's replacement services loss may not exceed $200 per week.]

[(i) ALTERNATIVE B: Reparations for work loss, replacement services loss, dependent's economic loss, and dependent's replacement services loss may not exceed the amount by which the victim's income is reduced below $200 per week.]

[(j) Reparations payable to a victim and to all other claimants sustaining economic loss because of injury to or death of that victim may not exceed [$50,000] in the aggregate.]

§ 6. Notice to Attorney General; Function of Attorney General

Promptly upon receipt of an application for reparations, the Board shall forward a copy of the application and all supporting papers to the [Attorney General], who in appropriate cases may investigate the claim, appear in hearings on the claim, and present evidence in opposition to or support of an award.

§ 7. Informal Disposition; Contested Case

Unless precluded by law, informal disposition may be made of a claim by stipulation, agreed settlement, consent order, or default. A claim not so disposed of is a contested case.

§ 8. Contested Cases; Notice; Hearing; Records

(a) In a contested case, all parties shall be afforded an opportunity for hearing after reasonable notice.

(b) The notice of hearing shall include:

(1) a statement of the time, place, and nature of the hearing;

(2) a statement of the legal authority and jurisdiction under which the hearing is to be held;

(3) a reference to the particular sections of the statutes and rules involved; and

(4) a short and plain statement of the matters asserted.

To the extent that the board is unable to state the matters at the time the notice is served, the initial notice may be limited to a statement of the issues involved. Thereafter upon application a more definite statement shall be furnished.

(c) Every interested person shall be afforded an opportunity to appear and be heard and to offer evidence and argument on any issue relevant to his interest, and examine witnesses and offer evidence in reply to any matter of an evidentiary nature in the record relevant to his interest.

(d) A record of the proceedings shall be made and shall include:

(1) the application and supporting documents;

(2) all pleadings, motions, and intermediate rulings;

(3) evidence offered, received, or considered;

(4) a statement of matters officially noticed;

(5) all staff memoranda or data submitted to the Board in connection with its consideration of the case; and

(6) offers of proof, objections, and rulings.

(e) Oral proceedings or any part thereof shall be transcribed on request of any party, who shall pay transcription costs unless otherwise ordered by the Board.

(f) Determinations of the Board shall be made in writing, supported by findings of fact and conclusions of law based exclusively on the record, and mailed promptly to all parties.

§ 9. Evidence of Physical Condition

(a) There is no privilege, except privileges arising from the attorney-client relationship, as to communications or records relevant to an issue of the physical, mental, or emotional condition of the claimant or victim in a proceeding under this Act in which that condition is an element.

(b) If the mental, physical, or emotional condition of a victim or claimant is material to a claim, the Board may order the victim or claimant to submit to a mental or physical examination by a physician or psychologist, and may order an autopsy of a deceased victim. The order may be made for good cause shown upon notice to the person to be examined and to all persons who have appeared. The order shall specify the time, place, manner, conditions, and scope of the examination or autopsy and the person by whom it is to be made, and shall require the person to file with the Board a detailed written report of the examination or autopsy. The report shall set out his findings, including results of all tests made, diagnosis, prognoses, and other conclusions and reports of earlier examinations of the same conditions.

(c) On request of the person examined, the Board shall furnish him a copy of the report. If the victim is deceased, the Board, on request, shall furnish the claimant a copy of the report.

(d) The Board may require the claimant to supplement the application with any reasonably available medical or psychological reports relating to the injury for which reparations are claimed.

§ 10. Enforcement of Board's Orders

If a person refuses to comply with an order under this Act or asserts a privilege, except privileges arising from the attorney-client relationship, to withhold or suppress evidence relevant to a claim, the Board may make any just order including denial of the claim, but may not find the person in contempt. If necessary to carry out any of its powers and duties, the Board may petition the [ ] Court for an appropriate order, but the Court may not find a person in contempt for refusal to submit to a medical or physical examination.

§ 11. Award and Payment of Reparations

(a) An award may be made whether or not any person is prosecuted or convicted. Proof of conviction of a person whose acts give rise to a claim is conclusive evidence that the crime was committed, unless an application for rehearing, an appeal of the conviction, or certiorari is pending, or a rehearing or new trial has been ordered.

(b) The Board may suspend the proceedings pending disposition of a criminal prosecution that has been commenced or is imminent, but may make a tentative award under Section 15.

§ 12. Attorney's Fees

As part of an order, the Board shall determine and award reasonable attorney's fees, commensurate with services rendered, to be paid by the State to the attorney representing the claimant. Additional attorney's fees may be awarded by a court in the event of review. Attorney's fees may be denied on a finding that the claim or appeal is frivolous. Awards of attorney's fees shall be in addition to awards of reparations and may be made whether or not reparations are awarded. It is unlawful for an attorney to contract for or receive any larger sum than the amount allowed.

§ 13. Subrogation; Actions; Allocation of Expenses

(a) If reparations are awarded, the State is subrogated to all the claimant's rights to receive or recover benefits or advantages, for economic loss for which and to the extent only that reparations are awarded, from a source which is or, if readily available to the victim or claimant would be, a collateral source.

(b) As a prerequisite to bringing an action to recover damages related to criminally injurious conduct for which reparations are claimed or awarded, the claimant shall give the Board prior written notice of the proposed action. After receiving the notice, the Board shall promptly (1) join in the action as a party plaintiff to recover reparations awarded, (2) require the claimant to bring the action in his individual name, as a trustee in behalf of the State, to recover reparations awarded, or (3) reserve its rights and do neither in the proposed action. If, as requested by the Board, the claimant brings the action as trustee and recovers reparations awarded by the Board, he may deduct from the reparations recovered in behalf of the State the reasonable expenses, including attorney's fees, allocable by the court for that recovery.

(c) If a judgment or verdict indicates separately economic loss and non-economic detriment, payments on the judgment shall be allocated between them in proportion to the amounts indicated. In an action in a court of this State arising out of criminally injurious conduct, the judge, on timely motion, shall direct the jury to return a special verdict, indicating separately the awards for non-economic detriment, punitive damages, and economic loss.

§ 14. Manner of Payment; Non-assignability and Exemptions

(a) The Board may provide for the payment of an award in a lump sum or in installments. The part of an award equal to the amount of economic loss accrued to the date of the award shall be paid in a lump sum. An award for allowable expense that would accrue after the award is made may not be paid in a lump sum. Except as provided in subsection (b), the part of an award that may not be paid in a lump sum shall be paid in installments.

(b) At the instance of the claimant, the Board may commute future economic loss, other than allowable expense, to a lump sum but only upon a finding by the Board that:

(1) the award in a lump sum will promote the interests of the claimant; or

(2) the present value of all future economic loss other than allowable expense, does not exceed [$1,000].

(c) An award for future economic loss payable in installments may be made only for a period as to which the Board can reasonably determine future economic loss. The Board may reconsider and modify an award for future economic loss payable in installments, upon its finding that a material and substantial change of circumstances has occurred.

(d) An award is not subject to execution, attachment, garnishment, or other process, except that an award for allowable expense is not exempt from a claim of a creditor to the extent that he provided products, services, or accommodations the costs of which are included in the award.

(e) An assignment or agreement to assign a right to reparations for loss accruing in the future is unenforceable, except (1) an assignment of a right to reparations for work loss to secure payment of alimony, maintenance, or child support; or (2) an assignment of a right to reparations for allowable expense to the extent that the benefits are for the cost of products, services, or accommodations necessitated by the injury or death on which the claim is based and are provided or to be provided by the assignee.

§ 15. Tentative Awards

If the Board determines that the claimant will suffer financial hardship unless a tentative award is made, and it appears likely that a final award will be made, an amount may be paid to the claimant, to be deducted from the final award or repaid by and recoverable from the claimant to the extent that it exceeds the final award.

§ 16. Reconsideration and Review of Board Decisions

(a) The Board, on its own motion or on request of the claimant, may reconsider a decision making or denying an award or determining its amount. The Board shall reconsider at least annually every award being paid in installments. An order on reconsideration of an award shall not require refund of amounts previously paid unless the award was obtained by fraud.

(b) The right of reconsideration does not affect the finality of a Board decision for the purpose of judicial review.

(c) A final decision of the Board is subject to judicial review on appeal by the claimant, the [Attorney General], or the offender [in the same manner and to the same extent as the decision of a state trial court of general jurisdiction].

§ 17. Reports

The Board shall prepare and transmit [annually] to the Governor and the Legislature a report of its activities, including the name of the claimant, a brief description of the facts, and the amount of reparations awarded in each case, and a statistical summary of claims and awards made and denied.

§ 18. Uniformity of Application and Construction

This Act shall be applied and construed to effectuate its general purpose to make uniform the law with respect to the subject of this Act among those states enacting it.

§ 19. Severability

If any provision of this Act or the application thereof to any person is held invalid, the invalidity does not affect other provisions or applications of the Act which can be given effect without the invalid provision or application, and to this end the provisions of this Act are severable.

§ 20. Title

This Act may be cited as the Uniform Crime Victims Reparations Act.

UNIFORM LAW COMMISSIONERS' MODEL INSANITY DEFENSE AND POST–TRIAL DISPOSITION ACT

Table of Jurisdictions Wherein Act Has Been Adopted

Jurisdiction	Laws	Effective Date	Statutory Citation
North Dakota..........1985, c. 173			NDCC 12.1–04.1–01 to 12.1–04.1–26.

Historical Note

The Uniform Law Commissioners' Model Insanity Defense and Post–Trial Disposition Act was approved by the National Conference of Commissioners on Uniform State Laws in 1984.

PREFATORY NOTE

History

The conclusion that some insane persons are not criminally responsible originated as a judge-made facet of criminal law. The modern starting point is the famous M'Naghten Case, 8 Eng.Rep. 718 (1843), from which the M'Naghten Rule derived. In recent years, as criminal law has been re-examined and codified, some provisions on the insanity defense were incorporated into statutes. A major impetus was the American Law Institute's Model Penal Code (1962), which formulated a statement of the responsibility of persons suffering from mental disease or defect. The ALI's formulation was widely adopted by legislatures or by courts. Within the past decade, a number of legislatures added a provision allowing a finding that an accused person was guilty but mentally ill.

Public debate about the insanity defense intensified after John Hinckley was found not guilty of attempted assassination of President Reagan and related offenses. The House of Delegates of the American Bar Association resolved in February 1983 that (i) there should be a defense of nonresponsibility for crime which focuses solely on whether the defendant, as a result of mental disease or defect, was unable to appreciate the wrongfulness of that conduct at the time of the offense charged, and (ii) the prosecution should have the burden of proof by a preponderance of the evidence. The House of Delegates opposed enactment of statutes allowing a verdict of guilty but mentally ill.

Other major organizations have put forward position statements on criminal responsibility and related matters. Included are the Board of Trustees of the American Psychiatric Association (December 1982); the National Commission on the Insanity Defense, an independent body established by the National Mental Health Association (March 1983); the House of Delegates of the American Medical Association (December 1983); and the Council of Representatives of the American Psychological Association (January 1984); the ABA Standing Committee on Criminal Justice Standards (Criminal Justice Mental Health Standards, adopted by the House of Delegates, July 1984).

The Drafting Committee began its work on the Model Act in 1982. Throughout its work, the Drafting Committee has been assisted by the participation of liaison representatives of four major organizations concerned with this matter. Dr. Richard G. Lonsdorf, Associate Professor of Psychiatry and Law at the University of Pennsylvania Law School, served as the representative of the National Commission on the Insanity Defense. Dr. Loren H. Roth, Professor of Psychiatry at the University of Pittsburgh, provided the views of the American Psychiatric Association. The liaison representative of the American Psychological Association was Dr. Bruce Bennett of Northbrook, Illinois. Dean Steven Goldberg, University of Minnesota Law School, provided liaison with the American Bar Association Standing Committee on Criminal Justice Standards. The work of the Conference was greatly advanced through the invaluable contributions of these individuals.

Copies of the Model Act were submitted to many organizations with special interest in criminal law and criminal law enforcement. Included were the National Association of Attorneys General, the National District Attorneys Association, the National Association of Criminal Defense Lawyers, Inc., the National Legal Aid and Defender Association, and the International Association of Chiefs of Police. Each organization was invited to express its views on the Act.

The Model Act was adopted by the National Conference of Commissioners on Uniform State Laws at its annual meeting in Keystone, Colorado, in August 1984.

Scope Of The Act

Present law on nonresponsibility for crime by reason of mental illness or defect is in flux. Considerable legislative and rule-making activity has been taking place in the states and in the United States. State and

137

federal courts have been engaged in re-examination of common law doctrines. Respected organizations have promulgated recent statements of policy on these questions. Scholars have been making major contributions to the academic literature in this field.

One product of this considerable activity is deeper appreciation of the complex nature of the questions arising when a defendant's mental condition at the time of an alleged offense becomes an issue to be resolved at trial. Generally, an inquiry into mental condition requires utilization of experts who can testify meaningfully only after a one-on-one interview of the defendant. Numerous problems arise in providing for effective pretrial examination by experts for both the prosecution and the defense. Special safeguards are needed to assure against prosecution overreaching of defendants in court-ordered examinations, a concern that invokes sensitive areas of constitutional law as applied in criminal prosecutions. Traditional criminal codes fail to provide adequately, if at all, for the post-verdict disposition of persons found not criminally responsible by reason of mental illness or defect.

In addition to resolving the manifold problems of defining and implementing an insanity defense, criminal law is adapting to the growing recognition that a defendant's mental condition at the time of alleged criminal conduct may be very significant in determining whether that defendant acted with the state of mind required to commit the offense charged (mens rea). With few exceptions for crimes of strict liability, crimes are defined in terms that require a prosecutor to prove that an accused person had a particular state of mind. Persons suffering from mental illness or defect may lack capacity to form the relevant state of mind, or their mental condition may be probative on whether the relevant state of mind actually existed at the time of the conduct in question. From the beginning of its work, the Drafting Committee concluded that the Act should address both the insanity defense and the issues of mens rea that arise when a defendant's mental condition is brought into issue.

The Uniform Law Commissioners' Model Act addressed to these questions will be useful to legislators and rule makers who seek to frame the positive law of their respective jurisdictions. This is not a subject on which uniformity among states is a principal objective. The purposes of the Act can be substantially achieved even though it is not adopted in its entirety by every state. The Model Act calls attention to the issues that must be addressed and provides a means of dealing with those questions in an appropriate way that represents the best judgment of the Conference.

Comment Concerning Adoption

The provisions in this Model Act include both substantive and procedural matters. Articles III, IV and V, in particular, are largely procedural. In the event that procedural provisions in this Model Act are properly the subject of rules of court rather than statute under state law, these provisions should be proposed as additions or changes to the rules.

1984 ACT

ARTICLE I
SCOPE

ARTICLE II
DEFENSE OF ABSENCE OF
CRIMINAL RESPONSIBILITY

ARTICLE III
AUTHORIZATION FOR
EXPERTS AND EXAMINATION

ARTICLE IV
CONDUCT OF EXAMINATION ORDERED
AT REQUEST OF PROSECUTOR

ARTICLE V
EXCHANGE OF REPORTS AND
DOCUMENTS BEFORE TRIAL

ARTICLE VI
USE OF INFORMATION OBTAINED
FROM EXAMINATION ORDERED AT
REQUEST OF PROSECUTOR

ARTICLE I

SCOPE

§ 101. Scope of Act

This [Act] governs the defense of absence of criminal responsibility and provides for post-verdict disposition of an individual found not criminally responsible. It also governs the obtaining of evidence through post-arrest examination of a defendant by a mental-health professional on the issue of state of mind as an element of the crime charged and the use of that evidence.

ARTICLE II

DEFENSE OF ABSENCE OF CRIMINAL RESPONSIBILITY

§ 201. Standard for Absence of Criminal Responsibility

An individual is not criminally responsible if at the time of the alleged offense, as a result of mental illness or defect, the individual was substantially unable to appreciate the wrongfulness of the alleged conduct.

§ 202. Limitation on Mental Illness or Defect

For purposes of this [Act], neither repeated criminal or similar antisocial conduct nor impairment of mental condition caused primarily by voluntary use of alcoholic or psychoactive substances immediately before or contemporaneously with the criminal conduct charged, in itself constitutes mental illness or defect at the time of the crime charged. Evidence of the conduct or impairment may be probative in conjunction with other evidence to establish mental illness or defect.

ARTICLE III

AUTHORIZATION FOR EXPERTS AND EXAMINATION

§ 301. Court Authorization of State–Funded Mental–Health Services for Certain Defendants

A defendant who is unable to pay for the services of a mental-health professional, and to whom those services are not otherwise available, may apply to the court for assistance. Upon a showing of a likely need for examination on the question of absence of criminal responsibility or absence of requisite state of mind as a result of the defendant's mental condition, the court shall authorize reasonable expenditures from public funds for the defendant's retention of the services of one or more mental-health professionals. Upon request by the defendant, the application and the proceedings on the application must be ex parte and in camera, but any order under this section authorizing expenditures must be made part of the public record.

§ 302. Notice of Defense of Absence of Criminal Responsibility

(a) If the defendant intends to introduce at trial evidence obtained from examination of the defendant by a mental-health professional after the time of the alleged offense to show that defendant lacked the state of mind required for the crime charged, the defendant shall notify the prosecutor in writing and file a copy of the notice with the court.

(b) The defendant shall file the notice within the time prescribed for pretrial motions or at such earlier or later time as the court directs. For cause shown, the court may allow late filing of the notice and grant additional time to the parties to prepare for trial or may make other appropriate orders.

§ 304. Examination at Request of Prosecutor

(a) If the defendant has given notice under Section 302 or 303 of intent to introduce evidence obtained by a mental-health professional from examination of the defendant after the time of the alleged offense, the court, upon application by the prosecutor and after opportunity for response by the defendant, shall order that the defendant be examined by one or more mental-health professionals retained by the prosecutor. The court shall include in the order provisions as to the time, place, and conditions of the examination.

(b) If the parties agree to examination of the defendant by a mental-health professional retained by the prosecutor without order of the court, Sections 401, 402, 403, 501, 502, 503, 504, 601 and 602 apply to the examination.

ARTICLE IV

CONDUCT OF EXAMINATION ORDERED AT REQUEST OF PROSECUTOR

§ 401. Explanation to Defendant

At the beginning of each examination conducted under Section 304, the mental-health professional shall inform the defendant that (i) the examination is being made at the request of the prosecutor, (ii) the purpose of the examination is to obtain information about the defendant's mental condition at the time of the alleged offense, and (iii) information obtained from the examination may be used at trial and, if the defendant is found not criminally responsible by reason of mental illness or defect, in subsequent proceedings concerning commitment or other disposition.

§ 402. Scope of Examination

An examination of the defendant conducted under Section 304 may consist of such interviewing, clinical evaluation, and psychological testing as the mental-health professional considers appropriate, within the limits of nonexperimental, generally accepted medical, psychiatric, or psychological practices.

§ 403. Recording of Examination

(a) An examination of the defendant conducted under Section 304 must be audio-recorded and, if ordered by the court, video-recorded. The manner of recording may be specified by rule or by court order in individual cases.

(b) Within [7] days after completion of an examination conducted under Section 304, the mental-health professional conducting the examination shall deliver a copy of the recording of the examination, under seal, to the court and a copy of the recording to the defendant. The recording may not be disclosed except in accordance with this [Act].

§ 404. Consequence of Deliberate Failure of Defendant to Cooperate

If the defendant without just cause deliberately fails to participate or to respond to questions in an examination conducted under Section 304, the prosecutor before trial may apply to the court for appropriate relief. The court may consider the recording of the examination as evidence on the application, but proceedings concerning the recording must be in camera and out of the presence of counsel.

ARTICLE V

EXCHANGE OF REPORTS AND DOCUMENTS BEFORE TRIAL

§ 501. Reports by Mental–Health Professionals and Expert Witnesses

A mental-health professional retained by the prosecutor and a mental-health professional whom the defendant intends to call to testify at trial shall prepare a written report concerning examination of the defendant and other pretrial inquiry by or under the supervision of the mental-health professional. Any other individual whom either party intends to call at trial as an expert witness on any aspect of defendant's mental condition shall prepare a written report. A report under this section must contain:

(1) the specific issues addressed;

(2) the identity of individuals interviewed and records or other information used;

(3) the procedures, tests, and techniques used;

(4) the date and time of examination of the defendant, the explanation concerning the examination given to the defendant, and the identity of each individual present during an examination;

(5) the relevant information obtained and findings made;

(6) matters concerning which the mental-health professional was unable to obtain relevant information and the reasons therefor; and

(7) the conclusions reached and the reasoning on which the conclusions were based.

§ 502. Exchange of Reports and Production of Documents

Not less than [15] days before trial, the prosecutor shall furnish to the defendant reports prepared pursuant to Section 501, and the defendant shall furnish to the prosecutor reports by each mental-health professional or other expert on any aspect of the defendant's mental condition whom the defendant intends to call at trial. Upon application by either party and after hearing, the court may require production of documents prepared, completed, or used in the examination or inquiry by the mental-health professional or other expert.

§ 503. Use of Reports at Trial

Use at trial of a report prepared by a mental-health professional or other expert is governed by the rules of evidence. A report of a mental-health professional or other expert furnished by defendant pursuant to Section 501 may not be used at trial unless the defendant has called the mental-health professional or other expert who prepared the report to testify.

§ 504. Notice of Expert Witnesses

Not less than [20] days before trial, each party shall give written notice to the other of the name and qualifications of each mental-health professional or other individual the respective party intends to call as an expert witness at trial on the issue of absence of criminal responsibility or requisite state of mind as an element of the crime charged. For good cause shown, the court may permit later addition to or deletion from the list of individuals designated as expert witnesses.

ARTICLE VI

USE OF INFORMATION OBTAINED FROM EXAMINATION
ORDERED AT REQUEST OF PROSECUTOR

§ 601. Use of Evidence Obtained from Examination

(a) Except as provided in subsection (b) and in Sections 404 and 907, information obtained as a result of examination of a defendant by a mental-health professional conducted under Section 304 is not admissible over objection of the defendant in any proceeding against the defendant.

(b) Subject to the limitation in Section 602, information obtained from an examination of the defendant by a mental-health professional conducted under Section 304 is admissible at trial to rebut evidence introduced by the defendant obtained from an examination of the defendant by a mental-health professional or to impeach the defendant on defendant's testimony as to mental condition at the time of the alleged offense.

§ 602. Use of Recording of Examination

Except as provided in Section 404, recording of an examination of the defendant concerning the defendant's mental condition at the time of the crime charged may be referred to or otherwise used only on cross-examination for the purpose of impeachment of the mental-health professional who conducted the examination, and then on re-direct examination of that witness to the extent permitted by the rules of evidence. The defendant shall make the recording available to the prosecutor before any use of it pursuant to this section. If the recording is so used, this section does not preclude its use for the purpose of impeachment of the defendant in any other criminal, civil, or administrative proceeding.

ARTICLE VII

TRIAL

§ 701. Bifurcation of Issue of Absence of Criminal Responsibility

[Upon application of the defendant, the court may order that issues as to the commission of the crime charged be tried separately from the issue of absence of criminal responsibility.]

§ 702. Burden of Going Forward and Burden of Proof

(a) The burden of going forward with evidence on the defense of absence of criminal responsibility is on the defendant. At the close of the defendant's case, the prosecutor may move for an order that the defense of absence of criminal responsibility is not an issue in the case. The court shall deny the motion if evidence tending to prove absence of criminal responsibility has been introduced.

(b) The prosecutor has the burden of proving beyond a reasonable doubt the criminal responsibility of the defendant.

§ 703. Jury Instruction on Disposition Following Verdict of Absence of Criminal Responsibility

On request of the defendant in a trial by jury of the issue of absence of criminal responsibility for criminal conduct, the court shall instruct the jury as to the dispositional provisions applicable to the defendant if the jury returns a verdict of not criminally responsible by reason of mental illness or defect.

§ 704. Form of Verdict or Finding

If the issue of absence of criminal responsibility is submitted to the trier of fact:

(a) [In a unitary trial,] the trier of fact shall first determine whether the prosecutor has proven that the defendant committed the crime charged. [In a bifurcated trial, the trier of fact shall separately determine whether the prosecution has proven (i) that the defendant committed the crime charged and (ii) that the defendant was criminally responsible. Each determination must be made at the conclusion of the phase of the trial at which the respective issue was tried.] If the trier of fact concludes that the prosecutor failed to prove that the defendant committed the crime charged, the appropriate verdict or finding is "not guilty".

(b) If the trier of fact determines that the defendant committed the crime charged and that the defendant was criminally responsible for that crime, the appropriate verdict or finding is "guilty".

(c) If the trier of fact determines that the defendant committed the crime but was not criminally responsible for that crime, the appropriate verdict or finding is a statement of the crime the defendant is found to have committed and that the defendant is "not criminally responsible by reason of mental illness or defect".

ARTICLE VIII

POST–TRIAL MOTIONS AND APPEAL

§ 801. Post–Trial Motions and Appeal From Verdict or Finding of Not Criminally Responsible

(a) A defendant found not criminally responsible by reason of mental illness or defect may seek post-trial relief in the trial court and may appeal on issues pertaining to the verdict or finding that the defendant committed a crime.

(b) In the case of a verdict or finding of not criminally responsible by reason of mental illness or defect, if the verdict or finding that the defendant committed a crime is vacated or set aside and the defendant is retried, unless the defendant elects to waive the defense, the verdict or finding of absence of criminal responsibility is conclusive in the retrial.

ARTICLE IX

DISPOSITION OF PERSONS FOUND NOT RESPONSIBLE BY REASON OF MENTAL ILLNESS OR DEFECT

§ 901. Jurisdiction of Court

(a) Unless earlier discharged by order of the court pursuant to Section 903, 905, or 906, an individual found not criminally responsible by reason of mental illness or defect is subject to the jurisdiction of the court for a period equal to the maximum term of imprisonment that could have been imposed for the most serious crime of which the individual was charged but found not criminally responsible.

(b) Upon expiration of its jurisdiction under this [Act] or earlier discharge by its order, the court may order that a proceeding for involuntary commitment be initiated pursuant to the [statute on civil commitment of individuals who are mentally ill or defective].

§ 902. Proceeding Following Verdict or Finding

After entry of a verdict of finding that an individual is not criminally responsible by reason of mental illness or defect, the court shall:

(1) make a finding, based upon the verdict or finding provided in Section 704, of the expiration date of its jurisdiction; and

(2) order the individual committed to a state mental hospital or other suitable facility for examination. The order may set terms of custody during the period of examination.

§ 903. Initial Order of Disposition; Commitment to [Mental Hospital or Other Suitable Facility]; Conditional Release; Discharge

(a) The court shall conduct a dispositional hearing within [90] days after an order of commitment pursuant to Section 902 is entered, unless upon application of the prosecutor or the individual committed, the court for cause shown extends the time for the hearing. The court shall enter an initial order of disposition within [10] days after the hearing is concluded.

(b) In a proceeding under this section, unless excused by order of the court, defense counsel at the trial shall represent the individual committed.

(c) If the court finds that the individual committed lacks sufficient financial resources to retain the services of a mental-health professional and that those services are not otherwise available, it shall authorize reasonable expenditures from public funds for the individual's retention of the services of one or more mental-health professionals to examine the individual and make other inquiry concerning the individual's mental condition.

(d) In a proceeding under this section, the individual committed has the burden of proof by a preponderance of the evidence. The court shall enter an order in accordance with the following rules:

(1) If the court finds that the individual is not mentally ill or defective or that there is not a substantial risk, as a result of mental illness or defect, that the individual will commit a criminal act, it shall order the individual discharged from further constraint under this [Act].

(2) If the court finds that the individual is mentally ill or defective and that there is a substantial risk, as a result of mental illness or defect, that the individual will commit a criminal act of violence threatening another person with bodily injury or property damage and that the individual is not a proper subject for conditional release, it shall order the individual committed to [a mental hospital or other suitable facility designated by the commissioner of mental health] for custody and treatment. If the court finds that the risk that the individual will commit an act of violence threatening another person with bodily injury or property damage will be controlled adequately with supervision and treatment if the individual is conditionally released and that necessary supervision and treatment are available, it shall order the individual released subject to conditions the court considers appropriate for the protection of society.

(3) If the court finds that the individual is mentally ill or defective and that there is a substantial risk, as a result of mental illness or defect, that the individual will commit a criminal act not included in subsection (2), it may order the person to report to any state or local mental-health facility for noncustodial evaluation and treatment and to accept nonexperimental, generally accepted medical, psychiatric, or psychological treatment recommended by the facility.

§ 904. Terms of Commitment; Periodic Review of Commitment

(a) Unless an order of commitment of an individual to [a hospital or facility] provides for special terms as to custody during commitment, the [superintendent] may determine from time to time the nature of the constraints necessary within the [hospital or facility] to carry out the court's order. In an order of commitment, the court may authorize the [superintendent] to allow the individual a limited leave of absence from the [hospital or facility] on terms the court may direct.

(b) In an order of commitment of an individual to [a hospital or facility] under this [Act], the court shall set a date for review of the status of the individual. The date set must be within [one year] after the date of the order.

(c) At least [60] days before a date for review fixed in a court order, the [superintendent] of the [hospital or facility] shall inquire as to whether the individual is presently represented by counsel and file with the court a written report of the facts ascertained. If the individual is not represented by counsel, the court shall appoint counsel to consult with the individual and, if appropriate, to apply to the court for appointment of counsel to represent the individual in a proceeding for conditional release or discharge.

(d) If the court finds in a review that the individual lacks sufficient financial resources to retain the services of a mental-health professional and that those services are otherwise not available, the court shall authorize reasonable expenditures from public funds for the individual's retention of the services of one or more mental-health professionals to examine the individual and make other inquiry concerning the individual's mental condition. In proceedings brought before the next date for review, the court may authorize expenditures from public funds for that purpose.

(e) If an application for review of the status of the individual has not been filed by the date for review, the [superintendent] shall file a motion for a new date to be set by the court. The date set must be within [one year] after the previous date for review.

§ 905. Modification of Order of Commitment; Conditional Release or Discharge; Release Plan

(a) After commitment of an individual to [a hospital or facility] under this [Act], the [superintendent] may apply to the court for modification of the terms of an order of commitment or for an order of conditional release or discharge. The application must be accompanied by a report setting forth the facts supporting the application and, if the application is for conditional release, a plan for supervision and treatment of the individual.

(b) An individual who has been committed to [a hospital or facility] under this [Act], or another person acting on the individual's behalf, may apply to the court for modification of the terms of a commitment order or for an order of conditional release or discharge. If the application is being considered by the court at the time of review of the order of commitment, the court shall require a report from the [superintendent] of the [hospital or facility].

(c) The court shall consider and dispose of an application promptly. In a proceeding under this section, the applicant has the burden of proof by a preponderance of the evidence. The court shall enter an order in accordance with the following rules:

(1) If the court finds that the individual is not mentally ill or defective or that there is not a substantial risk that the individual will commit, as a result of mental illness or defect, a criminal act, it shall order the individual discharged from further constraint under this [Act].

(2) If the court finds that the individual is mentally ill or defective, but that there is not a substantial risk that the individual will commit, as a result of mental illness or defect, a criminal act of violence threatening another individual with bodily injury or inflicting property damage, it shall vacate the order committing the individual to [a hospital or facility]. If the court finds that there is a substantial risk, that the individual will commit, as a result of mental illness or defect, a nonviolent criminal act, it may order the individual to report to any state or local mental-health facility for noncustodial evaluation and treatment and to accept nonexperimental, generally accepted medical, psychiatric, or psychological treatment recommended by the facility.

(3) If the court finds that the individual is mentally ill or defective, but that the risk that the individual will commit, as a result of mental illness or defect, a criminal act of violence threatening another individual with bodily injury or inflicting property damage will be controlled adequately with supervision and treatment and that necessary supervision and treatment are available, it shall order the individual released subject to conditions it considers appropriate for the protection of society.

(d) In any proceeding for modification of an order of commitment to [a hospital or facility], if the individual has been represented by counsel and the application for modification of the order of commitment is denied after a plenary hearing, the court shall set a new date for periodic review of the status of the individual. The date set must be within [one year] after the date of the order.

§ 906. Conditional Release; Modification; Revocation; Discharge

(a) In an order for conditional release of an individual, the court shall designate a facility or a person to be responsible for supervision of the individual.

(b) As a condition of release, the court may (i) require the individual to report to any state or local mental-health facility for evaluation and treatment, (ii) require the individual to accept nonexperimental, generally accepted medical, psychiatric, or psychological treatment recommended by the facility, and (iii) impose other conditions reasonably necessary for protection of society.

(c) The person or the director of a facility responsible for supervision of an individual released shall furnish reports to the court, at intervals prescribed by the court, concerning the mental condition of the individual. Copies of reports submitted to the court must be furnished to the individual and to the prosecutor.

(d) If there is reasonable cause to believe that the individual released presents an imminent threat to cause bodily injury to another, the director of the facility or the person responsible for supervision of the individual pursuant to an order of conditional release may take the individual into custody, or request that the individual be taken into custody.

An individual taken into custody under this subsection must be accorded an emergency hearing before the court not later than the next court day to determine whether the individual should be retained in custody pending a further order pursuant to subsection (e).

(e) Upon application by an individual conditionally released, by the director of the facility or person responsible for supervision of the individual pursuant to an order of conditional release, or by the prosecutor, the court shall determine whether to continue, modify or terminate the order. The court shall consider and dispose of an application promptly. In a proceeding under this section, the applicant has the burden of proof by a preponderance of the evidence. The court shall enter an order in accordance with the following rules:

(1) If the court finds that the individual is not mentally ill or defective or that there is not a substantial risk that the individual will commit, as a result of mental illness or defect, a criminal act, it shall order that the individual be discharged from further constraint under this [Act].

(2) If the court finds that the individual is mentally ill or defective but that there is not a substantial risk that the individual will commit, as a result of mental illness or defect, a criminal act of violence threatening another individual with bodily injury or inflicting property damage, the court may modify the conditions of release as appropriate for the protection of society.

(3) If the court finds that the individual is mentally ill or defective and that there is a substantial risk that the individual will commit, as a result of mental illness or defect, a criminal act of violence threatening another individual with bodily injury or inflicting property damage and that the individual is no longer a proper subject for conditional release, the court shall order the individual committed to [a mental hospital or other suitable facility designated by the commissioner of mental health] for custody and treatment. If the court finds that the individual is mentally ill or defective and that there is a substantial risk that the individual will commit, as a result of mental

illness or defect, a nonviolent criminal act, the court may order the individual to report to any state or local mental-health facility for noncustodial evaluation and treatment and to accept nonexperimental, generally accepted medical, psychiatric, or psychological treatment recommended by the facility.

§ 907. Procedures Under Article

(a) An applicant for a court order under this Article shall deliver a copy of the application and any accompanying documents to the individual committed, the prosecutor, the [superintendent] of the [hospital or facility] to which the individual has been committed or the person or the director of a facility responsible for supervision of the individual conditionally released. The rules of civil procedure, adapted by the court to the circumstances of a post-verdict proceeding, apply to a proceeding under this Article.

(b) In a proceeding under this Article for an initial order of disposition, in a proceeding for modification or termination of an order of commitment to a [hospital or facility] initiated by the individual at the time of a review, or in a proceeding in which the status of the individual might be adversely affected, the individual has a right to counsel. If the court finds that the individual lacks sufficient financial resources to retain counsel and that counsel is not otherwise available, it shall appoint counsel to represent the individual.

(c) In a proceeding under this Article, the rules of evidence apply. If relevant evidence adduced in the criminal trial of the individual and information obtained by court-ordered examinations of the individual pursuant to Section 303 or 902 are admissible.

(d) A final order of the court is appealable to [the court of appeals].

ARTICLE X

GENERAL PROVISIONS

§ 1001. Short Title

This [Act] may be cited as the Uniform Law Commissioners' Model Insanity Defense and Post-Trial Disposition Act.

§ 1002. Severability

If any provision of this [Act] or its application to any person or circumstances is held invalid, the invalidity does not affect other provisions or applications of the [Act] which can be given effect without the invalid provision or application, and to this end the provisions of this [Act] are severable.

§ 1003. Repeal

The following acts and parts of acts are repealed:

  (1)

  (2)

  (3)

UNIFORM CRIMINAL–HISTORY RECORDS ACT

Historical Note

The Uniform Criminal History Records Act was approved by the National Conference of Commissioners on Uniform State Laws in 1986.

PREFATORY NOTE

The Uniform Criminal–History Records Act provides first for the collection in a single, statewide, centralized compilation of all criminal-history records in the state, recording all arrests and charges under the criminal law of the state and the subsequent history of the processing of those charges through final disposition or completion of sentence, and second, provides rules to govern the dissemination of those records from the central repository, to aid the police, other law enforcement agencies, and the courts, and to meet the justifiable public needs for information about an individual's past convictions of crime or his current involvement as a defendant in criminal proceedings.

The Act is a needed response to technological developments in information management and retrieval that have made feasible a comprehensive statewide system of criminal-history records. The potential contribution of such a system to efficient law enforcement has been widely recognized, often, however, through the establishment of hastily designed or makeshift arrangements. The Act provides for controls to regularize the process of compilation, to lay down clear lines of responsibility for reporting information to the central repository, to require prompt submission of reports, to verify the accuracy of the records, and to safeguard their physical security, since the utility of the system is directly dependent upon the correctness and completeness of the content of its records.

The principal purpose of centralized criminal-history records is to serve the needs of criminal law enforcement agencies, and the files are thus made available upon authorized request to police departments, prosecutors, correctional authorities, parole boards, and probation departments, for example, as well as to courts, to aid in sentencing or conditioning pre-trial release, and to the governor, for pardoning or clemency.

Exchanges of information with other states or the federal government are regulated and in general fostered by the Act. Consistency and uniformity in state laws can facilitate such interstate cooperation and contribute importantly to effective law enforcement in the nation as a whole.

The private sector may also have a legitimate interest in certain kinds of information about an individual's involvement in criminal proceedings. The Act therefore facilitates, for example, the screening of applicants for private employment in sensitive positions, by allowing any person, including a prospective employer as well as the press, a government agency, or any private citizen, to obtain certain information from the central files concerning a named subject clearly identified in the request. Under policies holding that public disgrace is an appropriate component of punishment for crime, past convictions are disclosable to the public. Pending prosecutions and recent nonconviction dispositions are also available from the central records for a period of one year after the latest reportable event in the processing of the arrest or charge, as matters of current events. Older nonconviction information is restricted to criminal law enforcement purposes.

The Act also undertakes to protect the interests of the individual subject by conferring a personal right to examine the subject's record as maintained, to demand correction of inaccurate information, and to be notified of disclosures of the records to members of the public. Civil and criminal sanctions are provided for specified violations of the protective provisions of the Act.

The purpose of the Act, as a whole, is to deal comprehensively with statewide criminal-history record systems, addressing the salient issues, and providing clear guides that take due account of the interests of law enforcement, the individual, and the public at large.

1986 ACT

§ 1. Definitions

Unless the context otherwise requires, as used in this [Act]:

(1) "Agency" means a political subdivision or combination of subdivisions, a department, institution, board, commission, district, council, bureau, office, officer, official, governing authority, or other instrumentality of state or local government, or a corporation or other establishment owned, operated, or managed by or on behalf of the state or any political subdivision, but the term does not include the [name of state legislature] or a court of this State.

(2) "Central repository" means the [office or department].

(3) "Criminal-history record" means a record of reportable events maintained by the central repository but the term does not include an intelligence or investigative record.

(4) "Criminal law enforcement agency" means an agency authorized by law, as one of its primary functions, to arrest, prosecute, incarcerate, parole, supervise, or rehabilitate criminal offenders, but the term does not include the [office of public defender].

(5) "Reportable event" means any of the following occurrences concerning an individual arrested for or charged with a criminal offense other than a petty offense or traffic violation excluded under Section 2(b)(4) or an offense adjudicated under the [juvenile court act]:

(i) an arrest;

(ii) a disposition after an arrest without the filing of a formal criminal charge;

(iii) the filing of a formal criminal charge;

(iv) the disposition of a formal criminal charge, including any sentence imposed, and a modification of the disposition or sentence;

(v) commitment after conviction to a place of detention;

(vi) release from punitive detention; or

(vii) completion of sentence.

(6) "Subject" means an individual who is the subject of a criminal-history record.

§ 2. Central Repository

(a) The central repository shall collect and maintain, as criminal-history records, the information required to be reported to it by this [Act].

The central repository may, but need not, retain information received concerning offenses under the laws of another jurisdiction.

(b) The [central repository], by rule or regulation, shall:

(1) specify the method and details of reporting each reportable event;

(2) designate the criminal law enforcement agency or court in this State that is responsible for reporting a reportable event to the central repository;

(3) specify the nature and form of the information to be used in identifying the individual who is the subject of a reportable event;

(4) specify the petty offenses and petty traffic violations that are excluded from the definition of a reportable event; and

(5) develop and promulgate procedures and formats for reporting and exchanging information under this [Act].

(6) establish a schedule of fees it may charge for disclosure under this [Act].

(c) The central repository shall specify and make public the items of information that it uses to retrieve criminal-history records.

(d) The [central repository] may adopt any other rules or regulations necessary to carry out the purposes of this [Act].

§ 3. Examinations

In order to ensure the timeliness and accuracy of information in criminal-history records and to evaluate the procedures and facilities relating to the privacy, disclosure, and security of criminal-history records, the [central repository] shall regularly examine the records and practices of the central repository and those of criminal law enforcement agencies. In order to ensure the timeliness and accuracy of the information, the central repository may examine the public records of the courts of this State required to report information to the central repository.

§ 4. Reporting

The court or criminal law enforcement agency responsible for reporting shall report a reportable event to the central repository promptly, but not later than:

(1) 48 hours after an arrest; or

(2) 30 days after any other reportable event.

§ 5.   Disclosure to Agency or Court

(a) The central repository shall disclose a criminal-history record and the record of disclosures maintained under subsection (d) and Section 6(d):

    (1) to a criminal law enforcement agency that requests the record for its functions as a criminal law enforcement agency or for use in hiring or retaining its employees;

    (2) to a court of this State, upon request, to aid in a decision concerning sentence, probation, or release pending trial or appeal;

    (3) to the Governor, upon request, to aid in a decision concerning an exercise of the power of pardon, reprieve, commutation or reduction of sentence, executive clemency, or interstate extradition or rendition;

    (4) pursuant to any judicial, legislative, or administrative agency subpoena issued in this State; and

    (5) as constitutionally required or as expressly required by any statute of this State or the United States.

(b) If the central repository discloses a criminal-history record that contains information concerning offenses under the laws of a jurisdiction other than this State, the information that is disclosed must contain a warning that the information may be inaccurate or incomplete.

(c) If a criminal-history record is disclosable under subsection (a) to an agency or court in this State:

    (1) the central repository shall disclose the record for the requested purpose to a like agency or court in another state if that state has enacted the Uniform Criminal–History Records Act containing equivalent limitations on disclosure; and

    (2) the central repository may disclose the record for the requested purpose to a like agency or court in any other state or of the federal government.

(d) The central repository shall maintain a record of all disclosures made under this section during the preceding three years, noting the identity of the requester and the subject and the date of disclosure.

§ 6.   General Disclosure

(a) Upon request by any person under subsection (b) and subject to subsection (c), the central repository shall disclose information in a criminal-history record that has not been sealed or expunged and concerns an offense under the laws of this State for which:

    (1) the subject has been convicted; or

    (2) a reportable event has occurred within one year preceding the request.

(b) A request for disclosure must contain the name of the requester and of the subject and:

    (1) the fingerprints of the subject;

    (2) the personal identification number assigned to the subject by the central repository; [or]

    (3) at least two other items of information that the central repository uses to retrieve criminal-history records, as specified under Section 2(c) [; or

    (4) a specific reportable event identified by date and either agency or court].

(c) If the identifying information supporting a request for disclosure matches the criminal-history record of more than one individual, the central repository may not disclose any of the records.

(d) The central repository shall maintain a record of all disclosures made under this section during the preceding three years, noting the identity of the requester and the subject and the date of disclosure.

§ 7.   Disclosure to Subject

Upon a request by a subject or the subject's attorney, accompanied by the fingerprints of the subject, the central repository shall disclose to the person designated by the requester the entire criminal-history record of the subject and the record of disclosures maintained under Section 6(d).

§ 8.   Procedures for Requests

(a) A requester may submit a request for disclosure under Section 6 or 7 directly to the central repository or indirectly through a [local police department or sheriff's office], which shall transmit the request to the central repository within three days.

(b) Promptly, but not later than [14] days after receiving a request for disclosure under Section 6 or 7, the central repository shall:

(1) transmit the available information, including an explanation of any code or abbreviation, to the person designated by the requester;

(2) inform the requester that there is no available information; or

(3) inform the requester of any deficiency in the request.

(c) If a request for disclosure under Section 6 is not accompanied by fingerprints or a personal identification number, the information that is disclosed must contain a warning that the record may not pertain to the individual named in the request.

(d) Within 24 hours after receipt of a subpoena under Section 5(a)(4), the central repository shall mail a copy of the subpoena to the subject at the subject's last known address.

(e) If information in a criminal-history record is disclosed under Section 6 at the request of a person other than the subject, the central repository shall notify the subject by mailing, within three days, a notice of the disclosure to the subject's last known address by a form of mail deliverable to the addressee only. The notice must contain the identity of the requester, the date of disclosure, a statement of the right of the subject to disclosure of the record and to correct or amend any incomplete or inaccurate information, and a statement of the sanctions for a violation of this [Act].

(f) The central repository may charge a requester a reasonable fee for processing a request for disclosure under Section 6, 7, or 9 and for notifying the subject under subsection (e).

§ 9. Limited Disclosure for Research or Statistical Purposes

(a) The central repository may disclose criminal-history-record information in a form that identifies a subject for the purpose of developing, studying, or reporting aggregate or anonymous information not intended to be published in any way in which the identity of the subject is disclosed, if the central repository:

(1) determines that the purpose cannot reasonably be accomplished without use of the information in that form; and

(2) secures from the recipient of the records a written agreement that the recipient will establish safeguards to assure the integrity, confidentiality, and security of the records.

(b) A recipient of records under this section may not use the records for purposes other than those specified in the agreement or disclose information in a form that identifies a subject without the express written authorization of the subject.

§ 10. Prohibited Disclosure

(a) Except as authorized under this [Act], the central repository may not disclose (i) criminal-history-record information in a form that identifies or can readily be associated with the identity of the subject, or (ii) the record of disclosures maintained under Section 5(d) or 6(d).

(b) The central repository may not disclose whether criminal-history-record information exists if disclosure of existing information is prohibited under subsection (a). If disclosure is prohibited or there is no information, the central repository shall answer: "No information is available because either no information exists or disclosure is prohibited."

(c) A criminal law enforcement agency receiving a criminal-history record under Section 5(a)(1) or from a central repository in another jurisdiction may disclose the information in the record only for the limited purpose for which its receipt was authorized, but may disclose the information in compliance with a subpoena or to another criminal law enforcement agency for its functions as a criminal law enforcement agency.

§ 11. Correction of Records

(a) A subject may request in writing that the central repository correct or amend any incomplete or inaccurate information in the criminal-history record.

(b) Promptly, but not later than [14] days after receiving the request, the central repository shall:

(1) make the requested correction or amendment and inform the subject of the action; or

(2) inform the subject, in writing, of its refusal to correct or amend the information, of the reason for the refusal, and of the subject's right to [administrative review under [the administrative procedure act] and to] maintain an action pursuant to Section 13.

§ 12. Security

A criminal law enforcement agency and the central repository shall ensure that:

(1) direct access to criminal-history records is available only to authorized officers or employees;

(2) each officer or employee working with or having access to criminal-history records is familiar with the requirements of this [Act]; and

(3) criminal-history records are physically secure.

§ 13.　Sanctions and Remedies

(a) For a violation of Section 5, 6, 7, 8, or 11, the requester or subject may maintain an action to compel the central repository to disclose, correct, or amend information in a criminal-history record. The court may examine the information at issue in camera.

(b) For disclosure in violation of Section 9 or 10, the subject may maintain an action for appropriate relief against the central repository, criminal law enforcement agency, or the recipient of information under Section 9 and recover compensatory damages sustained as a result of the violation [, but not less than $1,000,] and reasonable attorney's fees. This subsection does not affect any other right or remedy under law.

(c) An officer or employee of the central repository, of a criminal law enforcement agency, or of a court, or an individual who receives information under Section 9, is guilty of a [misdemeanor] if the individual intentionally:

(1) discloses information in a criminal-history record in violation of this [Act] with knowledge that the disclosure is prohibited;

(2) reports an event as a reportable event or intentionally discloses information in a criminal-history record, with knowledge that the report or information has been falsified; or

(3) fails to report a reportable event or intentionally fails to disclose, correct, or amend information in a criminal-history record, for the purpose of causing harm to the subject and with knowledge that the report, disclosure, correction, or amendment is required.

(d) A person who, by conduct that would constitute the offense of [false pretenses or theft] if property were involved, gains access to a criminal-history record the disclosure of which is prohibited to that person is guilty of a [misdemeanor].

§ 14.　Application and Construction

This [Act] shall be applied and construed to effectuate its general purpose to make uniform the law with respect to the subject of this [Act] among States enacting it.

§ 15.　Short Title

This [Act] may be cited as the Uniform Criminal–History Records Act.

§ 16.　Severability

If any provision of this [Act] or its application to any person or circumstance is held invalid, the invalidity does not affect other provisions or applications of this [Act] which can be given effect without the invalid provision or application, and to this end the provisions of this [Act] are severable.

§ 17.　Time of Taking Effect

This [Act] takes effect _____

§ 18.　Repeal

The following acts and parts of acts are repealed:

(1)

(2)

(3)

UNIFORM MANDATORY DISPOSITION OF DETAINERS ACT

Table of Jurisdiction Wherein Act Has Been Adopted

Jurisdiction	Laws	Effective Date	Statutory Citation
Alabama	1978, No. 590	4–27–1978	Code 1975, §§ 15–9–80 to 15–9–88.
Arizona			17 A.R.S. Rules of Crim.Proc., rule 8.3(b).
Colorado	1969, p. 291	10–1–1969	C.R.S. 16–14–101 to 16–14–108.
Kansas	1970, c. 129	7–1–1970	K.S.A. 22–4301 to 22–4308.
Minnesota	1967, c. 294	5–4–1967	M.S.A. § 629.292.
Missouri	1959, H.B. 259	7–1–1971	V.A.M.S. §§ 217.450 to 217.485.
North Dakota	1971, c. 321		NDCC 29–33–01 to 29–33–08.
Utah	1965, c. 157		U.C.A.1953, §§ 77–29–1 to 77–29–4.

Historical Note

The Uniform Mandatory Disposition of Detainers Act was approved by the National Conference of Commissioners on Uniform State Laws, and the American Bar Association, in 1958.

Commissioners' Prefatory Note

At the instance of the Parole and Probation Compact Administrators' Association, a "Joint Committee on Detainers," was organized with representation from that body, the National Association of Attorneys General, the Section on Criminal Law of the American Bar Association, the National Conference of Commissioners on Uniform State Laws, and the American Correctional Association. The report of that Joint Committee set forth the problems inherent in detainers (i.e., warrants filed against persons already in custody) and recommended a set of guiding principles to govern public officials but did not approach the problem by drafting suggested legislation. Later, on the recommendation of the New York Joint Legislative Committee on Interstate Cooperation, the Council of State Governments undertook to revive the machinery of the old Joint Committee to re-examine the problem. In addition to the members of the old Committee, other organizations were asked to attend meetings and help formulate legislation, respecting (1) authority to parole to a detainer, (2) merger of sentence, (3) mandatory disposition of detainers within a state, and (4) an interstate compact or agreement to authorize mandatory disposition of detainers which are interstate in nature, with participation by the Federal government.

This Committee met three times and numerous suggestions were made from time to time to improve the preliminary drafts. Our Conference was represented on at least one of the drafting sessions. While the entire field of suggested legislation is of importance to the states, and may sometime become an appropriate subject for development by the Conference, we are now concerned only with the mandatory disposition of detainers. California has devised a method of obtaining prompt disposition of detainers by providing that prosecuting officials, upon the request of the prisoner, must move forward with trial of the charge which caused the detainer. Failing to do so within a reasonable time automatically brings about a dismissal of such charge and withdrawal of the detainer. This procedure is available to the prisoner both with regard to detainers lodged at the time imprisonment commences or during the continuance of the term of imprisonment. In other words, a sort of "statute of limitations" is applied to detainers to the end that valid charges will be ripened into trials whereas detainers merely lodged on suspicion or less will be dismissed. Competent authorities estimate that as many as 50% of warrants now lodged against prisoners are never intended to be prosecuted.

Interstate Agreement on Detainers

The following jurisdictions have enacted into law an agreement on detainers in substantially the form set forth in the following reprint of the New York statute.

Alabama (Code 1975, § 15–9–81)

Alaska (AS 33.35.010 to 33.35.040)

Arizona (A.R.S. §§ 31–481, 31–482)

Arkansas (Code 1987, §§ 16–95–101 to 16–95–107)

California (West's Ann.Cal.Penal Code §§ 1389 to 1389.8)

Colorado (C.R.S. 24–60–501 to 24–60–507)

Connecticut (C.G.S.A. §§ 54–186 to 54–192)

Delaware (11 Del.C. §§ 2540 to 2550)

District of Columbia (D.C.Code 1981, §§ 24–701 to 24–705)

Florida (West's F.S.A. §§ 941.45 to 941.50)

Georgia (O.C.G.A. §§ 42–6–20 to 42–6–25)

Hawaii (HRS §§ 834–1 to 834–6)

Idaho (I.C. §§ 19–5001 to 19–5008)

Illinois (S.H.A. ch. 38, ¶ 1003–8–9)

Indiana (West's A.I.C. 35–33–10–4)

Iowa (I.C.A. §§ 821.1 to 821.8)

Kansas (K.S.A. 22–4401 to 22–4408)

Kentucky (KRS 440.450 to 440.510)

Maine (34–A M.R.S.A. §§ 9601 to 9609)

Maryland (Code 1957, art. 27, §§ 616A to 616S)

Massachusetts (M.G.L.A. c. 276 App., §§ 1–1 to 1–8)

Michigan (M.C.L.A. §§ 780.601 to 780.608)

Minnesota (M.S.A. § 629.294)

Missouri (V.A.M.S. §§ 217.490 to 217.520)

Montana (MCA 46–31–101 to 46–31–204)

Nebraska (R.R.S.1943, §§ 29–759 to 29–765)

Nevada (N.R.S. 178.620 to 178.640)

New Hampshire (R.S.A. 606–A:1 to 606–A:6)

New Jersey (N.J.S.A. 2A:159A–1 to 2A:159A–15)

New Mexico (NMSA 1978, § 31–5–12)

New York (McKinney's CPL § 580.20)

North Carolina (G.S. §§ 15A–761 to 15A–767)

North Dakota (NDCC 29–34–01 to 29–34–08)

Ohio (R.C. §§ 2963.30 to 2963.35)

Oklahoma (22 Okl.St.Ann. §§ 1345 to 1349)

Oregon (ORS 135.775 to 135.793)

Pennsylvania (42 Pa.C.S.A. §§ 9101 to 9108)

Rhode Island (Gen.Laws 1956, §§ 13–13–1 to 13–13–8)

South Carolina (Code 1976, §§ 17–11–10 to 17–11–80)

South Dakota (SDCL 23–24A–1 to 23–24A–34)

Tennessee (T.C.A. §§ 40–31–101 to 40–31–108)

Texas (Vernon's Ann.Texas C.C.P. art. 51.14)

Utah (U.C.A.1953, 77–29–5 to 77–29–11)

Vermont, (28 V.S.A. §§ 1501 to 1509, 1531 to 1537)

Virginia (Code 1950, §§ 53.1–210 to 53.1–215)

Washington (West's RCWA 9.100.010 to 9.100.080)

West Virginia (Code, 62–14–1 to 62–14–7)

Wisconsin (W.S.A. 976.05, 976.06)

Wyoming (W.S.1977, §§ 7–15–101 to 7–15–107)

United States (18 U.S.C.A.App.)

"TEXT OF THE AGREEMENT ON DETAINERS

The contracting states solemnly agree that:

"ARTICLE I

"The party states find that charges outstanding against a prisoner, detainers based on untried indictments, informations or complaints, and difficulties in securing speedy trial of persons already incarcerated in other jurisdictions, produce uncertainties which obstruct programs of prisoner treatment and rehabilitation. Accordingly, it is the policy of the party states and the purpose of this agreement to encourage the expeditious and orderly disposition of such charges and determination of the proper status of any and all detainers based on untried indictments, informations or complaints. The party states also find that proceedings with reference to such charges and detainers, when emanating from another jurisdiction, cannot properly be had in the absence of cooperative procedures. It is the further purpose of this agreement to provide such cooperative procedures.

"ARTICLE II

"As used in this agreement:

"(a) 'State' shall mean a state of the United States; the United States of America; a territory or possession of the United States; the District of Columbia; the Commonwealth of Puerto Rico.

"(b) 'Sending state' shall mean a state in which a prisoner is incarcerated at the time that he initiates a request for final disposition pursuant to Article III hereof or at the time that a request for custody or availability is initiated pursuant to Article IV hereof.

"(c) 'Receiving state' shall mean the state in which trial is to be had on an indictment, information or complaint pursuant to Article III or Article IV hereof.

"ARTICLE III

"(a) Whenever a person has entered upon a term of imprisonment in a penal or correctional institution of a party state, and whenever during the continuance of the term of imprisonment there is pending in any other party state any untried indictment, information or complaint on the basis of which a detainer has been lodged against the prisoner, he shall be brought to trial within one hundred eighty days after he shall have caused to be delivered to the prosecuting officer and the appropriate court of the prosecuting officer's jurisdiction written notice of the place of his imprisonment and his request for a final disposition to be made of the indictment, information or complaint; provided that for good cause shown in open court, the prisoner or his counsel being present, the court having jurisdiction of the matter may grant any necessary or reasonable continuance. The request of the prisoner shall be accompanied by a certificate of the appropriate official having custody of the prisoner, stating the term of commitment under which the prisoner is being held, the time already served, the time remaining to be served on the sentence, the amount of good time earned, the time of parole eligibility of the prisoner, and any decisions of the state parole agency relating to the prisoner.

"(b) The written notice and request for final disposition referred to in paragraph (a) hereof shall be given or sent by the prisoner to the warden, commissioner of correction or other official having custody of him, who shall promptly forward it together with the certificate to the appropriate prosecuting official and court by registered or certified mail, return receipt requested.

"(c) The warden, commissioner of correction or other official having custody of the prisoner shall promptly inform him of the source and contents of any detainer lodged against him and shall also inform him of his right to make a request for final disposition of the indictment, information or complaint on which the detainer is based.

"(d) Any request for final disposition made by a prisoner pursuant to paragraph (a) hereof shall operate as a request for final disposition of all untried indictments, informations or complaints on the basis of which detainers have been lodged against the prisoner from the state to whose prosecuting official the request for final disposition is specifically directed. The warden, commissioner of correction or other official having custody of the prisoner shall forthwith notify all appropriate prosecuting officers and courts in the several jurisdictions within the state to which the prisoner's request for final disposition is being sent of the proceeding being initiated by the prisoner. Any notification sent pursuant to this paragraph shall be accompanied by copies of the prisoner's written notice, request, and the certificate. If trial is not had on any indictment, information or complaint contemplated hereby prior to the return of the prisoner to the original place of imprisonment, such indictment, information or complaint shall not be of any further force or effect, and the court shall enter an order dismissing the same with prejudice.

"(e) Any request for final disposition made by a prisoner pursuant to paragraph (a) hereof shall also be deemed to be a waiver of extradition with respect to any charge or proceeding contemplated thereby or included therein by reason of paragraph (d) hereof, and a waiver of extradition to the receiving state to serve any sentence there imposed upon him, after completion of his term of imprisonment in the sending state. The request for final disposition shall also constitute a consent by the prisoner to the production of his body in any court where his presence may be required in order to effectuate the purposes of this agreement and a further consent voluntarily to be returned to the original place of imprisonment in accordance with the provisions of this agreement. Nothing in this paragraph shall prevent the imposition of a concurrent sentence if otherwise permitted by law.

"(f) Escape from custody by the prisoner subsequent to his execution of the request for final disposition referred to in paragraph (a) hereof shall void the request.

"(a) The appropriate officer of the jurisdiction in which an untried indictment, information or complaint is pending shall be entitled to have a prisoner against whom he has lodged a detainer and who is serving a term of imprisonment in any party state made available in accordance with Article V(a) hereof upon presentation of a written request for temporary custody or availability to the appropriate authorities of the state in which the prisoner is incarcerated; provided that the court having jurisdiction of such indictment, information or complaint shall have duly approved, recorded and transmitted the request; and provided further that there shall be a period of thirty days after receipt by the appropriate authorities before the request be honored, within which period the governor of the sending state may disapprove the request for temporary custody or availability, either upon his own motion or upon motion of the prisoner.

"(b) Upon receipt of the officer's written request as provided in paragraph (a) hereof, the appropriate authorities having the prisoner in custody shall furnish the officer with a certificate stating the term of commitment under which the prisoner is being held, the time already served, the time remaining to be served on the sentence, the amount of good time earned, the time of parole eligibility of the prisoner, and any decisions of the state parole agency relating to the prisoner. Said authorities simultaneously shall furnish all other officers and appropriate courts in the receiving state who have lodged detainers against the prisoner with similar certificates and with notices informing them of the request for custody or availability and of the reasons therefor.

"(c) In respect of any proceeding made possible by this Article, trial shall be commenced within one hundred twenty days of the arrival of the prisoner in the receiving state, but for good cause shown in open court, the prisoner or his counsel being present, the court having jurisdiction of the matter may grant any necessary or reasonable continuance.

"(d) Nothing contained in this Article shall be construed to deprive any prisoner of any right which he may have to contest the legality of his delivery as provided in paragraph (a) hereof but such delivery may not be opposed or denied on the ground that the executive authority of the sending state has not affirmatively consented to or ordered such delivery.

"(e) If trial is not had on any indictment, information or complaint contemplated hereby prior to the prisoner's being returned to the original place of imprisonment pursuant to Article V(e) hereof, such indictment, information or complaint shall not be of any further force or effect, and the court shall enter an order dismissing the same with prejudice.

"ARTICLE V

"(a) In response to a request made under Article III or Article IV hereof, the appropriate authority in a sending state shall offer to deliver temporary custody of such prisoner to the appropriate authority in the state where such indictment, information or complaint is pending against such person in order that speedy and efficient prosecution may be had. If the request for final disposition is made by the prisoner, the offer of temporary custody shall accompany the written notice provided for in Article III of this agreement. In the case of a federal prisoner, the appropriate authority in receiving state shall be entitled to temporary custody as provided by this agreement or to the prisoner's presence in federal custody at the place for trial, whichever custodial arrangement may be approved by the custodian.

"(b) The officer or other representative of a state accepting an offer of temporary custody shall present the following upon demand:

"(1) Proper identification and evidence of his authority to act for the state into whose temporary custody the prisoner is to be given.

"(2) A duly certified copy of the indictment, information or complaint on the basis of which the detainer has been lodged and on the basis of which the request for temporary custody of the prisoner has been made.

"(c) If the appropriate authority shall refuse or fail to accept temporary custody of said person, or in the event that an action on the indictment, information or complaint on the basis of which the detainer has been lodged is not brought to trial within the period provided in Article III or Article IV hereof, the appropriate court of the jurisdiction where the indictment, information or complaint has been pending shall enter an order dismissing the same with prejudice, and any detainer based thereon shall cease to be of any force or effect.

"(d) The temporary custody referred to in this agreement shall be only for the purpose of permitting prosecution on the charge or charges contained in one or more untried indictments, informations or complaints which form the basis of the detainer or detainers or for prosecution on any other charge or charges arising out of the same transaction. Except for his attendance at court and while being transported to or from any place at which his presence may be required, the prisoner shall be held in a suitable jail or other facility regularly used for persons awaiting prosecution.

"(e) At the earliest practicable time consonant with the purposes of this agreement, the prisoner shall be returned to the sending state.

"(f) During the continuance of temporary custody or while the prisoner is otherwise being made available for trial as required by this agreement, time being served on the sentence shall continue to run but good time shall be earned by the prisoner only if, and to the extent that, the law and practice of the jurisdiction which imposed the sentence may allow.

"(g) For all purposes other than that for which temporary custody as provided in this agreement is exercised, the prisoner shall be deemed to remain in the custody of and subject to the jurisdiction of the sending state and any escape from temporary custody may be dealt with in the same manner as an escape from the original place of imprisonment or in any other manner permitted by law.

"(h) From the time that a party state receives custody of a prisoner pursuant to this agreement until such prisoner is returned to the territory and custody of the sending state, the state in which the one or more untried indictments, informations or complaints are pending or in which trial is being had shall be responsible for the prisoner and shall also pay all costs of transporting, caring for, keeping and returning the prisoner. The provisions of this paragraph shall govern unless the states concerned shall have entered into a supplementary agreement providing for a different allocation of costs and responsibilities as between or among themselves. Nothing herein contained shall be construed to alter or affect any internal relationship among the departments, agencies and officers of and in the government of a party state, or between a party state and its subdivisions, as to the payment of costs, or responsibilities therefor.

"ARTICLE VI

"(a) In determining the duration and expiration dates of the time periods provided in Articles III and IV of this agreement, the running of said time periods shall be tolled whenever and for as long as the prisoner is unable to stand trial, as determined by the court having jurisdiction of the matter.

"(b) No provision of this agreement, and no remedy made available by this agreement, shall apply to any person who is adjudged to be mentally ill.

"ARTICLE VII

"Each state party to this agreement shall designate an officer who, acting jointly with like officers of other party states, shall promulgate rules and regulations to carry out more effectively the terms and provisions of this agreement, and who shall provide, within and without the state, information necessary to the effective operation of this agreement.

"ARTICLE VIII

"This agreement shall enter into full force and effect as to a party state when such state has enacted the same into law. A state party to this agreement may withdraw herefrom by enacting a statute repealing the same. However, the withdrawal of any state shall not affect the status of any proceedings already initiated by inmates or by state officers at the time such withdrawal takes effect, nor shall it affect their rights in respect thereof.

"ARTICLE IX

"1. This agreement shall be liberally construed so as to effectuate its purposes. The provisions of this agreement shall be severable and if any phrase, clause, sentence or provision of this agreement is declared to be contrary to the constitution of any party state or of the United States or the applicability thereof to any government, agency, person or circumstance is held invalid, the validity of the remainder of this agreement and the applicability thereof to any government, agency, person or circumstance shall not be affected thereby. If this agreement shall be held contrary to the constitution of any state party hereto, the agreement shall remain in full force and effect as to the remaining states and in full force and effect as to the state affected as to all severable matters.

"2. The phrase 'appropriate court' as used in the agreement on detainers shall, with reference to the courts of this state, mean any court with criminal jurisdiction.

"3. All courts, departments, agencies, officers and employees of this state and its political subdivisions are hereby directed to enforce the agreement on detainers and to cooperate with one another and with other party states in enforcing the agreement and effectuating its purposes.

"4. Escape from custody while in another state pursuant to the agreement on detainers shall constitute an offense against the laws of this state to the same extent and degree as an escape from the institution in which the prisoner was confined immediately prior to having been sent to another state pursuant to the provisions of the agreement on detainers and shall be punishable in the same manner as an escape from said institution.

"5. It shall be lawful and mandatory upon the warden or other official in charge of a penal or correctional institution in this state to give over the person of any inmate thereof whenever so required by the operation of the agreement on detainers.

"6. The governor is hereby authorized and empowered to designate an administrator who shall perform the duties and functions and exercise the powers conferred upon such person by Article VII of the agreement on detainers.

"7. In order to implement Article IV(a) of the agreement on detainers, and in furtherance of its purposes, the appropriate authorities having custody of the prisoner shall, promptly upon receipt of the officer's written request, notify the prisoner and the governor in writing that a request for temporary custody has been made and such notification shall describe the source and contents of said request. The authorities having custody of the prisoner shall also advise him in writing of his rights to counsel, to make representations to the governor within thirty days, and to contest the legality of his delivery."

Table of Sections

Section

Note: Section headings have been editorially supplied.

Be it enacted ....

---

§ 1. Request for Disposition of Untried Charges; Notification to Prisoner of Charges; Effect of Failure to Notify

(a) Any person who is imprisoned in a penal or correctional institution of this state may request final disposition of any untried [indictment, information or complaint] pending against him in this state. The request shall be in writing addressed to the court in which the [indictment, information or complaint] is pending and to the [prosecuting official] charged with the duty of prosecuting it, and shall set forth the place of imprisonment.

(b) The [warden, commissioner of corrections or other official] having custody of prisoners shall promptly inform each prisoner in writing of the source and nature of any untried [indictment, information or complaint] against him of which the [warden, commissioner of corrections or other official] had knowledge [or notice] and of his right to make a request for final disposition thereof.

(c) Failure of the [warden, commissioner of corrections or other official] to inform a prisoner, as required by this section, within one year after a detainer has been filed at the institution shall entitle him to a final dismissal of the [indictment, information or complaint] with prejudice.

§ 2. Procedure on Receipt of Request

The request shall be delivered to the [warden, commissioner of corrections or other officials] having custody of the prisoner, who shall forthwith

(1) certify the term of commitment under which the prisoner is being held, the time already served on the sentence, the time remaining to be served, the good time earned, the time of parole eligibility of the prisoner, and any decisions of the [state parole agency] relating to the prisoner; and

(2) send by registered or certified mail, return receipt requested, one copy of the request [and certificate] to the court and one copy to the [prosecuting official] to whom it is addressed.

§ 3. Period Within Which Trial Must Be Brought

Within [ninety days] after the receipt of the request and certificate by the court and [prosecuting official] or within such additional time as the court for good cause shown in open court may grant, the prisoner or his counsel being present, the [indictment, information or complaint] shall be brought to trial; but the parties may stipulate for a continuance or a continuance may be granted on notice to the attorney of record and opportunity for him to be heard. If, after such a request, the [indictment, information or complaint] is not brought to trial within that period, no court of this state shall any longer have jurisdiction thereof, nor shall the untried [indictment, information or complaint] be of any further force or effect, and the court shall dismiss it with prejudice.

§ 4. Avoidance of Request on Escape of Prisoner

Escape from custody by any prisoner subsequent to his execution of a request for final disposition of an untried [indictment, information or complaint] voids the request.

§ 5. Mentally Ill Persons

This Act does not apply to any person adjudged to be mentally ill [or a defective delinquent].

§ 6. Informing Prisoners of Available Procedure

The [warden, commissioner of corrections or other official] having custody of prisoners shall arrange for all prisoners to be informed in writing of the provisions of this Act, and for a record thereof to be placed in the prisoner's file.

§ 7. Uniformity of Interpretation

This Act shall be so construed as to effectuate its general purpose to make uniform the law of those states which enact it.

§ 8. Short Title

This Act may be cited as the Uniform Mandatory Disposition of Detainers Act.

§ 9. Repeal

The following acts and parts of acts are hereby repealed:

(a)

(b)

(c)

§ 10. Time of Taking Effect

This Act shall take effect _____.

UNIFORM LAW COMMISSIONERS' MODEL SENTENCING AND CORRECTIONS ACT

Editor's Note: The Model Sentencing and Corrections Act was approved by the National Conference of Commissioners on Uniform State Laws in 1978. This Act is limited to the sentencing and correction of persons convicted of crimes but does not cover juvenile court proceedings.

Table of Sections

SENTENCING AND CORRECTIONS

ARTICLE 5. VICTIMS
PART 1. VICTIMS ASSISTANCE SERVICE PROGRAM

PART 2. [RESERVED FOR THE CRIME VICTIMS REPARATIONS ACT]
ARTICLE 6. TRANSITION AND APPLICATION
PART 1. TRANSITION

PART 2. APPLICATION

PREFATORY NOTE

In 1974 the National Conference of Commissioners of Uniform State Laws adopted and published its proposed Uniform Rules of Criminal Procedure. Drafted with the assistance of a grant from the Law Enforcement Assistance Administration, the Uniform Rules established the procedure governing the criminal justice system from prior to arrest to sentencing. In a few instances, rules regulating the process of sentencing were also included, but the basis for sentencing criminal offenders and the nature of correctional programs were not addressed. In 1973, a committee of the National Conference was formed to examine the possibility of carrying forward through the sentencing and correctional phases the work begun with the Uniform Rules. In 1974 LEAA provided the necessary funds for that project to proceed. This Act along with the Uniform Rules provides a basic structure for the operation of a criminal justice system. The Model Sentencing and Corrections Act is limited to the sentencing and correction of persons convicted of crimes. Juvenile court cases are not governed by this Act.

The project began at a propitious time. A year earlier the National Advisory Commission on Criminal Justice Standards and Goals had published its report on Corrections offering a wide-ranging set of recommendations for reform. Among them was the call for wholesale reform of the correctional laws of the fifty states. The drafting committee for the Model Sentencing and Corrections Act relied heavily on the pioneering work of the National Commission.

The fundamental bases for sentencing criminal offenders were also undergoing a major reexamination.

The traditional approach to sentencing, adopted by the National Commission and earlier by the American Bar Association in its Criminal Justice Standards, consisted of a system of judicial sentencing designed to tailor the sentence in each particular case to the needs of the offender and of society. Although there were recommendations to reduce or to structure the discretion of the sentencing court, the system proposed in those reports remained heavily discretionary. Parole also was a critical element of the envisioned system, although here again recommendations were offered to structure the discretion of paroling authorities.

As the drafting committee began its work, a series of proposals from a variety of different study groups began to suggest an abandonment of traditional practice. The universal feature of these proposals was the recognition that individualized sentencing had failed and should be replaced by a system that provides a higher degree of equal treatment. The indeterminate sentence with parole was to be replaced by a flat, determinate sentence. The discretion to select a particular sentence was to be severely restricted, either by legislative mandate or by other devices. Sentences were no longer to reflect the rehabilitative potential of the defendant but rather were to insure a punishment justly deserved for the offense committed. The National Conference built upon these proposals and Article 3 of this Act reflects, in part, their philosophy.

In the late 1960's the courts abandoned what had become known as the "hands off" doctrine under which courts refused to intervene to review the decisions of correctional administrators or the conditions of correctional programs. Instead, courts began to measure correctional practices against constitutional principles and in many instances the existing practices fell short.

Since these early beginnings nearly every aspect of correctional programs has been evaluated by courts. In some cases, dramatic change was ordered. It became clear, on the other hand, that dramatic change would not come easily through judicial decrees. Oftentimes, lack of funds prevented prisons from meeting minimum standards even where those in charge of the institution desired to make change. In a few cases federal courts actually took over the operation of a prison in order to correct unconstitutional conditions and practices.

There is general agreement that the rule of law must be applied to the correctional elements of the criminal justice system. There remains, however, disagreement as to how that is to be accomplished. The National Advisory Commission recognized the gains to be derived from a legislative codification of the rights of persons subject to correctional authority:

Legislatures should respond with a comprehensive statement of the rights lost by confinement and procedures designed to implement and enforce retained rights. Otherwise, the courts will continue the slow, painful, and expensive process of accomplishing this task through case-by-case litigation. The inevitable period of uncertainty, of abrupt change, and of allocation of valuable and scarce correctional resources to litigation can be minimized by carefully conceived legislation.

National Advisory Commission on Criminal Justice Standards and Goals, Corrections at 558 (1973) [hereinafter cited as Nat'l Advisory Comm'n]. The Model Sentencing and Corrections Act responds to these concerns and proposes detailed legislative direction for the treatment of offenders.

The National Advisory Commission also examined and evaluated existing legislative proposals relating to sentencing and corrections. Nat'l Advisory Comm'n, Corrections at 549. Most of the then available proposed codifications were developed before the courts had begun to impose constitutional standards on correctional programs. Other proposed legislation addressed relatively specific problems and did not provide a comprehensive or coordinated statutory framework for correctional reform. Although many of these earlier proposals including the American Law Institute's Model Penal Code and the Study Draft of a New Federal Criminal Code provided a starting point for committee deliberation, this Model Act goes far beyond earlier attempts to define statutorily the treatment of offenders. And the sentencing provisions of this Model Act are based on different premises than these earlier proposals.

Several major themes distinguish the Model Sentencing and Corrections Act:

—The Act unifies the various elements of the correctional system into one department of corrections in order to coordinate the deployment of scarce correctional resources and to make correctional programs consistent and effective.

—The Act implements the legislative responsibility for determining basic correctional purposes and policies and, in several sections, legislatively established criteria and goals for decision-making are announced.

—The Act seeks to reduce the unfairness and ineffectiveness occasioned by sentencing disparity. Rehabilitation is eliminated as a goal of sentencing. Sentences, based on the punishment deserved for the offense, are determined by courts in accordance with statutory and administrative guidelines. Appellate review of sentences is authorized. Parole is abolished.

—Although rehabilitation will no longer be a factor in determining sentences, within the sentence imposed the Act seeks to enhance the rehabilitative potential of correctional environments by authorizing a wide variety of programs and giving offenders a greater voice in, and accordingly a greater incentive for, their own self-improvement.

—The Act also seeks to recognize the interests of victims in the sentencing and correctional process.

—Most importantly, the Act strives to bring justice and the rule of law to the correctional process. Traditional mechanisms used to structure and limit governmental discretion in the free society are applied to sentencing and corrections. The fundamental rights of confined persons are defined and protected in an attempt to enhance individual liberty unless compelling justification exists for its restriction.

The Act is divided into six Articles. Article 1 contains general provisions including definitions and rule-making procedures. Article 2 establishes the organization of the Department of Corrections. The Article has avoided inflexible organizational provisions in favor of enacting general organizational structures and providing authority for the administrative creation of a more detailed organization. Article 3 deals with sentencing. The Article establishes the fundamental policies behind sentencing criminal defendants and the procedures for doing so. In addition, each sentencing alternative, from community supervision to continuous confinement, to fines and restitution are more fully implemented. Article 4 contains provisions directly related to the treatment of sentenced persons. The Article articulates the protected interests of confined persons as well as requiring the establishment of grievance procedures. Activities within correctional agencies which directly impact on persons in the custody of the department are carefully circumscribed. Article 5 establishes a program for assisting the victims of criminal offenses. Article 6 provides for the effective date of the Act and governs the transition from prior law to the provisions of the Act.

Many if not all of the provisions of this Act are fraught with controversy. The Committee is indebted to the wide-range of individuals and organizations that have contributed their suggestions and criticism throughout the drafting process. In many instances the Act confronts and seeks to alter long-standing traditions in both sentencing and corrections. The presence and patience of many individuals insured that the provisions of the Act were not casually adopted but are the result of extensive and, at times, intense debate.

The Committee is grateful to the LEAA's National Institute of Law Enforcement and Criminal Justice for the grants which have made the Committee's and Staff's work possible.

ARTICLE 1

GENERAL PROVISIONS

§ 1–101. [Definitions.]

As used in this Act, unless the context otherwise requires:

(1) "chief executive officer" means a warden, superintendent, or other administrative head of a facility or program;

(2) "confined person" means a person confined in a facility for any purpose;

(3) "correctional mediator" means the correctional mediator created by Part 2 of Article 4;

(4) "department" means the department of corrections;

(5) "director" means the director of corrections;

(6) "facility" means a prison, reformatory, jail, training school, reception center, community-corrections center, half-way house, or other residential institution, and surrounding grounds, administered by the department for persons in its custody, but does not include a short-term holding facility maintained and administered by a political subdivision of the State;

(7) "furlough" means an authorized leave of absence from a facility for a designated purpose and period of time;

(8) "offender" means a person sentenced for an offense, who has not been discharged;

(9) "person in the custody of the department" includes a confined person and a person supervised in the community;

(10) "person supervised in the community" means a person authorized to reside in the community subject to the supervision of the department;

(11) "pretrial detainee" means a person accused of an offense and detained before the imposition of a sentence;

(12) "pretrial detention facility" means a facility or part of a facility used for the care and custody of pretrial detainees; and

(13) "sentencing commission" means the sentencing commission created by Part 1 of Article 3.

§ 1–102. [Scope of Act.]

This Act governs the sentencing, care, custody, and treatment of persons accused of or sentenced for a violation of the criminal laws of this State or otherwise held in the custody of the department. This Act does not apply to:

(1) juveniles processed by a [juvenile, family court] except to the extent they are pretrial detainees in a pretrial detention facility; or

(2) programs, services, or facilities administered by the department exclusively for juveniles committed to its custody by a [juvenile, family court].

§ 1–103. [Adoption of Rules; Procedures.]

(a) For purposes of this Act, "rule" means the whole or part of a statement of general applicability and future effect designed to implement, interpret, or prescribe law or policy or describe the organization, procedure, or practice requirements of an agency.

(b) Whenever the director adopts a measure, other than a rule, which is binding on persons in the custody of the department, he shall publish the measure in a manner reasonably calculated to give notice of its contents to those persons likely to be affected by it.

(c) Whenever this Act specifically requires the director to implement a section of this Act by adoption of rules or whenever the director specifically designates a measure as a rule, the director shall, before adoption, amendment, or repeal:

(1) give at least 10 days' notice of his intended action to persons in the custody of the department and likely to be affected. The notice shall contain the time, the place, and the manner in which affected persons may present

their views. The director shall give actual notice to persons likely to be affected or,

(i) if the action is likely to affect confined persons, post notice in facilities in a location readily accessible to confined persons and generally used for distributing information to them; and

(ii) if the action is likely to affect persons supervised in the community, mail or otherwise distribute written notice to 10 percent or 100 persons, whichever is less, of the supervised persons likely to be affected;

(2) afford interested persons reasonable opportunity to submit data, views, or arguments in writing relating to the director's intended action. The director also shall set aside a reasonable time period for receiving oral testimony from interested persons. The director may designate a hearing officer to receive and summarize oral testimony for consideration by the director. The director or the hearing officer shall seek to hear a variety of representative views and may refuse oral testimony that is repetitive or irrelevant; and

(3) consider fully all submissions and, if the proposed action is taken, issue a concise statement of the principal reasons for taking the proposed action, incorporating therein the reasons for rejecting contrary views.

(d) If the director finds that an imminent peril to the health, safety, or welfare of any person requires action without compliance with subsection (c), he may proceed without prior notice or hearing. The action may be effective for a period of not more than 30 days, renewable once for an additional 30–day period.

(e) All rules and regulations in force on the effective date of this Act remain effective for 6 months unless readopted, amended, or repealed in accordance with this section. Thereafter, no rule is valid unless adopted in substantial compliance with this section.

(f) This section applies to rules adopted within the department, whether by the director, associate director, or a subordinate.

(g) The director or his delegate at least annually shall hold a hearing for persons in each facility or program to consider proposals by these persons for changes in the rules of the department.

(h) The director at least annually shall publish copies of the rules of the department affecting the status, activities, or conditions of confinement or supervision of persons in its custody and make them readily accessible to persons in the custody of the department and the public. At least one current copy of the rules applicable to that facility shall be kept in each facility.

(i) The requirements of this section are in addition to, and in the event of conflict control, any other provision of law applicable to the adoption and publication of rules by state agencies.

§ 1–104. [Judicial Review of Contested Cases.]

(a) A person who has exhausted all administrative remedies available within the department and who is aggrieved by a final decision in a proceeding for which judicial review is authorized is entitled to judicial review under this section.

(b) Proceedings for review must be instituted by filing a [petition; complaint] in the [District Court of _____ County] within [10] days after notice of the final decision of the department. Copies of the [petition; complaint] must be served upon the department.

(c) The filing of a [petition; complaint] does not itself stay enforcement of the department's decision. The department may grant or, upon its refusal to do so, the reviewing court may order a stay upon appropriate terms.

(d) If a [petition; complaint] for review on its face reflects that it is meritorious, the reviewing court shall order the department to transmit to the reviewing court in the form maintained by the department a copy of the entire record of the proceeding under review. By stipulation of all parties to the review proceeding, the record may be shortened.

(e) The review shall be conducted by the court without a jury and confined to the record. In cases of alleged irregularities in procedure before the department, not shown in the record, proof thereon may be taken in the court.

(f) The court may not substitute its judgment for that of the department as to the weight of the evidence on questions of fact. The court may affirm the decision of the department or remand the case for further proceedings. The court may reverse or modify the decision if substantial rights of the person have been prejudiced because the findings, inferences, conclusions, or decisions of the department are:

(1) in violation of a constitutional, statutory, or administrative provision;

(2) in excess of the authority of the department;

(3) clearly erroneous in view of the reliable, probative, and substantial evidence on the whole record; or

(4) arbitrary or capricious.

ARTICLE 2

ORGANIZATION AND AUTHORITY

PREFATORY NOTE

The provisions of Article 2 relate to the organization of the correctional system and the allocation and regulation of administrative authority. The thrust of the Article is to improve correctional programs, services, and facilities. Although it is recognized that statutory provisions alone cannot insure effective corrections, a sound legislative framework is a prerequisite to the administrative development of a workable program.

The major policy position implemented in this Article relating to organization is the unification of all adult correctional programs under one department of corrections. Historically, correctional agencies and thereby correctional programs have been fragmented within a jurisdiction with no overall direction. Until recently in many states each correctional facility operated as an independent governmental agency subject only to general supervision by a board of corrections. In many states community-based programs such as probation and parole are administered separately from the facility based correctional agency. In most states misdemeanant and pretrial detention facilities are operated by local law enforcement agencies. Article 2 and other provisions of this Act seek to bring all adult correctional programs within one agency—a unified department of corrections.

Most recent national studies of corrections have called for unification. Nat'l Advisory Comm'n on Criminal Justice Standards & Goals, Corrections Std. 16.4 (1973) [hereinafter cited as Nat'l Advisory Comm'n]; President's Comm'n on Law Enforcement & Adm. of Justice, The Challenge of Crime in a Free Society 161–62 (1967) [hereinafter cited as President's Comm'n on Law Enforcement]. See also Advisory Comm'n on Intergovernmental Relations, State–Local Relations in the Criminal Justice System 55 (1971) (unification of all programs except local jails); American Correctional Ass'n, Manual of Correctional Standards 151–170 (3d ed. 1966) (recommending central state correctional organization) [hereinafter cited as ACA Manual]. According to American Correctional Ass'n Directory: Juvenile and Adult Correctional Departments, Institutions, Agencies and Paroling Authorities (1975–76) [hereinafter cited as ACA Directory] twenty-two states have placed adult probation, parole, and institutions in one state agency although some retain overlapping local probation systems. Id. at 250–57. Four states place these three

programs in three separate agencies. The breakdown between state and local responsibility for various aspects of the correctional system is shown in the following table from the Directory. Id. at 257.

TABLE 1
No. of Jurisdictions with Indicated Responsibilities
(50 States, D.C., Canal Zone & Puerto Rico)

Program	Local Resp.	State Resp.	State/Local Resp.
Juvenile detention	43	8	2
Juvenile probation	26	8	19
Juvenile institutions	0	50	0
Juvenile aftercare	4	47	2
Misdemeanant probation	13	19	9
Adult probation	9	32	12
Jails	43	9	1
Adult institutions	0	53	0
Adult parole	0	53	0

See also, Cal.Bd. of Corrections, Coordinated California Corrections: The System (1971); Final Report of the Prison Study Comm., A Unified System of Correction (Conn.1957). Many states report plans for further unifying correctional activities. LEAA, Recent Criminal Justice Unification, Consolidation and Coordination Efforts (Jan. 1976).

The arguments in favor of unification are based on effectiveness and efficiency. Correctional programming should be consistent and coordinate, particularly when the same individual often is subject to more than one element of the correctional system. An offender subject at relatively short intervals to pretrial detention, probation, and confinement should not confront inconsistent philosophies or expectations. His gradual reintegration into the free society may require an overall program that builds on past experience.

Consolidated authority over correctional programs also will allow the efficient utilization and allocation of scarce resources. In many instances professional counselors can assist confined persons as well as persons on supervision in the community. Consolidation also provides economies of scale which allow greater flexibility in providing programs and services.

Unification also facilitates long-range planning, the development of training and personnel programs, and the research and evaluation of past efforts.

Legislative formulations have proposed various levels of unification and have served as models for the development of some of Article 2: Ill. United Code Correc., Ill.Ann.Stat., ch. 38, §§ 1001–1–1 to 1008–5–1 (Smith–Hurd 1973); Neb. Treatment & Corrections Act, Neb. Rev.Stat. § 83–170 59 1, 152 (Reissue 1976); Advisory Comm'n on Intergovernmental Relations, State Department of Correction Act (1971); ALI, Model Penal Code art. 401 (1962) [hereinafter cited as Model Penal Code]; Nat'l Council on Crime and Delinquency, Standard Act for State Correctional Services (1966) [hereinafter cited as Standard Act].

In keeping with the nature of a model law designed for implementation in fifty states, the organizational structure of the department has been kept flexible. The statute creates four divisions within the department and two independent offices. The program-based divisions—division of facility-based services, division of community-based services, and division of jail administration—are created primarily as legal devices to regulate sentencing practices. In Article 3, offenders are sentenced to a particular division within the department. The director, however, is authorized to appoint a single person as associate director of more than one division, and otherwise to coordinate the activities of the divisions. This may be appropriate in small states.

The division of medical services is created as a separate division for substantive reasons. Delivery of medical care often comes into conflict with the security and administrative needs of the facilities. The separate division provides medical personnel with some independence from facility administrators while at the same time retaining departmental control and responsibility for medical services.

The effectiveness of the office of correctional legal services depends on its independence from direct supervision by the department of corrections. Personnel of the office may have to contest actions of departmental personnel; they must retain the confidence of both administration and persons in the custody of the department.

Beyond these provisions, the director is given full authority to organize the department and to create additional divisions. Larger systems may develop separate divisions for research, planning, purchasing, administration or other activities.

The other major purpose of Article 2 is to allocate and regulate correctional authority.

Historically, the legislative delegation of authority to correctional administrators has been framed in relatively broad language. Indeed, in some jurisdictions facilities or agencies are created and their operation left to administrative discretion without further guidance. This type of statutory foundation can have adverse effects. First, left without legislative guidance or support, some correctional administrators may be hesitant to attempt new and promising ideas for fear of public or legislative discontent or from doubt as to the limits of their authority. Second, without legislative direction the thrust of correctional programming over time will be erratic with each new change in administration operating on its own perception of public policy. Third, legislative restraint on administrative discretion is necessary to insure that persons in the custody of the department are treated fairly.

Many of the provisions applied in Article 2 are derived from long-standing techniques utilized to regulate administrative discretion in other areas. The basic approach follows the recommendations in K. Davis, Discretionary Justice (1969). See also Nat'l Advisory Comm'n Correc. Std. 16.2; President's Comm'n on Law Enforcement at 179–181.

Article 2 contains provisions to confine, structure, and check administrative discretion without unduly interfering with the flexibility and authority needed to effectively administer correctional facilities and programs. In some provisions, legislatively established goals are established and relevant considerations and factors for decisionmaking are stated. In many instances throughout this Act the director is obligated to exercise his discretion through formally adopted rules. The procedure for adopting rules allows participation by persons subject to the rules. The existence of rules will facilitate uniform application of policies throughout the department and provide a measure of protection against arbitrary actions by subordinates. The public nature of the rules will assist in creating a greater public awareness of the operation of the department.

OVERVIEW OF ARTICLE 2

Part 1 establishes the centralized department of corrections and provides for its authority and responsibilities. Provisions in this part have general application throughout the programs of the department.

Parts 2, 3, and 4 create the operational divisions of the department. The division of facility-based services has responsibility for major correctional facilities including prisons and long-term confinement institutions. The division of community-based services provides a cluster of programs and services that have a general community orientation. This division would have custody over persons sentenced to community-supervision. It might also have administrative responsibility for half-way houses and other facilities not used for continuous confinement. The division of jail administration would administer facilities traditionally thought of as local jails which would include pretrial detention facilities and misdemeanant confinement institutions.

Part 5 establishes a division of medical services responsible for all aspects of medical services in department facilities.

Part 6 establishes an independent office of correctional legal services to provide legal assistance to confined persons. The office is authorized to provide both legal counsel and paralegal assistance.

Part 7 provides legislative direction for the planning and design of new correctional facilities.

Underlying all of these provisions is the implicit premise that persons in the custody of the department have the right to be treated fairly. In part, support for the premise is philosophical—that the measure of the greatness of a society can be found in the way it treats its offenders. In part, support for the premise is utilitarian—that fair treatment is a prerequisite for rehabilitation. In part, support for the premise is legal—that offenders are entitled to basic elements of fair treatment under the Constitution. And, in part, support for the premise is traditional—that governmental power always should be restrained, not necessarily because of proven abuse but because of the potential for abuse.

ARTICLE 2

ORGANIZATION AND AUTHORITY

PART 1

DEPARTMENT OF CORRECTIONS

§ 2–101. [Department of Corrections; Function.]

(a) A department of corrections is created [within the executive branch of government; Department of Human Resources]. It shall provide programs, services, and facilities required for the care, custody, and treatment of persons in the custody of the department.

(b) Pursuant to an arrangement with a court or prosecuting attorney, the department:

(1) shall supervise persons released before trial whenever supervision is a condition of release; and

(2) may provide access to or maintain programs for persons accused of a criminal offense but released before trial.

§ 2–102. [Director of Corrections; Appointment.]

The Governor shall appoint a director of corrections who has appropriate training and experience in corrections. The director shall serve for a term of [6; 4] years and until his successor has been appointed. The Governor may remove the director only for disability, neglect of duty, incompetence, or malfeasance in office. Before removal, the director is entitled to a hearing.

§ 2–103. [Powers of Director.]

The director shall:

(1) administer the department;

(2) establish, consolidate, or abolish administrative subdivisions not established by law; and he shall appoint and may remove according to law the heads thereof;

(3) delegate appropriate powers and duties to the heads of administrative subdivisions and the chief executive officers of facilities and programs;

(4) adopt rules, statements of general policy, interpretive memoranda, and other measures relating to the care, custody, and treatment of persons in the custody of the department, the administration of programs, services, and facilities, and the conduct of employees of the department;

(5) collect, develop, and maintain information concerning the programs, services, and facilities of the department;

(6) at the request of the sentencing commission, collect, develop, and transmit statistical information required by the commission for the exercise of its duties;

(7) cooperate with individuals or public or private agencies or organizations for the development and improvement of the personnel, programs, services, and facilities of the department;

(8) explain correctional programs and services to the public; and

(9) exercise all powers and perform all duties necessary and proper in discharging his responsibilities.

§ 2–104. [Public Accountability.]

(a) The director shall adopt rules encouraging visits to facilities and programs by public officials and authorizing public visits to facilities and public observance of programs. The rules must be consistent with the following:

(1) The Governor, Attorney–General, members of the [Legislature], members of the state

judiciary, members of the advisory committee, and members of the sentencing commission may visit any part of any facility at any reasonable time and conduct private interviews with any willing employee or confined person unless the director determines that a state of emergency exists.

(2) Individuals and groups of persons may visit facilities or observe programs at reasonable times.

(3) Visits must be conducted in a manner designed to preserve confined persons' reasonable expectations of privacy.

(b) The director shall transmit annually to the Governor a report on the department. The report must contain:

(1) a description and evaluation of the programs, services, and facilities of the department;

(2) any recommendation or proposal for the alteration, expansion, addition, or discontinuance of programs, services, or facilities;

(3) any recommendation for statutory change necessary to improve programs, services, or facilities; and

(4) any other information required by law, requested by the Governor, or determined to be useful by the director.

(c) Upon receipt, the Governor shall transmit a copy of the report to the [Legislature], each trial and appellate court having jurisdiction over criminal cases, and the sentencing commission, and he shall make copies available to the press and members of the public.

§ 2–105. [Programs and Services.]

(a) The director shall provide access to programs and services to meet the needs of persons in the custody of the department.

(b) The director may contract with any individual or public or private agency or organization to provide programs or services to persons in the custody of the department. The contract shall permit the director to evaluate periodically the programs or services and to cancel the contract whenever the programs or services are not satisfactory.

(c) The director shall avoid unnecessary duplication of programs or services available from other sources.

§ 2–106. [Coordination Within Department.]

In order to avoid unnecessary duplication the director may:

(1) require one division to provide programs, services, and facilities to persons in the custody of another division; and

(2) appoint one person to head more than one division.

§ 2–107. [Gifts and Grants.]

Subject to other provisions of law, the director may apply for, accept, receive, and use, for and on behalf of the State, any money, goods, or services given by any source for purposes consistent with the responsibilities of the department and may agree to covenants, terms, and conditions the director considers necessary or desirable.

§ 2–108. [Employment and Training.]

(a) The director shall adopt measures governing the employment, training, and promotion of employees of the department. The measures shall prescribe:

(1) qualifications for the various positions within the department;

(2) for each position, initial training and educational requirements to be completed within one year after initial employment by the department; and

(3) for each position, training and educational requirements to be completed annually and additional training and educational requirements for promotion within the department.

(b) A person may not be employed, promoted, or retained by the department unless he complies with the measures adopted pursuant to subsection (a). Those measures are in addition to rules or other provisions of law generally applicable to the employment, training, promotion, and retention of state employees.

(c) Notwithstanding any other provision of law:

(1) a person may not be denied employment within the department solely because of the fact of prior conviction; and

(2) a person may not be denied a position within the department solely because of a sexual difference from the persons supervised or assisted.

(d) The director shall:

(1) assure the availability of appropriate training programs;

(2) consult and cooperate with educational institutions for the development of general and specialized courses of study for employees of the department;

(3) consult and cooperate with other departments and agencies concerned with the employment or training of employees of the department; and

(4) develop a plan for the recruitment and employment of persons of the same race or national origin as persons in the custody of the department.

(e) The director may make loans, for the purpose of academic study or training in fields relating to corrections, to employees of the department or applicants for employment, and may grant leaves of absences to employees. The director shall establish rules for conditions and awards of the loans, which may include a provision forgiving the loan on condition that the recipient work for the department for a stated period after completion of his study or training.

(f) [Measures adopted pursuant to this section must be adopted in accordance with procedures for the adoption of rules governing similar rules for employees of other state agencies.]

§ 2–109.   [Advisory Committee.]

(a) A department of corrections advisory committee is created to advise the director concerning the policies and practices of the department. It consists of 9 members appointed by the [Governor] who have an interest in or knowledge of corrections. Members of the committee shall serve staggered terms of [6; 4] years.

(b) The committee shall elect a chairman from among its members and meet quarterly and at other times at the call of the chairman. Members of the committee shall serve without compensation but are entitled to be reimbursed for expenses necessarily incurred in the performance of their duties.

(c) The director annually shall report to the committee on the policies and practices of the department. The members of the committee shall take appropriate steps to familiarize themselves with the problems and concerns of the department and persons in its custody and make recommendations to the director related thereto.

§ 2–110.   [Records.]

The director shall establish and maintain a central file on each person in the custody of the department. If available and appropriate, each file shall include:

(1) the presentence report, the record of the sentencing hearing, and other information from the sentencing court;

(2) the admission summary;

(3) the classification report and recommendations;

(4) official records of conviction and commitment as well as any earlier criminal record;

(5) reports of disciplinary infractions and dispositions;

(6) progress reports and orientation reports;

(7) other pertinent data about background, conduct, associations, and family relationships; and

(8) an index of the nature and location of all other information about the person maintained by the department other than incidental references to the person in files not directly related to him.

PART 2

COMMUNITY–BASED SERVICES

§ 2–201.   [Division   of   Community–Based Services; Creation.]

The division of community-based services is created within the department. It shall administer programs, services, and facilities for:

(1) persons sentenced or transferred to its custody;

(2) persons released before trial whenever supervision is a condition of release and a court or prosecuting attorney requests the department to participate; and

(3) victims of criminal offenses as authorized by Article 5.

§ 2–202.   [Associate Director for Community–Based Services.]

The director shall appoint and may remove in accordance with law an associate director of corrections for community-based services who has appropriate experience in corrections or training in a relevant discipline at an accredited college or university.

§ 2–203. [Duties of Associate Director.]

Subject to approval of the director, the associate director shall:

(1) administer the division;

(2) adopt rules and other measures relating to the division;

(3) appoint, and he may remove in accordance with law, community-service officers, deputy officers, if required, and other employees required to provide adequate supervision and assistance to persons in the custody of the division;

(4) appoint, and he may remove in accordance with law, the chief executive officer of each facility or program within the division and other employees and delegate to them appropriate powers and duties;

(5) evaluate and improve the effectiveness of the personnel, programs, services, and facilities of the division;

(6) develop programs, services, and facilities to meet the needs of persons in the custody of the division and victims;

(7) acquire and utilize community resources and social services for the benefit of persons in the custody of the division and victims; and

(8) exercise all powers and perform all duties necessary and proper in discharging his responsibilities.

§ 2–204. [Powers of Community Service Officers.]

(a) A community service officer shall:

(1) assist and supervise persons in the custody of the division;

(2) make reports required by a sentencing court to determine the effectiveness of a program of the division or the progress of an individual participant in a program; and

(3) exercise all powers and perform all duties necessary and proper in discharging his responsibilities.

(b) A community service officer may not arrest a person under his supervision except to the extent private citizens may make arrests.

PART 3

FACILITY–BASED SERVICES

§ 2–301. [Division of Facility–Based Services; Creation.]

The division of facility-based services is created within the department. It shall administer programs, services, and facilities for:

(1) offenders convicted of felonies and sentenced to terms of continuous confinement; and

(2) persons sentenced, committed, or transferred to its custody.

§ 2–302. [Associate Director; Appointment.]

The director shall appoint, and he may remove in accordance with law, an associate director of corrections for facility-based services who has appropriate experience in corrections or training in a relevant discipline at an accredited college or university.

§ 2–303. [Duties of Associate Director.]

Subject to approval of the director, the associate director shall:

(1) administer the division;

(2) adopt rules and other measures relating to the division;

(3) appoint, and he may remove in accordance with law, the chief executive officer of each facility or program within the division and other employees and delegate to them appropriate powers and duties;

(4) evaluate and improve the effectiveness of the personnel, programs, services, and facilities of the division;

(5) develop programs, services, and facilities to meet the needs of persons in the custody of the division;

(6) acquire and utilize community resources and social services for the benefit of persons in custody of the division; and

(7) exercise all powers and perform all duties necessary and proper in discharging his responsibilities.

PART 4

JAIL ADMINISTRATION

§ 2–401. [Division of Jail Administration.]

The division of jail administration is created within the department. It shall administer programs, services, and facilities for:

(1) offenders convicted of misdemeanors and sentenced to terms of continuous confinement;

(2) pretrial detainees; and

(3) persons sentenced, committed, or transferred to its custody.

[The following optional section is provided for states that prefer not to bring local jails within a unified states department of corrections. The section would be substituted for the entire Part 4 of Article 2.]

[§ 2–401. [Facilities Operated by Local Governments.]

(a) This Act does not prevent political subdivisions of the State from maintaining and administering local facilities for persons convicted of misdemeanors or pretrial detainees and temporary holding facilities for the shortterm custody of persons held immediately following arrest and before [pretrial release or bail hearing].

(b) The director may contract with a political subdivision or a combination of subdivisions to maintain and administer on their behalf of a local facility listed in subsection (a). The subdivision or subdivisions shall bear the costs associated with the facility.

(c) The director shall:

(1) Upon the request of local officials, provide assistance with respect to the construction, maintenance, administration, and personnel of local facilities;

(2) establish standards for the construction, maintenance, administration, and personnel of local facilities and procedures for enforcement of the standards;

(3) periodically inspect local facilities;

(4) certify local facilities meeting these standards; and

(5) establish standards and procedures for the temporary certification of holding facilities to accommodate an unusually large number of persons confined as a result of riot or other disorder.

(d) A person may not be confined in a local facility unless it is certified by the director as meeting the standards established pursuant to this section. The director may obtain an order from the [appropriate court] enjoining use of a facility that is not certified.

(e) The director may adopt rules exempting a local facility from specific provisions of Article 4. Unless a local facility is exempted, Article 4 applies, and for that purpose a person confined therein is considered to be a "confined person".]

§ 2–402. [Associate Director for Jail Administration.]

The director shall appoint, and he may remove in accordance with law, an associate director of corrections for jail administration who has appropriate experience in corrections or training in a relevant discipline at an accredited college or university.

§ 2–403. [Duties of Associate Director.]

Subject to approval of the director, the associate director shall:

(1) administer the division;

(2) adopt rules and other measures relating to the division;

(3) classify each facility or part of each facility within the division as a place of confinement for offenders or pretrial detainees or as a holding facility administered on behalf of a political subdivision of the State;

(4) appoint, and he may remove in accordance with law, the chief executive officer of each facility or program within the division and other employees and delegate to them appropriate powers and duties;

(5) evaluate and improve the effectiveness of the personnel, programs, services, and facilities of the division;

(6) develop programs, services, and facilities to meet the needs of persons in the custody of the division;

(7) acquire and utilize community resources and social services for the benefit of persons in the custody of the division; and

(8) exercise all powers and perform all duties necessary and proper in discharging his responsibilities.

§ 2–404. [Temporary Holding Facilities.]

(a) This Act does not prevent political subdivisions of the State from maintaining and administering temporary holding facilities for the short-term custody of persons held immediately following arrest and before [pretrial release or bail hearing].

(b) If a state detention facility is not reasonably accessible, temporary holding facilities may be used to confine persons needed in a locality for a continuing investigation or a trial.

(c) The associate director may contract with a political subdivision or a combination of subdivisions to maintain and administer on their behalf a temporary holding facility. The subdivision or subdivisions shall bear the costs associated with the facility.

(d) The associate director shall:

(1) provide, upon the request of local officials, assistance with respect to the construction, maintenance, and administration of temporary holding facilities;

(2) establish standards for the construction, maintenance, administration, and personnel of temporary holding facilities and procedures for enforcement of the standards;

(3) periodically inspect temporary holding facilities;

(4) certify temporary holding facilities meeting these standards; and

(5) establish standards and procedures for the temporary certification of holding facilities to accommodate an unusually large number of persons confined as a result of riot or other disorder.

(e) A person may not be confined in a temporary holding facility unless it is certified by the associate director as meeting the standards established by the associate director. The associate director may obtain an order from the [appropriate court] enjoining use of a facility that is not certified.

[§ 2–405. [Transition to State Control.]

(a) Within 5 years after the effective date of this Act, sole responsibility for the care, custody, and treatment of offenders sentenced to confinement or community supervision and pretrial detainees must be transferred to the State. The associate director of corrections for jail administration shall develop a plan for the orderly transfer of functions to the State. The plan must:

(1) include a timetable for implementing this section;

(2) detail the financial resources required for implementation;

(3) describe the extent to which existing facilities maintained by political subdivisions will be integrated into the department of corrections and the extent to which regional facilities will be established;

(4) describe the way in which programs, services, and facilities for short-term offenders will be integrated with existing or projected programs, services, and facilities for long-term offenders; and

(5) make recommendations for additional legislation necessary to fully implement this section.

(b) In developing the plan, the associate director shall consult with representatives of political subdivisions.

(c) Within one year after the effective date of this Act, the associate director shall submit the plan to the Governor and the [Legislature, General Assembly]. One year after submission of the plan, the director may exercise all powers and perform all duties necessary to implement the plan.

(d) All officials of the State and its political subdivisions shall cooperate with the associate director in developing the plan required by this section and comply with the requests of the associate director necessary to implement the plan.

(e) Notwithstanding any other provision of law, the associate director may assume responsibility for a facility administered by a political subdivision at any time funds are available and the affected political subdivision agrees.

(f) As long as a facility remains under the control of a political subdivision, it may:

(1) receive offenders on behalf of the department in order to establish the date on which a sentence to confinement commences;

(2) confine persons from the jurisdiction served by the facility before the effective date of this Act; and

(3) confine persons from other jurisdictions if the chief executive officer of the facility agrees, in which case the director may compensate the political subdivision for the cost of the confinement.

(g) The director may adopt rules exempting a facility administered by a political subdivision from specific provisions of Article 4. Unless a facility is exempted, Article 4 applies, and for that purpose a person confined therein is a "confined person."]

PART 5

CORRECTIONAL MEDICAL SERVICES

§ 2–501. [Division of Correctional Medical Services; Creation.]

(a) A division of correctional medical services is created within the department. It shall provide medical care to confined persons.

(b) As used in this Part, "medical care" includes the diagnosis or treatment of physical, dental, or mental health problems.

§ 2–502. [Associate Director for Correctional Medical Services.]

The director shall appoint, and he may remove in accordance with law, an associate director for medical services who has appropriate experience in the delivery of medical care.

§ 2–503. [Powers of Associate Director.]

Subject to the approval of the director, the associate director shall:

(1) administer the division;

(2) assure that each confined person has access to needed routine and emergency medical care;

(3) in cooperation with the division of community-based services, seek to assist persons supervised in the community to obtain medical care;

(4) appoint, and he may remove in accordance with law, the chief medical officer of each facility and other employees of the division and may delegate to them appropriate powers and duties;

(5) purchase, or authorize the purchase of, all medical equipment used in facilities;

(6) in cooperation with other divisions of the department, establish medical training programs for both correctional employees and confined persons;

(7) adopt rules, consistent with standards established by the department of health, governing,

(i) the provision of medical treatment to confined persons;

(ii) the administration of hospitals and other medical quarters within facilities;

(iii) the maintenance and use of medical equipment;

(iv) the storage and dispensing of medication;

(v) nutritional standards; and

(vi) sanitation within facilities;

(8) evaluate all medical personnel, programs, equipment, or services within facilities; and

(9) exercise all powers and perform all duties necessary and proper in discharging his responsibilities.

PART 6
CORRECTIONAL LEGAL SERVICES

§ 2–601. [Office of Correctional Legal Services; Creation.]

An office of correctional legal services is created [within the office of a statewide public defender or other state agency providing legal services] [the office of the Governor]. It shall provide legal assistance to confined persons directly or by contract with public or private organizations. The [State Public Defender] [Governor] shall appoint and may remove in accordance with law an administrator of correctional legal services who has appropriate experience in the delivery of legal services.

§ 2–602. [Powers and Duties.]

(a) Unless he can arrange with other agencies to do so, the administrator shall provide assistance in legal matters to indigent persons in the custody of the department in the manner and to the extent required by this Act.

(b) If a confined person has a legal problem for which the office is not authorized to provide assistance, the administrator shall refer the person to other sources of legal assistance.

§ 2–603. [Provision of Support Services.]

The director shall provide the office of correctional legal services with access to adequate space and equipment in each facility to perform properly its functions.

PART 7
FACILITY DESIGN AND CONSTRUCTION

§ 2–701. [Definitions.]

As used in this Part, unless the context otherwise requires:

(1) "housing unit" means a structure containing one or more living units which is administered as a single unit and constructed to separate persons while in the unit from the sight and sound of persons in other housing units;

(2) "living unit" means a space consisting of living quarters and leisure space for confined persons which is administered as a single unit and constructed to separate persons living in the unit from the sight and sound of persons in other living units;

(3) "living quarters" means the space assigned exclusively to each confined person and includes a cell, room, or proportionate share of a dormitory or other space designed for multiple occupancy; and

(4) "new facility" or "new housing unit" means a facility or housing unit other than a facility or housing unit which on the effective date of this Act is in use as a facility or housing unit or for which the bids for construction have been let.

§ 2–702. [Facilities; Maintenance and Administration.]

The director is responsible for the maintenance and administration of all facilities and shall plan for the construction or acquisition of new facilities and the remodeling of existing facilities.

§ 2–703. [Planning New Facilities.]

(a) Whenever the director determines that a new facility or new housing unit is necessary, he shall:

(1) develop a program statement describing,

(i) the type, purpose, and maximum capacity of the facility or housing unit;

(ii) the need for the facility or housing unit, including reasons a less-secure facility or housing unit will not satisfy the requirements of the department;

(iii) the type of person to be housed in the facility or housing unit;

(iv) the nature of the programs to be developed in the facility or housing unit;

(v) the likely location of the facility or housing unit and the manner in which the location is compatible with the programs to be developed therein;

(vi) the manner in which the facility or housing unit will meet the design principles established for new facilities and housing units (Section 2–704); and

(vii) the projected cost of the facility or housing unit; and

(2) adopt or amend the program statement in the manner and in accordance with the procedures established for the adoption of rules of the department.

(b) Funds may not be expended or obligated toward the final design or construction of a new facility or housing unit unless the Governor certifies in writing to the [Legislature] that there has been substantial compliance with this section.

§ 2-704. [Design Principles for New Facilities.]

Whenever a new facility or new housing unit is constructed or otherwise acquired, its capacity and physical environment must facilitate security and the safety of confined persons, employees of the department, and the public. Consistent with the requirements of safety and security, the following design principles should be considered and, to the extent practicable, applied:

(1) There should be compliance with fire safety standards established by the [fire marshal] and health and sanitation standards established by the [department of health].

(2) Provision should be made for,

(i) appropriate space for counseling, education, vocational, work, and other programs and activities in which confined persons may participate;

(ii) appropriate space for visiting between confined persons and their visitors;

(iii) use of the facility by handicapped persons;

(iv) appropriate areas for unregimented dining;

(v) reasonable control of noise;

(vi) reasonable avoidance of sensory deprivation;

(vii) outdoor and indoor recreational areas;

(viii) reasonable access to natural light;

(ix) maximizing privacy and personal living space, including, to the extent feasible, single-occupancy living quarters;

(x) minimizing the need for regimentation, surveillance equipment, weapons, or obtrusive hardware; and

(xi) the facilitation and implementation of the provisions of this Act.

(3) A facility should not be designed for more than [400] confined persons. A living unit should not be designed for more than [30] persons. Housing or living units may share with other units dining areas, academic, vocational, and other program space as well as access to available employment.

(4) Living quarters should be designed to provide each occupant with at least [70] square feet.

(5) Whenever feasible the location of a facility should be selected on the basis of proximity to,

(i) the communities in which persons likely to be confined therein reside;

(ii) areas that have community resources to support treatment programs and provide employment and educational opportunities;

(iii) courts; and

(iv) public transportation.

§ 2-705. [Remodeling Existing Facilities.]

(a) Whenever an existing facility is remodeled, the design principles for new facilities should be considered.

(b) The director, subject to available funds, may remodel existing facilities to comply with the design principles for new facilities.

(c) Whenever the director determines to remodel an existing facility and the remodeling is likely to cost more than [$50,000], he shall develop, to the extent appropriate for the nature of the remodeling, a program statement comparable to that required for new facilities and otherwise comply with Section 2-703.

§ 2-706. [Other Provisions Preempted.]

The provisions of this Part are in addition to any other provision of law applicable to the construction or acquisition of state buildings.

ARTICLE 3

SENTENCING

PREFATORY NOTE

Article 3 contains provisions relating to the selection, imposition, and execution of sentences for violation of criminal laws. The major basic policy decisions reflected in the Article are:

—the recognition of just deserts rather than rehabilitation or individual predictions of dangerousness as the major factor in sentencing and release decisions;

—the reduction and structuring of judicial sentencing discretion by establishment of a presumptively appropriate sentence to be imposed unless there is good cause not to do so; and

—the adoption of a flat-sentencing system for sentences to confinement by abolition of parole.

For many years the American system of sentencing has sought to achieve four goals: deterrence, rehabilitation, incapacitation, and retribution. Both the American Law Institute and the American Bar Association have proposed that all of these goals are legitimately considered in an appropriate case. ABA, Standards Relating to Sentencing Alternatives and Procedures, § 2.2 (1968) (hereinafter cited as ABA Sentencing Standards); ALI, Model Penal Code § 305.9 (Proposed Official Draft 1962) [hereinafter cited as Model Penal Code]. See also Nat'l Council on Crime & Delinquency, Model Sentencing Act (rev. 1972) [hereinafter cited as Model Sentencing Act]; Nat'l Advisory Comm'n on Criminal Justice Standards and Goals, Corrections Std. 5.2 (1973) [hereinafter cited as Nat'l Advisory Comm'n].

This multigoal system of sentencing resulted in variations on one basic model within the states—judicial imposition of an indeterminate sentence and discretionary release by a parole board. This model sought to promote individualized treatment of offenders ("let the punishment fit the criminal not the crime"), to limit the coercive power of the state by requiring a utilitarian rather than a retributive end, and to protect society by applying just the right amount of coercion and cure to produce law abiding citizens and to deter others from criminal behavior.

The model also had practical advantages in administering correctional institutions. The parole release discretion provided a safety valve for overcrowded prisons. The system also allowed sentencing courts to announce relatively long sentences to satisfy public concern, but allowed the parole board to award early release to keep sentences within reasonable limits.

Recent examinations of the results of the sentencing system have called into question both its practical effectiveness and its theoretical justification. The thrust of the criticisms have been threefold:

—The current system is ineffective in that it neither rehabilitates offenders, isolates the offenders likely to commit future crimes, nor allows effective use of deterrence principles.

—The current system results in large scale disparity in sentences creating frustrations, tensions, and disrespect for the system in both the offenders and the public-at-large.

—The current system is philosophically unjust in that it oftentimes severs the relationship between the punishment imposed and the offense committed.

These arguments and proposals for change are fully discussed in the following sources which serve as the primary theoretical basis for the philosophy behind Article 3:

American Friends Service Comm., Struggle for Justice (1971); Citizens Inquiry on Parole and Criminal Justice, Prisons Without Walls (1975); M. Frankel, Criminal Sentences (1973); Lipton, Martinson, & Wilks, The Effectiveness of Correctional Treatment (1975); N. Morris, The Future of Imprisonment (1974); Twentieth Century Fund Task Force on Criminal Sentencing, Fair and Certain Punishment (1976); D. Fogel, "... We are the Living Proof ..." (1975); A. von Hirsch, Doing Justice (1976); Harris, Disquisition on the Need for a New Model for Criminal Sanctioning Systems, 77 W.Va. L.Rev. 263 (1975); McGee, A New Look at Sentencing; Part I, Fed. Probation, June 1974, at 3; McGee, A New Look at Sentencing: Part II, Fed. Probation, Sept. 1974, at 3. Report on New York Parole (1975).

The acceptance of the need for basic systemic change in criminal sentencing is also reflected in the following:

—Maine and Indiana have enacted flat-sentencing systems by eliminating parole in most instances. Me. Rev.Stat. tit. 17–A, §§ 1253–54 (Pamphlet 1977); Ind. Code Ann. § 35–50–2–4 et seq. (Burns Supp.1977).

—California has both enacted a presumptive sentencing system and abolished discretionary release. Cal.Penal Code, § 1170 et seq. (West Supp.1977).

—The Federal Parole Commission and Reorganization Act of 1976, 18 U.S.C.A., §§ 4201–4218 (West Supp. 1977) 18 U.S.C. ch. 311 (Supp.1977), made mandatory an earlier administrative decision to establish presumptive parole dates for federal prisoners.

—State legislatures are considering various forms of presumptive and flat sentencing proposals in, among others, Minnesota, Illinois, Ohio, Alaska and New Jersey.

—Several courts are experimenting with sentencing guidelines. See, Wilkins, Kress, Gotffredson, Calpin & Gelman, Sentencing Guidelines; Structuring Judicial Discretion (1976).

—The ABA Joint Comm. on the Legal Status of Prisoners has proposed for Association approval a modified flat sentencing system. 14 Am.Crim.L.Rev. 375 (1977) [hereinafter cited as ABA Joint Comm.]

The provisions of Article 3 reflect the use of "just desert" as the overriding philosophy justifying the imposition of criminal sanctions. This philosophy requires that the nature and severity of the sanction imposed to be deserved on the basis of the offense committed and certain limited mitigating and aggravating factors relating to the offender. This seeks to avoid the injustice that results from utilizing the other traditional purposes of punishment.

The use of rehabilitation as a relevant factor in sentencing has been accused of causing substantial disparity in sentencing.

[I]f rehabilitation is the goal, and persons differ in their capacity to be rehabilitated, then two persons who have committed precisely the same crime under precisely the same circumstances might receive very different sentences, thereby violating the offenders' and our sense of justice. ... Rigorously applied on the basis of existing evidence about what factors are associated with recidivism, this theory would mean that if two persons together rob a liquor store, the one who is a young black male from a broken family, with little education and a record of drug abuse, will be kept in prison indefinitely, while an older white male from an intact family, with a high school diploma and no drug experience, will be released almost immediately. Not only the young black male, but most fair-minded observers, would regard that outcome as profoundly unjust. J. Wilson, Thinking About Crime 171 (1975).

Recent studies have also called into question the effectiveness of coerced rehabilitation programs. Lipton, Martinson, and Wilks examined hundreds of studies testing the effectiveness of programs and concluded that in large measure they cannot be shown statistically to be successful. The rigidly structured environment of a prison does not provide a suitable educational experience for learning how to exist in a free society. See D. Glaser, The Effectiveness of a Prison and Parole System (1964). And even if rehabilitation worked, the justification for extending a sentence for rehabilitative purposes beyond what was "deserved" for the offense committed, breaks the tie between offense and sanction thus removing the offense as the justification for intervention into the life of the offender. The full implication of governmental intervention into the lives of its citizens unrelated to commission of a criminal offense, runs counter to traditional freedom values and limited governmental power.

The abandonment of rehabilitation as a factor in determining the nature or length of a sentence *does not* abandon rehabilitation as a goal of the correctional system. Within the sentence imposed based on just desert, the Act requires that offenders be provided with programs and services to better themselves.

Another traditional goal of punishment has been to restrain or incapacitate those offenders predicted as likely to commit future crimes. This goal has been implemented for the most part through the parole system in which the parole board is authorized to release offenders from confinement when they are no longer dangerous or have been rehabilitated. In addition many systems provide enhanced sentences for those predicted to be dangerous. Although the theory of the system is plausible, in practice attempts to predict dangerousness have not been successful. The knowledge necessary to predict who will commit future crimes is undeveloped. As Professor von Hirsch noted: "With a predictive instrument of so little discernment and a target population so small, the forecaster will be able to spot a significant percentage of the actual violators *only if a large number of false positives is also included.*" (emphasis in original). Doing Justice 22 (1976). This results in the unnecessary confinement of many offenders in order to isolate a few who are dangerous. The unreliability of our methods of prediction and the tendency to greatly overpredict likely recidivism suggests that predictive restraint should not be used to determine the nature or severity of the sanction imposed.

Within the limitations of the deserved punishment, deterrence of others is an appropriate goal to pursue. The present system largely relies for deterrent effect on the existence of an undifferentiated criminal sanction. Our knowledge and ability to fine tune the sentencing system for deterrence purposes is not well developed. Zimring & Hawkins, Deterrence (1973). In part, this results from the individualized treatment model which prevents any informed knowledge of criminal sanctions from being imparted to the public. The deterrence impact of a legislative increase in a sentence for a particular offense is largely muted by the discretionary sentencing practices of courts and parole boards.

Perhaps the major indictment of the current system is that it has lost public confidence. The sentencing system purports to do more than it can deliver—it claims to rehabilitate, isolate, and deter and thus attracts the blame for publicized crimes by ex-offenders and for the perceived increase in crime generally.

Discretionary release systems like parole also have counterproductive effects on the lives and attitudes of offenders. Persons subject to a parole board's discretion inevitably participate in a "con game" to convince the board they are ready for release. In addition, the uncertain nature of their sentence prohibits careful planning for release. Perhaps more important, however, the parole system intensifies disparity in sentences creating tension and hostility within correctional institutions and making actual rehabilitation more difficult.

OVERVIEW OF ARTICLE 3

The provisions of Article 3 attempt to speak to the concerns expressed with current sentencing practices. They are directed by the overriding attempt to reduce injustice and to implement a modest, attainable system of sentencing criminal offenders.

Part 1 of the Article establishes the general framework for sentencing. The purposes and principles of sentencing are articulated in the Act (Sections 3–101 and 3–102) and the sentencing alternatives and maximum possible sentences for categories of offenses are established.

A Sentencing Commission is created to develop sentencing guidelines. These guidelines will provide the presumptively appropriate sentence to be imposed in each case based on statutorily authorized factors relating to the offender and the severity of the offense. The guidelines will indicate the appropriate type of sentence, i.e., fine, community supervision, periodic confinement, continuous confinement, and the length of the sentence to be imposed. The sentencing court is obligated to impose the guidelines sentence unless it finds that some other sentence would better serve the purposes and principles of sentencing. The court must also enter on the record the reasons for departing from the guidelines.

Part 2 of the Article establishes the procedures for imposing sentences. A presentence report is required in all cases, but the court may order a shortened report where there are no contested issues of mitigation or aggravation. A sentencing hearing is required and appellate review of sentences is authorized. Provisions authorize the victim of the offense to participate and make his own views known regarding the sentence to be imposed.

Parts 3 through 6 of the Article provide statutory detail for the various types of sentences authorized by the Act. Part 3 implements sentences to community supervision. The Act uses the language "community supervision" as a substitute for what has traditionally been called "probation" referring to supervision in the community under conditions imposed by the court. Part 4 relates to fines.

Part 5 provides for the elements of a sentence to confinement. Three types of sentences involving confinement are authorized: split-sentences, periodic confinement, and continuous confinement. Split sentences are sentences involving confinement for not more than 90 days followed by a term of community supervision. Periodic confinement involves confinement only during specified days or parts of days and supervision in the community at other times. A sentence for continuous confinement requires the offender to serve his entire sentence in a facility. There is no parole or other discretionary release, but each offender may earn one day of good time for each day he serves in confinement by avoiding violations of prison rules. Good time credits can be forfeited in a disciplinary proceeding; they are not awarded for program participation or on the basis of official judgments regarding rehabilitative progress. No supervision is provided after release from confinement but the department is authorized to provide services and assistance to released offenders on a voluntary basis.

Part 6 authorizes granting of restitution to victims of the offense.

ARTICLE 3

SENTENCING

PART 1

GENERAL PROVISIONS

§ 3–101. [Purposes.]

The purposes of this Article are to:

(1) punish a criminal defendant by assuring the imposition of a sentence he deserves in relation to the seriousness of his offense;

(2) assure the fair treatment of all defendants by eliminating unjustified disparity in sentences, providing fair warning of the nature of the sentence to be imposed, and establishing fair procedures for the imposition of sentences; and

(3) prevent crime and promote respect for law by,

(i) providing an effective deterrent to others likely to commit similar offenses;

(ii) restraining defendants with a long-history of criminal conduct; and

(iii) promoting correctional programs that elicit the voluntary cooperation and participation of offenders.

181

§ 3–102. [Principles of Sentencing.]

To implement the purposes of this Article the following principles apply:

(1) The sentence imposed should be no greater than that deserved for the offense committed.

(2) Inequalities in sentences that are unrelated to a purpose of this Article should be avoided.

(3) The sentence imposed should be the least severe measure necessary to achieve the purpose for which the sentence is imposed.

(4) Sentences not involving confinement should be preferred unless:

(i) confinement is necessary to protect society by restraining a defendant who has a long history of criminal conduct;

(ii) confinement is necessary to avoid deprecating the seriousness of the offense or justly to punish the defendant;

(iii) confinement is particularly suited to provide an effective deterrent to others likely to commit similar offenses;

(iv) measures less restrictive than confinement have frequently or recently been applied unsuccessfully to the defendant; or

(v) the purposes of this Article would be fulfilled only by a sentence involving confinement.

(5) The potential or lack of potential for the rehabilitation or treatment of the defendant should not be considered in determining the sentence alternative or length of term to be imposed, but the length of a term of community supervision may reflect the length of a treatment or rehabilitation program in which participation is a condition of the sentence.

(6) The prediction of the potential for future criminality by a particular defendant, unless based on prior criminal conduct or acts designated as a crime under the law, should not be considered in determining his sentence alternative or the length of term to be imposed.

§ 3–103. [Sentencing Alternatives.]

(a) A person convicted of a felony or a misdemeanor in this State must be sentenced in accordance with this Act.

(b) The following sentencing alternatives are authorized:

(1) payment of a fine either alone or in addition to any other sentence authorized by this subsection;

(2) service of a term of community supervision;

(3) service of a split sentence of confinement followed by a term of community supervision;

(4) service of a term of periodic confinement;

(5) service of a term of continuous confinement;

(6) making restitution alone or in addition to any other sentence authorized by this subsection.

(c) This Article does not deprive a court of any authority conferred by law to decree a forfeiture of property, suspend or cancel a license, remove a person from office, or impose costs and other monetary obligations if specifically authorized by law.

[(d) This Article does not prevent a court from imposing a sentence of death specifically authorized by law.]

§ 3–104. [Maximum Sentences.]

(a) The maximum term of a sentence to continuous confinement imposed for conviction of an offense is:

(1) [unless a sentence of death is imposed,] for [murder in the first degree], [___ years], but the maximum is [2 times the maximum term for murder in the first degree] for a persistent offender or an especially aggravated offense;

(2) for Class A felonies other than [murder in the first degree], [___ years], but the maximum is [2 times the maximum term for Class A felonies other than murder in the first degree] for a persistent offender or an especially aggravated offense;

(3) for Class B felonies, [___ years], but the maximum is [2 times the maximum term for Class B felonies] for a persistent offender;

(4) for Class C felonies, [___ years], but the maximum is [2 times the maximum term for Class C felonies] for a persistent offender;

(5) for Class A misdemeanors, [___ year], but the maximum is [2 times the maximum term for Class A misdemeanors] for a persistent offender; and

(6) for Class B misdemeanors, [___ months], but the maximum is [2 times the maximum term for Class B misdemeanors] for a persistent offender.

(b) The maximum term of a sentence to periodic confinement, a split sentence of confinement and community supervision, or community supervision is [___ years] for a felony or [___ year] for a misdemeanor. For the purpose of determining the maximum term under this subsection, the term of a sentence to periodic confinement or a split sentence includes both the time spent in confinement and the time spent in the community under supervision.

(c) The maximum of a fine imposed for conviction of an offense is:

(1) for a Class A or a Class B felony, [$___];

(2) for a Class C felony, [$___];

(3) for a Class A misdemeanor, [$___]; and

(4) for a Class B misdemeanor, [$___].

(d) If the defendant is an organization, the maximum amount of a fine imposed for conviction of an offense is 50 times the amount authorized in subsection (c). As used in this subsection "organization" means a legal entity other than an individual.

(e) In lieu of a fine imposed under subsection (c) or (d), a defendant who has been convicted of an offense through which he derived pecuniary gain or by which he caused personal injury or property damage or loss may be sentenced to a fine not exceeding twice the gain derived or twice the injury, damage, or loss caused. Whenever a person is convicted of an offense that is one of several transactions constituting a continuing scheme of criminal activity, the court in determining the amount of gain, injury, damage, or loss under this subsection may consider that resulting from the entire scheme.

§ 3–105.   [Persistent Offenders]

(a) A "persistent offender" is a person who has at least 2 prior felony convictions for offenses committed within the 5 years immediately preceding commission of the instant offense. In establishing the 5–year period, time spent in confinement may not be included but convictions for offenses committed during the period of confinement must be counted as prior convictions.

(b) Convictions that have been set aside in post-conviction proceedings or for which a full executive pardon has been granted are not included as convictions for purposes of this section.

(c) The conviction for 2 or more felonies committed as part of a single course of conduct during which there was no substantial change in the nature of the criminal objective constitutes one conviction for purposes of this section, but offenses resulting in bodily harm to another person committed while attempting to escape detection or apprehension are not part of the same criminal objective.

(d) Consistent with this section, the sentencing commission may adopt more specific criteria relating to sentencing persistent offenders.

§ 3–106.   [Especially Aggravated Offenses.]

(a) An "especially aggravated offense" is:

(1) a felony resulting in death or great bodily harm or involving the threat of death or great bodily harm to another person if,

(i) the defendant knowingly created a great risk of death to more than one person;

(ii) the offense manifested exceptional depravity; or

(iii) the defendant was previously convicted of [murder] or a felony resulting in death or great bodily harm or involving the threat of death or great bodily harm to another person; or

(2) murder in the first degree if,

(i) the defendant committed the offense for himself or another for the purpose of pecuniary gain;

(ii) the offense was knowingly directed at an active or former judicial officer, prosecuting or defense attorney, law enforcement officer, correctional employee or fireman during or because of the exercise of his official duties; or

(iii) at the time the murder was committed, the defendant committed another murder.

(b) Consistent with this section, the sentencing commission may adopt more specific guidelines relating to sentencing for especially aggravated offenses.

§ 3-107. [Concurrent and Consecutive Sentences.]

(a) If multiple sentences are imposed on a defendant or if a sentence is imposed on a defendant already subject to an undischarged sentence, the sentences shall run consecutively; but the sentences shall run concurrently if (1) they are imposed for 2 or more offenses committed as part of a single course of conduct during which there was no substantial change in the nature of the criminal objective; or (2) one of the acts constituting a separate offense is taken into account to enhance a sentence on the other offense.

(b) Notwithstanding subsection (a), a sentence, when combined with all other undischarged sentences and remaining undischarged parts of prior sentences, may not exceed twice the maximum term of the most serious offense involved. The phrase "the maximum term of the most serious offense" as used in this subsection means the statutory maximum term of the offense carrying the longest maximum term, but does not include the additional term that could be imposed on a persistent offender or for an especially aggravated offense.

(c) Notwithstanding subsection (b) a sentence imposed on a defendant for an offense committed while serving a sentence of continuous confinement for a prior offense shall run consecutively to the remaining part of the sentence for the prior offense.

(d) In all cases in which consecutive sentences are imposed the sentencing court shall direct that the sentence most restrictive of the person's liberty shall be served first.

§ 3-108. [Mitigating Factors.]

If appropriate for the offense, mitigating factors may include:

(1) the defendant's criminal conduct neither caused nor threatened serious bodily harm;

(2) the defendant did not contemplate that his criminal conduct would cause or threaten serious bodily harm;

(3) the defendant acted under strong provocation;

(4) substantial grounds exist tending to excuse or justify the defendant's criminal conduct, though failing to establish a defense;

(5) the defendant played a minor role in the commission of the offense;

(6) before his detection, the defendant compensated or made a good faith attempt to compensate the victim of criminal conduct for the damage or injury the victim sustained;

(7) the defendant because of his youth or old age lacked substantial judgment in committing the offense;

(8) the defendant was motivated by a desire to provide necessities for his family or himself;

(9) the defendant was suffering from a mental or physical condition that significantly reduced his culpability for the offense;

(10) the defendant assisted authorities to uncover offenses committed by other persons or to detect or apprehend other persons who had committed offenses;

(11) the defendant, although guilty of the crime, committed the offense under such unusual circumstances that it is unlikely that a sustained intent to violate the law motivated his conduct; and

(12) any other factor consistent with the purposes of this Article and the principles of sentencing.

§ 3-109. [Aggravating Factors.]

If appropriate for the offense, aggravating factors, if not themselves necessary elements of the offense, may include:

(1) the defendant has a recent history of convictions or criminal behavior;

(2) the defendant was a leader of the criminal activity;

(3) the offense involved more than one victim;

(4) a victim was particularly vulnerable;

(5) a victim was treated with cruelty during the perpetration of the offense;

(6) the harm inflicted on a victim was particularly great;

(7) the offense was committed to gratify the defendant's desire for pleasure or excitement;

(8) the defendant has a recent history of unwillingness to comply with the conditions of a sentence involving supervision in the community; and

(9) any other factor consistent with the purposes of this Article and the principles of sentencing.

§ 3–110. [Sentencing Commission; Creation.]

A sentencing commission is created in the office of the Governor. It consists of the director of corrections and [8] additional members appointed by the Governor [with the advice and consent of the Senate]. Three members must be active trial judges of courts having criminal jurisdiction, one must be a prosecuting attorney, one must be a practicing attorney having substantial recent experience representing criminal defendants, and the remaining members must be from the public at large. The Governor shall designate one of the members of the commission as chairman.

[Alternatives for States in which active judges cannot sit on policy-making commissions in another branch of government.]

[ALTERNATIVE A]

[(a) A Sentencing Commission is created in the office of the Governor. It consists of the director of corrections and [5] additional members appointed by the Governor [with the advice and consent of the Senate]. One member must be a prosecuting attorney, one must be a practicing attorney having substantial recent experience representing criminal defendants, and the remaining members must be from the public-at-large. The Governor shall designate one of the members of the Commission as chairman.

(b) The [Chief Justice of the Supreme Court] shall appoint a judicial advisory panel consisting of [3; 5] active trial judges of courts having criminal jurisdiction. The panel shall meet with the commission and advise it on the discharge of its responsibilities. Members of the panel may not vote on matters before the commission.]

[ALTERNATIVE B]

[(a) A Sentencing Commission is created in the judicial branch. It consists of 5 trial judges serving on courts having criminal jurisdiction appointed by the [Chief Justice of the Supreme Court]. The [Chief Justice] shall designate one of the members of the commission as chairman.

(b) The [Chief Justice of the Supreme Court] shall appoint an advisory panel consisting of [5] members. One member must be a prosecuting attorney, one must be a practicing attorney hav-

ing substantial recent experience representing criminal defendants, and the remaining members must be from the public-at-large. The panel shall meet with the commission and advise it on the discharge of its responsibilities. Members of the panel may not vote on matters before the commission.]

§ 3–111. [Terms of Sentencing Commission.]

(a) The members of the sentencing commission shall serve for staggered terms of [6 or 4] years or until they cease to hold the office or position that qualified them for appointment and until their successors are appointed and have qualified, but of the members first appointed the chairman must be appointed for a term of [6 or 4] years and the other members must be appointed in equal numbers to 2- and 4-year terms. Their successors must be appointed in the manner provided for the members first appointed, and a vacancy occurring before expiration of a term must be similarly filled for the unexpired term. The [Governor or Chief Justice] may remove a member of the commission only for disability, neglect of duty, incompetence, or malfeasance in office. Before removal, the member is entitled to a hearing.

(b) Members of the commission [and the advisory panel] not employed by the State or its political subdivisions are entitled to receive a per diem to be established by the Governor for days actually spent in the performance of their duties and all members shall be reimbursed for expenses necessarily incurred in the performance of their duties.

§ 3–112. [Duties of Sentencing Commission.]

(a) The sentencing commission shall:

(1) appoint, and it may remove in accordance with law, an executive director having appropriate training and experience to conduct statistical studies of sentencing practices, interpret and explain social science information relating to sentencing, and construct sentencing guidelines as provided by this Act;

(2) appoint, and it may remove in accordance with law, other employees of the commission as required;

(3) adopt in a form determined by the commission sentencing guidelines as provided by this Act;

(4) collect, develop and maintain statistical information relating to sentencing practices and other dispositions of criminal complaints;

(5) cooperate with sentencing courts in developing instructional programs for judges relating to sentencing;

(6) explain sentencing practices and guidelines to the public; and

(7) exercise all powers and perform all duties necessary and proper in discharging its responsibilities.

Optional Provisions

[The following subsections are provided for states that have not classified offenses for sentencing purposes by legislation.]

[(b) The sentencing commission shall classify all criminal offenses on the basis of their severity into one of the following categories:

(1) Class A felonies, which shall include felonies characteristically involving aggravated forms of violence or the risk of violence against the person;

(2) Class B felonies, which shall include felonies characteristically involving less-severe offenses against the person, aggravated offenses against property, or aggravated offenses against public administration or order;

(3) Class C felonies, which shall include all felonies not otherwise classified as Class A or B;

(4) Class A misdemeanors, which shall include misdemeanors characteristically involving or risking aggravated breaches of the peace or those directed against a person or public administration or order; and

(5) Class B misdemeanors, which shall include all misdemeanors not otherwise classified as Class A.

(c) Notwithstanding subsection (b), the commission may classify as "infractions" minor offenses that do not provide for imprisonment as a possible penalty. A person convicted or otherwise found to have committed an offense classified as an "infraction" may not be sentenced in accordance with this Article but may be penalized in accordance with other applicable law.

(d) The commission shall classify immediately any new offense enacted into law for which the [Legislature] has not stated a classification.

(e) Rules of the commission classifying offenses pursuant to this section must be adopted pursuant to the same procedures and are effective in the same manner as sentencing guidelines.

(f) After the effective date of the classification of offenses by the commission, the substantive provision establishing the criminal offense continues to be effective, but persons convicted of the offense are subject to the penalties provided in this Act.]

§ 3–113. [Sentencing Guidelines; Non–Monetary Sentencing Alternatives.]

(a) The sentencing commission shall adopt guidelines for the following decisions relating to the imposition of sentences involving supervision or confinement:

(1) selection among the various sentencing alternatives; and

(2) determination of the length of terms for each of the alternatives.

(b) Guidelines adopted pursuant to subsection (a) establish for the sentencing court, on the basis of the combination of offense and defendant characteristics in each case, the presumptively appropriate sentencing alternative and the length of term to impose.

(c) For a sentence involving community supervision, the commission shall propose a maximum term of confinement to be imposed if the defendant violates the conditions of his supervision.

§ 3–114. [Monetary and Non–Monetary Conditions of Sentencing Guidelines.]

The sentencing commission may adopt guidelines for the following decisions relating to the imposition of sentences:

(1) imposition of a fine or a requirement to make restitution, including the amount thereof;

(2) imposition of conditions as part of a sentence involving community supervision; and

(3) imposition of sanctions for violation of conditions of community supervision.

§ 3–115. [Sentencing Guideline Requirements.]

(a) Sentencing guidelines shall be consistent with the purposes of this Article and the principles of sentencing.

(b) In adopting sentencing guidelines the commission shall take into account characteristics of offenses and of defendants that relate to the purposes of this Article and the principles of sentencing. It shall consider:

(1) the nature and characteristics of the offense;

(2) the severity of the offense in relation to other offenses;

(3) the characteristics of the defendant that mitigate or aggravate the seriousness of his criminal conduct and the punishment deserved therefor; and

(4) the available resources of the department.

(c) The sentencing commission shall include with each set of guidelines a statement of its estimate of the effect of the guidelines on the resources of the department.

§ 3-116. [Promulgation of Sentencing Guidelines.]

(a) The commission shall hold at least one public hearing before final adoption of sentencing guidelines. The commission shall publish its proposed guidelines at least 30 days before the hearing. The commission shall afford interested persons reasonable opportunity to present data, views, or arguments at the hearing relating to the proposed guidelines, or to submit data, views, or arguments in writing before the hearing. The commission shall consider fully all written and oral submissions respecting the proposed guidelines and, if the guidelines are adopted, issue a concise statement of the principal reasons for or against adoption, incorporating therein its reasons for rejecting contrary views.

(b) Upon adoption of the guidelines the commission shall file them in the office of the [appropriate state depository for filing of administrative actions].

(c) Guidelines adopted by the commission become effective 20 days after filing and apply to sentences for offenses thereafter committed.

(d) The commission may modify the guidelines and shall follow the procedures of this section in so doing. At least once every 2 years the commission shall hold a hearing, consistent with subsection (a), to allow the public to comment on existing guidelines.

PART 2

PROCEDURES FOR IMPOSING SENTENCE

§ 3-201. [Presentence Service Officers.]

(a) The director of corrections shall appoint presentence service officers for each [court, division of a court] having criminal jurisdiction. Presentence service officers shall conduct investigations and make reports and recommendations to sentencing courts relating to the imposition of sentences on criminal defendants.

(b) With permission of the [district, circuit] court, the presentence service officer may:

(1) assist courts or other judicial officers in developing information relating to the setting of bail or other pretrial release or detention decisions; and

(2) develop information about offenders relating to the selection of an offender for particular correctional programs.

[(c) The Supreme Court shall adopt rules providing for office space, supporting staff, equipment, and other administrative provisions for presentence service officers.]

§ 3-202. [Presentence Procedures.]

(a) If the prosecuting attorney believes that a defendant should be sentenced for an especially aggravated offense or as a persistent offender, he shall file a statement thereof with the court before trial or acceptance of a plea of admission.

(b) In all other cases, upon acceptance of a plea of admission or upon a verdict or finding of guilty the court may require that:

(1) the prosecuting attorney file a statement with the court setting forth any aggravating or mitigating factors he believes should be considered by the court; and

(2) the defendant file a statement with the court setting forth any mitigating factors he believes should be considered by the court.

§ 3-203. [Presentence Investigation and Report.]

(a) Upon acceptance of a plea of admission or upon a verdict or finding of guilty, the court shall in the case of a felony and may in the case of a misdemeanor direct the presentence service officer to make a presentence investigation and report. The presentence service officer shall conduct any investigation he deems appropriate or the court directs and independently verify the factual basis for any aggravating or mitigating factors asserted by the parties.

(b) With the concurrence of a defendant, a court may direct the presentence service officer to begin the presentence investigation before adjudication of the guilt of the defendant. Nothing discovered by the presentence investigation may be disclosed to the prosecution, the court, or the jury before acceptance of a plea of admission or a verdict or finding of guilty unless the defendant concurs.

§ 3–204. [Requirements of Presentence Reports.]

(a) The presentence report must set forth:

(1) the characteristics and circumstances of the offense committed by the defendant;

(2) information relating to any aggravating or mitigating factors asserted by the parties and its source;

(3) the defendant's record of prior convictions;

(4) information relating to any aggravating or mitigating factor which may affect the sentence imposed although not asserted by the parties and the source from which the information was obtained;

(5) past sentencing practices relating to persons in circumstances substantially similar to those of the defendant;

(6) an analysis of the guidelines of the sentencing commission applicable to the particular defendant;

(7) if a sentence not involving confinement is likely, information to assist the court in imposing conditions for community supervision, including the nature and extent of programs and resources available to the defendant;

(8) if requested by the court, information to assist the court in imposing a fine or restitution including the financial resources of the defendant, the financial needs of the defendant's

dependents, and the gain derived from or loss caused by the criminal activity of the defendant;

(9) any statement relating to sentencing submitted by the victim of the offense or the investigative agency; and

(10) consistent with the purposes of this Article and the principles of sentencing, any other information the presentence service officer or the court considers relevant.

(b) In misdemeanor cases and in cases in which neither party asserts the existence of aggravating or mitigating factors the court may direct the presentence service officer to include in the report only the information required in paragraphs (1), (6), (9), and (10) of subsection (a).

§ 3–205. [Disclosure of Presentence Reports.]

The presentence report must be filed with the court and copies made available to the parties before sentencing. The court may order that the presentence report or any part thereof not be available for public inspection.

§ 3–206. [Sentencing Hearing.]

(a) Before imposing sentence or making other disposition upon acceptance of a plea of admission or upon a verdict or finding of guilty, the court shall conduct a sentencing hearing without unreasonable delay. The court, upon the request of either party, shall postpone the sentencing hearing until at least 10 days after the filing of a presentence report.

(b) At the hearing the court shall afford the parties and the victim of the offense the opportunity to be heard and present evidence relevant to the sentencing of the defendant. The court may allow the parties to subpoena witnesses and call or cross-examine witnesses, including the person who prepared the presentence report and any person whose information contained in the presentence report is relevant to the sentencing decision.

(c) In imposing sentence the court shall:

(1) consider the evidence received at the trial and the sentencing hearing;

(2) consider the presentence report; and

(3) review the appropriate sentencing guidelines.

(d) In determining the appropriate guideline to follow the court shall consider the nature and characteristics of the criminal conduct involved without regard to the offense charged. However, in the event that the guideline sentence is greater than the maximum sentence provided for the class of offense charged, the court may sentence the offender to no more than the maximum for the class of offense charged.

(e) A record of the sentencing hearing must be kept and preserved in the same manner as trial records. The record of the sentencing hearing is part of the record of the case and must include specific findings of fact upon which application of the sentencing guidelines was based.

(f) Whenever a defendant is sentenced to the custody of the department, the sentencing court shall transmit to the director a copy of the defendant's presentence report and the record of the sentencing hearing.

§ 3–207. [Imposition of Sentence.]

(a) In imposing sentence the sentencing court shall follow the sentencing guidelines unless it concludes that another sentence better serves the purposes of this Article and the principles of sentencing.

(b) The court may not suspend the imposition or execution of a sentence except the court may suspend the execution of a sentence for a period not to exceed 30 days to allow a defendant to order his affairs. This section does not limit the power of a court to stay its sentencing order pending appeals.

(c) Whenever the court imposes a sentence not in accordance with the guidelines, it shall place in the record its findings of fact and reasons for deviating from the guidelines.

(d) In cases other than those involving especially aggravated offenses or persistent offenders, a sentence must be based on substantial evidence in the record of the sentencing hearing and the presentence report.

(e) A person may not be sentenced for an especially aggravated offense or as a persistent offender unless:

(1) the prosecuting attorney has filed the statement with the court required by Section 3–202;

(2) the court finds that facts necessary to support the sentence have been proved beyond a reasonable doubt; and

(3) the court places on the record its findings of fact justifying the sentence.

§ 3–208. [Appellate Review of Sentences.]

(a) Either party to a criminal case may appeal from the length or nature of the sentence imposed by the trial court. An appeal pursuant to this section must be taken within the same time and in the same manner as other appeals in criminal cases.

(b) An appeal from a sentence may be on one or more of the following grounds:

(1) The sentencing court misapplied the sentencing guidelines.

(2) The sentencing court deviated from the sentencing guidelines and the sentence imposed (i) is unduly disproportionate to sentences imposed for similar offenses on similar defendants, or (ii) does not serve the purposes of this Article and the principles of sentencing better than the sentence provided in the guidelines.

(3) The sentence was not imposed in accordance with this Act.

(4) The applied sentencing guidelines are inconsistent with the purposes of this Article and the principles of sentencing.

(c) If a sentence is appealed, the [Supreme Court; Court of Appeals] may:

(1) dismiss the appeal;

(2) affirm, reduce, increase, modify, vacate, or set aside the sentence imposed;

(3) remand the case or direct the entry of an appropriate sentence or order; or

(4) direct any further proceedings required under the circumstances.

PART 3

COMMUNITY SUPERVISION

§ 3–301. [Community Supervision; Nature.]

A sentence to community supervision requires the defendant to reside in the community subject to the supervision of the division of community-based services pursuant to conditions imposed by the sentencing court in accordance with this Act.

§ 3–302. [Term and Conditions.]

(a) Whenever a court sentences an offender to community supervision, the court shall specify the term of the supervision and may require the offender to comply with one or more of the following conditions:

(1) meet his family responsibilities;

(2) devote himself to a specific employment or occupation;

(3) perform without compensation services in the community for charitable or governmental agencies;

(4) undergo available medical or psychiatric treatment, and enter and remain in a specified institution whenever required for that purpose;

(5) pursue a prescribed secular course of study or vocational training;

(6) refrain from possessing a firearm or other dangerous weapon unless granted written permission;

(7) remain within prescribed geographical boundaries and notify the court or the community service officer of any change in his address or employment;

(8) report as directed to the court or a community-service officer; and

(9) satisfy any other conditions reasonably related to the purpose of his sentence and not unduly restrictive of his liberty, incompatible with his freedom of conscience, or otherwise prohibited by this Act.

(b) The court may order the associate director of the division of community-based services to:

(1) provide the offender with reasonable services, programs, or assistance as specified by the court;

(2) provide the offender with an amount of vouchers for purchasing services in the community up to the amount the offender would have received had he been sentenced to confinement; or

(3) report as directed to the court on the progress of the offender.

(c) The court shall comply with applicable guidelines of the sentencing commission and the provisions of Section 3–207 in exercising its powers pursuant to this section.

§ 3–303. [Provision of Programs and Services.]

Throughout an offender's term of community supervision the associate director of community-based services may provide him with:

(1) access on a voluntary basis to programs or services; and

(2) vouchers for the purchase of programs or services.

§ 3–304. [Expiration of Conditions.]

(a) Except for conditions requiring an offender sentenced to community supervision to refrain from possession of firearms, remain within prescribed geographical boundaries, or report to the court or a community service officer, all conditions expire at the end of 2 years.

(b) Notwithstanding subsection (a), if the court after a hearing finds that an offender violated a condition of his supervision within the 2-year period, one or more of the expired conditions may be reimposed for one additional period not exceeding 2 years.

(c) This section does not extend the applicability of conditions of supervision beyond the term of the sentence to community supervision imposed.

§ 3–305. [Discharge from Supervision.]

(a) During the term of community supervision, the sentencing court, on its own motion, or on application of the associate director of community-based services or the offender, may:

(1) modify any condition;

(2) remove a condition; or

(3) discharge the offender from further supervision.

(b) The court may not make the conditions of supervision more onerous than those originally imposed except pursuant to a revocation proceeding under this Act.

(c) Whenever the court finds that the division of community-based services is unwilling or unable to comply with an order issued it pursuant to Section 3-302, the court shall modify the order or discharge the offender from further supervision.

(d) The court shall discharge the offender from supervision when the term of community supervision and any extensions of that term have expired.

§ 3-306. [Transfer of Jurisdiction.]

(a) Whenever a court authorizes an offender sentenced to community supervision to reside in this State but outside the jurisdiction of the sentencing court, the court may:

(1) retain jurisdiction over the offender; or

(2) transfer jurisdiction over the offender to an appropriate court in the jurisdiction in which the offender will reside. A court to which jurisdiction is transferred has the same powers as the sentencing court.

(b) [Reserved for ratification of the Interstate Compact for the Supervision of Parolees and Probationers.]

§ 3-307. [Violation of Conditions.]

(a) Whenever a community service officer believes that an offender sentenced to community supervision has violated a condition of his supervision, he shall submit a written report to the sentencing court.

(b) Whenever the sentencing court believes that an offender sentenced to community supervision has violated a condition of his supervision, it may:

(1) suspend with an appropriate notation in the record any further proceeding on the alleged violation;

(2) instruct the community service officer to handle the matter informally without instituting formal revocation procedures;

(3) request the offender to meet informally with it to review the offender's obligations under the sentence;

(4) issue an order for the offender to appear at a time, date, and place for a hearing on the violation; or

(5) if the offender does not comply with the order to appear at the hearing or it otherwise appears unlikely that he will comply, issue a warrant for the arrest of the offender. Any law enforcement officer authorized to serve criminal process in this State to whom a warrant issued under this subsection is delivered shall execute the warrant by arresting the offender.

(c) An order or warrant issued under this section must be accompanied by written notice of:

(1) the conditions alleged to have been violated and the facts and circumstances surrounding the alleged violation;

(2) the right to a preliminary hearing upon detention and the rights and procedures applicable to that hearing;

(3) the right to a revocation hearing and the rights and procedures applicable to that hearing;

(4) the manner in which he may secure appointed legal counsel, if eligible; and

(5) the possible sanctions that may be ordered by the sentencing court if it finds a violation of the conditions of supervision has occurred.

(d) Whenever the court issues an order or warrant pursuant to this section, it shall notify the prosecuting attorney who shall represent the state.

§ 3-308. [Preliminary Hearing.]

(a) If an offender is not detained before a hearing on the alleged violation, he shall appear at the time, date, and place in the order directing him to appear.

(b) Upon the arrest and detention of an offender for violation of a condition of his supervision, a (magistrate) without unnecessary delay shall hold a preliminary hearing to determine whether there is probable cause to believe that a violation has occurred.

(c) At the preliminary hearing:

(1) the state and the offender may offer evidence, subpoena witnesses, call and cross-examine witnesses, and present arguments; and

(2) the offender is entitled to be represented by legal counsel and, if indigent, to have legal counsel appointed for him.

(d) If the [magistrate] determines from the evidence that there is probable cause to believe that the offender violated a condition of his supervision, he shall determine whether the offender is eligible for bail or other form of release in the manner authorized for a person accused of an offense and awaiting trial.

(e) If the [magistrate] determines there is not probable cause, he shall discharge the offender and further proceedings relating to the alleged violation terminates.

§ 3–309.   [Revocation Hearing.]

(a) Within 30 days after issuance of an order to appear or the arrest of the offender, the court having jurisdiction over the offender shall hold a hearing to determine whether a violation of a condition of supervision has occurred and, if so, whether revocation of community supervision is warranted.

(b) At the hearing:

(1) the state and the offender may offer evidence, subpoena witnesses, call and cross-examine witnesses, and present arguments;

(2) the offender is entitled to be represented by legal counsel and, if indigent, to have legal counsel appointed for him; and

(3) the court shall assure a full and complete record of the hearing.

(c) The court shall render a decision on the record at the hearing or in writing within 14 days after the hearing. The court shall place on the record its findings of fact and reasons for its decision.

§ 3–310.   [Sanctions for Violation.]

(a) If the court finds that the offender violated a condition of community supervision, it shall, consistent with what is reasonably likely to promote the purpose of the sentence and the effectiveness of a system of supervised release:

(1) continue supervision in the community under the conditions previously imposed;

(2) intensify supervision with an increased reporting requirement;

(3) impose additional conditions of supervision authorized by this Act;

(4) impose a fine not to exceed the fine that could originally have been imposed for the offense committed;

(5) extend the term of supervision;

(6) require service of a term of periodic confinement; or

(7) require service of a term of continuous confinement.

(b) The court shall comply with applicable guidelines of the sentencing commission and the provisions of Section 3–207 in exercising its powers under this section. An order under this section may not extend the total period of supervision and confinement beyond the maximum term of supervision authorized by law for the offense for which the offender was originally sentenced.

§ 3–311.   [Revocation Proceedings; Simultaneous Proceedings.]

(a) Whenever criminal proceedings are pending against an offender serving a term of community supervision for an offense arising out of a transaction also involving a violation of a condition of his supervision, a revocation hearing to revoke his supervision shall be stayed until the criminal proceedings are concluded.

(b) Testimony or other information given by an offender at a revocation hearing on a charge of violation of a condition of his community supervision or any information directly or indirectly derived from that testimony or information may not be used against the offender in any criminal prosecution.

(c) Evidence adduced at the criminal proceedings and the outcome of the proceedings is admissible at a revocation hearing if otherwise relevant.

§ 3–312.   [Appellate Review of Revocation Proceedings.]

Whenever a court imposes a penalty under Section 3–310 for violation of a condition of community supervision, the penalty shall be treated as an imposition of sentence for purposes of appellate review pursuant to Section 3–208.

PART 4

FINES

§ 3–401. [Fines; Imposition.]

(a) A court shall comply with applicable guidelines of the sentencing commission and the provisions of Section 3–207 in imposing fines.

(b) The court shall specify the time for payment of a fine and may permit payment in installments. The court may not establish a payment schedule extending beyond the statutory maximum term of community supervision that could have been imposed for the offense.

(c) In determining the amount and method of payment of a fine, the court shall consider the financial resources and future ability of the offender to pay the fine and the likely adverse effect a fine will have on his ability to make restitution and on dependents of the offender. The court may not impose a fine that will prevent the defendant from making court-ordered restitution.

(d) If an offender is sentenced to pay a fine, the court may not impose at the same time an alternative sentence of confinement to be served in the event the fine is not paid.

§ 3–402. [Trust for Civil Judgments.]

(a) Whenever a fine could be imposed on an offender based on gain derived from or loss caused by his offense, the court, as an alternative to imposing the fine, may require the offender to establish a trust and to pay into the trust an amount equal to the amount of the fine. The trust shall be established and a trustee appointed in a manner approved by the court.

(b) The provisions of the trust shall authorize the trustee to pay out of the trust any judgment obtained against the offender in a civil action, commenced within 3 years after the date the sentence becomes final, for loss arising out of the offense or any transaction which is part of the same continuous scheme of criminal activity. The trustee may make payments from the trust based on a settlement agreement between the offender and a victim if approved by the court. If the trust is insufficient to pay all claims arising out of the offense or scheme of criminal activity, the court may approve a formula for partial payment.

(c) If the court determines that it is unlikely the funds will be needed to pay civil judgments rendered against the offender, the court shall order the funds remaining in the trust to be paid to the State.

(d) The court may order the defendant to give notice of the availability and the terms of the trust to the class of persons or the members of the public likely to have suffered loss because of the offense or the scheme of which the offense was a part.

(e) Payment of any civil judgment from the trust satisfies the judgment to the extent of the payment. This section does not prevent a judgment creditor from enforcing the judgment or any unpaid portion directly against the offender. Payment directly by the offender of any civil judgment arising out of the offense subrogates the offender to the judgment creditor's claim against the trust.

(f) The trust is not an asset of the offender and is not subject to attachment, garnishment, or other enforcement proceedings.

(g) Failure to comply with an order pursuant to this section is treated in the same manner as nonpayment of a fine.

§ 3–403. [Modification or Waiver.]

An offender at any time may petition the sentencing court to adjust or otherwise waive payment of any fine imposed or any unpaid portion thereof. If the court finds that the circumstances upon which it based the imposition or amount and method of payment of the fine no longer exist or that it otherwise would be unjust to require payment of the fine as imposed, the court may adjust or waive payment of the unpaid portion thereof or modify the time or method of payment. The court may extend the payment schedule, but a payment schedule may not require a payment on a date beyond the statutory maximum term of community supervision that could have been imposed for the offense.

§ 3–404. [Nonpayment.]

(a) If an offender sentenced to pay a fine defaults in payment, the court upon the motion of the prosecuting attorney or its own motion may issue an order requiring him to show cause why he should not be confined for nonpayment. The court may order him to appear at a time, date, and place for a hearing or issue a warrant for his arrest. The order or warrant must be accompanied by written notice of his right to a hearing and the rights and procedures applicable thereto. The procedures and rights of the offender at the hearing are the same as those applicable to a hearing to revoke community supervision.

(b) Unless the offender shows that his default was not attributable to an intentional refusal to obey the sentence of the court or to a failure on his part to make a good faith effort to obtain the necessary funds for payment, the court may order the offender to serve a term of periodic or continuous confinement not to exceed [___ years] if imposed for conviction of a felony or [___ year] if imposed for conviction of a misdemeanor. The term runs consecutively with any other term of confinement being served by the offender. The court may provide in its order that payment or satisfaction of the fine at any time will entitle the offender to his release from confinement or, after entering the order, at any time for good cause shown may reduce the term of confinement, including payment or satisfaction of the fine.

(c) The court shall comply with applicable guidelines of the sentencing commission and the provisions of Section 3-207 in imposing confinement for nonpayment of a fine.

(d) If a fine is imposed on an organization, it is the duty of any person authorized to order the disbursement of assets of the organization, and his superiors, to pay the fine from assets of the organization under his control. The failure of a person to do so renders him subject to an order to show cause why he should not be confined.

(e) The court may order [community service officer] to supervise the payment of the fine and to report to the court a default in payment.

(f) A fine constitutes a judgment rendered in favor of the State. Following a default in the payment of a fine or any installment thereof, the sentencing court may order the fine to be collected by any method authorized for the enforcement of other money judgments rendered in favor of the State.

PART 5

CONFINEMENT

§ 3-501. [Sentences to Confinement; Good Time Reductions.]

(a) A sentence to a term of confinement must be for a definite period prescribed by this Act.

(b) An offender's term of continuous confinement must be reduced for good behavior by one day for each day or part of a day he serves unless withheld for disciplinary purposes under this Act.

(c) For split sentences, reductions for good behavior are credited only for time spent in confinement and reduce the portion of the sentence involving confinement. Good time may not be credited for sentences to periodic confinement.

(d) The director shall release an offender who has served the sentence imposed minus reductions for good behavior.

§ 3-502. [Computation of Term of Confinement.]

(a) A sentence to a term of confinement commences on the date the offender is received by the department pursuant to the sentence unless the sentence is to be served concurrently with another sentence to be served in the custody of another jurisdiction, in which case the term commences on the date he is received by the other jurisdiction or the date the sentence is imposed, whichever is later.

(b) An offender must be given credit against his sentence for all time spent in confinement before being received by the department pursuant to the sentence as a result of the offense for which the sentence was imposed.

(c) If an offender is arrested on one charge and later prosecuted on another charge growing out of conduct occurring before his arrest, he must be given credit against his sentence resulting from that prosecution for all time spent in confinement under the former charge which has not been credited against another sentence.

(d) If an offender is subject to multiple sentences and one is set aside as the result of direct or collateral attack, he must be given credit against his remaining sentences for all time served pursuant to the sentence set aside which has not been credited against another sentence.

(e) If a sentence is set aside and the offender is reprosecuted or resentenced for the same offense or for another offense based on the same conduct, he must be given credit against his new sentence for all time served pursuant to the prior sentence which has not been credited against another sentence.

(f) Credit given an offender for time served before being received by the department must include an additional credit for good time credited while confined. A person confined before commencement of his sentence earns good time reductions and otherwise is subject to Section 3–501(b) as if he were an offender.

§ 3–503. [Split Sentence.]

(a) A court may impose a split sentence of continuous confinement for not more than 180 days, or periodic confinement during a period of not more than 180 days, followed by a term of community supervision.

(b) In imposing a split sentence of continuous confinement and community supervision the court shall:

(1) specify that the term of confinement be served in the custody of the department's division of community-based services, or division of jail administration; and

(2) establish the term of the confinement and the term and conditions of community supervision.

(c) In imposing a split sentence of periodic confinement and community supervision the court shall:

(1) place the offender in the custody of the division of community-based services; and

(2) establish the term and conditions of the periodic confinement and community supervision.

(d) At the expiration of a term of continuous or periodic confinement, the offender shall be transferred to the custody of the division of community-based services for supervision in the community.

(e) The court shall comply with applicable guidelines of the sentencing commission and the provisions of Section 3–207 in exercising its powers under this section.

§ 3–504. [Periodic Confinement; Effect.]

Under a sentence to the custody of the division of community-based services for a term of periodic confinement the offender serves the sentence of confinement on specified days or during specified parts of days, or both; in a correctional facility with the remainder of the time to be spent at liberty in the community subject to the supervision of the division under conditions imposed by the sentencing court.

§ 3–505. [Term and Conditions of Periodic Confinement.]

(a) If the court sentences an offender to a term of periodic confinement, it may attach one or more of the conditions authorized for a sentence to community supervision and shall specify:

(1) the term of periodic confinement, which may not exceed the maximum sentence prescribed for the offense; and

(2) the days or parts of days the offender is to be confined.

(b) The court shall comply with applicable guidelines of the sentencing commission and the provisions of Section 3–207 in exercising its powers under this section.

§ 3–506. [Violation of Conditions of Periodic Confinement.]

Whenever an offender sentenced to a term of periodic confinement fails to return to his place of confinement at the time specified in his sentence or violates any condition imposed, he shall be treated as if he were in violation of a condition of community supervision.

§ 3–507. [Pre-release and Post-release Programs.]

(a) The director shall establish:

(1) a pre-release assistance program to assist confined persons about to be released; and

(2) a post-release assistance program for released persons.

(b) The pre-release and post-release assistance programs shall provide counseling and other services and, to the extent feasible, shall utilize existing resources from the community.

(c) A person released from confinement may participate in a post-release assistance program for one year after his release.

(d) Within legislative appropriation therefor, the director may provide economic assistance to released persons conditioned upon their participation in release assistance programs.

§ 3–508. [Release of Confined Persons.]

(a) Upon final release of a confined person from a facility after a period of confinement exceeding 6 months, the chief executive officer of the facility shall provide him, if he is unable to provide them himself, sufficient resources to meet the person's immediate needs including:

(1) clothing appropriate to the season of the year; and

(2) transportation to the place where he can reasonably be expected to reside.

(b) If at the time of release a confined person is too ill or feeble or otherwise unable to care for himself upon release, the chief executive officer shall make arrangements for his care.

§ 3–509. [Released Offender Loan Fund.]

(a) The director may establish and shall administer a released-offender loan fund to provide loans to offenders released from continuous confinement in order to facilitate their adjustment to the free community if their own financial resources are inadequate for that purpose. The loan fund may be composed of appropriated state money, money resulting from the repayment of loans, interest earned on loans and other investments made by the fund, and money contributed to the fund. Loans made by the fund may be at interest, but the director may establish an interest rate below the prevailing market rate if he believes it to be in the public interest.

(b) If the director establishes the fund, he shall adopt rules for its administration.

(c) The director with the approval of the Governor may contract with a private lending institution to administer the fund.

PART 6

RESTITUTION

§ 3–601. [Sentence of Restitution.]

(a) A sentencing court may sentence an offender to make restitution to the victim of the offense.

(b) Whenever the court believes that restitution may be a proper sentence or the victim of the offense or the prosecuting attorney requests, the court shall order the presentence service officer to include in the presentence report documentation regarding the nature and amount of the victim's pecuniary loss.

(c) The court shall specify the amount and time of payment or other restitution to the victim and may permit payment or performance in installments. The court may not establish a payment or performance schedule extending beyond the statutory maximum term of community supervision that could have been imposed for the offense.

(d) In determining the amount and method of payment or other restitution, the court shall consider the financial resources and future ability of the offender to pay or perform. The court may provide for payment to the victim up to but not in excess of the pecuniary loss caused by the offense. The defendant is entitled to assert any defense that he could raise in a civil action for the loss

sought to be compensated by the restitution order.

(e) For purposes of this section "pecuniary loss" means:

(1) all special damages, but not general damages, substantiated by evidence in the record, which a person could recover against the offender in a civil action arising out of the facts or events constituting the offender's criminal activities, including without limitation the money equivalent of loss resulting from property taken, destroyed, broken, or otherwise harmed and out-of-pocket losses, such as medical expenses;

(2) reasonable out-of-pocket expenses incurred by the victim resulting from the filing of charges or cooperating in the investigation and prosecution of the offense[.] [; and]

[(3) interest on the amount of pecuniary loss from the time of loss until payment is made.]

(f) An insurer or surety that has paid any part of the victim's pecuniary loss is not a victim for purposes of obtaining restitution.

(g) The court may order a community-service officer to supervise the making of restitution and to report to the court a default in payment.

§ 3–602. [Modification or Waiver.]

An offender at any time may petition the sentencing court to adjust or otherwise waive payment or performance of any ordered restitution or any unpaid or unperformed portion thereof. The court shall schedule a hearing and give the victim notice of the hearing, date, place, and time and inform the victim that he will have an opportunity to be heard. If the court finds that the circumstances upon which it based the imposition or amount and method of payment or other restitution ordered no longer exist or that it otherwise would be unjust to require payment or other restitution as imposed, the court may adjust or waive payment of the unpaid portion thereof or other restitution or modify the time or method of making restitution. The court may extend the restitution schedule, but not beyond the statutory maximum term of community supervision that could have been imposed for the offense.

§ 3–603. [Default.]

(a) If an offender sentenced to make restitution defaults for 60 days, the court upon the motion of the prosecuting attorney, the victim, or its own motion may issue an order requiring the offender to show cause why he should not be confined for failure to obey the sentence of the court. The court may order the offender to appear at a time, date, and place for a hearing or issue a warrant for his arrest. The order or warrant shall be accompanied by written notice of his right to a hearing and the rights and procedures applicable thereto. The procedures and rights of the offender at the hearing shall be the same as those applicable to a hearing to revoke community supervision.

(b) Unless the offender shows that his default was not attributable to an intentional refusal to obey the sentence of the court or to a failure on his part to make a good faith effort to obtain the necessary funds for payment, the court may order the offender to serve a term of periodic or continuous confinement not to exceed [___ years] if imposed for conviction of a felony or [___ years] if imposed for conviction of a misdemeanor. The term runs consecutively with any other term of confinement being served by the offender. The court may provide in its order that payment or

satisfaction of the restitution order at any time will entitle the offender to his release from confinement or, after entering the order, at any time for good cause shown may reduce the term of confinement, including payment or satisfaction of the restitution order.

(c) The court shall comply with applicable guidelines of the sentencing commission and the provisions of Section 3–207 in imposing confinement for nonpayment of a restitution order.

(d) If restitution is imposed on an organization, it is the duty of any person authorized to order the disbursement of assets of the organization, and his superiors, to pay the restitution from assets of the organization under his control. Failure to do so renders a person subject to an order to show cause why he should not be confined.

(e) An order to pay restitution constitutes a judgment rendered in favor of the State and following a default in the payment of restitution or any installment thereof, the sentencing court may order the restitution to be collected by any method authorized for the enforcement of other judgments for money rendered in favor of the State.

§ 3–604. [Victim's Compensation.]

(a) Whenever a victim is paid by a crime victim's reparation fund for loss arising out of a criminal act, the fund is subrogated to the rights of the victim to any restitution ordered by the court and to any funds paid into a trust in lieu of a fine to satisfy civil judgments.

(b) The rights of the crime victim's reparation fund are subordinate to the claims of victims who have suffered loss arising out of the offenses or any transaction which is part of the same continuous scheme of criminal activity.

§ 3–605. [Civil Actions.]

(a) This Act does not limit or impair the right of a victim to sue and recover damages from the offender in a civil action.

(b) The findings in the sentencing hearing and the fact that restitution was required or paid is not admissible as evidence in a civil action and has no legal effect on the merits of a civil action.

(c) Any restitution paid by the offender to the victim shall be set off against any judgment in favor of the victim in a civil action arising out of the facts or events which were the basis for the restitution. The court trying the civil action shall hold a separate hearing to determine the validity and amount of any set-off asserted by the defendant.

ARTICLE 4

TREATMENT OF CONVICTED AND CONFINED PERSONS

PREFATORY NOTE

Article 4 is the legislative embodiment of a prescriptive code of treatment of offenders. It reflects an express assumption of the philosophy that "a prisoner retains all the rights of an ordinary citizen except those expressly or by necessary implication taken from him by law." Coffee v. Reichard, 143 F.2d 413 (6th Cir. 1944). Accord, e.g., Morales v. Schmidt, 340 F.Supp. 544, 553–54 (W.D.Wis.1972); United States ex rel. Wolfish v. United States, 428 F.Supp. 333 (S.D.N.Y.1977) (opinion on motion for summary judgment). Cf. Procunier v. Martinez, 416 U.S. 396 (1974); Bounds v. Smith, 45 U.S.L.W. 4411 (1977). It is a philosophy supported by many authorities, and it is gaining increasing recognition by the courts. See e.g., ABA Joint Comm. on the Legal Status of Prisoners, Standards Relating to the Legal Status of Prisoners, § 1.1 and Commentary (Tent. Dr.1977) reprinted in 14 Am.Crim.L.Rev. 377 (1977) [hereinafter cited as ABA Joint Comm.]; S. Kranz, R. Bell, & M. Magruder, Model Rules and Regulations on Prisoners' Rights and Responsibilities 1–4 (1977) [hereinafter cited as Kranz]; Nat'l Advisory Comm'n on Criminal Justice Standards & Goals, Corrections 17–21 (1973) [hereinafter cited as Nat'l Advisory Comm'n]. It has, moreover, been enacted into law in at least one state. Cal.Penal Code, § 2601 (West 1976) (a confined offender is "deprived of such rights, and only such rights, as is necessary in order to provide for the reasonable security of the institution in which he is confined and for the reasonable protection of the public").

The legislative recognition that a confined person generally retains the rights of a free citizen is by no means meant to deprecate the legitimate interests of institutional security and public safety. There is throughout Article 4 an affirmation that these security and safety interests are and must be of paramount importance. Article 4 represents the view that security and safety can be maintained consistent with the treatment of confined persons that is mandated or encouraged in the various sections. Thus, the Article describes a just—and safe—correctional system in which attention is paid to the societal interest in humane treatment of confined persons as well as to the personal interests of confined persons themselves in the treatment provided them. By so describing the system, it is believed that society will more nearly achieve the goal of every correctional system—to return to society confined persons who will adjust to the outside world and not recidivate. As was stated by the ABA Joint Committee:

Virtually all prisoners will someday be released to a society in which ... they will daily be required to make choices and exercise self-restraint. If our institutions of confinement do not replace self-restraint for compelled restraint, and encourage choice rather than rote obedience, released prisoners will continue to be unable to deal with the "real" world.

ABA Joint Comm. at 418–19.

Provision of rehabilitative programs and services is mandated throughout the Act. See e.g., Section 2–105 supra. It is intended that confined persons will be encouraged to avail themselves of opportunities presented by these programs and services. And many of the provisions are clearly drafted to provide incentives to confined persons to foster their participation. See e.g., Sections 4–801 to 4–816 infra. Forced rehabilitation of offenders is, however, rejected as both denigrating to the individuals involved and not productive of long-term results. See e.g., ABA Joint Comm., §§ 3.4 and 5.7 and Commentary; Nat'l Advisory Comm'n Correc.Std. 2.9 and Commentary.

Part 1 contains a delineation of the most important of the protected interests that are retained by confined persons. Some of these interest, such as, for example, medical treatment and physical exercise, address basic needs. Other protected interests, such as access to the courts, law libraries, and legal assistance, reflect, to a large degree, what has already been mandated by the courts. The protected interests in Part 1, however, extend beyond basic needs and court mandates and include free-citizen rights whose extension to confined persons is consistent with safety and security. Part 2, by creating the office of correctional mediator, provides one method to relieve tensions and mediate disputes within facilities. Part 3 requires the adoption of grievance procedures, another method to relieve tensions and permit a dialogue for change—when change is necessary—within facilities. Part 4 deals with the assignment, classification, and transfer of persons in the custody of the department. These decisions have a substantial impact on the lives of confined persons; this Part describes procedures by which these decisions must be made. Part 5 deals with discipline within facilities. It prescribes a code of punishment proportionate to the seriousness of the offense and affords some degree of due process protection to the confined person charged with a disciplinary infraction. Part 6 deals with programs putting confined persons at risk. It reflects the belief that informed confined-persons consent is possible in a correctional setting that eliminates parole, earned good time, and coerced rehabilitation, and that provides real earning capacity to confined persons so that they have sources alternative to experimentation by which to obtain funds. Part 7 provides for implementation, on a limited basis at least at first, of a voucher program. The program is intended to increase the number and effectiveness of programs offered confined persons and to encourage confined persons to take full advantage of such programs by permitting them to choose those programs in which they will participate. Part 8 provides for the employment of confined persons at "real" wages and in a realistic work environment. It encourages provision of a full panoply of employment and vocational training opportunities and, in moving towards a goal of full employment for confined persons, permits employment of confined persons by private enterprise and payment of competitive wages. Part 9 deals with compensation for work-related offender injuries. Part 10 deals with the collateral consequences of a conviction. It acts to restore to ex-offenders those rights abridged by conviction or confinement and to protect him from employment discrimination when the employment he seeks is not directly related to the offense for which he was convicted.

ARTICLE 4

TREATMENT OF CONVICTED AND CONFINED PERSONS

PART 1

PROTECTED INTERESTS AND TREATMENT OF CONFINED PERSONS

§ 4-101. [Definitions.]

As used in this Part, unless the context otherwise requires:

(1) "clergyman" means a minister, priest, rabbi, accredited Christian Science Practitioner, or other similar functionary of a religious organization;

(2) "contraband" means a weapon, controlled substance, escape plan, or material which may not be lawfully possessed by the general public;

(3) "intercept" means to intentionally read a written communication or to intentionally hear an oral or recorded communication;

(4) "medical care" means the diagnosis and treatment of physical, dental, or mental health problems;

(5) "prohibited material" means material that the director classifies as prohibited material pursuant to this Act;

(6) "reading material" means a book, a single copy or subscription to a periodical, magazine, newspaper, newsletter, or pamphlet, whether or not reproduced by a printing press, or material that qualifies for second-class mailing privileges.

(7) "written communication" means a communication which is fixed in a tangible medium of expression; and

(8) "scanner" means a metal detector, x-ray machine, fluoroscope, or other non-intrusive method used to detect the presence of particular substances.

§ 4-102. [Protected Interests; General Provisions.]

(a) Whenever this Act specifically provides a confined person with a "protected interest," the director shall take appropriate measures to preserve and facilitate the full realization of that interest.

(b) The director may suspend or limit the realization of a protected interest otherwise provided by this Act during an emergency in a facility or part of a facility if the director finds that unusual conditions exist in a facility that imminently jeopardize the safety of the public or the security or safety within a facility and that extreme measures are necessary. The director shall rescind the suspension as soon as the emergency is over and, within 30 days after the emergency is over, submit to the Governor a written report describing the nature of the emergency and the measures taken.

(c) Consistent with the provisions of this Part that specifically require or prohibit the performance of an act by the director, the director may adopt measures that:

(1) limit the full realization of a protected interest if the measures are designed to protect the safety of the public or the security or safety within a facility; and

(2) regulate the time, place, and manner of the realization of a protected interest if the

measures are designed to assure the orderly administration of a facility.

(d) Whenever the director adopts measures pursuant to subsection (c), they must be:

(1) designed to create no greater restriction on the protected interest than reasonably necessary to accomplish the purpose for which they were adopted; and

(2) adopted in accordance with the procedures established for the adoption of rules.

§ 4–103.　[Prohibited Material.]

(a) The director may adopt rules:

(1) classifying material as prohibited material;

(2) preventing the introduction of prohibited material into a facility; and

(3) making the possession of prohibited material by a confined person a disciplinary infraction.

(b) The director may classify as prohibited material material other than contraband which:

(1) if possessed by confined persons, may jeopardize the safety of the public or the security or safety within a facility or unreasonably interfere with the realization of protected interests of other confined persons;

(2) is determined by the [department of health] to constitute an unreasonable health hazard; or

(3) is owned by another and possessed by a confined person without permission of the owner.

(c) Material may not be classified as prohibited material solely on the basis of its source or because other confined persons do not possess similar material.

§ 4–104.　[Physical Security.]

(a) A confined person has a protected interest in his own physical security.

(b) The director shall:

(1) take adequate measures designed to protect a confined person from assaults;

(2) adopt rules limiting the use of physical force by employees to those situations in which physical force is believed to be reasonably necessary to protect the safety of the public or security or safety within a facility;

(3) discipline a confined person or employee who commits an assault;

(4) request prosecuting authorities to prosecute felonies involving physical violence occurring within a facility or involving a confined person and cooperate with prosecuting authorities in the course of those prosecutions; and

(5) keep records and report annually to the Governor on the extent of injuries or deaths incurred by confined persons and employees within facilities.

§ 4–105.　[Medical Care.]

(a) A confined person has a protected interest in receiving needed routine and emergency medical care.

(b) The director shall assure that:

(1) a newly admitted confined person receives an examination by a person trained to ascertain visible or common symptoms of communicable disease and conditions requiring immediate medical attention by a physician;

(2) except as provided in Section 4–126, a confined person receives a thorough physical and dental examination in accordance with accepted medical practice and standards,

(i) within 2 weeks after his initial admission to a facility unless earlier released; and

(ii) thereafter, not less than every 2 years and, if the most recent examination was given more than one year earlier, upon final release from the facility;

(3) appropriately trained persons are,

(i) present at each facility or otherwise reasonably available on a daily basis to evaluate requests for medical care from confined persons, and

(ii) reasonably available to provide emergency medical care;

(4) a confined person has access to needed routine and emergency medical care in a timely manner consistent with accepted medical practice and standards;

(5) a confined person found to have a communicable disease is isolated from the general population of a facility to the extent required by accepted medical practice and standards;

(6) a confined person requiring medical care not available in the facility is transferred to a

hospital or other appropriate place providing the care; and

(7) medical records of confined persons are:

(i) maintained in a confidential and secure manner;

(ii) compiled and maintained in accordance with accepted medical practice and standards; and

(iii) retained for at least 5 years after the person is released from the facility.

(c) The director shall permit confined persons to utilize their own resources to obtain medical care from any licensed health profession. He may require that the medical care be provided in a way that is consistent with the person's classification and facility assignment and that least interferes with the established administrative procedures of the facility.

(d) Whenever the department provides medical care to a confined person it is entitled to recover insurance or other benefits available to the confined person to pay for medical care.

(e) An employee of the department may not impede or unreasonably delay the access of a confined person to medical care.

§ 4–106. [Right to Healthful Environment.]

(a) A confined person has a protected interest in a healthful, safe, and sanitary living environment. The [director] of the [department of health], after consultation with the director of corrections, shall designate the appropriate health, safety, and sanitation requirements applicable to facilities and describe what would be substantial compliance with those requirements.

(b) The [director] of the [department of health] shall order closed any facility or part of a facility that he finds is not fit for human habitation.

(c) The [director] of the [department of health] and persons from other relevant departments [and two members of the advisory committee] shall inspect each facility semiannually. The [director] of the [department of health] shall forward to the director of corrections a written report after each inspection. The report shall contain a description of the conditions of the facility, and either:

(1) a certification that the facility is in substantial compliance with health, safety and sanitation requirements; or

(2) a statement that the facility is not in substantial compliance with health, safety, and sanitation requirements, together with a list of the particular violations and a specification of which violations prevent the [director] of the [department of health] from certifying the facility as being in substantial compliance. The [director] of the [department of health] also shall specify the date for reinspection of the facility if reinspection is necessary to determine whether the facility has been brought into substantial compliance.

(d) If at the time of reinspection the facility or part of the facility is still not in substantial compliance, the [director] of the [department of health] shall order closed the facility or the substandard part of the facility or issue any other order necessary to assure that the facility is brought into compliance within a reasonable time.

(e) Immediately after the [director] of the [department of health] orders a facility or part of a facility to be closed, the director of corrections shall transfer persons confined therein to another suitable facility or to the division of community-based services for supervision in the community.

(f) Reports issued pursuant to subsection (c) must be available for public inspection.

[(g) Whenever the [director] of the [department of health] finds that a facility or part of a facility unreasonably endangers the health of the persons confined therein he shall notify the director of corrections. The director shall credit against the sentences of all persons confined therein one additional day for every 3 days spent in the facility or part of the facility from the date the director receives the notice from the [director] of the [department of health] until the [director] of the [department of health] certifies that the facility or part of the facility no longer unreasonably endangers health.]

§ 4–107. [Physical Exercise.]

A confined person has a protected interest in reasonable opportunities for physical exercise.

§ 4–108. [Legal Assistance.]

(a) A confined person has a protected interest in access to assistance in legal matters.

(b) The office of correctional legal services shall provide to each indigent person in the custody of the department and not otherwise represented assistance at state expense in any of the following:

(1) post-conviction proceedings testing the legality of conviction or confinement;

(2) court proceedings challenging conditions of confinement or other correctional supervision;

(3) revocation of conditional liberty or supervision;

(4) proceedings before discipline or classification committees to the extent authorized by this Act or the director; and

(5) civil proceedings in which a confined person is a defendant or may be bound by a proceeding he did not initiate.

(c) Assistance pursuant to subsection (b) must:

(1) include consultation regarding legal matters and, unless an attorney provided by the office believes the claim is clearly frivolous, representation in legal proceedings; and

(2) be provided by a licensed attorney or other person authorized to practice law or to give legal assistance. The office shall provide a sufficient number of persons other than licensed attorneys to consult with confined persons on other matters affecting their status in the department.

(d) Persons providing legal assistance to confined persons may have access to facilities and confined persons at any reasonable time unless the director determines that a state of emergency exists. An employee of the department may not impede or unreasonably delay the access of a confined person to legal assistance.

§ 4–109. [Participating in the Legal Process.]

(a) A confined person has a protected interest in participating in the legal process.

(b) The director shall permit a confined person to offer testimony by deposition and provide space for him to do so.

(c) The director shall comply with a court order directing a confined person to attend in this state a legal proceeding directly involving that person's interest.

(d) If a third person requests a confined person to attend a legal proceeding that does not directly involve the confined person's interest, the director may require, as a condition of assuring the confined person's attendance, that the third person make arrangements to pay all or part of the expense of attendance including the expense of any necessary escort.

(e) If a confined person requests permission to attend a legal proceeding involving his interests, the director may require, as a condition of his attendance, that the confined person pay all or part of the expense of attendance, including the expense of any necessary escort. In determining whether to assess the expense against a confined person the director shall consider the confined person's available funds as well as whether he initiated the proceedings.

§ 4–110. [Access to Legal Materials.]

(a) A confined person has a protected interest in access to legal materials.

(b) The director shall facilitate reasonable access to legal materials and, to the extent necessary, provide support services and maintain a collection of basic legal materials in each facility housing persons sentenced to continuous confinement.

§ 4–111. [Discrimination Based on Race, Religion, National Origin, or Sex.]

(a) A confined person has a protected interest in freedom from discrimination on the basis of race, religion, national origin, or sex.

(b) The director shall prevent any discrimination on the basis of race, religion, national origin, or sex. Confined persons of either sex may be assigned to the same facility, or they may be assigned to separate facilities if there is essential equality in living conditions, decisionmaking processes affecting the status and activities of confined persons, and the availability of community and institutional programs, including educational, employment, and vocational training opportunities.

§ 4–112. [Absentee Voting.]

A confined person otherwise eligible to vote has a protected interest in voting in elections. The director shall assure that confined persons otherwise eligible to vote are informed of the right to vote by absentee ballot and, if requested, assure that confined persons are assisted in any procedural steps required to cast the ballot.

§ 4–113. [Religious Freedom.]

A confined person has a protected interest in participating in the religious services of his faith and otherwise enjoying the free exercise of his religion. To facilitate the free exercise of religion the director shall:

(1) assure that each chief executive officer fairly allocates available funds among all religions represented at the facility and provides each confined person with nutritious meals that do not violate the dietary laws of his religion;

(2) permit a confined person to comply with the dress or appearance requirements of his religion and observe the religious holidays of his faith unless to do so would jeopardize the safety of the public or security or safety within the facility; and

(3) permit a confined person access to a clergyman acting in his professional capacity unless the clergyman has been excluded from the facility pursuant to this Act. A confidential communication by a confined person to a clergyman of a different faith is privileged to the same extent as a confidential communication by a person to a clergyman of his own faith.

§ 4–114. [Communications.]

(a) A confined person has a protected interest in communicating privately with other persons by means of oral and written communication.

(b) The director shall:

(1) provide, at the department's expense, to each confined person a reasonable amount of stationery and writing implements;

(2) promptly transmit, at the department's expense,

(i) all written communications from a confined person to his attorney, the director, the correctional mediator, or any federal or state court having jurisdiction over a legal matter in which he is involved;

(ii) a reasonable number of written communications from a confined person to the Governor and members of the [Legislature];

(iii) up to 5 additional one-ounce written communications per week from the confined person to other persons; and

(iv) all written communications delivered to the facility and addressed to the confined person; and

(3) provide confined persons with access to telephones and permit a confined person to place and receive emergency telephone calls and those to or from his attorney.

(c) The director may not:

(1) limit the number of written communications that may be sent by a confined person at his own expense or received by him;

(2) limit the persons with whom a confined person exchanges written communications except pursuant to Section 4–118; or

(3) limit to less than 2 the number of 3–minute nonemergency telephone calls a confined person may place weekly at his own expense.

(d) Notwithstanding subsection (c), if a confined person sends more than 10 written communications per week beyond those sent at the department's expense or a confined person receives more than 10 written communications per week in response to any act of the confined person designed to result in a large amount of written correspondence, the director may require the confined person to pay the costs of processing the additional correspondence.

§ 4–115. [Visitation.]

(a) A confined person has a protected interest in receiving visitors from the free community.

(b) The director shall:

(1) establish a visiting schedule for each facility which provides opportunity for confined persons to meet with visitors and includes hours on holidays and weekends and in the evenings;

(2) permit each confined person to have at least [5] hours of visitation weekly and to accumulate unused visiting hours within a [2–month] period for extended visits within the established visiting schedule; and

(3) permit each confined person, other than a person classified as dangerous, to have monthly a private visit for a substantial period of time. Private visits need not be given to a confined person who has been permitted a furlough to visit his family or friends within the preceding 3 months.

(c) The director shall adopt measures to prevent the introduction of contraband or prohibited material into the facility by visitors. The director shall:

(1) assure that each visitor is given reasonable notice of what constitutes contraband and prohibited materials;

(2) utilize procedures, such as subjecting visitors to scanners or requiring thorough searches of confined persons both before and after visits, that minimize the need for more intrusive searches of visitors themselves;

(3) prohibit any search of a visitor unless he consents to be searched; and

(4) permit the exclusion from the facility of any visitor who refuses to consent to a search or causes a scanner to react or there is reliable information that he is carrying contraband or prohibited material.

(d) The director may not restrict the persons a confined person may receive as visitors except pursuant to Section 4–118.

§ 4–116. [Preserving Parental Relationships.]

(a) The director shall:

(1) assist confined persons in (i) communicating with their children and otherwise keeping informed of their affairs, and (ii) participating in decisions relating to the custody, care, and instruction of their children; and

(2) provide any confined person or any person accused of an offense access to relevant information about child-care facilities available in the department, counseling, and other assistance in order to aid the person in making arrangements for his child.

(b) The director may:

(1) establish and maintain facilities or parts of facilities suitable for the care and housing of confined persons with their children;

(2) authorize periodic extended or overnight visits by children with a confined person;

(3) authorize a child, upon the request of the confined person, to reside with the person in a facility while the person is entitled to custody of the child or if the person gives birth to the child during confinement.

(c) In determining whether a child may reside in a facility or visit a facility on an extended or overnight basis pursuant to subsection (b), the following factors, among others, must be considered:

(1) the best interest of the child and the confined person;

(2) the length of sentence imposed on the confined person and the likelihood that the child could remain in the facility throughout the confined person's term;

(3) the nature and extent of suitable facilities within the department;

(4) available alternatives that would protect and strengthen the relationship between the child and the confined person; and

(5) the age of the child.

(d) A child may not reside in a facility or visit a facility on an extended or overnight basis if:

(1) the division of correctional medical services certifies that the confined person is physically or emotionally unable to care for the child;

(2) the [Department of Welfare] certifies that the conditions in the facility will result in a substantial detriment to the physical or emotional well-being of the child; or

(3) the [juvenile, family court] orders that the child not do so.

(e) Whenever a child is authorized to reside in a facility or visit a facility on an extended or overnight basis, the director shall provide for the child's basic needs including food, clothing, and medical care if the confined person is unable to do so. The department is subrogated to any rights the confined person has against any other person or organization on account of those expenses.

(f) Whenever the director allows a child to reside with a confined person in a facility he shall notify the [Department of Welfare] which may take any action authorized by law to protect the best interest of the child.

(g) This section does not limit or otherwise affect the power of a court to determine the nature and extent of parental rights of confined persons or to determine the custody of children.

§ 4–117. [Searches and Interception of Communications.]

(a) The director may authorize the opening and search for contraband or prohibited material of an envelope, package, or container sent to or by a confined person. This subsection does not authorize the interception of written communications.

(b) The director may permit the interception of communications:

(1) upon obtaining reliable information that a particular communication may jeopardize the safety of the public or security or safety within a facility;

(2) in pursuance of a plan formulated by the chief executive officer of each facility for conducting random interception of communications by or to confined persons which plan must be approved by the director as providing the least intrusive invasion of privacy necessary to the safety of the public and security and safety within a facility; or

(3) when otherwise authorized by law.

(c) Notwithstanding subsection (b), a communication may not be intercepted except pursuant to a court order or unless otherwise authorized by law if the communication is one which reasonably should be anticipated to be:

(1) a privileged communication between a confined person and his attorney, clergyman, or physician; or

(2) between a confined person and the Governor, Attorney–General, a member of the [Legislature], a member of the state judiciary, a member of the advisory committee, or a member of the sentencing commission.

(d) Whenever the director is authorized by this Act to prevent a person from communicating with a confined person, the director, in lieu thereof, may authorize communications between the persons to be intercepted if both parties agree to the interception.

(e) The chief executive officer shall designate specifically employees authorized to intercept communications.

(f) If a written communication is intercepted, it thereafter shall be transmitted promptly to its addressee unless to do so would jeopardize the safety of the public or the security or safety within a facility. Only that part of the communication which jeopardizes the safety of the public or the security or safety within the facility may be excised.

(g) The director shall maintain a record of each interception or excision of a communication which includes the date of its occurrence, the content thereof, the person authorizing the interception or excision and the factual basis for his doing so, and the name of the confined person involved.

§ 4-118. [Limiting Visitors and Correspondents.]

(a) The director may issue an order that:

(1) prevents a specific person from communicating with a confined person if,

(i) the person seeking to communicate with a confined person knowingly has violated the rules relating to communication with confined persons, and

(ii) less restrictive measures, such as intercepting communications between the person and confined persons, are not feasible.

(2) prevents a specific person from entering facilities or visiting confined persons if,

(i) the person has in the past knowingly violated the rules of a facility relating to visitation; or

(ii) the director has reliable information that if admitted to the facility, the person is likely to advocate unlawful acts or rule violations that jeopardize the safety of the public or security or safety within a facility.

(b) A person against whom an order is issued is entitled to a written statement of the basis for the order, an opportunity to contest the order at a hearing before the director or his delegate, and judicial review.

(c) A confined person affected by an order issued pursuant to this section must be informed in writing of the order, the person against whom it is issued, and the specific reason for the order.

(d) An order pursuant to this section may not continue for more than 180 days without further evaluation.

§ 4-119. [Searches.]

(a) A confined person has a protected interest in freedom from unreasonable searches.

(b) Searches within facilities are subject to the following limitations:

(1) Searches must be conducted solely to detect contraband, prohibited material, or evidence of a crime;

(2) The frequency and scope of random or general searches of facilities or confined per-

sons must conform to a plan approved in advance by the director as providing the least intrusive invasion of privacy necessary to the safety of the public and security and safety within the facility. The plan may include provisions for search of confined persons upon admittance to a facility, upon leaving and returning to a facility, and upon entering or leaving designated areas. The plan need not be published or adopted in compliance with the procedures governing the adoption of rules or other measures.

(c) Searches other than those authorized by the plan and directed at living quarters or a particular confined person must be conducted only upon obtaining reliable information that a search is necessary to detect contraband, prohibited material, or evidence of a crime. Except in an emergency, prior authorization to conduct such a search must be obtained from the chief executive officer or supervisory-level correctional employees to whom the chief executive officer has delegated the responsibility to authorize searches.

(d) A search requiring a confined person to remove his clothes must be conducted with due regard to the privacy and dignity of the confined person.

(e) A search requiring the examination of a body cavity other than visual observation of the mouth, nose, or ear must be conducted by medically trained personnel of the Division of Correctional Medical Services in the medical quarters of the facility, or, in the absence of medical quarters, in other quarters appropriate for conducting a private examination.

§ 4-120. [Searches and Interceptions; Notice and Disclosure.]

(a) Within a reasonable time after contraband or prohibited material is seized or the substance of a communication is excised, the chief executive officer shall give the confined person affected a receipt identifying the sender, if any, the person conducting the search or interception, and the nature of the material confiscated or the reason for excising the communication.

(b) Except for interceptions conducted pursuant to a plan authorizing random interceptions, whenever a communication is intercepted the chief executive officer shall give the confined person a statement identifying the communica-

tion intercepted and the reason for its interception.

(c) A correctional employee who intercepts a communication may divulge the substance of the communication only when necessary to the performance of his official duties.

(d) Notwithstanding subsections (a) and (b), the chief executive officer may delay disclosing to a confined person information concerning the excising or interception of his communications until the disclosure no longer interferes with the purpose for which the excising or interception was conducted.

§ 4-121. [Privacy and Accuracy of Records.]

(a) A confined person has a protected interest in the privacy and accuracy of records maintained about him by the department.

(b) The department may not disclose information about a person who is or has been in its custody except pursuant to the written consent of the person, unless disclosure would be:

(1) to employees of the department or other persons providing services to persons in the custody of the department who need the information in the performance of their duties;

(2) pursuant to an order of a court of competent jurisdiction;

(3) to the correctional mediator;

(4) to a recipient who has provided the department in advance with adequate written assurance that the record will be used solely as a statistical research or reporting record and the record is to be transferred in a form that is not individually identifiable;

(5) to any governmental agency for a civil or criminal law enforcement or correctional activity if the activity is authorized by law and the head of the agency has made a written request to the director specifying the particular information desired and the law enforcement activity for which the information is sought; or

(6) in an emergency, to any appropriate person if the information is necessary to protect the health or safety of any person.

(c) Notwithstanding subsection (b), the director may authorize the disclosure of information about a person who is or has been in the custody of the department in an individually identifiable form whenever there is no practical way to obtain the consent of the person to whom the information pertains and the recipient has provided the department with advance adequate written assurance that:

(1) the information will be used solely for research purposes and will not be disseminated in an identifiable form;

(2) the recipient is affiliated with an agency that assumes responsibility for maintaining the confidentiality of the information;

(3) the recipient has implemented physical, technical, and administrative safeguards necessary to protect the confidentiality of the information; and

(4) disclosure of the information in identifiable form is necessary to accomplish the purpose of research and the value of the research outweighs the risk of disclosure.

(d) Persons in the custody of the department may not have access to the files of other persons in the custody of the department.

(e) Nothing in this section precludes the director from disclosing the name, former address, date and place of birth, sex, race, or national origin, length of sentence, crime committed, place of confinement, or residence of a person in the custody of the department to any person who the director believes has a valid interest in obtaining the information.

§ 4–122. [Access to Files.]

(a) The director, upon the request of a person who is or has been in the custody of the department, shall authorize him to:

(1) gain access to his central file and other information about him maintained by the department and copy all or any portion thereof in a form comprehensible to him;

(2) designate an employee of the office of correctional legal services, legal counsel, or, with the approval of the director, any other person to review and copy or accompany him in reviewing his file;

(3) request amendment or deletion of information contained in his file on the basis that the information is,

(i) erroneous;

(ii) deceptive; or

(iii) irrelevant or unnecessary; and

(4) add information to his file not clearly irrelevant to the functions of the department.

(b) Whenever a person requests an amendment or deletion of information in his file, the director shall review the file, determine whether the amendment or deletion is justified, order any change in the file he considers appropriate, and notify the person involved of his action. If the person is not satisfied with the action of the director, he may supplement the disputed information with his own version or explanation which must accompany any disclosure of the information it supplements.

(c) Notwithstanding subsection (a), the director may deny a person access to those portions of his file which a court has indicated in writing or the director determines consist of:

(1) diagnostic opinion relating to physical or mental health problems the disclosure of which might affect adversely a course of on-going treatment;

(2) information obtained upon a promise of confidentiality if the promise was made before the effective date of this Act;

(3) information about a pending investigation of alleged disciplinary or criminal activity; or

(4) other information that, if disclosed, would create a substantial risk of physical harm to any person.

(d) If any material or document in a person's file includes information on more than one person, the person may inspect only the information relating to him.

(e) Whenever the director denies access to portions of a person's file, he shall summarize the factual basis for the information. Upon the person's request, the director shall fully disclose the file to the correctional mediator who, without disclosing the information to the person, shall make a full investigation to determine the accuracy of the information and report his findings to the director and the person involved.

(f) Except for employees of the department authorized by the director to examine files in the course of their duties, the director shall maintain a written record of those individuals who have examined the file of a confined person or to whom information in a confined person's file has been disclosed.

§ 4-123. [Lending Library; Reading Material; Radio and Television.]

(a) A confined person has a protected interest in access to a lending library, in the possession and use of reading material, and in the receipt of regularly scheduled radio and television transmissions. The director shall permit each confined person to:

(1) acquire reading material by purchase, loan, or gift from any source, but the chief executive officer may withhold from the intended recipient material jeopardizing the safety of the public or security of safety within a facility; and

(2) acquire, if not otherwise reasonably available within the facility, and use, subject to the rights of other confined persons, a receiving radio and television set.

(b) The chief executive officer shall inform a confined person in writing whenever reading material is withheld from him.

§ 4-124. [Facility News Medium.]

The director may provide a newspaper, radio, or other news medium through which confined persons may share information and opinions with other confined persons. If the director provides a news medium, each confined person has a protected interest in freedom from discrimination in access to the medium for the presentation of his views.

§ 4-125. [Organizations.]

(a) A confined person has a protected interest in forming, joining, or belonging to an organization whose purposes are lawful.

(b) The director shall assure that rules regulating meetings and other activities of an organization do not unfairly discriminate among organizations within the facility.

(c) The director shall permit reasonable participation in the meetings or other activities of an organization by invited persons from the free community unless to do so would jeopardize the safety of the public or the security or safety within a facility.

§ 4-126. [Refusing Participation in Treatment Programs.]

(a) A confined person has a protected interest to choose whether to participate in educational, rehabilitative, recreational, or other treatment programs.

(b) Subject to subsection (d), a confined person other than a confined offender may choose whether to undergo a medical examination or treatment.

(c) A confined offender may be required to undergo an examination or a course of treatment reasonably believed to be necessary for preservation of his physical or mental health or a course of counselling directed at the alleviation of chemical dependency.

(d) A confined person may be required to undergo medical examination or course of medical treatment if the examination or treatment is:

(1) required by order of a court;

(2) reasonably believed to be necessary to detect or treat communicable disease or otherwise to protect the health of other persons; or

(3) reasonably believed to be necessary in an emergency to save the life of the person.

§ 4-127. [Personal Property.]

(a) A confined person has a protected interest in the ownership, possession, and use in his living quarters or elsewhere of personal property other than contraband or prohibited material. The director may limit the amount of property a confined person may possess in a facility at any one time to an amount that can be reasonably accommodated in the space available. The director may provide storage space in the facility for material that would constitute a health or safety hazard if stored in a confined person's living quarters.

(b) The director shall assure that upon final release, each confined person receives his own personal property, except contraband, that is under the control of the department including his accumulated earnings and accrued interest thereon. Earnings and interest must be paid either in a lump sum or otherwise as determined by the chief executive officer to be in the best interest of the confined person. At least one-third of his accumulated earnings must be paid upon release and the entirety must be paid within 90 days after release.

PART 2

CORRECTIONAL MEDIATION

§ 4-201. [Office of Correctional Mediation; Correctional Mediator; Appointment.]

The office of correctional mediation is created [as an independent state agency] [in the state ombudsman's office] [in the Governor's office]. It consists of the correctional mediator and other employees. The Governor shall appoint the correctional mediator after consultation with the director and representative offenders and [with the advice and consent of the Legislature, Senate]. The correctional mediator must have appropriate training and experience to analyze questions of law, administration, and public policy. He shall serve a term of [6 or 4] years and until his successor is appointed and has qualified. The Governor may remove the correctional mediator only for disability, neglect of duty, incompetence, or malfeasance in office. Before removal, the mediator is entitled to a hearing.

§ 4-202. [Duties of Correctional Mediator.]

The correctional mediator shall:

(1) administer the office;

(2) adopt rules for the office;

(3) appoint, and he may remove in accordance with law, employees of the office and may delegate to them appropriate powers and duties;

(4) assure that a member of his staff is available on a daily basis, except holidays and weekends, to confined persons in each facility and periodically visits all facilities;

(5) assure that a member of his staff is available on a daily basis for contact by persons in the custody of the department;

(6) receive and respond to a petition filed by a person in the custody of the department;

(i) requesting information regarding his status or the conditions of his confinement or supervision;

(ii) suggesting changes in the policies or practices of the department or its employees; or

(iii) stating a grievance arising out of an act or practice of the department, its employees, or other persons;

(7) meet periodically with correctional officials, employees, and persons in the custody of the department to discuss the conduct and improvement of his office; and

(8) report annually on the administration of his office to the director, the Governor, and the [Legislature] and make copies available to the press and persons in the custody of the department.

§ 4-203. [Powers of Correctional Mediator.]

The correctional mediator may:

(1) investigate, on a petition or on his own motion, any administrative act or practice of the department or its employees without regard to whether it is the final action of the department;

(2) process any request for information directly or by referring it to the relevant agency or individual;

(3) forward, with or without his own evaluation, any suggestion from any person for change in the policies or practices of the department or its employees;

(4) follow up on any request for information or suggestion for change that has been forwarded or referred and request, and he is entitled to receive, a progress report on the position of the agency regarding a request for information or suggestion for change;

(5) refer a grievance to the appropriate grievance committee;

(6) prescribe:

(i) the method by which petitions are to be written, received, and acted upon;

(ii) the scope and manner of investigation; and

(iii) the form, frequency, and manner of distribution of his findings, conclusions, and recommendations;

(7) request, and is entitled to receive from the department, cooperation, assistance, and

information he considers necessary in discharging his responsibilities;

(8) request and is entitled to receive office space and equipment in any facility necessary in discharging his responsibilities;

(9) inspect the records and documents of the department;

(10) inspect premises within the department's control;

(11) visit and confer in private with any person in the custody of the department;

(12) administer oaths and receive sworn testimony; and

(13) issue a subpoena, enforceable by action in [an appropriate] court, to compel any person to appear, give sworn testimony, or produce documentary or other evidence relevant to a matter under investigation. A person required to provide information is entitled to receive the same fees and travel allowances and to be accorded the same privileges and immunities as are extended to witnesses in the courts of this State and he is entitled to have counsel present while being questioned.

§ 4–204. [Confidentiality of Files.]

(a) Unless otherwise privileged, the fact that sources of information requested by the correctional mediator from the department are regarded by it as confidential or that the information is restricted does not authorize withholding the information or its source from the mediator. Whenever the correctional mediator obtains information that is confidential or otherwise restricted, he shall maintain the confidentiality of the information. Reports or recommendations made on the basis of that information must preserve confidentiality.

(b) The department shall indicate to the correctional mediator which information obtained from the department is regarded by it as confidential or is restricted and the reason for or source of the confidentiality or restriction.

(c) If a person filing a petition with the correctional mediator so requests, the correctional mediator must not disclose to any person or agency outside his office the name, identity, or status of the person filing the petition.

(d) A person outside the office of correctional mediation may not have access to the files of the office.

§ 4–205. [Handling of Petitions.]

(a) The correctional mediator may receive and respond to a petition from any person who requests information, makes recommendations, or states a grievance regarding acts or practices of the department, its employees, or other persons. He shall conduct an investigation unless he concludes that:

(1) the petitioner has available to him a more appropriate administrative remedy he could reasonably be expected to use and, if the petitioner is a person in the custody of the department, the mediator shall assist him in initiating the other remedy;

(2) the petition relates to a matter outside his power;

(3) the petitioner's interest is insufficiently related to the subject matter;

(4) the petition is frivolous or not made in good faith; or

(5) other petitions are more worthy of attention.

(b) The correctional mediator's refusal to investigate a petition does not bar him from proceeding on his own motion to inquire into related matters.

(c) Whenever a petition is filed by a person in the custody of the department, the correctional mediator shall acknowledge receipt thereof in writing and thereafter periodically inform him of its status until it is resolved.

§ 4–206. [Recommendations of Correctional Mediator.]

(a) After considering a petition or conducting an investigation, the correctional mediator may recommend that the department:

(1) consider a matter further;

(2) modify or cancel a practice or policy;

(3) explain more fully a practice or policy; or

(4) take any other action.

(b) If the correctional mediator so requests, the department, within a reasonable time, shall inform him of the action taken on his recommendations or the reasons for not complying with them.

(c) If the correctional mediator believes that legislative action is desirable, he shall inform the [Legislature] of his views and may recommend statutory change.

(d) The correctional mediator may publish his conclusions and recommendations by transmitting them to the Governor, the [state Legislature] or any of its committees, the press, and others who may be concerned. Before publishing a conclusion or recommendation that expressly or impliedly criticizes an agency or individual, the correctional mediator shall consult with that agency or individual and include with his conclusions and recommendations any statement the agency or individual may desire concerning or explaining the matter involved.

§ 4–207. [Access to Correctional Mediator.]

A person or agency may not:

(1) adopt any rule or undertake any act or practice that would adversely affect a person for, or otherwise discourage or restrict him from filing a petition with the correctional mediator;

(2) open, read, refuse to forward, or delay the forwarding of any letter or other correspondence between a person and the office of correctional mediation; or

(3) impede, intercept, or interfere with the personal access to or other communication with representatives of the office of correctional mediation by a person in the custody of the department.

PART 3

GRIEVANCE PROCEDURES

§ 4–301. [Grievance Procedure; Rules.]

(a) The director shall adopt rules to facilitate communication between employees of the department and persons in their custody and to encourage the informal resolution of grievances. The rules must provide at least the following:

(1) a method for persons in the custody of the department to communicate in a confidential manner with the director;

(2) authority for employees informally to resolve grievances;

(3) a requirement that employees who are in direct contact with persons in the custody of the department receive training in resolving grievances; and

(4) a method for the periodic explanation of the policies of the department to persons in its custody.

(b) The director shall meet periodically with representative persons in the custody of the department to develop procedures for resolving grievances. The director may adopt any procedure for resolving grievances. Those procedures are in addition to, but do not restrict, a person's right to avail himself of the procedures required by this Act.

§ 4–302. [Grievance Committees; Creation.]

(a) The director shall adopt rules establishing a procedure for creating grievance committees for each facility or program of supervision and governing their operation. Consistent with the provisions of this Act, the rules creating and governing grievance committees may vary within or between facilities and programs.

(b) Each grievance committee must consist of an equal number of employees of the department and persons in the custody of the department. The director shall adopt rules for the selection of the members of grievance committees and for resolving an impasse if a grievance committee cannot reach a decision.

§ 4–303. [Jurisdiction of Grievance Committees.]

(a) A grievance committee has jurisdiction over any grievance relating to a policy or practice of the department, an act or practice of an employee of the department, or a condition of a facility or program if the grievance is:

(1) filed by a person or group of persons in the custody of the department;

(2) referred to the committee by the correctional mediator; or

(3) referred to the committee by a chief executive officer.

(b) A grievance committee has jurisdiction over any grievance relating to an act or practice of a confined person if the grievance is filed by an employee of the department or a confined person.

(c) Unless authorized by the director, a grievance committee may not review the findings and actions arising out of an adjudicatory hearing conducted by a disciplinary hearing officer or a classification committee and resulting in a decision affecting a specific individual or group of individuals. The grievance committee may review grievances directed at the policies, practices, or procedures of hearing officers or classification committees.

§ 4–304. [Procedures of Grievance Committees.]

The director shall adopt rules establishing procedures for the resolution of grievances by grievance committees. The procedures must be consistent with the following:

(1) Each person in the custody of the department has a right to file a grievance with a committee.

(2) The grievance committee shall conduct a hearing on each complaint not patently frivolous. Each party to the dispute may present at the hearing information relating to the merits of the grievance and counter information offered against him.

(3) The director may require a person to utilize any other grievance procedure established by the director pursuant to Section 4–301 as a condition of filing a grievance with a grievance committee established pursuant to Section 4–302. If the grievance is not resolved within 15 days, the person may file a grievance pursuant to Section 4–302.

(4) The grievance committee in all cases shall make written findings of fact and recommendations within a reasonable time and forward them to the parties and the chief executive officer of the facility or program involved.

(5) The chief executive officer of the facility or program shall review the findings of fact and recommendations and resolve the matter on the basis of the committee's findings of fact unless clearly erroneous. If the chief executive officer does not accept the committee's recommendations he shall state in writing to the committee and the parties involved his reasons for not doing so.

§ 4–305. [Appeal from Grievance Committee Decision.]

A person aggrieved by a decision arising out of grievance procedures may appeal the decision to the director. The director, on the basis of the entire record of the matter, shall:

(1) submit the matter to the correctional mediator for his findings and recommendations; or

(2) affirm or modify the decision of the chief executive officer.

§ 4–306. [Access to Grievance Procedures.]

The department and its employees may not adopt any rule or undertake any act or practice that would adversely affect a person for, or otherwise discourage or restrict him from, utilizing a grievance procedure.

§ 4–307. [Arbitration.]

The director may adopt rules for the arbitration of disputes between the department and persons in its custody by one or more persons outside the department.

PART 4

ASSIGNMENT, CLASSIFICATION, AND TRANSFER

§ 4–401. [Immediate Assignment.]

(a) Whenever a person is ordered to confinement in the custody of the department, the court may:

(1) order the person to report at a specific time to the appropriate facility designated by the director for receiving confined persons; or

(2) order the [sheriff, marshall, bailiff] to take the person without unnecessary delay to the appropriate facility designated by the director for receiving confined persons.

(b) Whenever a person is sentenced to confinement, he shall be sentenced to the custody of the department and not to a specific facility.

§ 4–402. [Classification of Facilities.]

(a) The director shall classify each facility or part of a facility as to the level of security it provides for persons confined therein. In making the classification the director shall consider:

(1) the extent of perimeter security at the facility:

(2) the freedom of movement by confined persons within the facility;

(3) the nature of programs in the facility; and

(4) the extent of regimentation of confined persons in the facility.

§ 4–403. [Temporary Initial Facility Assignment.]

The director shall adopt rules governing the temporary initial facility assignment of confined persons, to be determined by consideration of the following factors:

(1) the apparent requirements of security and safety;

(2) the availability of space within facilities;

(3) the desirability of keeping a confined person in a facility near the area in which he lived before confinement or to which he is likely to return after confinement; and

(4) the extent to which his presence is required in a particular locality.

§ 4–404. [Rules for Classification and Assignment.]

The director shall adopt rules governing the classification and assignment of confined persons. The rules governing classification must:

(1) establish one or more classification committees consisting of not less than 3 members whose backgrounds reflect differing functions and services performed in facilities;

(2) establish classification guidelines that indicate on the basis of the following factors the presumptively appropriate security classification for a confined person:

(i) the present offense or, if a pretrial detainee, the charged offense;

(ii) the past criminal record;

(iii) the past history of behavior or escape attempts while confined;

(iv) the results of any psychological or other evaluations;

(v) any recommendation made by the sentencing court; and

(vi) any other factor relevant to security classification;

(3) require that confined persons be classified in the least restrictive security classification consistent with the safety of the public or security and safety within a facility;

(4) presumptively classify persons convicted of misdemeanors in the least restrictive security classification; and

(5) require that the presumptive classification be adopted unless to do so would jeopardize the safety of the public or the security or safety within a facility.

§ 4–405. [Classification of Dangerous Persons.]

(a) The director shall adopt rules authorizing a classification committee to classify or reclassify a confined person as requiring a greater level of security than that generally provided in a maximum security facility if the committee, after a hearing, finds a present factual basis that the person presents a substantial risk to the safety of another person within the facility. A person so classified may be assigned to separate more secure housing within a facility.

(b) A classification committee shall review at least once every 30 days the necessity to continue the more secure housing. A person may be continued in more secure housing under this section only as long as necessary to avoid the risk to other persons.

§ 4–406. [Assignment to Facilities.]

(a) Factors to be considered in assigning a person to a facility include:

(1) the person's security classification;

(2) the availability of programs in the facilities;

(3) the location of family or other supportive relationships;

(4) the location in which the person intends to reside after release;

(5) the location of employment opportunities;

(6) the wishes of the person to be assigned;

(7) the relationships with other confined persons;

(8) any written pretrial agreement entered into by the person and the prosecuting attorney

concerning the facility to which the person would be assigned;

(9) any recommendation made by the sentencing court; and

(10) any other factor established by the director relevant to the selection of an appropriate facility.

(b) Consistent with his security classification, a pretrial detainee must be assigned to the available facility nearest to the location of his trial unless the detainee and the court in which his trial will take place agree that the assignment should be made under subsection (a).

(c) Consistent with his security classification, an offender sentenced to a term of continuous confinement of 6 months or less must be assigned to an available facility near his place of residence if he has a permanent place of residence in this State unless the offender agrees that the assignment should be made under subsection (a).

§ 4–407. [Separation of Confined Persons.]

(a) Rules for the assignment of confined persons, to the extent feasible, must facilitate the separation of:

(1) offenders from confined persons other than offenders;

(2) violent offenders from confined persons other than violent offenders; and

(3) first offenders from multiple offenders.

(b) Pretrial detainees, to the extent feasible, must be assigned to pretrial detention facilities.

(c) Offenders sentenced to a term of continuous confinement of more than 6 months must be assigned to a facility in the division of facility-based services, but the director may authorize the offender to be transferred to serve his last 90 days in a facility in the division of jail administration or community-based services if the offender consents and the transfer will assist his return to the free community.

§ 4–408. [Classification and Assignment; Procedure; Review.]

(a) A representative of a classification committee, within 10 days after a confined person arrives at a facility, shall meet with the confined person, explain the guidelines and factors relating to classification and assignment, and seek to develop a mutually agreeable security classification and permanent facility assignment.

(b) If an agreement is reached, it must be submitted to a classification committee for its approval or rejection.

(c) If an agreement is not reached or a classification committee does not approve the agreement, a confined person is entitled to a hearing before a classification committee within 30 days after arrival at a facility for the purpose of determining his security classification and permanent facility assignment.

(d) The classification committee shall review at least annually with each confined person his security classification and facility assignment unless the confined person waives the review in writing. An offender who has served one-sixth of his sentence is entitled presumptively to a reduction in his security classification unless:

(1) the offender is in the least restrictive security classification;

(2) the offender has committed a serious disciplinary infraction within the past year;

(3) the offender has a history of violent behavior or escape attempts while confined; or

(4) there are other exceptional circumstances that would make the reduction unreasonable.

(e) A confined person who contests the decision by the classification committee in its annual review of his security classification and facility assignment is entitled to a hearing before a classification committee within 30 days after the annual review.

§ 4–409. [Furloughs.]

(a) The director shall adopt rules governing the granting of furloughs of not more than 14 days duration to confined persons for any of the following purposes:

(1) to visit a close relative or friend who is seriously ill or to attend the funeral of a close relative or friend;

(2) to obtain medical, psychiatric, psychological, or other treatment;

(3) to appear in court as a party or a witness;

(4) to make preliminary contacts for employment, admission to an educational institution, or participation in any similar activity;

(5) to secure a residence for release or make any other preparation for release;

(6) to visit family or friends;

(7) to make arrangements for the care and custody of a child;

(8) to appear before any group whose purpose is to obtain a better understanding of crime or corrections, including appearances on television or radio; and

(9) any other purpose the director determines to be in the person's and the public's interest.

(b) The chief executive officer of a facility, consistent with the rules of the department, shall determine whether a confined person is to be accompanied on furlough by an employee of the department.

(c) The chief executive officer shall provide each person with a written explanation of the conditions of his furlough.

§ 4–410. [Rules for Granting Furloughs.]

(a) An appropriate classification committee may consider any confined person for a furlough.

(b) The classification committee shall afford the confined person an opportunity to appear before the committee and present pertinent information to assist the committee.

(c) In determining whether to grant a furlough the committee shall consider the wishes of the confined person and whether:

(1) the person has violated a condition of a previous furlough;

(2) the person has a recent history of violation of rules of other conditional release programs;

(3) the person has a recent history of violation of rules of a facility; and

(4) release of the person would be in his interest and the public interest.

(d) The grant or denial of a furlough may not be used as a reward or punishment for participation or failure to participate in educational, training, or other treatment programs within a facility.

(e) If the committee denies a furlough, it shall provide the person with a written explanation of the reasons for its action.

(f) A confined person on request is entitled to be considered for a furlough when he has completed one-third of his sentence and once every 60 days when he has less than 6 months left in confinement.

§ 4–411. [Protective Confinement; Conditions.]

(a) Whenever the safety of a confined person is in jeopardy, the chief executive officer shall, if feasible, order reasonable arrangements other than protective confinement to secure safety. Unless other reasonable arrangements are made, a confined person must be placed in more secure confinement for his own protection at his own request, and may be so placed on the order of the chief executive officer. A person in protective confinement may not be denied any protected interests or privileges to which he would have been entitled in less secure confinement unless essential to assure his protection.

(b) A person may not be kept in protective confinement for more than 30 days unless a classification committee, after a hearing, finds that the person prefers to remain in protective confinement or:

(1) the person is in danger of serious bodily harm from other persons:

(2) there is no other facility, within or outside the jurisdiction, to which the person can be transferred in which he would be in less danger; and

(3) the state has a particular interest in the person's safety which overrides his desire to leave protective confinement.

(c) The classification committee shall review the necessity for involuntary protective confinement at least every 30 days.

§ 4–412. [Classification Committees; Hearing Procedures.]

(a) The director shall adopt rules establishing hearing procedures for classification committees. The rules must be consistent with the following:

(1) A confined person has, but may waive in writing, the right to,

(i) written notice at least 7 days before the hearing of the contemplated action and the facts on which it is based;

(ii) subject to the limitations of Section 4–122(c), examine at least 3 days before the hearing all information in the committee's possession to be considered at the hearing;

(iii) legal assistance in preparing for the hearing and in contesting a material fact upon which classification is likely to be based other than a fact determined by a court at the trial of the offense or necessarily found as part of the conviction;

(iv) present relevant evidence and cross-examine persons giving adverse evidence.

(2) The classification committee must,

(i) preserve, in transcribable form, a record of the hearing, which must be retained until the time for appeal has expired or the appeal has been concluded; and

(ii) inform the confined person in writing of its decision and the reasons therefor.

(b) This section does not require a person to appear or be examined or information to be disclosed if a classification committee makes a written factual finding that to do so would subject a person to a substantial risk of physical harm.

§ 4–413. [Classification Decisions; Appeal.]

(a) A confined person may appeal any decision of the committee to the chief executive officer, who shall decide the appeal within 7 days.

(b) The affected person may appeal to the director, who shall decide the appeal within 30 days.

(c) Failure by the appropriate officer to act within the time provided entitles the confined person to treat the failure as an adverse decision.

(d) A confined person is entitled to judicial review of a decision to reclassify him to a more restrictive classification, transfer him from his permanent facility assignment, or classify him as requiring a greater level of security than that generally provided in a maximum security facility.

§ 4–414. [Change in Status.]

(a) A confined person may not be reclassified to a more restrictive classification unless:

(1) he has committed a disciplinary infraction resulting in confinement in his own living quarters, placement in separate housing for more than 10 days, loss of privileges for more than 40 days, or loss of good time;

(2) he is convicted of a new offense;

(3) his status changes from a pretrial detainee to an offender;

(4) new information becomes available that would have affected his initial classification and its relevance to his classification is not outweighed by his conduct in the facility since the initial classification; or

(5) he consents to the classification.

(b) A confined person may not be transferred to another facility unless:

(1) he is subject to reclassification pursuant to subsection (a);

(2) his transfer is necessary to allow him to receive special medical, psychological, psychiatric, or other similar treatment;

(3) his space in the facility would be more constructively utilized by another confined person and his transfer to another facility would not result in a substantially more onerous assignment;

(4) his transfer is necessary to allow him to return to a general population setting from protective confinement;

(5) the facility or part of a facility to which he is assigned is closed or its population is being reduced; or

(6) he consents to the transfer.

(c) Whenever a confined person is reclassified or transferred without his consent pursuant to this section, he is entitled to a hearing before a classification committee.

(d) Whenever a confined person is reclassified or transferred so as to affect adversely the conditions of his confinement, a classification committee shall review his classification and facility assignment within 6 months.

§ 4–415. [Mentally Ill Confined Persons; Commitment.]

(a) Whenever the chief executive officer believes that a confined person may be mentally ill or mentally retarded, as defined in [The Mental Health Code], and in need of treatment that cannot be provided by the department, he shall commence civil commitment proceedings in the [appropriate court] under [the Mental Health Code] to transfer the prisoner to [a facility to be designated by the Department of Mental Health].

(b) The sentence of a person so transferred continues to run, and he remains eligible for credit for good behavior under this Act.

(c) If a person so transferred is released pursuant to [the Mental Health Code] before expiration of his sentence, he shall be returned to the department to complete service of his sentence.

§ 4–416. [Persons Subject to Foreign Laws.]

(a) [With the approval of the Governor,] the director, consistent with the terms of any applicable international agreement, may accept custody of a resident of this State convicted of an offense under the laws of a foreign country and may release to the custody of a foreign country a national of that country convicted of an offense under the laws of this State.

(b) Whenever a resident of this State convicted under the laws of a foreign country is received into the custody of the department, he is subject to the provisions of this Act except to the extent they are inconsistent with an express provision of the international agreement authorizing his transfer or of any agreement entered into pursuant thereto.

PART 5

DISCIPLINE

§ 4–501. [Disciplinary Rules.]

(a) The director shall adopt rules governing the conduct of confined persons. Subject to the approval of the director, each chief executive officer may adopt supplementary rules pertaining to his facility. A violation of any of these rules constitutes a disciplinary infraction for which a confined person may be punished pursuant to this Part.

(b) The rules must:

(1) define with particularity the conduct regulated;

(2) establish the maximum punishment for each infraction proportionate to the seriousness of the infraction;

(3) establish, on the basis of the seriousness of the infraction and the past history of similar infractions committed by confined persons, the presumptive punishment to be imposed; and

(4) require that the presumptive punishment be imposed by a hearing officer unless he states in writing the reasons for imposing a different punishment.

§ 4–502. [Punishments for Disciplinary Infractions.]

(a) Punishments that may be imposed for a disciplinary infraction are:

(1) confinement in living quarters for not more than 30 days or placement in separate housing for not more than 90 days;

(2) loss of privileges for not more than 120 days;

(3) restrictions on the realization of the protected interest in physical exercise or use of personal property for not more than 120 days;

(4) forfeiture or withholding of good time reductions pursuant to this section;

(5) fines in an amount not exceeding $100; and

(6) restitution to the department or to an injured person in an amount not exceeding $100 for personal injury or property damage or loss caused by the infraction.

(b) This section does not authorize, either alone or as an incident of another punishment:

(1) restrictions on the realization of protected interests other than physical exercise or use of personal property;

(2) restriction on physical exercise to less than 7 hours per week;

(3) isolation from oral communication with other confined persons for more than 16 hours per day, but a person may be isolated in an emergency for not more than 24 consecutive hours if necessary;

(4) deprivations of cosmetic or hygienic implements, clothing appropriate to the season, or regular diet.

(c) Rules authorizing the forfeiture of accumulated good-time reductions or the withholding of future good-time reductions as a punishment for disciplinary infractions must be consistent with the following:

(1) the forfeiture or withholding of good time reductions may be imposed only if,

    (i) the disciplinary infraction involves conduct that is a felony or seriously jeopardizes the safety of the public or security or safety within the facility; or

    (ii) less severe measures have been imposed frequently and recently on the confined person for disciplinary infractions.

(2) The director may not authorize hearing officers to impose a forfeiture or withholding of good-time reductions of more than 90 days for a disciplinary infraction. The director may adopt rules specifying particularly aggravated infractions or circumstances for which a hearing officer may recommend, and the director may impose, a forfeiture or withholding in excess of 90 days but not to exceed 2 years or one-fourth of the confined person's sentence, whichever is less. The director may not delegate this authority.

(3) Notwithstanding the provisions of subsection (c)(2), one-fourth of any accumulated good-time reductions vests and is not subject to forfeiture.

(d) Cumulative punishments may not be imposed for 2 or more infractions committed as part of a single course of conduct.

(e) The fact that a punishment is available or imposed pursuant to this section does not prevent the imposition of applicable civil or criminal penalties or remedies authorized by law.

§ 4–503. [Dissemination of Disciplinary Rules.]

(a) The director shall publish annually a written rulebook containing the current rules establishing disciplinary infractions and their maximum and presumptive punishments. The director shall assure that each of the following are given a copy of the most recent rulebook:

    (1) each employee of the department and each confined person on the effective date of this Act;

    (2) each new confined person upon admission to a facility; and

    (3) each new employee at the outset of his employment.

(b) The director shall assure that employees and confined persons are kept currently informed of changes in the rules. The director shall either:

    (1) distribute a written copy of changes in the rules to each employee or confined person; or

    (2) post a written copy of rule changes in the facility in a location readily accessible to employees and confined persons and generally used for distributing information to them.

(c) Rules shall be translated into any language that is the sole language understood by a significant number of confined persons.

(d) Failure to give a reasonable notice of a rule establishing a disciplinary infraction is a defense to a charge of violation of the rule unless the conduct prohibited is also a criminal offense or actual knowledge of the rule by the confined person is proved by a preponderance of the evidence.

(e) The director may adopt methods in addition to written publication to assist employees and confined persons in understanding the rules establishing disciplinary infractions. Special efforts shall be taken orally to inform illiterate persons of the substance of the rules.

§ 4–504. [Administrative Punishments.]

The director shall adopt rules governing the imposition of administrative punishment by authorizing designated employees to allow a confined person charged with specified minor disciplinary infractions to accept a loss of privileges of not more than 10 days rather than be tried by a disciplinary hearing officer. Acceptance of that punishment terminates any further proceeding upon the charge.

§ 4–505. [Disciplinary Hearing Officers.]

(a) The Attorney General shall appoint and train disciplinary hearing officers and assign them to facilities on a rotating basis. The Attorney General may remove a hearing officer in accordance with law and for good cause. Before removal, a hearing officer is entitled to a hearing.

(b) A hearing officer is an employee of the Attorney General and not of the department. The director shall provide hearing officers with adequate space and equipment in each facility.

(c) A hearing officer shall conduct disciplinary hearings on all charges of disciplinary infractions against confined persons except those who accept administrative punishment.

(d) A hearing officer may administer oaths.

§ 4–506. [Disciplinary Charges; Initiation; Prosecution.]

(a) The director shall adopt rules governing the initiation and prosecution of disciplinary charges. The rules must establish:

(1) a method for filing charges alleging that a confined person has committed a disciplinary infraction;

(2) the manner in which charges are to be investigated and require that whenever a confined person files charges against another confined person the person filing the charges is notified of the outcome of the investigation;

(3) procedures for the prosecution of charges and authorize dismissal of charges without prosecution if appropriate; and

(4) a procedure for the development and filing of a report that contains,

(i) the names of the person filing or investigating the charges and the person charged; and

(ii) the time, date, place, and nature of the infraction alleged to have been committed including the facts and circumstances surrounding the alleged infraction and the names of persons present.

(b) A confined person charged with a disciplinary infraction is entitled to receive, at least 72 hours before a hearing on the alleged infraction:

(1) a copy of the report of the investigation of the charges;

(2) the text of the rule violated;

(3) a notice of the time and place of the hearing; and

(4) a notice of the maximum and presumptive punishment established for the alleged infraction.

(c) A confined person charged with an infraction is entitled to a hearing not later than 15 days after the report is filed with the hearing officer unless the person charged or the chief executive officer demonstrates to the hearing officer good cause for further delay.

(d) Hearings on charges against a person who is confined in his living quarters or placed in separate housing before the hearing must be given priority.

(e) This section does not require the disclosure to a confined person of information that a hearing officer determines, if disclosed, would subject another person to a substantial risk of physical harm.

§ 4–507. [Disciplinary Hearings; Procedure.]

(a) At the disciplinary hearing the person charged is entitled to:

(1) appear and give evidence;

(2) present witnesses, but the hearing officer may exclude a witness for good cause;

(3) examine any witness and call and examine the employee of the facility who brought or investigated the charge or who has information about the incident; and

(4) immunity from the use of his testimony or any evidence derived therefrom in any other proceeding in which he elects to exercise his rights against self-incrimination except in a prosecution for perjury arising out of that testimony.

(b) A person may not be confined in his own living quarters for more than 10 days, placed in separate housing for more than 10 days, deprived of privileges for more than 40 days, restricted in the realization of protected interests for more than 40 days, or deprived of good time, unless in addition to the rights enumerated in subsection (a), he is accorded the right:

(1) except as provided in subsection (c), to confront and cross-examine any person giving adverse information; and

(2) to representation by an employee of the office of correctional legal services, or by retained counsel.

(c) This section does not require a person to appear or be examined if the hearing officer makes a written factual finding that to do so would subject a person to a substantial risk of physical harm. If the hearing officer allows a person to forego appearance or examination and information the person has provided will be used against the person charged with an infraction, the hearing officer shall meet with the person giving adverse information and give the person charged a summary of the factual basis of his testimony.

(d) The hearing officer must preserve in a transcribable form a record of the hearing, which must be retained until the time for appeal has expired or the appeal has been concluded.

(e) A confined person may not be found guilty of a disciplinary infraction unless his guilt is established by a preponderance of the evidence in the record. If the hearing officer finds the person guilty, he shall inform the person in writing of his findings of fact, and, if he does not impose the presumptive punishment, the factual basis and reasons for the punishment imposed.

§ 4-508. [Appeal from Hearing Officer Decision.]

(a) A confined person may appeal to the chief executive officer of the facility from a decision finding him guilty or from the punishment imposed by a disciplinary hearing officer. The chief executive officer shall decide the appeal within 30 days if the imposition of the punishment is stayed pending the appeal and within 5 days in other cases.

(b) If the chief executive officer affirms any part of the hearing officer's decision, the confined person may appeal to the director, who shall affirm, modify, or reverse the decision within 30 days.

(c) Failure by the appropriate officer to act within the time provided entitles the confined person to treat such failure as an adverse decision.

(d) If the decision appealed from imposes punishment of confinement to a confined person's own living quarters for more than 10 days, placement in separate housing for more than 10 days, loss of privileges for more than 40 days, restrictions on protected interests for more than 40 days, or loss of good-time reductions, the confined person is entitled to judicial review.

§ 4-509. [Action Pending Disciplinary Infraction Hearing.]

The chief executive officer may order a person charged with a disciplinary infraction that jeopardizes the safety of the public or the safety or security within a facility to be confined in his living quarters or placed in separate housing pending the disciplinary hearing. This status may be continued pending an appeal. All time spent in this status must be credited against any punishment imposed.

§ 4-510. [Emergency Confinement.]

If necessary because of an emergency in the facility, the director, without complying with the procedures of this Part, may confine persons to their living quarters or place them in separate housing during the emergency and for 24 hours thereafter.

§ 4-511. [Disciplinary Infraction Amounting to Offense.]

(a) If a confined person is charged with a disciplinary infraction that also is a felony the following apply:

(1) The chief executive officer of the facility promptly shall notify in writing the prosecuting attorney and suspend any disciplinary proceeding pursuant to this Part involving the infraction, but the chief executive officer may temporarily confine the person to his living quarters or place him in separate housing.

(2) Within 10 days after delivery or receipt of notification, whichever is earlier, the prosecuting attorney shall inform the chief executive officer whether he intends to prosecute the charged person.

(3) If prosecution is intended, the charged person may be confined to his living quarters or placed in separate housing for no more than 90 days, but if an indictment is obtained or an information filed the confinement may continue for the duration of the criminal prosecution.

(4) If the prosecuting attorney does not intend to prosecute or the prosecution terminates, the disciplinary proceedings in the facility may be resumed.

(b) If a person is both sentenced to confinement and has good time forfeited or withheld in a disciplinary proceeding for the same course of conduct, any good time forfeited or withheld must be credited against the sentence imposed.

§ 4-512. [Offenses in Facilities; Prosecution.]

(a) The Attorney General may designate a representative from his office to [assist in the prosecution of] [prosecute] offenses charged against confined persons within facilities.

(b) The [department; Attorney General] shall pay the expenses of the prosecution of a confined person for an offense allegedly committed within a facility.

PART 6

PERSONS AT RISK

§ 4–601. [Programs Placing Confined Persons at Risk.]

(a) A research or development program that exposes a confined person participating as a subject to the risk of significant physical or psychological injury is a program placing a confined person at risk.

(b) Consistent with other provisions of law, the director shall adopt rules to evaluate and approve programs placing confined persons at risk. A program placing a confined person at risk may not be approved unless:

(1) a board of at least 2 persons appointed by the [director] and professionally competent to evaluate the program certifies in writing as to its professional validity;

(2) after consultation with the department of corrections advisory committee the director finds that,

(i) the potential benefits to the confined person or the importance of the knowledge to be gained outweigh the risk to the confined person;

(ii) the program offers no undue inducement to confined persons;

(iii) the confined person will be offered a wage comparable to the market wage for similar programs, or if there is no market wage, a reasonable wage based on the risk involved to the subject and the benefits to be gained by the person conducting the program; and

(iv) adequate assurance is provided in the program for payment of damages resulting from participation in the program, including provision for medical care, disability, rehabilitation, and future wage loss in an amount determined by the director as reasonably likely to cover the risks; and

(3) the director issues a written report containing the factual basis for the findings required in paragraph (2).

(c) The sponsors of the program are subject to liability to pay compensation for damages resulting from injury or death to a confined person:

(1) injured in a program with a potential direct therapeutic benefit for that person if the injury or death is caused by negligence or willful misconduct of persons operating the program; or

(2) injured in non-therapeutic programs without regard to the fault of the persons operating the program.

§ 4–602. [Information Provided; Consent; Review.]

(a) A confined person may not be a subject in a program placing him at risk unless he consents to participate after a program representative informs him of:

(1) the likelihood, nature, extent, and duration of known side effects and hazards of the program and how and to what extent they may be controlled;

(2) the extent to which there may be hazards of the program which are unknown;

(3) the extent to which the program is generally accepted or considered experimental by professionals in the relevant fields;

(4) his right to withdraw at any time, or, if peremptory withdrawal would or might cause injury, his right to a phased withdrawal; and

(5) if the program has a potential direct therapeutic benefit for the participant,

(i) the nature and seriousness of his disease or illness;

(ii) the reasonable alternative treatments available and the likelihood and degree of improvement, remission, control, or cure of alternative treatments;

(iii) the likelihood and degree of improvement, remission, control, or cure resulting from participation in the program; and

(iv) the likelihood, nature, and extent of changes in and intrusion upon the confined person's physical and mental processes resulting from participation in the program.

(b) The director shall appoint a reviewer to determine the validity of a confined person's consent. The reviewer shall interview each confined

221

person no sooner than 48 hours after he has given his consent.

(c) A confined person may not participate in a program placing him at risk unless the reviewer finds and reports in writing that the confined person understood the information provided him and exercised free choice with no undue inducement or element of fraud, deceit, duress, or other ulterior form of constraint.

PART 7

VOUCHER PROGRAM

§ 4-701. [Voucher Program; Gradual Implementation.]

(a) As used in this Act, "voucher program" means a program in which persons are given voucher credits that can be used to purchase specified treatment programs and services directly from either public or private agencies.

(b) To facilitate the availability of a wide variety of programs and services for persons in the custody of the department, the director shall:

(1) within one year after the effective date of this Act, establish an experimental voucher program for a limited number of offenders in the custody of the department; [and]

(2) provide for an independent evaluation of the effectiveness of the voucher program [; and][.]

[(3) within 5 years after the effective date of this Act, establish a voucher program available to all offenders sentenced to terms of confinement or supervision for one year or more.]

(c) The director may extend the voucher program to all persons in the custody of the department.

(d) Within 3 years after the effective date of this Act, the director shall transmit to the [Legislature] any independent evaluations and his own report on the effectiveness of the voucher program.

§ 4-702. [Establishment of Voucher Programs.]

In establishing a voucher program the director shall set forth:

(1) the form, method, and eligibility requirements for the distribution of vouchers;

(2) the programs for which vouchers may be used;

(3) a prohibition against transfer of vouchers among persons in the custody of the depart-

ment without the specific approval of the director;

(4) the method of redemption of vouchers by individuals or public or private agencies or organizations providing programs or services; and

(5) the standards and procedures for certification of providers of programs or services in return for vouchers.

§ 4-703. [Vouchers; Allocation and Use.]

(a) The director shall provide that each person eligible for vouchers will receive a periodic allocation of vouchers unless that person:

(1) has sufficient personal resources available to purchase programs and services; or

(2) has continually refused to utilize his allocation of vouchers and is unlikely to use them in the future.

(b) A person may use his vouchers to purchase programs or services relating to his care, rehabilitation, treatment, or adjustment to life in the free community including:

(1) academic programs;

(2) vocational training programs;

(3) medical or psychiatric services;

(4) counseling services, including personal, marital, employment, or financial counseling; and

(5) any other program or service approved by the director.

(c) The director may supplement the voucher allocation to any person or group of persons in the custody of the department if required to assure the availability of suitable programs or services. In doing so, the director may:

(1) allocate additional vouchers to individuals or groups of persons;

(2) contract to bear directly a portion of the costs of the program or service; or

(3) provide a portion of the program or service from the resources of the department.

(d) The director may authorize persons receiving vouchers to accumulate them over a period of time. All vouchers held by a person and not obligated toward the purchase of services expire at the discharge of the person's sentence.

§ 4–704. [Application to Receive Vouchers.]

(a) An individual or public or private agency or organization desiring to provide programs or services in exchange for vouchers shall apply to the department for certification. In determining the qualifications of an applicant, the director shall consider the nature and extent of the programs or services to be provided and the integrity and reputation of the applicant. An application may not be denied solely because the applicant provides programs or services already available from the department or elsewhere.

(b) Program or services provided directly to persons in the custody of the department solely in return for vouchers are not subject to [provisions requiring public bidding for state purchasing].

§ 4–705. [Redemption of Vouchers.]

Vouchers issued and used as provided in this Act are redeemable at face value by a provider of programs or services upon presentment to the [director, State Treasurer] pursuant to any applicable rules.

§ 4–706. [Payment as Condition for Programs or Services.]

The director may require the payment of vouchers as a condition to participation in academic or vocational training programs or receipt of counseling services offered by the department.

PART 8

EMPLOYMENT AND TRAINING OF CONFINED PERSONS

§ 4–801. [Director's Duties.]

To the extent feasible, the director shall:

(1) provide confined persons with opportunities to engage in productive activity by upgrading and expanding employment and vocational training opportunities available to confined persons in order that confined persons may develop marketable skills and good work habits;

(2) assist confined persons to develop a sense of responsibility by developing a realistic employment environment in which wages are comparable to those paid in the free community and requiring confined persons to assume financial obligations similar to those of persons in the free community; and

(3) assist confined persons in obtaining employment upon release.

§ 4–802. [Employment and Training of Confined Persons; Authority.]

To fulfill his responsibilities set forth in Section 4–801, the director may:

(1) establish and administer business, commercial, industrial, and agricultural enterprises and educational or vocational training programs for confined persons;

(2) permit private business, commercial, industrial, and agricultural enterprises to operate on the property of a facility;

(3) permit the employment of confined persons by public or private enterprises; and

(4) adopt measures relating to the development and maintenance of employment and training opportunities for confined persons while confined and upon release.

§ 4–803. [Employment or Training Outside Facility.]

(a) The director may establish criteria and procedures for authorizing confined persons under prescribed conditions to work at paid employment or participate in educational or vocational training programs in the free community.

(b) Confined persons employed in the free community or participating in training programs in the free community may be housed in facilities designated for those purposes.

§ 4–804. [Private Enterprise on Property of Facility.]

(a) The director may lease property at a facility to a private business, commercial, industrial, or agricultural enterprise agreeing to provide employment to confined persons.

(b) Before leasing to a private enterprise, the director shall:

(1) obtain a valuation from the [state assessor] [State Auditor] of the property to be leased; and

(2) prepare a written report describing the [State Assessor's] [State Auditor's] valuation of the property, terms and conditions of the lease, including the projected necessity for an adjustment of lease payments as provided in Section 4-805, and the director's reasons for approving the proposed lease. The report shall be reviewed by [the Attorney General] [State Purchasing Agent] and is effective upon approval by the Governor.

(c) In awarding leases, the director shall consider:

(1) the nature of the enterprise and its compatibility with the administration of the facility;

(2) the number of confined persons to be employed;

(3) the nature and prevailing wage for the employment offered and the availability of similar employment opportunities for confined persons upon release;

(4) the willingness and capability of the private enterprise to train confined persons for employment in the enterprise;

(5) the financial gain to be derived by the department from the lease; and

(6) the views of appropriate civic, business, and labor organizations.

ALTERNATIVE A

[(d) If a private enterprise leases property pursuant to this section, a tax must be imposed for the privilege of using the property in the same amount and to the same extent as if the private enterprise owned the property. It must be assessed to the private enterprise and be payable in the same manner as taxes assessed to owners of real and personal property, but the tax may not become a lien against state-owned property.]

ALTERNATIVE B

[(d) If a private enterprise leases property pursuant to this section, the director shall assure that the payments made by the private enterprise include an amount equivalent to the taxes which might otherwise have been lawfully levied. The

director, from payments made for the leased property by the private enterprise, may make payments in lieu of taxes to the [city, township, and county] in which the property is located.]

§ 4-805. [Adjustment for Additional Costs Incurred by Private Enterprise on Property of Facility.]

(a) If a private enterprise operating on the property of a facility incurs additional costs because of the nature and size of the confined-person work force or the location of the facility, the director may, whenever necessary and appropriate:

(1) provide services and other assistance to the private enterprise;

(2) permit the private enterprise to supplement the confined-person work force with other employees; and

(3) after obtaining approval by the [Governor] pursuant to subsection (b), forgive payments to be made by the private enterprise, or make direct payments to the private enterprise, equivalent to the unavoidable additional costs incurred by employing confined persons.

(b) Before forgiving or making payments to a private enterprise, the director shall prepare a written report describing the terms and conditions of the adjustment, including a statement as to whether the adjustment was contemplated at the time the lease was approved, and his reasons for approving the adjustment. The report must be reviewed by [the Attorney General] [State Purchasing Agent] and approved by the [Governor].

§ 4-806. [Private Enterprise on Property of Facility Not State Agency.]

(a) A private enterprise employing a confined person is not for that reason alone an agency of the State, and the enterprise remains subject to the laws, rules, and regulations of the State governing the operation of similar private enterprises.

(b) A confined person is an employee of the private enterprise employing him while he is acting within the scope of his employment.

§ 4-807. [Employment and Training Assignments.]

(a) The director shall adopt rules governing the eligibility of confined persons for assignment to employment and training positions. The rules must provide that a confined person's preference be considered in making an employment or training assignment.

(b) The director shall establish which classes of confined persons are eligible for employment in each enterprise based on the security classification of confined persons and the risk to security presented by employment in the enterprise. Until there are sufficient training or employment opportunities to accommodate all confined persons, the director may utilize additional factors in determining which confined persons are eligible for each enterprise, including:

(1) the amount of time remaining to be served on the sentence;

(2) the amount of time served on the sentence;

(3) the amount of time served without training or employment opportunities; and

(4) whether the confined person has, as a condition to employment by an enterprise, spent a specified period of time employed in general maintenance work or in other services essential to the administration of a facility.

(c) Decisions to employ, promote, or discharge individual confined persons must be made by the manager of the enterprise, but a confined person may become ineligible for employment by an enterprise because of a reclassification to a higher security level or a transfer to another facility.

(d) The director, to the extent possible, shall assure that educational and other programs are scheduled so as not to restrict a program participant's opportunities for employment.

§ 4–808. [Required Work.]

(a) A confined person may be required to keep his own living quarters clean and orderly.

(b) A confined offender may be required to perform general maintenance work in the facility and assist in providing other services essential to the administration of the facility such as food and laundry service.

(c) A confined offender may be required to work in a business, commercial, industrial, or agricultural enterprise operated by the department.

§ 4–809. [Enterprises Operated by Department.]

(a) The director shall adopt measures governing the administration of enterprises operated by the department. The director shall:

(1) provide for the pricing and marketing of goods and services produced by those enterprises;

(2) assure that goods and services produced by these enterprises do not unfairly compete with those produced by private enterprise; and

(3) require that each enterprise maintain separate, accurate, and complete records and accounts in accordance with accepted accounting practices for business enterprises.

(b) The director may provide for the management of the enterprises operated by the department[.] [and may, if appropriate, incorporate one or more enterprises in accordance with the law of this state.]

(c) The director may expend funds generated by enterprises operated by the department and other available funds to:

(1) pay the capital and operating expenses of the enterprise;

(2) expand the size and scope of the enterprises;

(3) increase the rate of wages paid to employees of the enterprises;

(4) supplement the wages paid to confined persons employed in general maintenance work or other essential services;

(5) establish a placement program to assist confined persons in obtaining employment upon release; and

(6) support other activities related to the employment and training of confined persons.

§ 4–810. [Handcrafts.]

The director may authorize confined persons to engage in handcrafts and to sell their products to the public.

§ 4–811. [Terms and Conditions of Employment.]

(a) A confined person employed by private enterprise, an agency of government other than the department, or in a business, commercial, industrial, or agricultural enterprise operated by the department is entitled to be paid at least the wages paid for work of a similar nature performed in private enterprise by employees having similar skills working under similar conditions in the locality in which the work is performed. The [State Commissioner of Labor] [director] shall certify the prevailing wage for each job for which the department or other governmental agency employs confined persons.

(b) Notwithstanding subsection (a), if an enterprise operated by the department does not produce sufficient income to support payment of prevailing wages, the director may authorize wage payments to be based on the productivity of the enterprise until such time as the income of the enterprise can support a prevailing wage rate.

(c) A confined person employed by the department for work other than in a business, commercial, industrial, or agricultural enterprise operated by the department is entitled to be paid at least the lowest of the following rates:

(1) the prevailing wage for similar services performed in private industry;

(2) the minimum wage as established by [federal; state] law; or

(3) a sum equivalent to the lowest hourly wage paid to confined persons employed in an enterprise operated by the department.

(d) A confined person may not be paid for keeping his own living quarters clean and orderly.

(e) Termination of employment resulting from final release from a facility of a confined person employed by private enterprise is a voluntary leaving of employment without good cause [attributable to the employer; attributable to work] for purposes of [state unemployment compensation act].

§ 4–812. [Disposition of Wages.]

(a) The director shall provide for the disposition of a confined person's wages. A confined person's monthly gross wages minus required payroll deductions and necessary work-related incidental expenses must be distributed in the following manner:

(1) 10 percent to be deposited in the account of the confined person to be used by him for any lawful purpose;

(2) 25 percent to be paid to the department toward monthly room, board, and other maintenance costs. The director may reduce or waive

these charges if he determines that their collection is unreasonable.

(3) 10 percent to be deposited for the confined person and held until his release; and

(4) the remainder to be paid in accordance with the following priority:

(i) first in accordance with the law otherwise applicable to the collection of civil obligations against wage payments, and

(ii) second at the direction of the confined person for any lawful purpose.

(b) Wages earned by confined persons must be paid to the director and are not subject to judicial process or assignment except as provided in this section.

§ 4–813. [Funds of Confined Persons Held by Department.]

Funds of a confined person held by the department for his release must be credited to the confined person and deposited in an interest-bearing state or federally insured account.

§ 4–814. [Employment Upon Release.]

(a) The director shall adopt measures designed to assist confined persons in obtaining employment upon release.

(b) Whenever the director is unable to find an opportunity for employment for a confined person upon release that is comparable in remuneration and general working conditions to the employment last provided him while confined, the director shall pay him weekly a sum equal to his last weekly wage until he is employed, but for not more than [4] weeks.

§ 4–815. [Correctional Employees; Financial Interest in Offender Employment.]

To supplement other provisions of law governing state employees, the director shall adopt rules to:

(1) define prohibited conflicts of interest by employees of the department arising out of the employment of persons in the custody of the department;

(2) require disclosure of any financial interest held by an employee of the department in a private enterprise providing employment to persons in the custody of the department; and

(3) prevent exploitation of the labor of confined persons.

§ 4–816. [Interstate Commerce.]

Goods produced in whole or in part by confined persons in this State may be transported and sold in the same manner as goods produced by free persons. Goods produced in whole or in part by persons confined in another state or territory may be transported and sold in this State in the same manner as goods produced by confined persons in this State may be transported or sold in that state or territory.

PART 9

COMPENSATION FOR WORK–RELATED INJURIES TO CONFINED PERSONS

§ 4–901. [Application of Worker's Compensation Act.]

Subject to the provisions of this Act, if a confined person is injured in the performance of his work in connection with the maintenance or operation of the facility or in any business, commercial, industrial, or agricultural enterprise, he is subject to the provisions of [here insert reference to state Worker's Compensation Act].

§ 4–902. [Insurance.]

The director may [acquire insurance from a private insurance carrier] [contribute to the state worker's compensation plan] to discharge the liability imposed by this Part. In the absence of insurance or other source of funds, liability imposed by this Part is payable from the general funds available to the department.

§ 4–903. [Compensation; Distribution.]

Compensation for disability paid pursuant to this Part shall be distributed in the same manner as wages earned by confined persons.

§ 4–904. [Liability for Compensation Continued After Release.]

The release of a person from the custody of the department does not terminate the liability of the department to pay compensation already awarded.

§ 4–905. [Liability for Compensation Limited; Subrogation.]

The department is not liable pursuant to this Part for injuries or death to a confined person arising out of his employment by private enterprise if worker's compensation benefits are provided for him by the private enterprise. The department is subrogated to a confined person's claim for worker's compensation against a private enterprise to the extent the department has provided medical or other services pursuant to the claim.

PART 10

COLLATERAL CONSEQUENCES OF CHARGE AND CONVICTION

§ 4–1001. [Rights Retained.]

(a) A person convicted of an offense does not suffer civil death or corruption of blood.

(b) Except as provided by [the Constitution of this State or] this Act, a person convicted of an offense does not sustain loss of civil rights or forfeiture of estate or property by reason of a conviction or confinement; he retains all rights, political, personal, civil, and otherwise, including the right to:

(1) be a candidate for, be elected or appointed to, or hold public office or employment;

(2) vote in elections;

(3) hold, receive, and transfer property;

(4) enter into contracts;

(5) sue and be sued;

(6) hold offices of private trust in accordance with law;

(7) execute affidavits and other judicial documents;

(8) marry, separate, obtain a dissolution or annulment of marriage, adopt children, or withhold consent to the adoption of children; and

(9) testify in legal proceedings.

(c) This section does not affect laws governing the right of a person to benefit from the death of his victim.

§ 4-1002. [Juror Eligibility.]

A confined offender and an offender convicted of a felony are disqualified to serve on a jury.

§ 4-1003. [Voting.]

A confined person otherwise eligible may vote by absentee ballot. For voting purposes, the residence of a confined person is the last legal residence before confinement.

§ 4-1004. [Forfeiture of Public Office.]

(a) Unless the qualification or provisions with respect to length of term and procedures for removal are prescribed by the Constitution of this State, a person forfeits any public office he holds or to which he has been elected if thereafter convicted of any of the following offenses:

(1)

(2)

(3)

(b) This section applies if the person was convicted of a comparable offense under the laws of another state or of the United States.

(c) If the sentence is imposed in this State, a person forfeits his public office on the date sentence is imposed or, if the sentence is imposed in another state or in a federal court, on the date a certification of the sentence is filed in the office of [Secretary of State]. An appeal or other proceeding taken to set aside or otherwise nullify the conviction or sentence does not affect the application of this section, but if the conviction is reversed the defendant must be restored to any public office forfeited under this Act from the time of the reversal to the end of the term for which he was appointed or elected and is entitled to the emoluments thereof from the time of the forfeiture.

§ 4-1005. [Discrimination; Direct Relationship.]

(a) This section applies only to acts of discrimination directed at persons who have been convicted of an offense and discharged from their sentence.

(b) It is unlawful discrimination, solely by reason of a conviction:

(1) for an employer to discharge, refuse to hire, or otherwise to discriminate against a person with respect to the compensation, terms, conditions, or privileges of his employment. For purposes of this section, "employer" means this State and its political subdivisions and a private individual or organization [employing 15 or more employees for each working day in each of 20 or more calendar weeks in the current or preceding calendar year];

(2) for a trade, vocational, or professional school to suspend, expel, refuse to admit, or otherwise discriminate against a person;

(3) for a labor organization or other organization in which membership is a condition of employment or of the practice of an occupation or profession to exclude or to expel from membership or otherwise to discriminate against a person; or

(4) for this State or any of its political subdivisions to suspend or refuse to issue or renew a license, permit, or certificate necessary to practice or engage in an occupation or profession.

(c) It is not unlawful discrimination to discriminate against a person because of a conviction if the underlying offense directly relates to the particular occupation, profession, or educational endeavor involved. In making the determination of direct relationship the following factors must be considered:

(1) whether the occupation, profession, or educational endeavor provides an opportunity for the commission of similar offenses;

(2) whether the circumstances leading to the offense will recur;

(3) whether the person has committed other offenses since conviction or his conduct since conviction makes it likely that he will commit other offenses;

(4) whether the person seeks to establish or maintain a relationship with an individual or organization with which his victim is associated or was associated at the time of the offense; and

(5) the time elapsed since release.

(d) [The State Equal Employment–Opportunity Commission has jurisdiction over allegations of violations of this section in a like manner with its jurisdiction over other allegations of discrimination.]

SENTENCING AND CORRECTIONS

ARTICLE 5

VICTIMS

PREFATORY NOTE

Offender assaults Victim and takes his money. Offender and Victim are neighbors; both are undereducated, unskilled, and unemployed. Under this Act, Offender, once he is placed in the custody of the department of corrections and until his release, is guided to educational opportunities, job training, and even a paying job; after release he will be assisted in finding gainful employment. The provisions in Article 5, which are designed to complete the correctional picture, begin to provide similar assistance to victims.

Victims have been described as the real "clients," of the criminal justice system" Comm'n on Victim Witness Assistance Nat'l Dist. Attorneys Ass'n, A Primer for Model Victim Witness Assistance Centers (Undated). Their role in the criminal justice system has become the focus of a growing awareness among commentators in law and related disciplines. *See, e.g.,* Marquette University Center for Criminal Justice & Social Policy, Victims and Witnesses (1976) [hereinafter cited as Marquette University Center]; Greacen, *Arbitration: A Toll for Criminal Cases?,* 2 Barrister 10 (Winter 1975); Hall, *The Role of the Victim in the Prosecution and Disposition of a Criminal Case,* 28 Vand.L.Rev. 931 (1975); Sander, *Varieties of Dispute Processing,* 70 F.R.D. 111 (1976). *See also* H. Hentig, The Criminal and His Victim (1948).

The system, however, has afforded its "clients" inadequate treatment at best. *E.g.,* Comm'n on Victim Witness Assistance, Nat'l Dist. Attorneys Ass'n, Help for Victims and Witnesses (1976) [hereinafter cited as Help for Victims and Witnesses]; Marquette University Center. Victims of crime may need, among other things, medical and counseling services, compensation for injury suffered and its consequences, employment training, assistance in claiming personal property used in evidence, information about the criminal trial process and their role in it and, perhaps most importantly, recognition that they do have a role, an important role, in that process. *See* Jones, *A Cost Analysis of Federal Victim Compensation,* in Sample Surveys of the Victims of Crime 189, 196 (W. Skogan ed. 1976); Help for Victims and Witnesses. Victimization studies indicate that much crime goes unreported by victims. *See, e.g.,* Crimes and Victims, A Report on the Dayton–San Jose Pilot Study of Victimization 23–24 (1974). Although many reasons are given for such non-reporting, id., it is clear that the present operation of the criminal justice system does little to encourage victim participation. Help for Victims and Witnesses.

Although the majority of states do not as yet have programs to provide compensation to the victims of crime, progress is being made in this area. The National Conference of Commissioners on Uniform State Laws adopted the Uniform Crime Victims Reparations Act in 1974. It has been enacted in Ohio and Minnesota. Several other states have instituted programs of crime victims reparations and the federal government is also considering enactment of such a program. S. 1437, 95th Cong., 1st Sess. ch. 41, §§ 4111–4115 (Criminal Code Reform Act of 1977). There has also been progress in the development of victim-witness assistance projects. The National District Attorneys Association, through funds provided by the Law Enforcement Assistance Administration, has established several such projects. Similar projects are being conducted by courts (the Vera Institute is operating one such project at the Brooklyn Criminal Court), local law enforcement agencies (an example is the Indianapolis Victims Assistance Project) and at least one university (Marquette University Center for Criminal Justice and Social Policy).

There is, however, no concerted, organized, and comprehensive effort to provide for the wide range of victim needs. Without such an effort victims will continue to be "revictimized" by the criminal justice system itself. *See, e.g.,* Marquette University Center, at 9–10; Comm'n on Victim Witness Assistance, Nat'l Dist. Attorneys Ass'n, What Happens Now? (Undated Brochure). What is required is a statewide commitment offering centralized responsibility with sufficient flexibility for regional implementation. A state department of corrections, with the community programs and facilities contemplated by this Act, would seem well-suited to fulfill this requirement and is of course, equipped to provide many of the services needed by victims since it is already providing similar service to offenders.

It is likely that the provisions of Article V, even when read with other sections in the Act designed in part to meet victim needs, *e.g.,* Section 3–205, Presentence Reports; Section 3–207, Sentencing Hearing; Section 3–602, Restitution, do not go far enough. Their primary thrust is to require the department to refer victims to services, *see* section 2–203(7), *supra,* rather than to provide the services within the department. It is therefore contemplated that experience with this provision may well lead states to authorize the direct provision of services to victims. It is further recognized that there are many other ways in which a legislature may choose to assist victims. *See, e.g.,* Cal.Penal Code, § 1413(b) (West Supp.1977) (authority to photograph evidence in lieu of retention of evidence). The provisions are presented, however, as a necessary beginning—and as a base upon which development and expansion of victims services can and should be raised.

ARTICLE 5

VICTIMS

PART 1

VICTIMS ASSISTANCE SERVICE PROGRAM

§ 5-101. [Victims Assistance Service Officer; Appointment.]

The associate director for community-based services shall appoint, and he may remove in accordance with law, a victims assistance service officer who has appropriate training in counseling or a related discipline at an accredited college or university.

§ 5-102. [Duties of Victims Assistance Service Officer.]

The victims assistance service officer shall:

(1) administer a victims assistance program to assist victims who incur physical or emotional injury or property damage due to the commission of an offense;

(2) cooperate with individuals or public or private agencies or organizations concerned with the treatment or assistance of persons in the program and refer victims and their immediate families to providers of services including:

    (i) medical care;

    (ii) employment placement;

    (iii) placement in educational, vocational, and rehabilitation programs;

    (iv) legal assistance; and

    (v) financial assistance;

(3) explain to a victim the criminal-trial process, court and police procedures, pre-trial release decisions, and other aspects of the legal system as they may affect him;

(4) if requested by the victim,

    (i) assist in filing a criminal complaint;

    (ii) assist the victim in preparing a sentence recommendation for inclusion in the presentence report; [and]

    [(iii) assist in filing and pursuing a claim with the crime victims reparations board; and]

(5) explain and publicize the victims assistance program to the public; and

(6) prepare and transmit to the director, for inclusion in his annual report to the governor, a written summary of the program, including the nature and number of cases handled and the nature and number of services provided.

§ 5-103. [Victim Attendance at Investigative or Criminal Trial Process.]

(a) If a victim attends any stage of the investigative or criminal trial process at the request of a law enforcement officer or the prosecuting attorney, he is entitled to receive the same fees provided for witnesses who appear in obedience to a subpoena in criminal cases in [the district court].

(b) A person may not discharge a victim from employment because of absences from the employment caused by attendance at a stage of the investigative or criminal trial process at the request of a law enforcement officer or the prosecuting attorney.

(c) A person who violates this section is liable in a civil action to the victim for loss caused by a wrongful discharge and reasonable attorney's fees, and he may also be required to show cause why he should not be held in contempt of court.

PART 2

[Reserved for the Uniform Crime Victims Reparations Act.]

COMMENT

The Uniform Crime Victims Reparations Act was adopted in 1973 by the National Conference of Commissioners on Uniform State Laws. It has been enacted in Ohio, Ohio Rev.Code Ann., § 2743.51 to 2743.52 (Page Supp.1976), and in substantially similar form in Minnesota, Minn.Stat.Ann., §§ 299B.01 to 299B.16 (West Supp.1978). Congress has under consideration a federal program for victim compensation S.1437, 95th Cong., 1st Sess. ch. 41, §§ 4111–4115 (Criminal Code Reform Act of 1977). In addition, there is a growing number of states that provide compensation to victims. *E.g.,* Uniform Crime Victims Reparations Act (1974); Alaska Stat., §§ 18.67.010 to 180 (1974); Cal.Gov't Code, §§ 13960–13966 (West Supp.1977); Haw.Rev.Stat. ch. 351 (Supp.1975); Ill.Ann.Stat. ch. 70, §§ 71 to 84 (Smith–Hurd Supp.1977); Md.Ann.Code art. 26A (Supp. 1977); Mass.Ann.Laws ch. 258A (Michie/Law Co-op Supp.1977–1978); Mich.Comp.Laws Ann., §§ 18.351 to .362 (West Supp.1977–1978); Nev.Rev.Stat. ch. 217 (1975); N.J.Stat.Ann., §§ 52:4B–1 to 21 (West Supp. 1977–1978); N.Y.Exec.Law, §§ 622–635 (McKinney 1972 & Supp.1977).

Compensation to crime victims is an important aspect of victims services. The victims provisions provided in Article V Part 1 have specifically avoided those kinds of services which by their nature should be included as among the functions of a Crime Victims Reparations Board (examples of this include the reimbursement of hospital costs for an examination conducted to gather evidence for a criminal prosecution and payment by the state, after investigation by a Crime Victim Reparations Board, of actual costs incurred in the criminal justice process).

A state enacting the Uniform Sentencing and Corrections Act should consider its integration with crime victims reparations. Responsibilities of the Board, for example, could be to present its views to the Sentencing Commission or particular sentencing hearings. The Board could make compensation payments to victims and then seek a restitution award from a particular, identified offender. Further, in a fully integrated system there are probably many ways in which the Victims Assistance Service Officer could work with the Board.

ARTICLE 6

TRANSITION AND APPLICATION

PART 1

TRANSITION

§ 6–101. [Effective Date of Act.]

(a) Except as provided in this section, this Act takes effect one year after the date of its enactment.

(b) For the purpose of preparing for the effective date of this Act, the following provisions of this Act become effective on the same date as acts without an expressed effective date:

(1) provisions authorizing the creation and the appointment of officers and employees of,

(i) the department of corrections and its divisions;

(ii) the office of correctional legal services;

(iii) the office of correctional mediation; and

(iv) the sentencing commission.

(2) provisions authorizing the adoption of rules and sentencing guidelines;

(3) provisions establishing the manner in which rules and sentencing guidelines are to be adopted; and

(4) provisions establishing requirements for the design and construction of new facilities and the remodeling of existing facilities.

(c) A rule or sentencing guideline does not become effective until the effective date of this Act.

(d) Appropriated funds may be expended before the effective date of this Act to develop and adopt rules and sentencing guidelines and to take other necessary action to prepare for the effective date of this Act.

§ 6–102. [Transition of Sentencing Provisions.]

(a) Except as provided in this section, sentences for offenses committed before the effective date of this Act must be imposed and served pursuant to the law in force for this purpose as if this Act were not enacted.

(b) A person whose offense has been committed but whose sentence has not been imposed before the effective date of this Act may elect to be sentenced under this Act.

(c) Within one year after the effective date of this Act, the [board of parole] or a hearing officer designated by the [board] shall hold a parole hearing for each person held in the custody of the department pursuant to a sentence imposed under prior law for which the possibility of parole by the [board] was provided. The [board] or hearing officer shall consider each case the available information relevant to the exercise of its parole powers pursuant to prior law.

(d) Within 10 days after the hearing, the [board] shall establish a release date, which must be the likely date the person would have been released under the law as it existed before the enactment of this Act. The [board] may establish an earlier release date if it believes that the prior parol practice would have resulted in confinement longer than the guidelines of the sentencing commission on similar offenders for similar offenses. The release date established may not be earlier than any minimum parole eligibility date applicable to the offender under prior law.

(e) A person sentenced to confinement under prior law must be released on the date established by the [board], subject to applicable, good-time reductions. Upon release, he is entitled to assistance as provided in this Act in lieu of any parole supervision required under prior law.

(f) A person sentenced pursuant to prior law is entitled to receive good-time reductions under this Act unless he elects to receive the good-time reductions authorized by prior law. Restoration of good-time reductions forfeited pursuant to prior law may be restored pursuant to prior law. Good time reductions earned after the effective date of this Act are subject to forfeiture and withholding, as provided by this Act.

(g) On the effective date of this Act, a person under parole supervision must be discharged from parole as if he had satisfactorily completed his sentence. A person confined as a result of a parole revocation must be given a release date pursuant to subsection (c).

(h) One year after the effective date of this Act:

(1) all powers and duties vested in and imposed on the [board of parole], including those in this section, are transferred to and imposed upon the sentencing commission for as long as required to determine the release dates of persons sentenced pursuant to prior law; and

(2) the [board of parole] is abolished.

(i) On the effective date of this Act, all powers and duties vested in and imposed on [any official or agency having powers or duties relating to sentencing other than a court, such as local probation departments, sheriffs, local jailers, local parole boards] necessary to determine the length or conditions of sentence imposed for an offense committed prior to the effective date of this Act are transferred to the director of corrections for as long as required for the confinement, supervision, or release of persons sentenced pursuant to prior law.

(j) Nothing in this Act authorizes an offender sentenced pursuant to prior law to be retained in the custody of the department or in confinement in a facility for a period of time longer than he could have been retained in custody or confinement pursuant to prior law.

(k) The legislature finds that it is in the best interest of the State to adjust sentences imposed under prior law to make them comparable to those that would be imposed under this Act whenever to do so does not extend the sentence of any particular offender. The legislature requests that the [Governor; Pardon Board] exercise [his; its] computation powers to effectuate that adjustment.

PART 2

APPLICATION

§ 6-201. [Short Title.]

This Act may be cited as the Model Sentencing and Corrections Act.

§ 6-202. [Severability.]

If any provision of this Act or its application to any person or circumstances is held invalid, the invalidity does not affect other provisions or applications of the Act which can be given effect without the invalid provision or application, and to this end the provisions of this Act are severable.

§ 6-203. [Repeal.]

The following acts and parts of acts are repealed:

(1)

(2)

(3)

and all other acts, or parts thereof, to the extent that they are inconsistent with this Act.

UNIFORM POST–CONVICTION PROCEDURE ACT

1966 ACT

Table of Jurisdictions Wherein Act Has Been Adopted

Jurisdiction	Laws	Effective Date	Statutory Citation
Idaho	1967, c. 25		I.C. §§ 19–4901 to 19–4911.
Iowa	1970, c. 1276	7–1–1970	I.C.A. §§ 663A.1 to 663A.11.
Maryland	1958, c. 44	4–4–1958 *	Code 1957, art. 27, §§ 645A to 645J.
Minnesota	1967, c. 336	5–11–1967	M.S.A. §§ 590.01 to 590.06.
Montana	1967, c. 196	1–1–1968	MCA 46–21–101 to 46–21–203.
Nevada	1967, c. 1447		N.R.S. 177.315 to 177.385.
Oklahoma	1970, c. 220	7–1–1970	22 Okl.St.Ann. §§ 1080 to 1089.
Oregon	1959, c. 636	2–26–1959 **	ORS 138.510 to 138.680.
Rhode Island	1974, c. 220		Gen.Laws 1956, §§ 10–9.1–1 to 10–9.1–9.
South Carolina	1969, (56) 158	5–1–1969	Code 1976, §§ 17–27–10 to 17–27–120.

* Date of approval.

The 1966 Uniform Post–Conviction Procedure Act was superseded by the 1980 Uniform Post–Conviction Procedure Act approved by the National Conference of Commissioners on Uniform State Laws in August 1980. The text of the new 1980 Act is set out infra.

Commissioners' Prefatory Note

Reason for Proposed Uniform Act

Great attention has been given in recent years to the federal habeas corpus jurisdiction and the federal-state conflicts believed to be engendered by the use of the federal writ by state prisoners. In 1964 over 6000 petitions for writs of habeas corpus were filed in the federal courts and more than half of these were for persons in custody pursuant to judgment of a state court. The total in 1964 increased by 1600 over 1963 and all but 11 of the increases were for persons in custody pursuant to judgment of a state court.

As long ago as 1934 the United States Supreme Court stated that the states must afford prisoners some method by which they may raise claims of denial of federal right. See Mooney v. Holohan, 294 U.S. 103, 55 S.Ct. 340, 79 L.Ed. 791. In 1949 it stated that the method must be clearly defined. Young v. Ragen, 337 U.S. 235, 69 S.Ct. 1073, 93 L.Ed. 1333. In Case v. Nebraska, 381 U.S. 336, 85 S.Ct. 1486, 14 L.Ed.2d 422 (1965), the United States Supreme Court held that absence of a post-conviction remedy may itself be a denial of due process under the 14th amendment.

Title 28 of the United States Code, Section 2254, provides that an application for a writ of habeas corpus "in behalf of a person in custody pursuant to the judgment of a state court shall not be granted unless it appears that the applicant has exhausted the remedies available in the courts of the state, or that there is either an absence of available state corrective process or the existence of circumstances rendering such process ineffective to protect the rights of the prisoner." This section continues with the statement that a prisoner has not exhausted his remedies "if he had a right to raise his question by any available procedure under state law." See also Darr v. Burford, 339 U.S. 200, 70 S.Ct. 587, 94 L.Ed. 761 (1950). Thus, many of the abuses which have arisen in connection with federal habeas corpus can be eliminated through constructive action at the state level. This was the conclusion of a special committee on habeas corpus of the Conference of Chief Justices of the states at its annual meeting in 1953. (Report of Special Committee on Habeas Corpus, Proceedings, Conference of Chief Justices, 1953, p. 11.) Thus, it is clear that the continuing use and, indeed, the rapid increase in federal habeas corpus petitions for prisoners in state custody is closely related to the adequacy of post-conviction process in the state courts.

At common law the writ of habeas corpus was the proper remedy when the convicting court did not have jurisdiction over the subject or the person. But unless the state has extended this remedy or provided another remedy, a claim that the conviction in a court which had jurisdiction occurred in disregard of constitutional right cannot be asserted. The writ will not lie when it is sought to impeach a record of conviction or to correct a record. Consequently, in those states which have a narrow view of habeas corpus and which have not provided another remedy, the post-conviction relief available to a prisoner is not as broad as the claims which may be made under the 14th amendment of the United States Constitution. In such states prisoners who have bona fide claims of infringement of constitutional right must resort to federal habeas corpus. The ancient common law writ of error coram nobis is equally beset, in many states, with technical restrictions on availability. Confusion exists when the writ will lie. Because of the multiplicity and inadequacy of many post-conviction remedies, long delays in criminal administration occur and when a claim of constitutional right is successfully asserted the judgment to this effect occurs only after years of imprisonment which has turned out to be illegal. A very substantial number of states lack a unified all-embracing system of post-conviction relief capable of affording the prisoner a forum for his claims based on the United States Constitution.

It is true that the states are faced with a dilemma. If a person has been unconstitutionally imprisoned while the numerous state remedies are pursued for from two to ten years, the situation is abhorrent to our sense of justice. On the other hand, if the greatest number of applications for post-conviction relief are groundless, the wear and tear on the judicial machinery resulting from years of litigation in thousands of cases becomes a matter of serious import to courts and judges. The element of expense is not to be ignored.

Even if there were no problem of tension between the federal and state systems, a minimum standard of criminal justice would seem to require an expeditious and simplified post-conviction remedy. Many states can achieve such a post-conviction remedy by adoption of appropriate rules of court. The present Act, as did its predecessor, the 1955 Uniform Post–Conviction Procedure Act, seeks to meet two objectives: to establish a post-conviction procedure which meets the minimum standards of justice; and to reduce the use of federal habeas corpus to review decisions of state courts to the extent this can be done by state law or by rule of court. The Act may be adapted to rule of court if the courts are so inclined or the Act may be enacted by legislatures.

What the Proposed Act Does

(1) It provides a single, unitary, post-conviction remedy to be used in place of all other state remedies (except direct review). Section 1(b).

(2) It provides a remedy for all grounds for attacking the validity of a conviction or sentence in a criminal case. The grounds included are a claim of a violation of the United States Constitution and the State Constitution and laws; a claim that the court lacked jurisdiction over the person or subject matter; a claim that the sentence was unlawful as in excess of the maximum authorized by law; a claim that there exists evidence of material facts not previously presented and heard which should in justice be heard; that the sentence has expired or that parole, probation, or conditional release has been unlawfully revoked; and any other ground heretofore available under any common law or statutory remedy. See section 1(a).

(3) It makes available discovery and other pre-trial devices used customarily in civil proceedings to bring to the attention of the court the evidentiary bases for the post-conviction claims. See section 7.

(4) It provides for the making of a record which fully and carefully records the proceedings so that the evidentiary basis for the findings of fact will be available on review. See section 7.

(5) It provides that orders of the court should state explicitly the legal basis for the decision. See section 7.

(6) It provides that the expenses of representation including legal services should be provided to applicants who are unrepresented and without funds to pay for their own lawyers even to the extent of legal aid in preparation of the application. See section 5.

(7) It restricts attempts to finally dispose of application for relief on the basis simply of the sufficiency of allegations and it prohibits disposition on the pleadings and record if there is a material issue of fact. See section 6.

(8) It permits the court to obtain improvement in presentation of claims by applicants through development by the court of standardized forms but it directs the court to consider substance and not defects in form in disposition of applications. See section 3.

(9) It requires an applicant to present all of his claims for attack on his conviction or sentence in his initial post-conviction proceeding. It provides that any ground finally adjudicated in one proceeding or not raised in that proceeding or not knowingly, voluntarily, and intelligently waived in the proceeding may not be the basis for a subsequent application, but it gives the court discretion to find that a ground for relief asserted in a subsequent application was, for sufficient reason, not asserted or was inadequately raised in that proceeding. It provides no fixed period after conviction in which an application for post-conviction relief may be sought. See section 8.

Will This Act Meet the Objectives?

A minimum standard of criminal justice requires expeditious and simplified post-conviction procedures and it is believed that the Act is consistent with standards of criminal justice.

A basic principle of this Act is that it is preferable to deal with claims on their merits rather than to seek an elaborate set of technical procedures to avoid considering claims which we may assume not to be meritorious. It is believed that it will be less burdensome to the courts and more effective in the long run for courts to decide that claims are not meritorious and so state in written conclusions than to try to administer procedural doctrines to "save" judicial time and effort.

There are several indications that an Act of the type here presented will aid in the reduction of applications for federal habeas corpus. As Mr. Justice Clark pointed out in Case v. Nebraska, 381 U.S. 336, 340, 85 S.Ct. 1486, 14 L.Ed.2d 422, the Illinois Post–Conviction Act on which this draft is partially based produced after its enactment a considerable drop in federal applications from state prisoners. The experience under the federal post-conviction procedure (entitled motion to vacate sentence), 28 U.S.C. § 225, would seem to support the same conclusion. While habeas corpus petitions in the federal court since enactment of the federal law in 1949 have increased, the increase in applications by federal prisoners is substantially less than the increase in applications by state prisoners. While federal applications increased 129%, state applications increased 174%.

Why is a Revision Needed Now?

Since 1955, when the original Act was promulgated by the National Conference, the cases in the United States Supreme Court have strengthened a requirement that state relief is not adequate if there is a dismissal of the claim without a full and fair evidentiary hearing on the merits when the claim is based on disputed facts. Moreover new grounds for attacking a conviction have developed. The 1966 revision proposed herein is designed to take care of these developments. It is believed that it is now flexible enough so that with sympathetic consideration of pleadings and methods of presenting issues, a prisoner will always be able to raise his claim in a state court and thus, as provided in 28 U.S.C. § 2254 there will be no occasion for federal habeas corpus, because a state remedy is available.

Why Uniformity?

Since federal and state procedures are closely linked, as indicated above, state procedures ought to be uniform to conform to the uniform federal procedures. The Report of the Special Committee on Habeas Corpus of the Conference of Chief Justices in 1953 gives perhaps the basic reason for uniformity:

"If any proposition can be stated dogmatically in this field it is this: the state courts must provide post-conviction corrective process which is at least as broad as the requirements which will be enforced by the federal courts in habeas corpus through the due process clause of the 14th amendment. A state can call this remedy whatever it wants, but it must provide some corrective process."

It may be added that the requisite uniformity can be obtained either by statute or by rules of court. Uniformity would not be sacrificed if the substance of the accompanying Act were promulgated by the supreme court of the state by rule.

What State Laws Should be Repealed

Section 1(b) of the Act makes the remedy provided a substitute for all common law-statutory or other remedies heretofore available for challenging the conviction or sentence (other than direct review). A state should consider repealing its existing statutes on habeas corpus, *coram nobis* and statutory remedies, if any. Whether these are repealed or not, the direction in section 1(b) would seem to require a court to treat an application under such a remedy as made under this Act and governed by its provisions as to pleadings and procedure.

1966 REVISED ACT

Be it enacted

---

§ 1. [Remedy—To Whom Available—Conditions]

(a) Any person who has been convicted of, or sentenced for, a crime and who claims:

(1) that the conviction or the sentence was in violation of the Constitution of the United States or the Constitution or laws of this state;

(2) that the court was without jurisdiction to impose sentence;

(3) that the sentence exceeds the maximum authorized by law;

(4) that there exists evidence of material facts, not previously presented and heard, that requires vacation of the conviction or sentence in the interest of justice;

(5) that his sentence has expired, his probation, parole, or conditional release unlawfully revoked, or he is otherwise unlawfully held in custody or other restraint; or

(6) that the conviction or sentence is otherwise subject to collateral attack upon any ground of alleged error heretofore available under any common law, statutory or other writ, motion, petition, proceeding, or remedy;

may institute, without paying a filing fee, a proceeding under this Act to secure relief.

(b) This remedy is not a substitute for nor does it affect any remedy incident to the proceedings in the trial court, or of direct review of the sentence or conviction. Except as otherwise provided in this Act, it comprehends and takes the place of all other common law, statutory, or other remedies heretofore available for challenging the validity of the conviction or sentence. It shall be used exclusively in place of them.

§ 2. [Exercise of Original Jurisdiction in Habeas Corpus]

[(The Supreme Court, Circuit Court, District Court) in which, by the Constitution of this state, original jurisdiction in habeas corpus is vested, may entertain in accordance with its rules a proceeding under this Act in the exercise of its original jurisdiction. In that event, this Act, to the extent applicable, governs the proceeding.]

§ 3. [Commencement of Proceedings— Verification—Filing—Service]

A proceeding is commenced by filing an application verified by the applicant with the clerk of the court in which the conviction took place. An application may be filed at any time. Facts within the personal knowledge of the applicant and the authenticity of all documents and exhibits included in or attached to the application must be sworn to affirmatively as true and correct. The [Supreme Court, Court of Appeals] may prescribe the form of the application and verification. The clerk shall docket the application upon its receipt and promptly bring it to the attention of the court and deliver a copy to the [prosecuting attorney, county attorney, state's attorney, attorney general].

§ 4. [Application—Contents]

The application shall identify the proceedings in which the applicant was convicted, give the date of the entry of the judgment and sentence complained of, specifically set forth the grounds upon which the application is based, and clearly state the relief desired. Facts within the personal knowledge of the applicant shall be set forth separately from other allegations of facts and shall be verified as provided in section 3 of this Act. Affidavits, records, or other evidence supporting its allegations shall be attached to the application or the application shall recite why they are not attached. The application shall identify all previous proceedings, together with the grounds therein asserted, taken by the appli-

cant to secure relief from his conviction or sentence. Argument, citations, and discussion of authorities are unnecessary.

§ 5. [Inability to Pay Costs]

If the applicant is unable to pay court costs and expenses of representation, including stenographic, printing, and legal services; these costs and expenses shall be made available to the applicant in the preparation of the application, in the trial court, and on review.

§ 6. [Pleadings and Judgment on Pleadings]

(a) Within [30] days after the docketing of the application, or within any further time the court may fix, the state shall respond by answer or by motion which may be supported by affidavits. At any time prior to entry of judgment the court may grant leave to withdraw the application. The court may make appropriate orders for amendment of the application or any pleading or motion, for pleading over, for filing further pleadings or motions, or for extending the time of the filing of any pleading. In considering the application the court shall take account of substance regardless of defects of form. If the application is not accompanied by the record of the proceedings challenged therein, the respondent shall file with its answer the record or portions thereof that are material to the questions raised in the application.

(b) When a court is satisfied, on the basis of the application, the answer or motion, and the record, that the applicant is not entitled to post-conviction relief and no purpose would be served by any further proceedings, it may indicate to the parties its intention to dismiss the application and its reasons for so doing. The applicant shall be given an opportunity to reply to the proposed dismissal. In light of the reply, or on default thereof, the court may order the application dismissed or grant leave to file an amended application or direct that the proceedings otherwise continue. Disposition on the pleadings and record is not proper if there exists a material issue of fact.

(c) The court may grant a motion by either party for summary disposition of the application when it appears from the pleadings, depositions, answers to interrogatories, and admissions and agreements of fact, together with any affidavits submitted, that there is no genuine issue of material fact and the moving party is entitled to judgment as a matter of law.

§ 7. [Hearing—Evidence—Order]

The application shall be heard in, and before any judge of, the court in which the conviction took place. A record of the proceedings shall be made and preserved. All rules and statutes applicable in civil proceedings including pre-trial and discovery procedures are available to the parties. The court may receive proof by affidavits, depositions, oral testimony, or other evidence and may order the applicant brought before it for the hearing. If the court finds in favor of the applicant, it shall enter an appropriate order with respect to the conviction or sentence in the former proceedings, and any supplementary orders as to rearraignment, retrial, custody, bail, discharge, correction of sentence, or other matters that may be necessary and proper. The court shall make specific findings of fact, and state expressly its conclusions of law, relating to each issue presented. This order is a final judgment.

§ 8. [Waiver of or Failure to Assert Claims]

All grounds for relief available to an applicant under this Act must be raised in his original, supplemental or amended application. Any ground finally adjudicated or not so raised, or knowingly, voluntarily and intelligently waived in the proceeding that resulted in the conviction or sentence or in any other proceeding the applicant has taken to secure relief may not be the basis for a subsequent application, unless the court finds a ground for relief asserted which for sufficient reason was not asserted or was inade-

quately raised in the original, supplemental, or amended application.

§ 9. [Review]

A final judgment entered under this Act may be reviewed by the [Supreme Court, Court of Appeals] of this state on [appeal, writ of error] brought either by the applicant within _____ or by the state within _____ from the entry of the judgment.

§ 10. [Uniformity of Interpretation]

This Act shall be so interpreted and construed as to effectuate its general purpose to make uniform the law of those states which enact it.

§ 11. [Short Title]

This Act may be cited as the Uniform Post–Conviction Procedure Act.

§ 12. [Severability]

If any provision of this Act or the application thereof to any person or circumstance is held invalid, the invalidity does not affect other provisions or applications of the Act which can be given effect without the invalid provision or application, and to this end the provisions of this Act are severable.

§ 13. [Repeal]

The following acts and parts of acts are repealed:

(1)

(2)

(3)

§ 14. [Time of Taking Effect]

This Act shall take effect _____.

1980 ACT

Table of Jurisdictions Wherein Act Has Been Adopted

Jurisdiction	Laws	Effective Date	Statutory Citation
North Dakota.........	1985, c. 366	See footnote[1]	NDCC 29–32.1–01 to 29–32.1–14.

[1] Governs all convictions occurring after June 30, 1985.

Historical Note

The new Uniform Post–Conviction Procedure Act was approved by the National Conference of Commissioners on Uniform State Laws in 1980. It supersedes the 1966 Post–Conviction and Procedure Act.

PREFATORY NOTE

The National Conference of Commissioners on Uniform State Laws promulgated the original Uniform Post–Conviction Procedure Act in 1955. A revision was prepared contemporaneously with the development by the American Bar Association of the first edition of its Standards of Criminal Justice. The 1966 Revised Act reflected the Standards on Post–Conviction Remedies.

The American Bar Association is presently completing a review and updating of its Criminal Justice Standards. During the decade since their original publication, the criminal justice system was intensively studied by many organizations. The product of those efforts was considered by the ABA in preparing the second edition of the Standards. Consequently, the National Conference of Commissioners on Uniform State Laws authorized preparation of a second revision of the Uniform Post–Conviction Procedure Act.

Table of Sections

Be it enacted ...

§ 1. [Remedy—To Whom Available—Conditions]

(a) A person who has been convicted of and sentenced for a crime may institute a proceeding applying for relief under this Act upon the ground that:

(1) the conviction was obtained or the sentence was imposed in violation of the Constitution or of the United States or of the Constitution or laws of this State;

(2) the conviction was obtained under a statute that is in violation of the Constitution of the United States or the Constitution of this State, or that the conduct for which the applicant was prosecuted is constitutionally protected;

(3) the court that rendered the judgment of conviction and sentence was without jurisdiction over the person of the applicant or the subject matter;

(4) the sentence is not authorized by law;

(5) evidence, not previously presented and heard, exists requiring vacation of the conviction or sentence in the interest of justice;

(6) a significant change in substantive or procedural law has occurred which, in the interest of justice, should be applied retrospectively;

(7) the sentence has expired, probation or parole or conditional release was unlawfully revoked, or the applicant is otherwise unlawfully in custody or restrained; or

(8) the conviction or sentence is otherwise subject to collateral attack upon any ground of alleged error available before the effective date

of this Act under any common law, statutory or other writ, motion, proceeding, or remedy.

(b) A proceeding under this Act is not a substitute for and does not affect any remedy incident to the prosecution in the trial court or direct review of the judgment of conviction or sentence in an appellate court. Except as otherwise provided in this Act, a proceeding under this Act replaces all other common law, statutory, or other remedies available before the effective date of this Act for collaterally challenging the validity of the judgment of conviction or sentence. It is to be used exclusively in place of them.

§ 2. [Exercise of Original Jurisdiction in Habeas Corpus]

A court in which original jurisdiction in habeas corpus is vested may entertain a habeas corpus proceeding under the Act. This Act, to the extent appropriate, governs the proceeding.

§ 3. [Commencement of Proceedings— Filing—Service]

(a) A proceeding is commenced by filing an application with the clerk of the court in which the conviction and sentence took place. The [State, People, Commonwealth] must be named as respondent. No filing fee is required.

(b) An application may be filed at any time.

(c) If an application is filed before the time for appeal from the judgment of conviction or sentence has expired, the court, on motion of the applicant, may extend the time for appeal until a final order has been entered in the proceeding under this Act.

(d) If an application is filed while an appeal or other review is pending, the appellant court, on motion of either party or on its own motion, may defer further action on the appeal or other review until the determination of the application by the trial court or may order the application [removed] [certified] and consolidated with the pending appeal or other review.

(e) Upon receipt of an application, the clerk shall forthwith file it, make an entry in the appropriate docket and deliver a copy to the prosecutor.

(f) If the applicant is not represented by counsel, the clerk shall notify the applicant that assistance of counsel may be available to persons unable to obtain counsel. The clerk shall also inform the applicant of the procedure for obtaining counsel.

(g) The application may be considered by any judge of the court in which the conviction took place.

§ 4. [Application—Contents]

(a) The application must identify the proceedings in which the applicant was convicted and sentenced, give the date of the judgment and sentence complained of, set forth a concise statement of each ground for relief, and specify the relief requested. Argument, citations, and discussion of authorities are unnecessary.

(b) The application must identify all proceedings for direct review of the judgment of conviction or sentence and all previous post-conviction proceedings taken by the applicant to secure relief from the conviction or sentence, the grounds asserted therein, and the orders or judgments entered. The application must refer to the portions of the record of prior proceedings pertinent to the alleged grounds for relief. If the cited record is not in the files of the court, the applicant shall attach that record or portions thereof to the application or state why it is not attached. Affidavits or other material supporting the application may be attached, but are unnecessary.

§ 5. [Appointment of Counsel—Applicant's Inability to Pay Costs and Litigation Expenses]

(a) If an applicant requests appointment of counsel and the court is satisfied that the applicant is unable to obtain adequate representation, the court shall appoint counsel to represent the applicant.

(b) Costs and expenses incident to a proceeding under this Act, including fees for appointed counsel, must be reimbursed in the same manner as are costs and expenses incurred in the defense of criminal prosecutions under [cite appropriate statute].

§ 6. [Response by Answer or Motion]

(a) Within [30] days after the docketing of an application or within any further time the court may allow, the state shall respond by answer or motion.

(b) The state may move to dismiss an application on the ground that it is evident from the application that the applicant is not entitled to post-conviction relief and no purpose would be served by any further proceedings. In considering the motion, the court shall take account of substance regardless of defects of form.

(c) The following defenses may be raised by answer or motion:

(1) The claim has been fully and finally determined in previous proceeding (Section 12(a)); and

(2) The application constitutes misuse of process (Section 12(b)).

§ 7. [Amended and Supplemental Pleadings]

(a) The court may make appropriate orders allowing amendment of the application or any pleading or motion, allowing further pleadings or motions, or extending the time for filing any pleading.

(b) At any time before the entry of judgment, the court, for good cause, may grant leave to withdraw the application without prejudice.

§ 8. [Discovery]

The court, for good cause, may grant leave to either party to use the discovery procedures available in criminal or civil proceedings. Discovery procedures may be used only to the extent and in the manner the court has ordered or to which the parties have agreed.

§ 9. [Summary Disposition]

(a) The court may grant a motion by either party for summary disposition if the application, pleadings, any previous proceeding, discovery, or other matters of record show that there is no genuine issue as to any material fact and the moving party is entitled to a judgment as a matter of law.

(b) If an evidentiary hearing is necessary, the court may determine which issues of material fact are in controversy and appropriately restrict the hearing.

§ 10. [Hearing—Evidence]

(a) Evidence must be presented in open court, recorded and preserved as part of the record of the proceedings.

(b) A certified record of previous proceedings may be used as evidence of facts and occurrences established therein, but use of that record does not preclude either party from offering additional evidence as to those facts and occurrences.

(c) The deposition of a witness may be received in evidence, without regard to the availability of the witness, if written notice of intention to use the deposition was given in advance of the hearing and the deposition was taken subject to the right of cross-examination.

§ 11. [Findings of Fact—Conclusions of Law—Order]

(a) The court shall make explicit findings on material questions of fact and state expressly its conclusions of law relating to each issue presented.

(c) If the court finds in favor of the applicant, it shall enter an appropriate order with respect to the conviction or sentence in the previous proceedings, and any supplementary orders as to rearraignment, retrial, custody, bail, discharge, correction of sentence, or other matters that may be necessary and proper.

§ 12. [Affirmative Defenses—Res Judicata—Misuse of Process]

(a) An application for post-conviction relief may be denied on the ground that the same claim or claims were fully and finally determined in a previous proceeding.

(b) A court may deny relief on the ground of misuse of process. An applicant misuses process if he:

(1) presents a claim for relief which he inexcusably failed to raise either in a proceeding leading to judgment of conviction and sentence or in a previous post-conviction proceeding; or

(2) files multiple applications containing a claim so lacking in factual support or legal basis as to be frivolous.

(c) Res judicata and misuse of process are affirmative defenses to be pleaded by the state. Burden of proof is also upon the state, but, as to any ground for relief which, by statute or rule of court, must be presented as a defense or objection at a specified stage of a criminal prosecution, the applicant must show good cause for non-compliance with the statute or rule.

§ 13. [Reimbursement of Costs and Litigation Expenses]

If an application is denied, the state may move for an order requiring the applicant to reimburse the state for costs and for litigation expenses paid for him from public funds. The court may grant the motion if it finds that the applicant's claim is so completely lacking in factual support or legal basis as to be frivolous or that the applicant has deliberately misused process. The court may require reimbursement of costs and expenses only to the extent reasonable in light of the applicant's present and probable future financial resources.

§ 14. [Review]

A final judgment entered under this Act may be reviewed by the [designate appellate court] upon [appeal, writ of error] filed either by the applicant within [___] days or by the state within [___] days after the entry of judgment.

§ 15. [Uniformity of Application and Construction]

This Act shall be applied and construed to effectuate its general purpose to make uniform the law with respect to the subject of this Act among states enacting it.

§ 16. [Short Title]

This Act may be cited as the Uniform Post–Conviction Procedure Act (1980).

§ 17. [Severability]

If any provision of this Act or its application to any person or circumstance is held invalid, the invalidity does not affect other provisions or application of the Act which can be given effect without the invalid provision or application, and to this end the provisions of this Act are severable.

§ 18. [Repeal]

The following acts and parts of acts are repealed:

(1)

(2)

(3)

§ 19. [Time of Taking Effect]

This Act takes effect _____.

*

THE FEDERAL MODEL

Table of Contents

*

FEDERAL RULES OF CRIMINAL PROCEDURE
INTRODUCTION

Federal Rules (of Civil Procedure, Evidence, as well as Criminal Procedure) have been variously emulated among the states. In any case, questions raised by a study of the Federal Rules are pertinent to an inquiry into any criminal procedural system in this country.

The general structure of the Federal Rules of Criminal Procedure is evident in the Table of Rules that precedes the main Rules text. Of particular benefit to a student of the Rules are the Committee and Amendment Notes that immediately follow the text of each Rule. These Notes detail the underlying rationale of the given Rule and specify the impetus for and substance of that Rule's evolution.

FEDERAL RULES OF CRIMINAL PROCEDURE FOR THE UNITED STATES DISTRICT COURTS

As Amended to February 1, 1989

Table of Rules

RULES OF CRIMINAL PROCEDURE

Appendix to Forms (Abrogated).

Analysis Applicable to Offenses Committed Prior to Nov. 1, 1987

Rules 35 and 38 of this analysis as in effect prior to amendment by Pub.L. 98–473 read as follows:

For applicability of sentencing provisions to offenses, see Effective Date and Savings Provisions, etc., note, section 235 of Pub.L. 98–473, as amended, set out under section 3551 of Title 18, Crimes and Criminal Procedure.

ORDERS OF THE SUPREME COURT OF THE UNITED STATES ADOPTING AND AMENDING RULES

ORDER OF DECEMBER 26, 1944

It is ordered that Rules of Criminal Procedure for the District Courts of the United States governing proceedings in criminal cases prior to and including verdict, finding of guilty or not guilty by the court, or plea of guilty, be prescribed pursuant to the Act of June 29, 1940, c. 445, 54 Stat. 688, 18 U.S.C.A. § 687. And the Chief Justice is authorized and directed to transmit the Rules as prescribed to the Attorney General and to request him, as provided in that Act, to report these Rules to the Congress at the beginning of the regular session in January 1945.

Mr. Justice Black states that he does not approve of the adoption of the Rules.

Mr. Justice Frankfurter does not join in the Court's action for reasons stated in a memorandum opinion.

MR. JUSTICE FRANKFURTER:

That the federal courts have power, or may be empowered, to make rules of procedure for the conduct of litigation has been settled for a century and a quarter (*Wayman v. Southard*, 10 Wheat. 1, 6 L.Ed. 253). And experience proves that justice profits if the responsibility for such rule making be vested in a small, standing rule-making body rather than be left to legislation generated by particular controversies. These views make me regret all the more not to be able to join my brethren in the adoption of the Rules of Criminal Procedure of the District Courts of the United States.

By withholding approval of the adoption of the rules I do not imply disapproval. I express no opinion on their merits. With all respect to contrary views, I believe that this Court is not an appropriate agency for formulating the rules of criminal procedure for the district courts.

From the beginning of the nation down to the Evarts Act of 1891, 26 Stat. 826, though less and less after the Civil War, the members of this Court rode circuit. They thus had intimate, first-hand experience with the duties and demands of trial courts. For the last fifty years the Justices have become necessarily removed from direct, day-by-day contact with trials in the district courts. To that extent they are largely denied the first-hand opportunities for realizing vividly what rules of procedure are best calculated to promote the largest measure of justice. These considerations are especially relevant to the for-mulation of rules for the conduct of criminal trials. These closely concern the public security as well as the liberties of citizens.

And this leads to another strong reason for not charging this Court with the duty of approving in advance a code of criminal procedure. Such a code can hardly escape provisions in which lurk serious questions for future adjudication by this Court. Every lawyer knows the difference be-tween passing on a question concretely raised by specific litigation and the formulation of abstract rules, however fully considered by members of the lower courts and the bar. I deem it unwise to prejudge, however unintentionally, questions that may in due course of litigation come before this Court by having this Court lay down rules in the abstract rather than deciding issues coming here with the impact of actuality and duly contested.

And there is one more important consideration. The business of this Court is increasing in volume and complexity. In the years ahead the number of cases will not decrease nor their difficulties lessen. The jurisdiction of this Court has already been cut almost to the bone. If the Court is not to be swamped, as it has been in the past, and is to do its best work, it must exercise rigorously its discretionary jurisdiction. Every additional duty, such as responsibility for fashioning progressive codes of procedure and keeping them current, makes inroads upon the discharge of functions which no one else can exercise.

Brief as is this statement, it can leave no room for doubt that the reasons which have con-strained me to withhold approval of adoption of the rules completely transcend judgment of their merits.

ORDER OF FEBRUARY 8, 1946

It is ordered on this 8th day of February, 1946 that the annexed Rules governing proceedings in criminal cases after verdict, finding of guilty or not guilty by the court, or pleas of guilty, be prescribed pursuant to the Act of February 24, 1933, c. 119 as amended [47 Stat. 904, U.S.Code Title 18 § 3772] for the District Courts of the United States, the United States Circuit Courts of Appeals, the United States Court of Appeals for the District of Columbia and the Supreme Court of the United States, and that said rules shall become effective on the 21st day of March, 1946.

It is further ordered that these Rules and the Rules heretofore promulgated by order dated De-cember 26, 1944 governing proceedings prior to and including verdict, finding of guilty or not guilty by the court, or plea of guilty, shall be consecutively numbered as indicated and shall be known as the Federal Rules of Criminal Proce-dure.

ORDER OF DECEMBER 27, 1948

The following order was adopted by the Su-preme Court on December 27, 1948.

1. That the title of the Federal Rules of Crimi-nal Procedure be, and it hereby is, amended to read as follows:

Rules of Criminal Procedure for the United States District Courts.

2. That Rules 17(e)(2), 41(b)(3), 41(g), 54(a)(1), 54(b), 54(c), 55, 56, and Rule 57(a), of the Federal Rules of Criminal Procedure be, and they hereby are, amended as hereinafter set forth.

[See the amendments made thereby under the re-spective rules, post]

3. That Forms 1 to 27, inclusive, contained in the Appendix of Forms to the Federal Rules of Criminal Procedure be, and they hereby are, amended as hereinafter specified.

[See the amendments made thereby under the re-spective forms, post]

4. That these amendments to the Federal Rules of Criminal Procedure shall take effect on the day following the final adjournment of the first regular session of the 81st Congress.

5. That The Chief Justice be authorized to transmit these amendments to the Attorney Gen-eral with the request that he report them to the

Congress at the beginning of the regular session of the 81st Congress in January, 1949.

ORDER OF DECEMBER 27, 1948

1. That the first sentence of Rule 37(a)(1) of the Federal Rules of Criminal Procedure be, and it hereby is, amended to read as follows:

[See the amendment made thereby under Rule 37, post]

2. That the first sentence of Rule 38(a)(3) of the Federal Rules of Criminal Procedure be, and it hereby is, amended to read as follows:

[See the amendment made thereby under Rule 38, post]

3. That Rule 38(c) of the Federal Rules of Criminal Procedure be, and it hereby is, amended to read as follows:

[See the amendment made thereby under Rule 38, post]

4. That Rule 39(b)(2) of the Federal Rules of Criminal Procedure be, and it hereby is, amended to read as follows:

[See the amendment made thereby under Rule 39, post]

5. That the foregoing amendments to the Federal Rules of Criminal Procedure shall take effect on January 1, 1949.

ORDER OF APRIL 12, 1954

That Rule 37 of the Federal Rules of Criminal Procedure be, and it hereby is, amended to read as follows:

[See the amendment made thereby under Rule 37, post]

That the foregoing amendment to the Federal Rules of Criminal Procedure shall take effect on July 1, 1954.

ORDER OF APRIL 9, 1956

1. That Rules 41(a), 46(a)(2), 54(a)(1), and 54(c) of the Rules of Criminal Procedure for the United States District Courts be, and they hereby are, amended as hereinafter set forth.

[See the amendments made thereby under the respective rules, post]

2. That the Chief Justice be authorized to report these amendments to Congress in accordance with the provisions of Title 18 U.S.C.A. § 3771.

ORDER OF FEBRUARY 28, 1966

1. That the Rules of Criminal Procedure for the United States District Courts be, and they hereby are, amended by including therein Rules 17.1 and 26.1 and amendments to Rules 4, 5, 6, 7, 11, 14, 16, 17, 18, 20, 21, 23, 24, 25, 28, 29, 30, 32, 33, 34, 35, 37, 38, 40, 44, 45, 46, 49, 54, 55, and 56, and to Form 26, as hereinafter set forth:

[See added and amended Rules, post]

2. That the foregoing amendments and additions to the Rules of Criminal Procedure shall take effect on July 1, 1966, and shall govern all criminal proceedings thereafter commenced and so far as just and practicable all proceedings then pending.

3. That the Chief Justice be, and he hereby is, authorized to transmit to the Congress the foregoing amendments and additions to the Rules of Criminal Procedure in accordance with the provisions of title 18 U.S.C., section 3771.

4. That Rule 19 and subdivision (c) of Rule 45 of the Rules of Criminal Procedure for the United States District Courts, promulgated by this court on December 26, 1944, effective March 21, 1946, are hereby rescinded, effective July 1, 1966.

MR. JUSTICE BLACK, dissenting.

The Amendments to the Federal Rules of Civil and Criminal Procedure today transmitted to the Congress are the work of very capable advisory committees. Those committees, not the Court, wrote the rules. Whether by this transmittal the individual members of the Court who voted to transmit the rules intended to express approval of the varied policy decisions the rules embody I am not sure. I am reasonably certain, however, that the Court's transmittal does not carry with it a decision that the amended rules are all constitutional. For such a decision would be the equivalent of an advisory opinion which, I assume the Court would unanimously agree, we are without constitutional power to give. And I agree with my Brother DOUGLAS that some of the proposed criminal rules go to the very border line if they do not actually transgress the constitutional right of a defendant not to be compelled to be a witness against himself. This phase of the criminal rules in itself so infects the whole collection of proposals that, without mentioning other objections, I am opposed to transmittal of the proposed amendments to the criminal rules.

I am likewise opposed to transmittal of the proposed revision of the civil rules. In the first place I think the provisions of 28 U.S.C. § 2072 (1964 ed.), under which these rules are transmitted and the corresponding section, 18 U.S.C. § 3771 (1964 ed.), relating to the criminal rules, both of which provide for giving transmitted rules the effect of law as though they had been properly enacted by Congress are unconstitutional for reasons I have previously stated.[1] And in prior dissents I have stated some of the basic reasons for my objections to repeated rules revisions[2] that tend to upset established meanings and need not repeat those grounds of objection here. The confusion created by the adoption of the present rules, over my objection, has been partially dispelled by judicial interpretations of them by this Court and others. New rules and extensive amendments to present rules will mean renewed confusion resulting in new challenges and new reversals and prejudicial "pretrial" dismissals of cases before a trial on the merits for failure of lawyers to understand and comply with new rules of uncertain meaning. Despite my continuing objection to the old rules, it seems to me that since they have at least gained some degree of certainty it would be wiser to "bear those ills we have than fly to others we know not of," unless, of course, we are reasonably sure that the proposed reforms of the old rules are badly needed. But I am not. The new proposals, at least some of them, have, as I view them, objectionable possibilities that cause me to believe our judicial system could get along much better without them.

The momentum given the proposed revision of the old rules by this Court's transmittal makes it practically certain that Congress, just as has this Court, will permit the rules to take effect exactly as they were written by the Advisory Committee on Rules. Nevertheless, I am including here a memorandum I submitted to the Court expressing objections to the Committee's proposals and suggesting changes should they be transmitted. These suggestions chiefly center around rules that grant broad discretion to trial judges with reference to class suits, pretrial procedures, and dismissal of cases with prejudice. Cases coming before the federal courts over the years now filling nearly 40 volumes of Federal Rules Decisions show an accumulation of grievances by lawyers and litigants about the way many trial judges exercise their almost unlimited discretionary powers to use pretrial procedures to dismiss cases without trials. In fact, many of these cases indicate a belief of many judges and legal commentators that the cause of justice is best served in the long run not by trials on the merits but by summary dismissals based on out of court affidavits, pretrial depositions, and other pretrial techniques. My belief is that open court trials on the merits where litigants have the right to prove their case or defense best comports with due process of law.

The proposed rules revisions, instead of introducing changes designed to prevent the continued abuse of pretrial power to dismiss cases summarily without trials, move in the opposite direction. Of course, each such dismissal results in removal of one more case from our congested court dockets, but that factor should not weigh more heavily in our system of justice than assuring a full-fledged due process trial of every bona fide lawsuit brought to vindicate an honest, substantial claim. It is to protect this ancient right of a person to have his case tried rather than summarily thrown out of court that I suggested to the Court that it recommended changes in the Committee's proposals of the nature set out in the following memorandum.

"Dear Brethren:

"I have gone over all the proposed amendments carefully and while there are probably

---

1. In a statement accompanying a previous transmittal of the civil rules, MR. JUSTICE DOUGLAS and I said:

"MR. JUSTICE BLACK and MR. JUSTICE DOUGLAS are opposed to the submission of these rules to the Congress under a statute which permits them to 'take effect' and to repeal 'all laws in conflict with such rules' without requiring any affirmative consideration, action, or approval of the rules by Congress or by the President. We believe that while some of the Rules of Civil Procedure are simply housekeeping details, many determine matters so substantially affecting the rights of litigants in lawsuits that in practical effect they are the equivalent of new legislation which, in our judgment, the Constitution requires to be initiated in and enacted by the Congress and approved by the President. The Constitution, as we read it, provides that all laws shall be enacted by the House, the Senate, and the President, not by the mere failure of Congress to reject proposals of an outside agency. * * * " (Footnotes omitted.) 374 U.S. 865–866.

2. 346 U.S. 946, 374 U.S. 865. And see 368 U.S. 1011 and 1012.

some good suggestions, it is my belief that the bad results that can come from the adoption of these amendments predominate over any good they can bring about. I particularly think that every member of the Court should examine with great care the amendments relating to class suits. It seems to me that they place too much power in the hands of the trial judges and that the rules might almost as well simply provide that 'class suits can be maintained either for or against particular groups whenever in the discretion of a judge he thinks it is wise.' The power given to the judge to dismiss such suits or to divide them up into groups at will subjects members of classes to dangers that could not follow from carefully prescribed legal standards enacted to control class suits.

"In addition, the rules as amended, in my judgment, greatly aggravate the evil of vesting judges with practically uncontrolled power to dismiss with prejudice cases brought by plaintiffs or defenses interposed by defendants. The power to dismiss a plaintiff's case or to render judgments by default against defendants can work great harm to both parties. There are many inherent urges in existence which may subconsciously incline a judge towards disposing of the cases before him without having to go through the burden of a trial. Mr. Chief Justice White, before he became Chief Justice, wrote an opinion in the case of Hovey v. Elliot, 167 U.S. 409 [17 S.Ct. 841, 42 L.Ed. 215], which pointed out grave constitutional questions raised by attempting to punish the parties by depriving them of the right to try their law suits or to defend against law suits brought against them by others.

"Rule 41 entitled 'Dismissal of Actions' points up the great power of judges to dismiss actions and provides an automatic method under which a dismissal must be construed as a dismissal 'with prejudice' unless the judge specifically states otherwise. For that reason I suggest to the Conference that if the Rules are accepted, including that one, the last sentence of Rule 41(b) be amended so as to provide that a simple order of dismissal by a judge instead of operating 'as an adjudication upon the merits,' as the amended rule reads, shall provide that such a dismissal 'does not operate as an adjudication upon the merits.'

"As a further guarantee against oppressive dismissals I suggest the addition of the following as subdivision (c) of Rule 41.

" 'No plaintiff's case shall be dismissed or defendant's right to defend be cut off because of the neglect, misfeasance, malfeasance, or failure of their counsel to obey any order of the court, until and unless such plaintiff or defendant shall have been personally served with notice of their counsel's delinquency, and not then unless the parties themselves do or fail to do something on their own part that can legally justify dismissal of the plaintiff's case or of the defendant's defense.'

"This proposed amendment is suggested in order to protect litigants, both plaintiffs and defendants, against being thrown out of court as a penalty for their lawyer's neglect or misconduct. The necessity for such a rule is shown, I think, by the dismissal in the plaintiff's case in Link v. Wabash R. Co., 370 U.S. 626 [82 S.Ct. 1386, 8 L.Ed.2d 734]. The usual argument against this suggestion is that a party to a law suit hires his lawyer and should therefore be responsible for everything his lawyer does in the conduct of his case. This may be a good argument with reference to affluent litigants who not only know the best lawyers but are able to hire them. It is a wholly unrealistic argument, however, to make with reference to individual persons who do not know the ability of various lawyers or who are not financially able to hire those at the top of the bar and who are compelled to rely on the assumption that a lawyer licensed by the State is competent. It seems to me to be an uncivilized practice to punish clients by throwing their cases out of court because of their lawyers' conduct. It may be supportable by good, sound, formal logic but I think has no support whatever in a procedural system supposed to work as far as humanly possible to the end of obtaining equal and exact justice.

"H.L.B."

For all the reasons stated above and in my previous objections to the transmittals of rules I dissent from the transmittals here.

MR. JUSTICE DOUGLAS, dissenting in part.

I reiterate today what I stated on an earlier occasion (374 U.S. 865, 869–870) (statement of Black and Douglas, JJ.), that the responsibility for promulgating Rules of the kind we send to Congress today should rest with the Judicial Conference and not the Court. It is the Judicial Conference, not the Court, which appoints the Advisory Committee on Criminal Rules which makes the actual recommendations.[1] Members of the Judicial Conference, being in large part judges of the lower courts and attorneys who are using the Rules day in and day out, are in a far better position to make a practical judgment upon their utility or inutility than we.

But since under the statute[2] the Rules go to Congress only on the initiative of the Court, I cannot be only a conduit. I think that placing our imprimatur on the amendments to the Rules entails a large degree of responsibility of judgment concerning them. Some of the Criminal Rules which we forward to Congress today are very bothersome—not in the sense that they may be unwieldy or unworkable—but in the sense that they may entrench on important constitutional rights of defendants.

In my judgment, the amendments to Rule 16 dealing with discovery require further reflection. To the extent that they expand the defendant's opportunities for discovery, they accord with the views of a great many commentators who have concluded that a civilized society ought not to tolerate the conduct of a criminal prosecution as a "game."[3] But the proposed changes in the Rule go further. Rule 16(c) would permit a trial judge to condition granting the defendant discovery on the defendant's willingness to permit the prosecution to discover "scientific or medical reports, books, papers, documents, tangible objects, or copies or portions thereof" which (1) are in the defendant's possession; (2) he intends to

produce at trial; and (3) are shown to be material to the preparation of the prosecution's case.[4]

The extent to which a court may compel the defendant to disclose information or evidence pertaining to his case without infringing the privilege against self-incrimination is a source of current controversy among judges, prosecutors, defense lawyers, and other legal commentators. A distinguished state court has concluded—although not without a strong dissent—that the privilege is not violated by discovery of the names of expert medical witnesses whose appearance at trial is contemplated by the defense.[5] I mean to imply no views on the point, except to note that a serious constitutional question lurks here.

The prosecution's opportunity to discover evidence in the possession of the defense is somewhat limited in the proposal with which we deal in that it is tied to the exercise by the defense of the right to discover from the prosecution. But *if* discovery, by itself, of information in the possession of the defendant would violate the privilege against self-incrimination, is it any less a violation if conditioned on the defendant's exercise of the opportunity to discover evidence? May benefits be conditioned on the abandonment of constitutional rights? See, e.g., *Sherbert v. Verner*, 374 U.S. 398, 403–406, 83 S.Ct. 1790, 1793–1795, 10 L.Ed.2d 965. To deny a defendant the opportunity to discovery—an opportunity not withheld from defendants who agree to prosecutorial discovery or from whom discovery is not sought— merely because the defendant chooses to exercise the constitutional right to refrain from self-incrimination arguably imposes a penalty upon the exercise of that fundamental privilege. It is said,

1. 28 U.S.C. § 331 (1964 ed.) which establishes the Judicial Conference of the United States, provides that the Conference shall "carry on a continuous study of the operation and effect of the general rules of practice and procedure * * * prescribed by the Supreme Court * * *." The Conference has resolved that a standing Committee on Rules of Practice and Procedure be appointed by the Chief Justice and that, in addition, five advisory committees be established to recommend to the Judicial Conference changes in the rules of practice and procedure for the federal courts. See Annual Report of the Proceedings of the Judicial Conference of the United States 6–7 (1958).

2. 18 U.S.C. § 3771 (1964 ed.).

3. See, *e.g.*, Brennan, The Criminal Prosecution: Sporting Event or Quest for Truth?, 1963 Wash.U.L.Q. 279; Louisell, Criminal Discovery: Dilemma Real or

Apparent?, 49 Calif.L.Rev. 56 (1961); Traynor, Ground Lost and Found in Criminal Discovery, 39 N.Y.U.L.Rev. 228 (1964).

4. The proposed rule explicitly provides that the prosecution may not discover nonmedical documents or reports "made by the defendant, or his attorneys or agents in connection with the investigation or defense of the case, or of statements made by the defendant, or by government or defense witnesses, or by prospective government or defense witnesses, to the defendant, his agents or attorneys."

5. *Jones v. Superior Court of Nevada County*, 58 Cal.2d 56, 22 Cal.Rptr. 879, 372 P.2d 919, 96 A.L.R.2d 1213. See Comment, 51 Calif.L.Rev. 135; Note, 76 Harv.L.Rev. 838 (1963). The case is more extensively treated in Louisell, Criminal Discovery and Self–Incrimination, 53 Calif.L.Rev. 89 (1965).

however, that fairness may require disclosure by a defendant who obtains information from the prosecution. Perhaps—but the proposed rule establishes no such standards. Its application is mechanical: if the defendant is allowed discovery, so, too, is the prosecution. No requirement is imposed, for example, that the subject matter of the material sought to be discovered by the prosecution be limited to that relating to the subject of the defendant's discovery.

The proposed addition of Rule 17.1 also suggests difficulties, perhaps of constitutional dimension. This rule would establish a pretrial conference procedure. The language of the rule and the Advisory Committee's comments suggest that under some circumstances, the conference might even take place in the absence of the defendants! Cf. *Lewis v. United States*, 146 U.S. 370, 13 S.Ct. 136, 36 L.Ed. 1011; Fed.Rules Crim.Proc. Rule 43.

The proposed amendment to Rule 32(c)(2) states that the trial judge "may" disclose to the defendant or his counsel the contents of a presentence report on which he is relying in fixing sentence. The imposition of sentence is of critical importance to a man convicted of crime. Trial judges need presentence reports so that they may have at their disposal the fullest possible information. See *Williams v. People of State of New York*, 337 U.S. 241, 69 S.Ct. 1079, 93 L.Ed. 1337. But while the formal rules of evidence do not apply to restrict the factors which the sentencing judge may consider, fairness would, in my opinion, require that the defendant be advised of the facts— perhaps very damaging to him—on which the judge intends to rely. The presentence report may be inaccurate, a flaw which may be of constitutional dimension. Cf. *Townsend v. Burke*, 334 U.S. 736, 68 S.Ct. 1252, 92 L.Ed. 1690. It may exaggerate the gravity of the defendant's prior offenses. The investigator may have made an incomplete investigation. See Tappan, Crime, Justice and Correction 556 (1960). There may be countervailing factors not disclosed by the probation report. In many areas we can rely on the sound exercise of discretion by the trial judge; but how can a judge know whether or not the

presentence report calls for a reply by the defendant? Its faults may not appear on the face of the document.

Some States require full disclosure of the report to the defense.[6] The proposed Model Penal Code takes the middle-ground and requires the sentencing judge to disclose to the defense the factual contents of the report so that there is an opportunity to reply.[7] Whatever should be the rule for the federal courts, it ought not to be one which permits a judge to impose sentence on the basis of information of which the defendant may be unaware and to which he has not been afforded an opportunity to reply.

I do not think we should approve Rules 16, 17.1, and 32(c)(2). Instead, we should refer them back to the Judicial Conference and the Advisory Committee for further consideration and reflection, where I believe they were approved only by the narrowest majority.

WILLIAM O. DOUGLAS.

ORDER OF DECEMBER 4, 1967

1. That the following rules, to be known as the Federal Rules of Appellate Procedure, be, and they hereby are, prescribed, pursuant to sections 3771 and 3772 of Title 18, United States Code, and sections 2072 and 2075 of Title 28, United States Code, to govern the procedure in appeals to United States courts of appeals from the United States district courts, in the review by United States courts of appeals of decisions of the Tax Court of the United States, in proceedings in the United States courts of appeals for the review or enforcement of orders of administrative agencies, boards, commissions and officers, and in applications for writs or other relief which a United States court of appeals or judge thereof is competent to give:

[See text of Rules of Appellate Procedure, post]

2. That the foregoing rules shall take effect on July 1, 1968, and shall govern all proceedings in appeals and petitions for review or enforcement of orders thereafter brought and in all such pro-

---

6. *E.g.*, Calif.Penal Code § 1203.

7. Model Penal Code § 7.07(5) (Proposed Official Draft, 1962). The Code provides that the sources of confidential information need not be disclosed. "Less disclosure than this hardly comports with elementary fairness." Comment to § 7.07 (Tent.Draft No. 2, 1954), at 55. A discarded draft of the amendment to Fed.

Rules Crim.Proc. Rule 32 would have allowed disclosure to defense counsel of the report, from which the confidential sources would be removed. A defendant not represented by counsel would be told of the "essential facts" in the report. See 8 Moore's Federal Practice ¶¶ 32.03[4], 32.09 (1965).

ceedings then pending, except to the extent that in the opinion of the court of appeals their application in a particular proceeding then pending would not be feasible or would work injustice, in which case the former procedure may be followed.

3. *[Certain Rules of Civil Procedure for the United States District Courts, amended]*

4. *[Certain Rules of Civil Procedure for the United States District Courts, and Form 27, abrogated]*

5. That Rules 45, 49, 56 and 57 of the Rules of Criminal Procedure for the United States District Courts be, and they hereby are, amended, effective July 1, 1968, as hereinafter set forth:

[See amendments made thereby under the respective rules, post]

6. That the chapter heading "VIII. APPEAL", all of Rules 37 and 39, and subdivisions (b) and (c) of Rule 38 of the Rules of Criminal Procedure for the United States District Courts, and Forms 26 and 27 annexed to the said rules, be, and they hereby are, abrogated, effective July 1, 1968.

7. That the Chief Justice be, and he hereby is, authorized to transmit to the Congress the foregoing new rules and amendments to and abrogation of existing rules, in accordance with the provisions of Title 18, U.S.C., § 3771, and Title 28, U.S.C., §§ 2072 and 2075.

ORDER OF MARCH 1, 1971

1. *[Certain Rules of Civil Procedure for the United States District Courts amended]*

2. That subdivision (a) of Rule 45 and all of Rule 56 of the Federal Rules of Criminal Procedure be, and they hereby are, amended, effective July 1, 1971, to read as follows:

[See amendments made thereby under the respective rules, post]

3. That subdivision (a) of Rule 26 and subdivision (a) of Rule 45 of the Federal Rules of Appellate Procedure be, and they hereby are, amended, effective July 1, 1971, to read as follows:

[See amendments made thereby under the respective rules, post]

4. That THE CHIEF JUSTICE be, and he hereby is, authorized to transmit to the Congress the foregoing amendments to the Rules of Civil, Criminal and Appellate Procedure, in accordance with the provisions of Title 18 U.S.C. § 3771, and Title 28 U.S.C. §§ 2072 and 2075.

Mr. Justice Black and Mr. Justice Douglas dissent.

ORDER OF APRIL 24, 1972

1. That Rules 1, 3, 4(b) & (c), 5, 5.1, 6(b), 7(c), 9(b), (c) & (d), 17(a) & (g), 31(e), 32(b), 38(a), 40, 41, 44, 46, 50, 54 and 55 of the Federal Rules of Criminal Procedure be, and they hereby are, amended effective October 1, 1972, to read as follows:

[See amendments made thereby under the respective rules, post]

2. That Rule 9(c) of the Federal Rules of Appellate Procedure be, and hereby is amended, effective October 1, 1972, to read as follows:

[See amendments made thereby under the respective rules, post]

3. That THE CHIEF JUSTICE be, and he hereby is, authorized to transmit to the Congress the foregoing amendments to Rules of Criminal and Appellate Procedure, in accordance with the provisions of Title 18, U.S.Code, § 3771 and § 3772.

Mr. Justice Douglas dissented to adoption of Rule 50(b) of the Federal Rules of Criminal Procedure.

ORDER OF NOVEMBER 20, 1972

1. That the rules hereinafter set forth, to be known as the Federal Rules of Evidence, be, and they hereby are, prescribed pursuant to Sections 3402, 3771, and 3772, Title 18, United States Code, and Sections 2072 and 2075, Title 28, United States Code, to govern procedure, in the proceedings and to the extent set forth therein, in the United States courts of appeals, the United States district courts, the District Court for the District of the Canal Zone and the district courts of Guam and the Virgin Islands, and before United States magistrates.

2. That the aforementioned Federal Rules of Evidence shall take effect on July 1, 1973, and shall be applicable to actions and proceedings brought thereafter and also to further procedure in actions and proceedings then pending, except to the extent that in the opinion of the court their application in a particular action or proceeding then pending would not be feasible or would work injustice in which event the former procedure applies.

3. *[Certain Rules of Civil Procedure for the United State District Courts amended]*

4. That subdivision (c) of Rule 32 of the Federal Rules of Civil Procedure be, and it hereby is, abrogated, effective July 1, 1973.

5. That Rules 26, 26.1 and 28 of the Federal Rules of Criminal Procedure be, and they hereby are, amended effective July 1, 1973, to read as hereinafter set forth.

[See amendments made thereby under the respective rules, post]

6. That the Chief Justice be, and he hereby is, authorized to transmit the foregoing new rules and amendments to and abrogation of existing rules to the Congress at the beginning of its next regular session, in accordance with the provisions of Title 18 U.S.C. § 3771 and Title 28 U.S.C. §§ 2072 and 2075.

CONGRESSIONAL ACTION ON PROPOSED RULES OF EVIDENCE AND 1972 AMENDMENTS TO FEDERAL RULES OF CIVIL PROCEDURE AND FEDERAL RULES OF CRIMINAL PROCEDURE

Pub.L. 93–12, Mar. 30, 1973, 87 Stat. 9, provided: "That notwithstanding any other provisions of law, the Rules of Evidence for United States Courts and Magistrates, the Amendments to the Federal Rules of Civil Procedure, and the Amendments to the Federal Rules of Criminal Procedure, which are embraced by the orders entered by the Supreme Court of the United States on Monday, November 20, 1972, and Monday, December 18, 1972, shall have no force or effect except to the extent, and with such amendments, as they may be expressly approved by Act of Congress."

Pub.L. 93–595, § 3, Jan. 2, 1975, 88 Stat. 1959, provided that: "The Congress expressly approves the amendments to the Federal Rules of Civil Procedure, and the amendments to the Federal Rules of Criminal Procedure, which are embraced by the orders entered by the Supreme Court of the United States on November 20, 1972, and December 18, 1972, and such amendments shall take effect on the one hundred and eightieth day beginning after the date of the enactment of this Act [Jan. 2, 1975]."

ORDER OF MARCH 18, 1974

1. *[Amended subdivision 14 of Official Bankruptcy Form 7]*

2. That subdivision (a) of Rule 41 and the first paragraph of Rule 50 of the Federal Rules of Criminal Procedure be, and they hereby are, amended, effective July 1, 1974, to read as follows:

[See amendments made thereby under the respective rules, post]

3. That THE CHIEF JUSTICE be, and he hereby is, authorized to transmit the foregoing amendments to Official Bankruptcy Form 7 and Rules 41 and 50 of the Federal Rules of Criminal Procedure to the Congress in accordance with Title 28, U.S.C. § 2075, and Title 18, § 3771.

ORDER OF APRIL 22, 1974

1. That the Rules of Criminal Procedure for the United States District Courts be, and they hereby are, amended by including therein Rules 12.1, 12.2, and 29.1 and amendments to Rules 4, 9(a), 11, 12, 15, 16, 17(f), 20, 32(a), 32(c), 32(e) and 43 as hereinafter set forth:

[See amendments made thereby under the respective rules, post]

2. That the foregoing amendments and additions to the Rules of Criminal Procedure shall take effect on August 1, 1974, and shall govern all criminal proceedings thereafter commenced and, insofar as just and practicable, in proceedings then pending.

3. That The Chief Justice be, and he hereby is, authorized to transmit to the Congress the foregoing amendments and additions to the Rules of Criminal Procedure in accordance with the provisions of title 18, United States Code, sections 3771 and 3772.

Mr. Justice Douglas is opposed to the Court being a mere conduit of Rules to Congress since the Court has had no hand in drafting them and has no competence to design them in keeping with the titles and spirit of the Constitution.

CONGRESSIONAL ACTION ON AMENDMENTS TO RULES PROPOSED APRIL 22, 1974

Pub.L. 93–361, July 30, 1974, 88 Stat. 397, provided: "That, notwithstanding the provisions of sections 3771 and 3772 of title 18 of the United

States Code, the effective date of the proposed amendments to the Federal Rules of Criminal Procedure which are embraced by the order entered by the United States Supreme Court on April 22, 1974, and which were transmitted to the Congress by the Chief Justice on April 22, 1974, is postponed until August 1, 1975."

Pub.L. 94–64, § 2, July 31, 1975, 89 Stat. 370, provided that: "The amendments proposed by the United States Supreme Court to the Federal Rules of Criminal Procedure which are embraced in the order of that Court on April 22, 1974, are approved except as otherwise provided in this Act and shall take effect on December 1, 1975. Except with respect to the amendment of Rule 11, insofar as it adds Rule 11(e)(6), which shall take effect on August 1, 1975, the amendments made by section 3 of this Act shall also take effect on December 1, 1975."

ORDER OF APRIL 26, 1976

1. That the Rules of Criminal Procedure for the United States District Courts be, and they hereby are, amended by including therein Rule 40.1 and amendments to Rules 6(e), 6(f), 23(b), 23(c), 24(b), 41(a), 41(c), and 50(b) as hereinafter set forth:

[See amendments made thereby under the respective rules, post, and Congressional Action on Amendments to Rules hereunder]

2. That the foregoing amendments and additions to the rules of procedure shall take effect on August 1, 1976, and shall govern all criminal proceedings thereafter commenced and, insofar as just and practicable, in proceedings then pending.

3. That The Chief Justice be, and he hereby is, authorized to transmit to the Congress the foregoing amendments and addition to the Rules of Criminal Procedure in accordance with the provisions of Title 18, United States Code, Sections 3771 and 3772.

CONGRESSIONAL ACTION ON AMENDMENTS TO RULES PROPOSED APRIL 26, 1976

Pub.L. 94–349, § 1, July 8, 1976, 90 Stat. 822, provided: "That, notwithstanding the provisions of sections 3771 and 3772 of title 18 of the United States Code, the amendments to rules 6(e), 23, 24, 40.1 and 41(c)(2) of the Rules of Criminal Procedure for the United States district courts which are embraced by the order entered by the United

States Supreme Court on April 26, 1976, and which were transmitted to the Congress on or about April 26, 1976, shall not take effect until August 1, 1977, or until and to the extent approved by Act of Congress, whichever is earlier. The remainder of the proposed amendments to the Federal Rules of Criminal Procedure [to rules 6(f), 41(a), 41(c)(1), and 50(b)] shall become effective August 1, 1976, pursuant to law."

Pub.L. 95–78, § 1, July 30, 1977, 91 Stat. 319, provided: "That notwithstanding the first section of the Act entitled 'An Act to delay the effective date of certain proposed amendments to the Federal Rules of Criminal Procedure and certain other rules promulgated by the United States Supreme Court' (Public Law 94–349, approved July 8, 1976) the amendments to rules 6(e), 23, 24, 40.1 and 41(c)(2) of the Rules of Criminal Procedure for the United States district courts which are embraced by the order entered by the United States Supreme Court on April 26, 1976, shall take effect only as provided in this Act."

Section 2(a) of Pub.L. 95–78 provided in part that "The amendment proposed by the Supreme Court to subdivision (e) of rule 6 of such Rules of Criminal Procedure is approved in modified form".

Section 2(b) of Pub.L. 95–78 provided "The amendments proposed by the Supreme Court to subdivisions (b) and (c) of rule 23 of such Rules of Criminal Procedure are approved."

Section 2(c) of Pub.L. 95–78 provided "The amendment proposed by the Supreme Court to rule 24 of such Rules of Criminal Procedure is disapproved and shall not take effect."

Section 2(d) of Pub.L. 95–78 provided "The amendment proposed by the Supreme Court to such Rules of Criminal Procedure, adding a new rule designated as rule 40.1, is disapproved and shall not take effect."

Section 2(e) of Pub.L. 95–78 provided in part that "The amendment proposed by the Supreme Court to subdivision (c) of rule 41 of such Rules of Criminal Procedure is approved in a modified form".

Section 4(b) of Pub.L. 95–78 provided that the amendments to the Federal Rules of Criminal Procedure shall take effect October 1, 1977.

ORDER OF APRIL 30, 1979

1. That the Rules of Criminal Procedure for the United States District Courts be, and they hereby are, amended by including therein Rules 26.2 and 32.1 and amendments to Rules 6(e), 7(c)(2), 9(a), 11(e)(2) and (6), 17(h), 18, 32(c)(3)(E) and 32(f), 35, 40, 41(a), (b) and (c), and 44(c) as hereinafter set forth:

[See amendments made thereby under the respective rules, post]

2. That the foregoing amendments and additions to the rules of procedure shall take effect on August 1, 1979, and shall govern all criminal proceedings thereafter commenced and, insofar as just and practicable, all proceedings then pending.

3. That THE CHIEF JUSTICE be, and he hereby is, authorized to transmit to the Congress the foregoing amendments and additions to the Rules of Criminal Procedure in accordance with the provisions of Title 18, United States Code, Sections 3771 and 3772.

CONGRESSIONAL ACTION ON AMENDMENTS TO RULES PROPOSED APRIL 30, 1979

Pub.L. 96–42, July 31, 1979, 93 Stat. 326, provided: "That notwithstanding any provision of section 3771 or 3772 of title 18 of the United States Code or of section 2072, 2075, or 2076 of title 28 of the United States Code to the contrary—

"(1) the amendments proposed by the United States Supreme Court and transmitted by the Chief Justice on April 30, 1979, to the Federal Rules of Criminal Procedure affecting rules 11(e)(6), 17(h), 32(f), and 44(c), and adding new rules 26.2 and 32.1, and the amendment so proposed and transmitted to the Federal Rules of Evidence affecting rule 410, shall not take effect until December 1, 1980, or until and then only to the extent approved by Act of Congress, whichever is earlier; and

"(2) the amendment proposed by the United States Supreme Court and transmitted by the Chief Justice on April 30, 1979, affecting rule 40 of the Federal Rules of Criminal Procedure shall take effect on August 1, 1979, with the following amendments:

"(A) In the matter designated as paragraph (1) of subdivision (d), strike out 'in accordance with Rule 32.1(a)'.

"(B) In the matter designated as paragraph (2) of subdivision (d), strike out 'in accordance with Rule 32.1(a)(1)'."

ORDER OF APRIL 28, 1982

1. That the Federal Rules of Criminal Procedure be, and they hereby are, amended by including therein amendments to Rule 1, 5(b), 9(a), 9(b)(1), 9(b)(2), 9(c)(1), 9(c)(2), 11(c)(1), 11(c)(4), 11(c)(5), 20(b), 40(d)(1), 40(d)(2), 45(a), 54(a), 54(b)(4) and 54(c) as hereinafter set forth:

[See amendments made thereby under the respective rules, post]

2. That subdivision (d) of Rule 9 of the Federal Rules of Criminal Procedure is hereby abrogated:

3. That the foregoing amendments to the Federal Rules of Criminal Procedure shall take effect on August 1, 1982, and shall govern all criminal proceedings thereafter commenced and, insofar as just and practicable, all proceedings then pending.

4. That THE CHIEF JUSTICE be, and he hereby is, authorized to transmit to the Congress the foregoing amendments to the Federal Rules of Criminal Procedure in accordance with the provisions of Sections 3771 and 3772 of Title 18, United States Code.

ORDER OF APRIL 28, 1983

1. That the Federal Rules of Criminal Procedure for the United States District Courts be, and they hereby are, amended by including therein new Rules 11(h), 12(i) and 12.2(e), and amendments to Rules 6(e) and (g), 11(a), 12.2(b), (c) and (d), 16(a), 23(b), 32(a), (c) and (d), 35(b) and 55, as hereinafter set forth:

[See amendments made thereby under the respective rules, post]

2. That Rule 58 of the Federal Rules of Criminal Procedure and the Appendix of Forms are hereby abrogated.

3. That the foregoing additions and amendments to the Federal Rules of Criminal Procedure, together with the abrogation of Rule 58 and the Official Forms, shall take effect on August 1, 1983 and shall govern all criminal proceedings thereafter commenced and, insofar as just and practicable, in proceedings then pending.

4. That THE CHIEF JUSTICE be, and he hereby is, authorized to transmit to the Congress the foregoing additions to and changes in the Federal Rules of Criminal Procedure in accordance with the provisions of Sections 3771 and 3772 of Title 18, United States Code.

JUSTICE O'CONNOR, dissenting.

With one minor reservation, I join the Court in its adoption of the proposed amendments. They represent the product of considerable effort by the Advisory Committee, and they will institute desirable reforms. My sole disagreement with the Court's action today lies in its failure to recommend correction of an apparent error in the drafting of Proposed Rule 12.2(e).

As proposed, Rule 12.2(e) reads:

"Evidence of an intention as to which notice was given under subdivision (a) or (b), later withdrawn, is not admissible in any civil or criminal proceeding against the person who gave notice of the intention."

Identical language formerly appeared in Fed. Rules Crim.Proc. 11(e)(6) and Fed.Rules Evid. 410, each of which stated that

"[Certain material] is not admissible in any civil or criminal proceeding against the defendant."

Those rules were amended, Supreme Court Order April 30, 1979, 441 U.S. 970, 987, 1007, Pub.Law 96–42, approved July 31, 1979, 93 Stat. 326. After the amendments, the relevant language read,

"[Certain material] is not, in any civil or criminal proceeding, admissible against the defendant."

As the Advisory Committee explained, this minor change was necessary to eliminate an ambiguity. Before the amendment, the word "against" could be read as referring either to the kind of proceeding in which the evidence was offered or to the purpose for which it was offered. Thus, for instance, if a person was a witness in a suit but not a party, it was unclear whether the evidence could be used to impeach him. In such a case, the *use* would be against the person, but the *proceeding* would not be against him. Similarly, if the person wished to introduce the evidence in a proceeding in which he was the defendant, the use, but not the proceeding, would be against him. To eliminate the ambiguity, the Advisory Committee proposed the amendment clarifying that the evidence was inadmissible

against the person, regardless of whether the particular proceeding was against the person. See Adv.Comm.Note to Fed.Rule Crim.Proc. 11(e)(6); Adv.Comm.Note to Fed.Rules Evid. 410.

The same ambiguity inheres in the proposed version of Rule 12.2(e). We should recommend that it be eliminated now. To that extent, I respectfully dissent.

ORDER OF APRIL 29, 1985

1. That the Federal Rules of Criminal Procedure for the United States District Courts be, and they hereby are, amended by including therein a new Rule 49(e) and amendments to Rules 6(e)(3)(A)(ii), 6(e)(3)(B) and (C), 11(c)(1), 12.1(f), 12.2(e), 35(b), 45(a) and 57, as hereinafter set forth:

[See amendments made thereby under the respective rules, post]

2. That the foregoing amendments to the Federal Rules of Criminal Procedure shall take effect on August 1, 1985 and shall govern all proceedings in criminal cases thereafter commenced and, insofar as just and practicable, all proceedings in criminal cases then pending. The amendment to Rule 35(b) shall be effective until November 1, 1986 when Section 215(b) of the Comprehensive Crime Control Act of 1984, Pub.L. 98–473, approved October 12, 1984, 98 Stat. 2015, goes into effect.

3. That THE CHIEF JUSTICE be, and he hereby is, authorized to transmit to the Congress the foregoing addition to and changes in the Federal Rules of Criminal Procedure in accordance with the provisions of Sections 3771 and 3772 of Title 18, United States Code.

ORDER OF MARCH 9, 1987

That the Federal Rules of Criminal Procedure for the United States District Courts be, and they hereby are, amended by including therein amendments to Criminal Rules 4, 5, 5.1, 6, 7, 10, 11, 12, 12.1, 12.2, 15, 16, 17, 17.1, 20, 21, 24, 25, 26.2, 30, 32, 32.1, 33, 38, 40, 41, 42, 43, 44, 45, 46, 49, and 51, as hereinafter set forth:

[See amendments made thereby under respective rules, post]

2. That the foregoing amendments to the Federal Rules of Criminal Procedure shall take effect on August 1, 1987 and shall govern all proceed-

ings in criminal cases thereafter commenced and, insofar as just and practicable, all proceedings in criminal cases then pending.

3. That THE CHIEF JUSTICE be, and he hereby is, authorized to transmit to the Congress the foregoing amendments to the Federal Rules of Criminal Procedure in accordance with the provisions of Sections 3771 and 3772 of Title 18, United States Code.

ORDER OF APRIL 25, 1988

That the Federal Rules of Criminal Procedure for the United States District Courts be, and they hereby are, amended by including therein amendments to Criminal Rules 30 and 56, as hereinafter set forth:

[See amendments made thereby under respective rules, post]

2. That the foregoing amendments to the Federal Rules of Criminal Procedure shall take effect on August 1, 1988 and shall govern all proceedings in criminal cases thereafter commenced and, insofar as just and practicable, all proceedings in criminal cases then pending.

3. That THE CHIEF JUSTICE be, and he hereby is, authorized to transmit to the Congress the foregoing amendments to the Federal Rules of Criminal Procedure in accordance with the provisions of Sections 3771 and 3772 of Title 18, United States Code.

I. SCOPE, PURPOSE, AND CONSTRUCTION

Rule 1. Scope

These rules govern the procedure in all criminal proceedings in the courts of the United States, as provided in Rule 54(a); and, whenever specifically provided in one of the rules, to preliminary, supplementary, and special proceedings before United States magistrates and at proceedings before state and local judicial officers.

(As amended Apr. 24, 1972, eff. Oct. 1, 1972; Apr. 28, 1982, eff. Aug. 1, 1982.)

NOTES OF ADVISORY COMMITTEE ON RULES

1. These rules are prescribed under the authority of two acts of Congress, namely: the act of June 29, 1940, ch. 445, 18 U.S.C. former § 687 (now § 3771) (Proceedings in criminal cases prior to and including verdict; power of Supreme Court to prescribe rules), and the act of November 21, 1941, ch. 492, 18 U.S.C. former § 689 (now §§ 3771, 3772) (Proceedings to punish for criminal contempt of court; application to sections 687 and 688).

2. The courts of the United States covered by the rules are enumerated in Rule 54(a). In addition to Federal courts in the continental United States they include district courts in Alaska, Hawaii, Puerto Rico and the Virgin Islands. In the Canal Zone only the rules governing proceedings after verdict, finding or plea of guilty are applicable.

3. While the rules apply to proceedings before commissioners when acting as committing magistrates, they do not govern when a commissioner acts as a trial magistrate for the trial of petty offenses committed on Federal reservations. That procedure is governed by rules adopted by order promulgated by the Supreme Court on January 6, 1941 (311 U.S. 733), pursuant to the act of October 9, 1940, ch. 785, secs. 1–5. See 18

U.S.C. former §§ 576–576d (now §§ 3401, 3402) (relating to trial of petty offenses on Federal reservations by United States commissioners).

1972 AMENDMENT

The rule is amended to make clear that the rules are applicable to courts of the United States and, where the rule so provides, to proceedings before United States magistrates and state or local judicial officers.

Primarily these rules are intended to govern proceedings in criminal cases triable in the United States District Court. Special rules have been promulgated, pursuant to the authority set forth in 28 U.S.C. § 636(c), for the trial of "minor offenses" before United States magistrates. (See Rules of Procedure for the Trial of Minor Offenses Before United States Magistrates (January 27, 1971).)

However, there is inevitably some overlap between the two sets of rules. The Rules of Criminal Procedure for the United States District Courts deal with preliminary, supplementary, and special proceedings which will often be conducted before United States magistrates. This is true, for example, with regard to rule 3—The Complaint; rule 4—Arrest Warrant or Summons Upon Complaint; rule 5—Initial Appearance Before the Magistrate; and rule 5.1—Preliminary Examination. It is also true, for example, of supplementary and special proceedings such as rule 40—Commitment to Another District, Removal; rule 41—Search and Seizure; and rule 46—Release from Custody. Other of these rules, where applicable, also apply to proceedings before United States magistrates. See Rules of Procedure for the Trial of Minor Offenses Before United States Magistrates, rule 1—Scope:

These rules govern the procedure and practice for the trial of minor offenses (including petty offenses) before

United States magistrates under Title 18, U.S.C. § 3401, and for appeals in such cases to judges of the district courts. To the extent that pretrial and trial procedure and practice are not specifically covered by these rules, the Federal Rules of Criminal Procedure apply as to minor offenses other than petty offenses. All other proceedings in criminal matters, other than petty offenses, before United States magistrates are governed by the Federal Rules of Criminal Procedure.

State and local judicial officers are governed by these rules, but only when the rule specifically so provides. This is the case of rule 3—The Complaint; rule 4—Arrest Warrant or Summons Upon Complaint; and rule 5—Initial Appearance Before the Magistrate. These rules confer authority upon the "magistrate," a term which is defined in new rule 54 as follows:

"Magistrate" includes a United States magistrate as defined in 28 U.S.C. §§ 631–639, a judge of the United States, another judge or judicial officer specifically empowered by statute in force in any territory or possession, the commonwealth of Puerto Rico, or the District of Columbia, to perform a function to which a particular rule relates, and a state or local judicial officer, authorized by 18 U.S.C. § 3041 to perform the functions prescribed in rules 3, 4, and 5.

Rule 41 provides that a search warrant may be issued by "a judge of a state court of record" and thus confers that authority upon appropriate state judicial officers.

The scope of rules 1 and 54 is discussed in C. Wright, Federal Practice and Procedure: Criminal §§ 21, 871–874 (1969, Supp.1971), and 8 and 8A J. Moore, Federal Practice chapters 1 and 54 (2d ed. Cipes 1970, Supp.1971).

1982 AMENDMENT

The amendment corrects an erroneous cross reference, from Rule 54(c) to Rule 54(a), and replaces the word "defined" with the more appropriate word "provided."

Rule 2. Purpose and Construction

These rules are intended to provide for the just determination of every criminal proceeding. They shall be construed to secure simplicity in procedure, fairness in administration and the elimination of unjustifiable expense and delay.

NOTES OF ADVISORY COMMITTEE ON RULES

Compare Federal Rules of Civil Procedure, 28 U.S.C., following § 2072, Rule 1 (Scope of Rules), last sentence: "They [the Federal Rules of Civil Procedure, 28 U.S.C., Appendix,] shall be construed to secure the just, speedy, and inexpensive determination of every action."

II. PRELIMINARY PROCEEDINGS

Rule 3. The Complaint

The complaint is a written statement of the essential facts constituting the offense charged. It shall be made upon oath before a magistrate. (As amended Apr. 24, 1972, eff. Oct. 1, 1972.)

NOTES OF ADVISORY COMMITTEE ON RULES

The rule generally states existing law and practice, 18 U.S.C. former § 591 (now § 3041) (Arrest and removal for trial); *United States v. Simon*, E.D.Pa., 248 F. 980; *United States v. Maresca*, S.D.N.Y., 266 F. 713, 719–721. It eliminates, however, the requirement of conformity to State law as to the form and sufficiency of the complaint. See, also, rule 57(b).

1972 AMENDMENT

The amendment deletes the reference to "commissioner or other officer empowered to commit persons charged with offenses against the United States" and substitutes therefor "magistrate."

The change is editorial in nature to conform the language of the rule to the recently enacted Federal Magistrates Act. The term "magistrate" is defined in rule 54.

Rule 4. Arrest Warrant or Summons upon Complaint

(a) Issuance. If it appears from the complaint, or from an affidavit or affidavits filed with the complaint, that there is probable cause to believe that an offense has been committed and that the defendant has committed it, a warrant for the arrest of the defendant shall issue to any officer authorized by law to execute it. Upon the request of the attorney for the government a summons instead of a warrant shall issue. More than one warrant or summons may issue on the same complaint. If a defendant fails to appear in response to the summons, a warrant shall issue.

(b) Probable Cause. The finding of probable cause may be based upon hearsay evidence in whole or in part.

(c) Form.

(1) Warrant. The warrant shall be signed by the magistrate and shall contain the name of the defendant or, if the defendant's name is unknown, any name or description by which the defendant can be identified with reasonable certainty. It shall describe the offense charged in the complaint. It shall command that the defendant be arrested and brought before the nearest available magistrate.

(2) Summons. The summons shall be in the same form as the warrant except that it shall summon the defendant to appear before a magistrate at a stated time and place.

(d) Execution or Service; and Return.

(1) By Whom. The warrant shall be executed by a marshal or by some other officer authorized by law. The summons may be served by any person authorized to serve a summons in a civil action.

(2) Territorial Limits. The warrant may be executed or the summons may be served at any place within the jurisdiction of the United States.

(3) Manner. The warrant shall be executed by the arrest of the defendant. The officer need not have the warrant at the time of the arrest but upon request shall show the warrant to the defendant as soon as possible. If the officer does not have the warrant at the time of the arrest, the officer shall then inform the defendant of the offense charged and of the fact that a warrant has been issued. The summons shall be served upon a defendant by delivering a copy to the defendant personally, or by leaving it at the defendant's dwelling house or usual place of abode with some person of suitable age and discretion then residing therein and by mailing a copy of the summons to the defendant's last known address.

(4) Return. The officer executing a warrant shall make return thereof to the magistrate or other officer before whom the defendant is brought pursuant to Rule 5. At the request of the attorney for the government any unexecuted warrant shall be returned to and canceled by the magistrate by whom it was issued. On or before the return day the person to whom a summons was delivered for service shall make return thereof to the magistrate before whom the summons is returnable. At the request of the attorney for the government made at any time while the complaint is pending, a warrant returned unexecuted and not canceled or a summons returned unserved or a duplicate thereof may be delivered by the magistrate to

the marshal or other authorized person for execution or service.

(As amended Feb. 28, 1966, eff. July 1, 1966; Apr. 24, 1972, eff. Oct. 1, 1972; Apr. 22, 1974, eff. Dec. 1, 1975; July 31, 1975, Pub.L. 94–64, § 3(1)–(3), 89 Stat. 370; Mar. 9, 1987, eff. Aug. 1, 1987.)

NOTES OF ADVISORY COMMITTEE ON RULES

Note to Subdivision (a). 1. The rule states the existing law relating to warrants issued by commissioner or other magistrate. United States Constitution, Amendment IV; 18 U.S.C. former § 591 (now § 3041) (Arrest and removal for trial).

2. The provision for summons is new, although a summons has been customarily used against corporate defendants, 28 U.S.C. former § 377 (now § 1651) (Power to issue writs); *United States v. John Kelso Co.,* 86 F. 304, N.D.Cal., 1898. See also, *Albrecht v. United States,* 273 U.S. 1, 8, 47 S.Ct. 250, 71 L.Ed. 505 (1927). The use of the summons in criminal cases is sanctioned by many States, among them Indiana, Maryland, Massachusetts, New York, New Jersey, Ohio, and others. See A.L.I. Code of Criminal Procedure (1931), Commentaries to secs. 12, 13, and 14. The use of the summons is permitted in England by 11 & 12 Vict., c. 42, sec. 1 (1848). More general use of a summons in place of a warrant was recommended by the National Commission on Law Observance and Enforcement, Report on Criminal Procedure (1931) 47. The Uniform Arrest Act, proposed by the Interstate Commission on Crime, provides for a summons. Warner, 28 Va.L.R. 315. See also, Medalie, 4 Lawyers Guild, R. 1, 6.

3. The provision for the issuance of additional warrants on the same complaint embodies the practice heretofore followed in some districts. It is desirable from a practical standpoint, since when a complaint names several defendants, it may be preferable to issue a separate warrant as to each in order to facilitate service and return, especially if the defendants are apprehended at different times and places. Berge, 42 Mich.L.R. 353, 356.

4. Failure to respond to a summons is not a contempt of court, but is ground for issuing a warrant.

Note to Subdivision (b). Compare Rule 9(b) and forms of warrant and summons, Appendix of Forms.

Note to Subdivision (c)(2). This rule and Rule 9(c)(1) modify the existing practice under which a warrant may be served only within the district in which it is issued. *Mitchell v. Dexter,* 244 F. 926 (C.C.A.1st, 1917); *Palmer v. Thompson,* 20 App.D.C. 273 (1902); but see *In re Christian,* 82 F. 885 (C.C.W.D.Ark., 1897); 2 Op.Atty.Gen. 564. When a defendant is apprehended in a district other than that in which the prosecution has been instituted, this change will eliminate some of the steps that are at present followed: the issuance of a warrant in the district where the prosecution is pending; the return of the warrant non est inventus; the filing of a complaint on the basis of the warrant and its return in the district in which the defendant is found; and the issuance of another warrant in the latter district. The warrant originally issued will have efficacy throughout the United States and will constitute authority for arresting the defendant wherever found. Waite, 27 Jour. of Am.Judicature Soc. 101, 103. The change will not modify or affect the rights of the defendant as to removal. See Rule 40. The authority of the marshal to serve process is not limited to the district for which he is appointed, 28 U.S.C. former § 503 (now § 569).

Note to Subdivision (c)(3). 1. The provision that the arresting officer need not have the warrant in his possession at the time of the arrest is rendered necessary by the fact that a fugitive may be discovered and apprehended by any one of many officers. It is obviously impossible for a warrant to be in the possession of every officer who is searching for a fugitive or who unexpectedly might find himself in a position to apprehend the fugitive. The rule sets forth the customary practice in such matters, which has the sanction of the courts. "It would be a strong proposition in an ordinary felony case to say that a fugitive from justice for whom a capias or warrant was outstanding could not be apprehended until the apprehending officer had physical possession of the capias or the warrant. If such were the law, criminals could circulate freely from one end of the land to the other, because they could always keep ahead of an officer with the warrant." *In re Kosopud,* N.D.Ohio, 272 Fed. 330, 336. Waite, 27 Jour. of Am.Judicature Soc. 101, 103. The rule, however, safeguards the defendant's rights in such case.

2. Service of summons under the rule is substantially the same as in civil actions under Federal Rules of Civil Procedure, Rule 4(d)(1), 28 U.S.C., Appendix.

Note to Subdivision (c)(4). Return of a warrant or summons to the commissioner or other officer is provided by 18 U.S.C. § 603 [§ 4084] (Writs; copy as jailer's authority). The return of all "copies of process" by the commissioner to the clerk of the court is provided by 18 U.S.C. former § 591 (now § 3041); and see Rule 5(c), infra.

1966 AMENDMENT

In *Giordenello v. United States,* 357 U.S. 480 (1958) it was held that to support the issuance of a warrant the complaint must contain in addition to a statement "of the essential facts constituting the offense" (Rule 3) a statement of the facts relied upon by the complainant to establish probable cause. The amendment permits the complainant to state the facts constituting probable cause in a separate affidavit in lieu of spelling them out in the complaint. See also *Jaben v. United States,* 381 U.S. 214 (1965).

1972 AMENDMENT

Throughout the rule the term "magistrate" is substituted for the term "commissioner." Magistrate is defined in rule 54 to include a judge of the United States, a United States magistrate, and those state and local judicial officers specified in 18 U.S.C. § 3041.

1974 AMENDMENT

The amendments are designed to achieve several objectives: (1) to make explicit the fact that the determination of probable cause may be based upon hearsay evidence; (2) to make clear that probable cause is a prerequisite to the issuance of a summons; and (3) to give priority to the issuance of a summons rather than a warrant.

Subdivision (a) makes clear that the normal situation is to issue a summons.

Subdivision (b) provides for the issuance of an arrest warrant in lieu of or in addition to the issuance of a summons.

Subdivision (b)(1) restates the provision of the old rule mandating the issuance of a warrant when a defendant fails to appear in response to a summons.

Subdivision (b)(2) provides for the issuance of an arrest warrant rather than a summons whenever "a valid reason is shown" for the issuance of a warrant. The reason may be apparent from the face of the complaint or may be provided by the federal law enforcement officer or attorney for the government. See comparable provision in rule 9.

Subdivision (b)(3) deals with the situation in which conditions change after a summons has issued. It affords the government an opportunity to demonstrate the need for an arrest warrant. This may be done in the district in which the defendant is located if this is the convenient place to do so.

Subdivision (c) provides that a warrant or summons may issue on the basis of hearsay evidence. What constitutes probable cause is left to be dealt with on a case-to-case basis, taking account of the unlimited variations in source of information and in the opportunity of the informant to perceive accurately the factual data which he furnishes. See *e.g., Giordenello v. United States,* 357 U.S. 480, 78 S.Ct. 1245, 2 L.Ed.2d 1503 (1958); *Aguilar v. Texas,* 378 U.S. 108, 84 S.Ct. 1509, 12 L.Ed.2d 723 (1964); *United States v. Ventresca,* 380 U.S. 102, 85 S.Ct. 741, 13 L.Ed.2d 684 (1965); *Jaben v. United States,* 381 U.S. 214, 85 S.Ct. 1365, 14 L.Ed.2d 345 (1965); *McCray v. Illinois,* 386 U.S. 300, 87 S.Ct. 1056, 18 L.Ed.2d 62 (1967); *Spinelli v. United States,* 393 U.S. 410, 89 S.Ct. 584, 21 L.Ed.2d 637 (1969); *United States v. Harris,* 403 U.S. 573, 91 S.Ct. 2075, 29 L.Ed.2d 723 (1971); Note, The Informer's Tip as Probable Cause for Search or Arrest, 54 Cornell L.Rev. 958 (1969); C. Wright, Federal Practice and Procedure: Criminal § 52

(1969, Supp.1971); 8 S.J. Moore, Federal Practice ¶ 4.03 (2d ed. Cipes 1970, Supp.1971).

NOTES OF COMMITTEE ON THE JUDICIARY, HOUSE REPORT NO. 94–247

A. Amendments Proposed by the Supreme Court. Rule 4 of the Federal Rules of Criminal Procedure deals with arrest procedures when a criminal complaint has been filed. It provides in pertinent part:

> If it appears ... that there is probable cause ... a warrant for the arrest of the defendant shall issue to any officer authorized by law to execute it. Upon the *request* of the attorney for the government a summons instead of a warrant *shall* issue. [emphasis added]

The Supreme Court's amendments make a basic change in Rule 4. As proposed to be amended, Rule 4 gives priority to the issuance of a summons instead of an arrest warrant. In order for the magistrate to issue an arrest warrant, the attorney for the government must show a "valid reason."

B. Committee Action. The Committee agrees with and approves the basic change in Rule 4. The decision to take a citizen into custody is a very important one with far-reaching consequences. That decision ought to be made by a neutral official (a magistrate) rather than by an interested party (the prosecutor).

It has been argued that undesirable consequences will result if this change is adopted—including an increase in the number of fugitives and the introduction of substantial delays in our system of criminal justice. [See testimony of Assistant Attorney General W. Vincent Rakestraw in Hearings on Proposed Amendments to Federal Rules of Criminal Procedure Before the Subcommittee on Criminal Justice of the House Committee on the Judiciary, 93d Cong., 2d Sess., Serial No. 61, at 41–43 (1974) [hereinafter cited as "Hearing I"].] The Committee has carefully considered these arguments and finds them to be wanting. [The Advisory Committee on Criminal Rules has thoroughly analyzed the arguments raised by Mr. Rakestraw and convincingly demonstrated that the undesirable consequences predicted will not necessarily result. See Hearings on Proposed Amendments to Federal Rules of Criminal Procedure Before the Subcommittee on Criminal Justice of the House Committee on the Judiciary, 94th Congress, 1st Session, Serial No. 6, at 208–09 (1975) [hereinafter cited "Hearings II"].] The present rule permits the use of a summons in lieu of a warrant. The major difference between the present rule and the proposed rule is that the present rule vests the decision to issue a summons or a warrant in the prosecutor, while the proposed rule vests that decision in a judicial officer. Thus, the basic premise underlying the arguments against the proposed rule is the notion that only the prosecutor can be trusted to act responsibly in deciding whether a summons or a warrant shall issue.

The Committee rejects the notion that the federal judiciary cannot be trusted to exercise discretion wisely and in the public interest.

The Committee recast the language of Rule 4(b). No change in substance is intended. The phrase "valid reason" was changed to "good cause," a phrase with which lawyers are more familiar. [Rule 4, both as proposed by the Supreme Court and as changed by the Committee, does not in any way authorize a magistrate to issue a summons or a warrant sua sponte, nor does it enlarge, limit or change in any way the law governing warrantless arrests.]

The Committee deleted two sentences from Rule 4(c). These sentences permitted a magistrate to question the complainant and other witnesses under oath and required the magistrate to keep a record or summary of such a proceeding. The Committee does not intend this change to discontinue or discourage the practice of having the complainant appear personally or the practice of making a record or summary of such an appearance. Rather, the Committee intended to leave Rule 4(c) neutral on this matter, neither encouraging nor discouraging these practices.

The Committee added a new section that provides that the determination of good cause for the issuance of a warrant in lieu of a summons shall not be grounds for a motion to suppress evidence. This provision does not apply when the issue is whether there was probable cause to believe an offense has been committed. This provision does not in any way expand or limit the so-called "exclusionary rule."

CONFERENCE COMMITTEE NOTES, HOUSE REPORT NO. 94–414

Rule 4(e)(3) deals with the manner in which warrants and summonses may be served. The House version provides two methods for serving a summons: (1) personal service upon the defendant, or (2) service by leaving it with someone of suitable age at the defendant's dwelling *and* by mailing it to the defendant's last known address. The Senate version provides three methods: (1) personal service, (2) service by leaving it with someone of suitable age at the defendant's dwelling, or (3) service by mailing it to defendant's last known address.

1987 AMENDMENT

The amendments are technical. No substantive change is intended.

Rule 5. Initial Appearance Before the Magistrate

(a) In General. An officer making an arrest under a warrant issued upon a complaint or any person making an arrest without a warrant shall take the arrested person without unnecessary delay before the nearest available federal magistrate or, in the event that a federal magistrate is not reasonably available, before a state or local judicial officer authorized by 18 U.S.C. § 3041. If a person arrested without a warrant is brought before a magistrate, a complaint shall be filed forthwith which shall comply with the requirements of Rule 4(a) with respect to the showing of probable cause. When a person, arrested with or without a warrant or given a summons, appears initially before the magistrate, the magistrate shall proceed in accordance with the applicable subdivisions of this rule.

(b) Misdemeanors. If the charge against the defendant is a misdemeanor triable by a United States magistrate under 18 U.S.C. § 3401, the United States magistrate shall proceed in accordance with the Rules of Procedure for the Trial of Misdemeanors Before United States Magistrates.

(c) Offenses Not Triable by the United States Magistrate. If the charge against the defendant is not triable by the United States magistrate, the defendant shall not be called upon to plead. The magistrate shall inform the defendant of the complaint against the defendant and of any affidavit filed therewith, of the defendant's right to retain counsel or to request the assignment of counsel if the defendant is unable to obtain counsel, and of the general circumstances under which the defendant may secure pretrial release. The magistrate shall inform the defendant that the defendant is not required to make a statement and that any statement made by the defendant may be used against the defendant. The magistrate shall also inform the defendant of the right to a preliminary examination. The magistrate shall allow the defendant reasonable time and opportunity to consult counsel and shall detain or conditionally release the defendant as provided by statute or in these rules.

A defendant is entitled to a preliminary examination, unless waived, when charged with any offense, other than a petty offense, which is to be tried by a judge of the district court. If the defendant waives preliminary examination, the magistrate shall forthwith hold the defendant to answer in the district court. If the defendant does not waive the preliminary examination, the magistrate shall schedule a preliminary examination. Such examination shall be held within a reasonable time but in any event not later than

10 days following the initial appearance if the defendant is in custody and no later than 20 days if the defendant is not in custody, provided, however, that the preliminary examination shall not be held if the defendant is indicted or if an information against the defendant is filed in district court before the date set for the preliminary examination. With the consent of the defendant and upon a showing of good cause, taking into account the public interest in the prompt disposition of criminal cases, time limits specified in this subdivision may be extended one or more times by a federal magistrate. In the absence of such consent by the defendant, time limits may be extended by a judge of the United States only upon a showing that extraordinary circumstances exist and that delay is indispensable to the interests of justice.

(As amended Feb. 28, 1966, eff. July 1, 1966; Apr. 24, 1972, eff. Oct. 1, 1972; Apr. 28, 1982, eff. Aug. 1, 1982; Oct. 12, 1984, Pub.L. 98–473, Title II, § 209(a), 98 Stat. 1986; Mar. 9, 1987, eff. Aug. 1, 1987.)

NOTES OF ADVISORY COMMITTEE ON RULES

Note to Subdivision (a). 1. The time within which a prisoner must be brought before a committing magistrate is defined differently in different statutes. The rule supersedes all statutory provisions on this point and fixes a single standard, i.e., "without unnecessary delay", 18 U.S.C. former § 593 (Operating illicit distillery; arrest; bail); 18 U.S.C. former § 595 (Persons arrested taken before nearest officer for hearing); 5 U.S.C. former § 300a (now 18 U.S.C. §§ 3052, 3107) (Division of Investigation; authority of officers to serve warrants and make arrests); 16 U.S.C. former § 10 (Arrests by employees of park service for violations of laws and regulations); 16 U.S.C. § 706 (Migratory Bird Treaty Act; arrests; search warrants); D.C.Code (1940), Title 4, sec. 140 (Arrests without warrant); see, also, 33 U.S.C. former § 436, §§ 446, 452; 46 U.S.C. former § 708 (now 18 U.S.C. § 2279). What constitutes "unnecessary delay", i.e., reasonable time within which the prisoner should be brought before a committing magistrate, must be determined in the light of all the facts and circumstances of the case. The following authorities discuss the question what constitutes reasonable time for this purpose in various situations: *Carroll v. Parry,* 48 App.D.C. 453; *Janus v. United States,* 38 F.2d 431, C.C.A.9th; *Commonwealth v. Di Stasio,* 294 Mass. 273, 1 N.E.2d 189; *State v. Freeman,* 86 N.C. 683; *Peloquin v. Hibner,* 231 Wis. 77, 285 N.W. 380; see, also, Warner, 28 Va.L.R. 315, 339–341.

2. The rule also states the prevailing State practice, A.L.I. Code of Criminal Procedure (1931), Commentaries to secs. 35, 36.

Note to Subdivisions (b) and (c). 1. These rules prescribe a uniform procedure to be followed at preliminary hearings before a commissioner. They supersede the general provisions of 18 U.S.C. former § 591 (now § 3041) (Arrest and removal for trial). The procedure prescribed by the rules is that generally prevailing. See *Wood v. United States*, 128 F. 265, 271–272, App. D.C.; A.L.I. Code of Criminal Procedure (1931), secs. 39–60 and Commentaries thereto; Manual for United States Commissioners, pp. 6–10, published by Administrative Office of the United States Courts.

2. Pleas before a commissioner are excluded, as a plea of guilty at this stage has no legal status or function except to serve as a waiver of preliminary examination. It has been held inadmissible in evidence at the trial, if the defendant was not represented by counsel when the plea was entered. *Wood v. United States*, 128 F.2d 265, App.D.C. The rule expressly provides for a waiver of examination, thereby eliminating any necessity for a provision as to plea.

1966 AMENDMENT

The first change is designed to insure that under the revision made in Rule 4(a) the defendant arrested on a warrant will receive the same information concerning the basis for the issuance of the warrant as would previously have been given him by the complaint itself.

The second change obligates the commissioner to inform the defendant of his right to request the assignment of counsel if he is unable to obtain counsel. Cf. the amendment to Rule 44, and the Advisory Committee's Note thereon.

1972 AMENDMENT

There are a number of changes made in rule 5 which are designed to improve the editorial clarity of the rule; to conform the rule to the Federal Magistrates Act; and to deal explicitly in the rule with issues as to which the rule was silent and the law uncertain.

The principal editorial change is to deal separately with the initial appearance before the magistrate and the preliminary examination. They are dealt with together in old rule 5. They are separated in order to prevent confusion as to whether they constitute a single or two separate proceedings. Although the preliminary examination can be held at the time of the initial appearance, in practice this ordinarily does not occur. Usually counsel need time to prepare for the preliminary examination and as a consequence a separate date is typically set for the preliminary examination.

Because federal magistrates are reasonably available to conduct initial appearances, the rule is drafted on the assumption that the initial appearance is before a federal magistrate. If experience under the act indicates that there must be frequent appearances before state or local judicial officers it may be desirable to draft an additional rule, such as the following, detailing the procedure for an initial appearance before a state or local judicial officer:

Initial Appearance Before a State or Local Judicial Officer. If a United States magistrate is not reasonably available under rule 5(a), the arrested person shall be brought before a state or local judicial officer authorized by 18 U.S.C. § 3041, and such officer shall inform the person of the rights specified in rule 5(c) and shall authorize the release of the arrested person under the terms provided for by these rules and by 18 U.S.C. § 3146. The judicial officer shall immediately transmit any written order of release and any papers filed before him to the appropriate United States magistrate of the district and order the arrested person to appear before such United States magistrate within three days if not in custody or at the next regular hour of business of the United States magistrate if the arrested person is retained in custody. Upon his appearance before the United States magistrate, the procedure shall be that prescribed in rule 5.

Several changes are made to conform the language of the rule to the Federal Magistrates Act.

(1) The term "magistrate," which is defined in new rule 54, is substituted for the term "commissioner." As defined, "magistrate" includes those state and local judicial officers specified in 18 U.S.C. § 3041, and thus the initial appearance may be before a state or local judicial officer when a federal magistrate is not reasonably available. This is made explicit in subdivision (a).

(2) Subdivision (b) conforms the rule to the procedure prescribed in the Federal Magistrates Act when a defendant appears before a magistrate charged with a "minor offense" as defined in 18 U.S.C. § 3401(f): "misdemeanors punishable under the laws of the United States, the penalty for which does not exceed imprisonment for a period of one year, or a fine of not more than $1,000, or both, except that such term does not include ... [specified exceptions]."

If the "minor offense" is tried before a United States magistrate, the procedure must be in accordance with the Rules of Procedure for the Trial of Minor Offenses Before United States Magistrates (January 27, 1971).

(3) Subdivision (d) makes clear that a defendant is not entitled to a preliminary examination if he has been indicted by a grand jury prior to the date set for the preliminary examination or, in appropriate cases, if any information is filed in the district court prior to that date. See C. Wright, Federal Practice and Procedure: Criminal § 80, pp. 137–140 (1969, Supp.1971). This is also provided in the Federal Magistrates Act, 18 U.S.C. § 3060(e).

Rule 5 is also amended to deal with several issues not dealt with in old rule 5:

Subdivision (a) is amended to make clear that a complaint, complying with the requirements of rule 4(a), must be filed whenever a person has been arrested without a warrant. This means that the complaint, or an affidavit or affidavits filed with the complaint, must show probable cause. As provided in rule 4(a) the showing of probable cause "may be based upon hearsay evidence in whole or in part."

Subdivision (c) provides that defendant should be notified of the general circumstances under which he is entitled to pretrial release under the Bail Reform Act of 1966 (18 U.S.C. §§ 3141–3152). Defendants often do not in fact have counsel at the initial appearance and thus, unless told by the magistrate, may be unaware of their right to pretrial release. See C. Wright, Federal Practice and Procedure: Criminal § 78 N. 61 (1969).

Subdivision (c) makes clear that a defendant who does not waive his right to trial before a judge of the district court is entitled to a preliminary examination to determine probable cause for any offense except a petty offense. It also, by necessary implication, makes clear that a defendant is not entitled to a preliminary examination if he consents to be tried on the issue of guilt or innocence by the United States magistrate, even though the offense may be one not heretofore triable by the United States commissioner and therefore one as to which the defendant had a right to a preliminary examination. The rationale is that the preliminary examination serves only to justify holding the defendant in custody or on bail during the period of time it takes to bind the defendant over to the district court for trial. See *State v. Solomon*, 158 Wis. 146, 147 N.W. 640 (1914). A similar conclusion is reached in the New York Proposed Criminal Procedure Law. See McKinney's Session Law News, April 10, 1969, at p. A–119.

Subdivision (c) also contains time limits within which the preliminary examination must be held. These are taken from 18 U.S.C. § 3060. The provisions for the extension of the prescribed time limits are the same as the provisions of 18 U.S.C. § 3060 with two exceptions: The new language allows delay consented to by the defendant only if there is "a showing of good cause, taking into account the public interest in the prompt disposition of criminal cases." This reflects the view of the Advisory Committee that delay, whether prosecution or defense induced, ought to be avoided whenever possible. The second difference between the new rule and 18 U.S.C. § 3060 is that the rule allows the decision to grant a continuance to be made by a United States magistrate as well as by a judge of the United States. This reflects the view of the Advisory Committee that the United States magistrate should have sufficient judicial competence to make decisions such as that contemplated in subdivision (c).

1982 AMENDMENT

The amendment of subdivision (b) reflects the recent amendment of 18 U.S.C. § 3401(a), by the Federal Magistrate Act of 1979, to read: "When specially designated to exercise such jurisdiction by the district court or courts he serves, any United States magistrate shall have jurisdiction to try persons accused of, and sentence persons convicted of, misdemeanors committed within that judicial district."

1987 AMENDMENT

The amendments are technical. No substantive change is intended.

Rule 5.1   Preliminary Examination

(a) Probable Cause Finding. If from the evidence it appears that there is probable cause to believe that an offense has been committed and that the defendant committed it, the federal magistrate shall forthwith hold the defendant to answer in district court. The finding of probable cause may be based upon hearsay evidence in whole or in part. The defendant may cross-examine adverse witnesses and may introduce evidence. Objections to evidence on the ground that it was acquired by unlawful means are not properly made at the preliminary examination. Motions to suppress must be made to the trial court as provided in Rule 12.

(b) Discharge of Defendant. If from the evidence it appears that there is no probable cause to believe that an offense has been committed or that the defendant committed it, the federal magistrate shall dismiss the complaint and discharge the defendant. The discharge of the defendant shall not preclude the government from instituting a subsequent prosecution for the same offense.

(c) Records. After concluding the proceeding the federal magistrate shall transmit forthwith to the clerk of the district court all papers in the proceeding. The magistrate shall promptly make or cause to be made a record or summary of such proceeding.

(1) On timely application to a federal magistrate, the attorney for a defendant in a criminal case may be given the opportunity to have the recording of the hearing on preliminary examination made available to that attorney in connection with any further hearing or preparation for trial. The court may, by local rule, appoint the place for and define the conditions

under which such opportunity may be afforded counsel.

(2) On application of a defendant addressed to the court or any judge thereof, an order may issue that the federal magistrate make available a copy of the transcript, or of a portion thereof, to defense counsel. Such order shall provide for prepayment of costs of such transcript by the defendant unless the defendant makes a sufficient affidavit that the defendant is unable to pay or to give security therefor, in which case the expense shall be paid by the Director of the Administrative Office of the United States Courts from available appropriated funds. Counsel for the government may move also that a copy of the transcript, in whole or in part, be made available to it, for good cause shown, and an order may be entered granting such motion in whole or in part, on appropriate terms, except that the government need not prepay costs nor furnish security therefor.

(Added Apr. 24, 1972, eff. Oct. 1, 1972, and amended Mar. 9, 1987, eff. Aug. 1, 1987.)

NOTES OF ADVISORY COMMITTEE ON RULES

Rule 5.1 is, for the most part, a clarification of old rule 5(c).

Under the new rule, the preliminary examination must be conducted before a "federal magistrate" as defined in rule 54. Giving state or local judicial officers authority to conduct a preliminary examination does not seem necessary. There are not likely to be situations in which a "federal magistrate" is not "reasonably available" to conduct the preliminary examination, which is usually not held until several days after the initial appearance provided for in rule 5.

Subdivision (a) makes clear that a finding of probable cause may be based on "hearsay evidence in whole or in part." The propriety of relying upon hearsay at the preliminary examination has been a matter of some uncertainty in the federal system. See C. Wright, Federal Practice and Procedure: Criminal § 80 (1969, Supp.1971); 8 J. Moore, Federal Practice ¶ 504[4] (2d ed. Cipes 1970, Supp.1971); *Washington v. Clemmer*, 339 F.2d 715, 719 (D.C.Cir.1964); *Washington v. Clemmer*, 339 F.2d 725, 728 (D.C.Cir.1964); *Ross v. Sirica*, 380 F.2d 557, 565 (D.C.Cir.1967); *Howard v. United States*, 389 F.2d 287, 292 (D.C.Cir.1967); Weinberg and Weinberg, The Congressional Invitation to Avoid the Preliminary Hearing: An Analysis of Section 303 of the Federal Magistrates Act of 1968, 67 Mich.L.Rev. 1361, especially n. 92 at 1383 (1969); D. Wright, The Rules of Evidence Applicable to Hearings in Probable Cause, 37

Conn.B.J. 561 (1963), Comment, Preliminary Examination—Evidence and Due Process, 15 Kan.L.Rev. 374, 379–381 (1967).

A grand jury indictment may properly be based upon hearsay evidence. *Costello v. United States*, 350 U.S. 359 (1956); 8 J. Moore, Federal Practice ¶ 6.03[2] (2d ed. Cipes 1970, Supp.1971). This being so, there is practical advantage in making the evidentiary requirements for the preliminary examination as flexible as they are for the grand jury. Otherwise there will be increased pressure upon United States Attorneys to abandon the preliminary examination in favor of the grand jury indictment. See C. Wright, Federal Practice and Procedure: Criminal § 80 at p. 143 (1969). New York State, which also utilizes both the preliminary examination and the grand jury, has under consideration a new Code of Criminal Procedure which would allow the use of hearsay at the preliminary examination. See McKinney's Session Law News, April 10, 1969, pp. A119–A120.

For the same reason, subdivision (a) also provides that the preliminary examination is not the proper place to raise the issue of illegally obtained evidence. This is current law. In *Giordenello v. United States*, 357 U.S. 480, 484 (1958), the Supreme Court said: [T]he Commissioner here had no authority to adjudicate the admissibility at petitioner's later trial of the heroin taken from his person. That issue was for the trial court. This is specifically recognized by Rule 41(e) of the Criminal Rules, which provides that a defendant aggrieved by an unlawful search and seizure may " * * * move the district court * * * to suppress for use as evidence anything so obtained on the ground that * * * " the arrest warrant was defective on any of several grounds.

Dicta in *Costello v. United States*, 350 U.S. 359, 363–364 (1956), and *United States v. Blue*, 384 U.S. 251, 255 (1966), also support the proposed rule. In *United States ex rel. Almeida v. Rundle*, 383 F.2d 421, 424 (3d Cir.1967), the court, in considering the adequacy of an indictment said:

On this score, it is settled law that (1) "[an] indictment returned by a legally constituted nonbiased grand jury, * * * is enough to call for a trial of the charge on the merits and satisfies the requirements of the Fifth Amendment.", *Lawn v. United States*, 355 U.S. 399, 349, 78 S.Ct. 311, 317, 2 L.Ed.2d 321 (1958); (2) an indictment cannot be challenged "on the ground that there was inadequate or incompetent evidence before the grand jury", *Costello v. United States*, 350 U.S. 359, 363, 76 S.Ct. 406, 408, 100 L.Ed. 397 (1956); and (3) a prosecution is not abated, nor barred, even where "tainted evidence" has been submitted to a grand jury, *United States v. Blue*, 384 U.S. 251, 86 S.Ct. 1416, 16 L.Ed.2d 510 (1966). See also C. Wright, Federal Practice and Procedure: Criminal § 80 at 143 n. 5 (1969, Supp.1971); 8 J. Moore, Federal Practice ¶ 6.03[3] (2d ed. Cipes 1970, Supp.1971). The Manual for United States Commissioners (Administrative Office of United

States Courts, 1948) provides at pp. 24–25: "Motions for this purpose [to suppress illegally obtained evidence] may be made and heard only before a district judge. Commissioners are not empowered to consider or act upon such motions."

It has been urged that the rules of evidence at the preliminary examination should be those applicable at the trial because the purpose of the preliminary examination should be, not to review the propriety of the arrest or prior detention, but rather to determine whether there is evidence sufficient to justify subjecting the defendant to the expense and inconvenience of trial. See Weinberg and Weinberg, The Congressional Invitation to Avoid the Preliminary Hearing: An Analysis of Section 303 of the Federal Magistrates Act of 1968, 67 Mich.L.Rev. 1361, 1396–1399 (1969). The rule rejects this view for reasons largely of administrative necessity and the efficient administration of justice. The Congress has decided that a preliminary examination shall not be required when there is a grand jury indictment (18 U.S.C. § 3060). Increasing the procedural and evidentiary requirements applicable to the preliminary examination will therefore add to the administrative pressure to avoid the preliminary examination. Allowing objections to evidence on the ground that evidence has been illegally obtained would require two determinations of admissibility, one before the United States magistrate and one in the district court. The objective is to reduce, not increase, the number of preliminary motions.

To provide that a probable cause finding may be based upon hearsay does not preclude the magistrate from requiring a showing that admissible evidence will be available at the time of trial. See Comment, Criminal Procedure—Grand Jury—Validity of Indictment Based Solely on Hearsay Questioned When Direct Testimony Is Readily Available, 43 N.Y.U.L.Rev. 578 (1968); *United States v. Umans,* 368 F.2d 725 (2d Cir.1966), cert. dismissed as improvidently granted 389 U.S. 80 (1967); *United States v. Andrews,* 381 F.2d 377, 378 (2d Cir. 1967); *United States v. Messina,* 388 F.2d 393, 394 n. 1 (2d Cir.1968); *United States v. Beltram,* 388 F.2d 449 (2d Cir.1968); and *United States v. Arcuri,* 282 F.Supp. 347 (E.D.N.Y.1968). The fact that a defendant is not entitled to object to evidence alleged to have been illegally obtained does not deprive him of an opportunity for a pretrial determination of the admissibility of evidence. He can raise such an objection prior to trial in accordance with the provisions of rule 12.

Subdivision (b) makes it clear that the United States magistrate may not only discharge the defendant but may also dismiss the complaint. Current federal law authorizes the magistrate to discharge the defendant but he must await authorization from the United States Attorney before he can close his records on the case by dismissing the complaint. Making dismissal of the complaint a separate procedure accomplishes no worthwhile objective, and the new rule makes it clear that the magistrate can both discharge the defendant and file the record with the clerk.

Subdivision (b) also deals with the legal effect of a discharge of a defendant at a preliminary examination. This issue is not dealt with explicitly in the old rule. Existing federal case law is limited. What cases there are seem to support the right of the government to issue a new complaint and start over. See *e.g., Collins v. Loisel,* 262 U.S. 426 (1923); *Morse v. United States,* 267 U.S. 80 (1925). State law is similar. See *People v. Dillon,* 197 N.Y. 254, 90 N.E. 820 (1910); *Tell v. Wolke,* 21 Wis.2d 613, 124 N.W.2d 655 (1963). In the *Tell* case the Wisconsin court stated the common rationale for allowing the prosecutor to issue a new complaint and start over:

The state has no appeal from errors of law committed by a magistrate upon preliminary examination and the discharge on a preliminary would operate as an unchallengeable acquittal. * * * The only way an error of law committed on the preliminary examination prejudicial to the state may be challenged or corrected is by a preliminary examination on a second complaint. (21 Wis.2d at 619–620.)

Subdivision (c) is based upon old rule 5(c) and upon the Federal Magistrates Act, 18 U.S.C. § 3060(f). It provides methods for making available to counsel the record of the preliminary examination. See C. Wright, Federal Practice and Procedure: Criminal § 82 (1969, Supp.1971). The new rule is designed to eliminate delay and expense occasioned by preparation of transcripts where listening to the tape recording would be sufficient. Ordinarily the recording should be made available pursuant to subdivision (c)(1). A written transcript may be provided under subdivision (c)(2) at the discretion of the court, a discretion which must be exercised in accordance with *Britt v. North Carolina,* 404 U.S. 226, 30 L.Ed.2d 400, 405 (1971):

A defendant who claims the right to a free transcript does not, under our cases, bear the burden of proving inadequate such alternatives as may be suggested by the State or conjured up by a court in hindsight. In this case, however, petitioner has conceded that he had available an informal alternative which appears to be substantially equivalent to a transcript. Accordingly, we cannot conclude that the court below was in error in rejecting his claim.

1987 AMENDMENT

The amendments are technical. No substantive change is intended.

III. INDICTMENT AND INFORMATION

Rule 6. The Grand Jury

(a) Summoning Grand Juries.

(1) **Generally.** The court shall order one or more grand juries to be summoned at such time as the public interest requires. The grand jury shall consist of not less than 16 nor more than 23 members. The court shall direct that a sufficient number of legally qualified persons be summoned to meet this requirement.

(2) **Alternate Jurors.** The court may direct that alternate jurors may be designated at the time a grand jury is selected. Alternate jurors in the order in which they were designated may thereafter be impanelled as provided in subdivision (g) of this rule. Alternate jurors shall be drawn in the same manner and shall have the same qualifications as the regular jurors, and if impanelled shall be subject to the same challenges, shall take the same oath and shall have the same functions, powers, facilities and privileges as the regular jurors.

(b) Objections to Grand Jury and to Grand Jurors.

(1) **Challenges.** The attorney for the government or a defendant who has been held to answer in the district court may challenge the array of jurors on the ground that the grand jury was not selected, drawn or summoned in accordance with law, and may challenge an individual juror on the ground that the juror is not legally qualified. Challenges shall be made before the administration of the oath to the jurors and shall be tried by the court.

(2) **Motion to Dismiss.** A motion to dismiss the indictment may be based on objections to the array or on the lack of legal qualification of an individual juror, if not previously determined upon challenge. It shall be made in the manner prescribed in 28 U.S.C. § 1867(e) and shall be granted under the conditions prescribed in that statute. An indictment shall not be dismissed on the ground that one or more members of the grand jury were not legally qualified if it appears from the record kept pursuant to subdivision (c) of this rule that 12 or more jurors, after deducting the number not legally qualified, concurred in finding the indictment.

(c) Foreperson and Deputy Foreperson.

The court shall appoint one of the jurors to be foreperson and another to be deputy foreperson. The foreperson shall have power to administer oaths and affirmations and shall sign all indictments. The foreperson or another juror designated by the foreperson shall keep record of the number of jurors concurring in the finding of every indictment and shall file the record with the clerk of the court, but the record shall not be made public except on order of the court. During the absence of the foreperson, the deputy foreperson shall act as foreperson.

(d) Who May Be Present.

Attorneys for the government, the witness under examination, interpreters when needed and, for the purpose of taking the evidence, a stenographer or operator of a recording device may be present while the grand jury is in session, but no person other than the jurors may be present while the grand jury is deliberating or voting.

(e) Recording and Disclosure of Proceedings.

(1) **Recording of Proceedings.** All proceedings, except when the grand jury is deliberating or voting, shall be recorded stenographically or by an electronic recording device. An unintentional failure of any recording to reproduce all or any portion of a proceeding shall not affect the validity of the prosecution. The recording or reporter's notes or any transcript prepared therefrom shall remain in the custody or control of the attorney for the government unless otherwise ordered by the court in a particular case.

(2) **General Rule of Secrecy.** A grand juror, an interpreter, a stenographer, an operator of a recording device, a typist who transcribes recorded testimony, an attorney for the government, or any person to whom disclosure is made under paragraph (3)(A)(ii) of this subdivision shall not disclose matters occurring before the grand jury, except as otherwise provided for in these rules. No obligation of secrecy may be imposed on any person except in accordance with this rule. A knowing violation of Rule 6 may be punished as a contempt of court.

(3) Exceptions.

(A) Disclosure otherwise prohibited by this rule of matters occurring before the grand jury, other than its deliberations and the vote of any grand juror, may be made to—

(i) an attorney for the government for use in the performance of such attorney's duty; and

(ii) such government personnel (including personnel of a state or subdivision of a state) as are deemed necessary by an attorney for the government to assist an attorney for the government in the performance of such attorney's duty to enforce federal criminal law.

(B) Any person to whom matters are disclosed under subparagraph (A)(ii) of this paragraph shall not utilize that grand jury material for any purpose other than assisting the attorney for the government in the performance of such attorney's duty to enforce federal criminal law. An attorney for the government shall promptly provide the district court, before which was impaneled the grand jury whose material has been so disclosed, with the names of the persons to whom such disclosure has been made, and shall certify that the attorney has advised such persons of their obligation of secrecy under this rule.

(C) Disclosure otherwise prohibited by this rule of matters occurring before the grand jury may also be made—

(i) when so directed by a court preliminarily to or in connection with a judicial proceeding;

(ii) when permitted by a court at the request of the defendant, upon a showing that grounds may exist for a motion to dismiss the indictment because of matters occurring before the grand jury;

(iii) when the disclosure is made by an attorney for the government to another federal grand jury; or

(iv) when permitted by a court at the request of an attorney for the government, upon a showing that such matters may disclose a violation of state criminal law, to an appropriate official of a state or subdivision of a state for the purpose of enforcing such law.

If the court orders disclosure of matters occurring before the grand jury, the disclosure shall be made in such manner, at such time, and under such conditions as the court may direct.

(D) A petition for disclosure pursuant to subdivision (e)(3)(C)(i) shall be filed in the district where the grand jury convened. Unless the hearing is ex parte, which it may be when the petitioner is the government, the petitioner shall serve written notice of the petition upon (i) the attorney for the government, (ii) the parties to the judicial proceeding if disclosure is sought in connection with such a proceeding, and (iii) such other persons as the court may direct. The court shall afford those persons a reasonable opportunity to appear and be heard.

(E) If the judicial proceeding giving rise to the petition is in a federal district court in another district, the court shall transfer the matter to that court unless it can reasonably obtain sufficient knowledge of the proceeding to determine whether disclosure is proper. The court shall order transmitted to the court to which the matter is transferred the material sought to be disclosed, if feasible, and a written evaluation of the need for continued grand jury secrecy. The court to which the matter is transferred shall afford the aforementioned persons a reasonable opportunity to appear and be heard.

(4) Sealed Indictments. The federal magistrate to whom an indictment is returned may direct that the indictment be kept secret until the defendant is in custody or has been released pending trial. Thereupon the clerk shall seal the indictment and no person shall disclose the return of the indictment except when necessary for the issuance and execution of a warrant or summons.

(5) Closed Hearing. Subject to any right to an open hearing in contempt proceedings, the court shall order a hearing on matters affecting a grand jury proceeding to be closed to the extent necessary to prevent disclosure of matters occurring before a grand jury.

(6) Sealed Records. Records, orders and subpoenas relating to grand jury proceedings shall be kept under seal to the extent and for such time as is necessary to prevent disclosure of matters occurring before a grand jury.

(f) Finding and Return of Indictment. An indictment may be found only upon the concurrence of 12 or more jurors. The indictment shall be returned by the grand jury to a federal magistrate in open court. If a complaint or information is pending against the defendant and 12 jurors do not concur in finding an indictment, the foreperson shall so report to a federal magistrate in writing forthwith.

(g) Discharge and Excuse. A grand jury shall serve until discharged by the court, but no grand jury may serve more than 18 months unless the court extends the service of the grand jury for a period of six months or less upon a determination that such extension is in the public interest. At any time for cause shown the court may excuse a juror either temporarily or permanently, and in the latter event the court may impanel another person in place of the juror excused.

(As amended Feb. 28, 1966, eff. July 1, 1966; Apr. 24, 1972, eff. Oct. 1, 1972; Apr. 26, 1976, eff. Aug. 1, 1976; July 30, 1977, Pub.L. 95–78, § 2(a), 91 Stat. 319; Apr. 30, 1979, eff. Aug. 1, 1979; Apr. 28, 1983, eff. Aug. 1, 1983; Pub.L. 98–483, Title II, § 215(f), Oct. 12, 1984, 98 Stat. 2016; Apr. 29, 1985, eff. Aug. 1, 1985; Mar. 9, 1987, eff. Aug. 1, 1987.)

Subd. (e)(3)(C)(IV) of this Rule Applicable to Offenses Committed Prior to Nov. 1, 1987

Subd. (e)(3)(C)(IV) of this rule as in effect prior to amendment by Pub.L. 98–473 read as follows:

(iv) when permitted by a court at the request of an attorney for the government, upon a showing that such matters may disclose a violation of state criminal law, to an appropriate official of a state or subdivision of a state for the purpose of enforcing such law.

For applicability of sentencing provisions to offenses, see Effective Date and Savings Provisions, etc., note, section 235 of Pub.L. 98–473, as amended, set out under section 3551 of Title 18, Crimes and Criminal Procedure. See also Codification note below.

NOTES OF ADVISORY COMMITTEE ON RULES

Note to Subdivision (a). 1. The first sentence of this rule vests in the court full discretion as to the number of grand juries to be summoned and as to the times when they should be convened. This provision supersedes the existing law, which limits the authority of the court to summon more than one grand jury at the same time. At present two grand juries may be convened simultaneously only in a district which has a city or borough of at least 300,000 inhabitants, and three grand juries only in the Southern District of New York, 28 U.S.C. former § 421 (Grand juries; when, how and by whom summoned; length of service). This statute has been construed, however, as only limiting the authority of the court to summon more than one grand jury for a single place of holding court, and as not circumscribing the power to convene simultaneously several grand juries at different points within the same district, *Morris v. United States,* 128 F.2d 912, C.C.A. 5th; *United States v. Perlstein,* 39 F.Supp. 965, D.N.J.

2. The provision that the grand jury shall consist of not less than 16 and not more than 23 members continues existing law, 28 U.S.C. former § 419 (now 18 U.S.C. § 3321) (Grand jurors; number when less than required number).

3. The rule does not affect or deal with the method of summoning and selecting grand juries. Existing statutes on the subjects are not superseded. See 28 U.S.C. former §§ 411–426 (now §§ 1861–1870). As these provisions of law relate to jurors for both criminal and civil cases, it seemed best not to deal with this subject.

Note to Subdivision (b)(1). Challenges to the array and to individual jurors, although rarely invoked in connection with the selection of grand juries, are nevertheless permitted in the Federal courts and are continued by this rule, *United States v. Gale,* 109 U.S. 65, 69–70, 3 S.Ct. 1, 27 L.Ed. 857; *Clawson v. United States,* 114 U.S. 477, 5 S.Ct. 949, 29 L.Ed. 179; *Agnew v. United States,* 165 U.S. 36, 44, 17 S.Ct. 235, 41 L.Ed. 624. It is not contemplated, however, that defendants held for action of the grand jury shall receive notice of the time and place of the impaneling of a grand jury, or that defendants in custody shall be brought to court to attend at the selection of the grand jury. Failure to challenge is not a waiver of any objection. The objection may still be interposed by motion under Rule 6(b)(2).

Note to Subdivision (b)(2). 1. The motion provided by this rule takes the place of a plea in abatement, or motion to quash. *Crowley v. United States,* 194 U.S. 461, 469–474, 24 S.Ct. 731, 48 L.Ed. 1075; *United States v. Gale, supra.*

2. The second sentence of the rule is a restatement of 18 U.S.C. former § 554(a) (Indictments and presentments; objection on ground of unqualified juror barred where twelve qualified jurors concurred; record of number concurring), and introduces no change in existing law.

Note to Subdivision (c). 1. This rule generally is a restatement of existing law, 18 U.S.C. former § 554(a) and 28 U.S.C. former § 420. Failure of the foreman to sign or endorse the indictment is an irregularity and is not fatal, *Frisbie v. United States,* 157 U.S. 160, 163–165, 15 S.Ct. 586, 39 L.Ed. 657.

2. The provision for the appointment of a deputy foreman is new. Its purpose is to facilitate the transaction of business if the foreman is absent. Such a provision is found in the law of at least one State, N.Y.Code Criminal Procedure, sec. 244.

Note to Subdivision (d). This rule generally continues existing law. See 18 U.S.C. former § 556 (Indictments and presentments; defects of form); and 5 U.S.C. § 310 [28 § 515(a)] (Conduct of legal proceedings).

Note to Subdivision (e). 1. This rule continues the traditional practice of secrecy on the part of members of the grand jury, except when the court permits a disclosure, *Schmidt v. United States,* 115 F.2d 394, C.C.A.6th; *United States v. American Medical Association,* 26 F.Supp. 429, D.C.; Cf. *Atwell v. United States,* 162 Fed. 97, C.C.A.4th; and see 18 U.S.C. former § 554(a) (Indictments and presentments; objection on ground of unqualified juror barred where twelve qualified jurors concurred; record of number concurring). Government attorneys are entitled to disclosure of grand jury proceedings, other than the deliberations and the votes of the jurors, inasmuch as they may be present in the grand jury room during the presentation of evidence. The rule continues this practice.

2. The rule does not impose any obligation of secrecy on witnesses. The existing practice on this point varies among the districts. The seal of secrecy on witnesses seems an unnecessary hardship and may lead to injustice if a witness is not permitted to make a disclosure to counsel or to an associate.

3. The last sentence authorizing the court to seal indictments continues present practice.

Note to Subdivision (f). This rule continues existing law, 18 U.S.C. former § 554 (Indictments and presentments; by twelve grand jurors). The purpose of the last sentence is to provide means for a prompt release of a defendant if in custody, or exoneration of bail if he is on bail, in the event that the grand jury considers the case of a defendant held for its action and finds no indictment.

Note to Subdivision (g). Under existing law a grand jury serves only during the term for which it is summoned, but the court may extend its period of service for as long as 18 months, 28 U.S.C. former § 421. During the extended period, however, a grand jury may conduct only investigations commenced during the original term. The rule continues the 18 months' maximum for the period of service of a grand jury, but provides for such service as a matter of course, unless the court terminates it at an earlier date. The matter is left in the discretion of the court, as it is under existing law. The expiration of a term of court as a time limitation is elsewhere entirely eliminated (Rule 45(c)) and specific time limitations are substituted therefor. This was previously done by the Federal Rules of Civil Procedure for the civil side of the courts

(Federal Rules of Civil Procedure, Rule 6(c), 28 U.S.C., Appendix). The elimination of the requirement that at an extended period the grand jury may continue only investigations previously commenced, will obviate such a controversy as was presented in *United States v. Johnson,* 319 U.S. 503, 63 S.Ct. 1233, 87 L.Ed. 1546, rehearing denied 320 U.S. 808, 64 S.Ct. 25, 88 L.Ed. 488.

1966 AMENDMENT

Subdivision (d).—The amendment makes it clear that recording devices may be used to take evidence at grand jury sessions.

Subdivision (e).—The amendment makes it clear that the operator of a recording device and a typist who transcribes recorded testimony are bound to the obligation of secrecy.

Subdivision (f).—A minor change conforms the language to what doubtless is the practice. The need for a report to the court that no indictment has been found may be present even though the defendant has not been "held to answer." If the defendant is in custody or has given bail, some official record should be made of the grand jury action so that the defendant can be released or his bail exonerated.

1972 AMENDMENT

Subdivision (b)(2) is amended to incorporate by express reference the provisions of the Jury Selection and Service Act of 1968. That act provides in part:

The procedures prescribed by this section shall be the exclusive means by which a person accused of a Federal crime [or] the Attorney General of the United States * * * may challenge any jury on the ground that such jury was not selected in conformity with the provisions of this title. [28 U.S.C. § 1867(c)]

Under rule 12(e) the judge shall decide the motion before trial or order it deferred until after verdict. The authority which the judge has to delay his ruling until after verdict gives him an option which can be exercised to prevent the unnecessary delay of a trial in the event that a motion attacking a grand jury is made on the eve of the trial. In addition, rule 12(c) gives the judge authority to fix the time at which pretrial motions must be made. Failure to make a pretrial motion at the appropriate time may constitute a waiver under rule 12(f).

1976 AMENDMENT

Under the proposed amendment to rule 6(f), an indictment may be returned to a federal magistrate. ("Federal magistrate" is defined in rule 54(c) as including a United States magistrate as defined in 28 U.S.C. §§ 631–639 and a judge of the United States.) This change will foreclose the possibility of noncompliance with the Speedy Trial Act timetable because of the nonavailability of a judge. Upon the effective date of certain provisions of the Speedy Trial Act of 1974, the timely return of indictments will become a matter of critical importance; for the year commencing July 1, 1976, indictments must be returned within 60 days of arrest or summons, for the year following within 45 days, and thereafter within 30 days. 18 U.S.C. §§ 3161(b) and (f), 3163(a). The problem is acute in a one-judge district where, if the judge is holding court in another part of the district, or is otherwise absent, the return of the indictment must await the later reappearance of the judge at the place where the grand jury is sitting.

A corresponding change has been made to that part of subdivision (f) which concerns the reporting of a "no bill," and to that part of subdivision (e) which concerns keeping an indictment secret.

The change in the third sentence of rule 6(f) is made so as to cover all situations in which by virtue of a pending complaint or information the defendant is in custody or released under some form of conditional release.

1977 AMENDMENT

The proposed definition of "attorneys for the government" in subdivision (e) is designed to facilitate an increasing need, on the part of government attorneys, to make use of outside expertise in complex litigation. The phrase "other government personnel" includes, but is not limited to, employees of administrative agencies and government departments.

Present subdivision (e) provides for disclosure "to the attorneys for the government for use in the performance of their duties." This limitation is designed to further "the long established policy that maintains the secrecy of the grand jury in federal courts." United States v. Procter and Gamble Co., 356 U.S. 677 (1958).

As defined in rule 54(c), " 'Attorney for the government' means the Attorney General, an authorized assistant of the Attorney General, a United States Attorney, an authorized assistant of a United States Attorney and when applicable to cases arising under the laws of Guam * * *." The limited nature of this definition is pointed out in In re Grand Jury Proceedings, 309 F.2d 440 (3d Cir.1962) at 443:

The term attorneys for the government is restrictive in its application. * * * If it had been intended that the attorneys for the administrative agencies were to have free access to matters occurring before a grand jury, the rule would have so provided.

The proposed amendment reflects the fact that there is often government personnel assisting the Justice Department in grand jury proceedings. In In re Grand Jury Investigation of William H. Pflaumer & Sons, Inc., 53 F.R.D. 464 (E.D.Pa.1971), the opinion quoted the United States Attorney.

It is absolutely necessary in grand jury investigations involving analysis of books and records, for the government attorneys to rely upon investigative personnel (from the government agencies) for assistance.

See also 8 J. Moore, Federal Practice ¶ 6.05 at 6–28 (2d ed. Cipes, 1969):

The rule [6(e)] has presented a problem however, with respect to attorneys and nonattorneys who are assisting in preparation of a case for the grand jury. * * * These assistants often cannot properly perform their work without having access to grand jury minutes.

Although case law is limited, the trend seems to be in the direction of allowing disclosure to government personnel who assist attorneys for the government in situations where their expertise is required. This is subject to the qualification that the matters disclosed be used only for the purposes of the grand jury investigation. The court may inquire as to the good faith of the assisting personnel, to ensure that access to material is not merely a subterfuge to gather evidence unattainable by means other than the grand jury. This approach was taken in In re Grand Jury Investigation of William H. Pflaumer & Sons, Inc., 53 F.R.D. 464 (E.D.Pa.1971); In re April 1956 Term Grand Jury, 239 F.2d 263 (7th Cir.1956); United States v. Anzelimo, 319 F.Supp. 1106 (D.C.La.1970). Another case, Application of Kelly, 19 F.R.D. 269 (S.D.N.Y.1956), assumed, without deciding, that assistance given the attorney for the government by IRS and FBI agents was authorized.

The change at line 27 reflects the fact that under the Bail Reform Act of 1966 some persons will be released without requiring bail. See 18 U.S.C. §§ 3146, 3148.

Under the proposed amendment to rule 6(f), an indictment may be returned to a federal magistrate. ("Federal magistrate" is defined in rule 54(c) as including a United States magistrate as defined in 28 U.S.C. §§ 631–639 and a judge of the United States.) This change will foreclose the possibility of noncompliance with the Speedy Trial Act timetable because of the nonavailability of a judge. Upon the effective date of certain provisions of the Speedy Trial Act of 1974, the timely return of indictments will become a matter of critical importance; for the year commencing July 1, 1976, indictments must be returned within 60 days of arrest or summons, for the year following within 45 days, and thereafter within 30 days. 18 U.S.C. §§ 3161(b) and (f), 3163(a). The problem is acute in a one-judge district where, if the judge is holding court in another part of the district or is otherwise absent, the return of the indictment must await the later reappearance of the judge at the place where the grand jury is sitting.

A corresponding change has been made to that part of subdivision (f) which concerns the reporting of a "no bill," and to that part of subdivision (e) which concerns keeping an indictment secret.

The change in the third sentence of rule 6(f) is made so as to cover all situations in which by virtue of a pending complaint or information the defendant is in custody or released under some form of conditional release.

Notes of Committee on the Judiciary, Senate Report No. 95–354. Amendments Proposed by the Supreme Court.

Rule 6(e) currently provides that "disclosure of matters occurring before the grand jury other than its deliberations and the vote of any juror may be made to the attorneys for the government for use in the performance of their duties." Rule 54(c) defines attorneys for the government to mean "the Attorney General, an authorized assistant to the Attorney General, a United States attorney, and an authorized assistant of the United States attorney, and when applicable to cases arising under the laws of Guam, means the Attorney General of Guam...."

The Supreme Court proposal would change Rule 6(e) by adding the following new language:

For purposes of this subdivision, "attorneys for the government" includes those enumerated in Rule 54(c); it also includes such other government personnel as are necessary to assist the attorneys for the government in the performance of their duties.

It would also make a series of changes in the rule designed to make its provisions consistent with other provisions in the Rules and the Bail Reform Act of 1966.

The Advisory Committee note states that the proposed amendment is intended "to facilitate an increasing need, on the part of Government attorneys to make use of outside expertise in complex litigation". The note indicated that:

Although case law is limited, the trend seems to be in the direction of allowing disclosure to Government personnel who assist attorneys for the Government in situations where their expertise is required. This is subject to the qualification that the matter disclosed be used only for the purposes of the grand jury investigation.

It is past history at this point that the Supreme Court proposal attracted substantial criticism, which seemed to stem more from the lack of precision in defining, and consequent confusion and uncertainty concerning, the intended scope of the proposed change than from a fundamental disagreement with the objective.

Attorneys for the Government in the performance of their duties with a grand jury must possess the authority to utilize the services of other government employees. Federal crimes are "investigated" by the FBI, the IRS, or by Treasury agents and not by government prosecutors or the citizens who sit on grand juries. Federal agents gather and present information relating to criminal behavior to prosecutors who analyze and evaluate it and present it to grand juries. Often the prosecutors need the assistance of the agents in evaluating evidence. Also, if further investigation is required during or after grand jury proceedings, or even during the course of criminal trials, the Federal agents must do it. There is no reason for a barrier of secrecy to exist between the facets of the criminal justice system upon which we all depend to enforce the criminal laws.

The parameters of the authority of an attorney for the government to disclose grand jury information in the course of performing his own duties is not defined by Rule 6. However, a commonsense interpretation prevails, permitting "Representatives of other government agencies actively assisting United States attorneys in a grand jury investigation ... access to grand jury material in the performance of their duties." Yet projected against this current practice, and the weight of case law, is the anomalous language of Rule 6(e) itself, which, in its present state of uncertainty, is spawning some judicial decisions highly restrictive of the use of government experts that require the government to "show the necessity (to the Court) for each particular person's aid rather than showing merely a general necessity for assistance, expert or otherwise" and that make Rule 6(e) order subject to interlocutory appeal.

In this state of uncertainty, the Committee believes it is timely to redraft subdivision (e) of Rule 6 to make it clear.

Paragraph (1) as proposed by the Committee states the general rule that a grand jury, an interpreter, a stenographer, an operator of a recording device, a typist who transcribes recorded testimony, an attorney for the government, or government personnel to whom disclosure is made under paragraph (2)(A)(ii) shall not disclose matters occurring before the grand jury except as otherwise provided in these rules. It also expressly provides that a knowing violation of Rule 6 may be punished as a contempt of court. In addition, it carries forward the current provision that no obligation of secrecy may be imposed on any person except in accordance with this Rule.

Having stated the general rule of nondisclosure, paragraph (2) sets forth exemptions from nondisclosure. Subparagraph (A) of paragraph (2) provides that disclosure otherwise prohibited, other than the grand jury deliberations and the vote of any grand juror, may be made to an attorney for the government for use in the performance of his duty and to such personnel as are deemed necessary by an attorney for the government to assist an attorney for the government in the performance of such attorney's duty to enforce Federal criminal law. In order to facilitate resolution of subsequent claims of improper disclosure, subparagraph (B) further provides that the names of government personnel designated to assist the attorney for the government shall be promptly provided to the district court and such personnel shall not utilize grand jury material for any purpose other than assisting the attorney for the government in the performance of such attorney's duty to enforce Federal criminal law. Although not expressly required by the rule, the Committee contemplates that the names of such personnel will generally be furnished to the court before disclosure is made to them. Subparagraph (C) permits disclosure as directed by a court preliminarily to or in connection with a judicial proceeding or, at the request of the defendant, upon a showing that grounds may exist for dismissing the indictment because of matters occurring before the grand jury. Paragraph (3) carries forward the last sentence of current Rule 6(e) with the technical changes recommended by the Supreme Court.

The Rule as redrafted is designed to accommodate the belief on the one hand that Federal prosecutors should be able, without the time-consuming requirement of prior judicial interposition, to make such disclosures of grand jury information to other government personnel as they deem necessary to facilitate the performance of their duties relating to criminal law enforcement. On the other hand, the Rule seeks to allay the concerns of those who fear that such prosecutorial power will lead to misuse of the grand jury to enforce non-criminal Federal laws by (1) providing a clear prohibition, subject to the penalty of contempt and (2) requiring that a court order under paragraph (C) be obtained to authorize such a disclosure. There is, however, no intent to preclude the use of grand jury-developed evidence for civil law enforcement purposes. On the contrary, there is no reason why such use is improper, assuming that the grand jury was utilized for the legitimate purpose of a criminal investigation. Accordingly, the Committee believes and intends that the basis for a court's refusal to issue an order under paragraph (C) to enable the government to disclose grand jury information in a non-criminal proceeding should be no more restrictive than is the case today under prevailing court decisions. It is contemplated that the judicial hearing in connection with an application for a court order by the government under subparagraph (3)(C)(i) should be *ex parte* so as to preserve, to the maximum extent possible, grand jury secrecy.

Congressional Modification of Proposed Amendment

Section 2(a) of Pub.L. 95–78 provided in part that the amendment proposed by the Supreme Court [in its order of Apr. 26, 1976] to subdivision (e) of rule 6 of the Federal Rules of Criminal Procedure [subd. (e) of this rule] is approved in a modified form.

Effective Date of 1977 Amendment

Amendment of this rule by order of the United States Supreme Court on Apr. 26, 1976, modified and approved by Pub.L. 95–78, effective Oct. 1, 1977, under section 4 of Pub.L. 95–78.

1979 AMENDMENT

Note to Subdivision (e)(1). Proposed subdivision (e)(1) requires that all proceedings, except when the grand jury is deliberating or voting, be recorded. The existing rule does not require that grand jury proceedings be recorded. The provision in rule 6(d) that "a stenographer or operator of a recording device may be present while the grand jury is in session" has been taken to mean that recordation is permissive and not mandatory; see *United States v. Aloisio,* 440 F.2d 705 (7th Cir.1971), collecting the cases. However, the cases rather frequently state that recordation of the proceedings is the better practice; see *United States v. Aloisio,* supra; *United States v. Cramer,* 447 F.2d 210 (2d Cir. 1971); *Schlinsky v. United States,* 379 F.2d 735 (1st Cir.1967); and some cases require the district court, after a demand, to exercise discretion as to whether the proceedings should be recorded. *United States v. Price,* 474 F.2d 1223 (9th Cir.1973); *United States v. Thoresen,* 428 F.2d 654 (9th Cir.1970). Some district courts have adopted a recording requirement. See, e.g. *United States v. Aloisio,* supra; *United States v. Gramolini,* 301 F.Supp. 39 (D.R.I.1969). Recording of grand jury proceedings is currently a requirement in a number of states. See, e.g., Cal.Pen.Code §§ 938–938.3; Iowa Code Ann. § 772.4; Ky.Rev.Stat.Ann. § 28.460; and Ky.R. Crim.P. § 5.16(2).

The assumption underlying the proposal is that the cost of such recording is justified by the contribution made to the improved administration of criminal justice. See *United States v. Gramolini,* supra, noting; "Nor can it be claimed that the cost of recordation is prohibitive; in an electronic age, the cost of recordation must be categorized as miniscule." For a discussion of the success of electronic recording in Alaska, see Reynolds, *Alaska's Ten Years of Electronic Reporting,* 56 A.B.A.J. 1080 (1970).

Among the benefits to be derived from a recordation requirement are the following:

(1) Ensuring that the defendant may impeach a prosecution witness on the basis of his prior inconsistent statements before the grand jury. As noted in the opinion of Oakes, J., in *United States v. Cramer:* "First, since *Dennis v. United States,* 384 U.S. 855, 86 S.Ct. 1840, 16 L.Ed.2d 973 (1966), a defendant has been entitled to examine the grand jury testimony of witnesses against him. On this point, the Court was unanimous, holding that there was 'no justification' for the District of Columbia Court of Appeals' 'relying upon [the] "assumption" ' that 'no inconsistencies would have come to light.' The Court's decision was based on the general

proposition that '[i]n our adversary system for determining guilt or innocence, it is rarely justifiable for the prosecution to have exclusive access to a storehouse of relevant facts.' In the case at bar the prosecution *did* have exclusive access to the grand jury testimony of the witness Sager, by virtue of being present, and the defense had none—to determine whether there were any inconsistencies with, say, his subsequent testimony as to damaging admissions by the defendant and his attorney Richard Thaler. The Government claims, and it is supported by the majority here, that there is no problem since defendants were given the benefit of Sager's subsequent statements including these admissions as Jencks Act materials. But assuming this to be true, it does not cure the basic infirmity that the defense could not know whether the witness testified inconsistently before the grand jury."

(2) Ensuring that the testimony received by the grand jury is trustworthy. In *United States v. Cramer,* Oakes, J., also observed: "The recording of testimony is in a very real sense a circumstantial guaranty of trustworthiness. Without the restraint of being subject to prosecution for perjury, a restraint which is wholly meaningless or nonexistent if the testimony is unrecorded, a witness may make baseless accusations founded on hearsay or false accusations, all resulting in the indictment of a fellow citizen for a crime."

(3) Restraining prosecutorial abuses before the grand jury. As noted in *United States v. Gramolini:* "In no way does recordation inhibit the grand jury's investigation. True, recordation restrains certain prosecutorial practices which might, in its absence be used, but that is no reason not to record. Indeed, a sophisticated prosecutor must acknowledge that there develops between a grand jury and the prosecutor with whom the jury is closeted a rapport—a dependency relationship—which can easily be turned into an instrument of influence on grand jury deliberations. Recordation is the most effective restraint upon such potential abuses."

(4) Supporting the case made by the prosecution at trial. Oakes, J., observed in *United States v. Cramer:* "The benefits of having grand jury testimony recorded do not all inure to the defense. See, e.g., *United States v. DeSisto,* 329 F.2d 929, 934 (2d Cir.), cert. denied, 377 U.S. 979, 84 S.Ct. 1885, 12 L.Ed.2d 747 (1964) (conviction sustained in part on basis of witnesses's prior sworn testimony before grand jury)." Fed.R.Evid. 801(d)(1)(A) excludes from the category of hearsay the prior inconsistent testimony of a witness given before a grand jury. *United States v. Morgan,* 555 F.2d 238 (9th Cir.1977). See also *United States v. Carlson,* 547 F.2d 1346 (8th Cir.1976), admitting under Fed.R.Evid. 804(b)(5) the grand jury testimony of a witness who refused to testify at trial because of threats by the defendant.

Commentators have also supported a recording requirement. 8 Moore, Federal Practice par. 6.02[2][d] (2d ed. 1972) states: "Fairness to the defendant would seem to compel a change in the practice, particularly in view of the 1970 amendment to 18 U.S.C. § 3500 making grand jury testimony of government witnesses available at trial for purposes of impeachment. The requirement of a record may also prove salutary in controlling overreaching or improper examination of witnesses by the prosecutor." Similarly, 1 Wright, Federal Practice and Procedure—Criminal § 103 (1969), states that the present rule "ought to be changed, either by amendment or by judicial construction. The Supreme Court has emphasized the importance to the defense of access to the transcript of the grand jury proceedings [citing *Dennis*]. A defendant cannot have that advantage if the proceedings go unrecorded." American Bar Association, Report of the Special Committee on Federal Rules of Procedure, 52 F.R.D. 87, 94–95 (1971), renews the committee's 1965 recommendation "that all accusatorial grand jury proceedings either be transcribed by a reporter or recorded by electronic means."

Under proposed subdivision (e)(1), if the failure to record is unintentional, the failure to record would not invalidate subsequent judicial proceedings. Under present law, the failure to compel production of grand jury testimony where there is no record is not reversible error. See *Wyatt v. United States,* 388 F.2d 395 (10th Cir.1968).

The provision that the recording or reporter's notes or any transcript prepared therefrom are to remain in the custody or control (as where the notes are in the immediate possession of a contract reporter employed by the Department of Justice) of the attorney for the government is in accord with present practice. It is specifically recognized, however, that the court in a particular case may have reason to order otherwise.

It must be emphasized that the proposed changes in rule 6(e) deal only with the recording requirement, and in no way expand the circumstances in which disclosure of the grand jury proceedings is permitted or required. "Secrecy of grand jury proceedings is not jeopardized by recordation. The making of a record cannot be equated with disclosure of its contents, and disclosure is controlled by other means." *United States v. Price,* 474 F.2d 1223 (9th Cir.1973). Specifically, the proposed changes do not provide for copies of the grand jury minutes to defendants as a matter of right, as is the case in some states. See, e.g., Cal.Pen.Code § 938.1; Iowa Code Ann. § 772.4. The matter of disclosure continues to be governed by other provisions, such as rule 16(a) (recorded statements of the defendant), 18 U.S.C. § 3500 (statements of government witnesses), and the unchanged portions of rule 6(e), and the cases interpreting these provisions. See, e.g., *United States v. Howard,* 433 F.2d 1 (5th Cir.1970), and *Beatrice Foods Co. v. United States,* 312 F.2d 29 (8th Cir.1963), concerning the showing which must be made of improper matters occurring before the grand jury before disclosure is required.

Likewise, the proposed changes in rule 6(e) are not intended to make any change regarding whether a defendant may challenge a grand jury indictment. The Supreme Court has declined to hold that defendants may challenge indictments on the ground that they are not supported by sufficient or competent evidence. *Costello v. United States*, 350 U.S. 359 (1956); *Lawn v. United States*, 355 U.S. 339 (1958); *United States v. Blue*, 384 U.S. 251 (1966). Nor are the changes intended to permit the defendant to challenge the conduct of the attorney for the government before the grand jury absent a preliminary factual showing of serious misconduct.

Note to Subdivision (e)(3)(C). The sentence added to subdivision (e)(3)(C) gives express recognition to the fact that if the court orders disclosure, it may determine the circumstances of the disclosure. For example, if the proceedings are electronically recorded, the court would have discretion in an appropriate case to deny defendant the right to a transcript at government expense. While it takes special skills to make a stenographic record understandable, an electronic recording can be understood by merely listening to it, thus avoiding the expense of transcription.

1983 AMENDMENT

Rule 6(e)(3)(C)

New subdivision (e)(3)(C)(iii) recognizes that it is permissible for the attorney for the government to make disclosure of matters occurring before one grand jury to another federal grand jury. Even absent a specific provision to that effect, the courts have permitted such disclosure in some circumstances. See, e.g., *United States v. Socony–Vacuum Oil Co.*, 310 U.S. 150 (1940); *United States v. Garcia*, 420 F.2d 309 (2d Cir.1970). In this kind of situation, "[s]ecrecy of grand jury materials should be protected almost as well by the safeguards at the second grand jury proceeding, including the oath of the jurors, as by judicial supervision of the disclosure of such materials." *United States v. Malatesta*, 583 F.2d 748 (5th Cir.1978).

Rule 6(e)(3)(D)

In *Douglas Oil Co. v. Petrol Stops Northwest*, 441 U.S. 211 (1979), the Court held on the facts there presented that it was an abuse of discretion for the district judge to order disclosure of grand jury transcripts for use in civil proceedings in another district where that judge had insufficient knowledge of those proceedings to make a determination of the need for disclosure. The Court suggested a "better practice" on those facts, but declared that "procedures to deal with the many variations are best left to the rulemaking procedures established by Congress."

The first sentence of subdivision (e)(3)(D) makes it clear that when disclosure is sought under subdivision (e)(2)(C)(i), the petition is to be filed in the district where the grand jury was convened, whether or not it is the district of the "judicial proceeding" giving rise to the petition. Courts which have addressed the question have generally taken this view, e.g., *Illinois v. Sarbaugh*, 522 F.2d 768 [552 F.2d 768] (7th Cir.1977). As stated in *Douglas Oil*,

> those who seek grand jury transcripts have little choice other than to file a request with the court that supervised the grand jury, as it is the only court with control over the transcripts.

Quite apart from the practical necessity, the policies underlying Rule 6(e) dictate that the grand jury's supervisory court participate in reviewing such requests, as it is in the best position to determine the continuing need for grand jury secrecy. Ideally, the judge who supervised the grand jury should review the request for disclosure, as he will have firsthand knowledge of the grand jury's activities. But even other judges of the district where the grand jury sat may be able to discover facts affecting the need for secrecy more easily than would judges from elsewhere around the country. The records are in the custody of the District Court, and therefore are readily available for references. Moreover, the personnel of that court—particularly those of the United States Attorney's Office who worked with the grand jury—are more likely to be informed about the grand jury proceedings than those in a district that had no prior experience with the subject of the request.

The second sentence requires the petitioner to serve notice of his petition upon several persons who, by the third sentence, are recognized as entitled to appear and be heard on the matter. The notice requirement ensures that all interested parties, if they wish, may make a timely appearance. Absent such notice, these persons, who then might only learn of the order made in response to the motion after it was entered, have had to resort to the cumbersome and inefficient procedure of a motion to vacate the order. *In re Special February 1971 Grand Jury v. Conlisk*, 490 F.2d 894 (7th Cir.1973).

Though some authority is to be found that parties to the judicial proceeding giving rise to the motion are not entitled to intervene, in that "the order to produce was not directed to" them, *United States v. American Oil Co.*, 456 F.2d 1043, (3d Cir.1972), that position was rejected in *Douglas Oil*, where it was noted that such persons have standing "to object to the disclosure order, as release of the transcripts to their civil adversaries could result in substantial injury to them." As noted in *Illinois v. Sarbaugh*, supra, while present rule 6(e) "omits to state whether any one is entitled to object to disclosure," the rule

> seems to contemplate a proceeding of some kind, judicial proceedings are not normally *ex parte*, and persons in the situation of the intervenors [parties to the civil proceeding] are likely to be the only ones to object to an order for disclosure. If they are not

allowed to appear, the advantages of an adversary proceeding are lost.

If the judicial proceeding is a class action, notice to the representative is sufficient.

The amendment also recognizes that the attorney for the government in the district where the grand jury convened also has an interest in the matter and should be allowed to be heard. It may sometimes be the case, as in *Douglas Oil,* that the prosecutor will have relatively little concern for secrecy, at least as compared with certain parties to the civil proceeding. Nonetheless, it is appropriate to recognize that generally the attorney for the government is entitled to be heard so that he may represent what *Douglas Oil* characterizes as "the public interest in secrecy," including the government's legitimate concern about "the possible effect upon the functioning of future grand juries" of unduly liberal disclosure.

The second sentence leaves it to the court to decide whether any other persons should receive notice and be allowed to intervene. This is appropriate, for the necessity for and feasibility of involving others may vary substantially from case to case. In *Douglas Oil,* it was noted that the individual who produced before the grand jury the information now sought has an interest in the matter:

> Fear of future retribution or social stigma may act as powerful deterrents to those who would come forward and aid the grand jury in the performance of its duties. Concern as to the future consequences of frank and full testimony is heightened where the witness is an employee of a company under investigation.

Notice to such persons, however is by no means inevitably necessary, and in some cases the information sought may have reached the grand jury from such a variety of sources that it is not practicable to involve these sources in the disclosure proceeding. Similarly, while *Douglas Oil* notes that rule 6(e) secrecy affords "protection of the innocent accused from disclosure of the accusation made against him before the grand jury," it is appropriate to leave to the court whether that interest requires representation directly by the grand jury target at this time. When deemed necessary to protect the identity of such other persons, it would be a permissible alternative for the government or the court directly to give notice to these other persons, and thus the rule does not foreclose such action.

The notice requirement in the second sentence is inapplicable if the hearing is to be *ex parte.* The legislative history of rule 6(e) states: "It is contemplated that the judicial hearing in connection with an application for a court order by the government, under subparagraph (3)(C)(i) should be *ex parte* so as to preserve, to the maximum extent possible, grand jury secrecy." S.Rep. No. 95–354, 1977 U.S.Code Cong. &

Admin.News p. 532. Although such cases are distinguishable from other cases arising under this subdivision because internal regulations limit further disclosure of information disclosed to the government, the rule provides only that the hearing "may" be *ex parte* when the petitioner is the government. This allows the court to decide that matter based upon the circumstances of the particular case. For example, an *ex parte* proceeding is much less likely to be appropriate if the government acts as petitioner as an accommodation to, e.g., a state agency.

Rule 6(e)(3)(E)

Under the first sentence in new subdivision (e)(3)(E), the petitioner or any intervenor might seek to have the matter transferred to the federal district court where the judicial proceeding giving rise to the petition is pending. Usually it will be the petitioner, who is seeking disclosure, who will desire the transfer, but this is not inevitably the case. An intervenor might seek transfer on the ground that the other court, with greater knowledge of the extent of the need, would be less likely to conclude "that the material * * * is needed to avoid a possible injustice" (the test under *Douglas Oil*). The court may transfer on its own motion, for as noted in *Douglas Oil,* if transfer is the better course of action it should not be foreclosed "merely because the parties have failed to specify the relief to which they are entitled."

It must be emphasized that transfer is proper only if the proceeding giving rise to the petition "is in federal district court in another district." If, for example, the proceeding is located in another district but is at the state level, a situation encompassed within rule 6(e)(3)(C)(i), *In re Special February 1971 Grand Jury v. Conlisk,* supra, there is no occasion to transfer. Ultimate resolution of the matter cannot be placed in the hands of the state court, and in such a case the federal court in that place would lack what *Douglas Oil* recognizes as the benefit to be derived from transfer: "firsthand knowledge of the litigation in which the transcripts allegedly are needed." Formal transfer is unnecessary in intradistrict cases, even when the grand jury court and judicial proceeding court are not in the same division.

As stated in the first sentence, transfer by the court is appropriate "unless it can reasonably obtain sufficient knowledge of the proceeding to determine whether disclosure is proper." (As reflected by the "whether disclosure is proper" language, the amendment makes no effort to define the disclosure standard; that matter is currently governed by *Douglas Oil* and the authorities cited therein, and is best left to elaboration by future case law.) The amendment expresses a preference for having the disclosure issue decided by the grand jury court. Yet, it must be recognized, as stated in *Douglas Oil,* that often this will not be possible because the judges of the court having custody of the grand jury transcripts will have no first-hand knowledge of the litigation in which the transcripts allegedly are needed, and no practical means by which such knowledge can be obtained. In such a case, a judge in the district of the grand jury cannot weigh in an informed manner the need for disclosure against the need for maintaining grand jury secrecy.

The penultimate sentence provides that upon transfer the transferring court shall order transmitted the material sought to be disclosed and also a written evaluation of the need for continuing grand jury secrecy. Because the transferring court is in the best position to assess the interest in continued grand jury secrecy in the particular instance, it is important that the court which will now have to balance that interest against the need for disclosure receive the benefit of the transferring court's assessment. Transmittal of the material sought to be disclosed will not only facilitate timely disclosure if it is thereafter ordered, but will also assist the other court in deciding how great the need for disclosure actually is. For example, with that material at hand the other court will be able to determine if there is any inconsistency between certain grand jury testimony and testimony received in the other judicial proceeding. The rule recognizes, however, that there may be instances in which transfer of everything sought to be disclosed is not feasible. See, e.g., *In re 1975–2 Grand Jury Investigation,* 566 F.2d 1293 (5th Cir.1978) (court ordered transmittal of "an inventory of the grand jury subpoenas, transcripts, and documents," as the materials in question were "exceedingly voluminous, filling no less than 55 large file boxes and one metal filing cabinet").

The last sentence makes it clear that in a case in which the matter is transferred to another court, that court should permit the various interested parties specified in the rule to be heard. Even if those persons were previously heard before the court which ordered the transfer, this will not suffice. The order of transfer did not decide the ultimate issue of "whether a particularized need for disclosure outweighs the interest in continued grand jury secrecy," *Douglas Oil,* supra, which is what now remains to be resolved by the court to which transfer was made. Cf. *In re 1975–2 Grand Jury Investigation,* supra, holding that a transfer order is not appealable because it does not determine the ultimate question of disclosure, and thus "[n]o one has yet been aggrieved and no one will become aggrieved until [the court to which the matter was transferred] acts."

Rule 6(e)(5)

This addition to rule 6 would make it clear that certain hearings which would reveal matters which have previously occurred before a grand jury or are likely to occur before a grand jury with respect to a pending or ongoing investigation must be conducted in camera in whole or in part in order to prevent public disclosure of such secret information. One such hearing is that conducted under subdivision (e)(3)(D), for it will at least sometimes be necessary to consider and assess some of the "matters occurring before the grand jury" in order to decide the disclosure issue. Two other kinds of hearings at which information about a particular grand jury investigation might need to be discussed are those at which the question is whether to grant a grand jury witness immunity or whether to order a grand jury witness to comply fully with the terms of a subpoena directed to him.

A recent GAO study established that there is considerable variety in the practice as to whether such hearings are closed or open, and that open hearings often seriously jeopardize grand jury secrecy:

> For judges to decide these matters, the witness' relationship to the case under investigation must be discussed. Accordingly, the identities of witnesses and targets, the nature of expected testimony, and the extent to which the witness is cooperating are often revealed during preindictment proceedings. Because the matters discussed can compromise the purposes of grand jury secrecy, some judges close the preindictment proceedings to the public and the press; others do not. When the proceeding is open, information that may otherwise be kept secret under rule 6(e) becomes available to the public and the press....

> Open preindictment proceedings are a major source of information which can compromise the purposes of grand jury secrecy. In 25 cases we were able to establish links between open proceedings and later newspaper articles containing information about the identities of witnesses and targets and the nature of grand jury investigations.

Comptroller General, More Guidance and Supervision Needed over Federal Grand Jury Proceedings 8–9 (Oct. 16, 1980).

The provisions of rule 6(e)(5) do not violate any constitutional right of the public or media to attend such pretrial hearings. There is no Sixth Amendment right in the public to attend pretrial proceedings, *Gannett Co., Inc. v. DePasquale,* 443 U.S. 368 (1979), and *Richmond Newspapers, Inc. v. Virginia,* 448 U.S. 555, (1980), only recognizes a First Amendment "right to attend criminal trials." *Richmond Newspapers* was based largely upon the "unbroken, uncontradicted history" of public trials, while in *Gannett* it was noted "there exists no persuasive evidence that at common law members of the public had any right to attend pretrial proceedings." Moreover, even assuming some public right to attend certain pretrial proceedings, see *United States v. Criden,* 675 F.2d 550 (3d Cir.1982), that right is not absolute; it must give way, as stated in *Richmond Newspapers,* to "an overriding interest" in a particular case in favor of a closed proceeding. By permitting closure only "to the extent necessary to prevent disclosure of matters occurring before a grand jury," rule 6(e)(5) recognizes the longstanding interest in the secrecy of grand jury proceedings. Counsel or others allowed to be present at the closed hearing may be put under a protective order by the court.

Subdivision (e)(5) is expressly made "subject to any right to an open hearing in contempt proceedings." This will accommodate any First Amendment right which might be deemed applicable in that context because of the proceedings' similarities to a criminal trial, cf. *United States v. Criden,* supra, and also any Fifth or Sixth Amendment right of the contemnor. The latter right clearly exists as to a criminal contempt proceeding, *In re Oliver,* 333 U.S. 257 (1948), and some authority is to be found recognizing such a right in civil contempt proceedings as well. *In re Rosahn,* 671 F.2d 690 (2d Cir.1982). This right of the contemnor must be requested by him and, in any event, does not require that the entire contempt proceedings, including recitation of the substance of the questions he has refused to answer, be public. *Levine v. United States,* 362 U.S. 610 (1960).

Rule 6(e)(6)

Subdivision (e)(6) provides that records, orders and subpoenas relating to grand jury proceedings shall be kept under seal to the extent and for so long as is necessary to prevent disclosure of matters occurring before a grand jury. By permitting such documents as grand jury subpoenas and immunity orders to be kept under seal, this provision addresses a serious problem of grand jury secrecy and expressly authorizes a procedure now in use in many but not all districts. As reported in Comptroller General, More Guidance and Supervision Needed over Federal Grand Jury Proceedings 10, 14 (Oct. 16, 1980):

> In 262 cases, documents presented at open preindictment proceedings and filed in public files revealed details of grand jury investigations. These documents are, of course, available to anyone who wants them, including targets of investigations. [There are] two documents commonly found in public files which usually reveal the identities of witnesses and targets. The first document is a Department of Justice authorization to a U.S. attorney to apply to the court for a grant of immunity for a witness. The second document is the court's order granting the witness immunity from prosecution and compelling him to testify and produce requested information. * * *

Subpoenas are the fundamental documents used during a grand jury's investigation because through subpoenas, grand juries can require witnesses to testify and produce documentary evidence for their consideration. Subpoenas can identify witnesses, potential targets, and the nature of an investigation. Rule 6(e) does not provide specific guidance on whether a grand jury's subpoena should be kept secret. Additionally, case law has not consistently stated whether the subpoenas are protected by rule 6(e).

District courts still have different opinions about whether grand jury subpoenas should be kept secret. Out of 40 Federal District Courts we contacted, 36 consider these documents to be secret. However, 4 districts do make them available to the public.

Rule 6(g)

In its present form, subdivision 6(g) permits a grand jury to serve no more than 18 months after its members have been sworn, and absolutely no exceptions are permitted. (By comparison, under the Organized Crime Control Act of 1970, Title I, 18 U.S.C. §§ 3331–3334, special grand juries may be extended beyond their basic terms of 18 months if their business has not been completed.) The purpose of the amendment is to permit some degree of flexibility as to the discharge of grand juries where the public interest would be served by an extension.

As noted in *United States v. Fein,* 504 F.2d 1170 (2d Cir.1974), upholding the dismissal of an indictment returned 9 days after the expiration of the 18–month period but during an attempted extension, under the present inflexible rule "it may well be that criminal proceedings which would be in the public interest will be frustrated and that those who might be found guilty will escape trial and conviction." The present inflexible rule can produce several undesirable consequences, especially when complex fraud, organized crime, tax or antitrust cases are under investigation: (i) wastage of a significant amount of time and resources by the necessity of presenting the case once again to a successor grand jury simply because the matter could not be concluded before the term of the first grand jury expired; (ii) precipitous action to conclude the investigation before the expiration date of the grand jury; and (iii) potential defendants may be kept under investigation for a longer time because of the necessity to present the matter again to another grand jury.

The amendment to subdivision 6(g) permits extension of a regular grand jury only "upon a determination that such extension is in the public interest." This permits some flexibility, but reflects the fact that extension of regular grand juries beyond 18 months is to be the exception and not the norm. The intention of the amendment is to make it possible for a grand jury to have sufficient extra time to wind up an investigation when, for example, such extension becomes necessary because of the unusual nature of the case or unforeseen developments.

Because terms of court have been abolished, 28 U.S.C. § 138, the second sentence of subdivision 6(g) has been deleted.

1985 AMENDMENT

Rule 6(e)(3)(A)(ii)

Rule 6(e)(3)(A)(ii) currently provides that an attorney for the government may disclose grand jury information, without prior judicial approval, to other government personnel whose assistance the attorney for the government deems necessary in conducting the grand jury investigation. Courts have differed over whether employees of state and local governments are "government personnel" within the meaning of the rule. Compare *In re Miami Federal Grand Jury No. 79–9*, 478 F.Supp. 490 (S.D.Fla.1979), and *In re Grand Jury Proceedings*, 445 F.Supp. 349 (D.R.I.1978) (state and local personnel not included); with *In re 1979 Grand Jury Proceedings*, 479 F.Supp. 93 (E.D.N.Y.1979) (state and local personnel included). The amendment clarifies the rule to include state and local personnel.

It is clearly desirable that federal and state authorities cooperate, as they often do, in organized crime and racketeering investigations, in public corruption and major fraud cases, and in various other situations where federal and state criminal jurisdictions overlap. Because of such cooperation, government attorneys in complex grand jury investigations frequently find it necessary to enlist the help of a team of government agents. While the agents are usually federal personnel, it is not uncommon in certain types of investigations that federal prosecutors wish to obtain the assistance of state law enforcement personnel, which could be uniquely beneficial. The amendment permits disclosure to those personnel in the circumstances stated.

It must be emphasized that the disclosure permitted is limited. The disclosure under this subdivision is permissible only in connection with the attorney for the government's "duty to enforce federal criminal law" and only to those personnel "deemed necessary ... to assist" in the performance of that duty. Under subdivision (e)(3)(B), the material disclosed may not be used for any other purpose, and the names of persons to whom disclosure is made must be promptly provided to the court.

Rule 6(e)(3)(B)

The amendment to subdivision (e)(3)(B) imposes upon the attorney for the government the responsibility to certify to the district court that he has advised those persons to whom disclosure was made under subdivision (e)(3)(A)(ii) of their obligation of secrecy under Rule 6. Especially with the amendment of subdivision (e)(3)(A)(ii) to include personnel of a state or subdivision of a state, who otherwise would likely be unaware of this obligation of secrecy, the giving of such advice is an important step in ensuring against inadvertent breach of grand jury secrecy. But because not all federal government personnel will otherwise know of this obligation, the giving of the advice and certification thereof is required as to *all* persons receiving disclosure under subdivision (e)(3)(A)(ii).

Rule 6(e)(3)(C)

It sometimes happens that during a federal grand jury investigation evidence will be developed tending to show a violation of state law. When this occurs, it is very frequently the case that this evidence cannot be communicated to the appropriate state officials for further investigation. For one thing, any state officials who might seek this information must show particularized need. *Illinois v. Abbott & Associates*, 103 S.Ct. 1356 (1983). For another, and more significant, it is often the case that the information relates to a state crime outside the context of any pending or even contemplated state judicial proceeding, so that the "preliminarily to or in connection with a judicial proceeding" requirement of subdivision (e)(3)(C)(i) cannot be met.

This inability lawfully to disclose evidence of a state criminal violation—evidence legitimately obtained by the grand jury—constitutes an unreasonable barrier to the effective enforcement of our two-tiered system of criminal laws. It would be removed by new subdivision (e)(3)(C)(iv), which would allow a court to permit disclosure to a state or local official for the purpose of enforcing state law when an attorney for the government so requests and makes the requisite showing.

The federal court has been given control over any disclosure which is authorized, for subdivision (e)(3)(C) presently states that "the disclosure shall be made in such manner, at such time, and under such conditions as the court may direct." The Committee is advised that it will be the policy of the Department of Justice under this amendment to seek such disclosure only upon approval of the Assistant Attorney General in charge of the Criminal Division. There is no intention, by virtue of this amendment, to have federal grand juries act as an arm of the state.

1987 AMENDMENT

New subdivision (a)(2) gives express recognition to a practice now followed in some district courts, namely, that of designating alternate grand jurors at the time the grand jury is selected. (A person so designated does not attend court and is not paid the jury attendance fees and expenses authorized by 28 U.S.C. § 1871 unless subsequently impanelled pursuant to Rule 6(g).) Because such designation may be a more efficient procedure than election of additional grand jurors later as need arises under subdivision (g), the amendment makes it clear that it is a permissible step in the grand jury selection process.

This amendment is not intended to work any change in subdivision (g). In particular, the fact that one or more alternate jurors either have or have not been previously designated does not limit the district court's discretion under subdivision (g) to decide whether, if a juror is excused temporarily or permanently, another person should replace him to assure the continuity of the grand jury and its ability to obtain a quorum in order to complete its business.

The amendments are technical. No substantive change is intended.

Editorial Notes

Codification. Pub.L. 98–473, Title II, §§ 215(f), 235, Oct. 12, 1984, 98 Stat. 2016, 2031, as amended by Pub.L. 99–217, § 4, Dec. 26, 1985, 99 Stat. 1728, provided that, effective Nov. 1, 1987, subd. (e)(3)(C) of this rule is amended by adding the following subdivision:

"(iv) when permitted by a court at the request of an attorney for the government, upon a showing that such matters may disclose a violation of state criminal law, to an appropriate official of a state or subdivision of a state for the purpose of enforcing such law.".

Such amendment duplicates amendment made by Supreme Court of the United States order dated Apr. 29, 1985, eff. Aug. 1, 1985.

Effective Date and Savings Provisions of 1984 Amendment. Amendment by Pub.L. 98–473 effective on the first day of first calendar month beginning thirty six months after Oct. 12, 1984, applicable only to offenses committed after taking effect of sections 211 to 239 of Pub.L. 98–473, and except as otherwise provided for therein, see section 235 of Pub.L. 98–473, as amended, set out as a note under section 3551 of Title 18, Crimes and Criminal Procedure.

Rule 7. The Indictment and the Information

(a) Use of Indictment or Information. An offense which may be punished by death shall be prosecuted by indictment. An offense which may be punished by imprisonment for a term exceeding one year or at hard labor shall be prosecuted by indictment or, if indictment is waived, it may be prosecuted by information. Any other offense may be prosecuted by indictment or by information. An information may be filed without leave of court.

(b) Waiver of Indictment. An offense which may be punished by imprisonment for a term exceeding one year or at hard labor may be prosecuted by information if the defendant, after having been advised of the nature of the charge and of the rights of the defendant, waives in open court prosecution by indictment.

(c) Nature and Contents.

(1) In General. The indictment or the information shall be a plain, concise and definite written statement of the essential facts constituting the offense charged. It shall be signed by the attorney for the government. It need not contain a formal commencement, a formal conclusion or any other matter not necessary to such statement. Allegations made in one count may be incorporated by reference in another count. It may be alleged in a single count that the means by which the defendant committed the offense are unknown or that the defendant committed it by one or more specified means. The indictment or information shall state for each count the official or customary citation of the statute, rule, regulation or other provision of law which the defendant is alleged therein to have violated.

(2) Criminal Forfeiture. No judgment of forfeiture may be entered in a criminal proceeding unless the indictment or the information shall allege the extent of the interest or property subject to forfeiture.

(3) Harmless Error. Error in the citation or its omission shall not be ground for dismissal of the indictment or information or for reversal of a conviction if the error or omission did not mislead the defendant to the defendant's prejudice.

(d) Surplusage. The court on motion of the defendant may strike surplusage from the indictment or information.

(e) Amendment of Information. The court may permit an information to be amended at any time before verdict or finding if no additional or different offense is charged and if substantial rights of the defendant are not prejudiced.

(f) Bill of Particulars. The court may direct the filing of a bill of particulars. A motion for a bill of particulars may be made before arraignment or within ten days after arraignment or at such later time as the court may permit. A bill of particulars may be amended at any time subject to such conditions as justice requires.

(As amended Feb. 28, 1966, eff. July 1, 1966; Apr. 24, 1972, eff. Oct. 1, 1972; Apr. 30, 1979, eff. Aug. 1, 1979; Mar. 9, 1987, eff. Aug. 1, 1987.)

NOTES OF ADVISORY COMMITTEE ON RULES

Note to Subdivision (a). 1. This rule gives effect to the following provision of the Fifth Amendment to the Constitution of the United States: "No person shall be held to answer for a capital, or otherwise infamous crime, unless on a presentment or indictment of a Grand Jury * * *". An infamous crime has been defined as a crime punishable by death or by imprisonment in a penitentiary or at hard labor, *Ex parte Wilson*, 114 U.S. 417, 427, 5 S.Ct. 935, 29 L.Ed. 89;

United States v. Moreland, 258 U.S. 433, 42 S.Ct. 368, 66 L.Ed. 700, 24 A.L.R. 992. Any sentence of imprisonment for a term of over one year may be served in a penitentiary, if so directed by the Attorney General, 18 U.S.C. former § 753f (now §§ 4082, 4083) (Commitment of persons by any court of the United States and the juvenile court of the District of Columbia; place of confinement; transfers). Consequently any offense punishable by imprisonment for a term of over one year is an infamous crime.

2. Petty offenses and misdemeanors for which no infamous punishment is prescribed may now be prosecuted by information, 18 U.S.C. former § 541 (now § 1) (Felonies and misdemeanors); *Duke v. United States,* 301 U.S. 492, 57 S.Ct. 835, 81 L.Ed. 1243.

3. For a discussion of the provision for waiver of indictment, see Note to Rule 7(b), infra.

4. Presentment is not included as an additional type of formal accusation, since presentments as a method of instituting prosecutions are obsolete, at least as concerns the Federal courts.

Note to Subdivision (b). 1. Opportunity to waive indictment and to consent to prosecution by information will be a substantial aid to defendants, especially those who, because of inability to give bail, are incarcerated pending action of the grand jury, but desire to plead guilty. This rule is particularly important in those districts in which considerable intervals occur between sessions of the grand jury. In many districts where the grand jury meets infrequently a defendant unable to give bail and desiring to plead guilty is compelled to spend many days, and sometimes many weeks, and even months, in jail before he can begin the service of his sentence, whatever it may be, awaiting the action of a grand jury. Homer Cummings, 29 A.B.A.Jour. 654–655; Vanderbilt, 29 A.B.A.Jour. 376, 377; Robinson, 27 Jour. of the Am.Judicature Soc. 38, 45; Medalie, 4 Lawyers Guild R. (3)1, 3. The rule contains safeguards against improvident waivers.

The Judicial Conference of Senior Circuit Judges, in September 1941, recommended that "existing law or established procedure be so changed, that a defendant may waive indictment and plead guilty to an information filed by a United States attorney in all cases except capital felonies." Report of the Judicial Conference of Senior Circuit Judges (1941) 13. In September 1942 the Judicial Conference recommended that provision be made "for waiver of indictment and jury trial, so that persons accused of crime may not be held in jail needlessly pending trial." Id. (1942) 8.

Attorneys General of the United States have from time to time recommended legislation to permit defendants to waive indictment and to consent to prosecution by information. See Annual Report of the Attorney General of the United States (Mitchell) (1931) 3; Id. (Mitchell) (1932) 6; Id. (Cummings) (1933) 1, (1936) 2, (1937) 11, (1938) 9; Id. (Murphy) (1939) 7.

The Federal Juvenile Delinquency Act, 18 U.S.C. former §§ 921–929 (now §§ 5031, 5037), now permits a juvenile charged with an offense not punishable by death or life imprisonment to consent to prosecution by information on a charge of juvenile delinquency, 18 U.S.C. former § 922 (now §§ 5032, 5033).

2. On the constitutionality of this rule, see *United States v. Gill,* 55 F.2d 399, D.N.M., holding that the constitutional guaranty of indictment by grand jury may be waived by defendant. It has also been held that other constitutional guaranties may be waived by the defendant, e.g., *Patton v. United States,* 281 U.S. 276, 50 S.Ct. 253, 74 L.Ed. 854, 70 A.L.R. 263 (trial by jury); *Johnson v. Zerbst,* 304 U.S. 458, 465, 58 S.Ct. 1019, 82 L.Ed. 1461, 146 A.L.R. 357 (right of counsel); *Trono v. United States,* 199 U.S. 521, 534, 26 S.Ct. 121, 50 L.Ed. 292, 4 Ann.Cas. 773 (protection against double jeopardy); *United States v. Murdock,* 284 U.S. 141, 148, 52 S.Ct. 63, 76 L.Ed. 210, 82 A.L.R. 1376 (privilege against self-incrimination); *Diaz v. United States,* 223 U.S. 442, 450, 32 S.Ct. 250, 56 L.Ed. 500, Ann.Cas.1913C, 1138 (right of confrontation).

Note to Subdivision (c). 1. This rule introduces a simple form of indictment, illustrated by Forms 1 to 11 in the Appendix of Forms. Cf. Rule 8(a) of the Federal Rules of Civil Procedure, 28 U.S.C. following § 2072. For discussion of the effect of this rule and a comparison between the present form of indictment and the simple form introduced by this rule, see Vanderbilt, 29 A.B.A.Jour. 376, 377; Homer Cummings, 29 A.B.A.Jour. 654, 655; Holtzoff, 3 F.R.D. 445, 448–449; Holtzoff, 12 Geo. Washington L.R. 119, 123–126; Medalie, 4 Lawyers Guild R. (3)1, 3.

2. The provision contained in the fifth sentence that it may be alleged in a single count that the means by which the defendant committed the offense are unknown, or that he committed it by one or more specified means, is intended to eliminate the use of multiple counts for the purpose of alleging the commission of the offense by different means or in different ways. Cf. Federal Rules of Civil Procedure, Rule 8(e)(2), 28 U.S.C., Appendix.

3. The law at present regards citations to statutes or regulations as not a part of the indictment. A conviction may be sustained on the basis of a statute or regulation other than that cited. *Williams v. United States,* 168 U.S. 382, 389, 18 S.Ct. 92, 42 L.Ed. 509; *United States v. Hutcheson,* 312 U.S. 219, 229, 61 S.Ct. 463, 85 L.Ed. 788. The provision of the rule, in view of the many statutes and regulations, is for the benefit of the defendant and is not intended to cause a dismissal of the indictment, but simply to provide a means by which he can be properly informed without danger to the prosecution.

Note to Subdivision (d). This rule introduces a means of protecting the defendant against immaterial or irrelevant allegations in an indictment or information, which may, however, be prejudicial. The authority of the court to strike such surplusage is to be limited to doing so on defendant's motion, in the light of the rule that the guaranty of indictment by a grand jury implies that an indictment may not be amended, *Ex parte Bain*, 121 U.S. 1, 7 S.Ct. 781, 30 L.Ed. 849. By making such a motion, the defendant would, however, waive his rights in this respect.

Note to Subdivision (e). This rule continues the existing law that, unlike an indictment, an information may be amended, *Muncy v. United States*, 289 Fed. 780, C.C.A. 4th.

Note to Subdivision (f). This rule is substantially a restatement of existing law on bills of particulars.

1966 AMENDMENT

The amendment to the first sentence eliminating the requirement of a showing of cause is designed to encourage a more liberal attitude by the courts toward bills of particulars without taking away the discretion which courts must have in dealing with such motions in individual cases. For an illustration of wise use of this discretion see the opinion by Justice Whittaker written when he was a district judge in *United States v. Smith*, 16 F.R.D. 372 (W.D.Mo.1954).

The amendment to the second sentence gives discretion to the court to permit late filing of motions for bills of particulars in meritorious cases. Use of late motions for the purpose of delaying trial should not, of course, be permitted. The courts have not been agreed as to their power to accept late motions in the absence of a local rule or a previous order. See *United States v. Miller*, 217 F.Supp. 760 (E.D.Pa.1963); *United States v. Taylor*, 25 F.R.D. 225 (E.D.N.Y.1960); *United States v. Sterling*, 122 F.Supp. 81 (E.D.Pa.1954) (all taking a limited view of the power of the court). But cf. *United States v. Brown*, 179 F.Supp. 893 (E.D.N.Y.1959) (exercising discretion to permit an out of time motion).

1972 AMENDMENT

Subdivision (c)(2) is new. It is intended to provide procedural implementation of the recently enacted criminal forfeiture provision of the Organized Crime Control Act of 1970, Title IX, § 1963, and the Comprehensive Drug Abuse Prevention and Control Act of 1970, Title II, § 408(a)(2).

The Congress viewed the provisions of the Organized Crime Control Act of 1970 as reestablishing a limited common law criminal forfeiture. S.Rep. No. 91–617, 91st Cong., 1st Sess. 79–80 (1969). The legislative history of the Comprehensive Drug Abuse Prevention and Control Act of 1970 indicates a congressional purpose to have similar procedures apply to the forfeiture of prof-

its or interests under that act. H.Rep. No. 91–1444 (part I), 91st Cong., 2d Sess. 81–85 (1970).

Under the common law, in a criminal forfeiture proceeding the defendant was apparently entitled to notice, trial, and a special jury finding on the factual issues surrounding the declaration of forfeiture which followed his criminal conviction. Subdivision (c)(2) provides for notice. Changes in rules 31 and 32 provide for a special jury finding and for a judgment authorizing the Attorney General to seize the interest or property forfeited.

1979 AMENDMENT

The amendment to rule 7(c)(2) is intended to clarify its meaning. Subdivision (c)(2) was added in 1972, and, as noted in the Advisory Committee Note thereto, was "intended to provide procedural implementation of the recently enacted criminal forfeiture provision of the Organized Crime Control Act of 1970, Title IX, § 1963, and the Comprehensive Drug Abuse Prevention and Control Act of 1970, Title II, § 408(a)(2)." These provisions reestablished a limited common law criminal forfeiture, necessitating the addition of subdivision (c)(2) and corresponding changes in rules 31 and 32, for at common law the defendant in a criminal forfeiture proceeding was entitled to notice, trial, and a special jury finding on the factual issues surrounding the declaration of forfeiture which followed his criminal conviction.

Although there is some doubt as to what forfeitures should be characterized as "punitive" rather than "remedial," see Note, 62 Cornell L.Rev. 768 (1977), subdivision (c)(2) is intended to apply to those forfeitures which are criminal in the sense that they result from a special verdict under rule 31(e) and a judgment under rule 32(b)(2), and not to those resulting from a separate in rem proceeding. Because some confusion in this regard has resulted from the present wording of subdivision (c)(2), *United States v. Hall*, 521 F.2d 406 (9th Cir.1975), a clarifying amendment is in order.

1987 AMENDMENT

The amendments are technical. No substantive change is intended.

Rule 8. Joinder of Offenses and of Defendants

(a) Joinder of Offenses. Two or more offenses may be charged in the same indictment or information in a separate count for each offense if the offenses charged, whether felonies or misdemeanors or both, are of the same or similar character or are based on the same act or transaction or on two or more acts or transactions connected together or constituting parts of a common scheme or plan.

(b) Joinder of Defendants. Two or more defendants may be charged in the same indictment or information if they are alleged to have participated in the same act or transaction or in the same series of acts or transactions constituting an offense or offenses. Such defendants may be charged in one or more counts together or separately and all of the defendants need not be charged in each count.

NOTES OF ADVISORY COMMITTEE ON RULES

Note to Subdivision (a). This rule is substantially a restatement of existing law, 18 U.S.C. former § 557 (Indictments and presentments; joinder of charges).

Note to Subdivision (b). The first sentence of the rule is substantially a restatement of existing law, 9 Edmunds, Cyclopedia of Federal Procedure, 2d Ed., 4116. The second sentence formulates a practice now approved in some circuits. *Caringella v. United States,* 78 F.2d 563, 567, C.C.A.7th.

Rule 9. Warrant or Summons Upon Indictment or Information

(a) Issuance. Upon the request of the attorney for the government the court shall issue a warrant for each defendant named in an information supported by a showing of probable cause under oath as is required by Rule 4(a), or in an indictment. Upon the request of the attorney for the government a summons instead of a warrant shall issue. If no request is made, the court may issue either a warrant or a summons in its discretion. More than one warrant or summons may issue for the same defendant. The clerk shall deliver the warrant or summons to the marshal or other person authorized by law to execute or serve it. If a defendant fails to appear in response to the summons, a warrant shall issue. When a defendant arrested with a warrant or given a summons appears initially before a magistrate, the magistrate shall proceed in accordance with the applicable subdivisions of Rule 5.

(b) Form.

(1) Warrant. The form of the warrant shall be as provided in Rule 4(c)(1) except that it shall be signed by the clerk, it shall describe the offense charged in the indictment or information and it shall command that the defendant be arrested and brought before the nearest available magistrate. The amount of bail may be fixed by the court and endorsed on the warrant.

(2) Summons. The summons shall be in the same form as the warrant except that it shall summon the defendant to appear before a magistrate at a stated time and place.

(c) Execution or Service; and Return.

(1) Execution or Service. The warrant shall be executed or the summons served as provided in Rule 4(d)(1), (2) and (3). A summons to a corporation shall be served by delivering a copy to an officer or to a managing or general agent or to any other agent authorized by appointment or by law to receive service of process and, if the agent is one authorized by statute to receive service and the statute so requires, by also mailing a copy to the corporation's last known address within the district or at its principal place of business elsewhere in the United States. The officer executing the warrant shall bring the arrested person without unnecessary delay before the nearest available federal magistrate or, in the event that a federal magistrate is not reasonably available, before a state or local judicial officer authorized by 18 U.S.C. § 3041.

(2) Return. The officer executing a warrant shall make return thereof to the magistrate or other officer before whom the defendant is brought. At the request of the attorney for the government any unexecuted warrant shall be returned and cancelled. On or before the return day the person to whom a summons was delivered for service shall make return thereof. At the request of the attorney for the government made at any time while the indictment or information is pending, a warrant returned unexecuted and not cancelled or a summons returned unserved or a duplicate thereof may be delivered by the clerk to the marshal or other authorized person for execution or service.

[**(d) Remand to United States Magistrate for Trial of Minor Offenses]** (Abrogated Apr. 28, 1982, eff. Aug. 1, 1982).

(As amended Apr. 24, 1972, eff. Oct. 1, 1972; Apr. 22, 1974, eff. Dec. 1, 1975; July 31, 1975, Pub.L. 94–64, § 3(4), 89 Stat. 370; Dec. 12, 1975, Pub.L. 94–149, § 5, 89 Stat. 806; Apr. 30, 1979, eff. Aug. 1, 1979; Apr. 28, 1982, eff. Aug. 1, 1982.)

NOTES OF ADVISORY COMMITTEE ON RULES

1. See Note to Rule 4, supra.

2. The provision of Rule 9(a) that a warrant may be issued on the basis of an information only if the latter is supported by oath is necessitated by the Fourth Amendment to the Constitution of the United States. See *Albrecht v. United States,* 273 U.S. 1, 5, 47 S.Ct. 250, 71 L.Ed. 505.

3. The provision of Rule 9(b)(1) that the amount of bail may be fixed by the court and endorsed on the warrant states a practice now prevailing in many districts and is intended to facilitate the giving of bail by the defendant and eliminate delays between the arrest and the giving of bail, which might ensure if bail cannot be fixed until after arrest.

1972 AMENDMENT

Subdivision (b) is amended to make clear that the person arrested shall be brought before a United States magistrate if the information or indictment charges a "minor offense" triable by the United States magistrate.

Subdivision (c) is amended to reflect the office of United States magistrate.

Subdivision (d) is new. It provides for a remand to the United States magistrate of cases in which the person is charged with a "minor offense." The magistrate can then proceed in accordance with rule 5 to try the case if the right to trial before a judge of the district court is waived.

1974 AMENDMENT

Rule 9 is revised to give high priority to the issuance of a summons unless a "valid reason" is given for the issuance of an arrest warrant. See a comparable provision in rule 4.

Under the rule, a summons will issue by the clerk unless the attorney for the government presents a valid reason for the issuance of an arrest warrant. Under the old rule, it has been argued that the court must issue an arrest warrant if one is desired by the attorney for the government. See authorities listed in Frankel, Bench Warrants Upon the Prosecutor's Demand: A View From the Bench, 71 Colum.L.Rev. 403, 410 n. 25 (1971). For an expression of the view that this is undesirable policy, see Frankel, *supra,* pp. 410–415.

A summons may issue if there is an information supported by oath. The indictment itself is sufficient to establish the existence of probable cause. See C. Wright, Federal Practice and Procedure: Criminal § 151 (1969); 8 J. Moore, Federal Practice ¶ 9.02[2] at p. 9–4 (2d ed.) Cipes (1969); *Giordenello v. United States,* 357 U.S. 480, 78 S.Ct. 1245, 2 L.Ed.2d 1503 (1958). This is not necessarily true in the case of an information. See C. Wright, *supra,* § 151; 8 J. Moore, *supra,* ¶ 9.02. If the government requests a warrant rather than a summons, good practice would obviously require the judge to satisfy himself that there is probable cause.

This may appear from the information or from an affidavit filed with the information. Also a defendant can, at a proper time, challenge an information issued without probable cause.

NOTES OF COMMITTEE ON THE JUDICIARY, HOUSE REPORT NO. 94–247

A. Amendments Proposed by the Supreme Court. Rule 9 of the Federal Rules of Criminal Procedure is closely related to Rule 4. Rule 9 deals with arrest procedures after an information has been filed or an indictment returned. The present rule gives the prosecutor the authority to decide whether a summons or a warrant shall issue.

The Supreme Court's amendments to Rule 9 parallel its amendments to Rule 4. The basic change made in Rule 4 is also made in Rule 9.

B. Committee Action. For the reasons set forth above in connection with Rule 4, the Committee endorses and accepts the basic change in Rule 9. The Committee made changes in Rule 9 similar to the changes it made in Rule 4.

1975 AMENDMENT

Subd. (b)(1). Pub.L. 94–149 substituted reference to "rule 4(c)(1)" for "rule 4(b)(1)".

Subd. (c)(1). Pub.L. 94–149 substituted reference to "rule 4(d)(1), (2), and (3)" for "rule 4(c)(1), (2), and (3)".

1979 AMENDMENT

Subdivision (a) is amended to make explicit the fact that a warrant may issue upon the basis of an information only if the information or an affidavit filed with the information shows probable cause for the arrest. This has generally been assumed to be the state of the law even though not specifically set out in rule 9; see C. Wright, Federal Practice and Procedure: Criminal § 151 (1969); 8 J. Moore, Federal Practice par. 9.02[2] (2d ed. 1976).

In *Gerstein v. Pugh,* 420 U.S. 103 (1975), the Supreme Court rejected the contention "that the prosecutor's decision to file an information is itself a determination of probable cause that furnishes sufficient reason to detain a defendant pending trial," commenting:

Although a conscientious decision that the evidence warrants prosecution affords a measure of protection against unfounded detention, we do not think prosecutorial judgment standing alone meets the requirements of the Fourth Amendment. Indeed, we think the Court's previous decisions compel disapproval of [such] procedure. In *Albrecht v. United States,* 273 U.S. 1, 5, 47 S.Ct. 250, 251, 71 L.Ed. 505 (1927), the Court held that an arrest warrant issued solely upon a United States Attorney's information was invalid because the accompanying affidavits were defective. Although the Court's opinion did not explicitly state that the prosecutor's official oath could not furnish probable cause, that conclusion was implicit in the judgment that the arrest was illegal under the Fourth Amendment.

No change is made in the rule with respect to warrants issuing upon indictments. In *Gerstein*, the Court indicated it was not disturbing the prior rule that "an indictment, 'fair upon its face,' and returned by a 'properly constituted grand jury' conclusively determines the existence of probable cause and requires issuance of an arrest warrant without further inquiry." See *Ex parte United States*, 287 U.S. 241, 250 (1932).

The provision to the effect that a summons shall issue "by direction of the court" has been eliminated because it conflicts with the first sentence of the rule, which states that a warrant "shall" issue when requested by the attorney for the government, if properly supported. However, an addition has been made providing that if the attorney for the government does not make a request for either a warrant or summons, then the court may in its discretion issue either one. Other stylistic changes ensure greater consistency with comparable provisions in rule 4.

1982 AMENDMENT

The amendment of subdivision (a), by reference to Rule 5, clarifies what is to be done once the defendant is brought before the magistrate. This means, among other things, that no preliminary hearing is to be held in a Rule 9 case, as Rule 5(c) provides that no such hearing is to be had "if the defendant is indicted or if an information against the defendant is filed."

The amendment of subdivision (b) conforms Rule 9 to the comparable provisions in Rule 4(c)(1) and (2).

The amendment of subdivision (c) conforms Rule 9 to the comparable provisions in Rules 4(d)(4) and 5(a) concerning return of the warrant.

This subdivision (d), incorrect in its present form in light of the recent amendment of 18 U.S.C. § 3401(a), has been abrogated as unnecessary in light of the change to subdivision (a).

IV. ARRAIGNMENT AND PREPARATION FOR TRIAL

Rule 10. Arraignment

Arraignment shall be conducted in open court and shall consist of reading the indictment or information to the defendant or stating to the defendant the substance of the charge and calling on the defendant to plead thereto. The defendant shall be given a copy of the indictment or information before being called upon to plead. (As amended Mar. 9, 1987, eff. Aug. 1, 1987.)

NOTES OF ADVISORY COMMITTEE ON RULES

1. The first sentence states the prevailing practice.
2. The requirement that the defendant shall be given a copy of the indictment or information before he is called upon to plead, contained in the second sentence, is new.
3. Failure to comply with arraignment requirements has been held not to be jurisdictional, but a mere technical irregularity not warranting a reversal of a conviction, if not raised before trial, *Garland v. State of Washington*, 232 U.S. 642, 34 S.Ct. 456, 58 L.Ed. 772.

1987 AMENDMENT

The amendments are technical. No substantive change is intended.

Rule 11. Pleas

(a) Alternatives.

(1) In General. A defendant may plead not guilty, guilty, or nolo contendere. If a defen-dant refuses to plead or if a defendant corporation fails to appear, the court shall enter a plea of not guilty.

(2) Conditional Pleas. With the approval of the court and the consent of the government, a defendant may enter a conditional plea of guilty or nolo contendere, reserving in writing the right, on appeal from the judgment, to review of the adverse determination of any specified pretrial motion. A defendant who prevails on appeal shall be allowed to withdraw the plea.

(b) Nolo Contendere. A defendant may plead nolo contendere only with the consent of the court. Such a plea shall be accepted by the court only after due consideration of the views of the parties and the interest of the public in the effective administration of justice.

(c) Advice to Defendant. Before accepting a plea of guilty or nolo contendere, the court must address the defendant personally in open court and inform the defendant of, and determine that the defendant understands, the following:

(1) the nature of the charge to which the plea is offered, the mandatory minimum penalty provided by law, if any, and the maximum possible penalty provided by law, including the

effect of any special parole term or term of supervised release and, when applicable, that the court may also order the defendant to make restitution to any victim of the offense; and

(2) if the defendant is not represented by an attorney, that the defendant has the right to be represented by an attorney at every stage of the proceeding and, if necessary, one will be appointed to represent the defendant; and

(3) that the defendant has the right to plead not guilty or to persist in that plea if it has already been made, the right to be tried by a jury and at that trial the right to the assistance of counsel, the right to confront and cross-examine adverse witnesses, and the right against compelled self-incrimination; and

(4) that if a plea of guilty or nolo contendere is accepted by the court there will not be a further trial of any kind, so that by pleading guilty or nolo contendere the defendant waives the right to a trial; and

(5) if the court intends to question the defendant under oath, on the record, and in the presence of counsel about the offense to which the defendant has pleaded, that the defendant's answers may later be used against the defendant in a prosecution for perjury or false statement.

(d) Insuring That the Plea is Voluntary. The court shall not accept a plea of guilty or nolo contendere without first, by addressing the defendant personally in open court, determining that the plea is voluntary and not the result of force or threats or of promises apart from a plea agreement. The court shall also inquire as to whether the defendant's willingness to plead guilty or nolo contendere results from prior discussions between the attorney for the government and the defendant or the defendant's attorney.

(e) Plea Agreement Procedure.

(1) In General. The attorney for the government and the attorney for the defendant or the defendant when acting pro se may engage in discussions with a view toward reaching an agreement that, upon the entering of a plea of guilty or nolo contendere to a charged offense or to a lesser or related offense, the attorney for the government will do any of the following:

(A) move for dismissal of other charges; or

(B) make a recommendation, or agree not to oppose the defendant's request, for a particular sentence, with the understanding that such recommendation or request shall not be binding upon the court; or

(C) agree that a specific sentence is the appropriate disposition of the case.

The court shall not participate in any such discussions.

(2) Notice of Such Agreement. If a plea agreement has been reached by the parties, the court shall, on the record, require the disclosure of the agreement in open court or, on a showing of good cause, in camera, at the time the plea is offered. If the agreement is of the type specified in subdivision (e)(1)(A) or (C), the court may accept or reject the agreement, or may defer its decision as to the acceptance or rejection until there has been an opportunity to consider the presentence report. If the agreement is of the type specified in subdivision (e)(1)(B), the court shall advise the defendant that if the court does not accept the recommendation or request the defendant nevertheless has no right to withdraw the plea.

(3) Acceptance of a Plea Agreement. If the court accepts the plea agreement, the court shall inform the defendant that it will embody in the judgment and sentence the disposition provided for in the plea agreement.

(4) Rejection of a Plea Agreement. If the court rejects the plea agreement, the court shall, on the record, inform the parties of this fact, advise the defendant personally in open court or, on a showing of good cause, in camera, that the court is not bound by the plea agreement, afford the defendant the opportunity to then withdraw the plea, and advise the defendant that if the defendant persists in a guilty plea or plea of nolo contendere the disposition of the case may be less favorable to the defendant than that contemplated by the plea agreement.

(5) Time of Plea Agreement Procedure. Except for good cause shown, notification to the court of the existence of a plea agreement shall be given at the arraignment or at such other time, prior to trial, as may be fixed by the court.

(6) Inadmissibility of Pleas, Plea Discussions, and Related Statements. Except as otherwise provided in this paragraph, evidence of the following is not, in any civil or criminal proceeding, admissible against the defendant who made the plea or was a participant in the plea discussions:

    (A) a plea of guilty which was later withdrawn;

    (B) a plea of nolo contendere;

    (C) any statement made in the course of any proceedings under this rule regarding either of the foregoing pleas; or

    (D) any statement made in the course of plea discussions with an attorney for the government which do not result in a plea of guilty or which result in a plea of guilty later withdrawn.

However, such a statement is admissible (i) in any proceeding wherein another statement made in the course of the same plea or plea discussions has been introduced and the statement ought in fairness be considered contemporaneously with it, or (ii) in a criminal proceeding for perjury or false statement if the statement was made by the defendant under oath, on the record, and in the presence of counsel.

(f) Determining Accuracy of Plea. Notwithstanding the acceptance of a plea of guilty, the court should not enter a judgment upon such plea without making such inquiry as shall satisfy it that there is a factual basis for the plea.

(g) Record of Proceedings. A verbatim record of the proceedings at which the defendant enters a plea shall be made and, if there is a plea of guilty or nolo contendere, the record shall include, without limitation, the court's advice to the defendant, the inquiry into the voluntariness of the plea including any plea agreement, and the inquiry into the accuracy of a guilty plea.

(h) Harmless Error. Any variance from the procedures required by this rule which does not affect substantial rights shall be disregarded.

(As amended Feb. 28, 1966, eff. July 1, 1966; Apr. 22, 1974, eff. Dec. 1, 1975; July 31, 1975, Pub.L. 94–64, § 3(5)–(10), 89 Stat. 371, 372; Apr. 30, 1979, eff. Aug. 1, 1979, Dec. 1, 1980; Apr. 28, 1982, eff. Aug. 1, 1982; Apr. 28, 1983, eff. Aug. 1, 1983; Apr. 29, 1985, eff. Aug. 1, 1985; Mar. 9, 1987, eff. Aug. 1, 1987; Nov. 18, 1988, Pub.L. 100–690, Title VII, § 7076, 102 Stat. 4406.

NOTES OF ADVISORY COMMITTEE ON RULES

1. This rule is substantially a restatement of existing law and practice, 18 U.S.C. former § 564 (Standing mute); *Fogus v. United States*, 34 F.2d 97, C.C.A.4th (duty of court to ascertain that plea of guilty is intelligently and voluntarily made).

2. The plea of nolo contendere has always existed in the Federal courts, *Hudson v. United States*, 272 U.S. 451, 47 S.Ct. 127, 71 L.Ed. 347; *United States v. Norris*, 281 U.S. 619, 50 S.Ct. 424, 74 L.Ed. 1076. The use of the plea is recognized by the Probation Act, 18 U.S.C. former § 724 (now § 3651). While at times criticized as theoretically lacking in logical basis, experience has shown that it performs a useful function from a practical standpoint.

1966 AMENDMENT

The great majority of all defendants against whom indictments or informations are filed in the federal courts plead guilty. Only a comparatively small number go to trial. See United States Attorneys Statistical Report, Fiscal Year 1964, p. 1. The fairness and adequacy of the procedures on acceptance of pleas of guilty are of vital importance in according equal justice to all in the federal courts.

Three changes are made in the second sentence. The first change makes it clear that before accepting either a plea of guilty or nolo contendere the court must determine that the plea is made voluntarily with understanding of the nature of the charge. The second change expressly requires the court to address the defendant personally in the course of determining that the plea is made voluntarily and with understanding of the nature of the charge. The reported cases reflect some confusion over this matter. Compare *United States v. Diggs*, 304 F.2d 929 (6th Cir.1962); *Domenica v. United States*, 292 F.2d 483 (1st Cir.1961); *Gundlach v. United States*, 262 F.2d 72 (4th Cir.1958), cert. den., 360 U.S. 904 (1959); and *Julian v. United States*, 236 F.2d 155 (6th Cir.1956), which contain the implication that personal interrogation of the defendant is the better practice even when he is represented by counsel, with *Meeks v. United States*, 298 F.2d 204 (5th Cir.1962); *Nunley v. United States*, 294 F.2d 579 (10th Cir.1961), cert. den., 368 U.S. 991 (1962); and *United States v. Von der Heide*, 169 F.Supp. 560 (D.D.C.1959).

The third change in the second sentence adds the words "and the consequences of his plea" to state what clearly is the law. See e.g., *Von Moltke v. Gillies*, 332 U.S. 708, 724 (1948); *Kerchevel v. United States*, 274 U.S. 220, 223 (1927); *Munich v. United States*, 337 F.2d 356 (9th Cir.1964); *Pilkington v. United States*, 315 F.2d 204 (4th Cir.1963); *Smith v. United States*, 324 F.2d 436 (D.C.Cir.1963); but cf. *Marvel v. United States*, 335 F.2d 101 (5th Cir.1964).

A new sentence is added at the end of the rule to impose a duty on the court in cases where the defendant pleads guilty to satisfy itself that there is a factual basis for the plea before entering judgment. The court should satisfy itself, by inquiry of the defendant or the attorney for the government, or by examining the presentence report, or otherwise, that the conduct which the defendant admits constitutes the offense charged in the indictment or information or an offense included therein to which the defendant has pleaded guilty. Such inquiry should, e.g., protect a defendant who is in the position of pleading voluntarily with an understanding of the nature of the charge but without realizing that his conduct does not actually fall within the charge. For a similar requirement see Mich.Stat.Ann. § 28.1058 (1954); Mich.Sup.Ct. Rule 35A; *In re Valle*, 364 Mich. 471, 110 N.W.2d 673 (1961); *People v. Barrows*, 358 Mich. 267, 99 N.W.2d 347 (1959); *People v. Bumpus*, 355 Mich. 374, 94 N.W.2d 854 (1959); *People v. Coates*, 337 Mich. 56, 59 N.W.2d 83 (1953). See also *Stinson v. United States*, 316 F.2d 554 (5th Cir.1963). The normal consequence of a determination that there is not a factual basis for the plea would be for the court to set aside the plea and enter a plea of not guilty.

For a variety of reasons it is desirable in some cases to permit entry of judgment upon a plea of nolo contendere without inquiry into the factual basis for the plea. The new third sentence is not, therefore, made applicable to pleas of nolo contendere. It is not intended by this omission to reflect any view upon the effect of a plea of nolo contendere in relation to a plea of guilty. That problem has been dealt with by the courts. See e.g., *Lott v. United States*, 367 U.S. 421, 426 (1961).

1974 AMENDMENT

The amendments to rule 11 are designed to achieve two principal objectives:

(1) Subdivision (c) prescribes the advice which the court must give to insure that the defendant who pleads guilty has made an informed plea.

(2) Subdivision (e) provides a plea agreement procedure designed to give recognition to the propriety of plea discussions; to bring the existence of a plea agreement out into the open in court; and to provide methods for court acceptance or rejection of a plea agreement.

Other less basic changes are also made. The changes are discussed in the order in which they appear in the rule.

Subdivision (b) retains the requirement that the defendant obtain the consent of the court in order to plead nolo contendere. It adds that the court shall, in deciding whether to accept the plea, consider the views of the prosecution and of the defense and also the larger public interest in the administration of criminal justice.

Although the plea of nolo contendere has long existed in the federal courts, *Hudson v. United States*, 272 U.S. 451, 47 S.Ct. 127, 71 L.Ed. 347 (1926), the desirability of the plea has been a subject of disagreement. Compare Lane–Reticker, Nolo Contendere in North Carolina, 34 N.C.L.Rev. 280, 290–291 (1956), with Note. The Nature and Consequences of the Plea of Nolo Contendere, 33 Neb.L.Rev. 428, 434 (1954), favoring the plea. The American Bar Association Project on Standards for Criminal Justice takes the position that "the case for the nolo plea is not strong enough to justify a minimum standard supporting its use," but because "use of the plea contributes in some degree to the avoidance of unnecessary trials" it does not proscribe use of the plea. ABA, Standards Relating to Pleas of Guilty § 1.1(a) Commentary at 16 (Approved Draft, 1968).

A plea of nolo contendere is, for purposes of punishment, the same as the plea of guilty. See discussion of the history of the nolo plea in North Carolina v. Alford, 400 U.S. 25, 35–36 n. 8, 91 S.Ct. 160, 27 L.Ed.2d 162 (1970). Note, The Nature and Consequences of the Plea of Nolo Contendere, 33 Neb.L.Rev. 428, 430 (1954). A judgment upon the plea is a conviction and may be used to apply multiple offender statutes. Lenvin and Meyers, Nolo Contendere: Its Nature and Implications, 51 Yale L.J. 1255, 1265 (1942). Unlike a plea of guilty, however, it cannot be used against a defendant as an admission in a subsequent criminal or civil case. 4 Wigmore § 1066(4), at 58 (3d ed. 1940, Supp.1970); Rules of Evidence for United States Courts and Magistrates, rule 803(22) (Nov.1971). See Lenvin and Meyers, Nolo Contendere: Its Nature and Implications, 51 Yale L.J. 1255 (1942); ABA Standards Relating to Pleas of Guilty §§ 1.1(a) and (b), Commentary at 15–18 (Approved Draft, 1968).

The factors considered relevant by particular courts in determining whether to permit the plea of nolo contendere vary. Compare *United States v. Bagliore*, 182 F.Supp. 714, 716 (E.D.N.Y.1960), where the view is taken that the plea should be rejected unless a compelling reason for acceptance is established, with *United States v. Jones*, 119 F.Supp. 288, 290 (S.D.Cal.1954), where the view is taken that the plea should be accepted in the absence of a compelling reason to the contrary.

A defendant who desires to plead nolo contendere will commonly want to avoid pleading guilty because the plea of guilty can be introduced as an admission in subsequent civil litigation. The prosecution may oppose the plea of nolo contendere because it wants a definite resolution of the defendant's guilt or innocence either for correctional purposes or for reasons of subsequent litigation. ABA Standards Relating to Pleas of Guilty § 1.1(b) Commentary at 16–18 (Approved Draft, 1968). Under subdivision (b) of the new rule the balancing of the interests is left to the trial judge, who is mandated to take into account the larger public interest in the effective administration of justice.

Subdivision (c) prescribes the advice which the court must give to the defendant as a prerequisite to the acceptance of a plea of guilty. The former rule required that the court determine that the plea was made with "understanding of the nature of the charge and the consequences of the plea." The amendment identifies more specifically what must be explained to the defendant and also codifies, in the rule, the requirements of *Boykin v. Alabama*, 395 U.S. 238, 89 S.Ct. 1709, 23 L.Ed.2d 274 (1969), which held that a defendant must be apprised of the fact that he relinquishes certain constitutional rights by pleading guilty.

Subdivision (c) retains the requirement that the court address the defendant personally. See *McCarthy v. United States*, 394 U.S. 459, 466, 89 S.Ct. 1166, 22 L.Ed.2d 418 (1969). There is also an amendment to rule 43 to make clear that a defendant must be in court at the time of the plea.

Subdivision (c)(1) retains the current requirement that the court determine that the defendant understands the nature of the charge. This is a common requirement. See ABA Standards Relating to Pleas of Guilty § 1.4(a) (Approved Draft, 1968); Illinois Supreme Court Rule 402(a)(1) (1970), Ill.Rev.Stat.1973, ch. 110A, § 402(a)(1). The method by which the defendant's understanding of the nature of the charge is determined may vary from case to case, depending on the complexity of the circumstances and the particular defendant. In some cases, a judge may do this by reading the indictment and by explaining the elements of the offense to the defendants. Thompson, The Judge's Responsibility on a Plea of Guilty, 62 W.Va.L.Rev. 213, 220 (1960); Resolution of Judges of U.S. District Court for D.C., June 24, 1959.

Former rule 11 required the court to inform the defendant of the "consequences of the plea." Subdivision (c)(2) changes this and requires instead that the court inform the defendant of and determine that he understands "the mandatory minimum penalty provided by law, if any, and the maximum possible penalty provided by law for the offense to which the plea is offered." The objective is to insure that a defendant knows what minimum sentence the judge must impose and what maximum sentence the judge may impose. This information is usually readily ascertainable from the face of the statute defining the crime, and thus it is feasible for the judge to know specifically what to tell the defendant. Giving this advice tells a defendant the shortest mandatory sentence and also the longest possible sentence for the offense to which he is pleading guilty.

It has been suggested that it is desirable to inform a defendant of additional consequences which might follow from his plea of guilty. *Durant v. United States*, 410 F.2d 689 (1st Cir.1969), held that a defendant must be informed of his ineligibility for parole. *Trujillo v. United States*, 377 F.2d 266 (5th Cir.1967), cert. denied 389 U.S. 899, 88 S.Ct. 224, 19 L.Ed.2d 221 (1967), held that advice about eligibility for parole is not required. It has been suggested that a defendant be advised that a jury might find him guilty only of a lesser included offense. C. Wright, Federal Practice and Procedure: Criminal § 173 at 374 (1969). See contra Dorrough v. United States, 385 F.2d 887 (5th Cir.1967). The ABA Standards Relating to Pleas of Guilty § 1.4(c)(iii) (Approved Draft, 1968) recommend that the defendant be informed that he may be subject to additional punishment if the offense charged is one for which a different or additional punishment is authorized by reason of the defendant's previous conviction.

Under the rule the judge is not required to inform a defendant about these matters, though a judge is free to do so if he feels a consequence of a plea of guilty in a particular case is likely to be of real significance to the defendant. Currently, certain consequences of a plea of guilty, such as parole eligibility, may be so complicated that it is not feasible to expect a judge to clearly advise the defendant. For example, the judge may impose a sentence under 18 U.S.C. § 4202 making the defendant eligible for parole when he has served one third of the judicially imposed maximum; or, under 18 U.S.C. § 4208(a)(1), making parole eligibility after a specified period of time less than one third of the maximum; or, under 18 U.S.C. § 4208(a)(2), leaving eligibility to the discretion of the parole board. At the time the judge is required to advise the defendant of the consequences of his plea, the judge will usually not have seen the presentence report and thus will have no basis for giving a defendant any very realistic advice as to when he might be eligible for parole. Similar complications exist with regard to other, particularly collateral, consequences of a plea of guilty in a given case.

Subdivisions (c)(3) and (4) specify the constitutional rights that the defendant waives by a plea of guilty or nolo contendere. These subdivisions are designed to satisfy the requirements of understanding waiver set forth in *Boykin v. Alabama*, 395 U.S. 238, 89 S.Ct. 1709, 23 L.Ed.2d 274 (1969). Subdivision (c)(3) is intended to require that the judge inform the defendant and determine that he understands that he waives his fifth amendment rights. The rule takes the position that the defendant's right not to incriminate himself is best explained in terms of his right to plead not guilty and to persist in that plea if it has already been made. This is language identical to that adopted in Illinois for the same purpose. See Illinois Supreme Court Rule 402(a)(3) (1970), Ill.Rev.Stat.1973, ch. 110A, § 402(a)(3).

Subdivision (c)(4) assumes that a defendant's right to have his guilt proved beyond a reasonable doubt and the right to confront his accusers are best explained by indicating that the right to trial is waived. Specifying that there will be no future trial of any kind makes this fact clear to those defendants who, though knowing they have waived trial by jury, are under the mistaken impression that some kind of trial will follow. Illinois has recently adopted similar language. Illinois Supreme Court Rule 402(a)(4) (1970), Ill.Rev.Stat.1973, ch. 110A, § 402(a)(4). In explaining to a defendant that he waives his right to trial, the judge may want to explain some of the aspects of trial such as the right to confront witnesses, to subpoena witnesses, to testify in his own behalf, or, if he chooses, not to testify. What is required, in this respect, to conform to *Boykin* is left to future case-law development.

Subdivision (d) retains the requirement that the court determine that a plea of guilty or nolo contendere is voluntary before accepting it. It adds the requirement that the court also inquire whether the defendant's willingness to plead guilty or nolo contendere results from prior plea discussions between the attorney for the government and the defendant or his attorney. See *Santobello v. New York,* 404 U.S. 257, 261–262, 92 S.Ct. 495, 30 L.Ed.2d 427 (1971): "The plea must, of course, be voluntary and knowing and if it was induced by promises, the essence of those promises must in some way be made known." Subdivisions (d) and (e) afford the court adequate basis for rejecting an improper plea agreement induced by threats or inappropriate promises.

The new rule specifies that the court personally address the defendant in determining the voluntariness of the plea.

By personally interrogating the defendant, not only will the judge be better able to ascertain the plea's voluntariness, but he will also develop a more complete record to support his determination in a subsequent post-conviction attack. * * * Both of these goals are undermined in proportion to the degree the district judge resorts to "assumptions" not based upon recorded responses to his inquiries. *McCarthy v. United States,* 394 U.S. 459, 466, 467, 89 S.Ct. 1166, 22 L.Ed.2d 418 (1969).

Subdivision (e) provides a plea agreement procedure. In doing so it gives recognition to the propriety of plea discussions and plea agreements provided that they are disclosed in open court and subject to acceptance or rejection by the trial judge.

Although reliable statistical information is limited, one recent estimate indicated that guilty pleas account for the disposition of as many as 95% of all criminal cases. ABA Standards Relating to Pleas of Guilty, pp. 1–2 (Approved Draft, 1968). A substantial number of these are the result of plea discussions. The President's Commission on Law Enforcement and Administration of Justice, Task Force Report: The Courts 9 (1967); D. Newman, Conviction: The Determination of Guilt or Innocence Without Trial 3 (1966); L. Weinreb, Criminal Process 437 (1969); Note, Guilty Plea Bargaining: Com-

promises by Prosecutors To Secure Guilty Pleas, 112 U.Pa.L.Rev. 865 (1964).

There is increasing acknowledgement of both the inevitability and the propriety of plea agreements. See, e.g., ABA Standards Relating to Pleas of Guilty § 3.1 (Approved Draft, 1968); Illinois Supreme Court Rule 402 (1970), Ill.Rev.Stat.1973, ch. 110A, § 402.

In *Brady v. United States,* 397 U.S. 742, 752–753, 90 S.Ct. 1463, 25 L.Ed.2d 747 (1970), the court said:

Of course, that the prevalence of guilty pleas is explainable does not necessarily validate those pleas or the system which produces them. But we cannot hold that it is unconstitutional for the State to extend a benefit to a defendant who in turn extends a substantial benefit to the State and who demonstrates by his plea that he is ready and willing to admit his crime and to enter the correctional system in a frame of mind that affords hope for success in rehabilitation over a shorter period of time than might otherwise be necessary.

In *Santobello v. New York,* 404 U.S. 257, 260, 92 S.Ct. 495, 498, 30 L.Ed.2d 427 (1971), the court said:

The disposition of criminal charges by agreement between the prosecutor and the accused, sometimes loosely called "plea bargaining," is an essential component of the administration of justice. Properly administered, it is to be encouraged.

Administratively, the criminal justice system has come to depend upon pleas of guilty and, hence, upon plea discussions. See, e.g., President's Commission on Law Enforcement and Administration of Justice, Task Force Report. The Courts 9 (1967); Note, Guilty Plea Bargaining: Compromises By Prosecutors To Secure Guilty Pleas, 112 U.Pa.L.Rev. 865 (1964). But expediency is not the basis for recognizing the propriety of a plea agreement practice. Properly implemented, a plea agreement procedure is consistent with both effective and just administration of the criminal law. *Santobello v. New York,* 404 U.S. 257, 92 S.Ct. 495, 30 L.Ed.2d 427. This is the conclusion reached in the ABA Standards Relating to Pleas of Guilty § 1.8 (Approved Draft, 1968); the ABA Standards Relating to The Prosecution Function and The Defense Function pp. 243–253 (Approved Draft, 1971); and the ABA Standards Relating to the Function of the Trial Judge, § 4.1 (App.Draft, 1972). The Supreme Court of California recently recognized the propriety of plea bargaining. See *People v. West,* 3 Cal.3d 595, 91 Cal.Rptr. 385, 477 P.2d 409 (1970). A plea agreement procedure has recently been decided in the District of Columbia Court of General Sessions upon the recommendation of the United States Attorney. See 51 F.R.D. 109 (1971).

Where the defendant by his plea aids in insuring prompt and certain application of correctional measures, the proper ends of the criminal justice system are furthered because swift and certain punishment serves the ends of both general deterrence and the rehabilitation of the individual defendant. Cf. Note, The Influence of the Defendant's Plea on Judicial Determination of Sentence, 66 Yale L.J. 204, 211 (1956). Where the defendant has acknowledged his guilt and shown a willingness to assume responsibility for his conduct, it has been thought proper to recognize this in sentencing. See also ALI, Model Penal Code § 7.01 (P.O.D.1962); NPPA Guides for Sentencing (1957). Granting a charge reduction in return for a plea of guilty may give the sentencing judge needed discretion, particularly where the facts of a case do not warrant the harsh consequences of a long mandatory sentence or collateral consequences which are unduly severe. A plea of guilty avoids the necessity of a public trial and may protect the innocent victim of a crime against the trauma of direct and cross-examination.

Finally, a plea agreement may also contribute to the successful prosecution of other more serious offenders. See D. Newman, Conviction: The Determination of Guilt or Innocence Without Trial, chs. 2 and 3 (1966); Note, Guilty Plea Bargaining: Compromises By Prosecutors To Secure Guilty Pleas, 112 U.Pa.L.Rev. 865, 881 (1964).

Where plea discussions and agreements are viewed as proper, it is generally agreed that it is preferable that the fact of the plea agreement be disclosed in open court and its propriety be reviewed by the trial judge.

We have previously recognized plea bargaining as an ineradicable fact. Failure to recognize it tends not to destroy it but to drive it underground. We reiterate what we have said before: that when plea bargaining occurs it ought to be spread on the record [The Bench Book prepared by the Federal Judicial Center for use by United States District Judges now suggests that the defendant be asked by the court "if he believes there is any understanding or if any predictions have been made to him concerning the sentence he will receive." Bench Book for United States District Judges, Federal Judicial Center (1969) at 1.05.3.] and publicly disclosed. *United States v. Williams,* 407 F.2d 940 (4th Cir.1969). * * * In the future we think that the district judges should not only make the general inquiry under Rule 11 as to whether the plea of guilty has been coerced or induced by promises, but should specifically inquire of counsel whether plea bargaining has occurred. Logically the general inquiry should elicit information about plea bargaining, but it seldom has in the past. *Raines v. United States,* 423 F.2d 526, 530 (4th Cir.1970).

In the past, plea discussions and agreements have occurred in an informal and largely invisible manner. Enker, Perspectives on Plea Bargaining, in President's Commission on Law Enforcement and Administration of Justice, Task Force Report: The Courts 108, 115 (1967). There has often been a ritual of denial that any promises have been made, a ritual in which judges, prosecutors, and defense counsel have participated. ABA Standards Relating to Pleas of Guilty § 3.1, Com-

mentary at 60–69 (Approved Draft 1968); Task Force Report: The Courts 9. Consequently, there has been a lack of effective judicial review of the propriety of the agreements, thus increasing the risk of real or apparent unfairness. See ABA Standards Relating to Pleas of Guilty § 3.1, Commentary at 60 et seq.; Task Force Report: The Courts 9–13.

The procedure described in subdivision (e) is designed to prevent abuse of plea discussions and agreements by providing appropriate and adequate safeguards.

Subdivision (e)(1) specifies that the "attorney for the government and the attorney for the defendant or the defendant when acting pro se may" participate in plea discussions. The inclusion of "the defendant when acting pro se" is intended to reflect the fact that there are situations in which a defendant insists upon representing himself. It may be desirable that an attorney for the government not enter plea discussions with a defendant personally. If necessary, counsel can be appointed for purposes of plea discussions. (Subdivision (d) makes it mandatory that the court inquire of the defendant whether his plea is the result of plea discussions between him and the attorney for the government. This is intended to enable the court to reject an agreement reached by an unrepresented defendant unless the court is satisfied that acceptance of the agreement adequately protects the rights of the defendant and the interests of justice.) This is substantially the position of the ABA Standards Relating to Pleas of Guilty § 3.1(a), Commentary at 65–66 (Approved Draft, 1968). Apparently, it is the practice of most prosecuting attorneys to enter plea discussions only with defendant's counsel. Note, Guilty Plea Bargaining: Compromises By Prosecutors To Secure Guilty Pleas, 112 U.Pa.L.Rev. 865, 904 (1964). Discussions without benefit of counsel increase the likelihood that such discussions may be unfair. Some courts have indicated that plea discussions in the absence of defendant's attorney may be constitutionally prohibited. See *Anderson v. North Carolina,* 221 F.Supp. 930, 935 (W.D.N.C.1963); *Shape v. Sigler,* 230 F.Supp. 601, 606 (D.Neb.1964).

Subdivision (e)(1) is intended to make clear that there are four possible concessions that may be made in a plea agreement. First, the charge may be reduced to a lesser or related offense. Second, the attorney for the government may promise to move for dismissal of other charges. Third, the attorney for the government may agree to recommend or not oppose the imposition of a particular sentence. Fourth, the attorneys for the government and the defense may agree that a given sentence is an appropriate disposition of the case. This is made explicit in subdivision (e)(2) where reference is made to an agreement made "in the expectation that a specific sentence will be imposed." See Note, Guilty Plea Bargaining: Compromises By Prosecutors To Secure Guilty Pleas, 112 U.Pa.L.Rev. 865, 898 (1964).

Subdivision (e)(1) prohibits the court from participating in plea discussions. This is the position of the ABA Standards Relating to Pleas of Guilty § 3.3(a) (Approved Draft, 1968).

It has been stated that it is common practice for a judge to participate in plea discussions. See D. Newman, Conviction: The Determination of Guilt or Innocence Without Trial 32–52, 78–104 (1966); Note, Guilty Plea Bargaining: Compromises By Prosecutors To Secure Guilty Pleas, 112 U.Pa.L.Rev. 865, 891, 905 (1964).

There are valid reasons for a judge to avoid involvement in plea discussions. It might lead the defendant to believe that he would not receive a fair trial, were there a trial before the same judge. The risk of not going along with the disposition apparently desired by the judge might induce the defendant to plead guilty, even if innocent. Such involvement makes it difficult for a judge to objectively assess the voluntariness of the plea. See ABA Standards Relating to Pleas of Guilty § 3.3(a), Commentary at 72–74 (Approved Draft, 1968); Note, Guilty Plea Bargaining: Compromises By Prosecutors To Secure Guilty Pleas, 112 U.Pa.L.Rev. 865, 891–892 (1964); Comment, Official Inducements to Plead Guilty: Suggested Morals for a Marketplace, 32 U.Chi.L.Rev. 167, 180–183 (1964); Informal Opinion No. 779 ABA Professional Ethics Committee ("A judge should not be a party to advance arrangements for the determination of sentence, whether as a result of a guilty plea or a finding of guilt based on proof."), 51 A.B.A.J. 444 (1965). As has been recently pointed out:

The unequal positions of the judge and the accused, one with the power to commit to prison and the other deeply concerned to avoid prison, at once raise a question of fundamental fairness. When a judge becomes a participant in plea bargaining he brings to bear the full force and majesty of his office. His awesome power to impose a substantially longer or even maximum sentence in excess of that proposed is present whether referred to or not. A defendant needs no reminder that if he rejects the proposal, stands upon his right to trial and is convicted, he faces a significantly longer sentence. *United States ex rel. Elksnis v. Gilligan,* 256 F.Supp. 244, 254 (S.D.N.Y.1966).

On the other hand, one commentator has taken the position that the judge may be involved in discussions either after the agreement is reached or to help elicit facts and an agreement. Enker, Perspectives on Plea Bargaining, in President's Commission on Law Enforcement and Administration of Justice, Task Force Report: The Courts 108, 117–118 (1967).

The amendment makes clear that the judge should not participate in plea discussions leading to a plea agreement. It is contemplated that the judge may participate in such discussions as may occur when the plea agreement is disclosed in open court. This is the position of the recently adopted Illinois Supreme Court Rule 402(d)(1) (1970), Ill.Rev.Stat.1973, ch. 110A,

§ 402(d)(1). As to what may constitute "participation," contrast *People v. Earegood,* 12 Mich.App. 256, 268–269, 162 N.W.2d 802, 809–810 (1968), with *Kruse v. State,* 47 Wis.2d 460, 177 N.W.2d 322 (1970).

Subdivision (e)(2) provides that the judge shall require the disclosure of any plea agreement in open court. In *People v. West,* 3 Cal.3d 595, 91 Cal.Rptr. 385, 477 P.2d 409 (1970), the court said:

[T]he basis of the bargain should be disclosed to the court and incorporated in the record. * * *

Without limiting that court to those we set forth, we note four possible methods of incorporation: (1) the bargain could be stated orally and recorded by the court reporter, whose notes then must be preserved or transcribed; (2) the bargain could be set forth by the clerk in the minutes of the court; (3) the parties could file a written stipulation stating the terms of the bargain; (4) finally, counsel or the court itself may find it useful to prepare and utilize forms for the recordation of plea bargains. 91 Cal.Rptr. 393, 394, 477 P.2d at 417, 418.

The District of Columbia Court of General Sessions is using a "Sentence–Recommendation Agreement" form.

Upon notice of the plea agreement, the court is given the option to accept or reject the agreement or defer its decision until receipt of the presentence report.

The judge may, and often should, defer his decision until he examines the presentence report. This is made possible by rule 32 which allows a judge, with the defendant's consent, to inspect a presentence report to determine whether a plea agreement should be accepted. For a discussion of the use of conditional plea acceptance, see ABA Standards Relating to Pleas of Guilty § 3.3(b), Commentary at 74–76, and Supplement, Proposed Revisions § 3.3(b) at 2–3 (Approved Draft, 1968); Illinois Supreme Court Rule 402(d)(2) (1970), Ill. Rev.Stat.1973, ch. 110A, § 402(d)(2).

The plea agreement procedure does not attempt to define criteria for the acceptance or rejection of a plea agreement. Such a decision is left to the discretion of the individual trial judge.

Subdivision (e)(3) makes it mandatory, if the court decides to accept the plea agreement, that it inform the defendant that it will embody in the judgment and sentence the disposition provided in the plea agreement, or one more favorable to the defendant. This serves the purpose of informing the defendant immediately that the agreement will be implemented.

Subdivision (e)(4) requires the court, if it rejects the plea agreement, to inform the defendant of this fact and to advise the defendant personally, in open court, that the court is not bound by the plea agreement. The defendant must be afforded an opportunity to withdraw his plea and must be advised that if he persists in his guilty plea or plea of nolo contendere, the disposition of the case may be less favorable to him than that contemplated by the plea agreement. That the defendant should have the opportunity to withdraw his plea if the court rejects the plea agreement is the position taken in ABA Standards Relating to Pleas of Guilty, Supplement, Proposed Revisions § 2.1(a)(ii)(5) (Approved Draft, 1968). Such a rule has been adopted in Illinois. Illinois Supreme Court Rule 402(d)(2) (1970), Ill.Rev.Stat. 1973, ch. 110A, § 402(d)(2).

If the court rejects the plea agreement and affords the defendant the opportunity to withdraw the plea, the court is not precluded from accepting a guilty plea from the same defendant at a later time, when such plea conforms to the requirements of rule 11.

Subdivision (e)(5) makes it mandatory that, except for good cause shown, the court be notified of the existence of a plea agreement at the arraignment or at another time prior to trial fixed by the court. Having a plea entered at this stage provides a reasonable time for the defendant to consult with counsel and for counsel to complete any plea discussions with the attorney for the government. ABA Standards Relating to Pleas of Guilty § 1.3 (Approved Draft, 1968). The objective of the provision is to make clear that the court has authority to require a plea agreement to be disclosed sufficiently in advance of trial so as not to interfere with the efficient scheduling of criminal cases.

Subdivision (e)(6) is taken from rule 410, Rules of Evidence for United States Courts and Magistrates (Nov.1971). See Advisory Committee Note thereto. See also the ABA Standards Relating to Pleas of Guilty § 2.2 (Approved Draft, 1968); Illinois Supreme Court Rule 402(f) (1970), Ill.Rev.Stat.1973, ch. 110A, § 402(f).

Subdivision (f) retains the requirement of old rule 11 that the court should not enter judgment upon a plea of guilty without making such an inquiry as will satisfy it that there is a factual basis for the plea. The draft does not specify that any particular type of inquiry be made. See *Santobello v. New York*, 404 U.S. 257, 261, 92 S.Ct. 495, 30 L.Ed.2d 427 (1971); "Fed.Rule Crim.Proc. 11, governing pleas in federal courts, now makes clear that the sentencing judge must develop, on the record, the factual basis for the plea, as, for example, by having the accused describe the conduct that gave rise to the charge." An inquiry might be made of the defendant, of the attorneys for the government and the defense, of the presentence report when one is available, or by whatever means is appropriate in a specific case. This is the position of the ABA Standards Relating to Pleas of Guilty § 1.6 (Approved Draft, 1968). Where inquiry is made of the defendant himself it may be desirable practice to place the defendant under oath. With regard to a determination that there is a factual basis for a plea of guilty to a "lessor or related offense," compare ABA Standards Relating to Pleas of Guilty § 3.1(b)(ii), Commentary at 67–68 (Approved Draft, 1968), with ALI, Model Penal Code § 1.07(5) (P.O.D.1962). The rule does not speak directly to the issue of whether a judge may

accept a plea of guilty where there is a factual basis for the plea but the defendant asserts his innocence. *North Carolina v. Alford*, 400 U.S. 25, 91 S.Ct. 160, 27 L.Ed.2d 162 (1970). The procedure in such case would seem to be to deal with this as a plea of nolo contendere, the acceptance of which would depend upon the judge's decision as to whether acceptance of the plea is consistent with "the interest of the public in the effective administration of justice" [new rule 11(b)]. The defendant who asserts his innocence while pleading guilty or nolo contendere is often difficult to deal with in a correctional setting, and it may therefore be preferable to resolve the issue of guilt or innocence at the trial stage rather than leaving that issue unresolved, thus complicating subsequent correctional decisions. The rule is intended to make clear that a judge may reject a plea of nolo contendere and require the defendant either to plead not guilty or to plead guilty under circumstances in which the judge is able to determine that the defendant is in fact guilty of the crime to which he is pleading guilty.

Subdivision (g) requires that a verbatim record be kept of the proceedings. If there is a plea of guilty or nolo contendere, the record must include, without limitation, the court's advice to the defendant, the inquiry into the voluntariness of the plea and the plea agreement, and the inquiry into the accuracy of the plea. Such a record is important in the event of a post-conviction attack. ABA Standards Relating to Pleas of Guilty § 1.7 (Approved Draft, 1968). A similar requirement was adopted in Illinois: Illinois Supreme Court Rule 402(e) (1970), Ill.Rev.Stat.1973, ch. 110A, § 402(e).

NOTES OF COMMITTEE ON THE JUDICIARY, HOUSE REPORT NO. 94–247

A. Amendments Proposed by the Supreme Court. Rule 11 of the Federal Rules of Criminal Procedure deals with pleas. The Supreme Court has proposed to amend this rule extensively.

Rule 11 provides that a defendant may plead guilty, not guilty, or nolo contendere. The Supreme Court's amendments to Rule 11(b) provide that a nolo contendere plea "shall be accepted by the court only after due consideration of the views of the parties and the interest of the public in the effective administration of justice."

The Supreme Court amendments to Rule 11(c) spell out the advice that the court must give to the defendant before accepting the defendant's plea of guilty or nolo contendere. The Supreme Court amendments to Rule 11(d) set forth the steps that the court must take to insure that a guilty or nolo contendere plea has been voluntarily made.

The Supreme Court amendments to Rule 11(e) establish a plea agreement procedure. This procedure permits the parties to discuss disposing of a case without a trial and sets forth the type of agreements that the parties can reach concerning the disposition of the case. The procedure is not mandatory; a court is free not to permit the parties to present plea agreements to it.

The Supreme Court amendments to Rule 11(f) require that the court, before entering judgment upon a plea of guilty, satisfy itself that "there is a factual basis for the plea." The Supreme Court amendments to Rule 11(g) require that a verbatim record be kept of the proceedings at which the defendant enters a plea.

B. Committee Action. The proposed amendments to Rule 11, particularly those relating to the plea negotiating procedure, have generated much comment and criticism. No observer is entirely happy that our criminal justice system must rely to the extent it does on negotiating dispositions of cases. However, crowded court dockets make plea negotiating a fact that the Federal Rules of Criminal Procedure should contend with. The Committee accepts the basic structure and provisions of Rule 11(e).

Rule 11(e) as proposed permits each federal court to decide for itself the extent to which it will permit plea negotiations to be carried on within its own jurisdiction. No court is compelled to permit any plea negotiations at all. Proposed Rule 11(e) regulates plea negotiations and agreements if, and to the extent that, the court permits such negotiations and agreements. [Proposed Rule 11(e) has been criticized by some federal judges who read it to mandate the court to permit plea negotiations and the reaching of plea agreements. The Advisory Committee stressed during its testimony that the rule does not mandate that a court permit any form of plea agreement to be presented to it. See, e.g., the remarks of United States Circuit Judge William H. Webster in Hearings II, at 196. See also the exchange of correspondence between Judge Webster and United States District Judge Frank A. Kaufman in Hearings II, at 289–90.]

Proposed Rule 11(e) contemplates 4 different types of plea agreements. First, the defendant can plead guilty or nolo contendere in return for the prosecutor's reducing the charge to a less serious offense. Second, the defendant can plead guilty or nolo contendere in return for the prosecutor dropping, or not bringing, a charge or charges relating to other offenses. Third, the defendant can plead guilty or nolo contendere in return for the prosecutor's recommending a sentence. Fourth, the defendant and prosecutor can agree that a particular sentence is the appropriate disposition of the case. [It is apparent, though not explicitly stated, that Rule 11(e) contemplates that the plea agreement may bind the defendant to do more than just plead guilty or nolo contendere. For example, the plea agreement may bind the defendant to cooperate with the prosecution in a different investigation. The Committee intends by its approval of Rule 11(e) to permit the parties to agree on such terms in a plea agreement.]

The Committee added language in subdivisions (e)(2) and (e)(4) to permit a plea agreement to be disclosed to the court, or rejected by it, in camera. There must be a showing of good cause before the court can conduct such proceedings in camera. The language does not address itself to whether the showing of good cause may be made in open court or in camera. That issue is left for the courts to resolve on a case-by-case basis. These changes in subdivisions (e)(2) and (e)(4) will permit a fair trial when there is substantial media interest in a case and the court is rejecting a plea agreement.

The Committee added an exception to subdivision (e)(6). That subdivision provides:

Evidence of a plea of guilty, later withdrawn, or a plea of nolo contendere, or of an offer to plead guilty or nolo contendere to the crime charged or any other crime, or of statements made in connection with any of the foregoing pleas or offers, is not admissible in any civil or criminal proceeding against the person who made the plea or offer.

The Committee's exception permits the use of such evidence in a perjury or false statement prosecution where the plea, offer, or related statement was made by the defendant on the record, under oath and in the presence of counsel. The Committee recognizes that even this limited exception may discourage defendants from being completely candid and open during plea negotiations and may even result in discouraging the reaching of plea agreements. However, the Committee believes that, on balance, it is more important to protect the integrity of the judicial process from willful deceit and untruthfulness. [The Committee does not intend its language to be construed as mandating or encouraging the swearing-in of the defendant during proceedings in connection with the disclosure and acceptance or rejection of a plea agreement.]

The Committee recast the language of Rule 11(c), which deals with the advice given to a defendant before the court can accept his plea of guilty or nolo contendere. The Committee acted in part because it believed that the warnings given to the defendant ought to include those that *Boykin v. Alabama*, 395 U.S. 238 (1969), said were constitutionally required. In addition, and as a result of its change in subdivision (e)(6), the Committee thought it only fair that the defendant be warned that his plea of guilty (later withdrawn) or nolo contendere, or his offer of either plea, or his statements made in connection with such pleas or offers, could later be used against him in a perjury trial if made under oath, on the record, and in the presence of counsel.

CONFERENCE COMMITTEE NOTES, HOUSE REPORT NO. 94–414

Note to Subdivision (c). Rule 11(c) enumerates certain things that a judge must tell a defendant before the judge can accept that defendant's plea of guilty or nolo contendere. The House version expands upon the list originally proposed by the Supreme Court. The Senate version adopts the Supreme Court's proposal.

The Conference adopts the House provision.

Note to Subdivision (e)(1). Rule 11(e)(1) outlines some general considerations concerning the plea agreement procedure. The Senate version makes nonsubstantive change in the House version.

The Conference adopts the Senate provision.

Note to Subdivision (e)(6). Rule 11(e)(6) deals with the use of statements made in connection with plea agreements. The House version permits a limited use of pleas of guilty, later withdrawn, or nolo contendere, offers of such pleas, and statements made in connection with such pleas or offers. Such evidence can be used in a perjury or false statement prosecution if the plea, offer, or related statement was made under oath, on the record, and in the presence of counsel. The Senate version permits evidence of voluntary and reliable statements made in court on the record to be used for the purpose of impeaching the credibility of the declarant or in a perjury or false statement prosecution.

The Conference adopts the House version with changes. The Conference agrees that neither a plea nor the offer of a plea ought to be admissible for any purpose. The Conference-adopted provision, therefore, like the Senate provision, permits only the use of statements made in connection with a plea of guilty, later withdrawn, or a plea of nolo contendere, or in connection with an offer of a guilty or nolo contendere plea.

1979 AMENDMENT

Note to Subdivision (e)(2). The amendment to rule 11(e)(2) is intended to clarify the circumstances in which the court may accept or reject a plea agreement, with the consequences specified in subdivision (e)(3) and (4). The present language has been the cause of some confusion and has led to results which are not entirely consistent. Compare *United States v. Sarubbi,* 416 F.Supp. 633 (D.N.J.1976); with *United States v. Hull,* 413 F.Supp. 145 (E.D.Tenn.1976).

Rule 11(e)(1) specifies three types of plea agreements, namely, those in which the attorney for the government might

(A) move for dismissal of other charges; or

(B) make a recommendation, or agree not to oppose the defendant's request, for a particular sentence, with the understanding that such recommendation or request shall not be binding upon the court; or

(C) agree that a specific sentence is the appropriate disposition of the case.

A (B) type of plea agreement is clearly of a different order than the other two, for an agreement to recommend or not to oppose is discharged when the prosecutor performs as he agreed to do. By comparison, critical to a type (A) or (C) agreement is that the defendant receive the contemplated charge dismissal or agreed-to sentence. Consequently, there must ultimately be an acceptance or rejection by the court of a type (A) or (C) agreement so that it may be determined whether the defendant shall receive the bargained-for concessions or shall instead be afforded an opportunity to withdraw his plea. But this is not so as to a type (B) agreement; there is no "disposition provided for" in such a plea agreement so as to make the acceptance provisions of subdivision (e)(3) applicable, nor is there a need for rejection with opportunity for withdrawal under subdivision (e)(4) in light of the fact that the defendant knew the nonbinding character of the recommendation or request. *United States v. Henderson,* 565 F.2d 1119 (9th Cir.1977); *United States v. Savage,* 561 F.2d 554 (4th Cir.1977).

Because a type (B) agreement is distinguishable from the others in that it involves only a recommendation or request not binding upon the court, it is important that the defendant be aware that this is the nature of the agreement into which he has entered. The procedure contemplated by the last sentence of amended subdivision (e)(2) will establish for the record that there is such awareness. This provision conforms to ABA Standards Relating to Pleas of Guilty § 1.5 (Approved Draft, 1968), which provides that "the court must advise the defendant personally that the recommendations of the prosecuting attorney are not binding on the court."

Sometimes a plea agreement will be partially but not entirely of the (B) type, as where a defendant, charged with counts 1, 2 and 3, enters into an agreement with the attorney for the government wherein it is agreed that if defendant pleads guilty to count 1, the prosecutor will recommend a certain sentence as to that count and will move for dismissal of counts 2 and 3. In such a case, the court must take particular care to ensure that the defendant understands which components of the agreement involve only a (B) type recommendation and which do not. In the above illustration, that part of the agreement which contemplates the dismissal of counts 2 and 3 is an (A) type agreement, and thus under rule 11(e) the court must either accept the agreement to dismiss these counts or else reject it and allow the defendant to withdraw his plea. If rejected, the defendant must be allowed to withdraw the plea on count 1 even if the type (B) promise to recommend a certain sentence on that count is kept, for a multi-faceted plea agreement is nonetheless a single agreement. On the other hand, if counts 2 and 3 are dismissed and the sentence recommendation is made, then the defendant is not entitled to withdraw his plea even if the sentence recommendation is not accepted by the court, for the defendant received all he was entitled to under the various components of the plea agreement.

Note to Subdivision (e)(6). The major objective of the amendment to rule 11(e)(6) is to describe more precisely, consistent with the original purpose of the provision, what evidence relating to pleas or plea discussions is inadmissible. The present language is susceptible to interpretation which would make it applicable to a wide variety of statements made under various circumstances other than within the context of those plea discussions authorized by rule 11(e) and intended to be protected by subdivision (e)(6) of the rule. See *United States v. Herman,* 544 F.2d 791 (5th Cir.1977), discussed herein.

Fed.R.Ev. 410, as originally adopted by Pub.L. 93–595, provided in part that "evidence of a plea of guilty, later withdrawn, or a plea of nolo contendere, or of an offer to plead guilty or nolo contendere to the crime charged or any other crime, or of statements made in connection with any of the foregoing pleas or offers, is not admissible in any civil or criminal action, case, or proceeding against the person who made the plea or offer." (This rule was adopted with the proviso that it "shall be superseded by any amendment to the Federal Rules of Criminal Procedure which is inconsistent with this rule.") As the Advisory Committee Note explained: "Exclusion of offers to plead guilty or nolo has as its purpose the promotion of disposition of criminal cases by compromise." The amendment of Fed.R.Crim.P. 11, transmitted to Congress by the Supreme Court in April 1974, contained a subdivision (e)(6) essentially identical to the rule 410 language quoted above, as a part of a substantial revision of rule 11. The most significant feature of this revision was the express recognition given to the fact that the "attorney for the government and the attorney for the defendant or the defendant when acting pro se may engage in discussions with a view toward reaching" a plea agreement. Subdivision (e)(6) was intended to encourage such discussions. As noted in H.R.Rep. No. 94–247, 94th Cong., 1st Sess. 7 (1975), the purpose of subdivision (e)(6) is to not "discourage defendants from being completely candid and open during plea negotiations." Similarly, H.R.Rep. No. 94–414, 94th Cong., 1st Sess. 10 (1975), states that "Rule 11(e)(6) deals with the use of statements made in connection with plea agreements." (Rule 11(e)(6) was thereafter enacted, with the addition of the proviso allowing use of statements in a prosecution for perjury, and with the qualification that the inadmissible statements must also be "relevant to" the inadmissible pleas or offers. Pub.L. 94–64; Fed.R.Ev. 410 was then amended to conform. Pub.L. 94–149.)

While this history shows that the purpose of Fed. R.Ev. 410 and Fed.R.Crim.P. 11(e)(6) is to permit the unrestrained candor which produces effective plea discussions between the "attorney for the government and the attorney for the defendant or the defendant when acting pro se," given visibility and sanction in rule 11(e), a literal reading of the language of these two rules could reasonably lead to the conclusion that a broader rule of inadmissibility obtains. That is, because "statements" are generally inadmissible if "made in connection with, and relevant to" an "offer to plead guilty," it might be thought that an otherwise voluntary admission to law enforcement officials is rendered inadmissible merely because it was made in the hope of obtaining leniency by a plea. Some decisions interpreting rule 11(e)(6) point in this direction. See *United States v. Herman,* 544 F.2d 791 (5th Cir.1977) (defendant in custody of two postal inspectors during continuance of removal hearing instigated conversation with them and at some point said he would plead guilty to armed robbery if the murder charge was dropped; one inspector stated they were not "in position" to make any deals in this regard; held, defendant's statement inadmissible under rule 11(e)(6) because the defendant "made the statements during the course of a conversation in which he sought concessions from the government in return for a guilty plea"); *United States v. Brooks,* 536 F.2d 1137 (6th Cir.1976) (defendant telephoned postal inspector and offered to plead guilty if he got 2–year maximum; statement inadmissible).

The amendment makes inadmissible statements made "in the course of any proceedings under this rule regarding" either a plea of guilty later withdrawn or a plea of nolo contendere, and also statements "made in the course of plea discussions with an attorney for the government which do not result in a plea of guilty or which result in a plea of guilty later withdrawn." It is not limited to statements by the defendant himself, and thus would cover statements by defense counsel regarding defendant's incriminating admissions to him. It thus fully protects the plea discussion process authorized by rule 11 without attempting to deal with confrontations between suspects and law enforcement agents, which involve problems of quite different dimensions. See, e.g., ALI Model Code of Pre–Arraignment Procedure, art. 140 and § 150.2(8) (Proposed Official Draft, 1975) (latter section requires exclusion if "a law enforcement officer induces any person to make a statement by promising leniency"). This change, it must be emphasized, does not compel the conclusion that statements made to law enforcement agents, especially when the agents purport to have authority to bargain, are inevitably admissible. Rather, the point is that such cases are not covered by the per se rule of 11(e)(6) and thus must be resolved by that body of law dealing with police interrogations.

If there has been a plea of guilty later withdrawn or a plea of nolo contendere, subdivision (e)(6)(C) makes inadmissible statements made "in the course of any proceedings under this rule" regarding such pleas. This includes, for example, admissions by the defendant when he makes his plea in court pursuant to rule 11 and also admissions made to provide the factual basis pursuant to subdivision (f). However, subdivision (e)(6)(C) is not limited to statements made in court. If the court were to defer its decision on a plea agreement pending examination of the presentence report, as authorized by subdivision (e)(2), statements made to the probation officer in connection with the preparation of that report would come within this provision.

This amendment is fully consistent with all recent and major law reform efforts on this subject. ALI Model Code of Pre–Arraignment Procedure § 350.7 (Proposed Official Draft, 1975), and ABA Standards Relating to Pleas of Guilty § 3.4 (Approved Draft, 1968) both provide:

> Unless the defendant subsequently enters a plea of guilty or nolo contendere which is not withdrawn, the fact that the defendant or his counsel and the prosecuting attorney engaged in plea discussions or made a plea agreement should not be received in evidence against or in favor of the defendant in any criminal or civil action or administrative proceedings.

The Commentary to the latter states:

> The above standard is limited to discussions and agreements with the prosecuting attorney. Sometimes defendants will indicate to the police their willingness to bargain, and in such instances these statements are sometimes admitted in court against the defendant. *State v. Christian,* 245 S.W.2d 895 (Mo.1952). If the police initiate this kind of discussion, this may have some bearing on the admissibility of the defendant's statement. However, the policy considerations relevant to this issue are better dealt with in the context of standards governing in-custody interrogation by the police.

Similarly, Unif.R.Crim.P. 441(d) (Approved Draft, 1974), provides that except under limited circumstances "no discussion between the parties or statement by the defendant or his lawyer under this Rule," i.e., the rule providing "the parties may meet to discuss the possibility of pretrial diversion * * * or of a plea agreement," are admissible. The amendment is likewise consistent with the typical state provision on this subject; see, e.g., Ill.S.Ct.Rule 402(f).

The language of the amendment identifies with more precision than the present language the necessary relationship between the statements and the plea or discussion. See the dispute between the majority and concurring opinions in *United States v. Herman,* 544 F.2d 791 (5th Cir.1977), concerning the meanings and effect of the phrases "connection to" and "relevant to" in the present rule. Moreover, by relating the statements to "plea discussions" rather than "an offer to plead," the amendment ensures "that even an attempt to open plea bargaining [is] covered under the same rule of inadmissibility." *United States v. Brooks,* 536 F.2d 1137 (6th Cir.1976).

The last sentence of Rule 11(e)(6) is amended to provide a second exception to the general rule of nonadmissibility of the described statements. Under the amendment, such a statement is also admissible "in any proceeding wherein another statement made in the course of the same plea or plea discussions has been introduced and the statement ought in fairness be considered contemporaneously with it." This change is necessary so that, when evidence of statements made in the course of or as a consequence of a certain plea or plea discussions are introduced under circumstances not prohibited by this rule (e.g., not "against" the person who made the plea), other statements relating to the same plea or plea discussions may also be admitted when relevant to the matter at issue. For example, if a defendant upon a motion to dismiss a prosecution on some ground were able to admit certain statements made in aborted plea discussions in his favor, then other relevant statements made in the same plea discussions should be admissible against the defendant in the interest of determining the truth of the matter at issue. The language of the amendment follows closely that in Fed.R.Evid. 106, as the considerations involved are very similar.

The phrase "in any civil or criminal proceeding" has been moved from its present position, following the word "against," for purposes of clarity. An ambiguity presently exists because the word "against" may be read as referring either to the kind of proceeding in which the evidence is offered or the purpose for which it is offered. The change makes it clear that the latter construction is correct. No change is intended with respect to provisions making evidence rules inapplicable in certain situations. See, e.g., Fed.R.Evid. 104(a) and 1101(d).

Unlike ABA Standards Relating to Pleas of Guilty § 3.4 (Approved Draft, 1968), and ALI Model Code of Pre–Arraignment Procedure § 350.7 (Proposed Official Draft, 1975), rule 11(e)(6) does not also provide that the described evidence is inadmissible "in favor of" the defendant. This is not intended to suggest, however, that such evidence will inevitably be admissible in the defendant's favor. Specifically, no disapproval is intended of such decisions as *United States v. Verdoorn,* 528 F.2d 103 (8th Cir.1976), holding that the trial judge properly refused to permit the defendants to put into evidence at their trial the fact the prosecution had attempted to plea bargain with them, as "meaningful dialogue between the parties would, as a practical matter, be impossible if either party had to assume the risk that plea offers would be admissible in evidence."

1982 AMENDMENT

Note to Subdivision (c)(1). Subdivision (c)(1) has been amended by specifying "the effect of any special parole term" as one of the matters about which a defendant who has tendered a plea of guilty or nolo contendere is to be advised by the court. This amendment does not make any change in the law, as the courts are in agreement that such advice is presently required by Rule 11. See, e.g., *Moore v. United States,* 592 F.2d 753 (4th Cir.1979); *United States v. Eaton,* 579 F.2d 1181 (10th Cir.1978); *Richardson v. United States,* 577 F.2d 447 (8th Cir.1978); *United States v. Del Prete,* 567 F.2d 928 (9th Cir.1978); *United States v. Watson,* 548 F.2d 1058 (D.C.Cir.1977); *United States v. Crusco,* 536 F.2d 21 (2d Cir.1976); *United States v. Yazbeck,* 524 F.2d 641 (1st Cir.1975); *United States v. Wolak,* 510 F.2d 164 (6th Cir.1975). In *United States v. Timmreck,* 441 U.S. 780, 99 S.Ct. 2085, 60 L.Ed.2d 634 (1979), the Supreme Court assumed that the judge's failure in that case to describe the mandatory special parole term constituted "a failure to comply with the formal requirements of the Rule."

The purpose of the amendment is to draw more specific attention to the fact that advice concerning special parole terms is a necessary part of Rule 11 procedure. As noted in *Moore v. United States, supra:*

> Special parole is a significant penalty. * * * Unlike ordinary parole, which does not involve supervision beyond the original prison term set by the court and the violation of which cannot lead to confinement beyond that sentence, special parole increases the possible period of confinement. It entails the possibility that a defendant may have to serve his original sentence plus a substantial additional period, without credit for time spent on parole. Explanation of special parole in open court is therefore essential to comply with the Rule's mandate that the defendant be informed of "the maximum possible penalty provided by law."

As the aforecited cases indicate, in the absence of specification of the requirement in the rule it has sometimes happened that such advice has been inadvertently omitted from Rule 11 warnings.

The amendment does not attempt to enumerate all of the characteristics of the special parole term which the judge ought to bring to the defendant's attention. Some flexibility in this respect must be preserved although it is well to note that the unique characteristics of this kind of parole are such that they may not be readily perceived by laymen. *Moore v. United States, supra,* recommends that in an appropriate case the judge

> inform the defendant and determine that he understands the following:
>
> (1) that a special parole term will be added to any prison sentence he receives;
>
> (2) the minimum length of the special parole term that must be imposed and the absence of a statutory maximum;
>
> (3) that special parole is entirely different from— and in addition to—ordinary parole; and
>
> (4) that if the special parole is violated, the defendant can be returned to prison for the remainder of his sentence and the full length of his special parole term.

The amendment should not be read as meaning that a failure to comply with this particular requirement will inevitably entitle the defendant to relief. See *United States v. Timmreck, supra.* Likewise, the amendment makes no change in the existing law to the effect

> that many aspects of traditional parole need not be communicated to the defendant by the trial judge under the umbrella of Rule 11. For example, a defendant need not be advised of all conceivable consequences such as when he may be considered for parole or that, if he violates his parole, he will again be imprisoned.

Bunker v. Wise, 550 F.2d 1155, 1158 (9th Cir.1977).

Note to Subdivision (c)(4). The amendment to subdivision (c)(4) is intended to overcome the present conflict between the introductory language of subdivision (c), which contemplates the advice being given "[b]efore accepting a plea of guilty or nolo contendere," and thus presumably after the plea has been tendered, and the "if he pleads" language of subdivision (c)(4) which suggests the plea has not been tendered.

As noted by Judge Doyle in *United States v. Sinagub,* 468 F.Supp. 353 (W.D.Wis.1979):

> Taken literally, this wording of subsection (4) of 11(c) suggests that before eliciting any plea at an arraignment, the court is required to insure that a defendant understands that if he or she pleads guilty or nolo contendere, the defendant will be waiving the right to trial. Under subsection (3) of 11(c), however, there is no requirement that at this pre-plea stage, the court must insure that the defendant understands that he or she enjoys the right to a trial and, at trial, the right to the assistance of counsel, the right to confront and cross-examine witnesses against him or her, and the right not to be compelled to incriminate himself or herself. It would be incongruous to require that at the pre-plea stage the court insure that the defendant understands that if he enters a plea of guilty or nolo contendere he will be waiving a right, the existence and nature of which need not be explained until after such a plea has been entered. I conclude that the insertion of the words "that if he pleads guilty or nolo contendere," as they appear in subsection (4) of 11(c), was an accident of draftsmanship which occurred in the course of Congressional rewriting of 11(c) as it has been approved by the Supreme Court. Those words are to be construed consistently with the words "Before accepting a plea of guilty or nolo contendere," as they appear in the opening language of 11(c), and consistently with the omission of the words "that if he pleads" from subsections (1), (2), and (3) of 11(c). That is, as they appear in subsection (4) of 11(c), the words, "that if he pleads guilty or nolo contendere" should be construed to mean "that if his plea of guilty or nolo contendere is accepted by the court."

Although this is a very logical interpretation of the present language, the amendment will avoid the necessity to engage in such analysis in order to determine the true meaning of subdivision (c)(4).

Note to Subdivision (c)(5). Subdivision (c)(5), in its present form, may easily be read as contemplating that in *every* case in which a plea of guilty or nolo contendere is tendered, warnings must be given about the possible use of defendant's statements, obtained under oath, on the record and in the presence of counsel, in a later prosecution for perjury or false statement. The language has prompted some courts to reach the remarkable result that a defendant who pleads guilty or nolo contendere without receiving those warnings *must* be allowed to overturn his plea on appeal even though he was never questioned under oath, on the record, in the presence of counsel about the offense to which he pleaded. *United States v. Artis,* No. 78–5012 (4th Cir. March 12, 1979); *United States v. Boone,* 543 F.2d 1090 (4th Cir.1976). Compare *United States v. Michaelson,* 552 F.2d 472 (2d Cir.1977) (failure to give subdivision (c)(5) warnings not a basis for reversal, "at least when, as here, defendant was not put under oath before questioning about his guilty plea"). The present language of subdivision (c)(5) may also have contributed to the conclusion, not otherwise supported by the rule, that "Rule 11 requires that the defendant be under oath for the entirety of the proceedings" conducted pursuant to that rule and that failure to place the defendant under oath would itself make necessary overturning the plea on appeal. *United States v. Aldridge,* 553 F.2d 922 (5th Cir.1977).

When questioning of the kind described in subdivision (c)(5) is not contemplated by the judge who is receiving the plea, no purpose is served by giving the (c)(5) warnings, which in such circumstances can only confuse the defendant and detract from the force of the other warnings required by Rule 11. As correctly noted in *United States v. Sinagub, supra,*

> subsection (5) of section (c) of Rule 11 is qualitatively distinct from the other sections of the Rule. It does not go to whether the plea is knowingly or voluntarily made, nor to whether the plea should be accepted and judgment entered. Rather, it does go to the possible consequences of an event which may or may not occur during the course of the arraignment hearing itself, namely, the administration of an oath to the defendant. Whether this event is to occur is wholly within the control of the presiding judge. If the event is not to occur, it is pointless to inform the defendant of its consequences. If a presiding judge intends that an oath not be administered to a defendant during an arraignment hearing, but alters that intention at some point, only then would the need arise to inform the defendant of the possible consequences of the administration of the oath.

The amendment to subdivision (c)(5) is intended to make it clear that this is the case.

The amendment limits the circumstances in which the warnings must be given, but does not change the fact, as noted in *Sinagub* that these warnings are "qualitatively distinct" from the other advice required by Rule 11(c). This being the case, a failure to give the subdivision (c)(5) warnings even when the defendant *was* questioned under oath, on the record and in the presence of counsel would in no way affect the validity of the defendant's plea. Rather, this failure bears upon the admissibility of defendant's answers pursuant to subdivision (e)(6) in a later prosecution for perjury or false statement.

1983 AMENDMENT

Rule 11(a)

There are many defenses, objections and requests which a defendant must ordinarily raise by pretrial motion. See, e.g., 18 U.S.C. § 3162(a)(2); Fed.R.Crim.P. 12(b). Should that motion be denied, interlocutory appeal of the ruling by the defendant is seldom permitted. See *United States v. MacDonald,* 435 U.S. 850 (1978) (defendant may not appeal denial of his motion to dismiss based upon Sixth Amendment speedy trial grounds); *DiBella v. United States,* 369 U.S. 121 (1962) (defendant may not appeal denial of pretrial motion to suppress evidence); compare *Abney v. United States,* 431 U.S. 651 (1977) (interlocutory appeal of denial of motion to dismiss on double jeopardy grounds permissible). Moreover, should the defendant thereafter plead guilty or nolo contendere, this will usually foreclose later appeal with respect to denial of the pretrial motion. "When a criminal defendant has solemnly admitted in open court that he is in fact guilty of the offense with which he is charged, he may not thereafter raise independent claims relating to the deprivation of constitutional rights that occurred prior to the entry of the guilty plea." *Tollett v. Henderson,* 411 U.S. 258 (1973). Though a nolo plea differs from a guilty plea in other respects, it is clear that it also constitutes a waiver of all nonjurisdictional defects in a manner equivalent to a guilty plea. *Lott v. United States,* 367 U.S. 421 (1961).

As a consequence, a defendant who has lost one or more pretrial motions will often go through an entire trial simply to preserve the pretrial issues for later appellate review. This results in a waste of prosecutorial and judicial resources, and causes delay in the trial of other cases, contrary to the objectives underlying the Speedy Trial Act of 1974, 18 U.S.C. § 3161 et seq. These unfortunate consequences may be avoided by the conditional plea device expressly authorized by new subdivision (a)(2).

The development of procedures to avoid the necessity for trials which are undertaken for the sole purpose of preserving pretrial objections has been consistently favored by the commentators. See ABA Standards Relating to the Administration of Criminal Justice, standard 21–1.3(c) (2d ed. 1978); Model Code of Pre–Arraignment Procedure § SS 290.1(4)(b) (1975); Uniform Rules of Criminal Procedure, rule 444(d) (Approved Draft, 1974); 1 C. Wright, Federal Practice and Procedure—Criminal § 175 (1969); 3 W. LaFave, Search and Seizure § 11.1 (1978). The Supreme Court has characterized the New York practice, whereby appeals from suppression motions may be appealed notwithstanding a guilty plea, as a "commendable effort to relieve the problem of congested trial calendars in a manner that does not diminish the opportunity for the assertion of rights guaranteed by the Constitution." *Lefkowitz v. Newsome*, 420 U.S. 283, 293 (1975). That Court has never discussed conditional pleas as such, but has permitted without comment a federal appeal on issues preserved by a conditional plea. *Jaben v. United States*, 381 U.S. 214 (1965).

In the absence of specific authorization by statute or rule for a conditional plea, the circuits have divided on the permissibility of the practice. Two circuits have actually approved the entry of conditional pleas, *United States v. Burke*, 517 F.2d 377 (2d Cir.1975); *United States v. Moskow*, 588 F.2d 882 (3d Cir.1978); and two others have praised the conditional plea concept, *United States v. Clark*, 459 F.2d 977 (8th Cir.1972); *United States v. Dorsey*, 449 F.2d 1104 (D.C.Cir.1971). Three circuits have expressed the view that a conditional plea is logically inconsistent and thus improper, *United States v. Brown*, 499 F.2d 829 (7th Cir.1974); *United States v. Sepe*, 472 F.2d 784, aff'd en banc, 486 F.2d 1044 (5th Cir.1973); *United States v. Cox*, 464 F.2d 937 (6th Cir.1972); three others have determined only that conditional pleas are not now authorized in the federal system, *United States v. Benson*, 579 F.2d 508 (9th Cir.1978); *United States v. Nooner*, 565 F.2d 633 (10th Cir.1977); *United States v. Matthews*, 472 F.2d 1173 (4th Cir.1973); while one circuit has reserved judgment on the issue, *United States v. Warwar*, 478 F.2d 1183 (1st Cir.1973). (At the state level, a few jurisdictions by statute allow appeal from denial of a motion to suppress notwithstanding a subsequent guilty plea, Cal.Penal Code § 1538.5(m); N.Y.Crim.Proc.Law § 710.20(1); Wis. Stat.Ann. § 971.31(10), but in the absence of such a provision the state courts are also in disagreement as to whether a conditional plea is permissible; see cases collected in Comment, 26 U.C.L.A.L.Rev. 360, 373 (1978).)

The conditional plea procedure provided for in subdivision (a)(2) will, as previously noted, serve to conserve prosecutorial and judicial resources and advance speedy trial objectives. It will also produce much needed uniformity in the federal system on this matter; see *United States v. Clark*, supra, noting the split of authority and urging resolution by statute or rule. Also, the availability of a conditional plea under specified circumstances will aid in clarifying the fact that traditional, unqualified pleas do constitute a waiver of nonjurisdic-

tional defects. See *United States v. Nooner*, supra (defendant sought appellate review of denial of pretrial suppression motion, despite his prior unqualified guilty plea, claiming the Second Circuit conditional plea practice led him to believe a guilty plea did not bar appeal of pretrial issues).

The obvious advantages of the conditional plea procedure authorized by subdivision (a)(2) are not outweighed by any significant or compelling disadvantages. As noted in Comment, supra, at 375: "Four major arguments have been raised by courts disapproving of conditioned pleas. The objections are that the procedure encourages a flood of appellate litigation, militates against achieving finality in the criminal process, reduces effectiveness of appellate review due to the lack of a full trial record, and forces decision on constitutional questions that could otherwise be avoided by invoking the harmless error doctrine." But, as concluded therein, those "arguments do not withstand close analysis." Ibid.

As for the first of those arguments, experience in states which have permitted appeals of suppression motions notwithstanding a subsequent plea of guilty is most relevant, as conditional pleas are likely to be most common when the objective is to appeal that kind of pretrial ruling. That experience has shown that the number of appeals has not increased substantially. See Comment, 9 Hous.L.Rev. 305, 315–19 (1971). The minimal added burden at the appellate level is certainly a small price to pay for avoiding otherwise unnecessary trials.

As for the objection that conditional pleas conflict with the government's interest in achieving finality, it is likewise without force. While it is true that the conditional plea does not have the complete finality of the traditional plea of guilty or nolo contendere because "the essence of the agreement is that the legal guilt of the defendant exists only if the prosecution's case" survives on appeal, the plea

> continues to serve a partial state interest in finality, however, by establishing admission of the defendant's factual guilt. The defendant stands guilty and the proceedings come to an end if the reserved issue is ultimately decided in the government's favor.

Comment, 26 U.C.L.A.L.Rev. 360, 378 (1978).

The claim that the lack of a full trial record precludes effective appellate review may on occasion be relevant. Cf. *United States v. MacDonald*, supra (holding interlocutory appeal not available for denial of defendant's pretrial motion to dismiss on speedy trial grounds, and noting that "most speedy trial claims * * * are best considered only after the relevant facts have been developed at trial"). However, most of the objections which would likely be raised by pretrial motion and preserved for appellate review by a conditional plea are subject to appellate resolution without a trial record. Certainly this is true as to the very common motion to suppress evidence, as is indicated by the fact that appellate courts presently decide such issues upon interlocutory appeal by the government.

With respect to the objection that conditional pleas circumvent application of the harmless error doctrine, it must be acknowledged that "[a]bsent a full trial record, containing all the government's evidence against the defendant, invocation of the harmless error rule is arguably impossible." Comment, supra, at 380. But, the harmless error standard with respect to constitutional objections is sufficiently high, see *Chapman v. California*, 386 U.S. 18 (1967), that relatively few appellate decisions result in affirmance upon that basis. Thus it will only rarely be true that the conditional plea device will cause an appellate court to consider constitutional questions which could otherwise have been avoided by invocation of the doctrine of harmless error.

To the extent that these or related objections would otherwise have some substance, they are overcome by the provision in Rule 11(a)(2) that the defendant may enter a conditional plea only "with the approval of the court and the consent of the government." (In this respect, the rule adopts the practice now found in the Second Circuit.) The requirement of approval by the court is most appropriate, as it ensures, for example, that the defendant is not allowed to take an appeal on a matter which can only be fully developed by proceeding to trial; cf. *United States v. MacDonald,* supra. As for consent by the government, it will ensure that conditional pleas will be allowed only when the decision of the court of appeals will dispose of the case either by allowing the plea to stand or by such action as compelling dismissal of the indictment or suppressing essential evidence. Absent such circumstances, the conditional plea might only serve to postpone the trial and require the government to try the case after substantial delay, during which time witnesses may be lost, memories dimmed, and the offense grown so stale as to lose jury appeal. The government is in a unique position to determine whether the matter at issue would be case-dispositive, and, as a party to the litigation, should have an absolute right to refuse to consent to potentially prejudicial delay. Although it was suggested in *United States v. Moskow,* supra, that the government should have no right to prevent the entry of a conditional plea because a defendant has no comparable right to block government appeal of a pretrial ruling pursuant to 18 U.S.C. § 3731, that analogy is unconvincing. That statute requires the government to certify that the appeal is not taken for purposes of delay. Moreover, where the pretrial ruling is case-dispositive, § 3731 is the only mechanism by which the government can obtain appellate review, but a defendant may always obtain review by pleading not guilty.

Unlike the state statutes cited earlier, Rule 11(a)(2) is not limited to instances in which the pretrial ruling the defendant wishes to appeal was in response to defendant's motion to suppress evidence. Though it may be true that the conditional plea device will be most commonly employed as to such rulings, the objectives of the rule are well served by extending it to other pretrial rulings as well. See, e.g., ABA Standards, supra (declaring the New York provision "should be enlarged to include other pretrial defenses"); Uniform Rules of Criminal Procedure, rule 444(d) (Approved Draft, 1974) ("any pretrial motion which, if granted, would be dispositive of the case").

The requirement that the conditional plea be made by the defendant "reserving in writing the right to appeal from the adverse determination of any specified pretrial motion," though extending beyond the Second Circuit practice, will ensure careful attention to any conditional plea. It will document that a particular plea was in fact conditional, and will identify precisely what pretrial issues have been preserved for appellate review. By requiring this added step, it will be possible to avoid entry of a conditional plea without the considered acquiescence of the government (see *United States v. Burke,* supra, holding that failure of the government to object to entry of a conditional plea constituted consent) and post-plea claims by the defendant that his plea should be deemed conditional merely because it occurred after denial of his pretrial motions (see *United States v. Nooner,* supra).

It must be emphasized that the *only* avenue of review of the specified pretrial ruling permitted under a rule 11(a)(2) conditional plea is an appeal, which must be brought in compliance with Fed.R.App.P. 4(b). Relief via 28 U.S.C. § 2255 is not available for this purpose.

The Supreme Court has held that certain kinds of constitutional objections may be raised after a plea of guilty. *Menna v. New York,* 423 U.S. 61 (1975) (double jeopardy violation); *Blackledge v. Perry,* 417 U.S. 21 (1974) (due process violation by charge enhancement following defendant's exercise of right to trial de novo). Subdivision 11(a)(2) has no application to such situations, and should not be interpreted as either broadening or narrowing the *Menna–Blackledge* doctrine or as establishing procedures for its application.

Rule 11(h)

Subdivision (h) makes clear that the harmless error rule of Rule 52(a) is applicable to Rule 11. The provision does not, however, attempt to define the meaning of "harmless error," which is left to the case law. Prior to the amendments which took effect on Dec. 1, 1975, Rule 11 was very brief; it consisted of but four sentences. The 1975 amendments increased significantly the procedures which must be undertaken when a defendant tenders a plea of guilty or nolo contendere, but this change was warranted by the "two principal objectives" then identified in the Advisory Committee Note:

(1) ensuring that the defendant has made an informed plea; and (2) ensuring that plea agreements are brought out into the open in court. An inevitable consequence of the 1975 amendments was some increase in the risk that a trial judge, in a particular case, might inadvertently deviate to some degree from the procedure which a very literal reading of Rule 11 would appear to require.

This being so, it became more apparent than ever that Rule 11 should not be given such a crabbed interpretation that ceremony was exalted over substance. As stated in *United States v. Scarf,* 551 F.2d 1124 (8th Cir.1977), concerning amended Rule 11: "It is a salutary rule, and district courts are required to act in substantial compliance with it although * * * ritualistic compliance is not required." As similarly pointed out in *United States v. Saft,* 558 F.2d 1073 (2d Cir.1977),

the Rule does not say that compliance can be achieved only by reading the specified items *in haec verba.* Congress meant to strip district judges of freedom to decide *what* they must explain to a defendant who wishes to plead guilty, not to tell them precisely *how* to perform this important task in the great variety of cases that would come before them. While a judge who contents himself with literal application of the Rule will hardly be reversed, it cannot be supposed that Congress preferred this to a more meaningful explanation, provided that all the specified elements were covered.

Two important points logically flow from these sound observations. One concerns the matter of construing Rule 11: it is not to be read as requiring a litany or other ritual which can be carried out only by word-for-word adherence to a set "script." The other, specifically addressed in new subdivision (h), is that even when it may be concluded Rule 11 has not been complied with in all respects, it does not inevitably follow that the defendant's plea of guilty or nolo contendere is invalid and subject to being overturned by any remedial device then available to the defendant.

Notwithstanding the declaration in Rule 52(a) that "[a]ny error, defect, irregularity or variance which does not affect substantial rights shall be disregarded," there has existed for some years considerable disagreement concerning the applicability of the harmless error doctrine to Rule 11 violations. In large part, this is attributable to uncertainty as to the continued vitality and the reach of *McCarthy v. United States,* 394 U.S. 459 (1969). In *McCarthy,* involving a direct appeal from a plea of guilty because of noncompliance with Rule 11, the Court concluded

that prejudice inheres in a failure to comply with Rule 11, for noncompliance deprives the defendant of the Rule's procedural safeguards, which are designed to facilitate a more accurate determination of the voluntariness of his plea. Our holding [is] that a defendant whose plea has been accepted in violation

of Rule 11 should be afforded the opportunity to plead anew * * *.

McCarthy has been most frequently relied upon in cases where, as in that case, the defendant sought relief because of a Rule 11 violation by the avenue of direct appeal. It has been held that in such circumstances a defendant's conviction must be reversed whenever the "district court accepts his guilty plea without fully adhering to the procedure provided for in Rule 11," *United States v. Boone,* 543 F.2d 1090 (4th Cir.1976), and that in this context any reliance by the government on the Rule 52(a) harmless error concept "must be rejected." *United States v. Journet,* 544 F.2d 633 (2d Cir.1976). On the other hand, decisions are to be found taking a harmless error approach on direct appeal where it appeared the nature and extent of the deviation from Rule 11 was such that it could not have had any impact on the defendant's decision to plead or the fairness in now holding him to his plea. *United States v. Peters,* No. 77–1700 (4th Cir., Dec. 22, 1978) (where judge failed to comply fully with Rule 11(c)(1), in that defendant not correctly advised of maximum years of special parole term but was told it is at least 3 years, and defendant thereafter sentenced to 15 years plus 3–year special parole term, government's motion for summary affirmance granted, as "the error was harmless"); *United States v. Coronado,* 554 F.2d 166 (5th Cir.1977) (court first holds that charge of conspiracy requires some explanation of what conspiracy means to comply with Rule 11(c)(1), but then finds no reversible error "because the rule 11 proceeding on its face discloses, despite the trial court's failure sufficiently to make the required explication of the charges, that Coronado understood them").

But this conflict has not been limited to cases involving nothing more than a direct appeal following defendant's plea. For example, another type of case is that in which the defendant has based a post-sentence motion to withdraw his plea on a Rule 11 violation. Rule 32(d) says that such a motion may be granted "to correct manifest injustice," and some courts have relied upon this latter provision in holding that post-sentence plea withdrawal need not be permitted merely because Rule 11 was not fully complied with and that instead the district court should hold an evidentiary hearing to determine "whether manifest injustice will result if the conviction based on the guilty plea is permitted to stand." *United States v. Scarf,* 551 F.2d 1124 (8th Cir.1977). Others, however, have held that *McCarthy* applies and prevails over the language of Rule 32(d), so that "a failure to scrupulously comply with Rule 11 will invalidate a plea without a showing of manifest injustice." *United States v. Cantor,* 469 F.2d 435 (3d Cir. 1972).

Disagreement has also existed in the context of collateral attack upon pleas pursuant to 28 U.S.C. § 2255. On the one hand, it has been concluded that "[n]ot every violation of Rule 11 requires that the plea be set aside" in a § 2255 proceeding, and that "a guilty plea will be set aside on collateral attack only where to not do so would result in a miscarriage of justice, or where there exists exceptional circumstances justifying such relief." *Evers v. United States,* 579 F.2d 71 (10th Cir. 1978). The contrary view was that *McCarthy* governed in § 2255 proceedings because "the Supreme Court hinted at no exceptions to its policy of strict enforcement of Rule 11." *Timmreck v. United States,* 577 F.2d 377 (6th Cir.1978). But a unanimous Supreme Court resolved this conflict in *United States v. Timmreck,* 441 U.S. 780 (1979), where the Court concluded that the reasoning of *Hill v. United States,* 368 U.S. 424 (1962) (ruling a collateral attack could not be predicated on a violation of Rule 32(a))

is equally applicable to a formal violation of Rule 11.
* * *

Indeed, if anything, this case may be a stronger one for foreclosing collateral relief than the *Hill* case. For the concern with finality served by the limitation on collateral attack has special force with respect to convictions based on guilty pleas.

"Every inroad on the concept of finality undermines confidence in the integrity of our procedures; and, by increasing the volume of judicial work, inevitably delays and impairs the orderly administration of justice. The impact is greatest when new grounds for setting aside guilty pleas are approved because the vast majority of criminal convictions result from such pleas. Moreover, the concern that unfair procedures may have resulted in the conviction of an innocent defendant is only rarely raised by a petition to set aside a guilty plea."

This interest in finality is strongest in the collateral attack context the Court was dealing with in *Timmreck,* which explains why the Court there adopted the *Hill* requirement that in a § 2255 proceeding the rule violation must amount to "a fundamental defect which inherently results in a complete miscarriage of justice" or "an omission inconsistent with the rudimentary demands of fair procedure." The interest in finality of guilty pleas described in *Timmreck* is of somewhat lesser weight when a direct appeal is involved (so that the *Hill* standard is obviously inappropriate in that setting), but yet is sufficiently compelling to make unsound the proposition that reversal is required even where it is apparent that the Rule 11 violation was of the harmless error variety.

Though the *McCarthy* per se rule may have been justified at the time and in the circumstances which obtained when the plea in that case was taken, this is no longer the case. For one thing, it is important to recall that *McCarthy* dealt only with the much simpler pre-1975 version of Rule 11, which required only a brief procedure during which the chances of a minor, insignificant and inadvertent deviation were relatively slight. This means that the chances of a *truly* harmless error (which was not involved in *McCarthy* in any event, as the judge made *no* inquiry into the defendant's understanding of the nature of the charge, and the government had presented only the extreme argument that a court "could properly *assume* that petitioner was entering that plea with a complete understanding of the charge against him" merely from the fact he had stated he desired to plead guilty) are much greater under present Rule 11 than under the version before the Court in *McCarthy.* It also means that the more elaborate and lengthy procedures of present Rule 11, again as compared with the version applied in *McCarthy,* make it more apparent than ever that a guilty plea is not "a mere gesture, a temporary and meaningless formality reversible at the defendant's whim," but rather " 'a grave and solemn act,' which is 'accepted only with care and discernment.' " *United States v. Barker,* 514 F.2d 208 (D.C.Cir.1975), quoting from *Brady v. United States,* 397 U.S. 742 (1970). A plea of that character should not be overturned, even on direct appeal, when there has been a minor and technical violation of Rule 11 which amounts to harmless error.

Secondly, while *McCarthy* involved a situation in which the defendant's plea of guilty was before the court of appeals on direct appeal, the Supreme Court appears to have been primarily concerned with § 2255–type cases, for the Court referred exclusively to cases of that kind in the course of concluding that a per se rule was justified as to Rule 11 violations because of "the difficulty of achieving [rule 11's] purposes through a post-conviction voluntariness hearing." But that reasoning has now been substantially undercut by *United States v. Timmreck,* supra, for the Court there concluded § 2255 relief "is not available when all that is shown is a failure to comply with the formal requirements of the Rule," at least absent "other aggravating circumstances," which presumably could often only be developed in the course of a later evidentiary hearing.

Although all of the aforementioned considerations support the policy expressed in new subdivision (h), the Advisory Committee does wish to emphasize two important cautionary notes. The first is that subdivision (h) should *not* be read as supporting extreme or speculative harmless error claims or as, in effect, nullifying important Rule 11 safeguards. There would *not* be harmless error under subdivision (h) where, for example, as in *McCarthy,* there had been absolutely no inquiry by the judge into defendant's understanding of the nature of the charge and the harmless error claim of the government rests upon nothing more than the assertion that it may be "assumed" defendant possessed such understanding merely because he expressed a desire to plead guilty. Likewise, it would *not* be harmless error if the trial judge totally abdicated to the prosecutor the responsibility for giving to the defendant the various Rule 11 warnings, as this "results in the creation of an atmosphere of subtle coercion that clearly contravenes the policy behind Rule 11." *United States v. Crook,* 526 F.2d 708 (5th Cir.1976).

Indeed, it is fair to say that the kinds of Rule 11 violations which might be found to constitute harmless error upon direct appeal are fairly limited, as in such instances the matter "must be resolved solely on the basis of the Rule 11 transcript" and the other portions (e.g., sentencing hearing) of the limited record made in such cases. *United States v. Coronado,* supra. Illustrative are: where the judge's compliance with subdivision (c)(1) was not absolutely complete, in that some essential element of the crime was not mentioned, but the defendant's responses clearly indicate his awareness of that element, see *United States v. Coronado,* supra; where the judge's compliance with subdivision (c)(2) was erroneous in part in that the judge understated the maximum penalty somewhat, but the penalty actually imposed did not exceed that indicated in the warnings, see *United States v. Peters,* supra; and where the judge completely failed to comply with subdivision (c)(5), which of course has no bearing on the validity of the plea itself, cf. *United States v. Sinagub,* supra.

The second cautionary note is that subdivision (h) should *not* be read as an invitation to trial judges to take a more casual approach to Rule 11 proceedings. It is still true, as the Supreme Court pointed out in *McCarthy,* that thoughtful and careful compliance with Rule 11 best serves the cause of fair and efficient administration of criminal justice, as it

> will help reduce the great waste of judicial resources required to process the frivolous attacks on guilty plea convictions that are encouraged, and are more difficult to dispose of, when the original record is inadequate. It is, therefore, not too much to require that, before sentencing defendants to years of imprisonment, district judges take the few minutes necessary to inform them of their rights and to determine whether they understand the action they are taking.

Subdivision (h) makes *no change* in the responsibilities of the judge at Rule 11 proceedings, but instead merely rejects the extreme sanction of automatic reversal.

It must also be emphasized that a harmless error provision has been added to Rule 11 because some courts have read *McCarthy* as meaning that the general harmless error provision in Rule 52(a) cannot be utilized with respect to Rule 11 proceedings. Thus, the addition of subdivision (h) should *not* be read as suggesting that Rule 52(a) does not apply in other circumstances because of the absence of a provision comparable to subdivision (h) attached to other rules.

1985 AMENDMENT

Rule 11(c)(1)

Section 5 of the Victim and Witness Protection Act of 1982, Pub.L. No. 97–291, 96 Stat. 1248 (1982), adds 18

U.S.C. § 3579, providing that when sentencing a defendant convicted of a Title 18 offense or of violating various subsections of the Federal Aviation Act of 1958, the court "may order, in addition to or in lieu of any other penalty authorized by law, that the defendant make restitution to any victim of the offense." Under this law restitution is favored; if the court "does not order restitution, or orders only partial restitution, ... the court shall state on the record the reasons therefor." Because this restitution is deemed an aspect of the defendant's sentence, S.Rept. No. 97–532, 97th Cong., 2d Sess., 30–33 (1982), it is a matter about which a defendant tendering a plea of guilty or nolo contendere should be advised.

Because this new legislation contemplates that the amount of the restitution to be ordered will be ascertained later in the sentencing process, this amendment to Rule 11(c)(1) merely requires that the defendant be told of the court's power to order restitution. The exact amount or upper limit cannot and need not be stated at the time of the plea. Failure of a court to advise a defendant of the possibility of a restitution order would constitute harmless error under subdivision (h) if no restitution were thereafter ordered.

1987 AMENDMENT

The amendments are technical. No substantive change is intended.

Rule 12. Pleadings and Motions Before Trial; Defenses and Objections

(a) Pleadings and Motions. Pleadings in criminal proceedings shall be the indictment and the information, and the pleas of not guilty, guilty and nolo contendere. All other pleas, and demurrers and motions to quash are abolished, and defenses and objections raised before trial which heretofore could have been raised by one or more of them shall be raised only by motion to dismiss or to grant appropriate relief, as provided in these rules.

(b) Pretrial Motions. Any defense, objection, or request which is capable of determination without the trial of the general issue may be raised before trial by motion. Motions may be written or oral at the discretion of the judge. The following must be raised prior to trial:

(1) Defenses and objections based on defects in the institution of the prosecution; or

(2) Defenses and objections based on defects in the indictment or information (other than that it fails to show jurisdiction in the court or to charge an offense which objections shall be

noticed by the court at any time during the pendency of the proceedings); or

(3) Motions to suppress evidence; or

(4) Requests for discovery under Rule 16; or

(5) Requests for a severance of charges or defendants under Rule 14.

(c) Motion Date. Unless otherwise provided by local rule, the court may, at the time of the arraignment or as soon thereafter as practicable, set a time for the making of pretrial motions or requests and, if required, a later date of hearing.

(d) Notice by the Government of the Intention to Use Evidence.

(1) At the Discretion of the Government. At the arraignment or as soon thereafter as is practicable, the government may give notice to the defendant of its intention to use specified evidence at trial in order to afford the defendant an opportunity to raise objections to such evidence prior to trial under subdivision (b)(3) of this rule.

(2) At the Request of the Defendant. At the arraignment or as soon thereafter as is practicable the defendant may, in order to afford an opportunity to move to suppress evidence under subdivision (b)(3) of this rule, request notice of the government's intention to use (in its evidence in chief at trial) any evidence which the defendant may be entitled to discover under Rule 16 subject to any relevant limitations prescribed in Rule 16.

(e) Ruling on Motion. A motion made before trial shall be determined before trial unless the court, for good cause, orders that it be deferred for determination at the trial of the general issue or until after verdict, but no such determination shall be deferred if a party's right to appeal is adversely affected. Where factual issues are involved in determining a motion, the court shall state its essential findings on the record.

(f) Effect of Failure To Raise Defenses or Objections. Failure by a party to raise defenses or objections or to make requests which must be made prior to trial, at the time set by the court pursuant to subdivision (c), or prior to any extension thereof made by the court, shall constitute waiver thereof, but the court for cause shown may grant relief from the waiver.

(g) Records. A verbatim record shall be made of all proceedings at the hearing, including such findings of fact and conclusions of law as are made orally.

(h) Effect of Determination. If the court grants a motion based on a defect in the institution of the prosecution or in the indictment or information, it may also order that the defendant be continued in custody or that bail be continued for a specified time pending the filing of a new indictment or information. Nothing in this rule shall be deemed to affect the provisions of any Act of Congress relating to periods of limitations.

(i) Production of Statements at Suppression Hearing. Except as herein provided, rule 26.2 shall apply at a hearing on a motion to suppress evidence under subdivision (b)(3) of this rule. For purposes of this subdivision, a law enforcement officer shall be deemed a witness called by the government, and upon a claim of privilege the court shall excise the portions of the statement containing privileged matter.

(As amended Apr. 22, 1974, eff. Dec. 1, 1975; July 31, 1975, Pub.L. 94–64, § 3(11), (12), 89 Stat. 372; Apr. 28, 1983, eff. Aug. 1, 1983; Mar. 9, 1987, eff. Aug. 1, 1987.)

NOTES OF ADVISORY COMMITTEE ON RULES

Note to Subdivision (a). 1. This rule abolishes pleas to the jurisdiction, pleas in abatement, demurrers, special pleas in bar, and motions to quash. A motion to dismiss or for other appropriate relief is substituted for the purpose of raising all defenses and objections heretofore interposed in any of the foregoing modes. "This should result in a reduction of opportunities for dilatory tactics and, at the same time, relieve the defense of embarrassment. Many competent practitioners have been baffled and mystified by the distinctions between pleas in abatement, pleas in bar, demurrers, and motions to quash, and have, at times, found difficulty in determining which of these should be invoked." Homer Cummings, 29 A.B.A.Jour. 655. See also, Medalie, 4 Lawyers Guild R. (3)1, 4.

2. A similar change was introduced by the Federal Rules of Civil Procedure (Rule 7(a)) which has proven successful. It is also proposed by the A.L.I. Code of Criminal Procedure (Sec. 209).

Note to Subdivision (b)(1) and (2). These two paragraphs classify into two groups all objections and defenses to be interposed by motion prescribed by Rule 12(a). In one group are defenses and objections which must be raised by motion, failure to do so constituting a waiver. In the other group are defenses and objections which at the defendant's option may be raised by motion, failure to do so, however, not constituting a waiver. (Cf. Rule 12 of Federal Rules of Civil Procedure, 28 U.S.C., Appendix.)

In the first of these groups are included all defenses and objections that are based on defects in the institution of the prosecution or in the indictment and information, other than lack of jurisdiction or failure to charge an offense. All such defenses and objections must be included in a single motion. (Cf. Rule 12(g) of Federal Rules of Civil Procedure, 28 U.S.C., Appendix.) Among the defenses and objections in this group are the following: Illegal selection or organization of the grand jury, disqualification of individual grand jurors, presence of unauthorized persons in the grand jury room, other irregularities in grand jury proceedings, defects in indictment or information other than lack of jurisdiction or failure to state an offense, etc. The provision that these defenses and objections are waived if not raised by motion substantially continues existing law, as they are waived at present unless raised before trial by plea in abatement, demurrer, motion to quash, etc.

In the other group of objections and defenses, which the defendant at his option may raise by motion before trial, are included all defenses and objections which are capable of determination without a trial of the general issue. They include such matters as former jeopardy, former conviction, former acquittal, statute of limitations, immunity, lack of jurisdiction, failure of indictment or information to state an offense, etc. Such matters have been heretofore raised by demurrers, special pleas in bar and motions to quash.

Note to Subdivision (b)(3). This rule, while requiring the motion to be made before pleading, vests discretionary authority in the court to permit the motion to be made within a reasonable time thereafter. The rule supersedes 18 U.S.C. former § 556a (now §§ 3288, 3289), fixing a definite limitation of time for pleas in abatement and motions to quash. The rule also eliminates the requirement for technical withdrawal of a plea if it is desired to interpose a preliminary objection or defense after the plea has been entered. Under this rule a plea will be permitted to stand in the meantime.

Note to Subdivision (b)(4). This rule substantially restates existing law. It leaves with the court discretion to determine in advance of trial defenses and objections raised by motion or to defer them for determination at the trial. It preserves the right to jury trial in those cases in which the right is given under the Constitution or by statute. In all other cases it vests in the court authority to determine issues of fact in such manner as the court deems appropriate.

Note to Subdivision (b)(5). 1. The first sentence substantially restates existing law, 18 U.S.C. former § 561 (Indictments and presentments; judgment on demurrer), which provides that in case a demurrer to an indictment or information is overruled, the judgment shall be respondeat ouster.

2. The last sentence of the rule that "Nothing in this rule shall be deemed to affect the provisions of any act of Congress relating to periods of limitations" is intended to preserve the provisions of statutes which permit a reindictment if the original indictment is found defective or is dismissed for other irregularities and the statute of limitations has run in the meantime, 18 U.S.C. former § 587 (now § 3288) (Defective indictment; defect found after period of limitations; reindictment); Id. former sec. 588 (now § 3289) (Defective indictment; defect found before period of limitations; reindictment); Id. 18 U.S.C. former § 589 (now §§ 3288, 3289) (Defective indictment; defense of limitations to new indictment); Id. 18 U.S.C. former § 556a (now §§ 3288, 3289) (Indictments and presentments; objections to drawing or qualification of grand jury; time for filing; suspension of statute of limitations).

1974 AMENDMENT

Subdivision (a) remains as it was in the old rule. It "speaks only of defenses and objections that prior to the rules could have been raised by a plea, demurrer, or motion to quash" (C. Wright, Federal Practice and Procedure: Criminal § 191 at p. 397 (1969)), and this might be interpreted as limiting the scope of the rule. However, some courts have assumed that old rule 12 does apply to pretrial motions generally, and the amendments to subsequent subdivisions of the rule should make clear that the rule is applicable to pretrial motion practice generally. (See e.g., rule 12(b)(3), (4), (5) and rule 41(e).)

Subdivision (b) is changed to provide for some additional motions and requests which must be made prior to trial. Subdivisions (b)(1) and (2) are restatements of the old rule.

Subdivision (b)(3) makes clear that objections to evidence on the ground that it was illegally obtained must be raised prior to trial. This is the current rule with regard to evidence obtained as a result of an illegal search. See rule 41(e); C. Wright, Federal Practice and Procedure: Criminal § 673 (1969, Supp.1971). It is also the practice with regard to other forms of illegality such as the use of unconstitutional means to obtain a confession. See C. Wright, Federal Practice and Procedure: Criminal § 673 at p. 108 (1969). It seems apparent that the same principle should apply whatever the claimed basis for the application of the exclusionary rule of evidence may be. This is consistent with the court's statement in *Jones v. United States,* 362 U.S. 257, 264, 80 S.Ct. 725, 4 L.Ed.2d 697 (1960):

This provision of Rule 41(e), requiring the motion to suppress to be made before trial, is a crystallization of decisions of this Court requiring that procedure, and is designed **to eliminate from the trial disputes over police conduct not immediately relevant to the question of guilt.** (Emphasis added.)

Subdivision (b)(4) provides for a pretrial request for discovery by either the defendant or the government to the extent to which such discovery is authorized by rule 16.

Subdivision (b)(5) provides for a pretrial request for a severance as authorized in rule 14.

Subdivision (c) provides that a time for the making of motions shall be fixed at the time of the arraignment or as soon thereafter as practicable by court rule or direction of a judge. The rule leaves to the individual judge whether the motions may be oral or written. This and other amendments to rule 12 are designed to make possible and to encourage the making of motions prior to trial, whenever possible, and in a single hearing rather than in a series of hearings. This is the recommendation of the American Bar Association's Committee on Standards Relating to Discovery and Procedure Before Trial (Approved Draft, 1970); see especially §§ 5.2 and 5.3. It also is the procedure followed in those jurisdictions which have used the so-called "omnibus hearing" originated by Judge James Carter in the Southern District of California. See 4 Defender Newsletter 44 (1967); Miller, The Omnibus Hearing—An Experiment in Federal Criminal Discovery, 5 San Diego L.Rev. 293 (1968); American Bar Association, Standards Relating to Discovery and Procedure Before Trial, Appendices B, C, and D (Approved Draft, 1970). The omnibus hearing is also being used, on an experimental basis, in several other district courts. Although the Advisory Committee is of the view that it would be premature to write the omnibus hearing procedure into the rules, it is of the view that the single pretrial hearing should be made possible and its use encouraged by the rules.

There is a similar trend in state practice. See, e.g., *State ex rel. Goodchild v. Burke*, 27 Wis.2d 244, 133 N.W.2d 753 (1965); *State ex rel. Rasmussen v. Tahash*, 272 Minn. 539, 141 N.W.2d 3 (1965).

The rule provides that the motion date be set at "the arraignment or as soon thereafter as practicable." This is the practice in some federal courts including those using the omnibus hearing. (In order to obtain the advantage of the omnibus hearing, counsel routinely plead not guilty at the initial arraignment on the information or indictment and then may indicate a desire to change the plea to guilty following the omnibus hearing. This practice builds a more adequate record in guilty plea cases.) The rule further provides that the date may be set before the arraignment if local rules of court so provide.

Subdivision (d) provides a mechanism for insuring that a defendant knows of the government's intention to use evidence to which the defendant may want to object. On some occasions the resolution of the admissibility issue prior to trial may be advantageous to the government. In these situations the attorney for the government can make effective defendant's obligation

to make his motion to suppress prior to trial by giving defendant notice of the government's intention to use certain evidence. For example, in United States v. Desist, 384 F.2d 889, 897 (2d Cir.1967), the court said:

Early in the pre-trial proceedings, the Government commendably informed both the court and defense counsel that an electronic listening device had been used in investigating the case, and suggested a hearing be held as to its legality.

See also the "Omnibus Crime Control and Safe Streets Act of 1968," 18 U.S.C. § 2518(9):

The contents of any intercepted wire or oral communication or evidence derived therefrom shall not be received in evidence or otherwise disclosed in any trial, hearing, or other proceeding in a Federal or State court unless each party, not less than ten days before the trial, hearing, or proceeding, has been furnished with a copy of the court order, and accompanying application, under which the interception was authorized or approved.

In cases in which defendant wishes to know what types of evidence the government intends to use so that he can make his motion to suppress prior to trial, he can request the government to give notice of its intention to use specified evidence which the defendant is entitled to discover under rule 16. Although the defendant is already entitled to discovery of such evidence prior to trial under rule 16, rule 12 makes it possible for him to avoid the necessity of moving to suppress evidence which the government does not intend to use. No sanction is provided for the government's failure to comply with the court's order because the committee believes that attorneys for the government will in fact comply and that judges have ways of insuring compliance. An automatic exclusion of such evidence, particularly where the failure to give notice was not deliberate, seems to create too heavy a burden upon the exclusionary rule of evidence, especially when defendant has opportunity for broad discovery under rule 16. Compare ABA Project on Standards for Criminal Justice, Standards Relating to Electronic Surveillance (Approved Draft, 1971) at p. 116:

A failure to comply with the duty of giving notice could lead to the suppression of evidence. Nevertheless, the standards make it explicit that the rule is intended to be a matter of procedure which need not under appropriate circumstances automatically dictate that evidence otherwise admissible be suppressed.

Pretrial notice by the prosecution of its intention to use evidence which may be subject to a motion to suppress is increasingly being encouraged in state practice. See, e.g., *State ex rel. Goodchild v. Burke*, 27 Wis.2d 244, 264, 133 N.W.2d 753, 763 (1965):

In the interest of better administration of criminal justice we suggest that wherever practicable the prosecutor should within a reasonable time before trial notify the defense as to whether any alleged confession or admission will be offered in evidence at the trial. We also suggest, in cases where such notice is given by the prosecution, that the defense, if it intends to attack the confession or admission as involuntary, notify the prosecutor of a desire by the defense for a special determination on such issue.

See also *State ex rel. Rasmussen v. Tahash*, 272 Minn. 539, 553–556, 141 N.W.2d 3, 13–15 (1965):

At the time of arraignment when a defendant pleads not guilty, or as soon as possible thereafter, the state will advise the court as to whether its case against the defendant will include evidence obtained as the result of a search and seizure; evidence discovered because of a confession or statements in the nature of a confession obtained from the defendant; or confessions or statements in the nature of confessions.

Upon being so informed, the court will formally advise the attorney for the defendant (or the defendant himself if he refuses legal counsel) that he may, if he chooses, move the court to suppress the evidence so secured or the confession so obtained if his contention is that such evidence was secured or confession obtained in violation of defendant's constitutional rights. * * *

The procedure which we have outlined deals only with evidence obtained as the result of a search and seizure and evidence consisting of or produced by confession on the part of the defendant. However, the steps which have been suggested as a method of dealing with evidence of this type will indicate to counsel and to the trial courts that the pretrial consideration of other evidentiary problems, the resolution of which is needed to assure the integrity of the trial when conducted, will be most useful and that this court encourages the use of such procedures whenever practical.

Subdivision (e) provides that the court shall rule on a pretrial motion before trial unless the court orders that it be decided upon at the trial of the general issue or after verdict. This is the old rule. The reference to issues which must be tried by the jury is dropped as unnecessary, without any intention of changing current law or practice. The old rule begs the question of when a jury decision is required at the trial, providing only that a jury is necessary if "required by the Constitution or an act of Congress." It will be observed that subdivision (e) confers general authority to defer the determination of any pretrial motion until after verdict. However, in the case of a motion to suppress evidence the power should be exercised in the light of the possibility that if the motion is ultimately granted a retrial of the defendant may not be permissible.

Subdivision (f) provides that a failure to raise the objections or make the requests specified in subdivision (b) constitutes a waiver thereof, but the court is allowed to grant relief from the waiver if adequate cause is shown. See C. Wright, Federal Practice and Procedure: Criminal § 192 (1969), where it is pointed out that the old rule is unclear as to whether the waiver results only from a failure to raise the issue prior to trial or from the failure to do so at the time fixed by the judge for a hearing. The amendment makes clear that the defendant and, where appropriate, the government have an obligation to raise the issue at the motion date set by the judge pursuant to subdivision (c).

Subdivision (g) requires that a verbatim record be made of pretrial motion proceedings and requires the judge to make a record of his findings of fact and conclusions of law. This is desirable if pretrial rulings are to be subject to post-conviction review on the record. The judge may find and rule orally from the bench, so long as a verbatim record is taken. There is no necessity of a separate written memorandum containing the judge's findings and conclusions.

Subdivision (h) is essentially old rule 12(b)(5) except for the deletion of the provision that defendant may plead if the motion is determined adversely to him or, if he has already entered a plea, that that plea stands. This language seems unnecessary particularly in light of the experience in some district courts where a pro forma plea of not guilty is entered at the arraignment, pretrial motions are later made, and depending upon the outcome the defendant may then change his plea to guilty or persist in his plea of not guilty.

NOTES OF COMMITTEE ON THE JUDICIARY, HOUSE REPORT NO. 94–247

A. Amendments Proposed by the Supreme Court. Rule 12 of the Federal Rules of Criminal Procedure deals with pretrial motions and pleadings. The Supreme Court proposed several amendments to it. The more significant of these are set out below.

Subdivision (b) as proposed to be amended provides that the pretrial motions may be oral or written, at the court's discretion. It also provides that certain types of motions must be made before trial.

Subdivision (d) as proposed to be amended provides that the government, either on its own or in response to a request by the defendant, must notify the defendant of its intention to use certain evidence in order to give the defendant an opportunity before trial to move to suppress that evidence.

Subdivision (e) as proposed to be amended permits the court to defer ruling on a pretrial motion until the trial of the general issue or until after verdict.

Subdivision (f) as proposed to be amended provides that the failure before trial to file motions or requests or to raise defenses which must be filed or raised prior to trial, results in a waiver. However, it also provides that the court, for cause shown, may grant relief from the waiver.

Subdivision (g) as proposed to be amended requires that a verbatim record be made of the pretrial motion proceedings and that the judge make a record of his findings of fact and conclusions of law.

B. Committee Action. The Committee modified subdivision (e) to permit the court to defer its ruling on a pretrial motion until after the trial only for good cause. Moreover, the court cannot defer its ruling if to do so will adversely affect a party's right to appeal. The Committee believes that the rule proposed by the Supreme Court could deprive the government of its appeal rights under statutes like section 3731 of title 18 of the United States Code. Further, the Committee hopes to discourage the tendency to reserve rulings on pretrial motions until after verdict in the hope that the jury's verdict will make a ruling unnecessary.

The Committee also modified subdivision (h), which deals with what happens when the court grants a pretrial motion based upon a defect in the institution of the prosecution or in the indictment or information. The Committee's change provides that when such a motion is granted, the court may order that the defendant be continued in custody or that his bail be continued for a specified time. A defendant should not automatically be continued in custody when such a motion is granted. In order to continue the defendant in custody, the court must not only determine that there is probable cause, but it must also determine, in effect, that there is good cause to have the defendant arrested.

1983 AMENDMENT

Rule 12(i)

As noted in the recent decision of *United States v. Raddatz,* 447 U.S. 667 (1980), hearings on pretrial suppression motions not infrequently necessitate a determination of the credibility of witnesses. In such a situation, it is particularly important, as also highlighted by *Raddatz,* that the record include some other evidence which tends to either verify or controvert the assertions of the witness. (This is especially true in light of the *Raddatz* holding that a district judge, in order to make an independent evaluation of credibility, is not required to rehear testimony on which a magistrate based his findings and recommendations following a suppression hearing before the magistrate.) One kind of evidence which can often fulfill this function is prior statements of the testifying witness, yet courts have consistently held that in light of the Jencks Act, 18 U.S.C. § 3500, such production of statements cannot be compelled at a pretrial suppression hearing. *United States v. Spagnuolo,* 515 F.2d 818 (9th Cir.1975); *United States v. Sebastian,* 497 F.2d 1267 (2nd Cir.1974); *United States v. Montos,* 421 F.2d 215 (5th Cir.1970). This result, which finds no express Congressional approval in the legislative history of the Jencks Act, see *United States v. Sebastian,* supra; *United States v. Covello,* 410 F.2d 536

(2d Cir.1969), would be obviated by new subdivision (i) of rule 12.

This change will enhance the accuracy of the factual determinations made in the context of pretrial suppression hearings. As noted in *United States v. Sebastian,* supra, it can be argued

> most persuasively that the case for pre-trial disclosure is strongest in the framework of a suppression hearing. Since findings at such a hearing as to admissibility of challenged evidence will often determine the result at trial and, at least in the case of fourth amendment suppression motions, cannot be relitigated later before the trier of fact, pre-trial production of the statements of witnesses would aid defense counsel's impeachment efforts at perhaps the most crucial point in the case. * * * [A] government witness at the suppression hearing may not appear at trial so that defendants could never test his credibility with the benefits of Jencks Act material.

The latter statement is certainly correct, for not infrequently a police officer who must testify on a motion to suppress as to the circumstances of an arrest or search will not be called at trial because he has no information necessary to the determination of defendant's guilt. See, e.g., *United States v. Spagnuolo,* supra (dissent notes that "under the prosecution's own admission, it did not intend to produce at trial the witnesses called at the pre-trial suppression hearing"). Moreover, even if that person did testify at the trial, if that testimony went to a different subject matter, then under rule 26.2(c) only portions of prior statements covering the same subject matter need be produced, and thus portions which might contradict the suppression hearing testimony would not be revealed. Thus, while it may be true, as declared in *United States v. Montos,* supra, that "due process does not require premature production at pre-trial hearings on motions to suppress of statements ultimately subject to discovery under the Jencks Act," the fact of the matter is that those statements—or, the essential portions thereof—are not necessarily subject to later discovery.

Moreover, it is not correct to assume that somehow the problem can be solved by leaving the suppression issue "open" in some fashion for resolution once the trial is under way, at which time the prior statements will be produced. In *United States v. Spagnuolo,* supra, the court responded to the defendant's dilemma of inaccessible prior statements by saying that the suppression motion could simply be deferred until trial. But, under the current version of rule 12 this is not possible; subdivision (b) declares that motions to suppress "must" be made before trial, and subdivision (e) says such motions cannot be deferred for determination at trial "if a party's right to appeal is adversely affected," which surely is the case as to suppression motions. As for the possibility of the trial judge reconsidering the motion to suppress on the basis of prior statements produced at trial and casting doubt on the credibility of a suppression hearing witness, it is not a desirable or adequate solution. For one thing, as already noted, there is no assurance that the prior statements will be forthcoming. Even if they are, it is not efficient to delay the continuation of the trial to undertake a reconsideration of matters which could have been resolved in advance of trial had the critical facts then been available. Furthermore, if such reconsideration is regularly to be expected of the trial judge, then this would give rise on appeal to unnecessary issues of the kind which confronted the court in *United States v. Montos,* supra —whether the trial judge was obligated either to conduct a new hearing or to make a new determination in light of the new evidence.

The second sentence of subdivision (i) provides that a law enforcement officer is to be deemed a witness called by the government. This means that when such a federal, state or local officer has testified at a suppression hearing, the defendant will be entitled to any statement of the officer in the possession of the government and relating to the subject matter concerning which the witness has testified, without regard to whether the officer was in fact called by the government or the defendant. There is considerable variation in local practice as to whether the arresting or searching officer is considered the witness of the defendant or of the government, but the need for the prior statement exists in either instance.

The second sentence of subdivision (i) also provides that upon a claim of privilege the court is to excise the privileged matter before turning over the statement. The situation most likely to arise is that in which the prior statement of the testifying officer identifies an informant who supplied some or all of the probable cause information to the police. Under *McCray v. Illinois,* 386 U.S. 300 (1967), it is for the judge who hears the motion to decide whether disclosure of the informant's identity is necessary in the particular case. Of course, the government in any case may prevent disclosure of the informant's identity by terminating reliance upon information from that informant.

1987 AMENDMENT

The amendment is technical. No substantive change is intended.

Rule 12.1 Notice of Alibi

(a) Notice by Defendant. Upon written demand of the attorney for the government stating the time, date, and place at which the alleged offense was committed, the defendant shall serve within ten days, or at such different time as the court may direct, upon the attorney for the government a written notice of the defendant's intention to offer a defense of alibi. Such notice by the defendant shall state the specific place or places at which the defendant claims to have been at the time of the alleged offense and the names and addresses of the witnesses upon whom the defendant intends to rely to establish such alibi.

(b) Disclosure of Information and Witness. Within ten days thereafter, but in no event less than ten days before trial, unless the court otherwise directs, the attorney for the government shall serve upon the defendant or the defendant's attorney a written notice stating the names and addresses of the witnesses upon whom the government intends to rely to establish the defendant's presence at the scene of the alleged offense and any other witnesses to be relied on to rebut testimony of any of the defendant's alibi witnesses.

(c) Continuing Duty to Disclose. If prior to or during trial, a party learns of an additional witness whose identity, if known, should have been included in the information furnished under subdivision (a) or (b), the party shall promptly notify the other party or the other party's attorney of the existence and identity of such additional witness.

(d) Failure to Comply. Upon the failure of either party to comply with the requirements of this rule, the court may exclude the testimony of any undisclosed witness offered by such party as to the defendant's absence from or presence at, the scene of the alleged offense. This rule shall not limit the right of the defendant to testify.

(e) Exceptions. For good cause shown, the court may grant an exception to any of the requirements of subdivisions (a) through (d) of this rule.

(f) Inadmissibility of Withdrawn Alibi. Evidence of an intention to rely upon an alibi defense, later withdrawn, or of statements made in connection with such intention, is not, in any civil or criminal proceeding, admissible against the person who gave notice of the intention.

(Added Apr. 22, 1974, eff. Dec. 1, 1975; amended July 31, 1975, Pub.L. 94–64, § 3(13), 89 Stat. 372; Apr. 29, 1985, eff. Aug. 1, 1985; Mar. 9, 1987, eff. Aug. 1, 1987.)

NOTES OF ADVISORY COMMITTEE ON RULES

Rule 12.1 is new. See rule 87 of the United States District Court Rules for the District of Columbia for a somewhat comparable provision.

The Advisory Committee has dealt with the issue of notice of alibi on several occasions over the course of the past three decades. In the Preliminary Draft of the Federal Rules of Criminal Procedure, 1943, and the Second Preliminary Draft, 1944, an alibi-notice rule was proposed. But the Advisory Committee was closely divided upon whether there should be a rule at all and, if there were to be a rule, what the form of the rule should be. Orfield, The Preliminary Draft of the Federal Rules of Criminal Procedure, 22 Texas L.Rev. 37, 57–58 (1943). The principal disagreement was whether the prosecutor or the defendant should initiate the process. The Second Preliminary Draft published in 1944 required the defendant to initiate the process by a motion to require the government to state with greater particularity the time and place it would rely on. Upon receipt of this information, defendant was required to give his notice of alibi. This formulation was "vehemently objected" to by five members of the committee (out of a total of eighteen) and two alternative rule proposals were submitted to the Supreme Court. Both formulations—one requiring the prosecutor to initiate the process, the other requiring the defendant to initiate the process—were rejected by the Court. See Epstein, Advance Notice of Alibi, 55 J.Crim.L., C. & P.S. 29, 30 (1964), in which the view is expressed that the unresolved split over the rule "probably caused" the court to reject an alibi-notice rule.

Rule 12.1 embodies an intermediate position. The initial burden is upon the defendant to raise the defense of alibi, but he need not specify the details of his alibi defense until the government specifies the time, place, and date of alleged offense. Each party must, at the appropriate time, disclose the names and addresses of witnesses.

In 1962 the Advisory Committee drafted an alibi-notice rule and included it in the Preliminary Draft of December 1962, rule 12A at pp. 5–6. This time the Advisory Committee withdrew the rule without submitting it to the Standing Committee on Rules of Practice and Procedure. Wright, Proposed Changes in Federal Civil, Criminal, and Appellate Procedure, 35 F.R.D. 317, 326 (1964). Criticism of the December 1962 alibi-notice rule centered on constitutional questions and questions of general fairness to the defendant. See Everett, Discovery in Criminal Cases—In Search of a Standard, 1964 Duke L.J. 477, 497–499.

Doubts about the constitutionality of a notice-of-alibi rule were to some extent resolved by *Williams v. Florida*, 399 U.S. 78, 90 S.Ct. 1893, 26 L.Ed.2d 446 (1970). In that case the court sustained the constitutionality of the Florida notice-of-alibi statute, but left unresolved two important questions.

(1) The court said that it was not holding that a notice-of-alibi requirement was valid under conditions where a defendant does not enjoy "reciprocal discovery against the State." 399 U.S. at 82 n. 11, 90 S.Ct. 1893.

Under the revision of rule 16, the defendant is entitled to substantially enlarged discovery in federal cases, and it would seem appropriate to conclude that the rules will comply with the "reciprocal discovery" qualification of the *Williams* decision. [See, *Wardius v. Oregon*, 412 U.S. 470, 93 S.Ct. 2208, 37 L.Ed.2d 82 (1973) was decided after the approval of proposed Rule 12.1 by the Judicial Conference of the United States. In that case the Court held the Oregon Notice-of-Alibi statute unconstitutional because of the failure to give the defendant adequate reciprocal discovery rights.]

(2) The court said that it did not consider the question of the "validity of the threatened sanction, had petitioner chosen not to comply with the notice-of-alibi rule." 399 U.S. at 83 n. 14, 90 S.Ct. 1893. This issue remains unresolved. [See *Wardius v. Oregon*, 412 U.S. at 472, Note 4, 93 S.Ct. 2208.] Rule 12.1(e) provides that the court may exclude the testimony of any witness whose name has not been disclosed pursuant to the requirements of the rule. The defendant may, however, testify himself. Prohibiting from testifying a witness whose name was not disclosed is a common provision in state statutes. See Epstein, *supra*, at 35. It is generally assumed that the sanction is essential if the notice-of-alibi rule is to have practical significance. See Epstein, *supra*, at 36. The use of the term "may" is intended to make clear that the judge may allow the alibi witness to testify if, under the particular circumstances, there is cause shown for the failure to conform to the requirements of the rules. This is further emphasized by subdivision (f) which provides for exceptions whenever "good cause" is shown for the exception.

The Supreme Court of Illinois recently upheld an Illinois statute which requires a defendant to give notice of his alibi witnesses although the prosecution is not required to disclose its alibi rebuttal witnesses. *People v. Holiday*, 47 Ill.2d 300, 265 N.E.2d 634 (1970). Because the defense complied with the requirement, the court did not have to consider the propriety of penalizing noncompliance.

The requirement of notice of alibi seems to be an increasingly common requirement of state criminal procedure. State statutes and court rules are cited in 399 U.S. at 82 n. 11, 90 S.Ct. 1893. See also Epstein, *supra*.

Rule 12.1 will serve a useful purpose even though rule 16 now requires disclosure of the names and addresses of government and defense witnesses. There are cases in which the identity of defense witnesses may be known, but it may come as a surprise to the government that they intend to testify as to an alibi and there may be no advance notice of the details of the claimed alibi. The result often is an unnecessary interruption and delay in the trial to enable the government to conduct an appropriate investigation. The objective of rule 12.1 is to prevent this by providing a mechanism which will enable the parties to have specific information in advance of trial to prepare to meet the issue of alibi during the trial.

NOTES OF COMMITTEE ON THE JUDICIARY, HOUSE REPORT NO. 94–247

A. Amendments Proposed by the Supreme Court. Rule 12.1 is a new rule that deals with the defense of alibi. It provides that a defendant must notify the government of his intention to rely upon the defense of alibi. Upon receipt of such notice, the government must advise the defendant of the specific time, date, and place at which the offense is alleged to have been committed. The defendant must then inform the government of the specific place at which he claims to have been when the offense is alleged to have been committed, and of the names and addresses of the witnesses on whom he intends to rely to establish his alibi. The government must then inform the defendant of the names and addresses of the witnesses on whom it will rely to establish the defendant's presence at the scene of the crime. If either party fails to comply with the provisions of the rule, the court may exclude the testimony of any witness whose identity is not disclosed. The rule does not attempt to limit the right of the defendant to testify in his own behalf.

B. Committee Action. The Committee disagrees with the defendant-triggered procedures of the rule proposed by the Supreme Court. The major purpose of a notice-of-alibi rule is to prevent unfair surprise to the prosecution. The Committee, therefore, believes that it should be up to the prosecution to trigger the alibi defense discovery procedures. If the prosecution is worried about being surprised by an alibi defense, it can trigger the alibi defense discovery procedures. If the government fails to trigger the procedures and if the defendant raises an alibi defense at trial, then the government cannot claim surprise and get a continuance of the trial.

The Committee has adopted a notice-of-alibi rule similar to the one now used in the District of Columbia. [See Rule 2–5(b) of the Rules of the United States District Court for the District of Columbia. See also Rule 16–1 of the Rules of Criminal Procedure for the Superior Court of the District of Columbia.] The rule is prosecution-triggered. If the prosecutor notifies the defendant of the time, place, and date of the alleged offense, then the defendant has 10 days in which to notify the prosecutor of his intention to rely upon an alibi defense, specify where he claims to have been at the time of the alleged offense, and provide a list of his alibi witnesses. The prosecutor, within 10 days but no later than 10 days before trial, must then provide the defendant with a list of witnesses who will place the defendant at the scene of the alleged crime and those witnesses who will be used to rebut the defendant's alibi witnesses.

The Committee's rule does not operate only to the benefit of the prosecution. In fact, its rule will provide the defendant with more information than the rule proposed by the Supreme Court. The rule proposed by the Supreme Court permits the defendant to obtain a list of only those witnesses who will place him at the scene of the crime. The defendant, however, would get the names of these witnesses anyway as part of his discovery under Rule 16(a)(1)(E). The Committee rule not only requires the prosecution to provide the names of witnesses who place the defendant at the scene of the crime, but it also requires the prosecution to turn over the names of those witnesses who will be called in rebuttal to the defendant's alibi witnesses. This is information that the defendant is not otherwise entitled to discover.

1985 AMENDMENT

Rule 12.1(f)

This clarifying amendment is intended to serve the same purpose as a comparable change made in 1979 to similar language in Rule 11(e)(6). The change makes it clear that evidence of a withdrawn intent or of statements made in connection therewith is thereafter inadmissible against the person who gave the notice in any civil or criminal proceeding, without regard to whether the proceeding is against that person.

1987 AMENDMENT

The amendments are technical. No substantive change is intended.

Rule 12.2 Notice of Insanity Defense or Expert Testimony of Defendant's Mental Condition

(a) Defense of Insanity. If a defendant intends to rely upon the defense of insanity at the time of the alleged offense, the defendant shall, within the time provided for the filing of pretrial motions or at such later time as the court may direct, notify the attorney for the government in writing of such intention and file a copy of such notice with the clerk. If there is a failure to comply with the requirements of this subdivision, insanity may not be raised as a defense. The court may for cause shown allow late filing of the notice or grant additional time to the parties to prepare for trial or make such other order as may be appropriate.

(b) Expert Testimony of Defendant's Mental Condition. If a defendant intends to introduce expert testimony relating to a mental disease or defect or any other mental condition of the defendant bearing upon the issue of guilt, the defendant shall, within the time provided for the filing of pretrial motions or at such later time as the court may direct, notify the attorney for the government in writing of such intention and file a copy of such notice with the clerk. The court may for cause shown allow late filing of the notice or grant additional time to the parties to prepare for trial or make such other order as may be appropriate.

(c) Mental Examination of Defendant. In an appropriate case the court may, upon motion of the attorney for the government, order the defendant to submit to an examination pursuant to 18 U.S.C. 4241 or 4242. No statement made by the defendant in the course of any examination provided for by this rule, whether the examination be with or without the consent of the defendant, no testimony by the expert based upon such statement, and no other fruits of the statement shall be admitted in evidence against the defendant in any criminal proceeding except on an issue respecting mental condition on which the defendant has introduced testimony.

(d) Failure To Comply. If there is a failure to give notice when required by subdivision (b) of this rule or to submit to an examination when ordered under subdivision (c) of this rule, the court may exclude the testimony of any expert witness offered by the defendant on the issue of the defendant's guilt.

(e) Inadmissibility of Withdrawn Intention. Evidence of an intention as to which notice was given under subdivision (a) or (b), later withdrawn, is not, in any civil or criminal proceeding, admissible against the person who gave notice of the intention.

(Added Apr. 22, 1974, eff. Dec. 1, 1975; amended July 31, 1975, Pub.L. 94–64, § 3(14), 89 Stat. 373; Apr. 28, 1983, eff. Aug. 1, 1983; Oct. 12, 1984, Pub.L. 98–473, Title II, § 404, 98 Stat. 2067; Oct. 30, 1984, Pub.L. 98–596, § 11(a), (b), 98 Stat. 3138; Apr. 29, 1985, eff. Aug. 1, 1985; Nov. 10, 1986, Pub.L. 99–646, § 24, 100 Stat. 3597; Mar. 9, 1987, eff. Aug. 1, 1987.)

NOTES OF ADVISORY COMMITTEE ON RULES

Rule 12.2 is designed to require a defendant to give notice prior to trial of his intention (1) to rely upon the defense of insanity or (2) to introduce expert testimony of mental disease or defect on the theory that such mental condition is inconsistent with the mental state required for the offense charged. This rule does not deal with the issue of mental competency to stand trial.

The objective is to give the government time to prepare to meet the issue, which will usually require reliance upon expert testimony. Failure to give advance notice commonly results in the necessity for a continuance in the middle of a trial, thus unnecessarily delaying the administration of justice.

A requirement that the defendant give notice of his intention to rely upon the defense of insanity was proposed by the Advisory Committee in the Second Preliminary Draft of Proposed Amendments (March 1964), rule 12.1, p. 7. The objective of the 1964 proposal was explained in a brief Advisory Committee Note:

Under existing procedure although insanity is a defense, once it is raised the burden to prove sanity beyond a reasonable doubt rests with the government. *Davis v. United States,* 160 U.S. 469, 16 S.Ct. 353, 40 L.Ed. 499 (1895). This rule requires pretrial notice to the government of an insanity defense, thus permitting it to prepare to meet the issue. Furthermore, in *Lynch v. Overholser,* 369 U.S. 705, 82 S.Ct. 1063, 8 L.Ed.2d 211 (1962), the Supreme Court held that, at least in the face of a mandatory commitment statute, the defendant had a right to determine whether or not to raise the issue of insanity. The rule gives the defendant a method of raising the issue and precludes any problem of deciding whether or not the defendant relied on insanity.

The Standing Committee on Rules of Practice and Procedure decided not to recommend the proposed Notice of Insanity rule to the Supreme Court. Reasons were not given.

Requiring advance notice of the defense of insanity is commonly recommended as a desirable procedure. The Working Papers of the National Commission on Reform of Federal Criminal Laws, Vol. 1, p. 254 (1970), state in part:

It is recommended that procedural reform provide for advance notice that evidence of mental disease or defect will be relied upon in defense....

Requiring advance notice is proposed also by the American Law Institute's Model Penal Code, § 4.03 (P.O.D.1962). The commentary in Tentative Draft No. 4 at 193–194 (1955) indicates that, as of that time, six states required pretrial notice and an additional eight states required that the defense of insanity be specially pleaded.

For recent state statutes see N.Y. CPL § 250.10 (McKinney's Consol.Laws, c. 11–A, 1971) enacted in 1970 which provides that no evidence by a defendant of a mental disease negativing criminal responsibility shall be allowed unless defendant has served notice on the prosecutor of his intention to rely upon such defense. See also New Jersey Penal Code (Final Report of the New Jersey Criminal Law Revision Commission, Oct. 1971) § 2c: 4–3; New Jersey Court Rule 3:12;

State v. Whitlow, 45 N.J. 3, 22 n. 3, 210 T.2d 763 (1965), holding the requirement of notice to be both appropriate and not in violation of the privilege against self-incrimination.

Subdivision (a) deals with notice of the "defense of insanity." In this context the term insanity has a well-understood meaning. See, e.g., Tydings, A Federal Verdict of Not Guilty by Reason of Insanity and a Subsequent Commitment Procedure, 27 Md.L.Rev. 131 (1967). Precisely how the defense of insanity is phrased does, however, differ somewhat from circuit to circuit. See Study Draft of a New Federal Criminal Code, § 503 Comment at 37 (USGPO 1970). For a more extensive discussion of present law, see Working Papers of the National Commission on Reform of Federal Criminal Laws, Vol. 1, pp. 229–247 (USGPO 1970). The National Commission recommends the adoption of a single test patterned after the proposal of the American Law Institute's Model Penal Code. The proposed definition provides in part:

In any prosecution for an offense lack of criminal responsibility by reason of mental disease or defect is a defense. [Study Draft of a New Federal Criminal Code § 503 at 36–37.]

Should the proposal of the National Commission be adopted by the Congress, the language of subdivision (a) probably ought to be changed to read "defense of lack of criminal responsibility by reason of mental disease or defect" rather than "defense of insanity."

Subdivision (b) is intended to deal with the issue of expert testimony bearing upon the issue of whether the defendant had the "mental state required for the offense charged."

There is some disagreement as to whether it is proper to introduce evidence of mental disease or defect bearing not upon the defense of insanity, but rather upon the existence of the mental state required by the offense charged. The American Law Institute's Model Penal Code takes the position that such evidence is admissible [§ 4.02(1) (P.O.D.1962)]. See also *People v. Gorshen*, 51 Cal.2d 716, 336 P.2d 492 (1959).

The federal cases reach conflicting conclusions. See *Rhodes v. United States*, 282 F.2d 59, 62 (4th Cir.1960):

The proper way would have been to ask the witness to describe the defendant's mental condition and symptoms, his pathological beliefs and motivations, if he was thus afflicted, and to explain how these influenced or could have influenced his behavior, particularly his mental capacity knowingly to make the false statement charged, or knowingly to forge the signatures * * *.

Compare *Fisher v. United States*, 328 U.S. 463, 66 S.Ct. 1318, 90 L.Ed. 1382 (1946).

Subdivision (b) does not attempt to decide when expert testimony is admissible on the issue of the requisite mental state. It provides only that the defendant must give pretrial notice when he intends to introduce such evidence. The purpose is to prevent the need for a continuance when such evidence is offered without prior notice. The problem of unnecessary delay has arisen in jurisdictions which do not require prior notice of an intention to use expert testimony on the issue of mental state. Referring to this, the California Special Commission on Insanity and Criminal Offenders, First Report 30 (1962) said:

The abuses of the present system are great. Under a plea of "not guilty" without any notice to the people that the defense of insanity will be relied upon, defendant has been able to raise the defense upon the trial of the issue as to whether he committed the offense charged.

As an example of the delay occasioned by the failure to heretofore require a pretrial notice by the defendant, see *United States v. Albright*, 388 F.2d 719 (4th Cir. 1968), where a jury trial was recessed for 23 days to permit a psychiatric examination by the prosecution when the defendant injected a surprise defense of lack of mental competency.

Subdivision (c) gives the court the authority to order the defendant to submit to a psychiatric examination by a psychiatrist designated by the court. A similar provision is found in ALI, Model Penal Code § 4.05(1) (P.O.D. 1962). This is a common provision of state law, the constitutionality of which has been sustained. Authorities are collected in ALI, Model Penal Code, pp. 195–196 Tent. Draft No. 4, (1955). For a recent proposal, see the New Jersey Penal Code § 2c: 4–5 (Final Report of the New Jersey Criminal Law Revision Commission, Oct. 1971) authorizing appointment of "at least one qualified psychiatrist to examine and report upon the mental condition of the defendant." Any issue of self-incrimination which might arise can be dealt with by the court as, for example, by a bifurcated trial which deals separately with the issues of guilt and of mental responsibility. For statutory authority to appoint a psychiatrist with respect to competency to stand trial, see 18 U.S.C. § 4244.

Subdivision (d) confers authority on the court to exclude expert testimony in behalf of a defendant who has failed to give notice under subdivision (b) or who refuses to be examined by a court-appointed psychiatrist under subdivision (c). See *State v. Whitlow*, 45 N.J. 3, 23, 210 A.2d 763 (1965), which indicates that it is proper to limit or exclude testimony by a defense psychiatrist whenever defendant refuses to be examined.

NOTES OF COMMITTEE ON THE JUDICIARY, HOUSE REPORT NO. 94–247

A. Amendments Proposed by the Supreme Court. Rule 12.2 is a new rule that deals with defense based upon mental condition. It provides that: (1) The defendant must notify the prosecution in writing of his intention to rely upon the defense of insanity. If the defendant fails to comply, "insanity may not be raised as a defense." (2) If the defendant intends to introduce expert testimony relating to mental disease or defect on the issue whether he had the requisite mental state, he must notify the prosecution in writing. (3) The court, on motion of the prosecution, may order the defendant to submit to a psychiatric examination by a court-appointed psychiatrist. (4) If the defendant fails to undergo the court-ordered psychiatric examination, the court may exclude any expert witness the defendant offers on the issue of his mental state.

B. Committee Action. The Committee agrees with the proposed rule but has added language concerning the use of statements made to a psychiatrist during the course of a psychiatric examination provided for by Rule 12.2. The language provides:

No statement made by the accused in the course of any examination provided for by this rule, whether the examination shall be with or without the consent of the accused, shall be admitted in evidence against the accused before the judge who or jury which determines the guilt of the accused, prior to the determination of guilt.

The purpose of this rule is to secure the defendant's fifth amendment right against self-incrimination. See *State v. Raskin,* 34 Wis.2d 607, 150 N.W.2d 318 (1967). The provision is flexible and does not totally preclude the use of such statements. For example, the defendant's statement can be used at a separate determination of the issue of sanity or for sentencing purposes once guilt has been determined. A limiting instruction to the jury in a single trial to consider statements made to the psychiatrist only on the issue of sanity would not satisfy the requirements of the rule as amended. The prejudicial effect on the determination of guilt would be inescapable.

The Committee notes that the rule does not attempt to resolve the issue whether the court can constitutionally compel a defendant to undergo a psychiatric examination when the defendant is unwilling to undergo one. The provisions of subdivision (c) are qualified by the phrase, "In an appropriate case." If the court cannot constitutionally compel an unwilling defendant to undergo a psychiatric examination, then the provisions of subdivision (c) are inapplicable in every instance where the defendant is unwilling to undergo a court-ordered psychiatric examination. The Committee, by its approval of subdivision (c), intends to take no stand whatever on the constitutional question.

CONFERENCE COMMITTEE NOTES, HOUSE REPORT NO. 94–414

Rule 12.2(c) deals with court-ordered psychiatric examinations. The House version provides that no statement made by a defendant during a court-ordered psychiatric examination could be admitted in evidence against the defendant before the trier of fact that determines the issue of guilt prior to the determination of guilt. The Senate version deletes this provision.

The Conference adopts a modified House provision and restores to the bill the language of H.R. 6799 as it was originally introduced. The Conference adopted language provides that no statement made by the defendant during a psychiatric examination provided for by the rule shall be admitted against him on the issue of guilt in any criminal proceeding.

The Conference believes that the provision in H.R. 6799 as originally introduced in the House adequately protects the defendant's fifth amendment right against self-incrimination. The rule does not preclude use of statements made by a defendant during a court-ordered psychiatric examination. The statements may be relevant to the issue of defendant's sanity and admissible on that issue. However, a limiting instruction would not satisfy the rule if a statement is so prejudicial that a limiting instruction would be ineffective. Cf. Practice under 18 U.S.C. 4244.

1983 AMENDMENT

Rule 12.2(b)

Courts have recently experienced difficulty with the question of what kind of expert testimony offered for what purpose falls within the notice requirement of rule 12.2(b). See, e.g., *United States v. Hill,* 655 F.2d 512 (3d Cir.1980) (rule not applicable to tendered testimony of psychologist concerning defendant's susceptibility of inducement, offered to reinforce defendant's entrapment defense); *United States v. Webb,* 625 F.2d 709 (5th Cir.1980) (rule not applicable to expert testimony tendered to show that defendant lacked the "propensity to commit a violent act," as this testimony was offered "to prove that Webb did not commit the offense charged," shooting at a helicopter, "not that certain conduct was unaccompanied by criminal intent"); *United States v. Perl,* 584 F.2d 1316 (4th Cir.1978) (because entrapment defense properly withheld from jury, it was unnecessary to decide if the district court erred in holding rule applicable to tendered testimony of the doctor that defendant had increased susceptibility to suggestion as a result of medication he was taking); *United States v. Olson,* 576 F.2d 1267 (8th Cir.1978) (rule applicable to tendered testimony of an alcoholism and drug therapist that defendant was not responsible for his actions because of a problem with alcohol); *United States v. Staggs,* 553 F.2d 1073 (7th Cir.1977) (rule applicable to tendered testimony of psychologist that defendant, charged with assaulting federal officer, was more likely to hurt himself than to direct his aggressions toward others, as this testimony bears upon whether defendant intended to put victim in apprehension when he picked up the gun).

What these cases illustrate is that expert testimony about defendant's mental condition may be tendered in a wide variety of circumstances well beyond the situation clearly within rule 12.2(b), i.e., where a psychiatrist testifies for the defendant regarding his diminished capacity. In all of these situations and others like them, there is good reason to make applicable the notice provisions of rule 12.2(b). This is because in all circumstances in which the defendant plans to offer expert testimony concerning his mental condition at the time of the crime charged, advance disclosure to the government will serve "to permit adequate pretrial preparation, to prevent surprise at trial, and to avoid the necessity of delays during trial." 2 *A.B.A. Standards for Criminal Justice* 11–55 (2d 1980). Thus, while the district court in *United States v. Hill,* 481 F.Supp. 558 (E.D.Pa.1979), incorrectly concluded that present rule 12.2(b) covers testimony by a psychologist bearing on the defense of entrapment, the court quite properly concluded that the government would be seriously disadvantaged by lack of notice. This would have meant that the government would not have been equipped to cross-examine the expert, that any expert called by the government would not have had an opportunity to hear the defense expert testify, and that the government would not have had an opportunity to conduct the kind of investigation needed to acquire rebuttal testimony on defendant's claim that he was especially susceptible to inducement. Consequently, rule 12.2(b) has been expanded to cover all of the aforementioned situations.

Rule 12.2(c)

The amendment of the first sentence of subdivision (c), recognizing that the government may seek to have defendant subjected to a mental examination by an expert other than a psychiatrist, is prompted by the same considerations discussed above. Because it is possible that the defendant will submit to examination by an expert of his own other than a psychiatrist, it is necessary to recognize that it will sometimes be appropriate for defendant to be examined by a government expert other than a psychiatrist.

The last sentence of subdivision (c) has been amended to more accurately reflect the Fifth Amendment considerations at play in this context. See *Estelle v. Smith,* 451 U.S. 454 (1981), holding that self-incrimination protections are not inevitably limited to the guilt phase of a trial and that the privilege, when applicable, protects against use of defendant's statement and also the fruits thereof, including expert testimony based upon defendant's statements to the expert. *Estelle* also intimates that "a defendant can be required to submit to a sanity examination," and presumably some other form of mental examination, when "his silence may deprive the State of the only effective means it has of controverting his proof on an issue that he interjected into the case."

Rule 12.2(d)

The broader term "mental condition" is appropriate here in light of the above changes to subdivisions (b) and (c).

Rule 12.2(e)

New subdivision (e), generally consistent with the protection afforded in rule 12.1(f) with respect to notice of alibi, ensures that the notice required under subdivision (b) will not deprive the defendant of an opportunity later to elect not to utilize any expert testimony. This provision is consistent with *Williams v. Florida,* 399 U.S. 78 (1970), holding the privilege against self-incrimination is not violated by requiring the defendant to give notice of a defense where the defendant retains the "unfettered choice" of abandoning the defense.

1985 AMENDMENT

Rule 12.2(e)

This clarifying amendment is intended to serve the same purpose as a comparable change made in 1979 to similar language in Rule 11(e)(6). The change makes it clear that evidence of a withdrawn intent is thereafter inadmissible against the person who gave the notice in any civil or criminal proceeding, without regard to whether the proceeding is against that person.

1987 AMENDMENT

The amendments are technical. No substantive change is intended.

EDITORIAL NOTES

Codification. Amendments by 404(b), (c), and (d) of Pub.L. 98–473, which (1) deleted "other condition bearing upon the issue of whether he had the mental state required for the offense charged" in subdivision (b) and inserted in lieu thereof "any other mental condition bearing upon the issue of guilt", (2) deleted "to a psychiatric examination by a psychiatrist designated for this purpose in the order of the court" in subdivision (c) and inserted in lieu thereof "to an examination pursuant to 18 U.S.C. 4242", and (3) deleted "mental state" in subdivision (d) and inserted in lieu thereof "guilt", have not been executed to text. Subsecs. (b) and (d) of section 404 of Pub.L. 98–473 were not executed because both subsections were repealed by Pub.L. 98–596, § 11(b), Oct. 30, 1984, 98 Stat. 3138. Subsec. (c) of section 404 of Pub.L. 98–473 was not executed to text since it called for the deletion of non-existent language incapable of literal execution and the insertion of language identical to that inserted by section 11(a)(1) of Pub.L. 98–596.

Effective Date of 1984 Amendment. Section 11(c) of Pub.L. 98–596, Oct. 30, 1984, 98 Stat. 3138, provided: "The amendments and repeals made by subsections (a) and (b) of this section [to this rule and to Pub.L. 98–473, Title II, § 404(b), (d), Oct. 12, 1984, 98 Stat. 2067] shall apply on and after the enactment of the joint resolution entitled 'Joint resolution making continuing appropriations for the fiscal year 1985, and for other purposes', H.J.Res. 648, Ninety-eighth Congress [Pub.L. 98–473, Oct. 12, 1984, 98 Stat. 1837]."

Rule 12.3 Notice of Defense Based Upon Public Authority

(a) Notice by defendant; government response; disclosure of witnesses.

(1) Defendant's Notice and Government's Response. A defendant intending to claim a defense of actual or believed exercise of public authority on behalf of a law enforcement or Federal intelligence agency at the time of the alleged offense shall, within the time provided for the filing of pretrial motions or at such later time as the court may direct, serve upon the attorney for the Government a written notice of such intention and file a copy of such notice with the clerk. Such notice shall identify the law enforcement or Federal intelligence agency and any member of such agency on behalf of which and the period of time in which the defendant claims the actual or believed exercise of public authority occurred. If the notice identifies a Federal intelligence agency, the copy filed with the clerk shall be under seal. Within ten days after receiving the defendant's notice, but in no event less than twenty days before the trial, the attorney for the Government shall serve upon the defendant or the defendant's attorney a written response which shall admit or deny that the defendant exercised the public authority identified in the defendant's notice.

(2) Disclosure of Witnesses. At the time that the Government serves its response to the notice or thereafter, but in no event less than twenty days before the trial, the attorney for the Government may serve upon the defendant or the defendant's attorney a written demand for the names and addresses of the witnesses, if any, upon whom the defendant intends to rely in establishing the defense identified in the notice. Within seven days after receiving the Government's demand, the defendant shall serve upon the attorney for the Government a written statement of the names and addresses of any such witnesses. Within seven days after receiving the defendant's written statement, the attorney for the Government shall serve upon the defendant or the defendant's attorney a written statement of the names and addresses of the witnesses, if any, upon whom the

Government intends to rely in opposing the defense identified in the notice.

(3) Additional Time. If good cause is shown, the court may allow a party additional time to comply with any obligation imposed by this rule.

(b) Continuing duty to disclose. If, prior to or during trial, a party learns of any additional witness whose identity, if known, should have been included in the written statement furnished under subdivision (a)(2) of this rule, that party shall promptly notify in writing the other party or the other party's attorney of the name and address of any such witness.

(c) Failure to comply. If a party fails to comply with the requirements of this rule, the court may exclude the testimony of any undisclosed witness offered in support of or in opposition to the defense, or enter such other order as it deems just under the circumstances. This rule shall not limit the right of the defendant to testify.

(d) Protective procedures unaffected. This rule shall be in addition to and shall not supersede the authority of the court to issue appropriate protective orders, or the authority of the court to order that any pleading be filed under seal.

(e) Inadmissibility of withdrawn defense based upon public authority. Evidence of an intention as to which notice was given under subdivision (a), later withdrawn, is not, in any civil or criminal proceeding, admissible against the person who gave notice of the intention.

(Added Pub.L. 100–690, Title VI, § 6483, Nov. 18, 1988, 102 Stat. 4382.)

Rule 13. Trial Together of Indictments or Informations

The court may order two or more indictments or informations or both to be tried together if the offenses, and the defendants if there is more than one, could have been joined in a single indictment or information. The procedure shall be the same as if the prosecution were under such single indictment or information.

NOTES OF ADVISORY COMMITTEE ON RULES

This rule is substantially a restatement of existing law, 18 U.S.C. former § 557 (Indictments and presentments; joinder of charges); *Logan v. United States*, 144

U.S. 263, 296, 12 S.Ct. 617, 36 L.Ed. 429; *Showalter v. United States,* 260 Fed. 719, C.C.A.4th, certiorari denied 250 U.S. 672, 40 S.Ct. 14, 63 L.Ed. 1200; *Hostetter v. United States,* 16 F.2d 921, C.C.A.8th; *Capone v. United States,* 51 F.2d 609, 619–620, C.C.A.7th.

Rule 14. Relief from Prejudicial Joinder

If it appears that a defendant or the government is prejudiced by a joinder of offenses or of defendants in an indictment or information or by such joinder for trial together, the court may order an election or separate trials of counts, grant a severance of defendants or provide whatever other relief justice requires. In ruling on a motion by a defendant for severance the court may order the attorney for the government to deliver to the court for inspection *in camera* any statements or confessions made by the defendants which the government intends to introduce in evidence at the trial.

(As amended Feb. 28, 1966, eff. July 1, 1966.)

NOTES OF ADVISORY COMMITTEE ON RULES

This rule is a restatement of existing law under which severance and other similar relief is entirely in the discretion of the court, 18 U.S.C. former § 557 (Indictments and presentments; joinder of charges); *Pointer v. United States,* 151 U.S. 396, 14 S.Ct. 410, 38 L.Ed. 208; *Pierce v. United States,* 160 U.S. 355, 16 S.Ct. 321, 40 L.Ed. 454; *United States v. Ball,* 163 U.S. 662, 673, 16 S.Ct. 1192, 41 L.Ed. 300; *Stilson v. United States,* 250 U.S. 583, 40 S.Ct. 28, 63 L.Ed. 1154.

1966 AMENDMENT

A defendant may be prejudiced by the admission in evidence against a co-defendant of a statement or confession made by that co-defendant. This prejudice cannot be dispelled by cross-examination if the co-defendant does not take the stand. Limiting instructions to the jury may not in fact erase the prejudice. While the question whether to grant a severance is generally left within the discretion of the trial court, recent Fifth Circuit cases have found sufficient prejudice involved to make denial of a motion for severance reversible error. See *Schaffer v. United States,* 221 F.2d 17 (5th Cir.1955); *Barton v. United States,* 263 F.2d 894 (5th Cir.1959). It has even been suggested that when the confession of the co-defendant comes as a surprise at the trial, it may be error to deny a motion or a mistrial. See *Belvin v. United States,* 273 F.2d 583 (5th Cir.1960).

The purpose of the amendment is to provide a procedure whereby the issue of possible prejudice can be resolved on the motion for severance. The judge may direct the disclosure of the confessions or statements of the defendants to him for in camera inspection as an aid to determining whether the possible prejudice justifies ordering separate trials. Cf. note, Joint and Single Trials Under Rules 8 and 14 of the Federal Rules of Criminal Procedure, 74 Yale L.J. 551, 565 (1965).

Rule 15. Depositions

(a) **When Taken.** Whenever due to exceptional circumstances of the case it is in the interest of justice that the testimony of a prospective witness of a party be taken and preserved for use at trial, the court may upon motion of such party and notice to the parties order that testimony of such witness be taken by deposition and that any designated book, paper, document, record, recording, or other material not privileged, be produced at the same time and place. If a witness is detained pursuant to section 3144 of title 18, United States Code, the court on written motion of the witness and upon notice to the parties may direct that the witness' deposition be taken. After the deposition has been subscribed the court may discharge the witness.

(b) **Notice of Taking.** The party at whose instance a deposition is to be taken shall give to every party reasonable written notice of the time and place for taking the deposition. The notice shall state the name and address of each person to be examined. On motion of a party upon whom the notice is served, the court for cause shown may extend or shorten the time or change the place for taking the deposition. The officer having custody of a defendant shall be notified of the time and place set for the examination and shall, unless the defendant waives in writing the right to be present, produce the defendant at the examination and keep the defendant in the presence of the witness during the examination, unless, after being warned by the court that disruptive conduct will cause the defendant's removal from the place of the taking of the deposition, the defendant persists in conduct which is such as to justify exclusion from that place. A defendant not in custody shall have the right to be present at the examination upon request subject to such terms as may be fixed by the court, but a failure, absent good cause shown, to appear after notice and tender of expenses in accordance with subdivision (c) of this rule shall constitute a waiver of that right and of any objection to the taking and use of the deposition based upon that right.

(c) **Payment of Expenses.** Whenever a deposition is taken at the instance of the government, or whenever a deposition is taken at the instance of a defendant who is unable to bear the expenses of the taking of the deposition, the court may direct that the expense of travel and subsistence of the defendant and the defendant's attorney for attendance at the examination and the cost of the transcript of the deposition shall be paid by the government.

(d) How Taken. Subject to such additional conditions as the court shall provide, a deposition shall be taken and filed in the manner provided in civil actions except as otherwise provided in these rules, provided that (1) in no event shall a deposition be taken of a party defendant without that defendant's consent, and (2) the scope and manner of examination and cross-examination shall be such as would be allowed in the trial itself. The government shall make available to the defendant or the defendant's counsel for examination and use at the taking of the deposition any statement of the witness being deposed which is in the possession of the government and to which the defendant would be entitled at the trial.

(e) Use. At the trial or upon any hearing, a part or all of a deposition, so far as otherwise admissible under the rules of evidence, may be used as substantive evidence if the witness is unavailable, as unavailability is defined in Rule 804(a) of the Federal Rules of Evidence, or the witness gives testimony at the trial or hearing inconsistent with that witness' deposition. Any deposition may also be used by any party for the purpose of contradicting or impeaching the testimony of the deponent as a witness. If only a part of a deposition is offered in evidence by a party, an adverse party may require the offering of all of it which is relevant to the part offered and any party may offer other parts.

(f) Objections to Deposition Testimony. Objections to deposition testimony or evidence or parts thereof and the grounds for the objection shall be stated at the time of the taking of the deposition.

(g) Deposition by Agreement Not Precluded. Nothing in this rule shall preclude the taking of a deposition, orally or upon written questions, or the use of a deposition, by agreement of the parties with the consent of the court.

(As amended Apr. 22, 1974, eff. Dec. 1, 1975; July 31, 1975, Pub.L. 94–64, § 3(15)–(19), 89 Stat. 373, 374; Oct. 12, 1984, Pub.L. 98–473, Title II,

§ 209(b), 98 Stat. 1986; Mar. 9, 1987, eff. Aug. 1, 1987.)

NOTES OF ADVISORY COMMITTEE ON RULES

Note to Subdivision (a). 1. This rule continues the existing law permitting defendants to take depositions in certain limited classes of cases under dedimus potestatem and in perpetuam rei memoriam, 28 U.S.C. former § 644. This statute has been generally held applicable to criminal cases, *Clymer v. United States,* 38 F.2d 581, C.C.A.10th; *Wong Yim v. United States,* 118 F.2d 667, C.C.A.9th, certiorari denied 313 U.S. 589, 61 S.Ct. 1112, 85 L.Ed. 1544; *United States v. Cameron,* 15 Fed. 794, C.C.E.D.Mo.; *United States v. Hofmann,* 24 F.Supp. 847, S.D.N.Y. Contra, *Luxemberg v. United States,* 45 F.2d 497, C.C.A.4th, certiorari denied 283 U.S. 820, 51 S.Ct. 345, 75 L.Ed. 1436. The rule continues the limitation of the statute that the taking of depositions is to be restricted to cases in which they are necessary "in order to prevent a failure of justice."

2. Unlike the practice in civil cases in which depositions may be taken as a matter of right by notice without permission of the court (Rules 26(a) and 30, Federal Rules of Civil Procedure, 28 U.S.C., Appendix), this rule permits depositions to be taken only by order of the court, made in the exercise of discretion and on notice to all parties. It was contemplated that in criminal cases depositions would be used only in exceptional situations, as has been the practice heretofore.

3. This rule introduces a new feature in authorizing the taking of the deposition of a witness committed for failure to give bail (see Rule 46(b)). This matter is, however, left to the discretion of the court. The purpose of the rule is to afford a method of relief for such a witness, if the court finds it proper to extend it.

Note to Subdivision (b). This subdivision, as well as subdivisions (d) and (f), sets forth the procedure to be followed in the event that the court grants an order for the taking of a deposition. The procedure prescribed is similar to that in civil cases, Rules 28–31, Federal Rules of Civil Procedure, 28 U.S.C., Appendix.

Note to Subdivision (c). This rule introduces a new feature for the purpose of protecting the rights of an indigent defendant.

Note to Subdivision (d). See Note to Subdivision (b), supra.

Note to Subdivision (e). In providing when and for what purpose a deposition may be used at the trial, this rule generally follows the corresponding provisions of the Federal Rules of Civil Procedure, Rule 26(d)(3), 28 U.S.C., Appendix. The only difference is that in civil cases a deposition may be introduced at the trial if the witness is at a greater distance than 100 miles from the place of trial, while this rule requires that the witness be out of the United States. The distinction results from the fact that a subpoena in a civil case runs only within the district where issued or 100 miles from the place of trial (Rule 45(e)(1), Federal Rules of Civil Procedure, 28 U.S.C., Appendix), while a subpoena in a criminal case runs throughout the United States (see Rule 17(e)(1), infra).

Note to Subdivision (f). See Note to Subdivision (b), supra.

1974 AMENDMENT

Rule 15 authorizes the taking of depositions by the government. Under former rule 15 only a defendant was authorized to take a deposition.

The revision is similar to Title VI of the Organized Crime Control Act of 1970. The principal difference is that Title VI (18 U.S.C. § 3503) limits the authority of the government to take depositions to cases in which the Attorney General certifies that the "proceeding is against a person who is believed to have participated in an organized criminal activity." This limitation is not contained in rule 15.

Dealing with the issue of government depositions so soon after the enactment of 18 U.S.C. § 3503 is not inconsistent with the congressional purpose. On the floor of the House, Congressman Poff, a principal spokesman for the proposal, said that the House version was not designed to "limit the Judicial Conference of the United States in the exercise of its rule-making authority ... from addressing itself to other problems in this area or from adopting a broader approach." 116 Cong.Rec. 35293 (1970).

The recently enacted Title VI of the Organized Crime Control Act of 1970 (18 U.S.C. § 3503) is based upon earlier efforts of the Advisory Committee on Criminal Rules which has over the past twenty-five years submitted several proposals authorizing government depositions.

The earlier drafts of the Federal Rules of Criminal Procedure proposed that the government be allowed to take depositions. Orfield, The Federal Rules of Criminal Procedure, 33 Calif.L.Rev. 543, 559 (1945). The Fifth Draft of what became rule 15 (then rule 20) dated June 1942, was submitted to the Supreme Court for comment. The court had a number of unfavorable comments about allowing government depositions. These comments were not published. The only reference to the fact that the court made comments is in 2 Orfield, Criminal Procedure under the Federal Rules § 15:1 (1966); and Orfield, Depositions in Federal Criminal Procedure, 9 S.C.L.Q. 376, 380–381 (1957).

The Advisory Committee, in the 1940's continued to recommend the adoption of a provision authorizing government depositions. The final draft submitted to the Supreme Court contained a section providing:

The following additional requirements shall apply if the deposition is taken at the instance of the govern-

ment or of a witness. The officer having custody of a defendant shall be notified of the time and place set for examination, and shall produce him at the examination and keep him in the presence of the witness during the examination. A defendant not in custody shall be given notice and shall have the right to be present at the examination. The government shall pay in advance to the defendant's attorney and a defendant not in custody expenses of travel and subsistence for attendance at the examination.

See 2 Orfield, Criminal Procedure under the Federal Rules § 15:3, pp. 447–448 (1966); Orfield, Depositions in Federal Criminal Procedure, 9 S.C.L.Q. 376, 383 (1957).

The Supreme Court rejected this section in this entirety, thus eliminating the provision for depositions by the government. These changes were made without comment.

The proposal to allow government depositions was renewed in the amendments to the Federal Rules of Criminal Procedure in the early 1960's. The Preliminary Draft of Proposed Amendments to Rules of Criminal Procedure for the United States District Courts (December 1962) proposed to amend rule 15 by eliminating the words "of a defendant" from the first sentence of subdivision (a) and adding a subdivision (g) which was practically identical to the subdivision rejected by the Supreme Court in the original draft of the rules.

The Second Preliminary Draft of Proposed Amendments to Rules of Criminal Procedure for the United States District Courts (March 1964) continued to propose allowing governments depositions. Subdivision (g) was substantially modified, however.

The following additional requirements shall apply if the deposition is taken at the instance of the government or a witness. Both the defendant and his attorney shall be given reasonable advance notice of the time and place set for the examination. The officer having custody of a defendant shall be notified of the time and place set for the examination, and shall produce him at the examination and keep him in the presence of the witness during the examination. A defendant not in custody shall have the right to be present at the examination but his failure to appear after notice and tender of expenses shall constitute a waiver of that right. The government shall pay to the defendant's attorney and to a defendant not in custody expenses of travel and subsistence for attendance at the examination. The government shall make available to the defendant for his examination and use at the taking of the deposition any statement of the witness being deposed which is in the possession of the government and which the government would be required to make available to the defendant if the witness were testifying at the trial.

The proposal to authorize government depositions was rejected by the Standing Committee on Rules of Practice and Procedure, C. Wright, Federal Practice and Procedure § 241 at 477 (1969). 4 Barron, Federal Practice and Procedure (Supp.1967). The Report of the Judicial Conference, submitted to the Supreme Court for approval late in 1965, contained no proposal for an amendment to rule 15. See 39 F.R.D. 69, 168–211 (1966).

When the Organized Crime Control Act of 1970 was originally introduced in the Senate (S. 30) it contained a government deposition provision which was similar to the 1964 proposal of the Criminal Rules Advisory Committee, except that the original bill (S. 30) failed to provide standards to control the use of depositions at the trial. For an explanation and defense of the original proposal see McClellan, The Organized Crime Act (S. 30) or Its Critics: Which Threatens Civil Liberties?, 46 Notre Dame Lawyer 55, 100–108 (1970). This omission was remedied, prior to passage, with the addition of what is now 18 U.S.C. § 3503(f) which prescribes the circumstances in which a deposition can be used. The standards are the same as those in former rule 15(e) with the addition of language allowing the use of the deposition when "the witness refuses in the trial or hearing to testify concerning the subject of the deposition or the part offered."

Before the Organized Crime Control Act of 1970 was enacted an additional amendment was added providing that the right of the government to take a deposition is limited to cases in which the Attorney General certifies that the defendant is "believed to have participated in an organized criminal activity" [18 U.S.C. § 3503(a)]. The argument in favor of the amendment was that the whole purpose of the act was to deal with organized crime and therefore its provisions, including that providing for government depositions, should be limited to organized crime type cases.

There is another aspect of Advisory Committee history which is relevant. In January 1970, the Advisory Committee circulated proposed changes in rule 16, one of which gives the government, when it has disclosed the identity of its witnesses, the right to take a deposition and use it "in the event the witness has become unavailable without the fault of the government or if the witness has changed his testimony." [See Preliminary Draft of Proposed Amendments to the Federal Rules of Criminal Procedure for the United States District Courts, rule 16(a)(1)(vi) (January 1970).] This provision is now incorporated within rule 16(a)(1)(v).

Because neither the court nor the standing committee gave reasons for rejecting the government deposition proposal, it is not possible to know why they were not approved. To the extent that the rejection was based upon doubts as to the constitutionality of such a proposal, those doubts now seem resolved by *California v. Green*, 399 U.S. 149, 90 S.Ct. 1930, 26 L.Ed.2d 489 (1970).

On the merits, the proposal to allow the government to take depositions is consistent with the revision of rule 16 and with section 804(b)(1) of the Rules of Evidence for the United States Courts and Magistrates (November 1971) which provides that the following is not excluded by the hearsay rule if the declarant is unavailable:

(1) Former Testimony. Testimony given as a witness at another hearing of the same or a different proceeding, or in a deposition taken in compliance with law in the course of another proceeding, at the instance of or against a party with an opportunity to develop the testimony by direct, cross, or redirect examination, with motive and interest similar to those of the party against whom now offered.

Subdivision (a) is revised to provide that the government as well as the defendant is entitled to take a deposition. The phrase "whenever due to special circumstances of the case it is in the interest of justice," is intended to make clear that the decision by the court as to whether to order the taking of a deposition shall be made in the context of the circumstances of the particular case. The principal objective is the preservation of evidence for use at trial. It is not to provide a method of pretrial discovery nor primarily for the purpose of obtaining a basis for later cross-examination of an adverse witness. Discovery is a matter dealt with in rule 16. An obviously important factor is whether a deposition will expedite, rather than delay, the administration of criminal justice. Also important is the presence or absence of factors which determine the use of a deposition at the trial, such as the agreement of the parties to use of the deposition; the possible unavailability of the witness; or the possibility that coercion may be used upon the witness to induce him to change his testimony or not to testify. See rule 16(a)(1)(v).

Subdivision (a) also makes explicit that only the "testimony of a prospective witness of a party" can be taken. This means the party's own witness and does not authorize a discovery deposition of an adverse witness. The language "for use at trial" is intended to give further emphasis to the importance of the criteria for use specified in subdivision (e).

In subdivision (b) reference is made to the defendant in custody. If he is in state custody, a writ of habeas corpus ad testificandum (to produce the prisoner for purposes of testimony) may be required to accomplish his presence.

In subdivision (d) the language "except as otherwise provided in these rules" is meant to make clear that the subpoena provisions of rule 17 control rather than the provisions of the civil rules.

The use of the phrase "and manner" in subdivision (d)(2) is intended to emphasize that the authorization is not to conduct an adverse examination of an opposing witness.

In subdivision (e) the phrase "as substantive evidence" is added to make clear that the deposition can be used as evidence in chief as well as for purposes of impeachment.

Subdivision (e) also makes clear that the deposition can be used as affirmative evidence whenever the witness is available but gives testimony inconsistent with that given in the deposition. A California statute which contained a similar provision was held constitutional in *California v. Green,* 399 U.S. 149, 90 S.Ct. 1930, 26 L.Ed.2d 489 (1970). This is also consistent with section 801(d)(1) of the Rules of Evidence for United States Courts and Magistrates (Nov. 1971).

Subdivision (f) is intended to insure that a record of objections and the grounds for the objections is made at the time the deposition is taken when the witness is available so that the witness can be examined further, if necessary, on the point of the objection so that there will be an adequate record for the court's later ruling upon the objection.

Subdivision (g) uses the "unavailability" definition of the Rules of Evidence for the United States Courts and Magistrates, 804(a) (Nov.1971).

Subdivision (h) is intended to make clear that the court always has authority to order the taking of a deposition, or to allow the use of a deposition, where there is an agreement of the parties to the taking or to the use.

NOTES OF COMMITTEE ON THE JUDICIARY, HOUSE REPORT NO. 94-247

A. Amendments Proposed by the Supreme Court. Rule 15 of the Federal Rules of Criminal Procedure provides for the taking of depositions. The present rule permits only the defendant to move that a deposition of a prospective witness be taken. The court may grant the motion if it appears that (a) the prospective witness will be unable to attend or be prevented from attending the trial, (b) the prospective witness' testimony is material, and (c) the prospective witness' testimony is necessary to prevent a failure of justice.

The Supreme Court promulgated several amendments to Rule 15. The more significant amendments are described below.

Subdivision (a) as proposed to be amended permits either party to move the court for the taking of a deposition of a witness. However, a party may only move to take the deposition of one of its own witnesses, not one of the adversary party's witnesses.

Subdivision (c) as proposed to be amended provides that whenever a deposition is taken at the instance of the government or of an indigent defendant, the expenses of the taking of the deposition must be paid by the government.

Subdivision (e) as proposed to be amended provides that part or all of the deposition may be used at trial as substantive evidence if the witness is "unavailable" or if the witness gives testimony inconsistent with his deposition.

Subdivision (b) [1] as proposed to be amended defines "unavailable." "Unavailable" as a witness includes situations in which the deponent:

(1) is exempted by ruling of the judge on the ground of privilege from testifying concerning the subject matter of his deposition; or

(2) persists in refusing to testify concerning the subject matter of his deposition despite an order of the judge to do so; or

(3) testifies to a lack of memory of the subject matter of his deposition; or

(4) is unable to be present or to testify at the hearing because of death or then existing physical or mental illness or infirmity; or

(5) is absent from the hearing and the proponent of his deposition has been unable to procure his attendance by process or other reasonable means. A deponent is not unavailable as a witness if his exemption, refusal, claim of lack of memory, inability, or absence is due to the procurement or wrongdoing of the proponent of his deposition for the purpose of preventing the witness from attending or testifying.

B. Committee Action. The Committee narrowed the definition of "unavailability" in subdivision (g). The Committee deleted language from that subdivision that provided that a witness was "unavailable" if the court exempts him from testifying at the trial on the ground of privilege. The Committee does not want to encourage the use of depositions at trial, especially in view of the importance of having live testimony from a witness on the witness stand.

The Committee added a provision to subdivision (b) to parallel the provision of Rule 43(b)(2). This is to make it clear that a disruptive defendant may be removed from the place where a deposition is being taken.

The Committee added language to subdivision (c) to make clear that the government must pay for the cost of the transcript of a deposition when the deposition is taken at the instance of an indigent defendant or of the government. In order to use a deposition at trial, it must be transcribed. The proposed rule did not explicitly provide for payment of the cost of transcribing, and the Committee change rectifies this.

The Committee notes that subdivision (e) permits the use of a deposition when the witness "gives testimony at the trial or hearing inconsistent with his deposition." Since subdivision (e) refers to the rules of evidence, the

---

1. So in original. Probably should be "(g)".

Committee understands that the Federal Rules of Evidence will govern the admissibility and use of the deposition. The Committee, by adopting subdivision (e) as proposed to be amended by the Supreme Court, intends the Federal Rules of Evidence to govern the admissibility and use of the deposition.

The Committee believes that Rule 15 will not encourage trials by deposition. A deposition may be taken only in "exceptional circumstances" when "it is in the interest of justice that the testimony of a prospective witness of a party be taken and preserved. * * * " A deposition, once it is taken, is not automatically admissible at trial, however. It may only be used at trial if the witness is unavailable, and the rule narrowly defines unavailability. The procedure established in Rule 15 is similar to the procedure established by the Organized Crime Control Act of 1970 for the taking and use of depositions in organized crime cases. See 18 U.S.C. 3503.

CONFERENCE COMMITTEE NOTES, HOUSE REPORT NO. 94–414

Rule 15 deals with the taking of depositions and the use of depositions at trial. Rule 15(e) permits a deposition to be used if the witness is unavailable. Rule 15(g) defines that term.

The Supreme Court's proposal defines five circumstances in which the witness will be considered unavailable. The House version of the bill deletes a provision that said a witness is unavailable if he is exempted at trial, on the ground of privilege, from testifying about the subject matter of his deposition. The Senate version of the bill by cross reference to the Federal Rules of Evidence, restores the Supreme Court proposal.

The Conference adopts the Senate provision.

1987 AMENDMENT

The amendments are technical. No substantive change is intended.

Rule 16. Discovery and Inspection

(a) **Disclosure of Evidence by the Government.**

(1) Information Subject to Disclosure.

(A) **Statement of Defendant.** Upon request of a defendant the government shall permit the defendant to inspect and copy or photograph: any relevant written or recorded statements made by the defendant, or copies thereof, within the possession, custody or control of the government, the existence of which is known, or by the exercise of due diligence may become known, to the attorney for the government; the substance of any oral statement which the government intends to offer in evidence at the trial made by the defendant whether before or after arrest in response to interrogation by any person then known to the defendant to be a government agent; and recorded testimony of the defendant before a grand jury which relates to the offense charged. Where the defendant is a corporation, partnership, association or labor union, the court may grant the defendant, upon its motion, discovery of relevant recorded testimony of any witness before a grand jury who (1) was, at the time of that testimony, so situated as an officer or employee as to have been able legally to bind the defendant in respect to conduct constituting the offense, or (2) was, at the time of the offense, personally involved in the alleged conduct constituting the offense and so situated as an officer or employee as to have been able legally to bind the defendant in respect to that alleged conduct in which the witness was involved.

(B) **Defendant's Prior Record.** Upon request of the defendant, the government shall furnish to the defendant such copy of the defendant's prior criminal record, if any, as is within the possession, custody, or control of the government, the existence of which is known, or by the exercise of due diligence may become known, to the attorney for the government.

(C) **Documents and Tangible Objects.** Upon request of the defendant the government shall permit the defendant to inspect and copy or photograph books, papers, documents, photographs, tangible objects, buildings or places, or copies or portions thereof, which are within the possession, custody or control of the government, and which are material to the preparation of the defendant's defense or are intended for use by the government as evidence in chief at the trial, or were obtained from or belong to the defendant.

(D) **Reports of Examinations and Tests.** Upon request of a defendant the government shall permit the defendant to inspect and copy or photograph any results or reports of physical or mental examinations, and of scientific tests or experiments, or copies thereof, which are within the possession, custody, or control of the government, the existence of which is known, or by the exercise of due diligence may become known, to the attorney for the government, and which are material to the preparation of the defense or are intended for use by the government as evidence in chief at the trial.

(2) Information Not Subject to Disclosure. Except as provided in paragraphs (A), (B), and (D) of subdivision (a)(1), this rule does not authorize the discovery or inspection of reports, memoranda, or other internal government documents made by the attorney for the government or other government agents in connection with the investigation or prosecution of the case, or of statements made by government witnesses or prospective government witnesses except as provided in 18 U.S.C. § 3500.

(3) Grand Jury Transcripts. Except as provided in Rules 6, 12(i) and 26.2, and subdivision (a)(1)(A) of this rule, these rules do not relate to discovery or inspection of recorded proceedings of a grand jury.

[(4) Failure to Call Witness.] (Deleted Dec. 12, 1975)

(b) Disclosure of Evidence by the Defendant.

(1) Information Subject to Disclosure.

(A) Documents and Tangible Objects. If the defendant requests disclosure under subdivision (a)(1)(C) or (D) of this rule, upon compliance with such request by the government, the defendant, on request of the government, shall permit the government to inspect and copy or photograph books, papers, documents, photographs, tangible objects, or copies or portions thereof, which are within the possession, custody, or control of the defendant and which the defendant intends to introduce as evidence in chief at the trial.

(B) Reports of Examinations and Tests. If the defendant requests disclosure under subdivision (a)(1)(C) or (D) of this rule, upon compliance with such request by the government, the defendant, on request of the government, shall permit the government to inspect and copy or photograph any results or reports of physical or mental examinations and of scientific tests or experiments made in connection with the particular case, or copies thereof, within the possession or control of

the defendant, which the defendant intends to introduce as evidence in chief at the trial or which were prepared by a witness whom the defendant intends to call at the trial when the results or reports relate to that witness' testimony.

(2) Information Not Subject To Disclosure. Except as to scientific or medical reports, this subdivision does not authorize the discovery or inspection of reports, memoranda, or other internal defense documents made by the defendant, or the defendant's attorneys or agents in connection with the investigation or defense of the case, or of statements made by the defendant, or by government or defense witnesses, or by prospective government or defense witnesses, to the defendant, the defendant's agents or attorneys.

[(3) Failure to Call Witness.] (Deleted Dec. 12, 1975)

(c) Continuing Duty to Disclose. If, prior to or during trial, a party discovers additional evidence or material previously requested or ordered, which is subject to discovery or inspection under this rule, such party shall promptly notify the other party or that other party's attorney or the court of the existence of the additional evidence or material.

(d) Regulation of Discovery.

(1) Protective and Modifying Orders. Upon a sufficient showing the court may at any time order that the discovery or inspection be denied, restricted, or deferred, or make such other order as is appropriate. Upon motion by a party, the court may permit the party to make such showing, in whole or in part, in the form of a written statement to be inspected by the judge alone. If the court enters an order granting relief following such an ex parte showing, the entire text of the party's statement shall be sealed and preserved in the records of the court to be made available to the appellate court in the event of an appeal.

(2) Failure To Comply With a Request. If at any time during the course of the proceedings it is brought to the attention of the court that a party has failed to comply with this rule, the court may order such party to permit the discovery or inspection, grant a continuance, or prohibit the party from introducing evidence not disclosed, or it may enter such other order as it deems just under the circumstances. The court may specify the time, place and manner of making the discovery and inspection and may prescribe such terms and conditions as are just.

(e) Alibi Witnesses. Discovery of alibi witnesses is governed by Rule 12.1.

(As amended Feb. 28, 1966, eff. July 1, 1966; Apr. 22, 1974, eff. Dec. 1, 1975; July 31, 1975, Pub.L. 94–64, § 3(20)–(28), 89 Stat. 374, 375; Dec. 12, 1975, Pub.L. 94–149, § 5, 89 Stat. 806; Apr. 28, 1983, eff. Aug. 1, 1983; Mar. 9, 1987, eff. Aug. 1, 1987.)

NOTES OF ADVISORY COMMITTEE ON RULES

Whether under existing law discovery may be permitted in criminal cases is doubtful, *United States v. Rosenfeld,* 57 F.2d 74, C.C.A.2d, certiorari denied, 286 U.S. 556, 52 S.Ct. 642, 76 L.Ed. 1290. The courts have, however, made orders granting to the defendant an opportunity to inspect impounded documents belonging to him, *United States v. B. Goedde and Co.,* 40 Fed. Supp. 523, 534, E.D.Ill. The rule is a restatement of this procedure. In addition, it permits the procedure to be invoked in cases of objects and documents obtained from others by seizure or by process, on the theory that such evidential matter would probably have been accessible to the defendant if it had not previously been seized by the prosecution. The entire matter is left within the discretion of the court.

1966 AMENDMENT

The extent to which pretrial discovery should be permitted in criminal cases is a complex and controversial issue. The problems have been explored in detail in recent legal literature, most of which has been in favor of increasing the range of permissible discovery. See, e.g. Brennan, The Criminal Prosecution: Sporting Event or Quest for Truth, 1963 Wash.U.L.Q. 279; Everett, Discovery in Criminal Cases—In Search of a Standard, 1964 Duke L.J. 477; Fletcher, Pretrial Discovery in State Criminal Cases, 12 Stan.L.Rev. 293 (1960); Goldstein, The State and the Accused: Balance of Advantage in Criminal Procedure, 69 Yale L.J. 1149, 1172–1198 (1960); Krantz, Pretrial Discovery in Criminal Cases: A Necessity for Fair and Impartial Justice, 42 Neb.L.Rev. 127 (1962); Louisell, Criminal Discovery: Dilemma Real or Apparent, 49 Calif.L.Rev. 56 (1961); Louisell, The Theory of Criminal Discovery and the Practice of Criminal Law, 14 Vand.L.Rev. 921 (1961); Moran, Federal Criminal Rules Changes: Aid or Illusion for the Indigent Defendant? 51 A.B.A.J. 64 (1965); Symposium, Discovery in Federal Criminal Cases, 33 F.R.D. 47–128 (1963); Traynor, Ground Lost and Found in Criminal Discovery, 39 N.Y.U.L.Rev. 228 (1964); Developments in the Law—Discovery, 74 Harv.L.Rev. 940,

1051–1063. Full judicial exploration of the conflicting policy considerations will be found in *State v. Tune,* 13 N.J. 203, 98 A.2d 881 (1953) and *State v. Johnson,* 28 N.J. 133, 145 A.2d 313 (1958); cf. *State v. Murphy,* 36 N.J. 172, 175 A.2d 622 (1961); *State v. Moffa,* 36 N.J. 219, 176 A.2d 1 (1961). The rule has been revised to expand the scope of pretrial discovery. At the same time provisions are made to guard against possible abuses.

Subdivision (a).—The court is authorized to order the attorney for the government to permit the defendant to inspect and copy or photograph three different types of material:

(1) Relevant written or recorded statements or confessions made by the defendant, or copies thereof. The defendant is not required to designate because he may not always be aware that his statements or confessions are being recorded. The government's obligation is limited to production of such statements as are within the possession, custody or control of the government, the existence of which is known, or by the exercise of due diligence may become known, to the attorney for the government. Discovery of statements and confessions is in line with what the Supreme Court has described as the "better practice" (*Cicenia v. LaGay,* 357 U.S. 504, 511 (1958)), and with the law in a number of states. See e.g., Del.Rules Crim.Proc., Rule 16; Ill.Stat. Ch. 38, § 729; Md.Rules Proc., Rule 728; *State v. McGee,* 91 Ariz. 101, 370 P.2d 261 (1962); *Cash v. Superior Court,* 53 Cal.2d 72, 346 P.2d 407 (1959); *State v. Bickham,* 239 La. 1094, 121 So.2d 207, cert. den. 364 U.S. 874 (1960); *People v. Johnson,* 356 Mich. 619, 97 N.W.2d 739 (1959); *State v. Johnson,* supra; *People v. Stokes,* 24 Misc.2d 755, 204 N.Y.Supp.2d 827 (Ct.Gen. Sess.1960). The amendment also makes it clear that discovery extends to recorded as well as written statements. For state cases upholding the discovery of recordings, see, e.g., *People v. Cartier,* 51 Cal.2d 590, 335 P.2d 114 (1959); *State v. Minor,* 177 A.2d 215 (Del.Super.Ct.1962).

(2) Relevant results or reports of physical or mental examinations, and of scientific tests or experiments (including fingerprint and handwriting comparisons) made in connection with the particular case, or copies thereof. Again the defendant is not required to designate but the government's obligation is limited to production of items within the possession, custody or control of the government, the existence of which is known, or by the exercise of due diligence may become known, to the attorney for the government. With respect to results or reports of scientific tests or experiments the range of materials which must be produced by the government is further limited to those made in connection with the particular case. Cf. Fla.Stats. § 909.18; *State v. Superior Court,* 90 Ariz. 133, 367 P.2d 6 (1961); *People v. Cooper,* 53 Cal.2d 755, 770, 3 Cal.Rptr. 148,

157, 349 P.2d 1964, 973 (1960); *People v. Stokes,* supra, at 762, 204 N.Y.Supp.2d at 835.

(3) Relevant recorded testimony of a defendant before a grand jury. The policy which favors pretrial disclosure to a defendant of his statements to government agents also supports, pretrial disclosure of his testimony before a grand jury. Courts, however, have tended to require a showing of special circumstances before ordering such disclosure. See, e.g., *United States v. Johnson,* 215 F.Supp. 300 (D.Md.1963). Disclosure is required only where the statement has been recorded and hence can be transcribed.

Subdivision (b).—This subdivision authorizes the court to order the attorney for the government to permit the defendant to inspect the copy or photograph all other books, papers, documents, tangible objects, buildings or places, or copies or portions thereof, which are within the possession, custody or control of the government. Because of the necessarily broad and general terms in which the items to be discovered are described, several limitations are imposed:

(1) While specific designation is not required of the defendant, the burden is placed on him to make a showing of materiality to the preparation of his defense and that his request is reasonable. The requirement of reasonableness will permit the court to define and limit the scope of the government's obligation to search its files while meeting the legitimate needs of the defendant. The court is also authorized to limit discovery to portions of items sought.

(2) Reports, memoranda, and other internal government documents made by government agents in connection with the investigation or prosecution of the case are exempt from discovery. Cf. *Palermo v. United States,* 360 U.S. 343 (1959); *Ogden v. United States,* 303 F.2d 724 (9th Cir.1962).

(3) Except as provided for reports of examinations and tests in subdivision (a)(2), statements made by government witnesses or prospective government witnesses to agents of the government are also exempt from discovery except as provided by 18 U.S.C. § 3500.

Subdivision (c).—This subdivision permits the court to condition a discovery order under subdivision (a)(2) and subdivision (b) by requiring the defendant to permit the government to discover similar items which the defendant intends to produce at the trial and which are within his possession, custody or control under restrictions similar to those placed in subdivision (b) upon discovery by the defendant. While the government normally has resources adequate to secure the information necessary for trial, there are some situations in which mutual disclosure would appear necessary to prevent the defendant from obtaining an unfair advantage. For example, in cases where both prosecution and defense have employed experts to make psychiatric examinations, it seems as important for the government

to study the opinions of the experts to be called by the defendant in order to prepare for trial as it does for the defendant to study those of the government's witnesses. Or in cases (such as antitrust cases) in which the defendant is well represented and well financed, mutual disclosure so far as consistent with the privilege against self-incrimination would seem as appropriate as in civil cases. State cases have indicated that a requirement that the defendant disclose in advance of trial materials which he intends to use on his own behalf at the trial is not a violation of the privilege against self-incrimination. See *Jones v. Superior Court,* 58 Cal.2d 56, 22 Cal.Rptr. 879, 372 P.2d 919 (1962); *People v. Lopez,* 60 Cal.2d 223, 32 Cal.Rptr. 424, 384 P.2d 16 (1963); Traynor, Ground Lost and Found in Criminal Discovery, 39 N.Y.U.L.Rev. 228, 246 (1964); Comment, The Self-Incrimination Privilege: Barrier to Criminal Discovery, 51 Calif.L.Rev. 135 (1963); Note, 76 Harv.L.Rev. 828 (1963).

Subdivision (d).—This subdivision is substantially the same as the last sentence of the existing rule.

Subdivision (e).—This subdivision gives the court authority to deny, restrict or defer discovery upon a sufficient showing. Control of the abuses of discovery is necessary if it is to be expanded in the fashion proposed in subdivisions (a) and (b). Among the considerations to be taken into account by the court will be the safety of witnesses and others, a particular danger of perjury or witness intimidation, the protection of information vital to the national security, and the protection of business enterprises from economic reprisals.

For an example of a use of a protective order in state practice, see *People v. Lopez,* 60 Cal.2d 223, 32 Cal.Rptr. 424, 384 P.2d 16 (1963). See also Brennan, Remarks on Discovery, 33 F.R.D. 56, 65 (1963); Traynor, Ground Lost and Found in Criminal Discovery, 39 N.Y.U.L.Rev. 228, 244, 250.

In some cases it would defeat the purpose of the protective order if the government were required to make its showing in open court. The problem arises in its most extreme form where matters of national security are involved. Hence a procedure is set out where upon motion by the government the court may permit the government to make its showing, in whole or in part, in a written statement to be inspected by the court in camera. If the court grants relief based on such showing, the government's statement is to be sealed and preserved in the records of the court to be made available to the appellate court in the event of an appeal by the defendant, Cf. 18 U.S.C. § 3500.

Subdivision (f).—This subdivision is designed to encourage promptness in making discovery motions and to give the court sufficient control to prevent unnecessary delay and court time consequent upon a multiplication of discovery motions. Normally one motion should encompass all relief sought and a subsequent motion permitted only upon a showing of cause. Where pretrial hearings are used pursuant to Rule 17.1, discovery issues may be resolved at such hearings.

Subdivision (g).—The first sentence establishes a continuing obligation on a party subject to a discovery order with respect to material discovered after initial compliance. The duty provided is to notify the other party, his attorney or the court of the existence of the material. A motion can then be made by the other party for additional discovery and, where the existence of the material is disclosed shortly before or during the trial, for any necessary continuance.

The second sentence gives wide discretion to the court in dealing with the failure of either party to comply with a discovery order. Such discretion will permit the court to consider the reasons why disclosure was not made, the extent of the prejudice, if any, to the opposing party, the feasibility of rectifying that prejudice by a continuance, and any other relevant circumstances.

1974 AMENDMENT

Rule 16 is revised to give greater discovery to both the prosecution and the defense. Subdivision (a) deals with disclosure of evidence by the government. Subdivision (b) deals with disclosure of evidence by the defendant. The majority of the Advisory Committee is of the view that the two—prosecution and defense discovery—are related and that the giving of a broader right of discovery to the defense is dependent upon giving also a broader right of discovery to the prosecution.

The draft provides for a right of prosecution discovery independent of any prior request for discovery by the defendant. The Advisory Committee is of the view that this is the most desirable approach to prosecution discovery. See American Bar Association, Standards Relating to Discovery and Procedure Before Trial, pp. 7, 43–46 (Approved Draft, 1970).

The language of the rule is recast from "the court may order" or "the court shall order" to "the government shall permit" or "the defendant shall permit." This is to make clear that discovery should be accomplished by the parties themselves, without the necessity of a court order unless there is dispute as to whether the matter is discoverable or a request for a protective order under subdivision (d)(1). The court, however, has the inherent right to enter an order under this rule.

The rule is intended to prescribe the minimum amount of discovery to which the parties are entitled. It is not intended to limit the judge's discretion to order broader discovery in appropriate cases. For example, subdivision (a)(3) is not intended to deny a judge's discretion to order disclosure of grand jury minutes where circumstances make it appropriate to do so.

Subdivision (a)(1)(A) amends the old rule to provide, upon request of the defendant, the government shall permit discovery if the conditions specified in subdivision (a)(1)(A) exist. Some courts have construed the current language as giving the court discretion as to whether to grant discovery of defendant's statements. See *United States v. Kaminsky*, 275 F.Supp. 365 (S.D.N.Y.1967), denying discovery because the defendant did not demonstrate that his request for discovery was warranted; *United States v. Diliberto*, 264 F.Supp. 181 (S.D.N.Y.1967), holding that there must be a showing of actual need before discovery would be granted; *United States v. Louis Carreau, Inc.*, 42 F.R.D. 408 (S.D.N.Y. 1967), holding that in the absence of a showing of good cause the government cannot be required to disclose defendant's prior statements in advance of trial. In *United States v. Louis Carreau, Inc.*, at p. 412, the court stated that if rule 16 meant that production of the statements was mandatory, the word "shall" would have been used instead of "may." See also *United States v. Wallace*, 272 F.Supp. 838 (S.D.N.Y.1967); *United States v. Wood*, 270 F.Supp. 963 (S.D.N.Y.1967); *United States v. Leighton*, 265 F.Supp. 27 (S.D.N.Y. 1967); *United States v. Longarzo*, 43 F.R.D. 395 (S.D.N.Y.1967); *Loux v. United States*, 389 F.2d 911 (9th Cir. 1968); and the discussion of discovery in Discovery in Criminal Cases, 44 F.R.D. 481 (1968). Other courts have held that even though the current rules make discovery discretionary, the defendant need not show cause when he seeks to discover his own statements. See *United States v. Aadal*, 280 F.Supp. 859 (S.D.N.Y. 1967); *United States v. Federmann*, 41 F.R.D. 339 (S.D.N.Y.1967); and *United States v. Projansky*, 44 F.R.D. 550 (S.D.N.Y.1968).

The amendment making disclosure mandatory under the circumstances prescribed in subdivision (a)(1)(A) resolves such ambiguity as may currently exist, in the direction of more liberal discovery. See C. Wright, Federal Practice and Procedure: Criminal § 253 (1969, Supp.1971); Rezneck, The New Federal Rules of Criminal Procedure, 54 Geo.L.J. 1276 (1966); Fla.Stat.Ann. § 925.05 (Supp.1971–1972); N.J.Crim.Prac. Rule 35–11(a) (1967). This is done in the view that broad discovery contributes to the fair and efficient administration of criminal justice by providing the defendant with enough information to make an informed decision as to plea; by minimizing the undesirable effect of surprise at the trial; and by otherwise contributing to an accurate determination of the issue of guilt or innocence. This is the ground upon which the American Bar Association Standards Relating to Discovery and Procedure Before Trial (Approved Draft, 1970) has unanimously recommended broader discovery. The United States Supreme Court has said that the pretrial disclosure of a defendant's statements "may be the 'better practice.'" *Cicenia v. La Gay*, 357 U.S. 504, 511, 78 S.Ct. 1297, 2 L.Ed.2d 1523 (1958). See also *Leland v. Oregon*, 343 U.S. 790, 72 S.Ct. 1002, 96 L.Ed. 1302 (1952); *State v. Johnson*, 28 N.J. 133, 145 A.2d 313 (1958).

The requirement that the statement be disclosed prior to trial, rather than waiting until the trial, also contributes to efficiency of administration. It is during the pretrial stage that the defendant usually decides whether to plead guilty. See *United States v. Projansky,* supra. The pretrial stage is also the time during which many objections to the admissibility of types of evidence ought to be made. Pretrial disclosure ought, therefore, to contribute both to an informed guilty plea practice and to a pretrial resolution of admissibility questions. See ABA, Standards Relating to Discovery and Procedure Before Trial § 1.2 and Commentary pp. 40–43 (Approved Draft, 1970).

The American Bar Association Standards mandate the prosecutor to make the required disclosure even though not requested to do so by the defendant. The proposed draft requires the defendant to request discovery, although obviously the attorney for the government may disclose without waiting for a request, and there are situations in which due process will require the prosecution, on its own, to disclose evidence "helpful" to the defense. *Brady v. Maryland,* 373 U.S. 83, 83 S.Ct. 1194, 10 L.Ed.2d 215 (1963); *Giles v. Maryland,* 386 U.S. 66, 87 S.Ct. 793, 17 L.Ed.2d 737 (1967).

The requirement in subdivision (a)(1)(A) is that the government produce "statements" without further discussion of what "statement" includes. There has been some recent controversy over what "statements" are subject to discovery under the current rule. See Discovery in Criminal Cases, 44 F.R.D. 481 (1968); C. Wright, Federal Practice and Procedure: Criminal § 253, pp. 505–506 (1969, Supp.1971). The kinds of "statements" which have been held to be within the rule include "substantially verbatim and contemporaneous" statements, *United States v. Elife,* 43 F.R.D. 23 (S.D.N.Y.1967); statements which reproduce the defendant's "exact words," *United States v. Armantrout,* 278 F.Supp. 517 (S.D.N.Y.1968); a memorandum which was not verbatim but included the substance of the defendant's testimony, *United States v. Scharf,* 267 F.Supp. 19 (S.D.N.Y.1967); Summaries of the defendant's statements, *United States v. Morrison,* 43 F.R.D. 516 (N.D.Ill. 1967); and statements discovered by means of electronic surveillance, *United States v. Black,* 282 F.Supp. 35 (D.D.C.1968). The court in *United States v. Iovinelli,* 276 F.Supp. 629, 631 (N.D.Ill.1967), declared that "statements" as used in old rule 16 is not restricted to the "substantially verbatim recital of an oral statement" or to statements which are a "recital of past occurrences."

The Jencks Act, 18 U.S.C. § 3500, defines "statements" of government witnesses discoverable for purposes of cross-examination as: (1) a "written statement" signed or otherwise approved by a witness, (2) "a stenographic, mechanical, electrical, or other recording, or a transcription thereof, which is a substantially verbatim recital of an oral statement made by said witness to an agent of the government and recorded contemporane-

ously with the making of such oral statement." 18 U.S.C. § 3500(e). The language of the Jencks Act has most often led to a restrictive definition of "statements," confining "statements" to the defendant's "own words." See *Hanks v. United States,* 388 F.2d 171 (10th Cir.1968), and *Augenblick v. United States,* 377 F.2d 586, 180 Ct.Cl. 131 (1967).

The American Bar Association's Standards Relating to Discovery and Procedure Before Trial (Approved Draft, 1970) do not attempt to define "statements" because of a disagreement among members of the committee as to what the definition should be. The majority rejected the restrictive definition of "statements" contained in the Jencks Act, 18 U.S.C. § 3500(e), in the view that the defendant ought to be able to see his statement in whatever form it may have been preserved in fairness to the defendant and to discourage the practice, where it exists, of destroying original notes, after transforming them into secondary transcriptions, in order to avoid cross-examination based upon the original notes. See *Campbell v. United States,* 373 U.S. 487, 83 S.Ct. 1356, 10 L.Ed.2d 501 (1963). The minority favored a restrictive definition of "statements" in the view that the use of other than "verbatim" statements would subject witnesses to unfair cross-examination. See American Bar Association's Standards Relating to Discovery and Procedure Before Trial pp. 61–64 (Approved Draft, 1970). The draft of subdivision (a)(1)(A) leaves the matter of the meaning of the term unresolved and thus left for development on a case-by-case basis.

Subdivision (a)(1)(A) also provides for mandatory disclosure of a summary of any oral statement made by defendant to a government agent which the attorney for the government intends to use in evidence. The reasons for permitting the defendant to discover his own statements seem obviously to apply to the substance of any oral statement which the government intends to use in evidence at the trial. See American Bar Association Standards Relating to Discovery and Procedure Before Trial § 2.1(a)(ii) (Approved Draft, 1970). Certainly disclosure will facilitate the raising of objections to admissibility prior to trial. There have been several conflicting decisions under the current rules as to whether the government must disclose the substance of oral statements of the defendant which it has in its possession. Cf. *United States v. Baker,* 262 F.Supp. 657 (D.C.D.C.1966); *United States v. Curry,* 278 F.Supp. 508 (N.D.Ill.1967); *United States v. Morrison,* 43 F.R.D. 516 (N.D.Ill.1967); *United States v. Reid,* 43 F.R.D. 520 (N.D.Ill.1967); *United States v. Armantrout,* 278 F.Supp. 517 (S.D.N.Y.1968); and *United States v. Elife,* 43 F.R.D. 23 (S.D.N.Y.1967). There is, however, considerable support for the policy of disclosing the substance of the defendant's oral statement. Many courts have indicated that this is a "better practice" than denying such disclosure. E.g., *United States v. Curry,* supra; *Loux v.*

United States, 389 F.2d 911 (9th Cir.1968); and *United States v. Baker,* supra.

Subdivision (a)(1)(A) also provides for mandatory disclosure of any "recorded testimony" which defendant gives before a grand jury if the testimony "relates to the offense charged." The present rule is discretionary and is applicable only to those of defendant's statements which are "relevant."

The traditional rationale behind grand jury secrecy—protection of witnesses—does not apply when the accused seeks discovery of his own testimony. Cf. *Dennis v. United States,* 384 U.S. 855, 86 S.Ct. 1840, 16 L.Ed.2d 973 (1966); and *Allen v. United States,* 129 U.S.App.D. C. 61, 390 F.2d 476 (1968). In interpreting the rule many judges have granted defendant discovery without a showing of need or relevance. *United States v. Gleason,* 259 F.Supp. 282 (S.D.N.Y.1966); *United States v. Longarzo,* 43 F.R.D. 395 (S.D.N.Y.1967); and *United States v. United Concrete Pipe Corp.,* 41 F.R.D. 538 (N.D.Tex.1966). Making disclosure mandatory without a showing of relevance conforms to the recommendation of the American Bar Association Standards Relating to Discovery and Procedure Before Trial § 2.1(a)(iii) and Commentary pp. 64–66 (Approved Draft, 1970). Also see Note, Discovery by a Criminal Defendant of His Own Grand–Jury Testimony, 68 Columbia L.Rev. 311 (1968).

In a situation involving a corporate defendant, statements made by present and former officers and employees relating to their employment have been held discoverable as statements of the defendant. *United States v. Hughes,* 413 F.2d 1244 (5th Cir.1969). The rule makes clear that such statements are discoverable if the officer or employee was "able legally to bind the defendant in respect to the activities involved in the charges."

Subdivision (a)(1)(B) allows discovery of the defendant's prior criminal record. A defendant may be uncertain of the precise nature of his prior record and it seems therefore in the interest of efficient and fair administration to make it possible to resolve prior to trial any disputes as to the correctness of the relevant criminal record of the defendant.

Subdivision (a)(1)(C) gives a right of discovery of certain tangible objects under the specified circumstances. Courts have construed the old rule as making disclosure discretionary with the judge. Cf. *United States v. Kaminsky,* 275 F.Supp. 365 (S.D.N.Y.1967); *Gevinson v. United States,* 358 F.2d 761 (5th Cir.1966), cert. denied, 385 U.S. 823, 87 S.Ct. 51, 17 L.Ed.2d 60 (1966); and *United States v. Tanner,* 279 F.Supp. 457 (N.D.Ill.1967). The old rule requires a "showing of materiality to the preparation of his defense and that the request is reasonable." The new rule requires disclosure if any one of three situations exists: (a) the defendant shows that disclosure of the document or tangible object is material to the defense, (b) the government intends to use the

document or tangible object in its presentation of its case in chief, or (c) the document or tangible object was obtained from or belongs to the defendant.

Disclosure of documents and tangible objects which are "material" to the preparation of the defense may be required under the rule of *Brady v. Maryland,* 373 U.S. 83, 83 S.Ct. 1194, 10 L.Ed.2d 215 (1963), without an additional showing that the request is "reasonable." In *Brady* the court held that "due process" requires that the prosecution disclose evidence favorable to the accused. Although the Advisory Committee decided not to codify the Brady Rule, the requirement that the government disclose documents and tangible objects "material to the preparation of his defense" underscores the importance of disclosure of evidence favorable to the defendant.

Limiting the rule to situations in which the defendant can show that the evidence is material seems unwise. It may be difficult for a defendant to make this showing if he does not know what the evidence is. For this reason subdivision (a)(1)(C) also contains language to compel disclosure if the government intends to use the property as evidence at the trial or if the property was obtained from or belongs to the defendant. See ABA Standards Relating to Discovery and Procedure Before Trial § 2.1(a)(v) and Commentary pp. 68–69 (Approved Draft, 1970). This is probably the result under old rule 16 since the fact that the government intends to use the physical evidence at the trial is probably sufficient proof of "materiality." C. Wright, Federal Practice and Procedure: Criminal § 254 especially n. 70 at p. 513 (1969, Supp.1971). But it seems desirable to make this explicit in the rule itself.

Requiring disclosure of documents and tangible objects which "were obtained from or belong to the defendant" probably is also making explicit in the rule what would otherwise be the interpretation of "materiality." See C. Wright, Federal Practice and Procedure: Criminal § 254 at p. 510 especially n. 58 (1969, Supp.1971).

Subdivision (a)(1)(C) is also amended to add the word "photographs" to the objects previously listed. See ABA Standards Relating to Discovery and Procedure Before Trial § 2.1(a)(v) (Approved Draft, 1970).

Subdivision (a)(1)(D) makes disclosure of the reports of examinations and tests mandatory. This is the recommendation of the ABA Standards Relating to Discovery and Procedure Before Trial § 2.1(a)(iv) and Commentary pp. 66–68 (Approved Draft, 1970). The obligation of disclosure applies only to scientific tests or experiments "made in connection with the particular case." So limited, mandatory disclosure seems justified because: (1) it is difficult to test expert testimony at trial without advance notice and preparation; (2) it is not likely that such evidence will be distorted or misused if disclosed prior to trial; and (3) to the extent that a test may be favorable to the defense, its disclosure is mandated under the rule of *Brady v. Maryland,* supra.

Subdivision (a)(1)(E) is new. It provides for discovery of the names of witnesses to be called by the government and of the prior criminal record of these witnesses. Many states have statutes or rules which require that the accused be notified prior to trial of the witnesses to be called against him. See, e.g., Alaska R.Crim. Proc. 7(c); Ariz.R.Crim.Proc. 153, 17 A.R.S. (1956); Ark. Stat.Ann. § 43–1001 (1947); Cal.Pen.Code § 995n (West 1957); Colo.Rev.Stat.Ann. §§ 39–3–6, 39–4–2 (1963); Fla.Stat.Ann. § 906.29 (1944); Idaho Code Ann. § 19–1404 (1948); Ill.Rev.Stat. ch. 38, § 114–9 (1970); Ind.Ann.Stat. § 9–903 (1956), IC 1971, 35–1–16–3; Iowa Code Ann. § 772.3 (1950); Kan.Stat.Ann. § 62–931 (1964); Ky.R.Crim.Proc. 6.08 (1962); Mich.Stat.Ann. § 28.980, M.C.L.A. § 767.40 (Supp.1971); Minn.Stat. Ann. § 628.08 (1947); Mo.Ann.Stat. § 545.070 (1953); Mont.Rev.Codes Ann. § 95–1503 (Supp.1969); Neb.Rev. Stat. § 29–1602 (1964); Nev.Rev.Stat. § 173.045 (1967); Okl.Stat. tit. 22, § 384 (1951); Ore.Rev.Stat. § 132.580 (1969); Tenn.Code Ann. § 40–1708 (1955); Utah Code Ann. § 77–20–3 (1953). For examples of the ways in which these requirements are implemented, see *State v. Mitchell,* 181 Kan. 193, 310 P.2d 1063 (1957); *State v. Parr,* 129 Mont. 175, 283 P.2d 1086 (1955); *Phillips v. State,* 157 Neb. 419, 59 N.W. 598 (1953).

Witnesses' prior statements must be made available to defense counsel after the witness testifies on direct examination for possible impeachment purposes during trial: 18 U.S.C. § 3500.

The American Bar Association's Standards Relating to Discovery and Procedure Before Trial § 2.1(a)(i) (Approved Draft, 1970) require disclosure of both the names and the statements of prosecution witnesses. Subdivision (a)(1)(E) requires only disclosure, prior to trial, of names, addresses, and prior criminal record. It does not require disclosure of the witnesses' statements although the rule does not preclude the parties from agreeing to disclose statements prior to trial. This is done, for example, in courts using the so-called "omnibus hearing."

Disclosure of the prior criminal record of witnesses places the defense in the same position as the government, which normally has knowledge of the defendant's record and the record of anticipated defense witnesses. In addition, the defendant often lacks means of procuring this information on his own. See American Bar Association Standards Relating to Discovery and Procedure Before Trial § 2.1(a)(vi) (Approved Draft, 1970).

A principal argument against disclosure of the identity of witnesses prior to trial has been the danger to the witness, his being subjected either to physical harm or to threats designed to make the witness unavailable or to influence him to change his testimony. Discovery in Criminal cases, 44 F.R.D. 481, 499–500 (1968); Ratnoff, The New Criminal Deposition Statute in Ohio—Help or Hindrance to Justice?, 19 Case Western Reserve L.Rev. 279, 284 (1968). See, e.g., *United States v. Estep,* 151 F.Supp. 668, 672–673 (N.D.Tex.1957):

> Ninety percent of the convictions had in the trial court for sale and dissemination of narcotic drugs are linked to the work and the evidence obtained by an informer. If that informer is not to have his life protected there won't be many informers hereafter.

See also the dissenting opinion of Mr. Justice Clark in *Roviaro v. United States,* 353 U.S. 53, 66–67, 77 S.Ct. 623, 1 L.Ed.2d 639 (1957). Threats of market retaliation against witnesses in criminal antitrust cases are another illustration. *Bergen Drug Co. v. Parke, Davis & Company,* 307 F.2d 725 (3d Cir.1962); and *House of Materials, Inc. v. Simplicity Pattern Co.,* 298 F.2d 867 (2d Cir.1962). The government has two alternatives when it believes disclosure will create an undue risk of harm to the witness: It can ask for a protective order under subdivision (d)(1). See ABA Standards Relating to Discovery and Procedure Before Trial § 2.5(b) (Approved Draft, 1970). It can also move the court to allow the perpetuation of a particular witness's testimony for use at trial if the witness is unavailable or later changes his testimony. The purpose of the latter alternative is to make pretrial disclosure possible and at the same time to minimize any inducement to use improper means to force the witness either to not show up or to change his testimony before a jury. See rule 15.

Subdivision (a)(2) is substantially unchanged. It limits the discovery otherwise allowed by providing that the government need not disclose "reports, memoranda, or other internal government documents made by the attorney for the government or other government agents in connection with the investigation or prosecution of the case" or "statements made by government witnesses or prospective government witnesses." The only proposed change is that the "reports, memoranda, or other internal government documents made by the attorney for the government" are included to make clear that the work product of the government attorney is protected. See C. Wright, Federal Practice and Procedure: Criminal § 254 n. 92 (1969, Supp.1971); *United States v. Rothman,* 179 F.Supp. 935 (W.D.Pa.1959); Note, "Work Product" in Criminal Discovery, 1966 Wash.U.L.Q. 321; American Bar Association, Standards Relating to Discovery and Procedure Before Trial § 2.6(a) (Approved Draft, 1970); cf. *Hickman v. Taylor,* 329 U.S. 495, 67 S.Ct. 385, 91 L.Ed. 451 (1947). *Brady v. Maryland,* 373 U.S. 83, 83 S.Ct. 1194, 10 L.Ed.2d 215 (1963), requires the disclosure of evidence favorable to the defendant. This is, of course, not changed by this rule.

Subdivision (a)(3) is included to make clear that recorded proceedings of a grand jury are explicitly dealt with in rule 6 and subdivision (a)(1)(A) of rule 16 and thus are not covered by other provisions such as subdivision (a)(1)(C) which deals generally with discovery of documents in the possession, custody, or control of the government.

Subdivision (a)(4) is designed to insure that the government will not be penalized if it makes a full disclosure of all potential witnesses and then decides not to call one or more of the witnesses listed. This is not, however, intended to abrogate the defendant's right to comment generally upon the government's failure to call witnesses in an appropriate case.

Subdivision (b) deals with the government's right to discovery of defense evidence or, put in other terms, with the extent to which a defendant is required to disclose its evidence to the prosecution prior to trial. Subdivision (b) replaces old subdivision (c).

Subdivision (b) enlarges the right of government discovery in several ways: (1) it gives the government the right to discovery of lists of defense witnesses as well as physical evidence and the results of examinations and tests; (2) it requires disclosure if the defendant has the evidence under his control and intends to use it at trial in his case in chief, without the additional burden, required by the old rule, of having to show, in behalf of the government, that the evidence is material and the request reasonable; and (3) it gives the government the right to discovery without conditioning that right upon the existence of a prior request for discovery by the defendant.

Although the government normally has resources adequate to secure much of the evidence for trial, there are situations in which pretrial disclosure of evidence to the government is in the interest of effective and fair criminal justice administration. For example, the experimental "omnibus hearing" procedure (see discussion in Advisory Committee Note to rule 12) is based upon an assumption that the defendant, as well as the government, will be willing to disclose evidence prior to trial.

Having reached the conclusion that it is desirable to require broader disclosure by the defendant under certain circumstances, the Advisory Committee has taken the view that it is preferable to give the right of discovery to the government independently of a prior request for discovery by the defendant. This is the recommendation of the American Bar Association Standards Relating to Discovery and Procedure Before Trial, Commentary, pp. 43–46 (Approved Draft, 1970). It is sometimes asserted that making the government's right to discovery conditional will minimize the risk that government discovery will be viewed as an infringement of the defendant's constitutional rights. See discussion in C. Wright, Federal Practice and Procedure: Criminal § 256 (1969, Supp.1971); Moore, Criminal Discovery, 19 Hastings L.J. 865 (1968); Wilder, Prosecution Discovery and the Privilege Against Self–Incrimination, 6 Am.Cr.L.Q. 3 (1967). There are assertions that prosecution discovery, even if conditioned upon the defen-

dants being granted discovery, is a violation of the privilege. See statements of Mr. Justice Black and Mr. Justice Douglas, 39 F.R.D. 69, 272, 277–278 (1966); C. Wright, Federal Practice and Procedure: Criminal § 256 (1969, Supp.1971). Several states require defense disclosure of an intended defense of alibi and, in some cases, a list of witnesses in support of an alibi defense, without making the requirement conditional upon prior discovery being given to the defense. E.g., Ariz.R.Crim. P. 162(B), 17 A.R.S. (1956); Ind.Ann.Stat. § 9–1631 to 9–1633 (1956), IC 1971, 35–5–1–1 to 35–5–1–3; Mich. Comp.Laws Ann. §§ 768.20, 768.21 (1968); N.Y.CPL § 250.20 (McKinney's Consol.Laws, c. 11–A, 1971); and Ohio Rev.Code Ann. § 2945.58 (1954). State courts have refused to hold these statutes violative of the privilege against self-incrimination. See *State v. Thayer,* 124 Ohio St. 1, 176 N.E. 656 (1931), and *People v. Rakiec,* 260 App.Div. 452, 23 N.Y.S.2d 607, aff'd, 289 N.Y. 306, 45 N.E.2d 812 (1942). See also rule 12.1 and Advisory Committee Note thereto.

Some state courts have held that a defendant may be required to disclose, in advance of trial, evidence which he intends to use on his own behalf at trial without violating the privilege against self-incrimination. See *Jones v. Superior Court of Nevada County,* 58 Cal.2d 56, 22 Cal.Rptr. 879, 372 P.2d 919 (1962); *People v. Lopez,* 60 Cal.2d 223, 32 Cal.Rptr. 424, 384 P.2d 16 (1963); Comment, The Self–Incrimination Privilege: Barrier to Criminal Discovery?, 51 Calif.L.Rev. 135 (1963); Note, 76 Harv.L.Rev. 838 (1963). The courts in *Jones v. Superior Court of Nevada County,* supra, suggests that if mandatory disclosure applies only to those items which the accused intends to introduce in evidence at trial, neither the incriminatory nor the involuntary aspects of the privilege against self-incrimination are present.

On balance the Advisory Committee is of the view that an independent right of discovery for both the defendant and the government is likely to contribute to both effective and fair administration. See Louisell, Criminal Discovery and Self–Incrimination: Roger Traynor Confronts the Dilemma, 53 Calif.L.Rev. 89 (1965), for an analysis of the difficulty of weighing the value of broad discovery against the value which inheres in not requiring the defendant to disclose anything which might work to his disadvantage.

Subdivision (b)(1)(A) provides that the defendant shall disclose any documents and tangible objects which he has in his possession, custody, or control and which he intends to introduce in evidence in his case in chief.

Subdivision (b)(1)(B) provides that the defendant shall disclose the results of physical or mental examinations and scientific tests or experiments if (a) they were made in connection with a particular case; (b) the defendant has them under his control; and (c) he intends to offer them in evidence in his case in chief or which were prepared by a defense witness and the results or reports relate to the witness's testimony. In cases where both prosecution and defense have employed experts to conduct tests such as psychiatric examinations, it seems as important for the government to be able to study the results reached by defense experts which are to be called by the defendant as it does for the defendant to study those of government experts. See Schultz, Criminal Discovery by the Prosecution: Frontier Developments and Some Proposals for the Future, 22 N.Y.U.Intra.L.Rev. 268 (1967); American Bar Association, Standards Relating to Discovery and Procedure Before Trial § 3.2 (Supp., Approved Draft, 1970).

Subdivision (b)(1)(C) provides for discovery of a list of witnesses the defendant intends to call in his case in chief. State cases have indicated that disclosure of a list of defense witnesses does not violate the defendant's privilege against self-incrimination. See *Jones v. Superior Court of Nevada County,* supra, and *People v. Lopez,* supra. The defendant has the same option as does the government if it is believed that disclosure of the identity of a witness may subject that witness to harm or a threat of harm. The defendant can ask for a protective order under subdivision (d)(1) or can take a deposition in accordance with the terms of rule 15.

Subdivision (b)(2) is unchanged, appearing as the last sentence of subdivision (c) of old rule 16.

Subdivision (b)(3) provides that the defendant's failure to introduce evidence or call witnesses shall not be admissible in evidence against him. In states which require pretrial disclosure of witnesses' identity, the prosecution is not allowed to comment upon the defendant's failure to call a listed witness. See *O'Connor v. State,* 31 Wis.2d 684, 143 N.W.2d 489 (1966); *People v. Mancini,* 6 N.Y.2d 853, 188 N.Y.S.2d 559, 160 N.E.2d 91 (1959); and *State v. Cocco,* 73 Ohio App. 182, 55 N.E.2d 430 (1943). This is not, however, intended to abrogate the government's right to comment generally upon the defendant's failure to call witnesses in an appropriate case, other than the defendant's failure to testify.

Subdivision (c) is a restatement of part of old rule 16(g).

Subdivision (d)(1) deals with the protective order. Although the rule does not attempt to indicate when a protective order should be entered, it is obvious that one would be appropriate where there is reason to believe that a witness would be subject to physical or economic harm if his identity is revealed. See *Will v. United States,* 389 U.S. 90, 88 S.Ct. 269, 19 L.Ed.2d 305 (1967). The language "by the judge alone" is not meant to be inconsistent with *Alderman v. United States,* 394 U.S. 165, 89 S.Ct. 961, 22 L.Ed.2d 176 (1969). In *Alderman* the court points out that there may be appropriate occasions for the trial judge to decide questions relating to pretrial disclosure. See *Alderman v. United States,* 394 U.S. at 182 n. 14, 89 S.Ct. 961.

Subdivision (d)(2) is a restatement of part of old rule 16(g) and (d).

Old subdivision (f) of rule 16 dealing with time of motions is dropped because rule 12(c) provides the judge with authority to set the time for the making of pretrial motions including requests for discovery. Rule 12 also prescribes the consequences which follow from a failure to make a pretrial motion at the time fixed by the court. See rule 12(f).

NOTES OF COMMITTEE ON THE JUDICIARY, HOUSE REPORT NO. 94–247

A. Amendments Proposed by the Supreme Court. Rule 16 of the Federal Rules of Criminal Procedure regulates discovery by the defendant of evidence in possession of the prosecution, and discovery by the prosecution of evidence in possession of the defendant. The present rule permits the defendant to move the court to discover certain material. The prosecutor's discovery is limited and is reciprocal—that is, if the defendant is granted discovery of certain items, then the prosecution may move for discovery of similar items under the defendant's control.

As proposed to be amended, the rule provides that the parties themselves will accomplish discovery—no motion need be filed and no court order is necessary. The court will intervene only to resolve a dispute as to whether something is discoverable or to issue a protective order.

The proposed rule enlarges the scope of the defendant's discovery to include a copy of his prior criminal record and a list of the names and addresses, plus record of prior felony convictions, of all witnesses the prosecution intends to call during its case-in-chief. It also permits the defendant to discover the substance of any oral statement of his which the prosecution intends to offer at trial, if the statement was given in response to interrogation by any person known by defendant to be a government agent.

Proposed subdivision (a)(2) provides that Rule 16 does not authorize the defendant to discover "reports, memoranda, or other internal government documents made by the attorney for the government or other government agents in connection with the investigation or prosecution of the case...."

The proposed rule also enlarges the scope of the government's discovery of materials in the custody of the defendant. The government is entitled to a list of the names and addresses of the witnesses the defendant intends to call during his case-in-chief. Proposed subdivision (b)(2) protects the defendant from having to disclose "reports, memoranda, or other internal defense documents ... made in connection with the investigation or defense of the case...."

Subdivision (d)(1) of the proposed rule permits the court to deny, restrict, or defer discovery by either party, or to make such other order as is appropriate. Upon request, a party may make a showing that such an order is necessary. This showing shall be made to the judge alone if the party so requests. If the court enters an order after such a showing, it must seal the record of the showing and preserve it in the event there is an appeal.

B. Committee Action. The Committee agrees that the parties should, to the maximum possible extent, accomplish discovery themselves. The court should become involved only when it is necessary to resolve a dispute or to issue an order pursuant to subdivision (d).

Perhaps the most controversial amendments to this rule were those dealing with witness lists. Under present law, the government must turn over a witness list *only* in capital cases. [Section 3432 of title 18 of the United States Code provides: A person charged with treason or other capital offense shall at least three entire days before commencement of trial be furnished with a copy of the indictment and a list of the veniremen, and of the witnesses to be produced on the trial for proving the indictment, stating the place of abode of each venireman and witness.] The defendant never needs to turn over a list of his witnesses. The proposed rule requires both the government and the defendant to turn over witness lists in every case, capital or noncapital. Moreover, the lists must be furnished to the adversary party upon that party's request.

The proposed rule was sharply criticized by both prosecutors and defenders. The prosecutors feared that pretrial disclosure of prosecution witnesses would result in harm to witnesses. The defenders argued that a defendant cannot constitutionally be compelled to disclose his witnesses.

The Committee believes that it is desirable to promote greater pretrial discovery. As stated in the Advisory Committee Note,

> broader discovery by both the defense and the prosecution will contribute to the fair and efficient administration of criminal justice by aiding in informed plea negotiations, by minimizing the undersirable effect of surprise at trial, and by otherwise contributing to an accurate determination of the issue of guilt or innocence....

The Committee, therefore, endorses the principle that witness lists are discoverable. However, the Committee has attempted to strike a balance between the narrow provisions of existing law and the broad provisions of the proposed rule.

The Committee rule makes the procedures defendant-triggered. If the defendant asks for and receives a list of prosecution witnesses, then the prosecution may request a list of defense witnesses. The witness lists need not be turned over until 3 days before trial. The court can modify the terms of discovery upon a sufficient showing. Thus, the court can require disclosure of the

witness lists earlier than 3 days before trial, or can permit a party not to disclose the identity of a witness before trial.

The Committee provision promotes broader discovery and its attendant values—informed disposition of cases without trial, minimizing the undesirable effect of surprise, and helping insure that the issue of guilt or innocence is accurately determined. At the same time, it avoids the problems suggested by both the prosecutors and the defenders.

The major argument advanced by prosecutors is the risk of danger to their witnesses if their identities are disclosed prior to trial. The Committee recognizes that there may be a risk but believes that the risk is not as great as some fear that it is. Numerous states require the prosecutor to provide the defendant with a list of prosecution witnesses prior to trial. [These States include Alaska, Arizona, Arkansas, California, Colorado, Florida, Idaho, Illinois, Indiana, Iowa, Kansas, Kentucky, Michigan, Minnesota, Missouri, Montana, Nebraska, Nevada, Oklahoma, Oregon, Tennessee, and Utah. See Advisory Committee Note, House Document 93–292, at 60.] The evidence before the Committee indicates that these states have not experienced unusual problems of witness intimidation. [See the comments of the Standing Committee on Criminal Law and Procedure of the State Bar of California in Hearings II, at 302.]

Some federal jurisdictions have adopted an omnibus pretrial discovery procedure that calls upon the prosecutor to give the defendant its witness lists. One such jurisdiction is the Southern District of California. The evidence before the Committee indicates that there has been no unusual problems with witness intimidation in that district. Charles Sevilla, Chief Trial Attorney for the Federal Defenders of San Diego, Inc., which operates in the Southern District of California, testified as follows:

> The Government in one of its statements to this committee indicated that providing the defense with witness lists will cause coerced witness perjury. This does not happen. We receive Government witness lists as a matter of course in the Southern District, and it's a rare occasion when there is any overture by a defense witness or by a defendant to a Government witness. It simply doesn't happen except on the rarest of occasion. When the Government has that fear it can resort to the protective order. [Hearings II, at 42.]

Mr. Sevilla's observations are corroborated by the views of the U.S. Attorney for the Southern District of California:

> Concerning the modifications to Rule 16, we have followed these procedures informally in this district for a number of years. We were one of the districts selected for the pilot projects of the Omnibus Hearing

in 1967 or 1968. We have found that the courts in our district will not require us to disclose names of proposed witnesses when in our judgment to do so would not be advisable. Otherwise we routinely provide defense counsel with full discovery, including names and addresses of witnesses. We have not had any untoward results by following this program, having in mind that the courts will, and have, excused us from discovery where the circumstances warrant. [Hearings I, at 109.]

Much of the prosecutorial criticism of requiring the prosecution to give a list of its witnesses to the defendant reflects an unwillingness to trust judges to exercise sound judgment in the public interest. Prosecutors have stated that they frequently will open their files to defendants in order to induce pleas. [See testimony of Richard L. Thornburgh, United States Attorney for the Western District of Pennsylvania, in Hearings I, at 150.]

Prosecutors are willing to determine on their own when they can do this without jeopardizing the safety of witnesses. There is no reason why a judicial officer cannot exercise the same discretion in the public interest.

The Committee is convinced that in the usual case there is no serious risk of danger to prosecution witnesses from pretrial disclosure of their identities. In exceptional instances, there may be a risk of danger. The Committee rule, however, is capable of dealing with those exceptional instances while still providing for disclosure of witnesses in the usual case.

The Committee recognizes the force of the constitutional arguments advanced by defenders. Requiring a defendant, upon request, to give to the prosecution material which may be incriminating, certainly raises very serious constitutional problems. The Committee deals with these problems by having the defendant trigger the discovery procedures. Since the defendant has no constitutional right to discover any of the prosecution's evidence (unless it is exculpatory within the meaning of *Brady v. Maryland,* 373 U.S. 83 (1963)), it is permissible to condition his access to nonexculpatory evidence upon his turning over a list of defense witnesses. Rule 16 currently operates in this manner.

The Committee also changed subdivisions (a)(2) and (b)(2), which set forth "work product" exceptions to the general discovery requirements. The subsections proposed by the Supreme Court are cast in terms of the type of document involved (e.g., report), rather than in terms of the content (e.g., legal theory). The Committee recast these provisions by adopting language from Rule 26(b)(3) of the Federal Rules of Civil Procedure.

The Committee notes that subdivision (a)(1)(C) permits the defendant to discover certain items that "were obtained from or belong to the defendant." The Committee believes that, as indicated in the Advisory Committee Note [House Document 93-292, at 59], items that "were obtained from or belong to the defendant" are items that are material to the preparation of his defense.

The Committee added language to subdivision (a)(1)(B) to conform it to provisions in subdivision (a)(1)(A). The rule as changed by the Committee requires the prosecutor to give the defendant such copy of the defendant's prior criminal record as is within the prosecutor's "possession, custody, or control, the existence of which is known, or by the exercise of due diligence may become known" to the prosecutor. The Committee also made a similar conforming change in subdivision (a)(1)(E), dealing with the criminal records of government witnesses. The prosecutor can ordinarily discharge his obligation under these two subdivisions, (a)(1)(B) and (E), by obtaining a copy of the F.B.I. "rap sheet."

The Committee made an additional change in subdivision (a)(1)(E). The proposed rule required the prosecutor to provide the defendant with a record of the felony convictions of government witnesses. The major purpose for letting the defendant discover information about the record of government witnesses, is to provide him with information concerning the credibility of those witnesses. Rule 609(a) of the Federal Rules of Evidence permits a party to attack the credibility of a witness with convictions other than just felony convictions. The Committee, therefore, changed subdivision (a)(1)(E) to require the prosecutor to turn over a record of all criminal convictions, not just felony convictions.

The Committee changed subdivision (d)(1), which deals with protective orders. Proposed (d)(1) required the court to conduct an ex parte proceeding whenever a party so requested. The Committee changed the mandatory language to permissive language. A Court may, not must, conduct an ex parte proceeding if a party so requests. Thus, if a party requests a protective or modifying order and asks to make its showing ex parte, the court has two separate determinations to make. First, it must determine whether an ex parte proceeding is appropriate, bearing in mind that ex parte proceedings are disfavored and not to be encouraged. [An ex parte proceeding would seem to be appropriate if any adversary proceeding would defeat the purpose of the protective or modifying order. For example, the identity of a witness would be disclosed and the purpose of the protective order is to conceal that witness' identity.] Second, it must determine whether a protective or modifying order shall issue.

CONFERENCE COMMITTEE NOTES, HOUSE REPORT NO. 94-414

Rule 16 deals with pretrial discovery by the defendant and the government. The House and Senate versions of the bill differ on Rule 16 in several respects.

A. Reciprocal vs. Independent Discovery for the Government.—The House version of the bill provides that the government's discovery is reciprocal. If the defendant requires and receives certain items from the government, then the government is entitled to get similar items from the defendant. The Senate version of the bill gives the government an independent right to discover material in the possession of the defendant.

The Conference adopts the House provisions.

B. Rule 16(a)(1)(A).—The House version permits an organization to discover relevant recorded grand jury testimony of any witness who was, at the time of the acts charged or of the grand jury proceedings, so situated as an officer or employee as to have been able legally to bind it in respect to the activities involved in the charges. The Senate version limits discovery of this material to testimony of a witness who was, at the time of the grand jury proceeding, so situated as an officer or employee as to have been legally to bind the defendant in respect to the activities involved in the charges.

The Conferees share a concern that during investigations, ex-employees and ex-officers of potential corporate defendants are a critical source of information regarding activities of their former corporate employers. It is not unusual that, at the time of their testimony or interview, these persons may have interests which are substantially adverse to or divergent from the putative corporate defendant. It is also not unusual that such individuals, though no longer sharing a community of interest with the corporation, may nevertheless be subject to pressure from their former employers. Such pressure may derive from the fact that the ex-employees or ex-officers have remained in the same industry or related industry, are employed by competitors, suppliers, or customers of their former employers, or have pension or other deferred compensation arrangements with former employers.

The Conferees also recognize that considerations of fairness require that a defendant corporation or other legal entity be entitled to the grand jury testimony of a former officer or employee if that person was personally involved in the conduct constituting the offense and was able legally to bind the defendant in respect to the conduct in which he was involved.

The Conferees decided that, on balance, a defendant organization should not be entitled to the relevant grand jury testimony of a former officer or employee in every instance. However, a defendant organization should be entitled to it if the former officer or employee was personally involved in the alleged conduct constituting the offense and was so situated as to have been able legally to bind the defendant in respect to the alleged conduct. The Conferees note that, even in those situations where the rule provides for disclosure of the

testimony, the Government may, upon a sufficient showing, obtain a protective or modifying order pursuant to Rule 16(d)(1).

The Conference adopts a provision that permits a defendant organization to discover relevant grand jury testimony of a witness who (1) was, at the time of his testimony, so situated as an officer or employee as to have been able legally to bind the defendant in respect to conduct constituting the offense, or (2) was, at the time of the offense, personally involved in the alleged conduct constituting the offense and so situated as an officer or employee as to have been able legally to bind the defendant in respect to that alleged conduct in which he was involved.

C. Rules 16(a)(1)(E) and (b)(1)(C) (witness lists).—The House version of the bill provides that each party, the government and the defendant, may discover the names and addresses of the other party's witnesses 3 days before trial. The Senate version of the bill eliminates these provisions, thereby making the names and addresses of a party's witnesses nondiscoverable. The Senate version also makes a conforming change in Rule 16(d)(1). The Conference adopts the Senate version.

A majority of the Conferees believe it is not in the interest of the effective administration of criminal justice to require that the government or the defendant be forced to reveal the names and addresses of its witnesses before trial. Discouragement of witnesses and improper contact directed at influencing their testimony, were deemed paramount concerns in the formulation of this policy.

D. Rules 16(a)(2) and (b)(2).—Rules 16(a)(2) and (b)(2) define certain types of materials ("work product") not to be discoverable. The House version defines work product to be "the mental impressions, conclusions, opinions, or legal theories of the attorney for the government or other government agents." This is parallel to the definition in the Federal Rules of Civil Procedure. The Senate version returns to the Supreme Court's language and defines work product to be "reports, memoranda, or other internal government documents." This is the language of the present rule.

The Conference adopts the Senate provision.

The Conferees note that a party may not avoid a legitimate discovery request merely because something is labelled "report", "memorandum", or "internal document". For example if a document qualifies as a statement of the defendant within the meaning of the Rule 16(a)(1)(A), then the labelling of that document as "report", "memorandum", or "internal government document" will not shield that statement from discovery. Likewise, if the results of an experiment qualify as the results of a scientific test within the meaning of Rule 16(b)(1)(B), then the results of that experiment are not shielded from discovery even if they are labelled "report", "memorandum", or "internal defense document".

Rule 16(a)(3)

The added language is made necessary by the addition of Rule 26.2 and new subdivision (i) of Rule 12, which contemplate the production of statements, including those made to a grand jury, under specified circumstances.

1987 AMENDMENT

The amendments are technical. No substantive change is intended.

EDITORIAL NOTES

1975 Amendments. Subd. (a)(1). Pub.L. 94–64 amended subpars. (A), (B), and (D) generally, and deleted subpar. (E).

Subd. (a)(4). Pub.L. 94–149 deleted par. (4) reading "Failure to Call Witness. The fact that a witness' name is on a list furnished under this rule shall not be grounds for comment upon a failure to call the witness."

Subd. (b)(1). Pub.L. 94–64 amended subpars. (A) and (B) generally, and deleted subpar. (C).

Subd. (b)(3). Pub.L. 94–149 deleted par. (3) reading "Failure to Call Witness. The fact that a witness' name is on a list furnished under this rule shall not be grounds for a comment upon a failure to call a witness."

Subd. (c). Pub.L. 94–64 amended subd. (c) generally.

Subd. (d)(1). Pub.L. 94–64 amended par. (1) generally.

Rule 17. Subpoena

(a) For Attendance of Witnesses; Form; Issuance. A subpoena shall be issued by the clerk under the seal of the court. It shall state the name of the court and the title, if any, of the proceeding, and shall command each person to whom it is directed to attend and give testimony at the time and place specified therein. The clerk shall issue a subpoena, signed and sealed but otherwise in blank to a party requesting it, who shall fill in the blanks before it is served. A subpoena shall be issued by a United States magistrate in a proceeding before that magistrate, but it need not be under the seal of the court.

(b) Defendants Unable to Pay. The court shall order at any time that a subpoena be issued for service on a named witness upon an *ex parte* application of a defendant upon a satisfactory showing that the defendant is financially unable to pay the fees of the witness and that the presence of the witness is necessary to an adequate defense. If the court orders the subpoena to be issued the costs incurred by the process and the fees of the witness so subpoenaed shall be paid in the same manner in which similar costs and fees are paid in case of a witness subpoenaed in behalf of the government.

(c) For Production of Documentary Evidence and of Objects. A subpoena may also command the person to whom it is directed to produce the books, papers, documents or other objects designated therein. The court on motion made promptly may quash or modify the subpoena if compliance would be unreasonable or oppressive. The court may direct that books, papers, documents or objects designated in the subpoena be produced before the court at a time prior to the trial or prior to the time when they are to be offered in evidence and may upon their production permit the books, papers, documents or objects or portions thereof to be inspected by the parties and their attorneys.

(d) Service. A subpoena may be served by the marshal, by a deputy marshal or by any other person who is not a party and who is not less than 18 years of age. Service of a subpoena shall be made by delivering a copy thereof to the person named and by tendering to that person the fee for 1 day's attendance and the mileage allowed by law. Fees and mileage need not be tendered to the witness upon service of a subpoena issued in behalf of the United States or an officer or agency thereof.

(e) Place of Service.

(1) In United States. A subpoena requiring the attendance of a witness at a hearing or trial may be served at any place within the United States.

(2) Abroad. A subpoena directed to a witness in a foreign country shall issue under the circumstances and in the manner and be served as provided in Title 28, U.S.C., § 1783.

(f) For Taking Deposition; Place of Examination.

(1) Issuance. An order to take a deposition authorizes the issuance by the clerk of the court for the district in which the deposition is to be taken of subpoenas for the persons named or described therein.

(2) Place. The witness whose deposition is to be taken may be required by subpoena to attend at any place designated by the trial court, taking into account the convenience of the witness and the parties.

(g) Contempt. Failure by any person without adequate excuse to obey a subpoena served upon that person may be deemed a contempt of the court from which the subpoena issued or of the court for the district in which it issued if it was issued by a United States magistrate.

(h) Information Not Subject to Subpoena. Statements made by witnesses or prospective witnesses may not be subpoenaed from the government or the defendant under this rule, but shall be subject to production only in accordance with the provisions of Rule 26.2.

(As amended Dec. 27, 1948, eff. Oct. 20, 1949; Feb. 28, 1966, eff. July 1, 1966; Apr. 24, 1972, eff. Oct. 1, 1972; Apr. 22, 1974, eff. Dec. 1, 1975; July 31, 1975, Pub.L. 94–64, § 3(29), 89 Stat. 375, Apr. 30, 1979, eff. Dec. 1, 1980; Mar. 9, 1987, eff. Aug. 1, 1987.)

NOTES OF ADVISORY COMMITTEE ON RULES

Note to Subdivision (a). This rule is substantially the same as Rule 45(a) of the Federal Rules of Civil Procedure, 28 U.S.C. Appendix.

Note to Subdivision (b). This rule preserves the existing right of an indigent defendant to secure attendance of witnesses at the expense of the Government, 28 U.S.C. former § 656 (Witnesses for indigent defendants). Under existing law, however, the right is limited to witnesses who are within the district in which the court is held or within one hundred miles of the place of trial. No procedure now exists whereby an indigent defendant can procure at Government expense the attendance of witnesses found in another district and more than 100 miles of the place of trial. This limitation is abrogated by the rule so that an indigent defendant will be able to secure the attendance of witnesses at the expense of the Government no matter where they are located. The showing required by the rule to justify such relief is the same as that now exacted by 28 U.S.C. former § 656.

Note to Subdivision (c). This rule is substantially the same as Rule 45(b) of the Federal Rules of Civil Procedure, 28 U.S.C., Appendix.

Note to Subdivision (d). This rule is substantially the same as Rule 45(c) of the Federal Rules of Civil Procedure, 28 U.S.C., Appendix. The provision permitting persons other than the marshal to serve the subpoena, and requiring the payment of witness fees in Government cases is new matter.

Note to Subdivision (e). (1) This rule continues existing law, 28 U.S.C. § 654 (Witnesses; subpoenas; may run into another district). The rule is different in civil cases in that in such cases, unless a statute otherwise provides, a subpoena may be served only within the district or within 100 miles of the place of trial, 28

U.S.C. former § 654; Rule 45(e)(1) of the Federal Rules of Civil Procedure, 28 U.S.C., Appendix.

(2) This rule is substantially the same as Rule 45(e)(2) of the Federal Rules of Civil Procedure, 28 U.S.C., Appendix. See *Blackmer v. United States,* 284 U.S. 421, upholding the validity of the statute referred to in the rule.

Note to Subdivision (f). This rule is substantially the same as Rule 45(d) of the Federal Rules of Civil Procedure, 28 U.S.C., Appendix.

Note to Subdivision (g). This rule is substantially the same as Rule 45(f) of the Federal Rules of Civil Procedure, 28 U.S.C., Appendix.

1948 AMENDMENT

The amendment is to substitute proper reference to Title 28 in place of the repealed act.

1966 AMENDMENT

Subdivision (b).—Criticism has been directed at the requirement that an indigent defendant disclose in advance the theory of his defense in order to obtain the issuance of a subpoena at government expense while the government and defendants able to pay may have subpoenas issued in blank without any disclosure. See Report of the Attorney General's Committee on Poverty and the Administration of Criminal Justice (1963) p. 27. The Attorney General's Committee also urged that the standard of financial inability to pay be substituted for that of indigency. Id. at 40–41. In one case it was held that the affidavit filed by an indigent defendant under this subdivision could be used by the government at his trial for purposes of impeachment. *Smith v. United States,* 312 F.2d 867 (D.C.Cir.1962). There has also been doubt as to whether the defendant need make a showing beyond the face of his affidavit in order to secure issuance of a subpoena. *Greenwell v. United States,* 317 F.2d 108 (D.C.Cir.1963).

The amendment makes several changes. The references to a judge are deleted since applications should be made to the court. An ex parte application followed by a satisfactory showing is substituted for the requirement of a request or motion supported by affidavit. The court is required to order the issuance of a subpoena upon finding that the defendant is unable to pay the witness fees and that the presence of the witness is necessary to an adequate defense.

Subdivision (d).—The subdivision is revised to bring it into conformity with 28 U.S.C. § 1825.

1972 AMENDMENT

Subdivisions (a) and (g) are amended to reflect the existence of the "United States magistrate," a phrase defined in rule 54.

1974 AMENDMENT

Subdivision (f)(2) is amended to provide that the court has discretion over the place at which the deposition is to be taken. Similar authority is conferred by Civil Rule 45(d)(2). See C. Wright, Federal Practice and Procedure: Criminal § 278 (1969).

Ordinarily the deposition should be taken at the place most convenient for the witness but, under certain circumstances, the parties may prefer to arrange for the presence of the witness at a place more convenient to counsel.

NOTES OF COMMITTEE ON THE JUDICIARY, HOUSE REPORT NO. 94–247

A. Amendments Proposed by the Supreme Court. Rule 17 of the Federal Rules of Criminal Procedure deals with subpoenas. Subdivision (f)(2) as proposed by the Supreme Court provides:

The witness whose deposition is to be taken may be required by subpoena to attend at any place designated by the trial court.

B. Committee Action. The Committee added language to the proposed amendment that directs the court to consider the convenience of the witness and the parties when compelling a witness to attend where a deposition will be taken.

1979 AMENDMENT

This addition to rule 17 is necessary in light of proposed rule 26.2, which deals with the obtaining of statements of government and defense witnesses.

1987 AMENDMENT

The amendments are technical. No substantive change is intended.

Rule 17.1　Pretrial Conference

At any time after the filing of the indictment or information the court upon motion of any party or upon its own motion may order one or more conferences to consider such matters as will promote a fair and expeditious trial. At the conclusion of a conference the court shall prepare and file a memorandum of the matters agreed upon. No admissions made by the defendant or the defendant's attorney at the conference shall be used against the defendant unless the admissions are reduced to writing and signed by the defendant and the defendant's attorney. This rule shall not be invoked in the case of a defendant who is not represented by counsel.

(Added Feb. 28, 1966, eff. July 1, 1966, and amended Mar. 9, 1987, eff. Aug. 1, 1987.)

NOTES OF ADVISORY COMMITTEE ON RULES

This new rule establishes a basis for pretrial conferences with counsel for the parties in criminal cases within the discretion of the court. Pretrial conferences are now being utilized to some extent even in the absence of a rule. See, generally, Brewster, Criminal Pre–Trials—Useful Techniques, 29 F.R.D. 442 (1962); Estes, Pre–Trial Conferences in Criminal Cases, 23 F.R.D. 560 (1959); Kaufman, Pre–Trial in Criminal Cases, 42 J.Am.Jud.Soc. 150 (1959); Kaufman, The Appalachian Trial: Further Observations on Pre–Trial in Criminal Cases, 44 J.Am.Jud.Soc. 53 (1960); West, Criminal Pre–Trials—Useful Techniques, 29 F.R.D. 436 (1962); Handbook of Recommended Procedures for the Trial of Protracted Cases, 25 F.R.D. 399–403, 468–470 (1960). Cf.Mo.Sup.Ct. Rule 25.09; Rules Governing the N.J. Courts, § 3:5–3.

The rule is cast in broad language so as to accommodate all types of pretrial conferences. As the third sentence suggests, in some cases it may be desirable or necessary to have the defendant present. See Committee on Pretrial Procedure of the Judicial Conference of the United States, Recommended Procedures in Criminal Pretrials, 37 F.R.D. 95 (1965).

1987 AMENDMENT

The amendments are technical. No substantive change is intended.

V.　VENUE

Rule 18.　Place of Prosecution and Trial

Except as otherwise permitted by statute or by these rules, the prosecution shall be had in a district in which the offense was committed. The court shall fix the place of trial within the district with due regard to the convenience of the defendant and the witnesses and the prompt administration of justice.

(As amended Feb. 28, 1966, eff. July 1, 1966; Apr. 30, 1979, eff. Aug. 1, 1979.)

NOTES OF ADVISORY COMMITTEE ON RULES

1. The Constitution of the United States, Article III. Section 2, Paragraph 3, provides:

The Trial of all Crimes, except in Cases of Impeachment, shall be by Jury; and such Trial shall be held in the State where the said Crimes shall have been committed; but when not committed within any State, the

Trial shall be at such Place or Places as the Congress may by Law have directed.

Amendment VI provides:

In all criminal prosecutions, the accused shall enjoy the right to a speedy and public trial, by an impartial jury of the State and district wherein the crime shall have been committed, which district shall have been previously ascertained by law * * *

28 U.S.C. former § 114 (now §§ 1393, 1441) provides:

All prosecutions for crimes or offenses shall be had within the division of such districts where the same were committed, unless the court, or the judge thereof, upon the application of the defendant, shall order the cause to be transferred for prosecution to another division of the district.

The word "prosecutions," as used in this statute, does not include the finding and return of an indictment. The prevailing practice of impaneling a grand jury for the entire district at a session in some division and of distributing the indictments among the divisions in which the offenses were committed is deemed proper and legal, *Salinger v. Loisel*, 265 U.S. 224, 237, 44 S.Ct. 519, 68 L.Ed. 989. The court stated that this practice is "attended with real advantages." The rule is a restatement of existing law and is intended to sanction the continuance of this practice. For this reason, the rule requires that only the trial be held in the division in which the offense was committed and permits other proceedings to be had elsewhere in the same district.

2. Within the framework of the foregoing constitutional provisions and the provisions of the general statute, 28 U.S.C. former § 114 (now §§ 1393, 1441), supra, numerous statutes have been enacted to regulate the venue of criminal proceedings, particularly in respect to continuing offenses and offenses consisting of several transactions occurring in different districts. *Armour Packing Co. v. United States*, 209 U.S. 56, 73–77, 28 S.Ct. 428, 52 L.Ed. 681; *United States v. Johnson*, 323 U.S. 273, 65 S.Ct. 249, 89 L.Ed. 236. These special venue provisions are not affected by the rule. Among these statutes are the following:

U.S.C. Title 8 former:

§ 138 [now §§ 1326, 1328, 1329] (Importation of aliens for immoral purposes; attempt to reenter after deportation; penalty)

U.S.C. Title 15:

§ 78aa (Regulation of Securities Exchanges; jurisdiction of offenses and suits)

§ 79y (Control of Public Utility Holding Companies; jurisdiction of offenses and suits)

§ 80a–43 (Investment Companies; jurisdiction of offenses and suits)

§ 80b–14 (Investment Advisers; jurisdiction of offenses and suits)

§ 298 (Falsely Stamped Gold or Silver, etc., violations of law; penalty; jurisdiction of prosecutions)

§ 715i (Interstate Transportation of Petroleum Products; restraining violations; civil and criminal proceedings; jurisdiction of District Courts; review)

§ 717u (Natural Gas Act; jurisdiction of offenses; enforcement of liabilities and duties)

U.S.C. Title 18 former:

§ 39 [now §§ 5, 3241] (Enforcement of neutrality; United States defined; jurisdiction of offenses; prior offenses; partial invalidity of provisions)

§ 336 [now § 1302] (Lottery, or gift enterprise circulars not mailable; place of trial)

§ 338a [now §§ 876, 3239] (Mailing threatening communications)

§ 338b [now §§ 877, 3239] (Same; mailing in foreign country for delivery in the United States)

§ 345 [now § 1717] (Using or attempting to use mails for transmission of matter declared nonmailable by title; jurisdiction of offense)

§ 396e [now § 1762] (Transportation or importation of convict-made goods with intent to use in violation of local law; jurisdiction of violations)

§ 401 [now § 2421] (White slave traffic; jurisdiction of prosecutions)

§ 408 [now §§ 10, 2311 to 2313] (Motor vehicles; transportation, etc., of stolen vehicles)

§ 408d [now §§ 875, 3239] (Threatening communications in interstate commerce)

§ 408e [now § 1073] (Moving in interstate or foreign commerce to avoid prosecution for felony or giving testimony)

§ 409 [now §§ 659, 660, 2117] (Larceny, etc., of goods in interstate or foreign commerce; penalty)

§ 412 [now § 660] (Embezzlement, etc., by officers of carrier; jurisdiction; double jeopardy)

§ 418 [now § 3237] (National Stolen Property Act; jurisdiction)

§ 419d [now § 3237] (Transportation of stolen cattle in interstate or foreign commerce; jurisdiction of offense)

§ 420d [now § 1951] (Interference with trade and commerce by violence, threats, etc., jurisdiction of offenses)

§ 494 [now § 1654] (Arming vessel to cruise against citizen; trials)

§ 553 [now § 3236] (Place of committal of murder or manslaughter determined)

U.S.C. Title 21:

§ 17 (Introduction into, or sale in, State or Territory or District of Columbia of dairy or food products falsely labeled or branded; penalty; jurisdiction of prosecutions)

§ 118 (Prevention of introduction and spread of contagion; duty of district attorneys)

U.S.C. Title 28 former:

§ 101 [now 18 U.S.C. § 3235] (Capital cases)

§ 102 [now 18 U.S.C. § 3238] (Offenses on the high seas)

§ 103 [now 18 U.S.C. § 3237] (Offenses begun in one district and completed in another)

§ 121 [now 18 U.S.C. § 3240] (Creation of new district or division)

U.S.C. Title 47:

§ 33 (Submarine Cables; jurisdiction and venue of actions and offenses)

§ 505 (Special Provisions Relating to Radio; venue of trials)

U.S.C. Title 49:

§ 41 (Legislation Supplementary to Interstate Commerce Act; liability of corporation carriers and agents; offenses and penalties—(1) Liability of corporation common carriers; offenses; penalties; Jurisdiction)

§ 623 [now § 1473] (Civil Aeronautics Act; venue and prosecution of offenses)

1966 AMENDMENT

The amendment eliminates the requirement that the prosecution shall be in a division in which the offense was committed and vests discretion in the court to fix the place of trial at any place within the district with due regard to the convenience of the defendant and his witnesses.

The Sixth Amendment provides that the defendant shall have the right to a trial "by an impartial jury of the State and district wherein the crime shall have been committed, which district shall have been previously ascertained by law. * * *" There is no constitutional right to trial within a division. See *United States v. Anderson*, 328 U.S. 699, 704, 705 (1946); *Barrett v. United States*, 169 U.S. 218 (1898); *Lafoon v. United States*, 250 F.2d 958 (5th Cir.1958); *Carrillo v. Squier*, 137 F.2d 648 (9th Cir.1943); *McNealey v. Johnston*, 100 F.2d 280, 282 (9th Cir.1938). Cf. *Platt v. Minnesota Mining and Manufacturing Co.*, 376 U.S. 240 (1964).

The former requirement for venue within the division operated in an irrational fashion. Divisions have been created in only half of the districts, and the differentiation between those districts with and those without divisions often bears no relationship to comparative size or population. In many districts a single judge is required to sit in several divisions and only brief and infrequent terms may be held in particular divisions. As a consequence under the original rule there was often undue delay in the disposition of criminal cases—delay which was particularly serious with respect to defendants who had been unable to secure release on bail pending the holding of the next term of court.

If the court is satisfied that there exists in the place fixed for trial prejudice against the defendant so great as to render the trial unfair, the court may, of course, fix another place of trial within the district (if there be such) where such prejudice does not exist. Cf. Rule 21 dealing with transfers between districts.

1979 AMENDMENT

This amendment is intended to eliminate an inconsistency between rule 18, which in its present form has been interpreted not to allow trial in a division other than that in which the offense was committed except as dictated by the convenience of the defendant and witnesses, *Dupoint v. United States*, 388 F.2d 39 (5th Cir. 1968), and the Speedy Trial Act of 1974. This Act provides:

In any case involving a defendant charged with an offense, the appropriate judicial officer, at the earliest practicable time, shall, after consultation with the counsel for the defendant and the attorney for the Government, set the case for trial on a day certain, or list it for trial on a weekly or other short-term trial calendar at a place within the judicial district, so as to assure a speedy trial.

18 U.S.C. § 3161(a). This provision is intended to "permit the trial of a case at any place within the judicial district. This language was included in anticipation of problems which might occur in districts with statutory divisions, where it could be difficult to set trial outside the division." H.R.Rep. No. 93–1508, 93d Cong., 2d Sess. 29 (1974).

The change does not offend the venue or vicinage provisions of the Constitution. Article III, § 2, clause 3 places venue (the geographical location of the trial) "in the State where the said Crimes shall have been committed," while the Sixth Amendment defines the vicinage (the geographical location of the jurors) as "the State and district wherein the crime shall have been committed, which district shall have been previously ascertained by law." The latter provision makes "no reference to a division within a judicial district." *United States v. James*, 528 F.2d 999 (5th Cir.1976). "It follows *a fortiori* that when a district is not separated into divisions, * * * trial at any place within the district is allowable under the Sixth Amendment * * *." *United States v. Fernandez*, 480 F.2d 726 (2d Cir.1973). See also *Zicarelli v. Gray*, 543 F.2d 466 (3d Cir.1976) and cases cited therein.

Nor is the change inconsistent with the Declaration of Policy in the Jury Selection and Service Act of 1968, which reads:

It is the policy of the United States that all litigants in Federal courts entitled to trial by jury shall have the right to grand and petit juries selected at random from a fair cross section of the community in the district or division wherein the court convenes. 28 U.S.C. § 1861. This language does *not* mean that the Act requires "the trial court to convene not only in the district but also in the division wherein the offense occurred," as:

> There is no hint in the statutory history that the Jury Selection Act was intended to do more than provide improved judicial machinery so that grand and petit jurors would be selected at random by the use of objective qualification criteria to ensure a representative cross section of the district or division in which the grand or petit jury sits.

United States v. Cates, 485 F.2d 26 (1st Cir.1974).

The amendment to rule 18 does not eliminate either of the existing considerations which bear upon fixing the place of trial within a district, but simply adds yet another consideration in the interest of ensuring compliance with the requirements of the Speedy Trial Act of 1974. The amendment does not authorize the fixing of the place of trial for yet other reasons. Cf. *United States v. Fernandez,* 480 F.2d 726 (2d Cir.1973) (court in the exercise of its supervisory power held improper the fixing of the place of trial "for no apparent reason other than the convenience of the judge").

Rule 19. Rescinded Feb. 28, 1966, eff. July 1, 1966

1966 Rescission

Prior to rescission this rule read: "In a District consisting of two or more divisions the arraignment may be had, a plea entered, the trial conducted or sentence imposed, if the defendant consents, in any division at any time".

NOTES OF ADVISORY COMMITTEE ON RULES

Rule 19 is rescinded in view of the amendments being proposed to rule 18.

Rule 20. Transfer From the District for Plea and Sentence

(a) Indictment or Information Pending. A defendant arrested, held, or present in a district other than that in which an indictment or information is pending against that defendant may state in writing a wish to plead guilty or nolo contendere, to waive trial in the district in which the indictment or information is pending, and to consent to disposition of the case in the district in which that defendant was arrested, held, or present, subject to the approval of the United States attorney for each district. Upon receipt of the defendant's statement and of the written ap-

proval of the United States attorneys, the clerk of the court in which the indictment or information is pending shall transmit the papers in the proceeding or certified copies thereof to the clerk of the court for the district in which the defendant is arrested, held, or present, and the prosecution shall continue in that district.

(b) Indictment or Information Not Pending. A defendant arrested, held, or present, in a district other than the district in which a complaint is pending against that defendant may state in writing a wish to plead guilty or nolo contendere, to waive venue and trial in the district in which the warrant was issued, and to consent to disposition of the case in the district in which that defendant was arrested, held, or present, subject to the approval of the United States attorney for each district. Upon filing the written waiver of venue in the district in which the defendant is present, the prosecution may proceed as if venue were in such district.

(c) Effect of Not Guilty Plea. If after the proceeding has been transferred pursuant to subdivision (a) or (b) of this rule the defendant pleads not guilty, the clerk shall return the papers to the court in which the prosecution was commenced, and the proceeding shall be restored to the docket of that court. The defendant's statement that the defendant wishes to plead guilty or nolo contendere shall not be used against that defendant.

(d) Juveniles. A juvenile (as defined in 18 U.S.C. § 5031) who is arrested, held, or present in a district other than that in which the juvenile is alleged to have committed an act in violation of a law of the United States not punishable by death or life imprisonment may, after having been advised by counsel and with the approval of the court and the United States attorney for each district, consent to be proceeded against as a juvenile delinquent in the district in which the juvenile is arrested, held, or present. The consent shall be given in writing before the court but only after the court has apprised the juvenile of the juvenile's rights, including the right to be returned to the district in which the juvenile is alleged to have committed the act, and of the consequences of such consent.

(As amended Feb. 28, 1966, eff. July 1, 1966; Apr. 22, 1974, eff. Dec. 1, 1975; July 31, 1975, Pub.L.

94–64, § 3(30), 89 Stat. 375; Apr. 28, 1982, eff. Aug. 1, 1982; Mar. 9, 1987, eff. Aug. 1, 1987.)

NOTES OF ADVISORY COMMITTEE ON RULES

This rule introduces a new procedure in the interest of defendants who intend to plead guilty and are arrested in a district other than that in which the prosecution has been instituted. This rule would accord to a defendant in such a situation an opportunity to secure a disposition of the case in the district where the arrest takes place, thereby relieving him of whatever hardship may be involved in a removal to the place where the prosecution is pending. In order to prevent possible interference with the administration of justice, however, the consent of the United States attorneys involved is required.

1966 AMENDMENT

Rule 20 has proved to be most useful. In some districts, however, literal compliance with the procedures spelled out by the rule has resulted in unnecessary delay in the disposition of cases. This delay has been particularly troublesome where the defendant has been arrested prior to the filing of an indictment or information against him. See e.g., the procedure described in *Donovan v. United States,* 205 F.2d 557 (10th Cir.1953). Furthermore, the benefit of the rule has not been available to juveniles electing to be proceeded against under 18 U.S.C. §§ 5031–5037. In an attempt to clarify and simplify the procedure the rule has been recast into four subdivisions.

Subdivision (a).—This subdivision is intended to apply to the situation in which an indictment or information is pending at the time at which the defendant indicates his desire to have the transfer made. Two amendments are made to the present language of the rule. In the first sentence the words "or held" and "or is held" are added to make it clear that a person already in state or federal custody within a district may request a transfer of federal charges pending against him in another district. See 4 Barron, Federal Practice and Procedure 146 (1951). The words "after receiving a copy of the indictment or information" are deleted.

The defendant should be permitted, if he wishes, to initiate transfer proceedings under the Rule without waiting for a copy of the indictment or information to be obtained. The defendant is protected against prejudice by the fact that under subdivision (c) he can, in effect, rescind his action by pleading not guilty after the transfer has been completed.

Subdivision (b).—This subdivision is intended to apply to the situation in which no indictment or information is pending but the defendant has been arrested on a warrant issued upon a complaint in another district. Under the procedure set out he may initiate the transfer proceedings without waiting for the filing of an indictment or information in the district where the

complaint is pending. Also it is made clear that the defendant may validate an information previously filed by waiving indictment in open court when he is brought before the court to plead. See *United States v. East,* 5 F.R.D. 389. (N.D.Ind.1946); *Potter v. United States,* 36 F.R.D. 394 (W.D.Mo.1965). Here again the defendant is fully protected by the fact that at the time of pleading in the transferee court he may then refuse to waive indictment and rescind the transfer by pleading not guilty.

Subdivision (c).—The last two sentences of the original rule are included here. The last sentence is amended to forbid use against the defendant of his statement that he wishes to plead guilty or nolo contendere whether or not he was represented by counsel when it was made. Since under the amended rule the defendant may make his statement prior to receiving a copy of the indictment or information, it would be unfair to permit use of that statement against him.

Subdivision (d).—Under 18 U.S.C. § 5033 a juvenile who has committed an act in violation of the law of the United States in one district and is apprehended in another must be returned to the district "having cognizance of the alleged violation" before he can consent to being proceeded against as a juvenile delinquent. This subdivision will permit a juvenile after he has been advised by counsel and with the approval of the court and the United States attorney to consent to be proceeded against in the district in which he is arrested or held. Consent is required only of the United States attorney in the district of the arrest in order to permit expeditious handling of juvenile cases. If it is necessary to recognize special interests of particular districts where offenses are committed—e.g., the District of Columbia with its separate Juvenile Court (District of Columbia Code § 11–1551(a))—the Attorney General may do so through his Administrative control over United States Attorneys.

Subdivision (e).—This subdivision is added to make it clear that a defendant who appears in one district in response to a summons issued in the district where the offense was committed may initiate transfer proceedings under the rule.

1974 AMENDMENT

Rule 20 is amended to provide that a person "present" in a district other than the district in which he is charged with a criminal offense may, subject to the other provisions of rule 20, plead guilty in the district in which he is "present." See rule 6(b), Rules of Procedure for the Trial of Minor Offenses Before Magistrates.

Under the former rule, practice was to have the district in which the offense occurred issue a bench warrant authorizing the arrest of the defendant in the district in which he was located. This is a procedural complication which serves no interest of either the government or the defense and therefore can properly be dispensed with.

Making the fact that a defendant is "present" in the district an adequate basis for allowing him to plead guilty there makes it unnecessary to retain subdivision (e) which makes appearance in response to a summons equivalent to an arrest. Dropping (e) will eliminate some minor ambiguity created by that subdivision. See C. Wright, Federal Practice and Procedure: Criminal § 322 n. 26, p. 612 (1969, Supp.1971).

There are practical advantages which will follow from the change. In practice a person may turn himself in in a district other than that in which the prosecution is pending. It may be more convenient to have him plead in the district in which he is present rather than having him or the government incur the expense of his return to the district in which the charge is pending.

The danger of "forum shopping" can be controlled by the requirement that both United States Attorneys agree to the handling of the case under provisions of this rule.

NOTES OF COMMITTEE ON THE JUDICIARY, HOUSE REPORT NO. 94–247

A. Amendments Proposed by the Supreme Court. Rule 20 of the Federal Rules of Criminal Procedure deals with transferring a defendant from one district to another for the purpose of pleading and being sentenced. It deals with the situation where a defendant is located in one district (A) and is charged with a crime in another district (B). Under the present rule, if such a defendant desires to waive trial and plead guilty or nolo contendere, a judge in district B would issue a bench warrant for the defendant, authorizing his arrest in district A and his transport to district B for the purpose of pleading and being sentenced.

The Supreme Court amendments permit the defendant in the above example to plead guilty or nolo contendere in district A, if the United States Attorneys for districts A and B consent.

B. Committee Action. The Committee has added a conforming amendment to subdivision (d), which establishes procedures for dealing with defendants who are juveniles.

1982 AMENDMENT

This amendment to subdivision (b) is intended to expedite transfer proceedings under Rule 20. At present, considerable delay—sometimes as long as three or four weeks—occurs in subdivision (b) cases, that is, where no indictment or information is pending. This time is spent on the transmittal of defendant's statement to the district where the complaint is pending, the filing of an information or return of an indictment there, and the transmittal of papers in the case from

that district to the district where the defendant is present. Under the amendment, the defendant, by also waiving venue, would make it possible for charges to be filed in the district of his arrest or presence. This would advance the interests of both the prosecution and defendant in a timely entry of a plea of guilty. No change has been made in the requirement that the transfer occur with the consent of both United States attorneys.

1987 AMENDMENT

The amendments are technical. No substantive change is intended.

Rule 21. Transfer From the District for Trial

(a) For Prejudice in the District. The court upon motion of the defendant shall transfer the proceeding as to that defendant to another district whether or not such district is specified in the defendant's motion if the court is satisfied that there exists in the district where the prosecution is pending so great a prejudice against the defendant that the defendant cannot obtain a fair and impartial trial at any place fixed by law for holding court in that district.

(b) Transfer in Other Cases. For the convenience of parties and witnesses, and in the interest of justice, the court upon motion of the defendant may transfer the proceeding as to that defendant or any one or more of the counts thereof to another district.

(c) Proceedings on Transfer. When a transfer is ordered the clerk shall transmit to the clerk of the court to which the proceeding is transferred all papers in the proceeding or duplicates thereof and any bail taken, and the prosecution shall continue in that district.

(As amended Feb. 28, 1966, eff. July 1, 1966; Mar. 9, 1987, eff. Aug. 1, 1987.)

NOTES OF ADVISORY COMMITTEE ON RULES

Note to Subdivisions (a) and (b). 1. This rule introduces an addition to existing law. "Lawyers not thoroughly familiar with Federal practice are somewhat astounded to learn that they may not move for a change of venue, even if they are able to demonstrate that public feeling in the vicinity of the crime may render impossible a fair and impartial trial. This seems to be a defect in the federal law, which the proposed rules would cure." Homer Cummings, 29 A.B.A.Jour. 655; Medalie, 4 Lawyers Guild R. (3)1, 5.

2. The rule provides for two kinds of motions that may be made by the defendant for a change of venue.

The first is a motion on the ground that so great a prejudice exists against the defendant that he cannot obtain a fair and impartial trial in the district or division where the case is pending. Express provisions to a similar effect are found in many State statutes. See, e.g., Ala.Code (1940), Title 15, sec. 267; Cal.Pen. Code (Deering, 1941), sec. 1033; Conn.Gen.Stat. (1930), sec. 6445; Mass.Gen.Laws (1932) c. 277, sec. 51 (in capital cases); N.Y.Code of Criminal Procedure, sec. 344. The second is a motion for a change of venue in cases involving an offense alleged to have been committed in more than one district or division. In such cases the court, on defendant's motion, will be authorized to transfer the case to another district or division in which the commission of the offense is charged, if the court is satisfied that it is in the interest of justice to do so. The effect of this provision would be to modify the existing practice under which in such cases the Government has the final choice of the jurisdiction where the prosecution should be conducted. The matter will now be left in the discretion of the court.

3. The rule provides for a change of venue only on defendant's motion and does not extend the same right to the prosecution, since the defendant has a constitutional right to a trial in the district where the offense was committed. Constitution of the United States, Article III, Sec. 2, Par. 3; Amendment VI. By making a motion for a change of venue, however, the defendant waives this constitutional right.

4. This rule is in addition to and does not supersede existing statutes enabling a party to secure a change of judge on the ground of personal bias or prejudice, 28 U.S.C. former § 25 (now § 144); or enabling the defendant to secure a change of venue as of right in certain cases involving offenses committed in more than one district, 18 U.S.C. former § 338a(d) (now §§ 876, 3239) (Mailing threatening communications); Id. 18 U.S.C. § 403d(d) (now §§ 875, 3239) (Threatening communications in interstate commerce).

Note to Subdivision (c). Cf. 28 U.S.C. former § 114 (now §§ 1393, 1441) and Rule 20, supra.

1966 AMENDMENT

Subdivision (a).—All references to divisions are eliminated in accordance with the amendment to Rule 18 eliminating division venue. The defendant is given the right to a transfer only when he can show that he cannot obtain a fair and impartial trial at any place fixed by law for holding court in the district. Transfers within the district to avoid prejudice will be within the power of the judge to fix the place of trial as provided in

the amendments to Rule 18. It is also made clear that on a motion to transfer under this subdivision the court may select the district to which the transfer may be made. Cf. *United States v. Parr*, 17 F.R.D. 512, 519 (S.D.Tex.1955); *Parr v. United States*, 351 U.S. 513 (1956).

Subdivision (b).—The original rule limited change of venue for reasons other than prejudice in the district to those cases where venue existed in more than one district. Upon occasion, however, convenience of the parties and witnesses and the interest of justice would best be served by trial in a district in which no part of the offense was committed. See, e.g., *Travis v. United States*, 364 U.S. 631 (1961), holding that the only venue of a charge of making or filing a false non-Communist affidavit required by § 9(h) of the National Labor Relations Act is in Washington, D.C. even though all the relevant witnesses may be located at the place where the affidavit was executed and mailed. See also Barber, Venue in Federal Criminal Cases: A Plea for Return to Principle, 42 Tex.L.Rev. 39 (1963); Wright, Proposed Changes in Federal Civil, Criminal and Appellate Procedure, 35 F.R.D. 317, 329 (1964). The amendment permits a transfer in any case on motion of the defendant on a showing that it would be for the convenience of parties and witnesses, and in the interest of justice. Cf. 28 U.S.C. § 1404(a), stating a similar standard for civil cases. See also *Platt v. Minnesota Min. & Mfg. Co.*, 376 U.S. 240 (1964). Here, as in subdivision (a), the court may select the district to which the transfer is to be made. The amendment also makes it clear that the court may transfer all or part of the offenses charged in a multi-count indictment or information. Cf. *United States v. Choate*, 276 F.2d 724 (5th Cir.1960). References to divisions are eliminated in accordance with the amendment to Rule 18.

Subdivision (c).—The reference to division is eliminated in accordance with the amendment to Rule 18.

1987 AMENDMENT

The amendments are technical. No substantive change is intended.

Rule 22.   Time of Motion to Transfer

A motion to transfer under these rules may be made at or before arraignment or at such other time as the court or these rules may prescribe.

NOTES OF ADVISORY COMMITTEE ON RULES

Cf. Rule 12(b)(3).

VI. TRIAL

Rule 23. Trial by Jury or by the Court

(a) **Trial by Jury.** Cases required to be tried by jury shall be so tried unless the defendant waives a jury trial in writing with the approval of the court and the consent of the government.

(b) **Jury of Less Than Twelve.** Juries shall be of 12 but at any time before verdict the parties may stipulate in writing with the approval of the court that the jury shall consist of any number less than 12 or that a valid verdict may be returned by a jury of less than 12 should the court find it necessary to excuse one or more jurors for any just cause after trial commences. Even absent such stipulation, if the court finds it necessary to excuse a juror for just cause after the jury has retired to consider its verdict, in the discretion of the court a valid verdict may be returned by the remaining 11 jurors.

(c) **Trial Without a Jury.** In a case tried without a jury the court shall make a general finding and shall in addition, on request made before the general finding, find the facts specially. Such findings may be oral. If an opinion or memorandum of decision is filed, it will be sufficient if the findings of fact appear therein.

(As amended Feb. 28, 1966, eff. July 1, 1966; Apr. 26, 1976, eff. Oct. 1, 1977; Pub.L. 95–78, § 2(b), July 30, 1977, 91 Stat. 320; Apr. 28, 1983, eff. Aug. 1, 1983.)

NOTES OF ADVISORY COMMITTEE ON RULES

Note to Subdivision (a). 1. This rule is a formulation of the constitutional guaranty of trial by jury, Constitution of the United States, Article III, Sec. 2, Par. 3: "The Trial of all Crimes, except in Cases of Impeachment, shall be by Jury * * *"; Amendment VI: "In all criminal prosecutions, the accused shall enjoy the right to a speedy and public trial, by an impartial jury * * *." The right to a jury trial, however, does not apply to petty offenses, *District of Columbia v. Clawans,* 300 U.S. 617, 57 S.Ct. 660, 81 L.Ed. 843; *Schick v. United States,* 195 U.S. 65, 24 S.Ct. 826, 49 L.Ed. 99, 1 Ann.Cas. 585; Frankfurter and Corcoran, 39 Harv.L.R. 917. Cf. Rule 38(a) of the Federal Rules of Civil Procedure.

2. The provision for a waiver of jury trial by the defendant embodies existing practice, the constitutionality of which has been upheld, *Patton v. United States,* 281 U.S. 276, 50 S.Ct. 253, 74 L.Ed. 854, 70 A.L.R. 263; *Adams v. United States ex rel. McCann,* 317 U.S. 269, 63 S.Ct. 236, 87 L.Ed. 268, 143 A.L.R. 435; Cf. Rules 38 and 39 of Federal Rules of Civil Procedure, 28 U.S.C., Appendix. Many States by express statutory provision permit waiver of jury trial in criminal cases. See A.L.I. Code of Criminal Procedure Commentaries, pp. 807–811.

Note to Subdivision (b). This rule would permit either a stipulation before the trial that the case be tried by a jury composed of less than 12 or a stipulation during the trial consenting that the case be submitted to less than 12 jurors. The second alternative is useful in case it becomes necessary during the trial to excuse a juror owing to illness or for some other cause and no alternate juror is available. The rule is a restatement of existing practice, the constitutionality of which was approved in *Patton v. United States,* 281 U.S. 276, 50 S.Ct. 253, 74 L.Ed. 854, 70 A.L.R. 263.

Note to Subdivision (c). This rule changes existing law in so far as it requires the court in a case tried without a jury to make special findings of fact if requested. Cf. Connecticut practice, under which a judge in a criminal case tried by the court without a jury makes findings of fact, *State v. Frost,* 105 Conn. 326, 135 A. 446.

1966 AMENDMENT

This amendment adds to the rule a provision added to Civil Rule 52(a) in 1946.

1977 AMENDMENT

The amendment to subdivision (b) makes it clear that the parties, with the approval of the court, may enter into an agreement to have the case decided by less than twelve jurors if one or more jurors are unable or disqualified to continue. For many years the Eastern District of Virginia has used a form entitled, "Waiver of Alternate Jurors." In a substantial percentage of cases the form is signed by the defendant, his attorney, and the Assistant United States Attorney in advance of trial, generally on the morning of trial. It is handled automatically by the courtroom deputy clerk who, after completion, exhibits it to the judge.

This practice would seem to be authorized by existing rule 23(b), but there has been some doubt as to whether the pretrial stipulation is effective unless again agreed to by a defendant at the time a juror or jurors have to be excused. See 8 J. Moore, Federal Practice ¶ 23.04 (2d ed. Cipes, 1969); C. Wright, Federal Practice and Procedure: Criminal § 373 (1969). The proposed amendment is intended to make clear that the pretrial stipulation is an effective waiver, which need not be renewed at the time the incapacity or disqualification of the juror becomes known.

In view of the fact that a defendant can make an effective pretrial waiver of trial by jury or by a jury of twelve, it would seem to follow that he can also effectively waive trial by a jury of twelve in situations where a juror or jurors cannot continue to serve.

As has been the practice under rule 23(b), a stipulation addressed to the possibility that some jurors may later be excused need not be open-ended. That is, the stipulation may be conditioned upon the jury not being reduced below a certain size. See, e.g., *Williams v. United States,* 332 F.2d 36 (7th Cir.1964) (agreement to proceed if no more than 2 jurors excused for illness); *Rogers v. United States,* 319 F.2d 5 (7th Cir.1963) (same).

Subdivision (c) is changed to make clear the deadline for making a request for findings of fact and to provide that findings may be oral. The oral findings, of course, become a part of the record, as findings of fact are essential to proper appellate review on a conviction resulting from a nonjury trial. *United States v. Livingston,* 459 F.2d 797 (3d Cir.1972).

The meaning of current subdivision (c) has been in some doubt because there is no time specified within which a defendant must make a "request" that the court "find the facts specially." See, e.g., *United States v. Rivera,* 444 F.2d 136 (2d Cir.1971), where the request was not made until the sentence had been imposed. In the opinion the court said: This situation might have raised the interesting and apparently undecided question of when a request for findings under Fed.R.Crim.P. 23(c) is too late, since Rivera's request was not made until the day after sentence was imposed. See generally *Benchwick v. United States,* 297 F.2d 330, 335 (9th Cir.1961); *United States v. Morris,* 263 F.2d 594 (7th Cir.1959).

NOTES OF COMMITTEE ON THE JUDICIARY, SENATE REPORT NO. 95–354. AMENDMENTS PROPOSED BY THE SUPREME COURT

Subsection (b) of section 2 of the bill simply approves the Supreme Court proposed changes in subdivisions (b) and (c) of rule 23 for the reasons given by the Advisory Committee on Rules of Practice and Procedure to the Judicial Conference.

CONGRESSIONAL APPROVAL OF PROPOSED AMENDMENTS

Section 2(b) of Pub.L. 95–78 provided that: "The amendments proposed by the Supreme Court [in its order of Apr. 26, 1976] to subdivisions (b) and (c) of rule 23 of such Rules of Criminal Procedure [subd. (b) and (c) of this rule] are approved."

1983 AMENDMENT

Rule 23(b)

The amendment to subdivision (b) addresses a situation which does not occur with great frequency but which, when it does occur, may present a most difficult issue concerning the fair and efficient administration of justice. This situation is that in which, after the jury has retired to consider its verdict and any alternate jurors have been discharged, one of the jurors is seriously incapacitated or otherwise found to be unable to continue service upon the jury. The problem is acute when the trial has been a lengthy one and consequently the remedy of mistrial would necessitate a second expenditure of substantial prosecution, defense and court resources. See, e.g., *United States v. Meinster,* 484 F.Supp. 442 (S.D.Fla.1980), aff'd sub nom. *United States v. Phillips,* 664 F.2d 971 (5th Cir.1981) (juror had heart attack during deliberations after "well over four months of trial"); *United States v. Barone,* 83 F.R.D. 565 (S.D.Fla.1979) (juror removed upon recommendation of psychiatrist during deliberations after "approximately six months of trial").

It is the judgment of the Committee that when a juror is lost during deliberations, especially in circumstances like those in *Barone* and *Meinster,* it is essential that there be available a course of action other than mistrial. Proceeding with the remaining 11 jurors, though heretofore impermissible under rule 23(b) absent stipulation by the parties and approval of the court, *United States v. Taylor,* 507 F.2d 166 (5th Cir.1975), is constitutionally permissible. In *Williams v. Florida,* 399 U.S. 78 (1970), the Court concluded

the fact that the jury at common law was composed of precisely 12 is an historical accident, unnecessary to effect the purposes of the jury system and wholly without significance "except to mystics." * * * To read the Sixth Amendment as forever codifying a feature so incidental to the real purpose of the Amendment is to ascribe a blind formalism to the Framers which would require considerably more evidence than we have been able to discover in the history and language of the Constitution or in the reasoning of our past decisions. * * * Our holding does no more than leave these considerations to Congress and the States, unrestrained by an interpretation of the Sixth Amendment which would forever dictate the precise number which can constitute a jury.

Williams held that a six-person jury was constitutional because such a jury had the "essential feature of a jury," i.e., "the interposition between the accused and his accuser of the common-sense judgment of a group of laymen, and in the community participation and shared responsibility which results from that group's determination of guilt or innocence," necessitating only a group "large enough to promote group deliberation, free from outside attempts at intimidation, and to provide a fair possibility for obtaining a representative cross section of the community." This being the case, quite clearly the occasional use of a jury of slightly less than 12, as contemplated by the amendment to rule 23(b), is constitutional. Though the alignment of the Court and especially the separate opinion by Justice Powell in *Apodoca v. Oregon*, 406 U.S. 404 (1972), makes it at best uncertain whether less-than-unanimous verdicts would be constitutionally permissible in federal trials, it hardly follows that a requirement of unanimity of a group slightly less than 12 is similarly suspect.

The *Meinster* case clearly reflects the need for a solution other than mistrial. There twelve defendants were named in a 36–count, 100–page indictment for RICO offenses and related violations, and the trial lasted more than four months. Before the jury retired for deliberations, the trial judge inquired of defense counsel whether they would now agree to a jury of less than 12 should a juror later be unable to continue during the deliberations which were anticipated to be lengthy. All defense counsel rejected that proposal. When one juror was excused a day later after suffering a heart attack, all defense counsel again rejected the proposal that deliberations continue with the remaining 11 jurors. Thus, the solution now provided in rule 23(b), stipulation to a jury of less than 12, was not possible in that case, just as it will not be possible in any case in which defense counsel believe some tactical advantage will be gained by retrial. Yet, to declare a mistrial at that point would have meant that over four months of trial time would have gone for naught and that a comparable period of time would have to be expended on retrial. For a variety of reasons, not the least of which is the impact such a retrial would have upon that court's ability to comply with speedy trial limits in other cases, such a result is most undesirable.

That being the case, it is certainly understandable that the trial judge in *Meinster* (as in *Barone*) elected to substitute an alternate juror at that point. Given the rule 23(b) bar on a verdict of less than 12 absent stipulation, *United States v. Taylor*, supra, such substitution seemed the least objectionable course of action. But in terms of what change in the Federal Rules of Criminal Procedure is to be preferred in order to facilitate response to such situations in the future, the judgment of the Advisory Committee is that it is far better to permit the deliberations to continue with a jury of 11 than to make a substitution at that point.

In rejecting the substitution-of-juror alternative, the Committee's judgment is in accord with that of most commentators and many courts.

There have been proposals that the rule should be amended to permit an alternate to be substituted if a regular juror becomes unable to perform his duties after the case has been submitted to the jury. An early draft of the original Criminal Rules had contained such a provision, but it was withdrawn when the Supreme Court itself indicated to the Advisory Committee on Criminal Rules doubts as to the desira-

bility and constitutionality of such a procedure. These doubts are as forceful now as they were a quarter century ago. To permit substitution of an alternate after deliberations have begun would require either that the alternate participate though he has missed part of the jury discussion, or that he sit in with the jury in every case on the chance he might be needed. Either course is subject to practical difficulty and to strong constitutional objection.

Wright, *Federal Practice and Procedure* § 388 (1969). See also Moore, *Federal Practice* par. 24.05 (2d ed. Cipes 1980) ("The inherent coercive effect upon an alternate who joins a jury leaning heavily toward a guilty verdict may result in the alternate reaching a premature guilty verdict"); 3 *ABA Standards for Criminal Justice* § 15–2.7, commentary (2d ed. 1980) ("it is not desirable to allow a juror who is unfamiliar with the prior deliberations to suddenly join the group and participate in the voting without the benefit of earlier group discussion"); *United States v. Lamb*, 529 F.2d 1153 (9th Cir. 1975); *People v. Ryan*, 19 N.Y.2d 100, 224 N.E.2d 710 (1966). Compare *People v. Collins* 17 Cal.3d 687, 131 Cal.Rptr. 782, 522 P.2d 742 (1976); *Johnson v. State* 267 Ind. 256, 396 N.E.2d 623 (1977).

The central difficulty with substitution, whether viewed only as a practical problem or a question of constitutional dimensions (procedural due process under the Fifth Amendment or jury trial under the Sixth Amendment), is that there does not appear to be any way to nullify the impact of what has occurred without the participation of the new juror. Even were it required that the jury "review" with the new juror their prior deliberations or that the jury upon substitution start deliberations anew, it still seems likely that the continuing jurors would be influenced by the earlier deliberations and that the new juror would be somewhat intimidated by the others by virtue of being a newcomer to the deliberations. As for the possibility of sending in the alternates at the very beginning with instructions to listen but not to participate until substituted, this scheme is likewise attended by practical difficulties and offends "the cardinal principle that the deliberations of the jury shall remain private and secret in every case." *United States v. Virginia Erection Corp.*, 335 F.2d 868 (4th Cir.1964).

The amendment provides that if a juror is excused after the jury has retired to consider its verdict, it is within the discretion of the court whether to declare a mistrial or to permit deliberations to continue with 11 jurors. If the trial has been brief and not much would be lost by retrial, the court might well conclude that the unusual step of allowing a jury verdict by less than 12 jurors absent stipulation should not be taken. On the other hand, if the trial has been protracted the court is much more likely to opt for continuing with the remaining 11 jurors.

Rule 24. Trial Jurors

(a) Examination. The court may permit the defendant or the defendant's attorney and the attorney for the government to conduct the examination of prospective jurors or may itself conduct the examination. In the latter event the court shall permit the defendant or the defendant's attorney and the attorney for the government to supplement the examination by such further inquiry as it deems proper or shall itself submit to the prospective jurors such additional questions by the parties or their attorneys as it deems proper.

(b) Peremptory Challenges. If the offense charged is punishable by death, each side is entitled to 20 peremptory challenges. If the offense charged is punishable by imprisonment for more than one year, the government is entitled to 6 peremptory challenges and the defendant or defendants jointly to 10 peremptory challenges. If the offense charged is punishable by imprisonment for not more than one year or by fine or both, each side is entitled to 3 peremptory challenges. If there is more than one defendant, the court may allow the defendants additional peremptory challenges and permit them to be exercised separately or jointly.

(c) Alternate Jurors. The court may direct that not more than 6 jurors in addition to the regular jury be called and impanelled to sit as alternate jurors. Alternate jurors in the order in which they are called shall replace jurors who, prior to the time the jury retires to consider its verdict, become or are found to be unable or disqualified to perform their duties. Alternate jurors shall be drawn in the same manner, shall have the same qualifications, shall be subject to the same examination and challenges, shall take the same oath and shall have the same functions, powers, facilities and privileges as the regular jurors. An alternate juror who does not replace a regular juror shall be discharged after the jury retires to consider its verdict. Each side is entitled to 1 peremptory challenge in addition to those otherwise allowed by law if 1 or 2 alternate jurors are to be impanelled, 2 peremptory challenges if 3 or 4 alternate jurors are to be impanelled, and 3 peremptory challenges if 5 or 6 alternate jurors are to be impanelled. The additional peremptory challenges may be used against an alternate juror only, and the other peremptory challenges allowed by these rules may not be used against an alternate juror.

(As amended Feb. 28, 1966, eff. July 1, 1966; Mar. 9, 1987, eff. Aug. 1, 1987.)

NOTES OF ADVISORY COMMITTEE ON RULES

Note to Subdivision (a). This rule is similar to Rule 47(a) of the Federal Rules of Civil Procedure, 28 U.S.C., Appendix, and also embodies the practice now followed by many Federal courts in criminal cases. Uniform procedure in civil and criminal cases on this point seems desirable.

Note to Subdivision (b). This rule embodies existing law, 28 U.S.C. former § 424 (now § 1870) (Challenges), with the following modifications. In capital cases the number of challenges is equalized as between the defendant and the United States so that both sides have 20 challenges, which only the defendant has at present. While continuing the existing rule that multiple defendants are deemed a single party for purposes of challenges, the rule vests in the court discretion to allow additional peremptory challenges to multiple defendants and to permit such challenges to be exercised separately or jointly. Experience with cases involving numerous defendants indicates the desirability of this modification.

Note to Subdivision (c). This rule embodies existing law, 28 U.S.C. former § 417a (Alternate jurors), as well as the practice prescribed for civil cases by Rule 47(b) of the Federal Rules of Civil Procedure, 28 U.S.C., Appendix, except that the number of possible alternate jurors that may be impaneled is increased from two to four, with a corresponding adjustment of challenges.

1966 AMENDMENT

Experience has demonstrated that four alternate jurors may not be enough for some lengthy criminal trials. See e.g., *United States v. Bentvena,* 288 F.2d 442 (2d Cir.1961); Reports of the Proceedings of the Judicial Conference of the United States, 1961, p. 104. The amendment to the first sentence increases the number authorized from four to six. The fourth sentence is amended to provide an additional peremptory challenge where a fifth or sixth alternate juror is used.

The words "or are found to be" are added to the second sentence to make clear that an alternate juror may be called in the situation where it is first discovered during the trial that a juror was unable or disqualified to perform his duties at the time he was sworn. See *United States v. Goldberg,* 330 F.2d 30 (3rd Cir. 1964), cert. den. 377 U.S. 953 (1964).

1987 AMENDMENT

The amendments are technical. No substantive change is intended.

Rule 25. Judge; Disability

(a) During Trial. If by reason of death, sickness or other disability the judge before whom a jury trial has commenced is unable to proceed with the trial, any other judge regularly sitting in or assigned to the court, upon certifying familiarity with the record of the trial, may proceed with and finish the trial.

(b) After Verdict or Finding of Guilt. If by reason of absence, death, sickness or other disability the judge before whom the defendant has been tried is unable to perform the duties to be performed by the court after a verdict or finding of guilt, any other judge regularly sitting in or assigned to the court may perform those duties; but if that judge is satisfied that a judge who did not preside at the trial cannot perform those duties or that it is appropriate for any other reason, that judge may grant a new trial.

(As amended Feb. 28, 1966, eff. July 1, 1966; Mar. 9, 1987, eff. Aug. 1, 1987.)

NOTES OF ADVISORY COMMITTEE ON RULES

This rule is similar to Rule 63 of the Federal Rules of Civil Procedure, 28 U.S.C., Appendix. See also, 28 U.S.C. former § 776 (Bill of exceptions; authentication; signing of by judge).

1966 AMENDMENT

In September, 1963, the Judicial Conference of the United States approved a recommendation of its Committee on Court Administration that provision be made for substitution of a judge who becomes disabled during trial. The problem has become serious because of the increase in the number of long criminal trials. See 1963 Annual Report of the Director of the Administrative Office of the United States Courts, p. 114, reporting a 25% increase in criminal trials lasting more than one week in fiscal year 1963 over 1962.

Subdivision (a).—The amendment casts the rule into two subdivisions and in subdivision (a) provides for substitution of a judge during a jury trial upon his certification that he has familiarized himself with the record of the trial. For similar provisions see Alaska Rules of Crim.Proc., Rule 25; California Penal Code, § 1053.

Subdivision (b).—The words "from the district" are deleted to permit the local judge to act in those situations where a judge who has been assigned from within the district to try the case is, at the time for sentence, etc., back at his regular place of holding court which may be several hundred miles from the place of trial. It is not intended, of course, that substitutions shall be made where the judge who tried the case is available within a reasonable distance from the place of trial.

1987 AMENDMENT

The amendments are technical. No substantive change is intended.

Rule 26. Taking of Testimony

In all trials the testimony of witnesses shall be taken orally in open court, unless otherwise provided by an Act of Congress or by these rules, the Federal Rules of Evidence, or other rules adopted by the Supreme Court.

(As amended Nov. 20, 1972.)

NOTES OF ADVISORY COMMITTEE ON RULES

1. This rule contemplates the development of a uniform body of rules of evidence to be applicable in trials of criminal cases in the Federal courts. It is based on *Funk v. United States*, 290 U.S. 371, 54 S.Ct. 212, 78 L.Ed. 369, 93 A.L.R. 1136, and *Wolfle v. United States*, 291 U.S. 7, 54 S.Ct. 279, 78 L.Ed. 617, which indicated that in the absence of statute the Federal courts in criminal cases are not bound by the State law of evidence, but are guided by common law principles as interpreted by the Federal courts "in the light of reason and experience." The rule does not fetter the applicable law of evidence to that originally existing at common law. It is contemplated that the law may be modified and adjusted from time to time by judicial decisions. See Homer Cummings, 29 A.B.A.Jour. 655; Vanderbilt, 29 A.B.A.Jour. 377; Holtzoff, 12 George Washington, L.R. 119, 131–132; Holtzoff, 3 F.R.D. 445, 453; Howard, 51 Yale L.Jour. 763; Medalie, 4 Lawyers Guild R. (3)1, 5–6.

2. This rule differs from the corresponding rule for civil cases (Federal Rules of Civil Procedure, Rule 43(a), 28 U.S.C., Appendix), in that this rule contemplates a uniform body of rules of evidence to govern in criminal trials in the Federal courts, while the rule for civil cases prescribes partial conformity to State law and, therefore, results in a divergence as between various districts. Since in civil actions in which Federal jurisdiction is based on diversity of citizenship, the State substantive law governs the rights of the parties, uniformity of rules of evidence among different districts does not appear necessary. On the other hand, since all Federal crimes are statutory and all criminal prosecutions in the Federal courts are based on acts of Congress, uniform rules of evidence appear desirable if not essential in criminal cases, as otherwise the same facts under differing rules of evidence may lead to a conviction in one district and to an acquittal in another.

3. This rule expressly continues existing statutes governing the admissibility of evidence and the compe-

tency and privileges of witnesses. Among such statutes are the following:

8 U.S.C. former:

§ 138 [now §§ 1326, 1328, 1329] (Importation of aliens for immoral purposes; attempt to reenter after deportation; penalty)

28 U.S.C. former:

§ 632 [now 18 U.S.C. § 3481] (Competency of witnesses governed by State laws; defendants in criminal cases)

§ 633 (Competency of witnesses governed by State laws; husband or wife of defendant in prosecution for bigamy)

§ 634 [now 18 U.S.C. § 3486] (Testimony of witnesses before Congress)

§ 638 [now § 1731] (Comparison of handwriting to determine genuineness)

§ 695 [now § 1732] (Admissibility)

§ 695a [now 18 U.S.C. § 3491] (Foreign documents)

46 U.S.C.

§ 193 (Bills of lading to be issued; contents)

1972 AMENDMENT

The first sentence is retained, with appropriate narrowing of the title, since its subject is not covered in the Rules of Evidence. The second sentence is deleted because the Rules of Evidence govern admissibility of evidence, competency of witnesses, and privilege. The language is broadened, however, to take account of the Rules of Evidence and any other rules adopted by the Supreme Court.

EDITORIAL NOTES

References in Text. The Federal Rules of Evidence, referred to in text, are set out in this pamphlet.

Rule 26.1 Determination of Foreign Law

A party who intends to raise an issue concerning the law of a foreign country shall give reasonable written notice. The court, in determining foreign law, may consider any relevant material or source, including testimony, whether or not submitted by a party or admissible under the Federal Rules of Evidence. The court's determination shall be treated as a ruling on a question of law.

(Added Feb. 28, 1966, eff. July 1, 1966; amended Nov. 20, 1972.)

NOTES OF ADVISORY COMMITTEE ON RULES

The original Federal Rules of Criminal Procedure did not contain a provision explicitly regulating the determination of foreign law. The resolution of issues of foreign law, when relevant in federal criminal proceedings, falls within the general compass of Rule 26 which provides for application of "the [evidentiary] principles of the common law as they may be interpreted by the courts of the United States in the light of reason and experience." See Green, Preliminary Report on the Advisability and Feasibility of Developing Uniform Rules of Evidence for the United States District Courts 6–7, 17–18 (1962). Although traditional "commonlaw" methods for determining foreign-country law have proved inadequate, the courts have not developed more appropriate practices on the basis of this flexible rule. Cf. Green, op. cit. supra at 26–28. On the inadequacy of common-law procedures for determining foreign law, see, e.g., Nussbaum, Proving the Law of Foreign Countries, 3 Am.J.Comp.L. 60 (1954).

Problems of foreign law that must be resolved in accordance with the Federal Rules of Criminal Procedure are most likely to arise in places such as Washington, D.C., the Canal Zone, Guam, and the Virgin Islands, where the federal courts have general criminal jurisdiction. However, issues of foreign law may also arise in criminal proceedings commenced in other federal districts. For example, in an extradition proceeding, reasonable ground to believe that the person sought to be extradited is charged with, or was convicted of, a crime under the laws of the demanding state must generally be shown. See *Factor v. Laubenheimer,* 290 U.S. 276 (1933); *Fernandez v. Phillips,* 268 U.S. 311 (1925); Bishop International Law: Cases and Materials (2d ed. 1962). Further, foreign law may be invoked to justify non-compliance with a subpoena duces tecum, *Application of Chase Manhattan Bank,* 297 F.2d 611 (2d Cir.1962), and under certain circumstances, as a defense to prosecution. Cf. *American Banana Co. v. United Fruit Co.,* 213 U.S. 347 (1909). The content of foreign law may also be relevant in proceedings arising under 18 U.S.C. §§ 1201, 2312–2317.

Rule 26.1 is substantially the same as Civil Rule 44.1. A full explanation of the merits and practicability of the rule appear in the Advisory Committee's Note to Civil Rule 44.1. It is necessary here to add only one comment to the explanations there made. The second sentence of the rule frees the court from the restraints of the ordinary rules of evidence in determining foreign law. This freedom, made necessary by the peculiar nature of the issue of foreign law, should not constitute an unconstitutional deprivation of the defendant's rights to confrontation of witnesses. The issue is essentially one of law rather than of fact. Furthermore, the cases have held that the Sixth Amendment does not serve as a rigid barrier against the development of reasonable and necessary exceptions to the hearsay rule. See *Kay v. United States,* 255 F.2d 476, 480 (4th Cir.1958), cert. den., 358 U.S. 825 (1958); *Matthews v. United States,* 217 F.2d 409, 418 (5th Cir.1954); *United States v. Leathers,* 135 F.2d 507 (2d Cir.1943); and cf.,

Painter v. Texas, 85 S.Ct. 1065 (1965); *Douglas v. Alabama*, 85 S.Ct. 1074 (1965).

1972 AMENDMENT

Since the purpose is to free the judge, in determining foreign law, from restrictive evidentiary rules, the reference is made to the Rules of Evidence generally.

Rule 26.2   Production of Statements of Witnesses

(a) Motion for Production. After a witness other than the defendant has testified on direct examination, the court, on motion of a party who did not call the witness, shall order the attorney for the government or the defendant and the defendant's attorney, as the case may be, to produce, for the examination and use of the moving party, any statement of the witness that is in their possession and that relates to the subject matter concerning which the witness has testified.

(b) Production of Entire Statement. If the entire contents of the statement relate to the subject matter concerning which the witness has testified, the court shall order that the statement be delivered to the moving party.

(c) Production of Excised Statement. If the other party claims that the statement contains matter that does not relate to the subject matter concerning which the witness has testified, the court shall order that it be delivered to the court in camera. Upon inspection, the court shall excise the portions of the statement that do not relate to the subject matter concerning which the witness has testified, and shall order that the statement, with such material excised, be delivered to the moving party. Any portion of the statement that is withheld from the defendant over the defendant's objection shall be preserved by the attorney for the government, and, in the event of a conviction and an appeal by the defendant, shall be made available to the appellate court for the purpose of determining the correctness of the decision to excise the portion of the statement.

(d) Recess for Examination of Statement. Upon delivery of the statement to the moving party, the court, upon application of that party, may recess proceedings in the trial for the examination of such statement and for preparation for its use in the trial.

(e) Sanction for Failure to Produce Statement. If the other party elects not to comply with an order to deliver a statement to the moving party, the court shall order that the testimony of the witness be stricken from the record and that the trial proceed, or, if it is the attorney for the government who elects not to comply, shall declare a mistrial if required by the interest of justice.

(f) Definition. As used in this rule, a "statement" of a witness means:

(1) a written statement made by the witness that is signed or otherwise adopted or approved by the witness;

(2) a substantially verbatim recital of an oral statement made by the witness that is recorded contemporaneously with the making of the oral statement and that is contained in a stenographic, mechanical, electrical, or other recording or a transcription thereof; or

(3) a statement, however taken or recorded, or a transcription thereof, made by the witness to a grand jury.

(Added Apr. 30, 1979, eff. Dec. 1, 1980, and amended Mar. 9, 1987, eff. Aug. 1, 1987.)

NOTES OF ADVISORY COMMITTEE ON RULES

S. 1437, 95th Cong., 1st Sess. (1977), would place in the criminal rules the substance of what is now 18 U.S.C. § 3500 (the Jencks Act). Underlying this and certain other additions to the rules contemplated by S. 1437 is the notion that provisions which are purely procedural in nature should appear in the Federal Rules of Criminal Procedure rather than in Title 18. See Reform of the Federal Criminal Laws, Part VI: Hearings on S. 1, S. 716, and S. 1400, Subcomm. on Criminal Laws and Procedures, Senate Judiciary Comm., 93rd Cong., 1st Sess. (statement of Judge Albert B. Maris, at page 5503). Rule 26.2 is identical to the S. 1437 rule except as indicated by the marked additions and deletions. As those changes show, rule 26.2 provides for production of the statements of defense witnesses at trial in essentially the same manner as is now provided for with respect to the statements of government witnesses. Thus, the proposed rule reflects these two judgments: (i) that the subject matter—production of the statements of witnesses—is more appropriately dealt with in the criminal rules; and (ii) that in light of *United States v. Nobles*, 422 U.S. 225 (1975), it is important to establish procedures for the production of defense witnesses' statements as well. The rule is not intended to discourage the practice of voluntary disclosure at an earlier time so as to avoid delays at trial.

In *Nobles,* defense counsel sought to introduce the testimony of a defense investigator who prior to trial had interviewed prospective prosecution witnesses and had prepared a report embodying the essence of their conversation. When the defendant called the investigator to impeach eyewitness testimony identifying the defendant as the robber, the trial judge granted the prosecutor the right to inspect those portions of the investigator's report relating to the witnesses' statements, as a potential basis for cross-examination of the investigator. When the defense declined to produce the report, the trial judge refused to permit the investigator to testify. The Supreme Court unanimously upheld the trial court's actions, finding that neither the Fifth nor Sixth Amendments nor the attorney work product doctrine prevented disclosure of such a document at trial. Noting "the federal judiciary's inherent power to require the prosecution to produce the previously recorded statements of its witnesses so that the defense may get the full benefit of cross-examinations and the truth-finding process may be enhanced," the Court rejected the notion "that the Fifth Amendment renders criminal discovery 'basically a one-way street,'" and thus concluded that "in a proper case, the prosecution can call upon that same power for production of witness statements that facilitate 'full disclosure of all the [relevant] facts.'"

The rule, consistent with the reasoning in *Nobles,* is designed to place the disclosure of prior relevant statements of a defense witness in the possession of the defense on the same legal footing as is the disclosure of prior statements of prosecution witnesses in the hands of the government under the Jencks Act, 18 U.S.C. § 3500 (which S. 1437 would replace with the rule set out therein). See *United States v. Pulvirenti,* 408 F.Supp. 12 (E.D.Mich.1976), holding that under *Nobles* "[t]he obligation [of disclosure] placed on the defendant should be the reciprocal of that placed upon the government * * * [as] defined by the Jencks Act." Several state courts have likewise concluded that witness statements in the hands of the defense at trial should be disclosed on the same basis that prosecution witness statements are disclosed, in order to promote the concept of the trial as a search for truth. See, e.g., *People v. Sanders,* 110 Ill.App.2d 85, 249 N.E.2d 124 (1969); *State v. Montague,* 55 N.J. 371, 262 A.2d 398 (1970); *People v. Damon,* 24 N.Y.2d 256, 299 N.Y.S.2d 830, 247 N.E.2d 651 (1959).

The rule, with minor exceptions, makes the procedure identical for both prosecution and defense witnesses, including the provision directing the court, whenever a claim is made that disclosure would be improper because the statement contains irrelevant matter, to examine the statements in camera and excise such matter as should not be disclosed. This provision acts as a safeguard against abuse and will enable a defendant who believes that a demand is being improperly made to secure a swift and just resolution of the issue.

The treatment as to defense witnesses of necessity differs slightly from the treatment as to prosecution witnesses in terms of the sanction for a refusal to comply with the court's disclosure order. Under the Jencks Act and the rule proposed in S. 1437, if the prosecution refuses to abide by the court's order, the court is required to strike the witness's testimony unless in its discretion it determines that the more serious sanction of a mistrial in favor of the accused is warranted. Under this rule, if a defendant refuses to comply with the court's disclosure order, the court's only alternative is to enter an order striking or precluding the testimony of the witness, as was done in *Nobles.*

Under subdivision (a) of the rule, the motion for production may be made by "a party who did not call the witness." Thus, it also requires disclosure of statements in the possession of either party when the witness is called neither by the prosecution nor the defense but by the court pursuant to the Federal Rules of Evidence. Present law does not deal with this situation, which consistency requires be treated in an identical manner as the disclosure of statements of witnesses called by a party to the case.

1987 AMENDMENT

The amendments are technical. No substantive change is intended.

Rule 27. Proof of Official Record

An official record or an entry therein or the lack of such a record or entry may be proved in the same manner as in civil actions.

NOTES OF ADVISORY COMMITTEE ON RULES

This rule incorporates by reference Rule 44 of the Federal Rules of Civil Procedure, 28 U.S.C., Appendix, which provided a simple and uniform method of proving public records and entry or lack of entry therein. The rule does not supersede statutes regulating modes of proof in respect to specific official records. In such cases parties have the option of following the general rule or the pertinent statute. Among the many statutes are:

28 U.S.C. former:

§ 661 [now § 1733] (Copies of department or corporation records and papers; admissibility; seal)

§ 662 [now § 1733] (Same; in office of General Counsel of the Treasury)

§ 663 [now § 1733] (Instruments and papers of Comptroller of Currency; admissibility)

§ 664 [now § 1733] (Organization certificates of national banks; admissibility)

§ 665 [now § 1733] (Transcripts from books of Treasury in suits against delinquents; admissibility)

§ 666 [now § 1733] (Same; certificate by Secretary or Assistant Secretary)

§ 668 [now 18 U.S.C. § 3497] (Same; indictments for embezzlement of public moneys)

§ 669 (Copies of returns in returns office admissible)

§ 670 [now § 1743] (Admissibility of copies of statements of demands by Post Office Department)

§ 671 [now § 1733] (Admissibility of copies of post office records and statement of accounts)

§ 672 [See § 1733] (Admissibility of copies of records in General Land Office)

§ 673 [now § 1744] (Admissibility of copies of records, and so forth, of Patent Office)

§ 674 [now § 1745] (Copies of foreign letters patent as prima facie evidence)

§ 675 (Copies of specifications and drawings of patents admissible)

§ 676 [now § 1736] (Extracts from Journals of Congress admissible when injunction of secrecy removed)

§ 677 [now § 1740] (Copies of records in offices of United States consuls admissible)

§ 678 (Books and papers in certain district courts)

§ 679 (Records in clerks' offices, western district of North Carolina)

§ 680 (Records in clerks' offices of former district of California)

§ 681 [now § 1734] (Original records lost or destroyed; certified copy admissible)

§ 682 [now § 1734] (Same; when certified copy not obtainable)

§ 685 [now § 1735] (Same; certified copy of official papers)

§ 687 [now § 1738] (Authentication of legislative acts; proof of judicial proceedings of State)

§ 688 [now § 1739] (Proofs of records in offices not pertaining to courts)

§ 689 [now § 1742] (Copies of foreign records relating to land titles)

§§ 695a–695h [now 18 U.S.C. §§ 3491–3496; 22 U.S.C. § 1204; § 1741] (Foreign documents)

1 U.S.C. former:

§ 30 [now § 112] (Statutes at Large; contents; admissibility in evidence)

§ 30a [now § 113] ("Little and Brown's" edition of laws and treaties competent evidence of Acts of Congress)

§ 54 [now § 204] (Codes and Supplements as establishing prima facie the Laws of United States and District of Columbia, citation of Codes and Supplements)

§ 55 [now § 209] (Copies of Supplements to Code of Laws of United States and of District of Columbia

Code and Supplements; conclusive evidence of original)

5 U.S.C. former:

§ 490 [now 28 U.S.C. § 1733] (Records of Department of Interior; authenticated copies as evidence)

8 U.S.C. former:

§ 717(b) [now §§ 1435, 1482] (Former citizens of United States excepted from certain requirements; citizenship lost by spouse's alienage or loss of United States citizenship, or by entering armed forces of foreign state or acquiring its nationality)

§ 727(g) [now § 1443] (Administration of naturalization laws; rules and regulations; instruction in citizenship; forms; oaths; depositions; documents in evidence; photographic studio)

15 U.S.C. former:

§ 127 [now § 1057(e)] (Trade-marks; copies of records as evidence)

U.S.C. Title 20:

§ 52 (Smithsonian Institution; evidence of title to site and buildings)

25 U.S.C.:

§ 6 (Bureau of Indian Affairs; seal; authenticated and certified documents; evidence)

31 U.S.C.:

§ 46 (Laws governing General Accounting Office; copies of books, records, etc., thereof as evidence)

38 U.S.C. former:

§ 11g [now § 202] (Seal of Veterans' Administration; authentication of copies of records)

43 U.S.C.:

§ 57 (Authenticated copies or extracts from records as evidence)

§ 58 (Transcripts from records of Louisiana)

§ 59 (Official papers in office of surveyor general in California; papers; copies)

§ 83 (Transcripts of records as evidence)

44 U.S.C. former:

§ 300h [now §§ 397, 399] (National Archives; seal; reproduction of archives; fee; admissibility in evidence of reproductions)

§ 307 (Filing document as constructive notice; publication in Register as presumption of validity; judicial notice; citation)

47 U.S.C.:

§ 412 (Documents filed with Federal Communications Commission as public records; prima facie evidence; confidential records)

49 U.S.C.:

§ 16 (Orders of Commission and enforcement thereof; forfeitures—(13) copies of schedules, tariffs, contracts, etc., kept as public records; evidence)

Rule 28. Interpreters

The court may appoint an interpreter of its own selection and may fix the reasonable compensation of such interpreter. Such compensation shall be paid out of funds provided by law or by the government, as the court may direct.

(As amended Feb. 28, 1966, eff. July 1, 1966; Nov. 20, 1972.)

NOTES OF ADVISORY COMMITTEE ON RULES

The power of the court to call its own witnesses, though rarely invoked, is recognized in the Federal courts, *Young v. United States,* 107 F.2d 490, C.C.A.5th; *Litsinger v. United States,* 44 F.2d 45, C.C.A.7th. This rule provides a procedure whereby the court may, if it chooses, exercise this power in connection with expert witnesses. The rule is based, in part, on the Uniform Expert Testimony Act, drafted by the Commissioners on Uniform State Laws, Hand Book of the National Conference of Commissioners on Uniform State Laws (1937), 337; see, also, Wigmore—Evidence, 3d Ed., sec. 563; A.L.I.Code of Criminal Procedure, secs. 307–309; National Commission on Law of Observance and Enforcement—Report on Criminal Procedure, 37. Similar provisions are found in the statutes of a number of States: Wisconsin—Wis.Stat. (1941), sec. 357.12; Indiana—Ind.Stat.Ann. (Burns, 1933), sec. 9–1702; California—Cal.Pen.Code (Deering, 1941), sec. 1027.

1966 AMENDMENT

Subdivision (a).—The original rule is made a separate subdivision. The amendment permits the court to inform the witness of his duties in writing since it often constitutes an unnecessary inconvenience and expense to require the witness to appear in court for such purpose.

Subdivision (b).—This new subdivision authorizes the court to appoint and provide for the compensation of interpreters. General language is used to give discretion to the court to appoint interpreters in all appropriate situations. Interpreters may be needed to interpret the testimony of non-English speaking witnesses or to assist non-English speaking defendants in understanding the proceedings or in communicating with assigned counsel. Interpreters may also be needed where a witness or a defendant is deaf.

1972 AMENDMENT

Subdivision (a). This subdivision is stricken, since the subject of court-appointed expert witnesses is covered in Evidence Rule 706 in detail.

Subdivision (b). The provisions of subdivision (b) are retained. Although Evidence Rule 703 specifies the qualifications of interpreters and the form of oath to be administered to them, it does not cover their appointment or compensation.

Rule 29. Motion for Judgment of Acquittal

(a) Motion Before Submission to Jury. Motions for directed verdict are abolished and motions for judgment of acquittal shall be used in their place. The court on motion of a defendant or of its own motion shall order the entry of judgment of acquittal of one or more offenses charged in the indictment or information after the evidence on either side is closed if the evidence is insufficient to sustain a conviction of such offense or offenses. If a defendant's motion for judgment of acquittal at the close of the evidence offered by the government is not granted, the defendant may offer evidence without having reserved the right.

(b) Reservation of Decision on Motion. If a motion for judgment of acquittal is made at the close of all the evidence, the court may reserve decision on the motion, submit the case to the jury and decide the motion either before the jury returns a verdict or after it returns a verdict of guilty or is discharged without having returned a verdict.

(c) Motion After Discharge of Jury. If the jury returns a verdict of guilty or is discharged without having returned a verdict, a motion for judgment of acquittal may be made or renewed within 7 days after the jury is discharged or within such further time as the court may fix during the 7–day period. If a verdict of guilty is returned the court may on such motion set aside the verdict and enter judgment of acquittal. If no verdict is returned the court may enter judgment of acquittal. It shall not be necessary to the making of such a motion that a similar motion has been made prior to the submission of the case to the jury.

(d) Same: Conditional Ruling on Grant of Motion. If a motion for judgment of acquittal after verdict of guilty under this Rule is granted, the court shall also determine whether any motion for a new trial should be granted if the judgment of acquittal is thereafter vacated or reversed, specifying the grounds for such determination. If the motion for a new trial is granted conditionally, the order thereon does not affect the finality of the judgment. If the motion for a new trial has been granted conditionally and the judgment is reversed on appeal, the new trial shall proceed unless the appellate court has otherwise ordered. If such motion has been denied conditionally, the appellee on appeal may assert error in that denial, and if the judgment is reversed on appeal, subsequent proceedings shall be in accordance with the order of the appellate court.

(As amended Feb. 28, 1966, eff. July 1, 1966; Nov. 10, 1986, Pub.L. 99–646, § 54(a), 100 Stat. 3607.)

NOTES OF ADVISORY COMMITTEE ON RULES

Note to Subdivision (a). 1. The purpose of changing the name of a motion for a directed verdict to a motion for judgment of acquittal is to make the nomenclature accord with the realities. The change of nomenclature, however, does not modify the nature of the motion or enlarge the scope of matters that may be considered.

2. The second sentence is patterned on New York Code of Criminal Procedure, sec. 410.

3. The purpose of the third sentence is to remove the doubt existing in a few jurisdictions on the question whether the defendant is deemed to have rested his case if he moves for a directed verdict at the close of the prosecution's case. The purpose of the rule is expressly to preserve the right of the defendant to offer evidence in his own behalf, if such motion is denied. This is a restatement of the prevailing practice, and is also in accord with the practice prescribed for civil cases by Rule 50(a) of the Federal Rules of Civil Procedure, 28 U.S.C., Appendix.

Note to Subdivision (b). This rule is in substance similar to Rule 50(b) of the Federal Rules of Civil Procedure, 28 U.S.C., Appendix, and permits the court to render judgment for the defendant notwithstanding a verdict of guilty. Some Federal courts have recognized and approved the use of a judgment non obstante veredicto for the defendant in a criminal case, *Ex parte United States*, 101 F.2d 870, C.C.A.7th, affirmed by an equally divided court, *United States v. Stone*, 308 U.S. 519, 60 S.Ct. 177, 84 L.Ed. 441. The rule sanctions this practice.

1966 AMENDMENT

Subdivision (a).—A minor change has been made in the caption.

Subdivision (b).—The last three sentences are deleted with the matters formerly covered by them transferred to the new subdivision (c).

Subdivision (c).—The new subdivision makes several changes in the former procedure. A motion for judgment of acquittal may be made after discharge of the jury whether or not a motion was made before submission to the jury. No legitimate interest of the government is intended to be prejudiced by permitting the court to direct an acquittal on a post-verdict motion. The constitutional requirement of a jury trial in criminal cases is primarily a right accorded to the defendant. Cf. *Adams v. United States, ex rel. McCann*, 317 U.S. 269 (1942); *Singer v. United States*, 380 U.S. 24 (1965); Note, 65 Yale L.J. 1032 (1956).

The time in which the motion may be made has been changed to 7 days in accordance with the amendment to Rule 45(a) which by excluding Saturday from the days to be counted when the period of time is less than 7 days would make 7 days the normal time for a motion required to be made in 5 days. Also the court is authorized to extend the time as is provided for motions for new trial (Rule 33) and in arrest of judgment (Rule 34).

References in the original rule to the motion for a new trial as an alternate to the motion for judgment of acquittal and to the power of the court to order a new trial have been eliminated. Motions for new trial are adequately covered in Rule 33. Also the original wording is subject to the interpretation that a motion for judgment of acquittal gives the court power to order a new trial even though the defendant does not wish a new trial and has not asked for one.

EDITORIAL NOTES

Effective Date of 1986 Amendment. Section 54(b) of Pub.L. 99–646 provided that: "The amendments made by this section [enacting subd. (d) of this rule] shall take effect 30 days after the date of the enactment of this Act [Nov. 10, 1986]."

Rule 29.1   Closing Argument

After the closing of evidence the prosecution shall open the argument. The defense shall be permitted to reply. The prosecution shall then be permitted to reply in rebuttal.

(Added Apr. 22, 1974, eff. Dec. 1, 1975.)

NOTES OF ADVISORY COMMITTEE ON RULES

This rule is designed to control the order of closing argument. It reflects the Advisory Committee's view that it is desirable to have a uniform federal practice. The rule is drafted in the view that fair and effective administration of justice is best served if the defendant knows the arguments actually made by the prosecution in behalf of conviction before the defendant is faced with the decision whether to reply and what to reply.

NOTES OF COMMITTEE ON THE JUDICIARY, HOUSE REPORT NO. 94–247

A. Amendments Proposed by the Supreme Court. Rule 29.1 is a new rule that was added to regulate closing arguments. It prescribes that the government shall make its closing argument and then the defendant shall make his. After the defendant has argued, the government is entitled to reply in rebuttal.

B. Committee Action. The Committee endorses and adopts this proposed rule in its entirety. The Committee believes that as the Advisory Committee Note has stated, fair and effective administration of justice is best served if the defendant knows the arguments actually made by the prosecution in behalf of conviction before the defendant is faced with the decision whether to reply and what to reply. Rule 29.1 does not specifically address itself to what happens if the prosecution waives its initial closing argument. The Committee is of the view that the prosecutor, when he waives his initial closing argument, also waives his rebuttal. [See the remarks of Senior United States Circuit Judge J. Edward Lumbard in Hearings II, at 207.]

Rule 30. Instructions

At the close of the evidence or at such earlier time during the trial as the court reasonably directs, any party may file written requests that the court instruct the jury on the law as set forth in the requests. At the same time copies of such requests shall be furnished to all parties. The court shall inform counsel of its proposed action upon the requests prior to their arguments to the jury. The court may instruct the jury before or after the arguments are completed or at both times. No party may assign as error any portion of the charge or omission therefrom unless that party objects thereto before the jury retires to consider its verdict, stating distinctly the matter to which that party objects and the grounds of the objection. Opportunity shall be given to make the objection out of the hearing of the jury and, on request of any party, out of the presence of the jury.

(As amended Feb. 28, 1966, eff. July 1, 1966; Mar. 9, 1987, eff. Aug. 1, 1987; Apr. 25, 1988, eff. Aug. 1, 1988.)

NOTES OF ADVISORY COMMITTEE ON RULES

This rule corresponds to Rule 51 of the Federal Rules of Civil Procedure, 28 U.S.C., Appendix, the second sentence alone being new. It seemed appropriate that on a point such as instructions to juries there should be no difference in procedure between civil and criminal cases.

1966 AMENDMENT

The amendment requires the court, on request of any party, to require the jury to withdraw in order to permit full argument of objections to instructions.

1987 AMENDMENT

In its current form, Rule 30 requires that the court instruct the jury after the arguments of counsel. In some districts, usually where the state practice is otherwise, the parties prefer to stipulate to instruction before closing arguments. The purpose of the amendment is to give the court discretion to instruct the jury before or after closing arguments, or at both times. The amendment will permit courts to continue instructing the jury after arguments as Rule 30 had previously required. It will also permit courts to instruct before arguments in order to give the parties an opportunity to argue to the jury in light of the exact language used by the court. See generally Raymond, *Merits and Demerits of the Missouri System in Instructing Juries,* 5 St. Louis U.L.J. 317 (1959). Finally, the amendment plainly indicates that the court may instruct both before and after arguments, which assures that the court retains power to remedy omissions in pre-argument instructions or to add instructions necessitated by the arguments.

1988 AMENDMENT

The amendment is technical. No substantive change is intended.

EDITORIAL NOTES

Effective Date of 1988 Amendment. The Order of the Supreme Court dated April 25, 1988, provided in part: "That the foregoing amendments to the Federal Rules of Criminal Procedure [this rule and rule 56] shall take effect on August 1, 1988 and shall govern all proceedings in criminal cases thereafter commenced and, insofar as just and practicable, all proceedings in criminal cases then pending." See order preceding rule 1.

Rule 31. Verdict

(a) Return. The verdict shall be unanimous. It shall be returned by the jury to the judge in open court.

(b) Several Defendants. If there are two or more defendants, the jury at any time during its deliberations may return a verdict or verdicts with respect to a defendant or defendants as to whom it has agreed; if the jury cannot agree with respect to all, the defendant or defendants as to whom it does not agree may be tried again.

(c) Conviction of Less Offense. The defendant may be found guilty of an offense necessarily included in the offense charged or of an attempt to commit either the offense charged or an offense necessarily included therein if the attempt is an offense.

(d) Poll of Jury. When a verdict is returned and before it is recorded the jury shall be polled at the request of any party or upon the court's own motion. If upon the poll there is not unanimous concurrence, the jury may be directed to retire for further deliberations or may be discharged.

(e) Criminal Forfeiture. If the indictment or the information alleges that an interest or property is subject to criminal forfeiture, a special verdict shall be returned as to the extent of the interest or property subject to forfeiture, if any.

(As amended Apr. 24, 1972, eff. Oct. 1, 1972.)

NOTES OF ADVISORY COMMITTEE ON RULES

Note to Subdivision (a). This rule is a restatement of existing law and practice. It does not embody any regulation of sealed verdicts, it being contemplated that this matter would be governed by local practice in the various district courts. The rule does not affect the existing statutes relating to qualified verdicts in cases in which capital punishment may be imposed, 18 U.S.C. former § 408a (now § 1201) (Kidnapped persons); 18 U.S.C. former § 412a (now § 1992) (Wrecking trains);

18 U.S.C. former § 567 (now § 1111) (Verdicts; qualified verdicts).

Note to Subdivision (b). This rule is a restatement of existing law, 18 U.S.C. former § 566 (Verdicts; several joint defendants).

Note to Subdivision (c). This rule is a restatement of existing law, 18 U.S.C. former § 566 (Verdicts; less offense than charged).

Note to Subdivision (d). This rule is a restatement of existing law and practice, *Mackett v. United States,* 90 F.2d 462, 465, C.C.A.7th; *Bruce v. Chestnut Farms Chevy Chase Dairy,* 126 F.2d 224, App.D.C.

1972 AMENDMENT

Subdivision (e) is new. It is intended to provide procedural implementation of the recently enacted criminal forfeiture provision of the Organized Crime Control Act of 1970, Title IX, § 1963, and the Comprehensive Drug Abuse Prevention and Control Act of 1970, Title II, § 408(a)(2).

The assumption of the draft is that the amount of the interest or property subject to criminal forfeiture is an element of the offense to be alleged and proved. See Advisory Committee Note to rule 7(c)(2).

Although special verdict provisions are rare in criminal cases, they are not unknown. See *United States v. Spock,* 416 F.2d 165 (1st Cir.1969), especially footnote 41 where authorities are listed.

VII. JUDGMENT

Rule 32. Sentence and Judgment

(a) Sentence.

(1) Imposition of Sentence. Sentence shall be imposed without unnecessary delay, but the court may, upon a motion that is jointly filed by the defendant and by the attorney for the Government and that asserts a factor important to the sentencing determination is not capable of being resolved at that time, postpone the imposition of sentence for a reasonable time until the factor is capable of being resolved. Prior to the sentencing hearing, the court shall provide the counsel for the defendant and the attorney for the Government with notice of the probation officer's determination, pursuant to the provisions of subdivision (c)(2)(B), of the sentencing classifications and sentencing guideline range believed to be applicable to the case. At the sentencing hearing, the court shall afford the counsel for the defendant and the attorney for the Government an opportunity to comment upon the probation

officer's determination and on other matters relating to the appropriate sentence. Before imposing sentence, the court shall also—

(A) determine that the defendant and his counsel have had the opportunity to read and discuss the presentence investigation report made available pursuant to subdivision (c)(3)(A) or summary thereof made available pursuant to subdivision (c)(3)(B);

(B) afford counsel for the defendant an opportunity to speak on behalf of the defendant; and

(C) address the defendant personally and ask him if he wishes to make a statement in his own behalf and to present any information in mitigation of the sentence.

The attorney for the Government shall have an equivalent opportunity to speak to the court. Upon a motion that is jointly filed by the defendant and by the attorney for the Government, the court may hear in camera such a statement by the defendant, counsel for the defendant, or the attorney for the Government.

(2) Notification of Right to Appeal. After imposing sentence in a case which has gone to trial on a plea of not guilty, the court shall advise the defendant of the defendant's right to appeal, including any right to appeal the sentence, and of the right of a person who is unable to pay the cost of an appeal to apply for leave to appeal in forma pauperis. There shall be no duty on the court to advise the defendant of any right of appeal after sentence is imposed following a plea of guilty or nolo contendere, except that the court shall advise the defendant of any right to appeal his sentence. If the defendant so requests, the clerk of the court shall prepare and file forthwith a notice of appeal on behalf of the defendant.

(b) Judgment.

(1) In General. A judgment of conviction shall set forth the plea, the verdict or findings, and the adjudication and sentence. If the defendant is found not guilty or for any other reason is entitled to be discharged, judgment shall be entered accordingly. The judgment shall be signed by the judge and entered by the clerk.

(2) Criminal Forfeiture. When a verdict contains a finding of property subject to a criminal forfeiture, the judgment of criminal forfeiture shall authorize the Attorney General to seize the interest or property subject to forfeiture, fixing such terms and conditions as the court shall deem proper.

(c) Presentence Investigation.

(1) When Made. A probation officer shall make a presentence investigation and report to the court before the imposition of sentence unless the court finds that there is in the record information sufficient to enable the meaningful exercise of sentencing authority pursuant to 18 U.S.C. 3553, and the court explains this finding on the record.

The report shall not be submitted to the court or its contents disclosed to anyone unless the defendant has pleaded guilty or nolo contendere or has been found guilty, except that a judge may, with the written consent of the defendant, inspect a presentence report at any time.

(2) Report. The report of the presentence investigation shall contain—

(A) information about the history and characteristics of the defendant, including his prior criminal record, if any, his financial condition, and any circumstances affecting his behavior that may be helpful in imposing sentence or in the correctional treatment of the defendant;

(B) the classification of the offense and of the defendant under the categories established by the Sentencing Commission pursuant to section 994(a) of title 28, that the probation officer believes to be applicable to the defendant's case; the kinds of sentence and the sentencing range suggested for such a category of offense committed by such a category of defendant as set forth in the guidelines issued by the Sentencing Commission pursuant to 28 U.S.C. 994(a)(1); and an explanation by the probation officer of any factors that may indicate that a sentence of a different kind or of a different length from one within the applicable guideline would be more appropriate under all the circumstances;

(C) any pertinent policy statement issued by the Sentencing Commission pursuant to 28 U.S.C. 994(a)(2);

(D) verified information stated in a non-argumentative style containing an assessment of the financial, social, psychological, and medical impact upon, and cost to, any individual against whom the offense has been committed;

(E) unless the court orders otherwise, information concerning the nature and extent of nonprison programs and resources available for the defendant; and

(F) such other information as may be required by the court.

(3) Disclosure.

(A) At a reasonable time before imposing sentence the court shall permit the defendant and the defendant's counsel to read the report of the presentence investigation, including the information required by subdivision (c)(2) but not including any final recommendation as to sentence, but not to the extent that in the opinion of the court the report contains diagnostic opinions which, if disclosed, might seriously disrupt a program of rehabilitation; or sources of information obtained upon a promise of confidentiality; or any other information which, if disclosed, might result in harm, physical or otherwise, to the defendant or other persons. The court shall afford the defendant and the defendant's counsel an opportunity to comment on the report and, in the discretion of the court, to introduce testimony or other information relating to any alleged factual inaccuracy contained in it.

(B) If the court is of the view that there is information in the presentence report which should not be disclosed under subdivision (c)(3)(A) of this rule, the court in lieu of making the report or part thereof available shall state orally or in writing a summary of the factual information contained therein to be relied on in determining sentence, and shall give the defendant and the defendant's counsel an opportunity to comment thereon. The statement may be made to the parties in camera.

(C) Any material which may be disclosed to the defendant and the defendant's counsel shall be disclosed to the attorney for the government.

(D) If the comments of the defendant and the defendant's counsel or testimony or other information introduced by them allege any factual inaccuracy in the presentence investigation report or the summary of the report or part thereof, the court shall, as to each matter controverted, make (i) a finding as to the allegation, or (ii) a determination that no such finding is necessary because the matter controverted will not be taken into account in sentencing. A written record of such findings and determinations shall be appended to and accompany any copy of the presentence investigation report thereafter made available to the Bureau of Prisons.

(E) Any copies of the presentence investigation report made available to the defendant and the defendant's counsel and the attorney for the government shall be returned to the probation officer immediately following the imposition of sentence or the granting of probation, unless the court, in its discretion otherwise directs.

(F) The reports of studies and recommendations contained therein made by the Director of the Bureau of Prisons pursuant to 18 U.S.C. § 3552(b) shall be considered a presentence investigation within the meaning of subdivision (c)(3) of this rule.

(d) Plea Withdrawal. If a motion for withdrawal of a plea of guilty or nolo contendere is made before sentence is imposed, the court may permit withdrawal of the plea upon a showing by the defendant of any fair and just reason. At any later time, a plea may be set aside only on direct appeal or by motion under 28 U.S.C. § 2255.

(e) Probation. After conviction of an offense not punishable by death or by life imprisonment, the defendant may be placed on probation if permitted by law.

(f) [Revocation of Probation.] (Abrogated Apr. 30, 1979, eff. Dec. 1, 1980)

(As amended Feb. 28, 1966, eff. July 1, 1966; Apr. 24, 1972, eff. Oct. 1, 1972; Apr. 22, 1974, eff. Dec. 1, 1975, as amended Pub.L. 93–361, July 30, 1974, 88 Stat. 397 and Pub.L. 94–64, § 2, July 31, 1975, 89 Stat. 370; July 31, 1975, Pub.L. 94–64, § 3(31)–(34), 89 Stat. 376; Apr. 30, 1979, eff. Aug. 1, 1979, Dec. 1, 1980; Pub.L. 97–291, § 3, Oct. 12, 1982, 96 Stat. 1249; Apr. 28, 1983, eff. Aug. 1, 1983; Oct. 12, 1984, Pub.L. 98–473, Title II, § 215(a), 98 Stat. 2014; Nov. 10, 1986, Pub.L. 99–646, § 25, 100 Stat. 3597; Mar. 9, 1987, eff. Aug. 1, 1987.)

Rule Applicable to Offenses Committed Prior to Nov. 1, 1987

This rule as in effect prior to amendment by Pub.L. 98–473 read as follows:

Rule 32. Sentence and Judgment

(a) Sentence.

(1) Imposition of Sentence. Sentence shall be imposed without unreasonable delay. Before imposing sentence the court shall

(A) determine that the defendant and the defendant's counsel have had the opportunity to read and discuss the presentence investigation report made available pursuant to subdivision (c)(3)(A) or summary thereof made available pursuant to subdivision (c)(3)(B);

(B) afford counsel an opportunity to speak on behalf of the defendant; and

(C) address the defendant personally and ask the defendant if the defendant wishes to make a statement in the defendant's own behalf and to present any information in mitigation of punishment.

The attorney for the government shall have an equivalent opportunity to speak to the court.

(2) Notification of Right to Appeal. After imposing sentence in a case which has gone to trial on a plea of not guilty, the court shall advise the defendant of the defendant's right to appeal, and of the right of a person who is unable to pay the cost of an appeal to apply for leave to appeal in forma pauperis. There shall be no duty on the court to advise the defendant of any right of appeal after sentence is imposed following a plea of guilty or nolo contendere. If the defendant so requests, the clerk of the court shall prepare and file forthwith a notice of appeal on behalf of the defendant.

(b) Judgment.

(1) In General. A judgment of conviction shall set forth the plea, the verdict or findings, and the adjudication and sentence. If the defendant is found not guilty or for any other reason is entitled to be discharged, judgment shall be entered accordingly. The judgment shall be signed by the judge and entered by the clerk.

(2) Criminal Forfeiture. When a verdict contains a finding of property subject to a criminal forfeiture, the judgment of criminal forfeiture shall authorize the Attorney General to seize the interest or property subject to forfeiture, fixing such terms and conditions as the court shall deem proper.

(c) Presentence Investigation.

(1) When Made. The probation service of the court shall make a presentence investigation and report to the court before the imposition of sentence or the granting of probation unless, with the permission of the court, the defendant waives a presentence investigation and report, or the court finds that there is in the record information sufficient to enable the meaningful exercise of sentencing discretion, and the court explains this finding on the record.

The report shall not be submitted to the court or its contents disclosed to anyone unless the defendant has pleaded guilty or nolo contendere or has been found guilty, except that a judge may, with the written consent of the defendant, inspect a presentence report at any time.

(2) Report. The presentence report shall contain—

(A) any prior criminal record of the defendant;

(B) a statement of the circumstances of the commission of the offense and circumstances affecting the defendant's behavior;

(C) information concerning any harm, including financial, social, psychological, and physical harm, done to or loss suffered by any victim of the offense; and

(D) any other information that may aid the court in sentencing, including the restitution needs of any victim of the offense.

(3) Disclosure.

(A) At a reasonable time before imposing sentence the court shall permit the defendant and the defendant's counsel to read the report of the presentence investigation exclusive of any recommendation as to sentence, but not to the extent that in the opinion of the court the report contains diagnostic opinions which, if disclosed, might seriously disrupt a program of rehabilitation; or sources of information obtained upon a promise of confidentiality; or any other information which, if disclosed, might result in harm, physical or otherwise, to the defendant or other persons. The court shall afford the defendant and the defendant's counsel an opportunity to comment on the report and, in the discretion of the court, to introduce testimony or other information relating to any alleged factual inaccuracy contained in it.

(B) If the court is of the view that there is information in the presentence report which should not be disclosed under subdivision (c)(3)(A) of this rule, the court in lieu of making the report or part thereof available shall state orally or in writing a summary of the factual information contained therein to be relied on in determining sentence, and shall give the defendant and the defendant's counsel an opportunity to comment thereon. The statement may be made to the parties in camera.

(C) Any material which may be disclosed to the defendant and the defendant's counsel shall be disclosed to the attorney for the government.

(D) If the comments of the defendant and the defendant's counsel or testimony or other information introduced by them allege any factual inaccuracy in the presentence investigation report or the summary of the report or part thereof, the court shall, as to each matter controverted, make (i) a finding as to the allegation, or (ii) a determination that no such finding is necessary because the matter controverted will not be taken into account in sentencing. A written record of such findings and determinations shall be appended to and accompany any copy of the presentence investigation report thereafter made available to the Bureau of Prisons or the Parole Commission.

(E) Any copies of the presentence investigation report made available to the defendant and the defendant's counsel and the attorney for the government shall be returned to the probation officer immediately following the imposition of sentence or the granting of probation, unless the court, in its discretion otherwise directs.

(F) The reports of studies and recommendations contained therein made by the Director of the Bureau of Prisons or the Parole Commission pursuant to 18 U.S.C. §§ 4205(c), 4252, 5010(e), or 5037(c) shall be considered a presentence investigation within the meaning of subdivision (c)(3) of this rule.

(d) Plea Withdrawal. If a motion for withdrawal of a plea of guilty or nolo contendere is made before sentence is imposed, imposition of sentence is suspended, or disposition is had under 18 U.S.C. § 4205(c), the court may permit withdrawal of the plea upon a showing by the defendant of any fair and just reason. At any later time, a plea may be set aside only on direct appeal or by motion under 28 U.S.C. § 2255.

(e) Probation. After conviction of an offense not punishable by death or by life imprisonment, the defendant may be placed on probation if permitted by law.

(f) [Revocation of Probation.] (Abrogated Apr. 30, 1979, eff. Dec. 1, 1980)

For applicability of sentencing provisions to offenses, see Effective Date and Savings Provisions, etc., note, section 235 of Pub.L. 98–473, as amended, set out under section 3551 of Title 18, Crimes and Criminal Procedure.

NOTES OF ADVISORY COMMITTEE ON RULES

Note to Subdivision (a). This rule is substantially a restatement of existing procedure. Rule I of the Criminal Appeals Rules of 1933, 292 U.S. 661 [18 U.S.C. formerly following § 688]. See Rule 43 relating to the presence of the defendant.

Note to Subdivision (b). This rule is substantially a restatement of existing procedure. Rule I of the Criminal Appeals Rules of 1933, 292 U.S. 661 [18 U.S.C. formerly following § 688].

Note to Subdivision (c). The purpose of this provision is to encourage and broaden the use of presentence investigations, which are now being utilized to good advantage in many cases. See, "The Presentence Investigation" published by Administrative Office of the United States Courts, Division of Probation.

Note to Subdivision (d). This rule modifies existing practice by abrogating the ten-day limitation on a motion for leave to withdraw a plea of guilty. See Rule II(4) of the Criminal Appeals Rules of 1933, 292 U.S. 661 [18 U.S.C. formerly following § 688].

Note to Subdivision (e). See 18 U.S.C. former § 724 et seq. (now § 3651 et seq.).

1966 AMENDMENT

Subdivision (a)(1).—The amendment writes into the rule the holding of the Supreme Court that the court before imposing sentence must afford an opportunity to the defendant personally to speak in his own behalf. See *Green v. United States*, 365 U.S. 301 (1961); *Hill v. United States*, 368 U.S. 424 (1962). The amendment also provides an opportunity for counsel to speak on behalf of the defendant.

Subdivision (a)(2).—This amendment is a substantial revision and a relocation of the provision originally found in Rule 37(a)(2): "When a court after trial imposes sentence upon a defendant not represented by counsel, the defendant shall be advised of his right to appeal and if he so requests, the clerk shall prepare and file forthwith a notice of appeal on behalf of the defendant." The court is required to advise the defendant of his right to appeal in all cases which have gone to trial after plea of not guilty because situations arise in which a defendant represented by counsel at the trial is not adequately advised by such counsel of his right to appeal. Trial counsel may not regard his responsibility as extending beyond the time of imposition of sentence. The defendant may be removed from the courtroom immediately upon sentence and held in custody, under circumstances which make it difficult for counsel to advise him. See, e.g., *Hodges v. United States*, 368 U.S. 139 (1961). Because indigent defendants are most likely to be without effective assistance of counsel at this point in the proceedings, it is also provided that defendants be notified of the right of a person without funds to apply for leave to appeal in forma pauperis. The provision is added here because this rule seems the most appropriate place to set forth a procedure to be followed by the court at the time of sentencing.

Subdivision (c)(2).—It is not a denial of due process of law for a court in sentencing to rely on a report of a presentence investigation without disclosing such report to the defendant or giving him an opportunity to rebut it. *Williams v. New York*, 337 U.S. 241 (1949); *Williams v. Oklahoma*, 358 U.S. 576 (1959). However, the question whether as a matter of policy the defendant should be accorded some opportunity to see and refute allegations made in such reports has been the subject of heated controversy. For arguments favoring disclosure, see Tappan, Crime, Justice, and Correction, 558 (1960); Model Penal Code, 54–55 (Tent. Draft No. 2, 1954); Thomsen, Confidentiality of the Presentence Report: A Middle Position, 28 Fed.Prob., March 1964, p. 8; Wyzanski, A Trial Judge's Freedom and Responsibility, 65 Harv.L.Rev. 1281, 1291–2 (1952); Note, Employment of Social Investigation Reports in Criminal and Juvenile Proceedings, 58 Colum.L.Rev. 702 (1958); cf. Kadish, The Advocate and the Expert: Counsel in the Peno-Correctional Process, 45 Minn.L.Rev. 803, 806, (1961). For arguments opposing disclosure, see Barnett and Gronewold, Confidentiality of the Presentence Report, 26 Fed.Prob. March 1962, p. 26; Judicial Conference Committee on Administration of the Probation System, Judicial Opinion on Proposed Change in Rule 32(c) of the Federal Rules of Criminal Procedure—a Survey

(1964); Keve, The Probation Officer Investigates, 6–15 (1960); Parsons, The Presentence Investigation Report Must be Preserved as a Confidential Document, 28 Fed.Prob. March 1964, p. 3; Sharp, The Confidential Nature of Presentence Reports, 5 Cath.U.L.Rev. 127 (1955); Wilson, A New Arena is Emerging to Test the Confidentiality of Presentence Reports, 25 Fed.Prob. Dec. 1961, p. 6; Federal Judge's Views on Probation Practices, 24 Fed.Prob. March 1960, p. 10.

In a few jurisdictions the defendant is given a right of access to the presentence report. In England and California a copy of the report is given to the defendant in every case. English Criminal Justice Act of 1948, 11 & 12 Geo. 6, c. 58, § 43; Cal.Pen.C. § 1203. In Alabama the defendant has a right to inspect the report. Ala. Code, Title 42, § 23. In Ohio and Virginia the probation officer reports in open court and the defendant is given the right to examine him on his report. Ohio Rev.Code, § 2947.06; Va.Code, § 53–278.1. The Minnesota Criminal Code of 1963, § 609.115(4), provides that any presentence report "shall be open for inspection by the prosecuting attorney and the defendant's attorney prior to sentence and on the request of either of them a summary hearing in chambers shall be held on any matter brought in issue, but confidential sources of information shall not be disclosed unless the court otherwise directs." Cf. Model Penal Code § 7.07(5) (P.O.D. 1962): "Before imposing sentence, the Court shall advise the defendant or his counsel of the factual contents and the conclusions of any presentence investigation or psychiatric examination and afford fair opportunity, if the defendant so requests, to controvert them. The sources of confidential information need not, however, be disclosed."

Practice in the federal courts is mixed, with a substantial minority of judges permitting disclosure while most deny it. See the recent survey prepared for the Judicial Conference of the District of Columbia by the Junior Bar Section of the Bar Association of the District of Columbia, reported in Conference Papers on Discovery in Federal Criminal Cases, 33 F.R.D. 101, 125–127 (1963). See also Gronewold, Presentence Investigation Practices in the Federal Probation System, Fed.Prob. Sept. 1958, pp. 27, 31. For divergent judicial opinions see *Smith v. United States*, 223 F.2d 750, 754 (5th Cir.1955) (supporting disclosure); *United States v. Durham*, 181 F.Supp. 503 (D.D.C.1960) (supporting secrecy).

Substantial objections to compelling disclosure in every case have been advanced by federal judges, including many who in practice often disclose all or parts of presentence reports. See Judicial Conference Committee on the Administration of the Probation System, Judicial Opinion on Proposed Change in Rule 32(c) of the Federal Rules of Criminal Procedure—A Survey (1964). Hence, the amendment goes no further than to make it clear that courts may disclose all or part of the presentence report to the defendant or to his counsel. It is hoped that courts will make increasing use of their discretion to disclose so that defendants generally may be given full opportunity to rebut or explain facts in presentence reports which will be material factors in determining sentences. For a description of such a practice in one district, see Thomsen, Confidentiality of the Presentence Report: A Middle Position, 28 Fed. Prob., March 1964, p. 8.

It is also provided that any material disclosed to the defendant or his counsel shall be disclosed to the attorney for the government. Such disclosure will permit the government to participate in the resolution of any factual questions raised by the defendant.

Subdivision (f).—This new subdivision writes into the rule the procedure which the cases have derived from the provision in 18 U.S.C. § 3653 that a person arrested for violation of probation "shall be taken before the court" and that thereupon the court may revoke the probation. See *Escoe v. Zerbst*, 295 U.S. 490 (1935); *Brown v. United States*, 236 F.2d 253 (9th Cir. 1956) certiorari denied 356 U.S. 922 (1958). Compare Model Penal Code § 301.4 (P.O.D.1962); Hink, The Application of Constitutional Standards of Protection to Probation, 29 U.Chi.L.Rev. 483 (1962).

1972 AMENDMENT

Subdivision (b)(2) is new. It is intended to provide procedural implementation of the recently enacted criminal forfeiture provisions of the Organized Crime Control Act of 1970, Title IX, § 1963, and the Comprehensive Drug Abuse Prevention and Control Act of 1970, Title II, § 408(a)(2).

18 U.S.C. § 1963(c) provides for property seizure and disposition. In part it states:

(c) Upon conviction of a person under this section, the court shall authorize the Attorney General to seize all property or other interest declared forfeited under this section upon such terms and conditions as the court shall deem proper.

Although not specifically provided for in the Comprehensive Drug Abuse Prevention and Control Act of 1970, the provision of Title II, § 408(a)(2) forfeiting "profits" or "interest" will need to be implemented procedurally, and therefore new rule 32(b)(2) will be applicable also to that legislation.

For a brief discussion of the procedural implications of a criminal forfeiture, see Advisory Committee Note to rule 7(c)(2).

1974 AMENDMENT

Subdivision (a)(1) is amended by deleting the reference to commitment or release pending sentencing. This issue is dealt with explicitly in the proposed revision of rule 46(c).

Subdivision (a)(2) is amended to make clear that there is no duty on the court to advise the defendant of the right to appeal after sentence is imposed following a plea of guilty or nolo contendere.

To require the court to advise the defendant of a right to appeal after a plea of guilty, accepted pursuant to the increasingly stringent requirements of rule 11, is likely to be confusing to the defendant. See American Bar Association Standards Relating to Criminal Appeals § 2.1(b) (Approved Draft, 1970), limiting the court's duty to advice to "contested cases."

The Advisory Committee is of the opinion that such advice, following a sentence imposed after a plea of guilty, will merely tend to build false hopes and encourage frivolous appeals, with the attendant expense to the defendant or the taxpayers.

Former rule 32(a)(2) imposes a duty only upon conviction after "trial on a plea of not guilty." The few federal cases dealing with the question have interpreted rule 32(a)(2) to say that the court has no duty to advise defendant of his right to appeal after conviction following a guilty plea. *Burton v. United States,* 307 F.Supp. 448, 450 (D.Ariz.1970); *Alaway v. United States,* 280 F.Supp. 326, 336 (C.D.Calif.1968); *Crow v. United States,* 397 F.2d 284, 285 (10th Cir.1968).

Prior to the 1966 amendment of rule 32, the court's duty was even more limited. At that time [rule 37(a)(2)] the court's duty to advise was limited to those situations in which sentence was imposed after trial upon a not guilty plea of a defendant not represented by counsel. 8A J. Moore, Federal Practice ¶ 32.01[3] (2d ed. Cipes 1969); C. Wright, Federal Practice and Procedure: Criminal § 528 (1969); 5 L. Orfield, Criminal Procedure Under the Federal Rules § 32:11 (1967).

With respect to appeals in forma pauperis, see appellate rule 24.

Subdivision (c)(1) makes clear that a presentence report is required except when the court otherwise directs for reasons stated of record. The requirement of reasons on the record for not having a presentence report is intended to make clear that such a report ought to be routinely required except in cases where there is a reason for not doing so. The presentence report is of great value for correctional purposes and will serve as a valuable aid in reviewing sentences to the extent that sentence review may be authorized by future rule change. For an analysis of the current rule as it relates to the situation in which a presentence investigation is required, see C. Wright, Federal Practice and Procedure: Criminal § 522 (1969); 8A J. Moore, Federal Practice ¶ 32.03[1] (2d ed. Cipes 1969).

Subdivision (c)(1) is also changed to permit the judge, after obtaining defendant's consent, to see the presentence report in order to decide whether to accept a plea agreement, and also to expedite the imposition of sentence in a case in which the defendant has indicated that he may plead guilty or nolo contendere.

Former subdivision (c)(1) provides that "The report shall not be submitted to the court * * * unless the defendant has pleaded guilty * * *." This precludes a judge from seeing a presentence report prior to the acceptance of the plea of guilty. L. Orfield, Criminal Procedure Under the Federal Rules § 32:35 (1967); 8A J. Moore, Federal Practice ¶ 32.03[2], p. 32–22 (2d ed. Cipes 1969); C. Wright, Federal Practice and Procedure: Criminal § 523, p. 392 (1969); *Gregg v. United States,* 394 U.S. 489, 89 S.Ct. 1134, 22 L.Ed.2d 442 (1969).

Because many plea agreements will deal with the sentence to be imposed, it will be important, under rule 11, for the judge to have access to sentencing information as a basis for deciding whether the plea agreement is an appropriate one.

It has been suggested that the problem be dealt with by allowing the judge to indicate approval of the plea agreement subject to the condition that the information in the presentence report is consistent with what he has been told about the case by counsel. See American Bar Association, Standards Relating to Pleas of Guilty § 3.3 (Approved Draft, 1963); President's Commission on Law Enforcement and Administration of Justice. The Challenge of Crime in a Free Society 136 (1967).

Allowing the judge to see the presentence report prior to his decision as to whether to accept the plea agreement is, in the view of the Advisory Committee, preferable to a conditional acceptance of the plea. See Enker, Perspectives on Plea Bargaining, Appendix A of President's Commission on Law Enforcement and Administration of Justice, Task Force Report: The Courts at 117 (1967). It enables the judge to have all of the information available to him at the time he is called upon to decide whether or not to accept the plea of guilty and thus avoids the necessity of a subsequent appearance whenever the information is such that the judge decides to reject the plea agreement.

There is presently authority to have a presentence report *prepared* prior to the acceptance of the plea of guilty. In *Gregg v. United States,* 394 U.S. 489, 491, 89 S.Ct. 1134, 22 L.Ed.2d 442 (1969), the court said that the "language [of rule 32] clearly permits the preparation of a presentence report before guilty plea or conviction * * *." In footnote 3 the court said:

The history of the rule confirms this interpretation. The first Preliminary Draft of the rule would have required the consent of the defendant or his attorney to commence the investigation before the determination of guilt. Advisory Committee on Rules of Criminal Procedure, Fed.Rules Crim.Proc., Preliminary Draft 130, 133 (1943). The Second Preliminary Draft omitted this requirement and imposed no limitation on the time when the report could be made and submitted to the court. Advisory Committee on Rules of Criminal Procedure, Fed.Rules Crim.Proc. Second Preliminary Draft 126–128 (1944). The third and final draft, which was adopted as Rule 32, was evidently a compromise between those who opposed any time limitation, and those who preferred that the entire investigation be conducted after determination of guilt. See 5 L. Orfield, Criminal Procedure Under the Federal Rules § 32.2 (1967).

Where the judge rejects the plea agreement after seeing the presentence report, he should be free to recuse himself from later presiding over the trial of the case. This is left to the discretion of the judge. There are instances involving prior convictions where a judge may have seen a presentence report, yet can properly try a case on a plea of not guilty. *Webster v. United States,* 330 F.Supp. 1080 (D.C., 1971). Unlike the situation in *Gregg v. United States,* subdivision (e)(3) provides for disclosure of the presentence report to the defendant, and this will enable counsel to know whether the information thus made available to the judge is likely to be prejudicial. Presently trial judges who decide pretrial motions to suppress illegally obtained evidence are not, for that reason alone, precluded from presiding at a later trial.

Subdivision (c)(3)(A) requires disclosure of presentence information to the defense, exclusive of any recommendation of sentence. The court is required to disclose the report to defendant or his counsel unless the court is of the opinion that disclosure would seriously interfere with rehabilitation, compromise confidentiality, or create risk of harm to the defendant or others.

Any recommendation as to sentence should not be disclosed as it may impair the effectiveness of the probation officer if the defendant is under supervision on probation or parole.

The issue of disclosure of presentence information to the defense has been the subject of recommendations from the Advisory Committee in 1944, 1962, 1964, and 1966. The history is dealt with in considerable detail in C. Wright, Federal Practice and Procedure: Criminal § 524 (1969), and 8A J. Moore, Federal Practice ¶ 32.03[4] (2d ed. Cipes 1969).

In recent years, three prestigious organizations have recommended that the report be disclosed to the defense. See American Bar Association, Standards Relating to Sentencing Alternatives and Procedures § 4.4 (Approved Draft, 1968); American Law Institute Model Penal Code § 7.07(5) (P.O.D.1962); National Council on Crime and Delinquency, Model Sentencing Act § 4 (1963). This is also the recommendation of the President's Commission on Law Enforcement and Administration of Justice. The Challenge of Crime in a Free Society (1967) at p. 145.

In the absence of compelling reasons for nondisclosure of special information, the defendant and his counsel should be permitted to examine the entire presentence report.

The arguments for and against disclosure are well known and are effectively set forth in American Bar Association Standards Relating to Sentencing Alternatives and Procedures, § 4.4 Commentary at pp. 214–225 (Approved Draft, 1968). See also Lehrich, The Use and Disclosure of Presentence Reports in the United States, 47 F.R.D. 225 (1969).

A careful account of existing practices in Detroit, Michigan and Milwaukee, Wisconsin is found in R. Dawson, Sentencing (1969).

Most members of the federal judiciary have, in the past, opposed compulsory disclosure. See the view of District Judge Edwin M. Stanley, American Bar Association Standards Relating to Sentencing Alternatives and Procedures. Appendix A. (Appendix A also contains the results of a survey of all federal judges showing that the clear majority opposed disclosure.)

The Advisory Committee is of the view that accuracy of sentencing information is important not only to the defendant but also to effective correctional treatment of a convicted offender. The best way of insuring accuracy is disclosure with an opportunity for the defendant and counsel to point out to the court information thought by the defense to be inaccurate, incomplete, or otherwise misleading. Experience in jurisdictions which require disclosure does not lend support to the argument that disclosure will result in less complete presentence reports or the argument that sentencing procedures will become unnecessarily protracted. It is not intended that the probation officer would be subjected to any rigorous examination by defense counsel, or that he will even be sworn to testify. The proceedings may be very informal in nature unless the court orders a full hearing.

Subdivision (c)(3)(B) provides for situations in which the sentencing judge believes that disclosure should not be made under the criteria set forth in subdivision (c)(3)(A). He may disclose only a summary of that factual information "to be relied on in determining sentence." This is similar to the proposal of the American Bar Association Standards Relating to Sentencing Alternatives and Procedures § 4.4(b) and Commentary at pp. 216–224.

Subdivision (c)(3)(D) provides for the return of disclosed presentence reports to insure that they do not become available to unauthorized persons. See National Council on Crime and Delinquency, Model Sentencing Act § 4 (1963): "Such reports shall be part of the record but shall be sealed and opened only on order of the court."

Subdivision (c)(3)(E) makes clear that diagnostic studies under 18 U.S.C. §§ 4208(b), 5010(c), or 5034 are covered by this rule and also that 18 U.S.C. § 4252 is included within the disclosure provisions of subdivision (c). Section 4252 provides for the presentence examination of an "eligible offender" who is believed to be an addict to determine whether "he is an addict and is likely to be rehabilitated through treatment."

Both the Organized Crime Control Act of 1970 [§ 3775(b)] and the Comprehensive Drug Abuse Prevention and Control Act of 1970 [§ 409(b)] have special provisions for presentence investigation in the implementation of the dangerous special offender provision. It is however, unnecessary to incorporate them by reference in rule 32 because each contains a specific provision requiring disclosure of the presentence report. The judge does have authority to withhold some information "in extraordinary cases" provided notice is given the parties and the court's reasons for withholding information are made part of the record.

Subdivision (e) is amended to clarify the meaning.

NOTES OF COMMITTEE ON THE JUDICIARY, HOUSE REPORT NO. 94-247

A. Amendments Proposed by the Supreme Court Rule 32 of the Federal Rules of Criminal Procedure deals with sentencing matters.

Proposed subdivision (a)(2) provides that the court is not dutybound to advise the defendant of a right to appeal when the sentence is imposed following a plea of guilty or nolo contendere.

Proposed subdivision (e) provides that the probation service must make a presentence investigation and report unless the court orders otherwise "for reasons stated on the record." The presentence report will not be submitted to the court until after the defendant pleads nolo contendere or guilty, or is found guilty, unless the defendant consents in writing. Upon the defendant's request, the court must permit the defendant to read the presentence report, except for the recommendation as to sentence. However, the court may decline to let the defendant read the report if it contains (a) diagnostic opinion that might seriously disrupt a rehabilitation program, (b) sources of information obtained upon a promise of confidentiality, or (c) any other information that, if disclosed, might result in harm to the defendant or other persons. The court must give the defendant an opportunity to comment upon the presentence report. If the court decides that the defendant should not see the report, then it must provide the defendant, orally or in writing, a summary of the factual information in the report upon which it is relying in determining sentence. No party may keep the report or make copies of it.

B. Committee Action. The Committee added language to subdivision (a)(1) to provide that the attorney for the government may speak to the court at the time of sentencing. The language does not require that the attorney for the government speak but permits him to do so if he wishes.

The Committee recast the language of subdivision (c)(1), which defines when presentence reports must be obtained. The Committee's provision makes it more difficult to dispense with a presentence report. It requires that a presentence report be made unless (a) the defendant waives it, or (b) the court finds that the record contains sufficient information to enable the meaningful exercise of sentencing discretion and explains this finding on the record. The Committee believes that presentence reports are important aids to sentencing and should not be dispensed with easily.

The Committee added language to subdivision (c)(3)(A) that permits a defendant to offer testimony or information to rebut alleged factual inaccuracies in the presentence report. Since the presentence report is to be used by the court in imposing sentence and since the consequence of any significant inaccuracy can be very serious to the defendant, the Committee believes that it is essential that the presentence report be completely accurate in every material respect. The Committee's addition to subdivision (c)(3)(A) will help insure the accuracy of the presentence report.

The Committee added language to subdivision (c)(3)(D) that gives the court the discretion to permit either the prosecutor or the defense counsel to retain a copy of the presentence report. There may be situations when it would be appropriate for either or both of the parties to retain the presentence report. The Committee believes that the rule should give the court the discretion in such situations to permit the parties to retain their copies.

1979 AMENDMENT

Note to Subdivision (c)(3)(E). The amendment to rule 32(c)(3)(E) is necessary in light of recent changes in the applicable statutes.

Note to Subdivision (f). This subdivision is abrogated. The subject matter is now dealt with in greater detail in proposed new rule 32.1.

1983 AMENDMENT

Rule 32(a)(1)

Subdivision (a)(1) has been amended so as to impose upon the sentencing court the additional obligation of determining that the defendant and his counsel have had an opportunity to read the presentence investigation report or summary thereof. This change is consistent with the amendment of subdivision (c)(3), discussed below, providing for disclosure of the report (or, in the circumstances indicated, a summary thereof) to *both* defendant *and* his counsel *without request*. This amendment is also consistent with the findings of a recent empirical study that under present rule 32 meaningful disclosure is often lacking and "that some form of judicial prodding is necessary to achieve full disclosure." Fennell & Hall, *Due Process at Sentencing: An Empirical and Legal Analysis of the Disclosure of*

Presentence Reports in Federal Courts, 93 Harv.L.Rev. 1613, 1651 (1980):

The defendant's interest in an accurate and reliable presentence report does not cease with the imposition of sentence. Rather, these interests are implicated at later stages in the correctional process by the continued use of the presentence report as a basic source of information in the handling of the defendant. If the defendant is incarcerated, the presentence report accompanies him to the correctional institution and provides background information for the Bureau of Prisons' classification summary, which, in turn, determines the defendant's classification within the facility, his ability to obtain furloughs, and the choice of treatment programs. The presentence report also plays a crucial role during parole determination. Section 4207 of the Parole Commission and Reorganization Act directs the parole hearing examiner to consider, if available, the presentence report as well as other records concerning the prisoner. In addition to its general use as background at the parole hearing, the presentence report serves as the primary source of information for calculating the inmate's parole guideline score.

Though it is thus important that the defendant be aware *now* of all these potential uses, the Advisory Committee has considered but not adopted a requirement that the trial judge specifically advise the defendant of these matters. The Committee believes that this additional burden should not be placed upon the trial judge, and that the problem is best dealt with by a form attached to the presentence report, to be signed by the defendant, advising of these potential uses of the report. This suggestion has been forwarded to the Probation Committee of the Judicial Conference.

Rule 32(c)(3)(A), (B) & (C)

Three important changes are made in subdivision (c)(3): disclosure of the presentence report is no longer limited to those situations in which a request is made; disclosure is now provided to both defendant and his counsel; and disclosure is now required a reasonable time before sentencing. These changes have been prompted by findings in a recent empirical study that the extent and nature of disclosure of the presentence investigation report in federal courts under current rule 32 is insufficient to ensure accuracy of sentencing information. In 14 districts, disclosure is made only on request, and such requests are received in fewer than 50% of the cases. Forty-two of 92 probation offices do not provide automatic notice to defendant or counsel of the availability of the report; in 18 districts, a majority of the judges do not provide any notice of the availability of the report, and in 20 districts such notice is given only on the day of sentencing. In 28 districts, the report itself is not disclosed until the day of sentencing in a majority of cases. Thirty-one courts generally disclose the report only to counsel and not to the

defendant, unless the defendant makes a specific request. Only 13 districts disclose the presentence report to both defendant and counsel prior to the day of sentencing in 90% or more of the cases. Fennell & Hall, supra, at 1640–49.

These findings make it clear that rule 32 in its present form is failing to fulfill its purpose. Unless disclosure is made sufficiently in advance of sentencing to permit the assertion and resolution of claims of inaccuracy prior to the sentencing hearing, the submission of additional information by the defendant when appropriate, and informed comment on the presentence report, the purpose of promoting accuracy by permitting the defendant to contest erroneous information is defeated. Similarly, if the report is not made available to the defendant and his counsel in a timely fashion, and if disclosure is only made on request, their opportunity to review the report may be inadequate. Finally, the failure to disclose the report to the defendant, or to require counsel to review the report with the defendant, significantly reduces the likelihood that false statements will be discovered, as much of the content of the presentence report will ordinarily be outside the knowledge of counsel.

The additional change to subdivision (c)(3)(C) is intended to make it clear that the government's right to disclosure does not depend upon whether the defendant elects to exercise his right to disclosure.

Rule 32(c)(3)(D)

Subdivision (c)(3)(D) is entirely new. It requires the sentencing court, as to each matter controverted, either to make a finding as to the accuracy of the challenged factual proposition or to determine that no reliance will be placed on that proposition at the time of sentencing. This new provision also requires that a record of this action accompany any copy of the report later made available to the Bureau of Prisons or Parole Commission.

As noted above, the Bureau of Prisons and the Parole Commission made substantial use of the presentence investigation report. Under current practice, this can result in reliance upon assertions of fact in the report in the making of critical determinations relating to custody or parole. For example, it is possible that the Bureau or Commission, in the course of reaching a decision on such matters as institution assignment, eligibility for programs, or computation of salient factors, will place great reliance upon factual assertions in the report which are in fact untrue and which remained unchallenged at the time of sentencing because defendant or his counsel deemed the error unimportant in the sentencing context (e.g., where the sentence was expected to conform to an earlier plea agreement, or where the judge said he would disregard certain controverted matter in setting the sentence).

The first sentence of new subdivision (c)(3)(D) is intended to ensure that a record is made as to exactly what resolution occurred as to controverted matter. The second sentence is intended to ensure that this record comes to the attention of the Bureau or Commission when these agencies utilize the presentence investigation report. In current practice, "less than one-fourth of the district courts (twenty of ninety-two) communicate to the correctional agencies the defendant's challenges to information in the presentence report and the resolution of these challenges." Fennell & Hall, supra, at 1680.

New subdivision (c)(3)(D) does not impose an onerous burden. It does not even require the preparation of a transcript. As is now the practice in some courts, these findings and determinations can be simply entered onto a form which is then appended to the report.

Rule 32(c)(3)(E) & (F)

Former subdivisions (c)(3)(D) and (E) have been renumbered as (c)(3)(E) and (F). The only change is in the former, necessitated because disclosure is now to defendant and his counsel.

The issue of access to the presentence report at the institution was discussed by the Advisory Committee, but no action was taken on that matter because it was believed to be beyond the scope of the rule-making power. Rule 32 in its present form does not speak to this issue, and thus the Bureau of Prisons and the Parole Commission are free to make provision for disclosure to inmates and their counsel.

Rule 32(d)

The amendment to Rule 32(d) is intended to clarify (i) the standard applicable to plea withdrawal under this rule, and (ii) the circumstances under which the appropriate avenue of relief is other than a withdrawal motion under this rule. Both of these matters have been the source of considerable confusion under the present rule. In its present form, the rule declares that a motion to withdraw a plea of guilty or nolo contendere may be made only before sentence is imposed, but then states the standard for permitting withdrawal after sentence. In fact, "there is no limitation upon the time within which relief thereunder may, after sentencing, be sought." *United States v. Watson*, 548 F.2d 1058 (D.C.Cir.1977). It has been critically stated that "the Rule offers little guidance as to the applicable standard for a pre-sentence withdrawal of plea," *United States v. Michaelson*, 552 F.2d 472 (2d Cir.1977), and that as a result "the contours of [the presentence] standard are not easily defined." *Bruce v. United States*, 379 F.2d 113 (D.C.Cir.1967).

By replacing the "manifest injustice" standard with a requirement that, in cases to which it applied, the defendant must (unless taking a direct appeal) proceed under 28 U.S.C. § 2255, the amendment avoids language which has been a cause of unnecessary confusion.

Under the amendment, a defendant who proceeds too late to come under the more generous "fair and just reason" standard must seek relief under § 2255, meaning the applicable standard is that stated in *Hill v. United States*, 368 U.S. 424 (1962): "a fundamental defect which inherently results in a complete miscarriage of justice" or "an omission inconsistent with the rudimentary demands of fair procedure."

Some authority is to be found to the effect that the rule 32(d) "manifest injustice" standard is indistinguishable from the § 2255 standard. In *United States v. Hamilton*, 553 F.2d 63 (10th Cir.1977), for example, the court, after first concluding defendant was not entitled to relief under the § 2255 "miscarriage of justice" test, then held that "[n]othing is to be gained by the invocation of Rule 32(d)" and its "manifest injustice" standard. Some courts, however, have indicated that the rule 32(d) standard provides a somewhat broader basis for relief than § 2255. *United States v. Dabdoub–Diaz*, 599 F.2d 96 (5th Cir.1979); *United States v. Watson*, 548 F.2d 1058 (D.C.Cir.1977); *Meyer v. United States*, 424 F.2d 1181 (8th Cir.1970); *United States v. Kent*, 397 F.2d 446 (7th Cir.1968). It is noteworthy, however, that in *Dabdoub–Diaz*, *Meyer* and *Kent* the defendant did not prevail under either § 2255 or Rule 32(d), and that in *Watson*, though the § 2255 case was remanded for consideration as a 32(d) motion, defendant's complaint (that he was not advised of the special parole term, though the sentence he received did not exceed that he was warned about by the court) was one as to which relief had been denied even upon direct appeal from the conviction. *United States v. Peters*, No. 77–1700 (4th Cir. Dec. 22, 1978).

Indeed, it may more generally be said that the results in § 2255 and 32(d) guilty plea cases have been for the most part the same. Relief has often been granted or recognized as available via either of these routes for essentially the same reasons: that there exists a complete constitutional bar to conviction on the offense charged, *Brooks v. United States*, 424 F.2d 425 (5th Cir.1970) (§ 2255), *United States v. Bluso*, 519 F.2d 473 (4th Cir.1975) (Rule 32); that the defendant was incompetent at the time of his plea, *United States v. Masthers*, 539 F.2d 721 (D.C.Cir.1976) (§ 2255), *Kienlen v. United States*, 379 F.2d 20 (10th Cir.1967) (Rule 32); and that the bargain the prosecutor made with defendant was not kept, *Walters v. Harris*, 460 F.2d 988 (4th Cir.1972) (§ 2255), *United States v. Hawthorne*, 502 F.2d 1183 (3rd Cir.1974) (Rule 32). Perhaps even more significant is the fact that relief has often been denied under like circumstances whichever of the two procedures was used: a mere technical violation of Rule 11, *United States v. Timmreck*, 441 U.S. 780 (1979) (§ 2255), *United States v. Saft*, 558 F.2d 1073 (2d Cir.1977) (Rule 32); the mere fact defendants expected a lower sentence, *United States v. White*, 572 F.2d 1007 (4th Cir.1978) (§ 2255), *Masciola v. United States*, 469 F.2d 1057 (3rd Cir.1972)

(Rule 32); or mere familial coercion, *Wojtowicz v. United States,* 550 F.2d 786 (2d Cir.1977) (§ 2255), *United States v. Bartoli,* 572 F.2d 188 (8th Cir.1978) (Rule 32).

The one clear instance in which a Rule 32(d) attack might prevail when a § 2255 challenge would not is present in those circuits which have reached the questionable result that post-sentence relief under 32(d) is available not merely upon a showing of a "manifest injustice" but also for any deviation from literal compliance with Rule 11. *United States v. Cantor,* 469 F.2d 435 (3d Cir.1972). See Advisory Committee Note to Rule 11(h), noting the unsoundness of that position.

The change in Rule 32(d), therefore, is at best a minor one in terms of how post-sentence motions to withdraw pleas will be decided. It avoids the confusion which now obtains as to whether a § 2255 petition must be assumed to also be a 32(d) motion and, if so, whether this bears significantly upon how the matter should be decided. See, e.g., *United States v. Watson,* supra. It also avoids the present undesirable situation in which the mere selection of one of two highly similar avenues of relief, rule 32(d) or § 2255, may have significant procedural consequences, such as whether the government can take an appeal from the district court's adverse ruling (possible under § 2255 only). Moreover, because § 2255 and Rule 32(d) are properly characterized as the "two principal procedures for collateral attack of a federal plea conviction," Borman, *The Hidden Right to Direct Appeal From a Federal Conviction,* 64 Cornell L.Rev. 319, 327 (1979), this amendment is also in keeping with the proposition underlying the Supreme Court's decision in *United States v. Timmreck* supra, namely, that "the concern with finality served by the limitation on collateral attack has special force with respect to convictions based on guilty pleas." The amendment is likewise consistent with ALI Code of Pre-Arraignment Procedure § 350.9 (1975) ("Allegations of noncompliance with the procedures provided in Article 350 shall not be a basis for review of a conviction after the appeal period for such conviction has expired, unless such review is required by the Constitution of the United States or of this State or otherwise by the law of this State other than Article 350"); ABA Standards Relating to the Administration of Criminal Justice § 14–2.1 (2d ed. 1978) (using "manifest injustice" standard, but listing six specific illustrations each of which would be basis for relief under § 2255); Unif. R.Crim.P. 444(e) (Approved Draft, 1974) (Using "interest of justice" test, but listing five specific illustrations each of which would be basis for relief under § 2255).

The first sentence of the amended rule incorporates the "fair and just" standard which the federal courts, relying upon dictum in *Kercheval v. United States,* 274 U.S. 220 (1927), have consistently applied to presentence motions. See, e.g., *United States v. Strauss,* 563 F.2d 127 (4th Cir.1977); *United States v. Bradin,* 535 F.2d 1039 (8th Cir.1976); *United States v. Barker,* 514

F.2d 208 (D.C.Cir.1975). Under the rule as amended, it is made clear that the defendant has the burden of showing a "fair and just" reason for withdrawal of the plea. This is consistent with the prevailing view, which is that "the defendant has the burden of satisfying the trial judge that there are valid grounds for withdrawal," see *United States v. Michaelson,* supra, and cases cited therein. (Illustrative of a reason which would meet this test but would likely fall short of the § 2255 test is where the defendant now wants to pursue a certain defense which he for good reason did not put forward earlier, *United States v. Barker,* supra.)

Although "the terms 'fair and just' lack any pretense of scientific exactness," *United States v. Barker,* supra, guidelines have emerged in the appellate cases for applying this standard. Whether the movant has asserted his legal innocence is an important factor to be weighed, *United States v. Joslin,* 434 F.2d 526 (D.C.Cir. 1970), as is the reason why the defenses were not put forward at the time of original pleading. *United States v. Needles,* 472 F.2d 652 (2d Cir.1973). The amount of time which has passed between the plea and the motion must also be taken into account.

A swift change of heart is itself strong indication that the plea was entered in haste and confusion * * *. By contrast, if the defendant has long delayed his withdrawal motion, and has had the full benefit of competent counsel at all times, the reasons given to support withdrawal must have considerably more force.

United States v. Barker, supra.

If the defendant establishes such a reason, it is then appropriate to consider whether the government would be prejudiced by withdrawal of the plea. Substantial prejudice may be present for a variety of reasons. See *United States v. Jerry,* 487 F.2d 600 (3d Cir.1973) (physical evidence had been discarded); *United States v. Vasquez–Velasco,* 471 F.2d 294 (9th Cir.1973) (death of chief government witness); *United States v. Lombardozzi,* 436 F.2d 878 (2d Cir.1971) (other defendants with whom defendant had been joined for trial had already been tried in a lengthy trial); *Farnsworth v. Sanford,* 115 F.2d 375 (5th Cir.1940) (prosecution had dismissed 52 witnesses who had come from all over the country and from overseas bases).

There is currently some disparity in the manner in which presentence motions to withdraw a guilty plea are dealt with. Some courts proceed as if any desire to withdraw the plea before sentence is "fair and just" so long as the government fails to establish that it would be prejudiced by the withdrawal. Illustrative is *United States v. Savage,* 561 F.2d 554 (4th Cir.1977), where the defendant pleaded guilty pursuant to a plea agreement that the government would recommend a sentence of 5 years. At the sentencing hearing, the trial judge indicated his unwillingness to follow the government's recommendation, so the defendant moved to withdraw his plea. That motion was denied. On appeal, the court held that there had been no violation of Rule 11, in that refusal to accept the government's recommendation does not constitute a rejection of the plea agreement. But the court then proceeded to hold that absent any showing of prejudice by the government, "the defendant should be allowed to withdraw his plea"; only upon such a showing by the government must the court "weigh the defendant's reasons for seeking to withdraw his plea against the prejudice which the government will suffer." The other view is that there is no occasion to inquire into the matter of prejudice unless the defendant first shows a good reason for being allowed to withdraw his plea. As stated in *United States v. Saft,* 558 F.2d 1073 (2d Cir.1977): "The Government is not required to show prejudice when a defendant has shown no sufficient grounds for permitting withdrawal of a guilty plea, although such prejudice may be considered by the district court in exercising its discretion." The second sentence of the amended rule, by requiring that the defendant show a "fair and just" reason, adopts the *Saft* position and rejects that taken in *Savage.*

The *Savage* position, as later articulated in *United States v. Strauss,* supra, is that the "sounder view, supported by both the language of the rule and by the reasons for it, would be to allow withdrawal of the plea prior to sentencing unless the prosecution has been substantially prejudiced by reliance upon the defendant's plea." (Quoting 2 C. Wright, Federal Practice and Procedure § 538, at 474–75 (1969). Although that position may once have been sound, this is no longer the case in light of the recent revisions of Rule 11. Rule 11 now provides for the placing of plea agreements on the record, for full inquiry into the voluntariness of the plea, for detailed advice to the defendant concerning his rights and the consequences of his plea and a determination that the defendant understands these matters, and for a determination of the accuracy of the plea. Given the great care with which pleas are taken under this revised Rule 11, there is no reason to view pleas so taken as merely "tentative," subject to withdrawal before sentence whenever the government cannot establish prejudice.

Were withdrawal automatic in every case where the defendant decided to alter his tactics and present his theory of the case to the jury, the guilty plea would become a mere gesture, a temporary and meaningless formality reversible at the defendant's whim. In fact, however, a guilty plea is no such trifle, but "a grave and solemn act," which is "accepted only with care and discernment."

United States v. Barker, supra, quoting from *Brady v. United States,* 397 U.S. 742 (1970).

The facts of the *Savage* case reflect the wisdom of this position. In *Savage,* the defendant had entered into a plea agreement whereby he agreed to plead guilty in exchange for the government's promise to recommend a sentence of 5 years, which the defendant knew was not binding on the court. Yet, under the approach taken in *Savage,* the defendant remains free to renege on his plea bargain, notwithstanding full compliance therewith by the attorney for the government, if it later appears to him from the presentence report or the comments of the trial judge or any other source that the court will not follow the government's recommendation. Having bargained for a recommendation pursuant to Rule 11(e)(1)(B), the defendant should not be entitled, in effect, to unilaterally convert the plea agreement into a Rule 11(e)(1)(C) type of agreement (i.e., one with a guarantee of a specific sentence which, if not given, permits withdrawal of the plea).

The first sentence of subdivision (d) provides that the motion, to be judged under the more liberal "fair and just reason" test, must have been made before sentence is imposed, imposition of sentence is suspended, or disposition is had under 18 U.S.C. § 4205(c). The latter of these has been added to the rule to make it clear that the lesser standard also governs prior to the second stage of sentencing when the judge, pursuant to that statute, has committed the defendant to the custody of the Attorney General for study pending final disposition. Several circuits have left this issue open, e.g., *United States v. McCoy,* 477 F.2d 550 (5th Cir.1973); *Callaway v. United States,* 367 F.2d 140 (10th Cir.1966); while some have held that a withdrawal motion filed between tentative and final sentencing should be judged against the presentence standard, *United States v. Barker,* 514 F.2d 208 (D.C.Cir.1975); *United States v. Thomas* 415 F.2d 1216 (9th Cir.1969).

Inclusion of the § 4205(c) situation under the presentence standard is appropriate. As explained in *Barker.*

Two reasons of policy have been advanced to explain the near-presumption which Rule 32(d) erects against post-sentence withdrawal motions. The first is that post-sentence withdrawal subverts the "stability" of "final judgments." * * * The second reason is that the post-sentence withdrawal motion often constitutes a veiled attack on the judge's sentencing decision; to grant such motions in lenient fashion might undermine respect for the courts and fritter away the time and painstaking effort devoted to the sentence process.

* * * Concern for the "stability of final judgments" has little application to withdrawal motions filed between tentative and final sentencing under Section 4208(b) [now 4205(c)]. The point at which a defendant's judgment of conviction becomes "final" for purposes of appeal—whether at tentative or at final sentencing—is wholly within the defendant's discretion. * * * Concern for the integrity of the sentencing process is, however, another matter. The major point, in our view, is that tentative sentencing under Section 4208(b) [now 4205(c)] leaves the defendant ignorant of his final sentence. He will therefore be

unlikely to use a withdrawal motion as an oblique attack on the judge's sentencing policy. The relative leniency of the "fair and just" standard is consequently not out of place.

1987 AMENDMENT

The amendments are technical. No substantive change is intended.

EDITORIAL NOTES

Effective Date and Savings Provisions of 1984 Amendment. Amendment by Pub.L. 98–473 effective on the first day of first calendar month beginning thirty six months after Oct. 12, 1984, applicable only to offenses committed after taking effect of sections 211 to 239 of Pub.L. 98–473, and except as otherwise provided for therein, see section 235 of Pub.L. 98–473, as amended, set out as a note under section 3551 of Title 18, Crimes and Criminal Procedure.

Effective Date of 1982 Amendment. Amendment by Pub.L. 97–291 effective Oct. 12, 1982, see section 9(a) of Pub.L. 97–291 set out as a note under section 1512 of this title.

Rule 32.1 Revocation or Modification of Probation

(a) Revocation of Probation.

(1) Preliminary Hearing. Whenever a probationer is held in custody on the ground that the probationer has violated a condition of probation, the probationer shall be afforded a prompt hearing before any judge, or a United States magistrate who has been given authority pursuant to 28 U.S.C. § 636 to conduct such hearings, in order to determine whether there is probable cause to hold the probationer for a revocation hearing. The probationer shall be given

(A) notice of the preliminary hearing and its purpose and of the alleged violation of probation;

(B) an opportunity to appear at the hearing and present evidence in the probationer's own behalf;

(C) upon request, the opportunity to question witnesses against the probationer unless, for good cause, the federal magistrate decides that justice does not require the appearance of the witness; and

(D) notice of the probationer's right to be represented by counsel.

The proceedings shall be recorded stenographically or by an electronic recording device. If probable cause is found to exist, the probationer shall be held for a revocation hearing. The probationer may be released pursuant to Rule 46(c) pending the revocation hearing. If probable cause is not found to exist, the proceeding shall be dismissed.

(2) Revocation Hearing. The revocation hearing, unless waived by the probationer, shall be held within a reasonable time in the district of probation jurisdiction. The probationer shall be given

(A) written notice of the alleged violation of probation;

(B) disclosure of the evidence against the probationer;

(C) an opportunity to appear and to present evidence in the probationer's own behalf;

(D) the opportunity to question adverse witnesses; and

(E) notice of the probationer's right to be represented by counsel.

(b) Modification of Probation. A hearing and assistance of counsel are required before the terms or conditions of probation can be modified, unless the relief to be granted to the probationer upon the probationer's request or the court's own motion is favorable to the probationer, and the attorney for the government, after having been given notice of the proposed relief and a reasonable opportunity to object, has not objected. An extension of the term of probation is not favorable to the probationer for the purposes of this rule.

(Added Apr. 30, 1979, eff. Dec. 1, 1980, and amended Nov. 10, 1986, Pub.L. 99–646, § 12(b), 100 Stat. 3594; Mar. 9, 1987, eff. Aug. 1, 1987.)

NOTES OF ADVISORY COMMITTEE ON RULES

Rule 32.1(a)(1). Since *Morrissey v. Brewer,* 408 U.S. 471 (1972), and *Gagnon v. Scarpelli,* 411 U.S. 778 (1973), it is clear that a probationer can no longer be denied due process in reliance on the dictum in *Escoe v. Zerbst,* 295 U.S. 490, 492 (1935), that probation is an "act of grace." See Van Alstyne, The Demise of the Right–Privilege Distinction in Constitutional Law, 81 Harv.L. Rev. 1439 (1968); President's Commission on Law Enforcement and Administration of Justice, Task Force Report: Corrections 86 (1967).

Subdivision (a)(1) requires, consistent with the holding in *Scarpelli,* that a prompt preliminary hearing must be held whenever "a probationer is held in custody on the ground that he has violated a condition of his probation." See 18 U.S.C. § 3653 regarding arrest of the probationer with or without a warrant. If there is to be a revocation hearing but there has not been a holding in custody for a probation violation, there need not be a preliminary hearing. It was the fact of such a holding in custody "which prompted the Court to determine that a preliminary as well as a final revocation hearing was required to afford the petitioner due process of law," *United States v. Tucker,* 524 F.2d 77 (5th Cir.1975). Consequently, a preliminary hearing need not be held if the probationer was at large and was not arrested but was allowed to appear voluntarily, *United States v. Strada,* 503 F.2d 1081 (8th Cir.1974), or in response to a show cause order which "merely requires his appearance in court," *United States v. Langford,* 369 F.Supp. 1107 (N.D.Ill.1973); if the probationer was in custody pursuant to a new charge, *Thomas v. United States,* 391 F.Supp. 202 (W.D.Pa.1975), or pursuant to a final conviction of a subsequent offense, *United States v. Tucker,* supra; or if he was arrested but obtained his release.

Subdivision (a)(1)(A), (B) and (C) list the requirements for the preliminary hearing, as developed in *Morrissey* and made applicable to probation revocation cases in *Scarpelli.* Under (A), the probationer is to be given notice of the hearing and its purpose and of the alleged violation of probation. "Although the allegations in a motion to revoke probation need not be as specific as an indictment, they must be sufficient to apprise the probationer of the conditions of his probation which he is alleged to have violated, as well as the dates and events which support the charge." *Kartman v. Parratt,* 397 F.Supp. 531 (D.Nebr.1975). Under (B), the probationer is permitted to appear and present evidence in his own behalf. And under (C), *upon request* by the probationer, adverse witnesses shall be made available for questioning unless the magistrate determines that the informant would be subjected to risk of harm if his identity were disclosed.

Subdivision (a)(1)(D) provides for notice to the probationer of his right to be represented by counsel at the preliminary hearing. Although *Scarpelli* did not impose as a constitutional requirement a right to counsel in all instances, under 18 U.S.C. § 3006A(b) a defendant is entitled to be represented by counsel whenever charged "with a violation of probation."

The federal magistrate (see definition in rule 54(c)) is to keep a record of what transpires at the hearing and, if he finds probable cause of a violation, hold the probationer for a revocation hearing. The probationer may be released pursuant to rule 46(c) pending the revocation hearing.

Rule 32.1(a)(2). Subdivision (a)(2) mandates a final revocation hearing within a reasonable time to determine whether the probationer has, in fact, violated the conditions of his probation and whether his probation should be revoked. Ordinarily this time will be measured from the time of the probable cause finding (if a preliminary hearing was held) or of the issuance of an order to show cause. However, what constitutes a reasonable time must be determined on the facts of the particular case, such as whether the probationer is available or could readily be made available. If the probationer has been convicted of and is incarcerated for a new crime, and that conviction is the basis of the pending revocation proceedings, it would be relevant whether the probationer waived appearance at the revocation hearing.

The hearing required by rule 32.1(a)(2) is not a formal trial; the usual rules of evidence need not be applied. See *Morrissey v. Brewer,* supra ("the process should be flexible enough to consider evidence including letters, affidavits, and other material that would not be admissible in an adversary criminal trial"); Rule 1101(d)(e) of the Federal Rules of Evidence (rules not applicable to proceedings "granting or revoking probation"). Evidence that would establish guilt beyond a reasonable doubt is not required to support an order revoking probation. *United States v. Francischine,* 512 F.2d 827 (5th Cir.1975). This hearing may be waived by the probationer.

Subdivisions (a)(2)(A)–(E) list the rights to which a probationer is entitled at the final revocation hearing. The final hearing is less a summary one because the decision under consideration is the ultimate decision to revoke rather than a mere determination of probable cause. Thus, the probationer has certain rights not granted at the preliminary hearing: (i) the notice under (A) must be written; (ii) under (B) disclosure of all the evidence against the probationer is required; and (iii) under (D) the probationer does not have to specifically request the right to confront adverse witnesses, and the court may not limit the opportunity to question the witnesses against him.

Under subdivision (a)(2)(E) the probationer must be given notice of his right to be represented by counsel. Although *Scarpelli* holds that the Constitution does not compel counsel in all probation revocation hearings, under 18 U.S.C. § 3006A(b) a defendant is entitled to be represented by counsel whenever charged "with a violation of probation."

Revocation of probation is proper if the court finds a violation of the conditions of probation and that such violation warrants revocation. Revocation followed by imprisonment is an appropriate disposition if the court finds on the basis of the original offense and the intervening conduct of the probationer that:

(i) confinement is necessary to protect the public from further criminal activity by the offender; or

(ii) the offender is in need of correctional treatment which can most effectively be provided if he is confined; or

(iii) it would unduly depreciate the seriousness of the violation if probation were not revoked.

See American Bar Association, Standards Relating to Probation § 5.1 (Approved Draft, 1970).

If probation is revoked, the probationer may be required to serve the sentence originally imposed, or any lesser sentence, and if imposition of sentence was suspended he may receive any sentence which might have been imposed. 18 U.S.C. § 3653. When a split sentence is imposed under 18 U.S.C. § 3651 and probation is subsequently revoked, the probationer is entitled to credit for the time served in jail but not for the time he was on probation. *Thomas v. United States,* 327 F.2d 795 (10th Cir.), cert. denied 377 U.S. 1000 (1964); *Schley v. Peyton,* 280 F.Supp. 307 (W.D.Va.1968).

Rule 32.1(b). Subdivision (b) concerns proceedings on modification of probation (as provided for in 18 U.S.C. § 3651). The probationer should have the right to apply to the sentencing court for a clarification or change of conditions. American Bar Association, Standards Relating to Probation § 3.1(c) (Approved Draft, 1970). This avenue is important for two reasons: (1) the probationer should be able to obtain resolution of a dispute over an ambiguous term or the meaning of a condition without first having to violate it; and (2) in cases of neglect, overwork, or simply unreasonableness on the part of the probation officer, the probationer should have recourse to the sentencing court when a condition needs clarification or modification.

Probation conditions should be subject to modification, for the sentencing court must be able to respond to changes in the probationer's circumstances as well as new ideas and methods of rehabilitation. See generally ABA Standards, supra, § 3.3. The sentencing court is given the authority to shorten the term or end probation early upon its own motion without a hearing. And while the modification of probation is a part of the sentencing procedure, so that the probationer is ordinarily entitled to a hearing and presence of counsel, a modification favorable to the probationer may be accomplished without a hearing in the presence of defendant and counsel. *United States v. Bailey,* 343 F.Supp. 76 (W.D.Mo.1971).

1987 AMENDMENT

The amendments are technical. No substantive change is intended.

EDITORIAL NOTES

Effective Date of 1986 Amendment. Section 12(c)(2) of Pub.L. 99–646 provided that: "The amendments made by subsection (b) [amending subd. (b) of this rule] shall take effect 30 days after the date of enactment of this Act [Nov. 10, 1986]."

Rule 33. New Trial

The court on motion of a defendant may grant a new trial to that defendant if required in the interest of justice. If trial was by the court without a jury the court on motion of a defendant for a new trial may vacate the judgment if entered, take additional testimony and direct the entry of a new judgment. A motion for a new trial based on the ground of newly discovered evidence may be made only before or within two years after final judgment, but if an appeal is pending the court may grant the motion only on remand of the case. A motion for a new trial based on any other grounds shall be made within 7 days after verdict or finding of guilty or within such further time as the court may fix during the 7–day period.

(As amended Feb. 28, 1966, eff. July 1, 1966; Mar. 9, 1987, eff. Aug. 1, 1987.)

NOTES OF ADVISORY COMMITTEE ON RULES

This rule enlarges the time limit for motions for new trial on the ground of newly discovered evidence, from 60 days to two years; and for motions for new trial on other grounds from three to five days. Otherwise, it substantially continues existing practice. See Rule II of the Criminal Appeals Rules of 1933, 292 U.S. 661 [18 U.S.C. formerly following § 688]. Cf. Rule 59(a) of the Federal Rules of Civil Procedure, 28 U.S.C., Appendix.

1966 AMENDMENT

The amendments to the first two sentences make it clear that a judge has no power to order a new trial on his own motion, that he can act only in response to a motion timely made by a defendant. Problems of double jeopardy arise when the court acts on its own motion. See *United States v. Smith,* 331 U.S. 469 (1947). These amendments do not, of course, change the power which the court has in certain circumstances, prior to verdict or finding of guilty, to declare a mistrial and order a new trial on its own motion. See e.g., *Gori v. United States,* 367 U.S. 364 (1961); *Downum v. United States,* 372 U.S. 734 (1963); *United States v. Tateo,* 377 U.S. 463 (1964). The amendment to the last sentence changes the time in which the motion may be made to 7 days. See the Advisory Committee's Note to Rule 29.

1987 AMENDMENT

The amendment is technical. No substantive change is intended.

Rule 34.   Arrest of Judgment

The court on motion of a defendant shall arrest judgment if the indictment or information does not charge an offense or if the court was without jurisdiction of the offense charged. The motion in arrest of judgment shall be made within 7 days after verdict or finding of guilty, or after plea of guilty or *nolo contendere,* or within such further time as the court may fix during the 7–day period.

(As amended Feb. 28, 1966, eff. July 1, 1966.)

NOTES OF ADVISORY COMMITTEE ON RULES

This rule continues existing law except that it enlarges the time for making motions in arrest of judgment from 3 days to 5 days. See Rule II(2) of Criminal Appeals Rules of 1933, 292 U.S.C. 661 [18 U.S.C. formerly following § 688].

1966 AMENDMENT

The words "on motion of a defendant" are added to make clear here, as in Rule 33, that the court may act only pursuant to a timely motion by the defendant.

The amendment to the second sentence is designed to clarify an ambiguity in the rule as originally drafted. In *Lott v. United States,* 367 U.S. 421 (1961) the Supreme Court held that when a defendant pleaded nolo contendere the time in which a motion could be made under this rule did not begin to run until entry of the judgment. The Court held that such a plea was not a "determination of guilty." No reason of policy appears to justify having the time for making this motion commence with the verdict or finding of guilt but not with the acceptance of the plea of nolo contendere or the plea of guilty. The amendment changes the result in the *Lott* case and makes the periods uniform. The amendment also changes the time in which the motion may be made to 7 days. See the Advisory Committee's Note to Rule 29.

Rule 35.   Correction of Sentence

(a) Correction of a Sentence on Remand. The court shall correct a sentence that is determined on appeal under 18 U.S.C. 3742 to have been imposed in violation of law, to have been imposed as a result of an incorrect application of the sentencing guidelines, or to be unreasonable, upon remand of the case to the court—

    (1) for imposition of a sentence in accord with the findings of the court of appeals; or

    (2) for further sentencing proceedings if, after such proceedings, the court determines that the original sentence was incorrect.

(b) Correction of Sentence for Changed Circumstances. The court, on motion of the Government, may within one year after the imposition of a sentence, lower a sentence to reflect a defendant's subsequent, substantial assistance in the investigation or prosecution of another person who has committed an offense, in accordance with the guidelines and policy statements issued by the Sentencing Commission pursuant to section 994 of title 28, United States Code. The court's authority to lower a sentence under this subdivision includes the authority to lower such sentence to a level below that established by statute as a minimum sentence.

(As amended Feb. 28, 1966, eff. July 1, 1966; Apr. 30, 1979, eff. Aug. 1, 1979; Apr. 28, 1983, eff. Aug. 1, 1983; Oct. 12, 1984, Pub.L. 98–473, Title II, § 215(b), 98 Stat. 2015; Apr. 29, 1985, eff. Aug. 1, 1985; Oct. 27, 1986, Pub.L. 99–570, Title X, § 1009, 100 Stat. 3207–8.)

Rule Applicable to Offenses Committed Prior to Nov. 1, 1987

This rule as in effect prior to amendment by Pub.L. 98–473 read as follows:

Rule 35.   Correction or Reduction of Sentence

(a) Correction of Sentence. The court may correct an illegal sentence at any time and may correct a sentence imposed in an illegal manner within the time provided herein for the reduction of sentence.

(b) Reduction of Sentence. A motion to reduce a sentence may be made, or the court may reduce a sentence without motion, within 120 days after the sentence is imposed or probation is revoked, or within 120 days after receipt by the court of a mandate issued upon affirmance of the judgment or dismissal of the appeal, or within 120 days after entry of any order or judgment of the Supreme Court denying review of, or having the effect of upholding, a judgment of conviction or probation revocation. The court shall determine the motion within a reasonable time. Changing a sentence from a sentence of incarceration to a grant of probation shall constitute a permissible reduction of sentence under this subdivision.

For applicability of sentencing provisions to offenses, see Effective Date and Savings Provisions, etc., note, section 235 of Pub.L. 98–473, as amended, set out under section 3551 of Title 18, Crimes and Criminal Procedure. See, also, Codification note below.

NOTES OF ADVISORY COMMITTEE ON RULES

The first sentence of the rule continues existing law. The second sentence introduces a flexible time limitation on the power of the court to reduce a sentence, in lieu of the present limitation of the term of court. Rule 45(c) abolishes the expiration of a term of court as a time limitation, thereby necessitating the introduction of a specific time limitation as to all proceedings now governed by the term of court as a limitation. The Federal Rules of Civil Procedure (Rule 6(c)), 28 U.S.C. Appendix, abolishes the term of court as a time limitation in respect to civil actions. The two rules together thus do away with the significance of the expiration of a term of court which has largely become an anachronism.

1966 AMENDMENT

The amendment to the first sentence gives the court power to correct a sentence imposed in an illegal manner within the same time limits as those provided for reducing a sentence. In *Hill v. United States*, 368 U.S. 424 (1962) the court held that a motion to correct an illegal sentence was not an appropriate way for a defendant to raise the question whether when he appeared for sentencing the court had afforded him an opportunity to make a statement in his own behalf as required by Rule 32(a). The amendment recognizes the distinction between an illegal sentence, which may be corrected at any time, and a sentence imposed in an illegal manner, and provides a limited time for correcting the latter.

The second sentence has been amended to increase the time within which the court may act from 60 days to 120 days. The 60-day period is frequently too short to enable the defendant to obtain and file the evidence, information and argument to support a reduction in sentence. Especially where a defendant has been committed to an institution at a distance from the sentencing court, the delays involved in institutional mail inspection procedures and the time required to contact relatives, friends and counsel may result in the 60-day period passing before the court is able to consider the case.

The other amendments to the second sentence clarify ambiguities in the timing provisions. In those cases in which the mandate of the court of appeals is issued prior to action by the Supreme Court on the defendant's petition for certiorari, the rule created problems in three situations: (1) If the writ were denied, the last phrase of the rule left obscure the point at which the period began to run because orders of the Supreme Court denying applications for writs are not sent to the district courts. See *Johnson v. United States*, 235 F.2d 459 (5th Cir.1956). (2) If the writ were granted but later dismissed as improvidently granted, the rule did not provide any time period for reduction of sentence. (3) If the writ were granted and later the Court affirmed a judgment of the court of appeals which had affirmed

the conviction, the rule did not provide any time period for reduction of sentence. The amendment makes it clear that in each of these three situations the 120-period commences to run with the entry of the order or judgment of the Supreme Court.

The third sentence has been added to make it clear that the time limitation imposed by Rule 35 upon the reduction of a sentence does not apply to such reduction upon the revocation of probation as authorized by 18 U.S.C. § 3653.

1979 AMENDMENT

Rule 35 is amended in order to make it clear that a judge may, in his discretion, reduce a sentence of incarceration to probation. To the extent that this permits the judge to grant probation to a defendant who has already commenced service of a term of imprisonment, it represents a change in the law. See *United States v. Murray*, 275 U.S. 347 (1928) (Probation Act construed not to give power to district court to grant probation to convict after beginning of service of sentence, even in the same term of court); *Affronti v. United States*, 350 U.S. 79 (1955) (Probation Act construed to mean that after a sentence of consecutive terms on multiple counts of an indictment has been imposed and service of sentence for the first such term has commenced, the district court may not suspend sentence and grant probation as to the remaining term or terms). In construing the statute in *Murray* and *Affronti*, the Court concluded Congress could not have intended to make the probation provisions applicable during the *entire* period of incarceration (the only other conceivable interpretation of the statute), for this would result in undue duplication of the three methods of mitigating a sentence—probation, pardon and parole—and would impose upon district judges the added burden of responding to probation applications from prisoners throughout the service of their terms of imprisonment. Those concerns do not apply to the instant provisions, for the reduction may occur only within the time specified in subdivision (b). This change gives "meaningful effect" to the motion-to-reduce remedy by allowing the court "to consider all alternatives that were available at the time of imposition of the original sentence." *United States v. Golphin*, 362 F.Supp. 698 (W.D.Pa.1973).

Should the reduction to a sentence of probation occur after the defendant has been incarcerated more than six months, this would put into issue the applicability of 18 U.S.C. § 3651, which provides that initially the court "may impose a sentence in excess of six months and provide that the defendant be confined in a jail-type institution for a period not exceeding six months and that the execution of the remainder of the sentence be suspended and the defendant placed on probation for such period and upon such terms and conditions as the court deems best."

1983 AMENDMENT

Rule 35(b)

There is currently a split of authority on the question of whether a court may reduce a sentence within 120 days after revocation of probation when the sentence was imposed earlier but execution of the sentence had in the interim been suspended in part or in its entirety. Compare *United States v. Colvin,* 644 F.2d 703 (8th Cir.1981) (yes); *United States v. Johnson,* 634 F.2d 94 (3d Cir.1980) (yes); with *United States v. Rice,* 671 F.2d 455 (11th Cir.1982) (no); *United States v. Kahane,* 527 F.2d 491 (2d Cir.1975) (no). The Advisory Committee believes that the rule should be clarified in light of this split, and has concluded that as a policy matter the result reached in *Johnson* is preferable.

The Supreme Court declared in *Korematsu v. United States,* 319 U.S. 432, 435 (1943), that "the difference to the probationer between imposition of sentence followed by probation ... and suspension of the imposition of sentence [followed by probation]" is not a meaningful one. When imposition of sentence is suspended entirely at the time a defendant is placed on probation, that defendant has 120 days after revocation of probation and imposition of sentence to petition for leniency. The amendment to subdivision (b) makes it clear that similar treatment is to be afforded probationers for whom execution, rather than imposition, of sentence was originally suspended.

The change facilitates the underlying objective of rule 35, which is to "give every convicted defendant a second round before the sentencing judge, and [afford] the judge an opportunity to reconsider the sentence in the light of any further information about the defendant or the case which may have been presented to him in the interim." *United States v. Ellenbogan,* 390 F.2d 537, 543 (2d Cir.1968). It is only technically correct that a reduction may be sought when a suspended sentence is imposed. As noted in *Johnson,* supra, at 96:

> It frequently will be unrealistic for a defendant whose sentence has just been suspended to petition the court for the further relief of a reduction of that suspended sentence.

Just as significant, we doubt that sentencing judges would be very receptive to Rule 35 motions proffered at the time the execution of a term of imprisonment is suspended in whole or in part and the defendant given a term of probation. Moreover, the sentencing judge cannot know of events that might occur later and that might bear on what would constitute an appropriate term of imprisonment should the defendant violate his probation.... In particular, it is only with the revocation hearing that the judge is in a position to consider whether a sentence originally suspended pending probation should be reduced. The revocation hearing is thus the first point at which an offender can be afforded a realistic opportunity to plead for a light sentence. If the offender is to be provided two chances with the sentencing judge, to be meaningful this second sentence must occur subsequent to the revocation hearing.

1985 AMENDMENT

Rule 35(b)

This amendment to Rule 35(b) conforms its language to the nonliteral interpretation which most courts have already placed upon the rule, namely, that it suffices that the defendant's motion was made within the 120 days and that the court determines the motion within a reasonable time thereafter. *United States v. DeMier,* 671 F.2d 1200 (8th Cir.1982); *United States v. Smith,* 650 F.2d 206 (9th Cir.1981); *United States v. Johnson,* 634 F.2d 94 (3d Cir.1980); *United States v. Mendoza,* 581 F.2d 89 (5th Cir.1978); *United States v. Stollings,* 516 F.2d 1287 (4th Cir.1975). Despite these decisions, a change in the language is deemed desirable to remove any doubt which might arise from dictum in some cases, e.g., *United States v. Addonizio,* 442 U.S. 178, 189 (1979), that Rule 35 only "authorizes District Courts to reduce a sentence within 120 days" and that this time period "is jurisdictional, and may not be extended." See *United States v. Kajevic,* 711 F.2d 767 (7th Cir. 1983), following the *Addonizio* dictum.

As for the "reasonable time" limitation, reasonableness in this context "must be evaluated in light of the policies supporting the time limitations and the reasons for the delay in each case." *United States v. Smith,* supra, at 209. The time runs "at least for so long as the judge reasonably needs time to consider and act upon the motion." *United States v. Stollings,* supra, at 1288.

In some instances the court may decide to reduce a sentence even though no motion seeking such action is before the court. When that is the case, the amendment makes clear, the reduction must actually occur within the time specified.

This amendment does not preclude the filing of a motion by a defendant for further reduction of sentence after the court has reduced a sentence on its own motion, if filed within the 120 days specified in this rule.

EDITORIAL NOTES

Codification. Amendment of subsec. (b) by Supreme Court Order dated Apr. 29, 1985, eff. Aug. 1, 1985, which has been executed to text, to terminate Nov. 1, 1986, pursuant to section 2 of the Order, when section 215(b) of Pub.L. 98–473, Oct. 12, 1984, 98 Stat. 2015, becomes effective. Pub.L. 99–217, § 4, Dec. 26, 1985, 99 Stat. 1728, amended section 235(a)(1) of Pub.L. 98–473, which provided for effective date for section 215(b) of Pub.L. 98–473, to provide for effective date of Nov. 1, 1987.

See section 22 of Pub.L. 100–182, set out as a note below.

Effective Date of 1986 Amendment. Section 1009(b) of Pub.L. 99–570 provided that: "The amendment made by this section [amending subd. (a)] shall take effect on the date of the taking effect of rule 35(b) of the Federal Rules of Criminal Procedure, as amended by section 215(b) of the Comprehensive Crime Control Act of 1984 [Nov. 1, 1987]."

Effective Date and Savings Provisions of 1984 Amendment. Amendment by Pub.L. 98–473 effective on the first day of first calendar month beginning thirty six months after Oct. 12, 1984, applicable only to offenses committed after taking effect of sections 211 to 239 of Pub.L. 98–473, and except as otherwise provided for therein, see section 235 of Pub.L. 98–473, as amended, set out as a note under section 3551 of Title 18, Crimes and Criminal Procedure.

Application of Rule 35(b) to Conduct Occurring Before Effective Date of Sentencing Guidelines. Pub.L. 100–182, § 22, Dec. 7, 1987, 101 Stat. 1271, provided that: "The amendment to rule 35(b) of the Federal Rules of Criminal Procedure [subd. (b) of this rule] made by the order of the Supreme Court on April 29, 1985, shall apply with respect to all offenses committed before the taking effect of section 215(b) of the Comprehensive Crime Control Act of 1984 [section 215(b) of Pub.L. 98–473, which amended this rule]."

Authority to Lower Sentences Below Statutory Minimum for Old Offenses. Subd. (b) of this rule as amended by section 215(b) of Pub.L. 98–473 and subd. (b) of this rule as in effect before the taking effect of the initial set of guidelines promulgated by the United States Sentencing Commission pursuant to chapter 58 (§ 991 et seq.) of Title 28, Judiciary and Judicial Procedure, to apply in the case of an offense committed before the taking effect of such guidelines notwithstanding section 235 of Pub.L. 98–473, see section 24 of Pub.L. 100–182, set out as a note under section 3553 of Title 18, Crimes and Criminal Procedure.

Rule 36. Clerical Mistakes

Clerical mistakes in judgments, orders or other parts of the record and errors in the record arising from oversight or omission may be corrected by the court at any time and after such notice, if any, as the court orders.

NOTES OF ADVISORY COMMITTEE ON RULES

This rule continues existing law. *Rupinski v. United States,* 4 F.2d 17, C.C.A.6th. The rule is similar to Rule 60(a) of the Federal Rules of Civil Procedure, 28 U.S.C., Appendix.

[VIII.   APPEAL] (Abrogated Dec. 4, 1967, eff. July 1, 1968)

[Rule 37. Taking Appeal; and Petition for Writ of Certiorari.] (Abrogated Dec. 4, 1967, Eff. July 1, 1968)

NOTES OF ADVISORY COMMITTEE ON RULES

These are the criminal rules [Rules 37, 38(b), (c), 39] relating to appeals, the provisions of which are transferred to and covered by the Federal Rules of Appellate Procedure and (in the case of Rule 37(b) and (c), taking appeal to the Supreme Court and petition for review on writ of certiorari, respectively) by the Rules of the Supreme Court.

Rule 38. Stay of Execution

(a) Death. A sentence of death shall be stayed if an appeal is taken from the conviction or sentence.

(b) Imprisonment. A sentence of imprisonment shall be stayed if an appeal is taken from the conviction or sentence and the defendant is released pending disposition of appeal pursuant to Rule 9(b) of the Federal Rules of Appellate Procedure. If not stayed, the court may recommend to the Attorney General that the defendant be retained at, or transferred to, a place of confinement near the place of trial or the place where an appeal is to be heard, for a period reasonably necessary to permit the defendant to assist in the preparation of an appeal to the court of appeals.

(c) Fine. A sentence to pay a fine or a fine and costs, if an appeal is taken, may be stayed by the district court or by the court of appeals upon such terms as the court deems proper. The court may require the defendant pending appeal to deposit the whole or any part of the fine and costs in the registry of the district court, or to give bond for the payment thereof, or to submit to an examination of assets, and it may make any appropriate order to restrain the defendant from dissipating such defendant's assets.

(d) Probation. A sentence of probation may be stayed if an appeal from the conviction or sentence is taken. If the sentence is stayed, the court shall fix the terms of the stay.

(e) Criminal Forfeiture, Notice to Victims, and Restitution. A sanction imposed as part of the sentence pursuant to 18 U.S.C. 3554, 3555, or 3556 may, if an appeal of the conviction or sentence is taken, be stayed by the district court or by the court of appeals upon such terms as the court finds appropriate. The court may issue such orders as may be reasonably necessary to ensure compliance with the sanction upon disposition of the appeal, including the entering of a restraining order or an injunction or requiring a deposit in whole or in part of the monetary amount involved into the registry of the district court or execution of a performance bond.

(f) Disabilities. A civil or employment disability arising under a Federal statute by reason of the defendant's conviction or sentence, may, if an appeal is taken, be stayed by the district court or by the court of appeals upon such terms as the court finds appropriate. The court may enter a restraining order or an injunction, or take any other action that may be reasonably necessary to protect the interest represented by the disability pending disposition of the appeal.

(As amended Dec. 27, 1948, eff. Jan. 1, 1949; Feb. 28, 1966, eff. July 1, 1966; Dec. 4, 1967, eff. July 1, 1968; Apr. 24, 1972, eff. Oct. 1, 1972; Oct. 12, 1984, Pub.L. 98–473, Title II, § 215(c), 98 Stat. 2016; Mar. 9, 1987, eff. Aug. 1, 1987.)

Rule Applicable to Offenses Committed Prior to Nov. 1, 1987

This rule as in effect prior to amendment by Pub.L. 98–473 read as follows:

Rule 38. Stay of Execution, and Relief Pending Review

(a) Stay of Execution.

(1) **Death.** A sentence of death shall be stayed if an appeal is taken.

(2) **Imprisonment.** A sentence of imprisonment shall be stayed if an appeal is taken and the defendant is released pending disposition of appeal pursuant to Rule 9(b) of the Federal Rules of Appellate Procedure. If not stayed, the court may recommend to the Attorney General that the defendant be retained at, or transferred to, a place of confinement near the place of trial or the place where an appeal is to be heard, for a period reasonably necessary to permit the defendant to assist in the preparation of an appeal to the court of appeals.

(3) **Fine.** A sentence to pay a fine or a fine and costs, if an appeal is taken, may be stayed by the district court or by the court of appeals upon such terms as the court deems proper. The court may require the defendant pending appeal to deposit the whole or any part of the fine and costs in the registry of the district court, or to give bond for the payment thereof, or to submit to an examination of assets, and it may make any appropriate order to restrain the defendant from dissipating such defendant's assets.

(4) **Probation.** An order placing the defendant on probation may be stayed if an appeal is taken. If not stayed, the court shall specify when the term of probation shall commence. If the order is stayed the court shall fix the terms of the stay.

[**(b) Bail.**] (Abrogated Dec. 4, 1967, eff. July 1, 1968)

[**(c) Application for Relief Pending Review.**] (Abrogated Dec. 4, 1967, eff. July 1, 1968)

For applicability of sentencing provisions to offenses, see Effective Date and Savings Provisions, etc., note, section 235 of Pub.L. 98–473, as amended, set out under section 3551 of Title 18, Crimes and Criminal Procedure.

NOTES OF ADVISORY COMMITTEE ON RULES

This rule substantially continues existing law except that it provides that in case an appeal is taken from a judgment imposing a sentence of imprisonment, a stay shall be granted only if the defendant so elects, or is admitted to bail. Under the present rule the sentence is automatically stayed unless the defendant elects to commence service of the sentence pending appeal. The new rule merely changes the burden of making the election. See Rule V of the Criminal Appeals Rules, 1933, 292 U.S. 661 [18 U.S.C. formerly following § 688].

1966 AMENDMENT

A defendant sentenced to a term of imprisonment is committed to the custody of the Attorney General who is empowered by statute to designate the place of his confinement. 18 U.S.C. § 4082. The sentencing court has no authority to designate the place of imprisonment. See, e.g., *Hogue v. United States*, 287 F.2d 99 (5th Cir.1961), cert. den., 368 U.S. 932 (1961).

When the place of imprisonment has been designated, and notwithstanding the pendency of an appeal, the defendant is usually transferred from the place of his temporary detention within the district of his conviction unless he has elected "not to commence service of the sentence." This transfer can be avoided only if the defendant makes the election, a course sometimes advised by counsel who may deem it necessary to consult with the defendant from time to time before the appeal is finally perfected. However, the election deprives the defendant of a right to claim credit for the time spent in jail pending the disposition of the appeal because 18 U.S.C. § 3568 provides that the sentence of imprisonment commences, to run only from "the date on which such person is received at the penitentiary, reformatory, or jail for service of said sentence." See, e.g., *Shelton v. United States*, 234 F.2d 132 (5th Cir.1956).

The amendment eliminates the procedure for election not to commence service of sentence. In lieu thereof it is provided that the court may recommend to the Attorney General that the defendant be retained at or transferred to a place of confinement near the place of trial or the place where the appeal is to be heard for the period reasonably necessary to permit the defendant to assist in the preparation of his appeal to the court of appeals. Under this procedure the defendant would no longer be required to serve dead time in a local jail in order to assist in preparation of his appeal.

1968 AMENDMENT

Subdivisions (b) and (c) of this rule relate to appeals, the provisions of which are transferred to and covered by the Federal Rules of Appellate Procedure. See Advisory Committee Note under rule 37.

1972 AMENDMENT

Rule 38(a)(2) is amended to reflect rule 9(b), Federal Rules of Appellate Procedure. The criteria for the stay of a sentence of imprisonment pending disposition of an appeal are those specified in rule 9(c) which incorporates 18 U.S.C. § 3148 by reference.

The last sentence of subdivision (a)(2) is retained although easy access to the defendant has become less important with the passage of the Criminal Justice Act which provides for compensation to the attorney to travel to the place at which the defendant is confined. Whether the court will recommend confinement near the place of trial or place where the appeal is to be heard will depend upon a balancing of convenience against the possible advantage of confinement at a more remote correctional institution where facilities and program may be more adequate.

The amendment to subdivision (a)(4) gives the court discretion in deciding whether to stay the order placing the defendant on probation. It also makes mandatory the fixing of conditions for the stay if a stay is granted. The court cannot release the defendant pending appeal without either placing him on probation or fixing the conditions for the stay under the Bail Reform Act, 18 U.S.C. § 3148.

Former rule 38(a)(4) makes mandatory a stay of an order placing the defendant on probation whenever an appeal is noted. The court may or may not impose conditions upon the stay. See rule 46, Federal Rules of Criminal Procedure; and the Bail Reform Act, 18 U.S.C. § 3148.

Having the defendant on probation during the period of appeal may serve the objectives of both community protection and defendant rehabilitation. In current practice, the order of probation is sometimes stayed for an appeal period as long as two years. In a situation where the appeal is unsuccessful, the defendant must start under probation supervision after so long a time that the conditions of probation imposed at the time of initial sentencing may no longer appropriately relate either to the defendant's need for rehabilitation or to the community's need for protection. The purposes of probation are more likely to be served if the judge can exercise discretion, in appropriate cases, to require the defendant to be under probation during the period of appeal. The American Bar Association Project on Standards for Criminal Justice takes the position that prompt imposition of sentence aids in the rehabilitation of defendants, ABA Standards Relating to Pleas of Guilty § 1.8(a)(i), Commentary p. 40 (Approved Draft, 1968). See also Sutherland and Cressey, Principles of Criminology 336 (1966).

Under 18 U.S.C. § 3148 the court now has discretion to impose conditions of release which are necessary to protect the community against danger from the defendant. This is in contrast to release prior to conviction, where the only appropriate criterion is insuring the appearance of the defendant. 18 U.S.C. § 3146. Because the court may impose conditions of release to insure community protection, it seems appropriate to enable the court to do so by ordering the defendant to submit to probation supervision during the period of appeal, thus giving the probation service responsibility for supervision.

A major difference between probation and release under 18 U.S.C. § 3148 exists if the defendant violates the conditions imposed upon his release. In the event that release is under 18 U.S.C. § 3148, the violation of the condition may result in his being placed in custody pending the decision on appeal. If the appeal were unsuccessful, the order placing him on probation presumably would become effective at that time, and he would then be released under probation supervision. If the defendant were placed on probation, his violation of a condition could result in the imposition of a jail or prison sentence. If the appeal were unsuccessful, the jail or prison sentence would continue to be served.

1987 AMENDMENT

The amendments are technical. No substantive change is intended.

EDITORIAL NOTES

References in Text. The Federal Rules of Appellate Procedure, referred to in subsec. (b), are set out in this pamphlet.

Effective Date and Savings Provisions of 1984 Amendment. Amendment by Pub.L. 98–473 effective on the first day of first calendar month beginning thirty six months after Oct. 12, 1984, applicable only to offenses committed after taking effect of sections 211 to 239 of Pub.L. 98–473, and except as otherwise provided for therein, see section 235 of Pub.L. 98–473, as amended, set out as a note under section 3551 of Title 18, Crimes and Criminal Procedure.

[Rule 39. Supervision of Appeal.] (Abrogated Dec. 4, 1967, Eff. July 1, 1968)

NOTES OF ADVISORY COMMITTEE ON RULES

This rule relating to appeals is abrogated since the provisions of the rule are transferred to and covered by

the Federal Rules of Appellate Procedure. See Advisory Committee Note under rule 37.

IX. SUPPLEMENTARY AND SPECIAL PROCEEDINGS

Rule 40. Commitment to Another District

(a) Appearance Before Federal Magistrate. If a person is arrested in a district other than that in which the offense is alleged to have been committed, that person shall be taken without unnecessary delay before the nearest available federal magistrate. Preliminary proceedings concerning the defendant shall be conducted in accordance with Rules 5 and 5.1, except that if no preliminary examination is held because an indictment has been returned or an information filed or because the defendant elects to have the preliminary examination conducted in the district in which the prosecution is pending, the person shall be held to answer upon a finding that such person is the person named in the indictment, information or warrant. If held to answer, the defendant shall be held to answer in the district court in which the prosecution is pending, provided that a warrant is issued in that district if the arrest was made without a warrant, upon production of the warrant or a certified copy thereof.

(b) Statement by Federal Magistrate. In addition to the statements required by Rule 5, the federal magistrate shall inform the defendant of the provisions of Rule 20.

(c) Papers. If a defendant is held or discharged, the papers in the proceeding and any bail taken shall be transmitted to the clerk of the district court in which the prosecution is pending.

(d) Arrest of Probationer. If a person is arrested for a violation of probation in a district other than the district having probation jurisdiction, such person shall be taken without unnecessary delay before the nearest available federal magistrate. The federal magistrate shall:

(1) Proceed under Rule 32.1 if jurisdiction over the probationer is transferred to that district pursuant to 18 U.S.C. § 3605;

(2) Hold a prompt preliminary hearing if the alleged violation occurred in that district, and either (i) hold the probationer to answer in the district court of the district having probation jurisdiction or (ii) dismiss the proceedings and so notify that court; or

(3) Otherwise order the probationer held to answer in the district court of the district having probation jurisdiction upon production of certified copies of the probation order, the warrant, and the application for the warrant, and upon a finding that the person before the magistrate is the person named in the warrant.

(e) Arrest for Failure to Appear. If a person is arrested on a warrant in a district other than that in which the warrant was issued, and the warrant was issued because of the failure of the person named therein to appear as required pursuant to a subpoena or the terms of that person's release, the person arrested shall be taken without unnecessary delay before the nearest available federal magistrate. Upon production of the warrant or a certified copy thereof and upon a finding that the person before the magistrate is the person named in the warrant, the federal magistrate shall hold the person to answer in the district in which the warrant was issued.

(f) Release or Detention. If a person was previously detained or conditionally released, pursuant to chapter 207 of title 18, United States Code, in another district where a warrant, information, or indictment issued, the federal magistrate shall take into account the decision previously made and the reasons set forth therefor, if any, but will not be bound by that decision. If the federal magistrate amends the release or detention decision or alters the conditions of release, the magistrate shall set forth the reasons therefore [1] in writing.

(As amended Feb. 28, 1966, eff. July 1, 1966; Apr. 24, 1972, eff. Oct. 1, 1972; Apr. 30, 1979, eff. Aug. 1, 1979; July 31, 1979, Pub.L. 96–42, § 1(2), 93 Stat. 326; Apr. 28, 1982, eff. Aug. 1, 1982; Oct. 12, 1984, Pub.L. 98–473, Title II, §§ 209(c), 215(d),

98 Stat. 1986, 2016; Mar. 9, 1987, eff. Aug. 1, 1987.)

1. So in original.

Subd. (d) of this Rule Applicable to Offenses Committed Prior to Nov. 1, 1987

Subd. (d) of this rule as in effect prior to amendment by Pub.L. 98–473 read as follows:

(d) Arrest of Probationer. If a person is arrested for a violation of probation in a district other than the district having probation jurisdiction, such person shall be taken without unnecessary delay before the nearest available federal magistrate. The federal magistrate shall:

(1) Proceed under Rule 32.1 if jurisdiction over the probationer is transferred to that district pursuant to 18 U.S.C. § 3653;

(2) Hold a prompt preliminary hearing if the alleged violation occurred in that district, and either (i) hold the probationer to answer in the district court of the district having probation jurisdiction or (ii) dismiss the proceedings and so notify that court; or

(3) Otherwise order the probationer held to answer in the district court of the district having probation jurisdiction upon production of certified copies of the probation order, the warrant, and the application for the warrant, and upon a finding that the person before the magistrate is the person named in the warrant.

For applicability of sentencing provisions to offenses, see Effective Date and Savings Provisions, etc., note, section 235 of Pub.L. 98–473, as amended, set out under section 3551 of Title 18, Crimes and Criminal Procedure.

NOTES OF ADVISORY COMMITTEE ON RULES

1. This rule modifies and revamps existing procedure. The present practice has developed as a result of a series of judicial decisions, the only statute dealing with the subject being exceedingly general, 18 U.S.C. former § 591 (now § 3041) (Arrest and removal for trial):

For any crime or offense against the United States, the offender may, by any justice or judge of the United States, or by any United States commissioner, or by any chancellor, judge of a supreme or superior court, chief or first judge of common pleas, mayor of a city, justice of the peace, or other magistrate, of any State where he may be found, and agreeably to the usual mode of process against offenders in such State, and at the expense of the United States, be arrested and imprisoned, or bailed, as the case may be, for trial before such court of the United States as by law has cognizance of the offense. * * * Where any offender or witness is committed in any district other than that where the offense is to be tried, it shall be the duty of the judge of

the district where such offender or witness is imprisoned, seasonably to issue, and of the marshal to execute, a warrant for his removal to the district where the trial is to be had.

The scope of a removal hearing, the issues to be considered, and other similar matters are governed by judicial decisions, *Beavers v. Henkel,* 194 U.S. 73, 24 S.Ct. 605, 48 L.Ed. 882; *Tinsley v. Treat,* 205 U.S. 20, 27 S.Ct. 430, 51 L.Ed. 689; *Henry v. Henkel,* 235 U.S. 219; *Rodman v. Pothier,* 264 U.S. 399, 44 S.Ct. 360, 68 L.Ed. 759; *Morse v. United States,* 267 U.S. 80, 45 S.Ct. 209, 69 L.Ed. 522; *Fetters v. United States ex rel. Cunningham,* 283 U.S. 638, 51 S.Ct. 596, 75 L.Ed. 1321; *United States ex rel. Kassin v. Mulligan,* 295 U.S. 396, 55 S.Ct. 781, 79 L.Ed. 1501; see, also, 9 Edmunds, Cyclopedia of Federal Procedure 3905, et seq.

2. The purpose of removal proceedings is to accord safeguards to a defendant against an improvident removal to a distant point for trial. On the other hand, experience has shown that removal proceedings have at times been used by defendants for dilatory purposes and in attempting to frustrate prosecution by preventing or postponing transportation even as between adjoining districts and between places a few miles apart. The object of the rule is adequately to meet each of these two situations.

3. For the purposes of removal, all cases in which the accused is apprehended in a district other than that in which the prosecution is pending have been divided into two groups: first, those in which the place of arrest is either in another district of the same State, or if in another State, then less than 100 miles from the place where the prosecution is pending; and second, cases in which the arrest occurs in a State other than that in which the prosecution is pending and the place of arrest is 100 miles or more distant from the latter place.

In the first group of cases, removal proceedings are abolished. The defendant's right to the usual preliminary hearing is, of course, preserved, but the committing magistrate, if he holds defendant would bind him over to the district court in which the prosecution is pending. As ordinarily there are no removal proceedings in State prosecutions as between different parts of the same State, but the accused is transported by virtue of the process under which he was arrested, it seems reasonable that no removal proceedings should be required in the Federal courts as between districts in the same State. The provision as to arrest in another State but at a place less than 100 miles from the place where the prosecution is pending was added in order to preclude obstruction against bringing the defendant a short distance for trial.

In the second group of cases mentioned in the first paragraph, removal proceedings are continued. The practice to be followed in removal hearings will depend on whether the demand for removal is based upon an indictment or upon an information or complaint. In the latter case, proof of identity and proof of reasonable cause to believe the defendant guilty will have to be adduced in order to justify the issuance of a warrant of removal. In the former case, proof of identity coupled with a certified copy of the indictment will be sufficient, as the indictment will be conclusive proof of probable cause. The distinction is based on the fact that in case of an indictment, the grand jury, which is an arm of the court, has already found probable cause. Since the action of the grand jury is not subject to review by a district judge in the district in which the grand jury sits, it seems illogical to permit such review collaterally in a removal proceeding by a judge in another district.

4. For discussions of this rule see, Homer Cummings, 29 A.B.A.Jour. 654, 656; Holtzoff, 3 F.R.D. 445, 450–452; Holtzoff, 12 George Washington L.R. 119, 127–130; Holtzoff, The Federal Bar Journal, October 1944, 18–37; Berge, 42 Mich.L.R. 353, 374; Medalie, 4 Lawyers Guild R. (3)1, 4.

Note to Subdivision (b). The rule provides that all removal hearings shall take place before a United States commissioner or a Federal judge. It does not confer such jurisdiction on State or local magistrates. While theoretically under existing law State and local magistrates have authority to conduct removal hearings, nevertheless as a matter of universal practice, such proceedings are always conducted before a United States commissioner or a Federal judge, 9 Edmunds, Cyclopedia of Federal Procedure 3919.

1966 AMENDMENT

The amendment conforms to the change made in the corresponding procedure in Rule 5(b).

1972 AMENDMENT

Subdivision (a) is amended to make clear that the person shall be taken before the federal magistrate "without unnecessary delay." Although the former rule was silent in this regard, it probably would have been interpreted to require prompt appearance, and there is therefore advantage in making this explicit in the rule itself. See C. Wright, Federal Practice and Procedure: Criminal § 652 (1969, Supp.1971). Subdivision (a) is amended to also make clear that the person is to be brought before a "federal magistrate" rather than a state or local magistrate authorized by 18 U.S.C. § 3041. The former rules were inconsistent in this regard. Although rule 40(a) provided that the person may be brought before a state or local officer authorized by former rule 5(a), such state or local officer lacks authority to conduct a preliminary examination under rule 5(c), and a principal purpose of the appearance is to hold a preliminary examination where no prior indictment or information has issued. The Federal Magistrates Act should make it possible to bring a person before a federal magistrate. See C. Wright, Federal

Practice and Procedure: Criminal § 653, especially n. 35 (1969, Supp.1971).

Subdivision (b)(2) is amended to provide that the federal magistrate should inform the defendant of the fact that he may avail himself of the provisions of rule 20 if applicable in the particular case. However, the failure to so notify the defendant should not invalidate the removal procedure. Although the old rule is silent in this respect, it is current practice to so notify the defendant, and it seems desirable, therefore, to make this explicit in the rule itself.

The requirement that an order of removal under subdivision (b)(3) can be made only by a judge of the United States and cannot be made by a United States magistrate is retained. However, subdivision (b)(5) authorizes issuance of the warrant of removal by a United States magistrate if he is authorized to do so by a rule of district court adopted in accordance with 28 U.S.C. § 636(b):

Any district court * * * by the concurrence of a majority of all the judges * * * may establish rules pursuant to which any full-time United States magistrate * * * may be assigned * * * such additional duties as are not inconsistent with the Constitution and laws of the United States.

Although former rule 40(b)(3) required that the warrant of removal be issued by a judge of the United States, there appears no constitutional or statutory prohibition against conferring this authority upon a United States magistrate in accordance with 28 U.S.C. § 636(b). The background history is dealt with in detail in 8A J. Moore, Federal Practice ¶¶ 40.01 and 40.02 (2d ed. Cipes 1970, Supp.1971).

Subdivision (b)(4) makes explicit reference to provisions of the Bail Reform Act of 1966 by incorporating a cross-reference to 18 U.S.C. § 3146 and § 3148.

1979 AMENDMENT

This substantial revision of rule 40 abolishes the present distinction between arrest in a nearby district and arrest in a distant district, clarifies the authority of the magistrate with respect to the setting of bail where bail had previously been fixed in the other district, adds a provision dealing with arrest of a probationer in a district other than the district of supervision, and adds a provision dealing with arrest of a defendant or witness for failure to appear in another district.

Note to Subdivision (a). Under subdivision (a) of the present rule, if a person is arrested in a nearby district (another district in the same state, or a place less than 100 miles away), the usual rule 5 and 5.1 preliminary proceedings are conducted. But under subdivision (b) of the present rule, if a person is arrested in a distant district, then a hearing leading to a warrant of removal is held. New subdivision (a) would make no distinction between these two situations and would pro-

Rule 40 THE FEDERAL MODEL

vide for rule 5 and 5.1 proceedings in all instances in which the arrest occurs outside the district where the warrant issues or where the offense is alleged to have been committed.

This abolition of the distinction between arrest in a nearby district and arrest in a distant district rests upon the conclusion that the procedures prescribed in rules 5 and 5.1 are adequate to protect the rights of an arrestee wherever he might be arrested. If the arrest is without a warrant, it is necessary under rule 5 that a complaint be filed forthwith complying with the requirements of rule 4(a) with respect to the showing of probable cause. If the arrest is with a warrant, that warrant will have been issued upon the basis of an indictment or of a complaint or information showing probable cause, pursuant to rules 4(a) and 9(a). Under rule 5.1, dealing with the preliminary examination, the defendant is to be held to answer only upon a showing of probable cause that an offense has been committed and that the defendant committed it.

Under subdivision (a), there are two situations in which no preliminary examination will be held. One is where "an indictment has been returned or an information filed," which pursuant to rule 5(c) obviates the need for a preliminary examination. The other is where "the defendant elects to have the preliminary examination conducted in the district in which the prosecution is pending." A defendant might wish to elect that alternative when, for example, the law in that district is that the complainant and other material witnesses may be required to appear at the preliminary examination and give testimony. See *Washington v. Clemmer,* 339 F.2d 715 (D.C.Cir.1964).

New subdivision (a) continues the present requirement that if the arrest was without a warrant a warrant must thereafter issue in the district in which the offense is alleged to have been committed. This will ensure that in the district of anticipated prosecution there will have been a probable cause determination by a magistrate or grand jury.

Note to Subdivision (b). New subdivision (b) follows existing subdivision (b)(2) in requiring the magistrate to inform the defendant of the provisions of rule 20 applicable in the particular case. Failure to so notify the defendant should not invalidate the proceedings.

Note to Subdivision (c). New subdivision (c) follows existing subdivision (b)(4) as to transmittal of papers.

Note to Subdivision (d). New subdivision (d) has no counterpart in the present rule. It provides a procedure for dealing with the situation in which a probationer is arrested in a district other than the district of supervision, consistent with 18 U.S.C. § 3653, which provides in part:

If the probationer shall be arrested in any district other than that in which he was last supervised, he

shall be returned to the district in which the warrant was issued, unless jurisdiction over him is transferred as above provided to the district in which he is found, and in that case he shall be detained pending further proceedings in such district.

One possibility, provided for in subdivision (d)(1), is that of transferring jurisdiction over the probationer to the district in which he was arrested. This is permissible under the aforementioned statute, which provides in part:

Whenever during the period of his probation, a probationer heretofore or hereafter placed on probation, goes from the district in which he is being supervised to another district, jurisdiction over him may be transferred, in the discretion of the court, from the court for the district from which he goes to the court for the other district, with the concurrence of the latter court. Thereupon the court for the district to which jurisdiction is transferred shall have all power with respect to the probationer that was previously possessed by the court for the district from which the transfer is made, except that the period of probation shall not be changed without the consent of the sentencing court. This process under the same conditions may be repeated whenever during the period of his probation the probationer goes from the district in which he is being supervised to another district.

Such transfer may be particularly appropriate when it is found that the probationer has now taken up residence in the district where he was arrested or where the alleged occurrence deemed to constitute a violation of probation took place in the district of arrest. In current practice, probationers arrested in a district other than that of their present supervision are sometimes unnecessarily returned to the district of their supervision, at considerable expense and loss of time, when the more appropriate course of action would have been transfer of probation jurisdiction.

Subdivisions (d)(2) and (3) deal with the situation in which there is not a transfer of probation jurisdiction to the district of arrest. If the alleged probation violation occurred in the district of arrest, then, under subdivision (d)(2), the preliminary hearing provided for in rule 32.1(a)(1) is to be held in that district. This is consistent with the reasoning in *Morrissey v. Brewer,* 408 U.S. 471 (1972), made applicable to probation cases in *Gagnon v. Scarpelli,* 411 U.S. 778 (1973), where the Court stressed that often a parolee "is arrested at a place distant from the state institution, to which he may be returned before the final decision is made concerning revocation," and cited this as a factor contributing to the conclusion that due process requires "that some minimal inquiry be conducted at or reasonably near the place of the alleged parole violation or arrest and as promptly as convenient after arrest while information

386

is fresh and sources are available." As later noted in *Gerstein v. Pugh,* 420 U.S. 103 (1975):

> In *Morrissey v. Brewer,* * * * and *Gagnon v. Scarpelli* * * * we held that a parolee or probationer arrested prior to revocation is entitled to an informal preliminary hearing at the place of arrest, with some provision for live testimony. * * * That preliminary hearing, more than the probable cause determination required by the Fourth Amendment, serves the purpose of gathering and preserving live testimony, since the final revocation hearing frequently is held at some distance from the place where the violation occurred.

However, if the alleged violation did not occur in that district, then first-hand testimony concerning the violation is unlikely to be available there, and thus the reasoning of *Morrissey* and *Gerstein* does not call for holding the preliminary hearing in that district. In such a case, as provided in subdivision (d)(3), the probationer should be held to answer in the district court of the district having probation jurisdiction. The purpose of the proceeding there provided for is to ascertain the identity of the probationer and provide him with copies of the warrant and the application for the warrant. A probationer is subject to the reporting condition at all times and is also subject to the continuing power of the court to modify such conditions. He therefore stands subject to return back to the jurisdiction district without the necessity of conducting a hearing in the district of arrest to determine whether there is probable cause to revoke his probation.

Note to Subdivision (e). New subdivision (e) has no counterpart in the present rule. It has been added because some confusion currently exists as to whether present rule 40(b) is applicable to the case in which a bench warrant has issued for the return of a defendant or witness who has absented himself and that person is apprehended in a distant district. In *Bandy v. United States,* 408 F.2d 518 (8th Cir.1969), a defendant, who had been released upon his personal recognizance after conviction and while petitioning for certiorari and who failed to appear as required after certiorari was denied, objected to his later arrest in New York and removal to Leavenworth without compliance with the rule 40 procedures. The court concluded:

> The short answer to Bandy's first argument is found in *Rush v. United States,* 290 F.2d 709, 710 (5 Cir.1961): "The provisions of Rules 5 and 40, Federal Rules of Criminal Procedure, 18 U.S.C.A. may not be availed of by a prisoner in escape status * * *." As noted by Holtzoff, "Removal of Defendants in Federal Criminal Procedure", 4 F.R.D. 455, 458 (1946):
>
> "Resort need not be had, however, to this [removal] procedure for the purpose of returning a prisoner who has been recaptured after an escape from custody. It has been pointed out that in such a case the court may summarily direct his return under its general

power to issue writs not specifically provided for by statute, which may be necessary for the exercise of its jurisdiction and agreeable to the usages and principles of law. In fact, in such a situation no judicial process appears necessary. The prisoner may be retaken and administratively returned to the custody from which he escaped."

Bandy's arrest in New York was pursuant to a bench warrant issued by the United States District Court for the District of North Dakota on May 1, 1962, when Bandy failed to surrender himself to commence service of his sentence on the conviction for filing false income tax refunds. As a fugitive from justice, Bandy was not entitled upon apprehension to a removal hearing, and he was properly removed to the United States Penitentiary at Leavenworth, Kansas to commence service of sentence.

Consistent with *Bandy,* new subdivision (e) does not afford such a person all of the protections provided for in subdivision (a). However, subdivision (e) does ensure that a determination of identity will be made before that person is held to answer in the district of arrest.

Note to Subdivision (f). Although the matter of bail is dealt with in rule 46 and 18 U.S.C. §§ 3146 and 3148, new subdivision (f) has been added to clarify the situation in which a defendant makes his initial appearance before the United States magistrate and there is a warrant issued by a judge of a different district who has endorsed the amount of bail on the warrant. The present ambiguity of the rule is creating practical administrative problems. If the United States magistrate concludes that a lower bail is appropriate, the judge who fixed the original bail on the warrant has, on occasion, expressed the view that this is inappropriate conduct by the magistrate. If the magistrate, in such circumstances, does not reduce the bail to the amount supported by all of the facts, there may be caused unnecessary inconvenience to the defendant, and there would arguably be a violation of at least the spirit of the Bail Reform Act and the Eighth Amendment.

The Procedures Manual for United States Magistrates, issued under the authority of the Judicial Conference of the United States, provides in ch. 6, pp. 8–9:

> Where the arrest occurs in a "distant" district, the rules do not expressly limit the discretion of the magistrate in the setting of conditions of release. However, whether or not the magistrate in the district of arrest has authority to set his own bail under Rule 40, considerations of propriety and comity would dictate that the magistrate should not attempt to set bail in a lower amount than that fixed by a judge in another district. If an unusual situation should arise where it appears from all the information available to the magistrate that the amount of bail endorsed on the warrant is excessive, he should consult with a judge of his own district or with the judge in the

other district who fixed the bail in order to resolve any difficulties. (Where an amount of bail is merely recommended on the indictment by the United States attorney, the magistrate has complete discretion in setting conditions of release.)

Rule 40 as amended would encourage the above practice and hopefully would eliminate the present confusion and misunderstanding.

The last sentence of subdivision (f) requires that the magistrate set forth the reasons for his action in writing whenever he fixes bail in an amount different from that previously fixed. Setting forth the reasons for the amount of bail fixed, certainly a sound practice in all circumstances, is particularly appropriate when the bail differs from that previously fixed in another district. The requirement that reasons be set out will ensure that the "considerations of propriety and comity" referred to above will be specifically taken into account.

Pub.L. 96–42, § 1(a), July 31, 1979, 93 Stat. 326, deleted "in accordance with Rule 32.1(a)" from subd. (d)(1), and "in accordance with Rule 32.1(a)(1)" from subd. (d)(2).

1982 AMENDMENT

The amendment to 40(d) is intended to make it clear that the transfer provisions therein apply whenever the arrest occurs other than in the district of probation jurisdiction, and that if probable cause is found at a preliminary hearing held pursuant to Rule 40(d)(2) the probationer should be held to answer in the district having probation jurisdiction.

On occasion, the district of probation supervision and the district of probation jurisdiction will not be the same. See, e.g., *Cupp v. Byington,* 179 F.Supp. 669 (S.D.Ind.1960) (supervision in Southern District of Indiana, but jurisdiction never transferred from District of Nevada). In such circumstances, it is the district having *jurisdiction* which may revoke the defendant's probation. *Cupp v. Byington, supra;* 18 U.S.C. § 3653 ("the court for the district having jurisdiction over him * * * may revoke the probation"; if probationer goes to another district, "jurisdiction over him may be transferred," and only then does "the court for the district to which jurisdiction is transferred * * * have all the power with respect to the probationer that was previously possessed by the court for the district from which the transfer was made"). That being the case, that is the jurisdiction to which the probationer should be transferred as provided in Rule 40(d).

Because Rule 32.1 has now taken effect, a cross-reference to those provisions has been made in subdivision (d)(1) so as to clarify how the magistrate is to proceed if jurisdiction is transferred.

1987 AMENDMENT

The amendments are technical. No substantive change is intended.

EDITORIAL NOTES

Effective Date and Savings Provisions of 1984 Amendment. Amendment by Pub.L. 98–473 effective on the first day of first calendar month beginning thirty six months after Oct. 12, 1984, applicable only to offenses committed after taking effect of sections 211 to 239 of Pub.L. 98–473, and except as otherwise provided for therein, see section 235 of Pub.L. 98–473, as amended, set out as a note under section 3551 of Title 18, Crimes and Criminal Procedure.

Rule 41. Search and Seizure

(a) Authority to Issue Warrant. A search warrant authorized by this rule may be issued by a federal magistrate or a judge of a state court of record within the district wherein the property or person sought is located, upon request of a federal law enforcement officer or an attorney for the government.

(b) Property or Persons Which May Be Seized With a Warrant. A warrant may be issued under this rule to search for and seize any (1) property that constitutes evidence of the commission of a criminal offense; or (2) contraband, the fruits of crime, or things otherwise criminally possessed; or (3) property designed or intended for use or which is or has been used as the means of committing a criminal offense; or (4) person for whose arrest there is probable cause, or who is unlawfully restrained.

(c) Issuance and Contents.

(1) Warrant Upon Affidavit. A warrant other than a warrant upon oral testimony under paragraph (2) of this subdivision shall issue only on an affidavit or affidavits sworn to before the federal magistrate or state judge and establishing the grounds for issuing the warrant. If the federal magistrate or state judge is satisfied that grounds for the application exist or that there is probable cause to believe that they exist, that magistrate or state judge shall issue a warrant identifying the property or person to be seized and naming or describing the person or place to be searched. The finding of probable cause may be based upon hearsay evidence in whole or in part. Before ruling on a request for a warrant the federal magistrate or state judge may require the affiant to appear personally and may examine under oath the affiant and any witnesses the affiant may produce, provided that such proceeding shall be taken down by a court reporter or recording equipment and made part of the affidavit. The warrant shall be directed to a civil officer of the United States authorized to enforce or assist in enforcing any law thereof or to a person so authorized by the President of the United States. It shall command the officer to search, within a specified period of time not to exceed 10 days, the person or place named for the property or person specified. The warrant shall be served in the daytime, unless the issuing authority, by appropriate provision in the warrant, and for reasonable cause shown, authorizes its execution at times other than daytime. It shall designate a federal magistrate to whom it shall be returned.

(2) Warrant upon Oral Testimony.

(A) General Rule. If the circumstances make it reasonable to dispense with a written affidavit, a Federal magistrate may issue a warrant based upon sworn oral testimony communicated by telephone or other appropriate means.

(B) Application. The person who is requesting the warrant shall prepare a document to be known as a duplicate original warrant and shall read such duplicate original warrant, verbatim, to the Federal magistrate. The Federal magistrate shall enter, verbatim, what is so read to such magistrate on a document to be known as the original warrant. The Federal magistrate may direct that the warrant be modified.

(C) Issuance. If the Federal magistrate is satisfied that the circumstances are such as to make it reasonable to dispense with a written affidavit and that grounds for the application exist or that there is probable cause to believe that they exist, the Federal magistrate shall order the issuance of a warrant by directing the person requesting the warrant to sign the Federal magistrate's name on the duplicate original warrant. The Federal magistrate shall immediately sign the original warrant and enter on the face of the original warrant the exact time when the warrant was ordered to be issued. The finding of probable cause for a warrant upon oral testimony may be based on the same kind of

evidence as is sufficient for a warrant upon affidavit.

(D) Recording and Certification of Testimony. When a caller informs the Federal magistrate that the purpose of the call is to request a warrant, the Federal magistrate shall immediately place under oath each person whose testimony forms a basis of the application and each person applying for that warrant. If a voice recording device is available, the Federal magistrate shall record by means of such device all of the call after the caller informs the Federal magistrate that the purpose of the call is to request a warrant. Otherwise a stenographic or longhand verbatim record shall be made. If a voice recording device is used or a stenographic record made, the Federal magistrate shall have the record transcribed, shall certify the accuracy of the transcription, and shall file a copy of the original record and the transcription with the court. If a longhand verbatim record is made, the Federal magistrate shall file a signed copy with the court.

(E) Contents. The contents of a warrant upon oral testimony shall be the same as the contents of a warrant upon affidavit.

(F) Additional Rule for Execution. The person who executes the warrant shall enter the exact time of execution on the face of the duplicate original warrant.

(G) Motion to Suppress Precluded. Absent a finding of bad faith, evidence obtained pursuant to a warrant issued under this paragraph is not subject to a motion to suppress on the ground that the circumstances were not such as to make it reasonable to dispense with a written affidavit.

(d) Execution and Return with Inventory. The officer taking property under the warrant shall give to the person from whom or from whose premises the property was taken a copy of the warrant and a receipt for the property taken or shall leave the copy and receipt at the place from which the property was taken. The return shall be made promptly and shall be accompanied by a written inventory of any property taken. The inventory shall be made in the presence of the applicant for the warrant and the person from whose possession or premises the property was taken, if they are present, or in the presence of at least one credible person other than the applicant for the warrant or the person from whose possession or premises the property was taken, and shall be verified by the officer. The federal magistrate shall upon request deliver a copy of the inventory to the person from whom or from whose premises the property was taken and to the applicant for the warrant.

(e) Motion for Return of Property. A person aggrieved by an unlawful search and seizure may move the district court for the district in which the property was seized for the return of the property on the ground that such person is entitled to lawful possession of the property which was illegally seized. The judge shall receive evidence on any issue of fact necessary to the decision of the motion. If the motion is granted the property shall be restored and it shall not be admissible in evidence at any hearing or trial. If a motion for return of property is made or comes on for hearing in the district of trial after an indictment or information is filed, it shall be treated also as a motion to suppress under Rule 12.

(f) Motion to Suppress. A motion to suppress evidence may be made in the court of the district of trial as provided in Rule 12.

(g) Return of Papers to Clerk. The federal magistrate before whom the warrant is returned shall attach to the warrant a copy of the return, inventory and all other papers in connection therewith and shall file them with the clerk of the district court for the district in which the property was seized.

(h) Scope and Definition. This rule does not modify any act, inconsistent with it, regulating search, seizure and the issuance and execution of search warrants in circumstances for which special provision is made. The term "property" is used in this rule to include documents, books, papers and any other tangible objects. The term "daytime" is used in this rule to mean the hours from 6:00 a.m. to 10:00 p.m. according to local time. The phrase "federal law enforcement officer" is used in this rule to mean any government agent, other than an attorney for the government as defined in Rule 54(c), who is engaged in the enforcement of the criminal laws and is within any category of officers authorized by the Attorney General to request the issuance of a search warrant.

(As amended Dec. 27, 1948, eff. Oct. 20, 1949; Apr. 9, 1956, eff. July 8, 1956; Apr. 24, 1972, eff.

Oct. 1, 1972; Mar. 18, 1974, eff. July 1, 1974; Apr. 26, 1976, eff. Aug. 1, 1976; July 30, 1977, Pub.L. 95–78, § 2(e), 91 Stat. 320; Apr. 30, 1979, eff. Aug. 1, 1979; Mar. 9, 1987, eff. Aug. 1, 1987.)

NOTES OF ADVISORY COMMITTEE ON RULES

This rule is a codification of existing law and practice.

Note to Subdivision (a). This rule is a restatement of existing law, 18 U.S.C. former § 611.

Note to Subdivision (b). This rule is a restatement of existing law, 18 U.S.C. former § 612; *Conyer v. United States,* 80 F.2d 292, C.C.A.6th. This provision does not supersede or repeal special statutory provisions permitting the issuance of search warrants in specific circumstances. See Subdivision (g) and Note thereto, infra.

Note to Subdivision (c). This rule is a restatement of existing law, 18 U.S.C. former §§ 613–616, 620; *Dumbra v. United States,* 268 U.S. 435, 45 S.Ct. 546, 69 L.Ed. 1032.

Note to Subdivision (d). This rule is a restatement of existing law, 18 U.S.C. former §§ 621–624.

Note to Subdivision (e). This rule is a restatement of existing law and practice, with the exception hereafter noted, 18 U.S.C. former §§ 625, 626; *Weeks v. United States,* 232 U.S. 383, 34 S.Ct. 341, 58 L.Ed. 652; *Silverthorne Lumber Co. v. United States,* 251 U.S. 385, 40 S.Ct. 182, 64 L.Ed. 319; *Agello v. United States,* 269 U.S. 20, 46 S.Ct. 4, 70 L.Ed. 145; *Gouled v. United States,* 255 U.S. 298, 41 S.Ct. 261, 65 L.Ed. 647. While under existing law a motion to suppress evidence or to compel return of property obtained by an illegal search and seizure may be made either before a commissioner subject to review by the court on motion, or before the court, the rule provides that such motion may be made only before the court. The purpose is to prevent multiplication of proceedings and to bring the matter before the court in the first instance. While during the life of the Eighteenth Amendment when such motions were numerous it was a common practice in some districts for commissioners to hear such motions, the prevailing practice at the present time is to make such motions before the district court. This practice, which is deemed to be preferable, is embodied in the rule.

Note to Subdivision (f). This rule is a restatement of existing law, 18 U.S.C. former § 627; cf. Rule 5(c) (last sentence).

Note to Subdivision (g). While Rule 41 supersedes the general provisions of 18 U.S.C. former §§ 611–626 (now 18 U.S.C. §§ 3105, 3109), relating to search warrants, it does not supersede, but preserves, all other statutory provisions permitting searches and seizures in specific situations. Among such statutes are the following:

U.S.C. Title 18 former:

RULES OF CRIMINAL PROCEDURE

§ 287 [Rule 41] (Search warrant for suspected counterfeiture)

U.S.C. Title 19:

§ 1595 (Customs duties; searches and seizures)

U.S.C. Title 26 former:

§ 3117 [now § 5557] (Officers and agents authorized to investigate, issue search warrants, and prosecute for violations)

For statutes which incorporate by reference 18 U.S.C. former § 98, and therefore are now controlled by this rule, see, e.g.:

U.S.C. Title 18 former:

§ 12 (Subversive activities; undermining loyalty, discipline, or morale of armed forces; searches and seizures)

U.S.C. Title 26 former:

§ 3116 [now § 7302] (Forfeitures and seizures)

Statutory provision for a warrant for detention of war materials seized under certain circumstances is found in 22 U.S.C. § 402 [now § 401] (Seizure of war materials intended for unlawful export).

Other statutes providing for searches and seizures or entry without warrants are the following:

U.S.C. Title 19:

§ 482 (Search of vehicles and persons)

U.S.C. Title 25 former:

§ 246 [now 18 U.S.C. § 3113] (Searches and seizures)

U.S.C. Title 26 former:

§ 3601 [now § 7606] (Entry of premises for examination of taxable objects)

U.S.C. Title 29:

§ 211 (Investigations, inspections, and records)

U.S.C. Title 49:

§ 781 (Unlawful use of vessels, vehicles, and aircrafts; contraband article defined)

§ 782 (Seizure and forfeiture)

§ 784 (Application of related laws)

1948 AMENDMENT

The amendment is to substitute proper reference to Title 18 in place of the repealed acts.

To eliminate reference to sections of the Act of June 15, 1917, c. 30, which have been repealed by the Act of June 25, 1948, c. 645, which enacted Title 18.

1972 AMENDMENT

Subdivision (a) is amended to provide that a search warrant may be issued only upon the request of a federal law enforcement officer or an attorney for the government. The phrase "federal law enforcement officer" is defined in subdivision (h) in a way which will allow the Attorney General to designate the category of officers who are authorized to make application for a search warrant. The phrase "attorney for the government" is defined in rule 54.

The title to subdivision (b) is changed to make it conform more accurately to the content of the subdivision. Subdivision (b) is also changed to modernize the language used to describe the property which may be seized with a lawfully issued search warrant and to take account of a recent Supreme Court decision (*Warden v. Haden*, 387 U.S. 294 (1967)) and recent congressional action (18 U.S.C. § 3103a) which authorize the issuance of a search warrant to search for items of solely evidential value. 18 U.S.C. § 3103a provides that "a warrant may be issued to search for and seize any property that constitutes evidence of a criminal offense...."

Recent state legislation authorizes the issuance of a search warrant for evidence of crime. See, *e.g.*, Cal.Penal Code § 1524(4) (West Supp.1968); Ill.Rev.Stat. ch. 38, § 108–3 (1965); LSA C.Cr.P. art. 161 (1967); N.Y.CPL § 690.10(4) (McKinney, 1971); Ore.Rev.Stat. § 141.010 (1969); Wis.Stat. § 968.13(2) (1969).

The general weight of recent text and law review comment has been in favor of allowing a search for evidence. 8 Wigmore, Evidence § 2184a. (McNaughton rev. 1961); Kamisar, The Wiretapping–Eavesdropping Problem: A Professor's View, 44 Minn.L.Rev. 891 (1960); Kaplan, Search and Seizure: A No-Man's Land in the Criminal Law, 49 Calif.L.Rev. 474 (1961); Comments: 66 Colum.L.Rev. 355 (1966), 45 N.C.L.Rev. 512 (1967), 20 U.Chi.L.Rev. 319 (1953).

There is no intention to limit the protection of the fifth amendment against compulsory self-incrimination, so items which are solely "testimonial" or "communicative" in nature might well be inadmissible on those grounds. *Schmerber v. California*, 384 U.S. 757 (1966). The court referred to the possible fifth amendment limitation in *Warden v. Hayden, supra:*

This case thus does not require that we consider whether there are items of evidential value whose very nature precludes them from being the object of a reasonable search and seizure. [387 U.S. at 303].

See ALI Model Code of Pre–Arraignment Procedure § 551.03(2) and commentary at pp. 3–5 (April 30, 1971).

It seems preferable to allow the fifth amendment limitation to develop as cases arise rather than attempt to articulate the constitutional doctrine as part of the rule itself.

The amendment to subdivision (c) is intended to make clear that a search warrant may properly be based upon a finding of probable cause based upon hearsay. That a search warrant may properly be issued on the basis of hearsay is current law. See, *e.g., Jones v. United States*, 362 U.S. 257 (1960); *Spinelli v. United States*, 393 U.S.

410 (1969). See also *State v. Beal,* 40 Wis.2d 607, 162 N.W.2d 640 (1968), reversing prior Wisconsin cases which held that a search warrant could not properly issue on the basis of hearsay evidence.

The provision in subdivision (c) that the magistrate may examine the affiant or witnesses under oath is intended to assure him an opportunity to make a careful decision as to whether there is probable cause. It seems desirable to do this as an incident to the issuance of the warrant rather than having the issue raised only later on a motion to suppress the evidence. See L. Tiffany, D. McIntyre, and D. Rotenberg, Detection of Crime 118 (1967). If testimony is taken it must be recorded, transcribed, and made part of the affidavit or affidavits. This is to insure an adequate basis for determining the sufficiency of the evidentiary grounds for the issuance of the search warrant if that question should later arise.

The requirement that the warrant itself state the grounds for its issuance and the names of any affiants, is eliminated as unnecessary paper work. There is no comparable requirement for an arrest warrant in rule 4. A person who wishes to challenge the validity of a search warrant has access to the affidavits upon which the warrant was issued.

The former requirement that the warrant require that the search be conducted "forthwith" is changed to read "within a specified period of time not to exceed 10 days." The former rule contained an inconsistency between subdivision (c) requiring that the search be conducted "forthwith" and subdivision (d) requiring execution "within 10 days after its date." The amendment resolves this ambiguity and confers discretion upon the issuing magistrate to specify the time within which the search may be conducted to meet the needs of the particular case.

The rule is also changed to allow the magistrate to authorize a search at a time other than "daytime," where there is "reasonable cause shown" for doing so. To make clear what "daytime" means, the term is defined in subdivision (h).

Subdivision (d) is amended to conform its language to the Federal Magistrates Act. The language "The warrant may be executed and returned only within 10 days after its date" is omitted as unnecessary. The matter is now covered adequately in proposed subdivision (c) which gives the issuing officer authority to fix the time within which the warrant is to be executed.

The amendment to subdivision (e) and the addition of subdivision (f) are intended to require the motion to suppress evidence to be made in the trial court rather than in the district in which the evidence was seized as now allowed by the rule. In *DiBella v. United States,* 369 U.S. 121 (1962), the court, in effect, discouraged motions to suppress in the district in which the property was seized:

There is a decision in the Second Circuit, *United States v. Klapholz,* 230 F.2d 494 (1956), allowing the Government an appeal from an order granting a post-indictment motion to suppress, apparently for the single reason that the motion was filed in the district of seizure rather than of trial; but the case was soon thereafter taken by a District Court to have counseled declining jurisdiction of such motions for reasons persuasive against allowing the appeal: "This course will avoid a needless duplication of effort by two courts and provide a more expeditious resolution of the controversy besides avoiding the risk of determining prematurely and inadequately the admissibility of evidence at the trial.... A piecemeal adjudication such as that which would necessarily follow from a disposition of the motion here might conceivably result in prejudice either to the Government or the defendants, or both." *United States v. Lester,* 21 F.R.D. 30, 31 (D.C.S.D.N.Y.1957). Rule 41(e), of course, specifically provides for making of the motion in the district of seizure. On a summary hearing, however, the ruling there is likely always to be tentative. We think it accords most satisfactorily with sound administration of the Rules to treat such rulings as interlocutory. [369 U.S. at 132–133.]

As amended, subdivision (e) provides for a return of the property if (1) the person is entitled to lawful possession *and* (2) the seizure was illegal. This means that the judge in the district of seizure does not have to decide the legality of the seizure in cases involving contraband which, even if seized illegally, is not to be returned.

The five grounds for returning the property, presently listed in the rule, are dropped for two reasons—(1) substantive grounds for objecting to illegally obtained evidence (*e.g., Miranda*) are not ordinarily codified in the rules and (2) the categories are not entirely accurate. See *United States v. Howard,* 138 F.Supp. 376, 380 (D.Md.1956).

A sentence is added to subdivision (e) to provide that a motion for return of property, made in the district of trial, shall be treated also as a motion to suppress under rule 12. This change is intended to further the objective of rule 12 which is to have all pretrial motions disposed of in a single court appearance rather than to have a series of pretrial motions made on different dates, causing undue delay in administration.

Subdivision (f) is new and reflects the position that it is best to have the motion to suppress made in the court of the district of trial rather than in the court of the district in which the seizure occurred. The motion to suppress in the district of trial should be made in accordance with the provisions of rule 12.

Subdivision (g) is changed to conform to subdivision (c) which requires the return to be made before a federal judicial officer even though the search warrant may have been issued by a nonfederal magistrate.

Subdivision (h) is former rule 41(g) with the addition of a definition of the term "daytime" and the phrase "federal law enforcement officer."

1977 AMENDMENT

Rule 41(c)(2) is added to establish a procedure for the issuance of a search warrant when it is not reasonably practicable for the person obtaining the warrant to present a written affidavit to a magistrate or a state judge as required by subdivision (c)(1). At least two states have adopted a similar procedure, Ariz.Rev.Stat. Ann. §§ 13-1444(c)-1445(c) (Supp.1973); Cal.Pen.Code §§ 1526(b), 1528(b) (West Supp.1974), and comparable amendments are under consideration in other jurisdictions. See Israel, Legislative Regulation of Searches and Seizures: The Michigan Proposals, 73 Mich.L.Rev. 221, 258–63 (1975); Nakell, Proposed Revisions of North Carolina's Search and Seizure Law, 52 N.Car.L.Rev. 277, 306–11 (1973). It has been strongly recommended that "every State enact legislation that provides for the issuance of search warrants pursuant to telephoned petitions and affidavits from police officers." National Advisory Commission on Criminal Justice Standards and Goals, Report on Police 95 (1973). Experience with the procedure has been most favorable. Miller, Telephonic Search Warrants: The San Diego Experience, 9 The Prosecutor 385 (1974).

The trend of recent Supreme Court decisions had been to give greater priority to the use of a search warrant as the proper way of making a lawful search: It is a cardinal rule that, in seizing goods and articles, law enforcement agents must secure and use search warrants whenever reasonably practicable.... This rule rests upon the desirability of having magistrates rather than police officers determine when searches and seizures are permissible and what limitations should be placed upon such activities. *Trupiano v. United States,* 334 U.S. 699, 705 (1948), quoted with approval in *Chimel v. California,* 395 U.S. 752, 758 (1969). See also *Coolidge v. New Hampshire,* 403 U.S. 443 (1971); Note, *Chambers v. Maroney: New Dimensions in the Law of Search and Seizure* 46 Indiana L.J. 257, 262 (1971).

Use of search warrants can best be encouraged by making it administratively feasible to obtain a warrant when one is needed. One reason for the nonuse of the warrant has been the administrative difficulties involved in getting a warrant, particularly at times of the day when a judicial officer is ordinarily unavailable. See L. Tiffany, D. McIntyre, and D. Rotenberg, Detection of Crime 105–116 (1967); LaFave, Improving Police Performance Through the Exclusionary Rule, 30 Mo.L. Rev. 391, 411 (1965). Federal law enforcement officers are not infrequently confronted with situations in which the circumstances are not sufficiently "exigent" to justify the serious step of conducting a warrantless search of private premises, but yet there exists a signifi-cant possibility that critical evidence would be lost in the time it would take to obtain a search warrant by traditional means. See, e.g., *United States v. Johnson,* ___ F.2d ___ (D.C.Cir. June 16, 1975).

Subdivision (c)(2) provides that a warrant may be issued on the basis of an oral statement of a person not in the physical presence of the federal magistrate. Telephone, radio, or other electronic methods of communication are contemplated. For the warrant to properly issue, four requirements must be met:

(1) The applicant—a federal law enforcement officer or an attorney for the government, as required by subdivision (a)—must persuade the magistrate that the circumstances of time and place make it reasonable to request the magistrate to issue a warrant on the basis of oral testimony. This restriction on the issuance of a warrant recognizes the inherent limitations of an oral warranted procedure, the lack of demeanor evidence, and the lack of a written record for the reviewing magistrate to consider before issuing the warrant. See Comment, Oral Search Warrants: A New Standard of Warrant Availability, 21 U.C.L.A. Law Review 691, 701 (1974). Circumstances making it reasonable to obtain a warrant on oral testimony exist if delay in obtaining the warrant might result in the destruction or disappearance of the property [see *Chimel v. California,* 395 U.S. 752, 773–774 (1969) (White, dissenting); Landynski, The Supreme Court's Search for Fourth Amendment Standards: The Warrantless Search, 45 Conn.B.J. 2, 25 (1971)]; or because of the time when the warrant is sought, the distance from the magistrate of the person seeking the warrant, or both.

(2) The applicant must orally state facts sufficient to satisfy the probable cause requirement for the issuance of the search warrant. (See subdivision (c)(1).) This information may come from either the applicant federal law enforcement officer or the attorney for the government or a witness willing to make an oral statement. The oral testimony must be recorded at this time so that the transcribed affidavit will provide an adequate basis for determining the sufficiency of the evidence if that issue should later arise. See Kipperman, Inaccurate Search Warrant Affidavits as a Ground for Suppressing Evidence, 84 Harv.L.Rev. 825 (1971). It is contemplated that the recording of the oral testimony will be made by a court reporter, by a mechanical recording device, or by a verbatim contemporaneous writing by the magistrate. Recording a telephone conversation is no longer difficult with many easily operated recorders available. See 86:2 L.A. Daily Journal 1 (1973); Miller, Telephonic Search Warrants: The San Diego Experience, 9 The Prosecutor 385, 386 (1974).

(3) The applicant must read the contents of the warrant to the federal magistrate in order to enable the magistrate to know whether the requirements of

certainty in the warrant are satisfied. The magistrate may direct that changes be made in the warrant. If the magistrate approves the warrant as requested or as modified by the magistrate, he then issues the warrant by directing the applicant to sign the magistrate's name to the duplicate original warrant. The magistrate then causes to be made a written copy of the approved warrant. This constitutes the original warrant. The magistrate enters the time of issuance of the duplicate original warrant on the face of the original warrant.

(4) Return of the duplicate original warrant and the original warrant must conform to subdivision (d). The transcript of the sworn oral testimony setting forth the grounds for issuance of the warrant must be signed by affiant in the presence of the magistrate and filed with the court.

Because federal magistrates are likely to be accessible through the use of the telephone or other electronic devices, it is unnecessary to authorize state judges to issue warrants under subdivision (c)(2).

Although the procedure set out in subdivision (c)(2) contemplates resort to technology which did not exist when the Fourth Amendment was adopted, the Advisory Committee is of the view that the procedure complies with all of the requirements of the Amendment. The telephonic search warrant process has been upheld as constitutional by the courts, e.g., *People v. Peck*, 38 Cal.App.3d 993, 113 Cal.Rptr. 806 (1974), and has consistently been so viewed by commentators. See Israel, Legislative Regulation of Searches and Seizures: The Michigan Proposals, 73 Mich.L.Rev. 221, 260 (1975); Nakell, Proposed Revisions of North Carolina's Search and Seizure Law, 52 N.Car.L.Rev. 277, 310 (1973); Comment, Oral Search Warrants: A New Standard of Warrant Availability, 21 U.C.L.A.Rev. 691, 697 (1973).

Reliance upon oral testimony as a basis for issuing a search warrant is permissible under the Fourth Amendment. *Campbell v. Minnesota*, 487 F.2d 1 (8th Cir.1973); *United States ex rel. Gaugler v. Brierley*, 477 F.2d 516 (3d Cir.1973); *Tabasko v. Barton*, 472 F.2d 871 (6th Cir.1972); *Frazier v. Roberts*, 441 F.2d 1224 (8th Cir. 1971). Thus, the procedure authorized under subdivision (c)(2) is not objectionable on the ground that the oral statement is not transcribed in advance of the issuance of the warrant. *People v. Peck*, 38 Cal.App.3d 993, 113 Cal.Rptr. 806 (1974). Although it has been questioned whether oral testimony will suffice under the Fourth Amendment if some kind of contemporaneous record is not made of that testimony, see dissent from denial of certiorari in *Christofferson v. Washington*, 393 U.S. 1090 (1969), this problem is not present under the procedure set out in subdivision (c)(2).

The Fourth Amendment requires that warrants issue "upon probable cause, supported by Oath or affirmation." The significance of the oath requirement is "that someone must take the responsibility for the facts alleged, giving rise to the probable cause for the issuance of a warrant." *United States ex rel. Pugh v. Pate*, 401 F.2d 6 (7th Cir.1968); See also *Frazier v. Roberts*, 441 F.2d 1224 (8th Cir.1971). This is accomplished under the procedure required by subdivision (c)(2); the need for an oath under the Fourth Amendment does not "require a face to face confrontation between the magistrate and the affiant." *People v. Chavaz*, 27 Cal.App.3d 883, 104 Cal.Rptr. 247 (1972). See also *People v. Aguirre*, 26 Cal.App.3d 7, 103 Cal.Rptr. 153 (1972), noting it is unnecessary that "oral statements [be] taken in the physical presence of the magistrate."

The availability of the procedure authorized by subdivision (c)(2) will minimize the necessity of federal law enforcement officers engaging in other practices which, at least on occasion, might threaten to a greater extent those values protected by the Fourth Amendment. Although it is permissible for an officer in the field to relay his information by radio or telephone to another officer who has more ready access to a magistrate and who will thus act as the affiant, *Lopez v. United States*, 370 F.2d 8 (5th Cir.1966); *State v. Banks*, 250 N.C. 728, 110 S.E.2d 322 (1959), that procedure is less desirable than that permitted under subdivision (c)(2), for it deprives "the magistrate of the opportunity to examine the officer at the scene, who is in a much better position to answer questions relating to probable cause and the requisite scope of the search." Israel, Legislative Regulation of Searches and Seizures: The Michigan Proposals, 73 Mich.L.Rev. 221, 260 (1975). Or, in the absence of the subdivision (c)(2) procedure, officers might take "protective custody" of the premises and occupants for a significant period of time while a search warrant was sought by traditional means. The extent to which the "protective custody" procedure may be employed consistent with the Fourth Amendment is uncertain at best; see Griswold, Criminal Procedure, 1969—Is It a Means or an End?, 29 Md.L.Rev. 307, 317 (1969). The unavailability of the subdivision (c)(2) procedure also makes more tempting an immediate resort to a warrantless search in the hope that the circumstances will later be found to have been sufficiently "exigent" to justify such a step. See Miller, Telephonic Search Warrants: The San Diego Experience, 9 The Prosecutor 385, 386 (1974), noting a dramatic increase in police utilization of the warrant process following enactment of a telephonic warrant statute.

NOTES OF COMMITTEE ON THE JUDICIARY, SENATE REPORT NO. 95–354. AMENDMENTS PROPOSED BY THE SUPREME COURT

The committee agrees with the Supreme Court that it is desirable to encourage Federal law enforcement officers to seek search warrants in situations where they might otherwise conduct warrantless searches by providing for a telephone search warrant procedure with the basic characteristics suggested in the proposed Rule 41(c)(2). As the Supreme Court has observed, "It is a cardinal rule that, in seizing goods and articles, law enforcement agents must secure and use search warrants whenever reasonably practicable. After consideration of the Supreme Court version and a proposal set forth in H.R. 7888, the committee decided to use the language of the House bill as the vehicle, with certain modifications.

A new provision, as indicated in subparagraph (c)(2)(A), is added to establish a procedure for the issuance of a search warrant where the circumstances make it reasonable to dispense with a written affidavit to be presented in person to a magistrate. At least two States have adopted a similar procedure—Arizona and California—and comparable amendments are under consideration in other jurisdictions. Such a procedure has been strongly recommended by the National Advisory Commission on Criminal Justice Standards and Goals and State experience with the procedure has been favorable. The telephone search warrant process has been upheld as constitutional by the courts and has consistently been so viewed by commentators.

In recommending a telephone search warrant procedure, the Advisory Committee note on the Supreme Court proposal points out that the preferred method of conducting a search is with a search warrant. The note indicates that the rationale for the proposed change is to encourage Federal law enforcement officers to seek search warrants in situations when they might otherwise conduct warrantless searches. "Federal law enforcement officers are not infrequently confronted with situations in which the circumstances are not sufficiently 'exigent' to justify the serious step of conducting a warrantless search of private premises, but yet there exists a significant possibility that critical evidence would be lost in the time it would take to obtain a search warrant by traditional means."

Subparagraph (c)(2)(B) provides that the person requesting the warrant shall prepare a "duplicate original warrant" which will be read and recorded verbatim by the magistrate on an "original warrant." The magistrate may direct that the warrant be modified.

Subparagraph (c)(2)(C) provides that, if the magistrate is satisfied that the circumstances are such as to make it reasonable to dispense with a written affidavit and that grounds for the application exist or there is probable cause to believe that they exist, he shall order the issuance of the warrant by directing the requestor to sign the magistrate's name on the duplicate original warrant. The magistrate is required to sign the original warrant and enter the time of issuance thereon. The finding of probable cause may be based on the same type of evidence appropriate for a warrant upon affidavit.

Subparagraph (c)(2)(D) requires the magistrate to place the requestor and any witness under oath and, if a voice recording device is available, to record the proceeding. If a voice recording is not available, the proceeding must be recorded verbatim stenographically or in longhand. Verified copies must be filed with the court as specified.

Subparagraph (c)(2)(E) provides that the contents of the warrant upon oral testimony shall be the same as the contents of a warrant upon affidavit.

Subparagraph (c)(2)(F) provides that the person who executes the warrant shall enter the exact time of execution on the face of the duplicate original warrant. Unlike H.R. 7888, this subparagraph does not require the person who executes the warrant to have physical possession of the duplicate original warrant at the time of the execution of the warrant. The committee believes this would make an unwise and unnecessary distinction between execution of regular warrants issued on written affidavits and warrants issued by telephone that would limit the flexibility and utility of this procedure for no useful purpose.

Finally, subparagraph (c)(2)(G) makes it clear that, absent a finding of bad faith by the government, the magistrate's judgment that the circumstances made it reasonable to dispense with a written affidavit—a decision that does not go to the core question of whether there was probable cause to issue a warrant—is not a ground for granting a motion to suppress evidence.

CONGRESSIONAL MODIFICATION OF PROPOSED AMENDMENT

Section 2(e) of Pub.L. 95–78 provided in part that the amendment by the Supreme Court [in its order of Apr. 26, 1976] to subdivision (c) of rule 41 of the Federal Rules of Criminal Procedure [subd. (c) of this rule] is approved in a modified form.

1979 AMENDMENT

This amendment to Rule 41 is intended to make it possible for a search warrant to issue to search *for* a person under two circumstances: (i) when there is probable cause to arrest that person; or (ii) when that person is being unlawfully restrained. There may be instances in which a search warrant would be required to conduct a search in either of these circumstances. Even when a search warrant would not be required to enter a place to search for a person, a procedure for obtaining a warrant should be available so that law enforcement officers will be encouraged to resort to the preferred alternative of acquiring "an objective predetermination of probable cause," *Katz v. United States,* 389 U.S. 347, 88 S.Ct. 507, 19 L.Ed.2d 576 (1967), in this instance, that the person sought is at the place to be searched.

That part of the amendment which authorizes issuance of a search warrant to search for a person unlawfully restrained is consistent with ALI Model

Code of Pre–Arraignment Procedure § SS 210.3(1)(d) (Proposed Official Draft, 1975), which specifies that a search warrant may issue to search for "an individual * * * who is unlawfully held in confinement or other restraint." As noted in the Commentary thereto, id. at p. 507:

Ordinarily such persons will be held against their will and in that case the persons are, of course, not subject to "seizure." But they are, in a sense, "evidence" of crime, and the use of search warrants for these purposes presents no conceptual difficulties.

Some state search warrant provisions also provide for issuance of a warrant in these circumstances. See, e.g., Ill.Rev.Stat. ch. 38, § 108–3 ("Any person who has been kidnapped in violation of the laws of this State, or who has been kidnapped in another jurisdiction and is now concealed within this State").

It may be that very often exigent circumstances, especially the need to act very promptly to protect the life or well-being of the kidnap victim, would justify an immediate warrantless search for the person restrained. But this is not inevitably the case. Moreover, as noted above, there should be available a process whereby law enforcement agents may acquire in advance a judicial determination that they have cause to intrude upon the privacy of those at the place where the victim is thought to be located.

That part of the amendment which authorizes issuance of a search warrant to search for a person to be arrested is also consistent with ALI Model Code of Pre–Arraignment Procedure § SS 210.3(1)(d) (Proposed Official Draft, 1975), which states that a search warrant may issue to search for "an individual for whose arrest there is reasonable cause." As noted in the Commentary thereto, id. at p. 507, it is desirable that there be "explicit statutory authority for such searches." Some state search warrant provisions also expressly provide for the issuance of a search warrant to search for a person to be arrested. See, e.g., Del.Code Ann. tit. 11, § 2305 ("Persons for whom a warrant of arrest has been issued"). This part of the amendment to Rule 41 covers a defendant or witness for whom an arrest warrant has theretofore issued, or a defendant for whom grounds to arrest exist even though no arrest warrant has theretofore issued. It also covers the arrest of a deportable alien under 8 U.S.C. § 1252, whose presence at a certain place might be important evidence of criminal conduct by another person, such as the harboring of undocumented aliens under 8 U.S.C. § 1324(a)(3).

In *United States v. Watson*, 423 U.S. 411, 96 S.Ct. 820, 46 L.Ed.2d 598 (1976), the Court once again alluded to "the still unsettled question" of whether, absent exigent circumstances, officers acting without a warrant may enter private premises to make an arrest. Some courts have indicated that probable cause alone ordinarily is sufficient to support an arrest entry, *United States v. Fernandez*, 480 F.2d 726 (2d Cir.1973); *United States ex* *rel. Wright v. Woods*, 432 F.2d 1143 (7th Cir.1970). There exists some authority, however, that except under exigent circumstances a warrant is required to enter the defendant's own premises, *United States v. Calhoun*, 542 F.2d 1094 (9th Cir.1976); *United States v. Lindsay*, 506 F.2d 166 (D.C.Cir.1974); *Dorman v. United States*, 435 F.2d 385 (D.C.Cir.1970), or, at least, to enter the premises of a third party, *Virgin Islands v. Gereau*, 502 F.2d 914 (3d Cir.1974); *Fisher v. Volz*, 496 F.2d 333 (3d Cir.1974); *Huotari v. Vanderport*, 380 F.Supp. 645 (D.Minn.1974).

It is also unclear, assuming a need for a warrant, what kind of warrant is required, although it is sometimes assumed that an arrest warrant will suffice, e.g., *United States v. Calhoun*, supra; *United States v. James*, 528 F.2d 999 (5th Cir.1976). There is a growing body of authority, however, that what is needed to justify entry of the premises of a third party to arrest is a search warrant, e.g., *Virgin Islands v. Gereau*, supra; *Fisher v. Volz*, supra. The theory is that if the privacy of this third party is to be protected adequately, what is needed is a probable cause determination by a magistrate that the wanted person is presently within that party's premises. "A warrant for the arrest of a suspect may indicate that the police officer has probable cause to believe the suspect committed the crime; it affords no basis to believe the suspect is in some stranger's home." *Fisher v. Volz*, supra.

It has sometimes been contended that a search warrant should be required for a nonexigent entry to arrest even when the premises to be entered are those of the person to be arrested. Rotenberg & Tanzer, Searching for the Person to be Seized, 35 Ohio St.L.J. 56, 69 (1974). Case authority in support is lacking, and it may be that the protections of a search warrant are less important in such a situation because ordinarily "rudimentary police procedure dictates that a suspect's residence be eliminated as a possible hiding place before a search is conducted elsewhere." *People v. Sprovieri*, 95 Ill.App.2d 10, 238 N.E.2d 115 (1968).

Despite these uncertainties, the fact remains that in some circuits under some circumstances a search warrant is required to enter private premises to arrest. Moreover, the law on this subject is in a sufficient state of uncertainty that this position may be taken by other courts. It is thus important that Rule 41 clearly express that a search warrant for this purpose may issue. And even if future decisions head the other direction, the need for the amendment would still exist. It is clear that law enforcement officers "may not constitutionally enter the home of a private individual to search for another person, though he be named in a valid arrest warrant in their possession, absent probable cause to believe that the named suspect is present within at the time." *Fisher v. Volz*, supra. The cautious officer is entitled to a procedure whereby he may have this probable cause determination made by a neutral and detached magistrate in advance of the entry.

1987 AMENDMENT

The amendments are technical. No substantive change is intended.

Rule 42. Criminal Contempt

(a) Summary Disposition. A criminal contempt may be punished summarily if the judge certifies that the judge saw or heard the conduct constituting the contempt and that it was committed in the actual presence of the court. The order of contempt shall recite the facts and shall be signed by the judge and entered of record.

(b) Disposition Upon Notice and Hearing. A criminal contempt except as provided in subdivision (a) of this rule shall be prosecuted on notice. The notice shall state the time and place of hearing, allowing a reasonable time for the preparation of the defense, and shall state the essential facts constituting the criminal contempt charged and describe it as such. The notice shall be given orally by the judge in open court in the presence of the defendant or, on application of the United States attorney or of an attorney appointed by the court for that purpose, by an order to show cause or an order of arrest. The defendant is entitled to a trial by jury in any case in which an act of Congress so provides. The defendant is entitled to admission to bail as provided in these rules. If the contempt charged involves disrespect to or criticism of a judge, that judge is disqualified from presiding at the trial or hearing except with the defendant's consent. Upon a verdict or finding of guilt the court shall enter an order fixing the punishment.

(As amended Mar. 9, 1987, eff. Aug. 1, 1987.)

NOTES OF ADVISORY COMMITTEE ON RULES

The rule-making power of the Supreme Court with respect to criminal proceedings was extended to proceedings to punish for criminal contempt of court by the Act of November 21, 1941 (55 Stat. 779), 18 U.S.C. former § 689 (now §§ 3771, 3772).

Note to Subdivision (a). This rule is substantially a restatement of existing law, *Ex parte Terry,* 128 U.S. 289; *Cooke v. United States,* 267 U.S. 517, 534, 45 S.Ct. 390, 69 L.Ed. 767.

Note to Subdivision (b). This rule is substantially a restatement of the procedure prescribed in 28 U.S.C. former §§ 386–390 (now 18 U.S.C. §§ 401, 402, 3285, 3691), and 29 U.S.C. former § 111 (now 18 U.S.C. § 3692).

2. The requirement in the second sentence that the notice shall describe the criminal contempt as such is intended to obviate the frequent confusion between criminal and civil contempt proceedings and follows the suggestion made in *McCann v. New York Stock Exchange,* 80 F.2d 211, C.C.A.2d. See also *Nye v. United States,* 313 U.S. 33, 42–43, 61 S.Ct. 810, 85 L.Ed. 1172.

3. The fourth sentence relating to trial by jury preserves the right to a trial by jury in those contempt cases in which it is granted by statute, but does not enlarge the right or extend it to additional cases. The respondent in a contempt proceeding may demand a trial by jury as of right if the proceeding is brought under the Act of March 23, 1932, ch. 90, sec. 11, 47 Stat. 72, 29 U.S.C. former § 111 (now 18 U.S.C. § 3692) (Norris–La Guardia Act), or the Act of October 15, 1914, ch. 323, sec. 22, 38 Stat. 738, 28 U.S.C. § 387 (Clayton Act).

4. The provision in the sixth sentence disqualifying the judge affected by the contempt if the charge involves disrespect to or criticism of him, is based, in part, on 29 U.S.C. former § 112 (Contempts; demand for retirement of judge sitting in proceeding) and the observations of Chief Justice Taft in *Cooke v. United States,* 267 U.S. 517, 539, 45 S.Ct. 390, 69 L.Ed. 767.

5. Among the statutory provisions defining criminal contempts are the following:

U.S.C. Title 7:

§ 499m (Perishable Agricultural Commodities Act; investigation of complaints; procedure; penalties; etc. —(c) Disobedience to subpenas; remedy; contempt)

U.S.C. Title 9:

§ 7 (Witnesses before arbitrators; fees, compelling attendance)

U.S.C. Title 11:

§ 69 (Referees; contempts before)

U.S.C. Title 15:

§ 49 (Federal Trade Commission; documentary evidence; depositions; witnesses)

§ 78u (Regulation of Securities Exchanges; investigation; injunctions and prosecution of offenses)

§ 100 (Trademarks; destruction of infringing labels; service of injunction, and proceedings for enforcement)

§ 155 (China Trade Act; authority of registrar in obtaining evidence)

U.S.C. Title 17 former:

§ 36 [now § 112] (Injunctions; service and enforcement)

U.S.C. Title 19:

§ 1333 (Tariff Commission; testimony and production of papers—(b) Witnesses and evidence)

U.S.C. Title 22 former:

§ 270f (International Bureaus; Congresses, etc.; perjury; contempts; penalties)

U.S.C. Title 28 former:

§ 385 [now § 459; 18 U.S.C. § 401] (Administration of oaths; contempts)

§ 386 [now 18 U.S.C. §§ 402, 3691] (Contempts; when constituting also criminal offense)

§ 387 [now 18 U.S.C. § 402] (Same; procedure; bail; attachment; trial; punishment) (Clayton Act; jury trial; section)

§ 388 (Same; review of conviction)

§ 389 [now 18 U.S.C. §§ 402, 3691] (Same; not specifically enumerated)

§ 390 [now 18 U.S.C. § 3285] (Same; limitations)

§ 390a [now 18 U.S.C. § 402] ("Person" or "persons" defined)

§ 648 [now 18 U.S.C., Appendix, R. 17(f); 28 U.S.C., Appendix, R. 45(d)] (Depositions under dedimus potestatem; witnesses; when required to attend)

§ 703 (Punishment of witness for contempt)

§ 714 [now § 1784] (Failure of witness to obey subpena; order to show cause in contempt proceedings)

§ 715 [now § 1784] (Direction in order to show cause for seizure of property of witness in contempt)

§ 716 [now § 1784] (Service of order to show cause)

§ 717 [now § 1784] (Hearing on order to show cause; judgment; satisfaction)

§ 750 [now § 2405] (Garnishees in suits by United States against a corporation; garnishee failing to appear)

U.S.C. Title 29 former:

§ 111 [now 18 U.S.C. § 3692] (Contempts; speedy and public trial; jury) (Norris–La Guardia Act)

§ 112 [now 18 U.S.C., Appendix, R. 42] (Contempts; demands for retirement of judge sitting in proceeding)

§ 160 (Prevention of unfair labor practices—(h) Jurisdiction of courts unaffected by limitations prescribed in sections 101–115 of Title 29)

§ 161 (Investigatory powers of Board—(2) Court aid in compelling production of evidence and attendance of witnesses)

§ 209 (Fair Labor Standards Act; attendance of witnesses)

U.S.C. Title 33:

§ 927 (Longshoremen's and Harbor Workers' Compensation Act; powers of deputy commissioner)

U.S.C. Title 35 former:

§ 56 [now § 24] (Failing to attend or testify)

U.S.C. Title 47:

§ 409 (Federal Communications Commission; hearing; subpenas; oaths; witnesses; production of books and papers; contempts; depositions; penalties)

U.S.C. Title 48 former:

§ 1345a (Canal Zone; general jurisdiction of district court; issue of process at request of officials; witnesses; contempt)

U.S.C. Title 49:

§ 12 (Interstate Commerce Commission; authority and duties of commission; witnesses; depositions—(3) Compelling attendance and testimony of witnesses, etc.)

TAFT–HARTLEY INJUNCTIONS

Former section 112 of Title 29, Labor, upon which subd. (b) of this rule is in part based, as inapplicable to injunctions issued under the Taft–Hartley Act, see section 178 of said Title 29.

1987 AMENDMENT

The amendments are technical. No substantive change is intended.

X. GENERAL PROVISIONS

Rule 43. Presence of the Defendant

(a) Presence Required. The defendant shall be present at the arraignment, at the time of the plea, at every stage of the trial including the impaneling of the jury and the return of the verdict, and at the imposition of sentence, except as otherwise provided by this rule.

(b) Continued Presence Not Required. The further progress of the trial to and including the return of the verdict shall not be prevented and the defendant shall be considered to have waived the right to be present whenever a defendant, initially present,

(1) is voluntarily absent after the trial has commenced (whether or not the defendant has been informed by the court of the obligation to remain during the trial), or

(2) after being warned by the court that disruptive conduct will cause the removal of the defendant from the courtroom, persists in conduct which is such as to justify exclusion from the courtroom.

(c) Presence Not Required. A defendant need not be present in the following situations:

(1) A corporation may appear by counsel for all purposes.

(2) In prosecutions for offenses punishable by fine or by imprisonment for not more than one year or both, the court, with the written consent of the defendant, may permit arraignment, plea, trial, and imposition of sentence in the defendant's absence.

(3) At a conference or argument upon a question of law.

(4) At a reduction of sentence under Rule 35.

(As amended Apr. 22, 1974, eff. Dec. 1, 1975; July 31, 1975, Pub.L. 94–64, § 3(35), 89 Stat. 376; Mar. 9, 1987, eff. Aug. 1, 1987.)

NOTES OF ADVISORY COMMITTEE ON RULES

1. The first sentence of the rule setting forth the necessity of the defendant's presence at arraignment and trial is a restatement of existing law, *Lewis v. United States,* 146 U.S. 370, 13 S.Ct. 136, 36 L.Ed. 1011; *Diaz v. United States,* 223 U.S. 442, 455, 32 S.Ct. 250, 56 L.Ed. 500, Ann.Cas.1913C, 1138. This principle does not apply to hearings on motions made prior to or after trial, *United States v. Lynch,* 132 F.2d 111, C.C.A.3d.

2. The second sentence of the rule is a restatement of existing law that, except in capital cases, the defendant may not defeat the proceedings by voluntarily absenting himself after the trial has been commenced in his presence, *Diaz v. United States,* 223 U.S. 442, 455, 32 S.Ct. 250, 56 L.Ed. 500, Ann.Cas.1913C, 1138; *United States v. Noble,* 294 Fed. 689 (D.Mont.)—affirmed, 300 Fed. 689, C.C.A.9th; *United States v. Barracota,* 45 F.Supp. 38, S.D.N.Y.; *United States v. Vassalo,* 52 F.2d 699, E.D.Mich.

3. The fourth sentence of the rule empowering the court in its discretion, with the defendant's written consent, to conduct proceedings in misdemeanor cases in defendant's absence adopts a practice prevailing in some districts comprising very large areas. In such districts appearance in court may require considerable travel, resulting in expense and hardship not commensurate with the gravity of the charge, if a minor infraction is involved and a small fine is eventually imposed. The rule, which is in the interest of defendants in such situations, leaves it discretionary with the court to permit defendants in misdemeanor cases to absent themselves and, if so, to determine in what types of misdemeanors and to what extent. Similar provisions are found in the statutes of a number of States. See A.L.I. Code of Criminal Procedure, pp. 881–882.

4. The purpose of the last sentence of the rule is to resolve a doubt that at times has arisen as to whether it is necessary to bring the defendant to court from an institution in which he is confined, possibly at a distant point, if the court determines to reduce the sentence previously imposed. It seems in the interest of both the Government and the defendant not to require such presence, because of the delay and expense that are involved.

1974 AMENDMENT

The revision of rule 43 is designed to reflect *Illinois v. Allen,* 397 U.S. 337, 90 S.Ct. 1057, 25 L.Ed.2d 353 (1970). In *Allen,* the court held that "there are at least three constitutionally permissible ways for a trial judge to handle an obstreperous defendant like Allen: (1) bind and gag him, thereby keeping him present; (2) cite him for contempt; (3) take him out of the courtroom until he promises to conduct himself properly." 397 U.S. at 343–344, 90 S.Ct. 1057.

Since rule 43 formerly limited trial in absentia to situations in which there is a "voluntary absence after the trial has been commenced," it could be read as precluding a federal judge from exercising the third option held to be constitutionally permissible in *Allen.* The amendment is designed to make clear that the judge does have the power to exclude the defendant from the courtroom when the circumstances warrant such action.

The decision in *Allen,* makes no attempt to spell out standards to guide a judge in selecting the appropriate method to ensure decorum in the courtroom and there is no attempt to do so in the revision of the rule.

The concurring opinion of Mr. Justice Brennan stresses that the trial judge should make a reasonable effort to enable an excluded defendant "to communicate with his attorney and, if possible, to keep apprised of the progress of the trial." 397 U.S. at 351, 90 S.Ct. 1057. The Federal Judicial Center is presently engaged in experimenting with closed circuit television in courtrooms. The experience gained from these experiments may make closed circuit television readily available in federal courtrooms through which an excluded defendant would be able to hear and observe the trial.

The defendant's right to be present during the trial on a capital offense has been said to be so fundamental that it may not be waived. *Diaz v. United States,* 223 U.S. 442, 455, 32 S.Ct. 250, 56 L.Ed. 500 (1912) (dictum); *Near v. Cunningham,* 313 F.2d 929, 931 (4th Cir.1963); C. Wright, Federal Practice and Procedure: Criminal § 723 at 199 (1969, Supp.1971).

However, in *Illinois v. Allen, supra* the court's opinion suggests that sanctions such as contempt may be least effective where the defendant is ultimately facing a far more serious sanction such as the death penalty. 397 U.S. at 345, 90 S.Ct. 1057. The ultimate determination of when a defendant can waive his right to be present in a capital case (assuming a death penalty provision is held constitutional, see *Furman v. Georgia,* 408 U.S. 238, 92 S.Ct. 2726, 33 L.Ed.2d 346 (1972)) is left for further clarification by the courts.

Subdivision (b)(1) makes clear that voluntary absence may constitute a waiver even if the defendant has not been informed by the court of his obligation to remain during the trial. Of course, proof of voluntary absence will require a showing that the defendant knew of the fact that the trial or other proceeding was going on. C. Wright, Federal Practice and Procedure: Criminal § 723 n. 35 (1969). But it is unnecessary to show that he was specifically warned of his obligation to be present; a warning seldom is thought necessary in current practice. [See *Taylor v. United States,* 414 U.S. 17, 94 S.Ct. 194, 38 L.Ed.2d 174 (1973).]

Subdivision (c)(3) makes clear that the defendant need not be present at a conference held by the court and counsel where the subject of the conference is an issue of law.

The other changes in the rule are editorial in nature. In the last phrase of the first sentence, "these rules" is changed to read "this rule," because there are no references in any of the other rules to situations where the defendant is not required to be present. The phrase "at the time of the plea," is added to subdivision (a) to make perfectly clear that defendant must be present at the time of the plea. See rule 11(c)(5) which provides that the judge may set a time, other than arraignment, for the holding of a plea agreement procedure.

NOTES OF COMMITTEE ON THE JUDICIARY, HOUSE REPORT NO. 94–247

A. Amendments Proposed by the Supreme Court. Rule 43 of the Federal Rules of Criminal Procedure deals with the presence of the defendant during the proceedings against him. It presently permits a defendant to be tried in absentia only in non-capital cases where the defendant has voluntarily absented himself after the trial has begun.

The Supreme Court amendments provide that a defendant has waived his right to be present at the trial of a capital or noncapital case in two circumstances: (1) when he voluntarily absents himself after the trial has begun; and (2) where he "engages in conduct which is such as to justify his being excluded from the courtroom."

B. Committee Action. The Committee added language to subdivision (b)(2), which deals with excluding a disruptive defendant from the courtroom. The Advisory Committee Note indicates that the rule proposed by the Supreme Court was drafted to reflect the decision in *Illinois v. Allen,* 397 U.S. 337 (1970). The Committee found that subdivision (b)(2) as proposed did not full track the *Allen* decision. Consequently, language was added to that subsection to require the court to warn a disruptive defendant before excluding him from the courtroom.

1987 AMENDMENT

The amendments are technical. No substantive change is intended.

Rule 44. Right to and Assignment of Counsel

(a) Right to Assigned Counsel. Every defendant who is unable to obtain counsel shall be entitled to have counsel assigned to represent that defendant at every stage of the proceedings from initial appearance before the federal magistrate or the court through appeal, unless that defendant waives such appointment.

(b) Assignment Procedure. The procedures for implementing the right set out in subdivision (a) shall be those provided by law and by local rules of court established pursuant thereto.

(c) Joint Representation. Whenever two or more defendants have been jointly charged pursuant to Rule 8(b) or have been joined for trial pursuant to Rule 13, and are represented by the same retained or assigned counsel or by retained or assigned counsel who are associated in the practice of law, the court shall promptly inquire with respect to such joint representation and shall personally advise each defendant of the right to the effective assistance of counsel, including separate representation. Unless it appears that there is good cause to believe no conflict of interest is likely to arise, the court shall take such measures as may be appropriate to protect each defendant's right to counsel.

(As amended Feb. 28, 1966, eff. July 1, 1966; Apr. 24, 1972, eff. Oct. 1, 1972; Apr. 30, 1979, eff. Dec. 1, 1980; Mar. 9, 1987, eff. Aug. 1, 1987.)

NOTES OF ADVISORY COMMITTEE ON RULES

1. This rule is a restatement of existing law in regard to the defendant's constitutional right of counsel as defined in recent judicial decisions. The Sixth Amendment provides:

"In all criminal prosecutions, the accused shall enjoy the right * * * to have the Assistance of Counsel for his defense."

28 U.S.C. former § 394 (now § 1654) provides:

"In all the courts of the United States the parties may plead and manage their own causes personally, or by the assistance of such counsel or attorneys at law as, by the rules of the said courts, respectively, are permitted to manage and conduct causes therein."

18 U.S.C. former § 563 (now § 3005), which is derived from the act of April 30, 1790 (1 Stat. 118), provides:

"Every person who is indicted of treason or other capital crime, shall be allowed to make his full defense by counsel learned in the law; and the court before which he is tried or some judge thereof, shall immediately, upon his request, assign to him such counsel, not exceeding two, as he may desire, and they shall have free access to him at all seasonable hours."

The present extent of the right of counsel has been defined recently in *Johnson v. Zerbst*, 304 U.S. 458, 58 S.Ct. 1019, 82 L.Ed. 1461; *Walker v. Johnston*, 312 U.S. 275, 61 S.Ct. 574, 85 L.Ed. 830; and *Glasser v. United States*, 315 U.S. 60, 62 S.Ct. 457, 86 L.Ed. 680, rehearing denied 315 U.S. 827, 62 S.Ct. 629, 637, two cases, 86 L.Ed. 1222. The rule is a restatement of the principles enunciated in these decisions. See, also, Holtzoff, 20 N.Y.U.L.Q.R. 1.

2. The rule is intended to indicate that the right of the defendant to have counsel assigned by the court relates only to proceedings in court and, therefore, does not include preliminary proceedings before a committing magistrate. Although the defendant is not entitled to have counsel assigned to him in connection with preliminary proceedings, he is entitled to be represented by counsel retained by him, if he so chooses, Rule 5(b) (Proceedings before the Commissioner; Statement by the Commissioner) and Rule 40(b)(2) (Commitment to Another District; Removal—Arrest in Distant District—Statement by Commissioner or Judge). As to defendant's right of counsel in connection with the taking of depositions, see Rule 15(c) (Depositions—Defendant's Counsel and Payment of Expenses).

1966 AMENDMENT

A new rule is provided as a substitute for the old to provide for the assignment of counsel to defendants unable to obtain counsel during all stages of the proceeding. The Supreme Court has recently made clear the importance of providing counsel both at the earliest possible time after arrest and on appeal. See *Crooker v. California,* 357 U.S. 433 (1958); *Cicenia v. LaGay,* 357 U.S. 504 (1958); *White v. Maryland,* 373 U.S. 59 (1963); *Gideon v. Wainwright,* 372 U.S. 335 (1963); *Douglas v. California,* 372 U.S. 353 (1963). See also Association of the Bar of the City of New York, Special Committee to Study the Defender System, Equal Justice for the Accused (1959); Report of the Attorney General's Committee on Poverty and the Administration of Justice (1963); Beaney, Right to Counsel Before Arraignment, 45 Minn. L.Rev. 771 (1961); Boskey, The Right to Counsel in Appellate Proceedings, 45 Minn.L.Rev. 783 (1961); Douglas, The Right to Counsel—A Foreword, 45 Minn. L.Rev. 693 (1961); Kamisar, The Right to Counsel and the Fourteenth Amendment; A Dialogue on "The Most Pervasive Right" of an Accused, 30 U.Chi.L.Rev. 1 (1962); Kamisar, Betts v. Brady Twenty Years Later:

The Right to Counsel and Due Process Values, 61 Mich. L.Rev. 219 (1962); Symposium, The Right to Counsel, 22 Legal Aid Briefcase 4–48 (1963). Provision has been made by law for a Legal Aid Agency in the District of Columbia which is charged with the duty of providing counsel and courts are admonished to assign such counsel "as early in the proceeding as practicable." D.C. Code § 2–2202. Congress has now made provision for assignment of counsel and their compensation in all of the districts. Criminal Justice Act of 1964 (78 Stat. 552).

Like the original rule the amended rule provides a right to counsel which is broader in two respects than that for which compensation is provided in the Criminal Justice Act of 1964: (1) the right extends to petty offenses to be tried in the district courts, and (2) the right extends to defendants unable to obtain counsel for reasons other than financial. These rules do not cover procedures other than those in the courts of the United States and before United States commissioners. See Rule 1. Hence, the problems relating to the providing of counsel prior to the initial appearance before a court or commissioner are not dealt with in this rule. Cf. *Escobedo v. United States,* 378 U.S. 478 (1964); Enker and Elsen, Counsel for the Suspect: *Massiah v. United States* and *Escobedo v. Illinois,* 49 Minn.L.Rev. 47 (1964).

Subdivision (a). This subdivision expresses the right of the defendant unable to obtain counsel to have such counsel assigned at any stage of the proceedings from his initial appearance before the commissioner or court through the appeal, unless he waives such right. The phrase "from his initial appearance before the commissioner or court" is intended to require the assignment of counsel as promptly as possible after it appears that the defendant is unable to obtain counsel. The right to assignment of counsel is not limited to those financially unable to obtain counsel. If a defendant is able to compensate counsel but still cannot obtain counsel, he is entitled to the assignment of counsel even though not to free counsel.

Subdivision (b). This new subdivision reflects the adoption of the Criminal Justice Act of 1964. See Report of the Judicial Conference of the United States on the Criminal Justice Act of 1964, 36 F.R.D. 277 (1964).

1972 AMENDMENT

Subdivision (a) is amended to reflect the Federal Magistrates Act of 1968. The phrase "federal magistrate" is defined in rule 54.

1979 AMENDMENT

Rule 44(c) establishes a procedure for avoiding the occurrence of events which might otherwise give rise to a plausible post-conviction claim that because of joint representation the defendants in a criminal case were deprived of their Sixth Amendment right to the effective assistance of counsel. Although "courts have differed with respect to the scope and nature of the affirmative duty of the trial judge to assure that criminal defendants are not deprived of their right to the effective assistance of counsel by joint representation of conflicting interests," *Holloway v. Arkansas*, 98 S.Ct. 1173 (1978) (where the Court found it unnecessary to reach this issue), this amendment is generally consistent with the current state of the law in several circuits. As held in *United States v. Carrigan*, 543 F.2d 1053 (2d Cir.1976):

> When a potential conflict of interest arises, either where a court has assigned the same counsel to represent several defendants or where the same counsel has been retained by co-defendants in a criminal case, the proper course of action for the trial judge is to conduct a hearing to determine whether a conflict exists to the degree that a defendant may be prevented from receiving advice and assistance sufficient to afford him the quality of representation guaranteed by the Sixth Amendment. The defendant should be fully advised by the trial court of the facts underlying the potential conflict and be given the opportunity to express his views.

See also *United States v. Lawriw*, 568 F.2d 98 (8th Cir.1977) (duty on trial judge to make inquiry where joint representation by appointed or retained counsel, and "without such an inquiry a finding of knowing and intelligent waiver will seldom, if ever, be sustained by this Court"); *Abraham v. United States*, 549 F.2d 236 (2d Cir.1977); *United States v. Mari*, 526 F.2d 117 (2d Cir.1975); *United States v. Truglio*, 493 F.2d 574 (4th Cir.1974) (joint representation should cause trial judge "to inquire whether the defenses to be presented in any way conflict"); *United States v. DeBerry*, 487 F.2d 488 (2d Cir.1973); *United States ex rel. Hart v. Davenport*, 478 F.2d 203 (3d Cir.1973) (noting there "is much to be said for the rule ... which assumes prejudice and nonwaiver if there has been no on-the-record inquiry by the court as to the hazards to defendants from joint representation"); *United States v. Alberti*, 470 F.2d 878 (2d Cir.1973); *United States v. Foster*, 469 F.2d 1 (1st Cir.1972) (lack of sufficient inquiry shifts the burden of proof on the question of prejudice to the government); *Campbell v. United States*, 352 F.2d 359 (D.C.Cir.1965) (where joint representation, court "has a duty to ascertain whether each defendant has an awareness of the potential risks of that course and nevertheless has knowingly chosen it"). Some states have taken a like position; see, e.g., *State v. Olsen*, Minn.1977, 258 N.W. 2d 898.

This procedure is also consistent with that recommended in the ABA Standards Relating to the Function of the Trial Judge (Approved Draft, 1972), which provide in § 3.4(b):

> Whenever two or more defendants who have been jointly charged, or whose cases have been consolidated, are represented by the same attorney, the trial judge should inquire into potential conflicts which may jeopardize the right of each defendant to the fidelity of his counsel.

Avoiding a conflict-of-interest situation is in the first instance a responsibility of the attorney. If a lawyer represents "multiple clients having potentially differing interests, he must weigh carefully the possibility that his judgment may be impaired or his loyalty divided if he accepts or continues the employment," and he is to "resolve all doubts against the propriety of the representation." Code of Professional Responsibility, Ethical Consideration 5–15. See also ABA Standards Relating to the Defense Function § 3.5(b) (Approved Draft, 1971), concluding that the "potential for conflict of interest in representing multiple defendants is so grave that ordinarily a lawyer should decline to act for more than one of several co-defendants except in unusual situations when, after careful investigation, it is clear that no conflict is likely to develop and when the several defendants give an informed consent to such multiple representation."

It by no means follows that the inquiry provided for by rule 44(c) is unnecessary. For one thing, even the most diligent attorney may be unaware of facts giving rise to a potential conflict. Often "counsel must operate somewhat in the dark and feel their way uncertainly to an understanding of what their clients may be called upon to meet upon a trial" and consequently "are frequently unable to foresee developments which may require changes in strategy." *United States v. Carrigan*, supra (concurring opinion). "Because the conflicts are often subtle it is not enough to rely upon counsel, who may not be totally disinterested, to make sure that each of his joint clients has made an effective waiver." *United States v. Lawriw*, supra.

Moreover, it is important that the trial judge ascertain whether the effective and fair administration of justice would be adversely affected by continued joint representation, even when an actual conflict is not then apparent. As noted in *United States v. Mari*, supra (concurring opinion):

> Trial court insistence that, except in extraordinary circumstances, codefendants retain separate counsel will in the long run ... prove salutary not only to the administration of justice and the appearance of justice but the cost of justice; habeas corpus petitions, petitions for new trials, appeals and occasionally retrials ... can be avoided. Issues as to whether there is an actual conflict of interest, whether the conflict has resulted in prejudice, whether there has been a waiver, whether the waiver is intelligent and knowledgeable, for example, can all be avoided. Where a conflict that first did not appear subsequently arises in or before trial, ... continuances or mistrials can be

saved. Essentially by the time a case ... gets to the appellate level the harm to the appearance of justice has already been done, whether or not reversal occurs; at the trial level it is a matter which is so easy to avoid.

A rule 44(c) inquiry is required whether counsel is assigned or retained. It "makes no difference whether counsel is appointed by the court or selected by the defendants; even where selected by the defendants the same dangers of potential conflict exist, and it is also possible that the rights of the public to the proper administration of justice may be affected adversely." *United States v. Mari,* supra (concurring opinion). See also *United States v. Lawriw,* supra. When there has been "no discussion as to possible conflict initiated by the court," it cannot be assumed that the choice of counsel by the defendants "was intelligently made with knowledge of any possible conflict." *United States v. Carrigan,* supra. As for assigned counsel, it is provided by statute that "the court shall appoint separate counsel for defendants having interests that cannot properly be represented by the same counsel, or when other good cause is shown." 18 U.S.C. § 3006(A)(b). Rule 44(c) is not intended to prohibit the automatic appointment of separate counsel in the first instance, see *Ford v. United States,* 379 F.2d 123 (D.C.Cir.1967); *Lollar v. United States,* 376 F.2d 243 (D.C.Cir.1967), which would obviate the necessity for an inquiry.

Under rule 44(c), an inquiry is called for when the joined defendants are represented by the same attorney and also when they are represented by attorneys "associated in the practice of law." This is consistent with Code of Professional Responsibility, Disciplinary Rule 5–105(D) (providing that if "a lawyer is required to decline employment or to withdraw from employment" because of a potential conflict, "no partner or associate of his or his firm may accept or continue such employment"); and ABA Standards Relating to the Defense Function § 3.5(b) (Approved Draft, 1971) (applicable to "a lawyer or lawyers who are associated in practice"). Attorneys representing joined defendants should so advise the court if they are associated in the practice of law.

The rule 44(c) procedure is not limited to cases expected to go to trial. Although the more dramatic conflict situations, such as when the question arises as to whether the several defendants should take the stand, *Morgan v. United States,* 396 F.2d 110 (2d Cir. 1968), tend to occur in a trial context, serious conflicts may also arise when one or more of the jointly represented defendants pleads guilty.

The problem is that even where as here both codefendants pleaded guilty there are frequently potential conflicts of interest ... [T]he prosecutor may be inclined to accept a guilty plea from one codefendant which may harm the interests of the other. The contrast in the dispositions of the cases may have a harmful impact on the codefendant who does not initially plead guilty; he may be pressured into pleading guilty himself rather than face his codefendant's bargained-for testimony at a trial. And it will be his own counsel's recommendation to the initially pleading codefendant which will have contributed to this harmful impact upon him ... [I]n a given instance it would be at least conceivable that the prosecutor would be willing to accept pleas to lesser offenses from two defendants in preference to a plea of guilty by one defendant to a greater offense.

United States v. Mari, supra (concurring opinion). To the same effect is ABA Standards Relating to the Defense Function at 213–14.

It is contemplated that under rule 44(c) the court will make appropriate inquiry of the defendants and of counsel regarding the possibility of a conflict of interest developing. Whenever it is necessary to make a more particularized inquiry into the nature of the contemplated defense, the court should "pursue the inquiry with defendants and their counsel on the record but in chambers" so as "to avoid the possibility of prejudicial disclosures to the prosecution." *United States v. Foster,* supra. It is important that each defendant be "fully advised of the facts underlying the potential conflict and is given an opportunity to express his or her views." *United States v. Alberti,* supra. The rule specifically requires that the court personally advise each defendant of his right to effective assistance of counsel, including separate representation. See *United States v. Foster,* supra, requiring that the court make a determination that jointly represented defendants "understand that they may retain separate counsel, or if qualified, may have such counsel appointed by the court and paid for by the government."

Under rule 44(c), the court is to take appropriate measures to protect each defendant's right to counsel unless it appears "there is good cause to believe no conflict of interest is likely to arise" as a consequence of the continuation of such joint representation. A less demanding standard would not adequately protect the Sixth Amendment right to effective assistance of counsel or the effective administration of criminal justice. Although joint representation "is not per se violative of constitutional guarantees of effective assistance of counsel, *Holloway v. Arkansas,* supra, it would not suffice to require the court to act only when a conflict of interest is then apparent, for it is not possible to "anticipate with complete accuracy the course that a criminal trial may take." *Fryar v. United States,* 404 F.2d 1071 (10th Cir.1968). This is particularly so in light of the fact that if a conflict later arises and a defendant thereafter raises a Sixth Amendment objection, a court must grant relief without indulging "in nice calculations as to the amount of prejudice arising from its denial." *Glasser v. United States,* 315 U.S. 60 (1942). This is because, as the Supreme Court more recently noted in *Holloway v.*

Arkansas, supra, "in a case of joint representation of conflicting interests the evil ... is in what the advocate finds himself compelled to refrain from doing," and this makes it "virtually impossible" to assess the impact of the conflict.

Rule 44(c) does not specify what particular measures must be taken. It is appropriate to leave this within the court's discretion, for the measures which will best protect each defendant's right to counsel may well vary from case to case. One possible course of action is for the court to obtain a knowing, intelligent and voluntary waiver of the right to separate representation, for, as noted in *Holloway v. Arkansas*, supra, "a defendant may waive his right to the assistance of an attorney unhindered by a conflict of interests." See *United States v. DeBerry*, supra, holding that defendants should be jointly represented only if "the court has ascertained that ... each understands clearly the possibilities of a conflict of interest and waives any rights in connection with it." It must be emphasized that a "waiver of the right to separate representation should not be accepted by the court unless the defendants have each been informed of the probable hazards; and the voluntary character of their waiver is apparent." ABA Standards Relating to the Function of the Trial Judge at 45. *United States v. Garcia*, supra, spells out in significant detail what should be done to assure an adequate waiver:

As in Rule 11 procedures, the district court should address each defendant personally and forthrightly advise him of the potential dangers of representation by counsel with a conflict of interest. The defendant must be at liberty to question the district court as to the nature and consequences of his legal representation. Most significantly, the court should seek to elicit a narrative response from each defendant that he has been advised of his right to effective representation, that he understands the details of his attorney's possible conflict of interest and the potential perils of such a conflict, that he has discussed the matter with his attorney or if he wishes with outside counsel, and that he voluntarily waives his Sixth Amendment protections. It is, of course, vital that the wavier be established by "clear, unequivocal, and unambiguous language." ... Mere assent in response to a series of questions from the bench may in some circumstances constitute an adequate waiver, but the court should nonetheless endeavor to have each defendant personally articulate in detail his intent to forego this significant constitutional protection. Recordation of the waiver colloque between defendant and judge, will also serve the government's interest by assisting in shielding any potential conviction from collateral attack, either on Sixth Amendment grounds or on a Fifth or Fourteenth Amendment "fundamental fairness" basis.

See also Hyman, Joint Representation of Multiple Defendants in a Criminal Trial: The Court's Headache, 5 Hofstra L.Rev. 315, 334 (1977).

Another possibility is that the court will order that the defendants be separately represented in subsequent proceedings in the case.

Though the court must remain alert to and take account of the fact that "certain advantages might accrue from joint representation," *Holloway v. Arkansas*, supra, it need not permit the joint representation to continue merely because the defendants express a willingness to so proceed. That is, there will be cases where the court should require separate counsel to represent certain defendants despite the expressed wishes of such defendants. Indeed, failure of the trial court to require separate representation may ... require a new trial, even though the defendants have expressed a desire to continue with the same counsel. The right to effective representation by counsel whose loyalty is undivided is so paramount in the proper administration of criminal justice that it must in some cases take precedence over all other considerations, including the expressed preference of the defendants concerned and their attorney.

United States v. Carrigan, supra (concurring opinion). See also *United States v. Lawriw*, supra; *Abraham v. United States*, supra; ABA Standards Relating to the Defense Function at 213, concluding that in some circumstances "even full disclosure and consent of the client may not be an adequate protection." As noted in *United States v. Dolan*, 570 F.2d 1177 (3d Cir.1978), such an order may be necessary where the trial judge is

not satisfied that the wavier is proper. For example, a defendant may be competent enough to stand trial, but not competent enough to understand the complex, subtle, and sometimes unforeseeable dangers inherent in multiple representation. More importantly, the judge may find that the waiver cannot be intelligently made simply because he is not in a position to inform the defendant of the foreseeable prejudices multiple representation might entail for him.

As concluded in *Dolan*, "exercise of the court's supervisory powers by disqualifying an attorney representing multiple criminal defendants in spite of the defendants' express desire to retain that attorney does not necessarily abrogate defendant's sixth amendment rights". It does not follow from the absolute right of self-representation recognized in *Faretta v. California*, 422 U.S. 806 (1975), that there is an *absolute* right to counsel of one's own choice. Thus,

when a trial court finds an actual conflict of interest which impairs the ability of a criminal defendant's chosen counsel to conform with the ABA Code of Professional Responsibility, the court should not be required to tolerate an inadequate representation of a defendant. Such representation not only constitutes a breach of professional ethics and invites disrespect for the integrity of the court, but it is also detrimental to the independent interest of the trial judge to be free from future attacks over the adequacy of the waiver or the fairness of the proceedings in his own court and the subtle problems implicating the defendant's comprehension of the waiver. Under such circumstances, the court can elect to exercise its supervisory authority over members of the bar to enforce the ethical standard requiring an attorney to decline multiple representation.

United States v. Dolan, supra. See also Geer, Conflict of Interest and Multiple Defendants in a Criminal Case: Professional Responsibilities of the Defense Attorney, 62 Minn.L.Rev. 119 (1978); Note, Conflict of Interests in Multiple Representation of Criminal Co–Defendants, 68 J.Crim.L. & C. 226 (1977).

The failure in a particular case to conduct a rule 44(c) inquiry would not, standing alone, necessitate the reversal of a conviction of a jointly represented defendant. However, as is currently the case, a reviewing court is more likely to assume a conflict resulted from the joint representation when no inquiry or an inadequate inquiry was conducted. *United States v. Carrigan,* supra; *United States v. DeBerry,* supra. On the other hand, the mere fact that a rule 44(c) inquiry was conducted in the early stages of the case does not relieve the court of all responsibility in this regard thereafter. The obligation placed upon the court by rule 44(c) is a continuing one, and thus in a particular case further inquiry may be necessary on a later occasion because of new developments suggesting a potential conflict of interest.

1987 AMENDMENT

The amendments are technical. No substantive change is intended.

Rule 45. Time

(a) **Computation.** In computing any period of time the day of the act or event from which the designated period of time begins to run shall not be included. The last day of the period so computed shall be included, unless it is a Saturday, a Sunday, or a legal holiday, or, when the act to be done is the filing of some paper in court, a day on which weather or other conditions have made the office of the clerk of the district court inaccessible, in which event the period runs until the end of the next day which is not one of the aforementioned days. When a period of time prescribed or allowed is less than 11 days, intermediate Saturdays, Sundays and legal holidays shall be excluded in the computation. As used in these rules, "legal holiday" includes New Year's Day, Birthday of Martin Luther King, Jr., Washington's Birthday, Memorial Day, Independence Day, Labor Day, Columbus Day, Veterans Day, Thanksgiving Day, Christmas Day, and any other day appointed as a holiday by the President or the Congress of the United States, or by the state in which the district court is held.

(b) **Enlargement.** When an act is required or allowed to be done at or within a specified time, the court for cause shown may at any time in its discretion (1) with or without motion or notice, order the period enlarged if request therefor is made before the expiration of the period originally prescribed or as extended by a previous order or (2) upon motion made after the expiration of the specified period permit the act to be done if the failure to act was the result of excusable neglect; but the court may not extend the time for taking any action under Rules 29, 33, 34 and 35, except to the extent and under the conditions stated in them.

[(c) Unaffected by Expiration of Term.] (Rescinded Feb. 28, 1966, eff. July 1, 1966.)

(d) **For Motions; Affidavits.** A written motion, other than one which may be heard *ex parte,* and notice of the hearing thereof shall be served not later than 5 days before the time specified for the hearing unless a different period is fixed by rule or order of the court. For cause shown such an order may be made on *ex parte* application. When a motion is supported by affidavit, the affidavit shall be served with the motion; and opposing affidavits may be served not less than 1 day before the hearing unless the court permits them to be served at a later time.

(e) **Additional Time After Service by Mail.** Whenever a party has the right or is required to do an act within a prescribed period after the service of a notice or other paper upon that party and the notice or other paper is served by mail, 3 days shall be added to the prescribed period.

(As amended Feb. 28, 1966, eff. July 1, 1966; Dec. 4, 1967, eff. July 1, 1968; Mar. 1, 1971, eff. July 1, 1971; Apr. 28, 1982, eff. Aug. 1, 1982; Apr. 29, 1985, eff. Aug. 1, 1985; Mar. 9, 1987, eff. Aug. 1, 1987.)

NOTES OF ADVISORY COMMITTEE ON RULES

The rule is in substance the same as Rule 6 of the Federal Rules of Civil Procedure, 28 U.S.C., Appendix. It seems desirable that matters covered by this rule should be regulated in the same manner for civil and criminal cases, in order to preclude possibility of confusion.

Note to Subdivision (a). This rule supersedes the method of computing time prescribed by Rule 13 of the Criminal Appeals Rules, promulgated on May 7, 1934, 292 U.S. 661.

Note to Subdivision (c). This rule abolishes the expiration of a term of court as a time limitation for the taking of any step in a criminal proceeding, as is done for civil cases by Rule 6(c) of the Federal Rules of Civil Procedure, 28 U.S.C., Appendix. In view of the fact that the duration of terms of court varies among the several districts and the further fact that the length of time for the taking of any step limited by a term of court depends on the stage within the term when the time begins to run, specific time limitations have been substituted for the taking of any step which previously had to be taken within the term of court.

Note to Subdivision (d). Cf. Rule 47 (Motions) and Rule 49 (Service and filing of papers).

1966 AMENDMENT

Subdivision (a). This amendment conforms the subdivision with the amendments made effective on July 1, 1963, to the comparable provision in Civil Rule 6(a). The only major change is to treat Saturdays as legal holidays for the purpose of computing time.

Subdivision (b). The amendment conforms the subdivision to the amendments made effective in 1948 to the comparable provision in Civil Rule 6(b). One of these conforming changes, substituting the words "extend the time" for the words "enlarge the period" clarifies the ambiguity which gave rise to the decision in *United States v. Robinson*, 361 U.S. 220 (1960). The amendment also, in connection with the amendments to Rules 29 and 37, makes it clear that the only circumstances under which extensions can be granted under Rules 29, 33, 34, 35, 37(a)(2) and 39(c) are those stated in them.

Subdivision (c). Subdivision (c) of Rule 45 is rescinded as unnecessary in view of the 1963 amendment to 28 U.S.C. § 138 eliminating terms of court.

1968 AMENDMENT

The amendment eliminates inappropriate references to Rules 37 and 39 which are to be abrogated.

1971 AMENDMENT

The amendment adds Columbus Day to the list of legal holidays to conform the subdivision to the Act of June 28, 1968, 82 Stat. 250, which constituted Columbus Day a legal holiday effective after January 1, 1971.

The Act, which amended Title 5, U.S.C., § 6103(a), changes the day on which certain holidays are to be observed. Washington's Birthday, Memorial Day and Veterans Day are to be observed on the third Monday in February, the last Monday in May and the fourth Monday in October, respectively, rather than, as heretofore, on February 22, May 30, and November 11, respectively. Columbus Day is to be observed on the second Monday in October. New Year's Day, Independence Day, Thanksgiving Day and Christmas continue to be observed on the traditional days.

1982 AMENDMENT

The amendment to subdivision (a) takes account of the fact that on rare occasion severe weather conditions or other circumstances beyond control will make it impossible to meet a filing deadline under Rule 45(a). Illustrative is an incident which occurred in Columbus, Ohio during the "great blizzard of 1978," in which weather conditions deteriorated to the point where personnel in the clerk's office found it virtually impossible to reach the courthouse, and where the GSA Building Manager found it necessary to close and secure the entire building. The amendment covers that situation and also similar situations in which weather or other conditions made the clerk's office, though open, not readily accessible to the lawyer. Whether the clerk's office was in fact "inaccessible" on a given date is to be determined by the district court. Some state time computation statutes contain language somewhat similar to that in the amendment; see, e.g., Md.Code Ann. art. 94, § 2.

1985 AMENDMENT

The rule is amended to extend the exclusion of intermediate Saturdays, Sundays, and legal holidays to the computation of time periods less than 11 days. Under the current version of the Rule, parties bringing motions under rules with 10–day periods could have as few as 5 working days to prepare their motions. This change corresponds to the change being made in the comparable provision in Fed.R.Civ.P. 6(a).

The Birthday of Martin Luther King, Jr., which becomes a legal holiday effective January 1986, has been added to the list of legal holidays enumerated in the Rule.

1987 AMENDMENT

The amendments are technical. No substantive change is intended.

Rule 46.   Release from Custody

(a) Release Prior to Trial. Eligibility for release prior to trial shall be in accordance with 18 U.S.C. §§ 3142 and 3144.

(b) Release During Trial. A person released before trial shall continue on release during trial under the same terms and conditions as were previously imposed unless the court determines that other terms and conditions or termination of release are necessary to assure such person's presence during the trial or to assure that such person's conduct will not obstruct the orderly and expeditious progress of the trial.

(c) Pending Sentence and Notice of Appeal. Eligibility for release pending sentence or pending notice of appeal or expiration of the time allowed for filing notice of appeal, shall be in accordance with 18 U.S.C. § 3143. The burden of establishing that the defendant will not flee or pose a danger to any other person or to the community rests with the defendant.

(d) Justification of Sureties. Every surety, except a corporate surety which is approved as provided by law, shall justify by affidavit and may be required to describe in the affidavit the property by which the surety proposes to justify and the encumbrances thereon, the number and amount of other bonds and undertakings for bail entered into by the surety and remaining undischarged and all the other liabilities of the surety. No bond shall be approved unless the surety thereon appears to be qualified.

(e) Forfeiture.

(1) Declaration. If there is a breach of condition of a bond, the district court shall declare a forfeiture of the bail.

(2) Setting Aside. The court may direct that a forfeiture be set aside in whole or in part, upon such conditions as the court may impose, if a person released upon execution of an appearance bond with a surety is subsequently surrendered by the surety into custody or if it otherwise appears that justice does not require the forfeiture.

(3) Enforcement. When a forfeiture has not been set aside, the court shall on motion enter a judgment of default and execution may issue thereon. By entering into a bond the obligors submit to the jurisdiction of the district court and irrevocably appoint the clerk of the court as their agent upon whom any papers affecting their liability may be served. Their liability may be enforced on motion without the necessity of an independent action. The motion and such notice of the motion as the court prescribes may be served on the clerk of the court, who shall forthwith mail copies to the obligors to their last known addresses.

(4) Remission. After entry of such judgment, the court may remit it in whole or in part under the conditions applying to the setting aside of forfeiture in paragraph (2) of this subdivision.

(f) Exoneration. When the condition of the bond has been satisfied or the forfeiture thereof has been set aside or remitted, the court shall exonerate the obligors and release any bail. A surety may be exonerated by a deposit of cash in the amount of the bond or by a timely surrender of the defendant into custody.

(g) Supervision of Detention Pending Trial. The court shall exercise supervision over the detention of defendants and witnesses within the district pending trial for the purpose of eliminating all unnecessary detention. The attorney for the government shall make a biweekly report to the court listing each defendant and witness who has been held in custody pending indictment, arraignment or trial for a period in excess of ten days. As to each witness so listed the attorney for the government shall make a statement of the reasons why such witness should not be released with or without the taking of a deposition pursuant to Rule 15(a). As to each defendant so listed the attorney for the government shall make a statement of the reasons why the defendant is still held in custody.

(h) Forfeiture of Property. Nothing in this rule or in chapter 207 of title 18, United States Code, shall prevent the court from disposing of any charge by entering an order directing forfeiture of property pursuant to 18 U.S.C. 3142(c)(2)(K) if the value of the property is an amount that would be an appropriate sentence after conviction of the offense charged and if such forfeiture is authorized by statute or regulation.

(As amended Apr. 9, 1956, eff. July 8, 1956; Feb. 28, 1966, eff. July 1, 1966; Apr. 24, 1972, eff. Oct. 1, 1972; Oct. 12, 1984, Pub.L. 98–473, Title II, § 209(d), 98 Stat. 1987; Mar. 9, 1987, eff. Aug. 1, 1987.)

NOTES OF ADVISORY COMMITTEE ON RULES

Note to Subdivision (a)(1). This rule is substantially a restatement of existing law, 18 U.S.C. former §§ 596, 597 (now § 3141).

Note to Subdivision (a)(2). This rule is substantially a restatement of Rule 6 of Criminal Appeals Rules, with the addition of a reference to bail pending certiorari. This rule does not supersede 18 U.S.C. former § 682 (now § 3731) (Appeals; on behalf of the United States; rules of practice and procedure), which provides for the admission of the defendant to bail on his own recognizance pending an appeal taken by the Government.

Note to Subdivision (b). This rule is substantially a restatement of existing law, 28 U.S.C. former § 657.

Note to Subdivision (d). This rule is a restatement of existing practice, and is based in part on 6 U.S.C. § 15 (Bonds or notes of United States in lieu of recognizance, stipulation, bond, guaranty, or undertaking; place of deposit; return to depositor; contractors' bonds).

Note to Subdivision (e). This rule is similar to Sec. 79 of A.L.I. Code of Criminal Procedure introducing, however, an element of flexibility. Corporate sureties are regulated by 6 U.S.C. §§ 6–14.

Note to Subdivision (f). 1. With the exception hereafter noted, this rule is substantially a restatement of existing law in somewhat greater detail than contained in 18 U.S.C. former § 601 (Remission of penalty of recognizance).

2. Subdivision (f)(2) changes existing law in that it increases the discretion of the court to set aside a forfeiture. The power of the court under 18 U.S.C. former § 601 was limited to cases in which the defendant's default had not been willful.

3. The second sentence of paragraph (3) is similar to Rule 73(f) of the Federal Rules of Civil Procedure, 28 U.S.C., Appendix. This paragraph also substitutes simple motion procedure for enforcing forfeited bail bonds for the procedure by scire facias, which was abolished by Rule 81(b) of the Federal Rules of Civil Procedure, 28 U.S.C., Appendix.

Note to Subdivision (g). This rule is a restatement of existing law and practice. It is based in part on 18 U.S.C. former § 599 (now § 3142) (Surrender by bail).

1966 AMENDMENT

Subdivision (c). The more inclusive word "terms" is substituted for "amount" in view of the amendment to subdivision (d) authorizing releases without security on such conditions as are necessary to insure the appearance of the defendant. The phrase added at the end of this subdivision is designed to encourage commissioners and judges to set the terms of bail so as to eliminate unnecessary detention. See *Stack v. Boyle,* 342 U.S. 1 (1951); *Bandy v. United States,* 81 S.Ct. 197 (1960); *Bandy v. United States,* 82 S.Ct. 11 (1961); *Carbo v. United States,* 82 S.Ct. 662 (1962); review den. 369 U.S. 868 (1962).

Subdivision (d). The amendments are designed to make possible (and to encourage) the release on bail of a greater percentage of indigent defendants than now are released. To the extent that other considerations make it reasonably likely that the defendant will appear it is both good practice and good economics to release him

on bail even though he cannot arrange for cash or bonds in even small amounts. In fact it has been suggested that it may be a denial of constitutional rights to hold indigent prisoners in custody for no other reason than their inability to raise the money for a bond. *Bandy v. United States,* 81 S.Ct. 197 (1960).

The first change authorizes the acceptance as security of a deposit of cash or government securities in an amount less than the face amount of the bond. Since a defendant typically purchases a bail bond for a cash payment of a certain percentage of the face of the bond, a direct deposit with the court of that amount (returnable to the defendant upon his appearance) will often be equally adequate as a deterrent to flight. Cf. Ill.Code Crim.Proc. § 110–7 (1963).

The second change authorizes the release of the defendant without financial security on his written agreement to appear when other deterrents appear reasonably adequate. See the discussion of such deterrents in *Bandy v. United States,* 81 S.Ct. 197 (1960). It also permits the imposition of nonfinancial conditions as the price of dispensing with security for the bond. Such conditions are commonly used in England. Devin, The Criminal Prosecution in England, 89 (1958). See the suggestion in Note, Bail: An Ancient Practice Reexamined, 70 Yale L.J. 966, 975 (1961) that such conditions " * * * might include release in custody of a third party, such as the accused's employer, minister, attorney, or a private organization; release subject to a duty to report periodically to the court or other public official; or even release subject to a duty to return to jail each night." Willful failure to appear after forfeiture of bail is a separate criminal offense and hence an added deterrent to flight. 18 U.S.C. § 3146.

For full discussion and general approval of the changes made here see Report of the Attorney General's Committee on Poverty and the Administration of Criminal Justice 58–89 (1963).

Subdivision (h). The purpose of this new subdivision is to place upon the court in each district the responsibility for supervising the detention of defendants and witnesses and for eliminating all unnecessary detention. The device of the report by the attorney for the government is used because in many districts defendants will be held in custody in places where the court sits only at infrequent intervals and hence they cannot be brought personally before the court without substantial delay. The magnitude of the problem is suggested by the facts that during the fiscal year ending June 30, 1960, there were 23,811 instances in which persons were held in custody pending trial and that the average length of detention prior to disposition (i.e., dismissal, acquittal, probation, sentence to imprisonment, or any other method of removing the case from the court docket) was 25.3 days. Federal Prisons 1960, table 22, p. 60. Since 27,645 of the 38,855 defendants whose cases were terminated during the fiscal year ending June 30, 1960, pleaded guilty (United States Attorneys Statistical Report, October 1960, p. 1 and table 2), it would appear that the greater part of the detention reported occurs prior to the initial appearance of the defendant before the court.

1972 AMENDMENT

The amendments are intended primarily to bring rule 46 into general conformity with the Bail Reform Act of 1966 and to deal in the rule with some issues not now included within the rule.

Subdivision (a) makes explicit that the Bail Reform Act of 1966 controls release on bail prior to trial. 18 U.S.C. § 3146 refers to release of a defendant. 18 U.S.C. § 3149 refers to release of a material witness.

Subdivision (b) deals with an issue not dealt with by the Bail Reform Act of 1966 or explicitly in former rule 46, that is, the issue of bail during trial. The rule gives the trial judge discretion to continue the prior conditions of release or to impose such additional conditions as are adequate to insure presence at trial or to insure that his conduct will not obstruct the orderly and expeditious progress of the trial.

Subdivision (c) provides for release during the period between a conviction and sentencing and for the giving of a notice of appeal or of the expiration of the time allowed for filing notice of appeal. There are situations in which defense counsel may informally indicate an intention to appeal but not actually give notice of appeal for several days. To deal with this situation the rule makes clear that the district court has authority to release under the terms of 18 U.S.C. § 3148 pending notice of appeal (*e.g.*, during the ten days after entry of judgment; see rule 4(b) of the Rules of Appellate Procedure). After the filing of notice of appeal, release by the district court shall be in accordance with the provisions of rule 9(b) of the Rules of Appellate Procedure. The burden of establishing that grounds for release exist is placed upon the defendant in the view that the fact of conviction justifies retention in custody in situations where doubt exists as to whether a defendant can be safely released pending either sentence or the giving of notice of appeal.

Subdivisions (d), (e), (f), and (g) remain unchanged. They were formerly lettered (e), (f), (g), and (h).

1987 AMENDMENT

The amendments are technical. No substantive change is intended.

Rule 47. Motions

An application to the court for an order shall be by motion. A motion other than one made during a trial or hearing shall be in writing unless the court permits it to be made orally. It shall state the grounds upon which it is made and shall set forth the relief or order sought. It may be supported by affidavit.

NOTES OF ADVISORY COMMITTEE ON RULES

1. This rule is substantially the same as the corresponding civil rule (first sentence of Rule 7(b)(1), Federal Rules of Civil Procedure), 28 U.S.C., Appendix, except that it authorizes the court to permit motions to be made orally and does not require that the grounds upon which a motion is made shall be stated "with particularity," as is the case with the civil rule.

2. This rule is intended to state general requirements for all motions. For particular provisions applying to specific motions, see Rules 6(b)(2), 12, 14, 15, 16, 17(b) and (c), 21, 22, 29 and Rule 41(e). See also Rule 49.

3. The last sentence providing that a motion may be supported by affidavit is not intended to permit "speaking motions" (e.g. motion to dismiss an indictment for insufficiency supported by affidavits), but to authorize the use of affidavits when affidavits are appropriate to establish a fact (e.g. authority to take a deposition or former jeopardy).

Rule 48. Dismissal

(a) By Attorney for Government. The Attorney General or the United States attorney may by leave of court file a dismissal of an indictment, information or complaint and the prosecution shall thereupon terminate. Such a dismissal may not be filed during the trial without the consent of the defendant.

(b) By Court. If there is unnecessary delay in presenting the charge to a grand jury or in filing an information against a defendant who has been held to answer to the district court, or if there is unnecessary delay in bringing a defendant to trial, the court may dismiss the indictment, information or complaint.

NOTES OF ADVISORY COMMITTEE ON RULES

Note to Subdivision (a). 1. The first sentence of this rule will change existing law. The common-law rule that the public prosecutor may enter a nolle prosequi in his discretion, without any action by the court, prevails in the Federal courts, *Confiscation Cases*, 7 Wall. 454, 457; *United States v. Woody*, 2 F.2d 262 (D.Mont.). This provision will permit the filing of a nolle prosequi only by leave of court. This is similar to the rule now prevailing in many States. A.L.I. Code of Criminal Procedure, Commentaries, pp. 895–897.

2. The rule confers the power to file a dismissal by leave of court on the Attorney General, as well as on

the United States attorney, since under existing law the Attorney General exercises "general superintendence and direction" over the United States attorneys "as to the manner of discharging their respective duties," 5 U.S.C. former § 317 (now 28 U.S.C. §§ 507, 547). Moreover it is the administrative practice for the Attorney General to supervise the filing of a nolle prosequi by United States attorneys. Consequently it seemed appropriate that the Attorney General should have such power directly.

3. The rule permits the filing of a dismissal of an indictment, information or complaint. The word "complaint" was included in order to resolve a doubt prevailing in some districts as to whether the United States attorney may file a nolle prosequi between the time when the defendant is bound over by the United States commissioner and the finding of an indictment. It has been assumed in a few districts that the power does not exist and that the United States attorney must await action of the grand jury, even if he deems it proper to dismiss the prosecution. This situation is an unnecessary hardship to some defendants.

4. The second sentence is a restatement of existing law, *Confiscation Cases,* 7 Wall. 454–457; *United States v. Shoemaker,* 27 Fed. Cases No. 16,279, C.C.Ill. If the trial has commenced, the defendant has a right to insist on a disposition on the merits and may properly object to the entry of a nolle prosequi.

Note to Subdivision (b). This rule is a restatement of the inherent power of the court to dismiss a case for want of prosecution. *Ex parte Altman,* 34 F.Supp. 106, S.D.Cal.

Rule 49. Service and Filing of Papers

(a) Service: When Required. Written motions other than those which are heard *ex parte,* written notices, designations of record on appeal and similar papers shall be served upon each of the parties.

(b) Service: How Made. Whenever under these rules or by an order of the court service is required or permitted to be made upon a party represented by an attorney, the service shall be made upon the attorney unless service upon the party personally is ordered by the court. Service upon the attorney or upon a party shall be made in the manner provided in civil actions.

(c) Notice of Orders. Immediately upon the entry of an order made on a written motion subsequent to arraignment the clerk shall mail to each party a notice thereof and shall make a note in the docket of the mailing. Lack of notice of the entry by the clerk does not affect the time to appeal or relieve or authorize the court to relieve

a party for failure to appeal within the time allowed, except as permitted by Rule 4(b) of the Federal Rules of Appellate Procedure.

(d) Filing. Papers required to be served shall be filed with the court. Papers shall be filed in the manner provided in civil actions.

(e) Filing of Dangerous Offender Notice. A filing with the court pursuant to 18 U.S.C. § 3575(a) or 21 U.S.C. § 849(a) shall be made by filing the notice with the clerk of the court. The clerk shall transmit the notice to the chief judge or, if the chief judge is the presiding judge in the case, to another judge or United States magistrate in the district, except that in a district having a single judge and no United States magistrate, the clerk shall transmit the notice to the court only after the time for disclosure specified in the aforementioned statutes and shall seal the notice as permitted by local rule.

(As amended Feb. 28, 1966, eff. July 1, 1966; Dec. 4, 1967, eff. July 1, 1968; Apr. 29, 1985, eff. Aug. 1, 1985; Mar. 9, 1987, eff. Aug. 1, 1987.)

NOTES OF ADVISORY COMMITTEE ON RULES

Note to Subdivision (a). This rule is substantially the same as Rule 5(a) of the Federal Rules of Civil Procedure, 28 U.S.C., Appendix, with such adaptations as are necessary for criminal cases.

Note to Subdivision (b). The first sentence of this rule is in substance the same as the first sentence of Rule 5(b) of the Federal Rules of Civil Procedure. The second sentence incorporates by reference the second and third sentences of Rule 5(b) of the Federal Rules of Civil Procedure, 28 U.S.C., Appendix.

Note to Subdivision (c). This rule is an adaptation for criminal proceedings of Rule 77(d) of the Federal Rules of Civil Procedure, 28 U.S.C., Appendix. No consequence attaches to the failure of the clerk to give the prescribed notice, but in a case in which the losing party in reliance on the clerk's obligation to send a notice failed to file a timely notice of appeal, it was held competent for the trial judge, in the exercise of sound discretion, to vacate the judgment because of clerk's failure to give notice and to enter a new judgment, the term of court not having expired. *Hill v. Hawes,* 320 U.S. 520, 64 S.Ct. 334, 88 L.Ed. 283, rehearing denied 321 U.S. 801, 64 S.Ct. 515, 88 L.Ed. 1088.

Note to Subdivision (d). This rule incorporates by reference Rule 5(d) and (e) of the Federal Rules of Civil Procedure, 28 U.S.C., Appendix.

1966 AMENDMENT

Subdivision (a). The words "adverse parties" in the original rule introduced a question of interpretation.

When, for example, is a co-defendant an adverse party? The amendment requires service on each of the parties thus avoiding the problem of interpretation and promoting full exchange of information among the parties. No restriction is intended, however, upon agreements among co-defendants or between the defendants and the government restricting exchange of papers in the interest of eliminating unnecessary expense. Cf. the amendment made effective July 1, 1963, to Civil Rule 5(a).

Subdivision (c). The words "affected thereby" are deleted in order to require notice to all parties. Cf. the similar change made effective July 1, 1963, to Civil Rule 77(d).

The sentence added at the end of the subdivision eliminates the possibility of extension of the time to appeal beyond the provision for a 30 day extension on a showing or "excusable neglect" provided in Rule 37(a)(2). Cf. the similar change made in Civil Rule 77(d) effective in 1948. The question has arisen in a number of cases whether failure or delay in giving notice on the part of the clerk results in an extension of the time for appeal. The "general rule" has been said to be that in the event of such failure or delay "the time for taking an appeal runs from the date of later actual notice or receipt of the clerk's notice rather than from the date of entry of the order." *Lohman v. United States,* 237 F.2d 645, 646 (6th Cir.1956). See also *Rosenbloom v. United States,* 355 U.S. 80 (1957) (permitting an extension). In two cases it has been held that no extension results from the failure to give notice of entry of judgments (as opposed to orders) since such notice is not required by Rule 49(d). *Wilkinson v. United States,* 278 F.2d 604 (10th Cir.1960), cert. den. 363 U.S. 829; *Hyche v. United States,* 278 F.2d 915 (5th Cir.1960), cert. den. 364 U.S. 881. The excusable neglect extension provision in Rule 37(a)(2) will cover most cases where failure of the clerk to give notice of judgments or orders has misled the defendant. No need appears for an indefinite extension without time limit beyond the 30 day period.

1968 AMENDMENT

The amendment corrects the reference to Rule 37(a)(2), the pertinent provisions of which are contained in Rule 4(b) of the Federal Rules of Appellate Procedure.

1985 AMENDMENT

18 U.S.C. § 3575(a) and 21 U.S.C. § 849(a), dealing respectively with dangerous special offender sentencing and dangerous special drug offender sentencing, provide for the prosecutor to file notice of such status "with the court" and for the court to "order the notice sealed" under specified circumstances, but also declare that disclosure of this notice shall not be made "to the presiding judge without the consent of the parties" before verdict or plea of guilty or nolo contendere. It has been noted that these provisions are "regrettably

unclear as to where, in fact, such notice is to be filed" and that possibly filing with the chief judge is contemplated. *United States v. Tramunti,* 377 F.Supp. 6 (S.D. N.Y.1974). But such practice has been a matter of dispute when the chief judge would otherwise have been the presiding judge in the case, *United States v. Gaylor,* No. 80–5016 (4th Cir.1981), and "it does not solve the problem in those districts where there is only one federal district judge appointed," *United States v. Tramunti, supra.*

The first sentence of subdivision (e) clarifies that the filing of such notice with the court is to be accomplished by filing with the clerk of the court, which is generally the procedure for filing with the court; see subdivision (d) of this rule. Except in a district having a single judge and no United States magistrate, the clerk will then, as provided in the second sentence, transmit the notice to the chief judge or to some other judge or a United States magistrate if the chief judge is scheduled to be the presiding judge in the case, so that the determination regarding sealing of the notice may be made without the disclosure prohibited by the aforementioned statutes. But in a district having a single judge and no United States magistrate this prohibition means the clerk may not disclose the notice to the court at all until the time specified by statute. The last sentence of subdivision (e) contemplates that in such instances the clerk will seal the notice if the case falls within the local rule describing when "a public record may prejudice fair consideration of a pending criminal matter," the determination called for by the aforementioned statutes. The local rule might provide, for example, that the notice is to be sealed upon motion by any party.

1987 AMENDMENT

The amendment is technical. No substantive change is intended.

EDITORIAL NOTES

References in Text. The Federal Rules of Appellate Procedure, referred to in subdiv. (c), are set out in this pamphlet.

Rule 50. Calendars; Plan for Prompt Disposition

(a) Calendars. The district courts may provide for placing criminal proceedings upon appropriate calendars. Preference shall be given to criminal proceedings as far as practicable.

(b) Plans for Achieving Prompt Disposition of Criminal Cases. To minimize undue delay and to further the prompt disposition of criminal cases, each district court shall conduct a continuing study of the administration of criminal justice in the district court and before United States magistrates of the district and shall prepare plans for the prompt disposition of criminal cases in accordance with the provisions of Chapter 208 of Title 18, United States Code.

(As amended Apr. 24, 1972, eff. Oct. 1, 1972; Mar. 18, 1974, eff. July 1, 1974; Apr. 26, 1976, eff. Aug. 1, 1976.)

NOTES OF ADVISORY COMMITTEE ON RULES

This rule is a restatement of the inherent residual power of the court over its own calendars, although as a matter of practice in most districts the assignment of criminal cases for trial is handled by the United States attorney. Cf. Federal Rules of Civil Procedure, Rules 40 and 78, 28 U.S.C., Appendix. The direction that preference shall be given to criminal proceedings as far as practicable is generally recognized as desirable in the orderly administration of justice.

1972 AMENDMENT

The addition to the rule proposed by subdivision (b) is designed to achieve the more prompt disposition of criminal cases.

Preventing undue delay in the administration of criminal justice has become an object of increasing interest and concern. This is reflected in the Congress. See, e.g., 116 Cong.Rec. S7291-97 (daily ed. May 18, 1970) (remarks of Senator Ervin). Bills have been introduced fixing specific time limits. See S. 3936, H.R. 14822, H.R. 15888, 91st Cong., 2d Sess. (1970).

Proposals for dealing with the problem of delay have also been made by the President's Commission on Law Enforcement and Administration of Justice, Task Force Report: The Courts (1967) especially pp. 84–90, and by the American Bar Association Project on Standards for Criminal Justice, Standards Relating to Speedy Trial (Approved Draft, 1968). Both recommend specific time limits for each stage in the criminal process as the most effective way of achieving prompt disposition of criminal cases. See also Note, Nevada's 1967 Criminal Procedure Law from Arrest to Trial: One State's Response to a Widely Recognized Need, 1969 Utah L.Rev. 520, 542 No. 114.

Historically, the right to a speedy trial has been thought of as a protection for the defendant. Delay can cause a hardship to a defendant who is in custody awaiting trial. Even if afforded the opportunity for pretrial release, a defendant nonetheless is likely to suffer anxiety during a period of unwanted delay, and he runs the risk that his memory and those of his witnesses may suffer as time goes on.

Delay can also adversely affect the prosecution. Witnesses may lose interest or disappear or their memories may fade thus making them more vulnerable to cross-examination. See Note, The Right to a Speedy Criminal Trial, 57 Colum.L.Rev. 846 (1957).

There is also a larger public interest in the prompt disposition of criminal cases which may transcend the interest of the particular prosecutor, defense counsel, and defendant. Thus there is need to try to expedite criminal cases even when both prosecution and defense may be willing to agree to a continuance or continuances. It has long been said that it is the certain and prompt imposition of a criminal sanction rather than its severity that has a significant deterring effect upon potential criminal conduct. See Banfield and Anderson, Continuances in the Cook County Criminal Courts, 35 U.Chi.L.Rev. 259, 259–63 (1968).

Providing specific time limits for each stage of the criminal justice system is made difficult, particularly in federal courts, by the widely varying conditions which exist between the very busy urban districts on the one hand and the far less busy rural districts on the other hand. In the former, account must be taken of the extremely heavy caseload, and the prescription of relatively short time limits is realistic only if there is provided additional prosecutorial and judicial manpower. In some rural districts, the availability of a grand jury only twice a year makes unrealistic the provision of short time limits within which an indictment must be returned. This is not to say that prompt disposition of criminal cases cannot be achieved. It means only that the achieving of prompt disposition may require solutions which vary from district to district. Finding the best methods will require innovation and experimentation. To encourage this, the proposed draft mandates each district court to prepare a plan to achieve the prompt disposition of criminal cases in the district. The method prescribed for the development and approval of the district plans is comparable to that prescribed in the Jury Selection and Service Act of 1968, 28 U.S.C. § 1863(a).

Each plan shall include rules which specify time limits and a means for reporting the status of criminal cases. The appropriate length of the time limits is left to the discretion of the individual district courts. This permits each district court to establish time limits that are appropriate in light of its criminal caseload, frequency of grand jury meetings, and any other factors which affect the progress of criminal actions. Where local conditions exist which contribute to delay, it is contemplated that appropriate efforts will be made to eliminate those conditions. For example, experience in some rural districts demonstrates that grand juries can be kept on call thus eliminating the grand jury as a cause for prolonged delay. Where manpower shortage is a major cause for delay, adequate solutions will require congressional action. But the development and analysis of the district plans should disclose where manpower shortages exist; how large the shortages are; and what is needed, in the way of additional manpower, to achieve the prompt disposition of criminal cases.

The district court plans must contain special provision for prompt disposition of cases in which there is reason to believe that the pretrial liberty of a defendant poses danger to himself, to any other person, or to the community. Prompt disposition of criminal cases may provide an alternative to the pretrial detention of potentially dangerous defendants. See 116 Cong.Rec. S7291–97 (daily ed. May 18, 1970) (remarks of Senator Ervin). Prompt disposition of criminal cases in which the defendant is held in pretrial detention would ensure that the deprivation of liberty prior to conviction would be minimized.

Approval of the original plan and any subsequent modification must be obtained from a reviewing panel made up of one judge from the district submitting the plan (either the chief judge or another active judge appointed by him) and the members of the judicial council of the circuit. The makeup of this reviewing panel is the same as that provided by the Jury Selection and Service Act of 1968, 28 U.S.C. § 1863(a). This reviewing panel is also empowered to direct the modification of a district court plan.

The Circuit Court of Appeals for the Second Circuit recently adopted a set of rules for the prompt disposition of criminal cases. See 8 Cr.L. 2251 (Jan. 13, 1971). These rules, effective July 5, 1971, provide time limits for the early trial of high risk defendants, for court control over the granting of continuances, for criteria to control continuance practice, and for sanction against the prosecution or defense in the event of noncompliance with prescribed time limits.

1976 AMENDMENT

This amendment to rule 50(b) takes account of the enactment of The Speedy Trial Act of 1974, 18 U.S.C. §§ 3152–3156, 3161–3174. As the various provisions of the Act take effect, see 18 U.S.C. § 3163, they and the district plans adopted pursuant thereto will supplant the plans heretofore adopted under rule 50(b). The first such plan must be prepared and submitted by each district court before July 1, 1976. 18 U.S.C. § 3165(e)(1).

That part of rule 50(b) which sets out the necessary contents of district plans has been deleted, as the somewhat different contents of the plans required by the Act are enumerated in 18 U.S.C. § 3166. That part of rule 50(b) which describes the manner in which district plans are to be submitted, reviewed, modified and reported upon has also been deleted, for these provisions now appear in 18 U.S.C. § 3165(c) and (d).

Rule 51. Exceptions Unnecessary

Exceptions to rulings or orders of the court are unnecessary and for all purposes for which an exception has heretofore been necessary it is sufficient that a party, at the time the ruling or order of the court is made or sought, makes known to the court the action which that party desires the court to take or that party's objection to the action of the court and the grounds therefor; but if a party has no opportunity to object to a ruling or order, the absence of an objection does not thereafter prejudice that party.

(As amended Mar. 9, 1987, eff. Aug. 1, 1987.)

NOTES OF ADVISORY COMMITTEE ON RULES

1. This rule is practically identical with Rule 46 of the Federal Rules of Civil Procedure, 28 U.S.C., Appendix. It relates to a matter of trial practice which should be the same in civil and criminal cases in the interest of avoiding confusion. The corresponding civil rule has been construed in *Ulm v. Moore–McCormack Lines, Inc.,* 115 F.2d 492, C.C.A.2d, and *Bucy v. Nevada Construction Company,* 125 F.2d 213, 218, C.C.A.9th. See, also, Orfield, 22 Texas L.R. 194, 221. As to the method of taking objections to instructions to the jury, see Rule 30.

2. Many States have abolished the use of exceptions in criminal and civil cases. See, e.g., Cal.Pen.Code (Deering, 1941), sec. 1259; Mich.Stat.Ann. (Henderson, 1938), secs. 28.1046, 28.1053; Ohio Gen.Code Ann. (Page, 1938), secs. 11560, 13442–7; Oreg.Comp.Laws Ann. (1940), secs. 5–704, 26–1001.

1987 AMENDMENT

The amendments are technical. No substantive change is intended.

Rule 52. Harmless Error and Plain Error

(a) **Harmless Error.** Any error, defect, irregularity or variance which does not affect substantial rights shall be disregarded.

(b) **Plain Error.** Plain errors or defects affecting substantial rights may be noticed although they were not brought to the attention of the court.

NOTES OF ADVISORY COMMITTEE ON RULES

Note to Subdivision (a). This rule is a restatement of existing law, 28 U.S.C. former § 391 (second sentence): "On the hearing of any appeal, certiorari, writ of error, or motion for a new trial, in any case, civil or criminal, the court shall give judgment after an examination of the entire record before the court, without regard to technical errors, defects, or exceptions which do not affect the substantial rights of the parties"; 18 U.S.C. former § 556; "No indictment found and presented by a grand jury in any district or other court of the United States shall be deemed insufficient, nor shall the trial, judgment, or other proceeding thereon be affected by reason of any defect or imperfection in matter of form only, which shall not tend to the prejudice of the defendant, * * *." A similar provision is found in Rule 61 of the Federal Rules of Civil Procedure, 28 U.S.C., Appendix.

Note to Subdivision (b). This rule is a restatement of existing law, *Wiborg v. United States,* 163 U.S. 632, 658, 16 S.Ct. 1127, 1197, 2 cases, 41 L.Ed. 289; *Hemphill v. United States,* 112 F.2d 505, C.C.A.9th, reversed 312 U.S. 657, 61 S.Ct. 729, 85 L.Ed. 1106, conformed to 120 F.2d 115, certiorari denied 314 U.S. 627, 62 S.Ct. 111, 86 L.Ed. 503. Rule 27 of the Rules of the Supreme Court, 28 U.S.C. foll. § 354, provides that errors not specified will be disregarded, "save as the court, at its option, may notice a plain error not assigned or specified." Similar provisions are found in the rules of several circuit courts of appeals.

Rule 53.　Regulation of Conduct in the Court Room

The taking of photographs in the court room during the progress of judicial proceedings or radio broadcasting of judicial proceedings from the court room shall not be permitted by the court.

NOTES OF ADVISORY COMMITTEE ON RULES

While the matter to which the rule refers has not been a problem in the Federal courts as it has been in some State tribunals, the rule was nevertheless included with a view to giving expression to a standard which should govern the conduct of judicial proceedings, Orfield, 22 Texas L.R. 194, 222–3; Robbins, 21 A.B.A.Jour. 301, 304. See, also, Report of the Special Committee on Cooperation between Press, Radio and Bar, as to Publicity Interfering with Fair Trial of Judicial and Quasi–Judicial Proceedings (1937), 62 A.B.A.Rep. 851, 862–865; (1932) 18 A.B.A.Jour. 762; (1926) 12 Id. 488; (1925) 11 Id. 64.

Rule 54.　Application and Exception

(a) Courts. These rules apply to all criminal proceedings in the United States District Courts; in the District Court of Guam; in the District Court for the Northern Mariana Islands, except as otherwise provided in articles IV and V of the covenant provided by the Act of March 24, 1976 (90 Stat. 263); in the District Court of the Virgin Islands; and (except as otherwise provided in the Canal Zone Code) in the United States District Court for the District of the Canal Zone; in the United States Courts of Appeals; and in the Supreme Court of the United States; except that all offenses shall continue to be prosecuted in the District Court of Guam and in the District Court of the Virgin Islands by information as heretofore except such as may be required by local law to be prosecuted by indictment by grand jury.

(b) Proceedings.

(1) Removed Proceedings. These rules apply to criminal prosecutions removed to the United States district courts from state courts and govern all procedure after removal, except that dismissal by the attorney for the prosecution shall be governed by state law.

(2) Offenses Outside a District or State. These rules apply to proceedings for offenses committed upon the high seas or elsewhere out of the jurisdiction of any particular state or district, except that such proceedings may be had in any district authorized by 18 U.S.C. § 3238.

(3) Peace Bonds. These rules do not alter the power of judges of the United States or of United States magistrates to hold to security of the peace and for good behavior under Revised Statutes, § 4069, 50 U.S.C. § 23, but in such cases the procedure shall conform to these rules so far as they are applicable.

(4) Proceedings Before United States Magistrates. Proceedings involving misdemeanors before United States magistrates are governed by the Rules of Procedure for the Trial of Misdemeanors before United States Magistrates.

(5) Other Proceedings. These rules are not applicable to extradition and rendition of fugitives; civil forfeiture of property for violation of a statute of the United States; or the collection of fines and penalties. Except as provided in Rule 20(d) they do not apply to proceedings under 18 U.S.C., Chapter 403—Juvenile Delinquency—so far as they are inconsistent with that chapter. They do not apply to summary trials for offenses against the navigation laws under Revised Statutes §§ 4300–4305, 33 U.S.C. §§ 391–396, or to proceedings involving disputes between seamen under Revised Statutes, §§ 4079–4081, as amended, 22 U.S.C. §§ 256–258, or to proceedings for fishery offenses under the Act of June 28, 1937, c. 392, 50 Stat. 325–327, 16 U.S.C. §§ 772–772i, or to proceedings against a witness in a foreign country under 28 U.S.C. § 1784.

(c) Application of Terms. As used in these rules the following terms have the designated meanings.

"Act of Congress" includes any act of Congress locally applicable to and in force in the District of Columbia, in Puerto Rico, in a territory or in an insular possession.

"Attorney for the government" means the Attorney General, an authorized assistant of the Attorney General, a United States Attorney, an authorized assistant of a United States Attorney, when applicable to cases arising under the laws of Guam the Attorney General of Guam or such other person or persons as may be authorized by the laws of Guam to act therein, and when applicable to cases arising under the laws of the Northern Mariana Islands the Attorney General of the Northern Mariana Islands or any other person or persons as may be authorized by the laws of the Northern Marianas to act therein.

"Civil action" refers to a civil action in a district court.

The words "demurrer," "motion to quash," "plea in abatement," "plea in bar" and "special plea in bar," or words to the same effect, in any act of Congress shall be construed to mean the motion raising a defense or objection provided in Rule 12.

"District court" includes all district courts named in subdivision (a) of this rule.

"Federal magistrate" means a United States magistrate as defined in 28 U.S.C. §§ 631–639, a judge of the United States or another judge or judicial officer specifically empowered by statute in force in any territory or possession, the Commonwealth of Puerto Rico, or the District of Columbia, to perform a function to which a particular rule relates.

"Judge of the United States" includes a judge of a district court, court of appeals, or the Supreme Court.

"Law" includes statutes and judicial decisions.

"Magistrate" includes a United States magistrate as defined in 28 U.S.C. §§ 631–639, a judge of the United States, another judge or judicial officer specifically empowered by statute in force in any territory or possession, the Commonwealth of Puerto Rico, or the District of Columbia, to perform a function to which a particular rule relates, and a state or local judicial officer, autho-

rized by 18 U.S.C. § 3041 to perform the functions prescribed in Rules 3, 4, and 5.

"Oath" includes affirmations.

"Petty offense" has the meaning set forth in 18 U.S.C. 19.

"State" includes District of Columbia, Puerto Rico, territory and insular possession.

"United States magistrate" means the officer authorized by 28 U.S.C. §§ 631–639.

(As amended Dec. 27, 1948, eff. Oct. 20, 1949; Apr. 9, 1956, eff. July 8, 1956; Feb. 28, 1966, eff. July 1, 1966; Apr. 24, 1972, eff. Oct. 1, 1972; Apr. 28, 1982, eff. Aug. 1, 1982; Oct. 12, 1984, Pub.L. 98–473, Title II, §§ 209(e), 215(e), 98 Stat. 1987, 2016; Nov. 18, 1988, Pub.L. 100–690, Title VII, § 7089(c), 102 Stat. 4409.)

Subd. (c) of this Rule Applicable to Offenses Committed Prior to Nov. 1, 1987

Subd. (c) of this rule as in effect prior to amendment by Pub.L. 98–473 § 215(e), reads as follows:

(c) Application of Terms. As used in these rules the following terms have the designated meanings.

"Act of Congress" includes any act of Congress locally applicable to and in force in the District of Columbia, in Puerto Rico, in a territory or in an insular possession.

"Attorney for the government" means the Attorney General, an authorized assistant of the Attorney General, a United States Attorney, an authorized assistant of a United States Attorney, when applicable to cases arising under the laws of Guam the Attorney General of Guam or such other person or persons as may be authorized by the laws of Guam to act therein, and when applicable to cases arising under the laws of the Northern Mariana Islands the Attorney General of the Northern Mariana Islands or any other person or persons as may be authorized by the laws of the Northern Marianas to act therein.

"Civil action" refers to a civil action in a district court.

The words "demurrer," "motion to quash," "plea in abatement," "plea in bar" and "special plea in bar," or words to the same effect, in any act of Congress shall be construed to mean the motion raising a defense or objection provided in Rule 12.

"District court" includes all district courts named in subdivision (a) of this rule.

"Federal magistrate" means a United States magistrate as defined in 28 U.S.C. §§ 631–639, a judge of the United States or another judge or judicial officer specifically empowered by statute in force in any territory or possession, the Commonwealth of Puerto Rico, or the

District of Columbia, to perform a function to which a particular rule relates.

"Judge of the United States" includes a judge of a district court, court of appeals, or the Supreme Court.

"Law" includes statutes and judicial decisions.

"Magistrate" includes a United States magistrate as defined in 28 U.S.C. §§ 631–639, a judge of the United States, another judge or judicial officer specifically empowered by statute in force in any territory or possession, the Commonwealth of Puerto Rico, or the District of Columbia, to perform a function to which a particular rule relates, and a state or local judicial officer, authorized by 18 U.S.C. § 3041 to perform the functions prescribed in Rules 3, 4, and 5.

"Oath" includes affirmations.

"Petty offense" is defined in 18 U.S.C. § 1(3).

"State" includes District of Columbia, Puerto Rico, territory and insular possession.

"United States magistrate" means the officer authorized by 28 U.S.C. §§ 631–639.

For applicability of sentencing provisions to offenses, see Effective Date and Savings Provisions, etc., note, section 235 of Pub.L. 98–473, as amended, set out under section 3551 of Title 18, Crimes and Criminal Procedure.

NOTES OF ADVISORY COMMITTEE ON RULES

Note to Subdivision (a)(1). 1. The act of June 28, 1940 (54 Stat. 688; 18 U.S.C. former § 687 (now § 3771)), authorizing the Supreme Court to prescribe rules of criminal procedure for the district courts of the United States in respect to proceedings prior to and including verdict or finding of guilty or not guilty or plea of guilty, is expressly applicable to the district courts of Alaska, Hawaii, Puerto Rico, Canal Zone, Virgin Islands, the Supreme Courts of Hawaii and Puerto Rico, and the United States Court for China. This is likewise true of the act of February 24, 1933 (47 Stat. 904; 18 U.S.C. former § 688 (now § 3772)), authorizing the Supreme Court to prescribe rules in respect to proceedings after verdict or finding or after plea of guilty. In this respect these two statutes differ from the act of June 19, 1934 (48 Stat. 1064; 28 U.S.C. former §§ 723b, 723c (now § 2072)), authorizing the Supreme Court to prescribe rules of civil procedure. The last-mentioned Act comprises only district courts of the United States and the courts of the District of Columbia. The phrase "district courts of the United States" was held not to include district courts in the territories and insular possessions, *Mookini v. United States*, 303 U.S. 201, 58 S.Ct. 543, 82 L.Ed. 748, conformed to 95 F.2d 960. By subsequent legislation the Federal Rules of Civil Procedure were extended to the District Court of the United States for Hawaii and to appeals therefrom (act of June 19, 1939; 53 Stat. 841; 48 U.S.C. former § 646) and to the District Court of the United

States for Puerto Rico and to appeals therefrom (act of February 12, 1940; 54 Stat. 22; 48 U.S.C. former § 873a).

2. While the specific reference in the rule to the District Court of the United States for the District of Columbia is probably superfluous, since that court has the same powers and exercises the same jurisdiction as other district courts of the United States in addition to such local powers and jurisdiction as have been conferred upon it by statute (D.C.Code, 1940, Title 11, § 305), nevertheless it was listed in the rule in view of the fact that the Federal Rules of Civil Procedure contain a somewhat similar provision (Rule 81(d), 28 U.S.C., Appendix).

3. The United States Court for China has been omitted from the rule in view of the fact that the court has recently been abolished with the abandonment by the United States of its extraterritorial jurisdiction in China.

4. Although, as indicated above, the rule-making power of the Supreme Court in respect to criminal cases extends to the Supreme Courts of Hawaii and Puerto Rico, the rules are not made applicable to those two courts, in view of the fact that they are purely local appellate courts having no appellate jurisdiction over the district courts of the United States in those territories. Alaska and Hawaii have dual systems of courts: local courts exercising purely local jurisdiction and United States district courts exercising Federal jurisdiction. The Supreme Court of each of the two territories hears appeals only from the local courts.

5. Alaska.—There is a district court for the Territory of Alaska consisting of four divisions, established on a territorial basis, 48 U.S.C. §§ 101, 101a. As the only court in the Territory, it acts in a dual capacity: it has jurisdiction over cases arising under the laws of the United States as well as those arising under local laws. Although a legislative rather than a constitutional court, it is, nevertheless, deemed a court of the United States and has the jurisdiction of district courts of the United States, 48 U.S.C. §§ 101, 101a; *Steamer Coquitlam v. United States*, 163 U.S. 346, 16 S.Ct. 1117, 41 L.Ed. 184; *McAllister v. United States*, 141 U.S. 174, 179, 11 S.Ct. 949, 35 L.Ed. 693; *Ex parte Krause*, 228 Fed. 547, 549, W.D.Wash. Criminal procedure is now regulated by acts of Congress, by the Alaska Code of Criminal Procedure (Alaska Comp.Laws, 1933, pp. 959–1018), and by rules promulgated by the district court.

6. Hawaii.—Hawaii has a dual system of courts. The United States District Court for the Territory of Hawaii, a legislative court, has the jurisdiction of district courts of the United States and proceeds therein "in the same manner as a district court," 48 U.S.C. former §§ 641, 642. In addition, there are circuit courts having jurisdiction over cases arising under local

laws. Appeals from the circuit courts run to the Supreme Court of the Territory, 48 U.S.C. § 631. These rules are made applicable to the district court, but not to the local courts. The Federal Rules of Civil Procedure have been made applicable to the district court and to appeals therefrom, 48 U.S.C. former § 646.

7. Puerto Rico.—Puerto Rico has a dual system of courts. The District Court of the United States for Puerto Rico, a legislative court, has jurisdiction of all cases cognizable in the district courts of the United States and proceeds "In the same manner," 48 U.S.C. § 863.

In addition, there are local courts for the trial of cases arising under local law, appeals therefrom running to the Supreme Court of the Territory. These rules are made applicable to the district court, but not to the local courts. The Federal Rules of Civil Procedure, 28 U.S.C., Appendix, have been extended to the district court, 48 U.S.C. former § 873a.

8. Virgin Islands.—In the Virgin Islands there is a District Court of the Virgin Islands, a legislative court, consisting of two divisions and exercising both Federal and local jurisdiction, 48 U.S.C. §§ 1405z, 1406. Heretofore the rules of practice and procedure have been prescribed "by law or ordinance or by rules and regulations of the district judge not inconsistent with law or ordinance," 48 U.S.C. § 1405z.

9. Canal Zone.—In the Canal Zone there is a United States District Court for the District of the Canal Zone, a legislative court, exercising both Federal and local jurisdiction, 48 U.S.C. former §§ 1344, 1345. Criminal procedure is regulated by the Code of Criminal Procedure of the Canal Zone (Canal Zone Code, Title 6; 48 Stat. 1122), and by rules of practice and procedure prescribed by the district judge, 48 U.S.C. former § 1344. There are no grand juries in the district, all prosecutions being instituted by information. In the light of these circumstances and because of the peculiar status of the Canal Zone and its quasi-military nature, these rules have been made applicable to its district court, only with respect to proceedings after verdict or finding of guilty or plea of guilty.

10. By order dated March 31, 1941, effective July 1, 1941, the Supreme Court extended the rules of practice and procedure after plea of guilty, verdict or finding of guilty, in criminal cases, to the district courts of Alaska, Hawaii, Puerto Rico, Canal Zone, and Virgin Islands, and all subsequent proceedings in such cases in the United States circuit courts of appeals and in the Supreme Court of the United States, 312 U.S. 721.

Note to Subdivision (a)(2). 1. Rules 3, 4, and 5, supra, relate to proceedings before United States commissioners.

2. Justices and judges of the United States, as well as United States commissioners, may issue warrants and conduct proceedings as committing magistrates, 18

U.S.C. former § 591 (now § 3041) (Arrest and removal for trial); 9 Edmunds, Cyclopedia of Federal Procedure, 2d Ed., secs. 3800, 3819.

3. In the District of Columbia judges of the Municipal Court have authority to issue warrants and conduct proceedings as committing magistrates, D.C. Code, 1940, Title 11, secs. 602, 755. These proceedings are governed by these rules. The Municipal Court of the District of Columbia is also a local court for the trial of misdemeanors, but when so acting it is not a court of the United States. These rules, therefore, do not apply to such proceedings.

4. State and local judges and magistrates may issue warrants and act as committing magistrates in Federal cases, 18 U.S.C. former § 591 (now § 3041). Only a very small proportion of cases are brought before them, however, and then ordinarily only in an emergency. Since these judicial officers may not be familiar with Federal procedure, these rules have not been made applicable to such proceedings.

Note to Subdivision (b)(1). 1. Certain types of State criminal prosecutions, principally those in which defendant is an officer appointed under or acting by authority of a revenue law of the United States and is prosecuted on account of an act done under color of his office, are removable to a Federal court on defendant's motion, 28 U.S.C. former § 74 (now §§ 1443, 1446, 1447) (Removal of suits from State courts; causes against persons denied civil rights); former sec. 76 (now §§ 1442, 1446, 1447) (Removal of suits from State courts; suits and prosecutions against revenue officers). In such cases the Federal court applies the substantive law of the State, but follows Federal procedure; *State of Tennessee v. Davis*, 100 U.S. 257, 25 L.Ed. 648; *Carter v. Tennessee*, 18 F.2d 850, C.C.A. 6th; *Miller v. Kentucky*, 40 F.2d 820, C.C.A.6th. See also, *State of Maryland v. Soper*, 270 U.S. 9, 46 S.Ct. 185, 70 L.Ed. 449. The rule is, therefore, a restatement of existing law, except that it does not affect whatever power the State prosecutor may have as to dismissal.

2. The rule does not affect the mode of removing a case from a State to a Federal court and leaves undisturbed the statutes governing this matter, 28 U.S.C. former §§ 74–76 (now §§ 1442, 1443, 1446, 1447).

Note to Subdivision (b)(2). This rule should be read in conjunction with Rule 18, which provides that "Except as otherwise permitted by statute or by these rules, the prosecution shall be held in a district in which the offense was committed * * *".

Note to Subdivision (b)(4). United States commissioners specially designated for that purpose by the court by which they are appointed have trial jurisdiction over petty offenses committed on Federal reservations if the defendant waives his right to be tried in the district court and consents to be tried before the commissioner. Act of October 9, 1940, 54 Stat. 1058, 18

U.S.C. former § 576 (now § 3401). A petty offense is an offense the penalty for which does not exceed confinement in a common jail without hard labor for a period of six months or a fine of $500, or both, 18 U.S.C. former § 541 (now § 1). Appeals from convictions by commissioners lie to the district court, 18 U.S.C. former § 576a (now § 3402). These rules do not apply to trials before United States commissioners in such cases, since rules of procedure and practice in such matters were specially prescribed by the Supreme Court on January 6, 1941, 311 U.S. 733 et seq. The substantive law applicable in such cases with respect to offenses other than so-called Federal offenses is governed by 18 U.S.C. former § 468 (now § 13) (Laws of States adopted for punishing wrongful acts; effect of repeal). In addition, National Park commissioners have limited trial jurisdiction with respect to offenses committed in National Parks. Trials before commissioners in such cases are not governed by these rules, although when a National Park commissioner conducts a proceeding as a committing magistrate, these rules are applicable.

Among the statutes relating to jurisdiction of and proceedings before National Park commissioners are the following:

U.S.C. Title 16:

§ 10 (Arrests by employees of park service for violation of laws and regulations)

§ 10a (Arrests by employees for violation of regulations made under § 9a)

§ 27 [now 28 U.S.C. §§ 131, 631, 632] (Yellowstone National Park; commissioner; jurisdiction and powers)

§ 66 [now 28 U.S.C. §§ 631, 632] (Yosemite and Sequoia National Parks; commissioners; appointment; jurisdiction)

§ 70 [now 18 U.S.C. §§ 3041, 3141; 18 U.S.C., App., Rules 4, 5(c), 9] (Same; arrests by commissioners for certain offenses; holding persons arrested for trial; bail)

§ 101 [now 18 U.S.C. §§ 3041, 3141; 18 U.S.C., App., Rule 4; 28 U.S.C., App., Rule 4] (Mount Rainier National Park; commissioner; arrest; bail)

§ 102 [now 18 U.S.C. § 3053; 18 U.S.C., App., Rule 4; 28 U.S.C., App., Rule 4] (Same; commissioner; direction of process of; arrests by other officers)

§ 117b [now 18 U.S.C. § 13] (Mesa Verde National Park; application of Colorado laws to offenses)

§ 117f [now 18 U.S.C. §§ 3041, 3141; 18 U.S.C., App., Rules 4, 5(c), 9] (Same; criminal offenses not covered by section 117c; jurisdiction of commissioner)

§ 117g [now 18 U.S.C. § 3053; 18 U.S.C., App., Rule 4; 28 U.S.C., App., Rule 4] (Same; process to whom issued; arrests without process)

§ 129 [now 28 U.S.C. §§ 631, 632] (Crater Lake National Park; commissioner; appointment; powers and duties)

§ 130 [now 18 U.S.C. §§ 3041, 3141; 18 U.S.C., App., Rules 4, 5(c), 9] (Same; commissioner; arrests by; bail)

§ 131 [18 § 3053; 18 Rule 4; 28 Rule 4] (Same; commissioner; direction of process; arrest without process)

§ 172 [28 §§ 631, 632] (Glacier National Park; commissioner; jurisdiction; powers and duties)

§ 173 [18 §§ 3041, 3141; 18 Rules 4, 5(c), 9] (Same; commissioner; arrest of offenders, confinement, and bail)

§ 174 [18 § 3053; 28 Rule 4] (Same; commissioner; process directed to marshal; arrest without process)

§ 198b [18 § 13] (Rocky Mountain National Park; punishment of offenses; Colorado laws when followed)

§ 198e [28 §§ 631, 632] (Same; United States Commissioner; appointment; jurisdiction; issuing process; appeals; rules of procedure)

§ 198f [18 §§ 3041, 3141; 18 Rules 4, 5(c), 9] (Same; United States Commissioner; arrest of persons for offenses not covered by section 198c; bail)

§ 198g [18 § 3053; 18 Rule 4; 28 Rule 4] (Same; United States Commissioner; process to whom directed; arrest without process)

§ 204b [18 § 13] (Lassen Volcanic National Park; application of California laws to offenses)

§ 204e [28 §§ 631, 632] (Same; United States Commissioner; appointment; jurisdiction of offenses; appeals; rules of procedure)

§ 204f [18 §§ 3041, 3141; 18 Rules 4, 5(c), 9] (Same; criminal offenses not covered by section 204c; jurisdiction of commissioner)

§ 204g [18 § 3053; 18 Rule 4; 28 Rule 4] (Same; process to whom issued; arrests without process)

§ 376 [28 § 632] (Hot Springs National Park; prosecutions for violations of law or rules and regulations)

§ 377 [18 §§ 3041, 3141; 18 Rules 4, 5(c), 9] (Same; prosecutions for other offenses)

§ 378 [18 § 3053; 18 Rule 4; 28 Rule 4] (Same; process directed to marshal; arrests by others)

§ 381 [18 § 3041] (Same; execution of sentence on conviction)

§ 382 [18 § 3041] (Same; imprisonment for nonpayment of fines or costs)

§ 395b [18 § 13] (Hawaii National Park; application of Hawaiian laws to offenses)

§ 395e [28 §§ 631, 632] (Same; United States Commissioner; appointment; jurisdiction of offenses; appeals; rules of procedure; acting commissioners)

§ 395f [18 §§ 3041, 3141; 18 Rules 4, 5(c), 9] (Same; criminal offenses not covered by section 395c; jurisdiction of commissioner)

§ 395g [18 § 3053; 18 Rule 4] (Same; process to whom issued; arrests without process)

§ 403c–1 (Shenandoah National Park and Great Smoky Mountains National Park; notice of assumption of police jurisdiction over Shenandoah Park by United States; exceptions)

§ 403c–5 [28 §§ 631, 632] (Same; United States Commissioner; appointment; jurisdiction of offenses; appeals; rules of procedure)

§ 403c–6 [28 § 632] (Same; jurisdiction of other commissioners)

§ 403c–7 [18 §§ 3041, 3141; 18 Rules 4, 5(c), 9] (Same; commissioner's jurisdiction of offenses not covered by section 403c–2)

§ 403c–8 [18 § 3053; 18 Rule 4; 28 Rule 4] (Same; process to whom directed, arrest without process)

§ 415 (National Military Parks; arrest and prosecution of offenders)

Note to Subdivision (b)(5). 1. Foreign extradition proceedings are governed by the following statutes:

U.S.C. Title 18 former:

§ 651 [§ 3184] (Fugitives from foreign country)

§ 652 [§ 3185] (Fugitives from country under control of United States)

§ 653 [§ 3186] (Surrender of fugitive)

§ 654 [§ 3188] (Time allowed for extradition)

§ 655 [§ 3190] (Evidence on hearing)

§ 656 [§ 3191] (Witnesses for indigent defendants)

§ 657 [§ 3189] (Place and character of hearing)

§ 658 [§ 3181] (Continuance of provisions limited)

§ 659 [§ 3192] (Protection of accused)

§ 660 [§ 3193] (Agent receiving offenders; powers)

Interstate rendition or extradition proceedings are governed by the following statutes:

U.S.C. Title 18 former:

§ 662 [§§ 3182, 3195] (Fugitives from State or Territory)

§ 662c [§§ 752, 3183, 3195] (Fugitives from State or Territory; arrest and removal)

§ 662d [§§ 3187, 3195] (Fugitives from State or Territory; provisional arrest and detention)

2. Proceedings relating to forfeiture of property used in connection with a violation of a statute of the United States are governed by various statutes, among which are following:

U.S.C. Title 16:

§ 26 (Yellowstone Park; regulations for hunting and fishing in; punishment for violation; forfeitures)

§ 65 (Yosemite and Sequoia National Parks; seizure and forfeiture of guns, traps, teams, horses, and so forth)

§ 99 (Mount Rainier National Park; protection of game and fish; forfeitures of guns, traps, teams, and so forth)

§ 117d (Mesa Verde National Park; forfeiture of property used for unlawful purpose)

§ 128 (Crater Lake National Park; hunting and fishing; forfeitures or seizure of guns, traps, teams, etc., for violating regulations)

§ 171 (Glacier National Park; hunting and fishing; forfeitures and seizures of guns, traps, teams, and so forth)

§ 198d (Rocky Mountain National Park; forfeiture of property used in commission of offenses)

§ 204d (Lassen Volcanic National Park; forfeiture of property used for unlawful purposes)

§ 635 (Importing illegally taken skins; forfeiture)

§ 706 (Arrests; search warrants)

§ 727 (Upper Mississippi River Wild Life and Fish Refuge; powers of employees of Department of the Interior; searches and seizures)

§ 772e (Penalties and forfeitures)

U.S.C. Title 18 former:

§ 286 [§ 492] (Forfeiture of counterfeit obligations, etc.; failure to deliver)

§ 645 [§ 3611] (Confiscation of firearms possessed by convicted felons)

§ 646 [§ 3617] (Remission or mitigation of forfeitures under liquor laws; possession pending trial)

§ 647 [§ 3616] (Use of confiscated motor vehicles)

U.S.C. Title 19:

§ 483 [§ 1595a] (Forfeitures; penalty for aiding unlawful importation)

§ 1592 (Fraud; penalty against goods)

§ 1602 (Seizure; report to collector)

§ 1603 (Seizure; collector's reports)

§ 1604 (Seizure; prosecution)

§ 1605 (Seizure; custody)

§ 1606 (Seizure; appraisement)

§ 1607 (Seizure; value $1,000 or less)

§ 1608 (Seizure; claims; judicial condemnation)

§ 1609 (Seizure; summary of forfeiture and sale)

§ 1610 (Seizure; value more than $1,000)

§ 1611 (Seizure; sale unlawful)

§ 1612 (Seizure; summary sale)

§ 1613 (Disposition of proceeds of forfeited property)

§ 1614 (Release of seized property)

§ 1615 (Burden of proof in forfeiture proceedings)

§ 1703 (Seizure and forfeiture of vessels)

§ 1705 (Destruction of forfeited vessel)

U.S.C. Title 21:

§ 334 (Seizure)

§ 337 (Proceedings in name of United States; provision as to subpenas)

U.S.C. Title 22:

§ 401 (Seizure of war materials intended for unlawful export generally; forfeiture)

§ 402 (Seizure of war materials intended for unlawful export generally; warrant for detention of seized property)

§ 403 (Seizure of war materials intended for unlawful export generally; petition for restoration of seized property)

§ 404 (Seizure of war materials intended for unlawful export generally; libel and sale of seized property)

§ 405 (Seizure of war materials intended for unlawful export generally; method of trial; bond for redelivery)

§ 406 (Seizure of war materials intended for unlawful export generally; sections not to interfere with foreign trade)

U.S.C. Title 26:

§ 3116 [§ 7302] (Forfeitures and seizures)

3. Collection of fines and penalties is accomplished in the same manner as the collection of a civil judgment. See Rule 69(a) of the Federal Rules of Civil Procedure, 28 U.S.C., Appendix. For mode of discharging indigent convicts imprisoned for non-payment of fine, see 18 U.S.C. former § 641 (now § 3569).

4. The Federal Juvenile Delinquency Act, 18 U.S.C. former §§ 921–929 (now §§ 5031–5037), authorizes prosecution of a juvenile delinquent on the charge of juvenile delinquency, if the juvenile consents to this procedure. In such cases the court may be convened at any time and place, in chambers or otherwise, and the trial is without a jury. The purpose of excepting proceedings under the act is to make inapplicable to them the requirement of an arraignment in open court (Rule 10) and other similar provisions.

5. As habeas corpus proceedings are regarded as civil proceedings, they are not governed by these rules. The procedure in such cases is prescribed by 28 U.S.C. former §§ 451–466 (now §§ 2241–2243, 2251–2253). Appeals in habeas corpus proceedings are governed by the Federal Rules of Civil Procedure (Rule 81(a)(2) of the Federal Rules of Civil Procedure, 28 U.S.C., Appendix).

Note to Subdivision (c). 1. This rule is analogous to Rule 81(e) of the Federal Rules of Civil Procedure, 28 U.S.C. following § 2072.

2. 1 U.S.C. §§ 1–6, containing general rules of construction, should be read in conjunction with this rule.

3. In connection with the definition of "attorney for the Government", see the following statutes:

U.S.C. Title 5:

§ 291 (Establishment of Department)

§ 293 (Solicitor General)

§ 294 (Assistant to Attorney General)

§ 295 (Assistant Attorneys General)

§ 309 (Conduct and argument of cases by Attorney General and Solicitor General)

§ 310 (Conduct of legal proceedings)

§ 311 (Performance of duty by officers of Department)

§ 312 [28 §§ 503, 507, 508] (Counsel to aid district attorneys)

§ 315 (Appointment and oath of special attorneys or counsel)

U.S.C. Title 28 former:

§ 481 [§ 501] (District attorneys)

§ 483 [§ 502] (Assistant district attorneys)

§ 485 [§ 507] (District attorneys; duties)

4. The last sentence of this rule has particular reference to 18 U.S.C. former § 682 (now § 3731). (Appeals; on behalf of the United States; rules of practice and procedure), which authorizes the United States to appeal in criminal cases from a decision on a motion to quash, a demurrer or a special plea in bar, if the defendant has not been placed in jeopardy. It is intended that the right of the Government to appeal in such cases should not be affected as the result of the substitution of a motion under Rule 12 for a demurrer, motion to quash and a special plea in bar. The rule is equally applicable to any other statute employing the same terminology.

1948 AND 1956 AMENDMENTS

To conform to the nomenclature of revised Title 28 with respect to district courts and courts of appeals (28 U.S.C. §§ 132(a), 43(a); to eliminate special reference to the district courts for the District of Columbia, Hawaii and Puerto Rico which are now United States district courts for all purposes (28 U.S.C. §§ 88, 91, 119, 132, 133, 451), and to eliminate special reference to the court of appeals for the District of Columbia which is now a United States court of appeals for all purposes (28 U.S.C. §§ 41, 43).

The amendment to paragraph (1) is to incorporate nomenclature of Revised Title 28 and in paragraphs (2), (3), (4), and (5) to insert proper reference to Titles 18 and 28 in place of repealed acts.

Under revised Title 28 the justices of the United States Court of Appeals and District Court for the District of Columbia become circuit and district judges (see 28 U.S.C. §§ 44, 133) and the use of the descriptive phrase "senior circuit judge" is abandoned in favor of the title "chief judge" in all circuits including the District of Columbia.

1966 AMENDMENT

Subdivision (a). The first change reflects the granting of statehood to Alaska. The second change conforms to Section 3501 of the Canal Zone Code.

Subdivision (b). The change is made necessary by the new provision in Rule 20(d).

1972 AMENDMENT

Subdivisions (a) and (b) are amended to delete the references to "Commissioners" and to substitute, where appropriate, the phrase "United States magistrates."

Subdivision (a)(2) is deleted. In its old form it makes reference to "rules applicable to criminal proceedings before commissioners," which are now replaced by the Rules of Procedure for the Trial of Minor Offenses before United States Magistrates (1971). Rule 1 of the magistrates' rules provides that they are applicable to cases involving "minor offenses" as defined in 18 U.S.C. § 3401 "before United States magistrates." Cases involving "minor offenses" brought before a judge of the district court will be governed by the Rules of Criminal Procedure for the United States District Courts.

The last sentence of old subdivision (a)(2) is stricken for two reasons: (1) Whenever possible, cases should be brought before a United States magistrate rather than before a state or local judicial officer authorized by 18 U.S.C. § 3041. (2) When a state or local judicial officer is involved, he should conform to the federal rules.

Subdivision (b)(4) makes clear that minor offense cases before United States magistrates are governed by the Rules of Procedure for the Trial of Minor Offenses before United States Magistrates (1971). See rule 1 of the magistrates' rules.

In subdivision (b)(5) the word "civil" is added before the word "forfeiture" to make clear that the rules do apply to criminal forfeitures. This is clearly the intention of Congress. See Senate Report No. 91–617, 91st Cong., 1st Sess., Dec. 16, 1969, at 160:

Subsection (a) provides the remedy of criminal forfeiture. Forfeiture trials are to be governed by the Fed.R. Crim.P. But see Fed.R.Crim.P. 54(b)(5).

Subdivision (c) is amended to list the defined terms in alphabetical order to facilitate the use of the rule. There are added six new definitions.

"Federal magistrate" is a phrase to be used whenever the rule is intended to confer authority on any federal judicial officer including a United States magistrate.

"Judge of the United States" is a phrase defined to include district court, court of appeals, and supreme court judges. It is used in the rules to indicate that only a judge (not to include a United States magistrate) is authorized to act.

"Magistrate" is a term used when both federal and state judicial officers may be authorized to act. The scope of authority of state or local judicial officers is clarified by the enumeration of those rules (3, 4, and 5) under which they are authorized to act.

"United States magistrate" is a phrase which refers to the federal judicial officer created by the Federal Magistrates Act (28 U.S.C. §§ 631–639).

Also added are cross references to the statutory definitions of "minor offense" and "petty offense."

1982 AMENDMENT

Subdivision (a). The amendment of subdivision (a) conforms to 48 U.S.C. § 1694(c), which provides that "the rules heretofore or hereafter promulgated and made effective by the Congress or the Supreme Court of the United States pursuant to Titles 11, 18, and 28 shall apply to the District Court for the Northern Mariana Islands and appeals therefrom where appropriate, except as otherwise provided in articles IV and V of the covenant provided by the Act of March 24, 1976 (90 Stat. 263)." The reference is to the "Covenant To Establish a Commonwealth of the Northern Mariana Islands in Political Union with the United States of America." Article IV of the covenant provides that except when exercising "the jurisdiction of a district court of the United States," the District Court will be considered a court of the Northern Mariana Islands for the purposes of determining the requirements of indictment by grand jury or trial by jury." Article V provides that "neither trial by jury nor indictment by grand jury shall be required in any civil action or criminal prosecution based on local law, except when required by local law."

Subdivision (b)(4). This change is necessitated by the recent amendment of 18 U.S.C. § 3401 by the Federal Magistrate Act of 1979.

Subdivision (c). The first amendment to subdivision (c) conforms to 48 U.S.C. § 1694(c), which states: "The terms 'attorney for the government' and 'United States Attorney' as used in the Federal Rules of Criminal Procedure (Rule 54(c)) shall, when applicable to cases arising under the laws of the Northern Mariana Islands, include the attorney general of the Northern Mariana Islands or any other person or persons as may be authorized by the laws of the Northern Marianas to act therein."

The second amendment to subdivision (c) eliminates any reference to minor offenses. By virtue of the recent amendment of 18 U.S.C. § 3401 by the Federal Magistrate Act of 1979, the term "minor offense" is no longer utilized in the statute. It is likewise no longer used in these rules. See amendments to Rules 5(b) and 9(d).

EDITORIAL NOTES

Effective Date and Savings Provisions of 1984 Amendment. Amendment by Pub.L. 98–473 effective on the first day of first calendar month beginning thirty six months after Oct. 12, 1984, applicable only to offenses committed after taking effect of sections 211 to 239 of Pub.L. 98–473, and except as otherwise provided for therein, see section 235 of Pub.L. 98–473, as amended, set out as a note under section 3551 of Title 18, Crimes and Criminal Procedure.

Rule 55. Records

The clerk of the district court and each United States magistrate shall keep records in criminal proceedings in such form as the Director of the Administrative Office of the United States Courts may prescribe. The clerk shall enter in the records each order or judgment of the court and the date such entry is made.

(As amended Dec. 27, 1948, eff. Oct. 20, 1949; Feb. 28, 1966, eff. July 1, 1966; Apr. 24, 1972, eff. Oct. 1, 1972; Apr. 28, 1983, eff. Aug. 1, 1983.)

NOTES OF ADVISORY COMMITTEE ON RULES

The Federal Rules of Civil Procedure Rule 79, 28 U.S.C., Appendix, prescribed in detail the books and records to be kept by the clerk in civil cases. Subsequently to the effective date of the civil rules, however, the act establishing the Administrative Office of the United States Courts became law (act of August 7, 1939; 53 Stat. 1223; 28 U.S.C. former §§ 444–450 (now §§ 332–333, 456, 601–610)). One of the duties of the Director of that Office is to have charge, under the supervision and direction of the Conference of Senior Circuit Judges, of all administrative matters relating to the offices of the clerks and other clerical and administrative personnel of the courts, 28 U.S.C. former § 446 (now §§ 604, 609). In view of this circumstance it seemed best not to prescribe the records to be kept by the clerks of the district courts and by the United States commissioners, in criminal proceedings, but to vest the power to do so in the Director of the Administrative Office of the United States Courts with the approval of the Conference of Senior Circuit Judges.

1948 AMENDMENT

To incorporate nomenclature provided for by Revised Title 28 U.S.C., § 331.

1966 AMENDMENT

Rule 37(a)(2) provides that for the purpose of commencing the running of the time for appeal a judgment or order is entered "when it is entered in the criminal docket." The sentence added here requires that such a docket be kept and that it show the dates on which judgments or orders are entered therein. Cf. Civil Rule 79(a).

1983 AMENDMENT

The Advisory Committee Note to original Rule 55 observes that, in light of the authority which the Director and Judicial Conference have over the activities of clerks, "it seems best not to prescribe the records to be kept by clerks." Because of current experimentation with automated record-keeping, this approach is more appropriate than ever before. The amendment will make it possible for the Director to permit use of more sophisticated record-keeping techniques, including those which may obviate the need for a "criminal docket" book. The reference to the Judicial Conference has been stricken as unnecessary. See 28 U.S.C. § 604.

Rule 56. Courts and Clerks

The district court shall be deemed always open for the purpose of filing any proper paper, of issuing and returning process and of making motions and orders. The clerk's office with the clerk or a deputy in attendance shall be open during business hours on all days except Saturdays, Sundays, and legal holidays, but a court may provide by local rule or order that its clerk's office shall be open for specified hours on Saturdays or particular legal holidays other than New Year's Day, Birthday of Martin Luther King, Jr., Washington's Birthday, Memorial Day, Independence Day, Labor Day, Columbus Day, Veterans Day, Thanksgiving Day, and Christmas Day.

(As amended Dec. 27, 1948, eff. Oct. 20, 1949; Feb. 28, 1966, eff. July 1, 1966; Dec. 4, 1967, eff. July 1, 1968; Mar. 1, 1971, eff. July 1, 1971; Apr. 25, 1988, eff. Aug. 1, 1988.)

NOTES OF ADVISORY COMMITTEE ON RULES

1. The first sentence of this rule is substantially the same as Rule 77(a) of the Federal Rules of Civil Procedure, 28 U.S.C., Appendix, except that it is applicable to circuit courts of appeals as well as to district courts.

2. In connection with this rule, see 28 U.S.C. former § 14 (Monthly adjournments for trial of criminal causes) and 28 U.S.C. former § 15 (now § 141) (Special terms). These sections "indicate a policy of avoiding the hardships consequent upon a closing of the court during vacations," *Abbott v. Brown*, 241 U.S. 606, 611, 36 S.Ct. 689, 60 L.Ed. 1199.

3. The second sentence of the rule is identical with the first sentence of Rule 77(c) of the Federal Rules of Civil Procedure, 28 U.S.C., Appendix.

4. The term "legal holidays" includes Federal holidays as well as holidays prescribed by the laws of the State where the clerk's office is located.

1948 AMENDMENT

To incorporate nomenclature provided for by Revised Title 28, U.S.C. § 43(a).

1966 AMENDMENT

The change is in conformity with the changes made in Rule 45. See the similar changes in Civil Rule 77(c) made effective July 1, 1963.

1968 AMENDMENT

The provisions relating to courts of appeals are included in Rule 47 of the Federal Rules of Appellate Procedure.

1971 AMENDMENT

The amendment adds Columbus Day to the list of legal holidays. See the Note accompanying the amendment of Rule 45(a).

1988 AMENDMENT

The amendment is technical. No substantive change is intended.

EDITORIAL NOTES

Effective Date of 1988 Amendment. The Order of the Supreme Court dated April 25, 1988, provided in part: "That the foregoing amendments to the Federal Rules of Criminal Procedure [this rule and rule 30] shall take effect on August 1, 1988 and shall govern all proceedings in criminal cases thereafter commenced and, insofar as just and practicable, all proceedings in criminal cases then pending." See order preceding rule 1.

Rule 57. Rules by District Courts

Each district court by action of a majority of the judges thereof may from time to time, after giving appropriate public notice and an opportunity to comment, make and amend rules governing its practice not inconsistent with these rules. A local rule so adopted shall take effect upon the date specified by the district court and shall remain in effect unless amended by the district court or abrogated by the judicial council of the circuit in which the district is located. Copies of the rules and amendments so made by any district court shall upon their promulgation be furnished to the judicial council and the Administrative Office of the United States Courts and be made available to the public. In all cases not provided for by rule, the district judges and magistrates may regulate their practice in any manner not inconsistent with these rules or those of the district in which they act.

(As amended Dec. 27, 1948, eff. Oct. 20, 1949; Dec. 4, 1967, eff. July 1, 1968; Apr. 29, 1985, eff. Aug. 1, 1985.)

NOTES OF ADVISORY COMMITTEE ON RULES

Note to Subdivision (a). This rule is substantially a restatement of 28 U.S.C. former § 731 (now § 2071) (Rules of practice in district courts). A similar provision is found in Rule 83 of the Federal Rules of Civil Procedure, 28 U.S.C., Appendix.

Note to Subdivision (b). 1. One of the purposes of this rule is to abrogate any existing requirement of conformity to State procedure on any point whatsoever. The Federal Rules of Civil Procedure, 28 U.S.C., Appendix, have been held to repeal the Conformity Act, 28 U.S.C. former § 724, *Sibbach v. Wilson,* 312 U.S. 1, 10, 61 S.Ct. 422, 85 L.Ed. 479.

2. While the rules are intended to constitute a comprehensive procedural code for criminal cases in the Federal courts, nevertheless it seemed best not to endeavor to prescribe a uniform practice as to some matters of detail, but to leave the individual courts free to regulate them, either by local rules or by usage. Among such matters are the mode of impaneling a jury, the manner and order of interposing challenges to jurors, the manner of selecting the foreman of a trial jury, the matter of sealed verdicts, the order of counsel's arguments to the jury, and other similar details.

1948 AMENDMENT

To incorporate nomenclature provided for by Revised Title 28, U.S.C., § 43(a).

1968 AMENDMENT

The provisions relating to the court of appeals are included in Rule 47 of the Federal Rules of Appellate Procedure.

1985 AMENDMENT

Rule 57 has been reformulated to correspond to Fed. R.Civ.P. 83, including the proposed amendments thereto. The purpose of the reformulation is to emphasize that the procedures for adoption of local rules by a district court are the same under both the civil and the criminal rules. In particular, the major purpose of the reformulation is to enhance the local rulemaking process by requiring appropriate public notice of proposed rules and an opportunity to comment on them. See Committee Note to Fed.R.Civ.P. 83.

[Rule 58.   Forms.] (Abrogated Apr. 28, 1983, Eff. Aug. 1, 1983)

Rule 58 and the Appendix of Forms are unnecessary and have been abrogated. Forms of indictment and information are made available to United States Attorneys' offices by the Department of Justice. Forms used by the courts are made available by the Director of the Administrative Office of the United States Courts.

Rule 59.   Effective Date

These rules take effect on the day which is 3 months subsequent to the adjournment of the first regular session of the 79th Congress, but if that day is prior to September 1, 1945, then they take effect on September 1, 1945. They govern all criminal proceedings thereafter commenced and so far as just and practicable all proceedings then pending.

NOTES OF ADVISORY COMMITTEE ON RULES

This rule is based on act of June 29, 1940 (54 Stat. 688; 18 U.S.C. former § 687 (now § 3771)). It is substantially the same as Rule 86 of the Federal Rules of Civil Procedure, 28 U.S.C., Appendix.

Rule 60.   Title

These rules may be known and cited as the Federal Rules of Criminal Procedure.

NOTES OF ADVISORY COMMITTEE ON RULES

This rule is similar to Rule 85 of the Federal Rules of Civil Procedure, 28 U.S.C., Appendix, which reads as follows:

These rules may be known and cited as the Federal Rules of Civil Procedure.

HABEAS CORPUS PROVISIONS

Table of Contents

INTRODUCTION

Reprinted from Krantz, Corrections and Prisoners' Rights, 3rd Ed. (1988).

STATE REMEDIES

Largely influenced by the Uniform Post–Conviction Procedure Act and Standards enunciated by the American Bar Association Project on Criminal Justice, most states have installed an avenue of procedures for post-conviction review. For the most part, however, state habeas corpus hearings are limited to inquiries into the legality of imprisonment. See Rogers v. Warden (1968). This is because state habeas corpus statutes typically focus only on persons who are illegally imprisoned. A few state courts have interpreted their statutes to allow writs to be used to secure relief from shocking conditions or invalid regulations. See, e.g., Commonwealth ex rel. Bryant v. Hendrick (1971), where the Court found state habeas corpus to be the appropriate remedy for attacking conditions of cruel and unusual punishment in the Philadelphia prison system. To the extent that state habeas corpus is available to attack prison conditions, however, it is likely that state courts will initially require that prisoners exhaust any available administrative remedy first. See People ex rel. Willis v. Department of Corrections (1972).

Arguably, numerous other state judicial and administrative remedies should be available for use in prisoners' rights cases. For equitable relief, states typically have judicial remedies such as declaratory judgments, injunctions, and writs of mandamus, prohibition, and quo warranto. In states such as California, they have been liberally used. Also, Massachusetts enacted a counterpart to the Federal Civil Rights Act in 1979, Mass.Gen. Laws Ann. c. 12 §§ 11H and I (1979).

Generally, though, these judicial options have not been successfully used in most jurisdictions. This could be so for many reasons—the procedures surrounding these remedies are often complicated, narrowly defined, and utilized only in rare circumstances (for example, a writ of mandamus is normally considered to be an extraordinary writ to be granted in few cases); prisoners and their lawyers are more familiar with and more comfortable in federal courts; the opportunities for discovery may be more restrictive; the remedial options under state law may be far more limited; and the possibilities that attorneys fees may be awarded may be less likely. See Koren, Boston, Alexander and Manville, *A Primer for Jail Litigators: Some Practical Suggestions for Surviving and Prevailing in Your Lawsuit* in Robbins, Prisoners and the Law (1987) at 17–11.

THE FEDERAL MODEL

FEDERAL HABEAS CORPUS

Aside from § 1983 of the Federal Civil Rights Act *, state prisoners essentially have only one other way to have their complaints heard in the federal courts—federal habeas corpus. (But consider the authority of the United States Attorney General to intervene in cases where state prisoners are subjected to "egregious or flagrant conditions" under the Institutionalized Persons Act, 42 U.S.C.A. § 1997.) Under 28 U.S.C.A. § 2254, the federal courts can entertain an application for a writ of habeas corpus by a state prisoner being held in custody in violation of the Constitution or laws of the United States. (28 U.S.C.A. § 2255 and is the federal counterpart to § 2254, and is available to federal prisoners). Historically, the only relief which could be granted in habeas corpus cases was immediate physical release from all constraints. This was because the only issue cognizable under the Great Writ was whether or not the trial court had jurisdiction to hear the case. Frank v. Mangum (1915). Since *Frank*, however, there has been a tremendous expansion in what an inmate could allege in proving that his custody was in violation of the federal Constitution or federal laws, e.g., that a statute under which a person is convicted is unconstitutional, that a person was denied constitutional rights at trial, or that a person is unlawfully confined in the wrong institution. See Preiser v. Rodriguez (1973).

Moreover, the view of the scope of federal habeas corpus has broadened considerably in recent years in prison conditions cases. Beginning with Coffin v. Reichard (1944), courts began to accept the view that federal habeas corpus is appropriate under certain circumstances to consider the *nature* as well as the *fact* of confinement. In *Coffin*, the court expressed the law to be as follows:

A prisoner is entitled to the writ of habeas corpus when, though lawfully in custody, he is deprived of some right to which he is lawfully entitled even in his confinement, the deprivation of which serves to make his imprisonment more burdensome than the law allows or curtails his liberty to a greater extent than the law permits.

In Armstrong v. Cardwell (1972), the court supported this interpretation of the permissible scope of federal habeas corpus by pointing out that federal courts have authority in issuing a writ to do more than simply order a prisoner's release. This stems from 28 U.S.C.A. § 2243, which provides that "the court shall summarily hear and determine the facts, and dispose of the matter as law and justice require."

Although the Supreme Court has not yet defined the permissible use of federal habeas corpus in the scope suggested by *Coffin*, it appears to be moving in that direction. In Johnson v. Avery (1969), the Court permitted the writ to be used to invalidate a prison regulation prohibiting legal work by jail-house lawyers and to release a prisoner from disciplinary confinement for violating the regulation. See also Wilwording v. Swenson (1971), where the Court indicated federal habeas corpus could be used to challenge prison

* 42 U.S.C.A. § 1983 provides:

Every person who, under color of any statute, ordinance, regulation, custom or usage, of any State or Territory, subjects or causes to be subjected, any citizen of the United States or other person within the jurisdiction thereof to the deprivation of any rights, privileges or immunities secured by the Constitution and laws, shall be liable to the party injured in an action at law, suit in equity, or other proper proceeding for redress.

Jurisdiction to hear § 1983 cases is vested in the federal courts under 42 U.S.C.A. § 1343. State courts also have concurrent jurisdiction over claims under the Federal Civil Rights Act. See Martinez v. California (1980). In summary, the requisites under § 1983 are that: (1) a person or persons; (2) acting under color of state law; (3) deprive(s) one or more of federally protected rights.

conditions. In Preiser v. Rodriguez (1973) the Court held that the writ could be used to attack the duration as well as the fact of confinement. Thus, habeas corpus could be used for the purpose of shortening the length of actual confinement in prison. The Court went on to say that habeas corpus arguably may be available to challenge other unlawful prison conditions:

> When a prisoner is put under additional and unconstitutional restraints during his lawful custody, it is arguable that habeas corpus will lie to remove the constraints making the custody illegal.

The Court refused to decide whether habeas corpus should be expanded to this extent, however, since the issue was not before it. It did determine, though, that, even if the scope of habeas corpus were expanded, damages would not be an appropriate or available federal remedy under it.

Under § 2254(b), a writ of habeas corpus cannot be granted "unless it appears that the applicant has exhausted the remedies available in the courts of the State, or that there is either an absence of available State corrective process or the existence of circumstances rendering such process ineffective to protect the rights of the prisoner." It has been determined under this and other provisions that exhaustion must include both available state judicial and state administrative remedies. See Preiser v. Rodriguez (1973).

The exhaustion requirement relates to all possible claims. In Rose v. Lundy (1982), the Supreme Court held that a federal district court must dismiss a habeas petition that contains any unexhausted claims. The petitioner is then given the choice of amending his petition by striking the unexhausted claims or going back and exhausting them in the proper State forum before continuing in federal court.

It is not yet clear what impact *Lundy* will have on reducing the effective use of federal habeas corpus.

In Wilwording v. Swenson (1971), a case decided ten years before, the Supreme Court made it clear that § 2254 should not be read to erect "insuperable or successive barriers to the invocation of federal habeas corpus." In that case, the prisoners applied for federal relief on their living conditions and disciplinary measures after their state habeas corpus petitions were dismissed. The state argued that § 2254 had not been satisfied since the prisoners had not invoked other possible state alternatives such as "a suit for injunction, a writ of prohibition, or mandamus or a declaratory judgment in the state courts, or perhaps other relief under the State Administrative Procedure Act." In its per curiam opinion, the Court held that the petitioners were not required to file repetitious applications in state court. Further, the Court stated that the mere possibility of success in additional proceedings did not bar federal relief. Finally, the Court quoted, with approval from an earlier concurring opinion by Justice Rutledge in Marino v. Ragen (1947):

> The exhaustion-of-state-remedies rule should not be stretched to the absurdity of requiring exhaustion of * * * separate remedies when at the outset a petitioner cannot intelligently select the proper way, and in conclusion he may find only that none of the [alternatives] is appropriate or effective.

Given the Court's attitude in *Wilwording,* the exhaustion of remedies requirement, in spite of Rose v. Lundy, should not, in theory, create insuperable obstacles today in being able to utilize the federal writ quickly to obtain relief for unlawful prison conditions. For few states now possess state judicial remedies which can be effectively used to challenge conditions of confinement. The Supreme Court's finding in *Wilwording* that it was not referred to a single instance, regardless of the state remedy invoked, in which the Missouri courts had granted a hearing to prisoners on the conditions of their confinement is undoubtedly typical of a majority of the states. The same is true of available administrative remedies in most jurisdictions.

In both *Preiser* and *Lundy,* the Supreme Court made it clear that the doctrine of comity mandated a total exhaustion requirement. The notion underlying this doctrine is that the states should be given the initial opportunity to correct problems arising within their own institutions before the federal courts are asked to intervene. This suggests that the federal courts (by narrowing the permissible use of § 1983 among other ways) will be putting increasing pressure on the states to establish their own judicial and administrative remedies for prisoners' rights cases. Once these remedies begin to emerge, whether they are effective or not, the exhaustion of remedies requirement will become an increasing hardship in obtaining appropriate relief for prisoners with legitimate complaints.

For a concise summary of the law of corrections and prisoners' rights, surveying the entire correctional process from pretrial diversion to the restoration of offenders' rights upon release, see Krantz' Corrections and Prisoners' Rights in a Nutshell, 3rd Ed., Nutshell Series (West Publishing Company, St. Paul, 1988) ... from pages 255–256 and 281–288 of which this INTRODUCTION is drawn.

TITLE 28
JUDICIARY AND JUDICIAL PROCEDURE

Act June 25, 1948, c. 646, § 1, 62 Stat. 869
As amended to February 1, 1989

CHAPTER 153—HABEAS CORPUS

SENATE REVISION AMENDMENT

Chapter catchline was changed by Senate amendment. See 80th Congress Senate Report No. 1559.

EDITORIAL NOTES

Codification. Section 250(b) of Pub.L. 95–598, Nov. 6, 1978, 92 Stat. 2672, amended the table of sections by inserting the following item:

2256. Habeas corpus from bankruptcy courts. Section 113 of Pub.L. 98–353, July 10, 1984, 98 Stat. 343, (effective June 27, 1984 pursuant to section 122(c) of Pub.L. 98–353) provided that this amendment "shall not be effective". Section 121 of Pub.L. 98–353 (effective on July 10, 1984 pursuant to section 122(a) of Pub.L. 98–353) provided that this amendment shall take effect on July 10, 1984.

Cross Reference

Rules Governing Section 2254 Cases in the United States District Courts and Rules Governing Proceedings in the United States District Courts under Section 2255 of Title 28, United States Code, are set out in this pamphlet, ante.

§ 2241. Power to grant writ

(a) Writs of habeas corpus may be granted by the Supreme Court, any justice thereof, the district courts and any circuit judge within their respective jurisdictions. The order of a circuit judge shall be entered in the records of the district court of the district wherein the restraint complained of is had.

(b) The Supreme Court, any justice thereof, and any circuit judge may decline to entertain an application for a writ of habeas corpus and may transfer the application for hearing and determination to the district court having jurisdiction to entertain it.

(c) The writ of habeas corpus shall not extend to a prisoner unless—

(1) He is in custody under or by color of the authority of the United States or is committed for trial before some court thereof; or

(2) He is in custody for an act done or omitted in pursuance of an Act of Congress, or an order, process, judgment or decree of a court or judge of the United States; or

(3) He is in custody in violation of the Constitution or laws or treaties of the United States; or

(4) He, being a citizen of a foreign state and domiciled therein is in custody for an act done or omitted under any alleged right, title, authority, privilege, protection, or exemption claimed under the commission, order or sanction of any foreign state, or under color thereof, the validity and effect of which depend upon the law of nations; or

(5) It is necessary to bring him into court to testify or for trial.

(d) Where an application for a writ of habeas corpus is made by a person in custody under the judgment and sentence of a State court of a State which contains two or more Federal judicial districts, the application may be filed in the district court for the district wherein such person is in custody or in the district court for the district within which the State court was held which convicted and sentenced him and each of such district courts shall have concurrent jurisdiction to entertain the application. The district court for the district wherein such an application is filed in the exercise of its discretion and in furtherance of justice may transfer the application to the other district court for hearing and determination.

(As amended May 24, 1949, c. 139, § 112, 63 Stat. 105; Sept. 19, 1966, Pub.L. 89–590, 80 Stat. 811.)

REVISION NOTES
1948 ACT

Based on title 28, U.S.C., 1940 ed., §§ 451, 452, 453 (R.S. §§ 751, 752, 753; Mar. 3, 1911, ch. 231, § 291, 36 Stat. 1167; Feb. 13, 1925, ch. 229, § 6, 43 Stat. 940).

Section consolidates sections 451, 452 and 453 of title 28, U.S.C., 1940 ed., with changes in phraseology necessary to effect the consolidation.

Words "for the purpose of an inquiry into the cause of restraint of liberty" in section 452 of title 28, U.S.C., 1940 ed., were omitted as merely descriptive of the writ.

Subsection (b) was added to give statutory sanction to orderly and appropriate procedure. A circuit judge who unnecessarily entertains applications which should be addressed to the district court, thereby disqualifies himself to hear such matters on appeal and to that extent limits his usefulness as a judge of the court of appeals. The Supreme Court and Supreme Court Justices should not be burdened with applications for writs cognizable in the district courts.

1949 ACT

This section inserts commas in certain parts of the text of subsection (b) of section 2241 of title 28, U.S.C., for the purpose of proper punctuation.

§ 2242. Application

Application for a writ of habeas corpus shall be in writing signed and verified by the person for whose relief it is intended or by someone acting in his behalf.

It shall allege the facts concerning the applicant's commitment or detention, the name of the person who has custody over him and by virtue of what claim or authority, if known.

It may be amended or supplemented as provided in the rules of procedure applicable to civil actions.

If addressed to the Supreme Court, a justice thereof or a circuit judge it shall state the reasons for not making application to the district court of the district in which the applicant is held.

REVISION NOTES

Based on title 28, U.S.C., 1940 ed., § 454 (R.S. § 754).

Words "or by someone acting in his behalf" were added. This follows the actual practice of the courts, as set forth in *United States ex rel. Funaro v. Watchorn*, C.C.1908, 164 F. 152; *Collins v. Traeger*, C.C.A.1928, 27 F.2d 842, and cases cited.

The third paragraph is new. It was added to conform to existing practice as approved by judicial decisions. See Dorsey v. Gill (App.D.C.) 148 F.2d 857, 865, 866. See also Holiday v. Johnston, 61 S.Ct. 1015, 313 U.S. 342, 85 L.Ed. 1392.

Changes were made in phraseology.

§ 2243. Issuance of writ; return; hearing; decision

A court, justice or judge entertaining an application for a writ of habeas corpus shall forthwith award the writ or issue an order directing the respondent to show cause why the writ should not be granted, unless it appears from the application that the applicant or person detained is not entitled thereto.

The writ, or order to show cause shall be directed to the person having custody of the person detained. It shall be returned within three days unless for good cause additional time, not exceeding twenty days, is allowed.

The person to whom the writ or order is directed shall make a return certifying the true cause of the detention.

When the writ or order is returned a day shall be set for hearing, not more than five days after the return unless for good cause additional time is allowed.

Unless the application for the writ and the return present only issues of law the person to whom the writ is directed shall be required to produce at the hearing the body of the person detained.

The applicant or the person detained may, under oath, deny any of the facts set forth in the return or allege any other material facts.

The return and all suggestions made against it may be amended, by leave of court, before or after being filed.

The court shall summarily hear and determine the facts, and dispose of the matter as law and justice require.

REVISION NOTES

Based on title 28, U.S.C., 1940 ed., §§ 455, 456, 457, 458, 459, 460, and 461 (R.S. §§ 755–761).

Section consolidates sections 455–461 of title 28, U.S.C., 1940 ed.

The requirement for return within 3 days "unless for good cause additional time, not exceeding 20 days is allowed" in the second paragraph, was substituted for the provision of such section 455 which allowed 3 days for return if within 20 miles, 10 days if more than 20 but not more than 100 miles, and 20 days if more than 100 miles distant.

Words "unless for good cause additional time is allowed" in the fourth paragraph, were substituted for words "unless the party petitioning requests a longer time" in section 459 of title 28, U.S.C., 1940 ed.

The fifth paragraph providing for production of the body of the detained person at the hearing is in conformity with Walker v. Johnston, 1941, 61 S.Ct. 574, 312 U.S. 275, 85 L.Ed. 830.

Changes were made in phraseology.

§ 2244. Finality of determination

(a) No circuit or district judge shall be required to entertain an application for a writ of habeas corpus to inquire into the detention of a person pursuant to a judgment of a court of the United States if it appears that the legality of such detention has been determined by a judge or court of the United States on a prior application for a writ of habeas corpus and the petition presents no new ground not theretofore presented and determined, and the judge of court is satisfied that the ends of justice will not be served by such inquiry.

(b) When after an evidentiary hearing on the merits of a material factual issue, or after a hearing on the merits of an issue of law, a person in custody pursuant to the judgment of a State court has been denied by a court of the United States or a justice or judge of the United States release from custody or other remedy on an application for a writ of habeas corpus, a subsequent application for a writ of habeas corpus in behalf of such person need not be entertained by a court of the United States or a justice or judge of the United States unless the application alleges and is predicated on a factual or other ground not adjudicated on the hearing of the earlier application for the writ, and unless the court, justice, or judge is satisfied that the applicant has not on the earlier application deliberately withheld the newly asserted ground or otherwise abused the writ.

(c) In a habeas corpus proceeding brought in behalf of a person in custody pursuant to the judgment of a State court, a prior judgment of the Supreme Court of the United States on an appeal or review by a writ of certiorari at the instance of the prisoner of the decision of such State court, shall be conclusive as to all issues of fact or law with respect to an asserted denial of a Federal right which constitutes ground for discharge in a habeas corpus proceeding, actually adjudicated by the Supreme Court therein, unless the applicant for the writ of habeas corpus shall plead and the court shall find the existence of a material and controlling fact which did not appear in the record of the proceeding in the Supreme Court and the court shall further find that the applicant for the writ of habeas corpus could not have caused such fact to appear in such record by the exercise of reasonable diligence.

(As amended Nov. 2, 1966, Pub.L. 89–711, § 1, 80 Stat. 1104.)

REVISION NOTES

This section makes no material change in existing practice. Notwithstanding the opportunity open to litigants to abuse the writ, the courts have consistently refused to entertain successive "nuisance" applications for habeas corpus. It is derived from H.R. 4232 introduced in the first session of the Seventy-ninth Congress by Chairman Hatton Sumners of the Committee on the Judiciary and referred to that Committee.

The practice of suing out successive, repetitious, and unfounded writs of habeas corpus imposes an unnecessary burden on the courts. See Dorsey v. Gill, 1945, 148 F.2d 857, 862, in which Miller, J., notes that "petitions for the writ are used not only as they should be to protect unfortunate persons against miscarriages of justice, but also as a device for harassing court, custodial, and enforcement officers with a multiplicity of repetitious, meritless requests for relief. The most extreme example is that of a person who, between July 1, 1939, and April 1944 presented in the District Court 50 petitions for writs of habeas corpus; another person has presented 27 petitions; a third, 24; a fourth, 22; a fifth, 20. One hundred nineteen persons have presented 597 petitions—an average of 5."

§ 2245. Certificate of trial judge admissible in evidence

On the hearing of an application for a writ of habeas corpus to inquire into the legality of the detention of a person pursuant to a judgment the certificate of the judge who presided at the trial resulting in the judgment, setting forth the facts occurring at the trial, shall be admissible in evidence. Copies of the certificate shall be filed with the court in which the application is pending and in the court in which the trial took place.

REVISION NOTES

This section makes no substantive change in existing law. It is derived from H.R. 4232 introduced in the first session of the Seventy-ninth Congress by Chairman Sumners of the House Committee on the Judiciary. It clarifies existing law and promotes uniform procedure.

§ 2246. Evidence; depositions; affidavits

On application for a writ of habeas corpus, evidence may be taken orally or by deposition, or, in the discretion of the judge, by affidavit. If affidavits are admitted any party shall have the right to propound written interrogatories to the affiants, or to file answering affidavits.

REVISION NOTES

This section is derived from H.R. 4232 introduced in the first session of the Seventy-ninth Congress by Chairman Sumners of the House Committee on the Judiciary. It clarifies existing practice without substantial change.

§ 2247. Documentary evidence

On application for a writ of habeas corpus documentary evidence, transcripts of proceedings upon arraignment, plea and sentence and a transcript of the oral testimony introduced on any previous similar application by or in behalf of the same petitioner, shall be admissible in evidence.

REVISION NOTES

Derived from H.R. 4232, Seventy-ninth Congress, first session. It is declaratory of existing law and practice.

§ 2248. Return or answer; conclusiveness

The allegations of a return to the writ of habeas corpus or of an answer to an order to show cause in a habeas corpus proceeding, if not traversed, shall be accepted as true except to the extent that the judge finds from the evidence that they are not true.

REVISION NOTES

Derived from H.R. 4232, Seventy-ninth Congress, first session. At common law the return was conclusive and could not be controverted but it is now almost universally held that the return is not conclusive of the facts alleged therein. 39 C.J.S. pp. 664–666, §§ 98, 99.

§ 2249. Certified copies of indictment, plea and judgment; duty of respondent

On application for a writ of habeas corpus to inquire into the detention of any person pursuant to a judgment of a court of the United States, the respondent shall promptly file with the court certified copies of the indictment, plea of petitioner and the judgment, or such of them as may be material to the questions raised, if the petitioner fails to attach them to his petition, and same shall be attached to the return to the writ, or to the answer to the order to show cause.

REVISION NOTES

Derived from H.R. 4232, Seventy-ninth Congress, first session. It conforms to the prevailing practice in habeas corpus proceedings.

§ 2250. Indigent petitioner entitled to documents without cost

If on any application for a writ of habeas corpus an order has been made permitting the petitioner to prosecute the application in forma pauperis, the clerk of any court of the United States shall furnish to the petitioner without cost certified copies of such documents or parts of the record on file in his office as may be required by order of the judge before whom the application is pending.

REVISION NOTES

Derived from H.R. 4232, Seventy-ninth Congress, first session. It conforms to the prevailing practice.

§ 2251. Stay of State court proceedings

A justice or judge of the United States before whom a habeas corpus proceeding is pending, may, before final judgment or after final judgment of discharge, or pending appeal, stay any proceeding against the person detained in any State court or by or under the authority of any State for any matter involved in the habeas corpus proceeding.

After the granting of such a stay, any such proceeding in any State court or by or under the authority of any State shall be void. If no stay is granted, any such proceeding shall be as valid as if no habeas corpus proceedings or appeal were pending.

REVISION NOTES

Based on title 28, U.S.C., 1940 ed., § 465 (R.S. § 766; Mar. 3, 1893, ch. 226, 27 Stat. 751; Feb. 13, 1925, ch. 229, § 8(c), 43 Stat. 940; June 19, 1934, ch. 673, 48 Stat. 1177).

Provisions relating to proceedings pending in 1934 were deleted as obsolete.

A provision requiring an appeal to be taken within 3 months was omitted as covered by sections 2101 and 2107 of this title.

Changes were made in phraseology.

§ 2252. Notice

Prior to the hearing of a habeas corpus proceeding in behalf of a person in custody of State officers or by virtue of State laws notice shall be served on the attorney general or other appropriate officer of such State as the justice or judge at the time of issuing the writ shall direct.

REVISION NOTES

Based on title 28, U.S.C., 1940 ed., § 462 (R.S. § 762).

Section 462 of title 28, U.S.C., 1940 ed., was limited to alien prisoners described in section 453 of title 28, U.S.C., 1940 ed. The revised section extends to all cases of all prisoners under State custody or authority, leaving it to the justice or judge to prescribe the notice to State officers, to specify the officer served, and to satisfy himself that such notice has been given.

Provision for making due proof of such service was omitted as unnecessary. The sheriff's or marshal's return is sufficient.

Changes were made in phraseology.

§ 2253. Appeal

In a habeas corpus proceeding before a circuit or district judge, the final order shall be subject to review, on appeal, by the court of appeals for the circuit where the proceeding is had.

There shall be no right of appeal from such an order in a proceeding to test the validity of a warrant to remove, to another district or place for commitment or trial, a person charged with a criminal offense against the United States, or to test the validity of his detention pending removal proceedings.

An appeal may not be taken to the court of appeals from the final order in a habeas corpus proceeding where the detention complained of arises out of process issued by a State court, unless the justice or judge who rendered the order or a circuit justice or judge issues a certificate of probable cause.

(As amended May 24, 1949, c. 139, § 113, 63 Stat. 105; Oct. 31, 1951, c. 655, § 52, 65 Stat. 727.)

1948 ACT
REVISION NOTES

Based on title 28, U.S.C., 1940 ed., §§ 463(a) and 466 (Mar. 10, 1908, ch. 76, 36 Stat. 40; Feb. 13, 1925, ch. 229, §§ 6, 13, 43 Stat. 940, 942; June 29, 1938, ch. 806, 52 Stat. 1232).

This section consolidates paragraph (a) of section 463, and section 466 of title 28, U.S.C., 1940 ed.

The last two sentences of section 463(a) of title 28, U.S.C., 1940 ed., were omitted. They were repeated in section 452 of title 28, U.S.C., 1940 ed. (See reviser's note under section 2241 of this title).

Changes were made in phraseology.

1949 ACT

This section corrects a typographical error in the second paragraph of section 2253 of title 28.

§ 2254. State custody; remedies in State courts

(a) The Supreme Court, a Justice thereof, a circuit judge, or a district court shall entertain an application for a writ of habeas corpus in behalf of a person in custody pursuant to the judgment of a State court only on the ground that he is in custody in violation of the Constitution or laws or treaties of the United States.

(b) An application for a writ of habeas corpus in behalf of a person in custody pursuant to the judgment of a State court shall not be granted unless it appears that the applicant has exhausted the remedies available in the courts of the State, or that there is either an absence of available State corrective process or the existence of circumstances rendering such process ineffective to protect the rights of the prisoner.

(c) An applicant shall not be deemed to have exhausted the remedies available in the courts of the State, within the meaning of this section, if he has the right under the law of the State to raise, by any available procedure, the question presented.

(d) In any proceeding instituted in a Federal court by an application for a writ of habeas corpus by a person in custody pursuant to the judgment of a State court, a determination after a hearing on the merits of a factual issue, made by a State court of competent jurisdiction in a proceeding to which the applicant for the writ and the State or an officer or agent thereof were parties, evidenced by a written finding, written opinion, or other reliable and adequate written indicia, shall be presumed to be correct, unless the applicant shall establish or it shall otherwise appear, or the respondent shall admit—

(1) that the merits of the factual dispute were not resolved in the State court hearing;

(2) that the factfinding procedure employed by the State court was not adequate to afford a full and fair hearing;

(3) that the material facts were not adequately developed at the State court hearing;

(4) that the State court lacked jurisdiction of the subject matter or over the person of the applicant in the State court proceeding;

(5) that the applicant was an indigent and the State court, in deprivation of his constitutional right, failed to appoint counsel to represent him in the State court proceeding;

(6) that the applicant did not receive a full, fair, and adequate hearing in the State court proceeding; or

(7) that the applicant was otherwise denied due process of law in the State court proceeding;

(8) or unless that part of the record of the State court proceeding in which the determination of such factual issue was made, pertinent to a determination of the sufficiency of the evidence to support such factual determination,

is produced as provided for hereinafter, and the Federal court on a consideration of such part of the record as a whole concludes that such factual determination is not fairly supported by the record:

And in an evidentiary hearing in the proceeding in the Federal court, when due proof of such factual determination has been made, unless the existence of one or more of the circumstances respectively set forth in paragraphs numbered (1) to (7), inclusive, is shown by the applicant, otherwise appears, or is admitted by the respondent, or unless the court concludes pursuant to the provisions of paragraph numbered (8) that the record in the State court proceeding, considered as a whole, does not fairly support such factual determination, the burden shall rest upon the applicant to establish by convincing evidence that the factual determination by the State court was erroneous.

(e) If the applicant challenges the sufficiency of the evidence adduced in such State court proceeding to support the State court's determination of a factual issue made therein, the applicant, if able, shall produce that part of the record pertinent to a determination of the sufficiency of the evidence to support such determination. If the applicant, because of indigency or other reason is unable to produce such part of the record, then the State shall produce such part of the record and the Federal court shall direct the State to do so by order directed to an appropriate State official. If the State cannot provide such pertinent part of the record, then the court shall determine under the existing facts and circumstances what weight shall be given to the State court's factual determination.

(f) A copy of the official records of the State court, duly certified by the clerk of such court to be a true and correct copy of a finding, judicial opinion, or other reliable written indicia showing such a factual determination by the State court shall be admissible in the Federal court proceeding.

(As amended Nov. 2, 1966, Pub.L. 89–711, § 2, 80 Stat. 1105.)

REVISION NOTES

This new section is declaratory of existing law as affirmed by the Supreme Court. (See Ex parte Hawk, 1944, 64 S.Ct. 448, 321 U.S. 114, 88 L.Ed. 572.)

Senate amendment to this section, Senate Report No. 1559, amendment No. 47, has three declared purposes, set forth as follows:

"The first is to eliminate from the prohibition of the section applications in behalf of prisoners in custody under authority of a State officer but whose custody has not been directed by the judgment of a State court. If the section were applied to applications by persons detained solely under authority of a State officer it would unduly hamper Federal courts in the protection of Federal officers prosecuted for acts committed in the course of official duty.

"The second purpose is to eliminate, as a ground of Federal jurisdiction to review by habeas corpus judgments of State courts, the proposition that the State court has denied a prisoner a 'fair adjudication of the legality of his detention under the Constitution and laws of the United States.' The Judicial Conference believes that this would be an undesirable ground for Federal jurisdiction in addition to exhaustion of State remedies or lack of adequate remedy in the State courts because it would permit proceedings in the Federal court on this ground before the petitioner had exhausted his State remedies. This ground would, of course, always be open to a petitioner to assert in the Federal court after he had exhausted his State remedies or if he had no adequate State remedy.

"The third purpose is to substitute detailed and specific language for the phrase 'no adequate remedy available.' That phrase is not sufficiently specific and precise, and its meaning should, therefore, be spelled out in more detail in the section as is done by the amendment."

Cross References

Rules Governing Section 2254 Cases in the United States District Courts are set out ante.

§ 2255. Federal custody; remedies on motion attacking sentence

A prisoner in custody under sentence of a court established by Act of Congress claiming the right to be released upon the ground that the sentence was imposed in violation of the Constitution or laws of the United States, or that the court was without jurisdiction to impose such sentence, or that the sentence was in excess of the maximum authorized by law, or is otherwise subject to collateral attack, may move the court which imposed the sentence to vacate, set aside or correct the sentence.

A motion for such relief may be made at any time.

Unless the motion and the files and records of the case conclusively show that the prisoner is entitled to no relief, the court shall cause notice thereof to be served upon the United States attorney, grant a prompt hearing thereon, determine the issues and make findings of fact and conclusions of law with respect thereto. If the court finds that the judgment was rendered without jurisdiction, or that the sentence imposed was not authorized by law or otherwise open to collateral attack, or that there has been such a denial or infringement of the constitutional rights of the prisoner as to render the judgment vulnerable to collateral attack, the court shall vacate and set the judgment aside and shall discharge the prisoner or resentence him or grant a new trial or correct the sentence as may appear appropriate.

A court may entertain and determine such motion without requiring the production of the prisoner at the hearing.

The sentencing court shall not be required to entertain a second or successive motion for similar relief on behalf of the same prisoner.

An appeal may be taken to the court of appeals from the order entered on the motion as from a final judgment on application for a writ of habeas corpus.

An application for a writ of habeas corpus in behalf of a prisoner who is authorized to apply for relief by motion pursuant to this section, shall not be entertained if it appears that the applicant has failed to apply for relief, by motion, to the court which sentenced him, or that such court has denied him relief, unless it also appears that the remedy by motion is inadequate or ineffective to test the legality of his detention.

(As amended May 24, 1949, c. 139, § 114, 63 Stat. 105.)

1948 ACT
REVISION NOTES

This section restates, clarifies and simplifies the procedure in the nature of the ancient writ of error coram nobis. It provides an expeditious remedy for correcting erroneous sentences without resort to habeas corpus. It has the approval of the Judicial Conference of the United States. Its principal provisions are incorporated in H.R. 4233, Seventy-ninth Congress.

1949 ACT

This amendment conforms language of section 2255 of title 28, U.S.C., with that of section 1651 of such title and makes it clear that the section is applicable in the district courts in the Territories and possessions.

Cross References

Rules Governing Section 2255 Proceedings in the United States District Courts are set out ante.

[§ 2256. Omitted]

EDITORIAL NOTES

Codification. Section 250(a) of Pub.L. 95–598, Nov. 6, 1978, 92 Stat. 2672, added this section. Section 113 of Pub.L. 98–353, July 10, 1984, 98 Stat. 343, (effective June 27, 1984 pursuant to section 122(c) of Pub.L. 98–353) provided that this amendment "shall not be effective". Section 121 of Pub.L. 98–353 (effective on July 10, 1984 pursuant to section 122(a) of Pub.L. 98–353) provided that this amendment shall take effect on July 10, 1984. Section 2256 reads as follows:

"**§ 2256. Habeas corpus from bankruptcy courts**

"A bankruptcy court may issue a writ of habeas corpus—

"(1) when appropriate to bring a person before the court—

"(A) for examination;

"(B) to testify; or

"(C) to perform a duty imposed on such person under this title; or

"(2) ordering the release of a debtor in a case under title 11 in custody under the judgment of a Federal or State court if—

"(A) such debtor was arrested or imprisoned on process in any civil action;

"(B) such process was issued for the collection of a debt—

"(i) dischargeable under title 11; or

"(ii) that is or will be provided for in a plan under chapter 11 or 13 of title 11; and

"(C) before the issuance of such writ, notice and a hearing have been afforded the adverse party of such debtor in custody to contest the issuance of such writ."

Prior Provisions. A prior section 2256, added Pub. L. 95–144, § 3, Oct. 28, 1977, 91 Stat. 1220, which related to jurisdiction of proceedings relating to transferred offenders, was transferred to section 3244 of Title 18, Crimes and Criminal Procedure, by Pub.L. 95–598, Title III, § 314(j), Nov. 6, 1978, 92 Stat. 2677.

RULES GOVERNING SECTION 2254 CASES IN THE UNITED STATES DISTRICT COURTS

Effective February 1, 1977
As amended to May 1, 1988

APPENDIX OF FORMS

Model form for use in applications for habeas corpus under 28 U.S.C. § 2254.

Model form for use in 28 U.S.C. § 2254 cases involving a Rule 9 issue.

Cross Reference

For statutory provisions respecting habeas corpus, see Chapter 153 (section 2241 et seq.) of Title 28, Judiciary and Judicial Procedure, set out in this pamphlet, post.

ORDERS OF THE SUPREME COURT OF THE UNITED STATES ADOPTING AND AMENDING RULES GOVERNING CASES IN THE UNITED STATES DISTRICT COURTS UNDER SECTION 2254 OF TITLE 28, UNITED STATES CODE

ORDER OF APRIL 26, 1976

1. That the rules and forms governing proceedings in the United States District Courts under Section 2254 and Section 2255 of Title 28, United States Code, as approved by the Judicial Conference of the United States be, and they hereby are, prescribed pursuant to Section 2072 of Title 28, United States Code and Sections 3771 and 3772 of Title 18, United States Code.

2. That the aforementioned rules and forms shall take effect August 1, 1976, and shall be applicable to all proceedings then pending except to the extent that in the opinion of the court their application in a particular proceeding would not be feasible or would work injustice.

3. That THE CHIEF JUSTICE be, and he hereby is, authorized to transmit the aforementioned rules and forms governing Section 2254 and Section 2255 proceedings to the Congress in accordance with the provisions of Section 2072 of Title 28 and Sections 3771 and 3772 of Title 18, United States Code.

CONGRESSIONAL ACTION ON PROPOSED RULES AND FORMS GOVERNING PROCEEDING UNDER 28 U.S.C. §§ 2254 and 2255

Pub.L. 94–349, § 2, July 8, 1976, 90 Stat. 822, provided: "That, notwithstanding the provisions of section 2072 of title 28 of the United States Code, the rules and forms governing section 2254 cases in the United States district courts and the rules and forms governing section 2255 proceedings in the United States district courts which are embraced by the order entered by the United States Supreme Court on April 26, 1976, and which were transmitted to the Congress on or about April 26, 1976, shall not take effect until thirty days after the adjournment sine die of the 94th Congress, or until and to the extent approved by Act of Congress, whichever is earlier."

Pub.L. 94–426, § 1, Sept. 28, 1976, 90 Stat. 1334, provided: "That the rules governing section 2254 cases in the United States district courts and the rules governing section 2255 proceedings for the United States district courts, as proposed by the United States Supreme Court, which were delayed by the Act entitled 'An Act to delay the effective date of certain proposed amendments to the Federal Rules of Criminal Procedure and certain other rules promulgated by the United States Supreme Court' (Public Law 94–349), are approved with the amendments set forth in section 2 of this Act and shall take effect as so amended, with respect to petitions under section 2254 and motions under section 2255 of title 28 of the United States Code filed on or after February 1, 1977."

ORDER OF APRIL 30, 1979

1. That Rule 10 of the Rules Governing Proceedings in the United States District Courts on application under Section 2254 of Title 28, United States Code, be, and hereby is, amended to read as follows:

[See text of Rule 10 below]

2. That Rules 10 and 11 of the Rules Governing Proceedings in the United States District Courts on a motion under Section 2255 of Title 28, United States Code, be, and they hereby are, amended to read as follows:

Rule 10. Powers of magistrates

The duties imposed upon the judge of the district court by these rules may be performed by a United States magistrate pursuant to 28 U.S.C. § 636.

Rule 11. Time for appeal

The time for appeal from an order entered on a motion for relief made pursuant to these rules is as provided in Rule 4(a) of the Federal Rules of Appellate Procedure. Nothing in these rules shall be construed as extending the time to appeal from the original judgment of conviction in the district court.

ORDER OF APRIL 28, 1982

1. That the rules and forms governing proceedings in the United States district courts under Section 2254 and Section 2255 of Title 28, United States Code, be, and they hereby are, amended by including therein an amendment to Rule 2(c) of the rules for Section 2254 cases, an amendment to Rule 2(b) of the rules for Section 2255 proceedings, and amendments to the model forms for use in applications under Section 2254 and motions under Section 2255, as hereinafter set forth:

[See amendments made thereby under: Rule 2 and Forms for Habeas Corpus Applications and Rule 9 Issues, Post; and Rule 2 and Forms for Motions and Rule 9 Issue Motions of Rules Governing 28 U.S.C. § 2255 Proceedings, set out following Rule 35 of Federal Rules of Criminal Procedure, Ante.]

2. That the aforementioned amendments shall take effect August 1, 1982, and shall be applicable to all proceedings thereafter commenced and, insofar as just and practicable, all proceedings then pending.

3. That THE CHIEF JUSTICE be, and he hereby is, authorized to transmit the aforementioned amendments to the Congress in accordance with Section 2072 of Title 28 and Sections 3771 and 3772 of Title 18, United States Code.

Rule 1. Scope of Rules

(a) **Applicable to cases involving custody pursuant to a judgment of a state court.** These rules govern the procedure in the United States district courts on applications under 28 U.S.C. § 2254:

(1) by a person in custody pursuant to a judgment of a state court, for a determination that such custody is in violation of the Constitution, laws, or treaties of the United States; and

(2) by a person in custody pursuant to a judgment of either a state or a federal court, who makes application for a determination that custody to which he may be subject in the future under a judgment of a state court will be in violation of the Constitution, laws, or treaties of the United States.

(b) **Other situations.** In applications for habeas corpus in cases not covered by subdivision (a), these rules may be applied at the discretion of the United States district court.

ADVISORY COMMITTEE NOTE

Rule 1 provides that the habeas corpus rules are applicable to petitions by persons in custody pursuant to a judgment of a state court. See *Preiser v. Rodriguez,* 411 U.S. 475, 484 (1973). Whether the rules ought to apply to other situations (*e.g.,* person in active military service, *Glazier v. Hackel,* 440 F.2d 592 (9th Cir.1971); or a reservist called to active duty but not reported, *Hammond v. Lenfest,* 398 F.2d 705 (2d Cir.1968)) is left to the discretion of the court.

The basic scope of habeas corpus is prescribed by statute. 28 U.S.C. § 2241(c) provides that the "writ of habeas corpus shall not extend to a prisoner unless * * * (h)e is *in custody* in violation of the Constitution." 28 U.S.C. § 2254 deals specifically with state custody, providing that habeas corpus shall apply only "in behalf of a person in custody pursuant to a judgment of a state court * * *."

In *Preiser v. Rodriguez, supra,* the court said: "It is clear ... that the essence of habeas corpus is an attack by a person in custody upon the legality of that custody, and that the traditional function of the writ is to secure release from illegal custody." 411 U.S. at 484.

Initially the Supreme Court held that habeas corpus was appropriate only in those situations in which petitioner's claim would, if upheld, result in an immediate release from a present custody. *McNally v. Hill,* 293 U.S. 131 (1934). This was changed in *Peyton v. Rowe,* 391 U.S. 54 (1968), in which the court held that habeas corpus was a proper way to attack a consecutive sentence to be served in the future, expressing the view that consecutive sentences resulted in present custody under both judgments, not merely the one imposing the first sentence. This view was expanded in *Carafas v. LaVallee,* 391 U.S. 234 (1968), to recognize the propriety of habeas corpus in a case in which petitioner was in custody when the petition had been originally filed but had since been unconditionally released from custody.

See also *Preiser v. Rodriguez,* 411 U.S. at 486 et seq.

Since *Carafas,* custody has been construed more liberally by the courts so as to make a § 2255 motion or habeas corpus petition proper in more situations. "In custody" now includes a person who is: on parole, *Jones v. Cunningham,* 371 U.S. 236 (1963); at large on his own recognizance but subject to several conditions pending execution of his sentence, *Hensley v. Municipal Court,* 411 U.S. 345 (1973); or released on bail after conviction pending final disposition of his case, *Lefkowitz v. Newsome,* 95 S.Ct. 886 (1975). See also *United States v. Re,* 372 F.2d 641 (2d Cir.), cert. denied, 388 U.S. 912 (1967) (on probation); *Walker v. North Carolina,* 262 F.Supp. 102 (W.D.N.C.1966), aff'd per curiam, 372 F.2d 129 (4th Cir.), cert. denied, 388 U.S. 917 (1967) (recipient of a conditionally suspended sentence); *Burris v. Ryan,* 397 F.2d 553 (7th Cir.1968); *Marden v. Purdy,* 409 F.2d 784 (5th Cir.1969) (free on bail); *United States ex rel. Smith v. Dibella,* 314 F.Supp. 446 (D.Conn. 1970) (release on own recognizance); *Choung v. California,* 320 F.Supp. 625 (E.D.Cal.1970) (federal stay of state court sentence); *United States ex rel. Meadows v. New York,* 426 F.2d 1176 (2d Cir.1970), cert. denied, 401 U.S. 941 (1971) (subject to parole detainer warrant); *Capler v. City of Greenville,* 422 F.2d 299 (5th Cir.1970) (released on appeal bond); *Glover v. North Carolina,* 301 F.Supp. 364 (E.D.N.C.1969) (sentence served, but as convicted felon disqualified from engaging in several activities).

The courts are not unanimous in dealing with the above situations, and the boundaries of custody remain somewhat unclear. In *Morgan v. Thomas,* 321 F.Supp. 565 (S.D.Miss.1970), the court noted:

It is axiomatic that actual physical custody or restraint is not required to confer habeas jurisdiction. Rather, the term is synonymous with restraint of liberty. The real question is how much restraint of one's liberty is necessary before the right to apply for the writ comes into play. * * *

It is clear however, that something more than moral restraint is necessary to make a case for habeas corpus.

321 F.Supp. at 573

Hammond v. Lenfest, 398 F.2d 705 (2d Cir.1968), reviewed prior "custody" doctrine and reaffirmed a generalized flexible approach to the issue. In speaking about 28 U.S.C. § 2241, the first section in the habeas corpus statutes, the court said:

While the language of the Act indicates that a writ of habeas corpus is appropriate only when a petitioner is "in custody," * * * the Act "does not attempt to mark the boundaries of 'custody' nor in any way other than by use of that word attempt to limit the situations in which the writ can be used." * * * And,

recent Supreme Court decisions have made clear that "[i]t [habeas corpus] is not now and never has been a static, narrow, formalistic remedy; its scope has grown to achieve its grand purpose—the protection of individuals against erosion of their right to be free from wrongful restraints upon their liberty." * * * "[B]esides physical imprisonment, there are other restraints on a man's liberty, restraints not shared by the public generally, which have been thought sufficient in the English-speaking world to support the issuance of habeas corpus."

398 F.2d at 710–711

There is, as of now, no final list of the situations which are appropriate for habeas corpus relief. It is not the intent of these rules or notes to define or limit "custody."

It is, however, the view of the Advisory Committee that claims of improper conditions of custody or confinement (not related to the propriety of the custody itself), can better be handled by other means such as 42 U.S.C. § 1983 and other related statutes. In *Wilwording v. Swenson,* 404 U.S. 249 (1971), the court treated a habeas corpus petition by a state prisoner challenging the conditions of confinement as a claim for relief under 42 U.S.C. § 1983, the Civil Rights Act. Compare *Johnson v. Avery,* 393 U.S. 483 (1969).

The distinction between duration of confinement and conditions of confinement may be difficult to draw. Compare *Preiser v. Rodriguez,* 411 U.S. 475 (1973), with *Clutchette v. Procunier,* 497 F.2d 809 (9th Cir.1974), modified, 510 F.2d 613 (1975).

Rule 2.   Petition

(a) **Applicants in present custody.** If the applicant is presently in custody pursuant to the state judgment in question, the application shall be in the form of a petition for a writ of habeas corpus in which the state officer having custody of the applicant shall be named as respondent.

(b) **Applicants subject to future custody.** If the applicant is not presently in custody pursuant to the state judgment against which he seeks relief but may be subject to such custody in the future, the application shall be in the form of a petition for a writ of habeas corpus with an added prayer for appropriate relief against the judgment which he seeks to attack. In such a case the officer having present custody of the applicant and the attorney general of the state in which the judgment which he seeks to attack was entered shall each be named as respondents.

(c) **Form of petition.** The petition shall be in substantially the form annexed to these rules, except that any district court may by local rule require that petitions filed with it shall be in a form prescribed by the local rule. Blank petitions in the prescribed form shall be made available without charge by the clerk of the district court to applicants upon their request. It shall specify all the grounds for relief which are available to the petitioner and of which he has or by the exercise of reasonable diligence should have knowledge and shall set forth in summary form the facts supporting each of the grounds thus specified. It shall also state the relief requested. The petition shall be typewritten or legibly handwritten and shall be signed under penalty of perjury by the petitioner.

(d) Petition to be directed to judgments of one court only. A petition shall be limited to the assertion of a claim for relief against the judgment or judgments of a single state court (sitting in a county or other appropriate political subdivision). If a petitioner desires to attack the validity of the judgments of two or more state courts under which he is in custody or may be subject to future custody, as the case may be, he shall do so by separate petitions.

(e) Return of insufficient petition. If a petition received by the clerk of a district court does not substantially comply with the requirements of rule 2 or rule 3, it may be returned to the petitioner, if a judge of the court so directs, together with a statement of the reason for its return. The clerk shall retain a copy of the petition.

(As amended Pub.L. 94–426, § 2(1), (2), Sept. 28, 1976, 90 Stat. 1334; Apr. 28, 1982, eff. Aug. 1, 1982.)

ADVISORY COMMITTEE NOTE

Rule 2 describes the requirements of the actual petition, including matters relating to its form, contents, scope, and sufficiency. The rule provides more specific guidance for a petitioner and the court than 28 U.S.C. § 2242, after which it is patterned.

Subdivision (a) provides that an applicant challenging a state judgment, pursuant to which he is presently in custody, must make his application in the form of a petition for a writ of habeas corpus. It also requires that the state officer having custody of the applicant be named as respondent. This is consistent with 28 U.S.C. § 2242, which says in part, "[Application for a writ of habeas corpus] shall allege * * * the name of the person who has custody over [the applicant] * * *." The proper person to be served in the usual case is either

the warden of the institution in which the petitioner is incarcerated (*Sanders v. Bennett*, 148 F.2d 19 (D.C.Cir. 1945)) or the chief officer in charge of state penal institutions.

Subdivision (b) prescribes the procedure to be used for a petition challenging a judgment under which the petitioner will be subject to custody in the future. In this event the relief sought will usually not be released from present custody, but rather for a declaration that the judgment being attacked is invalid. Subdivision (b) thus provides for a prayer for "appropriate relief." It is also provided that the attorney general of the state of the judgment as well as the state officer having actual custody of the petitioner shall be named as respondents. This is appropriate because no one will have custody of the petitioner in the state of the judgment being attacked, and the habeas corpus action will usually be defended by the attorney general. The attorney general is in the best position to inform the court as to who the proper party respondent is. If it is not the attorney general, he can move for a substitution of party.

Since the concept of "custody" requisite to the consideration of a petition for habeas corpus has been enlarged significantly in recent years, it may be worthwhile to spell out the various situations which might arise and who should be named as respondent(s) for each situation.

(1) The applicant is in jail, prison, or other actual physical restraint due to the state action he is attacking. The named respondent shall be the state officer who has official custody of the petitioner (for example, the warden of the prison).

(2) The applicant is on probation or parole due to the state judgment he is attacking. The named respondents shall be the particular probation or parole officer responsible for supervising the applicant, and the official in charge of the parole or probation agency, or the state correctional agency, as appropriate.

(3) The applicant is in custody in any other manner differing from (1) and (2) above due to the effects of the state action he seeks relief from. The named respondent should be the attorney general of the state wherein such action was taken.

(4) The applicant is in jail, prison, or other actual physical restraint but is attacking a state action which will cause him to be kept in custody in the future rather than the government action under which he is presently confined. The named respondents shall be the state or federal officer who has official custody of him at the time the petition is filed and the attorney general of the state whose action subjects the petitioner to future custody.

(5) The applicant is in custody, although not physically restrained, and is attacking a state action which will result in his future custody rather than the government action out of which his present custody arises. The

named respondent(s) shall be the attorney general of the state whose action subjects the petitioner to future custody, as well as the government officer who has present official custody of the petitioner if there is such an officer and his identity is ascertainable.

In any of the above situations the judge may require or allow the petitioner to join an additional or different party as a respondent if to do so would serve the ends of justice.

As seen in rule 1 and paragraphs (4) and (5) above, these rules contemplate that a petitioner currently in federal custody will be permitted to apply for habeas relief from a state restraint which is to go into effect in the future. There has been disagreement in the courts as to whether they have jurisdiction of the habeas application under these circumstances (compare *Piper v. United States,* 306 F.Supp. 1259 (D.Conn.1969), with *United States ex rel. Meadows v. New York,* 426 F.2d 1176 (2d Cir.1970), cert. denied, 401 U.S. 941 (1971)). This rule seeks to make clear that they do have such jurisdiction.

Subdivision (c) provides that unless a district court requires otherwise by local rule, the petition must be in the form annexed to these rules. Having a standard prescribed form has several advantages. In the past, petitions have frequently contained mere conclusions of law, unsupported by any facts. Since it is the relationship of the facts to the claim asserted that is important, these petitions were obviously deficient. In addition, lengthy and often illegible petitions, arranged in no logical order, were submitted to judges who have had to spend hours deciphering them. For example, in *Passic v. Michigan,* 98 F.Supp. 1015, 1016 (E.D.Mich.1951), the court dismissed a petition for habeas corpus, describing it as "two thousand pages of irrational, prolix and redundant pleadings * * *."

Administrative convenience, of benefit to both the court and the petitioner, results from the use of a prescribed form. Judge Hubert L. Will briefly described the experience with the use of a standard form in the Northern District of Illinois:

> Our own experience, though somewhat limited, has been quite satisfactory. * * *

> In addition, [petitions] almost always contain the necessary basic information * * *. Very rarely do we get the kind of hybrid federal-state habeas corpus petition with civil rights allegations thrown in which were not uncommon in the past. * * * [W]hen a real constitutional issue is raised it is quickly apparent * * *.

> 33 F.R.D. 363, 384

Approximately 65 to 70% of all districts have adopted forms or local rules which require answers to essentially the same questions as contained in the standard form annexed to these rules. All courts using forms have indicated the petitions are time-saving and more legible.

The form is particularly helpful in getting information about whether there has been an exhaustion of state remedies or, at least, where that information can be obtained.

The requirement of a standard form benefits the petitioner as well. His assertions are more readily apparent, and a meritorious claim is more likely to be properly raised and supported. The inclusion in the form of the ten most frequently raised grounds in habeas corpus petitions is intended to encourage the applicant to raise all his asserted grounds in one petition. It may better enable him to recognize if an issue he seeks to raise is cognizable under habeas corpus and hopefully inform him of those issues as to which he must first exhaust his state remedies.

Some commentators have suggested that the use of forms is of little help because the questions usually are too general, amounting to little more than a restatement of the statute. They contend the blanks permit a prisoner to fill in the same ambiguous answers he would have offered without the aid of a form. See Comment, Developments in the Law—Federal Habeas Corpus, 83 Harv.L.Rev. 1038, 1177–1178 (1970). Certainly, as long as the statute requires factual pleading, the adequacy of a petition will continue to be affected largely by the petitioner's intelligence and the legal advice available to him. On balance, however, the use of forms has contributed enough to warrant mandating their use.

Giving the petitioner a list of often-raised grounds may, it is said, encourage perjury. See Comment, Developments in the Law—Federal Habeas Corpus, 83 Harv.L.Rev. 1038, 1178 (1970). Most inmates are aware of, or have access to, some common constitutional grounds for relief. Thus, the risk of perjury is not likely to be substantially increased and the benefit of the list for some inmates seems sufficient to outweigh any slight risk that perjury will increase. There is a penalty for perjury, and this would seem the most appropriate way to try to discourage it.

Legal assistance is increasingly available to inmates either through paraprofessional programs involving law students or special programs staffed by members of the bar. See Jacob and Sharma, Justice After Trial: Prisoners' Need for Legal Services in the Criminal–Correctional Process, 18 Kan.L.Rev. 493 (1970). In these situations, the prescribed form can be filled out more competently, and it does serve to ensure a degree of uniformity in the manner in which habeas corpus claims are presented.

Subdivision (c) directs the clerk of the district court to make available to applicants upon request, without charge, blank petitions in the prescribed form.

Subdivision (c) also requires that all available grounds for relief be presented in the petition, including those grounds of which, by the exercise of reasonable diligence, the petitioner should be aware. This is reinforced by rule 9(b), which allows dismissal of a second petition which fails to allege new grounds or, if new grounds are alleged, the judge finds an inexcusable failure to assert the ground in the prior petition.

Both subdivision (c) and the annexed form require a legibly handwritten or typewritten petition. As required by 28 U.S.C. § 2242, the petition must be signed and sworn to by the petitioner (or someone acting in his behalf).

Subdivision (d) provides that a single petition may assert a claim only against the judgment or judgments of a single state court (*i.e.,* a court of the same county or judicial district or circuit). This permits, but does not require, an attack in a single petition on judgments based upon separate indictments or on separate counts even though sentences were imposed on separate days by the same court. A claim against a judgment of a court of a different political subdivision must be raised by means of a separate petition.

Subdivision (e) allows the clerk to return an insufficient petition to the petitioner, and it must be returned if the clerk is so directed by a judge of the court. Any failure to comply with the requirements of rule 2 or 3 is grounds for insufficiency. In situations where there may be arguable noncompliance with another rule, such as rule 9, the judge, not the clerk, must make the decision. If the petition is returned it must be accompanied by a statement of the reason for its return. No petitioner should be left to speculate as to why or in what manner his petition failed to conform to these rules.

Subdivision (e) also provides that the clerk shall retain one copy of the insufficient petition. If the prisoner files another petition, the clerk will be in a better position to determine the sufficiency of the new petition. If the new petition is insufficient, comparison with the prior petition may indicate whether the prisoner has failed to understand the clerk's prior explanation for its insufficiency, so that the clerk can make another, hopefully successful, attempt at transmitting this information to the petitioner. If the petitioner insists that the original petition was in compliance with the rules, a copy of the original petition is available for the consideration of the judge. It is probably better practice to make a photocopy of a petition which can be corrected by the petitioner, thus saving the petitioner the task of completing an additional copy.

1982 AMENDMENT

Note to Subdivision (c). The amendment takes into account 28 U.S.C. § 1746, enacted after adoption of the § 2254 rules. Section 1746 provides that in lieu of an affidavit an unsworn statement may be given under penalty of perjury in substantially the following form if executed within the United States, its territories, possessions or commonwealths: "I declare (or certify, verify, or state) under penalty of perjury that the foregoing is true and correct. Executed on (date). (Signature)." The statute is "intended to encompass prisoner litigation," and the statutory alternative is especially appropriate in such cases because a notary might not be readily available. *Carter v. Clark,* 616 F.2d 228 (5th Cir.1980). The § 2254 forms have been revised accordingly.

EDITORIAL NOTES

1976 Amendment. Subd. (c). Pub.L. 94–426, § 2(1), inserted "substantially" following "The petition shall be in", and struck out requirement that the petition follow the prescribed form.

Subd. (e). Pub.L. 94–426, § 2(2), inserted "substantially" following "district court does not", and struck out provision which permitted the clerk to return a petition for noncompliance without a judge so directing.

Rule 3. Filing Petition

(a) Place of filing; copies; filing fee. A petition shall be filed in the office of the clerk of the district court. It shall be accompanied by two conformed copies thereof. It shall also be accompanied by the filing fee prescribed by law unless the petitioner applies for and is given leave to prosecute the petition in forma pauperis. If the petitioner desires to prosecute the petition in forma pauperis, he shall file the affidavit required by 28 U.S.C. § 1915. In all such cases the petition shall also be accompanied by a certificate of the warden or other appropriate officer of the institution in which the petitioner is confined as to the amount of money or securities on deposit to the petitioner's credit in any account in the institution, which certificate may be considered by the court in acting upon his application for leave to proceed in forma pauperis.

(b) Filing and service. Upon receipt of the petition and the filing fee, or an order granting leave to the petitioner to proceed in forma pauperis, and having ascertained that the petition appears on its face to comply with rules 2 and 3, the clerk of the district court shall file the petition and enter it on the docket in his office. The filing of the petition shall not require the respondent to answer the petition or otherwise move with respect to it unless so ordered by the court.

ADVISORY COMMITTEE NOTE

Rule 3 sets out the procedures to be followed by the petitioner and the court in filing the petition. Some of its provisions are currently dealt with by local rule or practice, while others are innovations. Subdivision (a) specifies the petitioner's responsibilities. It requires that the petition, which must be accompanied by two conformed copies thereof, be filed in the office of the clerk of the district court. The petition must be accompanied by the filing fee prescribed by law (presently $5; see 28 U.S.C. § 1914(a)), unless leave to prosecute the petition in forma pauperis is applied for and granted. In the event the petitioner desires to prosecute the petition in forma pauperis, he must file the affidavit required by 28 U.S.C. § 1915, together with a certificate showing the amount of funds in his institutional account.

Requiring that the petition be filed in the office of the clerk of the district court provides an efficient and uniform system of filing habeas corpus petitions.

Subdivision (b) requires the clerk to file the petition. If the filing fee accompanies the petition, it may be filed immediately, and, if not, it is contemplated that prompt attention will be given to the request to proceed in forma pauperis. The court may delegate the issuance of the order to the clerk in those cases in which it is clear from the petition that there is full compliance with the requirements to proceed in forma pauperis.

Requiring the copies of the petition to be filed with the clerk will have an impact not only upon administrative matters, but upon more basic problems as well. In districts with more than one judge, a petitioner under present circumstances may send a petition to more than one judge. If no central filing system exists for each district, two judges may independently take different action on the same petition. Even if the action taken is consistent, there may be needless duplication of effort.

The requirement of an additional two copies of the form of the petition is a current practice in many courts. An efficient filing system requires one copy for use by the court (central file), one for the respondent (under 3(b), the respondent receives a copy of the petition whether an answer is required or not), and one for petitioner's counsel, if appointed. Since rule 2 provides that blank copies of the petition in the prescribed form are to be furnished to the applicant free of charge, there should be no undue burden created by this requirement.

Attached to copies of the petition supplied in accordance with rule 2 is an affidavit form for the use of petitioners desiring to proceed in forma pauperis. The form requires information concerning the petitioner's financial resources.

In forma pauperis cases, the petition must also be accompanied by a certificate indicating the amount of funds in the petitioner's institution account. Usually the certificate will be from the warden. If the petitioner is on probation or parole, the court might want to require a certificate from the supervising officer. Petitions by persons on probation or parole are not numerous enough, however, to justify making special provision for this situation in the text of the rule.

The certificate will verify the amount of funds credited to the petitioner in an institution account. The district court may by local rule require that any amount credited to the petitioner, in excess of a stated maximum, must be used for the payment of the filing fee. Since prosecuting an action in forma pauperis is a privilege (see *Smart v. Heinze,* 347 F.2d 114, 116 (9th Cir.1965)), it is not to be granted when the petitioner has sufficient resources.

Subdivision (b) details the clerk's duties with regard to filing the petition. If the petition does not appear on its face to comply with the requirements of rules 2 and 3, it may be returned in accordance with rule 2(e). If it appears to comply, it must be filed and entered on the docket in the clerk's office. However, under this subdivision the respondent is not required to answer or otherwise move with respect to the petition unless so ordered by the court.

Rule 4. Preliminary Consideration by Judge

The original petition shall be presented promptly to a judge of the district court in accordance with the procedure of the court for the assignment of its business. The petition shall be examined promptly by the judge to whom it is assigned. If it plainly appears from the face of the petition and any exhibits annexed to it that the petitioner is not entitled to relief in the district court, the judge shall make an order for its summary dismissal and cause the petitioner to be notified. Otherwise the judge shall order the respondent to file an answer or other pleading within the period of time fixed by the court or to take such other action as the judge deems appropriate. In every case a copy of the petition and any order shall be served by certified mail on the respondent and the attorney general of the state involved.

ADVISORY COMMITTEE NOTE

Rule 4 outlines the options available to the court after the petition is properly filed. The petition must be promptly presented to and examined by the judge to whom it is assigned. If it plainly appears from the face of the petition and any exhibits attached thereto that the petitioner is not entitled to relief in the district court, the judge must enter an order summarily dismissing the petition and cause the petitioner to be notified. If summary dismissal is not ordered, the judge must order the respondent to file an answer or to otherwise plead to the petition within a time period to be fixed in the order.

28 U.S.C. § 2243 requires that the writ shall be awarded, or an order to show cause issued, "unless it appears from the application that the applicant or person detained is not entitled thereto." Such consideration may properly encompass any exhibits attached to the petition, including, but not limited to, transcripts, sentencing records, and copies of state court opinions. The judge may order any of these items for his consideration if they are not yet included with the petition. See 28 U.S.C. § 753(f) which authorizes payment for transcripts in habeas corpus cases.

It has been suggested that an answer should be required in every habeas proceeding, taking into account the usual petitioner's lack of legal expertise and the important functions served by the return. See Developments in the Law—Federal Habeas Corpus, 83 Harv.L. Rev. 1038, 1178 (1970). However, under § 2243 it is the duty of the court to screen out frivolous applications and eliminate the burden that would be placed on the respondent by ordering an unnecessary answer. *Allen v. Perini*, 424 F.2d 134, 141 (6th Cir.1970). In addition, "notice" pleading is not sufficient, for the petition is expected to state facts that point to a "real possibility of constitutional error." See *Aubut v. State of Maine*, 431 F.2d 688, 689 (1st Cir.1970).

In the event an answer is ordered under rule 4, the court is accorded greater flexibility than under § 2243 in determining within what time period an answer must be made. Under § 2243, the respondent must make a return within three days after being so ordered, with additional time of up to forty days allowed under the Federal Rules of Civil Procedure, Rule 81(a)(2), for good cause. In view of the widespread state of work overload in prosecutors' offices (see, *e.g., Allen*, 424 F.2d at 141), additional time is granted in some jurisdictions as a matter of course. Rule 4, which contains no fixed time requirement, gives the court the discretion to take into account various factors such as the respondent's workload and the availability of transcripts before determining a time within which an answer must be made.

Rule 4 authorizes the judge to "take such other action as the judge deems appropriate." This is designed to afford the judge flexibility in a case where either dismissal or an order to answer may be inappropriate. For example, the judge may want to authorize the respondent to make a motion to dismiss based upon information furnished by respondent, which may show that petitioner's claims have already been decided on the merits in a federal court; that petitioner has failed to exhaust state remedies; that the petitioner is not in custody within the meaning of 28 U.S.C. § 2254; or that a decision in the matter is pending in state court. In these situations, a dismissal may be called for on procedural grounds, which may avoid burdening the respondent with the necessity of filing an answer on the substantive merits of the petition. In other situations, the judge may want to consider a motion from respondent to make the petition more certain. Or the judge may want to dismiss some allegations in the petition, requiring the respondent to answer only those claims which appear to have some arguable merit.

Rule 4 requires that a copy of the petition and any order be served by certified mail on the respondent and the attorney general of the state involved. See 28 U.S.C. § 2252. Presently, the respondent often does not receive a copy of the petition unless the court directs an answer under 28 U.S.C. § 2243. Although the attorney general is served, he is not required to answer if it is more appropriate for some other agency to do so. Although the rule does not specifically so provide, it is assumed that copies of the court orders to respondent will be mailed to petitioner by the court.

Rule 5.   Answer; Contents

The answer shall respond to the allegations of the petition. In addition it shall state whether the petitioner has exhausted his state remedies including any post-conviction remedies available to him under the statutes or procedural rules of the state and including also his right of appeal both from the judgment of conviction and from any adverse judgment or order in the post-conviction proceeding. The answer shall indicate what transcripts (of pretrial, trial, sentencing, and post-conviction proceedings) are available, when they can be furnished, and also what proceedings have been recorded and not transcribed. There shall be attached to the answer such portions of the transcripts as the answering party deems relevant. The court on its own motion or upon request of the petitioner may order that further portions of the existing transcripts be furnished or that certain portions of the non-transcribed proceedings be transcribed and furnished. If a transcript is neither available nor procurable, a narrative summary of the evidence may be submitted. If the petitioner appealed from the judgment of conviction or from an adverse judgment or order in a post-conviction proceeding, a copy of the petitioner's brief on appeal and of the opinion of the appellate court, if any, shall also be filed by the respondent with the answer.

ADVISORY COMMITTEE NOTE

Rule 5 details the contents of the "answer". (This is a change in terminology from "return," which is still used below when referring to prior practice.) The answer plays an obviously important role in a habeas proceeding:

The return serves several important functions: it permits the court and the parties to uncover quickly the disputed issues; it may reveal to the petitioner's attorney grounds for release that the petitioner did not know; and it may demonstrate that the petitioner's claim is wholly without merit.

Developments in the Law—Federal Habeas Corpus, 83 Harv.L.Rev. 1083, 1178 (1970).

The answer must respond to the allegations of the petition. While some districts require this by local rule (see, *e.g.,* E.D.N.C.R. 17(B)), under 28 U.S.C. § 2243 little specificity is demanded. As a result, courts occasionally receive answers which contain only a statement certifying the true cause of detention, or a series of delaying motions such as motions to dismiss. The requirement of the proposed rule that the "answer shall respond to the allegations of the petition" is intended to ensure that a responsive pleading will be filed and thus the functions of the answer fully served.

The answer must also state whether the petitioner has exhausted his state remedies. This is a prerequisite to eligibility for the writ under 28 U.S.C. § 2254(b) and applies to every ground the petitioner raises. Most form petitions now in use contain questions requiring information relevant to whether the petitioner has exhausted his remedies. However, the exhaustion requirement is often not understood by the unrepresented petitioner. The attorney general has both the legal expertise and access to the record and thus is in a much better position to inform the court on the matter of exhaustion of state remedies. An alleged failure to exhaust state remedies as to any ground in the petition may be raised by a motion by the attorney general, thus avoiding the necessity of a formal answer as to that ground.

The rule requires the answer to indicate what transcripts are available, when they can be furnished, and also what proceedings have been recorded and not transcribed. This will serve to inform the court and petitioner as to what factual allegations can be checked against the actual transcripts. The transcripts include pretrial transcripts relating, for example, to pretrial motions to suppress; transcripts of the trial or guilty plea proceeding; and transcripts of any post-conviction proceedings which may have taken place. The respondent is required to furnish those portions of the transcripts which he believes relevant. The court may order the furnishing of additional portions of the transcripts upon the request of petitioner or upon the court's own motion.

Where transcripts are unavailable, the rule provides that a narrative summary of the evidence may be submitted.

Rule 5 (and the general procedure set up by this entire set of rules) does not contemplate a traverse to the answer, except under special circumstances. See advisory committee note to rule 9. Therefore, the old common law assumption of verity of the allegations of a return until impeached, as codified in 28 U.S.C. § 2248, is no longer applicable. The meaning of the section, with its exception to the assumption "to the extent that the judge finds from the evidence that they (the allegations) are not true," has given attorneys and courts a great deal of difficulty. It seems that when the petition and return pose an issue of fact, no traverse is required; *Stewart v. Overholser,* 186 F.2d 339 (D.C.Cir.1950).

We read § 2248 of the Judicial Code as not requiring a traverse when a factual issue has been clearly framed by the petition and the return or answer. This section provides that the allegations of a return or answer to an order to show cause shall be accepted as true if not traversed, except to the extent the judge finds from the evidence that they are not true. This contemplates that where the petition and return or answer do present an issue of fact material to the legality of detention, evidence is required to resolve that issue despite the absence of a traverse. This reference to evidence assumes a hearing on issues raised by the allegations of the petition and the return or answer to the order to show cause.

186 F.2d at 342, n. 5

In actual practice, the traverse tends to be a mere pro forma refutation of the return, serving little if any expository function. In the interests of a more streamlined and manageable habeas corpus procedure, it is not required except in those instances where it will serve a truly useful purpose. Also, under rule 11 the court is given the discretion to incorporate Federal Rules of Civil Procedure when appropriate, so civil rule 15(a) may be used to allow the petitioner to amend his petition when the court feels this is called for by the contents of the answer.

Rule 5 does not indicate who the answer is to be served upon, but it necessarily implies that it will be mailed to the petitioner (or to his attorney if he has one). The number of copies of the answer required is left to the court's discretion. Although the rule requires only a copy of petitioner's brief on appeal, respondent is free also to file a copy of respondent's brief. In practice, courts have found it helpful to have a copy of respondent's brief.

Rule 6.   Discovery

(a) Leave of court required. A party shall be entitled to invoke the processes of discovery available under the Federal Rules of Civil Procedure if, and to the extent that, the judge in the exercise of his discretion and for good cause shown grants leave to do so, but not otherwise. If necessary for effective utilization of discovery procedures, counsel shall be appointed by the judge for a petitioner who qualifies for the appointment of counsel under 18 U.S.C. § 3006A(g).

(b) Requests for discovery. Requests for discovery shall be accompanied by a statement of the interrogatories or requests for admission and a list of the documents, if any, sought to be produced.

(c) Expenses. If the respondent is granted leave to take the deposition of the petitioner or any other person the judge may as a condition of taking it direct that the respondent pay the expenses of travel and subsistence and fees of counsel for the petitioner to attend the taking of the deposition.

ADVISORY COMMITTEE NOTE

This rule prescribes the procedures governing discovery in habeas corpus cases. Subdivision (a) provides that any party may utilize the processes of discovery available under the Federal Rules of Civil Procedure (rules 26–37) if, and to the extent that, the judge allows. It also provides for the appointment of counsel for a petitioner who qualifies for this when counsel is necessary for effective utilization of discovery procedures permitted by the judge.

Subdivision (a) is consistent with *Harris v. Nelson*, 394 U.S. 286 (1969). In that case the court noted,

[I]t is clear that there was no intention to extend to habeas corpus, as a matter of right, the broad discovery provisions * * * of the new [Federal Rules of Civil Procedure].

394 U.S. at 295

However, citing the lack of methods for securing information in habeas proceedings, the court pointed to an alternative.

Clearly, in these circumstances * * * the courts may fashion appropriate modes of procedure, by analogy to existing rules or otherwise in conformity with judicial usage. * * * Their authority is expressly confirmed in the All Writs Act, 28 U.S.C. § 1651.

394 U.S. at 299

The court concluded that the issue of discovery in habeas corpus cases could best be dealt with as part of an effort to provide general rules of practice for habeas corpus cases:

In fact, it is our view that the rulemaking machinery should be invoked to formulate rules of practice with respect to federal habeas corpus and § 2255 proceedings, on a comprehensive basis and not merely one confined to discovery. The problems presented by these proceedings are materially different from those dealt with in the Federal Rules of Civil Procedure and the Federal Rules of Criminal Procedure, and reliance upon usage and the opaque language of

Civil Rule 81(a)(2) is transparently inadequate. In our view the results of a meticulous formulation and adoption of special rules for federal habeas corpus and § 2255 proceedings would promise much benefit.

394 U.S. at 301 n. 7

Discovery may, in appropriate cases, aid in developing facts necessary to decide whether to order an evidentiary hearing or to grant the writ following an evidentiary hearing:

We are aware that confinement sometimes induces fantasy which has its basis in the paranoia of prison rather than in fact. But where specific allegations before the court show reason to believe that the petitioner may, if the facts are fully developed, be able to demonstrate that he is confined illegally and is therefore entitled to relief, it is the duty of the court to provide the necessary facilities and procedures for an adequate inquiry. Obviously, in exercising this power, the court may utilize familiar procedures, as appropriate, whether these are found in the civil or criminal rules or elsewhere in the "usages and principles."

Granting discovery is left to the discretion of the court, discretion to be exercised where there is a showing of good cause why discovery should be allowed. Several commentators have suggested that at least some discovery should be permitted without leave of court. It is argued that the courts will be burdened with weighing the propriety of requests to which the discovered party has no objection. Additionally, the availability of protective orders under Fed.R.Civ.R., Rules 30(b) and 31(d) will provide the necessary safeguards. See Developments in the Law—Federal Habeas Corpus, 83 Harv.L.Rev. 1038, 1186–87 (1970); Civil Discovery in Habeas Corpus, 67 Colum.L.Rev. 1296, 1310 (1967).

Nonetheless, it is felt the requirement of prior court approval of all discovery is necessary to prevent abuse, so this requirement is specifically mandated in the rule.

While requests for discovery in habeas proceedings normally follow the granting of an evidentiary hearing, there may be instances in which discovery would be appropriate beforehand. Such an approach was advocated in *Wagner v. United States*, 418 F.2d 618, 621 (9th Cir.1969), where the opinion stated the trial court could permit interrogatories, provide for deposing witnesses, "and take such other prehearing steps as may be appropriate." While this was an action under § 2255, the reasoning would apply equally well to petitions by state prisoners. Such pre-hearing discovery may show an evidentiary hearing to be unnecessary, as when there are "no disputed issues of law or fact." 83 Harv.L.Rev. 1038, 1181 (1970). The court in Harris alluded to such a possibility when it said "the court may * * * authorize such proceedings with respect to development, *before or in conjunction with the hearing* of the facts

* * *." [emphasis added] 394 U.S. at 300. Such pre-hearing discovery, like all discovery under rule 6, requires leave of court. In addition, the provisions in rule 7 for the use of an expanded record may eliminate much of the need for this type of discovery. While probably not as frequently sought or granted as discovery in conjunction with a hearing, it may nonetheless serve a valuable function.

In order to make pre-hearing discovery meaningful, subdivision (a) provides that the judge should appoint counsel for a petitioner who is without counsel and qualifies for appointment when this is necessary for the proper utilization of discovery procedures. Rule 8 provides for the appointment of counsel at the evidentiary hearing stage (see rule 8(b) and advisory committee note), but this would not assist the petitioner who seeks to utilize discovery to stave off dismissal of his petition (see rule 9 and advisory committee note) or to demonstrate that an evidentiary hearing is necessary. Thus, if the judge grants a petitioner's request for discovery prior to making a decision as to the necessity for an evidentiary hearing, he should determine whether counsel is necessary for the effective utilization of such discovery and, if so, appoint counsel for the petitioner if the petitioner qualifies for such appointment.

This rule contains very little specificity as to what types and methods of discovery should be made available to the parties in a habeas proceeding, or how, once made available, these discovery procedures should be administered. The purpose of this rule is to get some experience in how discovery would work in actual practice by letting district court judges fashion their own rules in the context of individual cases. When the results of such experience are available it would be desirable to consider whether further, more specific codification should take place.

Subdivision (b) provides for judicial consideration of all matters subject to discovery. A statement of the interrogatories, or requests for admission sought to be answered, and a list of any documents sought to be produced, must accompany a request for discovery. This is to advise the judge of the necessity for discovery and enable him to make certain that the inquiry is relevant and appropriately narrow.

Subdivision (c) refers to the situation where the respondent is granted leave to take the deposition of the petitioner or any other person. In such a case the judge may direct the respondent to pay the expenses and fees of counsel for the petitioner to attend the taking of the deposition, as a condition granting the respondent such leave. While the judge is not required to impose this condition subdivision (c) will give the court the means to do so. Such a provision affords some protection to the indigent petitioner who may be prejudiced by his inability to have counsel, often court-appointed, present at the taking of a deposition. It is recognized that under 18 U.S.C. § 3006A(g), court-appointed counsel in a

§ 2254 proceeding is entitled to receive up to $250 and reimbursement for expenses reasonably incurred. (Compare Fed.R.Crim.P. 15(c).) Typically, however, this does not adequately reimburse counsel if he must attend the taking of depositions or be involved in other pre-hearing proceedings. Subdivision (c) is intended to provide additional funds, if necessary, to be paid by the state government (respondent) to petitioner's counsel.

Although the rule does not specifically so provide, it is assumed that a petitioner who qualifies for the appointment of counsel under 18 U.S.C. § 3006A(g) and is granted leave to take a deposition will be allowed witness costs. This will include recording and transcription of the witness's statement. Such costs are payable pursuant to 28 U.S.C. § 1825. See Opinion of Comptroller General, February 28, 1974.

Subdivision (c) specifically recognizes the right of the respondent to take the deposition of the petitioner. Although the petitioner could not be called to testify against his will in a criminal trial, it is felt the nature of the habeas proceeding, along with the safeguards accorded by the Fifth Amendment and the presence of counsel, justify this provision. See 83 Harv.L.Rev. 1038, 1183–84 (1970).

Rule 7.   Expansion of Record

(a) **Direction for expansion.** If the petition is not dismissed summarily the judge may direct that the record be expanded by the parties by the inclusion of additional materials relevant to the determination of the merits of the petition.

(b) **Materials to be added.** The expanded record may include, without limitation, letters predating the filing of the petition in the district court, documents, exhibits, and answers under oath, if so directed, to written interrogatories propounded by the judge. Affidavits may be submitted and considered as a part of the record.

(c) **Submission to opposing party.** In any case in which an expanded record is directed, copies of the letters, documents, exhibits, and affidavits proposed to be included shall be submitted to the party against whom they are to be offered, and he shall be afforded an opportunity to admit or deny their correctness.

(d) **Authentication.** The court may require the authentication of any material under subdivision (b) or (c).

ADVISORY COMMITTEE NOTE

This rule provides that the judge may direct that the record be expanded. The purpose is to enable the judge to dispose of some habeas petitions not dismissed on the pleadings, without the time and expense required for an evidentiary hearing. An expanded record may also be helpful when an evidentiary hearing is ordered.

The record may be expanded to include additional material relevant to the merits of the petition. While most petitions are dismissed either summarily or after a response has been made, of those that remain, by far the majority require an evidentiary hearing. In the fiscal year ending June 30, 1970, for example, of 8,423 § 2254 cases terminated, 8,231 required court action. Of these, 7,812 were dismissed before a prehearing conference and 469 merited further court action (*e.g.*, expansion of the record, prehearing conference, or an evidentiary hearing). Of the remaining 469 cases, 403 required an evidentiary hearing, often time-consuming, costly, and, at least occasionally, unnecessary. See Director of the Administrative Office of the United States Courts, Annual Report, 245a–245c (table C4) (1970). In some instances these hearings were necessitated by slight omissions in the state record which might have been cured by the use of an expanded record.

Authorizing expansion of the record will, hopefully, eliminate some unnecessary hearings. The value of this approach was articulated in *Raines v. United States,* 423 F.2d 526, 529–530 (4th Cir.1970):

> Unless it is clear from the pleadings and the files and records that the prisoner is entitled to no relief, the statute makes a hearing mandatory. We think there is a permissible intermediate step that may avoid the necessity for an expensive and time consuming evidentiary hearing in every Section 2255 case. It may instead be perfectly appropriate, depending upon the nature of the allegations, for the district court to proceed by requiring that the record be expanded to include letters, documentary evidence, and, in an appropriate case, even affidavits. *United States v. Carlino,* 400 F.2d 56 (2nd Cir.1968); *Mirra v. United States,* 379 F.2d 782 (2nd Cir.1967); *Accardi v. United States,* 379 F.2d 312 (2nd Cir.1967). When the issue is one of credibility, resolution on the basis of affidavits can rarely be conclusive, but that is not to say they may not be helpful.

In *Harris v. Nelson,* 394 U.S. 286, 300 (1969), the court said:

> At any time in the proceedings * * * *either on [the court's] own motion* or upon cause shown by the petitioner, it may issue such writs and take or authorize such proceedings * * * *before* or in conjunction with the hearing of the facts * * * [emphasis added]

Subdivision (b) specifies the materials which may be added to the record. These include, without limitation, letters predating the filing of the petition in the district court, documents, exhibits, and answers under oath directed to written interrogatories propounded by the judge. Under this subdivision affidavits may be submitted and considered part of the record. Subdivision (b) is consistent with 28 U.S.C. §§ 2246 and 2247 and

the decision in *Raines* with regard to types of material that may be considered upon application for a writ of habeas corpus. See *United States v. Carlino,* 400 F.2d 56, 58 (2d Cir.1968), and *Machibroda v. United States,* 368 U.S. 487 (1962).

Under subdivision (c) all materials proposed to be included in the record must be submitted to the party against whom they are to be offered.

Under subdivision (d) the judge can require authentication if he believes it desirable to do so.

Rule 8.　Evidentiary Hearing

(a) Determination by court. If the petition is not dismissed at a previous stage in the proceeding, the judge, after the answer and the transcript and record of state court proceedings are filed, shall, upon a review of those proceedings and of the expanded record, if any, determine whether an evidentiary hearing is required. If it appears that an evidentiary hearing is not required, the judge shall make such disposition of the petition as justice shall require.

(b) Function of the magistrate.

(1) When designated to do so in accordance with 28 U.S.C. § 636(b), a magistrate may conduct hearings, including evidentiary hearings, on the petition, and submit to a judge of the court proposed findings of fact and recommendations for disposition.

(2) The magistrate shall file proposed findings and recommendations with the court and a copy shall forthwith be mailed to all parties.

(3) Within ten days after being served with a copy, any party may serve and file written objections to such proposed findings and recommendations as provided by rules of court.

(4) A judge of the court shall make a de novo determination of those portions of the report or specified proposed findings or recommendations to which objection is made. A judge of the court may accept, reject, or modify in whole or in part any findings or recommendations made by the magistrate.

(c) Appointment of counsel; time for hearing. If an evidentiary hearing is required the judge shall appoint counsel for a petitioner who qualifies for the appointment of counsel under 18 U.S.C. § 3006A(g) and the hearing shall be conducted as promptly as practicable, having regard for the need of counsel for both parties for adequate time for investigation and preparation. These rules do not limit the appointment of counsel under 18 U.S.C. § 3006A at any stage of the case if the interest of justice so requires.

(As amended Pub.L. 94–426, § 2(5), Sept. 28, 1976, 90 Stat. 1334; Pub.L. 94–577, § 2(a)(1), (b)(1), Oct. 21, 1976, 90 Stat. 2730, 2731.)

ADVISORY COMMITTEE NOTE

This rule outlines the procedure to be followed by the court immediately prior to and after the determination of whether to hold an evidentiary hearing.

The provisions are applicable if the petition has not been dismissed at a previous stage in the proceeding [including a summary dismissal under rule 4; a dismissal pursuant to a motion by the respondent; a dismissal after the answer and petition are considered; or a dismissal after consideration of the pleadings and an expanded record].

If dismissal has not been ordered, the court must determine whether an evidentiary hearing is required. This determination is to be made upon a review of the answer, the transcript and record of state court proceedings, and if there is one, the expanded record. As the United States Supreme Court noted in *Townsend v. Sam*, 372 U.S. 293, 319 (1963):

Ordinarily [the complete state-court] record—including the transcript of testimony (or if unavailable some adequate substitute, such as a narrative record), the pleadings, court opinions, and other pertinent documents—is indispensable to determining whether the habeas applicant received a full and fair state-court evidentiary hearing resulting in reliable findings.

Subdivision (a) contemplates that all of these materials, if available, will be taken into account. This is especially important in view of the standard set down in *Townsend* for determining *when* a hearing in the federal habeas proceeding is mandatory.

The appropriate standard * * * is this: Where the facts are in dispute, the federal court in habeas corpus must hold an evidentiary hearing if the habeas applicant did not receive a full and fair evidentiary hearing in a state court, either at the time of the trial or in a collateral proceeding.

372 U.S. at 312

The circumstances under which a federal hearing is mandatory are now specified in 28 U.S.C. § 2254(d). The 1966 amendment clearly places the burden on the petitioner, when there has already been a state hearing, to show that it was not a fair or adequate hearing for one or more of the specifically enumerated reasons, in order to force a federal evidentiary hearing. Since the function of an evidentiary hearing is to try issues of fact (372 U.S. at 309), such a hearing is unnecessary when only issues of law are raised. See, *e.g.*, *Yeaman v. United States*, 326 F.2d 293 (9th Cir.1963).

In situations in which an evidentiary hearing is not mandatory, the judge may nonetheless decide that an evidentiary hearing is desirable:

The purpose of the test is to indicate the situations in which the holding of an evidentiary hearing is mandatory. In all other cases where the material facts are in dispute, the holding of such a hearing is in the discretion of the district judge.

372 U.S. at 318

If the judge decides that an evidentiary hearing is neither required nor desirable, he shall make such a disposition of the petition "as justice shall require." Most habeas petitions are dismissed before the pre-hearing conference stage (see Director of the Administrative Office of the United States Courts, Annual Report 245a–245c (table C4) (1970)) and of those not dismissed, the majority raise factual issues that necessitate an evidentiary hearing. If no hearing is required, most petitions are dismissed, but in unusual cases the court may grant the relief sought without a hearing. This includes immediate release from custody or nullification of a judgment under which the sentence is to be served in the future.

Subdivision (b) provides that a magistrate, when so empowered by rule of the district court, may recommend to the district judge that an evidentiary hearing be held or that the petition be dismissed, provided he gives the district judge a sufficiently detailed description of the facts so that the judge may decide whether or not to hold an evidentiary hearing. This provision is not inconsistent with the holding in *Wingo v. Wedding*, 418 U.S. 461 (1974), that the Federal Magistrates Act did not change the requirement of the habeas corpus statute that federal judges personally conduct habeas evidentiary hearings, and that consequently a local district court rule was invalid insofar as it authorized a magistrate to hold such hearings. 28 U.S.C. § 636(b) provides that a district court may by rule authorize any magistrate to perform certain additional duties, including preliminary review of applications for posttrial relief made by individuals convicted of criminal offenses, and submission of a report and recommendations to facilitate the decision of the district judge having jurisdiction over the case as to whether there should be a hearing.

As noted in *Wingo*, review "by Magistrates of applications for post-trial relief is thus limited to review for the purpose of proposing, not holding, evidentiary hearings."

Utilization of the magistrate as specified in subdivision (b) will aid in the expeditious and fair handling of habeas petitions.

A qualified, experienced magistrate will, it is hoped, acquire an expertise in examining these [post-conviction review] applications and summarizing their important contents for the district judge, thereby facilitating his decisions. Law clerks are presently charged with this responsibility by many judges, but judges have noted that the normal 1–year clerkship does not afford law clerks the time or experience necessary to attain real efficiency in handling such applications.

S.Rep. No. 371, 90th Cong., 1st Sess., 26 (1967)

Under subdivision (c) there are two provisions that differ from the procedure set forth in 28 U.S.C. § 2243. These are the appointment of counsel and standard for determining how soon the hearing will be held.

If an evidentiary hearing is required the judge must appoint counsel for a petitioner who qualified for appointment under the Criminal Justice Act. Currently, the appointment of counsel is not recognized as a right at any stage of a habeas proceeding. See, e.g., United States ex rel. Marshall v. Wilkins, 338 F.2d 404 (2d Cir.1964). Some district courts have, however, by local rule, required that counsel must be provided for indigent petitioners in cases requiring a hearing. See, e.g., D.N.M.R. 21(f), E.D.N.Y.R. 26(d). Appointment of counsel at this stage is mandatory under subdivision (c). This requirement will not limit the authority of the court to provide counsel at an earlier stage if it is thought desirable to do so as is done in some courts under current practice. At the evidentiary hearing stage, however, an indigent petitioner's access to counsel should not depend on local practice and, for this reason, the furnishing of counsel is made mandatory.

Counsel can perform a valuable function benefiting both the court and the petitioner. The issues raised can be more clearly identified if both sides have the benefit of trained legal personnel. The presence of counsel at the prehearing conference may help to expedite the evidentiary hearing or make it unnecessary, and counsel will be able to make better use of available prehearing discovery procedures. Compare ABA Project on Standards for Criminal Justice, Standards Relating to Post–Conviction Remedies § 4.4, p. 66 (Approved Draft 1968). At a hearing, the petitioner's claims are more likely to be effectively and properly presented by counsel.

Under 18 U.S.C. § 3006A(g), payment is allowed counsel up to $250, plus reimbursement for expenses reasonably incurred. The standards of indigency under this section are less strict than those regarding eligibility to prosecute a petition in forma pauperis, and thus many who cannot qualify to proceed under 28 U.S.C. § 1915 will be entitled to the benefits of counsel under 18 U.S.C. § 3006A(g). Under rule 6(c), the court may order the respondent to reimburse counsel from state funds for fees and expenses incurred as the result of the utilization of discovery procedures by the respondent.

Subdivision (c) provides that the hearing shall be conducted as promptly as possible, taking into account

"the need of counsel for both parties for adequate time for investigation and preparation." This differs from the language of 28 U.S.C. § 2243, which requires that the day for the hearing be set "not more than five days after the return unless for good cause additional time is allowed." This time limit fails to take into account the function that may be served by a prehearing conference and the time required to prepare adequately for an evidentiary hearing. Although "additional time" is often allowed under § 2243, subdivision (c) provides more flexibility to take account of the complexity of the case, the availability of important materials, the workload of the attorney general, and the time required by appointed counsel to prepare.

While the rule does not make specific provision for a prehearing conference, the omission is not intended to cast doubt upon the value of such a conference:

> The conference may limit the questions to be resolved, identify areas of agreement and dispute, and explore evidentiary problems that may be expected to arise. * * * [S]uch conferences may also disclose that a hearing is unnecessary * * *.

ABA Project on Standards for Criminal Justice, Standards Relating to Post–Conviction Remedies § 4.6, commentary pp. 74–75. (Approved Draft, 1968.)

See also Developments in the Law—Federal Habeas Corpus, 83 Harv.L.Rev. 1038, 1188 (1970).

The rule does not contain a specific provision on the subpoenaing of witnesses. It is left to local practice to determine the method for doing this. The implementation of 28 U.S.C. § 1825 on the payment of witness fees is dealt with in an opinion of the Comptroller General, February 28, 1974.

EDITORIAL NOTES

1976 Amendment. Subsec. (b). Pub.L. 94–577, § 2(a)(1), substituted provisions which authorized magistrates, when designated to do so in accordance with section 636(b) of this title, to conduct hearings, including evidentiary hearings, on the petition and to submit to a judge of the court proposed findings of fact and recommendations for disposition, which directed the magistrate to file proposed findings and recommendations with the court with copies furnished to all parties, which allowed parties thus served 10 days to file written objections thereto, and which directed a judge of the court to make de novo determinations of the objected-to portions and to accept, reject, or modify the findings or recommendations for provisions under which the magistrate had been empowered only to recommend to the district judge that an evidentiary hearing be held or that the petition be dismissed.

Subsec. (c). Pub.L. 94–577, § 2(b)(1), substituted "and the hearing shall be conducted" for "and shall conduct the hearing".

Pub.L. 94–426 provided that these rules not limit the appointment of counsel under section 3006A of title 18, if the interest of justice so require.

Rule 9. Delayed or Successive Petitions

(a) Delayed petitions. A petition may be dismissed if it appears that the state of which the respondent is an officer has been prejudiced in its ability to respond to the petition by delay in its filing unless the petitioner shows that it is based on grounds of which he could not have had knowledge by the exercise of reasonable diligence before the circumstances prejudicial to the state occurred.

(b) Successive petitions. A second or successive petition may be dismissed if the judge finds that it fails to allege new or different grounds for relief and the prior determination was on the merits or, if new and different grounds are alleged, the judge finds that the failure of the petitioner to assert those grounds in a prior petition constituted an abuse of the writ.

(As amended Pub.L. 94–426, § 2(7), (8), Sept. 28, 1976, 90 Stat. 1335.)

ADVISORY COMMITTEE NOTE

This rule is intended to minimize abuse of the writ of habeas corpus by limiting the right to assert stale claims and to file multiple petitions. Subdivision (a) deals with the delayed petition. Subdivision (b) deals with the second or successive petition.

Subdivision (a) provides that a petition attacking the judgment of a state court may be dismissed on the grounds of delay if the petitioner knew or should have known of the existence of the grounds he is presently asserting in the petition and the delay has resulted in the state being prejudiced in its ability to respond to the petition. If the delay is more than five years after the judgment of conviction, prejudice is presumed, although this presumption is rebuttable by the petitioner. Otherwise, the state has the burden of showing such prejudice.

The assertion of stale claims is a problem which is not likely to decrease in frequency. Following the decisions in *Jones v. Cunningham,* 371 U.S. 236 (1963), and *Benson v. California,* 328 F.2d 159 (9th Cir.1964), the concept of custody expanded greatly, lengthening the time period during which a habeas corpus petition may be filed. The petitioner who is not unconditionally discharged may be on parole or probation for many years. He may at some date, perhaps ten or fifteen years after conviction, decide to challenge the state court judgment. The grounds most often troublesome to the courts are ineffective counsel, denial of right of appeal, plea of guilty unlawfully induced, use of a coerced confession, and illegally constituted jury. The latter four grounds are often interlocked with the allegation of ineffective counsel. When they are asserted after the passage of many years, both the attorney for the defendant and the state have difficulty in ascertaining what the facts are. It often develops that the defense attorney has little or no recollection as to what took place and that many of the participants in the trial are dead or their whereabouts unknown. The court reporter's notes may have been lost or destroyed, thus eliminating any exact record of what transpired. If the case was decided on a guilty plea, even if the record is intact, it may not satisfactorily reveal the extent of the defense attorney's efforts in behalf of the petitioner. As a consequence, there is obvious difficulty in investigating petitioner's allegations.

The interest of both the petitioner and the government can best be served if claims are raised while the evidence is still fresh. The American Bar Association has recognized the interest of the state in protecting itself against stale claims by limiting the right to raise such claims after completion of service of a sentence imposed pursuant to a challenged judgment. See ABA Standards Relating to Post–Conviction Remedies § 2.4(c), p. 45 (Approved Draft, 1968). Subdivision (a) is not limited to those who have completed their sentence. Its reach is broader, extending to all instances where delay by the petitioner has prejudiced the state, subject to the qualifications and conditions contained in the subdivision.

In *McMann v. Richardson,* 397 U.S. 759 (1970), the court made reference to the issue of the stale claim:

> What is at stake in this phase of the case is not the integrity of the state convictions obtained on guilty pleas, *but whether, years later,* defendants must be permitted to withdraw their pleas, which were perfectly valid when made, and be given another choice between admitting their guilt and putting the State to its proof. [Emphasis added.]

397 U.S. at 773

The court refused to allow this, intimating its dislike of collateral attacks on sentences long since imposed which disrupt the state's interest in finality of convictions which were constitutionally valid when obtained.

Subdivision (a) is not a statute of limitations. Rather, the limitation is based on the equitable doctrine of laches. "Laches is such delay in enforcing one's rights as works disadvantage to another." 30A C.J.S. Equity § 112, p. 19. Also, the language of the subdivision, "a petition *may* be dismissed" [emphasis added], is permissive rather than mandatory. This clearly allows the court which is considering the petition to use discretion in assessing the equities of the particular situation.

The use of a flexible rule analogous to laches to bar the assertion of stale claims is suggested in ABA Standards Relating to Post–Conviction Remedies § 2.4, commentary at 48 (Approved Draft, 1968). Additionally, in *Fay v. Noia*, 372 U.S. 391 (1963), the Supreme Court noted:

> Furthermore, habeas corpus has traditionally been regarded as governed by equitable principles. *United States ex rel. Smith v. Baldi*, 344 U.S. 561, 573 (dissenting opinion). Among them is the principle that a suitor's conduct in relation to the matter at hand may disentitle him to the relief he seeks.

> 372 U.S. at 438

Finally, the doctrine of laches has been applied with reference to another postconviction remedy, the writ of coram nobis. See 24 C.J.S. Criminal Law § 1606(25), p. 779.

The standard used for determining if the petitioner shall be barred from asserting his claim is consistent with that used in laches provisions generally. The petitioner is held to a standard of reasonable diligence. Any inference or presumption arising by reason of the failure to attack collaterally a conviction may be disregarded where (1) there has been a change of law or fact (new evidence) or (2) where the court, in the interest of justice, feels that the collateral attack should be entertained and the prisoner makes a proper showing as to why he has not asserted a particular ground for relief.

Subdivision (a) establishes the presumption that the passage of more than five years from the time of the judgment of conviction to the time of filing a habeas petition is prejudicial to the state. "Presumption" has the meaning given it by Fed.R.Evid. 301. The prisoner has "the burden of going forward with evidence to rebut or meet the presumption" that the state has not been prejudiced by the passage of a substantial period of time. This does not impose too heavy a burden on the petitioner. He usually knows what persons are important to the issue of whether the state has been prejudiced. Rule 6 can be used by the court to allow petitioner liberal discovery to learn whether witnesses have died or whether other circumstances prejudicial to the state have occurred. Even if the petitioner should fail to overcome the presumption of prejudice to the state, he is not automatically barred from asserting his claim. As discussed previously, he may proceed if he neither knew nor, by the exercise of reasonable diligence, could have known of the grounds for relief.

The presumption of prejudice does not come into play if the time lag is not more than five years.

The time limitation should have a positive effect in encouraging petitioners who have knowledge of it to assert all their claims as soon after conviction as possible. The implementation of this rule can be substantially furthered by the development of greater legal

resources for prisoners. See ABA Standards Relating to Post–Conviction Remedies § 3.1, pp. 49–50 (Approved Draft, 1968).

Subdivision (a) does not constitute an abridgement or modification of a substantive right under 28 U.S.C. § 2072. There are safeguards for the hardship case. The rule provides a flexible standard for determining when a petition will be barred.

Subdivision (b) deals with the problem of successive habeas petitions. It provides that the judge may dismiss a second or successive petition (1) if it fails to allege new or different grounds for relief or (2) if new or different grounds for relief are alleged and the judge finds the failure of the petitioner to assert those grounds in a prior petition is inexcusable.

In *Sanders v. United States*, 373 U.S. 1 (1963), the court, in dealing with the problem of successive applications, stated:

> Controlling weight *may* be given to denial of a prior application for federal habeas corpus or § 2255 relief only if (1) the same ground presented in the subsequent application was determined adversely to the applicant on the prior application, (2) the prior determination was on the merits, and (3) the ends of justice would not be served by reaching the merits of the subsequent application. [Emphasis added.]

> 373 U.S. at 15

The requirement is that the prior determination of the same ground has been on the merits. This requirement is in 28 U.S.C. § 2244(b) and has been reiterated in many cases since *Sanders*. See *Gains v. Allgood*, 391 F.2d 692 (5th Cir.1968); *Hutchinson v. Craven*, 415 F.2d 278 (9th Cir.1969); *Brown v. Peyton*, 435 F.2d 1352 (4th Cir.1970).

With reference to a successive application asserting a new ground or one not previously decided on the merits, the court in *Sanders* noted:

> In either case, full consideration of the merits of the new application can be avoided only if there has been an abuse of the writ * * * and this the Government has the burden of pleading. * * *

> Thus, for example, if a prisoner deliberately withholds one of two grounds for federal collateral relief at the time of filing his first application, * * * he may be deemed to have waived his right to a hearing on a second application presenting the withheld ground.

> 373 U.S. at 17–18

Subdivision (b) has incorporated this principle and requires that the judge find petitioner's failure to have asserted the new grounds in the prior petition to be inexcusable.

Sanders, 18 U.S.C. § 2244, and subdivision (b) make it clear that the court has discretion to entertain a successive application.

The burden is on the government to plead abuse of the writ. See *Sanders v. United States,* 373 U.S. 1, 10 (1963); *Dixon v. Jacobs,* 427 F.2d 589, 596 (D.C.Cir. 1970); cf. *Johnson v. Copinger,* 420 F.2d 395 (4th Cir. 1969). Once the government has done this, the petitioner has the burden of proving that he has not abused the writ. In *Price v. Johnston,* 334 U.S. 266, 292 (1948), the court said:

[I]f the Government chooses * * * to claim that the prisoner has abused the writ of *habeas corpus,* it rests with the Government to make that claim with clarity and particularity in its return to the order to show cause. That is not an intolerable burden. The Government is usually well acquainted with the facts that are necessary to make such a claim. Once a particular abuse has been alleged, the prisoner has the burden of answering that allegation and of proving that he has not abused the writ.

Subdivision (b) is consistent with the important and well established purpose of habeas corpus. It does not eliminate a remedy to which the petitioner is rightfully entitled. However, in *Sanders,* the court pointed out:

Nothing in the traditions of habeas corpus requires the federal courts to tolerate needless piecemeal litigation, or to entertain collateral proceedings whose only purpose is to vex, harass, or delay.

373 U.S. at 18

There are instances in which petitioner's failure to assert a ground in a prior petition is excusable. A retroactive change in the law and newly discovered evidence are examples. In rare instances, the court may feel a need to entertain a petition alleging grounds that have already been decided on the merits. *Sanders,* 373 U.S. at 1, 16. However, abusive use of the writ should be discouraged, and instances of abuse are frequent enough to require a means of dealing with them. For example, a successive application, already decided on the merits, may be submitted in the hope of getting before a different judge in multijudge courts. A known ground may be deliberately withheld in the hope of getting two or more hearings or in the hope that delay will result in witnesses and records being lost. There are instances in which a petitioner will have three or four petitions pending at the same time in the same court. There are many hundreds of cases where the application is at least the second one by the petitioner. This subdivision is aimed at screening out the abusive petitions from this large volume, so that the more meritorious petitions can get quicker and fuller consideration.

The form petition, supplied in accordance with rule 2(c), encourages the petitioner to raise all of his available grounds in one petition. It sets out the most common grounds asserted so that these may be brought to his attention.

Some commentators contend that the problem of abuse of the writ of habeas corpus is greatly overstated:

Most prisoners, of course, are interested in being released as soon as possible; only rarely will one inexcusably neglect to raise all available issues in his first federal application. The purpose of the "abuse" bar is apparently to deter repetitious applications from those few bored or vindictive prisoners * * *.

83 Harv.L.Rev. at 1153–1154

See also ABA Standards Relating to Post–Conviction Remedies § 6.2, commentary at 92 (Approved Draft, 1968), which states: "The occasional, highly litigious prisoner stands out as the rarest exception." While no recent systematic study of repetitious applications exists, there is no reason to believe that the problem has decreased in significance in relation to the total number of § 2254 petitions filed. That number has increased from 584 in 1949 to 12,088 in 1971. See Director of the Administrative Office of the United States Courts, Annual Report, table 16 (1971). It is appropriate that action be taken by rule to allow the courts to deal with this problem, whatever its specific magnitude. The bar set up by subdivision (b) is not one of rigid application, but rather is within the discretion of the courts on a case-by-case basis.

If it appears to the court after examining the petition and answer (where appropriate) that there is a high probability that the petition will be barred under either subdivision of rule 9, the court ought to afford petitioner an opportunity to explain his apparent abuse. One way of doing this is by the use of the form annexed hereto. The use of a form will ensure a full airing of the issue so that the court is in a better position to decide whether the petition should be barred. This conforms with *Johnson v. Copinger,* 420 F.2d 395 (4th Cir.1969), where the court stated:

[T]he petitioner is obligated to present facts demonstrating that his earlier failure to raise his claims is excusable and does not amount to an abuse of the writ. However, it is inherent in this obligation placed upon the petitioner that he must be given an opportunity to make his explanation, if he has one. If he is not afforded such an opportunity, the requirement that he satisfy the court that he has not abused the writ is meaningless. Nor do we think that a procedure which allows the imposition of a forfeiture for abuse of the writ, without allowing the petitioner an opportunity to be heard on the issue, comports with the minimum requirements of fairness.

420 F.2d at 399

Use of the recommended form will contribute to an orderly handling of habeas petitions and will contribute to the ability of the court to distinguish the excusable from the inexcusable delay or failure to assert a ground for relief in a prior petition.

1976 Amendment. Subsec. (a). Pub.L. 94–426, § 2(7), struck out provision which established a rebuttable presumption of prejudice to the state if the petition was filed more than five years after conviction and started the running of the five year period, where a petition challenged the validity of an action after conviction, from the time of the order of such action.

Subsec. (b). Pub.L. 94–426, § 2(8), substituted "constituted an abuse of the writ" for "is not excusable".

Rule 10. Powers of Magistrates

The duties imposed upon the judge of the district court by these rules may be performed by a United States magistrate pursuant to 28 U.S.C. § 636.

(As amended Pub.L. 94–426, § 2(11), Sept. 28, 1976, 90 Stat. 1335; Apr. 30, 1979, eff. Aug. 1, 1979.)

ADVISORY COMMITTEE NOTE

Under this rule the duties imposed upon the judge of the district court by rules 2, 3, 4, 6, and 7 may be performed by a magistrate if and to the extent he is empowered to do so by a rule of the district court. However, when such duties involve the making of an order under rule 4 disposing of the petition, that order must be made by the court. The magistrate in such instances must submit to the court his report as to the facts and his recommendation with respect to the order.

The Federal Magistrates Act allows magistrates, when empowered by local rule, to perform certain functions in proceedings for post-trial relief. See 28 U.S.C. § 636(b)(3). The performance of such functions, when authorized, is intended to "afford some degree of relief to district judges and their law clerks, who are presently burdened with burgeoning numbers of habeas corpus petitions and applications under 28 U.S.C. § 2255." Committee on the Judiciary, The Federal Magistrates Act, S.Rep. No. 371, 90th Cong., 1st sess., 26 (1967).

Under 28 U.S.C. § 636(b), any district court, by the concurrence of a majority of all the judges of such district court, may establish rules pursuant to which any full-time United States magistrate * * * may be assigned within the territorial jurisdiction of such court such additional duties as are not inconsistent with the Constitution and laws of the United States.

The proposed rule recognizes the limitations imposed by 28 U.S.C. § 636(b) upon the powers of magistrates to act in federal postconviction proceedings. These limitations are: (1) that the magistrate may act only pursuant to a rule passed by the majority of the judges in the

district court in which the magistrate serves, and (2) that the duties performed by the magistrate pursuant to such rule be consistent with the Constitution and laws of the United States.

It has been suggested that magistrates be empowered by law to hold hearings and make final decisions in habeas proceedings. See Proposed Reformation of Federal Habeas Corpus Procedure: Use of Federal Magistrates, 54 Iowa L.Rev. 1147, 1158 (1969). However, the Federal Magistrates Act does not authorize such use of magistrates. *Wingo v. Wedding,* 418 U.S. 461 (1974). See advisory committee note to rule 8. While the use of magistrates can help alleviate the strain imposed on the district courts by the large number of unmeritorious habeas petitions, neither 28 U.S.C. § 636(b) nor this rule contemplate the abdication by the court of its decision-making responsibility. See also Developments in the Law—Federal Habeas Corpus, 83 Harv.L.Rev. 1038, 1188 (1970).

Where a full-time magistrate is not available, the duties contemplated by this rule may be assigned to a part-time magistrate.

1979 AMENDMENT

This amendment conforms the rule to subsequently enacted legislation clarifying and further defining the duties which may be assigned to a magistrate, 18 U.S.C. § 636, as amended in 1976 by Pub.L. 94–577. To the extent that rule 10 is more restrictive than § 636, the limitations are of no effect, for the statute expressly governs "[n]otwithstanding any provision of law to the contrary."

The reference to particular rules is stricken, as under § 636(b)(1)(A) a judge may designate a magistrate to perform duties under other rules as well (e.g., order that further transcripts be furnished under rule 5; appoint counsel under rule 8). The reference to "established standards and criteria" is stricken, as § 636(4) requires each district court to "establish rules pursuant to which the magistrates shall discharge their duties." The exception with respect to a rule 4 order dismissing a petition is stricken, as that limitation appears in § 636(b)(1)(B) and is thereby applicable to certain other actions under these rules as well (e.g., determination of a need for an evidentiary hearing under rule 8; dismissal of a delayed or successive petition under rule 9).

1976 Amendment. Pub.L. 94–426 inserted "and to the extent the district court has established standards and criteria for the performance of such duties" following "rule of the district court".

Rule 11. Federal Rules of Civil Procedure; Extent of Applicability

The Federal Rules of Civil Procedure, to the extent that they are not inconsistent with these rules, may be applied, when appropriate, to petitions filed under these rules.

ADVISORY COMMITTEE NOTE

Habeas corpus proceedings are characterized as civil in nature. See *e.g., Fisher v. Baker,* 203 U.S. 174, 181 (1906). However, under Fed.R.Civ.P. 81(a)(2), the applicability of the civil rules to habeas corpus actions has been limited, although the various courts which have considered this problem have had difficulty in setting out the boundaries of this limitation. See *Harris v. Nelson,* 394 U.S. 286 (1969) at 289, footnote 1. Rule 11 is intended to conform with the Supreme Court's approach in the *Harris* case. There the court was dealing with the petitioner's contention that Civil Rule 33 granting the right to discovery via written interrogatories is wholly applicable to habeas corpus proceedings. The court held:

> We agree with the Ninth Circuit that Rule 33 of the Federal Rules of Civil Procedure is not applicable to habeas corpus proceedings and that 28 U.S.C. § 2246 does not authorize interrogatories except in limited circumstances not applicable to this case; but we conclude that, in appropriate circumstances, a district court, confronted by a petition for habeas corpus which establishes a prima facie case for relief, may use or authorize the use of suitable discovery procedures, including interrogatories, reasonably fashioned to elicit facts necessary to help the court to "dispose of the matter as law and justice require" 28 U.S.C. § 2243.

394 U.S. at 290

The court then went on to consider the contention that the "conformity" provision of Rule 81(a)(2) should be rigidly applied so that the civil rules would be applicable only to the extent that habeas corpus practice had conformed to the practice in civil actions at the time of the adoption of the Federal Rules of Civil Procedure on September 16, 1938. The court said:

> Although there is little direct evidence, relevant to the present problem, of the purpose of the "conformity" provision of Rule 81(a)(2), the concern of the draftsmen, as a general matter, seems to have been to

provide for the continuing applicability of the "civil" rules in their new form to those areas of practice in habeas corpus and other enumerated proceedings in which the "specified" proceedings had theretofore utilized the modes of civil practice. Otherwise, those proceedings were to be considered outside of the scope of the rules without prejudice, of course, to the use of particular rules by analogy or otherwise, where appropriate.

394 U.S. at 294

The court then reiterated its commitment to judicial discretion in formulating rules and procedures for habeas corpus proceedings by stating:

> [T]he habeas corpus jurisdiction and the duty to exercise it being present, the courts may fashion appropriate modes of procedure, by analogy to existing rules or otherwise in conformity with judicial usage.

Where their duties require it, this is the inescapable obligation of the courts. Their authority is expressly confirmed in the All Writs Act, 28 U.S.C. § 1651.

394 U.S. at 299

Rule 6 of these proposed rules deals specifically with the issue of discovery in habeas actions in a manner consistent with *Harris.* Rule 11 extends this approach to allow the court considering the petition to use any of the rules of civil procedure (unless inconsistent with these rules of habeas corpus) when in its discretion the court decides they are appropriate under the circumstances of the particular case. The court does not have to rigidly apply rules which would be inconsistent or inequitable in the overall framework of habeas corpus. Rule 11 merely recognizes and affirms their discretionary power to use their judgment in promoting the ends of justice.

Rule 11 permits application of the civil rules only when it would be appropriate to do so. Illustrative of an inappropriate application is that rejected by the Supreme Court in *Pitchess v. Davis,* 95 S.Ct. 1748 (1975), holding that Fed.R.Civ.P. 60(b) should not be applied in a habeas case when it would have the effect of altering the statutory exhaustion requirement of 28 U.S.C. § 2254.

APPENDIX OF FORMS

MODEL FORM FOR USE IN APPLICATIONS FOR HABEAS CORPUS UNDER 28 U.S.C. § 2254

Name _____

Prison number _____

Place of confinement _____

United States District Court __ District of _____

Case No. _____

(To be supplied by Clerk of U.S. District Court)

_____, PETITIONER

(Full name)

v.

_____, RESPONDENT

(Name of Warden, Superintendent, Jailor, or authorized person having custody of petitioner)

and

THE ATTORNEY GENERAL OF THE STATE OF

_____

ADDITIONAL RESPONDENT.

(If petitioner is attacking a judgment which imposed a sentence to be served in the *future*, petitioner must fill in the name of the state where the judgment was entered. If petitioner has a sentence to be served in the *future* under a federal judgment which he wishes to attack, he should file a motion under 28 U.S.C. § 2255, in the federal court which entered the judgment.)

PETITION FOR WRIT OF HABEAS CORPUS BY A PERSON IN STATE CUSTODY

Instructions—Read Carefully

(1) This petition must be legibly handwritten or typewritten, and signed by the petitioner under penalty of perjury. Any false statement of a material fact may serve as the basis for prosecution and conviction for perjury. All questions must be answered concisely in the proper space on the form.

(2) Additional pages are not permitted except with respect to the *facts* which you rely upon to support your grounds for relief. No citation of authorities need be furnished. If briefs or arguments are submitted, they should be submitted in the form of a separate memorandum.

(3) Upon receipt of a fee of $5 your petition will be filed if it is in proper order.

(4) If you do not have the necessary filing fee, you may request permission to proceed *in forma pauperis*, in which event you must execute the declaration on the last page, setting forth information establishing your inability to prepay the fees and costs or give security therefor. If you wish to proceed *in forma pauperis*, you must have an authorized officer at the penal institution complete the certificate as to the amount of money and securities on deposit to your credit in any account in the institution. If your prison account exceeds $_____, you must pay the filing fee as required by the rule of the district court.

(5) Only judgments entered by one court may be challenged in a single petition. If you seek to challenge judgments entered by different courts either in the same state or in different

states, you must file separate petitions as to each court.

(6) Your attention is directed to the fact that you must include all grounds for relief and all facts supporting such grounds for relief in the petition you file seeking relief from any judgment of conviction.

(7) When the petition is fully completed, *the original and two copies* must be mailed to the Clerk of the United States District Court whose address is

_____

(8) Petitions which do not conform to these instructions will be returned with a notation as to the deficiency.

PETITION

1. Name and location of court which entered the judgment of conviction under attack _____

_____

2. Date of judgment of conviction _____

3. Length of sentence _____

4. Nature of offense involved (all counts) _____

_____

_____

_____

5. What was your plea? (Check one)

(a) Not guilty ☐

(b) Guilty ☐

(c) Nolo contendere ☐

If you entered a guilty plea to one count or indictment, and a not guilty plea to another count or indictment, give details:

_____

_____

_____

6. Kind of trial: (Check one)

(a) Jury ☐

(b) Judge only ☐

7. Did you testify at the trial?
Yes ☐ No ☐

8. Did you appeal from the judgment?
Yes ☐ No ☐

9. If you did appeal, answer the following:

(a) Name of court _____

(b) Result _____

(c) Date of result _____

10. Other than a direct appeal from the judgment of conviction and sentence, have you previously filed any petitions, applications, or motions with respect to this judgment in any court, state or federal?

Yes ☐ No ☐

11. If your answer to 10 was "yes," give the following information:

(a)(1) Name of court _____

(2) Nature of proceeding _____
_____

(3) Grounds raised _____
_____
_____
_____
_____
_____

(4) Did you receive an evidentiary hearing on your petition, application or motion?

Yes ☐ No ☐

(5) Result _____

(6) Date of result _____

(b) As to any second petition, application or motion give the same information:

(1) Name of court _____

(2) Nature of proceeding _____
_____

(3) Grounds raised _____
_____
_____
_____
_____
_____

(4) Did you receive an evidentiary hearing on your petition, application or motion?

Yes ☐ No ☐

(5) Result _____

(6) Date of result _____

(c) As to any third petition, application or motion, give the same information:

(1) Name of court _____

(2) Nature of proceeding _____
_____

(3) Grounds raised _____
_____
_____
_____
_____

(4) Did you receive an evidentiary hearing on your petition, application, or motion?

Yes ☐ No ☐

(5) Result _____

(6) Date of result _____

(d) Did you appeal to the highest state court having jurisdiction the result of action taken on any petition, application or motion?

(1) First petition, etc. Yes ☐ No ☐

(2) Second petition, etc. Yes ☐ No ☐

(3) Third petition, etc. Yes ☐ No ☐

(e) If you did *not* appeal from the adverse action on any petition, application or motion, explain briefly why you did not:

_____
_____
_____

12. State *concisely* every ground on which you claim that you are being held unlawfully. Summarize *briefly* the *facts* supporting each ground. If necessary, you may attach pages stating additional grounds and *facts* supporting same.

Caution: In order to proceed in the federal court, you must ordinarily first exhaust your state court remedies as to each ground on which you request action by the federal court. If you fail to set forth all grounds in this petition, you may be barred from presenting additional grounds at a later date.

For your information, the following is a list of the most frequently raised grounds for relief in habeas corpus proceedings. Each statement preceded by a letter constitutes a separate ground for possible relief. You may raise any grounds which you may have other than those listed if you have exhausted your state court remedies with respect to them. However, *you should raise in this petition all available grounds* (relating to this conviction) on which you base your allegations that you are being held in custody unlawfully.

Do not check any of these listed grounds. If you select one or more of these grounds for relief, you must allege facts. The petition will be returned to you if you merely check (a) through (j) or any one of these grounds.

(a) Conviction obtained by plea of guilty which was unlawfully induced or not made voluntarily with understanding of the nature of the charge and the consequences of the plea.

(b) Conviction obtained by use of coerced confession.

(c) Conviction obtained by use of evidence gained pursuant to an unconstitutional search and seizure.

(d) Conviction obtained by use of evidence obtained pursuant to an unlawful arrest.

(e) Conviction obtained by a violation of the privilege against self-incrimination.

(f) Conviction obtained by the unconstitutional failure of the prosecution to disclose to the defendant evidence favorable to the defendant.

(g) Conviction obtained by a violation of the protection against double jeopardy.

(h) Conviction obtained by action of a grand or petit jury which was unconstitutionally selected and impaneled.

(i) Denial of effective assistance of counsel.

(j) Denial of right of appeal.

    A. Ground one: _____
_____

        Supporting FACTS (tell your story *briefly* without citing cases or law): __
_____
_____
_____
_____
_____
_____

    B. Ground two: _____
_____

        Supporting FACTS (tell your story *briefly* without citing cases or law): __
_____
_____
_____
_____
_____
_____

    C. Ground three: _____
_____

        Supporting FACTS (tell your story *briefly* without citing cases or law): __
_____
_____

_____
_____
_____
_____

    D. Ground four: _____
_____

        Supporting FACTS (tell your story *briefly* without citing cases or law): __
_____
_____
_____
_____
_____
_____

13. If any of the grounds listed in 12A, B, C, and D were not previously presented in any other court, state or federal, state *briefly* what grounds were not so presented, and give your reasons for not presenting them:

_____
_____
_____

14. Do you have any petition or appeal now pending in any court, either state or federal, as to the judgment under attack?

Yes ☐ No ☐

15. Give the name and address, if known, of each attorney who represented you in the following stages of the judgment attacked herein:

    (a) At preliminary hearing _____

    (b) At arraignment and plea _____

    (c) At trial _____
_____

    (d) At sentencing _____

    (e) On appeal _____

    (f) In any post-conviction proceeding _____
_____

    (g) On appeal from any adverse ruling in a post-conviction proceeding _____
_____

16. Were you sentenced on more than one count of an indictment, or on more than one indictment, in the same court and at the same time?

Yes ☐ No ☐

17. Do you have any future sentence to serve after you complete the sentence imposed by the judgment under attack?

Yes ☐ No ☐

(a) If so, give name and location of court which imposed sentence to be served in the future: _____

_____

(b) And give date and length of sentence to be served in the future: _____

_____

(c) Have you filed, or do you contemplate filing, any petition attacking the judgment which imposed the sentence to be served in the future?

Yes ☐ No ☐

Wherefore, petitioner prays that the Court grant petitioner relief to which he may be entitled in this proceeding.

_____
Signature of Attorney (if any)

I declare (or certify, verify, or state) under penalty of perjury that the foregoing is true and correct. Executed on _____

(date)

_____
Signature of Petitioner

IN FORMA PAUPERIS DECLARATION

[Insert appropriate court]

_____   DECLARATION IN
(Petitioner)   SUPPORT
v.   OF REQUEST
                            TO PROCEED
_____   IN FORMA
(Respondent(s))   PAUPERIS

I, _____, declare that I am the petitioner in the above entitled case; that in support of my motion to proceed without being required to prepay fees, costs or give security therefor, I state that because of my poverty I am unable to pay the costs of said proceeding or to give security therefor; that I believe I am entitled to relief.

1. Are you presently employed? Yes ☐ No ☐

a. If the answer is "yes," state the amount of your salary or wages per month, and give the name and address of your employer.

_____

_____

b. If the answer if "no," state the date of last employment and the amount of the salary and wages per month which you received.

_____

_____

2. Have you received within the past twelve months any money from any of the following sources?

a. Business, profession or form of self-employment?

Yes ☐ No ☐

b. Rent payments, interest or dividends?

Yes ☐ No ☐

c. Pensions, annuities or life insurance payments?

Yes ☐ No ☐

d. Gifts or inheritances?

Yes ☐ No ☐

e. Any other sources?

Yes ☐ No ☐

If the answer to any of the above is "yes," describe each source of money and state the amount received from each during the past twelve months.

_____

_____

_____

_____

3. Do you own cash, or do you have money in a checking or savings account?

Yes ☐ No ☐ (Include any funds in prison accounts.)

If the answer is "yes," state the total value of the items owned.

_____

_____

4. Do you own any real estate, stocks, bonds, notes, automobiles, or other valuable property

(excluding ordinary household furnishings and clothing)?

Yes ☐ No ☐

If the answer is "yes," describe the property and state its approximate value.

_____

_____

_____

5. List the persons who are dependent upon you for support, state your relationship to those persons, and indicate how much you contribute toward their support.

_____

_____

I declare (or certify, verify, or state) under penalty of perjury that the foregoing is true and correct. Executed on _____.

(date)

_____

Signature of Petitioner

Certificate

I hereby certify that the petitioner herein has the sum of $_____ on account to his credit at the _____ institution where he is confined. I further certify that petitioner likewise has the following securities to his credit according to the records of said _____ institution:

_____

_____

_____

_____

_____

AUTHORIZED OFFI-
CER OF INSTITUTION

(As amended Apr. 28, 1982, eff. Aug. 1, 1982.)

MODEL FORM FOR USE IN 28 U.S.C. § 2254
CASES INVOLVING A RULE 9 ISSUE

Form No. 9

United States District Court,

_____ District of _____

Case No. _____

_____, PETITIONER

v.

_____, RESPONDENT

and

_____, ADDITIONAL RESPONDENT

Petitioner's Response as to Why His Petition Should Not Be Barred Under Rule 9

Explanation and Instructions—Read Carefully

(I) Rule 9. Delayed or successive petitions

(a) Delayed petitions. A petition may be dismissed if it appears that the state of which the respondent is an officer has been prejudiced in its ability to respond to the petition by delay in its filing unless the petitioner shows that it is based on grounds of which he could not have had knowledge by the exercise of reasonable diligence before the circumstances prejudicial to the state occurred.

(b) Successive petitions. A second or successive petition may be dismissed if the judge finds that it fails to allege new or different grounds for relief and the prior determination was on the merits or, if new and different grounds are alleged, the judge finds that the failure of the petitioner to assert those grounds in a prior petition constituted an abuse of the writ.

(II) Your petition for habeas corpus has been found to be subject to dismissal under rule 9( ) for the following reason(s):

_____

_____

_____

_____

(III) This form has been sent so that you may explain why your petition contains the defect(s) noted in (II) above. It is required that you fill out this form and send it back to the court within _____ days. Failure to do so will result in the automatic dismissal of your petition.

(IV) When you have fully completed this form, the original and two copies must be mailed to the Clerk of the United States District Court whose address is

_____

(V) This response must be legibly handwritten or typewritten, and signed by the petitioner, under penalty of perjury. Any false statement of a material fact may serve as the basis for prosecution and conviction for perjury. All questions must be answered concisely in the proper space on the form.

(VI) Additional pages are not permitted except with respect to the *facts* which you rely upon in item 4 or 5 in the response. Any citation of authorities should be kept to an absolute minimum and is only appropriate if there has been a change in the law since the judgment you are attacking was rendered.

(VII) Respond to 4 *or* 5 below, not to both, unless (II) above indicates that you must answer both sections.

RESPONSE

1. Have you had the assistance of an attorney, other law-trained personnel, or writ writers since the conviction your petition is attacking was entered?

Yes ☐   No ☐

2. If you checked "yes," above, specify as precisely as you can the period(s) of time during which you received such assistance, up to and including the present.

———————————————————

3. Describe the nature of the assistance, including the names of those who rendered it to you.

———————————————————
———————————————————
———————————————————
———————————————————

4. If your petition is in jeopardy because of delay prejudicial to the state under rule 9(a), explain why you feel the delay has not been prejudicial and/or why the delay is excusable under the terms of 9(a). This should be done by relying upon FACTS, not your opinions or conclusions.

———————————————————
———————————————————
———————————————————
———————————————————

5. If your petition is in jeopardy under rule 9(b) because it asserts the same grounds as a previous petition, explain why you feel it deserves a reconsideration. If its fault under rule 9(b) is that it asserts new grounds which should have been included in a prior petition, explain why you are raising these grounds now rather than previously. Your explanation should rely on FACTS, not your opinions or conclusions.

———————————————————
———————————————————
———————————————————
———————————————————
———————————————————
———————————————————
———————————————————

I declare (or certify, verify, or state) under penalty of perjury that the foregoing is true and correct. Executed on —————.

(date)

———————————————————
Signature of Petitioner

(As amended Apr. 28, 1982, eff. Aug. 1, 1982.)

RULES GOVERNING PROCEEDINGS IN THE UNITED STATES DISTRICT COURTS UNDER SECTION 2255 OF TITLE 28, UNITED STATES CODE

Effective February 1, 1977
As amended to May 1, 1988

Cross Reference

For statutory provisions respecting habeas corpus, see Chapter 153 (section 2241 et seq.) of Title 28 Judiciary and Judicial Procedure, set out in this pamphlet, post.

ORDERS OF THE SUPREME COURT OF THE UNITED STATES ADOPTING AND AMENDING RULES GOVERNING PROCEEDINGS IN THE UNITED STATES DISTRICT COURTS UNDER SECTION 2255 OF TITLE 28, UNITED STATES CODE

ORDER OF APRIL 26, 1976

1. That the rules and forms governing proceedings in the United States District Courts under Section 2254 and Section 2255 of Title 28, United States Code, as approved by the Judicial Conference of the United States be, and they hereby are, prescribed pursuant to Section 2072 of Title 28, United States Code and Sections 3771 and 3772 of Title 18, United States Code.

2. That the aforementioned rules and forms shall take effect August 1, 1976, and shall be applicable to all proceedings then pending except to the extent that in the opinion of the court their application in a particular proceeding would not be feasible or would work injustice.

3. That THE CHIEF JUSTICE be, and he hereby is, authorized to transmit the aforementioned rules and forms governing Section 2254 and Section 2255 proceedings to the Congress in accordance with the provisions of Section 2072 of Title 28 and Sections 3771 and 3772 of Title 18, United States Code.

CONGRESSIONAL ACTION ON PROPOSED RULES AND FORMS GOVERNING PROCEEDING UNDER 28 U.S.C. §§ 2254 and 2255

Pub.L. 94–349, § 2, July 8, 1976, 90 Stat. 822, provided: "That, notwithstanding the provisions of section 2072 of title 28 of the United States Code, the rules and forms governing section 2254 cases in the United States district courts and the rules and forms governing section 2255 proceedings in the United States district courts which are embraced by the order entered by the United States Supreme Court on April 26, 1976, and which were transmitted to the Congress on or about April 26, 1976, shall not take effect until thirty days after the adjournment sine die of the 94th Congress, or until and to the extent approved by Act of Congress, whichever is earlier."

Pub.L. 94–426, § 1, Sept. 28, 1976, 90 Stat. 1334, provided: "That the rules governing section 2254 cases in the United States district courts and the rules governing section 2255 proceedings for the United States district courts, as proposed by the United States Supreme Court, which were delayed by the Act entitled 'An Act to delay the effective date of certain proposed amendments to the Federal Rules of Criminal Procedure and certain other rules promulgated by the United States Supreme Court' (Public Law 94–349), are approved with the amendments set forth in section 2 of this Act and shall take effect as so amended, with respect to petitions under section 2254 and motions under section 2255 of title 28 of the United States Code filed on or after February 1, 1977."

462

ORDER OF APRIL 30, 1979

1. That Rule 10 of the Rules Governing Proceedings in the United States District Courts on application under Sections 2254 of Title 28, United States Code, be, and hereby is, amended to read as follows:

Rule 10. Powers of magistrates

The duties imposed upon the judge of the district court by these rules may be performed by a United States magistrate pursuant to 28 U.S.C. § 636.

2. That Rules 10 and 11 of the Rules Governing Proceedings in the United States District Courts on a motion under Section 2255 of Title 28, United States Code, be, and they hereby are, amended to read as follows:

[See text of Rules 10 and 11 below]

ORDER OF APRIL 28, 1982

1. That the rules and forms governing proceedings in the United States district courts under Section 2254 and Section 2255 of Title 28, United States Code, be, and they hereby are, amended by including therein an amendment to Rule 2(c) of the rules for Section 2254 cases, an amendment to Rule 2(b) of the rules for Section 2255 proceedings, and amendments to the model forms for use in applications under Section 2254 and motions under Section 2255, as hereinafter set forth:

[See amendments made thereby under: Rule 2 and Forms for Motions and Rule 9 Issue Motions, Post; and Rule 2 and Forms for Habeas Corpus Applications and Rule 9 Issues of Rules Governing 28 U.S.C. § 2254 Cases, set out following Rule 22 of Federal Rules of Appellate Procedure, Post.]

2. That the aforementioned amendments shall take effect August 1, 1982, and shall be applicable to all proceedings thereafter commenced and, insofar as just and practicable, all proceedings then pending.

3. That THE CHIEF JUSTICE be, and he hereby is, authorized to transmit the aforementioned amendments to the Congress in accordance with Section 2072 of Title 28 and Sections 3771 and 3772 of Title 18, United States Code.

Rule 1. Scope of Rules

These rules govern the procedure in the district court on a motion under 28 U.S.C. § 2255.

(1) by a person in custody pursuant to a judgment of that court for a determination that the judgment was imposed in violation of the Constitution or laws of the United States, or that the court was without jurisdiction to impose such judgment, or that the sentence was in excess of the maximum authorized by law, or is otherwise subject to collateral attack; and

(2) by a person in custody pursuant to a judgment of a state or other federal court and subject to future custody under a judgment of the district court for a determination that such future custody will be in violation of the Constitution or laws of the United States, or that the district court was without jurisdiction to impose such judgment, or that the sentence was in excess of the maximum authorized by law, or is otherwise subject to collateral attack.

ADVISORY COMMITTEE NOTE

The basic scope of this postconviction remedy is prescribed by 28 U.S.C. § 2255. Under these rules the person seeking relief from federal custody files a motion to vacate, set aside, or correct sentence, rather than a petition for habeas corpus. This is consistent with the terminology used in section 2255 and indicates the difference between this remedy and federal habeas for a state prisoner. Also, habeas corpus is available to the person in federal custody if his "remedy by motion is inadequate or ineffective to test the legality of his detention."

Whereas sections 2241–2254 (dealing with federal habeas for those in state custody) speak of the district court judge "issuing the writ" as the operative remedy, section 2255 provides that, if the judge finds the movant's assertions to be meritorious, he "shall discharge the prisoner or resentence him or grant a new trial or correct the sentence as may appear appropriate." This is possible because a motion under § 2255 is a further step in the movant's criminal case and not a separate civil action, as appears from the legislative history of section 2 of S. 20, 80th Congress, the provisions of which were incorporated by the same Congress in title 28 U.S.C. as § 2255. In reporting S. 20 favorably the Senate Judiciary Committee said (Sen.Rep. 1526, 80th Cong. 2d Sess., p. 2):

The two main advantages of such motion remedy over the present habeas corpus are as follows:

First, habeas corpus is a separate civil action and not a further step in the criminal case in which petitioner is sentenced (*Ex parte Tom Tong*, 108 U.S. 556, 559 (1883)). It is not a determination of guilt or innocence of the charge upon which petitioner was sentenced. Where a prisoner sustains his right to discharge in habeas corpus, it is usually because some right—such as lack of counsel—has been denied which reflects no determination of his guilt or innocence but affects solely the fairness of his earlier criminal trial. Even under the broad power in the statute "to dispose of the party as law and justice require" (28 U.S.C.A., sec. 461), the court or judge is by no means in the same advantageous position in habeas corpus to do justice as would be so if the matter were determined in the criminal proceeding (see *Medley*, petitioner, 134 U.S. 160, 174 (1890)). For instance, the judge (by habeas corpus) cannot grant a new trial in the criminal case. Since the motion remedy is in the criminal proceeding, this section 2 affords the opportunity and expressly gives the broad powers to set aside the judgment and to "discharge the prisoner or resentence him or grant a new trial or correct the sentence as may appear appropriate."

The fact that a motion under § 2255 is a further step in the movant's criminal case rather than a separate civil action has significance at several points in these rules. See, *e.g.*, advisory committee note to rule 3 (re no filing fee), advisory committee note to rule 4 (re availability of files, etc., relating to the judgment), advisory committee note to rule 6 (re availability of discovery under criminal procedure rules), advisory committee note to rule 11 (re no extension of time for appeal), and advisory committee note to rule 12 (re applicability of federal criminal rules). However, the fact that Congress has characterized the motion as a further step in the criminal proceedings does *not* mean that proceedings upon such a motion are of necessity governed by the legal principles which are applicable at a criminal trial regarding such matters as counsel, presence, confrontation, self-incrimination, and burden of proof.

The challenge of decisions such as the revocation of probation or parole are not appropriately dealt with under 28 U.S.C. § 2255, which is a continuation of the original criminal action. Other remedies, such as habeas corpus, are available in such situations.

Although rule 1 indicates that these rules apply to a motion for a determination that the judgment was imposed "in violation of the ... laws of the United States," the language of 28 U.S.C. § 2255, it is not the intent of these rules to define or limit what is encompassed within that phrase. *See Davis v. United States,* 417 U.S. 333 (1974), holding that it is not true "that every asserted error of law can be raised on a § 2255 motion," and that the appropriate inquiry is "whether the claimed error of law was a fundamental defect which inherently results in a complete miscarriage of justice, 'and whether [i]t ... present[s] exceptional circumstances where the need for the remedy afforded by the writ of habeas corpus is apparent.' "

For a discussion of the "custody" requirement and the intended limited scope of this remedy, see advisory committee note to § 2254 rule 1.

Rule 2. Motion

(a) **Nature of application for relief.** If the person is presently in custody pursuant to the federal judgment in question, or if not presently in custody may be subject to such custody in the future pursuant to such judgment, the application for relief shall be in the form of a motion to vacate, set aside, or correct the sentence.

(b) **Form of motion.** The motion shall be in substantially the form annexed to these rules, except that any district court may by local rule require that motions filed with it shall be in a form prescribed by the local rule. Blank motions in the prescribed form shall be made available without charge by the clerk of the district court to applicants upon their request. It shall specify all the grounds for relief which are available to the movant and of which he has or, by the exercise of reasonable diligence, should have knowledge and shall set forth in summary form the facts supporting each of the grounds thus specified. It shall also state the relief requested. The motion shall be typewritten or legibly handwritten and shall be signed under penalty of perjury by the petitioner.

(c) **Motion to be directed to one judgment only.** A motion shall be limited to the assertion of a claim for relief against one judgment only of the district court. If a movant desires to attack the validity of other judgments of that or any other district court under which he is in custody or may be subject to future custody, as the case may be, he shall do so by separate motions.

(d) **Return of insufficient motion.** If a motion received by the clerk of a district court does not substantially comply with the requirements of rule 2 or rule 3, it may be returned to the movant, if a judge of the court so directs, together with a statement of the reason for its return. The clerk shall retain a copy of the motion. (As amended Pub.L. 94–426, § 2(3), (4), Sept. 28, 1976, 90 Stat. 1334; Apr. 28, 1982, eff. Aug. 1, 1982.)

ADVISORY COMMITTEE NOTE

Under these rules the application for relief is in the form of a motion rather than a petition (see rule 1 and advisory committee note). Therefore, there is no requirement that the movant name a respondent. This is consistent with 28 U.S.C. § 2255. The United States Attorney for the district in which the judgment under attack was entered is the proper party to oppose the motion since the federal government is the movant's adversary of record.

If the movant is attacking a federal judgment which will subject him to future custody, he must be in present custody (see rule 1 and advisory committee note) as the result of a state or federal governmental action. He need not alter the nature of the motion by trying to include the government officer who presently has official custody of him as a pseudo-respondent, or third-party plaintiff, or other fabrication. The court hearing his motion attacking the future custody can exercise jurisdiction over those having him in present custody without the use of artificial pleading devices.

There is presently a split among the courts as to whether a person currently in state custody may use a § 2255 motion to obtain relief from a federal judgment under which he will be subjected to custody in the future. Negative, see *Newton v. United States,* 329 F.Supp. 90 (S.D.Tex.1971); affirmative, see *Desmond v. The United States Board of Parole,* 397 F.2d 386 (1st Cir.1968), *cert. denied,* 393 U.S. 919 (1968); and *Paalino v. United States,* 314 F.Supp. 875 (C.D.Cal.1970). It is intended that these rules settle the matter in favor of the prisoner's being able to file a § 2255 motion for relief under those circumstances. The proper district in which to file such a motion is the one in which is situated the court which rendered the sentence under attack.

Under rule 35, Federal Rules of Criminal Procedure, the court may correct an illegal sentence or a sentence imposed in an illegal manner, or may reduce the sentence. This remedy should be used, rather than a motion under these § 2255 rules, whenever applicable, but there is some overlap between the two proceedings which has caused the courts difficulty.

The movant should not be barred from an appropriate remedy because he has misstyled his motion. See *United States v. Morgan,* 346 U.S. 502, 505 (1954). The court should construe it as whichever one is proper under the circumstances and decide it on its merits. For a § 2255 motion construed as a rule 35 motion, see *Heflin v. United States,* 358 U.S. 415 (1959); and *United States v. Coke,* 404 F.2d 836 (2d Cir.1968). For writ of error coram nobis treated as a rule 35 motion, see *Hawkins v. United States,* 324 F.Supp. 223 (E.D.Texas, Tyler Division 1971). For a rule 35 motion treated as a § 2255 motion, see *Moss v. United States,* 263 F.2d 615 (5th Cir.1959); *Jones v. United States,* 400 F.2d 892 (8th Cir.1968), cert. denied 394 U.S. 991 (1969); and *United States v. Brown,* 413 F.2d 878 (9th Cir.1969), cert. denied 397 U.S. 947 (1970).

One area of difference between § 2255 and rule 35 motions is that for the latter there is no requirement that the movant be "in custody." *Heflin v. United States,* 358 U.S. 415, 418, 422 (1959); *Duggins v. United States,* 240 F.2d 479, 483 (6th Cir.1957). Compare with rule 1 and advisory committee note for § 2255 motions. The importance of this distinction has decreased since *Peyton v. Rowe,* 391 U.S. 54 (1968), but it might still make a difference in particular situations.

A rule 35 motion is used to attack the sentence imposed not the basis for the sentence. The court in *Gilinsky v. United States,* 335 F.2d 914, 916 (9th Cir. 1964), stated, "a Rule 35 motion presupposes a valid conviction. * * * [C]ollateral attack on errors allegedly committed at trial is not permissible under Rule 35." By illustration the court noted at page 917: "a Rule 35 proceeding contemplates the correction of a sentence of a court having jurisdiction. * * * [J]urisdictional defects * * * involve a collateral attack, they must ordinarily be presented under 28 U.S.C. § 2255." In *United States v. Semet,* 295 F.Supp. 1084 (E.D.Okla.1968), the prisoner moved under rule 35 and § 2255 to invalidate the sentence he was serving on the grounds of his failure to understand the charge to which he pleaded guilty. The court said:

> As regards Defendant's Motion under Rule 35, said Motion must be denied as it presupposes a valid conviction of the offense with which he was charged and may be used only to attack the sentence. It may not be used to examine errors occurring prior to the imposition of sentence.

295 F.Supp. at 1085

See also: *Moss v. United States,* 263 F.2d at 616; *Duggins v. United States,* 240 F.2d at 484; *Migdal v. United States,* 298 F.2d 513, 514 (9th Cir.1961); *Jones v. United States,* 400 F.2d at 894; *United States v. Coke,* 404 F.2d at 847; and *United States v. Brown,* 413 F.2d at 879.

A major difficulty in deciding whether rule 35 or § 2255 is the proper remedy is the uncertainty as to what is meant by an "illegal sentence." The Supreme Court dealt with this issue in *Hill v. United States,* 368 U.S. 424 (1962). The prisoner brought a § 2255 motion to vacate sentence on the ground that he had not been given a Fed.R.Crim.P. 32(a) opportunity to make a statement in his own behalf at the time of sentencing. The majority held this was not an error subject to collateral attack under § 2255. The five-member majority considered the motion as one brought pursuant to rule 35, but denied relief, stating:

> [T]he narrow function of Rule 35 is to permit correction at any time of an illegal *sentence,* not to re-examine errors occurring at the trial or other proceedings prior to the imposition of sentence. The sentence in this case was not illegal. The punishment meted out was not in excess of that prescribed by the relevant statutes, multiple terms were not imposed for the same offense, nor were the terms of the sentence itself legally or constitutionally invalid in any other respect.

368 U.S. at 430

The four dissenters felt the majority definition of "illegal" was too narrow.

> [Rule 35] provides for the correction of an "illegal sentence" without regard to the reasons why that sentence is illegal and contains not a single word to support the Court's conclusion that only a sentence

illegal by reason of the punishment it imposes is "illegal" within the meaning of the Rule I would have thought that a sentence imposed in an illegal manner—whether the amount or form of the punishment meted out constitutes an additional violation of law or not—would be recognized as an "illegal sentence" under any normal reading of the English language.

368 U.S. at 431–432

The 1966 amendment of rule 35 added language permitting correction of a sentence imposed in an "illegal manner." However, there is a 120–day time limit on a motion to do this, and the added language does not clarify the intent of the rule or its relation to § 2255.

The courts have been flexible in considering motions under circumstances in which relief might appear to be precluded by *Hill v. United States.* In *Peterson v. United States,* 432 F.2d 545 (8th Cir.1970), the court was confronted with a motion for reduction of sentence by a prisoner claiming to have received a harsher sentence than his codefendants because he stood trial rather than plead guilty. He alleged that this violated his constitutional right to a jury trial. The court ruled that, even though it was past the 120–day time period for a motion to reduce sentence, the claim was still cognizable under rule 35 as a motion to correct an illegal sentence.

The courts have made even greater use of § 2255 in these types of situations. In *United States v. Lewis,* 392 F.2d 440 (4th Cir.1968), the prisoner moved under § 2255 and rule 35 for relief from a sentence he claimed was the result of the judge's misunderstanding of the relevant sentencing law. The court held that he could not get relief under rule 35 because it was past the 120 days for correction of a sentence imposed in an illegal manner and under *Hill v. United States* it was not an illegal sentence. However, § 2255 was applicable because of its "otherwise subject to collateral attack" language. The flaw was not a mere trial error relating to the finding of guilt, but a rare and unusual error which amounted to "exceptional circumstances" embraced in § 2255's words "collateral attack." See 368 U.S. at 444 for discussion of other cases allowing use of § 2255 to attack the sentence itself in similar circumstances, especially where the judge has sentenced out of a misapprehension of the law.

In *United States v. McCarthy,* 433 F.2d 591, 592 (1st Cir.1970), the court allowed a prisoner who was past the time limit for a proper rule 35 motion to use § 2255 to attack the sentence which he received upon a plea of guilty on the ground that it was induced by an unfulfilled promise of the prosecutor to recommend leniency. The court specifically noted that under § 2255 this was a proper collateral attack on the sentence and there was no need to attack the conviction as well.

The court in *United States v. Malcolm,* 432 F.2d 809, 814, 818 (2d Cir.1970), allowed a prisoner to challenge his sentence under § 2255 without attacking the conviction. It held rule 35 inapplicable because the sentence was not illegal on its face, but the manner in which the sentence was imposed raised a question of the denial of due process in the sentencing itself which was cognizable under § 2255.

The flexible approach taken by the courts in the above cases seems to be the reasonable way to handle these situations in which rule 35 and § 2255 appear to overlap. For a further discussion of this problem, see C. Wright, Federal Practice and Procedure: Criminal §§ 581–587 (1969, Supp.1975).

See the advisory committee note to rule 2 of the § 2254 rules for further discussion of the purposes and intent of rule 2 of these § 2255 rules.

1982 AMENDMENT

Note to Subdivision (b). The amendment takes into account 28 U.S.C. § 1746, enacted after adoption of the § 2255 rules. Section 1746 provides that in lieu of an affidavit an unsworn statement may be given under penalty of perjury in substantially the following form if executed within the United States, its territories, possessions or commonwealths: "I declare (or certify, verify, or state) under penalty of perjury that the foregoing is true and correct. Executed on (date). (Signature)." The statute is "intended to encompass prisoner litigation," and the statutory alternative is especially appropriate in such cases because a notary might not be readily available. *Carter v. Clark,* 616 F.2d 228 (5th Cir.1980). The § 2255 forms have been revised accordingly.

Rule 3.   Filing Motion

(a) Place of filing; copies. A motion under these rules shall be filed in the office of the clerk of the district court. It shall be accompanied by two conformed copies thereof.

(b) Filing and service. Upon receipt of the motion and having ascertained that it appears on its face to comply with rules 2 and 3, the clerk of the district court shall file the motion and enter it on the docket in his office in the criminal action in which was entered the judgment to which it is directed. He shall thereupon deliver or serve a copy of the motion together with a notice of its filing on the United States Attorney of the district in which the judgment under attack was entered. The filing of the motion shall not require said United States Attorney to answer the motion or otherwise move with respect to it unless so ordered by the court.

ADVISORY COMMITTEE NOTE

There is no filing fee required of a movant under these rules. This is a change from the practice of charging $15 and is done to recognize specifically the nature of a § 2255 motion as being a continuation of the criminal case whose judgment is under attack.

The long-standing practice of requiring a $15 filing fee has followed from 28 U.S.C. § 1914(a) whereby "parties instituting any civil action * * * pay a filing fee of $15, except that on an application for a writ of habeas corpus the filing fee shall be $5." This has been held to apply to a proceeding under § 2255 despite the rationale that such a proceeding is a motion and thus a continuation of the criminal action. (See note to rule 1.)

A motion under Section 2255 is a civil action and the clerk has no choice but to charge a $15.00 filing fee unless by leave of court it is filed in forma pauperis. *McCune v. United States,* 406 F.2d 417, 419 (6th Cir.1969).

Although the motion has been considered to be a new civil action in the nature of habeas corpus for filing purposes, the reduced fee for habeas has been held not applicable. The Tenth Circuit considered the specific issue in *Martin v. United States,* 273 F.2d 775 (10th Cir.1960), cert. denied, 365 U.S. 853 (1961), holding that the reduced fee was exclusive to habeas petitions.

Counsel for Martin insists that, if a docket fee must be paid, the amount is $5 rather than $15 and bases his contention on the exception contained in 28 U.S.C. § 1914 that in habeas corpus the fee is $5. This reads into § 1914 language which is not there. While an application under § 2255 may afford the same relief as that previously obtainable by habeas corpus, it is not a petition for a writ of habeas corpus. A change in § 1914 must come from Congress.

273 F.2d at 778

Although for most situations § 2255 is intended to provide to the federal prisoner a remedy equivalent to habeas corpus as used by state prisoners, there is a major distinction between the two. Calling a § 2255 request for relief a motion rather than a petition militates toward charging no new filing fee, not an increased one. In the absence of convincing evidence to the contrary, there is no reason to suppose that Congress did not mean what it said in making a § 2255 action a motion. Therefore, as in other motions filed in a criminal action, there is no requirement of a filing fee. It is appropriate that the present situation of docketing a § 2255 motion as a new action and charging a $15 filing fee be remedied by the rule when the whole question of § 2255 motions is thoroughly thought through and organized.

Even though there is no need to have a forma pauperis affidavit to proceed with the action since there is no requirement of a fee for filing the motion the affidavit remains attached to the form to be supplied potential movants. Most such movants are indigent, and this is a convenient way of getting this into the official record so that the judge may appoint counsel, order the government to pay witness fees, allow docketing of an appeal, and grant any other rights to which an indigent is entitled in the course of a § 2255 motion, when appropriate to the particular situation, without the need for an indigency petition and adjudication at such later point in the proceeding. This should result in a streamlining of the process to allow quicker disposition of these motions.

For further discussion of this rule, see the advisory committee note to rule 3 of the § 2254 rules.

Rule 4. Preliminary Consideration by Judge

(a) Reference to judge; dismissal or order to answer. The original motion shall be presented promptly to the judge of the district court who presided at the movant's trial and sentenced him, or, if the judge who imposed sentence was not the trial judge, then it shall go to the judge who was in charge of that part of the proceedings being attacked by the movant. If the appropriate judge is unavailable to consider the motion, it shall be presented to another judge of the district in accordance with the procedure of the court for the assignment of its business.

(b) Initial consideration by judge. The motion, together with all the files, records, transcripts, and correspondence relating to the judgment under attack, shall be examined promptly by the judge to whom it is assigned. If it plainly appears from the face of the motion and any annexed exhibits and the prior proceedings in the case that the movant is not entitled to relief in the district court, the judge shall make an order for its summary dismissal and cause the movant to be notified. Otherwise, the judge shall order the United States Attorney to file an answer or other pleading within the period of time fixed by the court or to take such other action as the judge deems appropriate.

ADVISORY COMMITTEE NOTE

Rule 4 outlines the procedure for assigning the motion to a specific judge of the district court and the options available to the judge and the government after the motion is properly filed.

The long-standing majority practice in assigning motions made pursuant to § 2255 has been for the trial judge to determine the merits of the motion. In cases where the § 2255 motion is directed against the sentence, the merits have traditionally been decided by the judge who imposed sentence. The reasoning for this was first noted in *Currell v. United States*, 173 F.2d 348–349 (4th Cir.1949):

> Complaint is made that the judge who tried the case passed upon the motion. Not only was there no impropriety in this, but it is highly desirable in such cases that the motions be passed on by the judge who is familiar with the facts and circumstances surrounding the trial, and is consequently not likely to be misled by false allegations as to what occurred.

This case, and its reasoning, has been almost unanimously endorsed by other courts dealing with the issue.

Commentators have been critical of having the motion decided by the trial judge. See Developments in the Law—Federal Habeas Corpus, 83 Harv.L.Rev. 1038, 1206–1208 (1970).

> [T]he trial judge may have become so involved with the decision that it will be difficult for him to review it objectively. Nothing in the legislative history suggests that "court" refers to a specific judge, and the procedural advantages of section 2255 are available whether or not the trial judge presides at the hearing.
>
> The theory that Congress intended the trial judge to preside at a section 2255 hearing apparently originated in *Carvell v. United States*, 173 F.2d 348 (4th Cir.1949) (per curiam), where the panel of judges included Chief Judge Parker of the Fourth Circuit, chairman of the Judicial Conference committee which drafted section 2255. But the legislative history does not indicate that Congress wanted the trial judge to preside. Indeed the advantages of section 2255 can all be achieved if the case is heard in the sentencing district, regardless of which judge hears it. According to the Senate committee report the purpose of the bill was to make the proceeding a part of the criminal action so the court could resentence the applicant, or grant him a new trial. (A judge presiding over a habeas corpus action does not have these powers.) In addition, Congress did not want the cases heard in the district of confinement because that tended to concentrate the burden on a few districts, and made it difficult for witnesses and records to be produced.

> 83 Harv.L.Rev. at 1207–1208

The Court of Appeals for the First Circuit has held that a judge other than the trial judge should rule on the 2255 motion. See *Halliday v. United States*, 380 F.2d 270 (1st Cir.1967).

There is a procedure by which the movant can have a judge other than the trial judge decide his motion in courts adhering to the majority rule. He can file an affidavit alleging bias in order to disqualify the trial judge. And there are circumstances in which the trial judge will, on his own, disqualify himself. See, *e.g.*, *Webster v. United States*, 330 F.Supp. 1080 (1972). However, there has been some questioning of the effectiveness of this procedure. See Developments in the Law—Federal Habeas Corpus, 83 Harv.L.Rev. 1038, 1200–1207 (1970).

Subdivision (a) adopts the majority rule and provides that the trial judge, or sentencing judge if different and appropriate for the particular motion, will decide the motion made pursuant to these rules, recognizing that, under some circumstances, he may want to disqualify himself. A movant is not without remedy if he feels this is unfair to him. He can file an affidavit of bias. And there is the right to appellate review if the trial judge refuses to grant his motion. Because the trial judge is thoroughly familiar with the case, there is obvious administrative advantage in giving him the first opportunity to decide whether there are grounds for granting the motion.

Since the motion is part of the criminal action in which was entered the judgment to which it is directed, the files, records, transcripts, and correspondence relating to that judgment are automatically available to the judge in his consideration of the motion. He no longer need order them incorporated for that purpose.

Rule 4 has its basis in § 2255 (rather than 28 U.S.C. § 2243 in the corresponding habeas corpus rule) which does not have a specific time limitation as to when the answer must be made. Also, under § 2255, the United States Attorney for the district is the party served with the notice and a copy of the motion and required to answer (when appropriate). Subdivision (b) continues this practice since there is no respondent involved in the motion (unlike habeas) and the United States Attorney, as prosecutor in the case in question, is the most appropriate one to defend the judgment and oppose the motion.

The judge has discretion to require an answer or other appropriate response from the United States Attorney. See advisory committee note to rule 4 of the § 2254 rules.

Rule 5. Answer; Contents

(a) Contents of answer. The answer shall respond to the allegations of the motion. In addition it shall state whether the movant has used any other available federal remedies including any prior post-conviction motions under these rules or those existing previous to the adoption of the present rules. The answer shall also state whether an evidentiary hearing was accorded the movant in a federal court.

(b) Supplementing the answer. The court shall examine its files and records to determine whether it has available copies of transcripts and briefs whose existence the answer has indicated.

If any of these items should be absent, the government shall be ordered to supplement its answer by filing the needed records. The court shall allow the government an appropriate period of time in which to do so, without unduly delaying the consideration of the motion.

ADVISORY COMMITTEE NOTE

Unlike the habeas corpus statutes (see 28 U.S.C. §§ 2243, 2248) § 2255 does not specifically call for a return or answer by the United States Attorney or set any time limits as to when one must be submitted. The general practice, however, if the motion is not summarily dismissed, is for the government to file an answer to the motion as well as counter-affidavits, when appropriate. Rule 4 provides for an answer to the motion by the United States Attorney, and rule 5 indicates what its contents should be.

There is no requirement that the movant exhaust his remedies prior to seeking relief under § 2255. However, the courts have held that such a motion is inappropriate if the movant is simultaneously appealing the decision.

We are of the view that there is no jurisdictional bar to the District Court's entertaining a Section 2255 motion during the pendency of a direct appeal but that the orderly administration of criminal law precludes considering such a motion absent extraordinary circumstances.

Womack v. United States, 395 F.2d 630, 631 (D.C.Cir. 1968)

Also see *Masters v. Eide,* 353 F.2d 517 (8th Cir.1965). The answer may thus cut short consideration of the motion if it discloses the taking of an appeal which was omitted from the form motion filed by the movant.

There is nothing in § 2255 which corresponds to the § 2248 requirement of a traverse to the answer. Numerous cases have held that the government's answer and affidavits are not conclusive against the movant, and if they raise disputed issues of fact a hearing must be held. *Machibroda v. United States,* 368 U.S. 487, 494, 495 (1962); *United States v. Salerno,* 290 F.2d 105, 106 (2d Cir.1961); *Romero v. United States,* 327 F.2d 711, 712 (5th Cir.1964); *Scott v. United States,* 349 F.2d 641, 642, 643 (6th Cir.1965); *Schiebelhut v. United States,* 357 F.2d 743, 745 (6th Cir.1966); and *Del Piano v. United States,* 362 F.2d 931, 932, 933 (3d Cir.1966). None of these cases make any mention of a traverse by the movant to the government's answer. As under rule 5 of the § 2254 rules, there is no intention here that such a traverse be required, except under special circumstances. See advisory committee note to rule 9.

Subdivision (b) provides for the government to supplement its answers with appropriate copies of transcripts or briefs if for some reason the judge does not already have them under his control. This is because the government will in all probability have easier access to such papers than the movant, and it will conserve the court's time to have the government produce them rather than the movant, who would in most instances have to apply in forma pauperis for the government to supply them for him anyway.

For further discussion, see the advisory committee note to rule 5 of the § 2254 rules.

Rule 6. Discovery

(a) Leave of court required. A party may invoke the processes of discovery available under the Federal Rules of Criminal Procedure or the Federal Rules of Civil Procedure or elsewhere in the usages and principles of law if, and to the extent that, the judge in the exercise of his discretion and for good cause shown grants leave to do so, but not otherwise. If necessary for effective utilization of discovery procedures, counsel shall be appointed by the judge for a movant who qualifies for appointment of counsel under 18 U.S.C. § 3006A(g).

(b) Requests for discovery. Requests for discovery shall be accompanied by a statement of the interrogatories or requests for admission and a list of the documents, if any, sought to be produced.

(c) Expenses. If the government is granted leave to take the deposition of the movant or any other person, the judge may as a condition of taking it direct that the government pay the expenses of travel and subsistence and fees of counsel for the movant to attend the taking of the deposition.

ADVISORY COMMITTEE NOTE

This rule differs from the corresponding discovery rule under the § 2254 rules in that it includes the processes of discovery available under the Federal Rules of Criminal Procedure as well as the civil. This is because of the nature of a § 2255 motion as a continuing part of the criminal proceeding (see advisory committee note to rule 1) as well as a remedy analogous to habeas corpus by state prisoners.

See the advisory committee note to rule 6 of the § 2254 rules. The discussion there is fully applicable to discovery under these rules for § 2255 motions.

Rule 7. Expansion of Record

(a) Direction for expansion. If the motion is not dismissed summarily, the judge may direct that the record be expanded by the parties by the inclusion of additional materials relevant to the determination of the merits of the motion.

(b) Materials to be added. The expanded record may include, without limitation, letters predating the filing of the motion in the district court, documents, exhibits, and answers under oath, if so directed, to written interrogatories propounded by the judge. Affidavits may be submitted and considered as a part of the record.

(c) Submission to opposing party. In any case in which an expanded record is directed, copies of the letters, documents, exhibits, and affidavits proposed to be included shall be submitted to the party against whom they are to be offered, and he shall be afforded an opportunity to admit or deny their correctness.

(d) Authentication. The court may require the authentication of any material under subdivision (b) or (c).

ADVISORY COMMITTEE NOTE

It is less likely that the court will feel the need to expand the record in a § 2255 proceeding than in a habeas corpus proceeding, because the trial (or sentencing) judge is the one hearing the motion (see rule 4) and should already have a complete file on the case in his possession. However, rule 7 provides a convenient method for supplementing his file if the case warrants it.

See the advisory committee note to rule 7 of the § 2254 rules for a full discussion of reasons and procedures for expanding the record.

Rule 8. Evidentiary Hearing

(a) Determination by court. If the motion has not been dismissed at a previous stage in the proceeding, the judge, after the answer is filed and any transcripts or records of prior court actions in the matter are in his possession, shall, upon a review of those proceedings and of the expanded record, if any, determine whether an evidentiary hearing is required. If it appears that an evidentiary hearing is not required, the judge shall make such disposition of the motion as justice dictates.

(b) Function of the magistrate.

(1) When designated to do so in accordance with 28 U.S.C. § 636(b), a magistrate may conduct hearings, including evidentiary hearings, on the motion, and submit to a judge of the court proposed findings and recommendations for disposition.

(2) The magistrate shall file proposed findings and recommendations with the court and a copy shall forthwith be mailed to all parties.

(3) Within ten days after being served with a copy, any party may serve and file written objections to such proposed findings and recommendations as provided by rules of court.

(4) A judge of the court shall make a de novo determination of those portions of the report or specified proposed findings or recommendations to which objection is made. A judge of the court may accept, reject, or modify in whole or in part any findings or recommendations made by the magistrate.

(c) Appointment of counsel; time for hearing. If an evidentiary hearing is required, the judge shall appoint counsel for a movant who qualifies for the appointment of counsel under 18 U.S.C. § 3006A(g) and the hearing shall be conducted as promptly as practicable, having regard for the need of counsel for both parties for adequate time for investigation and preparation. These rules do not limit the appointment of counsel under 18 U.S.C. § 3006A at any stage of the proceeding if the interest of justice so requires.
(As amended Pub.L. 94–426, § 2(6), Sept. 28, 1976, 90 Stat. 1335; Pub.L. 94–577, § 2(a)(2), (b)(2), Oct. 21, 1976, 90 Stat. 2730, 2731.)

ADVISORY COMMITTEE NOTE

The standards for § 2255 hearings are essentially the same as for evidentiary hearings under a habeas petition, except that the previous federal fact-finding proceeding is in issue rather than the state's. Also § 2255 does not set specific time limits for holding the hearing, as does § 2243 for a habeas action. With these minor differences in mind, see the advisory committee note to rule 8 of § 2254 rules, which is applicable to rule 8 of these § 2255 rules.

Rule 9. Delayed or Successive Motions

(a) Delayed motions. A motion for relief made pursuant to these rules may be dismissed if it appears that the government has been prejudiced in its ability to respond to the motion by delay in its filing unless the movant shows that it is based on grounds of which he could not have had knowledge by the exercise of reasonable diligence before the circumstances prejudicial to the government occurred.

(b) Successive motions. A second or successive motion may be dismissed if the judge finds that it fails to allege new or different grounds for relief and the prior determination was on the merits or, if new and different grounds are alleged, the judge finds that the failure of the movant to assert those grounds in a prior motion constituted an abuse of the procedure governed by these rules.

(As amended Pub.L. 94–426, § 2(9), (10), Sept. 28, 1976, 90 Stat. 1335.)

ADVISORY COMMITTEE NOTE

Unlike the statutory provisions on habeas corpus (28 U.S.C. §§ 2241–2254), § 2255 specifically provides that "a motion for such relief may be made *at any time.*" [Emphasis added.] Subdivision (a) provides that delayed motions may be barred from consideration if the government has been prejudiced in its ability to respond to the motion by the delay and the movant's failure to seek relief earlier is not excusable within the terms of the rule. Case law, dealing with this issue, is in conflict.

Some courts have held that the literal language of § 2255 precludes any possible time bar to a motion brought under it. In *Heflin v. United States,* 358 U.S. 415 (1959), the concurring opinion noted:

The statute [28 U.S.C. § 2255] further provides: "A motion * * * may be made at any time." This * * * simply means that, as in habeas corpus, there is no statute of limitations, no *res judicata,* and that the doctrine of laches is inapplicable.

358 U.S. at 420

McKinney v. United States, 208 F.2d 844 (D.C.Cir.1953) reversed the district court's dismissal of a § 2255 motion for being too late, the court stating:

McKinney's present application for relief comes late in the day: he has served some fifteen years in prison. But tardiness is irrelevant where a constitutional issue is raised and where the prisoner is still confined.

208 F.2d at 846, 847

In accord, see: *Juelich v. United States,* 300 F.2d 381, 383 (5th Cir.1962); *Conners v. United States,* 431 F.2d 1207, 1208 (9th Cir.1970); *Sturrup v. United States,* 218 F.Supp. 279, 281 (E.D.N.Car.1963); and *Banks v. United States,* 319 F.Supp. 649, 652 (S.D.N.Y.1970).

It has also been held that delay in filing a § 2255 motion does not bar the movant because of lack of reasonable diligence in pressing the claim.

The statute [28 U.S.C. § 2255], when it states that the motion may be made at any time, excludes the addition of a showing of diligence in delayed filings. A number of courts have considered contentions similar to those made here and have concluded that there are no time limitations. This result excludes the requirement of diligence which is in reality a time limitation.

Haier v. United States, 334 F.2d 441, 442 (10th Cir.1964)

Other courts have recognized that delay may have a negative effect on the movant. In *Raines v. United States,* 423 F.2d 526 (4th Cir.1970), the court stated:

[B]oth petitioners' silence for extended periods, one for 28 months and the other for nine years, serves to render their allegations less believable. "Although a delay in filing a section 2255 motion is not a controlling element * * * it may merit some consideration * * *."

423 F.2d at 531

In *Aiken v. United States,* 191 F.Supp. 43, 50 (M.D.N. Car.1961), aff'd 296 F.2d 604 (4th Cir.1961), the court said: "While motions under 28 U.S.C. § 2255 may be made at any time, the lapse of time affects the good faith and credibility of the moving party." For similar conclusions, see: *Parker v. United States,* 358 F.2d 50, 54 n. 4 (7th Cir.1965), cert. denied, 386 U.S. 916 (1967); *Le Clair v. United States,* 241 F.Supp. 819, 824 (N.D.Ind. 1965); *Malone v. United States,* 299 F.2d 254, 256 (6th Cir.1962), cert. denied, 371 U.S. 863 (1962); *Howell v. United States,* 442 F.2d 265, 274 (7th Cir.1971); and *United States v. Wiggins,* 184 F.Supp. 673, 676 (D.C.Cir. 1960).

There have been holdings by some courts that a delay in filing a § 2255 motion operates to increase the burden of proof which the movant must meet to obtain relief. The reasons for this, as expressed in *United States v. Bostic,* 206 F.Supp. 855 (D.C.Cir.1962), are equitable in nature.

Obviously, the burden of proof on a motion to vacate a sentence under 28 U.S.C. § 2255 is on the moving party. ... The burden is particularly heavy if the issue is one of fact and a long time has elapsed since the trial of the case. While neither the statute of limitations nor laches can bar the assertion of a constitutional right, nevertheless, the passage of time may make it impracticable to retry a case if the motion is granted and a new trial is ordered. No doubt, at times such a motion is a product of an afterthought. Long delay may raise a question of good faith.

206 F.Supp. at 856–857

See also *United States v. Wiggins,* 184 F.Supp. at 676.

A requirement that the movant display reasonable diligence in filing a § 2255 motion has been adopted by some courts dealing with delayed motions. The court in *United States v. Moore,* 166 F.2d 102 (7th Cir.1948), cert. denied, 334 U.S. 849 (1948), did this, again for equitable reasons.

[W]e agree with the District Court that the petitioner has too long slept upon his rights. * * * [A]pparently there is no limitation of time within which

* * * a motion to vacate may be filed, except that an applicant must show reasonable diligence in presenting his claim. * * *

The reasons which support the rule requiring diligence seem obvious. * * * Law enforcement officials change, witnesses die, memories grow dim. The prosecuting tribunal is put to a disadvantage if an unexpected retrial should be necessary after long passage of time.

166 F.2d at 105

In accord see *Desmond v. United States,* 333 F.2d 378, 381 (1st Cir.1964), on remand, 345 F.2d 225 (1st Cir. 1965).

One of the major arguments advanced by the courts which would penalize a movant who waits an unduly long time before filing a § 2255 motion is that such delay is highly prejudicial to the prosecution. In *Desmond v. United States,* writing of a § 2255 motion alleging denial of effective appeal because of deception by movant's own counsel, the court said:

> [A]pplications for relief such as this must be made promptly. It will not do for a prisoner to wait until government witnesses have become unavailable as by death, serious illness or absence from the country, or until the memory of available government witnesses has faded. It will not even do for a prisoner to wait any longer than is reasonably necessary to prepare appropriate moving papers, however inartistic, after discovery of the deception practiced upon him by his attorney.

333 F.2d at 381

In a similar vein are *United States v. Moore* and *United States v. Bostic,* supra, and *United States v. Wiggins,* 184 F.Supp. at 676.

Subdivision (a) provides a flexible, equitable time limitation based on laches to prevent movants from withholding their claims so as to prejudice the government both in meeting the allegations of the motion and in any possible retrial. It includes a reasonable diligence requirement for ascertaining possible grounds for relief. If the delay is found to be excusable, or nonprejudicial to the government, the time bar is inoperative.

Subdivision (b) is consistent with the language of § 2255 and relevant case law.

The annexed form is intended to serve the same purpose as the comparable one included in the § 2254 rules.

For further discussion applicable to this rule, see the advisory committee note to rule 9 of the § 2254 rules.

Rule 10. Powers of Magistrates

The duties imposed upon the judge of the district court by these rules may be performed by a United States magistrate pursuant to 28 U.S.C. § 636.

(As amended Pub.L. 94–426, § 2(12), Sept. 28, 1976, 90 Stat. 1335; Apr. 30, 1979, eff. Aug. 1, 1979.)

ADVISORY COMMITTEE NOTES

See the advisory committee note to rule 10 of the § 2254 rules for a discussion fully applicable here as well.

1979 AMENDMENT

This amendment conforms the rule to 18 U.S.C. § 636. See Advisory Committee Note to rule 10 of the Rules Governing Section 2254 Cases in the United States District Courts.

Rule 11. Time for Appeal

The time for appeal from an order entered on a motion for relief made pursuant to these rules is as provided in Rule 4(a) of the Federal Rules of Appellate Procedure. Nothing in these rules shall be construed as extending the time to appeal from the original judgment of conviction in the district court.

(As amended Apr. 30, 1979, eff. Aug. 1, 1979.)

ADVISORY COMMITTEE NOTES

Rule 11 is intended to make clear that, although a § 2255 action is a continuation of the criminal case, the bringing of a § 2255 action does not extend the time.

1979 AMENDMENT

Prior to the promulgation of the Rules Governing Section 2255 Proceedings, the courts consistently held that the time for appeal in a section 2255 case is as provided in Fed.R.App.P. 4(a), that is, 60 days when the government is a party, rather than as provided in appellate rule 4(b), which says that the time is 10 days in criminal cases. This result has often been explained on the ground that rule 4(a) has to do with civil cases and that "proceedings under section 2255 are civil in nature." E.g., *Rothman v. United States,* 508 F.2d 648 (3d Cir.1975). Because the new section 2255 rules are based upon the premise "that a motion under § 2255 is a further step in the movant's criminal case rather than a separate civil action," see Advisory Committee Note to rule 1, the question has arisen whether the new rules have the effect of shortening the time for appeal to that provided in appellate rule 4(b). A sentence has been added to rule 11 in order to make it clear that this is not the case.

Even though section 2255 proceedings are a further step in the criminal case, the added sentence correctly states current law. In *United States v. Hayman,* 342

472

U.S. 205 (1952), the Supreme Court noted that such appeals "are governed by the civil rules applicable to appeals from final judgments in habeas corpus actions." In support, the Court cited *Mercado v. United States,* 183 F.2d 486 (1st Cir.1950), a case rejecting the argument that because § 2255 proceedings are criminal in nature the time for appeal is only 10 days. The *Mercado* court concluded that the situation was governed by that part of 28 U.S.C. § 2255 which reads: "An appeal may be taken to the court of appeals from the order entered on the motion as from a final judgment on application for a writ of habeas corpus." Thus, because appellate rule 4(a) is applicable in habeas cases, it likewise governs in § 2255 cases even though they are criminal in nature.

Rule 12. Federal Rules of Criminal and Civil Procedure; Extent of Applicability

If no procedure is specifically prescribed by these rules, the district court may proceed in any lawful manner not inconsistent with these rules, or any applicable statute, and may apply the Federal Rules of Criminal Procedure or the Federal Rules of Civil Procedure, whichever it deems most appropriate, to motions filed under these rules.

ADVISORY COMMITTEE NOTE

This rule differs from rule 11 of the § 2254 rules in that it includes the Federal Rules of Criminal Procedure as well as the civil. This is because of the nature of a § 2255 motion as a continuing part of the criminal proceeding (see advisory committee note to rule 1) as well as a remedy analogous to habeas corpus by state prisoners.

Since § 2255 has been considered analogous to habeas as respects the restrictions in Fed.R.Civ.P. 81(a)(2) (see *Sullivan v. United States,* 198 F.Supp. 624 (S.D.N.Y. 1961)), rule 12 is needed. For discussion, see the advisory committee note to rule 11 of the § 2254 rules.

EDITORIAL NOTES

References in Text. The Federal Rules of Criminal Procedure, referred to in text, are set out in this pamphlet.

The Federal Rules of Civil Procedure, referred to in text, are classified generally to the Appendix to Title 28, U.S.C.A., Judiciary and Judicial Procedure.

APPENDIX OF FORMS

MODEL FORM FOR MOTIONS UNDER 28 U.S.C. § 2255

Name _____

Prison Number _____

Place of Confinement _____

United States District Court _____ District of _____ Case No. _____ (to be supplied by Clerk of U.S. District Court)

United States,

v.

_____

(full name of movant)

(If movant has a sentence to be served in the *future* under a federal judgment which he wishes to attack, he should file a motion in the federal court which entered the judgment.)

MOTION TO VACATE, SET ASIDE, OR CORRECT SENTENCE BY A PERSON IN FEDERAL CUSTODY

Instructions—Read Carefully

(1) This motion must be legibly handwritten or typewritten, and signed by the movant under penalty of perjury. Any false statement of a material fact may serve as the basis for prosecution and conviction for perjury. All questions must be answered concisely in the proper space on the form.

(2) Additional pages are not permitted except with respect to the *facts* which you rely upon to support your grounds for relief. No citation of authorities need be furnished. If briefs or arguments are submitted, they should be submitted in the form of a separate memorandum.

(3) Upon receipt, your motion will be filed if it is in proper order. No fee is required with this motion.

(4) If you do not have the necessary funds for transcripts, counsel, appeal, and other costs connected with a motion of this type, you may request permission to proceed *in forma pau-*

peris in which event you must execute the declaration on the last page, setting forth information establishing your inability to pay the costs. If you wish to proceed *in forma pauperis,* you must have an authorized officer at the penal institution complete the certificate as to the amount of money and securities on deposit to your credit in any account in the institution.

(5) Only judgments entered by one court may be challenged in a single motion. If you seek to challenge judgments entered by different judges or divisions either in the same district or in different districts, you must file separate motions as to each such judgment.

(6) Your attention is directed to the fact that you must include all grounds for relief and all facts supporting such grounds for relief in the motion you file seeking relief from any judgment of conviction.

(7) When the motion is fully completed, the *original* and *two copies* must be mailed to the Clerk of the United States District Court whose address is _____

_____

(8) Motions which do not conform to these instructions will be returned with a notation as to the deficiency.

MOTION

1. Name and location of court which entered the judgment of conviction under attack _____

2. Date of judgment of conviction _____

3. Length of sentence _____

4. Nature of offense involved (all counts) _____

_____

_____

5. What was your plea? (Check one)

   (a) Not guilty ☐

   (b) Guilty ☐

   (c) Nolo contendere ☐

If you entered a guilty plea to one count or indictment, and a not guilty plea to another count or indictment, give details:

_____

_____

_____

6. Kind of trial: (Check one)

   (a) Jury   ☐

   (b) Judge only ☐

7. Did you testify at the trial?

Yes ☐ No ☐

8. Did you appeal from the judgment of conviction?

Yes ☐ No ☐

9. If you did appeal, answer the following:

   (a) Name of court _____

   (b) Result _____

   (c) Date of result _____

10. Other than a direct appeal from the judgment of conviction and sentence, have you previously filed any petitions, applications or motions with respect to this judgment in any federal court?

Yes ☐ No ☐

11. If your answer to 10 was "yes," give the following information:

   (a) (1) Name of court _____

      (2) Nature of proceeding _____

      _____

      (3) Grounds raised _____

      _____

      _____

      _____

      _____

      (4) Did you receive an evidentiary hearing on your petition, application or motion?

      Yes ☐ No ☐

      (5) Result _____

      (6) Date of result _____

   (b) As to any second petition, application or motion give the same information:

      (1) Name of court _____

      (2) Nature of proceeding _____

      _____

      (3) Grounds raised _____

      _____

      _____

      _____

      _____

      (4) Did you receive an evidentiary hearing on your petition, application or motion?

      Yes ☐ No ☐

(5) Result _____

(6) Date of result _____

(c) As to any third petition, application or motion, give the same information:

(1) Name of court _____

(2) Nature of proceeding _____
_____

(3) Grounds raised _____
_____
_____
_____
_____

(4) Did you receive an evidentiary hearing on your petition, application or motion?

Yes ☐ No ☐

(d) Did you appeal, to an appellate federal court having jurisdiction, the result of action taken on any petition, application or motion?

(1) First petition, etc. Yes ☐ No ☐

(2) Second petition, etc. Yes ☐ No ☐

(3) Third petition, etc. Yes ☐ No ☐

(e) If you did *not* appeal from the adverse action on any petition, application or motion, explain briefly why you did not:

_____
_____
_____

12. State *concisely* every ground on which you claim that you are being held unlawfully. Summarize *briefly* the facts supporting each ground. If necessary, you may attach pages stating additional grounds and *facts* supporting same.

CAUTION: If you fail to set forth all grounds in this motion, you may be barred from presenting additional grounds at a later date.

For your information, the following list is a list of the most frequently raised grounds for relief in these proceedings. Each statement preceded by a letter constitutes a separate ground for possible relief. You may raise any grounds which you have other than those listed. However, *you should raise in this motion all available grounds* (relating to this conviction) on which you based your allegations that you are being held in custody unlawfully.

Do not check any of these listed grounds. If you select one or more of these grounds for relief, you must allege facts. The motion will be returned to you if you merely check (a) through (j) or any one of the grounds.

(a) Conviction obtained by plea of guilty which was unlawfully induced or not made voluntarily or with understanding of the nature of the charge and the consequences of the plea.

(b) Conviction obtained by use of coerced confession.

(c) Conviction obtained by use of evidence gained pursuant to an unconstitutional search and seizure.

(d) Conviction obtained by use of evidence obtained pursuant to an unlawful arrest.

(e) Conviction obtained by a violation of the privilege against self-incrimination.

(f) Conviction obtained by the unconstitutional failure of the prosecution to disclose to the defendant evidence favorable to the defendant.

(g) Conviction obtained by a violation of the protection against double jeopardy.

(h) Conviction obtained by action of a grand or petit jury which was unconstitutionally selected and impanelled.

(i) Denial of effective assistance of counsel.

(j) Denial of right of appeal.

A. Ground one: _____
_____

Supporting FACTS (tell your story *briefly* without citing cases or law): _____
_____
_____
_____
_____
_____

B. Ground two: _____

Supporting FACTS (tell your story *briefly* without citing cases or law): _____
_____
_____
_____
_____
_____

THE FEDERAL MODEL

C. Ground three: _____
_____

Supporting FACTS (tell your story *briefly* without citing cases or law): _____
_____
_____
_____
_____
_____

D. Ground four: _____
_____

Supporting FACTS (tell your story *briefly* without citing cases or law): _____
_____
_____
_____
_____
_____

13. If any of the grounds listed in 12A, B, C, and D were not previously presented, state *briefly* what grounds were not so presented, and give your reasons for not presenting them: _
_____
_____
_____
_____

14. Do you have any petition or appeal now pending in any court as to the judgment under attack?

Yes ☐ No ☐

15. Give the name and address, if known, of each attorney who represented you in the following stages of the judgment attacked herein:

(a) At preliminary hearing _____
_____

(b) At arraignment and plea _____
_____

(c) At trial _____
_____

(d) At sentencing _____
_____

(e) On appeal _____
_____

(f) In any post-conviction proceeding _____
_____

(g) On appeal from any adverse ruling in a post-conviction proceeding _____
_____

16. Were you sentenced on more than one count of an indictment, or on more than one indictment, in the same court and at approximately the same time?

Yes ☐ No ☐

17. Do you have any future sentence to serve after you complete the sentence imposed by the judgment under attack?

Yes ☐ No ☐

(a) If so, give name and location of court which imposed sentence to be served in the future: _____
_____
_____

(b) And give date and length of sentence to be served in the future: _____

(c) Have you filed, or do you contemplate filing, any petition attacking the judgment which imposed the sentence to be served in the future?

Yes ☐ No ☐

Wherefore, movant prays that the Court grant him all relief to which he may be entitled in this proceeding.

_____
Signature of Attorney (if any)

I declare (or certify, verify, or state) under penalty of perjury that the foregoing is true and correct. Executed on _____

(date)

_____
Signature of Movant

IN FORMA PAUPERIS DECLARATION

[Insert appropriate court]

United States v.	DECLARATION IN SUPPORT OF REQUEST TO PROCEED *IN FORMA PAUPERIS*
(Movant)	

I, _____, declare that I am the movant in the above entitled case; that in support of my motion

476

to proceed without being required to prepay fees, costs or give security therefor, I state that because of my poverty, I am unable to pay the costs of said proceeding or to give security therefor; that I believe I am entitled to relief.

1. Are you presently employed? Yes ☐ No ☐

  a. If the answer is "yes," state the amount of your salary or wages per month, and give the name and address of your employer.

  _____

  b. If the answer is "no," state the date of last employment and the amount of the salary and wages per month which you received.

  _____

2. Have you received within the past twelve months any money from any of the following sources?

  a. Business, profession or form of self-employment?

  Yes ☐ No ☐

  b. Rent payments, interest or dividends?

  Yes ☐ No ☐

  c. Pensions, annuities or life insurance payments?

  Yes ☐ No ☐

  d. Gifts or inheritances?

  Yes ☐ No ☐

  e. Any other sources?

  Yes ☐ No ☐

  If the answer to any of the above is "yes," describe each source of money and state the amount received from each during the past twelve months. _____

  _____

3. Do you own any cash, or do you have money in a checking or savings account?

  Yes ☐ No ☐ (Include any funds in prison accounts)

  If the answer is "yes," state the total value of the items owned. _____

  _____

4. Do you own real estate, stocks, bonds, notes, automobiles, or other valuable property (excluding ordinary household furnishings and clothing)?

  Yes ☐ No ☐

  If the answer is "yes," describe the property and state its approximate value. _____

  _____

5. List the persons who are dependent upon you for support, state your relationship to those persons, and indicate how much you contribute toward their support. _____

  _____

  I declare (or certify, verify, or state) under penalty of perjury that the foregoing is true and correct. Executed on _____

  (date)

  _____
  Signature of Movant

CERTIFICATE

I hereby certify that the movant herein has the sum of $_____ on account to his credit at the _____ institution where he is confined. I further certify that movant likewise has the following securities to his credit according to the records of said _____ institution: _____

_____

_____

_____

_____
Authorized Officer of Institution

(As amended Apr. 28, 1982, eff. Aug. 1, 1982.)

MODEL FORM FOR USE IN 28 U.S.C. § 2255 CASES INVOLVING A RULE 9 ISSUE

Form No. 9

United States District Court

_____ District of _____

Case No. _____

United States

v.

(Name of Movant)

Movant's Response as to Why His Motion
Should Not be Barred Under Rule 9

Explanation and Instructions—Read Carefully

(I) Rule 9. Delayed or successive motions.

(a) **Delayed motions.** A motion for relief
made pursuant to these rules may be dismissed if
it appears that the government has been prejudiced in its ability to respond to the motion by
delay in its filing unless the movant shows that it
is based on grounds of which he could not have
had knowledge by the exercise of reasonable diligence before the circumstances prejudicial to the
government occurred.

(b) **Successive motions.** A second or successive motion may be dismissed if the judge finds
that it fails to allege new or different grounds for
relief and the prior determination was on the
merits or, if new and different grounds are alleged, the judge finds that the failure of the
movant to assert those grounds in a prior motion
constituted an abuse of the procedure governed
by these rules.

(II) Your motion to vacate, set aside, or correct
sentence has been found to be subject to dismissal under rule 9( ) for the following rea-
son(s):

_____

_____

_____

_____

_____

(III) This form has been sent so that you may
explain why your motion contains the de-
fect(s) noted in (II) above. It is required that
you fill out this form and send it back to the
court within — days. Failure to do so will
result in the automatic dismissal of your
motion.

(IV) When you have fully completed this form,
the original and two copies must be mailed
to the Clerk of the United States District
Court whose address is _____

_____

(V) This response must be legibly handwritten or
typewritten, and signed by the movant, under
penalty of perjury. Any false statement of a
material fact may serve as the basis for prose-

cution and conviction for perjury. All questions must be answered concisely in the proper space on the form.

(VI) Additional pages are not permitted except
with respect to the *facts* which you rely upon
in item 4 or 5 in the response. Any citation
of authorities should be kept to an absolute
minimum and is only appropriate if there
has been a change in the law since the
judgment you are attacking was rendered.

(VII) Respond to 4 *or* 5, not to both, unless (II)
above indicates that you must answer both
sections.

RESPONSE

1. Have you had the assistance of an attorney,
   other law-trained personnel, or writ writers
   since the conviction your motion is attacking
   was entered?

   Yes ☐   No ☐

2. If you checked "yes" above, specify as precisely as you can the period(s) of time during
   which you received such assistance, up to and
   including the present. _____

   _____

3. Describe the nature of the assistance, including the names of those who rendered it to
   you. _____

   _____

   _____

   _____

4. If your motion is in jeopardy because of delay
   prejudicial to the government under rule 9(a),
   explain why you feel the delay has not been
   prejudicial and/or why the delay is excusable
   under the terms of 9(a). This should be done
   by relying upon FACTS, not your opinions or
   conclusions. _____

   _____

   _____

   _____

   _____

5. If your motion is in jeopardy under rule 9(b)
   because it asserts the same grounds as a
   previous motion, explain why you feel it deserves a reconsideration. If its fault under
   rule 9(b) is that it asserts new grounds which
   should have been included in a prior motion,
   explain why you are raising these grounds

now rather than previously. Your explanation should rely on FACTS, not your opinions or conclusions. _____

_____

_____

_____

_____

_____

_____

I declare (or certify, verify, or state) under penalty of perjury that the foregoing is true and correct. Executed on _____

           (date)

_____

      Signature of Movant

(As amended Apr. 28, 1982, eff. Aug. 1, 1982.)

*

FEDERAL RULES OF APPELLATE PROCEDURE

INTRODUCTION

While there is no explicit constitutional right to appeal from a criminal conviction, all jurisdictions, state and federal, provide convicts the opportunity to seek the review of a higher court. In the federal context, the civil and criminal appellate mechanism is governed by the Federal Rules of Appellate Procedure.

Among the Appellate Rules, several provisions are specifically aimed at the criminal appeal, as is evident in the table of contents that precedes the main Rules text. Of particular benefit to a student of the Rules are the Committee and Amendment Notes that immediately follow the text of each Rule. These Notes detail the underlying rationale of the given Rule and specify the impetus for and substance of that Rule's evolution.

FEDERAL RULES OF APPELLATE PROCEDURE

As amended to February 1, 1989

Table of Rules

RULES OF APPELLATE PROCEDURE

ORDERS OF THE SUPREME COURT OF THE UNITED STATES ADOPTING AND AMENDING RULES

ORDER OF DECEMBER 4, 1967

1. That the following rules, to be known as the Federal Rules of Appellate Procedure, be, and they hereby are, prescribed, pursuant to sections 3771 and 3772 of Title 18, United States Code, and sections 2072 and 2075 of Title 28, United States Code, to govern the procedure in appeals to United States courts of appeals from the United States district courts, in the review by United States courts of appeals of decisions of the Tax Court of the United States, in proceedings in the United States courts of appeals for the review or enforcement of orders of administrative agencies, boards, commissions and officers, and in applications for writs or other relief which a United States court of appeals or judge thereof is competent to give:

[See text of Rules of Appellate Procedure, post]

2. That the foregoing rules shall take effect on July 1, 1968, and shall govern all proceedings in appeals and petitions for review or enforcement of orders thereafter brought and in all such proceedings then pending, except to the extent that in the opinion of the court of appeals their application in a particular proceeding then pending would not be feasible or would work injustice, in which case the former procedure may be followed.

3. That Rules 6, 9, 41, 77 and 81 of the Rules of Civil Procedure for the United States District Courts be, and they hereby are, amended, effective July 1, 1968, as hereinafter set forth:

[For text of amendments, see pamphlet containing Federal Rules of Civil Procedure]

4. That the chapter heading "IX. APPEALS", all of Rules 72, 73, 74, 75 and 76 of the Rules of Civil Procedure for the United States District Courts, and Form 27 annexed to the said rules, be, and they hereby are, abrogated, effective July 1, 1968.

5. That Rules 45, 49, 56 and 57 of the Rules of Criminal Procedure for the United States District Courts be, and they hereby are, amended, effective July 1, 1968, as hereinafter set forth:

[See amendments made thereby under the Rules of Criminal Procedure, ante]

6. That the chapter heading "VIII. APPEAL", all of Rules 37 and 39, and subdivisions (b) and (c) of Rule 38, of the Rules of Criminal Procedure for the United States District Courts, and Forms 26 and 27 annexed to the said rules, be, and they hereby are, abrogated, effective July 1, 1968.

7. That the Chief Justice be, and he hereby is, authorized to transmit to the Congress the foregoing new rules and amendments to and abrogation of existing rules, in accordance with the provisions of Title 18, U.S.C. § 3771, and Title 28, U.S.C. §§ 2072 and 2075.

ORDER OF MARCH 30, 1970

1. That subdivisions (a) and (c) of Rule 30 and subdivision (a) of Rule 31 of the Federal Rules of Appellate Procedure be, and they hereby are, amended as follows:

[See the amendments made thereby under the respective rules, post]

2. That the foregoing amendments to the Federal Rules of Appellate Procedure shall take effect on July 1, 1970, and shall govern all proceedings in actions brought thereafter and also in all further proceedings in actions then pending, except to the extent that in the opinion of the court their application in a particular action then pending would not be feasible or would work injustice, in which event the former procedure applies.

3. That the Chief Justice be, and he hereby is, authorized to transmit to the Congress the foregoing amendments to existing rules, in accordance with the provisions of Title 18, U.S.C., § 3772, and Title 28, U.S.C., §§ 2072 and 2075.

ORDER OF MARCH 1, 1971

1. That subdivision (a) of Rule 6, paragraph (4) of subdivision (a) of Rule 27, paragraph (6) of subdivision (b) of Rule 30, subdivision (c) of Rule 77, and paragraph (2) of subdivision (a) of Rule 81 of the Federal Rules of Civil Procedure be, and hereby are, amended, effective July 1, 1971, to read as follows:

[For text of amendments, see pamphlet containing Federal Rules of Civil Procedure]

2. That subdivision (a) of Rule 45 and all of Rule 56 of the Federal Rules of Criminal Procedure be, and they hereby are, amended, effective July 1, 1971, to read as follows:

[See amendments made thereby under the respective Rules of Criminal Procedure, ante]

3. That subdivision (a) of Rule 26 and subdivision (a) of Rule 45 of the Federal Rules of Appellate Procedure be, and they hereby are, amended, effective July 1, 1971, to read as follows:

[See amendments made thereby under the respective rules, post]

4. That THE CHIEF JUSTICE be, and he hereby is, authorized to transmit to the Congress the foregoing amendments to the Rules of Civil, Criminal and Appellate Procedure, in accordance with the provisions of Title 18, U.S.C., § 3771, and Title 28, U.S.C., §§ 2072 and 2075.

Mr. Justice Black and Mr. Justice Douglas dissent.

ORDER OF APRIL 24, 1972

1. That Rules 1, 3, 4(b) & (c), 5, 5.1, 6(b), 7(c), 9(b), (c) & (d), 17(a) & (g), 31(e), 32(b), 38(a), 40, 41, 44, 46, 50, 54 and 55 of the Federal Rules of Criminal Procedure by, and they hereby are, amended effective October 1, 1972, to read as follows:

[See amendments made thereby under the respective Rules of Criminal Procedure, ante]

2. That Rule 9(c) of the Federal Rules of Appellate Procedure be, and hereby is amended, effective October 1, 1972, to read as follows:

[See amendments made thereby under the respective rules, post]

3. That THE CHIEF JUSTICE be, and he hereby is, authorized to transmit to the Congress the foregoing amendments to Rules of Criminal and Appellate Procedure, in accordance with the provisions of Title 18, U.S. Code, §§ 3771 and 3772.

Mr. Justice Douglas dissented to adoption of Rule 50(b) of the Federal Rules of Criminal Procedure.

ORDER OF APRIL 30, 1979

1. That the Federal Rules of Appellate Procedure be, and they hereby are, amended by including therein amendments to Rules 1(a), 3(c), (d) and (e), 4(a), 5(d), 6(d), 7, 10(b), 11(a), (b), (c) and (d), 12, 13(a), 24(b), 27(b), 28(g) and (j), 34(a) and (b), 35(b) and (c), 39(c) and (d), and 40 as hereinafter set forth:

[See amendments made thereby under the respective rules, post]

2. That the foregoing amendments to the Federal Rules of Appellate Procedure shall take effect on August 1, 1979, and shall govern all appellate proceedings thereafter commenced and, insofar as just and practicable, all proceedings then pending.

3. That THE CHIEF JUSTICE be, and he hereby is, authorized to transmit to the Congress the foregoing amendments to the Federal Rules of Appellate Procedure in accordance with the provisions of Section 3772 of Title 18, United States Code, and Sections 2072 and 2075 of Title 28, United States Code.

ORDER OF MARCH 10, 1986

1. That the Federal Rules of Appellate Procedure be, and they hereby are, amended by including therein new Appellate Rules 3.1, 5.1 and 15.1 and amendments to Appellate Rules 3(d), 8(b), 10(b) and (c), 11(b), 12(a), 19, 23(b) and (c), 24(a), 25(a) and (b), 26(a) and (c), 28(c) and (j), 30(a), (b) and (c), 31(a) and (c), 34(a) and (e), 39(c) and (d), 43(a) and (c), 45(a), (b), and (d), and 46(a) and (b), as hereinafter set forth:

[See amendments made thereby under the respective rules, post]

2. That the foregoing additions to and changes in the Federal Rules of Appellate Procedure, shall take effect on July 1, 1986 and shall govern all proceedings in appellate actions thereafter commenced and, insofar as just and practicable, all proceedings in appellate actions then pending.

3. That THE CHIEF JUSTICE be, and he hereby is, authorized to transmit to the Congress the foregoing additions to and changes in the rules of appellate procedure in accordance with the provisions of Section 3772 of Title 18 and Section 2072 of Title 28, United States Code.

TITLE I

APPLICABILITY OF RULES

Rule 1. Scope of Rules

(a) **Scope of Rules.** These rules govern procedure in appeals to United States courts of appeals from the United States district courts and the United States Tax Court; in proceedings in the courts of appeals for review or enforcement of orders of administrative agencies, boards, commissions and officers of the United States; and in applications for writs or other relief which a court of appeals or a judge thereof is competent to give. When these rules provide for the making of a motion or application in the district court, the procedure for making such motion or application shall be in accordance with the practice of the district court.

(b) **Rules Not to Affect Jurisdiction.** These rules shall not be construed to extend or limit the jurisdiction of the courts of appeals as established by law.

(As amended Apr. 30, 1979, eff. Aug. 1, 1979.)

NOTES OF ADVISORY COMMITTEE ON APPELLATE RULES

These rules are drawn under the authority of 28 U.S.C. § 2072, as amended by the Act of November 6, 1966, 80 Stat. 1323 (1 U.S. Code Cong. & Ad. News, p. 1546 (1966)) (Rules of Civil Procedure); 28 U.S.C. § 2075 (Bankruptcy Rules); and 18 U.S.C. §§ 3771 (Procedure to and including verdict) and 3772 (Procedure after verdict). Those statutes combine to give to the Supreme Court power to make rules of practice and procedure for all cases within the jurisdiction of the courts of appeals. By the terms of the statutes, after the rules have taken effect all laws in conflict with them are of no further force or effect. Practice and procedure in the eleven courts of appeals are now regulated by rules promulgated by each court under the authority of 28 U.S.C. § 2071. Rule 47 expressly authorizes the courts of appeals to make rules of practice not inconsistent with these rules.

As indicated by the titles under which they are found, the following rules are of special application: Rules 3 through 12 apply to appeals from judgments and orders of the district courts; Rules 13 and 14 apply to appeals from decisions of the Tax Court (Rule 13 establishes an appeal as the mode of review of decisions of the Tax Court in place of the present petition for review); Rules 15 through 20 apply to proceedings for review or enforcement of orders of administrative agencies, boards, commissions and officers. Rules 22 through 24 regulate habeas corpus proceedings and appeals in forma pauperis. All other rules apply to all proceedings in the courts of appeals.

1979 AMENDMENT

The Federal Rules of Appellate Procedure were designed as an integrated set of rules to be followed in appeals to the courts of appeals, covering all steps in the appellate process, whether they take place in the district court or in the court of appeals, and with their adoption Rules 72–76 of the F.R.C.P. were abrogated. In some instances, however, the F.R.A.P. provide that a motion or application for relief may, or must, be made in the district court. See Rules 4(a), 10(b), and 24. The proposed amendment would make it clear that when this is so the motion or application is to be made in the form and manner prescribed by the F.R.C.P. or F.R.Cr. P. and local rules relating to the form and presentation of motions and is not governed by Rule 27 of the F.R.A.P. See Rule 7(b) of the F.R.C.P. and Rule 47 of the F.R.Cr.P.

Rule 2. Suspension of Rules

In the interest of expediting decision, or for other good cause shown, a court of appeals may, except as otherwise provided in Rule 26(b), suspend the requirements or provisions of any of these rules in a particular case on application of a party or on its own motion and may order proceedings in accordance with its direction.

NOTES OF ADVISORY COMMITTEE ON APPELLATE RULES

The primary purpose of this rule is to make clear the power of the courts of appeals to expedite the determination of cases of pressing concern to the public or to the litigants by prescribing a time schedule other than that provided by the rules. The rule also contains a general authorization to the courts to relieve litigants of the consequences of default where manifest injustice would otherwise result. Rule 26(b) prohibits a court of appeals from extending the time for taking appeal or seeking review.

TITLE II

APPEALS FROM JUDGMENTS AND ORDERS OF DISTRICT COURTS

Rule 3. Appeal as of Right—How Taken

(a) **Filing the Notice of Appeal.** An appeal permitted by law as of right from a district court to a court of appeals shall be taken by filing a notice of appeal with the clerk of the district court within the time allowed by Rule 4. Failure of an appellant to take any step other than the timely filing of a notice of appeal does not affect the validity of the appeal, but is ground only for such action as the court of appeals deems appropriate, which may include dismissal of the appeal. Appeals by permission under 28 U.S.C. § 1292(b) and appeals by allowance in bankruptcy shall be taken in the manner prescribed by Rule 5 and Rule 6, respectively.

(b) **Joint or Consolidated Appeals.** If two or more persons are entitled to appeal from a judgment or order of a district court and their interests are such as to make joinder practicable, they may file a joint notice of appeal, or may join in appeal after filing separate timely notices of appeal, and they may thereafter proceed on appeal as a single appellant. Appeals may be consolidated by order of the court of appeals upon its own motion or upon motion of a party, or by stipulation of the parties to the several appeals.

(c) **Content of the Notice of Appeals.** The notice of appeal shall specify the party or parties taking the appeal; shall designate the judgment, order or part thereof appealed from; and shall name the court to which the appeal is taken. Form 1 in the Appendix of Forms is a suggested form of a notice of appeal. An appeal shall not be dismissed for informality of form or title of the notice of appeal.

(d) **Service of the Notice of Appeal.** The clerk of the district court shall serve notice of the filing of a notice of appeal by mailing a copy thereof to counsel of record of each party other than the appellant, or, if a party is not represented by counsel, to the last known address of that party; and the clerk shall transmit forthwith a copy of the notice of appeal and of the docket entries to the clerk of the court of appeals named in the notice. When an appeal is taken by a defendant in a criminal case, the clerk shall also serve a copy of the notice of appeal upon the defendant, either by personal service or by mail addressed to the defendant. The clerk shall note on each copy served the date on which the notice of appeal was filed. Failure of the clerk to serve notice shall not affect the validity of the appeal. Service shall be sufficient notwithstanding the death of a party or the party's counsel. The clerk shall note in the docket the names of the parties to whom the clerk mails copies, with the date of mailing.

(e) Payment of Fees. Upon the filing of any separate or joint notice of appeal from the district court, the appellant shall pay to the clerk of the district court such fees as are established by statute, and also the docket fee prescribed by the Judicial Conference of the United States, the latter to be received by the clerk of the district court on behalf of the court of appeals.

(As amended Apr. 30, 1979, eff. Aug. 1, 1979; Mar. 10, 1986, eff. July 1, 1986.)

NOTES OF ADVISORY COMMITTEE ON APPELLATE RULES

General Note. Rule 3 and Rule 4 combine to require that a notice of appeal be filed with the clerk of the district court within the time prescribed for taking an appeal. Because the timely filing of a notice of appeal is "mandatory and jurisdictional," United States v. Robinson, 361 U.S. 220, 224, 80 S.Ct. 282, 4 L.Ed.2d 259 (1960), compliance with the provisions of those rules is of the utmost importance. But the proposed rules merely restate, in modified form, provisions now found in the civil and criminal rules (FRCP 5(e), 73; FRCrP 37), and decisions under the present rules which dispense with literal compliance in cases in which it cannot fairly be exacted should control interpretation of these rules. Illustrative decisions are: Fallen v. United States, 378 U.S. 139, 84 S.Ct. 1689, 12 L.Ed.2d 760 (1964) (notice of appeal by a prisoner, in the form of a letter delivered, well within the time fixed for appeal, to prison authorities for mailing to the clerk of the district court held timely filed notwithstanding that it was received by the clerk after expiration of the time for appeal; the appellant "did all he could" to effect timely filing); Richey v. Wilkins, 335 F.2d 1 (2d Cir. 1964) (notice filed in the court of appeals by a prisoner without assistance of counsel held sufficient); Halfen v. United States, 324 F.2d 52 (10th Cir. 1963) (notice mailed to district judge in time to have been received by him in normal course held sufficient); Riffle v. United States, 299 F.2d 802 (5th Cir. 1962) (letter of prisoner to judge of court of appeals held sufficient). Earlier cases evidencing "a liberal view of papers filed by indigent and incarcerated defendants" are listed in Coppedge v. United States, 369 U.S. 438, 442, n. 5, 82 S.Ct. 917, 8 L.Ed.2d 21 (1962).

Subdivision (a). The substance of this subdivision is derived from FRCP 73(a) and FRCrP 37(a)(1). The proposed rule follows those rules in requiring nothing other than the filing of a notice of appeal in the district court for the perfection of the appeal. The petition for allowance (except for appeals governed by Rules 5 and 6), citations, assignments of error, summons and severance—all specifically abolished by earlier modern rules —are assumed to be sufficiently obsolete as no longer to require pointed abolition.

Subdivision (b). The first sentence is derived from FRCP 74. The second sentence is added to encourage consolidation of appeals whenever feasible.

Subdivision (c). This subdivision is identical with corresponding provisions in FRCP 73(b) and FRCrP 37(a)(1).

Subdivision (d). This subdivision is derived from FRCP 73(b) and FRCrP 37(a)(1). The duty of the clerk to forward a copy of the notice of appeal and of the docket entries to the court of appeals in a criminal case extended to habeas corpus and 28 U.S.C. § 2255 proceedings.

1979 AMENDMENT

Note to Subdivision (c). The proposed amendment would add the last sentence. Because of the fact that the timely filing of the notice of appeal has been characterized as jurisdictional (See, e.g., Brainerd v. Beal (CA7th, 1974) 498 F.2d 901, in which the filing of a notice of appeal one day late was fatal), it is important that the right to appeal not be lost by mistakes of mere form. In a number of decided cases it has been held that so long as the function of notice is met by the filing of a paper indicating an intention to appeal, the substance of the rule has been complied with. See, e.g., Cobb v. Lewis (CA5th, 1974) 488 F.2d 41; Holley v. Capps (CA5th, 1972) 468 F.2d 1366. The proposed amendment would give recognition to this practice.

When a notice of appeal is filed, the clerk should ascertain whether any judgment designated therein has been entered in compliance with Rules 58 and 79(a) of the F.R.C.P. See Note to Rule 4(a)(6), infra.

Note to Subdivision (d). The proposed amendment would extend to civil cases the present provision applicable to criminal cases, habeas corpus cases, and proceedings under 28 U.S.C. § 2255, requiring the clerk of the district court to transmit to the clerk of the court of appeals a copy of the notice of appeal and of the docket entries, which should include reference to compliance with the requirements for payment of fees. See Note to (e), infra.

This requirement is the initial step in proposed changes in the rules to place in the court of appeals an increased practical control over the early steps in the appeal.

Note to Subdivision (e). Proposed new Rule 3(e) represents the second step in shifting to the court of appeals the control of the early stages of an appeal. See Note to Rule 3(d) above. Under the present rules the payment of the fee prescribed by 28 U.S.C. § 1917 is not covered. Under the statute, however, this fee is paid to the clerk of the district court at the time the notice of appeal is filed. Under present Rule 12, the "docket fee" fixed by the Judicial Conference of the United States under 28 U.S.C. § 1913 must be paid to the clerk of the court of appeals within the time fixed for transmission of the record, ". . . and the clerk shall thereupon enter the appeal upon the docket."

Under the proposed new Rule 3(e) both fees would be paid to the clerk of the district court at the time the notice of appeal is filed, the clerk of the district court receiving the docket fee on behalf of the court of appeals.

In view of the provision in Rule 3(a) that "[f]ailure of an appellant to taken any step other than the timely filing of a notice of appeal does not affect the validity of the appeal, but is ground only for such action as the court of appeals deems appropriate, which may include dismissal of the appeal," the case law indicates that the failure to prepay the statutory filing fee does not constitute a jurisdictional defect. See Parissi v. Telechron, 349 U.S. 46 (1955); Gould v. Members of N.J. Division of Water Policy & Supply, 555 F.2d 340 (3d Cir. 1977). Similarly, under present Rule 12, failure to pay the docket fee within the time prescribed may be excused by the court of appeals. See, e.g., Walker v. Mathews, 546 F.2d 814 (9th Cir.1976). Proposed new Rule 3(e) adopts the view of these cases, requiring that both fees be paid at the time the notice of appeal is filed, but subject to the provisions of Rule 26(b) preserving the authority of the court of appeals to permit late payment.

1986 AMENDMENT

The amendments to Rule 3(d) are technical. No substantive change is intended.

Rule 3.1 Appeals from Judgments Entered by Magistrates in Civil Cases

When the parties consent to a trial before a magistrate pursuant to 28 U.S.C. § 636(c)(1), an appeal from a judgment entered upon the direction of a magistrate shall be heard by the court of appeals pursuant to 28 U.S.C. § 636(c)(3), unless the parties, in accordance with 28 U.S.C. § 636(c)(4), consent to an appeal on the record to a judge of the district court and thereafter, by petition only, to the court of appeals. Appeals to the court of appeals pursuant to 28 U.S.C. § 636(c)(3) shall be taken in identical fashion as

appeals from other judgments of the district court.

(Added Mar. 10, 1986, eff. July 1, 1986.)

NOTES OF ADVISORY COMMITTEE ON APPELLATE RULES

Under the governing statute, 28 U.S.C. § 636(c)(3), the judgment of a magistrate becomes a judgment of the district court and is appealable to the court of appeals "as an appeal from any other judgment of a district court." This provision is designed to make this point explicit for the convenience of practitioners.

Rule 4. Appeal as of Right—When Taken

(a) Appeals in Civil Cases.

(1) In the civil case in which an appeal is permitted by law as of right from a district court to a court of appeals the notice of appeal required by Rule 3 shall be filed with the clerk of the district court within 30 days after the date of entry of the judgment or order appealed from; but if the United States or an officer or agency thereof is a party, the notice of appeal may be filed by any party within 60 days after such entry. If a notice of appeal is mistakenly filed in the court of appeals, the clerk of the court of appeals shall note thereon the date on which it was received and transmit it to the clerk of the district court and it shall be deemed filed in the district court on the date so noted.

(2) Except as provided in (a)(4) of this Rule 4, a notice of appeal filed after the announcement of a decision or order but before the entry of the judgment or order shall be treated as filed after such entry and on the day thereof.

(3) If a timely notice of appeal is filed by a party, any other party may file a notice of appeal within 14 days after the date on which the first notice of appeal was filed, or within the time otherwise prescribed by this Rule 4(a), whichever period last expires.

(4) If a timely motion under the Federal Rules of Civil Procedure is filed in the district court by any party: (i) for judgment under Rule 50(b); (ii) under Rule 52(b) to amend or make additional findings of fact, whether or not an alteration of the judgment would be required if the motion is granted; (iii) under Rule 59 to alter or amend the judgment; or (iv) under Rule 59 for a new trial, the time for appeal for all parties shall run from the entry of the order denying a new trial or

granting or denying any other such motion. A notice of appeal filed before the disposition of any of the above motions shall have no effect. A new notice of appeal must be filed within the prescribed time measured from the entry of the order disposing of the motion as provided above. No additional fees shall be required for such filing.

(5) The district court, upon a showing of excusable neglect or good cause, may extend the time for filing a notice of appeal upon motion filed not later than 30 days after the expiration of the time prescribed by this Rule 4(a). Any such motion which is filed before expiration of the prescribed time may be *ex parte* unless the court otherwise requires. Notice of any such motion which is filed after expiration of the prescribed time shall be given to the other parties in accordance with local rules. No such extension shall exceed 30 days past such prescribed time or 10 days from the date of entry of the order granting the motion, whichever occurs later.

(6) A judgment or order is entered within the meaning of this Rule 4(a) when it is entered in compliance with Rules 58 and 79(a) of the Federal Rules of Civil Procedure.

(b) Appeals in Criminal Cases. In a criminal case the notice of appeal by a defendant shall be filed in the district court within 10 days after the entry of (i) the judgment or order appealed from or (ii) a notice of appeal by the Government. A notice of appeal filed after the announcement of a decision, sentence or order but before entry of the judgment or order shall be treated as filed after such entry and on the day thereof. If a timely motion in arrest of judgment or for a new trial on any ground other than newly discovered evidence has been made, an appeal from a judgment of conviction may be taken within 10 days after the entry of an order denying the motion. A motion for a new trial based on the ground of newly discovered evidence will similarly extend the time for appeal from a judgment of conviction if the motion is made before or within 10 days after entry of the judgment. When an appeal by the government is authorized by statute, the notice of appeal shall be filed in the district court within 30 days after the entry of (i) the judgment or order appealed from or (ii) a notice of appeal by any defendant. A judgment or order is entered within the meaning of this subdivision when it is entered in the criminal docket. Upon a showing

of excusable neglect the district court may, before or after the time has expired, with or without motion and notice, extend the time for filing a notice of appeal for a period not to exceed 30 days from the expiration of the time otherwise prescribed by this subdivision.

(As amended Apr. 30, 1979, eff. Aug. 1, 1979; Nov. 18, 1988, Pub.L. 100–690, Title VII, § 7111, 102 Stat. 4419.)

NOTES OF ADVISORY COMMITTEE ON APPELLATE RULES

Subdivision (a). This subdivision is derived from FRCP 73(a) without any change of substance. The requirement that a request for an extension of time for filing the notice of appeal made after expiration of the time be made by motion and on notice codifies the result reached under the present provisions of FRCP 73(a) and 6(b). North Umberland Mining Co. v. Standard Accident Ins. Co., 193 F.2d 951 (9th Cir., 1952); Cohen v. Plateau Natural Gas Co., 303 F.2d 273 (10th Cir., 1962); Plant Economy, Inc. v. Mirror Insulation Co., 308 F.2d 275 (3d Cir., 1962).

Since this subdivision governs appeals in all civil cases, it supersedes the provisions of section 25 of the Bankruptcy Act (11 U.S.C. § 48). Except in cases to which the United States or an officer or agency thereof is a party, the change is a minor one, since a successful litigant in a bankruptcy proceeding may, under section 25, oblige an aggrieved party to appeal within 30 days after entry of judgment—the time fixed by this subdivision in cases involving private parties only—by serving him with notice of entry on the day thereof, and by the terms of section 25 an aggrieved party must in any event appeal within 40 days after entry of judgment. No reason appears why the time for appeal in bankruptcy should not be the same as that in civil cases generally. Furthermore, section 25 is a potential trap for the uninitiated. The time for appeal which it provides is not applicable to all appeals which may fairly be termed appeals in bankruptcy. Section 25 governs only those cases referred to in section 24 as "proceedings in bankruptcy" and "controversies arising in proceedings in bankruptcy." Lowenstein v. Reikes, 54 F.2d 481 (2d Cir., 1931), cert. den., 285 U.S. 539, 52 S.Ct. 311, 76 L.Ed. 932 (1932). The distinction between such cases and other cases which arise out of bankruptcy is often difficult to determine. See 2 Moore's Collier on Bankruptcy ¶ 24.12 through ¶ 24.36 (1962). As a result it is not always clear whether an appeal is governed by section 25 or by FRCP 73(a), which is applicable to such appeals in bankruptcy as are not governed by section 25.

In view of the unification of the civil and admiralty procedure accomplished by the amendments of the Federal Rules of Civil Procedure effective July 1, 1966, this subdivision governs appeals in those civil actions which involve admiralty or maritime claims and which prior to that date were known as suits in admiralty.

The only other change possibly effected by this subdivision is in the time for appeal from a decision of a district court on a petition for impeachment of an award of a board of arbitration under the Act of May 20, 1926, c. 347, § 9 (44 Stat. 585), 45 U.S.C. § 159. The act provides that a notice of appeal from such a decision shall be filed within 10 days of the decision. This singular provision was apparently repealed by the enactment in 1948 of 28 U.S.C. § 2107, which fixed 30 days from the date of entry of judgment as the time for appeal in all actions of a civil nature except actions in admiralty or bankruptcy matters or those in which the United States is a party. But it was not expressly repealed, and its status is in doubt. See 7 Moore's Federal Practice ¶ 73.09[2] (1966). The doubt should be resolved, and no reason appears why appeals in such cases should not be taken within the time provided for civil cases generally.

Subdivision (b). This subdivision is derived from FRCrP 37(a)(2) without change of substance.

1979 AMENDMENT

Note to Subdivision (a)(1). The words "(including a civil action which involves an admiralty or maritime claim and a proceeding in bankruptcy or a controversy arising therein)," which appear in the present rule are struck out as unnecessary and perhaps misleading in suggesting that there may be other categories that are not either civil or criminal within the meaning of Rule 4(a) and (b).

The phrases "within 30 days of such entry" and "within 60 days of such entry" have been changed to read "after" instead of "or." The change is for clarity only, since the word "of" in the present rule appears to be used to mean "after." Since the proposed amended rule deals directly with the premature filing of a notice of appeal, it was thought useful to emphasize the fact that except as provided, the period during which a notice of appeal may be filed is the 30 days, or 60 days as the case may be, following the entry of the judgment or order appealed from. See Notes to Rule 4(a)(2) and (4), below.

Note to Subdivision (a)(2). The proposed amendment to Rule 4(a)(2) would extend to civil cases the provisions of Rule 4(b), dealing with criminal cases, designed to avoid the loss of the right to appeal by filing the notice of appeal prematurely. Despite the absence of such a provision in Rule 4(a) the courts of appeals quite generally have held premature appeals effective. See, e.g., Matter of Grand Jury Empanelled Jan. 21, 1975, 541 F.2d 373 (3d Cir. 1976); Hodge v. Hodge, 507 F.2d 87 (3d Cir. 1976); Song Jook Suh v. Rosenberg, 437 F.2d 1098 (9th Cir. 1971); Ruby v. Secretary of the Navy, 365 F.2d 385 (9th Cir. 1966); Firchau v. Diamond Nat'l Corp., 345 F.2d 469 (9th Cir. 1965).

The proposed amended rule would recognize this practice but make an exception in cases in which a post trial motion has destroyed the finality of the judgment. See Note to Rule 4(a)(4) below.

Note to Subdivision (a)(4). The proposed amendment would make it clear that after the filing of the specified post trial motions, a notice of appeal should await disposition of the motion. Since the proposed amendments to Rules 3, 10, and 12 contemplate that immediately upon the filing of the notice of appeal the fees will be paid and the case docketed in the court of appeals, and the steps toward its disposition set in motion, it would be undesirable to proceed with the appeal while the district court has before it a motion the granting of which would vacate or alter the judgment appealed from. See, e.g., Kieth v. Newcourt, 530 F.2d 826 (8th Cir. 1976). Under the present rule, since docketing may not take place until the record is transmitted, premature filing is much less likely to involve waste effort. See, e.g., Stokes v. Peyton's Inc., 508 F.2d 1287 (5th Cir. 1975). Further, since a notice of appeal filed before the disposition of a post trial motion, even if it were treated as valid for purposes of jurisdiction, would not embrace objections to the denial of the motion, it is obviously preferable to postpone the notice of appeal until after the motion is disposed of.

The present rule, since it provides for the "termination" of the "running" of the appeal time, is ambiguous in its application to a notice of appeal filed prior to a post trial motion filed within the 10 day limit. The amendment would make it clear that in such circumstances the appellant should not proceed with the appeal during pendency of the motion but should file a new notice of appeal after the motion is disposed of.

Note to Subdivision (a)(5). Under the present rule it is provided that upon a showing of excusable neglect the district court at any time may extend the time for the filing of a notice of appeal for a period not to exceed 30 days from the expiration of the time otherwise prescribed by the rule, but that if the application is made after the original time has run, the order may be made only on motion with such notice as the court deems appropriate.

A literal reading of this provision would require that the extension be ordered and the notice of appeal filed within the 30 day period, but despite the surface clarity of the rule, it has produced considerable confusion. See the discussion by Judge Friendly in In re Orbitek, 520 F.2d 358 (2d Cir. 1975). The proposed amendment would make it clear that a motion to extend the time must be filed no later than 30 days after the expiration of the original appeal time, and that if the motion is timely filed the district court may act upon the motion at a later date, and may extend the time not in excess of 10 days measured from the date on which the order granting the motion is entered.

Under the present rule there is a possible implication that prior to the time the initial appeal time has run, the district court may extend the time on the basis of an informal application. The amendment would require that the application must be made by motion, though the motion may be made ex parte. After the expiration of the initial time a motion for the extension of the time must be made in compliance with the F.R.C.P. and local rules of the district court. See Note to proposed amended Rule 1, supra. And see Rules 6(d), 7(b) of the F.R.C.P.

The proposed amended rule expands to some extent the standard for the grant of an extension of time. The present rule requires a "showing of excusable neglect." While this was an appropriate standard in cases in which the motion is made after the time for filing the notice of appeal has run, and remains so, it has never fit exactly the situation in which the appellant seeks an extension before the expiration of the initial time. In such a case "good cause," which is the standard that is applied in the granting of other extensions of time under Rule 26(b) seems to be more appropriate.

Note to Subdivision (a)(6). The proposed amendment would call attention to the requirement of Rule 58 of the F.R.C.P. that the judgment constitute a separate document. See United States v. Indrelunas, 411 U.S. 216 (1973). When a notice of appeal is filed, the clerk should ascertain whether any judgment designated therein has been entered in compliance with Rules 58 and 79(a) and if not, so advise all parties and the district judge. While the requirement of Rule 48 is not jurisdictional, (see Bankers Trust Co. v. Mallis, 431 U.S. 928 (1977)), compliance is important since the time for the filing of a notice of appeal by other parties is measured by the time at which the judgment is properly entered.

Rule 5. Appeals by Permission Under 28 U.S.C. § 1292(b)

(a) Petition for Permission to Appeal. An appeal from an interlocutory order containing the statement prescribed by 28 U.S.C. § 1292(b) may be sought by filing a petition for permission to appeal with the clerk of the court of appeals within 10 days after the entry of such order in the district court with proof of service on all other parties to the action in the district court. An order may be amended to include the prescribed statement at any time, and permission to appeal may be sought within 10 days after entry of the order as amended.

(b) Content of Petition; Answer. The petition shall contain a statement of the facts neces-

sary to an understanding of the controlling question of law determined by the order of the district court; a statement of the question itself; and a statement of the reasons why a substantial basis exists for a difference of opinion on the question and why an immediate appeal may materially advance the termination of the litigation. The petition shall include or have annexed thereto a copy of the order from which appeal is sought and of any findings of fact, conclusions of law and opinion relating thereto. Within 7 days after service of the petition an adverse party may file an answer in opposition. The application and answer shall be submitted without oral argument unless otherwise ordered.

(c) Form of Papers; Number of Copies. All papers may be typewritten. Three copies shall be filed with the original, but the court may require that additional copies be furnished.

(d) Grant of Permission; Cost Bond; Filing of Record. Within 10 days after the entry of an order granting permission to appeal the appellant shall (1) pay to the clerk of the district court the fees established by statute and the docket fee prescribed by the Judicial Conference of the United States and (2) file a bond for costs if required pursuant to Rule 7. The clerk of the district court shall notify the clerk of the court of appeals of the payment of the fees. Upon receipt of such notice the clerk of the court of appeals shall enter the appeal upon the docket. The record shall be transmitted and filed in accordance with Rules 11 and 12(b). A notice of appeal need not be filed. (As amended Apr. 30, 1979, eff. Aug. 1, 1979.)

NOTES OF ADVISORY COMMITTEE ON APPELLATE RULES

This rule is derived in the main from Third Circuit Rule 11(2) which is similar to the rule governing appeals under 28 U.S.C. § 1292(b) in a majority of the circuits. The second sentence of subdivision (a) resolves a conflict over the question of whether the district court can amend an order by supplying the statement required by § 1292(b) at any time after entry of the order, with the result that the time fixed by the statute commences to run on the date of entry of the order as amended. Compare Milbert v. Bison Laboratories, 260 F.2d 431 (3d Cir., 1958) with Sperry Rand Corporation v. Bell Telephone Laboratories, 272 F.2d [29] (2d Cir. 1959), Hadjipateras v. Pacifica, S.A., 290 F.2d 697 (5th Cir. 1961), and Houston Fearless Corporation v. Teter, 313 F.2d 91 (10th Cir., 1962). The view taken by the Second, Fifth and Tenth Circuits seems theoretically and practically sound, and the rule adopts it. Although a majority of the circuits now require the filing of a notice of appeal following the grant of permission to appeal, filing of the notice serves no function other than to provide a time from which the time for transmitting the record and docketing the appeal begins to run.

1979 AMENDMENT

The proposed amendment adapts to the practice in appeals from interlocutory orders under 28 U.S.C. § 1292(b) the provisions of proposed Rule 3(e) above, requiring payment of all fees in the district court upon the filing of the notice of appeal. See Note to proposed amended Rule 3(e), supra.

Rule 5.1 Appeals by Permission Under 28 U.S.C. § 636(c)(5)

(a) Petition for Leave to Appeal; Answer or Cross Petition. An appeal from a district court judgment, entered after an appeal pursuant to 28 U.S.C. § 636(c)(4) to a judge of the district court from a judgment entered upon direction of a magistrate in a civil case, may be sought by filing a petition for leave to appeal. An appeal on petition for leave to appeal is not a matter of right, but its allowance is a matter of sound judicial discretion. The petition shall be filed with the clerk of the court of appeals within the time provided by Rule 4(a) for filing a notice of appeal, with proof of service on all parties to the action in the district court. A notice of appeal need not be filed. Within 14 days after service of the petition, a party may file an answer in opposition or a cross petition.

(b) Content of Petition; Answer. The petition for leave to appeal shall contain a statement of the facts necessary to an understanding of the questions to be presented by the appeal; a statement of those questions and of the relief sought; a statement of the reasons why in the opinion of the petitioner the appeal should be allowed; and a copy of the order, decree or judgment complained of and any opinion or memorandum relating thereto. The petition and answer shall be submitted to a panel of judges of the court of appeals without oral argument unless otherwise ordered.

(c) Form of Papers; Number of Copies. All papers may be typewritten. Three copies shall be filed with the original, but the court may require that additional copies be furnished.

(d) Allowance of the Appeal; Fees; Cost Bond; Filing of Record. Within 10 days after the entry of an order granting the appeal, the appellant shall (1) pay to the clerk of the district court the fees established by statute and the docket fee prescribed by the Judicial Conference of the United States and (2) file a bond for costs if required pursuant to Rule 7. The clerk of the district court shall notify the clerk of the court of appeals of the payment of the fees. Upon receipt of such notice, the clerk of the court of appeals shall enter the appeal upon the docket. The record shall be transmitted and filed in accordance with Rules 11 and 12(b).

(Added Mar. 10, 1986, eff. July 1, 1986.)

NOTES OF ADVISORY COMMITTEE ON APPELLATE RULES

When the initial appeal of a magistrate's decision is taken to the district court, the statute provides for a second discretionary appeal to the court of appeals. This rule provides the procedure for taking such an appeal.

Rule 6. Appeals by Allowance in Bankruptcy Proceedings

(a) Petition for Allowance. Allowance of an appeal under section 24 of the Bankruptcy Act (11 U.S.C. § 47) from orders, decrees, or judgments of a district court involving less than $500, or from an order making or refusing to make allowances of compensation or reimbursement under sections 250 or 498 thereof (11 U.S.C. § 650, § 898) shall be sought by filing a petition for allowance with the clerk of the court of appeals within the time provided by Rule 4(a) for filing a notice of appeal, with proof of service on all parties to the action in the district court. A notice of appeal need not be filed.

(b) Content of Petition; Answer. The petition shall contain a statement of the facts necessary to an understanding of the questions to be presented by the appeal; a statement of those questions and of the relief sought; a statement of the reasons why in the opinion of the petitioner the appeal should be allowed; and a copy of the order, decree or judgment complained of and of any opinion or memorandum relating thereto. Within 7 days after service of the petition an adverse party may file an answer in opposition. The petition and answer shall be submitted without oral argument unless otherwise ordered.

(c) Form of Papers; Number of Copies. All papers may be typewritten. Three copies shall be filed with the original, but the court may require that additional copies be furnished.

(d) Allowance of the Appeal; Fees; Cost Bond; Filing of Record. Within 10 days after the entry of an order granting permission to appeal the appellant shall (1) pay to the clerk of the district court the fees established by statute and the docket fee prescribed by the Judicial Conference of the United States and (2) file a bond for costs if required pursuant to Rule 7. The clerk of the district court shall notify the clerk of the court of appeals of the payment of the fees. Upon receipt of such notice the clerk of the court of appeals shall enter the appeal upon the docket. The record shall be transmitted and filed in accordance with Rules 11 and 12(b). A notice of appeal need not be filed.

(As amended Apr. 30, 1979, eff. Aug. 1, 1979.)

NOTES OF ADVISORY COMMITTEE ON APPELLATE RULES

This rule is substantially a restatement of present procedure. See D.C. Cir. Rule 34; 6th Cir. Rule 11; 7th Cir. Rule 10(d); 10th Cir. Rule 13.

Present circuit rules commonly provide that the petition for allowance of an appeal shall be filed within the time allowed by Section 25 of the Bankruptcy Act for taking appeals of right. For the reasons explained in the Note accompanying Rule 4, that rule makes the time for appeal in bankruptcy cases the same as that which obtains in other civil cases and thus supersedes Section 25. Thus the present rule simply continues the former practice of making the time for filing the petition in appeals by allowance the same as that provided for filing the notice of appeal in appeals of right.

1979 AMENDMENT

The proposed amendment adapts to the practice in appeals by allowance in bankruptcy proceedings the provisions of proposed Rule 3(e) above, requiring payment of all fees in the district court at the time of the filing of the notice of appeal. See Note to Rule 3(e), supra.

EDITORIAL NOTES

References in Text. The Bankruptcy Act, referred to in subd. (a), is Act July 1, 1898, c. 541, 30 Stat. 544, as amended. Sections 24, 250, and 498 of the Bankruptcy Act were classified to sections 47, 650, and 898, respectively, of former Title 11, prior to the repeal of the Bankruptcy Act by Pub.L. 95–598, Title IV, § 401(a), Nov. 6, 1978, 92 Stat. 2682. For selected provisions of the Bankruptcy Reform Act of 1978, see Pub.L. 95–598, Title 11, §§ 201–252, Title IV, §§ 401–411, Nov. 6, 1978, 92 Stat. 2657–2673, 2682–2688.

Rule 7.   Bond for Costs on Appeal in Civil Cases

The district court may require an appellant to file a bond or provide other security in such form and amount as it finds necessary to ensure payment of costs on appeal in a civil case. The provisions of Rule 8(b) apply to a surety upon a bond given pursuant to this rule.

(As amended Apr. 30, 1979, eff. Aug. 1, 1979.)

NOTES OF ADVISORY COMMITTEE ON APPELLATE RULES

This rule is derived from FRCP 73(c) without change in substance.

1979 AMENDMENT

The amendment would eliminate the provision of the present rule that requires the appellant to file a $250 bond for costs on appeal at the time of filing his notice of appeal. The $250 provision was carried forward in the F.R.App.P. from former Rule 73(c) of the F.R.Civ.P., and the $250 figure has remained unchanged since the adoption of that rule in 1937. Today it bears no relationship to actual costs. The amended rule would leave the question of the need for a bond for costs and its amount in the discretion of the court.

Rule 8.   Stay or Injunction Pending Appeal

(a) Stay Must Ordinarily Be Sought in the First Instance in District Court; Motion for Stay in Court of Appeals. Application for a stay of the judgment or order of a district court pending appeal, or for approval of a supersedeas bond, or for an order suspending, modifying, restoring or granting an injunction during the pendency of an appeal must ordinarily be made in the first instance in the district court. A motion for such relief may be made to the court of appeals or to a judge thereof, but the motion shall show that application to the district court for the relief sought is not practicable, or that the district court has denied an application, or has failed to afford the relief which the applicant requested, with the reasons given by the district court for its action. The motion shall also show the reasons for the relief requested and the facts relied upon, and if the facts are subject to dispute the motion shall be supported by affidavits or other sworn statements or copies thereof. With the motion shall be filed such parts of the record as are relevant. Reasonable notice of the motion shall be given to all parties. The motion shall be filed with the clerk and normally will be considered by a panel or division of the court, but in exceptional cases where such procedure would be impracticable due to the requirements of time, the application may be made to and considered by a single judge of the court.

(b) Stay May Be Conditioned Upon Giving of Bond; Proceedings Against Sureties. Relief available in the court of appeals under this rule may be conditioned upon the filing of a bond or other appropriate security in the district court. If security is given in the form of a bond or stipulation or other undertaking with one or more sureties, each surety submits to the jurisdiction of the district court and irrevocably appoints the clerk of the district court as the surety's agent upon whom any papers affecting the surety's liability on the bond or undertaking may be served. A surety's liability may be enforced on motion in the district court without the necessity of an independent action. The motion and such notice of the motion as the district court prescribes may be served on the clerk of the district court, who shall forthwith mail copies to the sureties if their addresses are known.

(c) Stays in Criminal Cases. Stays in criminal cases shall be had in accordance with the provisions of Rule 38(a) of the Federal Rules of Criminal Procedure.

(As amended Mar. 10, 1986, eff. July 1, 1986.)

NOTES OF ADVISORY COMMITTEE ON APPELLATE RULES

Subdivision (a). While the power of a court of appeals to stay proceedings in the district court during the pendency of an appeal is not explicitly conferred by statute, it exists by virtue of the all writs statute, 28 U.S.C. § 1651. Eastern Greyhound Lines v. Fusco, 310 F.2d 632 (6th Cir. 1962); United States v. Lynd, 301 F.2d 818 (5th Cir., 1962); Public Utilities Commission of Dist. of Col. v. Capital Transit Co., 94 U.S.App.D.C. 140, 214 F.2d 242 (1954). And the Supreme Court has termed the power "inherent" (In re McKenzie, 180 U.S. 536, 551, 21 S.Ct. 468, 45 L.Ed. 657 (1901)) and "part of its (the court of appeals) traditional equipment for the administration of justice." (Scripps-Howard Radio v. F.C.C., 316 U.S. 4, 9–10, 62 S.Ct. 875, 86 L.Ed. 1229 (1942)). The power of a single judge of the court of appeals to grant a stay pending appeal was recognized in In re McKenzie, supra. Alexander v. United States, 173 F.2d 865 (9th Cir., 1949) held that a single judge could not stay the judgment of a district court, but it noted the absence of a rule of court authorizing the

practice. FRCP 62(g) adverts to the grant of a stay by a single judge of the appellate court. The requirement that application be first made to the district court is the case law rule. Cumberland Tel. & Tel. Co. v. Louisiana Public Service Commission, 260 U.S. 212, 219, 43 S.Ct. 75, 67 L.Ed. 217 (1922); United States v. El–O–Pathic Pharmacy, 192 F.2d 62 (9th Cir., 1951); United States v. Hansell, 109 F.2d 613 (2d Cir., 1940). The requirement is explicitly stated in FRCrP 38(c) and in the rules of the First, Third, Fourth and Tenth Circuits. See also Supreme Court Rules 18 and 27.

The statement of the requirement in the proposed rule would work a minor change in present practice. FRCP 73(e) requires that if a bond for costs on appeal or a supersedeas bond is offered after the appeal is docketed, leave to file the bond must be obtained from the court of appeals. There appears to be no reason why matters relating to supersedeas and cost bonds should not be initially presented to the district court whenever they arise prior to the disposition of the appeal. The requirement of FRCP 73(e) appears to be a concession to the view that once an appeal is perfected, the district court loses all power over its judgment. See In re Federal Facilities Trust, 227 F.2d 651 (7th Cir., 1955) and cases—cited at 654–655. No reason appears why all questions related to supersedeas or the bond for costs on appeal should not be presented in the first instance to the district court in the ordinary case.

Subdivision (b). The provisions respecting a surety upon a bond or other undertaking are based upon FRCP 65.1.

1986 AMENDMENT

The amendments to Rule 8(b) are technical. No substantive change is intended.

Rule 9. Release in Criminal Cases

(a) Appeals from Orders Respecting Release Entered Prior to a Judgment of Conviction. An appeal authorized by law from an order refusing or imposing conditions of release shall be determined promptly. Upon entry of an order refusing or imposing conditions of release, the district court shall state in writing the reasons for the action taken. The appeal shall be heard without the necessity of briefs after reasonable notice to the appellee upon such papers, affidavits, and portions of the record as the parties shall present. The court of appeals or a judge thereof may order the release of the appellant pending the appeal.

(b) Release Pending Appeal from a Judgment of Conviction. Application for release after a judgment of conviction shall be made in the first instance in the district court. If the district court refuses release pending appeal, or imposes conditions of release, the court shall state in writing the reasons for the action taken. Thereafter, if an appeal is pending, a motion for release, or for modification of the conditions of release, pending review may be made to the court of appeals or to a judge thereof. The motion shall be determined promptly upon such papers, affidavits, and portions of the record as the parties shall present and after reasonable notice to the appellee. The court of appeals or a judge thereof may order the release of the appellant pending disposition of the motion.

(c) Criteria for Release. The decision as to release pending appeal shall be made in accordance with Title 18, U.S.C. § 3143. The burden of establishing that the defendant will not flee or pose a danger to any other person or to the community and that the appeal is not for purpose of delay and raises a substantial question of law or fact likely to result in reversal or in an order for a new trial rests with the defendant.

(As amended Apr. 24, 1972, eff. Oct. 1, 1972; Pub.L. 98–473, Title II, § 210, Oct. 12, 1984, 98 Stat. 1987.)

NOTES OF ADVISORY COMMITTEE ON APPELLATE RULES

1967 NOTE

Subdivision (a). The appealability of release orders entered prior to a judgment of conviction is determined by the provisions of 18 U.S.C. § 3147, as qualified by 18 U.S.C. § 3148, and by the rule announced in Stack v. Boyle, 342 U.S. 1, 72 S.Ct. 1, 96 L.Ed. 3 (1951), holding certain orders respecting release appealable as final orders under 28 U.S.C. § 1291. The language of the rule, "(a)n appeal authorized by law from an order refusing or imposing conditions of release," is intentionally broader than that used in 18 U.S.C. § 3147 in describing orders made appealable by that section. The summary procedure ordained by the rule is intended to apply to all appeals from orders respecting release, and it would appear that at least some orders not made appealable by 18 U.S.C. § 3147 are nevertheless appealable under the Stack v. Boyle rationale. See, for example, United States v. Foster, 278 F.2d 567 (2d Cir., 1960), holding appealable an order refusing to extend bail limits. Note also the provisions of 18 U.S.C. § 3148, which after withdrawing from persons charged with an offense punishable by death and from those who have been convicted of an offense the right of appeal granted by 18 U.S.C. § 3147, expressly preserves "other rights to judicial review of conditions of release or orders of detention."

The purpose of the subdivision is to insure the expeditious determination of appeals respecting release orders, an expedition commanded by 18 U.S.C. § 3147 and by the Court in *Stack v. Boyle,* supra. It permits such appeals to be heard on an informal record without the necessity of briefs and on reasonable notice. Equally important to the just and speedy disposition of these appeals is the requirement that the district court state the reasons for its decision. See Jones v. United States, 358 F.2d 543 (D.C.Cir. 1966); Rhodes v. United States, 275 F.2d 78 (4th Cir., 1960); United States v. Williams, 253 F.2d 144 (7th Cir., 1958).

Subdivision (b). This subdivision regulates procedure for review of an order respecting release at a time when the jurisdiction of the court of appeals has already attached by virtue of an appeal from the judgment of conviction. Notwithstanding the fact that jurisdiction has passed to the court of appeals, both 18 U.S.C. § 3148 and FRCrP 38(c) contemplate that the initial determination of whether a convicted defendant is to be released pending the appeal is to be made by the district court. But at this point there is obviously no need for a separate appeal from the order of the district court respecting release. The court of appeals or a judge thereof has power to effect release on motion as an incident to the pending appeal. See FRCrP 38(c) and 46(a)(2). But the motion is functionally identical with the appeal regulated by subdivision (a) and requires the same speedy determination if relief is to be effective. Hence the similarity of the procedure outlined in the two subdivisions.

1972 NOTE

Subdivision (c) is intended to bring the rule into conformity with 18 U.S.C. § 3148 and to allocate to the defendant the burden of establishing that he will not flee and that he poses no danger to any other person or to the community. The burden is placed upon the defendant in the view that the fact of his conviction justifies retention in custody in situations where doubt exists as to whether he can be safely released pending disposition of his appeal. Release pending appeal may also be denied if "it appears that an appeal is frivolous or taken for delay." 18 U.S.C. § 3148. The burden of establishing the existence of these criteria remains with the government.

Rule 10. The Record on Appeal

(a) Composition of the Record on Appeal. The original papers and exhibits filed in the district court, the transcript of proceedings, if any, and a certified copy of the docket entries prepared by the clerk of the district court shall constitute the record on appeal in all cases.

(b) The Transcript of Proceedings; Duty of Appellant to Order; Notice to Appellee if Partial Transcript is Ordered.

(1) Within 10 days after filing the notice of appeal the appellant shall order from the reporter a transcript of such parts of the proceedings not already on file as the appellant deems necessary, subject to local rules of the courts of appeals. The order shall be in writing and within the same period a copy shall be filed with the clerk of the district court. If funding is to come from the United States under the Criminal Justice Act, the order shall so state. If no such parts of the proceedings are to be ordered, within the same period the appellant shall file a certificate to that effect.

(2) If the appellant intends to urge on appeal that a finding or conclusion is unsupported by the evidence or is contrary to the evidence, the appellant shall include in the record a transcript of all evidence relevant to such finding or conclusion.

(3) Unless the entire transcript is to be included, the appellant shall, within the 10 days time provided in (b)(1) of this Rule 10, file a statement of the issues the appellant intends to present on the appeal and shall serve on the appellee a copy of the order or certificate and of the statement. If the appellee deems a transcript or other parts of the proceedings to be necessary, the appellee shall, within 10 days after the service of the order or certificate and the statement of the appellant, file and serve on the appellant a designation of additional parts to be included. Unless within 10 days after service of such designation the appellant has ordered such parts, and has so notified the appellee, the appellee may within the following 10 days either order the parts or move in the district court for an order requiring the appellant to do so.

(4) At the time of ordering, a party must make satisfactory arrangements with the reporter for payment of the cost of the transcript.

(c) Statement on the Evidence or Proceedings When No Report Was Made or When the Transcript is Unavailable. If no report of the evidence or proceedings at a hearing or trial was made, or if a transcript is unavailable, the appellant may prepare a statement of the evidence or proceedings from the best available means, including the appellant's recollection. The statement shall be served on the appellee, who may serve objections or proposed amendments thereto within 10 days after service. Thereupon the statement and any objections or proposed amendments shall be submitted to the district court for settlement and approval and as settled and approved shall be included by the clerk of the district court in the record on appeal.

(d) Agreed Statement as the Record on Appeal. In lieu of the record on appeal as defined in subdivision (a) of this rule, the parties may prepare and sign a statement of the case showing how the issues presented by the appeal arose and were decided in the district court and setting forth only so many of the facts averred and proved or sought to be proved as are essential to a decision of the issues presented. If the statement conforms to the truth, it, together with such additions as the court may consider necessary fully to present the issues raised by the appeal, shall be approved by the district court and shall then be certified to the court of appeals as the record on appeal and transmitted thereto by the clerk of the district court within the time provided by Rule 11. Copies of the agreed statement may be filed as the appendix required by Rule 30.

(e) Correction or Modification of the Record. If any difference arises as to whether the record truly discloses what occurred in the district court, the difference shall be submitted to and settled by that court and the record made to conform to the truth. If anything material to either party is omitted from the record by error or accident or is misstated therein, the parties by stipulation, or the district court either before or after the record is transmitted to the court of appeals, or the court of appeals, on proper suggestion or of its own initiative, may direct that the omission or misstatement be corrected, and if necessary that a supplemental record be certified and transmitted. All other questions as to the form and content of the record shall be presented to the court of appeals.

(As amended Apr. 30, 1979, eff. Aug. 1, 1979; Mar. 10, 1986, eff. July 1, 1986.)

NOTES OF ADVISORY COMMITTEE ON APPELLATE RULES

This rule is derived from FRCP 75(a), (b), (c) and (d) and FRCP 76, without change in substance.

1979 AMENDMENT

The proposed amendments to Rule 10(b) would require the appellant to place with the reporter a written order for the transcript of proceedings and file a copy with the clerk, and to indicate on the order if the transcript is to be provided under the Criminal Justice Act. If the appellant does not plan to order a transcript of any of the proceedings, he must file a certificate to that effect. These requirements make the appellant's steps in readying the appeal a matter of record and give the district court notice of requests for transcripts at the expense of the United States under the Criminal Justice Act. They are also the third step in giving the court of appeals some control over the production and transmission of the record. See Note to Rules 3(d), (e) above and Rule 11 below.

In the event the appellant orders no transcript, or orders a transcript of less than all the proceedings, the procedure under the proposed amended rule remains substantially as before. The appellant must serve on the appellee a copy of his order or in the event no order is placed, of the certificate to that effect, and a statement of the issues he intends to present on appeal, and the appellee may thereupon designate additional parts of the transcript to be included, and upon appellant's refusal to order the additional parts, may either order them himself or seek an order requiring the appellant to order them. The only change proposed in this procedure is to place a 10 day time limit on motions to require the appellant to order the additional portions.

Rule 10(b) is made subject to local rules of the courts of appeals in recognition of the practice in some circuits in some classes of cases, e.g., appeals by indigents in criminal cases after a short trial, of ordering immediate preparation of a complete transcript, thus making compliance with the rule unnecessary.

1986 AMENDMENT

The amendments to Rules 10(b) and (c) are technical. No substantive change is intended.

EDITORIAL NOTES

References in Text. The Criminal Justice Act, referred to in subd. (b)(1), probably means the Criminal Justice Act of 1964, Pub.L. 88–455, Aug. 20, 1964, 78 Stat. 552, which is classified to section 3006A of Title 18, U.S.C.A., Crimes and Criminal Procedure, set out post in this pamphlet.

Rule 11. Transmission of the Record

(a) **Duty of Appellant.** After filing the notice of appeal the appellant, or in the event that more than one appeal is taken, each appellant, shall comply with the provisions of Rule 10(b) and shall take any other action necessary to enable the clerk to assemble and transmit the record. A single record shall be transmitted.

(b) **Duty of Reporter to Prepare and File Transcript; Notice to Court of Appeals; Duty of Clerk to Transmit the Record.** Upon receipt of an order for a transcript, the reporter shall acknowledge at the foot of the order the fact that the reporter has received it and the date on which the reporter expects to have the transcript completed and shall transmit the order, so endorsed, to the clerk of the court of appeals. If the transcript cannot be completed within 30 days of receipt of the order the reporter shall request an extension of time from the clerk of the court of appeals and the action of the clerk of the court of appeals shall be entered on the docket and the parties notified. In the event of the failure of the reporter to file the transcript within the time allowed, the clerk of the court of appeals shall notify the district judge and take such other steps as may be directed by the court of appeals. Upon completion of the transcript the reporter shall file it with the clerk of the district court and shall notify the clerk of the court of appeals that the reporter has done so.

When the record is complete for purposes of the appeal, the clerk of the district court shall transmit it forthwith to the clerk of the court of appeals. The clerk of the district court shall number the documents comprising the record and shall transmit with the record a list of documents correspondingly numbered and identified with reasonable definiteness. Documents of unusual bulk or weight, physical exhibits other than documents, and such other parts of the record as the court of appeals may designate by local rule, shall not be transmitted by the clerk unless the clerk is directed to do so by a party or by the clerk of the court of appeals. A party must make advance arrangements with the clerks for the transportation and receipt of exhibits of unusual bulk or weight.

(c) **Temporary Retention of Record in District Court for Use in Preparing Appellate Papers.** Notwithstanding the provisions of (a) and (b) of this Rule 11, the parties may stipulate, or the district court on motion of any party may order, that the clerk of the district court shall temporarily retain the record for use by the parties in preparing appellate papers. In that event the clerk of the district court shall certify to the clerk of the court of appeals that the record, including the transcript or parts thereof, designated for inclusion and all necessary exhibits, is complete for purposes of the appeal. Upon receipt of the brief of the appellee, or at such earlier time as the parties may agree or the court may order, the appellant shall request the clerk of the district court to transmit the record.

(d) [Extension of Time for Transmission of the Record; Reduction of Time.] [Abrogated.]

(e) Retention of the Record in the District Court by Order of Court. The court of appeals may provide by rule or order that a certified copy of the docket entries shall be transmitted in lieu of the entire record, subject to the right of any party to request at any time during the pendency of the appeal that designated parts of the record be transmitted.

If the record or any part thereof is required in the district court for use there pending the appeal, the district court may make an order to that effect, and the clerk of the district court shall retain the record or parts thereof subject to the request of the court of appeals, and shall transmit a copy of the order and of the docket entries together with such parts of the original record as the district court shall allow and copies of such parts as the parties may designate.

(f) Stipulation of Parties that Parts of the Record be Retained in the District Court. The parties may agree by written stipulation filed in the district court that designated parts of the record shall be retained in the district court unless thereafter the court of appeals shall order or any party shall request their transmittal. The parts thus designated shall nevertheless be a part of the record on appeal for all purposes.

(g) Record for Preliminary Hearing in the Court of Appeals. If prior to the time the record is transmitted a party desires to make in the court of appeals a motion for dismissal, for release, for a stay pending appeal, for additional security on the bond on appeal or on a supersedeas bond, or for any intermediate order, the clerk of the district court at the request of any party shall transmit to the court of appeals such parts of the original record as any party shall designate.

(As amended Apr. 30, 1979, eff. Aug. 1, 1979; Mar. 10, 1986, eff. July 1, 1986.)

NOTES OF ADVISORY COMMITTEE ON APPELLATE RULES

Subdivisions (a) and (b). These subdivisions are derived from FRCP 73(g) and FRCP 75(e). FRCP 75(e) presently directs the clerk of the district court to transmit the record within the time allowed or fixed for its filing, which under the provisions of FRCP 73(g) is within 40 days from the date of filing the notice of appeal, unless an extension is obtained from the district court. The precise time at which the record must be transmitted thus depends upon the time required for delivery of the record from the district court to the court of appeals, since, to permit its timely filing, it must reach the court of appeals before expiration of the 40-day period of an extension thereof. Subdivision (a) of this rule provides that the record is to be transmitted within the 40-day period, or any extension thereof; subdivision (b) provides that transmission is effected when the clerk of the district court mails or otherwise forwards the record to the clerk of the court of appeals; Rule 12(b) directs the clerk of the court of appeals to file the record upon its receipt following timely docketing and transmittal. It can thus be determined with certainty precisely when the clerk of the district court must forward the record to the clerk of the court of appeals in order to effect timely filing: the final day of the 40-day period or of any extension thereof.

Subdivision (c). This subdivision is derived from FRCP 75(e) without change of substance.

Subdivision (d). This subdivision is derived from FRCP 73(g) and FRCrP 39(c). Under present rules the district court is empowered to extend the time for filing the record and docketing the appeal. Since under the proposed rule timely transmission now insures timely filing (see note to subdivisions (a) and (b) above) the power of the district court is expressed in terms of its power to extend the time for transmitting the record. Restriction of that power to a period of 90 days after the filing of the notice of appeal represents a change in the rule with respect to appeals in criminal cases. FRCrP 39(c) now permits the district court to extend the time for filing and docketing without restriction. No good reason appears for a difference between the civil and criminal rule in this regard, and subdivision (d) limits the power of the district court to extend the time for transmitting the record in all cases to 90 days from the date of filing the notice of appeal, just as its power is now limited with respect to docketing and filing in civil cases. Subdivision (d) makes explicit the power of the court of appeals to permit the record to be filed at any time. See Pyramid Motor Freight Corporation v. Ispass, 330 U.S. 695, 67 S.Ct. 954, 91 L.Ed. 1184 (1947).

Subdivisions (e), (f) and (g). These subdivisions are derived from FRCP 75(f), (a) and (g), respectively, without change of substance.

1979 AMENDMENT

Under present Rule 11(a) it is provided that the record shall be transmitted to the court of appeals within 40 days after the filing of the notice of appeal. Under present Rule 11(d) the district court, on request made during the initial time or any extension thereof, and cause shown, may extend the time for the transmission of the record to a point not more than 90 days after the filing of the first notice of appeal. If the district court is without authority to grant a request to extend the time, or denies a request for extension, the appellant may make a motion for extension of time in the court of appeals. Thus the duty to see that the record is transmitted is placed on the appellant. Aside from ordering the transcript within the time prescribed the appellant has no control over the time at which the record is transmitted, since all steps beyond this point are in the hands of the reporter and the clerk. The proposed amendments recognize this fact and place the duty directly on the reporter and the clerk. After receiving the written order for the transcript (See Note to Rule 10(b) above), the reporter must acknowledge its receipt, indicate when he expects to have it completed, and mail the order so endorsed to the clerk of the court of appeals. Requests for extensions of time must be made by the reporter to the clerk of the court of appeals and action on such requests is entered on the docket. Thus from the point at which the transcript is ordered the clerk of the court of appeals is made aware of any delays. If the transcript is not filed on time, the clerk of the court of appeals will notify the district judge.

Present Rule 11(b) provides that the record shall be transmitted when it is "complete for the purposes of the appeal." The proposed amended rule continues this requirement. The record is complete for the purposes of the appeal when it contains the original papers on file in the clerk's office, all necessary exhibits, and the transcript, if one is to be included. Cf. present Rule 11(c). The original papers will be in the custody of the clerk of the district court at the time the notice of appeal is filed. See Rule 5(e) of the F.R.C.P. The custody of exhibits is often the subject of local rules. Some of them require that documentary exhibits must be deposited with the clerk. See Local Rule 13 of the Eastern District of Virginia. Others leave exhibits with counsel, subject to order of the court. See Local Rule 33 of the Northern District of Illinois. If under local rules the custody of exhibits is left with counsel, the district court should make adequate provision for their preservation during the time during which an appeal may be taken, the prompt deposit with the clerk of such as under Rule 11(b) are to be transmitted to the court of appeals, and the availability of others in the event that the court of appeals should require their transmission. Cf. Local Rule 11 of the Second Circuit.

Usually the record will be complete with the filing of the transcript. While the proposed amendment requires transmission "forthwith" when the record is complete, it was not designed to preclude a local requirement by the court of appeals that the original papers and exhibits be transmitted when complete without awaiting the filing of the transcript.

The proposed amendments continue the provision in the present rule that documents of unusual bulk or weight and physical exhibits other than documents shall not be transmitted without direction by the parties or by the court of appeals, and the requirement that the parties make special arrangements for transmission and receipt of exhibits of unusual bulk or weight. In addition, they give recognition to local rules that make transmission of other record items subject to order of the court of appeals. See Local Rule 4 of the Seventh Circuit.

1986 AMENDMENT

The amendments to Rule 11(b) are technical. No substantive change is intended.

Rule 12. Docketing the Appeal; Filing of the Record

(a) **Docketing the Appeal.** Upon receipt of the copy of the notice of appeal and of the docket entries, transmitted by the clerk of the district court pursuant to Rule 3(d), the clerk of the court of appeals shall thereupon enter the appeal upon the docket. An appeal shall be docketed under the title given to the action in the district court, with the appellant identified as such, but if such title does not contain the name of the appellant, the appellant's name, identified as appellant, shall be added to the title.

(b) **Filing the Record, Partial Record, or Certificate.** Upon receipt of the record transmitted pursuant to Rule 11(b), or the partial record transmitted pursuant to Rule 11(e), (f), or (g), or the clerk's certificate under Rule 11(c), the clerk of the court of appeals shall file it and shall immediately give notice to all parties of the date on which it was filed.

(c) **[Dismissal for Failure of Appellant to Cause Timely Transmission or to Docket Appeal] [Abrogated]**

(As amended Apr. 30, 1979, eff. Aug. 1, 1979; Mar. 10, 1986, eff. July 1, 1986.)

NOTES OF ADVISORY COMMITTEE ON APPELLATE RULES

Subdivision (a). All that is involved in the docketing of an appeal is the payment of the docket fee. In practice, after the clerk of the court of appeals receives the record from the clerk of the district court he notifies the appellant of its receipt and requests payment of the fee. Upon receipt of the fee, the clerk enters the appeal upon the docket and files the record. The appellant is allowed to pay the fee at any time within the time allowed or fixed for transmission of the record and thereby to discharge his responsibility for docketing. The final sentence is added in the interest of facilitating future reference and citation and location of cases in indexes. Compare 3d Cir. Rule 10(2); 4th Cir. Rule 9(8); 6th Cir. Rule 14(1).

Subdivision (c). The rules of the circuits generally permit the appellee to move for dismissal in the event the appellant fails to effect timely filing of the record. See 1st Cir. Rule 21(3); 3d Cir. Rule 21(4); 5th Cir. Rule 16(1); 8th Cir. Rule 7(d).

1979 AMENDMENT

Note to Subdivision (a). Under present Rule 12(a) the appellant must pay the docket fee within the time fixed for the transmission of the record, and upon timely payment of the fee, the appeal is docketed. The proposed amendment takes the docketing out of the hands of the appellant. The fee is paid at the time the

notice of appeal is filed and the appeal is entered on the docket upon receipt of a copy of the notice of appeal and of the docket entries, which are sent to the court of appeals under the provisions of Rule 3(d). This is designed to give the court of appeals control of its docket at the earliest possible time so that within the limits of its facilities and personnel it can screen cases for appropriately different treatment, expedite the proceedings through prehearing conferences or otherwise, and in general plan more effectively for the prompt disposition of cases.

Note to Subdivision (b). The proposed amendment conforms the provision to the changes in Rule 11.

1986 AMENDMENT

The amendment to Rule 12(a) is technical. No substantive change is intended.

TITLE III

REVIEW OF DECISIONS OF THE UNITED STATES TAX COURT

Rule 13. Review of Decisions of the Tax Court

(a) How Obtained; Time for Filing Notice of Appeal. Review of a decision of the United States Tax Court shall be obtained by filing a notice of appeal with the clerk of the Tax Court within 90 days after the decision of the Tax Court is entered. If a timely notice of appeal is filed by one party, any other party may take an appeal by filing a notice of appeal within 120 days after the decision of the Tax Court is entered.

The running of the time for appeal is terminated as to all parties by a timely motion to vacate or revise a decision made pursuant to the Rules of Practice of the Tax Court. The full time for appeal commences to run and is to be computed from the entry of an order disposing of such motion, or from the entry of decision, whichever is later.

(b) Notice of Appeal—How Filed. The notice of appeal may be filed by deposit in the office of the clerk of the Tax Court in the District of Columbia or by mail addressed to the clerk. If a notice is delivered to the clerk by mail and is received after expiration of the last day allowed for filing, the postmark date shall be deemed to be the date of delivery, subject to the provisions of § 7502 of the Internal Revenue Code of 1954, as amended, and the regulations promulgated pursuant thereto.

(c) Content of the Notice of Appeal; Service of the Notice; Effect of Filing and Service of the Notice. The content of the notice of appeal, the manner of its service, and the effect of the filing of the notice and of its service shall be as prescribed by Rule 3. Form 2 in the Appendix of Forms is a suggested form of the notice of appeal.

(d) The Record on Appeal; Transmission of the Record; Filing of the Record. The provisions of Rules 10, 11 and 12 respecting the record and the time and manner of its transmission and filing and the docketing of the appeal in the court of appeals in cases on appeal from the district courts shall govern in cases on appeal from the Tax Court. Each reference in those rules and in Rule 3 to the district court and to the clerk of the district court shall be read as a reference to the Tax Court and to the clerk of the Tax Court respectively. If appeals are taken from a decision of the Tax Court to more than one court of appeals, the original record shall be transmitted to the court of appeals named in the first notice of appeal filed. Provision for the record in any other appeal shall be made upon appropriate application by the appellant to the court of appeals to which such other appeal is taken.

(As amended Apr. 30, 1979, eff. Aug. 1, 1979.)

NOTES OF ADVISORY COMMITTEE ON APPELLATE RULES

Subdivision (a). This subdivision effects two changes in practice respecting review of Tax Court decisions: (1) Section 7483 of the Internal Revenue Code, 68A Stat. 891, 26 U.S.C. § 7483, provides that review of a Tax Court decision may be obtained by filing a petition for review. The subdivision provides for review by the filing of the simple and familiar notice of appeal used to obtain review of district court judgments; (2) Section 7483, supra, requires that a petition for review be filed within 3 months after a decision is rendered, and provides that if a petition is so filed by one party, any other party may file a petition for review within 4 months after the decision is rendered. In the interest of fixing the time for review with precision, the proposed rule substitutes "90 days" and "120 days" for the statutory "3 months" and "4 months", respectively. The power of the Court to regulate these details of practice is clear. Title 28 U.S.C. § 2072, as amended by the Act of November 6, 1966, 80 Stat. 1323 (1 U.S.Code Cong. & Ad. News, p. 1546 (1966)), authorizes the Court to regulate "... practice and procedure in proceedings for the review by the courts of appeals of decisions of the Tax Court of the United States. ..."

The second paragraph states the settled teaching of the case law. See Robert Louis Stevenson Apartments, Inc. v. C.I.R., 337 F.2d 681, 10 A.L.R.3d 112 (8th Cir., 1964); Denholm & McKay Co. v. C.I.R., 132 F.2d 243 (1st Cir., 1942); Helvering v. Continental Oil Co., 63 App.D.C. 5, 68 F.2d 750 (1934); Burnet v. Lexington Ice & Coal Co., 62 F.2d 906 (4th Cir., 1933); Griffiths v. C.I.R., 50 F.2d 782 (7th Cir., 1931).

Subdivision (b). The subdivision incorporates the statutory provision (Title 26, U.S.C. § 7502) that timely mailing is to be treated as timely filing. The statute contains special provisions respecting other than ordinary mailing. If the notice of appeal is sent by registered mail, registration is deemed prima facie evidence that the notice was delivered to the clerk of the Tax Court, and the date of registration is deemed the postmark date. If the notice of appeal is sent by certified mail, the effect of certification with respect to prima facie evidence of delivery and the postmark date depends upon regulations of the Secretary of the Treasury. The effect of a postmark made other than by the United States Post Office likewise depends upon regulations of the Secretary. Current regulations are found in 26 CFR § 301.7502–1.

1979 AMENDMENT

The proposed amendment reflects the change in the title of the Tax Court to "United States Tax Court." See 26 U.S.C. § 7441.

Rule 14. Applicability of other Rules to Review of Decisions of the Tax Court

All provisions of these rules are applicable to review of a decision of the Tax Court, except that Rules 4–9, Rules 15–20, and Rules 22 and 23 are not applicable.

NOTES OF ADVISORY COMMITTEE ON APPELLATE RULES

The proposed rule continues the present uniform practice of the circuits of regulating review of decisions of the Tax Court by the general rules applicable to appeals from judgments of the district courts.

TITLE IV

REVIEW AND ENFORCEMENT OF ORDERS OF ADMINISTRATIVE AGENCIES, BOARDS, COMMISSIONS AND OFFICERS

Rule 15. Review or Enforcement of Agency Orders—How Obtained; Intervention

(a) **Petition for Review of Order; Joint Petition.** Review of an order of an administrative agency, board, commission or officer (hereinafter, the term "agency" shall include agency, board, commission or officer) shall be obtained by filing with the clerk of a court of appeals which is authorized to review such order, within the time prescribed by law, a petition to enjoin, set aside, suspend, modify or otherwise review, or a notice of appeal, whichever form is indicated by the applicable statute (hereinafter, the term "petition for review" shall include a petition to enjoin, set aside, suspend, modify or otherwise review, or a notice of appeal). The petition shall specify the parties seeking review and shall designate the respondent and the order or part thereof to be reviewed. Form 3 in the Appendix of Forms is a suggested form of a petition for review. In each case the agency shall be named respondent. The United States shall also be deemed a respondent if so required by statute, even though not so designated in the petition. If two or more persons are entitled to petition the same court for review of the same order and their interests are such as to make joinder practicable, they may file a joint petition for review and may thereafter proceed as a single petitioner.

(b) **Application for Enforcement of Order; Answer; Default; Cross-Application for En-**

forcement. An application for enforcement of an order of an agency shall be filed with the clerk of a court of appeals which is authorized to enforce the order. The application shall contain a concise statement of the proceedings in which the order was entered, the facts upon which venue is based, and the relief prayed. Within 20 days after the application is filed, the respondent shall serve on the petitioner and file with the clerk an answer to the application. If the respondent fails to file an answer within such time, judgment will be awarded for the relief prayed. If a petition is filed for review of an order which the court has jurisdiction to enforce, the respondent may file a cross-application for enforcement.

(c) **Service of Petition or Application.** A copy of a petition for review or of an application or cross-application for enforcement of an order shall be served by the clerk of the court of appeals on each respondent in the manner prescribed by Rule 3(d), unless a different manner of service is prescribed by an applicable statute. At the time of filing, the petitioner shall furnish the clerk with a copy of the petition or application for each respondent. At or before the time of filing a petition for review, the petitioner shall serve a copy thereof on all parties who shall have been admitted to participate in the proceedings before the agency other than respondents to be served by the clerk, and shall file with the clerk a list of those so served.

(d) **Intervention.** Unless an applicable statute provides a different method of intervention, a person who desires to intervene in a proceeding under this rule shall serve upon all parties to the proceeding and file with the clerk of the court of appeals a motion for leave to intervene. The motion shall contain a concise statement of the interest of the moving party and the grounds upon which intervention is sought. A motion for leave to intervene or other notice of intervention authorized by an applicable statute shall be filed within 30 days of the date on which the petition for review is filed.

NOTES OF ADVISORY COMMITTEE ON APPELLATE RULES

General Note. The power of the Supreme Court to prescribe rules of practice and procedure for the judicial review or enforcement of orders of administrative agencies, boards, commissions, and officers is conferred by 28 U.S.C. § 2072, as amended by the Act of November 6, 1966, § 1, 80 Stat. 1323 (1 U.S. Code Cong. & Ad. News,

p. 1546 (1966)). Section 11 of the Hobbs Administrative Orders Review Act of 1950, 64 Stat. 1132, reenacted as 28 U.S.C. § 2352 (28 U.S.C.A. § 2352 (Suppl.1966)), repealed by the Act of November 6, 1966, § 4, supra, directed the courts of appeals to adopt and promulgate, subject to approval by the Judicial Conference rules governing practice and procedure in proceedings to review the orders of boards, commissions and officers whose orders were made reviewable in the courts of appeals by the Act. Thereafter, the Judicial Conference approved a uniform rule, and that rule, with minor variations, is now in effect in all circuits. Third Circuit Rule 18 is a typical circuit rule, and for convenience it is referred to as the uniform rule in the notes which accompany rules under this Title.

Subdivision (a). The uniform rule (see General Note above) requires that the petition for review contain "a concise statement, in barest outline, of the nature of the proceedings as to which relief is sought, the facts upon which venue is based, the grounds upon which relief is sought, and the relief prayed." That language is derived from Section 4 of the Hobbs Administrative Orders Review Act of 1950, 64 Stat. 1130, reenacted as 28 U.S.C. § 2344 (28 U.S.C.A. § 2344 (Suppl.1966)). A few other statutes also prescribe the content of the petition, but the great majority are silent on the point. The proposed rule supersedes 28 U.S.C. § 2344 and other statutory provisions prescribing the form of the petition for review and permits review to be initiated by the filing of a simple petition similar in form to the notice of appeal used in appeals from judgments of district courts. The more elaborate form of petition for review now required is rarely useful either to the litigants or to the courts. There is no effective, reasonable way of obliging petitioners to come to the real issues before those issues are formulated in the briefs. Other provisions of this subdivision are derived from sections 1 and 2 of the uniform rule.

Subdivision (b). This subdivision is derived from sections 3, 4 and 5 of the uniform rule.

Subdivision (c). This subdivision is derived from section 1 of the uniform rule.

Subdivision (d). This subdivision is based upon section 6 of the uniform rule. Statutes occasionally permit intervention by the filing of a notice of intention to intervene. The uniform rule does not fix a time limit for intervention, and the only time limits fixed by statute are the 30-day periods found in the Communications Act Amendments, 1952, § 402(e), 66 Stat. 719, 47 U.S.C. § 402(e), and the Sugar Act of 1948, § 205(d), 61 Stat. 927, 7 U.S.C. § 1115(d).

Rule 15.1 Briefs and Oral Argument in National Labor Relations Board Proceedings

Each party adverse to the National Labor Relations Board in an enforcement or a review proceeding shall proceed first on briefing and at oral argument unless the court orders otherwise.

(Added Mar. 10, 1986, eff. July 1, 1986.)

NOTES OF ADVISORY COMMITTEE ON
APPELLATE RULES

This rule simply confirms the existing practice in most circuits.

Rule 16.　The Record on Review or Enforcement

(a) Composition of the Record. The order sought to be reviewed or enforced, the findings or report on which it is based, and the pleadings, evidence and proceedings before the agency shall constitute the record on review in proceedings to review or enforce the order of an agency.

(b) Omissions from or Misstatements in the Record. If anything material to any party is omitted from the record or is misstated therein, the parties may at any time supply the omission or correct the misstatement by stipulation, or the court may at any time direct that the omission or misstatement be corrected and, if necessary, that a supplemental record be prepared and filed.

NOTES OF ADVISORY COMMITTEE ON
APPELLATE RULES

Subdivision (a) is based upon 28 U.S.C. § 2112(b). There is no distinction between the record compiled in the agency proceeding and the record on review; they are one and the same. The record in agency cases is thus the same as that in appeals from the district court—the original papers, transcripts and exhibits in the proceeding below. Subdivision (b) is based upon section 8 of the uniform rule (see General Note following Rule 15).

Rule 17.　Filing of the Record

(a) Agency to File; Time for Filing; Notice of Filing. The agency shall file the record with the clerk of the court of appeals within 40 days after service upon it of the petition for review unless a different time is provided by the statute authorizing review. In enforcement proceedings the agency shall file the record within 40 days after filing an application for enforcement, but the record need not be filed unless the respondent has filed an answer contesting enforcement of the order, or unless the court otherwise orders. The court may shorten or extend the time above prescribed. The clerk shall give notice to all parties of the date on which the record is filed.

(b) Filing—What Constitutes. The agency may file the entire record or such parts thereof as the parties may designate by stipulation filed with the agency. The original papers in the agency proceeding or certified copies thereof may be filed. Instead of filing the record or designated parts thereof, the agency may file a certified list of all documents, transcripts of testimony, exhibits and other material comprising the record, or a list of such parts thereof as the parties may designate, adequately describing each, and the filing of the certified list shall constitute filing of the record. The parties may stipulate that neither the record nor a certified list be filed with the court. The stipulation shall be filed with the clerk of the court of appeals and the date of its filing shall be deemed the date on which the record is filed. If a certified list is filed, or if the parties designate only parts of the record for filing or stipulate that neither the record nor a certified list be filed, the agency shall retain the record or parts thereof. Upon request of the court or the request of a party, the record or any part thereof thus retained shall be transmitted to the court notwithstanding any prior stipulation. All parts of the record retained by the agency shall be a part of the record on review for all purposes.

NOTES OF ADVISORY COMMITTEE ON
APPELLATE RULES

Subdivision (a). This subdivision is based upon section 7 of the uniform rule (see General Note following Rule 15). That rule does not prescribe a time for filing the record in enforcement cases. Forty days are allowed in order to avoid useless preparation of the record or certified list in cases where the application for enforcement is not contested.

Subdivision (b). This subdivision is based upon 28 U.S.C. § 2112 and section 7 of the uniform rule. It permits the agency to file either the record itself or a certified list of its contents. It also permits the parties to stipulate against transmission of designated parts of the record without the fear that an inadvertent stipulation may "diminish" the record. Finally, the parties may, in cases where consultation of the record is unnecessary, stipulate that neither the record nor a certified list of its contents be filed.

Rule 18.　Stay Pending Review

Application for a stay of a decision or order of an agency pending direct review in the court of appeals shall ordinarily be made in the first instance to the agency. A motion for such relief may be made to the court of appeals or to a judge thereof, but the motion shall show that application to the agency for the relief sought is not practicable, or that application has been made to the agency and denied, with the reasons given by it for denial, or that the action of the agency did not afford the relief which the applicant had requested. The motion shall also show the reasons for the relief requested and the facts relied upon, and if the facts are subject to dispute the motion shall be supported by affidavits or other sworn statements or copies thereof. With the motion shall be filed such parts of the record as are relevant to the relief sought. Reasonable notice of the motion shall be given to all parties to the proceeding in the court of appeals. The court may condition relief under this rule upon the filing of a bond or other appropriate security. The motion shall be filed with the clerk and normally will be considered by a panel or division of the court, but in exceptional cases where such procedure would be impracticable due to the requirements of time, the application may be made to and considered by a single judge of the court.

NOTES OF ADVISORY COMMITTEE ON APPELLATE RULES

While this rule has no counterpart in present rules regulating review of agency proceedings, it merely assimilates the procedure for obtaining stays in agency proceedings with that for obtaining stays in appeals from the district courts. The same considerations which justify the requirement of an initial application to the district court for a stay pending appeal support the requirement of an initial application to the agency pending review. See Note accompanying Rule 8. Title 5, U.S.C. § 705 (5 U.S.C.A. § 705 (1966 Pamphlet)) confers general authority on both agencies and reviewing courts to stay agency action pending review. Many of the statutes authorizing review of agency action by the courts of appeals deal with the question of stays, and at least one, the Act of June 15, 1936, 49 Stat. 1499 (7 U.S.C. § 10a), prohibits a stay pending review. The proposed rule in nowise affects such statutory provisions respecting stays. By its terms, it simply indicates the procedure to be followed when a stay is sought.

Rule 19. Settlement of Judgments Enforcing Orders

When an opinion of the court is filed directing the entry of a judgment enforcing in part the order of an agency, the agency shall within 14 days thereafter serve upon the respondent and file with the clerk a proposed judgment in conformity with the opinion. If the respondent objects to the proposed judgment as not in conformity with the opinion, the respondent shall within 7 days thereafter serve upon the agency and file with the clerk a proposed judgment which the respondent deems to be in conformity with the opinion. The court will thereupon settle the judgment and direct its entry without further hearing or argument.

(As amended Mar. 10, 1986, eff. July 1, 1986.)

NOTES OF ADVISORY COMMITTEE ON APPELLATE RULES

This is section 12 of the uniform rule (see General Note following Rule 15) with changes in phraseology.

1986 AMENDMENT

The deletion of the words "in whole or" is designed to eliminate delay in the issuance of a judgment when the court of appeals has either enforced completely the order of an agency or denied completely such enforcement. In such a clear-cut situation, it serves no useful purpose to delay the issuance of the judgment until a proposed judgment is submitted by the agency and reviewed by the respondent. This change conforms the Rule to the existing practice in most circuits. Other amendments are technical and no substantive change is intended.

Rule 20. Applicability of other Rules to Review or Enforcement of Agency Orders

All provisions of these rules are applicable to review or enforcement of orders of agencies, except that Rules 3–14 and Rules 22 and 23 are not applicable. As used in any applicable rule, the term "appellant" includes a petitioner and the term "appellee" includes a respondent in proceedings to review or enforce agency orders.

NOTES OF ADVISORY COMMITTEE ON APPELLATE RULES

The proposed rule continues the present uniform practice of the circuits of regulating agency review or enforcement proceedings by the general rules applicable to appeals from judgments of the district courts.

TITLE V

EXTRAORDINARY WRITS

Rule 21. Writs of Mandamus and Prohibition Directed to a Judge or Judges and other Extraordinary Writs

(a) Mandamus or Prohibition to a Judge or Judges; Petition for Writ; Service and Filing. Application for a writ of mandamus or of prohibition directed to a judge or judges shall be made by filing a petition therefor with the clerk of the court of appeals with proof of service on the respondent judge or judges and on all parties to the action in the trial court. The petition shall contain a statement of the facts necessary to an understanding of the issues presented by the application; a statement of the issues presented and of the relief sought; a statement of the reasons why the writ should issue; and copies of any order or opinion or parts of the record which may be essential to an understanding of the matters set forth in the petition. Upon receipt of the prescribed docket fee, the clerk shall docket the petition and submit it to the court.

(b) Denial; Order Directing Answer. If the court is of the opinion that the writ should not be granted, it shall deny the petition. Otherwise, it shall order that an answer to the petition be filed by the respondents within the time fixed by the order. The order shall be served by the clerk on the judge or judges named respondents and on all other parties to the action in the trial court. All parties below other than the petitioner shall also be deemed respondents for all purposes. Two or more respondents may answer jointly. If the judge or judges named respondents do not desire to appear in the proceeding, they may so advise the clerk and all parties by letter, but the petition shall not thereby be taken as admitted. The clerk shall advise the parties of the dates on which briefs are to be filed, if briefs are required, and of the date of oral argument. The proceeding shall be given preference over ordinary civil cases.

(c) Other Extraordinary Writs. Application for extraordinary writs other than those provided for in subdivisions (a) and (b) of this rule shall be made by petition filed with the clerk of the court of appeals with proof of service on the parties named as respondents. Proceedings on such application shall conform, so far as is practicable, to the procedure prescribed in subdivisions (a) and (b) of this rule.

(d) Form of Papers; Number of Copies. All papers may be typewritten. Three copies shall be filed with the original, but the court may direct that additional copies be furnished.

NOTES OF ADVISORY COMMITTEE ON APPELLATE RULES

The authority of courts of appeals to issue extraordinary writs is derived from 28 U.S.C. § 1651. Subdivisions (a) and (b) regulate in detail the procedure surrounding the writs most commonly sought—mandamus or prohibition directed to a judge or judges. Those subdivisions are based upon Supreme Court Rule 31, with certain changes which reflect the uniform practice among the circuits (Seventh Circuit Rule 19 is a typical circuit rule). Subdivision (c) sets out a very general procedure to be followed in applications for the variety of other writs which may be issued under the authority of 28 U.S.C. § 1651.

TITLE VI

HABEAS CORPUS; PROCEEDINGS IN FORMA PAUPERIS

Rule 22. Habeas Corpus Proceedings

(a) Application for the Original Writ. An application for a writ of habeas corpus shall be made to the appropriate district court. If application is made to a circuit judge, the application will ordinarily be transferred to the appropriate district court. If an application is made to or transferred to the district court and denied, renewal of the application before a circuit judge is not favored; the proper remedy is by appeal to the court of appeals from the order of the district court denying the writ.

(b) Necessity of Certificate of Probable Cause for Appeal. In a habeas corpus proceeding in which the detention complained of arises out of process issued by a state court, an appeal by the applicant for the writ may not proceed unless a district or a circuit judge issues a certificate of probable cause. If an appeal is taken by the applicant, the district judge who rendered the judgment shall either issue a certificate of probable cause or state the reasons why such a certificate should not issue. The certificate or the statement shall be forwarded to the court of appeals with the notice of appeal and the file of the proceedings in the district court. If the district judge has denied the certificate, the applicant for the writ may then request issuance of the certificate by a circuit judge. If such a request is addressed to the court of appeals, it shall be deemed addressed to the judges thereof and shall be considered by a circuit judge or judges as the court deems appropriate. If no express request for a certificate is filed, the notice of appeal shall be deemed to constitute a request addressed to the judges of the court of appeals. If an appeal is taken by a state or its representative, a certificate of probable cause is not required.

NOTES OF ADVISORY COMMITTEE ON APPELLATE RULES

Subdivision (a). Title 28 U.S.C. § 2241(a) authorizes circuit judges to issue the writ of habeas corpus. Section 2241(b), however, authorizes a circuit judge to decline to entertain an application and to transfer it to the appropriate district court, and this is the usual practice. The first two sentences merely make present practice explicit. Title 28 U.S.C. § 2253 seems clearly to contemplate that once an application is presented to a district judge and is denied by him, the remedy is an appeal from the order of denial. But the language of 28 U.S.C. § 2241 seems to authorize a second original application to a circuit judge following a denial by a district judge. In re Gersing, 79 U.S.App.D.C. 245, 145 F.2d 481 (D.C.Cir., 1944) and Chapman v. Teets, 241 F.2d 186 (9th Cir., 1957) acknowledge the availability of such a procedure. But the procedure is ordinarily a waste of time for all involved, and the final sentence attempts to discourage it.

A court of appeals has no jurisdiction as a court to grant an original writ of habeas corpus, and courts of appeals have dismissed applications addressed to them. Loum v. Alvis, 263 F.2d 836 (6th Cir., 1959); In re Berry, 221 F.2d 798 (9th Cir., 1955); Posey v. Dowd, 134 F.2d 613 (7th Cir., 1943). The fairer and more expeditious practice is for the court of appeals to regard an application addressed to it as being addressed to one of its members, and to transfer the application to the appropriate district court in accordance with the provisions of this rule. Perhaps such a disposition is required by the rationale of In re Burwell, 350 U.S. 521, 76 S.Ct. 539, 100 L.Ed. 666 (1956).

Subdivision (b). Title 28 U.S.C. § 2253 provides that an appeal may not be taken in a habeas corpus proceeding where confinement is under a judgment of a state court unless the judge who rendered the order in the habeas corpus proceeding, or a circuit justice or judge, issues a certificate of probable cause. In the interest of insuring that the matter of the certificate will not be overlooked and that, if the certificate is denied, the reasons for denial in the first instance will be available on any subsequent application, the proposed rule requires the district judge to issue the certificate or to state reasons for its denial.

While 28 U.S.C. § 2253 does not authorize the court of appeals as a court to grant a certificate of probable cause, In re Burwell, 350 U.S. 521, 76 S.Ct. 539, 100 L.Ed. 666 (1956) makes it clear that a court of appeals may not decline to consider a request for the certificate addressed to it as a court but must regard the request as made to the judges thereof. The fourth sentence incorporates the Burwell rule.

Although 28 U.S.C. § 2253 appears to require a certificate of probable cause even when an appeal is taken by a state or its representative, the legislative history strongly suggests that the intention of Congress was to require a certificate only in the case in which an appeal is taken by an applicant for the writ. See United States ex rel. Tillery v. Cavell, 294 F.2d 12 (3d Cir., 1960). Four of the five circuits which have ruled on the point have so interpreted section 2253. United States ex rel. Tillery v. Cavell, supra; Buder v. Bell, 306 F.2d 71 (6th Cir.1962); United States ex rel. Calhoun v. Pate, 341 F.2d 885 (7th Cir., 1965); State of Texas v. Graves, 352 F.2d 514 (5th Cir., 1965). Cf. United States ex rel. Carrol v. LaVallee, 342 F.2d 641 (2d Cir., 1965). The final sentence makes it clear that a certificate of probable cause is not required of a state or its representative.

Rule 23. Custody of Prisoners in Habeas Corpus Proceedings

(a) Transfer of Custody Pending Review. Pending review of a decision in a habeas corpus proceeding commenced before a court, justice or judge of the United States for the release of a prisoner, a person having custody of the prisoner shall not transfer custody to another unless such transfer is directed in accordance with the provisions of this rule. Upon application of a custodian showing a need therefor, the court, justice or judge rendering the decision may make an order authorizing transfer and providing for the substitution of the successor custodian as a party.

(b) Detention or Release of Prisoner Pending Review of Decision Failing to Release. Pending review of a decision failing or refusing to release a prisoner in such a proceeding, the prisoner may be detained in the custody from which release is sought, or in other appropriate custody, or may be enlarged upon the prisoner's recognizance, with or without surety, as may appear fitting to the court or justice or judge rendering the decision, or to the court of appeals or to the Supreme Court, or to a judge or justice of either court.

(c) Release of Prisoner Pending Review of Decision Ordering Release. Pending review of a decision ordering the release of a prisoner in such a proceeding, the prisoner shall be enlarged upon the prisoner's recognizance, with or without surety, unless the court or justice or judge rendering the decision, or the court of appeals or the Supreme Court, or a judge or justice of either court shall otherwise order.

(d) Modification of Initial Order Respecting Custody. An initial order respecting the custody or enlargement of the prisoner and any recognizance or surety taken, shall govern review in the court of appeals and in the Supreme Court unless for special reasons shown to the court of appeals or to the Supreme Court, or to a judge or justice of either court, the order shall be modified, or an independent order respecting custody, enlargement or surety shall be made.

(As amended Mar. 10, 1986, eff. July 1, 1986.)

NOTES OF ADVISORY COMMITTEE ON APPELLATE RULES

The rule is the same as Supreme Court Rule 49, as amended on June 12, 1967, effective October 2, 1967 [see 1980 Revised Supreme Court Rule 41, effective June 30, 1980].

1986 AMENDMENT

The amendments to Rules 23(b) and (c) are technical. No substantive change is intended.

Rule 24. Proceedings in Forma Pauperis

(a) Leave to Proceed on Appeal in Forma Pauperis from District Court to Court of Appeals. A party to an action in a district court who desires to proceed on appeal in forma pauperis shall file in the district court a motion for leave so to proceed, together with an affidavit, showing, in the detail prescribed by Form 4 of the Appendix of Forms, the party's inability to pay fees and costs or to give security therefor, the party's belief that that party is entitled to redress, and a statement of the issues which that

party intends to present on appeal. If the motion is granted, the party may proceed without further application to the court of appeals and without prepayment of fees or costs in either court or the giving of security therefor. If the motion is denied, the district court shall state in writing the reasons for the denial.

Notwithstanding the provisions of the preceding paragraph, a party who has been permitted to proceed in an action in the district court in forma pauperis, or who has been permitted to proceed there as one who is financially unable to obtain adequate defense in a criminal case, may proceed on appeal in forma pauperis without further authorization unless, before or after the notice of appeal is filed, the district court shall certify that the appeal is not taken in good faith or shall find that the party is otherwise not entitled so to proceed, in which event the district court shall state in writing the reasons for such certification or finding.

If a motion for leave to proceed on appeal in forma pauperis is denied by the district court, or if the district court shall certify that the appeal is not taken in good faith or shall find that the party is otherwise not entitled to proceed in forma pauperis, the clerk shall forthwith serve notice of such action. A motion for leave so to proceed may be filed in the court of appeals within 30 days after service of notice of the action of the district court. The motion shall be accompanied by a copy of the affidavit filed in the district court, or by the affidavit prescribed by the first paragraph of this subdivision if no affidavit has been filed in the district court, and by a copy of the statement of reasons given by the district court for its action.

(b) Leave to Proceed on Appeal or Review in Forma Pauperis in Administrative Agency Proceedings. A party to a proceeding before an administrative agency, board, commission or officer (including, for the purpose of this rule, the United States Tax Court) who desires to proceed on appeal or review in a court of appeals in forma pauperis, when such appeal or review may be had directly in a court of appeals, shall file in the court of appeals a motion for leave so to proceed, together with the affidavit prescribed by the first paragraph of (a) of this Rule 24.

(c) Form of Briefs, Appendices and Other Papers. Parties allowed to proceed in forma pauperis may file briefs, appendices and other papers in typewritten form, and may request that the appeal be heard on the original record without the necessity of reproducing parts thereof in any form.

(As amended Apr. 30, 1979, eff. Aug. 1, 1979; Mar. 10, 1986, eff. July 1, 1986.)

NOTES OF ADVISORY COMMITTEE ON APPELLATE RULES

Subdivision (a). Authority to allow prosecution of an appeal in forma pauperis is vested in "[a]ny court of the United States" by 28 U.S.C. § 1915(a). The second paragraph of section 1915(a) seems to contemplate initial application to the district court for permission to proceed in forma pauperis, and although the circuit rules are generally silent on the question, the case law requires initial application to the district court. Hayes v. United States, 258 F.2d 400 (5th Cir., 1958), cert. den. 358 U.S. 856, 79 S.Ct. 87, 3 L.Ed.2d 89 (1958); Elkins v. United States, 250 F.2d 145 (9th Cir., 1957) see 364 U.S. 206, 80 S.Ct. 1437, 4 L.Ed.2d 1669 (1960); United States v. Farley, 238 F.2d 575 (2d Cir., 1956) see 354 U.S. 521, 77 S.Ct. 1371, 1 L.Ed.2d 1529 (1957). D.C.Cir. Rule 41(a) requires initial application to the district court. The content of the affidavit follows the language of the statute; the requirement of a statement of the issues comprehends the statutory requirement of a statement of "the nature of the ... appeal. ..." The second sentence is in accord with the decision in McGann v. United States, 362 U.S. 309, 80 S.Ct. 725, 4 L.Ed.2d 734 (1960). The requirement contained in the third sentence has no counterpart in present circuit rules, but it has been imposed by decision in at least two circuits. Ragan v. Cox, 305 F.2d 58 (10th Cir.1962); United States ex rel. Breedlove v. Dowd, 269 F.2d 693 (7th Cir., 1959).

The second paragraph permits one whose indigency has been previously determined by the district court to proceed on appeal in forma pauperis without the neces-

sity of a redetermination of indigency, while reserving to the district court its statutory authority to certify that the appeal is not taken in good faith, 28 U.S.C. § 1915(a), and permitting an inquiry into whether the circumstances of the party who was originally entitled to proceed in forma pauperis have changed during the course of the litigation. Cf. Sixth Circuit Rule 26.

The final paragraph establishes a subsequent motion in the court of appeals, rather than an appeal from the order of denial or from the certification of lack of good faith, as the proper procedure for calling in question the correctness of the action of the district court. The simple and expeditious motion procedure seems clearly preferable to an appeal. This paragraph applies only to applications for leave to appeal in forma pauperis. The order of a district court refusing leave to initiate an action in the district court in forma pauperis is reviewable on appeal. See Roberts v. United States District Court, 339 U.S. 844, 70 S.Ct. 954, 94 L.Ed. 1326 (1950).

Subdivision (b). Authority to allow prosecution in forma pauperis is vested only in a "court of the United States" (see Note to subdivision (a), above). Thus in proceedings brought directly in a court of appeals to review decisions of agencies or of the Tax Court, authority to proceed in forma pauperis should be sought in the court of appeals. If initial review of agency action is had in a district court, an application to appeal to a court of appeals in forma pauperis from the judgment of the district court is governed by the provisions of subdivision (a).

1979 AMENDMENT

The proposed amendment reflects the change in the title of the Tax Court to "United States Tax Court." See 26 U.S.C. § 7441.

1986 AMENDMENT

The amendments to Rule 24(a) are technical. No substantive change is intended.

TITLE VII

GENERAL PROVISIONS

Rule 25.   Filing and Service

(a) **Filing.** Papers required or permitted to be filed in a court of appeals shall be filed with the clerk. Filing may be accomplished by mail addressed to the clerk, but filing shall not be timely unless the papers are received by the clerk within the time fixed for filing, except that briefs and appendices shall be deemed filed on the day of mailing if the most expeditious form of delivery by mail, excepting special delivery, is utilized. If

a motion requests relief which may be granted by a single judge, the judge may permit the motion to be filed with the judge, in which even the judge shall note thereon the date of filing and shall thereafter transmit it to the clerk.

(b) **Service of All Papers Required.** Copies of all papers filed by any party and not required by these rules to be served by the clerk shall, at or before the time of filing, be served by a party or person acting for that party on all other parties to the appeal or review. Service on a party represented by counsel shall be made on counsel.

(c) Manner of Service. Service may be personal or by mail. Personal service includes delivery of the copy to a clerk or other responsible person at the office of counsel. Service by mail is complete on mailing.

(d) Proof of Service. Papers presented for filing shall contain an acknowledgment of service by the person served or proof of service in the form of a statement of the date and manner of service and of the names of the person served, certified by the person who made service. Proof of service may appear on or be affixed to the papers filed. The clerk may permit papers to be filed without acknowledgment or proof of service but shall require such to be filed promptly thereafter.

(As amended Mar. 10, 1986, eff. July 1, 1986.)

NOTES OF ADVISORY COMMITTEE ON APPELLATE RULES

The rule that filing is not timely unless the papers filed are received within the time allowed is the familiar one. Ward v. Atlantic Coast Line R.R. Co., 265 F.2d 75 (5th Cir., 1959), rev'd on other grounds 362 U.S. 396, 80 S.Ct. 789, 4 L.Ed.2d 820 (1960); Kahler-Ellis Co. v. Ohio Turnpike Commission, 225 F.2d 922 (6th Cir., 1955). An exception is made in the case of briefs and appendices in order to afford the parties the maximum time for their preparation. By the terms of the exception, air mail delivery must be used whenever it is the most expeditious manner of delivery.

A majority of the circuits now require service of all papers filed with the clerk. The usual provision in present rules is for service on "adverse" parties. In view of the extreme simplicity of service by mail, there seems to be no reason why a party who files a paper should not be required to serve all parties to the proceeding in the court of appeals, whether or not they may be deemed adverse. The common requirement of proof of service is retained, but the rule permits it to be made by simple certification, which may be endorsed on the copy which is filed.

1986 AMENDMENT

The amendments to Rules 25(a) and (b) are technical. No substantive change is intended.

Rule 26. Computation and Extension of Time

(a) Computation of Time. In computing any period of time prescribed by these rules, by an order of court, or by any applicable statute, the day of the act, event, or default from which the designated period of time begins to run shall not be included. The last day of the period shall be included, unless it is a Saturday, a Sunday, or a legal holiday, in which even the period extends until the end of the next day which is not a Saturday, a Sunday, or a legal holiday. When the period of time prescribed or allowed is less than 7 days, intermediate Saturdays, Sundays, and legal holidays shall be excluded in the computation. As used in this rule "legal holiday" includes New Year's Day, Birthday of Martin Luther King, Jr., Washington's Birthday, Memorial Day, Independence Day, Labor Day, Columbus Day, Veterans Day, Thanksgiving Day, Christmas Day, and any other day appointed as a holiday by the President or the Congress of the United States. It shall also include a day appointed as a holiday by the state wherein the district court which rendered the judgment or order which is or may be appealed from is situated, or by the state wherein the principal office of the clerk of the court of appeals in which the appeal is pending is located.

(b) Enlargement of Time. The court for good cause shown may upon motion enlarge the time prescribed by these rules or by its order for doing any act, or may permit an act to be done after the expiration of such time; but the court may not enlarge the time for filing a notice of appeal, a petition for allowance, or a petition for permission to appeal. Nor may the court enlarge the time prescribed by law for filing a petition to enjoin, set aside, suspend, modify, enforce or otherwise review, or a notice of appeal from, an order of an administrative agency, board, commission or officer of the United States, except as specifically authorized by law.

(c) Additional Time After Service by Mail. Whenever a party is required or permitted to do an act within a prescribed period after service of a paper upon that party and the paper is served by mail, 3 days shall be added to the prescribed period.

(As amended Mar. 1, 1971, eff. July 1, 1971; Mar. 10, 1986, eff. July 1, 1986.)

NOTES OF ADVISORY COMMITTEE ON APPELLATE RULES

1967 NOTE

The provisions of this rule are based upon FRCP 6(a), (b) and (e). See also Supreme Court Rule 34 and FRCrP

45. Unlike FRCP 6(b), this rule, read with Rule 27, requires that every request for enlargement of time be made by motion, with proof of service on all parties. This is the simplest, most convenient way of keeping all parties advised of developments. By the terms of Rule 27(b) a motion for enlargement of time under Rule 26(b) may be entertained and acted upon immediately, subject to the right of any party to seek reconsideration. Thus the requirement of motion and notice will not delay the granting of relief of a kind which a court is inclined to grant as of course. Specifically, if a court is of the view that an extension of time sought before expiration of the period originally prescribed or as extended by a previous order ought to be granted in effect ex parte, as FRCP 6(b) permits, it may grant motions seeking such relief without delay.

1971 NOTE

The amendment adds Columbus Day to the list of legal holidays to conform the subdivision to the Act of June 28, 1968, 82 Stat. 250, which constituted Columbus Day a legal holiday effective after January 1, 1971.

The Act, which amended Title 5, U.S.C. § 6103(a), changes the day on which certain holidays are to be observed. Washington's Birthday, Memorial Day and Veterans Day are to be observed on the third Monday in February, the last Monday in May and the fourth Monday in October, respectively, rather than, as heretofore, on February 22, May 30, and November 11, respectively. Columbus Day is to be observed on the second Monday in October. New Year's Day, Independence Day, Thanksgiving Day and Christmas continue to be observed on the traditional days.

1986 AMENDMENT

The Birthday of Martin Luther King, Jr. is added to the list of national holidays in Rule 26(a). The amendment to Rule 26(c) is technical. No substantive change is intended.

Rule 27. Motions

(a) Content of Motions; Response; Reply. Unless another form is elsewhere prescribed by these rules, an application for an order or other relief shall be made by filing a motion for such order or relief with proof of service on all other parties. The motion shall contain or be accompanied by any matter required by a specific provision of these rules governing such a motion, shall state with particularity the grounds on which it is based, and shall set forth the order or relief sought. If a motion is supported by briefs, affidavits or other papers, they shall be served and filed with the motion. Any party may file a response in opposition to a motion other than one for a procedural order [for which see subdivision (b)]

within 7 days after service of the motion, but motions authorized by Rules 8, 9, 18 and 41 may be acted upon after reasonable notice, and the court may shorten or extend the time for responding to any motion.

(b) Determination of Motions for Procedural Orders. Notwithstanding the provisions of (a) of this Rule 27 as to motions generally, motions for procedural orders, including any motion under Rule 26(b), may be acted upon at any time, without awaiting a response thereto, and pursuant to rule or order of the court, motions for specified types of procedural orders may be disposed of by the clerk. Any party adversely affected by such action may by application to the court request consideration, vacation or modification of such action.

(c) Power of a Single Judge to Entertain Motions. In addition to the authority expressly conferred by these rules or by law, a single judge of a court of appeals may entertain and may grant or deny any request for relief which under these rules may properly be sought by motion, except that a single judge may not dismiss or otherwise determine an appeal or other proceeding, and except that a court of appeals may provide by order or rule that any motion or class of motions must be acted upon by the court. The action of a single judge may be reviewed by the court.

(d) Form of Papers; Number of Copies. All papers relating to motions may be typewritten. Three copies shall be filed with the original, but the court may require that additional copies be furnished.

(As amended Apr. 30, 1979, eff. Aug. 1, 1979.)

NOTES OF ADVISORY COMMITTEE ON APPELLATE RULES

Subdivisions (a) and (b). Many motions seek relief of a sort which is ordinarily unopposed or which is granted as of course. The provision of subdivision (a) which permits any party to file a response in opposition to a motion within 7 days after its service upon him assumes that the motion is one of substance which ought not be acted upon without affording affected parties an opportunity to reply. A motion to dismiss or otherwise determine an appeal is clearly such a motion. Motions authorized by Rules 8, 9, 18 and 41 are likewise motions of substance; but in the nature of the relief sought, to afford an adversary an automatic delay of at least 7 days is undesirable, thus such motions may be acted upon after notice which is reasonable under the circumstances.

The term "motions for procedural orders" is used in subdivision (b) to describe motions which do not substantially affect the rights of the parties or the ultimate disposition of the appeal. To prevent delay in the disposition of such motions, subdivision (b) provides that they may be acted upon immediately without awaiting a response, subject to the right of any party who is adversely affected by the action to seek reconsideration.

Subdivision (c). Within the general consideration of procedure on motions is the problem of the power of a single circuit judge. Certain powers are granted to a single judge of a court of appeals by statute. Thus, under 28 U.S.C. § 2101(f) a single judge may stay execution and enforcement of a judgment to enable a party aggrieved to obtain certiorari; under 28 U.S.C. § 2251 a judge before whom a habeas corpus proceeding involving a person detained by state authority is pending may stay any proceeding against the person; under 28 U.S. C. § 2253 a single judge may issue a certificate of probable cause. In addition, certain of these rules expressly grant power to a single judge. See Rules 8, 9 and 18.

This subdivision empowers a single circuit judge to act upon virtually all requests for intermediate relief which may be made during the course of an appeal or other proceeding. By its terms he may entertain and act upon any motion other than a motion to dismiss or otherwise determine an appeal or other proceeding. But the relief sought must be "relief which under these rules may properly be sought by motion."

Examples of the power conferred on a single judge by this subdivision are: to extend the time for transmitting the record or docketing the appeal (Rules 11 and 12); to permit intervention in agency cases (Rule 15), or substitution in any case (Rule 43); to permit an appeal in forma pauperis (Rule 24); to enlarge any time period fixed by the rules other than that for initiating a proceeding in the court of appeals (Rule 26(b)); to permit the filing of a brief by amicus curiae (Rule 29); to authorize the filing of a deferred appendix (Rule 30(c)), or dispense with the requirement of an appendix in a specific case (Rule 30(f)), or permit carbon copies of briefs or appendices to be used (Rule 32(a)); to permit the filing of additional briefs (Rule 28(c)), or the filing of briefs of extraordinary length (Rule 28(g)); to postpone oral argument (Rule 34(a)), or grant additional time therefor (Rule 34(b)).

Certain rules require that application for the relief or orders which they authorize be made by petition. Since relief under those rules may not properly be sought by motion, a single judge may not entertain requests for such relief. Thus a single judge may not act upon requests for permission to appeal (see Rules 5 and 6); or for mandamus or other extraordinary writs (see Rule 21), other than for stays or injunctions *pendente lite,*

authority to grant which is "expressly conferred by these rules" on a single judge under certain circumstances (see Rules 8 and 18); or upon petitions for rehearing (see Rule 40).

A court of appeals may by order or rule abridge the power of a single judge if it is of the view that a motion or a class of motions should be disposed of by a panel. Exercise of any power granted a single judge is discretionary with the judge. The final sentence in this subdivision makes the disposition of any matter by a single judge subject to review by the court.

1979 AMENDMENT

The proposed amendment would give sanction to local rules in a number of circuits permitting the clerk to dispose of specified types of procedural motions.

Rule 28. Briefs

(a) Brief of the Appellant. The brief of the appellant shall contain under appropriate headings and in the order here indicated:

(1) A table of contents, with page references, and a table of cases (alphabetically arranged), statutes and other authorities cited, with references to the pages of the brief where they are cited.

(2) A statement of the issues presented for review.

(3) A statement of the case. The statement shall first indicate briefly the nature of the case, the course of proceedings, and its disposition in the court below. There shall follow a statement of the facts relevant to the issues presented for review, with appropriate references to the record (see subdivision (e)).

(4) An argument. The argument may be preceded by a summary. The argument shall contain the contentions of the appellant with respect to the issues presented, and the reasons therefor, with citations to the authorities, statutes and parts of the record relied on.

(5) A short conclusion stating the precise relief sought.

(b) Brief of the Appellee. The brief of the appellee shall conform to the requirements of subdivision (a)(1)–(4), except that a statement of the issues or of the case need not be made unless the appellee is dissatisfied with the statement of the appellant.

(c) Reply Brief. The appellant may file a brief in reply to the brief of the appellee, and if the appellee has cross-appealed, the appellee may file a brief in reply to the response of the appellant to the issues presented by the cross appeal. No further briefs may be filed except with leave of court. All reply briefs shall contain a table of contents, with page references, and a table of cases (alphabetically arranged), statutes and other authorities cited, with references to the pages of the reply brief where they are cited.

(d) References in Briefs to Parties. Counsel will be expected in their briefs and oral arguments to keep to a minimum references to parties by such designations as "appellant" and "appellee". It promotes clarity to use the designations used in the lower court or in the agency proceedings, or the actual names of parties, or descriptive terms such as "the employee," "the injured person," "the taxpayer," "the ship," "the stevedore," etc.

(e) References in Briefs to the Record. References in the briefs to parts of the record reproduced in the appendix filed with the brief of the appellant (see Rule 30(a)) shall be to the pages of the appendix at which those parts appear. If the appendix is prepared after the briefs are filed, references in the briefs to the record shall be made by one of the methods allowed by Rule 30(c). If the record is reproduced in accordance with the provisions of Rule 30(f), or if references are made in the briefs to parts of the record not reproduced, the references shall be to the pages of the parts of the record involved; e.g., Answer p. 7, Motion for Judgment p. 2, Transcript p. 231. Intelligible abbreviations may be used. If reference is made to evidence the admissibility of which is in controversy, reference shall be made to the pages of the appendix or of the transcript at which the evidence was identified, offered, and received or rejected.

(f) Reproduction of Statutes, Rules, Regulations, Etc. If determination of the issues presented requires the study of statutes, rules, regulations, etc. or relevant parts thereof, they shall be reproduced in the brief or in an addendum at the end, or they may be supplied to the court in pamphlet form.

(g) Length of Briefs. Except by permission of the court, or as specified by local rule of the court of appeals, principal briefs shall not exceed 50 pages, and reply briefs shall not exceed 25 pages, exclusive of pages containing the table of contents, tables of citations and any addendum containing statutes, rules, regulations, etc.

(h) Briefs in Cases Involving Cross Appeals. If a cross appeal is filed, the plaintiff in the court below shall be deemed the appellant for the purposes of this rule and Rules 30 and 31, unless the parties otherwise agree or the court otherwise orders. The brief of the appellee shall contain the issues and argument involved in his appeal as well as the answer to the brief of the appellant.

(i) Briefs in Cases Involving Multiple Appellants or Appellees. In cases involving more than one appellant or appellee, including cases consolidated for purposes of the appeal, any number of either may join in a single brief, and any appellant or appellee may adopt by reference any part of the brief of another. Parties may similarly join in reply briefs.

(j) Citation of Supplemental Authorities. When pertinent and significant authorities come to the attention of a party after the party's brief has been filed, or after oral argument but before decision, a party may promptly advise the clerk of the court, by letter, with a copy to all counsel, setting forth the citations. There shall be a reference either to the page of the brief or to a point argued orally to which the citations pertain, but the letter shall without argument state the reasons for the supplemental citations. Any response shall be made promptly and shall be similarly limited.

(As amended Apr. 30, 1979, eff. Aug. 1, 1979; Mar. 10, 1986, eff. July 1, 1986.)

NOTES OF ADVISORY COMMITTEE ON APPELLATE RULES

This rule is based upon Supreme Court Rule 40. For variations in present circuit rules on briefs see 2d Cir. Rule 17, 3d Cir. Rule 24, 5th Cir. Rule 24, and 7th Cir. Rule 17. All circuits now limit the number of pages of briefs, a majority limiting the brief to 50 pages of standard typographic printing. Fifty pages of standard typographic printing is the approximate equivalent of 70 pages of typewritten text, given the page sizes required by Rule 32 and the requirement set out there that text produced by a method other than standard typographic must be double spaced.

1979 AMENDMENT

Note to Subdivision (g). The proposed amendment eliminates the distinction appearing in the present rule between the permissible length in pages of printed and typewritten briefs, investigation of the matter having disclosed that the number of words on the printed page is little if any larger than the number on a page typed in standard elite type.

The provision is made subject to local rule to permit the court of appeals to require that typewritten briefs be typed in larger type and permit a correspondingly larger number of pages.

Note to Subdivision (j). Proposed new Rule 28(j) makes provision for calling the court's attention to authorities that come to the party's attention after the brief has been filed. It is patterned after the practice under local rule in some of the circuits.

1986 AMENDMENT

While Rule 28(g) can be read as requiring that tables of authorities be included in a reply brief, such tables are often not included. Their absence impedes efficient use of the reply brief to ascertain the appellant's response [sic] to a particular argument of the appellee or to the appellee's use of a particular authority. The amendment to Rule 28(c) is intended to make it clear that such tables are required in reply briefs.

The amendment to Rule 28(j) is technical. No substantive change is intended.

Rule 29.   Brief of an Amicus Curiae

A brief of an amicus curiae may be filed only if accompanied by written consent of all parties, or by leave of court granted on motion or at the request of the court, except that consent or leave shall not be required when the brief is presented by the United States or an officer or agency thereof, or by a State, Territory or Commonwealth. The brief may be conditionally filed with the motion for leave. A motion for leave shall identify the interest of the applicant and shall state the reasons why a brief of an amicus curiae is desirable. Save as all parties otherwise consent, any amicus curiae shall file its brief within the time allowed the party whose position as to affirmance or reversal the amicus brief will support unless the court for cause shown shall grant leave for later filing, in which event it shall specify within what period an opposing party may answer. A motion of an amicus curiae to participate in the oral argument will be granted only for extraordinary reasons.

NOTES OF ADVISORY COMMITTEE ON APPELLATE RULES

Only five circuits presently regulate the filing of the brief of an amicus curiae. See D.C. Cir. Rule 18(j); 1st Cir. Rule 23(10); 6th Cir. Rule 17(4); 9th Cir. Rule 18(9); 10th Cir. Rule 20. This rule follows the practice of a majority of circuits in requiring leave of court to file an amicus brief except under the circumstances stated therein. Compare Supreme Court Rule 42.

Rule 30.   Appendix to the Briefs

(a) Duty of Appellant To Prepare and File; Content of Appendix; Time for Filing; Number of Copies. The appellant shall prepare and file an appendix to the briefs which shall contain: (1) the relevant docket entries in the proceeding below; (2) any relevant portions of the pleadings, charge, findings or opinion; (3) the judgment, order or decision in question; and (4) any other parts of the record to which the parties wish to direct the particular attention of the court. Except where they have independent relevance, memoranda of law in the district court should not be included in the appendix. The fact that parts of the record are not included in the appendix shall not prevent the parties or the court from relying on such parts.

Unless filing is to be deferred pursuant to the provisions of subdivision (c) of this rule, the appellant shall serve and file the appendix with the brief. Ten copies of the appendix shall be filed with the clerk, and one copy shall be served on counsel for each party separately represented, unless the court shall by rule or order direct the filing or service of a lesser number.

(b) Determination of Contents of Appendix; Cost of Producing. The parties are encouraged to agree as to the contents of the appendix. In the absence of agreement, the appellant shall, not later than 10 days after the date on which the record is filed, serve on the appellee a designation of the parts of the record which the appellant intends to include in the appendix and a statement of the issues which the appellant intends to present for review. If the appellee deem it necessary to direct the particular attention of the court to parts of the record not designated by the appellant, the appellee shall, within 10 days after receipt of the designation, serve upon the appellant a designation of those parts. The appellant shall include in the appendix the parts thus designated. In designating parts of the record for inclusion in the appendix, the parties shall have regard for the fact that the entire record is always available to the court for reference and examination and shall not engage in unnecessary designation.

Unless the parties otherwise agree, the cost of producing the appendix shall initially be paid by the appellant, but if the appellant considers that parts of the record designated by the appellee for inclusion are unnecessary for the determination of the issues presented the appellant may so advise the appellee and the appellee shall advance the cost of including such parts. The cost of producing the appendix shall be taxed as costs in the case, but if either party shall cause matters to be included in the appendix unnecessarily the court may impose the cost of producing such parts on the party. Each circuit shall provide by local rule for the imposition of sanctions against attorneys who unreasonably and vexatiously increase the costs of litigation through the inclusion of unnecessary material in the appendix.

(c) Alternative Method of Designating Contents of the Appendix; How References to the Record May be Made in the Briefs When Alternative Method is Used. If the court shall so provide by rule for classes of cases or by order in specific cases, preparation of the appendix may be deferred until after the briefs have been filed, and the appendix may be filed 21 days after service of the brief of the appellee. If the preparation and filing of the appendix is thus deferred, the provisions of subdivision (b) of this Rule 30 shall apply, except that the designations referred to therein shall be made by each party at the time each brief is served, and a statement of the issues presented shall be unnecessary.

If the deferred appendix authorized by this subdivision is employed, references in the briefs to the record may be to the pages of the parts of the record involved, in which event the original paging of each part of the record shall be indicated in the appendix by placing in brackets the number of each page at the place in the appendix where that page begins. Or if a party desires to refer in a brief directly to pages of the appendix, that party may serve and file typewritten or page proof copies of the brief within the time required by Rule 31(a), with appropriate references to the pages of the parts of the record involved. In that event, within 14 days after the appendix is filed the party shall serve and file copies of the brief in the form prescribed by Rule 32(a) containing references to the pages of the appendix in place of or in addition to the initial references to the pages of the parts of the record involved. No other changes may be made in the brief as initially

served and filed, except that typographical errors may be corrected.

(d) Arrangement of the Appendix. At the beginning of the appendix there shall be inserted a list of the parts of the record which it contains, in the order in which the parts are set out therein, with references to the pages of the appendix at which each part begins. The relevant docket entries shall be set out following the list of contents. Thereafter, other parts of the record shall be set out in chronological order. When matter contained in the reporter's transcript of proceedings is set out in the appendix, the page of the transcript at which such matter may be found shall be indicated in brackets immediately before the matter which is set out. Omissions in the text of papers or of the transcript must be indicated by asterisks. Immaterial formal matters (captions, subscriptions, acknowledgments, etc.) shall be omitted. A question and its answer may be contained in a single paragraph.

(e) Reproduction of Exhibits. Exhibits designated for inclusion in the appendix may be contained in a separate volume, or volumes, suitably indexed. Four copies thereof shall be filed with the appendix and one copy shall be served on counsel for each party separately represented. The transcript of a proceeding before an administrative agency, board, commission or officer used in an action in the district court shall be regarded as an exhibit for the purpose of this subdivision.

(f) Hearing of Appeals on the Original Record Without the Necessity of an Appendix. A court of appeals may by rule applicable to all cases, or to classes of cases, or by order in specific cases, dispense with the requirement of an appendix and permit appeals to be heard on the original record, with such copies of the record, or relevant parts thereof, as the court may require.

(As amended Mar. 30, 1970, eff. July 1, 1970; Mar. 10, 1986, eff. July 1, 1986.)

NOTES OF ADVISORY COMMITTEE ON APPELLATE RULES

1967 NOTE

Subdivision (a). Only two circuits presently require a printed record (5th Cir. Rule 23(a); 8th Cir. Rule 10 (in civil appeals only)), and the rules and practice in those circuits combine to make the difference between a printed record and the appendix, which is now used in eight circuits and in the Supreme Court in lieu of the printed record, largely nominal. The essential characteristics of the appendix method are: (1) the entire record may not be reproduced; (2) instead, the parties are to set out in an appendix to the briefs those parts of the record which in their judgment the judges must consult in order to determine the issues presented by the appeal; (3) the appendix is not the record but merely a selection therefrom for the convenience of the judges of the court of appeals; the record is the actual trial court record, and the record itself is always available to supply inadvertent omissions from the appendix. These essentials are incorporated, either by rule or by practice, in the circuits that continue to require the printed record rather than the appendix. See 5th Cir. Rule 23(a)(9) and 8th Cir. Rule 10(a)–(d).

Subdivision (b). Under the practice in six of the eight circuits which now use the appendix method, unless the parties agree to use a single appendix, the appellant files with his brief an appendix containing the parts of the record which he deems it essential that the court read in order to determine the questions presented. If the appellee deems additional parts of the record necessary he must include such parts as an appendix to his brief. The proposed rules differ from that practice. By the new rule a single appendix is to be filed. It is to be prepared by the appellant, who must include therein those parts which he deems essential and those which the appellee designates as essential.

Under the practice by which each party files his own appendix the resulting reproduction of essential parts of the record is often fragmentary; it is not infrequently necessary to piece several appendices together to arrive at a usable reproduction. Too, there seems to be a tendency on the part of some appellants to reproduce less than what is necessary for a determination of the issues presented (see Moran Towing Corp. v. M.A. Gammino Construction Co., 363 F.2d 108 (1st Cir.1966); Walters v. Shari Music Publishing Corp., 298 F.2d 206 (2d Cir.1962) and cases cited therein; Morrison v. Texas Co., 289 F.2d 382 (7th Cir.1961) and cases cited therein), a tendency which is doubtless encouraged by the requirement in present rules that the appellee reproduce in his separately prepared appendix such necessary parts of the record as are not included by the appellant.

Under the proposed rule responsibility for the preparation of the appendix is placed on the appellant. If the appellee feels that the appellant has omitted essential portions of the record, he may require the appellant to include such portions in the appendix. The appellant is protected against a demand that he reproduce parts which he considers unnecessary by the provisions entitling him to require the appellee to advance the costs of reproducing such parts and authorizing denial of costs for matter unnecessarily reproduced.

Subdivision (c). This subdivision permits the appellant to elect to defer the production of the appendix to the briefs until the briefs of both sides are written, and authorizes a court of appeals to require such deferred filing by rule or order. The advantage of this method of preparing the appendix is that it permits the parties to determine what parts of the record need to be reproduced in the light of the issues actually presented by the briefs. Often neither side is in a position to say precisely what is needed until the briefs are completed. Once the argument on both sides is known, it should be possible to confine the matter reproduced in the appendix to that which is essential to a determination of the appeal or review. This method of preparing the appendix is presently in use in the Tenth Circuit (Rule 17) and in other circuits in review of agency proceedings, and it has proven its value in reducing the volume required to be reproduced. When the record is long, use of this method is likely to result in substantial economy to the parties.

Subdivision (e). The purpose of this subdivision is to reduce the cost of reproducing exhibits. While subdivision (a) requires that 10 copies of the appendix be filed, unless the court requires a lesser number, subdivision (e) permits exhibits necessary for the determination of an appeal to be bound separately, and requires only 4 copies of such a separate volume or volumes to be filed and a single copy to be served on counsel.

Subdivision (f). This subdivision authorizes a court of appeals to dispense with the appendix method of reproducing parts of the record and to hear appeals on the original record and such copies of it as the court may require.

Since 1962 the Ninth Circuit has permitted all appeals to be heard on the original record and a very limited number of copies. Under the practice as adopted in 1962, any party to an appeal could elect to have the appeal heard on the original record and two copies thereof rather than on the printed record theretofore required. The resulting substantial saving of printing costs led to the election of the new practice in virtually all cases, and by 1967 the use of printed records had ceased. By a recent amendment, the Ninth Circuit has abolished the printed record altogether. Its rules now provide that all appeals are to be heard on the original record, and it has reduced the number of copies required to two sets of copies of the transmitted original papers (excluding copies of exhibits, which need not be filed unless specifically ordered). See 9 Cir. Rule 10, as amended June 2, 1967, effective September 1, 1967. The Eighth Circuit permits appeals in criminal cases and in habeas corpus and 28 U.S.C. § 2255 proceedings to be heard on the original record and two copies thereof. See 8 Cir. Rule 8(i)–(j). The Tenth Circuit permits appeals in all cases to be heard on the original record and four copies thereof whenever the record consists of two hundred pages or less. See 10 Cir. Rule 17(a). This subdivision expressly authorizes the continuation of the practices in the Eighth, Ninth and Tenth Circuits.

The judges of the Court of Appeals for the Ninth Circuit have expressed complete satisfaction with the practice there in use and have suggested that attention be called to the advantages which it offers in terms of reducing cost.

1970 NOTE

Subdivision (a). The amendment of subdivision (a) is related to the amendment of Rule 31(a), which authorizes a court of appeals to shorten the time for filing briefs. By virtue of this amendment, if the time for filing the brief of the appellant is shortened the time for filing the appendix is likewise shortened.

Subdivision (c). As originally written, subdivision (c) permitted the appellant to elect to defer filing of the appendix until 21 days after service of the brief of the appellee. As amended, subdivision (c) requires that an order of court be obtained before filing of the appendix can be deferred, unless a court permits deferred filing by local rule. The amendment should not cause use of the deferred appendix to be viewed with disfavor. In cases involving lengthy records, permission to defer filing of the appendix should be freely granted as an inducement to the parties to include in the appendix only matter that the briefs show to be necessary for consideration by the judges. But the Committee is advised that appellants have elected to defer filing of the appendix in cases involving brief records merely to obtain the 21 day delay. The subdivision is amended to prevent that practice.

1986 AMENDMENT

Subdivision (a). During its study of the separate appendix [see Report of the Advisory Committee on the Federal Appellate Rules on the Operation of Rule 30, ___ FRD ___ (1985)], the Advisory Committee found that this document was frequently encumbered with memoranda submitted to the trial court. United States v. Noall, 587 F.2d 123, 125 n. 1 (2nd Cir.1978). See generally Drewett v. Aetna Cas. & Sur. Co., 539 F.2d 496, 500 (5th Cir.1976); Volkswagenwerk Aktiengesellschaft v. Church, 413 F.2d 1126, 1128 (9th Cir.1969). Inclusion of such material makes the appendix more bulky and therefore less useful to the appellate panel. It also can increase significantly the costs of litigation.

There are occasions when such trial court memoranda have independent relevance in the appellate litigation. For instance, there may be a dispute as to whether a particular point was raised or whether a concession was made in the district court. In such circumstances, it is appropriate to include pertinent sections of such memoranda in the appendix.

Subdivision (b). The amendment to subdivision (b) is designed to require the circuits, by local rule, to establish a procedural mechanism for the imposition of

sanctions against those attorneys who conduct appellate litigation in bad faith. Both 28 U.S.C. § 1927 and the inherent power of the court authorize such sanctions. See Brennan v. Local 357, International Brotherhood of Teamsters, 709 F.2d 611 (9th Cir.1983). See generally Roadway Express, Inc. v. Piper, 447 U.S. 752 (1980). While considerations of uniformity are important and doubtless will be taken into account by the judges of the respective circuits, the Advisory Committee believes that, at this time, the circuits need the flexibility to tailor their approach to the conditions of local practice. The local rule shall provide for notice and opportunity to respond before the imposition of any sanction.

Technical amendments also are made to subdivisions (a), (b) and (c) which are not intended to be substantive changes.

TAXATION OF FEES IN APPEALS IN WHICH THE REQUIREMENT OF AN APPENDIX IS DISPENSED WITH

The Judicial Conference of the United States at its session on October 28th and 29th approved the following resolution relating to fees to be taxed in the courts of appeals as submitted by the Judicial Council of the Ninth Circuit with the proviso that its application to any court of appeals shall be at the election of each such court:

For some time it has been the practice in the Ninth Circuit Court of Appeals to dispense with an appendix in an appellate record and to hear the appeal on the original record, with a number of copies thereof being supplied (Rule 30f, Federal Rules of Appellate Procedure). It has been the practice of the Court to tax a fee of $5 in small records and $10 in large records for the time of the clerk involved in preparing such appeals and by way of reimbursement for postage expense. Judicial Conference approval heretofore has not been secured and the Judicial Council of the Ninth Circuit now seeks to fix a flat fee of $15 to be charged as fees for costs to be charged by *any* court of appeals "in any appeal in which the requirement of an appendix is dispensed with pursuant to Rule 30f. Federal Rules of Appellate Procedure."

Rule 31. Filing and Service of Briefs

(a) Time for Serving and Filing Briefs. The appellant shall serve and file a brief within 40 days after the date on which the record is filed. The appellee shall serve and file a brief within 30 days after service of the brief of the appellant. The appellant may serve and file a reply brief within 14 days after service of the brief of the appellee, but, except for good cause shown, a reply brief must be filed at least 3 days before argument. If a court of appeals is prepared to consider cases on the merits promptly after briefs are filed, and its practice is to do so, it may shorten the periods prescribed above for serving and filing briefs, either by rule for all cases or for classes of cases, or by order for specific cases.

(b) Number of Copies to be Filed and Served. Twenty-five copies of each brief shall be filed with the clerk, unless the court by order in a particular case shall direct a lesser number, and two copies shall be served on counsel for each party separately represented. If a party is allowed to file typewritten ribbon and carbon copies of the brief, the original and three legible copies shall be filed with the clerk, and one copy shall be served on counsel for each party separately represented.

(c) Consequence of Failure to File Briefs. If an appellant fails to file a brief within the time provided by this rule, or within the time as extended, an appellee may move for dismissal of the appeal. If an appellee fails to file a brief, the appellee will not be heard at oral argument except by permission of the court.

(As amended Mar. 30, 1970, eff. July 1, 1970; Mar. 10, 1986, eff. July 1, 1986.)

NOTES OF ADVISORY COMMITTEE ON APPELLATE RULES

1967 NOTE

A majority of the circuits now require the brief of the appellant to be filed within 30 days from the date on which the record is filed. But in those circuits an exchange of designations is unnecessary in the preparation of the appendix. The appellant files with his brief an appendix containing the parts of the record which he deems essential. If the appellee considers other parts essential, he includes those parts in his own appendix. Since the proposed rule requires the appellant to file with his brief an appendix containing necessary parts of the record as designated by both parties, the rule allows the appellant 40 days in order to provide time for the exchange of designations respecting the content of the appendix (see Rule 30(b)).

1970 NOTE

The time prescribed by Rule 31(a) for preparing briefs —40 days to the appellant, 30 days to the appellee—is well within the time that must ordinarily elapse in most circuits before an appeal can be reached for consideration. In those circuits, the time prescribed by the Rule should not be disturbed. But if a court of appeals maintains a current calendar, that is, if an appeal can be heard as soon as the briefs have been filed, or if the practice of the court permits the submission of appeals

for preliminary consideration as soon as the briefs have been filed, the court should be free to prescribe shorter periods in the interest of expediting decision.

1986 AMENDMENT

The amendments to Rules 31(a) and (c) are technical. No substantive change is intended.

Rule 32. Form of Briefs, the Appendix and other Papers

(a) Form of Briefs and the Appendix. Briefs and appendices may be produced by standard typographic printing or by any duplicating or copying process which produces a clear black image on white paper. Carbon copies of briefs and appendices may not be submitted without permission of the court, except in behalf of parties allowed to proceed in forma pauperis. All printed matter must appear in at least 11 point type on opaque, unglazed paper. Briefs and appendices produced by the standard typographic process shall be bound in volumes having pages 6⅛ by 9¼ inches and type matter 4⅙ by 7⅙ inches. Those produced by any other process shall be bound in volumes having pages not exceeding 8½ by 11 inches and type matter not exceeding 6½ by 9½ inches, with double spacing between each line of text. In patent cases the pages of briefs and appendices may be of such size as is necessary to utilize copies of patent documents. Copies of the reporter's transcript and other papers reproduced in a manner authorized by this rule may be inserted in the appendix; such pages may be informally renumbered if necessary.

If briefs are produced by commercial printing or duplicating firms, or, if produced otherwise and the covers to be described are available, the cover of the brief of the appellant should be blue; that of the appellee, red; that of an intervenor or amicus curiae, green; that of any reply brief, gray. The cover of the appendix, if separately printed, should be white. The front covers of the briefs and of appendices, if separately printed, shall contain: (1) the name of the court and the number of the case; (2) the title of the case (see Rule 12(a)); (3) the nature of the proceeding in the court (e.g., Appeal; Petition for Review) and the name of the court, agency or board below; (4) the title of the document (e.g., Brief for Appellant, Appendix); and (5) the names and addresses of counsel representing the party on whose behalf the document is filed.

(b) Form of Other Papers. Petitions for rehearing shall be produced in a manner prescribed by subdivision (a). Motions and other papers may be produced in like manner, or they may be typewritten upon opaque, unglazed paper 8½ by 11 inches in size. Lines of typewritten text shall be double spaced. Consecutive sheets shall be attached at the left margin. Carbon copies may be used for filing and service if they are legible.

A motion or other paper addressed to the court shall contain a caption setting forth the name of the court, the title of the case, the file number, and a brief descriptive title indicating the purpose of the paper.

NOTES OF ADVISORY COMMITTEE ON APPELLATE RULES

Only two methods of printing are now generally recognized by the circuits—standard typographic printing and the offset duplicating process (multilith). A third, mimeographing, is permitted in the Fifth Circuit. The District of Columbia, Ninth, and Tenth Circuits permit records to be reproduced by copying processes. The Committee feels that recent and impending advances in the arts of duplicating and copying warrant experimentation with less costly forms of reproduction than those now generally authorized. The proposed rule permits, in effect, the use of any process other than the carbon copy process which produces a clean, readable page. What constitutes such is left in first instance to the parties and ultimately to the court to determine. The final sentence of the first paragraph of subdivision (a) is added to allow the use of multilith, mimeograph, or other forms of copies of the reporter's original transcript whenever such are available.

Rule 33. Prehearing Conference

The court may direct the attorneys for the parties to appear before the court or a judge thereof for a prehearing conference to consider the simplification of the issues and such other matters as may aid in the disposition of the proceeding by the court. The court or judge shall make an order which recites the action taken at the conference and the agreements made by the parties as to any of the matters considered and which limits the issues to those not disposed of by admissions or agreements of counsel, and such order when entered controls the subsequent course of the proceeding, unless modified to prevent manifest injustice.

NOTES OF ADVISORY COMMITTEE ON APPELLATE RULES

The uniform rule for review or enforcement of orders of administrative agencies, boards, commissions or officers (see the general note following Rule 15) authorizes a prehearing conference in agency review proceedings. The same considerations which make a prehearing conference desirable in such proceedings may be present in certain cases on appeal from the district courts. The proposed rule is based upon subdivision 11 of the present uniform rule for review of agency orders.

Rule 34. Oral Argument

(a) In General; Local Rule. Oral argument shall be allowed in all cases unless pursuant to local rule a panel of three judges, after examination of the briefs and record, shall be unanimously of the opinion that oral argument is not needed. Any such local rule shall provide any party with an opportunity to file a statement setting forth the reasons why oral argument should be heard. A general statement of the criteria employed in the administration of such local rule shall be published in or with the rule and such criteria shall conform substantially to the following minimum standard:

Oral Argument will be allowed unless

(1) the appeal is frivolous; or

(2) the dispositive issue or set of issues has been recently authoritatively decided; or

(3) the facts and legal arguments are adequately presented in the briefs and record and the decisional process would not be significantly aided by oral argument.

(b) Notice of Argument; Postponement. The clerk shall advise all parties whether oral argument is to be heard, and if so, of the time and place therefor, and the time to be allowed each side. A request for postponement of the argument or for allowance of additional time must be made by motion filed reasonably in advance of the date fixed for hearing.

(c) Order and Content of Argument. The appellant is entitled to open and conclude the argument. The opening argument shall include a fair statement of the case. Counsel will not be permitted to read at length from briefs, records or authorities.

(d) Cross and Separate Appeals. A cross or separate appeal shall be argued with the initial appeal at a single argument, unless the court otherwise directs. If a case involves a cross-appeal, the plaintiff in the action below shall be deemed the appellant for the purpose of this rule unless the parties otherwise agree or the court otherwise directs. If separate appellants support the same argument, care shall be taken to avoid duplication of argument.

(e) Non-Appearance of Parties. If the appellee fails to appear to present argument, the court will hear argument on behalf of the appellant, if present. If the appellant fails to appear, the court may hear argument on behalf of the appellee, if present. If neither party appears, the case will be decided on the briefs unless the court shall otherwise order.

(f) Submission on Briefs. By agreement of the parties, a case may be submitted for decision on the briefs, but the court may direct that the case be argued.

(g) Use of Physical Exhibits at Argument; Removal. If physical exhibits other than documents are to be used at the argument, counsel shall arrange to have them placed in the court room before the court convenes on the date of the argument. After the argument counsel shall cause the exhibits to be removed from the court room unless the court otherwise directs. If exhibits are not reclaimed by counsel within a reasonable time after notice is given by the clerk, they shall be destroyed or otherwise disposed of as the clerk shall think best.

(As amended Apr. 30, 1979, eff. Aug. 1, 1979; Mar. 10, 1986, eff. July 1, 1986.)

NOTES OF ADVISORY COMMITTEE ON APPELLATE RULES

A majority of circuits now limit oral argument to thirty minutes for each side, with the provision that additional time may be made available upon request. The Committee is of the view that thirty minutes to each side is sufficient in most cases, but that where additional time is necessary it should be freely granted on a proper showing of cause therefor. It further feels that the matter of time should be left ultimately to each court of appeals, subject to the spirit of the rule that a reasonable time should be allowed for argument. The term "side" is used to indicate that the time allowed by the rule is afforded to opposing interests rather than to individual parties. Thus if multiple appellants or appellees have a common interest, they constitute only a single side. If counsel for multiple parties who constitute a single side feel that additional time is necessary, they may request it. In other particulars this rule

follows the usual practice among the circuits. See 3d Cir. Rule 31; 6th Cir. Rule 20; 10th Cir. Rule 23.

1979 AMENDMENT

The proposed amendment, patterned after the recommendations in the Report of the Commission on Revision of the Federal Court Appellate System, *Structure and Internal Procedures: Recommendations for Change*, 1975, created by Public Law 489 of the 92nd Cong., 2nd Sess., 86 Stat. 807, sets forth general principles and minimum standards to be observed in formulating any local rule.

1986 AMENDMENT

The amendments to Rules 34(a) and (e) are technical. No substantive change is intended.

Rule 35. Determination of Causes by the Court in Banc

(a) When Hearing or Rehearing in Banc Will be Ordered. A majority of the circuit judges who are in regular active service may order that an appeal or other proceeding be heard or reheard by the court of appeals in banc. Such a hearing or rehearing is not favored and ordinarily will not be ordered except (1) when consideration by the full court is necessary to secure or maintain uniformity of its decisions, or (2) when the proceeding involves a question of exceptional importance.

(b) Suggestion of a Party for Hearing or Rehearing in Banc. A party may suggest the appropriateness of a hearing or rehearing in banc. No response shall be filed unless the court shall so order. The clerk shall transmit any such suggestion to the members of the panel and the judges of the court who are in regular active service but a vote need not be taken to determine whether the cause shall be heard or reheard in banc unless a judge in regular active service or a judge who was a member of the panel that rendered a decision sought to be reheard requests a vote on such a suggestion made by a party.

(c) Time for Suggestion of a Party for Hearing or Rehearing in Banc; Suggestion Does Not Stay Mandate. If a party desires to suggest that an appeal be heard initially in banc, the suggestion must be made by the date on which the appellee's brief is filed. A suggestion for a rehearing in banc must be made within the time prescribed by Rule 40 for filing a petition for rehearing, whether the suggestion is made in such petition or otherwise. The pendency of such a suggestion whether or not included in a petition for rehearing shall not affect the finality of the judgment of the court of appeals or stay the issuance of the mandate.

(As amended Apr. 30, 1979, eff. Aug. 1, 1979.)

NOTES OF ADVISORY COMMITTEE ON APPELLATE RULES

Statutory authority for in banc hearings is found in 28 U.S.C. § 46(c). The proposed rule is responsive to the Supreme Court's view in Western Pacific Ry. Corp. v. Western Pacific Ry. Co., 345 U.S. 247, 73 S.Ct. 656, 97 L.Ed. 986 (1953), that litigants should be free to suggest that a particular case is appropriate for consideration by all the judges of a court of appeals. The rule is addressed to the procedure whereby a party may suggest the appropriateness of convening the court in banc. It does not affect the power of a court of appeals to initiate in banc hearings *sua sponte*.

The provision that a vote will not be taken as a result of the suggestion of the party unless requested by a judge of the court in regular active service or by a judge who was a member of the panel that rendered a decision sought to be reheard is intended to make it clear that a suggestion of a party as such does not require any action by the court. See Western Pacific Ry. Corp. v. Western Pacific Ry. Co., supra, 345 U.S. at 262, 73 S.Ct. 656. The rule merely authorizes a suggestion, imposes a time limit on suggestions for rehearings in banc, and provides that suggestions will be directed to the judges of the court in regular active service.

In practice, the suggestion of a party that a case be reheard in banc is frequently contained in a petition for rehearing, commonly styled "petition for rehearing in banc." Such a petition is in fact merely a petition for a rehearing, with a suggestion that the case be reheard in banc. Since no response to the suggestion, as distinguished from the petition for rehearing, is required, the panel which heard the case may quite properly dispose of the petition without reference to the suggestion. In such a case the fact that no response has been made to the suggestion does not affect the finality of the judgment or the issuance of the mandate, and the final sentence of the rule expressly so provides.

1979 AMENDMENT

Under the present rule there is no specific provision for a response to a suggestion that an appeal be heard in banc. This has led to some uncertainty as to whether such a response may be filed. The proposed amendment would resolve this uncertainty.

While the present rule provides a time limit for suggestions for rehearing in banc, it does not deal with the timing of a request that the appeal be heard in banc initially. The proposed amendment fills this gap as

well, providing that the suggestion must be made by the date of which the appellee's brief is filed.

Provision is made for circulating the suggestions to members of the panel despite the fact that senior judges on the panel would not be entitled to vote on whether a suggestion will be granted.

Rule 36.   Entry of Judgment

The notation of a judgment in the docket constitutes entry of the judgment. The clerk shall prepare, sign and enter the judgment following receipt of the opinion of the court unless the opinion directs settlement of the form of the judgment, in which event the clerk shall prepare, sign and enter the judgment following final settlement by the court. If a judgment is rendered without an opinion, the clerk shall prepare, sign and enter the judgment following instruction from the court. The clerk shall, on the date judgment is entered, mail to all parties a copy of the opinion, if any, or of the judgment if no opinion was written, and notice of the date of entry of the judgment.

NOTES OF ADVISORY COMMITTEE ON APPELLATE RULES

This is the typical rule. See 1st Cir. Rule 29; 3rd Cir. Rule 32; 6th Cir. Rule 21. At present, uncertainty exists as to the date of entry of judgment when the opinion directs subsequent settlement of the precise terms of the judgment, a common practice in cases involving enforcement of agency orders. See Stern and Gressman, Supreme Court Practice, p. 203 (3d Ed., 1962). The principle of finality suggests that in such cases entry of judgment should be delayed until approval of the judgment in final form.

Rule 37.   Interest on Judgments

Unless otherwise provided by law, if a judgment for money in a civil case is affirmed, whatever interest is allowed by law shall be payable from the date the judgment was entered in the district court. If a judgment is modified or reversed with a direction that a judgment for money be entered in the district court, the mandate shall contain instructions with respect to allowance of interest.

NOTES OF ADVISORY COMMITTEE ON APPELLATE RULES

The first sentence makes it clear that if a money judgment is affirmed in the court of appeals, the interest which attaches to money judgments by force of law (see 28 U.S.C. § 1961 and § 2411) upon their initial entry is payable as if no appeal had been taken, whether or not the mandate makes mention of interest. There has been some confusion on this point. See Blair v. Durham, 139 F.2d 260 (6th Cir., 1943) and cases cited therein.

In reversing or modifying the judgment of the district court, the court of appeals may direct the entry of a money judgment, as, for example, when the court of appeals reverses a judgment notwithstanding the verdict and directs entry of judgment on the verdict. In such a case the question may arise as to whether interest is to run from the date of entry of the judgment directed by the court of appeals or from the date on which the judgment would have been entered in the district court except for the erroneous ruling corrected on appeal. In Briggs v. Pennsylvania R. Co., 334 U.S. 304, 68 S.Ct. 1039, 92 L.Ed. 1403 (1948), the Court held that where the mandate of the court of appeals directed entry of judgment upon a verdict but made no mention of interest from the date of the verdict to the date of the entry of the judgment directed by the mandate, the district court was powerless to add such interest. The second sentence of the proposed rule is a reminder to the court, the clerk and counsel of the Briggs rule. Since the rule directs that the matter of interest be disposed of by the mandate, in cases where interest is simply overlooked, a party who conceives himself entitled to interest from a date other than the date of entry of judgment in accordance with the mandate should be entitled to seek recall of the mandate for determination of the question.

Rule 38.   Damages for Delay

If a court of appeals shall determine that an appeal is frivolous, it may award just damages and single or double costs to the appellee.

NOTES OF ADVISORY COMMITTEE ON APPELLATE RULES

Compare 28 U.S.C. § 1912. While both the statute and the usual rule on the subject by courts of appeals (Fourth Circuit Rule 20 is a typical rule) speak of "damages for delay," the courts of appeals quite properly allow damages, attorney's fees and other expenses incurred by an appellee if the appeal is frivolous without requiring a showing that the appeal resulted in delay. See Dunscombe v. Sayle, 340 F.2d 311 (5th Cir., 1965), cert. den., 382 U.S. 814, 86 S.Ct. 32, 15 L.Ed.2d 62 (1965); Lowe v. Willacy, 239 F.2d 179 (9th Cir., 1956); Griffith Wellpoint Corp. v. Munro-Langstroth, Inc., 269 F.2d 64 (1st Cir., 1959); Ginsburg v. Stern, 295 F.2d 698 (3d Cir., 1961). The subjects of interest and damages are separately regulated, contrary to the present practice of combining the two (see Fourth Circuit Rule 20) to make it clear that the awards are distinct and independent. Interest is provided for by law; damages are awarded by the court in its discretion in the case of a

frivolous appeal as a matter of justice to the appellee and as a penalty against the appellant.

Rule 39.   Costs

(a) **To Whom Allowed.** Except as otherwise provided by law, if an appeal is dismissed, costs shall be taxed against the appellant unless otherwise agreed by the parties or ordered by the court; if a judgment is affirmed, costs shall be taxed against the appellant unless otherwise ordered; if a judgment is reversed, costs shall be taxed against the appellee unless otherwise ordered; if a judgment is affirmed or reversed in part, or is vacated, costs shall be allowed only as ordered by the court.

(b) **Costs For and Against the United States.** In cases involving the United States or an agency or officer thereof, if an award of costs against the United States is authorized by law, costs shall be awarded in accordance with the provisions of subdivision (a); otherwise, costs shall not be awarded for or against the United States.

(c) **Costs of Briefs, Appendices, and Copies of Records.** By local rule the court of appeals shall fix the maximum rate at which the cost of printing or otherwise producing necessary copies of briefs, appendices, and copies of records authorized by Rule 30(f) shall be taxable. Such rate shall not be higher than that generally charged for such work in the area where the clerk's office is located and shall encourage the use of economical methods of printing and copying.

(d) **Bill of Costs; Objections; Costs to be Inserted in Mandate or Added Later.** A party who desires such costs to be taxed shall state them in an itemized and verified bill of costs which the party shall file with the clerk, with proof of service, within 14 days after the entry of judgment. Objections to the bill of costs must be filed within 10 days of service on the party against whom costs are to be taxed unless the time is extended by the court. The clerk shall prepare and certify an itemized statement of costs taxed in the court of appeals for insertion in the mandate, but the issuance of the mandate shall not be delayed for taxation of costs and if the mandate has been issued before final determination of costs, the statement, or any amendment thereof, shall be added to the mandate upon request by the clerk of the court of appeals to the clerk of the district court.

(e) Costs on Appeal Taxable in the District Courts. Costs incurred in the preparation and transmission of the record, the cost of the reporter's transcript, if necessary for the determination of the appeal, the premiums paid for cost of supersedeas bonds or other bonds to preserve rights pending appeal, and the fee for filing the notice of appeal shall be taxed in the district court as costs of the appeal in favor of the party entitled to costs under this rule.

(As amended Apr. 30, 1979, eff. Aug. 1, 1979; Mar. 10, 1986, eff. July 1, 1986.)

NOTES OF ADVISORY COMMITTEE ON APPELLATE RULES

Subdivision (a). Statutory authorization for taxation of costs is found in 28 U.S.C. § 1920. The provisions of this subdivision follow the usual practice in the circuits. A few statutes contain specific provisions in derogation of these general provisions. (See 28 U.S.C. § 1928, which forbids the award of costs to a successful plaintiff in a patent infringement action under the circumstances described by the statute). These statutes are controlling in cases to which they apply.

Subdivision (b). The rules of the courts of appeals at present commonly deny costs to the United States except as allowance may be directed by statute. Those rules were promulgated at a time when the United States was generally invulnerable to an award of costs against it, and they appear to be based on the view that if the United States is not subject to costs if it loses, it ought not be entitled to recover costs if it wins.

The number of cases affected by such rules has been greatly reduced by the Act of July 18, 1966, 80 Stat. 308 (1 U.S. Code Cong. & Ad. News, p. 349 (1966), 89th Cong., 2d Sess., which amended 28 U.S.C. § 2412, the former general bar to the award of costs against the United States. Section 2412 as amended generally places the United States on the same footing as private parties with respect to the award of costs in civil cases. But the United States continues to enjoy immunity from costs in certain cases. By its terms amended section 2412 authorizes an award of costs against the United States only in civil actions, and it excepts from its general authorization of an award of costs against the United States cases which are "otherwise specifically provided (for) by statute." Furthermore, the Act of July 18, 1966, supra, provides that the amendments of section 2412 which it effects shall apply only to actions filed subsequent to the date of its enactment. The second clause continues in effect, for these and all other cases in which the United States enjoys immunity from costs, the presently prevailing rule that the United States may recover costs as the prevailing party only if it would have suffered them as the losing party.

Subdivision (c). While only five circuits (D.C. Cir. Rule 20(d); 1st Cir. Rule 31(4); 3d Cir. Rule 35(4); 4th Cir. Rule 21(4); 9th Cir. Rule 25, as amended June 2, 1967) presently tax the cost of printing briefs, the proposed rule makes the cost taxable in keeping with the principle of this rule that all cost items expended in the prosecution of a proceeding should be borne by the unsuccessful party.

Subdivision (e). The costs described in this subdivision are costs of the appeal and, as such, are within the undertaking of the appeal bond. They are made taxable in the district court for general convenience. Taxation of the cost of the reporter's transcript is specifically authorized by 28 U.S.C. § 1920, but in the absence of a rule some district courts have held themselves without authority to tax the cost. Perlman v. Feldmann, 116 F.Supp. 102 (D.Conn., 1953); Firtag v. Gendleman, 152 F.Supp. 226 (D.D.C., 1957); Todd Atlantic Shipyards Corps. v. The Southport, 100 F.Supp. 763 (E.D.S.C., 1951). Provision for taxation of the cost of premiums paid for supersedeas bonds is common in the local rules of district courts and the practice is established in the Second, Seventh, and Ninth Circuits. Berner v. British Commonwealth Pacific Air Lines, Ltd., 362 F.2d 799 (2d Cir., 1966); Land Oberoesterreich v. Gude, 93 F.2d 292 (2d Cir., 1937); In re Northern Ind. Oil Co., 192 F.2d 139 (7th Cir., 1951); Lunn v. F.W. Woolworth, 210 F.2d 159 (9th Cir., 1954).

1979 AMENDMENT

Note to Subdivision (c). The proposed amendment would permit variations among the circuits in regulating the maximum rates taxable as costs for printing or otherwise reproducing briefs, appendices, and copies of records authorized by Rule 30(f). The present rule has had a different effect in different circuits depending upon the size of the circuit, the location of the clerk's office, and the location of other cities. As a consequence there was a growing sense that strict adherence to the rule produces some unfairness in some of the circuits and the matter should be made subject to local rule.

Note to Subdivision (d). The present rule makes no provision for objections to a bill of costs. The proposed amendment would allow 10 days for such objections. Cf. Rule 54(d) of the F.R.C.P. It provides further that the mandate shall not be delayed for taxation of costs.

1986 AMENDMENT

The amendment to subdivision (c) is intended to increase the degree of control exercised by the courts of appeals over rates for printing and copying recoverable as costs. It further requires the courts of appeals to encourage cost-consciousness by requiring that, in fixing the rate, the court consider the most economical methods of printing and copying.

The amendment to subdivision (d) is technical. No substantive change is intended.

Rule 40.   Petition for Rehearing

(a) Time for Filing; Content; Answer; Action by Court if Granted. A petition for rehearing may be filed within 14 days after entry of judgment unless the time is shortened or enlarged by order or by local rule. The petition shall state with particularity the points of law or fact which in the opinion of the petitioner the court has overlooked or misapprehended and shall contain such argument in support of the petition as the petitioner desires to present. Oral argument in support of the petition will not be permitted. No answer to a petition for rehearing will be received unless requested by the court, but a petition for rehearing will ordinarily not be granted in the absence of such a request. If a petition for rehearing is granted the court may make a final disposition of the cause without reargument or may restore it to the calendar for reargument or resubmission or may make such other orders as are deemed appropriate under the circumstances of the particular case.

(b) Form of Petition; Length. The petition shall be in a form prescribed by Rule 32(a), and copies shall be served and filed as prescribed by Rule 31(b) for the service and filing of briefs. Except by permission of the court, or as specified by local rule of the court of appeals, a petition for rehearing shall not exceed 15 pages.

(As amended Apr. 30, 1979, eff. Aug. 1, 1979.)

NOTES OF ADVISORY COMMITTEE ON APPELLATE RULES

This is the usual rule among the circuits, except that the express prohibition against filing a reply to the petition is found only in the rules of the Fourth, Sixth and Eighth Circuits (it is also contained in Supreme Court Rule 58(3)). It is included to save time and expense to the party victorious on appeal. In the very rare instances in which a reply is useful, the court will ask for it.

1979 AMENDMENT

Note to Subdivision (a). The Standing Committee added to the first sentence of Rule 40(a) the words "or by local rule," to conform to current practice in the circuits. The Standing Committee believes the change noncontroversial.

Note to Subdivision (b). The proposed amendment would eliminate the distinction drawn in the present rule between printed briefs and those duplicated from typewritten pages in fixing their maximum length. See Note to Rule 28. Since petitions for rehearing must be prepared in a short time, making typographic printing less likely, the maximum number of pages is fixed at 15, the figure used in the present rule for petitions duplicated by means other than typographic printing.

Rule 41.   Issuance of Mandate; Stay of Mandate

(a) Date of Issuance. The mandate of the court shall issue 21 days after the entry of judgment unless the time is shortened or enlarged by order. A certified copy of the judgment and a copy of the opinion of the court, if any, and any direction as to costs shall constitute the mandate, unless the court directs that a formal mandate issue. The timely filing of a petition for rehearing will stay the mandate until disposition of the petition unless otherwise ordered by the court. If the petition is denied, the mandate shall issue 7 days after entry of the order denying the petition unless the time is shortened or enlarged by order.

(b) Stay of Mandate Pending Application for Certiorari. A stay of the mandate pending application to the Supreme Court for a writ of certiorari may be granted upon motion, reasonable notice of which shall be given to all parties. The stay shall not exceed 30 days unless the period is extended for cause shown. If during the period of the stay there is filed with the clerk of the court of appeals a notice from the clerk of the Supreme Court that the party who has obtained the stay has filed a petition for the writ in that court, the stay shall continue until final disposition by the Supreme Court. Upon the filing of a copy of an order of the Supreme Court denying the petition for writ of certiorari the mandate shall issue immediately. A bond or other security may be required as a condition to the grant or continuance of a stay of the mandate.

NOTES OF ADVISORY COMMITTEE ON APPELLATE RULES

The proposed rule follows the rule or practice in a majority of circuits by which copies of the opinion and the judgment serve in lieu of a formal mandate in the ordinary case. Compare Supreme Court Rule 59. Although 28 U.S.C. § 2101(c) permits a writ of certiorari to be filed within 90 days after entry of judgment, seven of the eight circuits which now regulate the matter of stays pending application for certiorari limit the initial stay of the mandate to the 30-day period provided in the proposed rule. Compare D.C. Cir. Rule 27(e).

Rule 42. Voluntary Dismissal

(a) **Dismissal in the District Court.** If an appeal has not been docketed, the appeal may be dismissed by the district court upon the filing in that court of a stipulation for dismissal signed by all the parties, or upon motion and notice by the appellant.

(b) **Dismissal in the Court of Appeals.** If the parties to an appeal or other proceeding shall sign and file with the clerk of the court of appeals an agreement that the proceeding be dismissed, specifying the terms as to payment of costs, and shall pay whatever fees are due, the clerk shall enter the case dismissed, but no mandate or other process shall issue without an order of the court. An appeal may be dismissed on motion of the appellant upon such terms as may be agreed upon by the parties or fixed by the court.

NOTES OF ADVISORY COMMITTEE ON APPELLATE RULES

Subdivision (a). This subdivision is derived from FRCP 73(a) without change of substance.

Subdivision (b). The first sentence is a common provision in present circuit rules. The second sentence is added. Compare Supreme Court Rule 60.

Rule 43. Substitution of Parties

(a) **Death of a Party.** If a party dies after a notice of appeal is filed or while a proceeding is otherwise pending in the court of appeals, the personal representative of the deceased party may be substituted as a party on motion filed by the representative or by any party with the clerk of the court of appeals. The motion of a party shall be served upon the representative in accordance with the provisions of Rule 25. If the deceased party has no representative, any party may suggest the death on the record and proceedings shall then be had as the court of appeals may direct. If a party against whom an appeal may be taken dies after entry of a judgment or order in the district court but before a notice of appeal is filed, an appellant may proceed as if death had not occurred. After the notice of appeal is filed substitution shall be effected in the court of appeals in accordance with this subdivision. If a party entitled to appeal shall die before filing a notice of appeal, the notice of appeal may be filed by that party's personal representative, or, if there is no personal representative by that party's attorney of record within the time prescribed by these rules. After the notice of appeal is filed substitution shall be effected in the court of appeals in accordance with this subdivision.

(b) **Substitution for Other Causes.** If substitution of a party in the court of appeals is necessary for any reason other than death, substitution shall be effected in accordance with the procedure prescribed in subdivision (a).

(c) **Public Officers; Death or Separation from Office.**

(1) When a public officer is a party to an appeal or other proceeding in the court of appeals in an official capacity and during its pendency dies, resigns or otherwise ceases to hold office, the action does not abate and the public officer's successor is automatically substituted as a party. Proceedings following the substitution shall be in the name of the substituted party, but any misnomer not affecting the substantial rights of the parties shall be disregarded. An order of substitution may be entered at any time, but the omission to enter such an order shall not affect the substitution.

(2) When a public officer is a party to an appeal or other proceeding in an official capacity that public officer may be described as a party by the public officer's official title rather than by name; but the court may require the public officer's name to be added.

(As amended Mar. 10, 1986, eff. July 1, 1986.)

NOTES OF ADVISORY COMMITTEE ON APPELLATE RULES

Subdivision (a). The first three sentences described a procedure similar to the rule on substitution in civil actions in the district court. See FRCP 25(a). The fourth sentence expressly authorizes an appeal to be taken against one who has died after the entry of judgment. Compare FRCP 73(b), which impliedly authorizes such an appeal.

The sixth sentence authorizes an attorney of record for the deceased to take an appeal on behalf of successors in interest if the deceased has no representative. At present, if a party entitled to appeal dies before the notice of appeal is filed, the appeal can presumably be taken only by his legal representative and must be taken within the time ordinarily prescribed. 13 Cyclopedia of Federal Procedure (3d Ed.) § 63.21. The states commonly make special provisions for the event of the death of a party entitled to appeal, usually by extending the time otherwise prescribed. Rules of Civil Procedure for Superior Courts of Arizona, Rule 73(t), 16 A.R.S.; New Jersey Rev. Rules 1:3–3; New York Civil

Practice Law and Rules, Sec. 1022; Wisconsin Statutes Ann. 274.01(2). The provision in the proposed rule is derived from California Code of Civil Procedure, Sec. 941.

Subdivision (c). This subdivision is derived from FRCP 25(d) and Supreme Court Rule 48, with appropriate changes.

1986 AMENDMENT

The amendments to Rules 43(a) and (c) are technical. No substantive change is intended.

Rule 44. Cases Involving Constitutional Questions Where United States is not a Party

It shall be the duty of a party who draws in question the constitutionality of any Act of Congress in any proceeding in a court of appeals to which the United States, or any agency thereof, or any officer or employee thereof, as such officer or employee, is not a party, upon the filing of the record, or as soon thereafter as the question is raised in the court of appeals, to give immediate notice in writing to the court of the existence of said question. The clerk shall thereupon certify such fact to the Attorney General.

NOTES OF ADVISORY COMMITTEE ON APPELLATE RULES

This rule is now found in the rules of a majority of the circuits. It is in response to the Act of August 24, 1937 (28 U.S.C. § 2403) which requires all courts of the United States to advise the Attorney General of the existence of an action or proceeding of the kind described in the rule.

Rule 45. Duties of Clerks

(a) General Provisions. The clerk of a court of appeals shall take the oath and give the bond required by law. Neither the clerk nor any deputy clerk shall practice as an attorney or counselor in any court while continuing in office. The court of appeals shall be deemed always open for the purpose of filing any proper paper, of issuing and returning process and of making motions and orders. The office of the clerk with the clerk or a deputy in attendance shall be open during business hours on all days except Saturdays, Sundays, and legal holidays, but a court may provide by local rule or order that the office of its clerk shall be open for specified hours on Saturdays or on particular legal holidays other than New Years Day, Birthday of Martin Luther King, Jr., Wash-

ington's Birthday, Memorial Day, Independence Day, Labor Day, Columbus Day, Veterans Day, Thanksgiving Day, and Christmas Day.

(b) The Docket; Calendar; Other Records Required. The clerk shall maintain a docket in such form as may be prescribed by the Director of the Administrative Office of the United States Courts. The clerk shall enter a record of all papers filed with the clerk and all process, orders and judgments. An index of cases contained in the docket shall be maintained as prescribed by the Director of the Administrative Office of the United States Courts.

The clerk shall prepare, under the direction of the court, a calendar of cases awaiting argument. In placing cases on the calendar for argument, the clerk shall give preference to appeals in criminal cases and to appeals and other proceedings entitled to preference by law.

The clerk shall keep such other books and records as may be required from time to time by the Director of the Administrative Office of the United States Courts with the approval of the Judicial Conference of the United States, or as may be required by the court.

(c) Notice of Orders or Judgments. Immediately upon the entry of an order or judgment the clerk shall serve a notice of entry by mail upon each party to the proceeding together with a copy of any opinion respecting the order or judgment, and shall make a note in the docket of the mailing. Service on a party represented by counsel shall be made on counsel.

(d) Custody of Records and Papers. The clerk shall have custody of the records and papers of the court. The clerk shall not permit any original record or paper to be taken from the clerk's custody except as authorized by the orders or instructions of the court. Original papers transmitted as the record on appeal or review shall upon disposition of the case be returned to the court or agency from which they were received. The clerk shall preserve copies of briefs and appendices and other printed papers filed. (As amended Mar. 1, 1971, eff. July 1, 1971; Mar. 10, 1986, eff. July 1, 1986.)

NOTES OF ADVISORY COMMITTEE ON APPELLATE RULES

1967 NOTE

The duties imposed upon clerks of the courts of appeals by this rule are those imposed by rule or practice in a majority of the circuits. The second sentence of subdivision (a) authorizing the closing of the clerk's office on Saturday and non-national legal holidays follows a similar provision respecting the district court clerk's office found in FRCP 77(c) and FRCrP 56.

1971 NOTE

The amendment adds Columbus Day to the list of legal holidays. See the Note accompanying the amendment of Rule 26(a).

1986 AMENDMENT

The amendment to Rule 45(b) permits the courts of appeals to maintain computerized dockets. The Committee believes that the Administrative Office of the United States Courts ought to have maximum flexibility in prescribing the format of this docket in order to ensure a smooth transition from manual to automated systems and subsequent adaptation to technological improvements.

The amendments to Rules 45(a) and (d) are technical. No substantive change is intended. The Birthday of Martin Luther King, Jr. has been added to the list of national holidays.

Rule 46. Attorneys

(a) Admission to the Bar of a Court of Appeals; Eligibility; Procedure for Admission. An attorney who has been admitted to practice before the Supreme Court of the United States, or the highest court of a state, or another United States court of appeals, or a United States district court (including the district courts for the Canal Zone, Guam and the Virgin Islands), and who is of good moral and professional character, is eligible for admission to the bar of a court of appeals.

An applicant shall file with the clerk of the court of appeals, on a form approved by the court and furnished by the clerk, an application for admission containing the applicant's personal statement showing eligibility for membership. At the foot of the application the applicant shall take and subscribe to the following oath or affirmation:

I, _____, do solemnly swear (or affirm) that I will demean myself as an attorney and counselor of this court, uprightly and according to law; and that I will support the Constitution of the United States.

Thereafter, upon written or oral motion of a member of the bar of the court, the court will act upon the application. An applicant may be admitted by oral motion in open court, but it is not necessary that the applicant appear before the court for the purpose of being admitted, unless the court shall otherwise order. An applicant shall upon admission pay to the clerk the fee prescribed by rule or order of the court.

(b) Suspension or Disbarment. When it is shown to the court that any member of its bar has been suspended or disbarred from practice in any other court of record, or has been guilty of conduct unbecoming a member of the bar of the court, the member will be subject to suspension or disbarment by the court. The member shall be afforded an opportunity to show good cause, within such time as the court shall prescribe, why the member should not be suspended or disbarred. Upon the member's response to the rule to show cause, and after hearing, if requested, or upon expiration of the time prescribed for a response if no response is made, the court shall enter an appropriate order.

(c) Disciplinary Power of the Court over Attorneys. A court a appeals may, after reasonable notice and an opportunity to show cause to the contrary, and after hearing, if requested, take any appropriate disciplinary action against any attorney who practices before it for conduct unbecoming a member of the bar or for failure to comply with these rules or any rule of the court.

(As amended Mar. 10, 1986, eff. July 1, 1986.)

NOTES OF ADVISORY COMMITTEE ON APPELLATE RULES

Subdivision (a). The basic requirement of membership in the bar of the Supreme Court, or of the highest court of a state, or in another court of appeals or a district court is found, with minor variations, in the rules of ten circuits. The only other requirement in those circuits is that the applicant be of good moral and professional character. In the District of Columbia Circuit applicants other than members of the District of Columbia District bar or the Supreme Court bar must claim membership in the bar of the highest court of a state, territory or possession for three years prior to application for admission (D.C.Cir. Rule 7). Members of the District of Columbia District bar and the Supreme Court bar again excepted, applicants for admission to the District of Columbia Circuit bar must meet precisely defined prelaw and law school study requirements (D.C.Cir. Rule 7½).

A few circuits now require that application for admission be made by oral motion by a sponsor member in open court. The proposed rule permits both the application and the motion by the sponsor member to be in writing, and permits action on the motion without the appearance of the applicant or the sponsor, unless the court otherwise orders.

Subdivision (b). The provision respecting suspension or disbarment is uniform. Third Circuit Rule 8(3) is typical.

Subdivision (c). At present only Fourth Circuit Rule 36 contains an equivalent provision. The purpose of this provision is to make explicit the power of a court of appeals to impose sanctions less serious than suspension or disbarment for the breach of rules. It also affords some measure of control over attorneys who are not members of the bar of the court. Several circuits permit a non-member attorney to file briefs and motions, membership being required only at the time of oral argument. And several circuits permit argument pro hac vice by non-member attorneys.

1986 AMENDMENT

The amendments to Rules 45(a) and (b) are technical. No substantive change is intended.

Rule 47.   Rules by Courts of Appeals

Each court of appeals by action of a majority of the circuit judges in regular active service may from time to time make and amend rules governing its practice not inconsistent with these rules. In all cases not provided for by rule, the courts of appeals may regulate their practice in any manner not inconsistent with these rules. Copies of all rules made by a court of appeals shall upon their promulgation be furnished to the Administrative Office of the United States Courts.

NOTES OF ADVISORY COMMITTEE ON APPELLATE RULES

This rule continues the authority now vested in individual courts of appeals by 28 U.S.C. § 2071 to make rules consistent with rules of practice and procedure promulgated by the Supreme Court.

Rule 48.   Title

These rules may be known and cited as the Federal Rules of Appellate Procedure.

APPENDIX OF FORMS

Form 1.
NOTICE OF APPEAL TO A COURT OF APPEALS FROM A JUDGMENT OR ORDER OF A DISTRICT COURT

United States District Court for the _____ District of _____

File Number _____

A.B., Plaintiff

　　v.　　　　　　Notice of Appeal

C.D., Defendant

Notice is hereby given that C. D., defendant above named, hereby appeals to the United States Court of Appeals for the _____ Circuit (from the final judgment) (from the order (describing it)) entered in this action on the ____ day of _____

1. The name of the Tax Court of the United States has been changed to United States Tax Court by Pub.L.

_____, 19___

(S) _____
_____
(Address)
Attorney for C. D.

Form 2.
NOTICE OF APPEAL TO A COURT OF APPEALS
FROM A DECISION OF THE TAX COURT

Tax Court of the United States
Washington, D. C.[1]

A.B., Petitioner

　　　　　　　　　Docket No. ____

　　v.

Commissioner of Internal Revenue, Respondent

91–172, 951, Dec. 30, 1969, 83 Stat. 730 (section 7441 of Title 26, Internal Revenue Code).

Notice of Appeal

Notice is hereby given that A. B. hereby appeals to the United States Court of Appeals for the _____ Circuit from [that part of] the decision of this court entered in the above captioned proceeding on the _____ day of _____ 19__ [relating to _____].

(S) _____

_____
(Address)
Counsel for A. B.

Form 3.

PETITION FOR REVIEW OF ORDER OF AN AGENCY, BOARD, COMMISSION OR OFFICER

United States Court of Appeals for
the _____ Circuit

A. B., Petitioner

                    Petition for Review
   v.

XYZ Commission,
  Respondent

A. B. hereby petitions the court for review of the Order of the XYZ Commission (describe the order) entered on _____, 19__

(s) _____
Attorney for Petitioner
Address: _____

Form 4.

AFFIDAVIT TO ACCOMPANY MOTION FOR LEAVE TO APPEAL IN FORMA PAUPERIS

United States District Court for the
_____
District of _____
United States of America
       v.   No. _____
A. B.

Affidavit in Support of Motion to Proceed on Appeal in Forma Pauperis

I, _____ being first duly sworn, depose and say that I am the _____, in the above-entitled case; that in support of my motion to proceed on appeal without being required to prepay fees, costs or give security therefor, I state that because of my poverty I am unable to pay the costs of said proceeding or to give security therefor; that I believe I am entitled to redress; and that the issues which I desire to present on appeal are the following:

I further swear that the responses which I have made to the questions and instructions below relating to my ability to pay the cost of prosecuting the appeal are true.

1. Are you presently employed?

    a. If the answer is yes, state the amount of your salary or wages per month and give the name and address of your employer.

    b. If the answer is no, state the date of your last employment and the amount of the salary and wages per month which you received.

2. Have you received within the past twelve months any income from a business, profession or other form of self-employment, or in the form of rent payments, interest, dividends, or other source?

    a. If the answer is yes, describe each source of income, and state the amount received from each during the past twelve months.

3. Do you own any cash or checking or savings account?

    a. If the answer is yes, state the total value of the items owned.

4. Do you own any real estate, stocks, bonds, notes, automobiles, or other valuable property (excluding ordinary household furnishings and clothing)?

    a. If the answer is yes, describe the property and state its approximate value.

5. List the persons who are dependent upon you for support and state your relationship to those persons.

I understand that a false statement or answer to any questions in this affidavit will subject me to penalties for perjury.

Let the applicant proceed without prepayment of costs or fees or the necessity of giving security therefor.

_____

SUBSCRIBED AND SWORN TO before me this _____ day of _____, 19__

_____

District Judge

SELECTED FEDERAL STATUTES

Table of Contents

INTRODUCTION

Reprinted from Abrams, Federal Criminal Law and Its Enforcement (1986).

Conduct comprising traditional crimes—the kind that makes up the normal caseload in state court systems—is also subject to prosecution in the federal courts under federal law when the offense occurs on federal property, or where federal moneys are affected or federal personnel are injured or killed. Thus murder, manslaughter and rape are federal crimes when committed "within the special ... territorial jurisdiction of the United States"; a provision punishing conspiracy to defraud the United States can be used to prosecute persons who have defrauded the government of federal moneys; and it is a crime to assault or kill a federal officer. In all such cases there is a direct federal interest in the prosecution.

Criminal conduct that does not involve such direct federal interests is also prosecuted by that federal government; the crimes involved are usually based in the commerce power. The Travel Act—which makes it a federal crime to travel interstate or use a facility of commerce with intent to carry on unlawful activity such as extortion, bribery or arson—illustrates this type of statute; it is aimed at criminal conduct which violates no direct federal interest and is of a sort that usually could as well be prosecuted at the state-local level. Federal criminal legislation of this type is sometimes justified on the ground that it permits federal prosecution where, because of the size of the criminal group or extensive interstate criminal activities, investigation and prosecution by the federal government rather than local law agencies is convenient. However, the definition of commerce power offenses is not restricted to instances where federal enforcement is more convenient, and the matters actually prosecuted are not limited to such cases. The result is that "local interest" crimes have proliferated in the federal criminal code, and the federal government has been increasingly involved in the business of investigating and prosecuting crime that could (should?) have been handled by state or local authorities.

True, the federal government cannot prosecute such local crimes unless there is a basis for federal jurisdiction, but the jurisdictional base typically "only very crudely marks off the area in which [there is justification for federal prosecution]." [1]; and as criminal legislation

---

1. Unless the federal government's concern is perceived simply as an enforcement aid to the states which is intended to operate occasionally without any principled basis [Is this an acceptable approach?], there are serious problems with making federal criminal jurisdiction turn simply on the fact that there has been transportation or movement across a state line. "The use of a particular jurisdictional circumstance in the definition of a federal crime only very crudely marks off the area in which ... [there is justification for federal prosecution]." Schwartz, *Federal Criminal Jurisdiction and Prosecutors' Discretion, 13 Law and Contemp.Probs. 64, 79 (1948)*

has increasingly used multiple bases drafted in broad terms, broadly interpreted, the jurisdictional limits on federal prosecution have weakened. The broader or more readily met the jurisdictional base is, the closer federal offenses of this type can come to duplicating the statutory coverage of the comparable state offenses.

As part of a continuing pattern of expansion, the number and extent of traditional crimes based in the commerce power has increased, either by way of changes in the jurisdictional coverage of existing crimes or by addition of new crime categories to the federal criminal code. Subject to the jurisdictional limit qualification (which, of course, varies in its significance from offense to offense) traditional crimes covered under federal law today without a direct federal interest include: various forms of theft, fraud, robbery, burglary, extortion, kidnapping, arson, bribery, loan sharking, murder, assault, threats, maiming, gambling, prostitution and drug offenses.

As you study various crime categories, consider the extent to which the statute under consideration is being used to prosecute conduct which does not involve a direct federal interest and which and how many local interest crimes have been thus absorbed into the federal criminal system.

The mail fraud statute, enacted in 1872, (18 U.S.C.A. § 1341) was the first federal criminal statute of broad scope used to prosecute criminal activity—fraudulent schemes— also dealt with under state law. In 1910, the Mann Act prohibiting interstate transportation of females for immoral purposes (18 U.S.C.A. § 2421) was enacted. The Harrison Act of 1914, was the start of federal criminal involvement with narcotic drugs (Ch. 1, 38 Stat. 785), and in 1919 the Dyer Act (18 U.S.C.A. § 2312) prohibiting interstate transportation of stolen motor vehicles became law. Between 1932 and 1935, a number of well-known federal crimes were enacted: the Anti–Racketeering Act of 1934 (18 U.S.C.A. § 1951); the Bank Robbery Act of 1934 (18 U.S.C.A. § 2113); The Fugitive Felon Act of 1932 (18 U.S.C.A. § 1073), and the Lindbergh Law—the Kidnapping Act of 1932 (18 U.S.C.A. § 1201). During the 1930's federal gun laws and additional narcotic drug laws were also added to the statute books.

In the 1950's, a wholesale expansion of federal criminal laws began.[2] Some examples illustrate the broad range of subjects touched upon. Congress began to adopt a series of criminal provisions aimed at gambling (for example, 15 U.S.C.A. § 1176), and over the course of the next two decades a number of anti-gambling provisions were enacted (for example, 18 U.S.C.A. § 1953). In 1959, a new enactment made the embezzlement of labor union funds a federal crime (29 U.S.C.A. § 501). In 1961, the Travel Act (18 U.S.C.A. § 1952) was passed. This was followed in 1962 by a provision relating to embezzlement from employee benefit plans (18 U.S.C.A. § 664). With the Gun Control Act of 1968, Congress extended the reach of federal gun control laws (18 U.S.C.A. §§ 921–928; 18 U.S.C.A.App. §§ 1201–1203). Provisions were also enacted relating to the illegal manufac-

Judge Henry Friendly has put the point more sharply:

Why should the federal government care if a Manhattan businessman takes his mistress to sleep with him in Greenwich, Connecticut, although it would not if the love-nest were in Port Chester, N.Y.? Why should it make a difference that a New York pimp chooses Newark, N.J., rather than Nyack, N.Y., as the place where his employees transact their business? If the house is in Nyack, why is the United States interested because the girls have traveled over the George Washington bridge and thence through New Jersey although it would not be if they crossed the Hudson over the New York Thruway?

Friendly, *Federal Jurisdiction, A General View* 58 (1973).

2. This paragraph is drawn in part from Abrams, Federal Criminal Law Enforcement, 2 Encyclopedia of Crime and Justice 779 (Free Press, New York, 1983) and is reprinted by permission.

ture and distribution of explosives and the transportation of switchblade knives (18 U.S.C.A. §§ 841–848; 15 U.S.C.A. § 1242). In 1968, too, traveling across a state line with the purpose of inciting a riot became a federal crime (18 U.S.C.A. §§ 2101–2102). In 1970, Congress passed several important pieces of substantive criminal legislation: RICO, the Racketeer–Influenced and Corrupt Organizations Statute (18 U.S.C.A. § 1961 et seq.); the illegal gambling business statute (18 U.S.C.A. § 1955), and a major revision of the drug laws—the Comprehensive Drug Abuse Prevention and Control Act (21 U.S.C.A. § 801 et seq.). In 1978, legislation was enacted relating to the sexual exploitation of children (18 U.S.C.A. §§ 2251–2253). Additionally, since the 1950's new federal criminal statutes have been enacted in the field of civil rights (for example, 18 U.S.C.A. § 245), consumer protection (15 U.S.C.A. § 1264), credit card fraud (15 U.S.C.A. § 1644), occupational safety (29 U.S.C.A. § 666), and traffic in contraband commercial items such as cigarettes, fireworks, and counterfeit phonograph records (18 U.S.C.A. §§ 2341–2346; § 836; § 2318). In 1984, Congress enacted a new crime package, the Comprehensive Crime Control Act of 1984 which, inter alia, contained provisions relating to the robbery or burglary of pharmacies; murder for hire; hostage-taking; crimes in aid of racketeering; and counterfeiting securities issued by a state. The wide-ranging Anti–Drug Abuse Acts of 1986 and 1988 contain provisions that mainly bear on drug offenses, although they also deal incidently with other crimes, too—e.g., the Travel Act, the RICO statute, the Bank Secrecy Act, mail and wire fraud statutes, and Money Laundering offenses.

This INTRODUCTION to federal criminal legislation is substantially adapted from Abrams' Federal Criminal Law and Its Enforcement, American Casebook Series (West Publishing Company, St. Paul, 1986), as supplemented, pages 63–65.

EDITOR'S NOTE

Reproducing the statutory text of a broad cross-section of federal crimes is beyond the scope of this pamphlet. (For a full rendition of the federal criminal code, see West's annual Federal Criminal Code and Rules.)

Serious drug offenses preoccupy criminal enforcement (and involve cooperative state-federal efforts) to such a degree that, among federal criminal statutes, the antidrug laws are invoked with extraordinary frequency ... and are set out here as a representative federal model.

Recognizing that "(t)he illegal importation, manufacture, distribution, and possession and improper use of controlled substances have a substantial and detrimental effect on the health and general welfare of the American people," Congress conceived The Comprehensive Drug Abuse Prevention and Control Act of 1970 (21 U.S.C.A. 801 et seq.), short title "Controlled Substances Act". This statute for the first time in a half century of federal legislative effort created a unified scheme covering both narcotic and dangerous drugs. Amendments have been wide-ranging, as federal criminal enforcement strategy evolves. [For a concise historical summary of federal drug control legislation, see Abrams, Federal Criminal Law and Its Enforcement, pp. 340–342 and current Supplement (West Publishing Company, St. Paul, 1986)]. The related Maritime Drug Law Enforcement Act (46 U.S.C.A. 1901 et seq.), money laundering provisions of Title 31, and provision for the civil commitment of addicted offenders (28 U.S.C.A. 2901–2906) complete the following collection of drug control laws.

With enactment of the Federal Comprehensive Drug Abuse Prevention and Control Act, it was imperative that the states update and revise their narcotic and dangerous drug laws. In 1970 the Uniform Law Commissioners approved the Uniform Controlled Substances Act "to achieve uniformity between the laws of the several States and those of the Federal government." All states, and the District of Columbia and the Virgin Islands, have since adopted the Uniform Act, their corresponding statutes listed immediately following the Table of Contents of the Comprehensive Drug Abuse Prevention and Control Act. Among the main objectives of the Uniform Controlled Substances Act was creation of a coordinated and codified system of drug control, modelled explicitly on the federal law, classifying drugs subject to control into several schedules. Since the Uniform Act largely overlaps the federal statute, the Uniform Act is not duplicated in this pamphlet.

TITLE 21
FOOD AND DRUGS

CHAPTER 13—DRUG ABUSE PREVENTION AND CONTROL

As amended to February 1, 1989

SUBCHAPTER I. CONTROL AND ENFORCEMENT
PART A. INTRODUCTORY PROVISIONS

PART B. AUTHORITY TO CONTROL; STANDARDS AND SCHEDULES

PART C. REGISTRATION OF MANUFACTURERS, DISTRIBUTORS, AND DISPENSERS OF CONTROLLED SUBSTANCES

PART D. OFFENSES AND PENALTIES

PART E. ADMINISTRATIVE AND ENFORCEMENT PROVISIONS

PART F. GENERAL PROVISIONS

SUBCHAPTER II. IMPORT AND EXPORT

538

Sec.

(d) Denial of application.

(e) Registration period.

(f) Rules and regulations.

(g) Scope of authorized activity.

(h) Separate registrations for each principal place of business.

(i) Emergency situations.

959. Possession, manufacture, or distribution for purposes of unlawful importation.

(a) Prohibition on controlled substance in schedule I or II.

(b) United States citizen on board any aircraft or any person on board United States owned or registered aircraft.

(c) Acts committed outside territorial jurisdiction of United States.

960. Prohibited acts A.

(a) Unlawful acts.

(b) Penalties.

(c) Repealed.

(d) Penalty for importation or exportation.

961. Prohibited acts B.

962. Second or subsequent offenses.

Sec.

(a) Term of imprisonment and fine.

(b) Determination of status.

(c) Procedures applicable.

963. Attempt and conspiracy.

964. Additional penalties.

965. Applicability of Part E of Subchapter I.

966. Authority of Secretary of the Treasury.

967. Smuggling of controlled substances; investigations; oaths; subpenas; witnesses; evidence; production of records; territorial limits; fees and mileage of witnesses.

968. Service of subpena; proof of service.

969. Contempt proceedings.

970. Criminal forfeitures.

971. Notification, suspension of shipment, and penalties with respect to importation and exportation of listed chemicals.

(a) Notification prior to transaction.

(b) Regular customers or suppliers.

(c) Suspension of importation or exportation; disqualification of regular customers or suppliers; hearing.

1. So in original.

Uniform Controlled Substances Act

Table of Jurisdictions Where the Uniform Controlled Substances Act has been Adopted.

The Code of the State of Maine contains provisions of both the Uniform Controlled Substances Act and the Uniform Narcotic Drug Act.

For text of Uniform Controlled Substances Act, and variation notes and annotation materials for

adopting jurisdictions, see Uniform Laws Annotated, Master Edition, Volume 9.

Jurisdiction	Statutory Citation
Alabama	Code 1975, §§ 20–2–1 to 20–2–93.
Alaska	AS 11.71.010 to 11.71.900, 17.30.010 to 17.30.900.
Arizona	A.R.S. §§ 36–2501 to 36–2553.
Arkansas	Code 1987, §§ 5–64–101 to 5–64–108.
California	West's Ann.Cal.Health & Safety Code, §§ 11000 to 11651.
Colorado	C.R.S. 12–22–301 to 12–22–322.
Connecticut	C.G.S.A. §§ 21a–240 to 21a–308.
Delaware	16 Del.C. §§ 4701 to 4796.
District of Columbia	D.C.Code 1981, §§ 33–501 to 33–567.
Florida	West's F.S.A. §§ 893.01 to 893.165.
Georgia	O.C.G.A. §§ 16–13–20 to 16–13–56.
Guam	9 G.C.A. §§ 67.10 to 67.98.
Hawaii	HRS §§ 329–1 to 329–58.

Jurisdiction	Statutory Citation
Idaho	I.C. §§ 37–2701 to 37–2751.
Illinois	S.H.A. ch. 56½, ¶¶ 1100 to 1603.
Indiana	West's A.I.C. 35–48–1–1 to 35–48–4–14.
Iowa	I.C.A. §§ 204.101 to 204.602.
Kansas	K.S.A. 65–4101 to 65–4140.
Kentucky	KRS 218A.010 to 218A.991.
Louisiana	LSA–R.S. 40:961 to 40:995.
Maine	17–A M.R.S.A. §§ 1101 to 1116; 22 M.R.S.A. §§ 2383, 2383–A.
Maryland	Code 1957, art. 27, §§ 276 to 302.
Massachusetts	M.G.L.A. c. 94C, §§ 1 to 48.
Michigan	M.C.L.A. §§ 333.7101 to 333.7545.
Minnesota	M.S.A. §§ 152.01 to 152.20.
Mississippi	Code 1972, §§ 41–29–101 to 41–29–185.
Missouri	V.A.M.S. §§ 195.010 to 195.320.
Montana	MCA 50–32–101 to 50–32–405.

Jurisdiction	Statutory Citation
Nebraska..............	R.R.S. 1943, § 28–401 et seq.
Nevada	N.R.S. 453.011 to 453.361.
New Jersey...........	N.J.S.A. 24:21–1 to 24:21–53.
New Mexico	NMSA 1978, §§ 30–31–1 to 30–31–41.
New York	McKinney's Public Health Law §§ 3300 to 3396.
North Carolina	G.S. §§ 90–86 to 90–113.8.
North Dakota........	NDCC 19–03.1–01 to 19–03.1–43.
Ohio	R.C. §§ 3719.01 to 3719.99.
Oklahoma	63 Okl.St.Ann. §§ 2–101 to 2–610.
Oregon..............	ORS 475.005 to 475.285, 475.992 to 475.995.
Pennsylvania.........	35 P.S. §§ 780–101 to 780–144.
Puerto Rico	24 L.P.R.A. §§ 2101 to 2607.
Rhode Island.........	Gen.Laws 1956, §§ 21–28–1.01 to 21–28–6.02.
South Carolina	Code 1976, §§ 44–53–110 to 44–53–590.
South Dakota........	SDCL 34–20B–1 to 34–20B–114.

Jurisdiction	Statutory Citation
Tennessee	T.C.A. §§ 39–6–401 to 39–6–419, 53–11–301 to 53–11–414.
Texas...............	Vernon's Ann.Civ.St. art. 4476–15.
Utah	U.C.A. 1953, §§ 58–37–1 to 58–37–19.
Virgin Islands	19 V.I.C. §§ 591 to 630a.
Virginia	Code 1950, § 54–54.1–3400 et seq.
Washington..........	West's RCWA §§ 69.50.101 to 69.50.607.
West Virginia	Code 60A–1–101 to 60A–6–605.
Wisconsin	W.S.A. 161.001 to 161.62.
Wyoming	W.S. 1977, §§ 35–7–1001 to 35–7–1057.

Savings Provisions of Pub.L. 98–473, Title II, c. II.
See section 235 of Pub.L. 98–473, Title II, c. II, Oct. 12, 1984, 98 Stat. 2031, as amended, set out as a note under section 3551 of Title 18, Crimes and Criminal Procedure.

SUBCHAPTER I

CONTROL AND ENFORCEMENT

Part A

Introductory Provisions

§ 801. Congressional findings and declarations: controlled substances

The Congress makes the following findings and declarations:

(1) Many of the drugs included within this subchapter have a useful and legitimate medical purpose and are necessary to maintain the health and general welfare of the American people.

(2) The illegal importation, manufacture, distribution, and possession and improper use of controlled substances have a substantial and detrimental effect on the health and general welfare of the American people.

(3) A major portion of the traffic in controlled substances flows through interstate and foreign commerce. Incidents of the traffic which are not an integral part of the interstate or foreign flow, such as manufacture, local distribution, and possession, nonetheless have a substantial and direct effect upon interstate commerce because—

(A) after manufacture, many controlled substances are transported in interstate commerce,

(B) controlled substances distributed locally usually have been transported in interstate commerce immediately before their distribution, and

(C) controlled substances possessed commonly flow through interstate commerce immediately prior to such possession.

(4) Local distribution and possession of controlled substances contribute to swelling the interstate traffic in such substances.

(5) Controlled substances manufactured and distributed intrastate cannot be differentiated from controlled substances manufactured and distributed interstate. Thus, it is not feasible to distinguish, in terms of controls, between controlled substances manufactured and distributed interstate and controlled substances manufactured and distributed intrastate.

(6) Federal control of the intrastate incidents of the traffic in controlled substances is essential to the effective control of the interstate incidents of such traffic.

(7) The United States is a party to the Single Convention on Narcotic Drugs, 1961, and other international conventions designed to establish effective control over international and domestic traffic in controlled substances.

(Pub.L. 91–513, Title II, § 101, Oct. 27, 1970, 84 Stat. 1242.)

EDITORIAL NOTES

References in Text. This subchapter, wherever referred to in this subchapter, was in the original "this title" which is Title II of Pub.L. 91–513, Oct. 27, 1970, 84 Stat. 1242, and is popularly known as the "Controlled Substances Act".

Joint Federal Task Force on Illegal Drug Laboratories. Pub.L. 100–690, Title II, § 2405, Nov. 18, 1988, 102 Stat. 4231, provided that:

"(a) **Establishment of Task Force.** There is established the Joint Federal Task Force on Illegal Drug Laboratories (hereafter in this section referred to as the 'Task Force').

"(b) **Appointment and Membership of Task Force.** The members of the Task Force shall be appointed by the Administrators of the Environmental Protection Agency and the Drug Enforcement Administration (hereafter in this section referred to as the 'Administrators'). The Task Force shall consist of at least 6 and not more than 20 members. Each Administrator shall appoint one-half of the members as follows: (1) the Administrator of the Environmental Protection Agency shall appoint members from among Emergency Response Technicians and other appropriate employees of the Agency; and (2) the Administrator of the Drug Enforcement Administration shall appoint members from among Special Agents assigned to field divisions and other appropriate employees of the Administration.

"(c) **Duties of Task Force.** The Task Force shall formulate, establish, and implement a program for the cleanup and disposal of hazardous waste produced by illegal drug laboratories. In formulating such program, the Task Force shall consider the following factors:

"(1) The volume of hazardous waste produced by illegal drug laboratories.

"(2) The cost of cleaning up and disposing of hazardous waste produced by illegal drug laboratories.

"(3) The effectiveness of the various methods of cleaning up and disposing of hazardous waste produced by illegal drug laboratories.

"(4) The coordination of the efforts of the Environmental Protection Agency and the Drug Enforcement Administration in cleaning up and disposing of hazardous waste produced by illegal drug laboratories.

"(5) The dissemination of information to law enforcement agencies that have responsibility for enforcement of drug laws.

"(d) **Guidelines.** The Task Force shall recommend to the Administrators guidelines for cleanup of illegal drug laboratories to protect the public health and environment. Not later than 180 days after the date of the enactment of this subtitle [Nov. 18, 1988], the Administrators shall formulate and publish such guidelines.

"(e) **Demonstration projects.—**

"(1) The Attorney General shall make grants to, and enter into contracts with, State and local governments for demonstration projects to clean up and safely dispose of substances associated with illegal drug laboratories which may present a danger to public health or the environment.

"(2) The Attorney General may not under this subsection make a grant or enter into a contract unless the applicant for such assistance agrees to comply with the guidelines issued pursuant to subsection (d).

"(3) The Attorney General shall, through grant or contract, provide for independent evaluations of the activities carried out pursuant to this subsection and shall recommend appropriate legislation to the Congress.

"(f) **Funding.** Of the amounts made available to carry out the Controlled Substances Act [21 U.S.C.A. § 801 et seq.] for fiscal year 1989, not less than $5,000,000 shall be made available to carry out subsections (d) and (e).

"(g) **Reports.** After consultation with the Task Force, the Administrators shall—

"(1) transmit to the President and to each House of Congress not later than 270 days after the date of the enactment of this subtitle [Nov. 18, 1988] a report describing the program established by the Task Force under subsection (c) (including an analysis of the factors specified in paragraphs (1) through (5) of that subsection);

"(2) periodically transmit to the President and to each House of Congress reports describing the implementation of the program established by the Task Force under subsection (c) (including an analysis of the factors specified in paragraphs (1) through (5) of that subsection) and the progress made in the cleanup and disposal of hazardous waste produced by illegal drug laboratories; and

"(3) transmit to each House of Congress a report describing the findings made as a result of the evaluations referred to in subsection (e)(3)."

Great Lakes Drug Interdiction. Pub.L. 100–690, Title VII, § 7404, Nov. 18, 1988, 102 Stat. 4484, provided that:

"(a) **Interagency agreement.** The Secretary of Transportation and the Secretary of the Treasury shall enter into an agreement for the purpose of increasing the effectiveness of maritime drug interdiction activities of the Coast Guard and the Customs Service in the Great Lakes area.

"(b) **Negotiations with Canada on drug enforcement cooperation.** The Secretary of State is encouraged to enter into negotiations with appropriate officials of the Government of Canada for the purpose of establishing an agreement between the United States and Canada which provides for increased cooperation and sharing of information between United States and Canadian law enforcement officials with respect to law enforcement efforts conducted on the Great Lakes between the United States and Canada."

GAO Study of Capabilities of United States to Control Drug Smuggling into United States. Section 1241 of Pub.L. 100–180, Div. A, Title XII, Dec. 4, 1987, 101 Stat. 1162, provided that:

"(a) Study requirement.—The Comptroller General of the United States shall conduct a comprehensive study regarding smuggling of illegal drugs into the United States and the current capabilities of the United States to deter such smuggling. In carrying out such study, the Comptroller General shall—

"(1) assess the national security implications of the smuggling of illegal drugs into the United States;

"(2) assess the magnitude, nature, and operational impact that current resource limitations have on the drug smuggling interdiction efforts of Federal law enforcement agencies and the capability of the Department of Defense to respond to requests for assistance from those law enforcement agencies;

"(3) assess the effect on military readiness, the costs that would be incurred, the operational effects on military and civilian agencies, the potential for improving drug interdiction operations, and the methods for implementing increased drug law enforcement assistance by the Department of Defense under section 825 of H.R. 1748 as passed the House of Representatives on May 20, 1987, as if such section were enacted into law and were to become effective on January 1, 1988;

"(4) assess results of a cooperative drug enforcement operation between the United States Customs Service and National Guard units from the States of Arizona, Utah, Missouri, and Wisconsin conducted along the United States-Mexico border beginning on August 29, 1987, and include in the assessment information relating to the cost of conducting the operation, the personnel and equipment used in such operation, the command and control relationships in such operation, and the legal issues involved in such operation;

"(5) determine whether giving the Armed Forces a more direct, active role in drug interdiction activities would enhance the morale and readiness of the Armed Forces;

"(6) determine what assets are currently available to and under consideration for the Department of Defense, the Department of Transportation, the Department of Justice, and the Department of the Treasury for the detection of airborne drug smugglers;

"(7) assess the current plan of the Customs Service for the coordinated use of such assets;

"(8) determine the cost effectiveness and the capability of the Customs Service to use effectively the information generated by the systems employed by or planned for the Department of Defense, the Coast Guard, and the Customs Service, respectively, to detect airborne drug smugglers;

"(9) determine the availability of current and anticipated tracking, pursuit, and apprehension resources to use the capabilities of such systems; and

"(10) at a minimum, assess the detection capabilities of the Over-the-Horizon Backscatter radar (OTH-B), ROTHR, aerostats, airships, and the E–3A, E–2C, P–3, and P–3 Airborne Early Warning aircraft (including any variant of the P–3 Airborne Early Warning aircraft).

"(b) Reports.—(1) Not later than April 30, 1988, the Comptroller General shall, as provided in paragraph (3), submit a report on the results of the study required by subsection (a) with respect to the elements of the study specified in paragraphs (1) through (5) of that subsection.

"(2) As soon as practicable after the report under paragraph (1) is submitted, and not later than March 31, 1989, the Comptroller General shall, as provided in paragraph (3), submit a report on the results of the study required by subsection (a) with respect to the elements of the study specified in paragraphs (6) through (10) of that subsection.

"(3) The reports under paragraphs (1) and (2) shall be submitted to—

"(A) the Committees on Armed Services, the Judiciary, Foreign Relations, and Appropriations of the Senate;

"(B) the Committees on Armed Services, the Judiciary, Foreign Affairs, and Appropriations of the House of Representatives;

"(C) the members of the Senate Caucus on International Narcotics Control; and

"(D) the Select Committee on Narcotics Abuse and Control of the House of Representatives.

"(4) The reports under this subsection shall be submitted in both classified and unclassified forms and shall include such comments and recommendations as the Comptroller General considers appropriate."

Compliance With Budget Act. Pub.L. 99–570, § 3, Oct. 27, 1986, 100 Stat. 3207–1, provided that: "Notwithstanding any other provision of this Act [see Tables volume], any spending authority and any credit authority provided under this Act shall be effective for any fiscal year only to such extent or in such amounts as are provided in appropriation Acts. For purposes of this Act, the term 'spending authority' has the meaning provided in section 401(c)(2) of the Congressional Budget

Act of 1974 [2 U.S.C.A. § 651(c)(2)] and the term 'credit authority' has the meaning provided in section 3(10) of the Congressional Budget Act of 1974 [2 U.S.C.A. § 622(10)]."

Drug Interdiction. Pub.L. 99–570, Title III, §§ 3001 to 3003, 3301, Oct. 27, 1986, 100 Stat. 3207–73, 3207–74, provided that:

"**Sec. 3001. Short title**

This title [enacting section 379 of Title 10, Armed Forces, sections 1590, 1628, 1629, and 2081 of Title 19, Customs Duties, and section 312a of Title 47, Telegraphs, Telephones, and Radiotelegraphs, amending section 959 of this title, sections 374 and 911 of Title 10, sections 507, 1401, 1433, 1436, 1454, 1459, 1497, 1509, 1584, 1585, 1586, 1594, 1595, 1595a, 1613, 1613b, 1619, and 1622 of Title 19, section 5316 of Title 31, Money and Finance, sections 1901, 1902, 1903, 1904, and 12109 of Title 46, Shipping, and sections 1401, 1472, 1474, and 1509 of Title 49, Transportation, repealing section 1460 of Title 19, enacting provisions set out as notes under this section, sections 371, 374, 525, and 9441 of Title 10, sections 1613b and 1654 of Title 19, section 403 of Title 23, Highways, section 1901 of Title 46, and sections 1509 and 11344 of Title 49, and repealing a provision set out as a note under section 89 of Title 14, Coast Guard] may be cited as the 'National Drug Interdiction Improvement Act of 1986'."

"**Sec. 3002. Findings**

"The Congress hereby finds that—

"(1) a balanced, coordinated, multifaceted strategy for combating the growing drug abuse and drug trafficking problem in the United States is essential in order to stop the flow and abuse of drugs within our borders;

"(2) a balanced, coordinated, multifaceted strategy for combating the narcotics drug abuse and trafficking in the United States should include—

"(A) increased investigations of large networks of drug smuggler organizations;

"(B) source country drug eradication;

"(C) increased emphasis on stopping narcotics traffickers in countries through which drugs are transshipped;

"(D) increased emphasis on drug education programs in the schools and workplace;

"(E) increased Federal Government assistance to State and local agencies, civic groups, school systems, and officials in their efforts to combat the drug abuse and trafficking problem at the local level; and

"(F) increased emphasis on the interdiction of drugs and drug smugglers at the borders of the United States, in the air, at sea, and on the land;

"(3) funds to support the interdiction of narcotics smugglers who threaten the transport of drugs through the air, on the sea, and across the land borders of the United States should be emphasized in the Federal Government budget process to the same extent as the other elements of a comprehensive antidrug effort are emphasized;

"(4) the Department of Defense and the use of its resources should be an integral part of a comprehensive, natonal [sic] drug interdiction program;

"(5) the Federal Government civilian agencies engaged in drug interdiction, particularly the United States Customs Service and the Coast Guard, currently lack the aircraft, ships, radar, command, control, communications, and intelligence (C3I) system, and manpower resources necessary to mount a comprehensive attack on the narcotics traffickers who threaten the United States;

"(6) the civilian drug interdiction agencies of the United States are currently interdicting only a small percentage of the illegal, drug smuggler penetrations in the United States every year;

"(7) the budgets for our civilian drug interdiction agencies, primarily the United States Customs Service and the Coast Guard, have not kept pace with those of the traditional investigative law enforcement agencies of the Department of Justice; and

"(8) since the amendment of the Posse Comitatus Act (18 U.S.C. 1385) [section 1385 of Title 18, Crimes and Criminal Procedure] in 1981, the Department of Defense has assisted in the effort to interdict drugs, but they can do more.

"**Sec. 3003. Purposes**

"It is the purpose of this title—

"(1) to increase the level of funding and resources available to civilian drug interdiction agencies of the Federal Government;

"(2) to increase the level of support from the Department of Defense as consistent with the Posse Comitatus Act [section 1385 of Title 18, Crimes and Criminal Procedure], for interdiction of the narcotics traffickers before such traffickers penetrate the borders of the United States; and

"(3) to improve other drug interdiction programs of the Federal Government."

"**Sec. 3301. Establishment of United States-Bahamas Drug Interdiction Task Force**

"(a) Authorization of Appropriations.—

"(1) Establishment of United States-Bahamas Drug Interdiction Task Force.—(A) There is authorized to be established a United States-Bahamas Drug Interdiction Task Force to be operated jointly by the United States Government and the Government of the Bahamas.

"(B) The Secretary of State, the Commandant of the Coast Guard, the Commissioner of Customs, the Attorney General, and the head of the National Narcotics Border Interdiction System (NNBIS), shall upon enactment of this Act [Oct. 27, 1986], immediately commence negotiations with the Government of the Bahamas to enter into a detailed agreement for the establishment and operation of a new drug interdiction task force, including plans for (i) the joint operation and maintenance of any drug interdiction assets authorized for the task force in this section and section 3141 [not classified to the Code], and (ii) any training and personnel enhancements authorized in this section and section 3141 [not classified to the Code].

"(C) The Attorney General shall report to the appropriate committees of Congress on a quarterly basis regarding the progress of the United States-Bahamas Drug Interdiction Task Force.

"(2) Amounts authorized.—There are authorized to be appropriated, in addition to any other amounts authorized to be appropriated in this title, $10,000,000 for the following:

"(A) $9,000,000 for 3 drug interdiction pursuit helicopters for use primarily for operations of the United States-Bahamas Drug Interdiction Task Force established under this section; and

"(B) $1,000,000 to enhance communications capabilities for the operation of a United States-Bahamas Drug Interdiction Task Force established under this section.

"(3) Coast Guard-Bahamas drug interdiction docking facility.—(A) There is authorized to be appropriated for acquisition, construction, and improvements for the Coast Guard for fiscal year 1987, $5,000,000, to be used for initial design engineering, and other activities for construction of a drug interdiction docking facility in the Bahamas to facilitate Coast Guard and Bahamian drug interdiction operations in and through the Bahama Islands. Of the amounts authorized to be appropriated in this subsection, such sums as may be necessary shall be available for necessary communication and air support.

"(B) The Commandant of the Coast Guard shall use such amounts appropriated pursuant to the authorization in this paragraph as may be necessary to establish a repair, maintenance, and boat lift facility to provide repair and maintenance services for both Coast Guard and Bahamian marine drug interdiction equipment, vessels, and related assets.

"(b) Concurrence by Secretary of State.—Programs authorized by this section may be carried out only with the concurrence of the Secretary of State."

Health Insurance Coverage for Drug and Alcohol Treatment. Pub.L. 99-570, Title VI, § 6006, Oct. 27, 1986, 100 Stat. 3207-160, provided:

"(a) Findings.—The Congress finds that—

"(1) drug and alcohol abuse are problems of grave concern and consequence in American society;

"(2) over 500,000 individuals are known heroin addicts; 5 million individuals use cocaine; and at least 7 million individuals regularly use prescription drugs, mostly addictive ones, without medical supervision;

"(3) 10 million adults and 3 million children and adolescents abuse alcohol, and an additional 30 to 40 million people are adversely affected because of close family ties to alcoholics;

"(4) the total cost of drug abuse to the Nation in 1983 was over $60,000,000,000; and

"(5) the vast majority of health benefits plans provide only limited coverage for treatment of drug and alcohol addiction, which is a fact that can discourage the abuser from seeking treatment or, if the abuser does seek treatment, can cause the abuser to face significant out of pocket expenses for the treatment.

"(b) Sense of Congress.—It is the sense of Congress that—

"(1) all employers providing health insurance policies should ensure that the policies provide adequate coverage for treatment of drug and alcohol addiction in recognition that the health consequences and costs for individuals and society can be as formidable as those resulting from other diseases and illnesses for which insurance coverage is much more adequate; and

"(2) State insurance commissioners should encourage employers providing health benefits plans to ensure that the policies provide more adequate coverage for treatment of drug and alcohol addiction."

Information on Drug Abuse at the Workplace. Pub.L. 99-570, Title IV, § 4303, Oct. 27, 1986, 100 Stat. 3207-154, provided that:

"(a) The Secretary of Labor shall collect such information as is available on the incidence of drug abuse in the workplace and efforts to assist workers, including counseling, rehabilitation and employee assistance programs. The Secretary shall conduct such additional research as is necessary to assess the impact and extent of drug abuse and remediation efforts. The Secretary shall submit the findings of such collection and research to the House Committee on Education and Labor and the Senate Committee on Labor and Human Services no later than two years from the date of enactment of this Act [Oct. 27, 1986].

"(b) There is authorized to be appropriated the aggregate sum of $3,000,000 for fiscal years 1987 and 1988, to remain available until expended, to enable the Secretary of Labor to carry out the purposes of this section."

Coordination of Interagency Drug Abuse Prevention Activities. Pub.L. 99–570, Title IV, § 4304, Oct. 27, 1986, 100 Stat. 3207-154, provided that:

"(a) The Secretary of Education, the Secretary of Health and Human Services, and the Secretary of Labor shall each designate an officer or employee of the Departments of Education, Health and Human Services, and Labor, respectively, to coordinate interagency drug abuse prevention activities to prevent duplication of effort.

"(b) Within one year after enactment of this Act [Oct. 27, 1986], a report shall be jointly submitted to the Congress by such Secretaries concerning the extent to which States and localities have been able to implement non-duplicative drug abuse prevention activities."

Substance Abuse Insurance Coverage Study. Pub.L. 99–570, Title VI, § 6005, Oct. 27, 1986, 100 Stat. 3207-160, as amended Pub.L. 100–690, Title II, § 2058(c), Nov. 18, 1988, 102 Stat. 4213, provided:

"(a) Study.—The Secretary of Health and Human Services shall contract with the Institute of Medicine of the National Academy of Sciences to conduct a study of (1) the extent to which the cost of drug abuse treatment is covered by private insurance, public programs, and other sources of payment, and (2) the adequacy of such coverage for the rehabilitation of drug abusers.

"(b) Report.—Not later than 18 months after the execution of the contract referred to in subsection (a), the Secretary of Health and Human Services shall transmit to the Congress a report of the results of the study conducted under subsection (a). The report shall include recommendations of means to meet the needs identified in such study."

EXECUTIVE ORDER NO. 11727

July 6, 1973, 38 F.R. 18357

DRUG LAW ENFORCEMENT

Reorganization Plan No. 2 of 1973 [set out in the Appendix to Title 5, Government Organization and Employees], which becomes effective on July 1, 1973, among other things establishes a Drug Enforcement Administration in the Department of Justice. In my message to the Congress transmitting that plan, I stated that all functions of the Office for Drug Abuse Law Enforcement (established pursuant to Executive Order No. 11641 of January 28, 1972) and the Office of National Narcotics Intelligence (established pursuant to Executive Order No. 11676 of July 27, 1972) would, together with other related functions, be merged in the new Drug Enforcement Administration.

Now, THEREFORE, by virtue of the authority vested in me by the Constitution and laws of the United States, including section 5317 of title 5 of the United States Code, as amended [section 5317 of Title 5, Government Organization and Employees], it is hereby ordered as follows:

Section 1. The Attorney General, to the extent permitted by law, is authorized to coordinate all activities of executive branch departments and agencies which are directly related to the enforcement of laws respecting narcotics and dangerous drugs. Each department and agency of the Federal Government shall, upon request and to the extent permitted by law, assist the Attorney General in the performance of functions assigned to him pursuant to this order, and the Attorney General may, in carrying out those functions, utilize the services of any other agencies, Federal and State, as may be available and appropriate.

Sec. 2. Executive Order No. 11641 of January 28, 1972, is revoked and the Attorney General shall provide for the reassignment of the functions of the Office for Drug Abuse Law Enforcement and for the abolishment of that Office.

Sec. 3. Executive Order No. 11676 of July 27, 1972, is hereby revoked and the Attorney General shall provide for the reassignment of the functions of the Office of National Narcotics Intelligence and for the abolishment of that Office.

Sec. 4. Section 1 of Executive Order No. 11708 of March 23, 1973, as amended, placing certain positions in level IV of the Executive Schedule is hereby further amended by deleting—

(1) "(6) Director, Office for Drug Abuse Law Enforcement, Department of Justice."; and

(2) "(7) Director, Office of National Narcotics Intelligence, Department of Justice."

Sec. 5. The Attorney General shall provide for the winding up of the affairs of the two offices and for the reassignment of their functions.

Sec. 6. This order shall be effective as of July 1, 1973.

RICHARD NIXON

§ 801a. Congressional findings and declarations: psychotropic substances

The Congress makes the following findings and declarations:

(1) The Congress has long recognized the danger involved in the manufacture, distribution, and use of certain psychotropic substances for nonscientific and nonmedical purposes, and has provided strong and effective legislation to control illicit trafficking and to regulate legitimate uses of psychotropic substances in this country. Abuse of psychotropic substances has become a phenomenon common to many countries, however, and is not confined to national borders. It is, therefore, essential that the

United States cooperate with other nations in establishing effective controls over international traffic in such substances.

(2) The United States has joined with other countries in executing an international treaty, entitled the Convention on Psychotropic Substances and signed at Vienna, Austria, on February 21, 1971, which is designed to establish suitable controls over the manufacture, distribution, transfer, and use of certain psychotropic substances. The Convention is not self-executing, and the obligations of the United States thereunder may only be performed pursuant to appropriate legislation. It is the intent of the Congress that the amendments made by this Act, together with existing law, will enable the United States to meet all of its obligations under the Convention and that no further legislation will be necessary for that purpose.

(3) In implementing the Convention on Psychotropic Substances, the Congress intends that, consistent with the obligations of the United States under the Convention, control of psychotropic substances in the United States should be accomplished within the framework of the procedures and criteria for classification of substances provided in the Comprehensive Drug Abuse Prevention and Control Act of 1970. This will insure that (A) the availability of psychotropic substances to manufacturers, distributors, dispensers, and researchers for useful and legitimate medical and scientific purposes will not be unduly restricted; (B) nothing in the Convention will interfere with bona fide research activities; and (C) nothing in the Convention will interfere with ethical medical practice in this country as determined by the Secretary of Health and Human Services on the basis of a consensus of the views of the American medical and scientific community. (Pub.L. 95–633, Title I, § 101, Nov. 10, 1978, 92 Stat. 3768; Pub.L. 96–88, Title V, § 509, Oct. 17, 1979, 93 Stat. 695.)

EDITORIAL NOTES

References in Text. This Act, referred to in par. (2), is Pub.L. 95–633, Nov. 10, 1978, 92 Stat. 2768, known as the Psychotropic Substances Act of 1978, which enacted this section and sections 830, and 852 of this title, amended sections 352, 802, 811, 812, 823, 827, 841 to 843, 872, 881, 952, 953, and 965 of Title 21, U.S.C.A., Food and Drugs, and section 242 of Title 42, U.S.C.A., The Public Health and Welfare, and enacted provisions set out as notes under this section and sections 801, 812, and 830 of Title 21.

The Comprehensive Drug Abuse Prevention and Control Act of 1970, referred to in par. (3), is Pub.L. 91–513, Oct. 27, 1970, 84 Stat. 1236, as amended, which is classified principally to this chapter.

Change of Name. "Secretary of Health and Human Services" was substituted for "Secretary of Health, Education, and Welfare" on authority of Pub.L. 96–88, Title V, § 509, Oct. 17, 1979, 93 Stat. 695, which is classified to section 3508 of Title 20, U.S.C.A., Education.

§ 802. Definitions

As used in this subchapter:

(1) The term "addict" means any individual who habitually uses any narcotic drug so as to endanger the public morals, health, safety, or welfare, or who is so far addicted to the use of narcotic drugs as to have lost the power of self-control with reference to his addiction.

(2) The term "administer" refers to the direct application of a controlled substance to the body of a patient or research subject by—

(A) a practitioner (or, in his presence, by his authorized agent), or

(B) the patient or research subject at the direction and in the presence of the practitioner,

whether such application be by injection, inhalation, ingestion, or any other means.

(3) The term "agent" means an authorized person who acts on behalf of or at the direction of a manufacturer, distributor, or dispenser; except that such term does not include a common or contract carrier, public warehouseman, or employee of the carrier or warehouseman, when acting in the usual and lawful course of the carrier's or warehouseman's business.

(4) The term "Drug Enforcement Administration" means the Drug Enforcement Administration in the Department of Justice.

(5) The term "control" means to add a drug or other substance, or immediate precursor, to a schedule under part B of this subchapter, whether by transfer from another schedule or otherwise.

(6) The term "controlled substance" means a drug or other substance, or immediate precursor, included in schedule I, II, III, IV, or V of part B of this subchapter. The term does not

include distilled spirits, wine, malt beverages, or tobacco, as those terms are defined or used in subtitle E of the Internal Revenue Code of 1954.

(7) The term "counterfeit substance" means a controlled substance which, or the container or labeling of which, without authorization, bears the trademark, trade name, or other identifying mark, imprint, number, or device, or any likeness thereof, of a manufacturer, distributor, or dispenser other than the person or persons who in fact manufactured, distributed, or dispensed such substance and which thereby falsely purports or is represented to be the product of, or to have been distributed by, such other manufacturer, distributor, or dispenser.

(8) The terms "deliver" or "delivery" mean the actual, constructive, or attempted transfer of a controlled substance or a listed chemical, whether or not there exists an agency relationship.

(9) The term "depressant or stimulant substance" means—

(A) a drug which contains any quantity of (i) barbituric acid or any of the salts of barbituric acid; or (ii) any derivative of barbituric acid which has been designated by the Secretary as habit forming under section 352(d) of this title; or

(B) a drug which contains any quantity of (i) amphetamine or any of its optical isomers; (ii) any salt of amphetamine or any salt of an optical isomer of amphetamine; or (iii) any substance which the Attorney General, after investigation, has found to be, and by regulation designated as, habit forming because of its stimulant effect on the central nervous system; or

(C) lysergic acid diethylamide; or

(D) any drug which contains any quantity of a substance which the Attorney General, after investigation, has found to have, and by regulation designated as having, a potential for abuse because of its depressant or stimulant effect on the central nervous system or its hallucinogenic effect.

(10) The term "dispense" means to deliver a controlled substance to an ultimate user or research subject by, or pursuant to the lawful order of, a practitioner, including the prescribing and administering of a controlled substance and the packaging, labeling, or compounding necessary to prepare the substance for such delivery. The term "dispenser" means a practitioner who so delivers a controlled substance to an ultimate user or research subject.

(11) The term "distribute" means to deliver (other than by administering or dispensing) a controlled substance or a listed chemical. The term "distributor" means a person who so delivers a controlled substance or a listed chemical.

(12) The term "drug" has the meaning given that term by section 321(g)(1) of this title.

(13) The term "felony" means any Federal or State offense classified by applicable Federal or State law as a felony.

(14) The term "isomer" means the optical isomer, except as used in schedule I(c) and schedule II(a)(4). As used in schedule I(c), the term "isomer" means any optical, positional, or geometric isomer. As used in schedule II(a)(4), the term "isomer" means any optical or geometric isomer.

(15) The term "manufacture" means the production, preparation, propagation, compounding, or processing of a drug or other substance, either directly or indirectly or by extraction from substances of natural origin, or independently by means of chemical synthesis or by a combination of extraction and chemical synthesis, and includes any packaging or repackaging of such substance or labeling or relabeling of its container; except that such term does not include the preparation, compounding, packaging, or labeling of a drug or other substance in conformity with applicable State or local law by a practitioner as an incident to his administration or dispensing of such drug or substance in the course of his professional practice. The term "manufacturer" means a person who manufactures a drug or other substance.

(16) The term "marihuana" means all parts of the plant Cannabis sativa L., whether growing or not; the seeds thereof; the resin extracted from any part of such plant; and every compound, manufacture, salt, derivative, mixture, or preparation of such plant, its seeds or resin. Such term does not include the mature stalks of such plant, fiber produced from such stalks, oil or cake made from the seeds of such

plant, any other compound, manufacture, salt, derivative, mixture, or preparation of such mature stalks (except the resin extracted therefrom), fiber, oil, or cake, or the sterilized seed of such plant which is incapable of germination.

(17) The term "narcotic drug" means any of the following whether produced directly or indirectly by extraction from substances of vegetable origin, or independently by means of chemical synthesis, or by a combination of extraction and chemical synthesis:

(A) Opium, opiates, derivatives of opium and opiates, including their isomers, esters, ethers, salts, and salts of isomers, esters, and ethers, whenever the existence of such isomers, esters, ethers, and salts is possible within the specific chemical designation. Such term does not include the isoquinoline alkaloids of opium.

(B) Poppy straw and concentrate of poppy straw.

(C) Coca leaves, except coca leaves and extracts of coca leaves from which cocaine, ecgonine, and derivatives of ecgonine or their salts have been removed.

(D) Cocaine, its salts, optical and geometric isomers, and salts of isomers.

(E) Ecgonine, its derivatives, their salts, isomers, and salts of isomers.

(F) Any compound, mixture, or preparation which contains any quantity of any of the substances referred to in subparagraphs (A) through (E).

(18) The term "opiate" means any drug or other substance having an addiction-forming or addiction-sustaining liability similar to morphine or being capable of conversion into a drug having such addiction-forming or addiction-sustaining liability.

(19) The term "opium poppy" means the plant of the species Papaver somniferum L., except the seed thereof.

(20) The term "poppy straw" means all parts, except the seeds, of the opium poppy, after mowing.

(21) The term "practitioner" means a physician, dentist, veterinarian, scientific investigator, pharmacy, hospital, or other person licensed, registered, or otherwise permitted, by the United States or the jurisdiction in which

he practices or does research, to distribute, dispense, conduct research with respect to, administer, or use in teaching or chemical analysis, a controlled substance in the course of professional practice or research.

(22) The term "production" includes the manufacture, planting, cultivation, growing, or harvesting of a controlled substance.

(23) The term "immediate precursor" means a substance—

(A) which the Attorney General has found to be and by regulation designated as being the principal compound used, or produced primarily for use, in the manufacture of a controlled substance;

(B) which is an immediate chemical intermediary used or likely to be used in the manufacture of such controlled substance; and

(C) the control of which is necessary to prevent, curtail, or limit the manufacture of such controlled substance.

(24) The term "Secretary", unless the context otherwise indicates, means the Secretary of Health and Human Services.

(25) The term "serious bodily injury" means bodily injury which involves—

(A) a substantial risk of death;

(B) protracted and obvious disfigurement; or

(C) protracted loss or impairment of the function of a bodily member, organ, or mental faculty.

(26) The term "State" means any State, territory, or possession of the United States, the District of Columbia, the Commonwealth of Puerto Rico, the Trust Territory of the Pacific Islands, and the Canal Zone.

(27) The term "ultimate user" means a person who has lawfully obtained, and who possesses, a controlled substance for his own use or for the use of a member of his household or for an animal owned by him or by a member of his household.

(28) The term "United States", when used in a geographic sense, means all places and waters, continental or insular, subject to the jurisdiction of the United States.

(29) The term "maintenance treatment" means the dispensing, for a period in excess of twenty-one days, of a narcotic drug in the treatment of an individual for dependence upon heroin or other morphine-like drugs.

(30) The term "detoxification treatment" means the dispensing, for a period not in excess of one hundred and eighty days, of a narcotic drug in decreasing doses to an individual in order to alleviate adverse physiological or psychological effects incident to withdrawal from the continuous or sustained use of a narcotic drug and as a method of bringing the individual to a narcotic drug-free state within such period.

(31) The term "Convention on Psychotropic Substances" means the Convention on Psychotropic Substances signed at Vienna, Austria, on February 21, 1971; and the term "Single Convention on Narcotic Drugs" means the Single Convention on Narcotic Drugs signed at New York, New York, on March 30, 1961.

(32)(A) Except as provided in subparagraph (B), the term "controlled substance analogue" means a substance—

(i) the chemical structure of which is substantially similar to the chemical structure of a controlled substance in schedule I or II;

(ii) which has a stimulant, depressant, or hallucinogenic effect on the central nervous system that is substantially similar to or greater than the stimulent[1], depressant, or hallucinogenic effect on the central nervous system of a controlled substance in schedule I or II; or

(iii) with respect to a particular person, which such person represents or intends to have a stimulent[1], depressant, or hallucinogenic effect on the central nervous system that is substantially similar to or greater than the stimulant, depressant, or hallucinogenic effect on the central nervous system of a controlled substance in schedule I or II.

(B) Such term does not include—

(i) a controlled substance;

(ii) any substance for which there is an approved new drug application;

(iii) with respect to a particular person any substance, if an exemption is in effect for investigational use, for that person, under

section 505 of the Federal Food, Drug, and Cosmetic Act (21 U.S.C. 355) [21 U.S.C.A. § 355] to the extent conduct with respect to such substance is pursuant to such exemption; or

(iv) any substance to the extent not intended for human consumption before such an exemption takes effect with respect to that substance.

(33) The term "listed chemical" means any listed precursor chemical or listed essential chemical.

(34) The term "listed precursor chemical" means a chemical specified by regulation of the Attorney General as a chemical that is used in manufacturing a controlled substance in violation of this title and is critical to the creation of the controlled substances, and such term includes (until otherwise specified by regulation of the Attorney General, as considered appropriate by the Attorney General or upon petition to the Attorney General by any person) the following:

(A) Anthranilic acid and its salts.

(B) Benzyl cyanide.

(C) Ephedrine, its salts, optical isomers, and salts of optical isomers.

(D) Ergonovine and its salts.

(E) Ergotamine and its salts.

(F) N–Acetylanthranilic acid and its salts.

(G) Norpseudoephedrine, its salts, optical isomers, and salts of optical isomers.

(H) Phenylacetic acid and its salts.

(I) Phenylpropanolamine, its salts, optical isomers, and salts of optical isomers.

(J) Piperidine and its salts.

(K) Pseudoephedrine, its salts, optical isomers, and salts of optical isomers.

(L) 3, 4–Methylenedioxyphenyl–2–propanone.

(35) The term "listed essential chemical" means a chemical specified by regulation of the Attorney General as a chemical that is used as a solvent, reagent, or catalyst in manufacturing a controlled substance in violation of this subchapter, and such term includes (until otherwise specified by regulation of the Attorney General, as considered appropriate by the At-

torney General or upon petition to the Attorney General by any person) the following chemicals:

(A) Acetic anhydride.

(B) Acetone.

(C) Benzyl chloride.

(D) Ethyl ether.

(E) Hydriodic acid.

(F) Potassium permanganate.

(G) 2–Butanone.

(H) Toluene.

(36) The term "regular customer" means, with respect to a regulated person, a customer with whom the regulated person has an established business relationship that is reported to the Attorney General.

(37) The term "regular supplier" means, with respect to a regulated person, a supplier with whom the regulated person has an established business relationship that is reported to the Attorney General.

(38) The term "regulated person" means a person who manufactures, distributes, imports, or exports a listed chemical, a tableting machine, or an encapsulating machine.

(39) The term "regulated transaction" means—

(A) a distribution, receipt, sale, importation or exportation of a threshold amount, including a cumulative threshold amount for multiple transactions (as determined by the Attorney General, in consultation with the chemical industry and taking into consideration the quantities normally used for lawful purposes), of a listed chemical, except that such term does not include—

(i) a domestic lawful distribution in the usual course of business between agents or employees of a single regulated person;

(ii) a delivery of a listed chemical to or by a common or contract carrier for carriage in the lawful and usual course of the business of the common or contract carrier, or to or by a warehouseman for storage in the lawful and usual course of the business of the warehouseman, except that if the carriage or storage is in connection with the distribution, importation, or exportation of a listed chemical to a third person, this clause does not

relieve a distributor, importer, or exporter from compliance with section 310;

(iii) any category of transaction specified by regulation of the Attorney General as excluded from this definition as unnecessary for enforcement of this subchapter or subchapter II of this chapter;

(iv) any transaction in a listed chemical that is contained in a drug that may be marketed or distributed lawfully in the United States under the Federal Food, Drug, and Cosmetic Act; or

(v) any transaction in a chemical mixture; and

(B) a distribution, importation, or exportation of a tableting machine or encapsulating machine.

(40) The term "chemical mixture" means a combination of two or more chemical substances, at least one of which is not a listed precursor chemical or a listed essential chemical, except that such term does not include any combination of a listed precursor chemical or a listed essential chemical with another chemical that is present solely as an impurity.

(Pub.L. 91–513, Title II, § 102, Oct. 27, 1970, 84 Stat. 1242; Pub.L. 93–281, § 2, May 14, 1974, 88 Stat. 124; Pub.L. 95–633, Title I, § 102(b), Nov. 10, 1978, 92 Stat. 3772; Pub.L. 96–88, Title V, § 509, Oct. 17, 1979, 93 Stat. 695; Pub.L. 96–132, § 16(a), Nov. 30, 1979, 93 Stat. 1049; Pub.L. 98–473, Title II, § 507(a), (b), Oct. 12, 1984, 98 Stat. 2071; Pub.L. 98–509, Title III, § 301(a), Oct. 19, 1984, 98 Stat. 2364; Pub.L. 99–570, Title I, §§ 1003(b), 1203, 1870, Oct. 27, 1986, 100 Stat. 3207–6, 3207–13, 3207–56; Pub.L. 99–646, § 83, Nov. 10, 1986, 100 Stat. 3619; Pub.L. 100–690, Title VI, § 6054, Nov. 18, 1988, 102 Stat. 4316.)

1. So in original. Probably should be "stimulant".

EDITORIAL NOTES

References in Text. "This subchapter", referred to in text, was in the original "this title" which is Title II of Pub.L. 91–513, Oct. 27, 1970, 84 Stat. 1242, and is popularly known as the "Controlled Substances Act". For complete classification of Title II to the Code, see Short Title note set out under section 801 of this title and Tables volume.

"Subchapter II of this chapter", referred to in text, was in the original "title III", meaning Title III of Pub.L. 91–513, Oct. 27, 1970, 84 Stat. 1285. Part A of

Title III comprises subchapter II of this chapter. For classification of Part B, consisting of sections 1101 to 1105 of Title III, see Tables volume.

The Federal Food, Drug, and Cosmetic Act, referred to in par. (39), is Act June 25, 1938, c. 675, 52 Stat. 1040, as amended, which is classified generally to chapter 9 (§ 301 et seq.) of this title. For complete classification of this Act to the Code, see section 301 of this title and Tables volume.

Subtitle E of the Internal Revenue Code of 1954, referred to in par. (6), is classified to section 5001 et seq. of Title 26, U.S.C.A., Internal Revenue Code.

Internal Revenue Code of 1954 in any law, etc., to include reference to Internal Revenue Code of 1986, except when inappropriate, see Pub.L. 99–514, § 2, Oct. 22, 1986, 100 Stat. 1095.

Schedule I or II, referred to in par. (32)(A), are set out in section 812(c) of this title.

Codifications. Amendment by section 83 of Pub.L. 99–646 to par. (14) was not executed in view of prior amendment to such par. by Pub.L. 99–570 making identical amendment.

Amendment by section 301(a) of Pub.L. 98–509, Oct. 19, 1984, 98 Stat. 2364, to par. (28) which substituted "one hundred and eighty" for "twenty-one" was executed to par. (29), which had been par. (28) prior to its redesignation by Pub.L. 98–473, Title II, § 507(a), Oct. 12, 1984, 98 Stat. 2071, as the probable intent of Congress.

Effective Date of 1988 Amendment. Section 6061 of Pub.L. 100–690 provided that: "Except as otherwise provided in this subtitle, this subtitle [enacting section 972 of this title, amending sections 802, 830, 841, 842, 843, 872, 876, 881, 960 and 961 of this title] shall take effect 120 days after the enactment of this Act [Nov. 18, 1988]."

Change of Name. "Secretary of Health and Human Services" was substituted for "Secretary of Health, Education, and Welfare" on authority of Pub.L. 96–88, Title V, § 509, Oct. 17, 1979, 93 Stat. 695, which is classified to section 3508 of Title 20, U.S.C.A., Education.

Promulgation of Regulations for Administration of Amendment by Alcohol Abuse, Drug Abuse, and Mental Health Amendments of 1984; Inclusion of Findings in Report. Section 301(b) of Pub.L. 98–509, Oct. 19, 1984, 98 Stat. 2364, provided that: "The Secretary of Health and Human Services shall, within ninety days of the date of the enactment of this Act [Oct. 19, 1984], promulgate regulations for the administration of section 102(28) of the Controlled Substances Act as amended by subsection (a) [probably par. 29 of this section] and shall include in the first report submitted under section 505(b) of the Public Health Service Act [section 290aa–4 of Title 42, The Public Health and Welfare] after the expiration of such ninety days the findings of the Secretary with respect to the effect of the amendment made by subsection (a) [amending par. (29) of this section]."

§ 803. Repealed. Pub.L. 95–137, § 1(b), Oct. 18, 1977, 91 Stat. 1169.

PART B

AUTHORITY TO CONTROL; STANDARDS AND SCHEDULES

§ 811. Authority and criteria for classification of substances

Rules and regulations of Attorney General; hearing

(a) The Attorney General shall apply the provisions of this subchapter to the controlled substances listed in the schedules established by section 812 of this title and to any other drug or other substance added to such schedules under this subchapter. Except as provided in subsections (d) and (e) of this section, the Attorney General may by rule—

(1) add to such a schedule or transfer between such schedules any drug or other substance if he—

(A) finds that such drug or other substance has a potential for abuse, and

(B) makes with respect to such drug or other substance the findings prescribed by subsection (b) of section 812 of this title for the schedule in which such drug is to be placed; or

(2) remove any drug or other substance from the schedules if he finds that the drug or other substance does not meet the requirements for inclusion in any schedule.

Rules of the Attorney General under this subsection shall be made on the record after opportunity for a hearing pursuant to the rulemaking procedures prescribed by subchapter II of chapter 5 of Title 5. Proceedings for the issuance, amendment, or repeal of such rules may be initiated by the Attorney General (1) on his own motion, (2) at the request of the Secretary, or (3) on the petition of any interested party.

Evaluation of drugs and other substances

(b) The Attorney General shall, before initiating proceedings under subsection (a) of this section to control a drug or other substance or to remove a drug or other substance entirely from the schedules, and after gathering the necessary data, request from the Secretary a scientific and medical evaluation, and his recommendations, as to whether such drug or other substance should be so controlled or removed as a controlled substance. In making such evaluation and recommendations, the Secretary shall consider the factors listed in paragraphs (2), (3), (6), (7), and (8) of subsection (c) of this section and any scientific or medical considerations involved in paragraphs (1), (4), and (5) of such subsection. The recommendations of the Secretary shall include recommendations with respect to the appropriate schedule, if any, under which such drug or other substance should be listed. The evaluation and the recommendations of the Secretary shall be made in writing and submitted to the Attorney General within a reasonable time. The recommendations of the Secretary to the Attorney General shall be binding on the Attorney General as to such scientific and medical matters, and if the Secretary recommends that a drug or other substance not be controlled, the Attorney General shall not control the drug or other substance. If the Attorney General determines that these facts and all other relevant data constitute substantial evidence of potential for abuse such as to warrant control or substantial evidence that the drug or other substance should be removed entirely from the schedules, he shall initiate proceedings for control or removal, as the case may be, under subsection (a) of this section.

Factors determinative of control or removal from schedules

(c) In making any finding under subsection (a) of this section or under subsection (b) of section 812 of this title, the Attorney General shall consider the following factors with respect to each drug or other substance proposed to be controlled or removed from the schedules:

(1) Its actual or relative potential for abuse.

(2) Scientific evidence of its pharmacological effect, if known.

(3) The state of current scientific knowledge regarding the drug or other substance.

(4) Its history and current pattern of abuse.

(5) The scope, duration, and significance of abuse.

(6) What, if any, risk there is to the public health.

(7) Its psychic or physiological dependence liability.

(8) Whether the substance is an immediate precursor of a substance already controlled under this subchapter.

International treaties, conventions, and protocols requiring control; procedures respecting changes in drug schedules of Convention on Psychotropic Substances

(d)(1) If control is required by United States obligations under international treaties, conventions, or protocols in effect on October 27, 1970, the Attorney General shall issue an order controlling such drug under the schedule he deems most appropriate to carry out such obligations, without regard to the findings required by subsection (a) of this section or section 812(b) of this title and without regard to the procedures prescribed by subsections (a) and (b) of this section.

(2)(A) Whenever the Secretary of State receives notification from the Secretary-General of the United Nations that information has been transmitted by or to the World Health Organization, pursuant to article 2 of the Convention on Psychotropic Substances, which may justify adding a drug or other substance to one of the schedules of the Convention, transferring a drug or substance from one schedule to another, or deleting it from the schedules, the Secretary of State shall immediately transmit the notice to the Secretary of Health and Human Services who shall publish it in the Federal Register and provide opportunity to interested persons to submit to him comments respecting the scientific and medical evaluations which he is to prepare respecting such drug or substance. The Secretary of Health and Human Services shall prepare for transmission through the Secretary of State to the World Health Organization such medical and scientific evaluations as may be appropriate regarding the possible action that could be proposed by the World Health Organization respecting the drug or substance with respect to which a notice was transmitted under this subparagraph.

(B) Whenever the Secretary of State receives information that the Commission on Narcotic Drugs of the United Nations proposes to decide whether to add a drug or other substance to one of the schedules of the Convention, transfer a drug or substance from one schedule to another, or delete it from the schedules, the Secretary of State shall transmit timely notice to the Secretary of Health and Human Services of such information who shall publish a summary of such information in the Federal Register and provide opportunity to interested persons to submit to him comments respecting the recommendation which he is to furnish, pursuant to this subparagraph, respecting such proposal. The Secretary of Health and Human Services shall evaluate the proposal and furnish a recommendation to the Secretary of State which shall be binding on the representative of the United States in discussions and negotiations relating to the proposal.

(3) When the United States receives notification of a scheduling decision pursuant to article 2 of the Convention on Psychotropic Substances that a drug or other substance has been added or transferred to a schedule specified in the notification or receives notification (referred to in this subsection as a "schedule notice") that existing legal controls applicable under this subchapter to a drug or substance and the controls required by the Federal Food, Drug, and Cosmetic Act do not meet the requirements of the schedule of the Convention in which such drug or substance has been placed, the Secretary of Health and Human Services, after consultation with the Attorney General, shall first determine whether existing legal controls under this subchapter applicable to the drug or substance and the controls required by the Federal Food, Drug, and Cosmetic Act, meet the requirements of the schedule specified in the notification or schedule notice and shall take the following action:

(A) If such requirements are met by such existing controls but the Secretary of Health and Human Services nonetheless believes that more stringent controls should be applied to the drug or substance, the Secretary shall recommend to the Attorney General that he initiate proceedings for scheduling the drug or substance, pursuant to subsec-

tions (a) and (b) of this section, to apply to such controls.

(B) If such requirements are not met by such existing controls and the Secretary of Health and Human Services concurs in the scheduling decision or schedule notice transmitted by the notification, the Secretary shall recommend to the Attorney General that he initiate proceedings for scheduling the drug or substance under the appropriate schedule pursuant to subsections (a) and (b) of this section.

(C) If such requirements are not met by such existing controls and the Secretary of Health and Human Services does not concur in the scheduling decision or schedule notice transmitted by the notification, the Secretary shall—

(i) if he deems that additional controls are necessary to protect the public health and safety, recommended to the Attorney General that he initiate proceedings for scheduling the drug or substance pursuant to subsections (a) and (b) of this section, to apply such additional controls;

(ii) request the Secretary of State to transmit a notice of qualified acceptance, within the period specified in the Convention, pursuant to paragraph 7 of article 2 of the Convention, to the Secretary-General of the United Nations;

(iii) request the Secretary of State to transmit a notice of qualified acceptance as prescribed in clause (ii) and request the Secretary of State to ask for a review by the Economic and Social Council of the United Nations, in accordance with paragraph 8 of article 2 of the Convention, of the scheduling decision; or

(iv) in the case of a schedule notice, request the Secretary of State to take appropriate action under the Convention to initiate proceedings to remove the drug or substance from the schedules under the Convention or to transfer the drug or substance to a schedule under the Convention different from the one specified in the schedule notice.

(4)(A) If the Attorney General determines, after consultation with the Secretary of Health and Human Services, that proceedings initiated under recommendations made under paragraph

(B) or (C)(i) of paragraph (3) will not be completed within the time period required by paragraph 7 of article 2 of the Convention, the Attorney General, after consultation with the Secretary and after providing interested persons opportunity to submit comments respecting the requirements of the temporary order to be issued under this sentence, shall issue a temporary order controlling the drug or substance under schedule IV or V, whichever is most appropriate to carry out the minimum United States obligations under paragraph 7 of article 2 of the Convention. As a part of such order, the Attorney General shall, after consultation with the Secretary, except such drug or substance from the application of any provision of part C of this subchapter which he finds is not required to carry out the United States obligations under paragraph 7 of article 2 of the Convention. In the case of proceedings initiated under subparagraph (B) of paragraph (3), the Attorney General, concurrently with the issuance of such order, shall request the Secretary of State to transmit a notice of qualified acceptance to the Secretary-General of the United Nations pursuant to paragraph 7 of article 2 of the Convention. A temporary order issued under this subparagraph controlling a drug or other substance subject to proceedings initiated under subsections (a) and (b) of this section shall expire upon the effective date of the application to the drug or substance of the controls resulting from such proceedings.

(B) After a notice of qualified acceptance of a scheduling decision with respect to a drug or other substance is transmitted to the Secretary-General of the United Nations in accordance with clause (ii) or (iii) of paragraph (3)(C) or after a request has been made under clause (iv) of such paragraph with respect to a drug or substance described in a schedule notice, the Attorney General, after consultation with the Secretary of Health and Human Services and after providing interested persons opportunity to submit comments respecting the requirements of the order to be issued under this sentence, shall issue an order controlling the drug or substance under schedule IV or V, whichever is most appropriate to carry out the minimum United States obligations under paragraph 7 of article 2 of the Convention in the case of a drug or substance for which a notice of qualified

acceptance was transmitted or whichever the Attorney General determines is appropriate in the case of a drug or substance described in a schedule notice. As a part of such order, the Attorney General shall, after consultation with the Secretary, except such drug or substance from the application of any provision of part C of this subchapter which he finds is not required to carry out the United States obligations under paragraph 7 of article 2 of the Convention. If, as a result of a review under paragraph 8 of article 2 of the Convention of the scheduling decision with respect to which a notice of qualified acceptance was transmitted in accordance with clause (ii) or (iii) of paragraph (3)(C)—

(i) the decision is reversed, and

(ii) the drug or substance subject to such decision is not required to be controlled under schedule IV or V to carry out the minimum United States obligations under paragraph 7 of article 2 of the Convention,

the order issued under this subparagraph with respect to such drug or substance shall expire upon receipt by the United States of the review decision. If, as a result of action taken pursuant to action initiated under a request transmitted under clause (iv) of paragraph (3)(C), the drug or substance with respect to which such action was taken is not required to be controlled under schedule IV or V, the order issued under this paragraph with respect to such drug or substance shall expire upon receipt by the United States of a notice of the action taken with respect to such drug or substance under the Convention.

(C) An order issued under subparagraph (A) or (B) may be issued without regard to the findings required by subsection (a) of this section or by section 812(b) of this title and without regard to the procedures prescribed by subsection (a) or (b) of this section.

(5) Nothing in the amendments made by the Psychotropic Substances Act of 1978 or the regulations or orders promulgated thereunder shall be construed to preclude requests by the Secretary of Health and Human Services or the Attorney General through the Secretary of State, pursuant to article 2 or other applicable provisions of the Convention, for review of scheduling decisions under such Convention, based on new or additional information.

Immediate precursors

(e) The Attorney General may, without regard to the findings required by subsection (a) of this section or section 812(b) of this title and without regard to the procedures prescribed by subsections (a) and (b) of this section, place an immediate precursor in the same schedule in which the controlled substance of which it is an immediate precursor is placed or in any other schedule with a higher numerical designation. If the Attorney General designates a substance as an immediate precursor and places it in a schedule, other substances shall not be placed in a schedule solely because they are its precursors.

Abuse potential

(f) If, at the time a new-drug application is submitted to the Secretary for any drug having a stimulant, depressant, or hallucinogenic effect on the central nervous system, it appears that such drug has an abuse potential, such information shall be forwarded by the Secretary to the Attorney General.

Non-narcotic substances sold over the counter without prescription; dextromethorphan

(g)(1) The Attorney General shall by regulation exclude any non-narcotic substance from a schedule if such substance may, under the Federal Food, Drug, and Cosmetic Act, be lawfully sold over the counter without a prescription.

(2) Dextromethorphan shall not be deemed to be included in any schedule by reason of enactment of this subchapter unless controlled after October 27, 1970 pursuant to the foregoing provisions of this section.

(3) The Attorney General may, by regulation, exempt any compound, mixture, or preparation containing a controlled substance from the application of all or any part of this subchapter if he finds such compound, mixture, or preparation meets the requirements of one of the following categories:

(A) A mixture, or preparation containing a nonnarcotic controlled substance, which mixture or preparation is approved for prescription use, and which contains one or more other active ingredients which are not listed in any schedule and which are included therein in such combinations, quantity, proportion, or concentration as to vitiate the potential for abuse.

(B) A compound, mixture, or preparation which contains any controlled substance, which is not for administration to a human being or animal, and which is packaged in such form or concentration, or with adulterants or denaturants, so that as packaged it does not present any significant potential for abuse.

Temporary scheduling to avoid imminent hazards to public safety

(h)(1) If the Attorney General finds that the scheduling of a substance in schedule I on a temporary basis is necessary to avoid an imminent hazard to the public safety, he may, by order and without regard to the requirements of subsection (b) of this section relating to the Secretary of Health and Human Services, schedule such substance in schedule I if the substance is not listed in any other schedule in section 812 of this title or if no exemption or approval is in effect for the substance under section 355 of this title. Such an order may not be issued before the expiration of thirty days from—

(A) the date of the publication by the Attorney General of a notice in the Federal Register of the intention to issue such order and the grounds upon which such order is to be issued, and

(B) the date the Attorney General has transmitted the notice required by paragraph (4).

(2) The scheduling of a substance under this subsection shall expire at the end of one year from the date of the issuance of the order scheduling such substance, except that the Attorney General may, during the pendency of proceedings under subsection (a)(1) of this section with respect to the substance, extend the temporary scheduling for up to six months.

(3) When issuing an order under paragraph (1), the Attorney General shall be required to consider, with respect to the finding of an imminent hazard to the public safety, only those factors set forth in paragraphs (4), (5), and (6) of subsection (c) of this section, including actual abuse, diversion from legitimate channels, and clandestine importation, manufacture, or distribution.

(4) The Attorney General shall transmit notice of an order proposed to be issued under paragraph (1) to the Secretary of Health and Human Services. In issuing an order under paragraph (1), the Attorney General shall take into consideration any comments submitted by the Secretary

in response to a notice transmitted pursuant to this paragraph.

(5) An order issued under paragraph (1) with respect to a substance shall be vacated upon the conclusion of a subsequent rulemaking proceeding initiated under subsection (a) of this section with respect to such substance.

(6) An order issued under paragraph (1) is not subject to judicial review.

(Pub.L. 91–513, Title II, § 201, Oct. 27, 1970, 84 Stat. 1245; Pub.L. 95–633, Title I, § 102(a), Nov. 10, 1978, 92 Stat. 3769; Pub.L. 96–88, Title V, § 509, Oct. 17, 1979, 93 Stat. 695; Pub.L. 98–473, Title II, §§ 508, 509(a), Oct. 12, 1984, 98 Stat. 2071, 2072.)

EDITORIAL NOTES

References in Text. The Federal Food, Drug, and Cosmetic Act, referred to in subsecs. (d)(3) and (g)(1), is Act June 25, 1938, c. 675, 52 Stat. 1040, as amended, which is classified generally to chapter 9 (section 301 et seq.) of Title 21, U.S.C.A., Food and Drugs.

Schedules IV and V, referred to in subsec. (d)(4)(A), (B), are set out in section 812(c) of this title.

The Psychotropic Substances Act of 1978, referred to in subsec. (d)(5), is Pub.L. 95–633, Nov. 11, 1978, 92 Stat. 3768, which enacted sections 801a, 830, and 852 of Title 21, U.S.C.A., Food and Drugs, amended this section and sections 352, 802, 812, 823, 827, 841 to 843, 872, 881, 952, 953, and 965 of Title 21 and section 242a of Title 42, U.S.C.A., The Public Health and Welfare, and enacted provisions set out as notes under sections 801, 801a, 812, and 830 of Title 21.

Change of Name. "Secretary of Health and Human Services" was substituted for "Secretary of Health, Education, and Welfare" on authority of Pub.L. 96–88, Title V, § 509, Oct. 17, 1979, 93 Stat. 695, which is classified to section 3508 of Title 20, U.S.C.A., Education.

Code of Federal Regulations

Administrative policies, practices, and procedures, see 21 CFR 1316.01 et seq.

Schedules, see 21 CFR 1308.01 et seq. and Table.

§ 812. Schedules of controlled substances

Establishment

(a) There are established five schedules of controlled substances, to be known as schedules I, II, III, IV, and V. Such schedules shall initially consist of the substances listed in this section. The schedules established by this section shall be updated and republished on a semiannual basis during the two-year period beginning one year after October 27, 1970 and shall be updated and republished on an annual basis thereafter.

Placement on schedules; findings required

(b) Except where control is required by United States obligations under an international treaty, convention, or protocol, in effect on October 27, 1970, and except in the case of an immediate precursor, a drug or other substance may not be placed in any schedule unless the findings required for such schedule are made with respect to such drug or other substance. The findings required for each of the schedules are as follows:

(1) Schedule I.—

(A) The drug or other substance has a high potential for abuse.

(B) The drug or other substance has no currently accepted medical use in treatment in the United States.

(C) There is a lack of accepted safety for use of the drug or other substance under medical supervision.

(2) Schedule II.—

(A) The drug or other substance has a high potential for abuse.

(B) The drug or other substance has a currently accepted medical use in treatment in the United States or a currently accepted medical use with severe restrictions.

(C) Abuse of the drug or other substances may lead to severe psychological or physical dependence.

(3) Schedule III.—

(A) The drug or other substance has a potential for abuse less than the drugs or other substances in schedules I and II.

(B) The drug or other substance has a currently accepted medical use in treatment in the United States.

(C) Abuse of the drug or other substance may lead to moderate or low physical dependence or high psychological dependence.

(4) Schedule IV.—

(A) The drug or other substance has a low potential for abuse relative to the drugs or other substances in schedule III.

(B) The drug or other substance has a currently accepted medical use in treatment in the United States.

(C) Abuse of the drug or other substance may lead to limited physical dependence or psychological dependence relative to the drugs or other substances in schedule III.

(5) Schedule V.—

(A) The drug or other substance has a low potential for abuse relative to the drugs or other substances in schedule IV.

(B) The drug or other substance has a currently accepted medical use in treatment in the United States.

(C) Abuse of the drug or other substance may lead to limited physical dependence or psychological dependence relative to the drugs or other substances in schedule IV.

Initial schedules of controlled substances

(c) Schedules I, II, III, IV, and V shall, unless and until amended pursuant to section 811 of this title, consist of the following drugs or other substances, by whatever official name, common or usual name, chemical name, or brand name designated:

Schedule I

(a) Unless specifically excepted or unless listed in another schedule, any of the following opiates, including their isomers, esters, ethers, salts, and salts of isomers, esters, and ethers, whenever the existence of such isomers, esters, ethers, and salts is possible within the specific chemical designation:

(1) Acetylmethadol.

(2) Allylprodine.

(3) Alphacetylmathadol.

(4) Alphameprodine.

(5) Alphamethadol.

(6) Benzethidine.

(7) Betacetylmethadol.

(8) Betameprodine.

(9) Betamethadol.

(10) Betaprodine.

(11) Clonitazene.

(12) Dextromoramide.

(13) Dextrorphan.

(14) Diampromide.

(15) Diethylthiambutene.

(16) Dimenoxadol.

(17) Dimepheptanol.

(18) Dimethylthiambutene.

(19) Dioxaphetyl butyrate.

(20) Dipipanone.

(21) Ethylmethylthiambutene.

(22) Etonitazene.

(23) Etoxeridine.

(24) Furethidine.

(25) Hydroxypethidine.

(26) Ketobemidone.

(27) Levomoramide.

(28) Levophenacylmorphan.

(29) Morpheridine.

(30) Noracymethadol.

(31) Norlevorphanol.

(32) Normethadone.

(33) Norpipanone.

(34) Phenadoxone.

(35) Phenampromide.

(36) Phenomorphan.

(37) Phenoperidine.

(38) Piritramide.

(39) Proheptazine.

(40) Properidine.

(41) Racemoramide.

(42) Trimeperidine.

(b) Unless specifically excepted or unless listed in another schedule, any of the following opium derivatives, their salts, isomers, and salts of isomers whenever the existence of such salts, isomers, and salts of isomers is possible within the specific chemical designation:

(1) Acetorphine.

(2) Acetyldihydrocodeine.

(3) Benzylmorphine.

(4) Codeine methylbromide.

(5) Codeine-N-Oxide.

(6) Cyprenorphine.

(7) Desomorphine.

(8) Dihydromorphine.

(9) Etorphine.

(10) Heroin.

(11) Hydromorphinol.

(12) Methyldesorphine.

(13) Methylhydromorphine.

(14) Morphine methylbromide.

(15) Morphine methylsulfonate.

(16) Morphine-N-Oxide.

(17) Myrophine.

(18) Nicocodeine.

(19) Nicomorphine.

(20) Normorphine.

(21) Pholcodine.

(22) Thebacon.

(c) Unless specifically excepted or unless listed in another schedule, any material, compound, mixture, or preparation, which contains any quantity of the following hallucinogenic substances, or which contains any of their salts, isomers, and salts of isomers whenever the existence of such salts, isomers, and salts of isomers is possible within the specific chemical designation:

(1) 3, 4-methylenedioxy amphetamine.

(2) 5-methoxy-3, 4-methylenedioxy amphetamine.

(3) 3, 4, 5-trimethoxy amphetamine.

(4) Bufotenine.

(5) Diethyltryptamine.

(6) Dimethyltryptamine.

(7) 4-methyl-2, 5-dimethoxyamphetamine.

(8) Ibogaine.

(9) Lysergic acid diethylamide.

(10) Marihuana.

(11) Mescaline.

(12) Peyote.

(13) N-ethyl-3-piperidyl benzilate.

(14) N-methyl-3-piperidyl benzilate.

(15) Psilocybin.

(16) Psilocyn.

(17) Tetrahydrocannabinols.

Schedule II

(a) Unless specifically excepted or unless listed in another schedule, any of the following substances whether produced directly or indirectly by extraction from substances of vegetable origin, or independently by means of chemical synthesis, or by a combination of extraction and chemical synthesis:

(1) Opium and opiate, and any salt, compound, derivative, or preparation of opium or opiate.

(2) Any salt, compound, derivative, or preparation thereof which is chemically equivalent or identical with any of the substances referred to in clause (1), except that these substances shall not include the isoquinoline alkaloids of opium.

(3) Opium poppy and poppy straw.

(4) Coca leaves except coca leaves and extracts of coca leaves from which cocaine, ecgonine, and derivatives of ecgonine or their salts have been removed; cocaine, its salts, optical and geometric isomers, and salts of isomers; ecgonine, its derivatives, their salts, isomers, and salts of isomers; or any compound, mixture, or preparation which contains any quantity of any of the substances referred to in this paragraph.

(b) Unless specifically excepted or unless listed in another schedule, any of the following opiates, including their isomers, esters, ethers, salts, and salts of isomers, esters and ethers, whenever the existence of such isomers, esters, ethers, and salts is possible within the specific chemical designation:

(1) Alphaprodine.

(2) Anileridine.

(3) Bezitramide.

(4) Dihydrocodeine.

(5) Diphenoxylate.

(6) Fentanyl.

(7) Isomethadone.

(8) Levomethorphan.

(9) Levorphanol.

(10) Metazocine.

(11) Methadone.

(12) Methadone-Intermediate, 4-cyano-2-dimethylamino-4, 4-diphenyl butane.

(13) Moramide-Intermediate, 2-methyl-3-morpholino-1, 1-diphenylpropane-carboxylic acid.

(14) Pethidine.

(15) Pethidine-Intermediate-A, 4-cyano-1-methyl-4-phenylpiperidine.

(16) Pethidine-Intermediate-B, ethyl-4-phenylpiperidine-4-carboxylate.

(17) Pethidine-Intermediate-C, 1-methyl-4-phenylpiperidine-4-carboxylic acid.

(18) Phenazocine.

(19) Piminodine.

(20) Racemethorphan.

(21) Racemorphan.

(c) Unless specifically excepted or unless listed in another schedule, any injectable liquid which contains any quantity of methamphetamine, including its salts, isomers, and salts of isomers.

Schedule III

(a) Unless specifically excepted or unless listed in another schedule, any material, compound, mixture, or preparation which contains any quantity of the following substances having a stimulant effect on the central nervous system:

(1) Amphetamine, its salts, optical isomers, and salts of its optical isomers.

(2) Phenmetrazine and its salts.

(3) Any substance (except an injectable liquid) which contains any quantity of methamphetamine, including its salts, isomers, and salts of isomers.

(4) Methylphenidate.

(b) Unless specifically excepted or unless listed in another schedule, any material, compound, mixture, or preparation which contains any quantity of the following substances having a depressant effect on the central nervous system:

(1) Any substance which contains any quantity of a derivative of barbituric acid, or any salt of a derivative of barbituric acid.

(2) Chorhexadol.

(3) Glutethimide.

(4) Lysergic acid.

(5) Lysergic acid amide.

(6) Methyprylon.

(7) Phencyclidine.

(8) Sulfondiethylmethane.

(9) Sulfonethylmethane.

(10) Sulfonmethane.

(c) Nalorphine.

(d) Unless specifically excepted or unless listed in another schedule, any material, compound, mixture, or preparation containing limited quantities of any of the following narcotic drugs, or any salts thereof:

(1) Not more than 1.8 grams of codeine per 100 milliliters or not more than 90 milligrams per dosage unit, with an equal or greater quantity of an isoquinoline alkaloid of opium.

(2) Not more than 1.8 grams of codeine per 100 milliliters or not more than 90 milligrams per dosage unit, with one or more active, nonnarcotic ingredients in recognized therapeutic amounts.

(3) Not more than 300 milligrams of dihydrocodeinone per 100 milliliters or not more than 15 milligrams per dosage unit, with a fourfold or greater quantity of an isoquinoline alkaloid of opium.

(4) Not more than 300 milligrams of dihydrocodeinone per 100 milliliters or not more than 15 milligrams per dosage unit, with one or more active, nonnarcotic ingredients in recognized therapeutic amounts.

(5) Not more than 1.8 grams of dihydrocodeine per 100 milliliters or not more than 90 milligrams per dosage unit, with one or more active, nonnarcotic ingredients in recognized therapeutic amounts.

(6) Not more than 300 milligrams of ethylmorphine per 100 milliliters or not more than 15 milligrams per dosage unit, with one or more active, nonnarcotic ingredients in recognized therapeutic amounts.

(7) Not more than 500 milligrams of opium per 100 milliliters or per 100 grams, or not more than 25 milligrams per dosage unit, with one or more active, nonnarcotic ingredients in recognized therapeutic amounts.

(8) Not more than 50 milligrams of morphine per 100 milliliters or per 100 grams with one or more active, nonnarcotic ingredients in recognized therapeutic amounts.

Schedule IV

(1) Barbital.

(2) Chloral betaine.

(3) Chloral hydrate.

(4) Ethchlorvynol.

(5) Ethinamate.

(6) Methohexital.

(7) Meprobamate.

(8) Methylphenobarbital.

(9) Paraldehyde.

(10) Petrichloral.

(11) Phenobarbital.

Schedule V

Any compound, mixture, or preparation containing any of the following limited quantities of narcotic drugs, which shall include one or more nonnarcotic active medicinal ingredients in sufficient proportion to confer upon the compound, mixture, or preparation valuable medicinal qualities other than those possessed by the narcotic drug alone:

(1) Not more than 200 milligrams of codeine per 100 milliliters or per 100 grams.

(2) Not more than 100 milligrams of dihydrocodeine per 100 milliliters or per 100 grams.

(3) Not more than 100 milligrams of ethylmorphine per 100 milliliters or per 100 grams.

(4) Not more than 2.5 milligrams of diphenoxylate and not less than 25 micrograms of atropine sulfate per dosage unit.

(5) Not more than 100 milligrams of opium per 100 milliliters or per 100 grams.

(Pub.L. 91–513, Title II, § 202, Oct. 27, 1970, 84 Stat. 1247; Pub.L. 95–633, Title I, § 103, Nov. 10, 1978, 92 Stat. 3772; Pub.L. 98–473, Title II, §§ 507(c), 509(b), Oct. 12, 1984, 98 Stat. 2071, 2072; Pub.L. 99–570, Title I, § 1867, Oct. 27, 1986, 100 Stat. 3207–55; Pub.L. 99–646, § 84, Nov. 10, 1986, 100 Stat. 3619.)

Amendment of Schedules

Subsection (c) of this section provides that Schedules I through V are subject to amendment pursuant to section 811 of Title 21, Food and Drugs. See 21 CFR part 1308 for revised schedules.

EDITORIAL NOTES

Placement of Pipradrol and SPA in Schedule IV to Carry Out Obligation Under Convention on Psychotropic Substances. Section 102(c) of Pub.L. 95–633 provided that: "For the purpose of carrying out the minimum United States obligations under paragraph 7 of article 2 of the Convention on Psychotropic Substances, signed at Vienna, Austria, on February 21, 1971, with respect to pipradrol and SPA (also known as (-)-1-dimethylamino-1,2-diphenylethane), the Attorney General shall by order, made without regard to sections 201 and 202 of the Controlled Substances Act [this section and section 811 of this title], place such drugs in schedule IV of such Act [see subsec. (c) of this section]."

Provision of section 102(c) of Pub.L. 95–633, set out above, effective July 15, 1980, the date the Convention on Psychotrophic Substances entered into force in the United States.

§ 813. Treatment of controlled substance analogues

A controlled substance analogue shall, to the extent intended for human consumption, be treated, for the purposes of any Federal law as a controlled substance in schedule I.

(Pub.L. 91–513, Title II, § 203, as added Pub.L. 99–570, Title I, § 1202, Oct. 27, 1986, 100 Stat. 3207–13; and amended Pub.L. 100–690, Title VI, § 6470(c), Nov. 18, 1988, 102 Stat. 4378.)

EDITORIAL NOTES

References in Text. Schedule I, referred to in text, is set out in section 812(c) of this title.

PART C

REGISTRATION OF MANUFACTURERS, DISTRIBUTORS, AND DISPENSERS OF CONTROLLED SUBSTANCES

§ 821. Rules and regulations

The Attorney General is authorized to promulgate rules and regulations and to charge reasonable fees relating to the registration and control of the manufacture, distribution, and dispensing of controlled substances.

(Pub.L. 91–513, Title II, § 301, Oct. 27, 1970, 84 Stat. 1253.)

Code of Federal Regulations

Administrative practices and procedures, see 21 CFR 10.1 et seq.

Personnel practices, see 21 CFR 19.1 et seq.

Public hearings, see 21 CFR 12.1 et seq. to 16.1 et seq.

§ 822. Persons required to register
Annual registration

(a)(1) Every person who manufactures or distributes any controlled substance, or who proposes to engage in the manufacture or distribution of any controlled substance, shall obtain annually a registration issued by the Attorney General in accordance with the rules and regulations promulgated by him.

(2) Every person who dispenses, or who proposes to dispense, any controlled substance, shall obtain from the Attorney General a registration issued in accordance with the rules and regulations promulgated by him. The Attorney General shall, by regulation, determine the period of such registrations. In no event, however, shall such registrations be issued for less than one year nor for more than three years.

Authorized activities

(b) Persons registered by the Attorney General under this subchapter to manufacture, distribute, or dispense controlled substances are authorized to possess, manufacture, distribute, or dispense such substances (including any such activity in the conduct of research) to the extent authorized by their registration and in conformity with the other provisions of this subchapter.

Exceptions

(c) The following persons shall not be required to register and may lawfully possess any controlled substance under this subchapter:

(1) An agent or employee of any registered manufacturer, distributor, or dispenser of any controlled substance if such agent or employee is acting in the usual course of his business or employment.

(2) A common or contract carrier or warehouseman, or an employee thereof, whose possession of the controlled substance is in the usual course of his business or employment.

(3) An ultimate user who possesses such substance for a purpose specified in section 802(25) of this title.

Waiver

(d) The Attorney General may, by regulation, waive the requirement for registration of certain manufacturers, distributors, or dispensers if he finds it consistent with the public health and safety.

Separate registration

(e) A separate registration shall be required at each principal place of business or professional practice where the applicant manufactures, distributes, or dispenses controlled substances.

Inspection

(f) The Attorney General is authorized to inspect the establishment of a registrant or applicant for registration in accordance with the rules and regulations promulgated by him.

(Pub.L. 91–513, Title II, § 302, Oct. 27, 1970, 84 Stat. 1253; Pub.L. 98–473, Title II, § 510, Oct. 12, 1984, 98 Stat. 2072.)

EDITORIAL NOTES

References in Text. "Section 802(25) of this title", referred to in subsec. (c)(3), probably should be a reference to "section 802(27) of this title" which defines the term "ultimate user".

Code of Federal Regulations

Administrative policies, practices, and procedures, see 21 CFR 1316.01 et seq.

General applicability, exceptions, etc., see 21 CFR 1307.01 et seq.

Registration requirements, see 21 CFR 1301.01 et seq.

§ 823. Registration requirements
Manufacturers of controlled substances in schedule I and II

(a) The Attorney General shall register an applicant to manufacture controlled substances in schedule I or II if he determines that such registration is consistent with the public interest and with United States obligations under international treaties, conventions, or protocols in effect on May 1, 1971. In determining the public interest, the following factors shall be considered:

(1) maintenance of effective controls against diversion of particular controlled substances and any controlled substance in schedule I or II compounded therefrom into other than legitimate medical, scientific, research, or industrial channels, by limiting the importation and bulk manufacture of such controlled substances to a number of establishments which can produce an adequate and uninterrupted supply of these substances under adequately competitive conditions for legitimate medical, scientific, research, and industrial purposes;

(2) compliance with applicable State and local law;

(3) promotion of technical advances in the art of manufacturing these substances and the development of new substances;

(4) prior conviction record of applicant under Federal and State laws relating to the manufacture, distribution, or dispensing of such substances;

(5) past experience in the manufacture of controlled substances, and the existence in the establishment of effective control against diversion; and

(6) such other factors as may be relevant to and consistent with the public health and safety.

Distributors of controlled substances in schedule I and II

(b) The Attorney General shall register an applicant to distribute a controlled substance in schedule I or II unless he determines that the issuance of such registration is inconsistent with the public interest. In determining the public interest, the following factors shall be considered:

(1) maintenance of effective control against diversion of particular controlled substances into other than legitimate medical, scientific, and industrial channels;

(2) compliance with applicable State and local law;

(3) prior conviction record of applicant under Federal or State laws relating to the manufacture, distribution, or dispensing of such substances;

(4) past experience in the distribution of controlled substances; and

(5) such other factors as may be relevant to and consistent with the public health and safety.

Limits of authorized activities

(c) Registration granted under subsections (a) and (b) of this section shall not entitle a registrant to (1) manufacture or distribute controlled substances in schedule I or II other than those specified in the registration, or (2) manufacture any quantity of those controlled substances in excess of the quota assigned pursuant to section 826 of this title.

Manufacturers of controlled substances in schedule III, IV, and V

(d) The Attorney General shall register an applicant to manufacture controlled substances in

schedule III, IV, or V, unless he determines that the issuance of such registration is inconsistent with the public interest. In determining the public interest, the following factors shall be considered:

(1) maintenance of effective controls against diversion of particular controlled substances and any controlled substance in schedule III, IV, or V compounded therefrom into other than legitimate medical, scientific, or industrial channels;

(2) compliance with applicable State and local law;

(3) promotion of technical advances in the art of manufacturing these substances and the development of new substances;

(4) prior conviction record of applicant under Federal or State laws relating to the manufacture, distribution, or dispensing of such substances;

(5) past experience in the manufacture, distribution, and dispensing of controlled substances, and the existence in the establishment of effective controls against diversion; and

(6) such other factors as may be relevant to and consistent with the public health and safety.

Distributors of controlled substances in schedule III, IV, and V

(e) The Attorney General shall register an applicant to distribute controlled substances in schedule III, IV, or V, unless he determines that the issuance of such registration is inconsistent with the public interest. In determining the public interest, the following factors shall be considered:

(1) maintenance of effective controls against diversion of particular controlled substances into other than legitimate medical, scientific, and industrial channels;

(2) compliance with applicable State and local law;

(3) prior conviction record of applicant under Federal or State laws relating to the manufacture, distribution, or dispensing of such substances;

(4) past experience in the distribution of controlled substances; and

(5) such other factors as may be relevant to and consistent with the public health and safety.

Research; pharmacies; research applications; construction of Article 7 of Convention on Psychotropic Substances

(f) The Attorney General shall register practitioners (including pharmacies, as distinguished from pharmacists) to dispense, or conduct research with, controlled substances in schedule II, III, IV, or V, if the applicant is authorized to dispense, or conduct research with respect to, controlled substances under the laws of the State in which he practices. The Attorney General may deny an application for such registration if he determines that the issuance of such registration would be inconsistent with the public interest. In determining the public interest, the following factors shall be considered:

(1) The recommendation of the appropriate State licensing board or professional disciplinary authority.

(2) The applicant's experience in dispensing, or conducting research with respect to controlled substances.

(3) The applicant's conviction record under Federal or State laws relating to the manufacture, distribution, or dispensing of controlled substances.

(4) Compliance with applicable State, Federal, or local laws relating to controlled substances.

(5) Such other conduct which may threaten the public health and safety.

Separate registration under this part for practitioners engaging in research with controlled substances in schedule II, III, IV, or V, who are already registered under this part in another capacity, shall not be required. Registration applications by practitioners wishing to conduct research with controlled substances in schedule I shall be referred to the Secretary, who shall determine the qualifications and competency of each practitioner requesting registration, as well as the merits of the research protocol. The Secretary, in determining the merits of each research protocol, shall consult with the Attorney General as to effective procedures to adequately safeguard against diversion of such controlled substances from legitimate medical or scientific use. Registration for the purpose of bona fide research with controlled substances in schedule I by a practitioner deemed qualified by the Secretary may be denied by the Attorney General only on a ground specified in section 824(a) of this title. Article 7 of the Convention on Psychotropic Substances shall not be construed to prohibit, or impose additional restrictions upon, research involving drugs or other substances scheduled under the convention which is conducted in conformity with this subsection and other applicable provisions of this subchapter.

Practitioners dispensing narcotic drugs for narcotic treatment; annual registration; separate registration; qualifications

(g) Practitioners who dispense narcotic drugs to individuals for maintenance treatment or detoxification treatment shall obtain annually a separate registration for that purpose. The Attorney General shall register an applicant to dispense narcotic drugs to individuals for maintenance treatment or detoxification treatment (or both)

(1) if the applicant is a practitioner who is determined by the Secretary to be qualified (under standards established by the Secretary) to engage in the treatment with respect to which registration is sought;

(2) if the Attorney General determines that the applicant will comply with standards established by the Attorney General respecting (A) security of stocks of narcotic drugs for such treatment, and (B) the maintenance of records (in accordance with section 827 of this title) on such drugs; and

(3) if the Secretary determines that the applicant will comply with standards established by the Secretary (after consultation with the Attorney General) respecting the quantities of narcotic drugs which may be provided for unsupervised use by individuals in such treatment.

(Pub.L. 91–513, Title II, § 303, Oct. 27, 1970, 84 Stat. 1253; Pub.L. 93–281, § 3, May 14, 1974, 88 Stat. 124; Pub.L. 95–633, Title I, § 109, Nov. 10, 1978, 92 Stat. 3773; Pub.L. 98–473, Title II, § 511, Oct. 12, 1984, 98 Stat. 2073.)

EDITORIAL NOTES

References in Text. Schedules I, II, III, IV, and V, referred to in text are set out in section 812(c) of this title.

Code of Federal Regulations

Registration requirements, see 21 CFR 1301.01 et seq.

Treatment of narcotic addicts, see 21 CFR 291.501 et seq.

§ 824. Denial, revocation, or suspension of registration

Grounds

(a) A registration pursuant to section 823 of this title to manufacture, distribute, or dispense a controlled substance may be suspended or revoked by the Attorney General upon a finding that the registrant—

(1) has materially falsified any application filed pursuant to or required by this subchapter or subchapter II of this chapter;

(2) has been convicted of a felony under this subchapter or subchapter II of this chapter or any other law of the United States, or of any State, relating to any substance defined in this subchapter as a controlled substance;

(3) has had his State license or registration suspended, revoked, or denied by competent State authority and is no longer authorized by State law to engage in the manufacturing, distribution, or dispensing of controlled substances or has had the suspension, revocation, or denial of his registration recommended by competent State authority;

(4) has committed such acts as would render his registration under section 823 of this title inconsistent with the public interest as determined under such section; or

(5) has been excluded (or directed to be excluded) from participation in a program pursuant to section 1320a–7(a) of Title 42.

A registration pursuant to section 823(g) of this title to dispense a narcotic drug for maintenance treatment or detoxification treatment may be suspended or revoked by the Attorney General upon a finding that the registrant has failed to comply with any standard referred to in section 823(g) of this title.

Limits of revocation or suspension

(b) The Attorney General may limit revocation or suspension of a registration to the particular controlled substance with respect to which grounds for revocation or suspension exist.

Service of show cause order; proceedings

(c) Before taking action pursuant to this section, or pursuant to a denial of registration under section 823 of this title, the Attorney General shall serve upon the applicant or registrant an order to show cause why registration should not be denied, revoked, or suspended. The order to show cause shall contain a statement of the basis thereof and shall call upon the applicant or registrant to appear before the Attorney General at a time and place stated in the order, but in no event less than thirty days after the date of receipt of the order. Proceedings to deny, revoke, or suspend shall be conducted pursuant to this section in accordance with subchapter II of chapter 5 of Title 5. Such proceedings shall be independent of, and not in lieu of, criminal prosecutions or other proceedings under this subchapter or any other law of the United States.

Suspension of registration in cases of imminent danger

(d) The Attorney General may, in his discretion, suspend any registration simultaneously with the institution of proceedings under this section, in cases where he finds that there is an imminent danger to the public health or safety. A failure to comply with a standard referred to in section 823(g) of this title may be treated under this subsection as grounds for immediate suspension of a registration granted under such section. A suspension under this subsection shall continue in effect until the conclusion of such proceedings, including judicial review thereof, unless sooner withdrawn by the Attorney General or dissolved by a court of competent jurisdiction.

Suspension and revocation of quotas

(e) The suspension or revocation of a registration under this section shall operate to suspend or revoke any quota applicable under section 826 of this title.

Disposition of controlled substances

(f) In the event the Attorney General suspends or revokes a registration granted under section 823 of this title, all controlled substances owned or possessed by the registrant pursuant to such registration at the time of suspension or the effective date of the revocation order, as the case may be, may, in the discretion of the Attorney General, be placed under seal. No disposition may be made of any controlled substances under seal until the time for taking an appeal has elapsed or until all appeals have been concluded except that a court, upon application therefor, may at any time order the sale of perishable controlled substances. Any such order shall require the deposit of the proceeds of the sale with the court. Upon a revocation order becoming final, all such controlled substances (or proceeds of sale deposited in court) shall be forfeited to the United States; and the Attorney General shall dispose of such controlled substances in accordance with section 881(e) of this title. All right, title, and interest in such controlled substances shall vest in the United States upon a revocation order becoming final.

Seizure or placement under seal of controlled substances

(g) The Attorney General may, in his discretion, seize or place under seal any controlled substances owned or possessed by a registrant whose registration has expired or who has ceased to practice or do business in the manner contemplated by his registration. Such controlled substances shall be held for the benefit of the registrant, or his successor in interest. The Attorney General shall notify a registrant, or his successor in interest, who has any controlled substance seized or placed under seal of the procedures to be followed to secure the return of the controlled substance and the conditions under which it will be returned. The Attorney General may not dispose of any controlled substance seized or placed under seal under this subsection until the expiration of one hundred and eighty days from the date such substance was seized or placed under seal.

(Pub.L. 91–513, Title II, § 304, Oct. 27, 1970, 84 Stat. 1255; Pub.L. 93–281, § 4, May 14, 1974, 88 Stat. 125; Pub.L. 98–473, Title II, §§ 304, 512, 513, Oct. 12, 1984, 98 Stat. 2050, 2073; Pub.L. 100–93, § 8(j), Aug. 18, 1987, 101 Stat. 695.)

EDITORIAL NOTES

References in Text. Subchapter II of this chapter, referred to in subsec. (a)(1), (2), was in the original "title III", meaning Title III of Pub.L. 91–513, Oct. 27, 1970, 84 Stat. 1285. Part A of Title III comprises subchapter II of this chapter. For classification of Part B, consisting of sections 1101 to 1105 of Title III, see U.S.C.A. Tables volume.

Effective Date of 1987 Amendment. Amendment by Pub.L. 100–93 effective at the end of the fourteen-day period beginning on Aug. 18, 1987, and inapplicable to administrative proceedings commenced before the end of such period, see section 15(a) of Pub.L. 100–93, set out as a note under section 1320a–7 of Title 42, The Public Health and Welfare.

Code of Federal Regulations

Registration requirements, see 21 CFR 1301.01 et seq.

§ 825. Labeling and packaging
Symbol

(a) It shall be unlawful to distribute a controlled substance in a commercial container unless such container, when and as required by regulations of the Attorney General, bears a label (as defined in section 321(k) of this title) containing an identifying symbol for such substance in accordance with such regulations. A different symbol shall be required for each schedule of controlled substances.

Unlawful distribution without identifying symbol

(b) It shall be unlawful for the manufacturer of any controlled substance to distribute such substance unless the labeling (as defined in section 321(m) of this title) of such substance contains, when and as required by regulations of the Attorney General, the identifying symbol required under subsection (a) of this section.

Warning on label

(c) The Secretary shall prescribe regulations under section 353(b) of this title which shall provide that the label of a drug listed in schedule II, III, or IV shall, when dispensed to or for a patient, contain a clear, concise warning that it is a crime to transfer the drug to any person other than the patient.

Containers to be securely sealed

(d) It shall be unlawful to distribute controlled substances in schedule I or II, and narcotic drugs in schedule III or IV, unless the bottle or other container, stopper, covering, or wrapper thereof is securely sealed as required by regulations of the Attorney General.

(Pub.L. 91–513, Title II, § 305, Oct. 27, 1970, 84 Stat. 1256.)

EDITORIAL NOTES

References in Text. Schedules I, II, III, and IV, referred to in subsecs. (c) and (d), are set out in section 812(c) of this title.

Code of Federal Regulations

Labeling and packaging requirements, see 21 CFR 1302.01 et seq.

§ 826. Production quotas for controlled substances

Establishment of total annual needs

(a) The Attorney General shall determine the total quantity and establish production quotas for each basic class of controlled substance in schedules I and II to be manufactured each calendar year to provide for the estimated medical, scientific, research, and industrial needs of the United States, for lawful export requirements, and for the establishment and maintenance of reserve stocks. Production quotas shall be established in terms of quantities of each basic class of controlled substance and not in terms of individual pharmaceutical dosage forms prepared from or containing such a controlled substance.

Individual production quotas; revised quotas

(b) The Attorney General shall limit or reduce individual production quotas to the extent necessary to prevent the aggregate of individual quotas from exceeding the amount determined necessary each year by the Attorney General under subsection (a) of this section. The quota of each registered manufacturer for each basic class of controlled substance in schedule I or II shall be revised in the same proportion as the limitation or reduction of the aggregate of the quotas. However, if any registrant, before the issuance of a limitation or reduction in quota, has manufactured in excess of his revised quota, the amount of the excess shall be subtracted from his quota for the following year.

Manufacturing quotas for registered manufacturers

(c) On or before October 1 of each year, upon application therefor by a registered manufacturer, the Attorney General shall fix a manufacturing quota for the basic classes of controlled substances in schedules I and II that the manufacturer seeks to produce. The quota shall be subject to the provisions of subsections (a) and (b) of this section. In fixing such quotas, the Attorney General shall determine the manufacturer's estimated disposal, inventory, and other requirements for the calendar year; and, in making his determination, the Attorney General shall consider the manufacturer's current rate of disposal, the trend of the national disposal rate during the preceding calendar year, the manufacturer's production cycle and inventory position, the economic availability of raw materials, yield and stability

problems, emergencies such as strikes and fires, and other factors.

Quotas for registrants who have not manufactured controlled substance during one or more preceding years

(d) The Attorney General shall, upon application and subject to the provisions of subsections (a) and (b) of this section, fix a quota for a basic class of controlled substance in schedule I or II for any registrant who has not manufactured that basic class of controlled substance during one or more preceding calendar years. In fixing such quota, the Attorney General shall take into account the registrant's reasonably anticipated requirements for the current year; and, in making his determination of such requirements, he shall consider such factors specified in subsection (c) of this section as may be relevant.

Quota increases

(e) At any time during the year any registrant who has applied for or received a manufacturing quota for a basic class of controlled substance in schedule I or II may apply for an increase in that quota to meet his estimated disposal, inventory, and other requirements during the remainder of that year. In passing upon the application the Attorney General shall take into consideration any occurrences since the filing of the registrant's initial quota application that may require an increased manufacturing rate by the registrant during the balance of the year. In passing upon the application the Attorney General may also take into account the amount, if any, by which the determination of the Attorney General under subsection (a) of this section exceeds the aggregate of the quotas of all registrants under this section.

Incidental production exception

(f) Notwithstanding any other provisions of this subchapter, no registration or quota may be required for the manufacture of such quantities of controlled substances in schedules I and II as incidentally and necessarily result from the manufacturing process used for the manufacture of a controlled substance with respect to which its manufacturer is duly registered under this subchapter. The Attorney General may, by regulation, prescribe restrictions on the retention and disposal of such incidentally produced substances.

(Pub.L. 91–513, Title II, § 306, Oct. 27, 1970, 84 Stat. 1257; Pub.L. 94–273, § 3(16), Apr. 21, 1976, 90 Stat. 377.)

EDITORIAL NOTES

References in Text. Schedules I and II, referred to in text, are set out in section 812(c) of this title.

Code of Federal Regulations

Quotas, see 21 CFR 1303.01 et seq.

§ 827. Records and reports of registrants

Inventory

(a) Except as provided in subsection (c) of this section—

(1) every registrant under this subchapter shall, on May 1, 1971, or as soon thereafter as such registrant first engages in the manufacture, distribution, or dispensing of controlled substances, and every second year thereafter, make a complete and accurate record of all stocks thereof on hand, except that the regulations prescribed under this section shall permit each such biennial inventory (following the initial inventory required by this paragraph) to be prepared on such registrant's regular general physical inventory date (if any) which is nearest to and does not vary by more than six months from the biennial date that would otherwise apply;

(2) on the effective date of each regulation of the Attorney General controlling a substance that immediately prior to such date was not a controlled substance, each registrant under this subchapter manufacturing, distributing, or dispensing such substance shall make a complete and accurate record of all stocks thereof on hand; and

(3) on and after May 1, 1971, every registrant under this subchapter manufacturing, distributing, or dispensing a controlled substance or substances shall maintain, on a current basis, a complete and accurate record of each such substance manufactured, received, sold, delivered, or otherwise disposed of by him, except that this paragraph shall not require the maintenance of a perpetual inventory.

Availability of records

(b) Every inventory or other record required under this section (1) shall be in accordance with, and contain such relevant information as may be required by, regulations of the Attorney General, (2) shall (A) be maintained separately from all other records of the registrant, or (B) alternatively, in the case of nonnarcotic controlled substances, be in such form that information required by the Attorney General is readily retrievable from the ordinary business records of the registrant, and (3) shall be kept and be available, for at least two years, for inspection and copying by officers or employees of the United States authorized by the Attorney General.

Nonapplicability

(c) The foregoing provisions of this section shall not apply—

(1)(A) to the prescribing of controlled substances in schedule II, III, IV, or V by practitioners acting in the lawful course of their professional practice unless such substance is prescribed in the course of maintenance or detoxification treatment of an individual; or

(B) to the administering of a controlled substance in schedule II, III, IV, or V unless the practitioner regularly engages in the dispensing or administering of controlled substances and charges his patients, either separately or together with charges for other professional services, for substances so dispensed or administered or unless such substance is administered in the course of maintenance treatment or detoxification treatment of an individual;

(2)(A) to the use of controlled substances, at establishments registered under this subchapter which keep records with respect to such substances, in research conducted in conformity with an exemption granted under section 355(i) or 360b(j) of this title;

(B) to the use of controlled substances, at establishments registered under this subchapter which keep records with respect to such substances, in preclinical research or in teaching; or

(3) to the extent of any exemption granted to any person, with respect to all or part of such provisions, by the Attorney General by or pursuant to regulation on the basis of a finding that the application of such provisions (or part thereof) to such person is not necessary for carrying out the purposes of this subchapter.

Nothing in the Convention on Psychotropic Substances shall be construed as superseding or otherwise affecting the provisions of paragraph (1)(B), (2), or (3) of this subsection.

Periodic reports to Attorney General

(d) Every manufacturer registered under section 823 of this title shall, at such time or times and in such form as the Attorney General may require, make periodic reports to the Attorney General of every sale, delivery, or other disposal by him of any controlled substance, and each distributor shall make such reports with respect to narcotic controlled substances, identifying by the registration number assigned under this subchapter the person or establishment (unless exempt from registration under section 822(d) of this title) to whom such sale, delivery, or other disposal was made.

Reporting and recordkeeping requirements of drug conventions

(e) In addition to the reporting and recordkeeping requirements under any other provision of this subchapter, each manufacturer registered under section 823 of this title shall, with respect to narcotic and nonnarcotic controlled substances manufactured by it, make such reports to the Attorney General, and maintain such records, as the Attorney General may require to enable the United States to meet its obligations under articles 19 and 20 of the Single Convention on Narcotic Drugs and article 16 of the Convention on Psychotropic Substances. The Attorney General shall administer the requirements of this subsection in such a manner as to avoid the unnecessary imposition of duplicative requirements under this subchapter on manufacturers subject to the requirements of this subsection.

Investigational uses of drugs; procedures

(f) Regulations under sections 355(i) and 360b(j) of this title, relating to investigational use of drugs, shall include such procedures as the Secretary, after consultation with the Attorney General, determines are necessary to insure the security and accountability of controlled substances used in research to which such regulations apply.

Change of address

(g) Every registrant under this subchapter shall be required to report any change of professional or business address in such manner as the Attorney General shall by regulation require.

(Pub.L. 91–513, Title II, § 307, Oct. 27, 1970, 84 Stat. 1258; Pub.L. 93–281, § 5, May 14, 1974, 88 Stat. 125; Pub.L. 95–633, Title I, §§ 104, 110, Nov. 10, 1978, 92 Stat. 3772, 3773; Pub.L. 98–473, Title II, §§ 514, 515, Oct. 12, 1984, 98 Stat. 2074.)

EDITORIAL NOTES

References in Text. Schedules II, III, IV, and V, referred to in subsec. (c)(1), are set out in section 812(c) of this title.

Code of Federal Regulations

Recordkeeping and reporting requirements, see 21 CFR 1304.01 et seq.

§ 828. Order forms

Unlawful distribution of controlled substances

(a) It shall be unlawful for any person to distribute a controlled substance in schedule I or II to another except in pursuance of a written order of the person to whom such substance is distributed, made on a form to be issued by the Attorney General in blank in accordance with subsection (d) of this section and regulations prescribed by him pursuant to this section.

Nonapplicability of provisions

(b) Nothing in subsection (a) of this section shall apply to—

(1) the exportation of such substances from the United States in conformity with subchapter II of this chapter;

(2) the delivery of such a substance to or by a common or contract carrier for carriage in the lawful and usual course of its business, or to or by a warehouseman for storage in the lawful and usual course of its business; but where such carriage or storage is in connection with the distribution by the owner of the substance to a third person, this paragraph shall not relieve the distributor from compliance with subsection (a) of this section.

Preservation and availability

(c)(1) Every person who in pursuance of an order required under subsection (a) of this section distributes a controlled substance shall preserve such order for a period of two years, and shall make such order available for inspection and copying by officers and employees of the United States duly authorized for that purpose by the Attorney General, and by officers or employees of States or their political subdivisions who are charged with the enforcement of State or local laws regulating the production, or regulating the distribution or dispensing, of controlled substances and who are authorized under such laws to inspect such orders.

(2) Every person who gives an order required under subsection (a) of this section shall, at or before the time of giving such order, make or cause to be made a duplicate thereof on a form to be issued by the Attorney General in blank in accordance with subsection (d) of this section and regulations prescribed by him pursuant to this section, and shall, if such order is accepted, preserve such duplicate for a period of two years and make it available for inspection and copying by the officers and employees mentioned in paragraph (1) of this subsection.

Issuance

(d)(1) The Attorney General shall issue forms pursuant to subsections (a) and (c)(2) of this section only to persons validly registered under section 823 of this title (or exempted from registration under section 822(d) of this title). Whenever any such form is issued to a person, the Attorney General shall, before delivery thereof, insert therein the name of such person, and it shall be unlawful for any other person (A) to use such form for the purpose of obtaining controlled substances or (B) to furnish such form to any person with intent thereby to procure the distribution of such substances.

(2) The Attorney General may charge reasonable fees for the issuance of such forms in such amounts as he may prescribe for the purpose of covering the cost to the United States of issuing such forms, and other necessary activities in connection therewith.

Unlawful acts

(e) It shall be unlawful for any person to obtain by means of order forms issued under this section controlled substances for any purpose other than their use, distribution, dispensing, or administration in the conduct of a lawful business in such substances or in the course of his professional practice or research.

(Pub.L. 91–513, Title II, § 308, Oct. 27, 1970, 84 Stat. 1259.)

EDITORIAL NOTES

References in Text. Schedules I and II, referred to in subsec. (a), are set out in section 812(c) of this title.

Subchapter II of this chapter, referred to in subsec. (b)(1), was in the original "title III", meaning Title III of Pub.L. 91–513, Oct. 27, 1970, 84 Stat. 1285. Part A of Title III comprises subchapter II of this chapter. For classification of Part B, consisting of sections 1101 to 1105 of Title III, see U.S.C.A. Tables volume.

Code of Federal Regulations

Forms requirements, see 21 CFR 1305.01 et seq.

§ 829. Prescriptions
Schedule II substances

(a) Except when dispensed directly by a practitioner, other than a pharmacist, to an ultimate user, no controlled substance in schedule II, which is a prescription drug as determined under the Federal Food, Drug, and Cosmetic Act, may be dispensed without the written prescription of a practitioner, except that in emergency situations, as prescribed by the Secretary by regulation after consultation with the Attorney General, such drug may be dispensed upon oral prescription in accordance with section 503(b) of that Act. Prescriptions shall be retained in conformity with the requirements of section 827 of this title. No prescription for a controlled substance in schedule II may be refilled.

Schedule III and IV substances

(b) Except when dispensed directly by a practitioner, other than a pharmacist, to an ultimate user, no controlled substance in schedule III or IV, which is a prescription drug as determined under the Federal Food, Drug, and Cosmetic Act, may be dispensed without a written or oral prescription in conformity with section 503(b) of that Act. Such prescriptions may not be filled or refilled more than six months after the date thereof or be refilled more than five times after the date of the prescription unless renewed by the practitioner.

Schedule V substances

(c) No controlled substance in schedule V which is a drug may be distributed or dispensed other than for a medical purpose.

Non-prescription drugs with abuse potential

(d) Whenever it appears to the Attorney General that a drug not considered to be a prescription drug under the Federal Food, Drug, and Cosmetic Act should be so considered because of its abuse potential, he shall so advise the Secretary and furnish to him all available data relevant thereto.

(Pub.L. 91–513, Title II, § 309, Oct. 27, 1970, 84 Stat. 1260.)

EDITORIAL NOTES

References in Text. Schedules II, III, IV, and V, referred to in text, are set out in section 812(c) of this title.

The Federal Food, Drug, and Cosmetic Act, referred to in subsecs. (a), (b), and (d), is Act June 25, 1938, c. 675, 52 Stat. 1040, as amended, which is classified generally to chapter 9 (section 301 et seq.) of Title 21 U.S.C.A., Food and Drugs. Section 503(b) of that Act is classified to section 353(b) of Title 21.

Code of Federal Regulations

Prescription requirements, see 21 CFR 1306.01 et seq.

§ 830. Regulation of listed chemicals and certain machines

Record of regulated transactions

(a)(1) Each regulated person who engages in a regulated transaction involving a listed chemical, a tableting machine, or an encapsulating machine shall keep a record of the transaction—

(A) for 4 years after the date of the transaction, if the listed chemical is a precursor chemical or if the transaction involves a tableting machine or an encapsulating machine; and

(B) for 2 years after the date of the transaction, if the listed chemical is an essential chemical.

(2) A record under this subsection shall be retrievable and shall include the date of the regulated transaction, the identity of each party to the regulated transaction, a statement of the quantity and form of the listed chemical, a description of the tableting machine or encapsulating machine, and a description of the method of transfer. Such record shall be available for inspection and copying by the Attorney General.

(3) It is the duty of each regulated person who engages in a regulated transaction to identify each other party to the transaction. It is the duty of such other party to present proof of identity to the regulated person. The Attorney General shall specify by regulation the types of documents and other evidence that constitute proof of identity for purposes of this paragraph.

Reports to Attorney General

(b) Each regulated person shall report to the Attorney General, in such form and manner as the Attorney General shall prescribe by regulation—

(1) any regulated transaction involving an extraordinary quantity of a listed chemical, an uncommon method of payment or delivery, or any other circumstance that the regulated person believes may indicate that the listed chemical will be used in violation of this subchapter;

(2) any proposed regulated transaction with a person whose description or other identifying characteristic the Attorney General furnishes in advance to the regulated person;

(3) any unusual or excessive loss or disappearance of a listed chemical under the control of the regulated person; and

(4) any regulated transaction in a tableting machine or an encapsulating machine.

Each report under paragraph (1) shall be made at the earliest practicable opportunity after the regulated person becomes aware of the circumstance involved. A regulated person may not complete a transaction with a person whose description or identifying characteristic is furnished to the regulated person under paragraph (2) unless the transaction is approved by the Attorney General. The Attorney General shall make available to regulated persons guidance documents describing transactions and circumstances for which reports are required under paragraph (1) and paragraph (3).

Confidentiality of information obtained by Attorney General; non-disclosure; exceptions

(c)(1) Except as provided in paragraph (2), any information obtained by the Attorney General under this section which is exempt from disclosure under section 552(a) of Title 5, by reason of section 552(b)(4) of Title 5, is confidential and may not be disclosed to any person.

(2) Information referred to in paragraph (1) may be disclosed only—

(A) to an officer or employee of the United States engaged in carrying out this subchapter, subchapter II of this chapter, or the customs laws;

(B) when relevant in any investigation or proceeding for the enforcement of this subchapter, subchapter II of this chapter, or the customs laws;

(C) when necessary to comply with an obligation of the United States under a treaty or other international agreement; or

(D) to a State or local official or employee in conjunction with the enforcement of controlled substances laws or precursor chemical laws.

(3) The Attorney General shall—

(A) take such action as may be necessary to prevent unauthorized disclosure of information by any person to whom such information is disclosed under paragraph (2); and

(B) issue guidelines that limit, to the maximum extent feasible, the disclosure of proprietary business information, including the names or identities of United States exporters of listed chemicals, to any person to whom such information is disclosed under paragraph (2).

(4) Any person who is aggrieved by a disclosure of information in violation of this section may bring a civil action against the violator for appropriate relief.

(5) Notwithstanding paragraph (4), a civil action may not be brought under such paragraph against investigative or law enforcement personnel of the Drug Enforcement Administration."

(Pub.L. 91–513, Title II, § 310, as added Pub.L. 95–633, Title II, § 202(a), Nov. 10, 1978, 92 Stat. 3774; and amended Pub.L. 100–690, Title VI, § 6052(a), Nov. 18, 1988, 102 Stat. 4313.)

EDITORIAL NOTES

Effective Date of 1988 Amendment. Amendment by section 6052 of Pub.L. 100–690 effective 120 days after Nov. 18, 1988, see section 6061 of Pub.L. 100–690, set out as a note under section 802 of this title.

Effective Date; Time to Submit Piperidine Report; Required Information. Section 203(a) of Pub.L. 95–633 provided that:

"(1) Except as provided under paragraph (2), the amendments may by this title [enacting this section and amending sections 841 to 843 of this title] shall take effect on the date of the enactment of this Act [Nov. 10, 1978].

"(2) Any person required to submit a report under section 310(a)(1) of the Controlled Substances Act [subsec. (a)(1) of this section] respecting a distribution, sale, or importation of piperidine during the 90 days after the date of the enactment of this Act [Nov. 10, 1978]

may submit such report any time up to 97 days after such date of enactment.

"(3) Until otherwise provided by the Attorney General by regulation, the information required to be reported by a person under section 310(a)(1) of the Controlled Substances Act (as added by section 202(a)(2) of this title) [subsec. (a)(1) of this section] with respect to the person's distribution, sale, or importation of piperidine shall—

"(A) be the information described in subparagraphs (A) and (B) of such section, and

"(B) except as provided in paragraph (2) of this subsection, be reported not later than seven days after the date of such distribution, sale, or importation."

Regulations for Piperidine Reporting. Section 203(b) of Pub.L. 95–633 provided that:

"The Attorney General shall—

"(1) first publish proposed interim regulations to carry out the requirements of section 310(a) of the Controlled Substances Act (as added by section 202(a)(2) of this title) [subsec. (a) of this section] not later than 30 days after the date of the enactment of this Act [Nov. 10, 1978], and

"(2) first promulgate final interim regulations to carry out such requirements not later than 75 days after the date of the enactment of this Act [Nov. 10, 1978], such final interim regulations to be effective with respect to distributions, sales, and importations of piperidine on and after the ninety-first day after the date of the enactment of this Act."

Report to President and Congress on Effectiveness of Title II of Pub.L. 95–633. Section 203(c) of Pub.L. 95–633 required the Attorney General, after consultation with the Secretary of Health, Education, and Welfare [now Secretary of Health and Human Services], to analyze and evaluate the impact and effectiveness of the amendments made by Title II of Pub.L. 95–633 [enacting this section and amending sections 841 to 843 of this title], including the impact on the illicit manufacture and use of phencyclidine and the impact of the requirements imposed by such amendments on legitimate distributions and uses of piperidine, and, not later than Mar. 1, 1980, to report to the President and the Congress on such analysis and evaluation and to include in such report such recommendations as he deemed appropriate.

Code of Federal Regulations

Identification requirements, see 21 CFR 1310.01 et seq.

PART D

OFFENSES AND PENALTIES

§ 841. Prohibited acts A

Unlawful acts

(a) Except as authorized by this subchapter, it shall be unlawful for any person knowingly or intentionally—

(1) to manufacture, distribute, or dispense, or possess with intent to manufacture, distribute, or dispense, a controlled substance; or

(2) to create, distribute, or dispense, or possess with intent to distribute or dispense, a counterfeit substance.

Penalties

(b) Except as otherwise provided in section 845, 845a, or 845b of this title, any person who violates subsection (a) of this section shall be sentenced as follows:

(1)(A) In the case of a violation of subsection (a) of this section involving—

(i) 1 kilogram or more of a mixture or substance containing a detectable amount of heroin;

(ii) 5 kilograms or more of a mixture or substance containing a detectable amount of—

(I) coca leaves, except coca leaves and extracts of coca leaves from which cocaine, ecgonine, and derivatives of ecgonine or their salts have been removed;

(II) cocaine, its salts, optical and geometric isomers, and salts of isomers;

(III) ecgonine, its derivatives, their salts, isomers, and salts of isomers; or

(IV) any compound, mixture, or preparation which contains any quantity of any of the substance [1] referred to in subclauses (I) through (III);

(iii) 50 grams or more of a mixture or substance described in clause (ii) which contains cocaine base;

(iv) 100 grams or more of phencyclidine (PCP) or 1 kilogram or more of a mixture or substance containing a detectable amount of phencyclidine (PCP);

(v) 10 grams or more of a mixture or substance containing a detectable amount of lysergic acid diethylamide (LSD);

(vi) 400 grams or more of a mixture or substance containing a detectable amount of N-phenyl-N-[1-(2-phenylethyl)-4-piperidinyl] propanamide or 100 grams or more of a mixture or substance containing a detectable amount of any analogue of N-phenyl-N-[1-(2-phenylethyl)-4-piperidinyl] propanamide;

(vii) 1000 kilograms or more of a mixture or substance containing a detectable amount of marihuana, or 1,000 or more marihuana plants regardless of weight; or

(viii) 100 grams or more of methamphetamine, its salts, isomers, and salts of its isomers or 100 grams or more of a mixture or substance containing a detectable amount of methamphetamine, its salts, isomers, or salts of its isomers;

such person shall be sentenced to a term of imprisonment which may not be less than 10 years or more than life and if death or serious bodily injury results from the use of such substance shall be not less than 20 years or more than life, a fine not to exceed the greater of that authorized in accordance with the provisions of Title 18, or $4,000,000 if the defendant is an individual or $10,000,000 if the defendant is other than an individual, or both. If any person commits such a violation after a prior conviction for a felony drug offense has become final, such person shall be sentenced to a term of imprisonment which may not be less than 20 years and not more than life imprisonment and if death or serious bodily injury results from the use of such substance shall be sentenced to life imprisonment, a fine not to exceed the greater of twice that authorized in accordance with the provisions of Title 18, or $8,000,000 if the defendant is an individual or $20,000,000 if the defendant is other than an individual, or both. If any person commits a violation of this subparagraph or of section 845, 845a, or 845b of this title after two or more prior convictions for a felony drug offense have become final, such person shall be sentenced to a mandatory term of life imprisonment without release and fined in accordance with the preceding sentence. For purposes of this subparagraph, the term "felony drug offense" means an offense that is a felony under any provision of this subchapter or any other Federal law that prohibits or restricts conduct relating to narcotic drugs, marihuana, or depressant or stimulant substances or a felony under any law of a State or a foreign country that prohibits or restricts conduct relating to narcotic drugs, marihuana, or depressant or stimulant substances. Any sentence under this subparagraph shall, in the absence of such a prior conviction, impose a term of supervised release of at least 5 years in addition to such term of imprisonment and shall, if there was such a prior conviction, impose a term of supervised release of at least 10 years in addition to such term of imprisonment. Notwithstanding any other provision of law, the court shall not place on probation or suspend the sentence of any person sentenced under this subparagraph. No person sentenced under this subparagraph shall be eligible for parole during the term of imprisonment imposed therein.

(B) In the case of a violation of subsection (a) of this section involving—

(i) 100 grams or more of a mixture or substance containing a detectable amount of heroin;

(ii) 500 grams or more of a mixture or substance containing a detectable amount of—

(I) coca leaves, except coca leaves and extracts of coca leaves from which cocaine, ecgonine, and derivatives of ecgonine or their salts have been removed;

(II) cocaine, its salts, optical and geometric isomers, and salts of isomers;

(III) ecgonine, its derivatives, their salts, isomers, and salts of isomers; or

(IV) any compound, mixture, or preparation which contains any quantity of any of the substance [1] referred to in subclauses (I) through (III);

(iii) 5 grams or more of a mixture or substance described in clause (ii) which contains cocaine base;

(iv) 10 grams or more of phencyclidine (PCP) or 100 grams or more of a mixture or substance containing a detectable amount of phencyclidine (PCP);

(v) 1 gram or more of a mixture or substance containing a detectable amount of lysergic acid diethylamide (LSD);

(vi) 40 grams or more of a mixture or substance containing a detectable amount of N-phenyl-N-[1-(2-phenylethyl)-4-piperidinyl] propanamide or 10 grams or more of a mixture or substance containing a detectable amount of any analogue of N-phenyl-N-[1-(2-phenylethyl)-4-piperidinyl] propanamide;

(vii) 100 kilograms or more of a mixture or substance containing a detectable amount of marihuana, or 100 or more marihuana plants regardless of weight; or

(viii) 10 grams or more of methamphetamine, its salts, isomers, and salts of its isomers or 100 grams or more of a mixture or substance containing a detectable amount of methamphetamine, its salts, isomers, or salts of its isomers;

such person shall be sentenced to a term of imprisonment which may not be less than 5 years and not more than 40 years and if death or serious bodily injury results from the use of such substance shall be not less than 20 years or more than life, a fine not to exceed the greater of that authorized in accordance with the provisions of Title 18, or $2,000,000 if the defendant is an individual or $5,000,000 if the defendant is other than an individual, or both. If any person commits such a violation after one or more prior convictions for an offense punishable under this paragraph, or for a felony under any other provision of this subchapter or subchapter II of this chapter or other law of a State, the United States, or a foreign country relating to narcotic drugs, marihuana, or depressant or stimulant substances, have become final, such person shall be sentenced to a term of imprisonment which may not be less than 10 years and not more than life imprisonment and if death or serious bodily injury results from the use of such substance shall be sentenced to life imprisonment, a fine not to exceed the greater of twice that authorized in accordance with the provisions of Title 18, or $4,000,000 if the defendant is an individual or $10,000,000 if the defendant is other than an individual, or both. Any sentence imposed under this subparagraph shall, in the absence of such a prior conviction, include a term of supervised release of at least 4 years in addition to such term of imprisonment and shall, if there was such a prior conviction, include a term of supervised release of at least 8 years in addition to such term of imprisonment. Notwithstanding any other provision of law, the court shall not place on probation or suspend the sentence of any person sentenced under this subparagraph. No person sentenced under this subparagraph shall be eligible for parole during the term of imprisonment imposed therein.

(C) In the case of a controlled substance in schedule I or II except as provided in subparagraphs (A), (B), and (D), such person shall be sentenced to a term of imprisonment of not more than 20 years and if death or serious bodily injury results from the use of such substance shall be sentenced to a term of imprisonment of not less than twenty years or more than life, a fine not to exceed the greater of that authorized in accordance with the provisions of Title 18, or $1,000,000 if the defendant is an individual or $5,000,000 if the defendant is other than an individual, or both. If any person commits such a violation after one or more prior convictions for an offense punishable under this paragraph, or for a felony under any other provision of this subchapter or subchapter II of this chapter or other law of a State, the United States or a foreign country relating to narcotic drugs, marihuana, or depressant or stimulant substances, have become final, such person shall be sentenced to a term of imprisonment of not more than 30 years and if death or serious bodily injury results from the use of such substance shall be sentenced to life imprisonment, a fine not to exceed the greater of twice that authorized in accordance with the provisions of Title 18, or $2,000,000 if the defendant is an individual or $10,000,000 if the defendant is other than an individual, or both. Any sentence imposing a term of imprisonment under this paragraph shall, in the absence of such a prior conviction, impose a term of supervised release of at least 3 years in addition to such term of imprisonment and shall, if there was such a prior conviction, impose a term of supervised release of at least 6 years in addition to such term of imprisonment. Notwithstanding any other provision of law, the court shall not place on probation or suspend the sentence of any person sentenced under the provisions of this subparagraph which provide for a mandatory term of imprisonment if death or serious bodily injury results, nor shall a person so sentenced be eligible for parole during the term of such a sentence.

(D) In the case of less than 50 kilograms of marihuana, except in the case of 50 or more marihuana plants regardless of weight, 10 kilograms of hashish, or one kilogram of hashish oil or in the case of any controlled substance in schedule III, such person shall, except as provided in paragraphs (4) and (5) of this subsection, be sentenced to a term of imprisonment of not more than 5 years, a fine not to exceed the greater of that authorized in accordance with the provisions of Title 18, or $250,000 if the defendant is an individual or $1,000,000 if the defendant is other than an individual, or both. If any person commits such a violation after one or more prior convictions of him for an offense punishable under this paragraph, or for a felony under any other provision of this subchapter or subchapter II of this chapter or other law of a State, the United States, or a foreign country relating to narcotic drugs, marihuana, or depressant or stimulant substances, have become final, such person shall be sentenced to a term of imprisonment of not more than 10 years, a fine not to exceed the greater of twice that authorized in accordance with the provisions of Title 18, or $500,000 if the defendant is an individual or $2,000,000 if the defendant is other than an individual, or both. Any sentence imposing a term of imprisonment under this paragraph shall, in the absence of such a prior conviction, impose a term of supervised release of at least 2 years in addition to such term of imprisonment and shall, if there was such a prior conviction, impose a term of supervised release of at least 4 years in addition to such term of imprisonment.

(2) In the case of a controlled substance in schedule IV, such person shall be sentenced to a term of imprisonment of not more than 3 years, a fine not to exceed the greater of that authorized in accordance with the provisions of Title 18, or $250,000 if the defendant is an individual or $1,000,000 if the defendant is other than an individual, or both. If any person commits such a violation after one or more prior convictions of him for an offense punishable under this paragraph, or for a felony under any other provision of this subchapter or subchapter II of this chapter or other law of a State, the United States, or a foreign country relating to narcotic drugs, marihuana, or depressant or stimulant substances, have become final, such person shall be sentenced to a term of imprisonment of not more than 6

years, a fine not to exceed the greater of twice that authorized in accordance with the provisions of Title 18, or $500,000 if the defendant is an individual or $2,000,000 if the defendant is other than an individual, or both. Any sentence imposing a term of imprisonment under this paragraph shall, in the absence of such a prior conviction, impose a term of supervised release of at least one year in addition to such term of imprisonment and shall, if there was such a prior conviction, impose a term of supervised release of at least 2 years in addition to such term of imprisonment.

(3) In the case of a controlled substance in schedule V, such person shall be sentenced to a term of imprisonment of not more than one year, a fine not to exceed the greater of that authorized in accordance with the provisions of Title 18, or $100,000 if the defendant is an individual or $250,000 if the defendant is other than an individual, or both. If any person commits such a violation after one or more convictions of him for an offense punishable under this paragraph, or for a crime under any other provision of this subchapter or subchapter II of this chapter or other law of a State, the United States, or a foreign country relating to narcotic drugs, marihuana, or depressant or stimulant substances, have become final, such person shall be sentenced to a term of imprisonment of not more than 2 years, a fine not to exceed the greater of twice that authorized in accordance with the provisions of Title 18, or $200,000 if the defendant is an individual or $500,000 if the defendant is other than an individual, or both.

(4) Notwithstanding paragraph (1)(D) of this subsection, any person who violates subsection (a) of this section by distributing a small amount of marihuana for no remuneration shall be treated as provided in section 844 of this title and section 3607 of Title 18.

(5) Any person who violates subsection (a) of this section by cultivating a controlled substance on Federal property shall be imprisoned as provided in this subsection and shall be fined any amount not to exceed—

(A) the amount authorized in accordance with this section;

(B) the amount authorized in accordance with the provisions of Title 18;

(C) $500,000 if the defendant is an individual; or

(D) $1,000,000 if the defendant is other than an individual;

or both.

(6) Any person who violates subsection (a) of this section, or attempts to do so, and knowingly or intentionally uses a poison, chemical, or other hazardous substance on Federal land, and, by such use—

(A) creates a serious hazard to humans, wildlife, or domestic animals,

(B) degrades or harms the environment or natural resources, or

(C) pollutes an aquifer, spring, stream, river, or body of water,

shall be fined in accordance with Title 18, or imprisoned not more than five years, or both.

(c) Repealed.   Pub.L.   98–473,   Title   II, § 224(a)(2), Oct. 12, 1984, 98 Stat. 2030

Offenses involving listed chemicals

(d) Any person who knowingly or intentionally—

(1) possesses a listed chemical with intent to manufacture a controlled substance except as authorized by this subchapter;

(2) possesses or distributes a listed chemical knowing, or having reasonable cause to believe, that the listed chemical will be used to manufacture a controlled substance except as authorized by this title; or

(3) with the intent of causing the evasion of the record-keeping or reporting requirements of section 830 of this title, or the regulations issued under that section, receives or distributes a reportable amount of any listed chemical in units small enough so that the making of records or filing of reports under that section is not required;

shall be fined in accordance with Title 18, or imprisoned not more than 10 years, or both.

Boobytraps on Federal property; penalties; definitions

(e)(1) Any person who assembles, maintains, places, or causes to be placed a boobytrap on Federal property where a controlled substance is being manufactured, distributed, or dispensed shall be sentenced to a term of imprisonment for not more than 10 years and shall be fined not more than $10,000.

(2) If any person commits such a violation after 1 or more prior convictions for an offense punishable under this subsection, such person shall be sentenced to a term of imprisonment of not more than 20 years and shall be fined not more than $20,000.

(3) For the purposes of this subsection, the term "boobytrap" means any concealed or camouflaged device designed to cause bodily injury when triggered by any action of any unsuspecting person making contact with the device. Such term includes guns, ammunition, or explosive devices attached to trip wires or other triggering mechanisms, sharpened stakes, and lines or wires with hooks attached.

Ten-year injunction as additional penalty

(f) In addition to any other applicable penalty, any person convicted of a felony violation of this section relating to the receipt, distribution, or importation of a listed chemical may be enjoined from engaging in any regulated transaction involving a listed chemical for not more than ten years.

Wrongful distribution or possession of listed chemicals

(g)(1) Whoever knowingly distributes a listed chemical in violation of this subchapter (other than in violation of a recordkeeping or reporting requirement of section 830 of this title) shall be fined under Title 18, or imprisoned not more than 5 years, or both.

(2) Whoever possesses any listed chemical, with knowledge that the recordkeeping or reporting requirements of section 830 of this title have not been adhered to, if, after such knowledge is acquired, such person does not take immediate steps to remedy the violation shall be fined under Title 18, or imprisoned not more than one year, or both.

(Pub.L. 91–513, Title II, § 401, Oct. 27, 1970, 84 Stat. 1260; Pub.L. 95–633, Title II, § 201, Nov. 10, 1978, 92 Stat. 3774; Pub.L. 96–359, § 8(c), Sept. 26, 1980, 94 Stat. 1194; Pub.L. 98–473, Title II, §§ 224(a), 502, 503(b)(1), (2), Oct. 12, 1984, 98 Stat. 2030, 2068, 2070; Pub.L. 98–473, § 224(a), as amended Pub.L. 99–570, Title I, § 1005(a), Oct. 27, 1986, 100 Stat. 3207–6; Pub.L. 99–570, Title I, §§ 1002, 1003(a), 1004(a), 1103, Title XV, § 15005, Oct. 27, 1986, 100 Stat. 3207–2, 3207–5, 3207–6,

3207–11, 3207–192; Pub.L. 100–690, Title VI, §§ 6055, 6254(h), 6452(a), 6470(g), (h), 6479, Nov. 18, 1988, 102 Stat. 4318, 4367, 4371, 4378, 4382.)

1 So in original. Probably should be "substances".

Subsecs. (b)(4) and (c) of this Section Applicable to Offenses Committed Prior to Nov. 1, 1987

Subsecs. (b)(4) and (c) of this section as in effect prior to amendment by Pub.L. 98–473, § 224(a), read as follows:

(b) Penalties

Except as otherwise provided in section 845, 845a, or 845b of this title, any person who violates subsection (a) of this section shall be sentenced as follows:

* * *

(4) Notwithstanding paragraph (1)(D) of this subsection, any person who violates subsection (a) of this section by distributing a small amount of marihuana for no remuneration shall be treated as provided in subsections (a) and (b) of section 844 of this title.

* * *

(c) Special parole term

A special parole term imposed under this section or section 845, 845a or 845b of this title may be revoked if its terms and conditions are violated. In such circumstances the original term of imprisonment shall be increased by the period of the special parole term and the resulting new term of imprisonment shall not be diminished by the time which was spent on special parole. A person whose special parole term has been revoked may be required to serve all or part of the remainder of the new term of imprisonment. A special parole term provided for in this section or section 845, 845a or 845b of this title shall be in addition to, and not in lieu of, any other parole provided for by law.

[See Codification note below.]

For applicability of sentencing provisions to offenses, see Effective Date and Savings Provisions, etc., note, section 235 of Pub.L. 98–473, as amended, set out under section 3551 of Title 18, Crimes and Criminal Procedure.

Editorial Notes

References in Text. "This subchapter", referred to in subsecs. (a), (b)(1), (2), (3), (5), (6), (d) and (g), was in the original "this title" which is Title II of Pub.L. 91–513, Oct. 27, 1970, 84 Stat. 1242, and is popularly known as the "Controlled Substances Act". For complete classification of Title II to the Code, see Short Title note set out under section 801 of this title and Tables volume.

Subchapter II of this chapter, referred to in text, was in the original "title III", meaning of Title III of Pub.L. 91–513, Oct. 27, 1970, 84 Stat. 1285. Part A of Title III comprises subchapter II of this chapter. For classification of Part B, consisting of sections 1101 to 1105 of Title III, see U.S.C.A. Tables volume.

Schedules I, II, III, IV, and V, referred to in subsec. (b)(1), (2), and (3), are set out in section 812(c) of this title.

Codification. Amendment by section 224(a)(5) of Pub.L. 98–473 prior to repeal by Pub.L. 99–570, § 1005(a)(2), deleting the last sentence of subsec. (b)(5), which read "Any sentence imposing a term of imprisonment under this paragraph shall, in the absence of such a prior conviction, impose a special parole term of at least 2 years in addition to such term of imprisonment and shall, if there was such a prior conviction, impose a special parole term of at least 4 years in addition to such term of imprisonment", did not take into account repeal of such subsec. (b)(5) by section 502(5) of Pub.L. 98–473 and addition of a new subsec. (b)(5) by section 502(6) of Pub.L. 98–473, thereby resulting in the deletion of a provision of subsec. (b)(5) which had been previously repealed.

The amendment to subsec. (c) by Pub.L. 99–570, § 1004(a), directing the substitution of "term of supervised release" for "special parole term" wherever appearing has not been executed to such subsec. (c) in view of repeal by Pub.L. 98–473, § 224(a)(2), eff. Nov. 1, 1987.

Repeals. Section 224(a)(1), (2), (3), and (5) of Pub.L. 98–473, cited to credit, was repealed by section 1005(a)(2) of Pub.L. 99–570. Such provisions of section 224(a) of Pub.L. 98–473, which were to take effect Nov. 1, 1987, as a result of repeal were never executed to text of section.

Effective Date of 1988 Amendment. Amendment by section 6055 of Pub.L. 100–690 effective 120 days after Nov. 18, 1988, see section 6061 of Pub.L. 100–690, set out as a note under section 802 of this title.

Effective Date of 1986 Amendment. Section 1004(b) of Pub.L. 99–570 provided that: "(b) The amendments made by this section [amending this section and sections 845, 845a, 960 and 962 of this title] shall take effect on the date of the taking effect of section 3583 of title 18, United States Code. [Nov. 1, 1987]."

Effective Date and Savings Provisions of 1984 Amendment. Amendment by Pub.L. 98–473 effective on the first day of first calendar month beginning thirty six months after Oct. 12, 1984, applicable only to offenses committed after taking effect of sections 211 to 239 of Pub.L. 98–473, and except as otherwise provided for therein, see section 235 of Pub.L. 98–473, as amended, set out as a note under section 3551 of Title 18, Crimes and Criminal Procedure.

§ 842. Prohibited acts B

Unlawful acts

(a) It shall be unlawful for any person—

(1) who is subject to the requirements of part C to distribute or dispense a controlled substance in violation of section 829 of this title;

(2) who is a registrant to distribute or dispense a controlled substance not authorized by his registration to another registrant or other authorized person or to manufacture a controlled substance not authorized by his registration;

(3) who is a registrant to distribute a controlled substance in violation of section 825 of this title;

(4) to remove, alter, or obliterate a symbol or label required by section 825 of this title;

(5) to refuse or fail to make, keep, or furnish any record, report, notification, declaration, order or order form, statement, invoice, or information required under this subchapter or subchapter II of this chapter;

(6) to refuse any entry into any premises or inspection authorized by this subchapter or subchapter II of this chapter;

(7) to remove, break, injure, or deface a seal placed upon controlled substances pursuant to section 824(f) or 881 of this title or to remove or dispose of substances so placed under seal;

(8) to use, to his own advantage, or to reveal, other than to duly authorized officers or employees of the United States, or to the courts when relevant in any judicial proceeding under this subchapter or subchapter II of this chapter, any information acquired in the course of an inspection authorized by this subchapter concerning any method or process which as a trade secret is entitled to protection, or to use to his own advantage or reveal (other than as authorized by section 830 of this title) any information that is confidential under such section;

(9) who is a regulated person to engage in a regulated transaction without obtaining the identification required by 830(a)(3) of this title; or

(10) to fail to keep a record or make a report under section 830 of this title.

Manufacture

(b) It shall be unlawful for any person who is a registrant to manufacture a controlled substance in schedule I or II which is—

(1) not expressly authorized by his registration and by a quota assigned to him pursuant to section 826 of this title; or

(2) in excess of a quota assigned to him pursuant to section 826 of this title.

Penalties

(c)(1) Except as provided in paragraph (2), any person who violates this section shall, with respect to any such violation, be subject to a civil penalty of not more than $25,000. The district courts of the United States (or, where there is no such court in the case of any territory or possession of the United States, then the court in such territory or possession having the jurisdiction of a district court of the United States in cases arising under the Constitution and laws of the United States) shall have jurisdiction in accordance with section 1355 of Title 28 to enforce this paragraph.

(2)(A) If a violation of this section is prosecuted by an information or indictment which alleges that the violation was committed knowingly and the trier of fact specifically finds that the violation was so committed, such person shall, except as otherwise provided in subparagraph (B) of this paragraph, be sentenced to imprisonment of not more than one year or a fine of not more than $25,000, or both.

(B) If a violation referred to in subparagraph (A) was committed after one or more prior convictions of the offender for an offense punishable under this paragraph (2), or for a crime under any other provision of this subchapter or subchapter II of this chapter or other law of the United States relating to narcotic drugs, marihuana, or depressant or stimulant substances, have become final, such person shall be sentenced to a term of imprisonment of not more than 2 years, a fine of $50,000, or both.

(c) Repealed.   Pub.L. 100–690, Title VI, § 6056(c), Nov. 18, 1988, 102 Stat. 4318

(3) Except under the conditions specified in paragraph (2) of this subsection, a violation of this section does not constitute a crime, and a judgment for the United States and imposition of a civil penalty pursuant to paragraph (1) shall not give rise to any disability or legal disadvantage based on conviction for a criminal offense.

(Pub.L. 91–513, Title II, § 402, Oct. 27, 1970, 84 Stat. 1262; Pub.L. 95–633, Title II, § 202(b)(1), (2), Nov. 10, 1978, 92 Stat. 3776; Pub.L. 100–690, Title VI, § 6056, Nov. 18, 1988, 102 Stat. 4318, 4319.)

Editorial Notes

References in Text. Subchapter II of this chapter, referred to in subsecs. (a)(5), (6), (8), and (c)(2)(B), was in the original "title III", meaning Title III of Pub.L. 91–513, Oct. 27, 1970, 84 Stat. 1285. Part A of Title III comprises subchapter II of this chapter. For classification of Part B, consisting of sections 1101 to 1105 of Title III, see U.S.C.A Tables volume.

Schedules I and II, referred to in subsec. (b), are set out in section 812(c), of this title.

Effective Date of 1988 Amendment. Amendment by section 6056 of Pub.L. 100–690, effective 120 days after Nov. 18, 1988, see section 6061 of Pub.L. 100–690, set out as a note under section 802 of this title.

§ 843. Prohibited acts C
Unlawful acts

(a) It shall be unlawful for any person knowingly or intentionally—

(1) who is a registrant to distribute a controlled substance classified in schedule I or II, in the course of his legitimate business, except pursuant to an order or an order form as required by section 828 of this title;

(2) to use in the course of the manufacture, distribution, or dispensing of a controlled substance, or to use for the purpose of acquiring or obtaining a controlled substance, a registration number which is fictitious, revoked, suspended, expired, or issued to another person;

(3) to acquire or obtain possession of a controlled substance by misrepresentation, fraud, forgery, deception, or subterfuge;

(4)(A) to furnish false or fraudulent material information in, or omit any material information from, any application, report, record, or other document required to be made, kept, or filed under this subchapter or subchapter II of this chapter, or (B) to present false or fraudulent identification where the person is receiving or purchasing a listed chemical and the person is required to present identification under section 830(a) of this title;

(5) to make, distribute, or possess any punch, die, plate, stone, or other thing designed to print, imprint, or reproduce the trademark, trade name, or other identifying mark, imprint, or device of another or any likeness of any of the foregoing upon any drug or container or

labeling thereof so as to render such drug a counterfeit substance;

(6) to possess any three-neck round-bottom flask, tableting machine, encapsulating machine, gelatin capsule, or equipment specially designed or modified to manufacture a controlled substance, with intent to manufacture a controlled substance except as authorized by this subchapter;

(7) to manufacture, distribute, or import any three-neck round-bottom flask, tableting machine, encapsulating machine, gelatin capsule, or equipment specially designed or modified to manufacture a controlled substance, knowing that it will be used to manufacture a controlled substance except as authorized by this subchapter; or

(8) to create a chemical mixture for the purpose of evading a requirement of section 830 of this title or to receive a chemical mixture created for that purpose.

Communication facility

(b) It shall be unlawful for any person knowingly or intentionally to use any communication facility in committing or in causing or facilitating the commission of any act or acts constituting a felony under any provision of this subchapter or subchapter II of this chapter. Each separate use of a communication facility shall be a separate offense under this subsection. For purposes of this subsection, the term "communication facility" means any and all public and private instrumentalities used or useful in the transmission of writing, signs, signals, pictures, or sounds of all kinds and includes mail, telephone, wire, radio, and all other means of communication.

Penalties

(c) Any person who violates this section shall be sentenced to a term of imprisonment of not more than 4 years, a fine of not more than $30,000, or both; except that if any person commits such a violation after one or more prior convictions of him for violation of this section, or for a felony under any other provision of this subchapter or subchapter II of this chapter or other law of the United States relating to narcotic drugs, marihuana, or depressant or stimulant substances, have become final, such person shall be sentenced to a term of imprisonment of not more than 8 years, a fine of not more than $60,000, or both.

Additional penalties

(d) In addition to any other applicable penalty, any person convicted of a felony violation of this section relating to the receipt, distribution, or importation of a listed chemical may be enjoined from engaging in any regulated transaction involving a listed chemical for not more than ten years.

(Pub.L. 91–513, Title II, § 403, Oct. 27, 1970, 84 Stat. 1263; Pub.L. 95–633, Title II, § 202(b)(3), Nov. 10, 1978, 92 Stat. 3776; Pub.L. 98–473, Title II, § 516, Oct. 12, 1984, 98 Stat. 2074; Pub.L. 99–570, Title I, § 1866(a), Oct. 27, 1986, 100 Stat. 3207–54; Pub.L. 100–690, Title VI, § 6057, Nov. 18, 1988, 102 Stat. 4319.)

EDITORIAL NOTES

References in Text. Schedules I and II, referred to in subsec. (a)(1), are set out in section 812(c) of this title.

Subchapter II of this chapter, referred to in subsecs. (a)(4)(A), (b), and (c), was in the original "title III", meaning Title III of Pub.L. 91–513, Oct. 27, 1970, 84 Stat. 1285. Part A of Title III comprises subchapter II of this chapter. For classification of Part B, consisting of sections 1101 to 1105 of Title III, see U.S.C.A. Tables volume.

"This subchapter", referred to in subsecs. (a)(4)(A), (6), (7), (b), and (c), was in the original "this title" which is Title II of Pub.L. 91–513, Oct. 27, 1970, 84 Stat. 1242, and is popularly known as the "Controlled Substances Act". For complete classification of Title II to the Code, see Short Title note set out under section 801 of this title and Tables volume.

Effective Date of 1988 Amendment. Amendment by section 6057 of Pub.L. 100–690, effective 120 days after Nov. 18, 1988, see section 6061 of Pub.L. 100–690, set out as a note under section 802 of this title.

§ 844. Penalty for simple possession

Simple possession

(a)[1] It shall be unlawful for any person knowingly or intentionally to possess a controlled substance unless such substance was obtained directly, or pursuant to a valid prescription or order, from a practitioner, while acting in the course of his professional practice, or except as otherwise authorized by this subchapter or subchapter II of this chapter. Any person who violates this subsection may be sentenced to a term of imprisonment of not more than 1 year, and shall be fined a minimum of $1,000, or both, except that if he commits such offense after a prior conviction under this subchapter or subchapter II of this chapter, or a prior conviction for any drug or narcotic offense chargeable under the law of any State, has become final, he shall be sentenced to a term of imprisonment for not less than 15 days but not more than 2 years, and shall be fined a minimum of $2,500, except, further, that if he commits such offense after two or more prior convictions under this subchapter or subchapter II of this chapter, or two or more prior convictions for any drug or narcotic offense chargeable under the law of any State, or a combination of two or more such offenses have become final, he shall be sentenced to a term of imprisonment for not less than 90 days but not more than 3 years, and shall be fined a minimum of $5,000. Notwithstanding the preceding sentence, a person convicted under this subsection for the possession of a mixture or substance which contains cocaine base shall be fined under Title 18, or imprisoned not less than 5 years and not more than 20 years, or both, if the conviction is a first conviction under this subsection and the amount of the mixture or substance exceeds 5 grams, if the conviction is after a prior conviction for the possession of such a mixture or substance under this subsection becomes final and the amount of the mixture or substance exceeds 3 grams, or if the conviction is after 2 or more prior convictions for the possession of such a mixture or substance under this subsection become final and the amount of the mixture or substance exceeds 1 gram. The imposition or execution of a minimum sentence required to be imposed under this subsection shall not be suspended or deferred. Further, upon conviction, a person who violates this subsection shall be fined the reasonable costs of the investigation and prosecution of the offense, including the costs of prosecution of an offense as defined in sections 1918 and 1920 of Title 28, except that this sentence shall not apply and a fine under this section need not be imposed if the court determines under the provision of Title 18 that the defendant lacks the ability to pay.

(b) Repealed Pub.L. 98–473, Title II, § 219(a), Oct. 12, 1984, 98 Stat. 2027.

Definition

(c) As used in this section, the term "drug or narcotic offense" means any offense which proscribes the possession, distribution, manufacture, cultivation, sale, transfer, or the attempt or con-

spiracy to possess, distribute, manufacture, cultivate, sell or transfer any substance the possession of which is prohibited under this subchapter.

(Pub.L. 91–513, Title II, § 404, Oct. 27, 1970, 84 Stat. 1264; Pub.L. 98–473, Title II, § 219, Oct. 12, 1984, 98 Stat. 2027; Pub.L. 99–570, Title I, § 1052, Oct. 27, 1986, 100 Stat. 3207–8; Pub.L. 100–690, Title VI, §§ 6371, 6480, Nov. 18, 1988, 102 Stat. 4370, 4382.)

1. So in original. Subsec. (a) designation, repealed by Pub.L. 98–473, has been editorially supplied.

Section Applicable to Offenses Committed Prior to Nov. 1, 1987

This section as in effect prior to amendment by Pub. L. 98–473 read as follows:

§ 844. Penalties

Simple possession

(a) It shall be unlawful for any person knowingly or intentionally to possess a controlled substance unless such substance was obtained directly, or pursuant to a valid prescription or order, from a practitioner, while acting in the course of his professional practice, or except as otherwise authorized by this subchapter or subchapter II of this chapter. Any person who violates this subsection may be sentenced to a term of imprisonment of not more than 1 year, and shall be fined a minimum of $1,000 but not more than $5,000, or both, except that if he commits such offense after a prior conviction under this subchapter or subchapter II of this chapter, or a prior conviction for any drug or narcotic offense chargeable under the law of any State, has become final, he shall be sentenced to a term of imprisonment for not less than 15 days but not more than 2 years, and shall be fined a minimum of $2,500 but not more than $10,000, except, further, that if he commits such offense after two or more prior convictions under this subchapter or subchapter II of this chapter, or two or more prior convictions for any drug or narcotic offense chargeable under the law of any State, or a combination of two or more such offenses have become final, he shall be sentenced to a term of imprisonment for not less than 90 days but not more than 3 years, and shall be fined a minimum of $5,000 but not more than $25,000. The imposition or execution of a minimum sentence required to be imposed under this subsection shall not be suspended or deferred. Further, upon conviction, a person who violates this subsection shall be fined the reasonable costs of the investigation and prosecution of the offense, including the costs of prosecution of an offense as defined in sections 1918 and 1920 of Title 28, except that this sentence shall not apply and a fine under this section need not be imposed if the court determines under the provision of Title 18 that the defendant lacks the ability to pay.

Probation; expungement of records relating to arrest, etc.

(b)(1) If any person who has not previously been convicted of violating subsection (a) of this section, any other provision of this subchapter or subchapter II of this chapter, or any other law of the United States relating to narcotic drugs, marihuana, or depressant or stimulant substances, is found guilty of a violation of subsection (a) of this section after trial or upon a plea of guilty, the court may, without entering a judgment of guilty and with the consent of such person, defer further proceedings and place him on probation upon such reasonable conditions as it may require and for such period, not to exceed one year, as the court may prescribe. Upon violation of a condition of the probation, the court may enter an adjudication of guilt and proceed as otherwise provided. The court may, in its discretion, dismiss the proceedings against such person and discharge him from probation before the expiration of the maximum period prescribed for such person's probation. If during the period of his probation such person does not violate any of the conditions of the probation, then upon expiration of such period the court shall discharge such person and dismiss the proceedings against him. Discharge and dismissal under this subsection shall be without court adjudication of guilt, but a nonpublic record thereof shall be retained by the Department of Justice solely for the purpose of use by the courts in determining whether or not, in subsequent proceedings, such person qualifies under this subsection. Such discharge or dismissal shall not be deemed a conviction for purposes of disqualifications or disabilities imposed by law upon conviction of a crime (including the penalties prescribed under this part for second or subsequent convictions) or for any other purpose. Discharge and dismissal under this section may occur only once with respect to any person.

(2) Upon the discharge of such person and dismissal of the proceedings against him under paragraph (1) of this subsection, such person, if he was not over twenty-one years of age at the time of the offense, may apply to the court for an order to expunge from all official records (other than the nonpublic records to be retained by the Department of Justice under paragraph (1)) all recordation relating to his arrest, indictment or information, trial, finding of guilty, and dismissal and discharge pursuant to this section. If the court determines, after hearing, that such person was dismissed and the proceedings against him discharged and that he was not over twenty-one years of age at the time of the offense, it shall enter such order. The effect of such order shall be to restore such person, in the contemplation of the law, to the status he occupied before such arrest or indictment or information. No person as to whom such order has been entered shall be held thereafter under any provision of any law to be guilty of perjury or otherwise giving a false statement by reason of his failures to recite or acknowledge such arrest, or indictment or information, or trial in response to any inquiry made of him for any purpose.

Definition

(c) As used in this section, the term "drug or narcotic offense" means any offense which proscribes the possession, distribution, manufacture, cultivation, sale, transfer, or the attempt or conspiracy to possess, distribute, manufacture, cultivate, sell or transfer any substance the possession of which is prohibited under this subchapter.

For applicability of sentencing provisions to offenses, see Effective Date and Savings Provisions, etc., note, section 235 of Pub.L. 98–473, as amended, set out under section 3551 of Title 18, Crimes and Criminal Procedure.

EDITORIAL NOTES

References in Text. "This subchapter", referred to in subsec. (a), was in the original "this title" which is Title II of Pub.L. 91–513, Oct. 27, 1970, 84 Stat. 1242, and is popularly known as the "Controlled Substances Act". For complete classification of Title II to the Code, see Short Title note set out under section 801 of this title and Tables volume.

"Subchapter II of this chapter", referred to in subsec. (a), was in the original "title III", meaning Title III of Pub.L. 91–513, Oct. 27, 1970, 84 Stat. 1285. Part A of Title III comprises subchapter II of this chapter. For classification of Part B, consisting of sections 1101 to 1105 of Title III, see Tables volume.

Effective Date and Savings Provisions of 1984 Amendment. Amendment by Pub.L. 98–473 effective on the first day of first calendar month beginning thirty six months after Oct. 12, 1984, applicable only to offenses committed after taking effect of sections 211 to 239 of Pub.L. 98–473, and except as otherwise provided for therein, see section 235 of Pub.L. 98–473, as amended, set out as a note under section 3551 of Title 18, Crimes and Criminal Procedure.

§ 844a. Civil penalty for possession of small amounts of certain controlled substances

In general

(a) Any individual who knowingly possesses a controlled substance that is listed in section 841(b)(1)(A) of this title in violation of section 844(b)(1)(A) of this title in an amount that, as specified by regulation of the Attorney General, is a personal use amount shall be liable to the United States for a civil penalty in an amount not to exceed $10,000 for each such violation.

Income and net assets

(b) The income and net assets of an individual shall not be relevant to the determination whether to assess a civil penalty under this section or to prosecute the individual criminally. However, in determining the amount of a penalty under this section, the income and net assets of an individual shall be considered.

Prior conviction

(c) A civil penalty may not be assessed under this section if the individual previously was convicted of a Federal or State offense relating to a controlled substance as defined in section 802 of this title.

Limitation on number of assessments

(d) A civil penalty may not be assessed on an individual under this section on more than two separate occasions.

Assessment

(e) A civil penalty under this section may be assessed by the Attorney General only by an order made on the record after opportunity for a hearing in accordance with section 554 of Title 5. The Attorney General shall provide written notice to the individual who is the subject of the proposed order informing the individual of the opportunity to receive such a hearing with respect to the proposed order. The hearing may be held only if the individual makes a request for the hearing before the expiration of the 30–day period beginning on the date such notice is issued.

Compromise

(f) The Attorney General may compromise, modify, or remit, with or without conditions, any civil penalty imposed under this section.

Judicial review

(g) If the Attorney General issues an order pursuant to subsection (e) of this section after a hearing described in such subsection, the individual who is the subject of the order may, before the expiration of the 30–day period beginning on the date the order is issued, bring a civil action in the appropriate district court of the United States. In such action, the law and the facts of the violation and the assessment of the civil penalty shall be determined de novo, and shall include the right of a trial by jury, the right to counsel, and the right to confront witnesses. The facts of the violation shall be proved beyond a reasonable doubt.

Civil action

(h) If an individual does not request a hearing pursuant to subsection (e) of this section and the Attorney General issues an order pursuant to such subsection, or if an individual does not under subsection (g) of this section seek judicial review of such an order, the Attorney General may commence a civil action in any appropriate district court of the United States for the purpose of recovering the amount assessed and an amount representing interest at a rate computed in accordance with section 1961 of Title 28. Such interest shall accrue from the expiration of the 30–day period described in subsection (g) of this section. In such an action, the decision of the Attorney General to issue the order, and the amount of the penalty assessed by the Attorney General, shall not be subject to review.

Limitation

(i) The Attorney General may not under this subsection commence proceeding against an individual after the expiration of the 5–year period beginning on the date on which the individual allegedly violated subsection (a) of this section.

Expungement procedures

(j) The Attorney General shall dismiss the proceedings under this section against an individual upon application of such individual at any time after the expiration of 3 years if—

(1) the individual has not previously been assessed a civil penalty under this section;

(2) the individual has paid the assessment;

(3) the individual has complied with any conditions imposed by the Attorney General;

(4) the individual has not been convicted of a Federal or State offense relating to a controlled substance as defined in section 802 of this title; and

(5) the individual agrees to submit to a drug test, and such test shows the individual to be drug free.

A nonpublic record of a disposition under this subsection shall be retained by the Department of Justice solely for the purpose of determining in any subsequent proceeding whether the person qualified for a civil penalty or expungement under this section. If a record is expunged under this subsection, an individual concerning whom such an expungement has been made shall not be held thereafter under any provision of law to be guilty of perjury, false swearing, or making a false statement by reason of his failure to recite or acknowledge a proceeding under this section or the results thereof in response to an inquiry made of him for any purpose.

(Pub.L. 100–690, Title VI, § 6486, Nov. 18, 1988, 102 Stat. 4384.)

EDITORIAL NOTES

Codification. Section was not enacted as part of the Controlled Substances Act, which comprises this subchapter.

Reference in the original of subsec. (a) to section 404 of that Act (21 U.S.C. 841(b)(1)(A)) has been translated as "section 844 of this title" as the probable intent of Congress.

§ 845. Distribution to persons under age twenty-one

First offense

(a) Except as provided in section 845a of this title, any person at least eighteen years of age who violates section 841(a)(1) of this title by distributing a controlled substance to a person under twenty-one years of age is (except as provided in subsection (b) of this section) punishable by (1) a term of imprisonment, or a fine, or both, up to twice that authorized by section 841(b) of this title, and (2) at least twice any term of supervised release authorized by section 841(b) of this title, for a first offense involving the same controlled substance and schedule. Except to the extent a greater minimum sentence is otherwise provided by section 841(b) of this title, a term of imprisonment under this subsection shall be not less than one year. The mandatory minimum sentencing provisions of this subsection shall not apply to offenses involving 5 grams or less of marihuana.

Second offense

(b) Except as provided in section 845a of this title, any person at least eighteen years of age who violates section 841(a)(1) of this title by distributing a controlled substance to a person under twenty-one years of age after a prior conviction under subsection (a) of this section (or under section 333(b) of this title as in effect prior to May 1, 1971) have become final, is punishable by (1) a term of imprisonment, or a fine, or both, up to three times that authorized by section 841(b) of this title, and (2) at least three times any term of supervised release authorized by section 841(b) of this title, for a second or subsequent offense involving the same controlled substance and schedule. Except to the extent a greater minimum sentence is otherwise provided by section 841(b) of this title, a term of imprisonment under this subsection shall not be less than one year. Penalties for third and subsequent convictions shall be governed by section 841(b)(1)(A) of this title.

(Pub.L. 91–513, Title II, § 405, Oct. 27, 1970, 84 Stat. 1265; Pub.L. 98–473, Title II, §§ 224(b), 503(b)(3), Oct. 12, 1984, 98 Stat. 2030, 2070; Pub.L. 98–473, § 224(b), as amended Pub.L. 99–570, Title I, § 1005(b)(1), Oct. 27, 1986, 100 Stat. 3207–6; Pub.L. 99–570, Title I, §§ 1004(a), 1105(a), (b), Oct. 27, 1986, 100 Stat. 3207–6, 3207–11; Pub.L. 100–690, Title VI, §§ 6452(b), 6455, 6456, Nov. 18, 1988, 102 Stat. 4371, 4372.)

EDITORIAL NOTES

Repeals. Section 224(b) of Pub.L. 98–473, cited to credit, was repealed by section 1005(b)(1) of Pub.L. 99–570. Such provisions of section 224(b) of Pub.L. 98–473, which were to take effect Nov. 1, 1987, as a result of repeal were never executed to text of section.

Effective Date of 1986 Amendment. Amendment by section 1004(a) of Pub.L. 99–570 to take effect on the date of the taking of effect of section 3583 of Title 18, Crimes and Criminal Procedure, Nov. 1, 1987, see section 1004(b) of Pub.L. 99–570, set out as a note under section 841 of this title.

Effective Date and Savings Provisions of 1984 Amendment. Amendment by Pub.L. 98–473, § 224(b), effective on the first day of first calendar month beginning thirty six months after Oct. 12, 1984, applicable only to offenses committed after taking effect of sections 211 to 239 of Pub.L. 98–473, and except as otherwise provided for therein, see section 235 of Pub.L. 98–473, as amended, set out as a note under section 3551 of Title 18, Crimes and Criminal Procedure.

§ 845a. Distribution or manufacturing in or near schools and colleges

Penalty

(a) Any person who violates section 841(a)(1) or section 856 of this title by distributing, possessing with intent to distribute, or manufacturing a controlled substance in or on, or within one thousand feet of, the real property comprising a public or private elementary, vocational, or secondary school or a public or private college, junior college, or university, or within 100 feet of a playground, public or private youth center, public swimming pool, or video arcade facility, is (except as provided in subsection (b) of this section) punishable (1) by a term of imprisonment, or fine, or both up to twice that authorized by section 841(b) of this title; and (2) at least twice any term of supervised release authorized by section 841(b) of this title for a first offense. Except to the extent a greater minimum sentence is otherwise provided by section 841(b) of this title, a term of imprisonment under this subsection shall be not less than one year. The mandatory minimum sentencing provisions of this paragraph shall not apply to offenses involving 5 grams or less of marihuana.

Second offenders

(b) Any person who violates section 841(a)(1) or section 856 of this title by distributing, possessing with intent to distribute, or manufacturing a controlled substance in or on, or within one thousand feet of, the real property comprising a public or private elementary, vocational, or secondary school or a public or private college, junior college, or university, or within 100 feet of a playground, public or private youth center, public swimming pool, or video arcade facility, after a prior conviction under subsection (a) of this section have become final is punishable (1) by the greater of (A) a term of imprisonment of not less than three years and not more than life imprisonment or (B) a term of imprisonment of up to three times that authorized by section 841(b) of this title for a first offense, or a fine up to three times that authorized by section 841(b) of this title for a first offense, or both, and (2) at least three times any term of supervised release authorized by section 841(b) of this title for a first offense. Penalties for third and subsequent convictions shall be governed by section 841(b)(1)(A) of this title.

Suspension of sentence; probation; parole

(c) In the case of any sentence imposed under subsection (b) of this section, imposition or execution of such sentence shall not be suspended and probation shall not be granted. An individual convicted under subsection (b) of this section shall not be eligible for parole under chapter 311 of Title 18 until the individual has served the minimum sentence required by such subsection.

Definitions

(d) For the purposes of this section—

(1) The term "playground" means any outdoor facility (including any parking lot appurtenant thereto) intended for recreation, open to the public, and with any portion thereof containing three or more separate apparatus intended for the recreation of children including, but not limited to, sliding boards, swingsets, and teeterboards.

(2) The term "youth center" means any recreational facility and/or gymnasium (including any parking lot appurtenant thereto), intended primarily for use by persons under 18 years of age, which regularly provides athletic, civic, or cultural activities.

(3) The term "video arcade facility" means any facility, legally accessible to persons under 18 years of age, intended primarily for the use of pinball and video machines for amusement containing a minimum of ten pinball and/or video machines.

(4) The term "swimming pool" includes any parking lot appurtenant thereto.

(Pub.L. 91–513, Title II, § 405A, as added Pub.L. 98–473, Title II, § 503(a), Oct. 12, 1984, 98 Stat. 2069, and amended Pub.L. 99–570, Title I, §§ 1004(a), 1104, 1105(c), 1841(b), 1866(b), (c), Oct. 27, 1986, 100 Stat. 3207–6, 3207–11, 3207–52, 3207–55; Pub.L. 99–646, § 28, Nov. 10, 1986, 100 Stat. 3598; Pub.L. 100–690, Title VI, §§ 6452(b)(1), 6457, 6458, Nov. 18, 1988, 102 Stat. 4371, 4373.)

EDITORIAL NOTES

Codification. Amendments to subsec. (b) of this section by Pub.L. 99–570, § 1866(b), which struck out "special term" and inserted in lieu thereof "term of supervised release", and by Pub.L. 99–646, § 28, which inserted "parole" after "(2) at least three times any special" were incapable of execution to the text. Amendment by Pub.L. 99–570, § 1004, is also incapable of execution to the text.

Effective Date of 1986 Amendment. Amendment by section 1004(a) of Pub.L. 99–570 to take effect on the date of the taking of effect of section 3583 of Title 18, Crimes and Criminal Procedure, Nov. 1, 1987, see section 1004(b) of Pub.L. 99–570, set out as a note under section 841 of this title.

§ 845b. Employment of persons under 18 years of age

Unlawfulness

(a) It shall be unlawful for any person at least eighteen years of age to knowingly and intentionally—

(1) employ, hire, use, persuade, induce, entice, or coerce, a person under eighteen years of age to violate any provision of this subchapter or subchapter II of this chapter;

(2) employ, hire, use, persuade, induce, entice, or coerce, a person under eighteen years of age to assist in avoiding detection or apprehension for any offense of this subchapter or subchapter II of this chapter by any Federal, State, or local law enforcement official; or

(3) receive a controlled substance from a person under 18 years of age, other than an immediate family member, in violation of this title or title III.

Penalties

(b) Any person who violates subsection (a) of this section is punishable by a term of imprisonment up to twice that otherwise authorized, or up to twice the fine otherwise authorized, or both, and at least twice any term of supervised release otherwise authorized for a first offense. Except to the extent a greater minimum sentence is otherwise provided, a term of imprisonment under this subsection shall not be less than one year.

Penalty for second offenses

(c) Any person who violates subsection (a) of this section after a prior conviction under subsection (a) of this section have become final, is punishable by a term of imprisonment up to three times that otherwise authorized, or up to three times the fine otherwise authorized, or both, and at least three times any term of supervised release otherwise authorized for a first offense. Except to the extent a greater minimum sentence is otherwise provided, a term of imprisonment under this subsection shall not be less than one year. Penalties for third and subsequent convictions shall be governed by section 841(b)(1)(A) of this title.

Penalty for providing or distributing controlled substance to underage person

(d) Any person who violates subsection (a)(1) or (2) of this section

(1) by knowingly providing or distributing a controlled substance or a controlled substance analogue to any person under eighteen years of age; or

(2) if the person employed, hired, or used is fourteen years of age or younger,

shall be subject to a term of imprisonment for not more than five years or a fine of not more than $50,000, or both, in addition to any other punishment authorized by this section.

Suspension of sentence; probation; parole

(e) In any case of any sentence imposed under this section, imposition or execution of such sentence shall not be suspended and probation shall not be granted. An individual convicted under this section of an offense for which a mandatory minimum term of imprisonment is applicable shall not be eligible for parole under section 4202 of Title 18 until the individual has served the mandatory term of imprisonment as enhanced by this section.

Distribution of controlled substance to pregnant individual

(f) Except as authorized by this subchapter, it shall be unlawful for any person to knowingly or intentionally provide or distribute any controlled substance to a pregnant individual in violation of any provision of this subchapter. Any person who violates this subsection shall be subject to the provisions of subsections (b), (c), and (e) of this section.

(Pub.L. 91–513, Title II, § 405B, as added Pub.L. 99–570, Title I, § 1102, Oct. 27, 1986, 100 Stat. 3207–10, and amended Pub.L. 100–690, Title VI, §§ 6452(b)(1), 6459, 6470(d), Nov. 18, 1988, 102 Stat. 4371, 4373, 4378.)

EDITORIAL NOTES

References in Text. "This subchapter", referred to in subsecs. (a) and (f), was in the original "this title" which is Title II of Pub.L. 91–513, Oct. 27, 1970, 84 Stat. 1242, and is popularly known as the "Controlled Substances Act". For complete classification of Title II to the Code, see Short Title note set out under section 801 of this title and Tables volume.

"Subchapter II of this chapter", referred to in subsec. (a), was in the original "title III", meaning Title III of Pub.L. 91–513, Oct. 27, 1970, 84 Stat. 1285. Part A of Title III comprises subchapter II of this chapter. For classification of Part B, consisting of sections 1101 to 1105 of Title III, see Tables volume.

§ 846. Attempt and conspiracy

Any person who attempts or conspires to commit any offense defined in this subchapter shall be subject to the same penalties as those prescribed for the offense, the commission of which was the object of the attempt or conspiracy.

(Pub.L. 91–513, Title II, § 406, Oct. 27, 1970, 84 Stat. 1265, amended Pub.L. 100–690, Title VI, § 6470(a), Nov. 18, 1988, 102 Stat. 4377.)

§ 847. Additional penalties

Any penalty imposed for violation of this subchapter shall be in addition to, and not in lieu of, any civil or administrative penalty or sanction authorized by law.

(Pub.L. 91–513, Title II, § 407, Oct. 27, 1970, 84 Stat. 1265.)

§ 848. Continuing criminal enterprise
Penalties; forfeitures

(a) Any person who engages in a continuing criminal enterprise shall be sentenced to a term of imprisonment which may not be less than 20 years and which may be up to life imprisonment, to a fine not to exceed the greater of that authorized in accordance with the provisions of Title 18, or $2,000,000 if the defendant is an individual or $5,000,000 if the defendant is other than an individual, and to the forfeiture prescribed in section 853 of this title; except that if any person engages in such activity after one or more prior convictions of him under this section have become final, he shall be sentenced to a term of imprisonment which may not be less than 30 years and which may be up to life imprisonment, to a fine not to exceed the greater of twice the amount authorized in accordance with the provisions of Title 18, or $4,000,000 if the defendant is an individual or $10,000,000 if the defendant is other than an individual, and to the forfeiture prescribed in section 853 of this title.

Conditions for life imprisonment for engaging in continuing criminal enterprise

(b) Any person who engages in a continuing criminal enterprise shall be imprisoned for life and fined in accordance with subsection (a) of this section, if—

(1) such person is the principal administrator, organizer, or leader of the enterprise or is one of several such principal administrators, organizers, or leaders; and

(2)(A) the violation referred to in subsection (d)(1) of this section involved at least 300 times the quantity of a substance described in subsection 841(b)(1)(B) of this title, or

(B) the enterprise, or any other enterprise in which the defendant was the principal or one of several principal administrators, organizers, or leaders, received $10 million dollars in gross receipts during any twelve-month period of its existence for the manufacture, importation, or distribution of a substance described in section 841(b)(1)(B) of this title.

Continuing criminal enterprise defined

(c) For purposes of subsection (a) of this section, a person is engaged in a continuing criminal enterprise if—

(1) he violates any provision of this subchapter or subchapter II of this chapter the punishment for which is a felony, and

(2) such violation is a part of a continuing series of violations of this subchapter or subchapter II of this chapter—

(A) which are undertaken by such person in concert with five or more other persons with respect to whom such person occupies a position of organizer, a supervisory position, or any other position of management, and

(B) from which such person obtains substantial income or resources.

Suspension of sentence and probation prohibited

(d) In the case of any sentence imposed under this section, imposition or execution of such sentence shall not be suspended, probation shall not be granted, and the Act of July 15, 1932 (D.C. Code, secs. 24–203 to 24–207), shall not apply.

Death penalty

(e)(1)[1] In addition to the other penalties set forth in this section—

(A) any person engaging in or working in furtherance of a continuing criminal enterprise, or any person engaging in an offense punishable under section 841(b)(1)(A) of this title or section 960(b)(1) who intentionally kills or counsels, commands, induces, procures, or causes the intentional killing of an individual and such killing results, shall be sentenced to any term of imprisonment, which shall not be less than 20 years, and which may be up to life imprisonment, or may be sentenced to death; and

(B) any person, during the commission of, in furtherance of, or while attempting to avoid apprehension, prosecution or service of a prison sentence for, a felony violation of this subchapter or subchapter II of this chapter who intentionally kills or counsels, commands, induces, procures, or causes the intentional killing of any Federal, State, or local law enforcement officer engaged in, or on account of, the performance of such officer's official duties and such killing results, shall be sentenced to any term of imprisonment, which shall not be less than 20 years, and which may be up to life imprisonment, or may be sentenced to death.

(2) As used in paragraph (1)(b), the term "law enforcement officer" means a public servant authorized by law or by a Government agency or Congress to conduct or engage in the prevention, investigation, prosecution or adjudication of an offense, and includes those engaged in corrections, probation, or parole functions.

Hearing required with respect to the death penalty

(g) A person shall be subjected to the penalty of death for any offense under this section only if a hearing is held in accordance with this section.

Notice by the Government in death penalty cases

(h)(1) Whenever the Government intends to seek the death penalty for an offense under this section for which one of the sentences provided is death, the attorney for the Government, a reasonable time before trial or acceptance by the court of a plea of guilty, shall sign and file with the court, and serve upon the defendant, a notice—

(A) that the Government in the event of conviction will seek the sentence of death; and

(B) setting forth the aggravating factors enumerated in subsection (n) of this section and any other aggravating factors which the Government will seek to prove as the basis for the death penalty.

(2) The court may permit the attorney for the Government to amend this notice for good cause shown.

Hearing before court or jury

(i)(1) When the attorney for the Government has filed a notice as required under subsection (h) of this section and the defendant is found guilty of or pleads guilty to an offense under subsection (e) of this section, the judge who presided at the trial or before whom the guilty plea was entered, or any other judge if the judge who presided at the trial or before whom the guilty plea was entered is unavailable, shall conduct a separate

sentencing hearing to determine the punishment to be imposed. The hearing shall be conducted—

(A) before the jury which determined the defendant's guilt;

(B) before a jury impaneled for the purpose of the hearing if—

(i) the defendant was convicted upon a plea of guilty;

(ii) the defendant was convicted after a trial before the court sitting without a jury;

(iii) the jury which determined the defendant's guilt has been discharged for good cause; or

(iv) after initial imposition of a sentence under this section, redetermination of the sentence under this section is necessary; or

(C) before the court alone, upon the motion of the defendant and with the approval of the Government.

(2) A jury impaneled under paragraph (1)(B) shall consist of 12 members, unless, at any time before the conclusion of the hearing, the parties stipulate with the approval of the court that it shall consist of any number less than 12.

Proof of aggravating and mitigating factors

(j) Notwithstanding rule 32(c) of the Federal Rules of Criminal Procedure, when a defendant is found guilty of or pleads guilty to an offense under subsection (e) of this section, no presentence report shall be prepared. In the sentencing hearing, information may be presented as to matters relating to any of the aggravating or mitigating factors set forth in subsections (m) and (n) of this section, or any other mitigating factor or any other aggravating factor for which notice has been provided under subsection (h)(1)(B) of this section. Where information is presented relating to any of the aggravating factors set forth in subsection (n) of this section, information may be presented relating to any other aggravating factor for which notice has been provided under subsection (h)(1)(B) of this section. Information presented may include the trial transcript and exhibits if the hearing is held before a jury or judge not present during the trial, or at the trial judge's discretion. Any other information relevant to such mitigating or aggravating factors may be presented by either the Government or the defendant, regardless of its admissibility under the rules governing admission of evidence at criminal trials, except that information may be excluded if its probative value is substantially outweighed by the danger of unfair prejudice, confusion of the issues, or misleading the jury. The Government and the defendant shall be permitted to rebut any information received at the hearing and shall be given fair opportunity to present argument as to the adequacy of the information to establish the existence of any of the aggravating or mitigating factors and as to appropriateness in that case of imposing a sentence of death. The Government shall open the argument. The defendant shall be permitted to reply. The Government shall then be permitted to reply in rebuttal. The burden of establishing the existence of any aggravating factor is on the Government, and is not satisfied unless established beyond a reasonable doubt. The burden of establishing the existence of any mitigating factor is on the defendant, and is not satisfied unless established by a preponderance of the evidence.

Return of findings

(k) The jury, or if there is no jury, the court, shall consider all the information received during the hearing. It shall return special findings identifying any aggravating factors set forth in subsection (n) of this section, found to exist. If one of the aggravating factors set forth in subsection (n)(1) of this section and another of the aggravating factors set forth in paragraphs (2) through (12) of subsection (n) of this section is found to exist, a special finding identifying any other aggravating factor for which notice has been provided under subsection (h)(1)(B) of this section, may be returned. A finding with respect to a mitigating factor may be made by one or more of the members of the jury, and any member of the jury who finds the existence of a mitigating factor may consider such a factor established for purposes of this subsection, regardless of the number of jurors who concur that the factor has been established. A finding with respect to any aggravating factor must be unanimous. If an aggravating factor set forth in subsection (n)(1) of this section is not found to exist or an aggravating factor set forth in subsection (n)(1) of this section is found to exist but no other aggravating factor set forth in subsection (n) is found to exist, the court shall impose a sentence, other than death, authorized by law. If an aggravating factor set forth in subsection (n)(1) of this section and one or more of the other aggravating factors set forth in

subsection (n) of this section are found to exist, the jury, or if there is no jury, the court, shall then consider whether the aggravating factors found to exist sufficiently outweigh any mitigating factor or factors found to exist, or in the absence of mitigating factors, whether the aggravating factors are themselves sufficient to justify a sentence of death. Based upon this consideration, the jury by unanimous vote, or if there is no jury, the court, shall recommend that a sentence of death shall be imposed rather than a sentence of life imprisonment without possibility of release or some other lesser sentence. The jury or the court, regardless of its findings with respect to aggravating and mitigating factors, is never required to impose a death sentence and the jury shall be so instructed.

Imposition of sentence

(*l*) Upon the recommendation that the sentence of death be imposed, the court shall sentence the defendant to death. Otherwise the court shall impose a sentence, other than death, authorized by law. A sentence of death shall not be carried out upon a person who is under 18 years of age at the time the crime was committed. A sentence of death shall not be carried out upon a person who is mentally retarded. A sentence of death shall not be carried out upon a person who, as a result of mental disability—

(1) cannot understand the nature of the pending proceedings, what such person was tried for, the reason for the punishment, or the nature of the punishment; or

(2) lacks the capacity to recognize or understand facts which would make the punishment unjust or unlawful, or lacks the ability to convey such information to counsel or to the court.

Mitigating factors

(m) In determining whether a sentence of death is to be imposed on a defendant, the finder of fact shall consider mitigating factors, including the following:

(1) The defendant's capacity to appreciate the wrongfulness of the defendant's conduct or to conform conduct to the requirements of law was significantly impaired, regardless of whether the capacity was so impaired as to constitute a defense to the charge.

(2) The defendant was under unusual and substantial duress, regardless of whether the

duress was of such a degree as to constitute a defense to the charge.

(3) The defendant is punishable as a principal (as defined in section 2 of Title 18) in the offense, which was committed by another, but the defendant's participation was relatively minor, regardless of whether the participation was so minor as to constitute a defense to the charge.

(4) The defendant could not reasonably have foreseen that the defendant's conduct in the course of the commission of murder, or other offense resulting in death for which the defendant was convicted, would cause, or would create a grave risk of causing, death to any person.

(5) The defendant was youthful, although not under the age of 18.

(6) The defendant did not have a significant prior criminal record.

(7) The defendant committed the offense under severe mental or emotional disturbance.

(8) Another defendant or defendants, equally culpable in the crime, will not be punished by death.

(9) The victim consented to the criminal conduct that resulted in the victim's death.

(10) That other factors in the defendant's background or character mitigate against imposition of the death sentence.

Aggravating factors for homicide

(n) If the defendant is found guilty of or pleads guilty to an offense under subsection (e) of this section, the following aggravating factors are the only aggravating factors that shall be considered, unless notice of additional aggravating factors is provided under subsection (h)(1)(B) of this section:

(1) The defendant—

(A) intentionally killed the victim;

(B) intentionally inflicted serious bodily injury which resulted in the death of the victim;

(C) intentionally engaged in conduct intending that the victim be killed or that lethal force be employed against the victim, which resulted in the death of the victim;

(D) intentionally engaged in conduct which—

(i) the defendant knew would create a grave risk of death to a person, other than one of the participants in the offense; and

(ii) resulted in the death of the victim.

(2) The defendant has been convicted of another Federal offense, or a State offense resulting in the death of a person, for which a sentence of life imprisonment or a sentence of death was authorized by statute.

(3) The defendant has previously been convicted of two or more State or Federal offenses punishable by a term of imprisonment of more than one year, committed on different occasions, involving the infliction of, or attempted infliction of, serious bodily injury upon another person.

(4) The defendant has previously been convicted of two or more State or Federal offenses punishable by a term of imprisonment of more than one year, committed on different occasions, involving the distribution of a controlled substance.

(5) In the commission of the offense or in escaping apprehension for a violation of subsection (e) of this section, the defendant knowingly created a grave risk of death to one or more persons in addition to the victims of the offense.

(6) The defendant procured the commission of the offense by payment, or promise of payment, of anything of pecuniary value.

(7) The defendant committed the offense as consideration for the receipt, or in the expectation of the receipt, of anything of pecuniary value.

(8) The defendant committed the offense after substantial planning and premeditation.

(9) The victim was particularly vulnerable due to old age, youth, or infirmity.

(10) The defendant had previously been convicted of violating this subchapter or subchapter II of this chapter for which a sentence of five or more years may be imposed or had previously been convicted of engaging in a continuing criminal enterprise.

(11) The violation of this subchapter in relation to which the conduct described in subsection (e) of this section occurred was a violation of section 845 of this title.

(12) The defendant committed the offense in an especially heinous, cruel, or depraved manner in that it involved torture or serious physical abuse to the victim.

Right of the defendant to justice without discrimination

(*o*)(1) In any hearing held before a jury under this section, the court shall instruct the jury that in its consideration of whether the sentence of death is justified it shall not consider the race, color, religious beliefs, national origin, or sex of the defendant or the victim, and that the jury is not to recommend a sentence of death unless it has concluded that it would recommend a sentence of death for the crime in question no matter what the race, color, religious beliefs, national origin, or sex of the defendant, or the victim, may be. The jury shall return to the court a certificate signed by each juror that consideration of the race, color, religious beliefs, national origin, or sex of the defendant or the victim was not involved in reaching his or her individual decision, and that the individual juror would have made the same recommendation regarding a sentence for the crime in question no matter what the race, color, religious beliefs, national origin, or sex of the defendant, or the victim, may be.

(2) Not later than one year from November 18, 1988, the Comptroller General shall conduct a study of the various procedures used by the several States for determining whether or not to impose the death penalty in particular cases, and shall report to the Congress on whether or not any or all of the various procedures create a significant risk that the race of a defendant, or the race of a victim against whom a crime was committed, influence the likelihood that defendants in those States will be sentenced to death. In conducting the study required by this paragraph, the General Accounting Office shall—

(A) use ordinary methods of statistical analysis, including methods comparable to those ruled admissible by the courts in race discrimination cases under title VII of the Civil Rights Act of 1964 [42 U.S.C.A. § 2000e et seq.];

(B) study only crimes occurring after January 1, 1976; and

(C) determine what, if any, other factors, including any relation between any aggravating or mitigating factors and the race of the victim or the defendant, may account for any evidence

that the race of the defendant, or the race of the victim, influences the likelihood that defendants will be sentenced to death. In addition, the General Accounting Office shall examine separately and include in the report, death penalty cases involving crimes similar to those covered under this section.

Sentencing in capital cases in which death penalty is not sought or imposed

(p) If a person is convicted for an offense under subsection (e) of this section and the court does not impose the penalty of death, the court may impose a sentence of life imprisonment without the possibility of parole.

Appeal in capital cases; counsel for financially unable defendants

(q)(1) In any case in which the sentence of death is imposed under this section, the sentence of death shall be subject to review by the court of appeals upon appeal by the defendant. Notice of appeal must be filed within the time prescribed for appeal of judgment in section 2107 of Title 28. An appeal under this section may be consolidated with an appeal of the judgment of conviction. Such review shall have priority over all other cases.

(2) On review of the sentence, the court of appeals shall consider the record, the evidence submitted during the trial, the information submitted during the sentencing hearing, the procedures employed in the sentencing hearing, and the special findings returned under this section.

(3) The court shall affirm the sentence if it determines that—

(A) the sentence of death was not imposed under the influence of passion, prejudice, or any other arbitrary factor; and

(B) the information supports the special finding of the existence of every aggravating factor upon which the sentence was based, together with, or the failure to find, any mitigating factors as set forth or allowed in this section.

In all other cases the court shall remand the case for reconsideration under this section. The court of appeals shall state in writing the reasons for its disposition of the review of the sentence.

(4)(A) Notwithstanding any other provision of law to the contrary, in every criminal action in which a defendant is charged with a crime which may be punishable by death, a defendant who is or becomes financially unable to obtain adequate representation or investigative, expert, or other reasonably necessary services at any time either—

    (i) before judgment; or

    (ii) after the entry of a judgment imposing a sentence of death but before the execution of that judgment;

shall be entitled to the appointment of one or more attorneys and the furnishing of such other services in accordance with paragraphs (5), (6), (7), (8), and (9).

(B) In any post conviction proceeding under section 2254 or 2255 of Title 28, seeking to vacate or set aside a death sentence, any defendant who is or becomes financially unable to obtain adequate representation or investigative, expert, or other reasonably necessary services shall be entitled to the appointment of one or more attorneys and the furnishing of such other services in accordance with paragraphs (5), (6), (7), (8), and (9).

(5) If the appointment is made before judgment, at least one attorney so appointed must have been admitted to practice in the court in which the prosecution is to be tried for not less than five years, and must have had not less than three years experience in the actual trial of felony prosecutions in that court.

(6) If the appointment is made after judgment, at least one attorney so appointed must have been admitted to practice in the court of appeals for not less than five years, and must have had not less than three years experience in the handling of appeals in that court in felony cases.

(7) With respect to paragraphs (5) and (6), the court, for good cause, may appoint another attorney whose background, knowledge, or experience would otherwise enable him or her to properly represent the defendant, with due consideration to the seriousness of the possible penalty and to the unique and complex nature of the litigation.

(8) Unless replaced by similarly qualified counsel upon the attorney's own motion or upon motion of the defendant, each attorney so appointed shall represent the defendant throughout every subsequent stage of available judicial proceedings, including pretrial proceedings, trial, sentencing, motions for new trial, appeals, applications,[2] for writ of certiorari to the Supreme Court of the United States, and all available post-conviction process, together with applications for stays of execution and other appropriate motions and procedures, and shall also represent the defendant in such competency proceedings and proceedings for executive or other clemency as may be available to the defendant.

(9) Upon a finding in ex parte proceedings that investigative, expert or other services are reasonably necessary for the representation of the defendant, whether in connection with issues relating to guilt or sentence, the court shall authorize the defendant's attorneys to obtain such services on behalf of the defendant and shall order the payment of fees and expenses therefore, under paragraph (10). Upon a finding that timely procurement of such services could not practicably await prior authorization, the court may authorize the provision of and payment for such services nunc pro tunc.

(10) Notwithstanding the rates and maximum limits generally applicable to criminal cases and any other provision of law to the contrary, the court shall fix the compensation to be paid to attorneys appointed under this subsection and the fees and expenses to be paid for investigative, expert, and other reasonably necessary services authorized under paragraph (9), at such rates or amounts as the court determines to be reasonably necessary to carry out the requirements of paragraphs (4) through (9).

Refusal to participate by State and Federal correctional employees

(r) No employee of any State department of corrections or the Federal Bureau of Prisons and no employee providing services to that department or bureau under contract shall be required, as a condition of that employment, or contractual obligation to be in attendance at or to participate in any execution carried out under this section if such participation is contrary to the moral or religious convictions of the employee. For purposes of this subsection, the term "participation in executions" includes personal preparation of the condemned individual and the apparatus used for execution and supervision of the activities of other personnel in carrying out such activities.

(Pub.L. 91–513, Title II, § 408, Oct. 27, 1970, 84 Stat. 1265; Pub.L. 98–473, Title II, §§ 224(b), 305, Oct. 12, 1984, 98 Stat. 2030, 2050; Pub.L. 98–473, § 224(b), formerly § 224(c), as amended Pub.L. 99–570, Title I, 1005(b)(2), Oct. 27, 1987, 100 Stat. 3207–6; Pub.L. 99–570, Title I, §§ 1252, 1253,

Oct. 27, 1986, 100 Stat. 3207–14, 3207–15; Pub.L. 100–690, Title VI, §§ 6481, Title VII, § 7001, Nov. 18, 1988, 102 Stat. 4382, 4387, 4388.)

1. See Codification note.

2. The phrase "applications, for writ of certiorari" so in original subsec. (q)(8).

Subsec. (d) of this Section Applicable to Offenses Committed Prior to Nov. 1, 1987

Subsec. (d) of this section as in effect prior to amendment by Pub.L. 98–473, § 224(b), read as follows:

Suspension of sentence and probation prohibited

(e) In the case of any sentence imposed under this section, imposition or execution of such sentence shall not be suspended, probation shall not be granted, and section 4202 of Title 18 and the Act of July 15, 1932 (D.C.Code, secs. 24–203 to 24–207), shall not apply.

For applicability of sentencing provisions to offenses, see Effective Date and Savings Provisions, etc., note, section 235 of Pub.L. 98–473, as amended, set out under section 3551 of Title 18, Crimes and Criminal Procedure.

EDITORIAL NOTES

References in Text. "This subchapter", referred to in text, was in the original "this title" which is Title II of Pub.L. 91–513, Oct. 27, 1970, 84 Stat. 1242, as amended, and is popularly known as the "Controlled Substances Act". For complete classification of Title II to the Code, see Short Title note set out under section 801 of this title and Tables volume.

"Subchapter II of this chapter", referred to in text, was in the original "title III", meaning Title III of Pub.L. 91–513, Oct. 27, 1970, 84 Stat. 1285. Part A of Title III comprises subchapter II of this chapter. For classification of Part B, consisting of sections 1101 to 1105 of Title III, see Tables volume.

The Civil Rights Act of 1964, referred to in subsec. (o)(2)(A), is Pub.L. 88–352, July 2, 1964, 78 Stat. 252, as amended. Title VII of the Civil Rights Act of 1964 is classified to subchapter VI (section 2000e et seq.) of chapter 21 of Title 42, The Public Health and Welfare. For complete classification of this Act to the Code, see Short Title note set out under section 2000a of Title 42 and Tables volume.

The Act of July 15, 1932 (D.C.Code, secs. 24–203 to 24–207), referred to in subsec. (d), is not classified to the U.S.C.A.

Codification. The language of section 7001(a)(1) of Pub.L. 100–690 directing the redesignation of subsec. (e) as (f), was incapable of execution in view of a prior redesignation of subsec. (e) as (d) by section 6481(b) of Pub.L. 100–690, leaving this section without a subsec. (f).

Effective Date and Savings Provisions of 1984 Amendment. Amendment by Pub.L. 98–473, § 224(b), effective on the first day of first calendar month beginning thirty six months after Oct. 12, 1984, applicable only to offenses committed after taking effect of sections 211 to 239 of Pub.L. 98–473, and except as otherwise provided for therein, see section 235 of Pub.L. 98–473, as amended, set out as a note under section 3551 of Title 18, Crimes and Criminal Procedure.

GAO Study of the Cost of Executions. Section 7002 of Pub.L. 100–690 provided that:

"(a) Study.—No later than three years after the date of the enactment of this Act [Nov. 18, 1988], the Comptroller General shall carry out a study to review the cost of implementing the procedures for imposing and carrying out a death sentence prescribed by this title [Title VII, subtitles A–O, of Pub.L. 100–690. See Tables volume for classifications to the Code].

"(b) Specific Requirement.—Such study shall consider, but not be limited to, information concerning impact on workload of the Federal prosecutors and judiciary and law enforcement necessary to obtain capital sentences and executions under this Act [see Short Title of 1988 Amendment note under section 1501 of this title].

"(c) Submission of Report.—Not later than four years after date of the enactment of this Act [Nov. 18, 1988], the Comptroller General shall submit to Congress a report describing the results of the study."

Code of Federal Regulations

Classification of inmates, see 28 CFR 524.10 et seq.

§ 849. Repealed. Pub.L. 98–473, Title II, § 219(a), Oct. 12, 1984, 98 Stat. 2027.

Section Applicable to Offenses Committed Prior to Nov. 1, 1987

This section as in effect prior to repeal by Pub.L. 98–473 read as follows:

§ 849. Dangerous special drug offender sentencing

Notice to court by United States attorney

(a) Whenever a United States attorney charged with the prosecution of a defendant in a court of the United States for an alleged felonious violation of any provision of this subchapter or subchapter II of this chapter committed when the defendant was over the age of twenty-one years has reasons to believe that the defendant is a dangerous special drug offender such United States attorney, a reasonable time before trial or acceptance by the court of a plea of guilty or nolo contendere, may sign and file with the court, and may amend, a notice (1) specifying that the defendant is a dangerous special drug offender who upon conviction for such felonious violation is subject to the imposition of a sentence under subsection (b) of this section, and (2) setting out with particularity the reasons why such attorney believes the defendant to be a dangerous special drug offender. In no case shall the fact that the defendant is alleged to be a dangerous special drug offender be an issue upon the trial of such felonious violation, be disclosed to the jury, or be disclosed before any plea of guilty or nolo contendere or verdict or finding of guilty to the presiding judge without the consent of the parties. If the court finds that the filing of the notice as a public record may prejudice fair consideration of a pending criminal matter, it may order the notice sealed and the notice shall not be subject to subpena or public inspection during the pendency of such criminal matter, except on order of the court, but shall be subject to inspection by the defendant alleged to be a dangerous special drug offender and his counsel.

Hearing; inspection of presentence report; counsel; process; examination of witnesses; penalty; sentence

(b) Upon any plea of guilty or nolo contendere or verdict or finding of guilty of the defendant of such felonious violation, a hearing shall be held, before sentence is imposed, by the court sitting without a jury. The court shall fix a time for the hearing, and notice thereof shall be given to the defendant and the United States at least ten days prior thereto. The court shall permit the United States and counsel for the defendant, or the defendant if he is not represented by counsel, to inspect the presentence report sufficiently prior to the hearing as to afford a reasonable opportunity for verification. In extraordinary cases, the court may withhold material not relevant to a proper sentence, diagnostic opinion which might seriously disrupt a program of rehabilitation, any source of information obtained on a promise of confidentiality, and material previously disclosed in open court. A court withholding all or part of a presentence report shall inform the parties of its action and place in the record the reasons therefor. The court may require parties inspecting all or part of a presentence report to give notice of any part thereof intended to be controverted. In connection with the hearing, the defendant and the United States shall be entitled to assistance of counsel, compulsory process, and cross-examination of such witnesses as appear at the hearing. A duly authenticated copy of a former judgment or commitment shall be prima facie evidence of such former judgment or commitment. If it appears by a preponderance of the information, including information submitted during the trial of such felonious violation and the sentencing hearing and so much of the presentence report as the court relies upon, that the defendant is a dangerous special drug offender, the court shall sentence the defendant to imprisonment for

an appropriate term not to exceed twenty-five years and not disproportionate in severity to the maximum term otherwise authorized by law for such felonious violation. Otherwise it shall sentence the defendant in accordance with the law prescribing penalties for such felonious violation. The court shall place in the record its findings, including an identification of the information relied upon in making such findings, and its reasons for the sentence imposed.

Sentences for life or for term exceeding twenty-five years

(c) This section shall not prevent the imposition and execution of a sentence of imprisonment for life or for a term exceeding twenty-five years upon any person convicted of an offense so punishable.

Mandatory minimum penalties

(d) Notwithstanding any other provision of this section, the court shall not sentence a dangerous special drug offender to less than any mandatory minimum penalty prescribed by law for such felonious violation. This section shall not be construed as creating any mandatory minimum penalty.

Special drug offender defined

(e) A defendant is a special drug offender for purposes of this section if—

(1) the defendant has previously been convicted in courts of the United States or a State or any political subdivision thereof for two or more offenses involving dealing in controlled substances, committed on occasions different from one another and different from such felonious violation, and punishable in such courts by death or imprisonment in excess of one year, for one or more of such convictions the defendant has been imprisoned prior to the commission of such felonious violation, and less than five years have elapsed between the commission of such felonious violation and either the defendant's release, or parole or otherwise, from imprisonment for one such conviction or his commission of the last such previous offense or another offense involving dealing in controlled substances and punishable by death or imprisonment in excess of one year under applicable laws of the United States or a State or any political subdivision thereof; or

(2) the defendant committed such felonious violation as part of a pattern of dealing in controlled substances which was criminal under applicable laws of any jurisdiction, which constituted a substantial source of his income, and in which he manifested special skill or expertise; or

(3) such felonious violation was, or the defendant committed such felonious violation in furtherance of, a conspiracy with three or more other persons to

engage in a pattern of dealing in controlled substances which was criminal under applicable laws of any jurisdiction, and the defendant did, or agreed that he would, initiate, organize, plan, finance, direct, manage, or supervise all or part of such conspiracy or dealing, or give or receive a bribe or use force in connection with such dealing.

A conviction shown on direct or collateral review or at the hearing to be invalid or for which the defendant has been pardoned on the ground of innocence shall be disregarded for purposes of paragraph (1) of this subsection. In support of findings under paragraph (2) of this subsection, it may be shown that the defendant has had in his own name or under his control income or property not explained as derived from a source other than such dealing. For purposes of paragraph (2) of this subsection, a substantial source of income means a source of income which for any period of one year or more exceeds the minimum wage, determined on the basis of a forty-hour week and fifty-week year, without reference to exceptions, under section 206(a)(1) of Title 29 for an employee engaged in commerce or in the production of goods for commerce, and which for the same period exceeds fifty percent of the defendant's declared adjusted gross income under section 62 of Title 26. For purposes of paragraph (2) of this subsection, special skill or expertise in such dealing includes unusual knowledge, judgment or ability, including manual dexterity, facilitating the initiation, organizing, planning, financing, direction, management, supervision, execution or concealment of such dealing, the enlistment of accomplices in such dealing, the escape from detection or apprehension for such dealing, or the disposition of the fruits or proceeds of such dealing. For purposes of paragraphs (2) and (3) of this subsection, such dealing forms a pattern if it embraces criminal acts that have the same or similar purposes, results, participants, victims, or methods of commission, or otherwise are interrelated by distinguishing characteristics and are not isolated events.

Dangerous defendants

(f) A defendant is dangerous for purposes of this section if a period of confinement longer than that provided for such felonious violation is required for the protection of the public from further criminal conduct by the defendant.

Appeal

(g) The time for taking an appeal from a conviction for which sentence is imposed after proceedings under this section shall be measured from imposition of the original sentence.

Review of sentence

(h) With respect to the imposition, correction, or reduction of a sentence after proceedings under this sec-tion, a review of the sentence on the record of the sentencing court may be taken by the defendant or the United States to a court of appeals. Any review of the sentence taken by the United States shall be taken at least five days before expiration of the time for taking a review of the sentence or appeal of the conviction by the defendant and shall be diligently prosecuted. The sentencing court may, with or without motion and notice, extend the time for taking a review of the sentence for a period not to exceed thirty days from the expiration of the time otherwise prescribed by law. The court shall not extend the time for taking a review of the sentence by the United States after the time has expired. A court extending the time for taking a review of the sentence by the United States shall extend the time for taking a review of the sentence or appeal of the conviction by the defendant for the same period. The taking of a review of the sentence by the United States shall be deemed the taking of a review of the sentence and an appeal of the conviction by the defendant. Review of the sentence shall include review of whether the procedure employed was lawful, the findings made were clearly erroneous, or the sentencing court's discretion was abused. The court of appeals on review of the sentence may, after considering the record, including the entire presentence report, information submitted during the trial of such felonious violation and the sentencing hearing, and the findings and reasons of the sentencing court, affirm the sentence, impose or direct the imposition of any sentence which the sentencing court could originally have imposed, or remand for further sentencing proceedings and imposition of sentence, except that a sentence may be made more severe only on review of the sentence taken by the United States and after hearing. Failure of the United States to take a review of the imposition of the sentence shall, upon review taken by the United States of the correction or reduction of the sentence, foreclose imposition of a sentence more severe than that previously imposed. Any withdrawal or dismissal of review of the sentence taken by the United States shall foreclose imposition of the sentence more severe than that reviewed but shall not otherwise foreclose the review of the sentence or the appeal of the conviction. The court of appeals shall state in writing the reasons for its disposition of the review of the sentence. Any review of the sentence taken by the United States may be dismissed on a showing of the abuse of the right of the United States to take such review.

(Pub.L. 91–513, Title II, § 409, Oct. 27, 1970, 84 Stat. 1266.)

For applicability of sentencing provisions to offenses, see Effective Date and Savings Provisions, etc., note, section 235 of Pub.L. 98–473, as amended, set out under section 3551 of Title 18, Crimes and Criminal Procedure.

Effective Date of Repeal; Savings Provisions. Repeal by Pub.L. 98–473 effective on the first day of first calendar month beginning thirty six months after Oct. 12, 1984, applicable only to offenses committed after taking effect of sections 211 to 239 of Pub.L. 98–473, and except as otherwise provided for therein, see section 235 of Pub.L. 98–473, as amended, set out as a note under section 3551 of Title 18, Crimes and Criminal Procedure.

§ 850. Information for sentencing

Except as otherwise provided in this subchapter or section 242a(a) of Title 42, no limitation shall be placed on the information concerning the background, character, and conduct of a person convicted of an offense which a court of the United States may receive and consider for the purpose of imposing an appropriate sentence under this subchapter or subchapter II of this chapter.

(Pub. L. 91–513, Title II, § 410, Oct. 27, 1970, 84 Stat. 1269.)

References in Text. Subchapter II of this chapter, referred to in text, was in the original "title III", meaning Title III of Pub. L. 91–513, Oct. 27, 1970, 84 Stat. 1285. Part A of Title III comprises subchapter II of this chapter. For classification of Part B, consisting of sections 1101 to 1105 of Title III, see U.S.C.A. Tables volume.

§ 851. Proceedings to establish prior convictions

Information filed by United States attorney

(a)(1) No person who stands convicted of an offense under this part shall be sentenced to increased punishment by reason of one or more prior convictions, unless before trial, or before entry of a plea of guilty, the United States attorney files an information with the court (and serves a copy of such information on the person or counsel for the person) stating in writing the previous convictions to be relied upon. Upon a showing by the United States attorney that facts regarding prior convictions could not with due diligence be obtained prior to trial or before entry of a plea of guilty, the court may postpone the trial or the taking of the plea of guilty for a reasonable period for the purpose of obtaining such facts. Clerical mistakes in the information may be amended at any time prior to the pronouncement of sentence.

(2) An information may not be filed under this section if the increased punishment which may be imposed is imprisonment for a term in excess of three years unless the person either waived or was afforded prosecution by indictment for the offense for which such increased punishment may be imposed.

Affirmation or denial of previous conviction

(b) If the United States attorney files an information under this section, the court shall after conviction but before pronouncement of sentence inquire of the person with respect to whom the information was filed whether he affirms or denies that he has been previously convicted as alleged in the information, and shall inform him that any challenge to a prior conviction which is not made before sentence is imposed may not thereafter be raised to attack the sentence.

Denial; written response; hearing

(c)(1) If the person denies any allegation of the information of prior conviction, or claims that any conviction alleged is invalid, he shall file a written response to the information. A copy of the response shall be served upon the United States attorney. The court shall hold a hearing to determine any issues raised by the response which would except the person from increased punishment. The failure of the United States attorney to include in the information the complete criminal record of the person or any facts in addition to the convictions to be relied upon shall not constitute grounds for invalidating the notice given in the information required by subsection (a)(1) of this section. The hearing shall be before the court without a jury and either party may introduce evidence. Except as otherwise provided in paragraph (2) of this subsection, the United States attorney shall have the burden of proof beyond a reasonable doubt on any issue of fact. At the request of either party, the court shall enter findings of fact and conclusions of law.

(2) A person claiming that a conviction alleged in the information was obtained in violation of the Constitution of the United States shall set forth his claim, and the factual basis therefor, with particularity in his response to the information. The person shall have the burden of proof by a preponderance of the evidence on any issue of fact raised by the response. Any challenge to

a prior conviction, not raised by response to the information before an increased sentence is imposed in reliance thereon, shall be waived unless good cause be shown for failure to make a timely challenge.

Imposition of sentence

(d)(1) If the person files no response to the information, or if the court determines, after hearing, that the person is subject to increased punishment by reason of prior convictions, the court shall proceed to impose sentence upon him as provided by this part.

(2) If the court determines that the person has not been convicted as alleged in the information, that a conviction alleged in the information is invalid, or that the person is otherwise not subject to an increased sentence as a matter of law, the court shall, at the request of the United States attorney, postpone sentence to allow an appeal from that determination. If no such request is made, the court shall impose sentence as provided by this part. The person may appeal from an order postponing sentence as if sentence had been pronounced and a final judgment of conviction entered.

Statute of limitations

(e) No person who stands convicted of an offense under this part may challenge the validity of any prior conviction alleged under this section which occurred more than five years before the date of the information alleging such prior conviction.

(Pub. L. 91–513, Title II, § 411, Oct. 27, 1970, 84 Stat. 1269.)

§ 852. Application of treaties and other international agreements

Nothing in the Single Convention on Narcotic Drugs, the Convention on Psychotropic Substances, or other treaties or international agreements shall be construed to limit the provision of treatment, education, or rehabilitation as alternatives to conviction or criminal penalty for offenses involving any drug or other substance subject to control under any such treaty or agreement.

(Pub. L. 91–513, Title II, § 412, as added Pub. L. 95–633, Title I, § 107(a), Nov. 10, 1978, 92 Stat. 3773.)

§ 853. Criminal forfeitures

Property subject to criminal forfeiture

(a) Any person convicted of a violation of this subchapter or subchapter II of this chapter punishable by imprisonment for more than one year shall forfeit to the United States, irrespective of any provision of State law—

(1) any property constituting, or derived from, any proceeds the person obtained, directly or indirectly, as the result of such violation;

(2) any of the person's property used, or intended to be used, in any manner or part, to commit, or to facilitate the commission of, such violation; and

(3) in the case of a person convicted of engaging in a continuing criminal enterprise in violation of section 848 of this title, the person shall forfeit, in addition to any property described in paragraph (1) or (2), any of his interest in, claims against, and property or contractual rights affording a source of control over, the continuing criminal enterprise.

The court, in imposing sentence on such person, shall order, in addition to any other sentence imposed pursuant to this subchapter or subchapter II of this chapter, that the person forfeit to the United States all property described in this subsection. In lieu of a fine otherwise authorized by this part, a defendant who derives profits or other proceeds from an offense may be fined not more than twice the gross profits or other proceeds.

Meaning of term "property"

(b) Property subject to criminal forfeiture under this section includes—

(1) real property, including things growing on, affixed to, and found in land; and

(2) tangible and intangible personal property, including rights, privileges, interests, claims, and securities.

Third party transfers

(c) All right, title, and interest in property described in subsection (a) of this section vests in the United States upon the commission of the act giving rise to forfeiture under this section. Any such property that is subsequently transferred to a person other than the defendant may be the subject of a special verdict of forfeiture and thereafter shall be ordered forfeited to the United States, unless the transferee establishes in a hearing pursuant to subsection (n) of this section that he is a bona fide purchaser for value of such property who at the time of purchase was reasonably without cause to believe that the property was subject to forfeiture under this section.

Rebuttable presumption

(d) There is a rebuttable presumption at trial that any property of a person convicted of a felony under this subchapter or subchapter II of this chapter is subject to forfeiture under this section if the United States establishes by a preponderance of the evidence that—

(1) such property was acquired by such person during the period of the violation of this subchapter or subchapter II of this chapter or within a reasonable time after such period; and

(2) there was no likely source for such property other than the violation of this subchapter or subchapter II of this chapter.

Protective orders

(e)(1) Upon application of the United States, the court may enter a restraining order or injunction, require the execution of a satisfactory performance bond, or take any other action to preserve the availability of property described in subsection (a) of this section for forfeiture under this section—

(A) upon the filing of an indictment or information charging a violation of this subchapter or subchapter II of this chapter for which criminal forfeiture may be ordered under this section and alleging that the property with respect to which the order is sought would, in the event of conviction, be subject to forfeiture under this section; or

(B) prior to the filing of such an indictment or information, if, after notice to persons appearing to have an interest in the property and opportunity for a hearing, the court determines that—

(i) there is a substantial probability that the United States will prevail on the issue of forfeiture and that failure to enter the order will result in the property being destroyed, removed from the jurisdiction of the court, or otherwise made unavailable for forfeiture; and

(ii) the need to preserve the availability of the property through the entry of the requested order outweighs the hardship on any party against whom the order is to be entered:

Provided, however, That an order entered pursuant to subparagraph (B) shall be effective for not more than ninety days, unless extended by the court for good cause shown or unless an indictment or information described in subparagraph (A) has been filed.

(2) A temporary restraining order under this subsection may be entered upon application of the United States without notice or opportunity for a hearing when an information or indictment has not yet been filed with respect to the property, if the United States demonstrates that there is probable cause to believe that the property with respect to which the order is sought would, in the event of conviction, be subject to forfeiture under this section and that provision of notice will jeopardize the availability of the property for forfeiture. Such a temporary order shall expire not more than ten days after the date on which it is entered, unless extended for good cause shown or unless the party against whom it is entered consents to an extension for a longer period. A hearing requested concerning an order entered under this paragraph shall be held at the earliest possible time and prior to the expiration of the temporary order.

(3) The court may receive and consider, at a hearing held pursuant to this subsection, evidence and information that would be inadmissible under the Federal Rules of Evidence.

Warrant of seizure

(f) The Government may request the issuance of a warrant authorizing the seizure of property subject to forfeiture under this section in the same manner as provided for a search warrant. If the court determines that there is probable cause to believe that the property to be seized would, in the event of conviction, be subject to forfeiture and that an order under subsection (e) of this section may not be sufficient to assure the availability of the property for forfeiture, the court shall issue a warrant authorizing the seizure of such property.

Execution

(g) Upon entry of an order of forfeiture under this section, the court shall authorize the Attorney General to seize all property ordered forfeited upon such terms and conditions as the court shall deem proper. Following entry of an order declaring the property forfeited, the court may, upon application of the United States, enter such appropriate restraining orders or injunctions, require the execution of satisfactory performance bonds, appoint receivers, conservators, appraisers, accountants, or trustees, or take any other action to protect the interest of the United States in the property ordered forfeited. Any income accruing to or derived from property ordered forfeited under this section may be used to offset ordinary and necessary expenses to the property which are required by law, or which are necessary to protect the interests of the United States or third parties.

Disposition of property

(h) Following the seizure of property ordered forfeited under this section, the Attorney General shall direct the disposition of the property by sale or any other commercially feasible means, making due provision for the rights of any innocent persons. Any property right or interest not exercisable by, or transferable for value to, the United States shall expire and shall not revert to the defendant, nor shall the defendant or any person acting in concert with him or on his behalf be eligible to purchase forfeited property at any sale held by the United States. Upon application of a person, other than the defendant or a person acting in concert with him or on his behalf, the court may restrain or stay the sale or disposition of the property pending the conclusion of any appeal of the criminal case giving rise to the forfeiture, if the applicant demonstrates that proceeding with the sale or disposition of the property will result in irreparable injury, harm, or loss to him.

Authority of the Attorney General

(i) With respect to property ordered forfeited under this section, the Attorney General is authorized to—

(1) grant petitions for mitigation or remission of forfeiture, restore forfeited property to victims of a violation of this subchapter or take any other action to protect the rights of innocent persons which is in the interest of justice and which is not inconsistent with the provisions of this section;

(2) compromise claims arising under this section;

(3) award compensation to persons providing information resulting in a forfeiture under this section;

(4) direct the disposition by the United States, in accordance with the provisions of section 881(e) of this title, of all property ordered forfeited under this section by public sale or any other commercially feasible means, making due provision for the rights of innocent persons; and

(5) take appropriate measures necessary to safeguard and maintain property ordered forfeited under this section pending its disposition.

Applicability of civil forfeiture provisions

(j) Except to the extent that they are inconsistent with the provisions of this section, the provisions of section 881(d) of this title shall apply to a criminal forfeiture under this section.

Bar on intervention

(k) Except as provided in subsection (n) of this section, no party claiming an interest in property subject to forfeiture under this section may—

(1) intervene in a trial or appeal of a criminal case involving the forfeiture of such property under this subchapter; or

(2) commence an action at law or equity against the United States concerning the validity of his alleged interest in the property subsequent to the filing of an indictment or information alleging that the property is subject to forfeiture under this section.

Jurisdiction to enter orders

(l) The district courts of the United States shall have jurisdiction to enter orders as provided in this section without regard to the location of any property which may be subject to forfeiture under this section or which has been ordered forfeited under this section.

Depositions

(m) In order to facilitate the identification and location of property declared forfeited and to facilitate the disposition of petitions for remission or mitigation of forfeiture, after the entry of an order declaring property forfeited to the United States, the court may, upon application of the United States, order that the testimony of any witness relating to the property forfeited be taken by deposition and that any designated book, paper, document, record, recording, or other material not privileged be produced at the same time and place, in the same manner as provided for the taking of depositions under Rule 15 of the Federal Rules of Criminal Procedure.

Third party interests

(n)(1) Following the entry of an order of forfeiture under this section, the United States shall publish notice of the order and of its intent to dispose of the property in such manner as the Attorney General may direct. The Government may also, to the extent practicable, provide direct written notice to any person known to have alleged an interest in the property that is the subject of the order of forfeiture as a substitute for published notice as to those persons so notified.

(2) Any person, other than the defendant, asserting a legal interest in property which has been ordered forfeited to the United States pursuant to this section may, within thirty days of the final publication of notice or his receipt of notice under paragraph (1), whichever is earlier, petition the court for a hearing to adjudicate the validity of his alleged interest in the property. The hearing shall be held before the court alone, without a jury.

(3) The petition shall be signed by the petitioner under penalty of perjury and shall set forth the nature and extent of the petitioner's right, title, or interest in the property, the time and circumstances of the petitioner's acquisition of the right, title, or interest in the property, any additional facts supporting the petitioner's claim, and the relief sought.

(4) The hearing on the petition shall, to the extent practicable and consistent with the interests of justice, be held within thirty days of the filing of the petition. The court may consolidate the hearing on the petition with a hearing on any other petition filed by a person other than the defendant under this subsection.

(5) At the hearing, the petitioner may testify and present evidence and witnesses on his own behalf, and cross-examine witnesses who appear at the hearing. The United States may present evidence and witnesses in rebuttal and in defense of its claim to the property and cross-examine witnesses who appear at the hearing. In addition to testimony and evidence presented at the hearing, the court shall consider the relevant portions of the record of the criminal case which resulted in the order of forfeiture.

(6) If, after the hearing, the court determines that the petitioner has established by a preponderance of the evidence that—

(A) the petitioner has a legal right, title, or interest in the property, and such right, title, or interest renders the order of forfeiture invalid in whole or in part because the right, title, or interest was vested in the petitioner rather than the defendant or was superior to any right, title, or interest of the defendant at the time of the commission of the acts which gave rise to the forfeiture of the property under this section; or

(B) the petitioner is a bona fide purchaser for value of the right, title, or interest in the property and was at the time of purchase reasonably without cause to believe that the property was subject to forfeiture under this section;

the court shall amend the order of forfeiture in accordance with its determination.

(7) Following the court's disposition of all petitions filed under this subsection, or if no such petitions are filed following the expiration of the period provided in paragraph (2) for the filing of such petitions, the United States shall have clear title to property that is the subject of the order of forfeiture and may warrant good title to any subsequent purchaser or transferee.

Construction

(o) The provisions of this section shall be liberally construed to effectuate its remedial purposes.

Forfeiture of substitute property

(p) If any of the property described in subsection (a) of this section, as a result of any act or omission of the defendant—

(1) cannot be located upon the exercise of due diligence;

(2) has been transferred or sold to, or deposited with, a third party;

(3) has been placed beyond the jurisdiction of the court;

(4) has been substantially diminished in value; or

(5) has been commingled with other property which cannot be divided without difficulty;

the court shall order the forfeiture of any other property of the defendant up to the value of any property described in paragraphs (1) through (5).

(Pub.L. 91–513, Title II, § 413, as added Pub.L. 98–473, Title II, § 303, Oct. 12, 1984, 98 Stat. 2044, and amended Pub.L. 98–473, Title II, § 2301(d)–(f), Oct. 12, 1984, 98 Stat. 2192, 2193; Pub.L. 99–570, Title I, §§ 1153(b), 1864, Oct. 27, 1986, 100 Stat. 3207–13, 3207–54.)

EDITORIAL NOTES

Codification. The language of section 1153(b) of Pub.L. 99–570, amending this section by the relettering of subsec. (p) as (q) and addition of a new subsec. (p) was executed by the addition of a new subsec. (p), but no relettering of prior subsec. (p) since such prior subsec. (p) had been relettered (o) by Pub.L. 98–473, Title II, § 2301(e)(2), Oct. 12, 1984, 98 Stat. 2193.

Amendment by section 1153(b) of Pub.L. 99–570 was executed to section 413 of the Comprehensive Drug Abuse Prevention and Control Act of 1970 (this section) as the probable intent of Congress, despite directory language purporting to require the amendment of section 413 of title II of the "Comprehensive Drug Abuse Prevention and Control Act of 1975".

The amendatory language of section 1864(1) of Pub.L. 99–570, directing the substitution of "subsection (n)" for "subsection (o)" in the second subsection (h) [originally enacted as (l) and relettered (h) by section 2301(e)(2) of Pub.L. 98–473] was executed to such relettered subsec. (h) which was subsequently relettered as (k) by section 1864(4) of Pub.L. 99–570.

The amendatory language of section 1864(3) of Pub.L. 99–570 directing the substitution of "this subchapter" for "this chapter" in subsec. (i)(1) was executed by the substitution of "this subchapter" for "this section" as the probable intent of Congress.

§ 853a. Denial of Federal benefits to drug traffickers and possessors

Drug traffickers

(a)(1) Any individual who is convicted of any Federal or State offense consisting of the distribution of controlled substances (as such terms are defined for purposes of the Controlled Substances Act) [21 U.S.C.A. § 801 et seq.] shall—

(A) at the discretion of the court, upon the first conviction for such an offense be ineligible for any or all Federal benefits for up to 5 years after such conviction;

(B) at the discretion of the court, upon a second conviction for such an offense be ineligible for any or all Federal benefits for up to 10 years after such conviction; and

(C) upon a third or subsequent conviction for such an offense be permanently ineligible for all Federal benefits.

(2) The benefits which are denied under this subsection shall not include benefits relating to long-term drug treatment programs for addiction for any person who, if there is a reasonable body of evidence to substantiate such declaration, declares himself to be an addict and submits himself to a long-term treatment program for addiction, or is deemed to be rehabilitated pursuant to rules established by the Secretary of Health and Human Services.

Drug possessors

(b)(1) Any individual who is convicted of any Federal or State offense involving the possession of a controlled substance (as such term is defined for purposes of the Controlled Substances Act) [21 U.S.C.A. 801 et seq.] shall—

(A) upon the first conviction for such an offense and at the discretion of the court—

(i) be ineligible for any or all Federal benefits for up to one year;

(ii) be required to successfully complete an approved drug treatment program which includes periodic testing to insure that the individual remains drug free;

(iii) be required to perform appropriate community service; or

(iv) any combination of clauses (i), (ii), or (iii); and

(B) upon a second or subsequent conviction for such an offense be ineligible for all Federal benefits for up to 5 years after such conviction as determined by the court. The court shall continue to have the discretion in subparagraph (A) above. In imposing penalties and conditions under subparagraph (A), the court may require that the completion of the conditions imposed by clause (ii) or (iii) be a requirement for the reinstatement of benefits under clause (i).

(2) The penalties and conditions which may be imposed under this subsection shall be waived in the case of a person who, if there is a reasonable body of evidence to substantiate such declaration, declares himself to be an addict and submits himself to a long-term treatment program for addiction, or is deemed to be rehabilitated pursu-

ant to rules established by the Secretary of Health and Human Services.

Suspension of period of eligibility

(c) The period of ineligibility referred to in subsections (a) and (b) of this section shall be suspended if the individual—

(A) completes a supervised drug rehabilitation program after becoming ineligible under this section;

(B) has otherwise been rehabilitated; or

(C) has made a good faith effort to gain admission to a supervised drug rehabilitation program, but is unable to do so because of inaccessibility or unavailability of such a program, or the inability of the individual to pay for such a program.

Definitions

(d) As used in this section—

(1) the term "Federal benefit"—

(A) means the issuance of any grant, contract, loan, professional license, or commercial license provided by an agency of the United States or by appropriated funds of the United States; and

(B) does not include any retirement, welfare, Social Security, health, disability, veterans benefit, public housing, or other similar benefit, or any other benefit for which payments or services are required for eligibility; and

(2) the term "veterans benefit" means all benefits provided to veterans, their families, or survivors by virtue of the service of a veteran in the Armed Forces of the United States.

Inapplicability of this section to Government witnesses

(e) The penalties provided by this section shall not apply to any individual who cooperates or testifies with the Government in the prosecution of a Federal or State offense or who is in a Government witness protection program.

Indian provision

(f) Nothing in this section shall be construed to affect the obligation of the United States to any Indian or Indian tribe arising out of any treaty, statute, Executive order, or the trust responsibility of the United States owing to such Indian or Indian tribe. Nothing in this subsection shall exempt any individual Indian from the sanctions provided for in this section, provided that no individual Indian shall be denied any benefit under Federal Indian programs comparable to those described in subsection (d)(1)(B) or (d)(2) of this section above.

Presidential report

(g)(1) On or before May 1, 1989, the President shall transmit to the Congress a report—

(A) delineating the role of State courts in implementing this section;

(B) describing the manner in which Federal agencies will implement and enforce the requirements of this section;

(C) detailing the means by which Federal and State agencies, courts, and law enforcement agencies will exchange and share the data and information necessary to implement and enforce the withholding of Federal benefits; and

(D) recommending any modifications to improve the administration of this section or otherwise achieve the goal of discouraging the trafficking and possession of controlled substances.

(2) No later than September 1, 1989, the Congress shall consider the report of the President and enact such changes as it deems appropriate to further the goals of this section.

Effective date

(h) The denial of Federal benefits set forth in this section shall take effect for convictions occurring after September 1, 1989.

(Pub.L. 100–690, Title V, § 5301, Nov. 18, 1988, 102 Stat. 4310.)

EDITORIAL NOTES

References in Text. The Controlled Substances Act, referred to in text, is title II of Pub.L. 91–513, Oct. 27, 1970, 84 Stat. 1242, as amended, which is classified principally to subchapter I (§ 801 et seq.) of this chapter. For complete classification of this Act to the Code, see Short Title note set out under section 801 of this title and Tables.

Codification. Section was enacted as part of the Anti–Drug Abuse Act of 1988 and not as part of the Comprehensive Drug Abuse Prevention and Control Act of 1970, which enacted this chapter, or the Controlled Substances Act, which comprises this subchapter.

§ 854.   Investment of illicit drug profits
Prohibition

(a) It shall be unlawful for any person who has received any income derived, directly or indirectly, from a violation of this subchapter or subchapter II of this chapter punishable by imprisonment for more than one year in which such person has participated as a principal within the meaning of section 2 of Title 18 to use or invest, directly or indirectly, any part of such income, or the proceeds of such income, in acquisition of any interest in, or the establishment or operation of, any enterprise which is engaged in, or the activities of which affect interstate or foreign commerce. A purchase of securities on the open market for purposes of investment, and without the intention of controlling or participating in the control of the issuer, or of assisting another to do so, shall not be unlawful under this section if the securities of the issuer held by the purchaser, the members of his immediate family, and his or their accomplices in any violation of this subchapter or subchapter II of this chapter after such purchase do not amount in the aggregate to 1 per centum of the outstanding securities of any one class, and do not confer, either in law or in fact, the power to elect one or more directors of the issuer.

Penalty

(b) Whoever violates this section shall be fined not more than $50,000 or imprisoned not more than ten years, or both.

"Enterprise" defined

(c) As used in this section, the term "enterprise" includes any individual, partnership, corporation, association, or other legal entity, and any union or group of individuals associated in fact although not a legal entity.

Construction

(d) The provisions of this section shall be liberally construed to effectuate its remedial purposes.

(Pub. L. 91–513, Title II, § 414, as added Pub. L. 98–473, Title II, § 303, Oct. 12, 1984, 98 Stat. 2049.)

§ 855.   Alternative fine

In lieu of a fine otherwise authorized by this part, a defendant who derives profits or other proceeds from an offense may be fined not more than twice the gross profits or other proceeds.

(Pub. L. 91–513, Title II, § 415, as added Pub. L. 98–473, Title II, § 2302, Oct. 12, 1984, 98 Stat. 2193.)

§ 856.   Establishment of manufacturing operations

(a) Except as authorized by this title, it shall be unlawful to—

(1) knowingly open or maintain any place for the purpose of manufacturing, distributing, or using any controlled substance;

(2) manage or control any building, room, or enclosure, either as an owner, lessee, agent, employee, or mortgagee, and knowingly and intentionally rent, lease, or make available for use, with or without compensation, the building, room, or enclosure for the purpose of unlawfully manufacturing, storing, distributing, or using a controlled substance.

(b) Any person who violates subsection (a) of this section shall be sentenced to a term of imprisonment of not more than 20 years or a fine of not more than $500,000, or both, or a fine of $2,000,000 for a person other than an individual.

(Pub.L. 91–513, Title II, § 416, as added Pub.L. 99–570, Title I, § 1841(a), Oct. 27, 1986, 100 Stat. 3207–52.)

§ 857.   Use of Postal Service for sale of drug paraphernalia
Unlawfulness

(a) It is unlawful for any person—

(1) to make use of the services of the Postal Service or other interstate conveyance as part of a scheme to sell drug paraphernalia;

(2) to offer for sale and transportation in interstate or foreign commerce drug paraphernalia; or

(3) to import or export drug paraphernalia.

Penalties

(b) Anyone convicted of an offense under subsection (a) of this section shall be imprisoned for not more than three years and fined not more than $100,000.

Seizure and forfeiture

(c) Any drug paraphernalia involved in any violation of subsection (a) of this section shall be subject to seizure and forfeiture upon the conviction of a person for such violation. Any such paraphernalia shall be delivered to the Administrator of General Services, General Services Administration, who may order such paraphernalia destroyed or may authorize its use for law enforcement or educational purposes by Federal, State, or local authorities.

Definition of "drug paraphernalia"

(d) The term "drug paraphernalia" means any equipment, product, or material of any kind which is primarily intended or designed for use in manufacturing, compounding, converting, concealing, producing, processing, preparing, injecting, ingesting, inhaling, or otherwise introducing into the human body a controlled substance, possession of which is unlawful under the Controlled Substances Act (title II of Public Law 91–513) [21 U.S.C.A. § 801 et seq.]. It includes items primarily intended or designed for use in ingesting, inhaling, or otherwise introducing marijuana, cocaine, hashish, hashish oil, PCP, or amphetamines into the human body, such as—

(1) metal, wooden, acrylic, glass, stone, plastic, or ceramic pipes with or without screens, permanent screens, hashish heads, or punctured metal bowls;

(2) water pipes;

(3) carburetion tubes and devices;

(4) smoking and carburetion masks;

(5) roach clips: meaning objects used to hold burning material, such as a marihuana cigarette, that has become too small or too short to be held in the hand;

(6) miniature spoons with level capacities of one-tenth cubic centimeter or less;

(7) chamber pipes;

(8) carburetor pipes;

(9) electric pipes;

(10) air-driven pipes;

(11) chillums;

(12) bongs;

(13) ice pipes or chillers;

(14) wired cigarette papers; or

(15) cocaine freebase kits.

Matters considered in determination of what constitutes drug paraphernalia

(e) In determining whether an item constitutes drug paraphernalia, in addition to all other logically relevant factors, the following may be considered:

(1) instructions, oral or written, provided with the item concerning its use;

(2) descriptive materials accompanying the item which explain or depict its use;

(3) national and local advertising concerning its use;

(4) the manner in which the item is displayed for sale;

(5) whether the owner, or anyone in control of the item, is a legitimate supplier of like or related items to the community, such as a licensed distributor or dealer of tobacco products;

(6) direct or circumstantial evidence of the ratio of sales of the item(s) to the total sales of the business enterprise;

(7) the existence and scope of legitimate uses of the item in the community; and

(8) expert testimony concerning its use.

Exemptions

(f) This section shall not apply to—

(1) any person authorized by local, State, or Federal law to manufacture, possess, or distribute such items; or

(2) any item that, in the normal lawful course of business, is imported, exported, transported, or sold through the mail or by any other means, and traditionally intended for use with tobacco products, including any pipe, paper, or accessory.

(Pub.L. 99–570, Title I, § 1822, Oct. 27, 1986, 100 Stat. 3207–51; Pub.L. 100–690, Title VI, § 6485, Nov. 18, 1988, 102 Stat. 4384.)

EDITORIAL NOTES

References in Text. The Controlled Substances Act, referred to in subsec. (d), in provisions preceding par. (1), is Title II of Pub.L. 91–513, Oct. 27, 1970, 84 Stat. 1242, as amended, which is classified principally to this subchapter. For complete classification of this Act to the Code, see Short Title note set out under section 801 of Title 21 and Tables volume.

Codification. Section was not enacted as part of the Controlled Substances Act, Pub.L. 91–513, Title II, which comprises this subchapter.

Effective Date. Section 1823 of Pub.L. 99–570 provided that: "This subtitle [enacting this section] shall become effective 90 days after the date of enactment of this Act [Oct. 27, 1986]."

§ 858. Endangering human life while illegally manufacturing a controlled substance

Whoever, while manufacturing a controlled substance in violation of this subchapter, or attempting to do so, or transporting or causing to be transported materials, including chemicals, to do so, creates a substantial risk of harm to human life shall be fined in accordance with Title 18, or imprisoned not more than 10 years, or both.

(Pub.L. 91–513, Title II, § 417, as added Pub.L. 100–690, Title VI, § 6301(a), Nov. 18, 1988, 102 Stat. 4370.)

EDITORIAL NOTES

References in Text. This subchapter, referred to in text, was in the original "this title" which is Title II of Pub.L. 91–513, Oct. 27, 1970, 84 Stat. 1242, and is popularly known as the "Controlled Substances Act". For complete classification of Title II to the Code, see Short Title note set out under section 801 of this title and Tables volume.

PART E

ADMINISTRATIVE AND ENFORCEMENT PROVISIONS

§ 871. Attorney General

Delegation of functions

(a) The Attorney General may delegate any of his functions under this subchapter to any officer or employee of the Department of Justice.

Rules and regulations

(b) The Attorney General may promulgate and enforce any rules, regulations, and procedures which he may deem necessary and appropriate for the efficient execution of his functions under this subchapter.

Acceptance of devises, bequests, gifts, and donations

(c) The Attorney General may accept in the name of the Department of Justice any form of devise, bequest, gift, or donation where the donor intends to donate property for the purpose of preventing or controlling the abuse of controlled substances. He may take all appropriate steps to secure possession of such property and may sell, assign, transfer, or convey any such property other than moneys.

(Pub. L. 91–513, Title II, § 501, Oct. 27, 1970, 84 Stat. 1270.)

Code of Federal Regulations

Office of the Attorney General, functions, etc., see 28 CFR 0.5 et seq.

Policies, practices, and procedures, see 21 CFR Chap. II.

§ 872. Education and research programs of Attorney General

Authorization

(a) The Attorney General is authorized to carry out educational and research programs directly related to enforcement of the laws under his jurisdiction concerning drugs or other substances which are or may be subject to control under this subchapter. Such programs may include—

(1) educational and training programs on drug abuse and controlled substances law enforcement for local, State, and Federal personnel;

(2) studies or special projects designed to compare the deterrent effects of various enforcement strategies on drug use and abuse;

(3) studies or special projects designed to assess and detect accurately the presence in the human body of drugs or other substances which are or may be subject to control under this subchapter, including the development of rapid field identification methods which would enable agents to detect microquantities of such drugs or other substances;

(4) studies or special projects designed to evaluate the nature and sources of the supply of illegal drugs throughout the country;

(5) studies or special projects to develop more effective methods to prevent diversion of controlled substances into illegal channels; and

(6) studies or special projects to develop information necessary to carry out his functions under section 811 of this title.

Contracts

(b) The Attorney General may enter into contracts for such educational and research activities without performance bonds and without regard to section 5 of Title 41.

Identification of research populations; authorization to withhold

(c) The Attorney General may authorize persons engaged in research to withhold the names and other identifying characteristics of persons who are the subjects of such research. Persons who obtain this authorization may not be compelled in any Federal, State, or local civil, criminal, administrative, legislative, or other proceeding to identify the subjects of research for which such authorization was obtained.

Effect of treaties and other international agreements on confidentiality

(d) Nothing in the Single Convention on Narcotic Drugs, the Convention on Psychotropic Substances, or other treaties or international agreements shall be construed to limit, modify, or prevent the protection of the confidentiality of patient records or of the names and other identifying characteristics of research subjects as provided by any Federal, State, or local law or regulation.

Use of controlled substances in research

(e) The Attorney General, on his own motion or at the request of the Secretary, may authorize the possession, distribution, and dispensing of controlled substances by persons engaged in research. Persons who obtain this authorization shall be exempt from State or Federal prosecution for possession, distribution, and dispensing of controlled substances to the extent authorized by the Attorney General.

Program to curtail diversion of precursor and essential chemicals

(f) The Attorney General shall maintain an active program, both domestic and international, to curtail the diversion of precursor chemicals and essential chemicals used in the illicit manufacture of controlled substances.

(Pub. L. 91–513, Title II, § 502, Oct. 27, 1970, 84 Stat. 1271; Pub. L. 95–633, Title I, § 108(a), Nov. 10, 1978, 92 Stat. 3773; Pub.L. 100–690, Title VI, § 6060, Nov. 18, 1988, 102 Stat. 4320.)

EDITORIAL NOTES

Effective Date of 1988 Amendment. Amendment by section 6060 of Pub.L. 100–690 effective 120 days after Nov. 18, 1988, see section 6061 of Pub.L. 100–690, set out as a note under section 802 of this title.

Code of Federal Regulations

Administrative policies, practices, and procedures, see 21 CFR 1316.01 et seq.

§ 873. Cooperative arrangements
Powers of Attorney General

(a) The Attorney General shall cooperate with local, State, and Federal agencies concerning traffic in controlled substances and in suppressing the abuse of controlled substances. To this end, he is authorized to—

(1) arrange for the exchange of information between governmental officials concerning the use and abuse of controlled substances;

(2) cooperate in the institution and prosecution of cases in the courts of the United States and before the licensing boards and courts of the several States;

(3) conduct training programs on controlled substance law enforcement for local, State, and Federal personnel;

(4) maintain in the Department of Justice a unit which will accept, catalog, file, and otherwise utilize all information and statistics, including records of controlled substance abusers and other controlled substance law offenders, which may be received from Federal, State, and local agencies, and make such information available for Federal, State, and local law enforcement purposes;

(5) conduct programs of eradication aimed at destroying wild or illicit growth of plant species from which controlled substances may be extracted;

(6) assist State and local governments in suppressing the diversion of controlled substances from legitimate medical, scientific, and commercial channels by—

(A) making periodic assessments of the capabilities of State and local governments to adequately control the diversion of controlled substances;

(B) providing advice and counsel to State and local governments on the methods by which such governments may strengthen their controls against diversion; and

(C) establishing cooperative investigative efforts to control diversion; and

(7) notwithstanding any other provision of law, enter into contractual agreements with

State and local law enforcement agencies to provide for cooperative enforcement and regulatory activities under this subchapter.

Requests by Attorney General for assistance from Federal agencies or instrumentalities

(b) When requested by the Attorney General, it shall be the duty of any agency or instrumentality of the Federal Government to furnish assistance, including technical advice, to him for carrying out his functions under this subchapter; except that no such agency or instrumentality shall be required to furnish the name of, or other identifying information about, a patient or research subject whose identity it has undertaken to keep confidential.

Descriptive and analytic reports by Attorney General to State agencies of distribution patterns of schedule II substances having highest rates of abuse

(c) The Attorney General shall annually (1) select the controlled substance (or controlled substances) contained in schedule II which, in the Attorney General's discretion, is determined to have the highest rate of abuse, and (2) prepare and make available to regulatory, licensing, and law enforcement agencies of States descriptive and analytic reports on the actual distribution patterns in such States of each such controlled substance.

Grants by Attorney General

(d)(1) The Attorney General may make grants, in accordance with paragraph (2), to State and local governments to assist in meeting the costs of—

(A) collecting and analyzing data on the diversion of controlled substances,

(B) conducting investigations and prosecutions of such diversions,

(C) improving regulatory controls and other authorities to control such diversions,

(D) programs to prevent such diversions,

(E) preventing and detecting forged prescriptions, and

(F) training law enforcement and regulatory personnel to improve the control of such diversions.

(2) No grant may be made under paragraph (1) unless an application therefor is submitted to the Attorney General in such form and manner as the Attorney General may prescribe. No grant may exceed 80 per centum of the costs for which the grant is made, and no grant may be made unless the recipient of the grant provides assurances satisfactory to the Attorney General that it will obligate funds to meet the remaining 20 per centum of such costs. The Attorney General shall review the activities carried out with grants under paragraph (1) and shall report annually to Congress on such activities.

(3) To carry out this subsection there is authorized to be appropriated $6,000,000 for fiscal year 1985 and $6,000,000 for fiscal year 1986.

(Pub. L. 91–513, Title II, § 503, Oct. 27, 1970, 84 Stat. 1271; Pub. L. 96–359, § 8(a), Sept. 26, 1980, 94 Stat. 1194; Pub.L. 98–473, Title II, § 517, Oct. 12, 1984, 98 Stat. 2074; Pub.L. 99–570, Title I, § 1868, Oct. 27, 1986, 100 Stat. 3207–55; Pub.L. 99–646, § 85, Nov. 10, 1986, 100 Stat. 3620.)

EDITORIAL NOTES

References in Text. "This subchapter", referred to in subsecs. (a)(7), (b), was in the original "this title" which is Title II of Pub.L. 91–513, Oct. 27, 1970, 84 Stat. 1242, and is popularly known as the "Controlled Substances Act". For complete classification of Title II to the Code, see Short Title note set out under section 801 of this title and Tables volume.

Codification. Pub.L. 99–570 and Pub.L. 99–646 made similar amendments by adding a new par. (7) to Subsec. (a). As originally enacted, Pub.L. 99–646 referred to "this Act" and Pub.L. 99–570 referred to "this title" and both have been editorially translated as "this Subchapter" in view of prior editorial treatment of references to the Controlled Substances Act.

§ 874. Advisory committees

The Attorney General may from time to time appoint committees to advise him with respect to preventing and controlling the abuse of controlled substances. Members of the committees may be entitled to receive compensation at the rate of $100 for each day (including traveltime) during which they are engaged in the actual performance of duties. While traveling on official business in the performance of duties for the committees, members of the committees shall be allowed expenses of travel, including per diem instead of subsistence, in accordance with subchapter I of chapter 57 of Title 5.

(Pub. L. 91–513, Title II, § 504, Oct. 27, 1970, 84 Stat. 1272.)

EDITORIAL NOTES

Termination of Advisory Committees. Advisory committees in existence on Jan. 5, 1973, to terminate not later than the expiration of two year period following Jan. 5, 1973, and advisory committees established after Jan. 5, 1973, to terminate not later than the expiration of two year period beginning on the date of their establishment, unless in the case of a committee established by the President or an officer of the Federal Government, such committee is renewed by appropriate action prior to the expiration of such two year period, or in the case of a committee established by Congress, its duration is otherwise provided by law, see section 14 of Pub. L. 92–463, Oct. 6, 1972, 86 Stat. 776, set out in the Appendix to Title 5, U.S.C.A., Government Organization and Employees.

§ 875.　Administrative hearings

Power of Attorney General

(a) In carrying out his functions under this subchapter, the Attorney General may hold hearings, sign and issue subpenas, administer oaths, examine witnesses, and receive evidence at any place in the United States.

Procedures applicable

(b) Except as otherwise provided in this subchapter, notice shall be given and hearings shall be conducted under appropriate procedures of subchapter II of chapter 5 of Title 5.

(Pub. L. 91–513, Title II, § 505, Oct. 27, 1970, 84 Stat. 1272.)

Code of Federal Regulations

Administrative policies, practices, and procedures, see 21 CFR 1316.01 et seq.

Registration requirements, see 21 CFR 1301.01 et seq.

§ 876.　Subpenas

Authorization of use by Attorney General

In any investigation relating to his functions under this subchapter with respect to controlled substances, listed chemicals, tableting machines, or encapsulating machines, the Attorney General may subpena witnesses, compel the attendance and testimony of witnesses, and require the production of any records (including books, papers, documents, and other tangible things which constitute or contain evidence) which the Attorney General finds relevant or material to the investigation. The attendance of witnesses and the production of records may be required from any place in any State or in any territory or other place subject to the jurisdiction of the United States at any designated place of hearing; except that a witness shall not be required to appear at any hearing more than 500 miles distant from the place where he was served with a subpena. Witnesses summoned under this section shall be paid the same fees and mileage that are paid witnesses in the courts of the United States.

Service

(b) A subpena issued under this section may be served by any person designated in the subpena to serve it. Service upon a natural person may be made by personal delivery of the subpena to him. Service may be made upon a domestic or foreign corporation or upon a partnership or other unincorporated association which is subject to suit under a common name, by delivering the subpena to an officer, to a managing or general agent, or to any other agent authorized by appointment or by law to receive service of process. The affidavit of the person serving the subpena entered on a true copy thereof by the person serving it shall be proof of service.

Enforcement

(c) In the case of contumacy by or refusal to obey a subpena issued to any person, the Attorney General may invoke the aid of any court of the United States within the jurisdiction of which the investigation is carried on or of which the subpenaed person is an inhabitant, or in which he carries on business or may be found, to compel compliance with the subpena. The court may issue an order requiring the subpenaed person to appear before the Attorney General to produce records, if so ordered, or to give testimony touching the matter under investigation. Any failure to obey the order of the court may be punished by the court as a contempt thereof. All process in any such case may be served in any judicial district in which such person may be found.

(Pub. L. 91–513, Title II, § 506, Oct. 27, 1970, 84 Stat. 1272; Pub.L. 100–690, Title VI, § 6058, Nov. 18, 1988, 102 Stat. 4319.)

EDITORIAL NOTES

Effective Date of 1988 Amendment. Amendment by section 6058 of Pub.L. 100–690 effective 120 days after Nov. 18, 1988, see section 6061 of Pub.L. 100–690, set out as a note under section 802 of this title.

§ 877.   Judicial review

All final determinations, findings, and conclusions of the Attorney General under this subchapter shall be final and conclusive decisions of the matters involved, except that any person aggrieved by a final decision of the Attorney General may obtain review of the decision in the United States Court of Appeals for the District of Columbia or for the circuit in which his principal place of business is located upon petition filed with the court and delivered to the Attorney General within thirty days after notice of the decision.   Findings of fact by the Attorney General, if supported by substantial evidence, shall be conclusive.

(Pub. L. 91–513, Title II, § 507, Oct. 27, 1970, 84 Stat. 1273.)

Code of Federal Regulations

Registration requirements, see 21 CFR 1301.01 et seq.

§ 878.   Powers of enforcement personnel

Officers or employees of Drug Enforcement Administration or any State or local law enforcement officer

(a) Any officer or employee of the Drug Enforcement Administration or any State or local law enforcement officer designated by the Attorney General may—

(1) carry firearms;

(2) execute and serve search warrants, arrest warrants, administrative inspection warrants, subpenas, and summonses issued under the authority of the United States;

(3) make arrests without warrant (A) for any offense against the United States committed in his presence, or (B) for any felony, cognizable under the laws of the United States, if he has probable cause to believe that the person to be arrested has committed or is committing a felony;

(4) make seizures of property pursuant to the provisions of this subchapter; and

(5) perform such other law enforcement duties as the Attorney General may designate.

Federal employee status

(b) State and local law enforcement officers performing functions under this section shall not be deemed Federal employees and shall not be subject to provisions of law relating to Federal employees, except that such officers shall be subject to section 3374(c) of Title 5.

(Pub. L. 91–513, Title II, § 508, Oct. 27, 1970, 84 Stat. 1273; Pub. L. 96–132, § 16(b), Nov. 30, 1979, 93 Stat. 1049; Pub. L. 99–570, Title I, § 1869, Oct. 27, 1986, 100 Stat. 3207–55; Pub. L. 99–646, § 86, Nov. 10, 1986, 100 Stat. 3620.)

EDITORIAL NOTES

References in Text. "This subchapter", referred to in subsec. (a)(4), was in the original "this title" which is Title II of Pub.L. 91–513, Oct. 27, 1970, 84 Stat. 1242, and is popularly known as the "Controlled Substances Act". For complete classification of Title II to the Code, see Short Title note set out under section 801 of this title and Tables volume.

Codification.   Amendment by section 1869(2) of Pub.L. 99–570, which directed that in subsec. (a) "or (with respect to offenses under this subchapter or subchapter II of this chapter) and State or local law enforcement officer" be inserted after "Drug Enforcement Administration" was not executed as the probable intent of Congress, in view of the subsequent amendment to subsec. (a) by section 86(2) of Pub.L. 99–646, which directed that "or any State or local law enforcement officer" be inserted after "Drug Enforcement Administration".

§ 879.   Search warrants

A search warrant relating to offenses involving controlled substances may be served at any time of the day or night if the judge or United States magistrate issuing the warrant is satisfied that there is probable cause to believe that grounds exist for the warrant and for its service at such time.

(Pub. L. 91–513, Title II, § 509, Oct. 27, 1970, 84 Stat. 1274; Pub. L. 93–481, § 3, Oct. 26, 1974, 88 Stat. 1455.)

§ 880.   Administrative inspections and warrants

Controlled premises defined

(a) As used in this section, the term "controlled premises" means—

(1) places where original or other records or documents required under this subchapter are kept or required to be kept, and

(2) places, including factories, warehouses, or other establishments, and conveyances, where persons registered under section 823 of this title (or exempted from registration under section 822(d) of this title) may lawfully hold,

manufacture, or distribute, dispense, administer, or otherwise dispose of controlled substances.

Grant of authority; scope of inspections

(b)(1) For the purpose of inspecting, copying, and verifying the correctness of records, reports, or other documents required to be kept or made under this subchapter and otherwise facilitating the carrying out of his functions under this subchapter, the Attorney General is authorized, in accordance with this section, to enter controlled premises and to conduct administrative inspections thereof, and of the things specified in this section, relevant to those functions.

(2) Such entries and inspections shall be carried out through officers or employees (hereinafter referred to as "inspectors") designated by the Attorney General. Any such inspector, upon stating his purpose and presenting to the owner, operator, or agent in charge of such premises (A) appropriate credentials and (B) a written notice of his inspection authority (which notice in the case of an inspection requiring, or in fact supported by, an administrative inspection warrant shall consist of such warrant), shall have the right to enter such premises and conduct such inspection at reasonable times.

(3) Except as may otherwise be indicated in an applicable inspection warrant, the inspector shall have the right—

(A) to inspect and copy records, reports, and other documents required to be kept or made under this subchapter;

(B) to inspect, within reasonable limits and in a reasonable manner, controlled premises and all pertinent equipment, finished and unfinished drugs and other substances or materials, containers, and labeling found therein, and, except as provided in paragraph (5)[1] of this subsection, all other things therein (including records, files, papers, processes, controls, and facilities) appropriate for verification of the records, reports, and documents referred to in clause (A) or otherwise bearing on the provisions of this subchapter; and

(C) to inventory any stock of any controlled substance therein and obtain samples of any such substance.

(4) Except when the owner, operator, or agent in charge of the controlled premises so consents in writing, no inspection authorized by this section shall extend to—

(A) financial data;

(B) sales data other than shipment data; or

(C) pricing data.

Situations not requiring warrants

(c) A warrant under this section shall not be required for the inspection of books and records pursuant to an administrative subpena issued in accordance with section 876 of this title, nor for entries and administrative inspections (including seizures of property)—

(1) with the consent of the owner, operator, or agent in charge of the controlled premises;

(2) in situations presenting imminent danger to health or safety;

(3) in situations involving inspection of conveyances where there is reasonable cause to believe that the mobility of the conveyance makes it impracticable to obtain a warrant;

(4) in any other exceptional or emergency circumstance where time or opportunity to apply for a warrant is lacking; or

(5) in any other situations where a warrant is not constitutionally required.

Administrative inspection warrants; issuance; execution; probable cause

(d) Issuance and execution of administrative inspection warrants shall be as follows:

(1) Any judge of the United States or of a State court of record, or any United States magistrate, may, within his territorial jurisdiction, and upon proper oath or affirmation showing probable cause, issue warrants for the purpose of conducting administrative inspections authorized by this subchapter or regulations thereunder, and seizures of property appropriate to such inspections. For the purposes of this section, the term "probable cause" means a valid public interest in the effective enforcement of this subchapter or regulations thereunder sufficient to justify administrative inspections of the area, premises, building, or conveyance, or contents thereof, in the circumstances specified in the application for the warrant.

(2) A warrant shall issue only upon an affidavit of an officer or employee having knowledge of the facts alleged, sworn to before the judge or magistrate and establishing the grounds for issuing the

warrant. If the judge or magistrate is satisfied that grounds for the application exist or that there is probable cause to believe they exist, he shall issue a warrant identifying the area, premises, building, or conveyance to be inspected, the purpose of such inspection, and, where appropriate, the type of property to be inspected, if any. The warrant shall identify the items or types of property to be seized, if any. The warrant shall be directed to a person authorized under subsection (b)(2) of this section to execute it. The warrant shall state the grounds for its issuance and the name of the person or persons whose affidavit has been taken in support thereof. It shall command the person to whom it is directed to inspect the area, premises, building, or conveyance identified for the purpose specified, and, where appropriate, shall direct the seizure of the property specified. The warrant shall direct that it be served during normal business hours. It shall designate the judge or magistrate to whom it shall be returned.

(3) A warrant issued pursuant to this section must be executed and returned within ten days of its date unless, upon a showing by the United States of a need therefor, the judge or magistrate allows additional time in the warrant. If property is seized pursuant to a warrant, the person executing the warrant shall give to the person from whom or from whose premises the property was taken a copy of the warrant and a receipt for the property taken or shall leave the copy and receipt at the place from which the property was taken. The return of the warrant shall be made promptly and shall be accompanied by a written inventory of any property taken. The inventory shall be made in the presence of the person executing the warrant and of the person from whose possession or premises the property was taken, if they are present, or in the presence of at least one credible person other than the person making such inventory, and shall be verified by the person executing the warrant. The judge or magistrate, upon request, shall deliver a copy of the inventory to the person from whom or from whose premises the property was taken and to the applicant for the warrant.

(4) The judge or magistrate who has issued a warrant under this section shall attach to the warrant a copy of the return and all papers filed in connection therewith and shall file them with the clerk of the district court of the United States

for the judicial district in which the inspection was made.

(Pub. L. 91–513, Title II, § 510, Oct. 27, 1970, 84 Stat. 1274.)

1. So in original. Probably should be "paragraph (4)".

Code of Federal Regulations

Administrative policies, practices, and procedures, see 21 CFR 1316.01 et seq.

§ 881. Forfeitures

Subject property

(a) The following shall be subject to forfeiture to the United States and no property right shall exist in them:

(1) All controlled substances which have been manufactured, distributed, dispensed, or acquired in violation of this subchapter.

(2) All raw materials, products, and equipment of any kind which are used, or intended for use, in manufacturing, compounding, processing, delivering, importing, or exporting any controlled substance in violation of this subchapter.

(3) All property which is used, or intended for use, as a container for property described in paragraph (1), (2), or (9).

(4) All conveyances, including aircraft, vehicles, or vessels, which are used, or are intended for use, to transport, or in any manner to facilitate the transportation, sale, receipt, possession, or concealment of property described in paragraph (1), (2), or (9), except that—

(A) no conveyance used by any person as a common carrier in the transaction of business as a common carrier shall be forfeited under the provisions of this section unless it shall appear that the owner or other person in charge of such conveyance was a consenting party or privy to a violation of this subchapter or subchapter II of this chapter;

(B) no conveyance shall be forfeited under the provisions of this section by reason of any act or omission established by the owner thereof to have been committed or omitted by any person other than such owner while such conveyance was unlawfully in the possession of a person other than the owner in violation of the criminal laws of the United States, or of any State; and

(C) no conveyance shall be forfeited under this paragraph to the extent of an interest of an owner, by reason of any act or omission established by that owner to have been committed or omitted without the knowledge, consent, or willful blindness of the owner.

(5) All books, records, and research, including formulas, microfilm, tapes, and data which are used, or intended for use, in violation of this subchapter.

(6) All moneys, negotiable instruments, securities, or other things of value furnished or intended to be furnished by any person in exchange for a controlled substance in violation of this subchapter, all proceeds traceable to such an exchange, and all moneys, negotiable instruments, and securities used or intended to be used to facilitate any violation of this subchapter, except that no property shall be forfeited under this paragraph, to the extent of the interest of an owner, by reason of any act or omission established by that owner to have been committed or omitted without the knowledge or consent of that owner.

(7) All real property, including any right, title, and interest (including any leasehold interest) in the whole of any lot or tract of land and any appurtenances or improvements, which is used, or intended to be used, in any manner or part, to commit, or to facilitate the commission of, a violation of this title punishable by more than one year's imprisonment, except that no property shall be forfeited under this paragraph, to the extent of an interest of an owner, by reason of any act or omission established by that owner to have been committed or omitted without the knowledge or consent of that owner.

(8) All controlled substances which have been possessed in violation of this subchapter.

(9) All listed chemicals, all drug manufacturing equipment, all tableting machines, all encapsulating machines, and all gelatin capsules, which have been imported, exported, manufactured, possessed, distributed, or intended to be distributed, imported, or exported, in violation of a felony provision of this subchapter or subchapter II of this chapter.

Seizure pursuant to Supplemental Rules for Certain Admiralty and Maritime Claims; issuance of warrant authorizing seizure

(b) Any property subject to civil forfeiture to the United States under this subchapter may be seized by the Attorney General upon process issued pursuant to the Supplemental Rules for Certain Admiralty and Maritime Claims by any district court of the United States having jurisdiction over the property, except that seizure without such process may be made when—

(1) the seizure is incident to an arrest or a search under a search warrant or an inspection under an administrative inspection warrant;

(2) the property subject to seizure has been the subject of a prior judgment in favor of the United States in a criminal injunction or forfeiture proceeding under this subchapter;

(3) the Attorney General has probable cause to believe that the property is directly or indirectly dangerous to health or safety; or

(4) the Attorney General has probable cause to believe that the property is subject to civil forfeiture under this subchapter.

In the event of seizure pursuant to paragraph (3) or (4) of this subsection, proceedings under subsection (d) of this section shall be instituted promptly.

The Government may request the issuance of a warrant authorizing the seizure of property subject to forfeiture under this section in the same manner as provided for a search warrant under the Federal Rules of Criminal Procedure.

Custody of Attorney General

(c) Property taken or detained under this section shall not be repleviable, but shall be deemed to be in the custody of the Attorney General, subject only to the orders and decrees of the court or the official having jurisdiction thereof. Whenever property is seized under any of the provisions of this subchapter, the Attorney General may—

(1) place the property under seal;

(2) remove the property to a place designated by him; or

(3) require that the General Services Administration take custody of the property and remove it, if practicable, to an appropriate location for disposition in accordance with law.

Other laws and proceedings applicable

(d) The provisions of law relating to the seizure, summary and judicial forfeiture, and condemnation of property for violation of the customs laws; the disposition of such property or the proceeds from the sale thereof; the remission or mitigation of such forfeitures; and the compromise of claims shall apply to seizures and forfeitures incurred, or alleged to have been incurred, under any of the provisions of this subchapter, insofar as applicable and not inconsistent with the provisions hereof; except that such duties as are imposed upon the customs officer or any other person with respect to the seizure and forfeiture of property under the customs laws shall be performed with respect to seizures and forfeitures of property under this subchapter by such officers, agents, or other persons as may be authorized or designated for that purpose by the Attorney General, except to the extent that such duties arise from seizures and forfeitures effected by any customs officer.

Disposition of forfeited property

(e)(1) Whenever property is civilly or criminally forfeited under this subchapter the Attorney General may—

(A) retain the property for official use or, in the manner provided with respect to transfers under section 1616a of Title 19, transfer the property to any Federal agency or to any State or local law enforcement agency which participated directly in the seizure or forfeiture of the property;

(B) sell any forfeited property which is not required to be destroyed by law and which is not harmful to the public;

(C) require that the General Services Administration take custody of the property and dispose of it in accordance with law;

(D) forward it to the Drug Enforcement Administration for disposition (including delivery for medical or scientific use to any Federal or State agency under regulations of the Attorney General); or

(E) transfer the forfeited personal property or the proceeds of the sale of any forfeited personal or real property to any foreign country which participated directly or indirectly in the seizure or forfeiture of the property, if such a transfer—

(i) has been agreed to by the Secretary of State;

(ii) is authorized in an international agreement between the United States and the foreign country; and

(iii) is made to a country which, if applicable, has been certified under section 2291(h) of Title 22.

(2)(A) The proceeds from any sale under subparagraph (B) of paragraph (1) and any moneys forfeited under this title shall be used to pay—

(i) all property expenses of the proceedings for forfeiture and sale including expenses of seizure, maintenance of custody, advertising, and court costs; and

(ii) awards of up to $100,000 to any individual who provides original information which leads to the arrest and conviction of a person who kills or kidnaps a Federal drug law enforcement agent.

Any award paid for information concerning the killing or kidnapping of a Federal drug law enforcement agent, as provided in clause (ii), shall be paid at the discretion of the Attorney General.

(B) The Attorney General shall forward to the Treasurer of the United States for deposit in accordance with section 524(c) of Title 28, any amounts of such moneys and proceeds remaining after payment of the expenses provided in subparagraph (A) except that, with respect to forfeitures conducted by the Postal Service, the Postal Service shall deposit in the Postal Service Fund, under section 2003(b)(7) of Title 39, such moneys and proceeds.

(3) The Attorney General shall assure that any property transferred to a State or local law enforcement agency under paragraph (1)(A)—

(A) has a value that bears a reasonable relationship to the degree of direct participation of the State or local agency in the law enforcement effort resulting in the forfeiture, taking into account the total value of all property forfeited and the total law enforcement effort with respect to the violation of law on which the forfeiture is based; and

(B) is not so transferred to circumvent any requirement of State law that prohibits forfeiture or limits use or disposition of property forfeited to State or local agencies.

Forfeiture and destruction of schedule I or II substances

(f)(1) All controlled substances in schedule I or II that are possessed, transferred, sold, or offered for sale in violation of the provisions of this subchapter shall be deemed contraband and seized and summarily forfeited to the United States. Similarly, all substances in schedule I or II, which are seized or come into the possession of the United States, the owners of which are unknown, shall be deemed contraband and summarily forfeited to the United States.

(2) The Attorney General may direct the destruction of all controlled substances in schedule I or II seized for violation of this subchapter under such circumstances as the Attorney General may deem necessary.

Plants

(g)(1) All species of plants from which controlled substances in schedules I and II may be derived which have been planted or cultivated in violation of this subchapter, or of which the owners or cultivators are unknown, or which are wild growths, may be seized and summarily forfeited to the United States.

(2) The failure, upon demand by the Attorney General or his duly authorized agent, of the person in occupancy or in control of land or premises upon which such species of plants are growing or being stored, to produce an appropriate registration, or proof that he is the holder thereof, shall constitute authority for the seizure and forfeiture.

(3) The Attorney General, or his duly authorized agent, shall have authority to enter upon any lands, or into any dwelling pursuant to a search warrant, to cut, harvest, carry off, or destroy such plants.

Vesting of title in United States

(h) All right, title, and interest in property described in subsection (a) of this section shall vest in the United States upon commission of the act giving rise to forfeiture under this section.

Stay of civil forfeiture proceedings

(i) The filing of an indictment or information alleging a violation of this subchapter or subchapter II of this chapter, or a violation of State or local law that could have been charged under this subchapter or subchapter II of this chapter, which is also related to a civil forfeiture proceeding under this section shall, upon motion of the United States and for good cause shown, stay the civil forfeiture proceeding.

Venue

(j) In addition to the venue provided for in section 1395 of Title 28 or any other provision of law, in the case of property of a defendant charged with a violation that is the basis for forfeiture of the property under this section, a proceeding for forfeiture under this section may be brought in the judicial district in which the defendant owning such property is found or in the judicial district in which the criminal prosecution is brought.

Agreement between Attorney General and Postal Service for performance of functions

(l)[1] The functions of the Attorney General under this section shall be carried out by the Postal Service pursuant to such agreement as may be entered into between the Attorney General and the Postal Service.

(Pub. L. 91–513, Title II, § 511, Oct. 27, 1970, 84 Stat. 1276; Pub. L. 95–633, Title III, § 301(a), Nov. 10, 1978, 92 Stat. 3777; Pub. L. 96–132, § 14, Nov. 30, 1979, 93 Stat. 1048; Pub.L. 98–473, Title II, §§ 306, 309, 518, Oct. 12, 1984, 98 Stat. 2050, 2051, 2075; Pub. L. 99–570, Title I, §§ 1006(c), 1865, 1992, Oct. 27, 1986, 100 Stat. 3207–7, 3207–54, 3207–60; Pub.L. 99–646, § 74, Nov. 10, 1986, 100 Stat. 3618; Pub.L. 100–690, Titles V, VI, §§ 5105, 6059, 6074, 6075, 6077(a), (b), 6253, Nov. 18, 1988, 102 Stat. 4301, 4320, 4323–4325, 4363.)

1. So in original.

EDITORIAL NOTES

References in Text. Subchapter II of this chapter, referred to in text, was in the original "title III", meaning Title III of Pub. L. 91–513, Oct. 27, 1970, 84 Stat. 1285. Part A of Title III compromises subchapter II of this chapter. For classification of Part B, consisting of sections 1101 to 1105 of Title III, see U.S.C.A. Tables volume.

The criminal laws of the United States, referred to in subsec. (a)(4)(B), are classified generally to Title 18, U.S.C.A., Crimes and Criminal Procedure, set out Ante.

The Supplemental Rules for Certain Admiralty and Maritime Claims, referred to in subsec. (b), are set out in Title 28, U.S.C.A., Judiciary and Judicial Procedure, and Federal Rules of Civil Procedure pamphlet, 1982 ed.

The Federal Rules of Criminal Procedure, referred to in subsec. (b), are set out in Title 18, U.S.C.A.

The customs laws, referred to in subsec. (d), are classified generally to Title 19, U.S.C.A., Customs Duties.

Schedules I and II, referred to in subsecs. (f) and (g)(1), are set out in section 812(c) of this title.

Codification. "Drug Enforcement Administration" was substituted for "Bureau of Narcotics and Dangerous Drugs" in subsec. (e)(4) to conform to congressional intent manifest in amendment of section 802(4) of this title by Pub. L. 96–132, § 16(a), Nov. 30, 1979, 93 Stat. 1049, now defining term "Drug Enforcement Administration" as used in this subchapter.

Effective Date of 1988 Amendment. Amendment by section 6059 of Pub.L. 100–690 effective 120 days after Nov. 18, 1988, see section 6061 of Pub.L. 100–690, set out as a note under section 802 of this title.

Section 6077(c) of Pub.L. 100–690 provided that: "Section 551(e)(3)(B) [probably means 511(e)(3)(B)] of the Controlled Substances Act, as enacted by subsection (a) [subsec. (e)(3)(B) of this section], shall apply with respect to fiscal years beginning after September 30, 1989."

Regulations for Expedited Administrative Forfeiture Procedures. Section 6079 of Pub.L. 100–690 provided that:

"(a) In General. Not later than 90 days after the date of enactment of this Act [Nov. 18, 1988], the Attorney General and the Secretary of the Treasury shall consult, and after providing a 30–day public comment period, shall prescribe regulations for expedited administrative procedures for seizures under section 511(a)(4), (6), and (7) of the Controlled Substances Act (21 U.S.C. 881(a)(4), (6), and (7)); section 596 of the Tariff Act of 1930 (19 U.S.C. 1595a(a)); and section 2 of the Act of August 9, 1939 (53 Stat. 1291; 49 U.S.C. App. 782) for violations involving the possession of personal use quantities of a controlled substance.

"(b) Specifications. The regulations prescribed pursuant to subsection (a) shall—

"(1) minimize the adverse impact caused by prolonged detention, and

"(2) provide for a final administrative determination of the case within 21 days of seizure, or provide a procedure by which the defendant can obtain release of the property pending a final determination of the case. Such regulations shall provide that the appropriate agency official rendering a final determination shall immediately return the property if the following conditions are established:

"(A) the owner or interested party did not know of or consent to the violation;

"(B) the owner establishes a valid, good faith interest in the seized property as owner or otherwise; and

"(C)(1) the owner establishes that the owner at no time had any knowledge or reason to believe that the property in which the owner claims an interest was being or would be used in a violation of the law; and

"(2) if the owner at any time had, or should have had, knowledge or reason to believe that the property in which the owner claims an interest was being or would be used in a violation of the law, that the owner did what reasonably could be expected to prevent the violation.

An owner shall not have the seized property returned under this subsection if the owner had not acted in a normal and customary manner to ascertain how the property would be used.

"(c) Notice. At the time of seizure or upon issuance of a summons to appear under subsection (d), the officer making the seizure shall furnish to any person in possession of the conveyance a written notice specifying the procedures under this section. At the earliest practicable opportunity after determining ownership of the seized conveyance, the head of the department or agency that seizes the conveyance shall furnish a written notice to the owner and other interested parties (including lienholders) of the legal and factual basis of the seizure.

"(d) Summons in Lieu of Seizure of Commercial Fishing Industry Vessels. Not later than 90 days after the enactment of this Act [Nov. 18, 1988], the Attorney General, the Secretary of the Treasury, and the Secretary of Transportation shall prescribe joint regulations, after a public comment period of at least 30 days, providing for issuance of a summons to appear in lieu of seizure of a commercial fishing industry vessel as defined in section 2101(11a), (11b), and (11c) of title 46, United States Code, for violations involving the possession of personal use quantities of a controlled substance. These regulations shall apply when the violation is committed on a commercial fishing industry vessel that is proceeding to or from a fishing area or intermediate port of call, or is actively engaged in fishing operations. The authority provided under this section shall not affect existing authority to arrest an individual for drug-related offenses or to release that individual into the custody of the vessel's master. Upon answering a summons to appear, the procedures set forth in subsections (a), (b), and (c) of this section shall apply. The jurisdiction of the district court for any forfeiture incurred shall not be affected by the use of a summons under this section.

"(e) Personal Use Quantities of a Controlled Substance. For the purposes of this section, personal use quantities of a controlled substance shall not include sweepings or other evidence of nonpersonal use amounts."

Code of Federal Regulations

Administrative policies, practices, and procedures, see 21 CFR 1316.01 et seq.

Inspection, search, and seizure, see 19 CFR 162.0 et seq.

§ 881–1. Expedited procedures for seized conveyances

Petition for expedited decision; determination

(a)(1) The owner of a conveyance may petition the Attorney General for an expedited decision with respect to the conveyance, if the conveyance is seized for a drug-related offense and the owner has filed the requisite claim and cost bond in the manner provided in section 1608 of Title 19. The Attorney General shall make a determination on a petition under this section expeditiously, including a determination of any rights or defenses available to the petitioner. If the Attorney General does not grant or deny a petition under this section within 20 days after the date on which the petition is filed, the conveyance shall be returned to the owner pending further forfeiture proceedings.

(2) With respect to a petition under this section, the Attorney General may—

(A) deny the petition and retain possession of the conveyance;

(B) grant the petition, move to dismiss the forfeiture action, if filed, and promptly release the conveyance to the owner; or

(C) advise the petitioner that there is not adequate information available to determine the petition and promptly release the conveyance to the owner.

(3) Release of a conveyance under subsection (a)(1) or (a)(2)(C) of this section does not affect any forfeiture action with respect to the conveyance.

(4) The Attorney General shall prescribe regulations to carry out this section.

Written notice of procedures

(b) At the time of seizure, the officer making the seizure shall furnish to any person in possession of the conveyance a written notice specifying the procedures under this section. At the earliest practicable opportunity after determining ownership of the seized conveyance, the head of the department or agency that seizes the conveyance shall furnish a written notice to the owner and other interested parties (including lienholders) of the legal and factual basis of the seizure.

Complaint for forfeiture

(c) Not later than 60 days after a claim and cost bond have been filed under section 1608 of Title 19 regarding a conveyance seized for a drug-related offense, the Attorney General shall file a complaint for forfeiture in the appropriate district court, except that the court may extend the period for filing for good cause shown or on agreement of the parties. If the Attorney General does not file a complaint as specified in the preceding sentence, the court shall order the return of the conveyance to the owner and the forfeiture may not take place.

Bond for release of conveyance

(d) Any owner of a conveyance seized for a drug-related offense may obtain release of the conveyance by providing security in the form of a bond to the Attorney General in an amount equal to the value of the conveyance unless the Attorney General determines the conveyance should be retained (1) as contraband, (2) as evidence of a violation of law, or (3) because, by reason of design or other characteristic, the conveyance is particularly suited for use in illegal activities.

(Pub.L. 91–513, Title II, § 511A, as added Pub.L. 100–690, Title VI, § 6080(a), Nov. 18, 1988, 102 Stat. 4326.)

§ 881a. Production control of controlled substances

Definitions

(a) As used in this section:

(1) The term "controlled substance" has the same meaning given such term in section 801(6) of this title.

(2) The term "Secretary" means the Secretary of Agriculture.

(3) The term "State" means each of the fifty States, the District of Columbia, the Commonwealth of Puerto Rico, Guam, the Virgin Islands of the United States, American Samoa, the Commonwealth of the Northern Mariana Islands, or the Trust Territory of the Pacific Islands.

Persons ineligible for Federal agricultural program benefits

(b) Notwithstanding any other provision of law, following December 23, 1985, any person who is convicted under Federal or State law of planting, cultivation, growing, producing, harvesting, or storing a controlled substance in any crop year shall be ineligible for—

(1) as to any commodity produced during that crop year, and the four succeeding crop years, by such person—

(A) any price support or payment made available under the Agricultural Act of 1949 (7 U.S.C. 1421 et seq.), the Commodity Credit Corporation Charter Act (15 U.S.C. 714 et seq.), or any other Act;

(B) a farm storage facility loan made under section 4(h) of the Commodity Credit Corporation Charter Act (15 U.S.C. 714b(h));

(C) crop insurance under the Federal Crop Insurance Act (7 U.S.C. 1501 et seq.);

(D) a disaster payment made under the Agricultural Act of 1949 (7 U.S.C. 1421 et seq.); or

(E) a loan made, insured or guaranteed under the Consolidated Farm and Rural Development Act (7 U.S.C. 1921 et seq.) or any other provision of law administered by the Farmers Home Administration; or

(2) a payment made under section 4 or 5 of the Commodity Credit Corporation Charter Act (15 U.S.C. 714b or 714c) for the storage of an agricultural commodity that is—

(A) produced during that crop year, or any of the four succeeding crop years, by such person; and

(B) acquired by the Commodity Credit Corporation.

Regulations

(c) Not later than 180 days after December 23, 1985, the Secretary shall issue such regulations as the Secretary determines are necessary to carry out this section, including regulations that—

(1) define the term "person";

(2) govern the determination of persons who shall be ineligible for program benefits under this section; and

(3) protect the interests of tenants and sharecroppers.

(Pub.L. 99–198, Title XVII, § 1764, Dec. 23, 1985, 99 Stat. 1652.)

EDITORIAL NOTES

Codification. Section was enacted as part of the Food Security Act of 1985, and not as part of the Controlled Substances Act, which comprises this subchapter.

Code of Federal Regulations

Denial of program eligibility for controlled substance violation, see 7 CFR 796.1 et seq.

§ 882.   Injunctions
Jurisdiction

(a) The district courts of the United States and all courts exercising general jurisdiction in the territories and possessions of the United States shall have jurisdiction in proceedings in accordance with the Federal Rules of Civil Procedure to enjoin violations of this subchapter.

Jury trial

(b) In case of an alleged violation of an injunction or restraining order issued under this section, trial shall, upon demand of the accused, be by a jury in accordance with the Federal Rules of Civil Procedure.

(Pub. L. 91–513, Title II, § 512, Oct. 27, 1970, 84 Stat. 1278.)

EDITORIAL NOTES

References in Text. The Federal Rules of Civil Procedure, referred to in text, are set out in Title 28, U.S.C.A., Judiciary and Judicial Procedure, and Federal Rules of Civil Procedure pamphlet, 1982 ed.

§ 883.   Enforcement proceedings

Before any violation of this subchapter is reported by the Administrator of the Drug Enforcement Administration to any United States attorney for institution of a criminal proceeding, the Administrator may require that the person against whom such proceeding is contemplated be given appropriate notice and an opportunity to present his views, either orally or in writing, with regard to such contemplated proceeding.

(Pub. L. 91–513, Title II, § 513, Oct. 27, 1970, 84 Stat. 1278; Pub. L. 96–132, § 16(c), Nov. 30, 1979, 93 Stat. 1049.)

Code of Federal Regulations

Administrative policies, practices, and procedures, see 21 CFR 1316.01 et seq.

§ 884.   Immunity and privilege
Refusal to testify

(a) Whenever a witness refuses, on the basis of his privilege against self-incrimination, to testify or provide other information in a proceeding before a court or grand jury of the United States, involving a violation of this subchapter, and the person presiding over the proceeding communicates to the witness an order issued under this section, the witness may not refuse to comply with the order on the basis of his privilege against self-incrimination. But no testimony or other information compelled under the order issued under subsection (b) of this section or any information obtained by the exploitation of such testimony or other information, may be used against the witness in any criminal case, including any criminal case brought in a court of a State, except a prosecution for perjury, giving a false statement, or otherwise failing to comply with the order.

Order of United States district court

(b) In the case of any individual who has been or may be called to testify or provide other information at any proceeding before a court or grand jury of the United States, the United States district court for the judicial district in which the proceeding is or may be held shall issue, upon the request of the United States attorney for such district, an order requiring such individual to give any testimony or provide any other information which he refuses to give or provide on the basis of his privilege against self-incrimination.

Request by United States attorney

(c) A United States attorney may, with the approval of the Attorney General or the Deputy Attorney General, the Associate Attorney General, or any Assistant Attorney General designated by the Attorney General, request an order under subsection (b) of this section when in his judgment—

(1) the testimony or other information from such individual may be necessary to the public interest; and

(2) such individual has refused or is likely to refuse to testify or provide other information on the basis of his privilege against self-incrimination.

(Pub. L. 91–513, Title II, § 514, Oct. 27, 1970, 84 Stat. 1278; Pub.L. 100–690, Title VII, § 7020(f), Nov. 18, 1988, 102 Stat. 4396.)

§ 885. Burden of proof; liabilities

Exemptions and exceptions; presumption in simple possession offenses

(a)(1) It shall not be necessary for the United States to negative any exemption or exception set forth in this subchapter in any complaint, information, indictment, or other pleading or in any trial, hearing, or other proceeding under this subchapter, and the burden of going forward with the evidence with respect to any such exemption or exception shall be upon the person claiming its benefit.

(2) In the case of a person charged under section 844(a) of this title with the possession of a controlled substance, any label identifying such substance for purposes of section 353(b)(2) of this title shall be admissible in evidence and shall be prima facie evidence that such substance was obtained pursuant to a valid prescription from a practitioner while acting in the course of his professional practice.

Registration and order forms

(b) In the absence of proof that a person is the duly authorized holder of an appropriate registration or order form issued under this subchapter, he shall be presumed not to be the holder of such registration or form, and the burden of going forward with the evidence with respect to such registration or form shall be upon him.

Use of vehicles, vessels, and aircraft

(c) The burden of going forward with the evidence to establish that a vehicle, vessel, or aircraft used in connection with controlled substances in schedule I was used in accordance with the provisions of this subchapter shall be on the persons engaged in such use.

Immunity of Federal, State, local and other officials

(d) Except as provided in sections 2234 and 2235 of Title 18, no civil or criminal liability shall be imposed by virtue of this subchapter upon any duly authorized Federal officer lawfully engaged in the enforcement of this subchapter, or upon any duly authorized officer of any State, territory, political subdivision thereof, the District of Columbia, or any possession of the United States, who shall be lawfully engaged in the enforcement of any law or municipal ordinance relating to controlled substances.

(Pub.L. 91–513, Title II, § 515, Oct. 27, 1970, 84 Stat. 1279.)

EDITORIAL NOTES

References in Text. Schedule I, referred to in subsec. (c), is set out in section 812(c) of this title.

§ 886.   Payments and advances

Payment to informers

(a) The Attorney General is authorized to pay any person, from funds appropriated for the Drug Enforcement Administration, for information concerning a violation of this subchapter, such sum or sums of money as he may deem appropriate, without reference to any moieties or rewards to which such person may otherwise be entitled by law.

Reimbursement for purchase of controlled substances

(b) Moneys expended from appropriations of the Drug Enforcement Administration for purchase of controlled substances and subsequently recovered shall be reimbursed to the current appropriation for the Administration.

Advance of funds for enforcement purposes

(c) The Attorney General is authorized to direct the advance of funds by the Treasury Department in connection with the enforcement of this subchapter.

Drug Pollution Fund

(d)(1) There is established in the Treasury a trust fund to be known as the "Drug Pollution Fund" (hereinafter referred to in this subsection as the "Fund"), consisting of amounts appropriated or credited to such Fund under section 841(b)(6) of this title.

(2) There are hereby appropriated to the Fund amounts equivalent to the fines imposed under section 841(b)(6) of this title.

(3) Amounts in the Fund shall be available, as provided in appropriations Acts, for the purpose of making payments in accordance with paragraph (4) for the clean up of certain pollution resulting from the actions referred to in section 841(b)(6) of this title.

(4)(A) The Secretary of the Treasury, after consultation with the Attorney General, shall make payments under paragraph (3), in such amounts as the Secretary determines appropriate, to the heads of executive agencies or departments that meet the requirements of subparagraph (B).

(B) In order to receive a payment under paragraph (3), the head of an executive agency or department shall submit an application in such form and containing such information as the Secretary of the Treasury shall by regulation require. Such application shall contain a description of the fine imposed under section 841(b)(6) of this title, the circumstances surrounding the imposition of such fine, and the type and severity of pollution that resulted from the actions to which such fine applies.

(5) For purposes of subchapter B of chapter 98 of Title 26, the Fund established under this paragraph shall be treated in the same manner as a trust fund established under subchapter A of such chapter.

(Pub.L. 91–513, Title II, § 516, Oct. 27, 1970, 84 Stat. 1279; Pub.L. 96–132, § 16(b), Nov. 30, 1979, 93 Stat. 1049; Pub.L. 100–690, Title VI, § 6254(i), Nov. 18, 1988, 102 Stat. 4367.)

EDITORIAL NOTES

Codification. "Administration" was substituted for "Bureau" in subsec. (b) as the probable intent of Congress in view of amendment by Pub.L. 96–132, which substituted "Drug Enforcement Administration" for "Bureau of Narcotics and Dangerous Drugs" in subsecs. (a) and (b).

§ 887.   Coordination and consolidation of post-seizure administration

The Attorney General and the Secretary of the Treasury shall take such action as may be necessary to develop and maintain a joint plan to coordinate and consolidate post-seizure administration of property seized under this subchapter, subchapter II of this chapter, or provisions of the customs laws relating to controlled substances.

(Pub.L. 91–513, Title II, § 517, as added Pub.L. 100–690, Title VI, § 6078(a), Nov. 18, 1988, 102 Stat. 4325.)

EDITORIAL NOTES

References in Text. "This subchapter", referred to in text, was in the original "this title" which is Title II of Pub.L. 91–513, Oct. 27, 1970, 84 Stat. 1242, and is popularly known as the "Controlled Substances Act". For complete classification of Title II to the Code, see Short Title note set out under section 801 of this title and Tables volume.

"Subchapter II of this chapter", referred to in text, was in the original "title III", meaning Title III of Pub.L. 91–513, Oct. 27, 1970, 84 Stat. 1285. Part A of Title III comprises subchapter II of this chapter. For classification of Part B, consisting of sections 1101 to 1105 of Title III, see Tables volume.

PART F

GENERAL PROVISIONS

§ 901. Severability of provisions

If a provision of this chapter is held invalid, all valid provisions that are severable shall remain in effect. If a provision of this chapter is held invalid in one or more of its applications, the provision shall remain in effect in all its valid applications that are severable.

(Pub.L. 91–513, Title II, § 706, Oct. 27, 1970, 84 Stat. 1284.)

EDITORIAL NOTES

References in Text. This chapter, referred to in text, was, in the original, this Act, meaning Pub.L. 91–513, Oct. 27, 1970, 84 Stat. 1236, the Comprehensive Drug Abuse Prevention and Control Act of 1970.

§ 902. Savings provisions

Nothing in this chapter, except this part and, to the extent of any inconsistency, sections 827(e) and 829 of this title, shall be construed as in any way affecting, modifying, repealing, or superseding the provisions of the Federal Food, Drug, and Cosmetic Act.

(Pub.L. 91–513, Title II, § 707, Oct. 27, 1970, 84 Stat. 1284.)

EDITORIAL NOTES

References in Text. This chapter, referred to in text, was, in the original, this Act, meaning Pub.L. 91–513, Oct. 27, 1970, 84 Stat. 1236, the Comprehensive Drug Abuse Prevention and Control Act of 1970.

The Federal Food, Drug, and Cosmetic Act, referred to in text, is Act June 25, 1938, c. 675, 52 Stat. 1040,

which is classified generally to chapter 9 (section 301 et seq.) of Title 21, U.S.C.A., Food and Drugs.

§ 903. Application of State law

No provision of this subchapter shall be construed as indicating an intent on the part of the Congress to occupy the field in which that provision operates, including criminal penalties, to the exclusion of any State law on the same subject matter which would otherwise be within the authority of the State, unless there is a positive conflict between that provision of this subchapter and that State law so that the two cannot consistently stand together.

(Pub.L. 91–513, Title II, § 708, Oct. 27, 1970, 84 Stat. 1284.)

§ 904. Payment of tort claims

Notwithstanding section 2680(k) of Title 28, the Attorney General, in carrying out the functions of the Department of Justice under this subchapter, is authorized to pay tort claims in the manner authorized by section 2672 of Title 28, when such claims arise in a foreign country in connection with the operations of the Drug Enforcement Administration abroad.

(Pub.L. 91–513, Title II, § 709, Oct. 27, 1970, 84 Stat. 1284; Pub.L. 93–481, § 1, Oct. 26, 1974, 88 Stat. 1455; Pub.L. 95–137, § 1(a), Oct. 18, 1977, 91 Stat. 1169; Pub.L. 96–132, §§ 13, 15, Nov. 30, 1979, 93 Stat. 1048; Pub.L. 97–414, § 9(g)(1), Jan. 4, 1983, 96 Stat. 2064.)

SUBCHAPTER II

IMPORT AND EXPORT

§ 951. Definitions

(a) For purposes of this subchapter—

(1) The term "import" means, with respect to any article, any bringing in or introduction of such article into any area (whether or not such bringing in or introduction constitutes an importation within the meaning of the tariff laws of the United States).

(2) The term "customs territory of the United States" has the meaning assigned to such term by general note 2 of the Harmonized Tariff Schedule of the United States.

(b) Each term defined in section 802 of this title shall have the same meaning for purposes of this subchapter as such term has for purposes of subchapter I of this chapter.

(Pub.L. 91–513, Title III, § 1001, Oct. 27, 1970, 84 Stat. 1285; Pub.L. 100–418, Title I, § 1214(m), Aug. 23, 1988, 102 Stat. 1158.)

EDITORIAL NOTES

References in Text. This subchapter, referred to in subsec. (b), was in the original "this title" meaning Title

III of Pub.L. 91–513, Oct. 27, 1970, 84 Stat. 1285. Part A of Title III comprises this subchapter. For classification of Part B, consisting of sections 1101 to 1105 of Pub.L. 91–513, see U.S.C.A. Tables volume.

Effective Date of 1988 Amendment. Amendment by Pub.L. 100–418 effective Jan. 1, 1989, and applicable with respect to articles entered on or after such date, see section 1217(b)(1) of Pub.L. 100–418, set out as a note under section 3001 of Title 19, Customs Duties.

Short Title. Section 1000 of Pub.L. 91–513 provided that: "This title [enacting this subchapter, amending sections 198a and 162 of Title 21, U.S.C.A., Food and Drugs, and following U.S.C.A. titles: section 4251 of Title 18, Crimes and Criminal Procedure, section 1584 of Title 19, Customs Duties, sections 4901, 4905, 6808, 7012, 7103, 7326, 7607, 7609, 7641, 7651, and 7655 of Title 26, Internal Revenue Code, section 2901 of Title 28, Judiciary and Judicial Procedure, sections 529d, 529e, and 529f of Title 31, Money and Finance, section 304m of Title 40, Public Buildings, Property, and Works, section 3411 of Title 42, The Public Health and Welfare, section 239a of Title 46, Shipping, and section 787 of Title 49, Transportation, repealing sections 171 to 174, 176 to 185, 188 to 188n, 191 to 193, 197, 198, 199, and 501 to 517 of Title 21, sections 1401 to 1407, and 3616 of Title 18, sections 4701 to 4707, 4711 to 4716, 4721 to 4726, 4731 to 4736, 4741 to 4746, 4751 to 4757, 4761, 4762, 4771 to 4776, 7237, 7238, and 7491 of Title 26, sections 529a and 529g of Title 31, section 1421m of Title 48, Territories and Insular Possessions, and enacting provisions set out as notes under this section and sections 171 and 957 of this title] may be cited as the 'Controlled Substances Import and Export Act'."

§ 952. Importation of controlled substances

Controlled substances in schedules I or II and narcotic drugs in schedules III, IV, or V; exceptions

(a) It shall be unlawful to import into the customs territory of the United States from any place outside thereof (but within the United States), or to import into the United States from any place outside thereof, any controlled substance in schedule I or II of subchapter I of this chapter, or any narcotic drug in schedule III, IV, or V of subchapter I of this chapter, except that—

    (1) such amounts of crude opium, poppy straw, concentrate of poppy straw, and coca leaves as the Attorney General finds to be necessary to provide for medical, scientific, or other legitimate purposes, and

    (2) such amounts of any controlled substance in schedule I or II or any narcotic drug in schedule III, IV, or V that the Attorney Gener-

al finds to be necessary to provide for the medical, scientific, or other legitimate needs of the United States—

    (A) during an emergency in which domestic supplies of such substance or drug are found by the Attorney General to be inadequate,

    (B) in any case in which the Attorney General finds that competition among domestic manufacturers of the controlled substance is inadequate and will not be rendered adequate by the registration of additional manufacturers under section 823 of this title, or

    (C) in any case in which the Attorney General finds that such controlled substance is in limited quantities exclusively for scientific, analytical, or research uses,

may be so imported under such regulations as the Attorney General shall prescribe. No crude opium may be so imported for the purpose of manufacturing heroin or smoking opium.

Nonnarcotic controlled substances in schedules III, IV, or V

(b) It shall be unlawful to import into the customs territory of the United States from any place outside thereof (but within the United States), or to import into the United States from any place outside thereof, any nonnarcotic controlled substance in schedule III, IV, or V, unless such nonnarcotic controlled substance—

    (1) is imported for medical, scientific, or other legitimate uses, and

    (2) is imported pursuant to such notification, or declaration, or in the case of any nonnarcotic controlled substance in schedule III, such import permit, notification, or declaration, as the Attorney General may by regulation prescribe, except that if a nonnarcotic controlled substance in schedule IV or V is also listed in schedule I or II of the Convention on Psychotropic Substances it shall be imported pursuant to such import permit requirements, prescribed by regulation of the Attorney General, as are required by the Convention.

Coca leaves

(c) In addition to the amount of coca leaves authorized to be imported into the United States under subsection (a) of this section, the Attorney General may permit the importation of additional amounts of coca leaves. All cocaine and ecgonine (and all salts, derivatives, and preparations from which cocaine or ecgonine may be synthesized or made) contained in such additional amounts of coca leaves imported under this subsection shall be destroyed under the supervision of an authorized representative of the Attorney General.

(Pub.L. 91–513, Title III, § 1002, Oct. 27, 1970, 84 Stat. 1285; Pub.L. 95–633, Title I, § 105, Nov. 10, 1978, 92 Stat. 3772; Pub.L. 98–473, Title II, §§ 519–521, Oct. 12, 1984, 98 Stat. 2075.)

Editorial Notes

References in Text. Schedules I, II, III, IV, and V of subchapter I of this chapter, referred to in subsecs. (a) and (b), are set out in section 812(c) of this title.

Code of Federal Regulations

Importation, search and seizure, see 19 CFR 162.0 et seq.

Policies and procedures, see 21 CFR 1312.01 et seq.

§ 953. Exportation of controlled substances

Narcotic drugs in schedules I, II, III, or IV

(a) It shall be unlawful to export from the United States any narcotic drug in schedule I, II, III, or IV unless—

(1) it is exported to a country which is a party to—

(A) the International Opium Convention of 1912 for the Suppression of the Abuses of Opium, Morphine, Cocaine, and Derivative Drugs, or to the International Opium Convention signed at Geneva on February 19, 1925; or

(B) the Convention for Limiting the Manufacture and Regulating the Distribution of Narcotic Drugs concluded at Geneva, July 13, 1931, as amended by the protocol signed at Lake Success on December 11, 1946, and the protocol bringing under international control drugs outside the scope of the convention of July 13, 1931, for limiting the manufacture and regulating the distribution of narcotic drugs (as amended by the protocol signed at Lake Success on December 11, 1946), signed at Paris, November 19, 1948; or

(C) the Single Convention on Narcotic Drugs, 1961, signed at New York, March 30, 1961;

(2) such country has instituted and maintains, in conformity with the conventions to which it is a party, a system for the control of imports of narcotic drugs which the Attorney General deems adequate;

(3) the narcotic drug is consigned to a holder of such permits or licenses as may be required under the laws of the country of import, and a permit or license to import such drug has been issued by the country of import;

(4) substantial evidence is furnished to the Attorney General by the exporter that (A) the narcotic drug is to be applied exclusively to medical or scientific uses within the country of import, and (B) there is an actual need for the narcotic drug for medical or scientific uses within such country; and

(5) a permit to export the narcotic drug in each instance has been issued by the Attorney General.

Exception for exportation for special scientific purposes

(b) Notwithstanding subsection (a) of this section, the Attorney General may authorize any narcotic drug (including crude opium and coca leaves) in schedule I, II, III, or IV to be exported from the United States to a country which is a party to any of the international instruments mentioned in subsection (a) of this section if the particular drug is to be applied to a special scientific purpose in the country of destination and the authorities of such country will permit the importation of the particular drug for such purpose.

Nonnarcotic controlled substances in schedule I or II

(c) It shall be unlawful to export from the United States any nonnarcotic controlled substance in schedule I or II unless—

(1) it is exported to a country which has instituted and maintains a system which the Attorney General deems adequate for the control of imports of such substances;

(2) the controlled substance is consigned to a holder of such permits or licenses as may be required under the laws of the country of import;

(3) substantial evidence is furnished to the Attorney General that (A) the controlled substance is to be applied exclusively to medical, scientific, or other legitimate uses within the

country to which exported, (B) it will not be exported from such country, and (C) there is an actual need for the controlled substance for medical, scientific, or other legitimate uses within the country; and

(4) a permit to export the controlled substance in each instance has been issued by the Attorney General.

Exception for exportation for special scientific purposes

(d) Notwithstanding subsection (c) of this section, the Attorney General may authorize any nonnarcotic controlled substance in schedule I or II to be exported from the United States if the particular substance is to be applied to a special scientific purpose in the country of destination and the authorities of such country will permit the importation of the particular drug for such purpose.

Nonnarcotic controlled substances in schedule III or IV; controlled substances in schedule V

(e) It shall be unlawful to export from the United States to any other country any nonnarcotic controlled substance in schedule III or IV or any controlled substances in schedule V unless—

(1) there is furnished (before export) to the Attorney General documentary proof that importation is not contrary to the laws or regulations of the country of destination for consumption for medical, scientific, or other legitimate purposes;

(2) it is exported pursuant to such notification or declaration, or in the case of any nonnarcotic controlled substance in schedule III, such export permit, notification, or declaration as the Attorney General may by regulation prescribe; and

(3) in the case of a nonnarcotic controlled substance in schedule IV or V which is also listed in schedule I or II of the Convention on Psychotropic Substances, it is exported pursuant to such export permit requirements, prescribed by regulation of the Attorney General, as are required by the Convention.

(Pub.L. 91–513, Title III, § 1003, Oct. 27, 1970, 84 Stat. 1286; Pub.L. 95–633, Title I, § 106, Nov. 10, 1978, 92 Stat. 3772; Pub.L. 98–473, Title II, § 522, Oct. 12, 1984, 98 Stat. 2076.)

EDITORIAL NOTES

References in Text. Schedules I, II, III, IV, and V, referred to in text, are set out in section 812(c) of this title.

Code of Federal Regulations

Policies and procedures, see 21 CFR 1312.01 et seq.

Search and seizure, see 19 CFR 162.0 et seq.

§ 954. Transshipment and in-transit shipment of controlled substances

Notwithstanding sections 952, 953, and 957 of this title—

(1) A controlled substance in schedule I may—

(A) be imported into the United States for transshipment to another country, or

(B) be transferred or transshipped from one vessel, vehicle, or aircraft to another vessel, vehicle, or aircraft within the United States for immediate exportation,

if and only if it is so imported, transferred, or transshipped (i) for scientific, medical, or other legitimate purposes in the country of destination, and (ii) with the prior written approval of the Attorney General (which shall be granted or denied within 21 days of the request).

(2) A controlled substance in schedule II, III, or IV may be so imported, transferred, or transshipped if and only if advance notice is given to the Attorney General in accordance with regulations of the Attorney General.

(Pub.L. 91–513, Title III, § 1004, Oct. 27, 1970, 84 Stat. 1287.)

EDITORIAL NOTES

References in Text. Schedules I, II, III, and IV, referred to in text, are set out in section 812(c) of this title.

Code of Federal Regulations

Policies and procedures, see 21 CFR 1312.01 et seq.

§ 955. Possession on board vessels, etc., arriving in or departing from United States

It shall be unlawful for any person to bring or possess on board any vessel or aircraft, or on board any vehicle of a carrier, arriving in or departing from the United States or the customs territory of the United States, a controlled substance in schedule I or II or a narcotic drug in schedule III or IV, unless such substance or drug is a part of the cargo entered in the manifest or part of the official supplies of the vessel, aircraft, or vehicle.

(Pub.L. 91–513, Title III, § 1005, Oct. 27, 1970, 84 Stat. 1287.)

EDITORIAL NOTES

References in Text. Schedules I, II, III, and IV, referred to in text, are set out in section 812(c) of this title.

§ 955a. Transferred

EDITORIAL NOTES

Codification. Section, Pub. L. 96–350, § 1, Sept. 15, 1980, 94 Stat. 1159; Pub. L. 99–570, Title III, § 3202, Oct. 27, 1986, 100 Stat. 3207–95; Pub. L. 99–640, § 17, Nov. 10, 1986, 100 Stat. 3552, which provided that sections 955a to 955d of this title be cited as the "Maritime Drug Law Enforcement Act", was transferred to section 1901 of Title 46, Shipping.

§ 955b. Transferred

EDITORIAL NOTES

Codification. Section, Pub. L. 96–350, § 2, Sept. 15, 1980, 94 Stat. 1160; Pub. L. 99–307, § 7, May 19, 1986, 100 Stat. 447; Pub. L. 99–570, Title III, § 3202, Oct. 27, 1986, 100 Stat. 3207–95; Pub. L. 99–640, § 17, Nov. 10, 1986, 100 Stat. 3552, which related to Congressional statement of findings on drug trafficking aboard vessels, was transferred to section 1902 of Title 46, Shipping.

§ 955c. Transferred

EDITORIAL NOTES

Codification. Section, Pub. L. 96–350, § 3, Sept. 15, 1980, 94 Stat. 1160; Pub. L. 99–570, Title III, § 3202, Oct. 27, 1986, 100 Stat. 3207–95; Pub. L. 99–640, § 17, Nov. 10, 1986, 100 Stat. 3552, which related to unlawful acts and definitions, was transferred to section 1903 of Title 46, Shipping.

§ 955d. Repealed. Pub. L. 99–570, Title III, § 3202, Oct. 27, 1986, 100 Stat. 3207–97

EDITORIAL NOTES

Section, Pub. L. 96–350, § 4, Sept. 15, 1980, 94 Stat. 1160, related to seizures or forfeitures of property. See section 1904 of Appendix to Title 46, Shipping.

§ 956. Exemption authority
Individual possessing controlled substance

(a) The Attorney General may by regulation exempt from sections 952(a) and (b), 953, 954, and 955 of this title any individual who has a controlled substance (except a substance in schedule I) in his possession for his personal medical use, or for administration to an animal accompanying him, if he lawfully obtained such substance and he makes such declaration (or gives such other notification) as the Attorney General may by regulation require.

Compound, mixture, or preparation

(b) The Attorney General may by regulation except any compound, mixture, or preparation containing any depressant or stimulant substance listed in paragraph (a) or (b) of schedule III or in schedule IV or V from the application of all or any part of this subchapter if (1) the compound, mixture, or preparation contains one or more active medicinal ingredients not having a depressant or stimulant effect on the central nervous system, and (2) such ingredients are included therein in such combinations, quantity, proportion, or concentration as to vitiate the potential for abuse of the substances which do have a depressant or stimulant effect on the central nervous system.

(Pub. L. 91–513, Title III, § 1006, Oct. 27, 1970, 84 Stat. 1288.)

EDITORIAL NOTES

References in Text. Schedules I, III, IV, and V, referred to in text, are set out in section 812(c) of this title.

Code of Federal Regulations

Inspection, search and seizure, see 19 CFR 162.0 et seq.

Registration requirements, see 21 CFR 1311.01 et seq.

§ 957. Persons required to register
Coverage

(a) No person may—

(1) import into the customs territory of the United States from any place outside thereof (but within the United States), or import into the United States from any place outside thereof, any controlled substance, or

(2) export from the United States any controlled substance in schedule I, II, III, IV, or V,

unless there is in effect with respect to such person a registration issued by the Attorney General under section 958 of this title, or unless such person is exempt from registration under subsection (b) of this section.

Exemptions

(b)(1) The following persons shall not be required to register under the provisions of this section and may lawfully possess a controlled substance:

(A) An agent or an employee of any importer or exporter registered under section 958 of this title if such agent or employee is acting in the usual course of his business or employment.

(B) A common or contract carrier or warehouseman, or an employee thereof, whose possession of any controlled substance is in the usual course of his business or employment.

(C) An ultimate user who possesses such substance for a purpose specified in section 802(25) of this title and in conformity with an exemption granted under section 956(a) of this title.

(2) The Attorney General may, by regulation, waive the requirement for registration of certain importers and exporters if he finds it consistent with the public health and safety; and may authorize any such importer or exporter to possess controlled substances for purposes of importation and exportation.

(Pub. L. 91–513, Title III, § 1007, Oct. 27, 1970, 84 Stat. 1288; Pub.L. 98–473, Title II, § 523, Oct. 12, 1984, 98 Stat. 2076.)

EDITORIAL NOTES

References in Text. Schedules I, II, III, and IV, referred to in subsec. (a)(2), are set out in section 812(c) of this title.

Code of Federal Regulations

Importation, search and seizure, see 19 CFR 162.0 et seq.

Registration requirements, see 21 CFR 1311.01 et seq.

§ 958. Registration requirements

Applicants to import or export controlled substances in schedule I or II

(a) The Attorney General shall register an applicant to import or export a controlled substance in schedule I or II if he determines that such registration is consistent with the public interest and with United States obligations under international treaties, conventions, or protocols in effect on May 1, 1971. In determining the public interest, the factors enumerated in paragraph (1) through (6) of section 823(a) of this title shall be considered.

Activity limited to specified substances

(b) Registration granted under this section shall not entitle a registrant to import or export controlled substances other than specified in the registration.

Applicants to import controlled substances in schedule III, IV, or V or to export controlled substances in schedule III or IV

(c) The Attorney General shall register an applicant to import a controlled substance in schedule III, IV, or V or to export a controlled substance in schedule III or IV, unless he determines that the issuance of such registration is inconsistent with the public interest. In determining the public interest, the factors enumerated in paragraphs (1) through (6) of section 823(d) of this title shall be considered.

Denial of application

(d)(1) The Attorney General may deny an application for registration under subsection (a) of this section if he is unable to determine that such registration is consistent with the public interest (as defined in subsection (a) of this section) and with the United States obligations under international treaties, conventions, or protocols in effect on May 1, 1971.

(2) The Attorney General may deny an application for registration under subsection (c) of this section, or revoke or suspend a registration under subsection (a) or (c) of this section, if he determines that such registration is inconsistent with the public interest (as defined in subsection (a) or (c) of this section) or with the United States obligations under international treaties, conventions, or protocols in effect on May 1, 1971.

(3) The Attorney General may limit the revocation or suspension of a registration to the particular controlled substance, or substances, with respect to which grounds for revocation or suspension exist.

(4) Before taking action pursuant to this subsection, the Attorney General shall serve upon the applicant or registrant an order to show cause as to why the registration should not be denied, revoked, or suspended. The order to show cause

shall contain a statement of the basis thereof and shall call upon the applicant or registrant to appear before the Attorney General, or his designee, at a time and place stated in the order, but in no event less than thirty days after the date of receipt of the order. Proceedings to deny, revoke, or suspend shall be conducted pursuant to this subsection in accordance with subchapter II of chapter 5 of Title 5. Such proceedings shall be independent of, and not in lieu of, criminal prosecutions or other proceedings under this subchapter or any other law of the United States.

(5) The Attorney General may, in his discretion, suspend any registration simultaneously with the institution of proceedings under this subsection, in cases where he finds that there is an imminent danger to the public health and safety. Such suspension shall continue in effect until the conclusion of such proceedings, including judicial review thereof, unless sooner withdrawn by the Attorney General or dissolved by a court of competent jurisdiction.

(6) In the event that the Attorney General suspends or revokes a registration granted under this section, all controlled substances owned or possessed by the registrant pursuant to such registration at the time of suspension or the effective date of the revocation order, as the case may be, may, in the discretion of the Attorney General, be seized or placed under seal. No disposition may be made of any controlled substances under seal until the time for taking an appeal has elapsed or until all appeals have been concluded, except that a court, upon application therefor, may at any time order the sale of perishable controlled substances. Any such order shall require the deposit of the proceeds of the sale with the court. Upon a revocation order becoming final, all such controlled substances (or proceeds of the sale thereof which have been deposited with the court) shall be forfeited to the United States; and the Attorney General shall dispose of such controlled substances in accordance with section 881(e) of this title.

Registration period

(e) No registration shall be issued under this subchapter for a period in excess of one year. Unless the regulations of the Attorney General otherwise provide, sections 822(f), 825, and 827 of this title shall apply to persons registered under this section to the same extent such sections apply to persons registered under section 823 of this title.

Rules and regulations

(f) The Attorney General is authorized to promulgate rules and regulations and to charge reasonable fees relating to the registration of importers and exporters of controlled substances under this section.

Scope of authorized activity

(g) Persons registered by the Attorney General under this section to import or export controlled substances may import or export (and, for the purpose of so importing or exporting, may possess) such substances to the extent authorized by their registration and in conformity with the other provisions of this subchapter and subchapter I of this chapter.

Separate registrations for each principal place of business

(h) A separate registration shall be required at each principal place of business where the applicant imports or exports controlled substances.

Emergency situations

(i) Except in emergency situations as described in section 952(a)(2)(A) of this title, prior to issuing a registration under this section to a bulk manufacturer of a controlled substance in schedule I or II, and prior to issuing a regulation under section 952(a) of this title authorizing the importation of such a substance, the Attorney General shall give manufacturers holding registrations for the bulk manufacture of the substance an opportunity for a hearing.

(Pub. L. 91–513, Title III, § 1008, Oct. 27, 1970, 84 Stat. 1289; Pub. L. 98–473, Title II, §§ 524, 525, Oct. 12, 1984, 98 Stat. 2076; Pub. L. 99–570, Title I, § 1866(d), Oct. 27, 1986, 100 Stat. 3207–55.)

EDITORIAL NOTES

References in Text. Schedules I, II, III, IV, and V, referred to in subsecs. (a), (b), (c), and (h), are set out in section 812(c) of this title.

This subchapter, referred to in subsec. (f), was in the original "this title" meaning Title III of Pub. L. 91–513, Oct. 27, 1970, 84 Stat. 1285. Part A of Title III comprises this subchapter. For classification of Part B, consisting of sections 1101 to 1105 of Title III, see U.S.C.A. Tables volume.

Code of Federal Regulations

Administrative policies, practices, and procedures, see 21 CFR 1316.01 et seq.

Labeling and packaging requirements, see 21 CFR 1302.01 et seq.

Recordkeeping and reporting requirements, see 21 CFR 1304.01 et seq.

Registration requirements, see 21 CFR 1311.01 et seq.

§ 959.   Possession, manufacture, or distribution for purposes of unlawful importation

Prohibition on controlled substance in schedule I or II

(a) It shall be unlawful for any person to manufacture or distribute a controlled substance in schedule I or II—

(1) intending that such substance will be unlawfully imported into the United States or into waters within a distance of 12 miles of the coast of the United States; or

(2) knowing that such substance will be unlawfully imported into the United States or into waters within a distance of 12 miles of the coast of the United States.

United States citizen on board any aircraft or any person on board United States owned or registered aircraft

(b) It shall be unlawful for any United States citizen on board any aircraft, or any person on board an aircraft owned by a United States citizen or registered in the United States, to—

(1) manufacture or distribute a controlled substance; or

(2) possess a controlled substance with intent to distribute.

Acts committed outside territorial jurisdiction of United States

(c) This section is intended to reach acts of manufacture or distribution committed outside the territorial jurisdiction of the United States. Any person who violates this section shall be tried in the United States district court at the point of entry where such person enters the United States, or in the United States District Court for the District of Columbia.

(Pub. L. 91–513, Title III, § 1009, Oct. 27, 1970, 84 Stat. 1289; Pub. L. 99–570, Title III, § 3161(a), Oct. 27, 1986, 100 Stat. 3207–94.)

EDITORIAL NOTES

References in Text. Schedules I and II, referred to in text, are set out in section 812(c) of this title.

§ 960.   Prohibited acts A

Unlawful acts

(a) Any person who—

(1) contrary to section 952, 953, or 957 of this title, knowingly or intentionally imports or exports a controlled substance,

(2) contrary to section 955 of this title, knowingly or intentionally brings or possesses on board a vessel, aircraft, or vehicle a controlled substance, or

(3) contrary to section 959 of this title, manufactures, possesses with intent to distribute, or distributes a controlled substance

shall be punished as provided in subsection (b) of this section.

Penalties

(b)(1) In the case of a violation of subsection (a) of this section involving—

(A) 1 kilogram or more of a mixture or substance containing a detectable amount of heroin;

(B) 5 kilograms or more of a mixture or substance containing a detectable amount of—

(i) coca leaves, except coca leaves and extracts of coca leaves from which cocaine, ecgonine, and derivatives of ecgonine or their salts have been removed;

(ii) cocaine, its salts, optical and geometric isomers, and salts or isomers;

(iii) ecgonine, its derivatives, their salts, isomers, and salts of isomers; or

(iv) any compound, mixture, or preparation which contains any quantity of any of the substances referred to in clauses (i) through (iii);

(C) 50 grams or more of a mixture or substance described in subparagraph (B) which contains cocaine base;

(D) 100 grams or more of phencyclidine (PCP) or 1 kilogram or more of a mixture or substance containing a detectable amount of phencyclidine (PCP);

(E) 10 grams or more of a mixture or substance containing a detectable amount of lysergic acid diethylamide (LSD);

(F) 400 grams or more of a mixture or substance containing a detectable amount of N-phenyl-N-[1-(2-phenylethyl)-4-piperidinyl] propanamide or 100 grams or more of a mixture or substance containing a detectable amount of any analogue of N-phenyl-N-[1-(2-phenylethyl)-4-piperidinyl] propanamide; or

(G) 1000 kilograms or more of a mixture or substance containing a detectable amount of marihuana;

the person committing such violation shall be sentenced to a term of imprisonment of not less than 10 years and not more than life and if death or serious bodily injury results from the use of such substance shall be sentenced to a term of imprisonment of not less than 20 years and not more than life, a fine not to exceed the greater of that authorized in accordance with the provisions of Title 18, or $4,000,000 if the defendant is an individual or $10,000,000 if the defendant is other than an individual, or both. If any person commits such a violation after one or more prior convictions for an offense punishable under this subsection, or for a felony under any other provision of this subchapter or subchapter I of this chapter or other law of a State, the United States, or a foreign country relating to narcotic drugs, marihuana, or depressant or stimulant substances, have become final, such person shall be sentenced to a term of imprisonment of not less than 20 years and not more than life imprisonment and if death or serious bodily injury results from the use of such substance shall be sentenced to life imprisonment, a fine not to exceed the greater of twice that authorized in accordance with the provisions of Title 18, or $8,000,000 if the defendant is an individual or $20,000,000 if the defendant is other than an individual, or both. Any sentence under this paragraph shall, in the absence of such a prior conviction, impose a term of supervised release of at least 5 years in addition to such term of imprisonment and shall, if there was such a prior conviction, impose a term of supervised release of at least 10 years in addition to such term of imprisonment. Notwithstanding any other provision of law, the court shall not place on probation or suspend the sentence of any person sentenced under this paragraph. No person sentenced under this paragraph shall be eligible for parole during the term of imprisonment imposed therein.

(2) In the case of a violation of subsection (a) of this section involving—

(A) 100 grams or more of a mixture or substance containing a detectable amount of heroin;

(B) 500 grams or more of a mixture or substance containing a detectable amount of—

(i) coca leaves, except coca leaves and extracts of coca leaves from which cocaine, ecgonine, and derivatives of ecgonine or their salts have been removed;

(ii) cocaine, its salts, optical and geometric isomers, and salts or isomers;

(iii) ecgonine, its derivatives, their salts, isomers, and salts of isomers; or

(iv) any compound, mixture, or preparation which contains any quantity of any of the substances referred to in clauses (i) through (iii);

(C) 5 grams or more of a mixture or substance described in subparagraph (B) which contains cocaine base;

(D) 10 grams or more of phencyclidine (PCP) or 100 grams or more of a mixture or substance containing a detectable amount of phencyclidine (PCP);

(E) 1 gram or more of a mixture or substance containing a detectable amount of lysergic acid diethylamide (LSD);

(F) 40 grams or more of a mixture or substance containing a detectable amount of N-phenyl-N-[1-(2-phenylethyl)-4-piperidinyl] propanamide or 10 grams or more of a mixture or substance containing a detectable amount of any analogue of N-phenyl-N-[1-(2-phenylethyl)-4-piperidinyl] propanamide; or

(G) 100 kilograms or more of a mixture or substance containing a detectable amount of marihuana;

the person committing such violation shall be sentenced to a term of imprisonment of not less than 5 years and not more than 40 years and if death or serious bodily injury results from the use of such substance shall be sentenced to a term of imprisonment of not less than twenty years and not more than life, a fine not to exceed the greater of that authorized in accordance with the provisions of Title 18, or $2,000,000 if the defendant is an individual or $5,000,000 if the defendant is other than an individual, or both. If any person commits such a violation after one or more prior convictions for an offense punishable under this subsection, or for a felony under any other provision of this subchapter or subchapter I of this chapter or other law of a State, the United States, or a foreign country relating to narcotic drugs, marihuana, or depressant or stimulant substances, have become final, such person shall be sentenced to a term of imprisonment of not less than 10 years and not more than life imprisonment and if death or serious bodily injury results from the use of such substance shall be sentenced to life imprisonment, a fine not to exceed the greater of twice that authorized in accordance with the provisions of Title 18, or $4,000,000 if the defendant is an individual or $10,000,000 if the defendant is other than an individual, or both. Any sentence imposed under this paragraph shall, in the absence of such a prior conviction, include a term of suspervised [1] release of at least 4 years in addition to such term of imprisonment and shall, if there was such a prior conviction, include a term of suspervised [1] release of at least 8 years in addition to such term of imprisonment. Notwithstanding any other provision of law, the court shall not place on probation or suspend the sentence of any person sentenced under this paragraph. No person sentenced under this paragraph shall be eligible for parole during the term of imprisonment imposed therein.

(3) In the case of a violation under subsection (a) of this section involving a controlled substance in schedule I or II, the person committing such violation shall, except as provided in paragraphs (1), (2), and (4), be sentenced to a term of imprisonment of not more than 20 years and if death or serious bodily injury results from the use of such substance shall be sentenced to a term of imprisonment of not less than twenty years and not more than life, a fine not to exceed the greater of that authorized in accordance with the provisions of Title 18, or $1,000,000 if the defendant is an individual or $5,000,000 if the defendant is other than an individual, or both. If any person commits such a violation after one or more prior convictions for an offense punishable under this subsection, or for a felony under any other provision of this subchapter or subchapter I of this chapter or other law of a State, the United States or a foreign country relating to narcotic drugs, marihuana, or depressant or stimulant sub-

stances, have become final, such person shall be sentenced to a term of imprisonment of not more than 30 years and if death or serious bodily injury results from the use of such substance shall be sentenced to life imprisonment, a fine not to exceed the greater of twice that authorized in accordance with the provisions of Title 18, or $2,000,000 if the defendant is an individual or $10,000,000 if the defendant is other than an individual, or both. Any sentence imposing a term of imprisonment under this paragraph shall, in the absence of such a prior conviction, impose a term of supervised release of at least 3 years in addition to such term of imprisonment and shall, if there was such a prior conviction, impose a term of supervised release of at least 6 years in addition to such term of imprisonment. Notwithstanding the prior sentence, and notwithstanding any other provision of law, the court shall not place on probation or suspend the sentence of any person sentenced under the provisions of this paragraph which provide for a mandatory term of imprisonment if death or serious bodily injury results, nor shall a person so sentenced be eligible for parole during the term of such a sentence.

(4) In the case of a violation under subsection (a) of this section with respect to less than 50 kilograms of marihuana, except in the case of 100 or more marihuana plants regardless of weight, less than 10 kilograms of hashish, less than one kilogram of hashish oil, or any quantity of a controlled substance in schedule III, IV, or V, the person committing such violation shall be imprisoned not more than five years, or be fined not to exceed the greater of that authorized in accordance with the provisions of Title 18, or $250,000 if the defendant is an individual or $1,000,000 if the defendant is other than an individual, or both. If a sentence under this paragraph provides for imprisonment, the sentence shall, in addition to such term of imprisonment, include (A) a term of supervised release of not less than two years if such controlled substance is in schedule I, II, III, or (B) a term of supervised release of not less than one year if such controlled substance is in schedule IV.

(c) **Repealed. Pub.L. 98–473, Title I, § 225, Oct. 12, 1984, 98 Stat. 2030.**

Penalty for importation or exportation

(d) Any person who knowingly or intentionally—

(1) imports or exports a listed chemical with intent to manufacture a controlled substance in violation of this subchapter or, in the case of an exportation, in violation of the law of the country to which the chemical is exported; or

(2) imports or exports a listed chemical knowing, or having reasonable cause to believe, that the listed chemical will be used to manufacture a controlled substance in violation of this subchapter or, in the case of an exportation, in violation of the law of the country to which the chemical is exported;

shall be fined in accordance with Title 18, or imprisoned not more than 10 years, or both.

(Pub. L. 91–513, Title III, § 1010, Oct. 27, 1970, 84 Stat. 1290; Pub.L. 98–473, Title II, § 225, formerly § 225(a), 504, Oct. 12, 1984, 98 Stat. 2030, 2070; Pub.L. 98–473, § 225 as amended Pub.L. 99–570, Title I, § 1005(c), Oct. 27, 1986, 100 Stat. 3207–6; Pub.L. 99–570, Title I, §§ 1004, 1302, 1866(e), Oct. 27, 1986, 100 Stat. 3207–6, 3207–15, 3207–55; Pub.L. 100–690, Title VI, §§ 6053(c), 6475, Nov. 18, 1988, 102 Stat. 4315, 4380.)

1. So in original.

Subsec. (c) of this Section Applicable to Offenses Committed Prior to Nov. 1, 1987

Subsec. (c) of this section as in effect prior to repeal by Pub.L. 98–473, § 225, read as follows:

Special parole term

(c) A special parole term imposed under this section or section 962 of this title may be revoked if its terms and conditions are violated. In such circumstances the original term of imprisonment shall be increased by the period of the special parole term and the resulting new term of imprisonment shall not be diminished by the time which was spent on special parole. A person whose special parole term has been revoked may be required to serve all or part of the remainder of the new term of imprisonment. The special term provided for in this section and in section 962 of this title is in addition to, and not in lieu of, any other parole provided for by law.

[See Codification note below.]

For applicability of sentencing provisions to offenses, see Effective Date and Savings Provisions, etc., note, section 235 of Pub.L. 98–473, as amended, set out under section 3551 of Title 18, Crimes and Criminal Procedure.

EDITORIAL NOTES

References in Text. Schedules I, II, III, and IV, referred to in subsec. (b), are set out in section 812(c) of this title.

"This subchapter" referred to in text, was in the original "this title" meaning Title III of Pub.L. 91–513, Oct. 27, 1970, 84 Stat. 1285. Part A of Title III comprises this subchapter. For classification of Part B, consisting of sections 1101 to 1105 of Pub.L. 91–513, see Tables volume.

Codification. The directory language of section 1005(c) of Pub.L. 99–570 provided for the amendment of section "1515 of the Controlled Substances Import and Export Act (21 U.S.C. 960)", which amendment has been executed to section 1010 of such Act (21 U.S.C.A. § 960) as the probable intent of Congress.

Amendment of subsec. (b)(3) [now (b)(4)] by section 1866(e) of Pub. L. 99–570, directing the striking out of "except as provided in paragraph (4)" has previously been executed by section 1302(a), (b)(1) of Pub.L. 99–570 which redesignated par. (3) as (4) and struck out the above quoted phrase.

The amendment to subsec. (c) by Pub.L. 99–570, § 1004(a), directing the substitution of "term of supervised release" for "special parole term" wherever appearing has not been executed to such subsec. (c) in view of repeal by Pub.L. 98–473, § 225, eff. Nov. 1, 1987.

Repeals. Section 225(a)(1) to (3) of Pub.L. 98–473, cited to credit, was amended by section 1005(c) of Pub.L. 99–570 to repeal pars. (1) and (2) and renumber par. (3) as section 225(a) of Pub.L. 98–473. Such provisions of section 225(a) of Pub.L. 98–473, which were to take effect Nov. 1, 1987, as a result of repeal were never executed to text of section.

Effective Date of 1988 Amendment. Amendment of section by section 6053(c) of Pub.L. 100–690 effective 120 days after Nov. 18, 1988, see section 6061 of Pub.L. 100–690, set out as a note under section 802 of this title.

Effective Date of 1986 Amendment. Amendment by section 1004(a) of Pub.L. 99–570 to take effect on the date of the taking of effect of section 3583 of Title 18, Crimes and Criminal Procedure, Nov. 1, 1987, see section 1004(b) of Pub.L. 99–570, set out as a note under section 841 of this title.

Effective Date and Savings Provisions of 1984 Amendment. Amendment by Pub.L. 98–473, § 225, effective on the first day of first calendar month beginning thirty six months after Oct. 12, 1984, applicable only to offenses committed after taking effect of sections 211 to 239 of Pub.L 98–473, and except as otherwise provided for therein, see section 235 of Pub.L. 98–473, as amended, set out as a note under section 3551 of Title 18, Crimes and Criminal Procedure.

§ 961.   Prohibited acts B

Any person who violates section 954 of this title or fails to notify the Attorney General of an importation or exportation under section 972 of this title shall be subject to the following penalties:

(1) Except as provided in paragraph (2), any such person shall, with respect to any such violation, be subject to a civil penalty of not more than $25,000. Sections 842(c)(1) and (c)(3) of this title shall apply to any civil penalty assessed under this paragraph.

(2) If such a violation is prosecuted by an information or indictment which alleges that the violation was committed knowingly or intentionally and the trier of fact specifically finds that the violation was so committed, such person shall be sentenced to imprisonment for not more than one year or a fine of not more than $25,000 or both.

(Pub. L. 91–513, Title III, § 1011, Oct. 27, 1970, 84 Stat. 1290; Pub.L. 100–690, Title VI, § 6053(d), Nov. 18, 1988, 102 Stat. 4316.)

EDITORIAL NOTES

Effective Date of 1988 Amendment. Amendment by section 6053(d) of Pub.L. 100–690 effective 120 days after Nov. 18, 1988, see section 6061 of Pub.L. 100–690, set out as a note under section 802 of this title.

§ 962.   Second or subsequent offenses

Term of imprisonment and fine

(a) Any person convicted of any offense under this subchapter is, if the offense is a second or subsequent offense, punishable by a term of imprisonment twice that otherwise authorized, by twice the fine otherwise authorized, or by both. If the conviction is for an offense punishable under section 960(b) of this title, and if it is the offender's second or subsequent offense, the court shall impose, in addition to any term of imprisonment and fine, twice the term of supervised release otherwise authorized.

Determination of status

(b) For purposes of this section, a person shall be considered convicted of a second or subsequent offense if, prior to the commission of such offense, one or more prior convictions of him for a felony under any provision of this subchapter or subchapter I of this chapter or other law of a State, the United States, or a foreign country relating to narcotic drugs, marihuana, or depressant or stimulant drugs, have become final.

Procedures applicable

(c) Section 851 of this title shall apply with respect to any proceeding to sentence a person under this section.

(Pub. L. 91–513, Title III, § 1012, Oct. 27, 1970, 84 Stat. 1290; Pub.L. 98–473, Title II, §§ 225(b), 505, Oct. 12, 1984, 98 Stat. 2030, 2070; Pub.L. 99–570, Title I, § 1004(a), Oct. 27, 1986, 100 Stat. 3207–6.)

EDITORIAL NOTES

References in Text. "This subchapter", referred to in subsec. (b), was in the original "this title" meaning Title III of Pub. L. 91–513, Oct. 27, 1970, 84 Stat. 1285. Part A of Title III comprises this subchapter. For classification of Part B, consisting of sections 1101 to 1105 of Title III, see U.S.C.A. Tables volume.

Repeals. Section 225(b) of Pub.L. 98–473, cited to credit, was repealed by section 1005(c) of Pub.L. 99–570. Such provisions of section 225(b) of Pub.L. 98–473, which were to take effect Nov. 1, 1987, as a result of repeal were never executed to text of section.

Effective Date of 1986 Amendment. Amendment by section 1004(a) of Pub.L. 99–570 to take effect on the date of the taking of effect of section 3583 of Title 18, Crimes and Criminal Procedure, Nov. 1, 1987, see section 1004(b) of Pub.L. 99–570, set out as a note under section 841 of this title.

Effective Date and Savings Provisions of 1984 Amendment. Amendment by Pub.L. 98–473, § 225(b), effective on the first day of first calendar month beginning thirty six months after Oct. 12, 1984, applicable only to offenses committed after taking effect of sections 211 to 239 of Pub.L. 98–473, and except as otherwise provided for therein, see section 235 of Pub.L. 98–473, as amended, set out as a note under section 3551 of Title 18, Crimes and Criminal Procedure.

§ 963.   Attempt and conspiracy

Any person who attempts or conspires to commit any offense defined in this subchapter shall be subject to the same penalties as those prescribed for the offense, the commission of which was the object of the attempt or conspiracy.

(Pub.L. 91–513, Title III, § 1013, Oct. 27, 1970, 84 Stat. 1291; Pub.L. 100–690, Title VI, § 6470(a), Nov. 18, 1988, 102 Stat. 4377.)

EDITORIAL NOTES

References in Text. This subchapter, referred to in text, was in the original "this title" meaning Title III of Pub. L. 91–513, Oct. 27, 1970, 84 Stat. 1285. Part A of Title III comprises this subchapter. For classification of Part B, consisting of sections 1101 to 1105 of Title III, see U.S.C.A. Tables volume.

§ 964. Additional penalties

Any penalty imposed for violation of this subchapter shall be in addition to, and not in lieu of, any civil or administrative penalty or sanction authorized by law.

(Pub. L. 91–513, Title III, § 1014, Oct. 27, 1970, 84 Stat. 1291.)

EDITORIAL NOTES

References in Text. This subchapter referred to in text, was in the original "this title" meaning Title III of Pub. L. 91–513, Oct. 27, 1970, 84 Stat. 1285. Part A of Title III comprises this subchapter. For classification of Part B, consisting of sections 1102 to 1105 of Title III, see U.S.C.A. Tables volume.

§ 965. Applicability of Part E of Subchapter I

Part E of subchapter I of this chapter shall apply with respect to functions of the Attorney General (and of officers and employees of the Bureau of Narcotics and Dangerous Drugs) under this subchapter, to administrative and judicial proceedings under this subchapter, and to violations of this subchapter, to the same extent that such part applies to functions of the Attorney General (and such officers and employees) under subchapter I of this chapter, to such proceedings under subchapter I of this chapter, and to violations of subchapter I of this chapter. For purposes of the application of this section to section 880 or 881 of this title, any reference in such section 880 or 881 of this title to "this subchapter" shall be deemed to be a reference to this subchapter, any reference to section 823 of this title shall be deemed to be a reference to section 958 of this title, and any reference to section 822(d) of this title shall be deemed to be a reference to section 957(b)(2) of this title.

(Pub. L. 91–513, Title III, § 1015, Oct. 27, 1970, 84 Stat. 1291; Pub. L. 95–633, Title III, § 301(b), Nov. 10, 1978, 92 Stat. 3778.)

EDITORIAL NOTES

References in Text. This subchapter referred to in text, was in the original "this title" meaning Title III of Pub. L. 91–513, Oct. 27, 1970, 84 Stat. 1285. Part A of Title III comprises this subchapter. For classification of Part B, consisting of sections 1101 to 1105 of Title III, see U.S.C.A. Tables volume.

Code of Federal Regulations

Administrative policies, practices, and procedures, see 21 CFR 1316.01 et seq.

§ 966. Authority of Secretary of the Treasury

Nothing in this chapter shall derogate from the authority of the Secretary of the Treasury under the customs and related laws.

(Pub. L. 91–513, Title III, § 1016, Oct. 27, 1970, 84 Stat. 1291.)

EDITORIAL NOTES

References in Text. This chapter, referred to in text, was, in the original, this Act, meaning Pub. L. 91–513, Oct. 27, 1970, 84 Stat. 1236, the Drug Abuse Prevention and Control Act of 1970.

The customs laws, referred to in text, are classified generally to Title 19, U.S.C.A., Customs Duties.

Code of Federal Regulations

Importation, search and seizure, see 19 CFR 162.0 et seq.

§ 967. Smuggling of controlled substances; investigations; oaths; subpenas; witnesses; evidence; production of records; territorial limits; fees and mileage of witnesses

For the purpose of any investigation which, in the opinion of the Secretary of the Treasury, is necessary and proper to the enforcement of section 545 of Title 18 (relating to smuggling goods into the United States) with respect to any controlled substance (as defined in section 802 of this title), the Secretary of the Treasury may administer oaths and affirmations, subpena witnesses, compel their attendance, take evidence, and require the production of records (including books, papers, documents, and tangible things which constitute or contain evidence) relevant or material to the investigation. The attendance of witnesses and the production of records may be required from any place within the customs territory of the United States, except that a witness shall not be required to appear at any hearing distant more than 100 miles from the place where he was served with subpena. Witnesses summoned by the Secretary shall be paid the same fees and mileage that are paid witnesses in the courts of the United States. Oaths and affirmations may be made at any place subject to the jurisdiction of the United States.

(Aug. 11, 1955, c. 800, § 1, 69 Stat. 684; Oct. 27, 1970, Pub.L. 91–513, Title III, § 1102(t), 84 Stat. 1294.)

EDITORIAL NOTES

Codification. This section was formerly classified to section 1034 of Title 31 prior to the general revision and enactment of Title 31, Money and Finance, by Pub.L. 97–258, § 1, Sept. 13, 1982, 96 Stat. 877.

Section was also formerly classified to section 198a of this title.

Section was not enacted as part of the Comprehensive Drug Abuse Prevention and Control Act of 1970 (Pub.L. 91–513, Oct. 27, 1970, 84 Stat. 1236) which comprises this chapter.

Effective Date of 1970 Amendment. Amendment by Pub.L. 91–513 effective the first day of the seventh calendar month that begins after Oct. 26, 1970, see section 1105(a) of Pub.L. 91–513.

Savings Provisions. Prosecutions for any violation of law occurring, and civil seizures or forfeitures and injunctive proceedings commenced, prior to the effective date of amendment of this section by section 1102 of Pub.L. 91–513, not to be affected or abated by reason thereof, see section 1103 of Pub.L. 91–513.

§ 968. Service of subpena; proof of service

A subpena of the Secretary of the Treasury may be served by any person designated in the subpena to serve it. Service upon a natural person may be made by personal delivery of the subpena to him. Service may be made upon a domestic or foreign corporation or upon a partnership or other unincorporated association which is subject to suit under a common name, by delivering the subpena to an officer, a managing or general agent, or to any other agent authorized by appointment or by law to receive service of process. The affidavit of the person serving the

subpena entered on a true copy thereof by the person serving it shall be proof of service.

(Aug. 11, 1955, c. 800, § 2, 69 Stat. 685.)

EDITORIAL NOTES

Codification. This section was formerly classified to section 1035 of Title 31 prior to the general revision and enactment of Title 31, Money and Finance, by Pub.L. 97–258, § 1, Sept. 13, 1982, 96 Stat. 877.

Section was also formerly classified to section 198b of this title.

Section was not enacted as part of the Comprehensive Drug Abuse Prevention and Control Act of 1970 (Pub.L. 91–513, Oct. 27, 1970, 84 Stat. 1236) which comprises this chapter.

§ 969. Contempt proceedings

In case of contumacy by, or refusal to obey a subpena issued to, any person, the Secretary of the Treasury may invoke the aid of any court of the United States within the jurisdiction of which the investigation is carried on or of which the subpenaed person is an inhabitant, carries on business or may be found, to compel compliance with the subpena of the Secretary of the Treasury. The court may issue an order requiring the subpenaed person to appear before the Secretary of the Treasury there to produce records, if so ordered, or to give testimony touching the matter under investigation. Any failure to obey the order of the court may be punished by the court as a contempt thereof. All process in any such case may be served in the judicial district whereof the subpenaed person is an inhabitant or wherever he may be found.

(Aug. 11, 1955, c. 800, § 3, 69 Stat. 685.)

EDITORIAL NOTES

Codification. This section was formerly classified to section 1036 of Title 31 prior to the general revision and enactment of Title 31, Money and Finance, by Pub.L. 97–258, § 1, Sept. 13, 1982, 96 Stat. 877.

Section was also formerly classified to section 198c of this title.

Section was not enacted as part of the Comprehensive Drug Abuse Prevention and Control Act of 1970 (Pub.L. 91–513, Oct. 27, 1970, 84 Stat. 1236) which comprises this chapter.

§ 970. Criminal forfeitures

Section 853 of this title, relating to criminal forfeitures, shall apply in every respect to a violation of this subchapter punishable by imprisonment for more than one year.

(Pub.L. 91–513, Title III, § 1017, as added Pub.L. 98–473, Title II, § 307, Oct. 12, 1984, 98 Stat. 2051.)

EDITORIAL NOTES

References in Text. This subchapter, referred to in text, was in the original "this title" meaning Title III of Pub.L. 91–513, Oct. 27, 1970, 84 Stat. 1285. Part A of Title III comprises this subchapter. For classification of Part B, consisting of sections 1101 to 1105 of Pub.L. 91–513, see U.S.C.A. Tables volume.

§ 971. Notification, suspension of shipment, and penalties with respect to importation and exportation of listed chemicals

Notification prior to transaction

(a) Each regulated person who imports or exports a listed chemical shall notify the Attorney General of the importation or exportation not later than 15 days before the transaction is to take place.

Regular customers or suppliers

(b)(1) The Attorney General shall provide by regulation for circumstances in which the requirement of subsection (a) of this section does not apply to a transaction between a regulated person and a regular customer or regular supplier of the regulated person. At the time of any importation or exportation constituting a transaction referred to in the preceding sentence, the regulated person shall notify the Attorney General of the transaction.

(2) The regulations under this subsection shall provide that the initial notification under subsection (a) of this section with respect to a customer or supplier of a regulated person shall, upon the expiration of the 15–day period, qualify the customer as a regular customer or regular supplier, unless the Attorney General otherwise notifies the regulated person in writing.

Suspension of importation or exportation; disqualification of regular customers or suppliers; hearing

(c)(1) The Attorney General may order the suspension of any importation or exportation of a listed chemical (other than a regulated transaction to which the requirement of subsection (a) of this section does not apply by reason of subsection (b)) of this section) or may disqualify any regular customer or regular supplier on the ground that the chemical may be diverted to the clandestine manufacture of a controlled substance. From and after the time when the Attorney General provides written notice of the order (including a statement of the legal and factual basis for the order) to the regulated person, the regulated person may not carry out the transaction.

(2) Upon written request to the Attorney General, a regulated person to whom an order applies under paragraph (1) is entitled to an agency hearing on the record in accordance with subchapter II of chapter 5 of Title 5. The hearing shall be held on an expedited basis and not later than 45 days after the request is made, except that the hearing may be held at a later time, if so requested by the regulated person.

(Pub.L. 91–513, Title III, § 1018, as added Pub.L. 100–690, Title VI, § 6053(a), Nov. 18, 1988, 102 Stat. 4314.)

EDITORIAL NOTES

Effective Dates and Special Rules. Section 6053(b) of Pub.L. 100–690 provided that:

"(1) Not later than 45 days after the date of the enactment of this Act [Nov. 18, 1988], the Attorney General shall forward to the Director of the Office of Management and Budget proposed regulations required by the amendment made by subsection (a) [enacting this section].

"(2) Not later than 55 days after the date of the enactment of this Act [Nov. 18, 1988], the Director of the Office of Management and Budget shall—

"(A) review such proposed regulations of the Attorney General; and

"(B) forward any comments and recommendations for modifications to the Attorney General.

"(3) Not later than 60 days after the date of the enactment of this Act [Nov. 18, 1988] the Attorney General shall publish the proposed final regulations required by the amendment made by subsection (a).

"(4) Not later than 120 days after the date of the enactment of this Act [Nov. 18, 1988] the Attorney General shall promulgate final regulations required by the amendment made by subsection (a).

"(5) Subsection (a) of section 1018 of the Controlled Substances Import and Export Act, as added by subsection (a) of this section, [subsec. (a) of this section] shall take effect 90 days after the promulgation of the final regulations under paragraph (4).

"(6) Each regulated person shall provide to the Attorney General the identity of any regular customer or regular supplier of the regulated person not later than 30 days after the promulgation of the final regulations under paragraph (4). Not later than 60 days after the end of such 30–day period, each regular customer and regular supplier so identified shall be a regular customer or regular supplier for purposes of any applicable exception from the requirement of subsection (a) of such section 1018 [subsec. (a) of this section], unless the the [sic] Attorney General otherwise notifies the regulated person in writing."

Section effective 120 days after Nov. 18, 1988, see section 6061 of Pub.L. 100–690, set out as a note under section 802 of this title.

TITLE 28
JUDICIARY AND JUDICIAL PROCEDURE

Act June 25, 1948, c. 646, § 1, 62 Stat. 869

As amended to February 1, 1989

CHAPTER 175

CIVIL COMMITMENT AND REHABILITATION OF NARCOTIC ADDICTS

§ 2901. Definitions

As used in this chapter—

(a) "Addict" means any individual who habitually uses any narcotic drug as defined by section 102(16) of the Controlled Substances Act so as to endanger the public morals, health, safety, or welfare, or who is so far addicted to the use of such narcotic drugs as to have lost the power of self-control with reference to his addiction.

(b) "Surgeon General" means the Surgeon General of the Public Health Service.

(c) "Crime of violence" includes voluntary manslaughter, murder, rape, mayhem, kidnaping, robbery, burglary or housebreaking in the night-time, extortion accompanied by threats of violence, assault with a dangerous weapon or assault with intent to commit any offense punishable by imprisonment for more than one year, arson punishable as a felony, or an attempt or conspiracy to commit any of the foregoing offenses.

(d) "Treatment" includes confinement and treatment in an institution and under supervised aftercare in the community and includes, but is not limited to, medical, educational, social, psychological, and vocational services, corrective and preventive guidance and training, and other reha-

bilitative services designed to protect the public and benefit the addict by eliminating his dependence on addicting drugs, or by controlling his dependence, and his susceptibility to addiction.

(e) "Felony" includes any offense in violation of a law of the United States classified as a felony under section 3581 of title 18 of the United States Code, and further includes any offense in violation of a law of any State, any possession or territory of the United States, the District of Columbia, the Canal Zone, or the Commonwealth of Puerto Rico, which at the time of the offense was classified as a felony by the law of the place where that offense was committed.

(f) "Conviction" and "convicted" mean the final judgment on a verdict or finding of guilty, a plea of guilty, or a plea of nolo contendere, but do not include a final judgment which has been expunged by pardon, reversed, set aside or otherwise rendered nugatory.

(g) "Eligible individual" means any individual who is charged with an offense against the United States, but does not include—

(1) an individual charged with a crime of violence.

(2) an individual charged with unlawfully importing, selling, or conspiring to import or sell, a narcotic drug.

(3) an individual against whom there is pending a prior charge of a felony which has not been finally determined or who is on probation or whose sentence following conviction on such a charge, including any time on parole, supervised release, or mandatory release, has not been fully served: *Provided,* That an individual on probation, parole, supervised release, or mandatory release shall be included if the authority authorized to require his return to custody consents to his commitment.

(4) an individual who has been convicted of a felony on two or more occasions.

(5) an individual who has been civilly committed under this Act, under the District of Columbia Code, or any State preceding because of narcotic addiction on three or more occasions.

(Added Pub.L. 89–793, Title I, § 101, Nov. 8, 1966, 80 Stat. 1438, and amended Pub.L. 91–513, Title III, § 1102(*l*), Oct. 27, 1970, 84 Stat. 1293; Pub.L. 92–420, § 2, Sept. 16, 1972, 86 Stat. 677; Pub.L. 98–473, Title II, § 228(c), Oct. 12, 1984, 98 Stat. 2030.)

EDITORIAL NOTES

References in Text. Section 102(16) of the Controlled Substances Act, referred to in subsec. (a), is set out as section 802(16) of Title 21 Food and Drugs.

"This Act", referred to in subsec. (g)(5), means Pub.L. 89–793, which enacted this chapter, chapter 314 of Title 18, and chapter 42 of Title 42, amended section 7237(d) of Title 26 and section 257 of Title 42, and enacted provisions set out as notes under section 4202 of Title 18 and section 3401 of Title 42.

Effective Date of 1984 Amendment. Amendment by Pub.L. 98–473 effective Oct. 12, 1984, see section 235(a)(1)(B)(ii)(IV) of Pub.L. 98–473, set out as an Effective Date note under section 3551 of Title 18, Crimes and Criminal Procedure. Pub.L. 99–646, § 35(2)(D), Nov. 10, 1986, 100 Stat. 3599, amended Pub.L. 99–473, § 235(a)(1)(B)(ii) to delete item (IV).

Effective Date of 1972 Amendment. Section 5 of Pub.L. 92–420 provided that: "This Act [amending subsec. (d) of this section, section 4251(c) of Title 18, and section 3411(b) of Title 42, and enacting provisions set out as note under this section] shall take effect immediately upon enactment [Sept. 16, 1972]. Sections 2 and 3 [amending section 4251(c) of Title 18 and section 3411(b) of Title 42 respectively] shall apply to any case pending

in a district court of the United States in which an appearance has not been made prior to the effective date [Sept. 16, 1972]."

Effective Date of 1970 Amendment. Amendment by Pub.L. 91–513 effective on the first day of the seventh calendar month that begins after the day immediately preceding the date of enactment of Pub.L. 91–513, which was approved on Oct. 27, 1970, see section 1105(a) of Pub.L. 91–513, set out as a note under section 951 of Title 21, Food and Drugs.

Savings Provisions. Prosecutions for any violation of law occurring, and civil seizures or forfeitures and injunctive proceedings commenced, prior to the effective date of amendment of this section by section 1102 of Pub.L. 91–513 not to be affected or abated by reason thereof, see section 1103 of Pub.L. 91–513.

§ 2902. Discretionary authority of court; examination, report, and determination by court; termination of civil commitment

(a) If the United States district court believes that an eligible individual is an addict, the court may advise him at his first appearance or thereafter at the sole discretion of the court that the prosecution of the criminal charge will be held in abeyance if he elects to submit to an immediate examination to determine whether he is an addict and is likely to be rehabilitated through treatment. In offering an individual an election, the court shall advise him that if he elects to be examined, he will be confined during the examination for a period not to exceed sixty days; that if he is determined to be an addict who is likely to be rehabilitated, he will be civilly committed to the Surgeon General for treatment; that he may not voluntarily withdraw from the examination or any treatment which may follow; that the treatment may last for thirty-six months; that during treatment, he will be confined in an institution and, at the discretion of the Surgeon General, he may be conditionally released for supervised aftercare treatment in the community; and that if he successfully completes treatment the charge will be dismissed, but if he does not, prosecution on the charge will be resumed. An individual upon being advised that he may elect to submit to an examination shall be permitted a maximum of five days within which to make his election. Except on a showing that a timely election could not have been made, an individual shall be barred from an election after the prescribed period. An individual who elects civil commitment shall be placed in the custody of the Attorney General or the Surgeon General, as the court directs, for an examination by the Surgeon General during a period not to exceed thirty days. This period may, upon notice to the court and the appropriate United States attorney, be extended by the Surgeon General for an additional thirty days.

(b) The Surgeon General shall report to the court the results of the examination and recommend whether the individual should be civilly committed. A copy of the report shall be made available to the individual and the United States attorney. If the court, acting on the report and other information coming to its attention, determines that the individual is not an addict or is an addict not likely to be rehabilitated through treatment, the individual shall be held to answer the abeyant charge. If the court determines that the individual is an addict and is likely to be rehabilitated through treatment, the court shall commit him to the custody of the Surgeon General for treatment, except that no individual shall be committed under this chapter if the Surgeon General certifies that adequate facilities or personnel for treatment are unavailable.

(c) Whenever an individual is committed to the custody of the Surgeon General for treatment under this chapter the criminal charge against him shall be continued without final disposition and shall be dismissed if the Surgeon General certifies to the court that the individual has successfully completed the treatment program. On receipt of such certification, the court shall discharge the individual from custody and dismiss the charge against him. If prior to such certification the Surgeon General determines that the individual cannot be further treated as a medical problem, he shall advise the court. The court shall thereupon terminate the commitment, and the pending criminal proceeding shall be resumed.

(d) An individual committed for examination or treatment shall not be released on bail or on his own recognizance.

(e) Whoever escapes or attempts to escape while committed to institutional custody for examination or treatment, or whoever rescues or attempts to rescue or instigates, aids, or assists the escape or attempt to escape of such a person, shall be subject to the penalties provided in sections 751 and 752 of title 18, United States Code.

(Added Pub.L. 89–793, Title I, § 101, Nov. 8, 1966, 80 Stat. 1439.)

§ **2903. Authority and responsibilities of the Surgeon General; institutional custody; aftercare; maximum period of civil commitment; credit toward sentence**

(a) An individual who is committed to the custody of the Surgeon General for treatment under this chapter shall not be conditionally released from institutional custody until the Surgeon General determines that he has made sufficient progress to warrant release to a supervisory aftercare authority. If the Surgeon General is unable to make such a determination at the expiration of twenty-four months after the commencement of institutional custody, he shall advise the court and the appropriate United States attorney whether treatment should be continued. The court may affirm the commitment or terminate it and resume the pending criminal proceeding.

(b) An individual who is conditionally released from institutional custody shall, while on release, remain in the legal custody of the Surgeon General and shall report for such supervised aftercare treatment as the Surgeon General directs. He shall be subject to home visits and to such physical examination and reasonable regulation of his conduct as the supervisory aftercare authority establishes, subject to the approval of the Surgeon General. The Surgeon General may, at any time, order a conditionally released individual to return for institutional treatment. The Surgeon General's order shall be a sufficient warrant for the supervisory aftercare authority, a probation officer, or any Federal officer authorized to serve criminal process within the United States to apprehend and return the individual to institutional custody as directed. If it is determined that an individual has returned to the use of narcotics, the Surgeon General shall inform the court of the conditions under which the return occurred and make a recommendation as to whether treatment should be continued. The court may affirm the commitment or terminate it and resume the pending criminal proceeding.

(c) The total period of treatment for any individual committed to the custody of the Surgeon General shall not exceed thirty-six months. If, at the expiration of such maximum period, the Surgeon General is unable to certify that the individual has successfully completed his treatment program the pending criminal proceeding shall be resumed.

(d) Whenever a pending criminal proceeding against an individual is resumed under this chapter, he shall receive full credit toward the service of any sentence which may be imposed for any time spent in the institutional custody of the Surgeon General or the Attorney General or any other time spent in institutional custody in connection with the matter for which sentence is imposed.

(Added Pub.L. 89–793, Title I, § 101, Nov. 8, 1966, 80 Stat. 1440.)

§ 2904.   Civil commitment not a conviction; use of test results

The determination of narcotic addiction and the subsequent civil commitment under this chapter shall not be deemed a criminal conviction. The results of any tests or procedures conducted by the Surgeon General or the supervisory aftercare authority to determine narcotic addiction may only be used in a further proceeding under this chapter. They shall not be used against the examined individual in any criminal proceeding except that the fact that he is a narcotic addict may be elicited on his cross-examination as bearing on his credibility as a witness.

(Added Pub.L. 89–793, Title I, § 101, Nov. 8, 1966, 80 Stat. 1441.)

§ 2905.   Delegation of functions by Surgeon General; use of Federal, State, and private facilities

(a) The Surgeon General may from time to time make such provision as he deems appropriate authorizing the performance of any of his functions under this chapter by any other officer or employee of the Public Health Service, or with the consent of the head of the Department or Agency concerned, by any Federal or other public or private agency or officer or employee thereof.

(b) The Surgeon General is authorized to enter into arrangements with any public or private agency or any person under which appropriate facilities or services of such agency or person will be made available, on a reimbursable basis or otherwise, for the examination or treatment of individuals who elect civil commitment under this chapter.

(Added Pub.L. 89–793, Title I, § 101, Nov. 8, 1966, 80 Stat. 1441.)

§ 2906.   Absence of offer by the court to a defendant of an election under section 2902(a) or any determination as to civil commitment, not reviewable on appeal or otherwise

The failure of a court to offer a defendant an election under section 2902(a) of this chapter, or a determination relative to civil commitment under this chapter shall not be reviewable on appeal or otherwise.

(Added Pub.L. 89–793, Title I, § 101, Nov. 8, 1966, 80 Stat. 1441.)

TITLE 31
MONEY AND FINANCE

CHAPTER 53

MONETARY TRANSACTIONS

SUBCHAPTER II

RECORDS AND REPORTS ON MONETARY INSTRUMENTS TRANSACTIONS

As amended to February 1, 1989

§ 5311. Declaration of purpose

It is the purpose of this subchapter (except section 5315) to require certain reports or records where they have a high degree of usefulness in criminal, tax, or regulatory investigations or proceedings.

(Pub.L. 97–258, Sept. 13, 1982, 96 Stat. 995.)

REVISION NOTES

Revised Section	Source (U.S.Code)	Source (Statutes at Large)
5311	31:1051	Oct. 26, 1970, Pub.L. 91–508, § 202, 84 Stat. 1118.

EDITORIAL NOTES

International Currency Transaction Reporting. Pub.L. 100–690, Title IV, § 4701, Nov. 18, 1988, 102 Stat. 4290, provided that:

"(a) Findings.—The Congress finds that—

"(1) the success of cash transaction and money laundering control statutes in the United States has been significant; and

"(2) the United States should play a leadership role in the development of an international system of a similar kind.

(b) Purpose.—It is the purpose of this section to urge the United States Government, to the maximum extent practicable, to seek the active cooperation of other countries in the enforcement of these statutes, since only a truly multilateral approach can be effective in eliminating bank haven loopholes through which money launderers can escape.

"(c) Establishment of International Agency.—The Congress urges the Secretary of the Treasury to negotiate with finance ministers of foreign countries to establish an international currency control agency to—

"(1) serve as a central source of information and database for international drug enforcement agencies;

"(2) collect and analyze currency transaction reports filed by member countries; and

639

"(3) encourage the adoption, by member countries, of uniform cash transaction and money laundering statutes.

(d) Maintenance of Domestic Effort.—While establishing a multilateral agency will be the most effective method of combating money laundering, the United States must itself continue to do everything it can to curb international money laundering."

Restrictions on Laundering of United States Currency. Pub.L. 100–690, Title IV, § 4702, Nov. 18, 1988, 102 Stat. 4291, provided that:

"(a) Findings.—The Congress finds that international currency transactions, especially in United States currency, that involve the proceeds of narcotics trafficking fuel trade in narcotics in the United States and worldwide and consequently are a threat to the national security of the United States.

"(b) Purpose.—The purpose of this section is to provide for international negotiations that would expand access to information on transactions involving large amounts of United States currency wherever those transactions occur worldwide.

"(c) Negotiations.—(1) The Secretary of the Treasury (hereinafter in this section referred to as the 'Secretary') shall enter into negotiations with the appropriate financial supervisory agencies and other officials of any foreign country the financial institutions of which do business in United States currency. Highest priority shall be attached to countries whose financial institutions the Secretary determines, in consultation with the Attorney General and the Director of National Drug Control Policy, may be engaging in currency transactions involving the proceeds of international narcotics trafficking, particularly United States currency derived from drug sales in the United States.

"(2) The purposes of negotiations under this subsection are—

"(A) to reach one or more international agreements to ensure that foreign banks and other financial institutions maintain adequate records of large United States currency transactions, and

"(B) to establish a mechanism whereby such records may be made available to United States law enforcement officials.

In carrying out such negotiations, the Secretary should seek to enter into and further cooperative efforts, voluntary information exchanges, the use of letters rogatory, and mutual legal assistance treaties.

"(d) Reports.—Not later than 1 year after the date of enactment of this Act [Nov. 18, 1988], the Secretary shall submit an interim report to the Committee on Banking, Finance and Urban Affairs of the House of Representatives and the Committee on Banking, Housing, and Urban Affairs of the Senate on progress in the negotiations under subsection (c). Not later than 2 years after such enactment, the Secretary shall submit a final report to such Committees and the President on the outcome of those negotiations and shall identify, in consultation with the Attorney General and the Director of National Drug Control Policy, countries—

"(1) with respect to which the Secretary determines there is evidence that the financial institutions in such countries are engaging in currency transactions involving the proceeds of international narcotics trafficking; and

"(2) which have not reached agreement with United States authorities on a mechanism for exchanging adequate records on international currency transactions in connection with narcotics investigations and proceedings.

"(e) Authority.—If after receiving the advice of the Secretary and in any case at the time of receipt of the Secretary's report, the Secretary determines that a foreign country—

"(1) has jurisdiction over financial institutions that are substantially engaging in currency transactions that effect the United States involving the proceeds of international narcotics trafficking;

"(2) such country has not reached agreement on a mechanism for exchanging adequate records on international currency transactions in connection with narcotics investigations and proceedings; and

"(3) such country is not negotiating in good faith to reach such an agreement,

the President shall impose appropriate penalties and sanctions, including temporarily or permanently—

"(1) prohibiting such persons, institutions or other entities in such countries from participating in any United States dollar clearing or wire transfer system; and

"(2) prohibiting such persons, institutions or entities in such countries from maintaining an account with any bank or other financial institution chartered under the laws of the United States or any State.

Any penalties or sanctions so imposed may be delayed or waived upon certification of the President to the Congress that it is in the national interest to do so. Financial institutions in such countries that maintain adequate records shall be exempt from such penalties and sanctions.

"(f) Definitions.—For the purposes of this section—

"(1) the term 'United States currency' means Federal Reserve Notes and United States coins.

"(2) The term 'adequate records' means records of United States' currency transactions in excess of $10,000 including the identification of the person initiating the transaction, the person's business or occupation, and the account or accounts affected by the transaction, or other records of comparable effect.

"(g) Sunset.—The authority given the President in subsection (e) shall expire on June 30, 1994."

§ 5312. Definitions and application

(a) In this subchapter—

(1) "financial agency" means a person acting for a person (except for a country, a monetary or financial authority acting as a monetary or financial authority, or an international financial institution of which the United States Government is a member) as a financial institution, bailee, depository trustee, or agent, or acting in a similar way related to money, credit, securities, gold, or a transaction in money, credit, securities, or gold.

(2) "financial institution" means—

(A) an insured bank (as defined in section 3(h) of the Federal Deposit Insurance Act (12 U.S.C. 1813(h)));

(B) a commercial bank or trust company;

(C) a private banker;

(D) an agency or branch of a foreign bank in the United States;

(E) an insured institution (as defined in section 401(a) of the National Housing Act (12 U.S.C. 1724(a)));

(F) a thrift institution;

(G) a broker or dealer registered with the Securities and Exchange Commission under the Securities Exchange Act of 1934 (15 U.S.C. 78a et seq.);

(H) a broker or dealer in securities or commodities;

(I) an investment banker or investment company;

(J) a currency exchange;

(K) an issuer, redeemer, or cashier of travelers' checks, checks, money orders, or similar instruments;

(L) an operator of a credit card system;

(M) an insurance company;

(N) a dealer in precious metals, stones, or jewels;

(O) a pawnbroker;

(P) a loan or finance company;

(Q) a travel agency;

(R) a licensed sender of money;

(S) a telegraph company;

(T) a business engaged in vehicle sales, including automobile, airplane, and boat sales;

(U) persons involved in real estate closings and settlements;

(V) the United States Postal Service;

(W) an agency of the United States Government or of a State or local government carrying out a duty or power of a business described in this paragraph;

(X) any business or agency which engages in any activity which the Secretary of the Treasury determines, by regulation, to be an activity which is similar to, related to, or a substitute for any activity in which any business described in this paragraph is authorized to engage; or

(Y) any other business designated by the Secretary whose cash transactions have a high degree of usefulness in criminal, tax, or regulatory matters.

(3) "monetary instruments" means—

(A) United States coins and currency; and

(B) as the Secretary may prescribe by regulation, coins and currency of a foreign country, travelers' checks, bearer negotiable instruments, bearer investment securities, bearer securities, stock on which title is passed on delivery, and similar material.

(4) "person", in addition to its meaning under section 1 of title 1, includes a trustee, a representative of an estate and, when the Secretary prescribes, a governmental entity.

(5) "United States" means the States of the United States, the District of Columbia, and, when the Secretary prescribes by regulation, the Commonwealth of Puerto Rico, the Virgin Islands, Guam, the Northern Mariana Islands, American Samoa, the Trust Territory of the Pacific Islands, a territory or possession of the United States, or a military or diplomatic establishment.

(b) In this subchapter—

(1) "domestic financial agency" and "domestic financial institution" apply to an action in

the United States of a financial agency or institution.

(2) "foreign financial agency" and "foreign financial institution" apply to an action outside the United States of a financial agency or institution.

(Pub.L. 97–258, Sept. 13, 1982, 96 Stat. 995; Pub. L. 99–570, Title I, § 1362, Oct. 27, 1986, 100 Stat. 3207–33; Pub.L. 100–690, Title VI, § 6185(a), (g)(1), Nov. 18, 1988, 102 Stat. 4354, 4357.)

REVISION NOTES

Revised Section	Source (U.S.Code)	Source (Statutes at Large)
5312(a)(1)...	31:1052(a), (b), (g), (i)......	Oct. 26, 1970, Pub.L. 91–508, § 203(a)–(i), (l), 84 Stat. 1118.
5312(a)(2)...	31:1052(e)....	
5312(a)(3)...	31:1052(l)....	
5312(a)(4)...	31:1052(c)....	
5312(a)(5)...	31:1052(d)....	
5312(b).....	31:1052(f), (h)	

In subsection (a)(1), the text of 31:1052(a) [former section 1052(a) of this title] is omitted as unnecessary. The text of 31:1052(b) [former section 1052(b) of this title] is omitted because of the restatement. The text of 31:1052(i) [former section 1052(i) of this title] is omitted as unnecessary because the source provision is restated where necessary in the revised subchapter.

In subsection (a)(2), (3), (4), and (5), the words "the Secretary ... prescribes" are substituted for "specified by the Secretary by regulation", "as the Secretary may by regulation specify", "specified by the Secretary", and "the Secretary shall by regulation specify" for consistency.

In subsection (a)(2) and (3), the words "for the purposes of the provision of this chapter to which the regulation relates" are omitted as surplus.

In subsection (a)(2), before subclause (A), the words "any person which does business in any one or more of the following capacities" are omitted as surplus. In subclause (F), the words "savings bank, building and loan association, credit union, industrial bank, or other" are omitted as surplus. In subclause (T), the words "agency of the United States Government or of a State or local government" are substituted for "Federal, State, or local government institution" for consistency. In subclause (U), the words "type of" are omitted as surplus. The word "agency" is substituted for "institution" for consistency.

In subsection (a)(3)(B)–(5), the word "prescribe" is substituted for "specify" for consistency in the revised title and with other titles of the United States Code.

In subsection (a)(3)(B), the words "in addition", and "and such types of" are omitted as surplus. The words "similar material" are substituted for "the equivalent thereof" for clarity.

In subsection (a)(4), the words "in addition to its meaning under section 1 of title 1" are substituted for "natural persons, partnerships, ... associations, corporations, and all entities cognizable as legal personalities" for consistency because 1:1 [section 1 of Title 1, General Provisions] is applicable to all laws unless otherwise provided. The words "a trustee, a representative of an estate" are substituted for "trusts, estates", and the word "entity" is substituted for "department or agency", for consistency.

The words "either for the purpose of this chapter generally or any particular requirement thereunder" are omitted as surplus.

In subsection (a)(5), the words "used in a geographic sense" are omitted because of the restatement. The words "either for the purposes of this chapter generally or any particular requirement thereunder" are omitted as surplus. The words "territory or" are added for consistency.

Subsection (b) is substituted for 31:1052(f) and (h) [former section 1052(f) and (h) of this title] to eliminate unnecessary words and for consistency.

EDITORIAL NOTES

References in Text. Section 3(h) of the Federal Deposit Insurance Act, referred to in subsec. (a)(2)(A), is section 3(h) of Act Sept. 21, 1950, c. 967, 64 Stat. 873, which is classified to section 1813(h) of Title 12, Banks and Banking.

Section 401(a) of the National Housing Act, referred to in subsec. (a)(2)(E), is section 401(a) of Act June 27, 1934, c. 847, Title IV, 48 Stat. 1255, which is classified to section 1724(a) of Title 12.

The Securities Exchange Act of 1934, referred to in subsec. (a)(2)(G), is Act June 6, 1934, c. 404, 48 Stat. 881, as amended, which is classified principally to chapter 2B (section 78a et seq.) of Title 15, Commerce and Trade. For complete classification of this Act to the Code, see section 78a of Title 15, and Tables volume.

§ 5313. Reports on domestic coins and currency transactions

(a) When a domestic financial institution is involved in a transaction for the payment, receipt, or transfer of United States coins or currency (or other monetary instruments the Secretary of the Treasury prescribes), in an amount, denomination, or amount and denomination, or under circumstances the Secretary prescribes by regulation, the institution and any other participant in the transaction the Secretary may prescribe shall file a report on the transaction at the time and in the way the Secretary prescribes. A participant acting for another person shall make the report as the agent or bailee of the person and identify the person for whom the transaction is being made.

(b) The Secretary may designate a domestic financial institution as an agent of the United States Government to receive a report under this section. However, the Secretary may designate a domestic financial institution that is not insured, chartered, examined, or registered as a domestic financial institution only if the institution consents. The Secretary may suspend or revoke a designation for a violation of this subchapter or a regulation under this subchapter (except a violation of section 5315 of this title or a regulation prescribed under section 5315), section 411 of the National Housing Act (12 U.S.C. 1730d), or section 21 of the Federal Deposit Insurance Act (12 U.S.C. 1829b).

(c)(1) A person (except a domestic financial institution designated under subsection (b) of this section) required to file a report under this section shall file the report—

(A) with the institution involved in the transaction if the institution was designated;

(B) in the way the Secretary prescribes when the institution was not designated; or

(C) with the Secretary.

(2) The Secretary shall prescribe—

(A) the filing procedure for a domestic financial institution designated under subsection (b) of this section; and

(B) the way the institution shall submit reports filed with it.

(Pub.L. 97–258, Sept. 13, 1982, 96 Stat. 996.)

REVISION NOTES

Revised Section	Source (U.S.Code)	Source (Statutes at Large)
5313(a)	31:1081	Oct. 26, 1970, Pub.L. 91–508, §§ 221–223, 84 Stat. 1122.
5313(b)	31:1082	
5313(c)	31:1083(a)	
	31:1083(b)	

In subsection (a), the words "coins or" are added, and the words "prescribe" and "prescribes" are substituted for "specify" in 31:1081 [former section 1081 of this title], and "require", for consistency. The words "other

parties thereto or" in 31:1082 [former section 1082 of this title] are omitted as surplus. The words "to the Secretary" in 31:1081 [former section 1081 of this title] are omitted as unnecessary and for clarity. The words "in such detail" are omitted as surplus. The words "A participant acting for another person shall make the report as the agent or bailee of the person and identify the person for whom the transaction is being made" are substituted for 31:1082 [former section 1082 of this title] (last sentence) for clarity and to eliminate unnecessary words.

In subsection (b), the words "in his discretion" and "individually or by class" are omitted as surplus. The word "Government" is added for consistency. The words "or a regulation under this subchapter", are added because of the restatement. The words "(except a violation of section 5315 of this title or a regulation prescribed under section 5315)" are added because 31:1141–1143 [former sections 1141 to 1143 of this title] was not enacted as a part of the Currency and Foreign Transactions Reporting Act [former section 1051 et seq. of this title] that is restated in this subchapter.

In subsection (c)(1), clause (A) is substituted for "with respect to a domestic financial institution ... with that institution" for clarity. Clause (C) is substituted for "any such person may, at his election and in lieu of filing the report in the manner hereinabove prescribed, file the report with the Secretary" to eliminate unnecessary words.

References in Text. Section 411 of the National Housing Act, referred to in subsec. (b), is section 411 of Act June 27, 1934, c. 847, Title IV, as added Oct. 26, 1970, Pub.L. 91–508, Title I, § 102, 84 Stat. 1116, which is classified to section 1730d of Title 12, Banks and Banking.

Section 21 of the Federal Deposit Insurance Act, referred to in subsec. (b), is section 2[21] of Act Sept. 21, 1950, c. 967, as added Oct. 26, 1970, Pub.L. 91–508, Title I, § 101, 84 Stat. 1114, which is classified to section 1829b of Title 12.

§ 5314. Records and reports on foreign financial agency transactions

(a) Considering the need to avoid impeding or controlling the export or import of monetary instruments and the need to avoid burdening unreasonably a person making a transaction with a foreign financial agency, the Secretary of the Treasury shall require a resident or citizen of the United States or a person in, and doing business in, the United States, to keep records, file reports, or keep records and file reports, when the resident, citizen, or person makes a transaction or maintains a relation for any person with a foreign financial agency. The records and reports shall contain the following information in the way and to the extent the Secretary prescribes:

(1) the identity and address of participants in a transaction or relationship.

(2) the legal capacity in which a participant is acting.

(3) the identity of real parties in interest.

(4) a description of the transaction.

(b) The Secretary may prescribe—

(1) a reasonable classification of persons subject to or exempt from a requirement under this section or a regulation under this section;

(2) a foreign country to which a requirement or a regulation under this section applies if the Secretary decides applying the requirement or regulation to all foreign countries is unnecessary or undesirable;

(3) the magnitude of transactions subject to a requirement or a regulation under this section;

(4) the kind of transaction subject to or exempt from a requirement or a regulation under this section; and

(5) other matters the Secretary considers necessary to carry out this section or a regulation under this section.

(c) A person shall be required to disclose a record required to be kept under this section or under a regulation under this section only as required by law.

(Pub.L. 97–258, Sept. 13, 1982, 96 Stat. 997.)

REVISION NOTES

Revised Section	Source (U.S. Code)	Source (Statutes at Large)
5314(a)	31:1121(a)	Oct. 26, 1970, Pub.L. 91–508, §§ 241, 242, 84 Stat. 1124.
5314(b)	31:1122	
5314(c)	31:1121(b)....	

In subsection (a), before clause (1), the words "currency or other", "legitimately", "by regulation", and "directly or indirectly" are omitted as surplus. The words "for any person" are substituted for "on behalf of himself or another" to eliminate unnecessary words.

The words "and to the extent" are substituted for "and in such detail" for clarity. In clauses (1) and (2), the words "participants" and "participant" are substituted for "parties" for consistency. In clause (2), the words "to the transaction or relationship" are omitted

as surplus. In clause (3), the words "if one or more of the parties are not acting solely as principals" are omitted as surplus. In clause (4), the words "including the amounts of money, credit, or other property involved" are omitted as surplus.

In subsection (b), the words "or a regulation under this section" are added because of the restatement. The words "or does not apply" and "uniform" in clause (2) are omitted as surplus. In clause (5), the words "carry out" are substituted for "the application of" for consistency.

In subsection (c), the words "produce or otherwise ... the contents of" and "in compliance with a subpena or summons duly authorized and issued or ... may otherwise be" are omitted as surplus. The words "under a regulation" are added because of the restatement.

§ 5315. Reports on foreign currency transactions

(a) Congress finds that—

(1) moving mobile capital can have a significant impact on the proper functioning of the international monetary system;

(2) it is important to have the most feasible current and complete information on the kind and source of capital flows, including transactions by large United States businesses and their foreign affiliates; and

(3) additional authority should be provided to collect information on capital flows under section 5(b) of the Trading With the Enemy Act (50 App. U.S.C. 5(b)) and section 8 of the Bretton Woods Agreement Act (22 U.S.C. 286f).

(b) In this section, "United States person" and "foreign person controlled by a United States person" have the same meanings given those terms in section 7(f)(2)(A) and (C), respectively, of the Securities and Exchange Act of 1934 (15 U.S.C. 78g(f)(2)(A), (C)).

(c) The Secretary of the Treasury shall prescribe regulations consistent with subsection (a) of this section requiring reports on foreign currency transactions conducted by a United States person or a foreign person controlled by a United States person. The regulations shall require that a report contain information and be submitted at the time and in the way, with reasonable exceptions and classifications, necessary to carry out this section.

(Pub.L. 97–258, Sept. 13, 1982, 96 Stat. 997.)

Revised Section	Source (U.S. Code)	Source (Statutes at Large)
5315(a)	31:1141	Sept. 21, 1973, Pub.L. 93–110, §§ 201, 202, 87 Stat. 353.
5315(b), (c)..	31:1142	

In subsection (a)(3), the words "it is desirable to emphasize this objective ... existing legal" are omitted as unnecessary.

In subsection (c), the words "(hereafter referred to as the 'Secretary')" are omitted because of the restatement. The words "under the authority of this subchapter and any other authority conferred by law" are omitted as surplus. The word "prescribe" is substituted for "supplement" for clarity. The words "the statement of findings under" and "the submission of" are omitted as surplus. The words "Reports required under this subchapter shall cover foreign currency transactions" are omitted because of the restatement. The words "such terms are" and "the policy of" are omitted as surplus.

References in Text. Section 5(b) of the Trading With the Enemy Act, referred to in subsec. (a)(3), is section 5(b) of Act Oct. 6, 1917, c. 106, 40 Stat. 415, which is classified to section 5(b) of the Appendix to Title 50, War and National Defense.

Section 5(b) of the Trading With the Enemy Act, referred to in subsec. (a)(3), is also classified to section 95a of Title 12, Banks and Banking.

Section 8 of the Bretton Woods Agreement Act, referred to in subsec. (a)(3), is section 8 of Act July 31, 1945, c. 339, 59 Stat. 515, which is classified to section 286f of Title 22, Foreign Relations and Intercourse.

Section 7(f)(2)(A) and (C) of the Securities and Exchange Act of 1934, referred to in subsec. (b), is section 7(f)(2)(A) and (C) of Act June 6, 1934, c. 404, Title I, 48 Stat. 886, which is classified to section 78g(f)(2)(A) and (C) of Title 15, Commerce and Trade.

International Information Exchange System: Study of Foreign Branches of Domestic Institutions. Pub.L. 99–570, Title XIII, § 1363, Oct. 27, 1986, 100 Stat. 3207–33, provided that:

"(a) **Discussions on International Information Exchange System.**—The Secretary of the Treasury, in consultation with the Board of Governors of the Federal Reserve System, shall initiate discussions with the central banks or other appropriate governmental authorities of other countries and propose that an information exchange system be established to assist the efforts of each participating country to eliminate the international flow of money derived from illicit drug operations and other criminal activities.

"(b) **Report on Discussions Required.**—Before the end of the 9–month period beginning on the date of the enactment of this Act [Oct. 27, 1986], the Secretary of the Treasury shall prepare and transmit a report to the Committee on Banking, Finance and Urban Affairs of the House of Representatives and the Committee on Banking, Housing, and Urban Affairs of the Senate on the results of discussions initiated pursuant to subsection (a).

"(c) **Study of Money Laundering Through Foreign Branches of Domestic Financial Institutions Required.**—The Secretary of the Treasury, in consultation with the Attorney General and the Board of Governors of the Federal Reserve System, shall conduct a study of—

"(1) the extent to which foreign branches of domestic institutions are used—

"(A) to facilitate illicit transfers of coins, currency, and other monetary instruments (as such term is defined in section 5312(a)(3) of title 31, United States Code [31 U.S.C.A. § 5312(a)(3)]) into and out of the United States; and

"(B) to evade reporting requirements with respect to any transfer of coins, currency, and other monetary instruments (as so defined) into and out of the United States;

"(2) the extent to which the law of the United States is applicable to the activities of such foreign branches; and

"(3) methods for obtaining the cooperation of the country in which any such foreign branch is located for purposes of enforcing the law of the United States with respect to transfers, and reports on transfers, of such monetary instruments into and out of the United States.

"(d) **Report on Study of Foreign Branches Required.**—Before the end of the 9–month period beginning on the date of the enactment of this Act [Oct. 27, 1986], the Secretary of the Treasury shall prepare and transmit a report to the Committee on Banking, Finance and Urban Affairs and the Committee on the Judiciary of the House of Representatives and the Committee on Banking, Housing, and Urban Affairs and the Committee on the Judiciary of the Senate on the results of the study conducted pursuant to subsection (c)."

§ 5316. Reports on exporting and importing monetary instruments

(a) Except as provided in subsection (c) of this section, a person or an agent or bailee of the person shall file a report under subsection (b) of this section when the person, agent, or bailee knowingly—

(1) transports, is about to transport, or has transported, monetary instruments of more than $10,000 at one time—

(A) from a place in the United States to or through a place outside the United States; or

(B) to a place in the United States from or through a place outside the United States; or

(2) receives monetary instruments of more than $10,000 at one time transported into the United States from or through a place outside the United States.

(b) A report under this section shall be filed at the time and place the Secretary of the Treasury prescribes. The report shall contain the following information to the extent the Secretary prescribes:

(1) the legal capacity in which the person filing the report is acting.

(2) the origin, destination, and route of the monetary instruments.

(3) when the monetary instruments are not legally and beneficially owned by the person transporting the instruments, or if the person transporting the instruments personally is not going to use them, the identity of the person that gave the instruments to the person transporting them, the identity of the person who is to receive them, or both.

(4) the amount and kind of monetary instruments transported.

(5) additional information.

(c) This section or a regulation under this section does not apply to a common carrier of passengers when a passenger possesses a monetary instrument, or to a common carrier of goods if the shipper does not declare the instrument.

(d) Cumulation of closely related events.— The Secretary of the Treasury may prescribe regulations under this section defining the term "at one time" for purposes of subsection (a). Such regulations may permit the cumulation of closely related events in order that such events may collectively be considered to occur at one time for the purposes of subsection (a).

(Pub.L. 97–258, Sept. 13, 1982, 96 Stat. 998; Pub. L. 98–473, Title II, § 901(c), Oct. 12, 1984, 98 Stat.

2135; Pub.L. 99–570, Title I, § 1358, Title III, § 3153, Oct. 27, 1986, 100 Stat. 3207–26, 3207–94.)

REVISION NOTES

Revised Section	Source (U.S. Code)	Source (Statutes at Large)
5316(a)	31:1101(a)	Oct. 26, 1970, Pub.L. 91–508, § 231, 84 Stat. 1122.
5316(b)	31:1101(b)	
5316(c)	31:1101(c)	

In subsection (a), before clause (1), the words "a person or an agent or bailee of the person shall" are substituted for "whoever, whether as principal, agent, or bailee, or by an agent or bailee" for consistency. The words "or reports" are omitted as unnecessary because of 1:1 [section 1 of Title 1, General Provisions]. In clause (2), the words "transported into the United States" are substituted for "at the termination of their transportation to the United States" for consistency and to eliminate unnecessary words.

In subsection (b), before clause (1), the word "required" is omitted as surplus. The word "prescribes" is substituted for "require" for consistency in the revised title and with other titles of the United States Code. The words "to the extent" are substituted for "in such detail" for clarity. In clause (1), the words "with respect to the monetary instruments transported" are omitted as surplus. In clause (3), the words "or if the person transporting the instruments personally is not going to use them" are substituted for "or are transported for any purpose other than the use in his own behalf of the person transporting the same" for clarity.

In subsection (c), the words "or a regulation under this section" are added because of the restatement.

EDITORIAL NOTES

Effective Date of Regulations Prescribed by 1986 Amendment. Section 1364(d) of Pub.L. 99–570 provided that: "Any regulation prescribed under the amendments made by section 1358 [amending this section] shall apply with respect to transactions completed after the effective date of such regulation."

§ 5317. Search and forfeiture of monetary instruments

(a) The Secretary of the Treasury may apply to a court of competent jurisdiction for a search warrant when the Secretary reasonably believes a monetary instrument is being transported and a report on the instrument under section 5316 of this title has not been filed or contains a material omission or misstatement. The Secretary shall include a statement of information in support of the warrant. On a showing of probable cause, the court may issue a search warrant for a designated person or a designated or described place or physical object. This subsection does not affect the authority of the Secretary under another law.

(b) Searches at border.—For purposes of ensuring compliance with the requirements of section 5316, a customs officer may stop and search, at the border and without a search warrant, any vehicle, vessel, aircraft, or other conveyance, any envelope or other container, and any person entering or departing from the United States.

(c) If a report required under section 5316 with respect to any monetary instrument is not filed (or if filed, contains a material omission or misstatement of fact), the instrument and any interest in property, including a deposit in a financial institution, traceable to such instrument may be seized and forfeited to the United States Government. A monetary instrument transported by mail or a common carrier, messenger, or bailee is being transported under this subsection from the time the instrument is delivered to the United States Postal Service, common carrier, messenger, or bailee through the time it is delivered to the addressee, intended recipient, or agent of the addressee or intended recipient without being transported further in, or taken out of, the United States.

(Pub.L. 97–258, Sept. 13, 1982, 96 Stat. 998; Pub. L. 98–473, Title II, § 901(d), Oct. 12, 1984, 98 Stat. 2135; Pub.L. 99–570, Title I, § 1355, Oct. 27, 1986, 100 Stat. 3207–22.)

REVISION NOTES

Revised Section	Source (U.S. Code)	Source (Statutes at Large)
5317(a)	31:1105	Oct. 26, 1970, Pub.L. 91–508, §§ 232, 235, 84 Stat. 1123.
5317(b)	31:1102	

In subsection (a), the words "The Secretary shall include a statement of information in support of the warrant" are substituted for 31:1105(a) [former section 1105(a) of this title] (last sentence) to eliminate unnecessary words and for consistency. The word "for" is substituted for "authorizing the search of . . . all of the following" to eliminate unnecessary words.

The words "or more" are omitted as unnecessary because the singular includes the plural under 1:1 [section 1 of Title 1, General Provisions]. The words "or

premises", "letters, parcels, packages, or other", and "vehicles" are omitted as surplus.

In subsection (b), the words "either" and "the possession of" are omitted as surplus. The words "United States Postal Service" are substituted for "postal service" for consistency with title 39 [Title 39, Postal Service]. The words "or retained in" are omitted as surplus.

EDITORIAL NOTES

Effective Date of 1986 Amendment. Section 1364(b) of Pub.L. 99–570 provided that: "The amendments made by sections 1355(b) [amending subsec. (c) of this section] and 1357(a) [amending section 5321(a) of this title by adding par. (4) thereto] shall apply with respect to violations committed after the end of the 3–month period beginning on the date of the enactment of this Act [Oct. 27, 1986]."

§ 5318. Compliance, exemptions, and summons authority

(a) General powers of Secretary.—The Secretary of the Treasury may (except under section 5315 of this title and regulations prescribed under section 5315)—

(1) except as provided in subsection (b)(2), delegate duties and powers under this subchapter to an appropriate supervising agency or the Postal Inspection Service and the Postal Service;

(2) require a class of domestic financial institutions to maintain appropriate procedures to ensure compliance with this subchapter and regulations prescribed under this subchapter;

(3) examine any books, papers, records, or other data of domestic financial institutions relevant to the recordkeeping or reporting requirements of this subchapter;

(4) summon a financial institution, an officer or employee of a financial institution (including a former officer or employee), or any person having possession, custody, or care of the reports and records required under this subchapter, to appear before the Secretary of the Treasury or his delegate at a time and place named in the summons and to produce such books, papers, records, or other data, and to give testimony, under oath, as may be relevant or material to an investigation described in subsection (b); and

(5) prescribe an appropriate exemption from a requirement under this subchapter and regulations prescribed under this subchapter. The

Secretary may revoke an exemption by actually or constructively notifying the parties affected. A revocation is effective during judicial review.

(b) Limitations on summons power.—

(1) Scope of power.—The Secretary of the Treasury may take any action described in paragraph (3) or (4) of subsection (a) only in connection with investigations for the purpose of civil enforcement of violations of this subchapter, section 21 of the Federal Deposit Insurance Act, section 411 of the National Housing Act, or chapter 2 of Public Law 91–508 (12 U.S.C. 1951 et seq.) or any regulation under any such provision.

(2) Authority to issue.—A summons may be issued under subsection (a)(4) only by, or with the approval of, the Secretary of the Treasury or a supervisory level delegate of the Secretary of the Treasury.

(c) Administrative aspects of summons.—

(1) Production at designated site.—A summons issued pursuant to this section may require that books, papers, records, or other data stored or maintained at any place be produced at any designated location in any State or in any territory or other place subject to the jurisdiction of the United States not more than 500 miles distant from any place where the financial institution operates or conducts business in the United States.

(2) Fees and travel expenses.—Persons summoned under this section shall be paid the same fees and mileage for travel in the United States that are paid witnesses in the courts of the United States.

(3) No liability for expenses.—The United States shall not be liable for any expense, other than an expense described in paragraph (2), incurred in connection with the production of books, papers, records, or other data under this section.

(d) Service of summons.—Service of a summons issued under this section may be by registered mail or in such other manner calculated to give actual notice as the Secretary may prescribe by regulation.

(e) Contumacy or refusal.—

(1) Referral to Attorney General.—In case of contumacy by a person issued a summons under paragraph (3) or (4) of subsection (a) or a refusal by such person to obey such summons, the Secretary of the Treasury shall refer the matter to the Attorney General.

(2) Jurisdiction of court.—The Attorney General may invoke the aid of any court of the United States within the jurisdiction of which—

(A) the investigation which gave rise to the summons is being or has been carried on;

(B) the person summoned is an inhabitant; or

(C) the person summoned carries on business or may be found, to compel compliance with the summons.

(3) Court order.—The court may issue an order requiring the person summoned to appear before the Secretary or his delegate to produce books, papers, records, and other data, to give testimony as may be necessary to explain how such material was compiled and maintained, and to pay the costs of the proceeding.

(4) Failure to comply with order.—Any failure to obey the order of the court may be punished by the court as a contempt thereof.

(5) Service of process.—All process in any case under this subsection may be served in any judicial district in which such person may be found.

(f) Written and signed statement required. —No person shall qualify for an exemption under subsection (a)(5) unless the relevant financial institution prepares and maintains a statement which—

(1) describes in detail the reasons why such person is qualified for such exemption; and

(2) contains the signature of such person.

(Pub.L. 97–258, Sept. 13, 1982, 96 Stat. 999; Pub. L. 99–570, Title I, § 1356(a), (b), (c)(2), Oct. 27, 1986, 100 Stat. 3207–23, 3207–24; Pub.L. 100–690, Title VI, §§ 6185(e), 6469(c), Nov. 18, 1988, 102 Stat. 4357, 4377.)

REVISION NOTES

Revised Section	Source (U.S. Code)	Source (Statutes at Large)
5318	31:1054(a), (b) (1st sentence)......	Oct. 26, 1970, Pub.L. 91–508, §§ 205(a), (b), (1st sentence), 206, 84 Stat. 1120.
	31:1055	

In the section, before clause (1), the words "have the responsibility to assure compliance with the requirements of this chapter" in 31:1054(a) [former section 1054(a) of this title] are omitted as unnecessary because of section 321 of the revised title [section 321 of this title]. The words "(except under section 5315 of this title and regulations prescribed under section 5315)" are added because 31:1141–1143 [former sections 1141 to 1143 of this title] was not enacted as a part of the Currency and Foreign Transactions Reporting Act [former section 1051 et seq. of this title] that is restated in this subchapter. In clause (1), the words "duties and powers" are substituted for "responsibilities" for consistency in the revised title and with other titles of the United States Code. The words "bank supervisory agency, or other" are omitted as surplus. In clause (2), the words "by regulation" and "as he may deem" are omitted as surplus. The words "and regulations prescribed under this subchapter" are added because of the restatement. In clause (3), the word "prescribe" is substituted for "make" in 31:1055 [former section 1055 of this title] for consistency in the revised title and with other titles of the Code. The words "otherwise imposed", 31:1055 [former section 1055 of this title] (1st sentence), and the words "in his discretion" are omitted as surplus.

EDITORIAL NOTES

References in Text. Section 21 of the Federal Deposit Insurance Act, referred to in subsec. (b)(1), is section 2[21] of Act Sept. 21, 1950, c. 967, as added Oct. 26, 1970, Pub.L. 91–508, Title I, § 101, 84 Stat. 1114, and amended, which is classified to section 1829b of Title 12, Banks and Banking.

Section 411 of the National Housing Act, referred to in subsec. (b)(1), is section 411 of Act June 27, 1934, c. 847, Title IV, as added Oct. 26, 1970, Pub.L. 91–508, Title I, § 102, 84 Stat. 1116, which is classified to section 1730d of Title 12.

Chapter 2 of Pub.L. 91–508 (12 U.S.C. 1951 et seq.), referred to in subsec. (b)(1), probably means Pub.L. 91–508, Title I, Chapter 2, § 121 et seq., Oct. 26, 1970, 84 Stat. 1116, which is classified to chapter 21 (section 1951 et seq.) of Title 12.

§ 5319. Availability of reports

The Secretary of the Treasury shall make information in a report filed under section 5313, 5314, or 5316 of this title available to an agency on request of the head of the agency. The report shall be available for a purpose consistent with those sections or a regulation prescribed under those sections. However, a report and records of reports are exempt from disclosure under section 552 of title 5.

(Pub.L. 97–258, Sept. 13, 1982, 96 Stat. 999.)

REVISION NOTES

Revised Section	Source (U.S. Code)	Source (Statutes at Large)
5319	31:1052(j)	Oct. 26, 1970, Pub.L. 91–508, §§ 203(j), 212, 84 Stat. 1120, 1121.
	31:1061	

The words "upon such conditions and pursuant to such procedures as he may by regulation prescribe" and "set forth" in 31:1061 [former section 1061 of this title], and the word "specifically" in 31:1052(j) [former section 1052(j) of this title], are omitted as surplus.

§ 5320. Injunctions

When the Secretary of the Treasury believes a person has violated, is violating, or will violate this subchapter or a regulation prescribed or order issued under this subchapter, the Secretary may bring a civil action in the appropriate district court of the United States or appropriate United States court of a territory or possession of the United States to enjoin the violation or to enforce compliance with the subchapter, regulation, or order. An injunction or temporary restraining order shall be issued without bond.

(Pub.L. 97–258, Sept. 13, 1982, 96 Stat. 999.)

REVISION NOTES

Revised Section	Source (U.S. Code)	Source (Statutes at Large)
5320	31:1057	Oct. 26, 1970, Pub.L. 91–508, § 208, 84 Stat. 1120.
	31:1143(b) (words before last comma)	Sept. 21, 1973, Pub.L. 93–110, § 203(b) (words before last comma), 87 Stat. 353.

The words "has violated, is violating, or will violate this subchapter" are substituted for "has engaged, is engaged, or is about to engage in any acts or practices constituting a violation of the provisions of this chapter" in 31:1057 [former section 1057 of this title] and "failed to submit a report required under any rule or regulation issued under this subchapter or has violated any rule or regulation issued hereunder" in 31:1143(b) [former section 1143(b) of this title] (words before last comma) to eliminate unnecessary words. The words "or a regulation prescribed" are added because of the restatement. The words "in his discretion" are omitted as surplus. The word "civil" is added because of rule 2 of the Federal Rules of Civil Procedure (28 App.U.S.C.) [rule 2, Federal Rules of Civil Procedure, Title 28, Judiciary and Judicial Procedure]. The word "possession" is substituted for "other place subject to the jurisdiction" for consistency in the revised title and with other titles of the United States Code. The words "or to enforce compliance with the subchapter, regulation, or order" are substituted for 31:1057 [former section 1057 of this title] (last sentence) and the words "a mandatory injunction commanding such person to comply with such rule or regulation" in 31:1143(b) [former section 1143(b) of this title] (words before last comma) to eliminate unnecessary words. The words "and upon a proper showing ... permanent or" are omitted as surplus.

§ 5321. Civil penalties

(a)(1) A domestic financial institution, and a partner, director, officer, or employee of a domestic financial institution, willfully violating this subchapter or a regulation prescribed under this subchapter (except sections 5314 and 5315 of this title or a regulation prescribed under sections 5314 and 5315) is liable to the United States Government for a civil penalty of not more than the greater of the amount (not to exceed $100,000) involved in the transaction (if any) or $25,000. For a violation of section 5318(a)(2) of this title or a regulation prescribed under section 5318(a)(2), a separate violation occurs for each day the violation continues and at each office, branch, or place of business at which a violation occurs or continues.

(2) The Secretary of the Treasury may impose an additional civil penalty on a person not filing a report, or filing a report containing a material omission or misstatement, under section 5316 of this title or a regulation prescribed under section 5316. A civil penalty under this paragraph may not be more than the amount of the monetary instrument for which the report was required. A civil penalty under this paragraph is reduced by an amount forfeited under section 5317(b) of this title.

(3) A person not filing a report under a regulation prescribed under section 5315 of this title or not complying with an injunction under section 5320 of this title enjoining a violation of, or enforcing compliance with, section 5315 or a regulation prescribed under section 5315, is liable to the Government for a civil penalty of not more than $10,000.

(4) Structured transaction violation.—

(A) Penalty authorized.—The Secretary of the Treasury may impose a civil money penalty on any person who willfully violates any provision of section 5324.

(B) Maximum amount limitation.—The amount of any civil money penalty imposed under subparagraph (A) shall not exceed the amount of the coins and currency (or such other monetary instruments as the Secretary may prescribe) involved in the transaction with respect to which such penalty is imposed.

(C) Coordination with forfeiture provision.—The amount of any civil money penalty imposed by the Secretary under subparagraph (A) shall be reduced by the amount of any forfeiture to the United States under section 5317(d) in connection with the transaction with respect to which such penalty is imposed.

(5) Foreign financial agency transaction violation.—

(A) Penalty authorized.—The Secretary of the Treasury may impose a civil money penalty on any person who willfully violates any provision of section 5314.

(B) Maximum amount limitation.—The amount of any civil money penalty imposed under subparagraph (A) shall not exceed—

(i) in the case of violation of such section involving a transaction, the greater of—

(I) the amount (not to exceed $100,000) of the transaction; or

(II) $25,000; and

(ii) in the case of violation of such section involving a failure to report the existence of an account or any identifying information required to be provided with respect to such account, the greater of—

(I) an amount (not to exceed $100,000) equal to the balance in the account at the time of the violation; or

(II) $25,000.

(6) Negligence.—The Secretary of the Treasury may impose a civil money penalty of not more than $500 on any financial institution which negligently violates any provision of this subchapter or any regulation prescribed under this subchapter.

(b) Time limitations for assessments and commencement of civil actions.—

(1) Assessments.—The Secretary of the Treasury may assess a civil penalty under subsection (a) at any time before the end of the 6-year period beginning on the date of the transaction with respect to which the penalty is assessed.

(2) Civil actions.—The Secretary may commence a civil action to recover a civil penalty assessed under subsection (a) at any time before the end of the 2-year period beginning on the later of—

(A) the date the penalty was assessed; or

(B) the date any judgment becomes final in any criminal action under section 5322 in connection with the same transaction with respect to which the penalty is assessed.

(c) The Secretary may remit any part of a forfeiture under subsection (c) or (d) of section 5317 of this title or civil penalty under subsection (a)(2) of this section.

(d) Criminal penalty not exclusive of civil penalty.—A civil money penalty may be imposed under subsection (a) with respect to any violation of this subchapter notwithstanding the fact that a criminal penalty is imposed with respect to the same violation.

(Pub.L. 97–258, Sept. 13, 1982, 96 Stat. 999; Pub. L. 98–473, Title II, § 901(a), Oct. 12, 1984, 98 Stat. 2135; Pub.L. 99–570, Title I, §§ 1356(c)(1), 1357(a)–(f), (h), Oct. 27, 1986, 100 Stat. 3207–24, 3207–25, 3207–26; Pub.L. 100–690, Title VI, § 6185(g)(2), Nov. 18, 1988, 102 Stat. 4357.)

REVISION NOTES

Revised Section	Source (U.S. Code)	Source (Statutes at Large)
5321(a)(1) . . .	31:1054(b) (last sentence related to civil penalties). . .	Oct. 26, 1970, Pub.L. 91–508, §§ 205(b) (last sentence related to civil penalties), 207, 233, 234, 84 Stat. 1120, 1123.
5321(a)(2) . . .	31:1056(a) 31:1103	
5321(a)(3) . . .	31:1143(a), (b) (words after last comma)	Sept. 21, 1973, Pub.L. 93–110, § 203(a), (b)
5321(b)	31:1056(b)	(words after last comma), 87 Stat. 353.
5321(c)	31:1104	

In subsection (a)(1), the words "or a regulation prescribed under this subchapter" are added because of the restatement. The words "(except section 5315 of this title or a regulation prescribed under section 5315)" are added because 31:1141–1143 [former sections 1141 to 1143 of this title] was not enacted as a part of the Currency and Foreign Transactions Reporting Act [former section 1051 et seq. of this title] that is restated in this subchapter. The words "is liable to the United States Government for" are substituted for "the Secretary may assess upon" in 31:1056(a) [former section 1056(a) of this title] for consistency in the revised title and with other titles of the United States Code. The words "the purposes of both civil and criminal penalties for" in 31:1054(b) [former section 1054(b) of this title] (last sentence) (related to civil penalties) are omitted, and the words "or a regulation prescribed under section 5318(2)" are added, because of the restatement. The words "the violation continues" are added for consistency in the revised title and with other titles of the Code. The word "separate" before "office" is omitted as surplus.

In subsection (a)(2), the word "impose" is substituted for "assess" for consistency in the revised title and with other titles of the Code. The word "additional" is substituted for 31:1103 [former section 1103 of this title] (last sentence words before last comma) to eliminate unnecessary words. The words "or a regulation prescribed under section 5316" are added because of the restatement. The words "amount of this", "to be filed", and "actually" are omitted as surplus.

Subsection (a)(3) is substituted for 31:1143(a) and (b) [former section 1143(a) and (b) of this title] (words after last comma) for clarity and consistency and because of the restatement.

In subsection (b), the words "in the discretion of", "in the name of the United States", and "of any person" are omitted as surplus.

In subsection (c), the words "in his discretion" and "upon such terms and conditions as he deems reasonable and just" are omitted as surplus. The word "civil" is added for clarity.

EDITORIAL NOTES

Effective Date of 1986 Amendment. Section 1364(c) of Pub.L. 99–570 provided that: "The amendments made by section 1357 (other than subsection (a) of such section) [amending this section and section 5322(b) of this title] shall apply with respect to violations committed after the date of the enactment of this Act [Oct. 27, 1986]."

Amendment to subsec. (a) of this section by section 1357(a) of Pub.L. 99–570, adding par. (4) thereto, to apply with respect to violations committed after the end of the 3–month period beginning on Oct. 27, 1986, see section 1364(b) of Pub.L. 99–570, set out as a note under section 5317 of this title.

§ 5322. Criminal penalties

(a) A person willfully violating this subchapter or a regulation prescribed under this subchapter (except section 5315 of this title or a regulation prescribed under section 5315) shall be fined not more than $250,000, or imprisonment [1] not more than five years, or both.

(b) A person willfully violating this subchapter or a regulation prescribed under this subchapter (except section 5315 of this title or a regulation prescribed under section 5315), while violating another law of the United States or as part of a pattern of any illegal activity involving more than $100,000 in a 12–month period, shall be fined not more than $500,000, imprisoned for not more than 10 years, or both.

(c) For a violation of section 5318(a)(2) of this title or a regulation prescribed under section 5318(a)(2), a separate violation occurs for each day the violation continues and at each office, branch, or place of business at which a violation occurs or continues.

(Pub.L. 97–258, Sept. 13, 1982, 96 Stat. 1000; Pub.L. 98–473, Title II, § 901(b), Oct. 12, 1984, 98 Stat. 2135; Pub.L. 99–570, Title I, §§ 1356(c)(1), 1357(g), Oct. 27, 1986, 100 Stat. 3207–24, 3207–26.)

1. So in original. "Imprisoned for" was probably intended.

REVISION NOTES

Revised Section	Source (U.S. Code)	Source (Statutes at Large)
5322(a)	31:1058	Oct. 26, 1970, Pub.L. 91–508, §§ 205(b) (last sentence related to criminal penalties), 209, 210, 84 Stat. 1120, 1121.
5322(b)	31:1059	
5322(c)	31:1054(b) (last sentence related to criminal penalties).	

In subsections (a) and (b), the words "(except section 5315 of this title or a regulation prescribed under section 5315)" are added because 31:1141–1143 [former sections 1141 to 1143 of this title] was not enacted as part of the Currency and Foreign Transactions Reporting Act [former section 1051 et seq. of this title] that is restated in the subchapter.

In subsection (a), the word "prescribed" is added for consistency.

In subsection (b), the words "or a regulation prescribed under this subchapter" are added because of the restatement. The words "committed" and "the commission of" are omitted as surplus. The words "United States" are substituted for "Federal" for consistency in the revised title and with other titles of the United States Code.

In subsection (c), the words "the purposes of both civil and criminal penalties for" are omitted because of the restatement. The word "separate" before "office" is omitted as surplus.

EDITORIAL NOTES

Effective Date of 1986 Amendment. Amendment to subsec. (b) of this section by section 1357(g) of Pub.L. 99–570 to apply with respect to violations committed after Oct. 27, 1986, see section 1364(c) of Pub.L. 99–570, set out as a note under section 5321 of this title.

§ 5323. Rewards for informants

(a) The Secretary may pay a reward to an individual who provides original information which leads to a recovery of a criminal fine, civil penalty, or forfeiture, which exceeds $50,000, for a violation of this chapter.

(b) The Secretary shall determine the amount of a reward under this section. The Secretary may not award more than 25 per centum of the net amount of the fine, penalty, or forfeiture collected or $150,000, whichever is less.

(c) An officer or employee of the United States, a State, or a local government who provides information described in subsection (a) in the performance of official duties is not eligible for a reward under this section.

(d) There are authorized to be appropriated such sums as may be necessary to carry out the provisions of this section.

(Added Pub.L. 98–473, Title II, § 901(e), Oct. 12, 1984, 98 Stat. 2135.)

§ 5324. Structuring transactions to evade reporting requirement prohibited

No person shall for the purpose of evading the reporting requirements of section 5313(a) with respect to such transaction—

(1) cause or attempt to cause a domestic financial institution to fail to file a report required under section 5313(a);

(2) cause or attempt to cause a domestic financial institution to file a report required under section 5313(a) that contains a material omission or misstatement of fact; or

(3) structure or assist in structuring, or attempt to structure or assist in structuring, any transaction with one or more domestic financial institutions.

(Added Pub.L. 99–570, Title I, § 1354(a), Oct. 27, 1986, 100 Stat. 3207–22.)

EDITORIAL NOTES

Effective Date. Section 1364(a) of Pub.L. 99–570 provided that: "The amendment made by section 1354 [enacting this section] shall apply with respect to transactions for the payment, receipt, or transfer of United States coins or currency or other monetary instruments completed after the end of the 3–month period beginning on the date of the enactment of this Act [Oct. 27, 1986]."

§ 5325. Identification required to purchase certain monetary instruments

(a) **In general.**—No financial institution may issue or sell a bank check, cashier's check, traveler's check, or money order to any individual in connection with a transaction or group of such contemporaneous transactions which involves United States coins or currency (or such other monetary instruments as the Secretary may prescribe) in amounts or denominations of $3,000 or more unless—

(1) the individual has a transaction account with such financial institution and the financial institution—

(A) verifies that fact through a signature card or other information maintained by such institution in connection with the account of such individual; and

(B) records the method of verification in accordance with regulations which the Secretary of the Treasury shall prescribe; or

(2) the individual furnishes the financial institution with such forms of identification as the Secretary of the Treasury may require in regulations which the Secretary shall prescribe and the financial institution verifies and records such information in accordance with regulations which such Secretary shall prescribe.

(b) **Report to Secretary upon request.**—Any information required to be recorded by any financial institution under paragraph (1) or (2) of subsection (a) shall be reported by such institution to the Secretary of the Treasury at the request of such Secretary.

(c) **Transaction account defined.**—For purposes of this section, the term "transaction account" has the meaning given to such term in section 19(b)(1)(C) of the Federal Reserve Act.

(Added Pub.L. 100–690, Title VI, § 6185(b), Nov. 18, 1988, 102 Stat. 4355.)

§ 5326. Records of certain domestic coin and currency transactions

(a) **In general.**—If the Secretary of the Treasury finds, upon the Secretary's own initiative or at the request of an appropriate Federal or State law enforcement official, that reasonable grounds exist for concluding that additional recordkeeping and reporting requirements are necessary to carry out the purposes of this subtitle and prevent evasions thereof, the Secretary may issue an order requiring any domestic financial institution or group of domestic financial institutions in a geographic area—

(1) to obtain such information as the Secretary may describe in such order concerning—

(A) any transaction in which such financial institution is involved for the payment, receipt, or transfer of United States coins or currency (or such other monetary instruments as the Secretary may describe in such order) the total amounts or denominations of which are equal to or greater than an amount which the Secretary may prescribe; and

(B) any other person participating in such transaction;

(2) to maintain a record of such information for such period of time as the Secretary may require; and

(3) to file a report with respect to any transaction described in paragraph (1)(A) in the manner and to the extent specified in the order.

(b) Maximum effective period for order.— No order issued under subsection (a) shall be effective for more than 60 days unless renewed pursuant to the requirements of subsection (a).

(Added Pub.L. 100–690, Title VI, § 6185(c), Nov. 18, 1988, 102 Stat. 4355.)

TITLE 46
SHIPPING, APPENDIX

CHAPTER 38

MARITIME DRUG LAW ENFORCEMENT

As amended to February 1, 1989

§ 1901. Short title

That this chapter may be cited as the "Maritime Drug Law Enforcement Act".

(Pub.L. 96–350, § 1, Sept. 15, 1980, 94 Stat. 1159; Pub.L. 99–570, Title III, § 3203, Oct. 27, 1986, 100 Stat. 3302; Pub.L. 99–640, § 17, Nov. 10, 1986, 100 Stat. 3552.)

Editorial Notes

Codification. Section was formerly classified to section 955a of Title 21, Food and Drugs.

§ 1902. Congressional declaration of findings

The Congress finds and declares that trafficking in controlled substances aboard vessels is a serious international problem and is universally condemned. Moreover, such trafficking presents a specific threat to the security and societal well-being of the United States.

(Pub.L. 96–350, § 2, Sept. 15, 1980, 94 Stat. 1160; Pub.L. 99–570, Title III, § 3202, Oct. 27, 1986, 100 Stat. 3302; Pub.L. 99–640, § 17, Nov. 10, 1986, 100 Stat. 3552).

Editorial Notes

Codification. Section was formerly classified to section 955b of Title 21, Food and Drugs.

Interdiction Procedures for Vessels of Foreign Registry. Section 2015 of Pub.L. 99–570, as amended Pub.L. 100–690, Title IV, § 4802(a)(1), Nov. 18, 1988, 102 Stat. 4294, provided that:

"(a) **Findings.**—The Congress finds that—

"(1) the interdiction by the United States Coast Guard of vessels suspected for carrying illicit narcotics can be a difficult procedure when the vessel is of foreign registry and is located beyond the customs waters of the United States;

"(2) before boarding and inspecting such a vessel, the Coast Guard must obtain consent from either the master of the vessel or the country of registry; and

"(3) this process, and obtaining the consent of the country of registry to further law enforcement action, may delay the interdiction of the vessel by 3 or 4 days.

"(b) **Negotiations concerning interdiction procedures.—**

"(1) The Congress urges the Secretary of State, in consultation with the Secretary of the department in which the Coast Guard is operating, to increase efforts to negotiate with relevant countries procedures which will facilitate interdiction of vessels suspected of carrying illicit narcotics.

"(2) If a country refuses to negotiate with respect to interdiction procedures, the President shall take appropriate actions directed against that country, which may include the denial of access to United States ports to vessels registered in that country.

"(3) The Secretary of State shall submit reports to the Congress semiannually identifying those countries which have failed to negotiate with respect to interdiction procedures."

§ 1903. Manufacture, distribution, or possession with intent to manufacture or distribute controlled substances on board vessels

(a) Vessels of United States or vessels subject to jurisdiction of United States

It is unlawful for any person on board a vessel of the United States, or on board a vessel subject to the jurisdiction of the United States, or who is a citizen of the United States or a resident alien of the United States on board any vessel, to knowingly or intentionally manufacture or distribute, or to possess with intent to manufacture or distribute, a controlled substance.

(b) "Vessel of the United States" defined

For purposes of this section, a "vessel of the United States" means—

(1) a vessel documented under chapter 121 of Title 46 or a vessel numbered as provided in chapter 123 of that title;

(2) a vessel owned in whole or part by—

(A) the United States or a territory, commonwealth, or possession of the United States;

(B) a State or political subdivision thereof;

(C) a citizen or national of the United States; or

(D) a corporation created under the laws of the United States or any State, the District of Columbia, or any territory, commonwealth, or possession of the United States;

unless the vessel has been granted the nationality of a foreign nation in accordance with article 5 of the 1958 Convention on the High Seas and a claim of nationality or registry for the vessel is made by the master or individual in charge at the time of the enforcement action by an officer or employee of the United States authorized to enforce applicable provisions of United States law; and

(3) a vessel that was once documented under the laws of the United States and, in violation of the laws of the United States, was either sold to a person not a citizen of the United States or placed under foreign registry or a foreign flag, whether or not the vessel has been granted the nationality of a foreign nation.

(c) "Vessel subject to the jurisdiction of the United States" and "vessel without nationality" defined; claim of nationality or registry

(1) For purposes of this section, a "vessel subject to the jurisdiction of the United States" includes—

(A) a vessel without nationality;

(B) a vessel assimilated to a vessel without nationality, in accordance with paragraph (2) of article 6 of the 1958 Convention on the High Seas;

(C) a vessel registered in a foreign nation where the flag nation has consented or waived objection to the enforcement of United States law by the United States;

(D) a vessel located within the customs waters of the United States; and

(E) a vessel located in the territorial waters of another nation, where the nation consents to the enforcement of United States law by the United States.

Consent or waiver of objection by a foreign nation to the enforcement of United States law by the United States under subparagraph (C) or (E) of this paragraph may be obtained by radio, telephone, or similar oral or electronic means, and may be proved by certification of the Secretary of State or the Secretary's designee.

(2) For purposes of this section, a "vessel without nationality" includes—

(A) a vessel aboard which the master or person in charge makes a claim of registry, which claim is denied by the flag nation whose registry is claimed; and

(B) any vessel aboard which the master or person in charge fails, upon request of an officer of the United States empowered to enforce applicable provisions of United States law, to make a claim of nationality or registry for that vessel.

A claim of registry under subparagraph (A) may be verified or denied by radio, telephone, or similar oral or electronic means. The denial of such claim of registry by the claimed flag nation may be proved by certification of the Secretary of State or the Secretary's designee.

(3) For purposes of this section, a claim of nationality or registry only includes:

(A) possession on board the vessel and production of documents evidencing the vessel's nationality in accordance with article 5 of the 1958 Convention on the High Seas;

(B) flying its flag nation's ensign or flag; or

(C) a verbal claim of nationality or registry by the master or person in charge of the vessel.

(d) Claim of failure to comply with international law; jurisdiction of court

A claim of failure to comply with international law in the enforcement of this chapter may be invoked solely by a foreign nation, and a failure to comply with international law shall not divest a court of jurisdiction or otherwise constitute a defense to any proceeding under this chapter.

(e) Exceptions; burden of proof

This section does not apply to a common or contract carrier or an employee thereof, who possesses or distributes a controlled substance in the lawful and usual course of the carrier's business or to a public vessel of the United States, or any person on board such a vessel who possesses or distributes a controlled substance in the lawful course of such person's duties, if the controlled substance is a part of the cargo entered in the vessel's manifest and is intended to be lawfully imported into the country of destination for scientific, medical, or other legitimate purposes. It shall not be necessary for the United States to negative the exception set forth in this subsection in any complaint, information, indictment, or other pleading or in any trial or other proceeding. The burden of going forward with the evidence with respect to this exception is upon the person claiming its benefit.

(f) Jurisdiction and venue

Any person who violates this section shall be tried in the United States district court at the point of entry where that person enters the United States, or in the United States District Court of the District of Columbia.

(g) Penalties

(1) Any person who commits an offense defined in this section shall be punished in accordance with the penalties set forth in section 1010 of the Comprehensive Drug Abuse Prevention and Control Act of 1970 (21 U.S.C. 960).

(2) Notwithstanding paragraph (1) of this subsection, any person convicted of an offense under this chapter shall be punished in accordance with the penalties set forth in section 1012 of the Comprehensive Drug Abuse Prevention and Control Act of 1970 (21 U.S.C. 962) if such offense is a second or subsequent offense as defined in section 1012(b) of that Act.

(h) Extension beyond territorial jurisdiction of United States

This section is intended to reach acts of possession, manufacture, or distribution committed outside the territorial jurisdiction of the United States.

(i) Definitions

The definitions in the Comprehensive Drug Abuse Prevention and Control Act of 1970 (21 U.S.C. 802) apply to terms used in this chapter.

(j) Attempt or conspiracy

Any person who attempts or conspires to commit any offense defined in this chapter is punishable by imprisonment or fine, or both, which may not exceed the maximum punishment prescribed for the offense, the commission of which was the object of the attempt or conspiracy.

(Pub.L. 96–350, § 3, Sept. 15, 1980, 94 Stat. 1160; Pub.L. 99–570, Title III, § 3202, Oct. 27, 1986, 100 Stat. 3302; Pub.L. 99–640, § 17, Nov. 10, 1986, 100 Stat. 3552; Pub.L. 100–690, Title VII, § 7402, Nov. 18, 1988, 102 Stat. 4483.)

EDITORIAL NOTES

Codification. Section was formerly classified to section 955c of Title 21, Food and Drugs.

§ 1904. Seizure or forfeiture of property

Any property described in section 881(a) of Title 21 that is used or intended for use to commit, or to facilitate the commission of, an offense under this chapter shall be subject to seizure and forfeiture in the same manner as similar property seized or forfeited under section 881 of Title 21.

(Pub.L. 96–350, § 4, Sept. 15, 1980, 94 Stat. 1160; Pub.L. 99–570, Title III, § 3202, Oct. 27, 1986, 100 Stat. 3302; Pub.L. 99–640, § 17, Nov. 10, 1986, 100 Stat. 3552.)

EDITORIAL NOTES

Codification. Section was formerly classified to section 955d of Title 21, Food and Drugs.

Pub.L. 99–570 originally directed that section 3 of Pub.L. 96–350 be amended but was executed to this section, section 4 of Pub.L. 96–350, as the probable intent of Congress, in view of the previous amendment to section 3 of Pub.L. 96–350 by Pub.L. 99–570.

FEDERAL RULES OF EVIDENCE

INTRODUCTION

The study of Evidence law is the study of the legal regulation of the proof used to persuade on fact questions in a trial. It is worth noting that, in many cases, Evidence law makes no distinction between civil and criminal lawsuits.

While Evidence law was originally almost entirely decisional law, it has become increasingly codified in statutes and rules of court. These often reflect provisions of the major codifications—i.e., the Federal Rules of Evidence or the 1974 Uniform Rules. Remember, no generalizations can substitute for careful consultation of the various pertinent sources in addressing a specific case in a specific jurisdiction. On the other hand, even authoritative law often leaves room for argument in the shadow of varying cases.

The most influential codification of Evidence law in recent years has been the Federal Rules of Evidence ("F.R.E."), 28 U.S.C.A. Rules Appendix, enacted by Congress to govern proceedings in federal courts, effective July 1, 1975. The Federal Rules draw heavily on the earlier California Evidence Code, and also on the Uniform Rules of Evidence (1953) of the National Conference of Commissioners on Uniform State Laws, promulgated as a model for state adoption. Although influential, the Uniform Rules were not widely adopted. In 1974 they were amended to substantially conform to the Federal Rules of Evidence. A growing number of states are now codifying along the lines of the Federal and Uniform Rules.

The Federal and Uniform Rules do not depart greatly from what was regarded as the better reasoned rulings found previously under the common law system.

In addition to strictly evidentiary sources, it should be recognized that state and federal constitutions exert some constraint on evidence rules and rulings, particularly in criminal cases.

For a concise survey of Evidence law, see Rothstein's Evidence in a Nutshell: State and Federal Rules, 2nd Ed., Nutshell Series (West Publishing Company, St. Paul, 1981) ... from pages 1–2 of which this INTRODUCTION is drawn. See also, Graham's Federal Rules of Evidence in a Nutshell, 2nd Ed., Nutshell Series (West Publishing Company, St. Paul, 1987).

RULES OF EVIDENCE FOR UNITED STATES COURTS AND MAGISTRATES

Effective July 1, 1975

(Including Amendments Effective November 18, 1988.)

Table of Rules

ARTICLE I. GENERAL PROVISIONS

ARTICLE II. JUDICIAL NOTICE

ARTICLE III. PRESUMPTIONS IN CIVIL ACTIONS AND PROCEEDINGS

ARTICLE IV. RELEVANCY AND ITS LIMITS

ARTICLE I

GENERAL PROVISIONS

RULE 101

SCOPE

These rules govern proceedings in the courts of the United States and before United States bankruptcy judges and United States magistrates, to the extent and with the exceptions stated in rule 1101.

[Amended effective October 1, 1987; November 1, 1988.]

RULE 102

PURPOSE AND CONSTRUCTION

These rules shall be construed to secure fairness in administration, elimination of unjustifiable expense and delay, and promotion of growth and development of the law of evidence to the end that the truth may be ascertained and proceedings justly determined.

RULE 103

RULINGS ON EVIDENCE

(a) Effect of Erroneous Ruling. Error may not be predicated upon a ruling which admits or excludes evidence unless a substantial right of the party is affected, and

(1) *Objection.* In case the ruling is one admitting evidence, a timely objection or motion to strike appears of record, stating the specific ground of objection, if the specific ground was not apparent from the context; or

(2) *Offer of Proof.* In case the ruling is one excluding evidence, the substance of the evidence was made known to the court by offer or was apparent from the context within which questions were asked.

(b) Record of Offer and Ruling. The court may add any other or further statement which shows the character of the evidence, the form in which it was offered, the objection made, and the ruling thereon. It may direct the making of an offer in question and answer form.

(c) Hearing of Jury. In jury cases, proceedings shall be conducted, to the extent practicable, so as to prevent inadmissible evidence from being suggested to the jury by any means, such as making statements or offers of proof or asking questions in the hearing of the jury.

(d) Plain Error. Nothing in this rule precludes taking notice of plain errors affecting substantial rights although they were not brought to the attention of the court.

RULE 104

PRELIMINARY QUESTIONS

(a) Questions of Admissibility Generally. Preliminary questions concerning the qualification of a person to be a witness, the existence of a privilege, or the admissibility of evidence shall be determined by the court, subject to the provisions of subdivision (b). In making its determination it is not bound by the rules of evidence except those with respect to privileges.

(b) Relevancy Conditioned on Fact. When the relevancy of evidence depends upon the fulfillment of a condition of fact, the court shall admit it upon, or subject to, the introduction of evidence sufficient to support a finding of the fulfillment of the condition.

(c) Hearing of Jury. Hearings on the admissibility of confessions shall in all cases be conducted out of the hearing of the jury. Hearings on other preliminary matters shall be so conducted when the interests of justice require, or when an accused is a witness and so requests.

(d) Testimony by Accused. The accused does not, by testifying upon a preliminary matter, become subject to cross-examination as to other issues in the case.

(e) Weight and Credibility. This rule does not limit the right of a party to introduce before the jury evidence relevant to weight or credibility.

[Amended effective October 1, 1987.]

RULE 105

LIMITED ADMISSIBILITY

When evidence which is admissible as to one party or for one purpose but not admissible as to another party or for another purpose is admitted, the court, upon request, shall restrict the evidence to its proper scope and instruct the jury accordingly.

RULE 106

REMAINDER OF OR RELATED WRITINGS OR RECORDED STATEMENTS

When a writing or recorded statement or part thereof is introduced by a party, an adverse party may require the introduction at that time of any other part or any other writing or recorded statement which ought in fairness to be considered contemporaneously with it.

[Amended effective October 1, 1987.]

ARTICLE II

JUDICIAL NOTICE

RULE 201

JUDICIAL NOTICE OF ADJUDICATIVE FACTS

(a) Scope of Rule. This rule governs only judicial notice of adjudicative facts.

(b) Kinds of Facts. A judicially noticed fact must be one not subject to reasonable dispute in that it is either (1) generally known within the territorial jurisdiction of the trial court or (2) capable of accurate and ready determination by resort to sources whose accuracy cannot reasonably be questioned.

(c) When Discretionary. A court may take judicial notice, whether requested or not.

(d) When Mandatory. A court shall take judicial notice if requested by a party and supplied with the necessary information.

(e) Opportunity to Be Heard. A party is entitled upon timely request to an opportunity to be heard as to the propriety of taking judicial notice and the tenor of the matter noticed. In the absence of prior notification, the request may be made after judicial notice has been taken.

(f) Time of Taking Notice. Judicial notice may be taken at any stage of the proceeding.

(g) Instructing Jury. In a civil action or proceeding, the court shall instruct the jury to accept as conclusive any fact judicially noticed. In a criminal case, the court shall instruct the jury that it may, but is not required to, accept as conclusive any fact judicially noticed.

ARTICLE III

PRESUMPTIONS IN CIVIL ACTIONS AND PROCEEDINGS

RULE 301

PRESUMPTIONS IN GENERAL IN CIVIL ACTIONS AND PROCEEDINGS

In all civil actions and proceedings not otherwise provided for by Act of Congress or by these rules, a presumption imposes on the party against whom it is directed the burden of going forward with evidence to rebut or meet the presumption, but does not shift to such party the burden of proof in the sense of the risk of nonpersuasion, which remains throughout the trial upon the party on whom it was originally cast.

RULE 302

APPLICABILITY OF STATE LAW IN CIVIL ACTIONS AND PROCEEDINGS

In civil actions and proceedings, the effect of a presumption respecting a fact which is an element of a claim or defense as to which State law supplies the rule of decision is determined in accordance with State law.

ARTICLE IV

RELEVANCY AND ITS LIMITS

RULE 401

DEFINITION OF "RELEVANT EVIDENCE"

"Relevant evidence" means evidence having any tendency to make the existence of any fact that is of consequence to the determination of the action more probable or less probable than it would be without the evidence.

RULE 402

RELEVANT EVIDENCE GENERALLY ADMISSIBLE; IRRELEVANT EVIDENCE INADMISSIBLE

All relevant evidence is admissible, except as otherwise provided by the Constitution of the United States, by Act of Congress, by these rules, or by other rules prescribed by the Supreme Court pursuant to statutory authority. Evidence which is not relevant is not admissible.

RULE 403

EXCLUSION OF RELEVANT EVIDENCE ON GROUNDS OF PREJUDICE, CONFUSION, OR WASTE OF TIME

Although relevant, evidence may be excluded if its probative value is substantially outweighed by the danger of unfair prejudice, confusion of the issues, or misleading the jury, or by considerations of undue delay, waste of time, or needless presentation of cumulative evidence.

RULE 404

CHARACTER EVIDENCE NOT ADMISSIBLE TO PROVE CONDUCT; EXCEPTIONS; OTHER CRIMES

(a) Character Evidence Generally. Evidence of a person's character or a trait of character is not admissible for the purpose of proving action in conformity therewith on a particular occasion, except:

(1) *Character of Accused.* Evidence of a pertinent trait of character offered by an accused, or by the prosecution to rebut the same;

(2) *Character of Victim.* Evidence of a pertinent trait of character of the victim of the crime offered by an accused, or by the prosecution to rebut the same, or evidence of a character trait of peacefulness of the victim offered by the prosecution in a homicide case to rebut evidence that the victim was the first aggressor;

(3) *Character of Witness.* Evidence of the character of a witness, as provided in rules 607, 608, and 609.

(b) Other Crimes, Wrongs, or Acts. Evidence of other crimes, wrongs, or acts is not admissible to prove the character of a person in order to show action in conformity therewith. It may, however, be admissible for other purposes, such as proof of motive, opportunity, intent, preparation, plan, knowledge, identity, or absence of mistake or accident.

[Amended effective October 1, 1987.]

RULE 405

METHODS OF PROVING CHARACTER

(a) Reputation or Opinion. In all cases in which evidence of character or a trait of character of a person is admissible, proof may be made by testimony as to reputation or by testimony in the form of an opinion. On cross-examination inquiry is allowable into relevant specific instances of conduct.

(b) Specific Instances of Conduct. In cases in which character or a trait of character of a person is an essential element of a charge, claim, or defense, proof may also be made of specific instances of that person's conduct.

[Amended effective October 1, 1987.]

RULE 406

HABIT; ROUTINE PRACTICE

Evidence of the habit of a person or of the routine practice of an organization, whether corroborated or not and regardless of the presence of eyewitnesses, is relevant to prove that the conduct of the person or organization on a particular occasion was in conformity with the habit or routine practice.

RULE 407

SUBSEQUENT REMEDIAL MEASURES

When, after an event, measures are taken which, if taken previously, would have made the event less likely to occur, evidence of the subsequent measures is not admissible to prove negligence or culpable conduct in connection with the event. This rule does not require the exclusion of evidence of subsequent measures when offered for another purpose, such as proving ownership, control, or feasibility of precautionary measures, if controverted, or impeachment.

RULE 408

COMPROMISE AND OFFERS TO COMPROMISE

Evidence of (1) furnishing or offering or promising to furnish, or (2) accepting or offering or promising to accept, a valuable consideration in compromising or attempting to compromise a claim which was disputed as to either validity or amount, is not admissible to prove liability for or invalidity of the claim or its amount. Evidence of conduct or statements made in compromise negotiations is likewise not admissible. This rule does not require the exclusion of any evidence otherwise discoverable merely because it is presented in the course of compromise negotiations. This rule also does not require exclusion when the evidence is offered for another purpose, such as proving bias or prejudice of a witness, negativing a contention of undue delay, or proving an effort to obstruct a criminal investigation or prosecution.

RULE 409

PAYMENT OF MEDICAL AND SIMILAR EXPENSES

Evidence of furnishing or offering or promising to pay medical, hospital, or similar expenses occasioned by an injury is not admissible to prove liability for the injury.

RULE 410

INADMISSIBILITY OF PLEAS, PLEA DISCUSSIONS, AND RELATED STATEMENTS

Except as otherwise provided in this rule, evidence of the following is not, in any civil or criminal proceeding, admissible against the defendant who made the plea or was a participant in the plea discussions:

(1) a plea of guilty which was later withdrawn;

(2) a plea of nolo contendere;

(3) any statement made in the course of any proceedings under Rule 11 of the Federal Rules of Criminal Procedure or comparable state procedure regarding either of the foregoing pleas; or

(4) any statement made in the course of plea discussions with an attorney for the prosecuting authority which do not result in a plea of guilty or which result in a plea of guilty later withdrawn.

However, such a statement is admissible (i) in any proceeding wherein another statement made in the course of the same plea or plea discussions has been introduced and the statement ought in fairness be considered contemporaneously with it, or (ii) in a criminal proceeding for perjury or false statement if the statement was made by the defendant under oath, on the record and in the presence of counsel.

[Amended December 12, 1975; April 30, 1979, effective December 1, 1980.]

RULE 411

LIABILITY INSURANCE

Evidence that a person was or was not insured against liability is not admissible upon the issue whether the person acted negligently or otherwise wrongfully. This rule does not require the exclusion of evidence of insurance against liability when offered for another purpose, such as proof of agency, ownership, or control, or bias or prejudice of a witness.

[Amended effective October 1, 1987.]

RULE 412

SEX OFFENSE CASES; RELEVANCE OF VICTIM'S PAST BEHAVIOR

(a) Notwithstanding any other provision of law, in a criminal case in which a person is accused of an offense under chapter 109A of title 18, United States Code, reputation or opinion evidence of the past sexual behavior of an alleged victim of such offense is not admissible.

(b) Notwithstanding any other provision of law, in a criminal case in which a person is accused of an offense under chapter 109A of title 18, United States Code, evidence of a victim's past sexual behavior other than reputation or opinion evidence is also not admissible, unless such evidence other than reputation or opinion evidence is—

(1) admitted in accordance with subdivisions (c)(1) and (c)(2) and is constitutionally required to be admitted; or

(2) admitted in accordance with subdivision (c) and is evidence of—

(A) past sexual behavior with persons other than the accused, offered by the accused upon the issue of whether the accused was or was not, with respect to the alleged victim, the source of semen or injury; or

(B) past sexual behavior with the accused and is offered by the accused upon the issue of whether the alleged victim consented to the sexual behavior with respect to which such offense is alleged.

(c)(1) If the person accused of committing an offense under chapter 109A of title 18, United States Code intends to offer under subdivision (b) evidence of specific instances of the alleged victim's past sexual behavior, the accused shall make a written motion to offer such evidence not later than fifteen days before the date on which the trial in which such evidence is to be offered is scheduled to begin, except that the court may allow the motion to be made at a later date, including during trial, if the court determines either that the evidence is newly discovered and could not have been obtained earlier through the exercise of due diligence or that the issue to which such evidence relates has newly arisen in the case. Any motion made under this paragraph shall be served on all other parties and on the alleged victim.

(2) The motion described in paragraph (1) shall be accompanied by a written offer of proof. If the court determines that the offer of proof contains evidence described in subdivision (b), the court shall order a hearing in chambers to determine if such evidence is admissible. At such hearing the parties may call witnesses, including the alleged victim, and offer relevant evidence. Notwithstanding subdivision (b) of rule 104, if the relevancy of the evidence which the accused seeks to offer in the trial depends upon the fulfillment of a condition of fact, the court, at the hearing in chambers or at a subsequent hearing in chambers scheduled for such purpose, shall accept evidence on the issue of whether such condition of fact is fulfilled and shall determine such issue.

(3) If the court determines on the basis of the hearing described in paragraph (2) that the evidence which the accused seeks to offer is relevant and that the probative value of such evidence outweighs the danger of unfair prejudice, such evidence shall be admissible in the trial to the extent an order made by the court specifies evidence which may be offered and areas with respect to which the alleged victim may be examined or cross-examined.

(d) For purposes of this rule, the term "past sexual behavior" means sexual behavior other than the sexual behavior with respect to which rape or assault with intent to commit rape is alleged.

[Added October 28, 1978; amended effective November 18, 1988.]

ARTICLE V

PRIVILEGES

RULE 501

GENERAL RULE

Except as otherwise required by the Constitution of the United States or provided by Act of Congress or in rules prescribed by the Supreme Court pursuant to statutory authority, the privilege of a witness, person, government, State, or political subdivision thereof shall be governed by the principles of the common law as they may be interpreted by the courts of the United States in the light of reason and experience. However, in civil actions and proceedings, with respect to an element of a claim or defense as to which State law supplies the rule of decision, the privilege of a witness, person, government, State, or political subdivision thereof shall be determined in accordance with State law.

ARTICLE VI

WITNESSES

RULE 601

GENERAL RULE OF COMPETENCY

Every person is competent to be a witness except as otherwise provided in these rules. However, in civil actions and proceedings, with respect to an element of a claim or defense as to which State law supplies the rule of decision, the competency of a witness shall be determined in accordance with State law.

RULE 602

LACK OF PERSONAL KNOWLEDGE

A witness may not testify to a matter unless evidence is introduced sufficient to support a finding that the witness has personal knowledge of the matter. Evidence to prove personal knowledge may, but need not, consist of the witness' own testimony. This rule is subject to the provisions of rule 703, relating to opinion testimony by expert witnesses.

[Amended effective October 1, 1987; November 1, 1988.]

RULE 603

OATH OR AFFIRMATION

Before testifying, every witness shall be required to declare that the witness will testify truthfully, by oath or affirmation administered in a form calculated to awaken the witness' conscience and impress the witness' mind with the duty to do so.

[Amended effective October 1, 1987.]

RULE 604

INTERPRETERS

An interpreter is subject to the provisions of these rules relating to qualification as an expert and the administration of an oath or affirmation to make a true translation.

[Amended effective October 1, 1987.]

RULE 605

COMPETENCY OF JUDGE AS WITNESS

The judge presiding at the trial may not testify in that trial as a witness. No objection need be made in order to preserve the point.

RULE 606

COMPETENCY OF JUROR AS WITNESS

(a) At the Trial. A member of the jury may not testify as a witness before that jury in the trial of the case in which the juror is sitting. If the juror is called so to testify, the opposing party shall be afforded an opportunity to object out of the presence of the jury.

(b) Inquiry into Validity of Verdict or Indictment. Upon an inquiry into the validity of a verdict or indictment, a juror may not testify as to any matter or statement occurring during the course of the jury's deliberations or to the effect of anything upon that or any other juror's mind or emotions as influencing the juror to assent to or dissent from the verdict or indictment or concerning the juror's mental processes in connection therewith, except that a juror may testify on the question whether extraneous prejudicial information was improperly brought to the jury's attention or whether any outside influence was improperly brought to bear upon any juror. Nor may a juror's affidavit or evidence of any statement by the juror concerning a matter about which the juror would be precluded from testifying be received for these purposes.

[Amended effective December 12, 1975; October 1, 1987.]

RULE 607

WHO MAY IMPEACH

The credibility of a witness may be attacked by any party, including the party calling the witness.

[Amended effective October 1, 1987.]

RULE 608

EVIDENCE OF CHARACTER AND CONDUCT OF WITNESS

(a) Opinion and Reputation Evidence of Character. The credibility of a witness may be attacked or supported by evidence in the form of opinion or reputation, but subject to these limitations: (1) the evidence may refer only to character for truthfulness or untruthfulness, and (2) evidence of truthful character is admissible only after the character of the witness for truthfulness has been attacked by opinion or reputation evidence or otherwise.

(b) Specific Instances of Conduct. Specific instances of the conduct of a witness, for the purpose of attacking or supporting the witness' credibility, other than conviction of crime as provided in rule 609, may not be proved by extrinsic evidence. They may, however, in the discretion of the court, if probative of truthfulness or untruthfulness, be inquired into on cross-examination of the witness (1) concerning the witness' character for truthfulness or untruthfulness, or (2) concerning the character for truthfulness or untruthfulness of another witness as to which character the witness being cross-examined has testified. The giving of testimony,

[Amended effective October 1, 1987; November 1, 1988.]

RULE 609

IMPEACHMENT BY EVIDENCE OF CONVICTION OF CRIME

(a) General Rule. For the purpose of attacking the credibility of a witness, evidence that the witness has been convicted of a crime shall be admitted if elicited from the witness or established by public record during cross-examination but only if the crime (1) was punishable by death or imprisonment in excess of one year under the law under which the witness was convicted, and the court determines that the probative value of admitting this evidence outweighs its prejudicial effect to the defendant, or (2) involved dishonesty or false statement, regardless of the punishment.

(b) Time Limit. Evidence of a conviction under this rule is not admissible if a period of more than ten years has elapsed since the date of the conviction or of the release of the witness from the confinement imposed for that conviction, whichever is the later date, unless the court determines, in the interests of justice, that the probative value of the conviction supported by specific facts and circumstances substantially outweighs its prejudicial effect. However, evidence of a conviction more than 10 years old as calculated herein, is not admissible unless the proponent gives to the adverse party sufficient advance written notice of intent to use such evidence to provide the adverse party with a fair opportunity to contest the use of such evidence.

(c) Effect of Pardon, Annulment, or Certificate of Rehabilitation. Evidence of a conviction is not admissible under this rule if (1) the conviction has been the subject of a pardon, annulment, certificate of rehabilitation, or other equivalent procedure based on a finding of the rehabilitation of the person convicted, and that person has not been convicted of a subsequent crime which was punishable by death or imprisonment in excess of one year, or (2) the conviction has been the subject of a pardon, annulment, or other equivalent procedure based on a finding of innocence.

(d) Juvenile Adjudications. Evidence of juvenile adjudications is generally not admissible under this rule. The court may, however, in a criminal case allow evidence of a juvenile adjudication of a witness other than the accused if conviction of the offense would be admissible to attack the credibility of an adult and the court is satisfied that admission in evidence is necessary for a fair determination of the issue of guilt or innocence.

(e) Pendency of Appeal. The pendency of an appeal therefrom does not render evidence of a conviction inadmissible. Evidence of the pendency of an appeal is admissible.

[Amended effective October 1, 1987.]

RULE 610

RELIGIOUS BELIEFS OR OPINIONS

Evidence of the beliefs or opinions of a witness on matters of religion is not admissible for the purpose of showing that by reason of their nature the witness' credibility is impaired or enhanced.

[Amended effective October 1, 1987.]

RULE 611

MODE AND ORDER OF INTERROGATION AND PRESENTATION

(a) Control by Court. The court shall exercise reasonable control over the mode and order of interrogating witnesses and presenting evidence so as to (1) make the interrogation and presentation effective for the ascertainment of the truth, (2) avoid needless consumption of time, and (3) protect witnesses from harassment or undue embarrassment.

(b) Scope of Cross-Examination. Cross-examination should be limited to the subject matter of the direct examination and matters affecting the credibility of the witness. The court may, in the exercise of discretion, permit inquiry into additional matters as if on direct examination.

(c) Leading Questions. Leading questions should not be used on the direct examination of a witness except as may be necessary to develop the witness' testimony. Ordinarily leading questions should be permitted on cross-examination. When a party calls a hostile witness, an adverse party, or a witness identified with an adverse party, interrogation may be by leading questions.

[Amended effective October 1, 1987.]

RULE 612

WRITING USED TO REFRESH MEMORY

Except as otherwise provided in criminal proceedings by section 3500 of title 18, United States Code, if a witness uses a writing to refresh memory for the purpose of testifying, either—

(1) while testifying, or

(2) before testifying, if the court in its discretion determines it is necessary in the interests of justice,

an adverse party is entitled to have the writing produced at the hearing, to inspect it, to cross-examine the witness thereon, and to introduce in evidence those portions which relate to the testimony of the witness. If it is claimed that the writing contains matters not related to the subject matter of the testimony the court shall examine the writing in camera, excise any portions not so related, and order delivery of the remainder to the party entitled thereto. Any portion withheld over objections shall be preserved and made available to the appellate court in the event of an appeal. If a writing is not produced or delivered pursuant to order under this rule, the court shall make any order justice requires, except that in criminal cases when the prosecution elects not to comply, the order shall be one striking the testimony or, if the court in its discretion determines that the interests of justice so require, declaring a mistrial.

[Amended effective October 1, 1987.]

RULE 613

PRIOR STATEMENTS OF WITNESSES

(a) Examining Witness Concerning Prior Statement. In examining a witness concerning a prior statement made by the witness, whether written or not, the statement need not be shown nor its contents disclosed to the witness at that time, but on request the same shall be shown or disclosed to opposing counsel.

(b) Extrinsic Evidence of Prior Inconsistent Statement of Witness. Extrinsic evidence of a prior inconsistent statement by a witness is not admissible unless the witness is afforded an opportunity to explain or deny the same and the opposite party is afforded an opportunity to interrogate the witness thereon, or the interests of justice otherwise require. This provision does not apply to admissions of a party-opponent as defined in rule 801(d)(2).

[Amended effective October 1, 1987; November 1, 1988.]

RULE 614

CALLING AND INTERROGATION OF WITNESSES BY COURT

(a) Calling by Court. The court may, on its own motion or at the suggestion of a party, call witnesses, and all parties are entitled to cross-examine witnesses thus called.

(b) Interrogation by Court. The court may interrogate witnesses, whether called by itself or by a party.

(c) Objections. Objections to the calling of witnesses by the court or to interrogation by it may be made at the time or at the next available opportunity when the jury is not present.

RULE 615

EXCLUSION OF WITNESSES

At the request of a party the court shall order witnesses excluded so that they cannot hear the testimony of other witnesses, and it may make the order of its own motion. This rule does not authorize exclusion of (1) a party who is a natural person, or (2) an officer or employee of a party which is not a natural person designated as its representative by its attorney, or (3) a person whose presence is shown by a party to be essential to the presentation of the party's cause.

[Amended effective October 1, 1987; November 1, 1988; November 18, 1988.]

ARTICLE VII

OPINIONS AND EXPERT TESTIMONY

RULE 701

OPINION TESTIMONY BY LAY WITNESSES

If the witness is not testifying as an expert, the witness' testimony in the form of opinions or inferences is limited to those opinions or inferences which are (a) rationally based on the perception of the witness and (b) helpful to a clear understanding of the witness' testimony or the determination of a fact in issue.

[Amended effective October 1, 1987.]

RULE 702

TESTIMONY BY EXPERTS

If scientific, technical, or other specialized knowledge will assist the trier of fact to understand the evidence or to determine a fact in issue, a witness qualified as an expert by knowledge, skill, experience, training, or education, may testify thereto in the form of an opinion or otherwise.

RULE 703

BASES OF OPINION TESTIMONY BY EXPERTS

The facts or data in the particular case upon which an expert bases an opinion or inference may be those perceived by or made known to the expert at or before the hearing. If of a type reasonably relied upon by experts in the particular field in forming opinions or inferences upon the subject, the facts or data need not be admissible in evidence.

[Amended effective October 1, 1987.]

RULE 704

OPINION ON ULTIMATE ISSUE

(a) Except as provided in subdivision (b), testimony in the form of an opinion or inference otherwise admissible is not objectionable because it embraces an ultimate issue to be decided by the trier of fact.

(b) No expert witness testifying with respect to the mental state or condition of a defendant in a criminal case may state an opinion or inference as to whether the defendant did or did not have the mental state or condition constituting an element of the crime charged or of a defense thereto. Such ultimate issues are matters for the trier of fact alone.

[Amended effective October 12, 1984.]

RULE 705

DISCLOSURE OF FACTS OR DATA UNDERLYING EXPERT OPINION

The expert may testify in terms of opinion or inference and gives reasons therefor without prior disclosure of the underlying facts or data, unless the court requires otherwise. The expert may in any event be required to disclose the underlying facts or data on cross-examination.

[Amended effective October 1, 1987.]

RULE 706

COURT APPOINTED EXPERTS

(a) Appointment. The court may on its own motion or on the motion of any party enter an order to show cause why expert witnesses should not be appointed, and may request the parties to submit nominations. The court may appoint any expert witnesses agreed upon by the parties, and may appoint expert witnesses of its own selection. An expert witness shall not be appointed by the court unless the witness consents to act. A witness so appointed shall be informed of the witness' duties by the court in writing, a copy of which shall be filed with the clerk, or at a conference in which the parties shall have opportunity to participate. A witness so appointed shall advise the parties of the witness' findings, if any; the witness' deposition may be taken by any party; and the witness may be called to testify by the court or any party. The witness shall be subject to cross-examination by each party, including a party calling the witness.

(b) Compensation. Expert witnesses so appointed are entitled to reasonable compensation in whatever sum the court may allow. The compensation thus fixed is payable from funds which may be provided by law in criminal cases and civil actions and proceedings involving just compensation under the fifth amendment. In other civil actions and proceedings the compensation shall be paid by the parties in such proportion and at such time as the court directs, and thereafter charged in like manner as other costs.

(c) Disclosure of Appointment. In the exercise of its discretion, the court may authorize disclosure to the jury of the fact that the court appointed the expert witness.

(d) Parties' Experts of Own Selection. Nothing in this rule limits the parties in calling expert witnesses of their own selection.

[Amended effective October 1, 1987.]

ARTICLE VIII

HEARSAY

RULE 801

DEFINITIONS

The following definitions apply under this article:

(a) Statement. A "statement" is (1) an oral or written assertion or (2) nonverbal conduct of a person, if it is intended by the person as an assertion.

(b) Declarant. A "declarant" is a person who makes a statement.

(c) Hearsay. "Hearsay" is a statement, other than one made by the declarant while testifying at the trial or hearing, offered in evidence to prove the truth of the matter asserted.

(d) Statements Which Are Not Hearsay. A statement is not hearsay if—

(1) *Prior Statement by Witness.* The declarant testifies at the trial or hearing and is subject to cross-examination concerning the statement, and the statement is (A) inconsistent with the declarant's testimony, and was given under oath subject to the penalty of perjury at a trial, hearing, or other proceeding, or in a deposition, or (B) consistent with the declarant's testimony and is offered to rebut an express or implied charge against the declarant of recent fabrication or improper influence or motive, or (C) one of identification of a person made after perceiving the person; or

(2) *Admission by Party–Opponent.* The statement is offered against a party and is (A) the party's own statement in either an individual or a representative capacity or (B) a statement of which the party has manifested an adoption or belief in its truth, or (C) a statement by a person authorized by the party to make a statement concerning the subject, or (D) a statement by the party's agent or servant concerning a matter within the scope of the agency or employment, made during the existence of the relationship, or (E) a statement by a coconspirator of a party during the course and in furtherance of the conspiracy.

[Amended effective October 16, 1975; October 1, 1987.]

RULE 802

HEARSAY RULE

Hearsay is not admissible except as provided by these rules or by other rules prescribed by the Supreme Court pursuant to statutory authority or by Act of Congress.

RULE 803

HEARSAY EXCEPTIONS; AVAILABILITY OF DECLARANT IMMATERIAL

The following are not excluded by the hearsay rule, even though the declarant is available as a witness:

(1) **Present Sense Impression.** A statement describing or explaining an event or condition made while the declarant was perceiving the event or condition, or immediately thereafter.

(2) **Excited Utterance.** A statement relating to a startling event or condition made while the declarant was under the stress of excitement caused by the event or condition.

(3) **Then Existing Mental, Emotional, or Physical Condition.** A statement of the declarant's then existing state of mind, emotion, sensation, or physical condition (such as intent, plan, motive, design, mental feeling, pain, and bodily health), but not including a statement of memory or belief to prove the fact remembered or believed unless it relates to the execution, revocation, identification, or terms of declarant's will.

(4) **Statements for Purposes of Medical Diagnosis or Treatment.** Statements made for purposes of medical diagnosis or treatment and describing medical history, or past or present symptoms, pain, or sensations, or the inception or general character of the cause or external source thereof insofar as reasonably pertinent to diagnosis or treatment.

(5) **Recorded Recollection.** A memorandum or record concerning a matter about which a witness once had knowledge but now has insufficient recollection to enable the witness to testify fully and accurately, shown to have been made or adopted by the witness when the matter was fresh in the witness' memory and to reflect that knowledge correctly. If admitted, the memorandum or record may be read into evidence but may not itself be received as an exhibit unless offered by an adverse party.

(6) **Records of Regularly Conducted Activity.** A memorandum, report, record, or data compilation, in any form, of acts, events, conditions, opinions, or diagnoses, made at or near the time by, or from information transmitted by, a person with knowledge, if kept in the course of a regularly conducted business activity, and if it was the regular practice of that business activity to make the memorandum, report, record, or data compilation, all as shown by the testimony of the custodian or other qualified witness, unless the source of information or the method or circumstances of preparation indicate lack of trustworthiness. The term "business" as used in this paragraph includes business, institution, association, profession, occupation, and calling of every kind, whether or not conducted for profit.

(7) **Absence of Entry in Records Kept in Accordance With the Provisions of Paragraph (6).** Evidence that a matter is not included in the memoranda reports, records, or data compilations, in any form, kept in accordance with the provisions of paragraph (6), to prove the

nonoccurrence or nonexistence of the matter, if the matter was of a kind of which a memorandum, report, record, or data compilation was regularly made and preserved, unless the sources of information or other circumstances indicate lack of trustworthiness.

(8) Public Records and Reports. Records, reports, statements, or data compilations, in any form, of public offices or agencies, setting forth (A) the activities of the office or agency, or (B) matters observed pursuant to duty imposed by law as to which matters there was a duty to report, excluding, however, in criminal cases matters observed by police officers and other law enforcement personnel, or (C) in civil actions and proceedings and against the Government in criminal cases, factual findings resulting from an investigation made pursuant to authority granted by law, unless the sources of information or other circumstances indicate lack of trustworthiness.

(9) Records of Vital Statistics. Records or data compilations, in any form, of births, fetal deaths, deaths, or marriages, if the report thereof was made to a public office pursuant to requirements of law.

(10) Absence of Public Record or Entry. To prove the absence of a record, report, statement, or data compilation, in any form, or the nonoccurrence or nonexistence of a matter of which a record, report, statement, or data compilation, in any form, was regularly made and preserved by a public office or agency, evidence in the form of a certification in accordance with rule 902, or testimony, that diligent search failed to disclose the record, report, statement, or data compilation, or entry.

(11) Records of Religious Organizations. Statements of births, marriages, divorces, deaths, legitimacy, ancestry, relationship by blood or marriage, or other similar facts of personal or family history, contained in a regularly kept record of a religious organization.

(12) Marriage, Baptismal, and Similar Certificates. Statements of fact contained in a certificate that the maker performed a marriage or other ceremony or administered a sacrament, made by a clergyman, public official, or other person authorized by the rules or practices of a religious organization or by law to perform the act certified, and purporting to have been issued at the time of the act or within a reasonable time thereafter.

(13) Family Records. Statements of fact concerning personal or family history contained in family Bibles, genealogies, charts, engravings on rings, inscriptions on family portraits, engravings on urns, crypts, or tombstones, or the like.

(14) Records of Documents Affecting an Interest in Property. The record of a document purporting to establish or affect an interest in property, as proof of the content of the original recorded document and its execution and delivery by each person by whom it purports to have been executed, if the record is a record of a public office and an applicable statute authorizes the recording of documents of that kind in that office.

(15) Statements in Documents Affecting an Interest in Property. A statement contained in a document purporting to establish or affect an interest in property if the matter stated was relevant to the purpose of the document, unless dealings with the property since the document was made have been inconsistent with the truth of the statement or the purport of the document.

(16) Statements in Ancient Documents. Statements in a document in existence twenty years or more the authenticity of which is established.

(17) Market Reports, Commercial Publications. Market quotations, tabulations, lists, directories, or other published compilations, generally used and relied upon by the public or by persons in particular occupations.

(18) Learned Treatises. To the extent called to the attention of an expert witness upon cross-examination or relied upon by the expert witness in direct examination, statements contained in published treatises, periodicals, or pamphlets on a subject of history, medicine, or other science or art, established as a reliable authority by the testimony or admission of the witness or by other expert testimony or by judicial notice. If admitted, the statements may be read into evidence but may not be received as exhibits.

(19) Reputation Concerning Personal or Family History. Reputation among members of a person's family by blood, adoption, or marriage, or among a person's associates, or in the community, concerning a person's birth, adoption, marriage, divorce, death, legitimacy, relationship by blood, adoption, or marriage, ancestry, or other similar fact of personal or family history.

(20) Reputation Concerning Boundaries or General History. Reputation in a community, arising before the controversy, as to boundaries of or customs affecting lands in the community, and reputation as to events of general history important to the community or State or nation in which located.

(21) Reputation as to Character. Reputation of a person's character among associates or in the community.

(22) Judgment of Previous Conviction. Evidence of a final judgment, entered after a trial or upon a plea of guilty (but not upon a plea of nolo contendere), adjudging a person guilty of a crime punishable by death or imprisonment in excess of one year, to prove any fact essential to sustain the judgment, but not including, when offered by the Government in a criminal prosecution for purposes other than impeachment, judgments against persons other than the accused. The pendency of an appeal may be shown but does not affect admissibility.

(23) Judgment as to Personal, Family, or General History, or Boundaries. Judgments as proof of matters of personal, family or general history, or boundaries, essential to the judgment, if the same would be provable by evidence of reputation.

(24) Other Exceptions. A statement not specifically covered by any of the foregoing exceptions but having equivalent circumstantial guarantees of trustworthiness, if the court determines that (A) the statement is offered as evidence of a material fact; (B) the statement is more probative on the point for which it is offered than any other evidence which the proponent can procure through reasonable efforts; and (C) the general purposes of these rules and the interests of justice will best be served by admission of the statement into evidence. However, a statement may not be admitted under this exception unless the proponent of it makes known to the adverse party sufficiently in advance of the trial or hearing to provide the adverse party with a fair opportunity to prepare to meet it, the proponent's intention to offer the statement and the particulars of it, including the name and address of the declarant.

[Amended effective December 12, 1975; October 1, 1987.]

RULE 804

HEARSAY EXCEPTIONS; DECLARANT UNAVAILABLE

(a) Definition of Unavailability. "Unavailability as a witness" includes situations in which the declarant—

(1) is exempted by ruling of the court on the ground of privilege from testifying concerning the subject matter of the declarant's statement; or

(2) persists in refusing to testify concerning the subject matter of the declarant's statement despite an order of the court to do so; or

(3) testifies to a lack of memory of the subject matter of the declarant's statement; or

(4) is unable to be present or to testify at the hearing because of death or then existing physical or mental illness or infirmity; or

(5) is absent from the hearing and the proponent of a statement has been unable to procure the declarant's attendance (or in the case of a hearsay exception under subdivision (b)(2), (3), or (4), the declarant's attendance or testimony) by process or other reasonable means.

A declarant is not unavailable as a witness if exemption, refusal, claim of lack of memory, inability, or absence is due to the procurement or wrongdoing of the proponent of a statement for the purpose of preventing the witness from attending or testifying.

(b) Hearsay Exceptions. The following are not excluded by the hearsay rule if the declarant is unavailable as a witness:

(1) *Former Testimony.* Testimony given as a witness at another hearing of the same or a different proceeding, or in a deposition taken in compliance with law in the course of the same or another proceeding, if the party against whom the testimony is now offered, or, in a civil action or proceeding, a predecessor in interest, had an opportunity and similar motive to develop the testimony by direct, cross, or redirect examination.

(2) *Statement Under Belief of Impending Death.* In a prosecution for homicide or in a civil action or proceeding, a statement made by a declarant while believing that the declarant's death was

imminent, concerning the cause or circumstances of what the declarant believed to be impending death.

(3) *Statement Against Interest.* A statement which was at the time of its making so far contrary to the declarant's pecuniary or proprietary interest, or so far tended to subject the declarant to civil or criminal liability, or to render invalid a claim by the declarant against another, that a reasonable person in the declarant's position would not have made the statement unless believing it to be true. A statement tending to expose the declarant to criminal liability and offered to exculpate the accused is not admissible unless corroborating circumstances clearly indicate the trustworthiness of the statement.

(4) *Statement of Personal or Family History.* (A) A statement concerning the declarant's own birth, adoption, marriage, divorce, legitimacy, relationship by blood, adoption, or marriage, ancestry, or other similar fact of personal or family history, even though declarant had no means of acquiring personal knowledge of the matter stated; or (B) a statement concerning the foregoing matters, and death also, of another person, if the declarant was related to the other by blood, adop-

tion, or marriage or was so intimately associated with the other's family as to be likely to have accurate information concerning the matter declared.

(5) *Other Exceptions.* A statement not specifically covered by any of the foregoing exceptions but having equivalent circumstantial guarantees of trustworthiness, if the court determines that (A) the statement is offered as evidence of a material fact; (B) the statement is more probative on the point for which it is offered than any other evidence which the proponent can procure through reasonable efforts; and (C) the general purposes of these rules and the interests of justice will best be served by admission of the statement into evidence. However, a statement may not be admitted under this exception unless the proponent of it makes known to the adverse party sufficiently in advance of the trial or hearing to provide the adverse party with a fair opportunity to prepare to meet it, the proponent's intention to offer the statement and the particulars of it, including the name and address of the declarant.

[Amended effective December 12, 1975; October 1, 1987; November 18, 1988.]

RULE 805

HEARSAY WITHIN HEARSAY

Hearsay included within hearsay is not excluded under the hearsay rule if each part of the combined statements conforms with an exception to the hearsay rule provided in these rules.

RULE 806

ATTACKING AND SUPPORTING CREDIBILITY OF DECLARANT

When a hearsay statement, or a statement defined in Rule 801(d)(2)(C), (D), or (E), has been admitted in evidence, the credibility of the declarant may be attacked, and if attacked may be supported, by any evidence which would be admissible for those purposes if declarant had testified as a witness. Evidence of a statement or conduct by the declarant at any time, inconsistent with the declarant's hearsay statement, is not subject to any requirement that the declarant may have been afforded an opportunity to deny or explain. If the party against whom a hearsay statement has been admitted calls the declarant as a witness, the party is entitled to examine the declarant on the statement as if under cross-examination.

[Amended effective October 1, 1987.]

ARTICLE IX

AUTHENTICATION AND IDENTIFICATION

RULE 901

REQUIREMENT OF AUTHENTICATION OR IDENTIFICATION

(a) General Provision. The requirement of authentication or identification as a condition precedent to admissibility is satisfied by evidence sufficient to support a finding that the matter in question is what its proponent claims.

(b) Illustrations. By way of illustration only, and not by way of limitation, the following are examples of authentication or identification conforming with the requirements of this rule:

(1) *Testimony of Witness With Knowledge.* Testimony that a matter is what it is claimed to be.

(2) *Nonexpert Opinion on Handwriting.* Nonexpert opinion as to the genuineness of handwriting, based upon familiarity not acquired for purposes of the litigation.

(3) *Comparison by Trier or Expert Witness.* Comparison by the trier of fact or by expert witnesses with specimens which have been authenticated.

(4) *Distinctive Characteristics and the Like.* Appearance, contents, substance, internal patterns, or other distinctive characteristics, taken in conjunction with circumstances.

(5) *Voice Identification.* Identification of a voice, whether heard firsthand or through mechanical or electronic transmission or recording, by opinion based upon hearing the voice at any time under circumstances connecting it with the alleged speaker.

(6) *Telephone Conversations.* Telephone conversations, by evidence that a call was made to the number assigned at the time by the telephone company to a particular person or business, if (A) in the case of a person, circumstances, including self-identification, show the person answering to be the one called, or (B) in the case of a business the call was made to a place of business and the conversation related to business reasonably transacted over the telephone.

(7) *Public Records or Reports.* Evidence that a writing authorized by law to be recorded or filed and in fact recorded or filed in a public office, or a purported public record, report, statement, or data compilation, in any form, is from the public office where items of this nature are kept.

(8) *Ancient Documents or Data Compilation.* Evidence that a document or data compilation, in any form, (A) is in such condition as to create no suspicion concerning its authenticity, (B) was in a place where it, if authentic, would likely be, and (C) has been in existence 20 years or more at the time it is offered.

(9) *Process or System.* Evidence describing a process or system used to produce a result and showing that the process or system produces an accurate result.

(10) *Methods Provided by Statute or Rule.* Any method of authentication or identification provided by Act of Congress or by other rules prescribed by the Supreme Court pursuant to statutory authority.

RULE 902

SELF–AUTHENTICATION

Extrinsic evidence of authenticity as a condition precedent to admissibility is not required with respect to the following:

(1) Domestic Public Documents Under Seal. A document bearing a seal purporting to be that of the United States, or of any State, district, Commonwealth, territory, or insular possession thereof, or the Panama Canal Zone, or the Trust Territory of the Pacific Islands, or of a political subdivision, department, officer, or agency thereof, and a signature purporting to be an attestation or execution.

(2) Domestic Public Documents Not Under Seal. A document purporting to bear the signature in the official capacity of an officer or employee of an entity included in paragraph (1) hereof, having no seal, if a public officer having a seal and having official duties in the district or political subdivision of the officer or employee certifies under seal that the signer has the official capacity and that the signature is genuine.

(3) Foreign Public Documents. A document purporting to be executed or attested in an official capacity by a person authorized by the laws of a foreign country to make the execution or attestation, and accompanied by a final certification as to the genuineness of the signature and official position (A) of the executing or attesting person, or (B) of any foreign official whose certificate of genuineness of signature and official position relates to the execution or attestation or is in a chain of certificates of genuineness of signature and official position relating to the execution or attestation. A final certification may be made by a secretary of embassy or legation, consul general, consul, vice consul, or consular agent of the United States, or a diplomatic or consular official of the foreign country assigned or accredited to the United States. If reasonable opportunity has been given to all parties to investigate the authenticity and accuracy of official documents, the court may, for good cause shown, order that they be treated as presumptively authentic without final certification or permit them to be evidenced by an attested summary with or without final certification.

(4) Certified Copies of Public Records. A copy of an official record or report or entry therein, or of a document authorized by law to be recorded or filed and actually recorded or filed in a public office, including data compilations in any form, certified as correct by the custodian or other person authorized to make the certification, by certificate complying with paragraph (1), (2), or (3) of this rule or complying with any Act of Congress or rule prescribed by the Supreme Court pursuant to statutory authority.

(5) Official Publications. Books, pamphlets, or other publications purporting to be issued by public authority.

(6) Newspapers and Periodicals. Printed materials purporting to be newspapers or periodicals.

(7) Trade Inscriptions and the Like. Inscriptions, signs, tags, or labels purporting to have been affixed in the course of business and indicating ownership, control, or origin.

(8) Acknowledged Documents. Documents accompanied by a certificate of acknowledgment executed in the manner provided by law by a notary public or other officer authorized by law to take acknowledgments.

(9) Commercial Paper and Related Documents. Commercial paper, signatures thereon, and documents relating thereto to the extent provided by general commercial law.

(10) Presumptions Under Acts of Congress. Any signature, document, or other matter declared by Act of Congress to be presumptively or prima facie genuine or authentic.

[Amended effective October 1, 1987; November 1, 1988.]

RULE 903

SUBSCRIBING WITNESS' TESTIMONY UNNECESSARY

The testimony of a subscribing witness is not necessary to authenticate a writing unless required by the laws of the jurisdiction whose laws govern the validity of the writing.

ARTICLE X

CONTENTS OF WRITINGS, RECORDINGS, AND PHOTOGRAPHS

RULE 1001

DEFINITIONS

For purposes of this article the following definitions are applicable:

(1) Writings and Recordings. "Writings" and "recordings" consist of letters, words, or numbers, or their equivalent, set down by handwriting, typewriting, printing, photostating, photographing, magnetic impulse, mechanical or electronic recording, or other form of data compilation.

(2) Photographs. "Photographs" include still photographs, X-ray films, video tapes, and motion pictures.

(3) Original. An "original" of a writing or recording is the writing or recording itself or any counterpart intended to have the same effect by a person executing or issuing it. An "original" of a photograph includes the negative or any print therefrom. If data are stored in a computer or similar device, any printout or other output readable by sight, shown to reflect the data accurately, is an "original".

(4) Duplicate. A "duplicate" is a counterpart produced by the same impression as the original, or from the same matrix, or by means of photography, including enlargements and miniatures, or by mechanical or electronic re-recording, or by chemical reproduction, or by other equivalent techniques which accurately reproduces the original.

RULE 1002

REQUIREMENT OF ORIGINAL

To prove the content of a writing, recording, or photograph, the original writing, recording, or photograph is required, except as otherwise provided in these rules or by Act of Congress.

RULE 1003

ADMISSIBILITY OF DUPLICATES

A duplicate is admissible to the same extent as an original unless (1) a genuine question is raised as to the authenticity of the original or (2) in the circumstances it would be unfair to admit the duplicate in lieu of the original.

RULE 1004

ADMISSIBILITY OF OTHER EVIDENCE OF CONTENTS

The original is not required, and other evidence of the contents of a writing, recording, or photograph is admissible if—

(1) Originals Lost or Destroyed. All originals are lost or have been destroyed, unless the proponent lost or destroyed them in bad faith; or

(2) Original Not Obtainable. No original can be obtained by any available judicial process or procedure; or

(3) Original in Possession of Opponent. At a time when an original was under the control of the party against whom offered, that party was put on notice, by the pleadings or otherwise, that the contents would be a subject of proof at the hearing, and that party does not produce the original at the hearing; or

(4) Collateral Matters. The writing, recording, or photograph is not closely related to a controlling issue.

[Amended effective October 1, 1987.]

RULE 1005

PUBLIC RECORDS

The contents of an official record, or of a document authorized to be recorded or filed and actually recorded or filed, including data compilations in any form, if otherwise admissible, may be proved by copy, certified as correct in accordance with rule 902 or testified to be correct by a witness who has compared it with the original. If a copy which complies with the foregoing cannot be obtained by the exercise of reasonable diligence, then other evidence of the contents may be given.

RULE 1006

SUMMARIES

The contents of voluminous writings, records, or photographs which cannot conveniently be examined in court may be presented in the form of a chart, summary, or calculation. The originals, or duplicates, shall be made available for examination or copying, or both, by other parties at a reasonable time and place. The court may order that they be produced in court.

RULE 1007

TESTIMONY OR WRITTEN ADMISSION OF PARTY

Contents of writings, recordings, or photographs may be proved by the testimony or deposition of the party against whom offered or by that party's written admission, without accounting for the nonproduction of the original.

[Amended effective October 1, 1987.]

RULE 1008

FUNCTIONS OF COURT AND JURY

When the admissibility of other evidence of contents of writings, recordings, or photographs under these rules depends upon the fulfillment of a condition of fact, the question whether the condition has been fulfilled is ordinarily for the court to determine in accordance with the provisions of rule 104. However, when an issue is raised (a) whether the asserted writing ever existed, or (b) whether another writing, recording, or photograph produced at the trial is the original, or (c) whether other evidence of contents correctly reflects the contents, the issue is for the trier of fact to determine as in the case of other issues of fact.

ARTICLE XI

MISCELLANEOUS RULES

RULE 1101

APPLICABILITY OF RULES

(a) Courts and Magistrates. These rules apply to the United States district courts, the District Court of Guam, the District Court of the Virgin Islands, the District Court for the Northern Mariana Islands, the United States courts of appeals, the United States Claims Court, and to United States bankruptcy judges and United States magistrates, in the actions, cases, and proceedings and to the extent hereinafter set forth. The terms "judge" and "court" in these Rules include United States bankruptcy judges and United States magistrates.

(b) Proceedings Generally. These rules apply generally to civil actions and proceedings, including admiralty and maritime cases, to criminal cases and proceedings, to contempt proceedings except those in which the court may act summarily, and to proceedings and cases under title 11, United States Code.

(c) Rule of Privilege. The rule with respect to privileges applies at all stages of all actions, cases, and proceedings.

(d) Rules Inapplicable. The rules (other than with respect to privileges) do not apply in the following situations:

(1) *Preliminary Questions of Fact.* The determination of questions of fact preliminary to admissibility of evidence when the issue is to be determined by the court under rule 104.

(2) *Grand Jury.* Proceedings before grand juries.

(3) *Miscellaneous Proceedings.* Proceedings for extradition or rendition; preliminary examinations in criminal cases; sentencing, or granting or revoking probation; issuance of warrants for arrest, criminal summonses, and search warrants; and proceedings with respect to release on bail or otherwise.

(e) Rules Applicable in Part. In the following proceedings these rules apply to the extent that matters of evidence are not provided for in the statutes which govern procedure therein or in other rules prescribed by the Supreme Court pursuant to statutory authority: the trial of minor and petty offenses by United States magistrates; review of agency actions when the facts are subject to trial de novo under section 706(2)(F) of title 5, United States Code; review of orders of the Secretary of Agriculture under section 2 of the Act entitled "An Act to authorize association of producers of agricultural products" approved February 18, 1922 (7 U.S.C. 292), and under sections 6 and 7(c) of the Perishable Agricultural Commodities Act, 1930 (7 U.S.C. 499f, 499g(c)); naturalization and revocation of naturalization under sections 310–318 of the Immigration and Nationality Act (8 U.S.C. 1421–1429); prize proceedings in admiralty under sections 7651–7681 of title 10, United States Code; review of orders of the Secretary of the Interior under section 2 of the Act entitled "An Act authorizing associations of producers of aquatic products" approved June 25, 1934 (15 U.S.C. 522); review of orders of petroleum control boards under section 5 of the Act entitled "An Act to regulate interstate and foreign commerce in petroleum and its products by prohibiting the shipment in such commerce of petroleum and its products produced in violation of State law, and for other purposes", approved February 22, 1935 (15 U.S.C. 715d); actions for fines, penalties, or forfeitures under part V of title IV of the Tariff Act of 1930 (19 U.S.C. 1581–1624), or under the Anti–Smuggling Act (19 U.S.C. 1701–1711); criminal libel for condemnation, exclusion of imports, or other proceedings under the Federal Food, Drug, and Cosmetic Act (21 U.S.C. 301–392); disputes between seamen under sections 4079, 4080, and 4081 of the Revised Statutes (22 U.S.C. 256–258); habeas corpus under sections 2241–2254 of title 28, United States Code; motions to vacate, set aside or correct sentence under section 2255 of title 28, United States Code; actions for penalties for refusal to transport destitute seamen under section 4578 of the Revised Statutes (46 U.S.C. 679); actions against the United States under the Act entitled "An Act authorizing suits against the United States in admiralty for damage caused by and salvage service rendered to public vessels belonging to the United States, and for other purposes", approved March 3, 1925 (46 U.S.C. 781–790), as implemented by section 7730 of title 10, United States Code.

[Amended effective December 12, 1975; October 1, 1982; April 1, 1984; October 1, 1987; November 1, 1988; November 18, 1988.]

RULE 1102

AMENDMENTS

Amendments to the Federal Rules of Evidence may be made as provided in section 2076 of title 28 of the United States Code.

RULE 1103

TITLE

These rules may be known and cited as the Federal Rules of Evidence.

FEDERAL SENTENCING GUIDELINES

INTRODUCTION

Reprinted from Krantz, Corrections and Prisoners' Rights (1988).

STATUTORY FRAMEWORK FOR SENTENCING

The primary source of authority for sentencing derives from the legislative branch. It is this branch, within constitutional boundaries, that must allocate sentencing authority among itself, the courts and correctional or other administrative agencies; set restrictions upon this authority; and, determine the criteria that should be used in making sentencing decisions. See, *President's Crime Commission, Task Force Report: The Courts 14 (1967).*

Maximum terms of sentences are normally fixed by statute. In the past, with few exceptions, however, as was noted earlier, sentencing courts had considerable latitude to select a sentence within a wide statutory range. For example, a judge may have unfettered discretion to sentence a convicted felon within ranges such as "any term up to 20 years" or "any term between 10 and 20 years." *President's Crime Commission, Task Force Report: The Courts 14 (1973).* For certain types of offenses (such as first degree murder or sale of heroin) or offenders (such as recidivists or dangerous offenders), the laws in many states provided for mandatory sentences. These laws compelled a trial judge to give a specified term (such as life imprisonment or at least 10 years) regardless what a judge's predilection may be or what may be appropriate under the circumstances.

In some jurisdictions, a judge has also been authorized or required to impose an "indeterminate sentence" (in which no maximum term is established) or an "indefinite sentence" (in which a maximum term is established). Under such provisions, it was then left to correctional officials to determine the actual length of a prison sentence. See, Prettyman, *The Indeterminate Sentence and the Right to Treatment,* 11 Am.Crim.L.Rev. 7 (1972). The primary rationale for this form of sentencing is that it provides flexibility and allows for the release of an offender by "correctional experts" as soon as he or she is rehabilitated and is "safe for society."

Many of the newer proposals for sentencing reform call for presumptive or determinate sentencing. Under them, it is common that:

[T]he legislature would set penalties for crimes defined in very specific and detailed language, and the judge would then be required to impose the penalty as called for by the statute which the defendant was convicted of violating, through aggravating or mitigating circumstances that might be present could be considered. Shane–Dubow, Brown & Olsen, *Sentencing Reform in the United States: History, Content, Effect* (1985) at 8.

A number of states, including some large urban states like California, have shifted to determinate sentencing. See, *Cal.Penal Code § 1170(a).* In 1984, Congress also adopted a more rigorous controlled sentencing system for the federal courts. The legislation defined the purposes of sentencing, eliminated parole, set maximum limits for various categories of crimes, and created a United States Sentencing Commission (composed of both judicial and non-judicial appointees) and delegated to it responsibility for setting sentencing policies and procedures. See, *Federal Comprehensive Crime Control Act of 1984, 18 U.S.C.A. § 3553; 28 U.S.C.A. §§ 991–994.* The Commission established federal sentencing guidelines which became effective in November, 1987.

These guidelines are empirically based. Federal crimes are given a numerical base offense level which defines seriousness of the offense. Burglary of a residence is given a base offense level, for example, of 17. The base offense level can be changed by considering factors such as vulnerability of victim and the importance of the sentenced offenders role in the crime.

Base offense level 17 has six possible gradations, ranging from 24–30 months to 51–63 months. Each of these gradations are keyed to points that are added or subtracted due to criminal history and patterns of behavior which reflect career criminal behavior.

If an offender has not had a prior record, the guidelines call for a sentence in the 24–30 month range. If he or she had two prior convictions in which there were sentences of imprisonment, for example, the range would change to a range of 30–37 months.

The guidelines also have explicit provisions about when a community based sentence such as probation is permitted. In addition, they specify when special offender characteristics such as age, education and vocational skills and family ties and responsibility may be taken into account. These factors are only occasionally considered germane. For a complete set of guidelines and supporting commentary, see, United States Sentencing Commission, *Federal Sentencing Guideline Manual* (West Publishing Company).

CRITICISMS OF DIFFERENT STATUTORY APPROACHES TO SENTENCING

Each statutory approach to sentencing has its detractors. First of all, the statutory scheme for penal sanctions that exists in most jurisdictions is unlike the determinate or presumptive approaches just described. It is rarely the result of rational, cohesive development. This was reflected by Judge Marvin Frankel in *Criminal Sentences 8–9 (1973)* and is still true now:

> Beyond their failure to impose meaningful limits upon the judges, our criminal codes have displayed bizarre qualities of illogic and incongruity. Studies in the recent past revealed such things as these: a Colorado statute providing a ten-year maximum for stealing a dog, while another Colorado statute prescribed six months and a $500 fine for killing a dog; * * * breaking into a car to steal from its glove compartment could result in up to fifteen years in California, while stealing the entire car carried a maximum of ten. The specific one I cite may have been repaired in recent revisions. Their essentially illustrative character remains a fair reflection of the haphazard, disorderly qualities of our criminal penalty provisions.

A review of criminal code reform underway nationally indicates that, aside from the movement to stimulate greater uniformity and reduce judicial discretion, some efforts are being made to group offenses into broader categories and provide a single range of prison sentences for all offenses within such categories. Within question, such reform efforts should be given high priority in those states that have not yet undertaken it.

Aside from the irrationality of criminal codes in general, it has been argued rather forcefully within recent years by persons at both ends of the political spectrum (and more recently by moderates as well) that judicial and administrative discretion in sentencing should be reduced or eliminated.

The primary reasons for this position are that substantial discretion: (1) provides enormous potential for abuse; and, (2) operates on the faulty premise that prisons can rehabilitate. See Frankel, *Criminal Sentences 86–102 (1973)* and Mitford, *Kind and Usual Punishment 79 (1973)*.

These concerns in the 1960s and 1970s sparked the movement towards determinate sentencing in which offenders committing a similar crime would receive the same punishment. Cf., Model Sentencing and Corrections Act. Those arguing for reforms, however, urged that determinate or more structured sentencing options be set at reasonable levels.

The American Bar Association Standards for Criminal Justice Relating to Sentencing Alternatives and Procedures (hereinafter referred to as ABA Standards) recommended, for example, that the maximum sentence for most offenses ought not to exceed ten years and normally should not exceed five. Longer sentences should be reserved, in the ABA's view, "for particularly serious offenses committed by particularly dangerous offenders." *ABA Standards Relating to Sentencing Alternatives and Procedures, Standard 18–2.1(e) (1979)*.

This approach to sentencing reform was generally not accepted and serves as one of many reasons why it has not taken long for greater legislative control over sentencing to have its detractors.

Those now hostile to these reforms have argued, first of all, that greater legislative specification of sentences invites the escalation of prison terms. In the current climate, the argument goes, legislators will try and outdo each other for political gain by racheting up the length of sentences. See, Shane–Dubow & Brown, Olsen, *Sentencing Return in the United States: History, Content and Effect (1985) at 9.*

Concern has also been raised about the sensibility of an empirical approach to sentencing such as the new federal scheme. The Sentencing Commission arrived at presumptive sentencing ranges by averaging past sentences for given federal crimes. It has been suggested that using averages "bastardizes" sentences and destroys any motion of proportionality. See, e.g., dissenting opinion of Professor Paul Robinson to U.S. Sentencing Commission Report 1988. Federal district court judges are beginning to criticize the guidelines as well. In United States v. Reich (1987), Judge Sweet complained about the maze of factfinding and tangential calculations that must be navigated. He added:

> But perhaps even more importantly, the idea of restraining discretion through grids, columns and various scores belittles the value of the social statement that attends the imposition of a criminal sentence. The formulae and the grid distance the offender from the sentencer—and from the reasons for punishment—by lending the process a false aura of scientific certainty.

Critics of determinate and presumptive sentencing also argue that these schemes do not really eliminate abuses of discretion. The abuses are simply shifted even further underground to the prosecutor as part of the charging or plea bargaining process where decision-making is even more hidden. See Shane–Dubow, Brown and Olsen, *Sentencing Reform in the United States: History, Content, and Effect (1985) at 10–11.* At an even more fundamental level, questions are being raised about sentencing guidelines and statutes which focus primarily on offense (and not offender) and punishment (and not rehabilitation). As Professor Francis Allen inquires, "if you forswear the rehabilitative ideal, where will the impetus come from to advance the essential decency of the system?" Allen, *The Decline of the Rehabilitative Ideal in American Criminal Justice, 27 Cleve.St.L.Rev. 147, 155–156 (1978).*

Sentencing schemes, which involve delegation of authority to develop guidelines to sentencing commissions, have also been attacked on constitutional grounds as well. When a commission is composed of members appointed by the legislative branch and the executive and also include judicial members, it was held by several courts that separation of powers principles may be violated. A year of tumultous uncertainty in the lower federal courts was ended in 1989, when the United States Supreme Court determined the Federal Sentencing Guidelines to be constitutional, since Congress neither (1) delegated excessive legislative power to the Commission nor (2) violated the separation-of-powers principle by placing the Commission in the Judicial Branch, by requiring federal judges to serve on the Commission and to share their authority with nonjudges, or by empowering the President to appoint Commission members and to remove them for cause. The Constitution's structural protections do not prohibit Congress from delegating to an expert body within the Judicial Branch the intricate task of formulating Sentencing Guidelines consistent with such significant statutory direction as is present here, nor from calling upon the accumulated wisdom and experience of the Judicial Branch in creating policy on a matter uniquely within the ken of judges. *See, Mistretta v. United States (1989).*

Thus, the new movement to reduce or eliminate the unfairness of indeterminate sentencing has been as controversial as the indeterminate sentencing schemes it was intended to replace.

For a concise summary of the law of corrections and prisoners' rights, surveying the entire correctional process from pretrial diversion to the restoration of offenders' rights upon release, see Krantz' Corrections and Prisoners' Rights in a Nutshell, 3rd Ed., Nutshell Series (West Publishing Company, St. Paul, 1988) ... from pages 13–20 of which this INTRODUCTION is drawn.

EXCERPTS FROM FEDERAL SENTENCING GUIDELINES MANUAL

Effective November 1, 1987

(Including Amendments Effective June 15, 1988)

CHAPTER ONE

INTRODUCTION AND GENERAL APPLICATION PRINCIPLES

PART A

INTRODUCTION

1. *Authority*

The United States Sentencing Commission ("Commission") is an independent agency in the judicial branch composed of seven voting and two non-voting, ex officio members. Its principal purpose is to establish sentencing policies and practices for the federal criminal justice system that will assure the ends of justice by promulgating detailed guidelines prescribing the appropriate sentences for offenders convicted of federal crimes.

The guidelines and policy statements promulgated by the Commission are issued pursuant to Section 994(a) of Title 28, United States Code.

2. *The Statutory Mission*

The Comprehensive Crime Control Act of 1984 foresees guidelines that will further the basic purposes of criminal punishment, i.e., deterring crime, incapacitating the offender, providing just punishment, and rehabilitating the offender. It delegates to the Commission broad authority to review and rationalize the federal sentencing process.

The statute contains many detailed instructions as to how this determination should be made, but the most important of them instructs the Commission to create categories of offense behavior and offender characteristics. An offense behavior category might consist, for example, of "bank robbery/committed with a gun/$2500 taken." An offender characteristic category might be "offender with one prior conviction who was not sentenced to imprisonment." The Commission is required to prescribe guidelines ranges that specify an appropriate sentence for each class of convicted persons, to be determined by coordinating the offense behavior categories with the offender characteristic categories. The statute contemplates the guidelines will establish a range of sentences for every coordination of categories. Where the guidelines call for imprisonment, the range must be narrow: the maximum imprisonment cannot exceed the minimum by more than the greater of 25 percent or 6 months. 28 U.S.C. § 994(b)(2).

The sentencing judge must select a sentence from within the guideline range. If, however, a particular case presents atypical features, the Act allows the judge to depart from the guidelines and sentence outside the range. In that case, the judge must specify reasons for departure. 18 U.S.C. § 3553(b). If the court sentences within the guideline range, an appellate court may review the sentence to see if the guideline was correctly applied. If the judge departs from the guideline range, an appellate court may review the reasonableness of the departure. 18 U.S.C. § 3742. The Act requires the offender to serve virtually all of any prison sentence imposed, for it abolishes parole and substantially restructures good behavior adjustments.

The law requires the Commission to send its initial guidelines to Congress by April 13, 1987, and under the present statute they take effect automatically on November 1, 1987. Pub.L. No. 98–473, § 235, reprinted at 18 U.S.C. § 3551. The Commission may submit guideline amendments each year to Congress between the beginning of a regular session and May 1. The amendments will take effect automatically 180 days after submission unless a law is enacted to the contrary. 28 U.S.C. § 994(p).

The Commission, with the aid of its legal and research staff, considerable public testimony and written commentary, has developed an initial set of guidelines which it now transmits to Congress. The Commission emphasizes, however, that it views the guideline-writing process as evolutionary. It expects, and the governing statute anticipates, that continuing research, experience, and analysis will result in modifications and revisions to the guidelines by submission of amendments to Congress. To this end, the Commission is established as a permanent agency to monitor sentencing practices in the federal courts throughout the nation.

3. The Basic Approach

To understand these guidelines and the rationale that underlies them, one must begin with the three objectives that Congress, in enacting the new sentencing law, sought to achieve. Its basic objective was to enhance the ability of the criminal justice system to reduce crime through an effective, fair sentencing system. To achieve this objective, Congress first sought *honesty* in sentencing. It sought to avoid the confusion and implicit deception that arises out of the present sentencing system which requires a judge to impose an indeterminate sentence that is automatically reduced in most cases by "good time" credits. In addition, the parole commission is permitted to determine how much of the remainder of any prison sentence an offender actually will serve. This usually results in a substantial reduction in the effective length of the sentence imposed, with defendants often serving only about one-third of the sentence handed down by the court.

Second, Congress sought *uniformity* in sentencing by narrowing the wide disparity in sentences imposed by different federal courts for similar criminal conduct by similar offenders. Third, Congress sought *proportionality* in sentencing through a system that imposes appropriately different sentences for criminal conduct of different severity.

Honesty is easy to achieve: The abolition of parole makes the sentence imposed by the court the sentence the offender will serve. There is a tension, however, between the mandate of uniformity (treat similar cases alike) and the mandate of proportionality (treat different cases differently) which, like the historical tension between law and equity, makes it difficult to achieve both goals simultaneously. Perfect uniformity—sentencing every offender to five years—destroys proportionality. Having only a few simple categories of crimes would make the guidelines uniform and easy to administer, but might lump together offenses that are different in important respects. For example, a single category for robbery that lumps together armed and unarmed robberies, robberies with and without injuries, robberies of a few dollars and robberies of millions, is far too broad.

At the same time, a sentencing system tailored to fit every conceivable wrinkle of each case can become unworkable and seriously compromise the certainty of punishment and its deterrent effect. A bank robber with (or without) a gun, which the robber kept hidden (or brandished), might have frightened (or merely warned), injured seriously (or less seriously), tied up (or simply pushed) a guard, a teller or a customer, at night (or at noon), for a bad (or arguably less bad) motive, in an effort to obtain money for other crimes (or for other purposes), in the company of a few (or many) other robbers, for the first (or fourth) time that day, while sober (or under the influence of drugs or alcohol), and so forth.

The list of potentially relevant features of criminal behavior is long; the fact that they can occur in multiple combinations means that the list of possible permutations of factors is virtually endless. The appropriate relationships among these different factors are exceedingly difficult to establish, for they are often context specific. Sentencing courts do not treat the occurrence of a simple bruise identically in all cases, irrespective of whether that bruise occurred in the context of a bank robbery or in the context of a breach of peace. This is so, in part, because the risk that such a harm will occur differs depending on the underlying offense with which it is connected (and therefore may already be counted, to a different degree, in the punishment for the underlying offense); and also because, in part, the relationship between punishment and multiple harms is not simply additive. The relation varies, depending on how much other harm has occurred. (Thus, one cannot easily assign points for each kind of harm and simply add them up, irrespective of context and total amounts.)

The larger the number of subcategories, the greater the complexity that is created and the less workable the system. Moreover, the subcategories themselves, sometimes too broad and sometimes too narrow, will apply and interact in unforeseen ways to unforeseen situations, thus failing to cure the unfairness of a simple, broad category system. Finally, and perhaps most importantly, probation officers and courts, in applying a complex system of subcategories, would have to make a host of decisions about whether the underlying facts are sufficient to bring the case within a particular subcategory. The greater the number of decisions required and the greater their complexity, the greater the risk that different judges will apply the guidelines differently to situations that, in fact, are similar, thereby reintroducing the very disparity that the guidelines were designed to eliminate.

In view of the arguments, it is tempting to retreat to the simple, broad-category approach and to grant judges the discretion to select the proper point along a broad sentencing range. Obviously, however, granting such broad discretion risks correspondingly broad disparity in sentencing, for different courts may exercise their discretionary powers in different ways. That is to say, such an approach risks a return to the wide disparity that Congress established the Commission to limit.

In the end, there is no completely satisfying solution to this practical stalemate. The Commission has had to simply balance the comparative virtues and vices of broad, simple categorization and detailed, complex subcategorization, and within the constraints established by that balance, minimize the discretionary powers of the sentencing court. Any ultimate system will, to a degree, enjoy the benefits and suffer from the drawbacks of each approach.

A philosophical problem arose when the Commission attempted to reconcile the differing perceptions of the purposes of criminal punishment. Most observers of the criminal law agree that the ultimate aim of the law itself, and of punishment in particular, is the control of crime. Beyond this point, however, the consensus seems to break down. Some argue that appropriate punishment should be defined primarily on the basis of the moral principle of "just deserts." Under this principle, punishment should be scaled to the offender's culpability and the resulting harms.

Thus, if a defendant is less culpable, the defendant deserves less punishment. Others argue that punishment should be imposed primarily on the basis of practical "crime control" considerations. Defendants sentenced under this scheme should receive the punishment that most effectively lessens the likelihood of future crime, either by deterring others or incapacitating the defendant.

Adherents of these points of view have urged the Commission to choose between them, to accord one primacy over the other. Such a choice would be profoundly difficult. The relevant literature is vast, the arguments deep, and each point of view has much to be said in its favor. A clear-cut Commission decision in favor of one of these approaches would diminish the chance that the guidelines would find the widespread acceptance they need for effective implementation. As a practical matter, in most sentencing decisions both philosophies may prove consistent with the same result.

For now, the Commission has sought to solve both the practical and philosophical problems of developing a coherent sentencing system by taking an empirical approach that uses data estimating the existing sentencing system as a starting point. It has analyzed data drawn from 10,000 presentence investigations, crimes as distinguished in substantive criminal statutes, the United States Parole Commission's guidelines and resulting statistics, and data from other relevant sources, in order to determine which distinctions are important in present practice. After examination, the Commission has accepted, modified, or rationalized the more important of these distinctions.

This empirical approach has helped the Commission resolve its practical problem by defining a list of relevant distinctions that, although of considerable length, is short enough to create a manageable set of guidelines. Existing categories are relatively broad and omit many distinctions that some may believe important, yet they include most of the major distinctions that statutes and presentence data suggest make a significant difference in sentencing decisions. Important distinctions that are ignored in existing practice probably occur rarely. A sentencing judge may take this unusual case into account by departing from the guidelines.

The Commission's empirical approach has also helped resolve its philosophical dilemma. Those who adhere to a just deserts philosophy may concede that the lack of moral consensus might make it difficult to say exactly what punishment is deserved for a particular crime, specified in minute detail. Likewise, those who subscribe to a philosophy of crime control may acknowledge that the lack of sufficient, readily available data might make it difficult to say exactly what punishment will best prevent that crime. Both groups might therefore recognize the wisdom of looking to those distinctions that judges and legislators have in fact made over the course of time. These established distinctions are ones that the community believes, or has found over time, to be important from either a moral or crime-control perspective.

The Commission has not simply copied estimates of existing practice as revealed by the data (even though establishing offense values on this basis would help eliminate disparity, for the data represent averages). Rather, it has departed from the data at different points for various important reasons. Congressional statutes, for example, may suggest or require departure, as in the case of the new drug law that imposes increased and mandatory minimum sentences. In addition, the data may reveal inconsistencies in treatment, such as punishing economic crime less severely than other apparently equivalent behavior.

Despite these policy-oriented departures from present practice, the guidelines represent an approach that begins with, and builds upon, empirical data. The guidelines will not please those who wish the Commission to adopt a single philosophical theory and then work deductively to establish a simple and perfect set of categorizations and distinctions. The guidelines may prove acceptable, however, to those who seek more modest, incremental improvements in the status quo, who believe the best is often the enemy of the good, and who recognize that these initial guidelines are but the first step in an evolutionary process. After spending considerable time and resources exploring alternative approaches, the Commission has developed these guidelines as a practical effort toward the achievement of a more honest, uniform, equitable, and therefore effective, sentencing system.

4. The Guidelines' Resolution of Major Issues

The guideline-writing process has required the Commission to resolve a host of important policy questions, typically involving rather evenly balanced sets of competing considerations. As an aid to understanding the guidelines, this introduction will briefly discuss several of those issues. Commentary in the guidelines explains others.

(a) Real Offense vs. Charge Offense Sentencing.

One of the most important questions for the Commission to decide was whether to base sentences upon the actual conduct in which the defendant engaged regardless of the charges for which he was indicted or convicted ("real offense" sentencing), or upon the conduct that constitutes the elements of the offense with which the defendant was charged and of which he was convicted ("charge offense" sentencing). A bank robber, for example, might have used a gun, frightened bystanders, taken $50,000, injured a teller, refused to stop when ordered, and raced away damaging property during escape. A pure real offense system would sentence on the basis of all identifiable conduct. A pure charge offense system would overlook some of the harms that did not constitute statutory elements of the offenses of which the defendant was convicted.

The Commission initially sought to develop a real offense system. After all, the present sentencing system is, in a sense, a real offense system. The sentencing court (and the parole commission) take account of the conduct in which the defendant actually engaged, as determined in a presentence report, at the sentencing hearing, or before a parole commission hearing officer. The Commission's initial efforts in this direction, carried out in the spring and early summer of 1986, proved unproductive mostly for practical reasons. To make such a system work, even to formalize and rationalize the status quo, would have required the Commission to decide precisely which harms to take into account, how to add them up, and what kinds of procedures the courts should use to determine the presence or absence of disputed factual elements. The Commission found no practical way to combine and account for the large number of diverse harms arising in different circumstances; nor did it find a practical way to reconcile the need for a fair adjudicatory procedure with the need for a speedy sentencing process, given the potential existence of hosts of adjudicated "real harm" facts in many typical cases. The effort proposed as a solution to these problems required the use of, for example, quadratic roots and other mathematical operations that the Commission considered too complex to be workable, and, in the Commission's view, risked return to wide disparity in practice.

The Commission therefore abandoned the effort to devise a "pure" real offense system and instead experimented with a "modified real offense system", which it published for public comment in a September 1986 preliminary draft.

This version also foundered in several major respects on the rock of practicality. It was highly complex and its mechanical rules for adding harms (e.g., bodily injury added the same punishment irrespective of context) threatened to work considerable unfairness. Ultimately, the Commission decided that it could not find a practical or fair and efficient way to implement either a pure or modified real offense system of the sort it originally wanted, and it abandoned that approach.

The Commission, in its January 1987 Revised Draft and the present guidelines, has moved closer to a "charge offense" system. The system is not, however, pure; it has a number of real elements. For one thing, the hundreds of overlapping and duplicative statutory provisions that make up the federal criminal law have forced the Commission to write guidelines that are descriptive of generic conduct rather than tracking purely statutory language. For another, the guidelines, both through specific offense characteristics and adjustments, take account of a number of important, commonly occurring real offense elements such as role in the offense, the presence of a gun, or the amount of money actually taken.

Finally, it is important not to overstate the difference in practice between a real and a charge offense system. The federal criminal system, in practice, deals mostly with drug offenses, bank robberies and white collar crimes (such as fraud, embezzlement, and bribery). For the most part, the conduct that an indictment charges approximates the real and relevant conduct in which the offender actually engaged.

The Commission recognizes its system will not completely cure the problems of a real offense system. It may still be necessary, for example, for a court to determine some particular real facts that will make a difference to the sentence.

Yet, the Commission believes that the instances of controversial facts will be far fewer; indeed, there will be few enough so that the court system will be able to devise fair procedures for their determination. See United States v. Fatico, 579 F.2d 707 (2d Cir.1978) (permitting introduction of hearsay evidence at sentencing hearing under certain conditions), on remand, 458 F.Supp. 388 (E.D.N.Y.1978), aff'd, 603 F.2d 1053 (2d Cir.1979) (holding that the government need not prove facts at sentencing hearing beyond a reasonable doubt), cert. denied, 444 U.S. 1073 (1980).

The Commission also recognizes that a charge offense system has drawbacks of its own. One of the most important is its potential to turn over to the prosecutor the power to determine the sentence by increasing or decreasing the number (or content) of the counts in an indictment. Of course, the defendant's actual conduct (that which the prosecutor can prove in court) imposes a natural limit upon the prosecutor's ability to increase a defendant's sentence. Moreover, the Commission has written its rules for the treatment of multicount convictions with an eye toward eliminating unfair treatment that might flow from count manipulation. For example, the guidelines treat a three-count indictment, each count of which charges sale of 100 grams of heroin, or theft of $10,000, the same as a single-count indictment charging sale of 300 grams of heroin or theft of $30,000. Further, a sentencing court may control any inappropriate manipulation of the indictment through use of its power to depart from the specific guideline sentence. Finally, the Commission will closely monitor problems arising out of count manipulation and will make appropriate adjustments should they become necessary.

(b) Departures.

The new sentencing statute permits a court to depart from a guideline-specified sentence only when it finds "an aggravating or mitigating circumstance ... that was not adequately taken into consideration by the Sentencing Commission ..." 18 U.S.C. § 3553(b). Thus, in principle, the Commission, by specifying that it had adequately considered a particular factor, could prevent a court from using it as grounds for departure. In this initial set of guidelines, however, the Commission does not so limit the courts' departure powers. The Commission intends the sentencing courts to treat each guideline as carving out a "heartland," a set of typical cases embodying the conduct that each guideline describes. When a court finds an atypical case, one to which a particular guideline linguistically applies but where conduct significantly differs from the norm, the court may consider whether a departure is warranted. Section 5H1.10 (Race, Sex, National Origin, Creed, Religion, Socio–Economic Status), the third sentence of § 5H1.4, and the last sentence of § 5K2.12, list a few factors that the court cannot take into account as grounds for departure. With those specific exceptions, however, the Commission does not intend to limit the kinds of factors (whether or not mentioned anywhere else in the guidelines) that could constitute grounds for departure in an unusual case.

The Commission has adopted this departure policy for two basic reasons. First is the difficulty of foreseeing and capturing a single set of guidelines that encompasses the vast range of human conduct potentially relevant to a sentencing decision. The Commission also recognizes that in the initial set of guidelines it need not do so. The Commission is a permanent body, empowered by law to write and rewrite guidelines, with progressive changes, over many years. By monitoring when courts depart from the guidelines and by analyzing their stated reasons for doing so, the Commission, over time, will be able to create more accurate guidelines that specify precisely where departures should and should not be permitted.

Second, the Commission believes that despite the courts' legal freedom to depart from the guidelines, they will not do so very often. This is because the guidelines, offense by offense, seek to take account of those factors that the Commission's sentencing data indicate make a significant difference in sentencing at the present time. Thus, for example, where the presence of actual physical injury currently makes an important difference in final sentences, as in the case of robbery, assault, or arson, the guidelines specifically instruct the judge to use this factor to augment the sentence. Where the guidelines do not specify an augmentation or diminution, this is generally because the sentencing data do not permit the Commission, at this time, to conclude that the factor is empirically important in relation to the particular offense. Of course, a factor (say physical injury) may nonetheless sometimes

occur in connection with a crime (such as fraud) where it does not often occur. If, however, as the data indicate, such occurrences are rare, they are precisely the type of events that the court's departure powers were designed to cover—unusual cases outside the range of the more typical offenses for which the guidelines were designed. Of course, the Commission recognizes that even its collection and analysis of 10,000 presentence reports are an imperfect source of data sentencing estimates. Rather than rely heavily at this time upon impressionistic accounts, however, the Commission believes it wiser to wait and collect additional data from our continuing monitoring process that may demonstrate how the guidelines work in practice before further modification.

It is important to note that the guidelines refer to three different kinds of departure. The first kind, which will most frequently be used, is in effect an interpolation between two adjacent, numerically oriented guideline rules. A specific offense characteristic, for example, might require an increase of four levels for serious bodily injury but two levels for bodily injury. Rather than requiring a court to force middle instances into either the "serious" or the "simple" category, the guideline commentary suggests that the court may interpolate and select a midpoint increase of three levels. The Commission has decided to call such an interpolation a "departure" in light of the legal views that a guideline providing for a range of increases in offense levels may violate the statute's 25 percent rule (though others have presented contrary legal arguments). Since interpolations are technically departures, the courts will have to provide reasons for their selection, and it will be subject to review for "reasonableness" on appeal. The Commission believes, however, that a simple reference by the court to the "mid-category" nature of the facts will typically provide sufficient reason. It does not foresee serious practical problems arising out of the application of the appeal provisions to this form of departure.

The second kind involves instances in which the guidelines provide specific guidance for departure, by analogy or by other numerical or non-numerical suggestions. For example, the commentary to § 2G1.1 (Transportation for Prostitution), recommends a downward adjustment of eight levels where commercial purpose was not involved. The Commission intends such suggestions as policy guidance for the courts. The Commission expects that most departures will reflect the suggestions, and that the courts of appeals may prove more likely to find departures "unreasonable" where they fall outside suggested levels.

A third kind of departure will remain unguided. It may rest upon grounds referred to in Chapter 5, Part H, or on grounds not mentioned in the guidelines. While Chapter 5, Part H lists factors that the Commission believes may constitute grounds for departure, those suggested grounds are not exhaustive. The Commission recognizes that there may be other grounds for departure that are not mentioned; it also believes there may be cases in which a departure outside suggested levels is warranted. In its view, however, such cases will be highly unusual.

(c) Plea Agreements.

Nearly ninety percent of all federal criminal cases involve guilty pleas, and many of these cases involve some form of plea agreement. Some commentators on early Commission guideline drafts have urged the Commission not to attempt any major reforms of the agreement process, on the grounds that any set of guidelines that threatens to radically change present practice also threatens to make the federal system unmanageable. Others, starting with the same facts, have argued that guidelines which fail to control and limit plea agreements would leave untouched a "loophole" large enough to undo the good that sentencing guidelines may bring. Still other commentators make both sets of arguments.

The Commission has decided that these initial guidelines will not, in general, make significant changes in current plea agreement practices. The court will accept or reject any such agreements primarily in accordance with the rules set forth in Fed.R.Crim.P. 11(e). The Commission will collect data on the courts' plea practices and will analyze this information to determine when and why the courts accept or reject plea agreements. In light of this information and analysis, the Commission will seek to further regulate the plea agreement process as appropriate.

The Commission nonetheless expects the initial set of guidelines to have a positive, rationalizing impact upon plea agreements for two reasons. First, the guidelines create a clear, definite expectation in respect to the sentence that a court will impose if a trial takes place. Insofar as a prosecutor and defense attorney seek to agree about a likely sentence or range of sentences, they will no longer work in the dark. This fact alone should help to reduce irrationality in respect to actual sentencing outcomes. Second, the guidelines create a norm to which judges will likely refer when they decide whether, under Rule 11(e), to accept or to reject a plea agreement or recommendation. Since they will have before them the norm, the relevant factors (as disclosed in the plea agreement), and the reason for the agreement, they will find it easier than at present to determine whether there is sufficient reason to accept a plea agreement that departs from the norm.

(d) Probation and Split Sentences.

The statute provides that the guidelines are to "reflect the general appropriateness of imposing a sentence other than imprisonment in cases in which the defendant is a first offender who has not been convicted of a crime of violence or an otherwise serious offense * * *" 28 U.S.C. § 994(j). Under present sentencing practice, courts sentence to probation an inappropriately high percentage of offenders guilty of certain economic crimes, such as theft, tax evasion, antitrust offenses, insider trading, fraud, and embezzlement, that in the Commission's view are "serious." If the guidelines were to permit courts to impose probation instead of prison in many or all such cases, the present sentences would continue to be ineffective.

The Commission's solution to this problem has been to write guidelines that classify as "serious" (and therefore subject to mandatory prison sentences) many offenses for which probation is now frequently given. At the same time, the guidelines will permit the sentencing court to impose short prison terms in many such cases. The Commission's view is that the definite prospect of prison, though the term is short, will act as a significant deterrent to many of these crimes, particularly when compared with the status quo where probation, not prison, is the norm.

More specifically, the guidelines work as follows in respect to a first offender. For offense levels one through six, the sentencing court may elect to sentence the offender to probation (with or without confinement conditions) or to a prison term. For offense levels seven through ten, the court may substitute probation for a prison term, but the probation must include confinement conditions (community confinement or intermittent confinement). For offense levels eleven and twelve, the court must impose at least one half the minimum confinement sentence in the form of prison confinement, the remainder to be served on supervised release with a condition of community confinement. The Commission, of course, has not dealt with the single acts of aberrant behavior that still may justify probation at higher offense levels through departures.

(e) Multi–Count Convictions.

The Commission, like other sentencing commissions, has found it particularly difficult to develop rules for sentencing defendants convicted of multiple violations of law, each of which makes up a separate count in an indictment. The reason it is difficult is that when a defendant engages in conduct that causes several harms, each additional harm, even if it increases the extent to which punishment is warranted, does not necessarily warrant a proportionate increase in punishment. A defendant who assaults others during a fight, for example, may warrant more punishment if he injures ten people than if he injures one, but his conduct does not necessarily warrant ten times the punishment. If it did, many of the simplest offenses, for reasons that are often fortuitous, would lead to life sentences of imprisonment—sentences that neither "just deserts" nor "crime control" theories of punishment would find justified.

Several individual guidelines provide special instructions for increasing punishment when the conduct that is the subject of that count involves multiple occurrences or has caused several harms. The guidelines also provide general rules for aggravating punishment in light of multiple harms charged separately in separate counts. These rules may produce occasional anomalies, but normally they will permit an appropriate degree of aggravation of punishment when multiple offenses that are the subjects of separate counts take place.

These rules are set out in Chapter Three, Part D. They essentially provide: (1) When the conduct involves fungible items, e.g., separate drug transactions or thefts of money, the amounts are added and the guidelines apply to the total amount. (2) When nonfungible harms are involved, the offense level for the most serious count is increased (according to a somewhat diminishing scale) to reflect the existence of other counts of conviction.

The rules have been written in order to minimize the possibility that an arbitrary casting of a single transaction into several counts will produce a longer sentence. In addition, the sentencing court will have adequate power to prevent such a result through departures where necessary to produce a mitigated sentence.

(f) Regulatory Offenses.

Regulatory statutes, though primarily civil in nature, sometimes contain criminal provisions in respect to particularly harmful activity. Such criminal provisions often describe not only substantive offenses, but also more technical, administratively-related offenses such as failure to keep accurate records or to provide requested information. These criminal statutes pose two problems. First, which criminal regulatory provisions should the Commission initially consider, and second, how should it treat technical or administratively-related criminal violations?

In respect to the first problem, the Commission found that it cannot comprehensively treat all regulatory violations in the initial set of guidelines. There are hundreds of such provisions scattered throughout the United States Code. To find all potential violations would involve examination of each individual federal regulation. Because of this practical difficulty, the Commission has sought to determine, with the assistance of the Department of Justice and several regulatory agencies, which criminal regulatory offenses are particularly important in light of the need for enforcement of the general regulatory scheme. The Commission has sought to treat these offenses in these initial guidelines. It will address the less common regulatory offenses in the future.

In respect to the second problem, the Commission has developed a system for treating technical recordkeeping and reporting offenses, dividing them into four categories.

First, in the simplest of cases, the offender may have failed to fill out a form intentionally, but without knowledge or intent that substantive harm would likely follow. He might fail, for example, to keep an accurate record of toxic substance transport, but that failure may not lead, nor be likely to lead, to the release or improper treatment of any toxic substance. Second, the same failure may be accompanied by a significant likelihood that substantive harm will occur; it may make a release of a toxic substance more likely. Third, the same failure may have led to substantive harm. Fourth, the failure may represent an effort to conceal a substantive harm that has occurred.

The structure of a typical guideline for a regulatory offense is as follows:

(1) The guideline provides a low base offense level (6) aimed at the first type of recordkeeping or reporting offense. It gives the court the legal authority to impose a punishment ranging from probation up to six months of imprisonment.

(2) Specific offense characteristics designed to reflect substantive offenses that do occur (in respect to some regulatory offenses), or that are likely to occur, increase the offense level.

(3) A specific offense characteristic also provides that a recordkeeping or reporting offense that conceals a substantive offense will be treated like the substantive offense.

The Commission views this structure as an initial effort. It may revise its approach in light of further experience and analysis of regulatory crimes.

(g) Sentencing Ranges.

In determining the appropriate sentencing ranges for each offense, the Commission began by estimating the average sentences now being served within each category. It also examined the sentence specified in congressional statutes, in the parole guidelines, and in other relevant, analogous sources. The Commission's forthcoming detailed report will contain a comparison between estimates of existing sentencing practices and sentences under the guidelines.

While the Commission has not considered itself bound by existing sentencing practice, it has not tried to develop an entirely new system of sentencing on the basis of theory alone. Guideline sentences in many instances will approximate existing practice, but adherence to the guidelines will help to eliminate wide disparity. For example, where a high percentage of persons now receive probation, a guideline may include one or more specific offense characteristics in an effort to distinguish those types of defendants who now receive probation from those who receive more severe sentences. In some instances, short sen-

tences of incarceration for all offenders in a category have been substituted for a current sentencing practice of very wide variability in which some defendants receive probation while others receive several years in prison for the same offense. Moreover, inasmuch as those who currently plead guilty often receive lesser sentences, the guidelines also permit the court to impose lesser sentences on those defendants who accept responsibility and those who cooperate with the government.

The Commission has also examined its sentencing ranges in light of their likely impact upon prison population. Specific legislation, such as the new drug law and the career offender provisions of the sentencing law, require the Commission to promulgate rules that will lead to substantial prison population increases. These increases will occur irrespective of any guidelines. The guidelines themselves, insofar as they reflect policy decisions made by the Commission (rather than legislated mandatory minimum, or career offender, sentences), will lead to an increase in prison population that computer models, produced by the Commission and the Bureau of Prisons, estimate at approximately 10 percent over a period of 10 years.

(h) The Sentencing Table.

The Commission has established a sentencing table. For technical and practical reasons it has 43 levels. Each row in the table contains levels that overlap with the levels in the preceding and succeeding rows. By overlapping the levels, the table should discourage unnecessary litigation. Both prosecutor and defendant will realize that the difference between one level and another will not necessarily make a difference in the sentence that the judge imposes. Thus, little purpose will be served in protracted litigation trying to determine, for example, whether $10,000 or $11,000 was obtained as a result of a fraud. At the same time, the rows work to increase a sentence proportionately. A change of 6 levels roughly doubles the sentence irrespective of the level at which one starts. The Commission, aware of the legal requirement that the maximum of any range cannot exceed the minimum by more than the greater of 25 percent or six months, also wishes to permit courts the greatest possible range for exercising discretion. The table overlaps offense levels meaningfully, works proportionately, and at the same time preserves the maximum degree of allowable discretion for the judge within each level.

Similarly, many of the individual guidelines refer to tables that correlate amounts of money with offense levels. These tables often have many, rather than a few levels. Again, the reason is to minimize the likelihood of unnecessary litigation. If a money table were to make only a few distinctions, each distinction would become more important and litigation as to which category an offender fell within would become more likely. Where a table has many smaller monetary distinctions, it minimizes the likelihood of litigation, for the importance of the precise amount of money involved is considerably less.

5. *A Concluding Note*

The Commission emphasizes that its approach in this initial set of guidelines is one of caution. It has examined the many hundreds of criminal statutes in the United States Code. It has begun with those that are the basis for a significant number of prosecutions. It has sought to place them in a rational order. It has developed additional distinctions relevant to the application of these provisions, and it has applied sentencing ranges to each resulting category. In doing so, it has relied upon estimates of existing sentencing practices as revealed by its own statistical analy-

ses, based on summary reports of some 40,000 convictions, a sample of 10,000 augmented presentence reports, the parole guidelines and policy judgments.

The Commission recognizes that some will criticize this approach as overly cautious, as representing too little a departure from existing practice. Yet, it will cure wide disparity. The Commission is a permanent body that can amend the guidelines each year. Although the data available to it, like all data, are imperfect, experience with these guidelines will lead to additional information and provide a firm empirical basis for revision.

Finally, the guidelines will apply to approximately 90 percent of all cases in the federal courts. Because of time constraints and the nonexistence of statistical information, some offenses that occur infrequently are not considered in this initial set of guidelines. They will, however, be addressed in the near future. Their exclusion from this initial submission does not reflect any judgment about their seriousness. The Commission has also deferred promulgation of guidelines pertaining to fines, probation and other sanctions for organizational defendants, with the exception of antitrust violations. The Commission also expects to address this area in the near future.

PART B

GENERAL APPLICATION PRINCIPLES

§ 1B1.1. Application Instructions

(a) Determine the guideline section in Chapter Two most applicable to the statute of conviction. See § 1B1.2 (Applicable Guidelines). The statutory index (Appendix A) provides a listing to assist in this determination. If more than one guideline is referenced for the particular statute, select the guideline most appropriate for the conduct of which the defendant was convicted.

(b) Determine the base offense level and apply any appropriate specific offense characteristics contained in the particular guideline in Chapter Two in the order listed.

(c) Apply the adjustments as appropriate related to victim, role, and obstruction of justice from Parts A, B, and C of Chapter Three.

(d) If there are multiple counts of conviction, repeat steps (a) through (c) for each count. Apply

Part D of Chapter Three to group the various counts and adjust the offense level accordingly.

(e) Apply the adjustment as appropriate for the defendant's acceptance of responsibility from Part E of Chapter Three. The resulting offense level is the total offense level.

(f) Compute the defendant's criminal history category as specified in Part A of Chapter Four. Determine from Part B of Chapter Four any other applicable adjustments.

(g) Determine the guideline range in Part A of Chapter Five that corresponds to the total offense level and criminal history category.

(h) For the particular guideline range, determine from Parts B through G of Chapter Five the sentencing requirements and options related to probation, imprisonment, supervision conditions, fines, and restitution.

(i) Refer to Parts H and K of Chapter Five, Specific Offender Characteristics and Departures, and to any other policy statements or commentary in the guidelines that might warrant consideration in imposing sentence.

General Principles Governing Chapter Two

§ 1B1.2. Applicable Guidelines

(a) The court shall apply the offense guideline section in Chapter Two (Offense Conduct) most applicable to the offense of conviction. Provided, however, in the case of conviction by a plea of guilty or nolo contendere containing a stipulation that specifically establishes a more serious offense than the offense of conviction, the court shall apply the guideline in such chapter most applicable to the stipulated offense. Similarly, stipulations to additional offenses are treated as if the defendant had been convicted of separate counts charging those offenses.

(b) After determining the appropriate offense guideline section pursuant to subsection (a) of this section, determine the applicable guideline range in accordance with § 1B1.3 (Relevant Conduct).

§ 1B1.3. Relevant Conduct (Factors that Determine the Guideline Range)

(a) Unless otherwise specified under the guidelines, conduct and circumstances relevant to the offense of conviction means:

acts or omissions committed or aided and abetted by the defendant, or by a person for whose conduct the defendant is legally accountable, that (1) are part of the same course of conduct, or a common scheme or plan, as the offense of conviction, or (2) are relevant to the defendant's state of mind or motive in committing the offense of conviction, or (3) indicate the defendant's degree of dependence upon criminal activity for a livelihood.

(b) Injury relevant to the offense of conviction means harm which is caused intentionally, recklessly or by criminal negligence in the course of conduct relevant to the offense of conviction.

§ 1B1.4. Information to be Used in Imposing Sentence (Selecting a Point Within the Guideline Range or Departing from the Guidelines)

In determining the sentence to impose within the guideline range, or whether a departure from the guidelines is warranted, the court may consider, without limitation, any information concerning the background, character and conduct of the defendant, unless otherwise prohibited by law. *See* 18 U.S.C. § 3661.

Commentary

Background: This section distinguishes between factors that determine the applicable guideline sentencing range (§ 1B1.3) and information that a court may consider in imposing sentence within that range. The section is based on 18 U.S.C. § 3661, which recodifies 18 U.S.C. § 3557. The recodification of this 1970 statute in 1984 with an effective date of 1987 (99 Stat. 1728), makes it clear that Congress intended that no limitation would be placed on the information that a court may consider in imposing an appropriate sentence under the future guideline sentencing system. A court is not precluded from considering information that the guidelines do not take into account. For example, if the defendant committed two robberies, but as part of a plea negotiation entered a guilty plea to only one, the robbery that was not taken into account by the guidelines would provide a reason for sentencing at the top of the guideline range. In addition, information that does not enter into the determination of the applicable guideline sentencing range may be considered in determining whether and to what extent to depart from the guidelines. Some policy statements do, however, express a Commission policy that certain factors should not be considered for any purpose, or should be considered only for limited purposes. *See, e.g.,* Chapter Five, Part H (Specific Offender Characteristics).

§ 1B1.5. Interpretation of References to Other Offense Guidelines

Unless otherwise expressly indicated, a reference to another guideline, or an instruction to apply another guideline, refers to the **entire** guideline, i.e., the base offense level plus all applicable adjustments for specific offense characteristics.

CHAPTER TWO

OFFENSE CONDUCT

OVERVIEW

Chapter Two pertains to offense conduct. The chapter is organized by offenses and divided into parts and related sections that may cover one statute or many. Each offense has a corresponding base offense level. When a particular offense warrants a more individualized sentence, specific offense characteristics are provided within the guidelines. Certain factors relevant to criminal conduct that are not provided in specific guidelines are set forth in Chapter Three, Part A (Victim–Related Adjustments) and Chapter Five, Part K (Departures). The statutes appearing at the beginning of each part are illustrative and do not necessarily include all the statutes covered by the guidelines in that part.

PART A

OFFENSES AGAINST THE PERSON

1. HOMICIDE

§ 2A1.1. First Degree Murder

(a) Base Offense Level: 43

* * *

§ 2A1.3. Voluntary Manslaughter

(a) Base Offense Level: 25

§ 2A1.4. Involuntary Manslaughter

(a) Base Offense Level:

(1) 10, if the conduct was criminally negligent; or

(2) 14, if the conduct was reckless.

* * *

2. ASSAULT

* * *

§ 2A2.1. Assault With Intent to Commit Murder; Conspiracy or Solicitation to Commit Murder; Attempted Murder

(a) Base Offense Level: 20

(b) Specific Offense Characteristics

(1) If an assault involved more than minimal planning, increase by 2 levels.

(2)(A) If a firearm was discharged, increase by 5 levels; (B) if a firearm or a dangerous weapon was otherwise used, increase by 4 levels; (C) if a firearm or other dangerous weapon was brandished or its use was threatened, increase by 3 levels.

(3) If the victim sustained bodily injury, increase the offense level according to the seriousness of the injury:

Degree of Bodily Injury	Increase in Level
(A) Bodily Injury	add 2
(B) Serious Bodily Injury	add 4
(C) Permanent or Life–Threatening Bodily Injury	add 6

Provided, however, that the cumulative adjustments from (2) and (3) shall not exceed 9 levels.

(4) If a conspiracy or assault was motivated by a payment or offer of money or other thing of value, increase by 2 levels.

§ 2A2.2. Aggravated Assault

(a) Base Offense Level: 15

(b) Specific Offense Characteristics

(1) If the assault involved more than minimal planning, increase by 2 levels.

(2)(A) If a firearm was discharged, increase by 5 levels; (B) if a firearm or a dangerous weapon was otherwise used, increase by 4 levels; (C) if a firearm or other dangerous weapon was brandished or its use was threatened, increase by 3 levels.

(3) If the victim sustained bodily injury, increase the offense level according to the seriousness of the injury:

Degree of Bodily Injury	Increase in Level
(A) Bodily Injury	add 2

Degree of Bodily Injury	Increase in Level
(B) Serious Bodily Injury	add 4
(C) Permanent or Life–Threatening Bodily Injury	add 6

Provided, however, that the cumulative adjustments from (2) and (3) shall not exceed 9 levels.

(4) If the assault was motivated by a payment or offer of money or other thing of value, increase by 2 levels.

§ 2A2.3. Minor Assault

(a) Base Offense Level:

(1) 6, if the conduct involved striking, beating, or wounding; or

(2) 3, otherwise.

* * *

3. CRIMINAL SEXUAL ABUSE

§ 2A3.1. Criminal Sexual Abuse; Attempt or Assault With the Intent to Commit Criminal Sexual Abuse

(a) Base Offense Level: 27

(b) Specific Offense Characteristics

(1) If the criminal sexual abuse was accomplished as defined in 18 U.S.C. § 2241 (including, but not limited to, the use or display of any dangerous weapon), increase by 4 levels.

(2)(A) If the victim had not attained the age of twelve years, increase by 4 levels; otherwise, (B) if the victim was under the age of sixteen, increase by 2 levels.

(3) If the victim was in the custody, care, or supervisory control of the defendant, was a corrections employee, or a person held in the custody of a correctional facility, increase by 2 levels.

(4)(A) If the victim sustained permanent or life-threatening bodily injury, increase by 4 levels; (B) if the victim sustained serious bodily injury, increase by 2 levels.

(5) If the victim was abducted, increase by 4 levels.

§ 2A3.2. Criminal Sexual Abuse of a Minor (Statutory Rape) or Attempt to Commit Such Acts

(a) Base Offense Level: 15

(b) Specific Offense Characteristic

(1) If the victim was in the custody, care, or supervisory control of the defendant, increase by 1 level.

§ 2A3.3. Criminal Sexual Abuse of a Ward (Statutory Rape) or Attempt to Commit Such Acts

(a) Base Offense Level: 9

§ 2A3.4. Abusive Sexual Contact or Attempt to Commit Abusive Sexual Contact

(a) Base Offense Level: 6

(b) Specific Offense Characteristics

(1) If the abusive sexual contact was accomplished as defined in 18 U.S.C. § 2241 (including, but not limited to, the use or display of any dangerous weapon), increase by 9 levels.

(2) If the abusive sexual contact was accomplished as defined in 18 U.S.C. § 2242, increase by 4 levels.

PART B

OFFENSES INVOLVING PROPERTY

1. THEFT, EMBEZZLEMENT, RECEIPT OF STOLEN PROPERTY, AND PROPERTY DESTRUCTION

* * *

§ 2B1.1 Larceny, Embezzlement, and Other Forms of Theft

(a) Base Offense Level: 4

(b) Specific Offense Characteristics

(1) If the loss exceeded $100, increase the offense level as follows:

Loss	Increase in Level
(A) $100 or less	no increase
(B) $101–$1,000	add 1
(C) $1,001–$2,000	add 2
(D) $2,001–$5,000	add 3
(E) $5,001–$10,000	add 4

Loss	Increase in Level
(F) $10,001–$20,000	add 5
(G) $20,001–$50,000	add 6
(H) $50,001–$100,000	add 7
(I) $100,001–$200,000	add 8
(J) $200,001–$500,000	add 9
(K) $500,001–$1,000,000	add 10
(L) $1,000,001–$2,000,000	add 11
(M) $2,000,001–$5,000,000	add 12
(N) over $5,000,000	add 13

(2) If a firearm, destructive device, or controlled substance was taken, increase by 1 level; but if the resulting offense level is less than 7, increase to level 7.

(3) If the theft was from the person of another, increase by 2 levels.

(4) If the offense involved more than minimal planning, increase by 2 levels.

(5) If undelivered United States mail was taken, and the offense level as determined above is less than level 6, increase to level 6.

(6) If the offense involved organized criminal activity, and the offense level as determined above is less than level 14, increase to level 14.

* * *

2. BURGLARY AND TRESPASS

§ 2B2.1.　Burglary of a Residence

(a) Base Offense Level: 17

(b) Specific Offense Characteristics

(1) If the offense involved more than minimal planning, increase by 2 levels.

(2) If the loss exceeded $2,500, increase the offense level as follows:

Loss	Increase in Level
(A) $2,500 or less	no increase
(B) $2,501–$10,000	add 1
(C) $10,001–$50,000	add 2
(D) $50,001–$250,000	add 3
(E) $250,001–$1,000,000	add 4
(F) $1,000,001–$5,000,000	add 5
(G) more than $5,000,000	add 6

(3) If obtaining a firearm, destructive device, or controlled substance was an object of the offense, increase by 1 level.

(4) If a firearm or other dangerous weapon was possessed, increase by 2 levels.

§ 2B2.2.　Burglary of Other Structures

(a) Base Offense Level: 12

(b) Specific Offense Characteristics

(1) If the offense involved more than minimal planning, increase by 2 levels.

(2) If the loss exceeded $2,500, increase by the corresponding number of levels from the table in § 2B2.1.

(3) If obtaining a firearm, destructive device, or controlled substance was an object of the offense, increase by 1 level.

(4) If a firearm or other dangerous weapon was possessed, increase by 2 levels.

§ 2B2.3.　Trespass

(a) Base Offense Level: 4

(b) Specific Offense Characteristics

(1) If the trespass occurred at a secured government facility, a nuclear energy facility, or a residence, increase by 2 levels.

(2) If a firearm or other dangerous weapon was possessed, increase by 2 levels.

* * *

3. ROBBERY, EXTORTION, AND BLACKMAIL

* * *

§ 2B3.1.　Robbery

(a) Base Offense Level: 18

(b) Specific Offense Characteristics

(1) If the loss exceeded $2,500, increase the offense level as follows:

Loss	Increase in Level
(A) $2,500 or less	no increase
(B) $2,501–$10,000	add 1
(C) $10,001–$50,000	add 2
(D) $50,001–$250,000	add 3
(E) $250,001–$1,000,000	add 4
(F) $1,000,001–$5,000,000	add 5
(G) more than $5,000,000	add 6

Treat the loss for a financial institution or post office as at least $5,000.

(2)(A) If a firearm was discharged increase by 5 levels; (B) if a firearm or a dangerous weapon was otherwise used, increase by 4 levels; (C) if a firearm or other dangerous weapon was brandished, displayed or possessed, increase by 3 levels.

(3) If any victim sustained bodily injury, increase the offense level according to the seriousness of the injury:

Degree of Bodily Injury	Increase in Level
(A) Bodily Injury	add 2
(B) Serious Bodily Injury	add 4
(C) Permanent or Life–Threatening Bodily Injury	add 6

Provided, however, that the cumulative adjustments from (2) and (3) shall not exceed 9 levels.

(4)(A) If any person was abducted to facilitate commission of the offense or to facilitate escape, increase by 4 levels; or (B) if any person was physically restrained to facilitate commission of the offense or to facilitate escape, increase by 2 levels.

(5) If obtaining a firearm, destructive device, or controlled substance was the object of the offense, increase by 1 level.

§ 2B3.2. Extortion by Force or Threat of Injury or Serious Damage

(a) Base Offense Level: 18

(b) Specific Offense Characteristics

(1) If the greater of the amount obtained or demanded exceeded $2,500, increase by the corresponding number of levels from the table in § 2B3.1.

(2)(A) If a firearm was discharged increase by 5 levels; (B) if a firearm or a dangerous weapon was otherwise used, increase by 4 levels; (C) if a firearm or other dangerous weapon was brandished, displayed or possessed, increase by 3 levels.

(3) If any victim sustained bodily injury, increase the offense level according to the seriousness of the injury:

Degree of Bodily Injury	Increase in Level
(A) Bodily Injury	add 2
(B) Serious Bodily Injury	add 4
(C) Permanent or Life–Threatening Bodily Injury	add 6

Provided, however, that the cumulative adjustments from (2) and (3) shall not exceed 9 levels.

(4)(A) If any person was abducted to facilitate commission of the offense or to facilitate escape, increase by 4 levels; or (B) if any person was physically restrained to facilitate commission of the offense or to facilitate escape, increase by 2 levels.

PART C

OFFENSES INVOLVING PUBLIC OFFICIALS

* * *

§ 2C1.1. Offering, Giving, Soliciting, or Receiving a Bribe; Extortion Under Color of Official Right

(a) Base Offense Level: 10

(b) Specific Offense Characteristics

Apply the greater:

(1) If the value of the bribe or the action received in return for the bribe exceeded $2,000, increase by the corresponding number of levels from the table in § 2F1.1 (Fraud and Deceit).

(2) If the offense involved a bribe for the purpose of influencing an elected official or any official holding a high level decision-making or sensitive position, increase by 8 levels.

PART D

OFFENSES INVOLVING DRUGS

1. UNLAWFUL MANUFACTURING, IMPORTING, EXPORTING, TRAFFICKING, OR POSSESSION; CONTINUING CRIMINAL ENTERPRISE

* * *

§ 2D1.1 Unlawful Manufacturing, Importing, Exporting, or Trafficking (Including Possession with Intent to Commit These Offenses)

(a) Base Offense Level:

(1) 43, for an offense that results in death or serious bodily injury with a prior conviction for a similar drug offense; or

* * *

(3) 6, for an offense that involves less than 250G Marijuana.

* * *

PART E

OFFENSES INVOLVING CRIMINAL ENTERPRISES AND RACKETEERING

1. RACKETEERING

§ 2E1.1. Unlawful Conduct Relating to Racketeer Influenced and Corrupt Organizations

(a) Base Offense Level (Apply the greater):

(1) 19; or

(2) the offense level applicable to the underlying racketeering activity.

* * *

2. EXTORTIONATE EXTENSION OF CREDIT

§ 2E2.1. Making, Financing, or Collecting an Extortionate Extension of Credit

(a) Base Offense Level: 20

(b) Specific Offense Characteristics

(1)

(A) If a firearm was discharged increase by 5 levels; or

(B) if a firearm or a dangerous weapon was otherwise used, increase by 4 levels; or

(C) if a firearm or other dangerous weapon was brandished, displayed or possessed, increase by 3 levels.

(2) If any victim sustained bodily injury, increase the offense level according to the seriousness of the injury:

Degree of Bodily Injury	Increase in Level
(A) Bodily Injury	add 2
(B) Serious Bodily Injury	add 4
(C) Permanent or Life–Threatening Bodily Injury	add 6

Provided, however, that the combined increase from (1) and (2) shall not exceed 9 levels.

(3)

(A) If any person was abducted to facilitate the commission of the offense or an escape from the scene of the crime, increase by 4 levels;

(B) if any person was physically restrained to facilitate commission of the offense or to facilitate escape, increase by 2 levels.

* * *

PART F

OFFENSES INVOLVING FRAUD OR DECEIT

§ 2F1.1. Fraud and Deceit

(a) Base Offense Level: 6

(b) Specific Offense Characteristics

(1) If the loss exceeded $2,000, increase the offense level as follows:

Loss	Increase in Level
(A) $2,000 or less	no increase
(B) $2,001–$5,000	add 1
(C) $5,001–$10,000	add 2
(D) $10,001–$20,000	add 3
(E) $20,001–$50,000	add 4
(F) $50,001–$100,000	add 5
(G) $100,001–$200,000	add 6
(H) $200,001–$500,000	add 7
(I) $500,001–$1,000,000	add 8
(J) $1,000,001–$2,000,000	add 9
(K) $2,000,001–$5,000,000	add 10
(L) over $5,000,000	add 11

(2) If the offense involved (A) more than minimal planning; (B) a scheme to defraud more than one victim; (C) a misrepresentation that the defendant was acting on behalf of a charitable, educational, religious or political organiza-tion, or a government agency; or (D) violation of any judicial or administrative order, injunction, decree or process; increase by 2 levels, but if the result is less than level 10, increase to level 10.

(3) If the offense involved the use of foreign bank accounts or transactions to conceal the true nature or extent of the fraudulent conduct, and the offense level as determined above is less than level 12, increase to level 12.

§ 2F1.2. Insider Trading

(a) Base Offense Level: 8

(b) Specific Offense Characteristic

(1) Increase by the number of levels from the table in § 2F1.1 corresponding to the gain resulting from the offense.

PART G

OFFENSES INVOLVING PROSTITUTION, SEXUAL EXPLOITATION OF MINORS, AND OBSCENITY

1. PROSTITUTION

§ 2G1.1. Transportation for the Purpose of Prostitution or Prohibited Sexual Conduct

(a) Base Offense Level: 14

(b) Specific Offense Characteristic

(1) If the defendant used physical force, or coercion by drugs or otherwise, increase by 4 levels.

* * *

3. OBSCENITY

§ 2G3.1. Importing, Mailing, or Transporting Obscene Matter

(a) Base Offense Level: 6

(b) Specific Offense Characteristics

(1) If the offense involved an act related to distribution for pecuniary gain, increase by the number of levels from the table in § 2F1.1 corresponding to the retail value of the material, but in no event by less than 5 levels.

(2) If the offense involved material that portrays sadomasochistic conduct or other depictions of violence, increase by 4 levels.

(c) Cross Reference

(1) If the offense involved a criminal enterprise, apply the appropriate guideline from Chapter Two, Part E (Offenses Involving Criminal Enterprises and Racketeering) if the resulting offense level is greater than that determined above.

§ 2G3.2. Obscene or Indecent Telephone Communications

(a) Base Offense Level: 6

PART H

OFFENSES INVOLVING INDIVIDUAL RIGHTS

1. CIVIL RIGHTS

* * *

§ 2H1.3. Use of Force or Threat of Force to Deny Benefits or Rights in Furtherance of Discrimination

(a) Base Offense Level (Apply the greatest):

(1) 10, if no injury occurred; or

(2) 15, if injury occurred; or

(3) 2 plus the offense level applicable to any underlying offense.

(b) Specific Offense Characteristic

(1) If the defendant was a public official at the time of the offense, increase by 4 levels.

* * *

PART K

OFFENSES INVOLVING PUBLIC SAFETY

* * *

2. FIREARMS

§ 2K2.1. Receipt, Possession, or Transportation of Firearms and Other Weapons by Prohibited Persons

(a) Base Offense Level: 9

(b) Specific Offense Characteristics

(1) If the firearm was stolen or had an altered or obliterated serial number, increase by 1 level.

(2) If the defendant obtained or possessed the firearm solely for sport or recreation, decrease by 4 levels.

PART L

OFFENSES INVOLVING IMMIGRATION, NATURALIZATION, AND PASSPORTS

1. IMMIGRATION

§ 2L1.1. Smuggling, Transporting, or Harboring an Unlawful Alien

(a) Base Offense Level: 9

(b) Specific Offense Characteristics

(1) If the defendant committed the offense other than for profit that the alien was excludable under 8 U.S.C. §§ 1182(a)(27), (28), (29), decrease by 3 levels.

(2) If the defendant previously has been convicted of smuggling, transporting, or harboring an unlawful alien, or a related offense, increase by 2 levels.

PART M

OFFENSES INVOLVING NATIONAL DEFENSE

1. TREASON

§ 2M1.1. Treason

(a) Base Offense Level:

(1) 43, if the conduct is tantamount to waging war against the United States; otherwise,

(2) the offense level applicable to the most analogous offense.

* * *

PART Q

OFFENSES INVOLVING THE ENVIRONMENT

1. ENVIRONMENT

§ 2Q1.1. Knowing Endangerment Resulting From Mishandling Hazardous or Toxic Substances, Pesticides or Other Pollutants

(a) Base Offense Level: 24

* * *

PART T

OFFENSES INVOLVING TAXATION

1. INCOME TAXES

§ 2T1.1. Tax Evasion

(a) Base Offense Level: Level from § 2T4.1 (Tax Table) corresponding to the tax loss.

* * *

4. TAX TABLE

§ 2T4.1. Tax Table

Tax Loss	Offense Level
(A) less than $2,000	6
(B) $2,000–$5,000	7
(C) $5,001–$10,000	8
(D) $10,001–$20,000	9
(E) $20,001–$40,000	10
(F) $40,001–$80,000	11
(G) $80,001–$150,000	12
(H) $150,001–$300,000	13
(I) $300,001–$500,000	14
(J) $500,001–$1,000,000	15
(K) $1,000,001–$2,000,000	16
(L) $2,000,001–$5,000,000	17
(M) more than $5,000,000	18

CHAPTER THREE

ADJUSTMENTS

PART A

VICTIM–RELATED ADJUSTMENTS

1. VICTIM-RELATED ADJUSTMENTS

The following adjustments are included in this Part because they may apply to a wide variety of offenses. They are to be treated as specific offense characteristics. Do not apply these adjustments if the offense guideline incorporates these factors either in the base offense level or as a specific offense characteristic.

§ 3A1.1. Vulnerable Victim

If the defendant knew or should have known that the victim of the offense was unusually vulnerable due to age, physical or mental condition, or that the victim was particularly susceptible to the criminal conduct, increase by 2 levels.

§ 3A1.2. Official Victim

If the victim was any law-enforcement or corrections officer, any other official as defined in 18 U.S.C. § 1114, or a member of the immediate family thereof, and the crime was motivated by such status, increase by 3 levels.

§ 3A1.3. Restraint of Victim

If the victim of a crime was physically restrained in the course of the offense, increase by 2 levels.

PART B—ROLE IN THE OFFENSE

Sections 3B1.1 and 3B1.2 address relative responsibility in cases involving more than one participant. Section 3B1.3 applies regardless of the number of participants.

§ 3B1.1. Aggravating Role

Based on the defendant's role in the offense, increase the offense level as follows:

(a) If the defendant was an organizer or leader of a criminal activity that involved five or more participants or was otherwise extensive, increase by 4 levels.

(b) If the defendant was a manager or supervisor (but not an organizer or leader) and the criminal activity involved five or more participants or was otherwise extensive, increase by 3 levels.

(c) If the defendant was an organizer, leader, manager, or supervisor in any criminal activity other than described in (a) or (b), increase by 2 levels.

* * *

§ 3B1.2.   Mitigating Role

Based on the defendant's role in the offense, decrease the offense level as follows:

(a) If the defendant was a minimal participant in any criminal activity, decrease by 4 levels.

(b) If the defendant was a minor participant in any criminal activity, decrease by 2 levels.

In cases falling between (a) and (b), decrease by 3 levels.

§ 3B1.3.   Abuse of Position of Trust or Use of Special Skill

If the defendant abused a position of public or private trust, or used a special skill, in a manner that significantly facilitated the commission or concealment of the offense, increase by 2 levels. This adjustment may not be employed in addition to that provided for in § 3B1.1, nor may it be employed if an abuse of trust or skill is included in the base offense level or specific offense characteristic.

§ 3B1.4.   In any other case, no adjustment is made for role in the offense.

* * *

PART E

ACCEPTANCE OF RESPONSIBILITY

§ 3E1.1.   Acceptance of Responsibility

(a) If the defendant clearly demonstrates a recognition and affirmative acceptance of personal responsibility for the criminal conduct, reduce the offense level by 2 levels.

(b) A defendant may be given consideration under this section without regard to whether his conviction is based upon a guilty plea or a finding of guilt by the court or jury or the practical certainty of conviction at trial.

(c) A defendant who enters a guilty plea is not entitled to a sentencing reduction under this section as a matter of right.

CHAPTER FOUR

CRIMINAL HISTORY AND CRIMINAL LIVELIHOOD

PART A

CRIMINAL HISTORY

INTRODUCTION

The Comprehensive Crime Control Act sets forth four purposes of sentencing. (See 18 U.S.C. § 3553(a)(2).) A defendant's record of past criminal conduct is directly relevant to those purposes. A defendant with a record of prior criminal behavior is more culpable than a first offender and thus deserving of greater punishment. General deterrence of criminal conduct dictates that a clear message be sent to society that repeated criminal behavior will aggravate the need for punishment with each recurrence. To protect the public from further crimes of the particular defendant, the likelihood of recidivism and future criminal behavior must be considered. Repeated criminal behavior is an indicator of a limited likelihood of successful rehabilitation.

The specific factors included in § 4A1.1 and § 4A1.3 are consistent with the extant empirical research assessing correlates of recidivism, and patterns of career criminal behavior. While empirical research has shown that other factors are correlated highly with the likelihood of recidivism, e.g., age, drug abuse, for policy reasons they were not here included at this time. The Commission has made no definitive judgment as to the reliability of the existing data. However, the Commission will review further data insofar as they become available in the future.

§ 4A1.1. Criminal History Category

The total points from items (a) through (e) determine the criminal history category in the Sentencing Table in Chapter Five, Part A.

(a) Add 3 points for each prior sentence of imprisonment exceeding one year and one month.

(b) Add 2 points for each prior sentence of imprisonment of at least sixty days not counted in (a).

(c) Add 1 point for each prior sentence not included in (a) or (b), up to a total of 4 points for this item.

(d) Add 2 points if the defendant committed the instant offense while under any criminal justice sentence, including probation, parole, supervised release, imprisonment, work release, or escape status.

(e) Add 2 points if the defendant committed the instant offense less than two years after release from imprisonment on a sentence counted under (a) or (b). If 2 points are added for item (d), add only 1 point for this item.

CHAPTER FIVE

DETERMINING THE SENTENCE

INTRODUCTION

For certain categories of offenses and offenders, the guidelines permit the court to impose either imprisonment or some other sanction or combination of sanctions. In determining the type of sentence to impose, the sentencing judge should consider the nature and seriousness of the conduct, the statutory purposes of sentencing, and the pertinent offender characteristics. A sentence is within the guidelines if it complies with each applicable section of this chapter. The court should impose a sentence sufficient, but not greater than necessary to comply with the statutory purposes of sentencing. 18 U.S.C. § 3553(a).

PART A

SENTENCING TABLE

The Sentencing Table used to determine the guideline range follows:

SENTENCING TABLE

Criminal History Category

Offense Level	I 0 or 1	II 2 or 3	III 4, 5, 6	IV 7, 8, 9	V 10, 11, 12	VI 13 or more
1	0–1	0–2	0–3	0–4	0–5	0–6
2	0–2	0–3	0–4	0–5	0–6	1–7
3	0–3	0–4	0–5	0–6	2–8	3–9
4	0–4	0–5	0–6	2–8	4–10	6–12
5	0–5	0–6	1–7	4–10	6–12	9–15
6	0–6	1–7	2–8	6–12	9–15	12–18
7	1–7	2–8	4–10	8–14	12–18	15–21
8	2–8	4–10	6–12	10–16	15–21	18–24
9	4–10	6–12	8–14	12–18	18–24	21–27
10	6–12	8–14	10–16	15–21	21–27	24–30
11	8–14	10–16	12–18	18–24	24–30	27–33
12	10–16	12–18	15–21	21–27	27–33	30–37
13	12–18	15–21	18–24	24–30	30–37	33–41
14	15–21	18–24	21–27	27–33	33–41	37–46
15	18–24	21–27	24–30	30–37	37–46	41–51

Offense Level	I 0 or 1	II 2 or 3	III 4, 5, 6	IV 7, 8, 9	V 10, 11, 12	VI 13 or more	
16		21–27	24–30	27–33	33–41	41–51	46–57
17		24–30	27–33	30–37	37–46	46–57	51–63
18		27–33	30–37	33–41	41–51	51–63	57–71
19		30–37	33–41	37–46	46–57	57–71	63–78
20		33–41	37–46	41–51	51–63	63–78	70–87
21		37–46	41–51	46–57	57–71	70–87	77–96
22		41–51	46–57	51–63	63–78	77–96	84–105
23		46–57	51–63	57–71	70–87	84–105	92–115
24		51–63	57–71	63–78	77–96	92–115	100–125
25		57–71	63–78	70–87	84–105	100–125	110–137
26		63–78	70–87	78–97	92–115	110–137	120–150
27		70–87	78–97	87–108	100–125	120–150	130–162
28		78–97	87–108	97–121	110–137	130–162	140–175
29		87–108	97–121	108–135	121–151	140–175	151–188
30		97–121	108–135	121–151	135–168	151–188	168–210
31		108–135	121–151	135–168	151–188	168–210	188–235
32		121–151	135–168	151–188	168–210	188–235	210–262
33		135–168	151–188	168–210	188–235	210–262	235–293
34		151–188	168–210	188–235	210–262	235–293	262–327
35		168–210	188–235	210–262	235–293	262–327	292–365
36		188–235	210–262	235–293	262–327	292–365	324–405
37		210–262	235–293	262–327	292–365	324–405	360–*life*
38		235–293	262–327	292–365	324–405	360–*life*	360–*life*
39		262–327	292–365	324–405	360–*life*	360–*life*	360–*life*
40		292–365	324–405	360–*life*	360–*life*	360–*life*	360–*life*
41		324–405	360–*life*	360–*life*	360–*life*	360–*life*	360–*life*
42		360–*life*	360–*life*	360–*life*	360–*life*	360–*life*	360–*life*
43		life	life	life	life	life	life

PART B

PROBATION

§ 5B1.1. Imposition of a Term of Probation

(a) Subject to the statutory restrictions in subsection (b) below, sentence of probation is authorized:

(1) if the minimum term of imprisonment in the range specified by the Sentencing Table in Part A, is zero months;

(2) if the minimum term of imprisonment specified by the Sentencing Table is at least one but not more than six months, provided that the court imposes a condition or combination of conditions requiring intermittent confinement or community confinement as provided in § 5C2.1(c)(2) (Imposition of a Term of Imprisonment).

§ 5B1.2. Term of Probation

(a) When probation is imposed, the term shall be:

(1) at least one year but not more than five years if the offense level is 6 or greater;

(2) no more than three years in any other case.

§ 5B1.3. Conditions of Probation

(a) If a term of probation is imposed, the court shall impose a condition that the defendant shall not commit another federal, state, or local crime during the term of probation. 18 U.S.C. § 3563(a)(1).

(b) The court may impose other conditions that (1) are reasonably related to the nature and circumstances of the offense, the history and characteristics of the defendant, and the purposes of sentencing and (2) involve only such deprivations of liberty or property as are reasonably necessary to effect the purposes of sentencing. 18 U.S.C. § 3563(b). Recommended conditions are set forth in § 5B1.4.

(c) If a term of probation is imposed for a felony, the court shall impose at least one of the following as a condition of probation: a fine, an order of restitution, or community service. 18 U.S.C. § 3563(a)(2).

(d) Intermittent confinement (custody for intervals of time) may be ordered as a condition of probation during the first year of probation. 18 U.S.C. § 3563(b)(11). Intermittent confinement shall be credited toward the guideline term of imprisonment at § 5C2.1 as provided in the schedule at § 5C2.1(e).

§ 5B1.4. Recommended Conditions of Probation and Supervised Release (Policy Statement)

(a) The following "standard" conditions (1–13) are generally recommended for both probation and supervised release:

(1) the defendant shall not leave the judicial district or other specified geographic area without the permission of the court or probation officer;

(2) the defendant shall report to the probation officer as directed by the court or probation officer and shall submit a truthful and complete written report within the first five days of each month;

(3) the defendant shall answer truthfully all inquiries by the probation officer and follow the instructions of the probation officer;

(4) the defendant shall support his dependents and meet other family responsibilities;

(5) the defendant shall work regularly at a lawful occupation unless excused by the probation officer for schooling, training, or other acceptable reasons;

(6) the defendant shall notify the probation officer within seventy-two hours of any change in residence or employment;

(7) the defendant shall refrain from excessive use of alcohol and shall not purchase, possess, use, distribute, or administer any narcotic or other controlled substance, or any paraphernalia related to such substances, except as prescribed by a physician;

(8) the defendant shall not frequent places where controlled substances are illegally sold, used, distributed, or administered, or other places specified by the court;

(9) the defendant shall not associate with any persons engaged in criminal activity, and shall not associate with any person convicted of a felony unless granted permission to do so by the probation officer;

(10) the defendant shall permit a probation officer to visit him at any time at home or elsewhere and shall permit confiscation of any contraband observed in plain view by the probation officer;

(11) the defendant shall notify the probation officer within seventy-two hours of being arrested or questioned by a law enforcement officer;

(12) the defendant shall not enter into any agreement to act as an informer or a special agent of a law enforcement agency without the permission of the court;

(13) as directed by the probation officer, the defendant shall notify third parties of risks that may be occasioned by the defendant's criminal record or personal history or characteristics, and shall permit the probation officer to make such notifications and to confirm the defendant's compliance with such notification requirement.

(b) The following "special" conditions of probation and supervised release (14–24) are either recommended or required by law under the circumstances described or may be appropriate in a particular case:

(14) Possession of Weapons

If the instant conviction is for a felony, or if the defendant was previously convicted of a felony or used a firearm or other dangerous weapon in the course of the instant offense, it is recommended that the court impose a condition prohibiting the defendant from possessing a firearm or other dangerous weapon.

(15) Restitution

If the court imposes an order of restitution, it is recommended that the court impose a condition requiring the defendant to make payment of restitution or adhere to a court ordered installment schedule for payment of restitution. See § 5E4.1 (Restitution).

(16) Fines

If the court imposes a fine, it is recommended that the court impose a condition requiring the defendant to pay the fine or adhere to a court ordered installment schedule for payment of the fine.

(17) Debt Obligations

If an installment schedule of payment of restitution or fines is imposed, it is recommended that the court impose a condition prohibiting the defendant from incurring new credit charges or opening additional lines of credit without approval of the probation officer unless the defendant is in compliance with the payment schedule.

(18) Access to Financial Information

If the court imposes an order of restitution, forfeiture, or notice to victims, or orders the defendant to pay a fine, it is recommended that the court impose a condition requiring the defendant to provide the probation officer access to any requested financial information.

(19) Community Confinement

Residence in a community treatment center, halfway house or similar facility may be imposed as a condition of probation or supervised release. See § 5F5.1 (Community Confinement).

(20) Home Detention

Home detention may be imposed as a condition of probation or supervised release. See § 5F5.2 (Home Detention).

(21) Community Service

Community service may be imposed as a condition of probation or supervised release. See § 5F5.3 (Community Service).

(22) Occupational Restrictions

Occupational Restrictions may be imposed as a condition of probation or supervised release. See § 5F5.5 (Occupational Restrictions).

(23) Substance Abuse Program Participation

If the court has reason to believe that the defendant is an abuser of narcotics, other controlled substances or alcohol, it is recommended that the court impose a condition requiring the defendant to participate in a program approved by the United States Probation Office for substance abuse, which program may include testing to determine whether the defendant has reverted to the use of drugs or alcohol.

(24) Mental Health Program Participation

If the court has reason to believe that the defendant is in need of psychological or psychiatric treatment, it is recommended that the court impose a condition requiring that the defendant participate in a mental health program approved by the United States Probation Office.

* * *

PART E

RESTITUTION, FINES, ASSESSMENTS, FORFEITURES

§ 5E4.1. Restitution

(a) Restitution shall be ordered for convictions under Title 18 of the United States Code or under 49 U.S.C. § 1472(h), (i), (j) or (n) in accordance with 18 U.S.C. § 3663(d), and may be ordered as a condition of probation or supervised release in any other case.

(b) If a defendant is ordered to make restitution and to pay a fine, the court shall order that any money paid by the defendant shall first be applied to satisfy the order of restitution.

§ 5E4.2. Fines for Individual Defendants

(a) Except as provided in subsection (f) below, the court shall impose a fine in all cases. If the guideline for the offense in Chapter Two pre-

scribes a different rule for imposing fines, that rule takes precedence over this subsection.

(b) Except as provided in subsections (f) and (i) below, or otherwise required by statute, the fine imposed shall be within the range specified in subsection (c) below.

(c)(1) The minimum of the fine range is the greater of:

(A) the amount shown in column A of the table below; or

(B) the pecuniary gain to the defendant, less restitution made or ordered.

(2) Except as specified in (4) below, the maximum of the fine range is the greater of:

(A) the amount shown in column B of the table below;

(B) twice the gross pecuniary loss caused by the offense; or

(C) three times the gross pecuniary gain to all participants in the offense.

(3)

Fine Table

Offense Level	A Minimum	B Maximum
1	$ 25	$ 250
2–3	$ 100	$ 1,000
4–5	$ 250	$ 2,500
6–7	$ 500	$ 5,000
8–9	$ 1,000	$ 10,000
10–11	$ 2,000	$ 20,000
12–13	$ 3,000	$ 30,000
14–15	$ 4,000	$ 40,000
16–17	$ 5,000	$ 50,000
18–19	$ 6,000	$ 60,000
20–22	$ 7,500	$ 75,000
23–25	$10,000	$100,000
26–28	$12,500	$125,000
29–31	$15,000	$150,000
32–34	$17,500	$175,000
35–37	$20,000	$200,000
38 and above	$25,000	$250,000

(4) Subsection (c)(2), limiting the maximum fine, does not apply if the defendant is convicted under a statute authorizing (A) a maximum fine greater than $250,000, or (B) a fine for each day of violation. In such cases, the court may impose a fine up to the maximum authorized by the statute.

(d) In determining the amount of the fine, the court shall consider:

(1) the need for the combined sentence to reflect the seriousness of the offense (including the harm or loss to the victim and the gain to the defendant), to promote respect for the law, to provide just punishment and to afford adequate deterrence;

(2) the ability of the defendant to pay the fine (including the ability to pay over a period of time) in light of his earning capacity and financial resources;

(3) the burden that the fine places on the defendant and his dependents relative to alternative punishments;

(4) any restitution or reparation that the defendant has made or is obligated to make;

(5) any collateral consequences of conviction, including civil obligations arising from the defendant's conduct;

(6) whether the defendant previously has been fined for a similar offense; and

(7) any other pertinent equitable considerations.

(e) The amount of the fine should always be sufficient to ensure that the fine, taken together with other sanctions imposed, is punitive.

(f) If the defendant establishes that (1) he is not able and, even with the use of a reasonable installment schedule, is not likely to become able to pay all or part of the fine required by the preceding provisions, or (2) imposition of a fine would unduly burden the defendant's dependents, the court may impose a lesser fine or waive the fine. In these circumstances, the court shall consider alternative sanctions in lieu of all or a portion of the fine, and must still impose a total combined sanction that is punitive. Although any additional sanction not proscribed by the guidelines is permissible, community service is the generally preferable alternative in such instances.

(g) If the defendant establishes that payment of the fine in a lump sum would have an unduly severe impact on him or his dependents, the court should establish an installment schedule for payment of the fine. The length of the installment schedule generally should not exceed twelve months, and shall not exceed the maximum term of probation authorized for the offense. The defendant should be required to pay a substantial installment at the time of sentencing. If the court authorizes a defendant sentenced to probation or supervised release to pay a fine on an installment schedule, the court shall require as a condition of probation or supervised release that the defendant pay the fine according to the schedule. The court also may impose a condition prohibiting the defendant from incurring new credit charges or opening additional lines of credit unless he is in compliance with the payment schedule.

(h) If the defendant knowingly fails to pay a delinquent fine, the court shall resentence him in accordance with 18 U.S.C. § 3614.

(i) Notwithstanding the provisions of subsection (c) of this section, but subject to the provisions of subsection (f) herein, the court shall impose an additional fine amount that is at least sufficient to pay the costs to the government of any imprisonment, probation, or supervised release ordered.

PART F

SENTENCING OPTIONS

§ 5F5.1. Community Confinement

Community confinement may be imposed as a condition of probation or supervised release.

§ 5F5.2. Home Detention

Home detention may be imposed as a condition of probation or supervised release.

§ 5F5.3. Community Service

(a) Community service may be ordered as a condition of probation or supervised release. If the defendant was convicted of a felony, the court must order one or more of the following sanctions: a fine, restitution, or community service. 18 U.S.C. § 3563(a)(2).

(b) With the consent of the victim of the offense, the court may order a defendant to perform services for the benefit of the victim in lieu of monetary restitution. 18 U.S.C. § 3663(b)(4).

* * *

§ 5F5.5. Occupational Restrictions

(a) The court may impose a condition of probation or supervised release prohibiting the defendant from engaging in a specified occupation, business, or profession, or limiting the terms on which the defendant may do so, only if it determines that:

    (1) a reasonably direct relationship existed between the defendant's occupation, business, or profession and the conduct relevant to the offense of conviction;

    (2) there is a risk that, absent such restriction, the defendant will continue to engage in unlawful conduct similar to that for which the defendant was convicted; and

    (3) imposition of such a restriction is reasonably necessary to protect the public.

(b) If the court decides to impose a condition of probation or supervised release restricting a defendant's engagement in a specified occupation, business, or profession, the court shall impose the condition for the minimum time and to the minimum extent necessary to protect the public.

* * *

PART H

SPECIFIC OFFENDER CHARACTERISTICS

INTRODUCTION

Congress has directed the Commission to consider whether certain specific offender characteristics "have any relevance to the nature, extent, place of service, or other incidents of an appropriate sentence" and to take them into account only to the extent they are determined relevant by the Commission. 28 U.S.C. § 994(d).

§ 5H1.1. Age (Policy Statement)

Age is not ordinarily relevant in determining whether a sentence should be outside the guidelines. Neither is it ordinarily relevant in determining the type of sentence to be imposed when the guidelines provide sentencing options. Age may be a reason to go below the guidelines when the offender is elderly and infirm and where a form of punishment (e.g., home confinement) might be equally efficient as and less costly than incarceration. If, independent of the consideration of age, a defendant is sentenced to probation or supervised release, age may be relevant in the determination of the length and conditions of supervision.

§ 5H1.2. Education and Vocational Skills (Policy Statement)

Education and vocational skills are not ordinarily relevant in determining whether a sentence should be outside the guidelines, but the extent to which a defendant may have misused special training or education to facilitate criminal activity is an express guideline factor. See § 3B1.3 (Abuse of Position of Trust or Use of

Special Skill) Neither are education and vocational skills relevant in determining the type of sentence to be imposed when the guidelines provide sentencing options. If, independent of consideration of education and vocational skills, a defendant is sentenced to probation or supervised release, these considerations may be relevant in the determination of the length and conditions of supervision for rehabilitative purposes, for public protection by restricting activities that allow for the utilization of a certain skill, or in determining the type or length of community service.

§ 5H1.3. Mental and Emotional Conditions (Policy Statement)

Mental and emotional conditions are not ordinarily relevant in determining whether a sentence should be outside the guidelines, except as provided in the general provisions in Chapter Five. Mental and emotional conditions, whether mitigating or aggravating, may be relevant in determining the length and conditions of probation or supervised release.

§ 5H1.4. Physical Condition, Including Drug Dependence and Alcohol Abuse (Policy Statement)

Physical condition is not ordinarily relevant in determining whether a sentence should be outside the guidelines or where within the guidelines a sentence should fall. However, an extraordinary physical impairment may be a reason to impose a sentence other than imprisonment.

Drug dependence or alcohol abuse is not a reason for imposing a sentence below the guidelines. Substance abuse is highly correlated to an increased propensity to commit crime. Due to this increased risk, it is highly recommended that a defendant who is incarcerated also be sentenced to supervised release with a requirement that the defendant participate in an appropriate substance abuse program. If participation in a substance abuse program is required, the length of supervised release should take into account the length of time necessary for the supervisory body to judge the success of the program.

This provision would also apply in cases where the defendant received a sentence of probation. The substance abuse condition is strongly recommended and the length of probation should be adjusted accordingly. Failure to comply would normally result in revocation of probation.

§ 5H1.5. Previous Employment Record (Policy Statement)

Employment record is not ordinarily relevant in determining whether a sentence should be outside the guidelines or where within the guidelines a sentence should fall. Employment record may be relevant in determining the type of sentence to be imposed when the guidelines provide for sentencing options. If, independent of the consideration of employment record, a defendant is sentenced to probation or supervised release, considerations of employment record may be relevant in the determination of the length and conditions of supervision.

§ 5H1.6. Family Ties and Responsibilities, and Community Ties (Policy Statement)

Family ties and responsibilities and community ties are not ordinarily relevant in determining whether a sentence should be outside the guidelines. Family responsibilities that are complied with are relevant in determining whether to impose restitution and fines. Where the guidelines provide probation as an option, these factors may be relevant in this determination. If a defendant is sentenced to probation or supervised release, family ties and responsibilities that are met may be relevant in the determination of the length and conditions of supervision.

§ 5H1.7. Role in the Offense (Policy Statement)

A defendant's role in the offense is relevant in determining the appropriate sentence. See Chapter Three, Part B (Role in the Offense).

§ 5H1.8. Criminal History (Policy Statement)

A defendant's criminal history is relevant in determining the appropriate sentence. See Chapter Four (Criminal History and Criminal Livelihood).

§ 5H1.9. Dependence Upon Criminal Activity for a Livelihood (Policy Statement)

The degree to which a defendant depends upon criminal activity for a livelihood is relevant in determining the appropriate sentence. See Chapter Four, Part B (Career Offenders and Criminal Livelihood).

§ 5H1.10. Race, Sex, National Origin, Creed, Religion and Socio–Economic Status (Policy Statement)

These factors are not relevant in the determination of a sentence.

PART K

DEPARTURES

1. SUBSTANTIAL ASSISTANCE TO AUTHORITIES

§ 5K1.1. Substantial Assistance to Authorities (Policy Statement)

Upon motion of the government stating that the defendant has made a good faith effort to provide substantial assistance in the investigation or prosecution of another person who has committed an offense, the court may depart from the guidelines.

(a) The appropriate reduction shall be determined by the court for reasons stated that may include, but are not limited to, consideration of the following conduct:

(1) the court's evaluation of the significance and usefulness of the defendant's assistance, taking into consideration the government's evaluation of the assistance rendered;

(2) the truthfulness, completeness, and reliability of any information or testimony provided by the defendant;

(3) the nature and extent of the defendant's assistance;

(4) any injury suffered, or any danger or risk of injury to the defendant or his family resulting from his assistance;

(5) the timeliness of the defendant's assistance.

§ 5K1.2. Refusal to Assist (Policy Statement)

A defendant's refusal to assist authorities in the investigation of other persons may not be considered as an aggravating sentencing factor.

2. GENERAL PROVISIONS: (POLICY STATEMENT)

Under 18 U.S.C. § 3553(b) the sentencing court may impose a sentence outside the range established by the applicable guideline, if the court finds "that there exists an aggravating or mitigating circumstance of a kind, or to a degree not adequately taken into consideration by the Sentencing Commission in formulating the guidelines." Circumstances that may warrant departure from the guidelines pursuant to this provision cannot, by their very nature, be comprehensively listed and analyzed in advance. The controlling decision as to whether and to what extent departure is warranted can only be made by the court at the time of sentencing. Nonetheless, the present section seeks to aid the court by identifying some of the factors that the Commission has not been able to fully take into account in formulating precise guidelines. Any case may involve factors in addition to those identified that have not been given adequate consideration by the Commission. Presence of any such factor may warrant departure from the guidelines, under some circumstances, in the discretion of the sentencing judge. Similarly, the court may depart from the guidelines, even though the reason for departure is listed elsewhere in the guidelines (e.g., as an adjustment or specific offense characteristic), if the court determines that, in light of unusual circumstances, the guideline level attached to that factor is inadequate.

Where the applicable guidelines, specific offense characteristics, and adjustments do take into consideration a factor listed in this part, departure from the guideline is warranted only if the factor is present to a degree substantially in excess of that which ordinarily is involved in the offense of conviction. Thus, disruption of a governmental function, § 5K2.7, would have to be quite serious to warrant departure from the guidelines when the offense of conviction is bribery or obstruction of justice. When the offense of conviction is theft, however, and when the theft caused disruption of a governmental function, departure from the applicable guideline more readily would be appropriate. Similarly, physical injury would not warrant departure from the guidelines when the offense of conviction is robbery because the robbery guideline includes a specific sentence adjustment based on the extent of any injury. However, because the robbery guideline does not deal with injury to more than one victim, departure would be warranted if several persons were injured. Also, a factor may be listed as a specific offense characteristic under one guideline but not under all guidelines. Simply because it was not listed does not mean that there may not be circumstances when that factor would be relevant to sentencing. For example, the use of a weapon has been listed as a specific offense characteristic under many guidelines, but not under immigration violations. Therefore, if a weapon is a relevant factor to sentencing for an immigration violation, the court may depart for this reason.

Harms identified as a possible basis for departure from the guidelines should be taken into account only when they are relevant to the offense of conviction, within the limitations set forth in the Overview to Chapter Two.

§ 5K2.1. Death (Policy Statement)

If death resulted, the court may increase the sentence above the authorized guideline range.

Loss of life does not automatically suggest a sentence at or near the statutory maximum. The sentencing judge must give consideration to matters that would normally distinguish among levels of homicide, such as the defendant's state of mind and the degree of planning or preparation. Other appropriate factors are whether multiple deaths resulted, and the means by which life was taken. The extent of the increase should depend on the dangerousness of the defendant's conduct, the extent to which death or serious injury was intended or knowingly risked, and the extent to which the offense level for the offense of conviction, as determined by the other Chapter Two guidelines, already reflects the risk of personal injury. For example, a substantial increase may be appropriate if the death was intended or knowingly risked or if the underlying offense was one for which base offense levels do not reflect an allowance for the risk of personal injury, such as fraud.

§ 5K2.2. Physical Injury (Policy Statement)

If significant physical injury resulted, the court may increase the sentence above the authorized

guideline range. The extent of the increase ordinarily should depend on the extent of the injury, the degree to which it may prove permanent, and the extent to which the injury was intended or knowingly risked. When the victim suffers a major, permanent disability and when such injury was intentionally inflicted, a substantial departure may be appropriate. If the injury is less serious or if the defendant (though criminally negligent) did not knowingly create the risk of harm, a less substantial departure would be indicated. In general, the same considerations apply as in § 5K2.1.

§ 5K2.3. Extreme Psychological Injury (Policy Statement)

If a victim or victims suffered psychological injury much more serious than that normally resulting from commission of the offense, the court may increase the sentence above the authorized guideline range. The extent of the increase ordinarily should depend on the severity of the psychological injury and the extent to which the injury was intended or knowingly risked. Normally, psychological injury would be sufficiently severe to warrant application of this adjustment only when there is a substantial impairment of the intellectual, psychological, emotional, or behavioral functioning of a victim, when the impairment is likely to be of an extended or continuous duration, and when the impairment manifests itself by physical or psychological symptoms or by changes in behavior patterns. The court should consider the extent to which such harm was likely, given the nature of the defendant's conduct.

§ 5K2.4. Abduction or Unlawful Restraint (Policy Statement)

If a person was abducted, taken hostage, or unlawfully restrained to facilitate commission of the offense or to facilitate the escape from the scene of the crime, the court may increase the sentence above the authorized guideline range.

§ 5K2.5. Property Damage or Loss (Policy Statement)

If the offense caused property damage or loss not taken into account within the guidelines, the court may increase the sentence above the authorized guideline range. The extent of the increase ordinarily should depend on the extent to which the harm was intended or knowingly risked and on the extent to which the harm to property is more serious than other harm caused or risked by the conduct relevant to the offense of conviction.

§ 5K2.6. Weapons and Dangerous Instrumentalities (Policy Statement)

If a weapon or dangerous instrumentality was used or possessed in the commission of the offense the court may increase the sentence above the authorized guideline range. The extent of the increase ordinarily should depend on the dangerousness of the weapon, the manner in which it was used, and the extent to which its use endangered others. The discharge of a firearm might warrant a substantial sentence increase.

§ 5K2.7. Disruption of Governmental Function (Policy Statement)

If the defendant's conduct resulted in a significant disruption of a governmental function, the court may increase the sentence above the authorized guideline range to reflect the nature and extent of the disruption and the importance of the governmental function affected. Departure from the guidelines ordinarily would not be justified when the offense of conviction is an offense such as bribery or obstruction of justice; in such cases interference with a governmental function is inherent in the offense, and unless the circumstances are unusual the guidelines will reflect the appropriate punishment for such interference.

§ 5K2.8. Extreme Conduct (Policy Statement)

If the defendant's conduct was unusually heinous, cruel, brutal, or degrading to the victim, the court may increase the sentence above the guideline range to reflect the nature of the conduct. Examples of extreme conduct include torture of a victim, gratuitous infliction of injury, or prolonging of pain or humiliation.

§ 5K2.9. Criminal Purpose (Policy Statement)

If the defendant committed the offense in order to facilitate or conceal the commission of another offense, the court may increase the sentence above the guideline range to reflect the actual seriousness of the defendant's conduct.

§ 5K2.10. Victim's Conduct (Policy Statement)

If the victim's wrongful conduct contributed significantly to provoking the offense behavior, the court may reduce the sentence below the guideline range to reflect the nature and circumstances of the offense. In deciding the extent of a sentence reduction, the court should consider:

(a) the size and strength of the victim, or other relevant physical characteristics, in comparison with those of the defendant;

(b) the persistence of the victim's conduct and any efforts by the defendant to prevent confrontation;

(c) the danger reasonably perceived by the defendant, including the victim's reputation for violence;

(d) the danger actually presented to the defendant by the victim; and

(e) any other relevant conduct by the victim that substantially contributed to the danger presented.

Victim misconduct ordinarily would not be sufficient to warrant application of this provision in the context of offenses under Chapter Two, Part A.3 (Criminal Sexual Abuse). In addition, this provision usually would not be relevant in the context of non-violent offenses. There may, however, be unusual circumstances in which substantial victim misconduct would warrant a reduced penalty in the case of a non-violent offense. For example, an extended course of provocation and harassment might lead a defendant to steal or destroy property in retaliation.

§ 5K2.11. Lesser Harms (Policy Statement)

Sometimes, a defendant may commit a crime in order to avoid a perceived greater harm. In such instances, a reduced sentence may be appropriate, provided that the circumstances significantly diminish society's interest in punishing the conduct, for example, in the case of a mercy killing. Where the interest in punishment or deterrence is not reduced, a reduction in sentence is not warranted. For example, providing defense secrets to a hostile power should receive no lesser punishment simply because the defendant believed that the government's policies were misdirected.

In other instances, conduct may not cause or threaten the harm or evil sought to be prevented by the law proscribing the offense at issue. For example, where a war veteran possessed a machine gun or grenade as a trophy, or a school teacher possessed controlled substances for display in a drug education program, a reduced sentence might be warranted.

§ 5K2.12. Coercion and Duress (Policy Statement)

If the defendant committed the offense because of serious coercion, blackmail or duress, under circumstances not amounting to a complete defense, the court may decrease the sentence below the applicable guideline range. The extent of the decrease ordinarily should depend on the reasonableness of the defendant's actions and on the extent to which the conduct would have been less harmful under the circumstances as the defendant believed them to be. Ordinarily coercion will be sufficiently serious to warrant departure only when it involves a threat of physical injury, substantial damage to property or similar injury resulting from the unlawful action of a third party or from a natural emergency. The Commission considered the relevance of economic hardship and determined that personal financial difficulties and economic pressures upon a trade or business do not warrant a decrease in sentence.

§ 5K2.13. Diminished Capacity (Policy Statement)

If the defendant committed a non-violent offense while suffering from significantly reduced mental capacity not resulting from voluntary use of drugs or other intoxicants, a lower sentence may be warranted to reflect the extent to which reduced mental capacity contributed to the commission of the offense, provided that the defendant's criminal history does not indicate a need for incarceration to protect the public.

§ 5K2.14. Public Welfare (Policy Statement)

If national security, public health, or safety was significantly endangered, the court may increase the sentence above the guideline range to reflect the nature and circumstances of the offense.

DISSENTING VIEW OF COMMISSIONER PAUL H. ROBINSON

[This is a summary of Commissioner Robinson's dissenting view.]

Introduction. The Sentencing Reform Act was intended to implement Congress' inspired vision of modern criminal sentencing. Comprehensive and binding guidelines were to bring rationality and greater consistency to federal sentencing. With the guidelines promulgated today, however, that vision dims. These guidelines may well produce more irrationality and more unwarranted disparity than exists today.

1. The Failure to Provide a Rational and Coherent Sentencing System.

The Failure to Define a Rational and Coherent Policy and to Provide Sentences Calculated to Achieve the Statutory Purposes of Sentencing. In direct violation of the Act, the guidelines do not establish sentences calculated to "assure the meeting of the purposes of sentencing [i.e., just punishment, deterrence, incapacitation of the dangerous, and rehabilitation]." They offer no sentencing philosophy; they adopt no coherent system of sentencing policies; they do not reflect serious consideration of existing research studies on how best to further the statutory purposes. Instead, the guidelines claim to simply continue past sentencing practices. In fact, the guidelines dramatically alter past practice, yet have no principled basis or explanation for the changes.

The Impropriety of Basing Guidelines on Mathematical Averages of Past Sentences. Sentences based on mathematical averages of past sentences are contrary to the Act and are "bastardized" sentences that are not likely to achieve any of the statutory purposes of sentencing. Further, the guidelines incorporate inaccurate measures of past practice to determine future practice.

The Failure to Rank Systematically Offenses According to Seriousness. As a concomitant to its failure to adopt a principled and rational approach to drafting, the guidelines fail to reflect a systematic ranking of offenses according to their seriousness. The failure results in clearly inappropriate treatment of many offenses.

The Failure to Provide Different Sentences for Cases that are Very Different in Seriousness: Promoting "Free" Harms and Ignoring Relevant Mitigations. The most basic function of any sentencing system is to provide appropriately different sentences for meaningfully different cases. Taking account of relevant aggravating and mitigating factors assures that additional harms will not go unpunished—that there are no "free" harms—and that significant mitigations will be reflected in an appropriately reduced sanction. The guidelines, however, routinely allow "free" harms, and overlook relevant mitigations. They do this by ignoring highly relevant and commonplace factors (e.g., an offender's causing physical injury, use of a weapon, or reduced culpable state of mind), by taking into account only the most serious factor when multiple factors exist, and by failing to provide an incremental penalty for each of different multiple offenses.

The Failure to Address the Problems of Fragmented and Overlapping Offenses. The guidelines are based on specific federal code sections, rather than on consolidated, nonoverlapping generic offense categories like those used by most states. This makes it impossible to formulate an appropriate sentence where an offender's conduct violates more than one specific code provision, a common occurrence.

2.   The Failure to Reduce (and the Potential for Increasing) Unwarranted Sentencing Disparity. The guidelines include so many invitations and directions to depart from the guidelines, in even commonplace cases, that the "guidelines" are little more than non-binding recommendations that are not likely to reduce disparity. Indeed, because the Parole Commission will no longer be adjusting the disparate sentences imposed by judges—as it does now, albeit in an inadequate way—it is very possible that unwarranted disparity will increase under these guidelines.

Requiring Departures, and Thus Inviting Disparity, by Adopting Skeletal Rather Than Comprehensive Guidelines. The Act permits judges to depart from the guidelines only if there exists a factor not adequately considered in drafting the guidelines. Departure was intended to be rare, however, because the guidelines were to be detailed and comprehensive. In fact, highly relevant and commonplace factors are omitted from the guidelines—even factors identified as relevant in previous drafts by the Commission. Because of these omissions, a judge must either give a sentence that is inappropriate because it does not reflect the relevant factor, or must depart from the guidelines and thereby create the disparity that the guidelines were intended to reduce.

Fostering Departures, and Thereby Disparity, by Using Vague and Ambiguous Standards. By using vague and ambiguous terms, frequently in key provisions, the guidelines invite disparity in application as different judges follow different interpretations.

Fostering Disparity by Inviting (and Directing) Extensive Departures Without the Guidance of an Articulated Sentencing Policy. The guidelines specifically invite (and in some cases direct) the court to depart from the guidelines in predictable and commonplace cases that the Commission has fully considered. Because much disparity results from differences in sentencing philosophy among judges, the guideline's failure to reflect a coherent sentencing policy, will further exacerbate the problem of unwarranted disparity under such a discretionary "departure system" of sentencing.

3.   The Failure to Prevent Plea–Bargaining from Subverting the Goals of the Guideline System. 87% of all cases in the federal system are disposed of through a plea bargain. The guidelines permit a judge to depart from the guidelines if the sentence is pursuant to a plea bargain and the judge feels there is a "justifiable reason" to depart. This guideline provision violates the Act, which does not allow departures simply because the judge feels there is a "justifiable reason." Further, by failing to prevent pleabargaining from subverting the system, the provision assures that the irrationality and disparity of current federal sentencing will continue under the guidelines. Such plea-bargained sentences will not achieve the statutory purposes of sentencing and are not likely to provide similar sentences for similar offenders.

4.   Impeding Future Refinement. The rationale for skeletal, non-binding guidelines is that such will provide a basis for refinement over time by the courts. But shifting guideline development to the courts is unwise, is inconsistent with the Act, and, in any case, would be ineffective because the guidelines are structured in a manner that will not permit the meaningful appellate review necessary for refinement.

The Failure to Provide an Adequate Foundation for Refinement. The lack of an articulated sentencing policy, the unwieldy and illogical structure of the guidelines, and the reliance on the antiquated, fragmented, and overlapping offense definitions of the federal code (rather than the consolidated generic offenses used in most state codes), each make the guidelines an inadequate foundation for future refinement.

The Impropriety of Relying on the Courts to Develop the Guidelines. It is inappropriate to rely on the judiciary to develop the guidelines. First, the guidelines fail to provide adequate direction for such development. Courts must necessarily consider issues on a case-by-case basis rather than from the system-wide perspective that is required. Courts cannot inform the policy-making process with the research studies that are needed and statutorily directed. Courts have had the opportunity to reduce or guide judicial discretion to avoid sentencing disparity in the past but have shown no willingness to do so. Finally, Congress has directed the Commission, not the courts, to structure and guide sentencing decisions.

The Failure to Permit Adequate Appellate Review. The guidelines assume that appellate review of departures will, over time, permit the courts to develop a "common law" of sentencing that will provide the substance and direction that they currently lack. But the failure to provide meaningful criteria for application, the failure to specify what factors have been taken into account in setting a given offense value, and the failure to articulate a rational sentencing policy, leaves sentencing judges unable to determine whether departure is appropriate and appellate judges unable to provide a principled review of a decision to depart. Further, there will be no appellate review of most departures, since departure pursuant to a plea-bargain sentence will not be subject to appellate review.

5. The Failure to Provide an Impact Assessment. Before promulgating guidelines that will govern the sentencing of over 100,000 federal offenders each year and that are likely to change the practice of federal prosecutors, defense counsel, probation officers, prison officials, magistrates, and judges, it would seem appropriate (and

it is feasible) to develop reliable estimates on how the guidelines will operate. Yet, the most basic effects of these guidelines have never been determined.

6. The Fundamental Failure of the Process. Many, if not most, of the guidelines' shortcomings have resulted from a lack of serious and informed deliberation and analysis. Because the guidelines do not embody a coherent policy-making process, the various drafts have lurched wildly from one extreme to the other, reacting to the criticisms of each previous draft. In the end, the final guidelines were drafted in three weeks and embody an approach significantly different from those previously considered—an approach that has been subject to little internal discussion or debate and no public comment or field-testing.

PRELIMINARY OBSERVATIONS OF THE COMMISSION ON COMMISSIONER ROBINSON'S DISSENT

May 1, 1987

The Commission, having just received today a fully detailed draft of Commissioner Robinson's dissent, but aware of his general views, makes the following preliminary observations.

1. Professor Robinson has strongly urged the Commission to adopt a highly detailed, mechanical guideline system that would aggravate punishments for each and every harm an offender causes and presumably lessen punishment for each and every relevant mitigating background factor. The Commission spent several months following the professor's lead in an effort to turn that approach into a set of workable guidelines. Professor Robinson embodied his approach in a "July 10" (1986) draft, which the Commission circulated widely within the criminal law community.

Despite the many valuable insights that his draft contained, the reaction was strongly and uniformly negative. The comments received ranged from "overly ambitious" and "ill advised" to "totally impractical" and "fraught with danger." Judge Jon O. Newman, a longtime advocate of sentencing guidelines, wrote the Commission that the Robinson approach

will likely fail to survive a Congressional veto and, even if allowed to become effective, will lead to a generation of needless litigation, a series of invalidated sentences, opportunities for manipulation by prosecutors and defense counsel, and a source of such confusion among judges as to make likely a clamor for return to the old system.

Judge Harold Tyler, who as Deputy Attorney General (under President Ford) directed the government's efforts to create sentencing reform legislation, wrote that he "doubt[ed] the necessity or wisdom of a complicated scoring system, at least initially." He said that the July 10, 1986, draft would be "politically unacceptable to Congress"; that it would create "real resistance on the part of * * * many sentencing judges"; that it would create "substantial practical problems" for the courts; and that its many gradations were "overly refined" and "not * * * necessary." Judge Marvin Frankel, whose initial studies of sentencing disparity helped to launch the guideline movement, wrote that however splendid in their conception and execution the July 10 draft may be, it is "too far ahead of the times for the goal of acceptance by the legislative and judicial people who will be considering" it.

In brief, the Commission found no significant support for the July 10, 1986, approach. The Commission then decided not to promulgate the draft; it concluded that its descriptions bore little or no relation to the actual statutory elements of an offense and that it was excessively impractical, a kind of academic fantasy. The Commission will publish the draft, however, among its working papers; those interested in the views that Professor Robinson states in his dissent should study it with care.

2. The reason that Professor Robinson's approach drew so little support from any quarter (academics included) is that it did not provide a practical solution to the problems viewed as important by the different segments of the criminal justice community. Those particularly concerned with lessening disparity in sentencing saw in the complexity of the July 10, 1986, draft, in its need for elaborate new factfinding, and in its use of complex mathematical formulae involving multiplication of quartic roots, the likelihood that different judges would apply the system differently to similar cases, thereby aggravating the disparity problem. Those professionally concerned with crime control saw in its factfinding demands the need for lengthy new hearings, complex arguments and appeals, all of which would significantly lessen the likelihood that convicted criminals would, in fact, receive appropriate punishment. Those particularly sensitive to the need for special treatment of unusual cases saw in its rigid, mechanical rules and near total absence of discretion, the elimination of a court's ability to deviate when, for example, unusual facts in a specific case cried out for special treatment.

Of course, it may be that there is a practical method of responding to Professor Robinson's present criticisms by taking the approach he advocates and, within a reasonable period of time, translating it into a practical set of guidelines. But nothing in the July 10, 1986, draft, nor in his work that we have seen since that time, convinces us that this is so.

3. What Professor Robinson means by a "rational and coherent sentencing system" is a system (preferably his system) that would radically revise what he calls the "archaic, fragmented" criminal code of the United States. He urges a "visionary" approach that would base guidelines upon "modern American criminal code" descriptions of conduct, many of which descriptions are found in recently revised state codes. The problem with this view, however, is that Congress, which has considered reform of the Criminal Code for more than a decade, has not enacted that reform into law. Thus, the Commission must apply federal statutory law as it now stands, whether or not visionaries believe that the existing statutes ought to be repealed or replaced. To put the matter bluntly, the Commission does not have the political mandate or the institutional authority to rewrite the United States Criminal Code under the guise of writing sentencing guidelines. The job of revising the Criminal Code belongs to Congress, not the Commission.

4. In our view, the actual effect of any major change upon a human institution inevitably involves uncertainty and the risk of unforeseen consequences. Professor Robinson may be certain about what changes will actually come about as a result of the guidelines we propose; we are not. We, therefore, strongly believe that our proposed changes should evolve from, not represent a sharp break with, existing practice. What we do, after all, will significantly affect the entire criminal justice system of the United States. And, lacking a crystal ball capable of telling us with precision what will actually occur, we act now perhaps less aggressively or ambitiously than Professor Robinson would like. We believe

it more responsible to proceed with caution, monitoring through data gathering and analysis the actual effects of our changes at each step, then revising, modifying, and advancing our work in light of what we learn.

5. We have read Professor Robinson's dissent with an awareness that our primary task is not to produce a perfect document, but rather to create a practical document in an area where every approach suffers some drawbacks. Thus, we have primarily been interested in the alternatives that Professor Robinson has been proposing. Viewing his dissent not in this light, however, but simply as a series of criticisms, our initial reaction is that the criticisms are wide of the mark. The dissent does not accurately characterize what the guidelines are trying to do; how, for example, they make use of the empirical data, or how and why they create some distinctions but not others. The dissent's use of guideline examples is misleading or mistaken.

The dissent, in our view, misunderstands both the statute and the guidelines. Regardless, the issue is not whether the Commission's present draft has some anomalies or disparities; some will be found. Nor is it whether the Commission has created the theoretically or academically "best" set of guidelines. The issue is whether we wish to perpetuate the current system, a system that creates anomalies and disparities daily by allowing each of hundreds of federal judges to sentence entirely on the basis of his or her own views. It is whether, with these initial guidelines, the Commission has laid a solid groundwork for further improvement and reform. The Commission is a permanent body that need not (and should not) try to complete its entire task in a single year. These initial guidelines begin a process that will create gradually but inevitably an ever fairer and more effective criminal justice system.

†